D0062311

China

Damian Harper, Steve Fallon, Katja Gaskell, Julie Grundvig,
Carolyn Heller, Thomas Huhti, Bradley Mayhew, Christopher Pitts

Contents

Destination China

China is unique among travel destinations. A journey through this colossus of a country is a mind-boggling encounter with the most populous and perhaps most culturally idiosyncratic nation on earth. Whatever China does to you – entertains, stimulates, beguiles or bemuses – you will witness a country undergoing a spectacular transformation. Long-range forecasts see China leapfrogging rival destinations to emerge as the world's leading tourist destination by 2020. Everyone is talking about China, so why not find out what all the fuss is about.

Tipped by pundits worldwide to shape – and perhaps lead – the 21st century, China is a land of ferocious contrasts. Shànghǎi's ambitious skyline is a triumphant statement, but it couldn't be further from the worldly renunciation acted out in Tibet's distant monasteries. The land is also a baffling tangle of tongues, from Tibetan to Uighur to Shànghǎihuà and, increasingly, badly spoken English.

If you're after history, indulge yourself on China's imperial monuments, stretching from Běijīng to Xī'ān and beyond. Seekers of modernity will find their requirements met in Hong Kong, Macau, Shànghǎi, Běijīng, Dàlián and Qīngdǎo, but if it's Chinese food that has seduced you, prepare for an aromatic adventure from highly spiced Húnán to the dainty morsels of Hong Kong and on to the Islamic dishes of the vast northwest.

Domestic tourism is in a state of supernova, showering sights around the land with much-needed investment (and less-needed noise pollution and litter). China remains huge and wild enough to satisfy your explorer instinct, and, crisscrossed with an extensive transport network, you won't be left high and dry. Enjoy your trip!

PHIL M WEYMOUTH

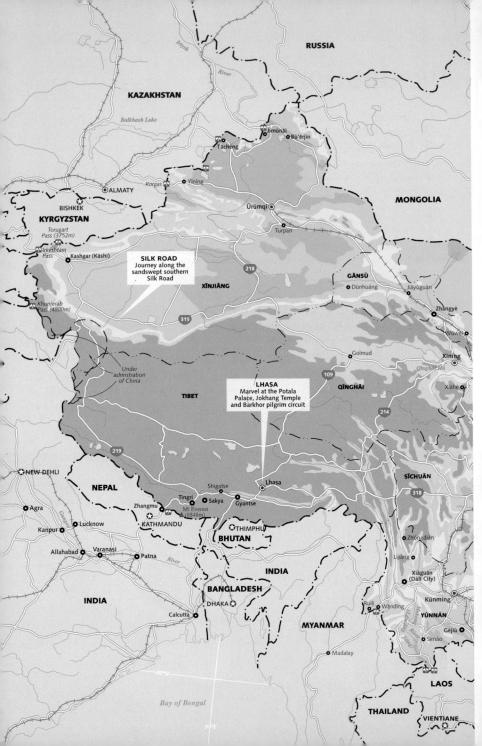

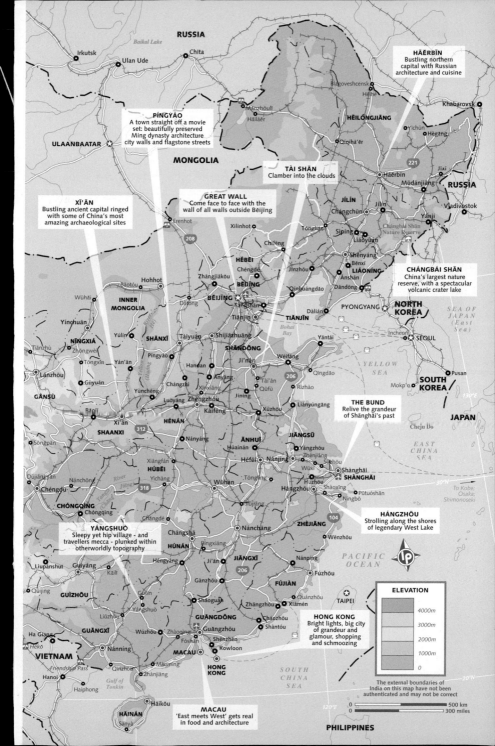

RUSSIA

Irkutsk
Ulan Ude
Chita
Baikal Lake

HÄERBIN
Bustling northern capital with Russian architecture and cuisine

Blagoveshchensk
Heihe
Khabarovsk

HÉILÓNGJIANG

Mǎnzhōulǐ
Hǎilǎěr
Yichūn
Hegǎng

Qiqihā'ěr
Jixi

PÍNGYÁO
A town straight off a movie set: beautifully preserved Ming dynasty architecture, city walls and flagstone streets

ULAANBAATAR

MONGOLIA

TÀI SHĀN
Clamber into the clouds

221
Hāěrbin
Mǔdānjiāng

RUSSIA

XĪ'ĀN
Bustling ancient capital ringed with some of China's most amazing archaeological sites

GREAT WALL
Come face to face with the wall of all walls outside Běijīng

JÍLÍN
Chángchūn
Jílín
Vladivostok
Yánjí

Erenhot

Xilinhot

208

Tōngliáo
Sìping
Liáoyuán

Chángbái Shān Nature Reserve

Chìfēng

Shěnyáng

HÉBĚI

Hohhot
Zhāngjiākǒu
Chengde
Jǐnzhōu
Bēnxī
Ānshān

CHÁNGBÁI SHĀN
China's largest nature reserve, with a spectacular volcanic crater lake

Wǔhǎi
Bāotóu
Dàtóng

BĚIJĪNG
Tángshān

Qínhuángdǎo
Dāndōng

INNER MONGOLIA

Dàlián

PYONGYANG

NORTH KOREA

SEA OF JAPAN (East Sea)

Yínchuān

Tiānjīn

TIĀNJĪN

Bohai Bay

Incheon
SEOUL

NÍNGXIÀ
Zhōngwèi

Yúlín

SHĀNXĪ
Tàiyuán
Shíjiāzhuāng

SHĀNDŌNG
Jǐ'nán
Weifāng
Yāntái

Tiānzhù

Tóngxīn
Yán'ān
Píngyáo

Qīngdǎo

SOUTH KOREA

Lánzhōu
Gùyuán

Hándān
Ānyáng
Tài'ān
Qūfù
Rìzhào

YELLOW SEA

Mokp'o
Pusan

GĀNSÙ
Báijī

Yúnchéng
Chángzhì
Xīnxiāng
Jīníng

THE BUND
Relive the grandeur of Shànghǎi's past

Luòyáng
Zhèngzhōu
Xúzhōu
Liányúngǎng

Cheju Do

JAPAN

Sōngpān
Xī'ān

312

SHAANXI
HÉNÁN
Kāifēng
Nányáng

ĀNHUĪ
Huáinán

JIĀNGSŪ
Yángzhōu
Zhènjiāng
Sūzhōu

EAST CHINA SEA

30°N

HÚBĚI
Xiāngfán
Yíchāng

Héféi
NÁNJĪNG
Wúxī

SHÀNGHǍI
Shànghǎi

130°E

Dūjiāngyàn
Nánchōng

River Yangzi

318

Wǔhàn
Tónglíng

Hángzhōu
Húzhōu
Shàoxīng

To Kobe; Osaka; Shimonoseki

Chéngdū
Chángdé

HÁNGZHŌU
Strolling along the shores of legendary West Lake

CHÓNGQÌNG
Chóngqìng

Jiǔjiāng

Pǔtuóshān
Níngbō

YÁNGSHUÒ
Sleepy yet hip village – and travellers mecca – plunked within otherworldly topography

HÚNÁN
Chángshā
Píngxiāng

JIĀNGXĪ
Nánchāng

ZHÈJIĀNG
104
Wēnzhōu

PACIFIC OCEAN

Liupánshuǐ
Guìyáng
Kǎilǐ

Héngyáng

Jí'ān

Nánpíng

Qūjìng
Yǎngshuò

Gànzhōu

206

FÚJIÀN
Fúzhōu

GUÌZHŌU
Liǔzhōu
Gùilín

Sháoguān
Zhāngzhōu
Xiàmén

Quánzhōu

TAIPEI

Ha Giang
Hékǒu

GUǍNGXĪ
Wúzhōu
Zhàoqìng

GUǍNGDŌNG
Guǎngzhōu
Shàntóu

HONG KONG
Bright lights, big city of grandeur and glamour, shopping and schmoozing

VIETNAM
Nánníng
Fóshān
Shēnzhèn
Kowloon

Friendship Pass
MACAU

Hanoi
Qīnzhōu
Zhànjiāng

HONG KONG

SOUTH CHINA SEA

20°N

Haiphong
Gulf of Tonkin

The external boundaries of India on this map have not been authenticated and may not be correct

HǍINÁN
Sānyà
Hǎikǒu

MACAU
'East meets West' gets real in food and architecture

PHILIPPINES

120°E

ELEVATION

4000m
3000m
2000m
1000m
0

0   500 km
0   300 miles

China harbours an amazing number of traditional villages where you can step back in time. Amble alongside the picturesque canals of **Zhōuzhuāng** (p250) in Jiāngsū. Escape into the terraced orchards and courtyard homes of **Chuāndǐxià** (p148) outside Běijīng or experience traditional Dong culture in Guìzhōu's colourful village of **Zhàoxìng** (p640). Trundle round **Píngyáo** (p395), a splendid portrait of traditional China, in Shānxī. **Yung Shue Wan** (p510) is Hong Kong village living at its 21st-century best: peace, solitude, restaurants, bars and even some shopping. Drop in on a local artist in **Tóngrén** (p880) and buy a *thangka* direct.

Miao houses with tiled roofs in Kǎilǐ (p637), Guìzhōu

Explore Hakka roundhouses in Yǒngdìng (p340) in remote southwestern Fújiàn

Black Dragon Pool Park (p669) in Lìjiāng, Yúnnán. Wander through Lìjiāng's cobbled streets and busy markets

Travellers interested in the tangible legacies of the colonial period will want to visit Macau for the magnificent ruins of the **Church of St Paul** (p537) and spend time in Hong Kong for the spectacle of the **Central business district** (p498). Enjoy the backstreets and villas of Shànghǎi's **French concession** (p278), travel to **Qīngdǎo** (p203) for its historic German haunts, peruse **Yantai Hill Park** (p212) in Yāntái or tour the pompous Treaty Port architecture of **Tiānjīn** (p150). For a further taste of yesteryear, stroll about the European-style villas of **Lúshān** (p470), **Jīgōng Shān** (p441) or **Gǔlàng Yǔ** (p339), admire the mouldering nobility of **Shamian Island** (p555), or explore the Russian heritage of Hāěrbīn's **Dàolǐqū district** (p379).

Admire the church of St Dominic (p534) in Macau

MICHAEL AW

RICHARD I'ANSON

Enjoy Macau's Portuguese architecture (p529)

Take an early morning stroll along the old-world Bund (p273) in Shànghǎi

GLENN BEANLAND

The Han Chinese heartland provinces are embellished with imperial remains and dynastic relics, such as Běijīng's **Ming City Wall** (p109). Admire the Buddhist carvings at the **Yungang Caves** (p403) outside Dàtóng or journey to the ancient dynastic capitals of **Hángzhōu** (p308), **Kāifēng** (p441) and **Lùoyáng** (p435). Roam among the riverside Buddhist statues at the **Longmen Caves** (p438) outside Lùoyáng and put aside a few days for a visit to **Xī'ān** (p409), where you can clamber up the city's Tang dynasty **pagodas** (p412). Visit the **Confucius Temple** (p198) in Qūfù and make your way up the slopes of sacred **Tài Shān** (p191).

DIANA MAYFIELD

The Three Pagodas (p662) reflected in a lake in Dàlǐ, Yúnnán

The gates leading to the Temple of Heaven (p109) in Běijīng

GRAHAM TWEEN

KEREN SU

Tower at the west end of the Great Wall at Jiāyùguān (p820) in Gānsù

BILL BACHMANN

Traverse restored sections of the Great Wall, such as at Jīnshānlǐng (p144) outside Běijīng

LEE FOSTER

Terracotta warrior in Emperor
Qin Shi Huang's tomb (p418)
outside Xī'ān, Shaanxi

One of the many ornate halls at the
Forbidden City (p110) in Běijīng

GLENN BEANLAND

The 17-arch bridge at the Summer Palace (p118) in Běijīng

GLENN BEANLAND

Admire the Bai architecture of **Xǐzhōu** (p665) or sample **Ruìlì's** (p702) borderland feel. Voyage south to Xīshuāngbǎnnà and trek from **Dàměnglóng to Bùlǎngshān** (p696), exploring Dai, Hani, Bulang and Lahu villages. Wander round **Lóngshèng** (p617) and **Sānjiāng** (p619), gateways to minority hamlets, before roaming into Guìzhōu to discover **Xījiāng** (p639) and more minority settlements. Travel between **Shàntóu** (p577) and **Cháozhōu** (p579), and pass fortified Hakka villages chock-a-block with traditional houses and ancient temples. Delve into Tibetan culture in **Qīnghǎi** (p875), **Sìchuān** (p708), **Yúnnán** (p642) and, of course, **Tibet** (p855). For a Central Asian experience, visit **Kashgar** (p793) or **Inner Mongolia** (p841).

Dai women (p687) during a temple festival

BRADLEY MAYHEW

BRADLEY MAYHEW

Bulang girls (p695) in the Xīshuāngbǎnnà region

The Lǐtáng Horse Festival (p746) in Sìchuān

BILL WASSMAN

LEE FOSTER

Hakka woman smoking a pipe on
Hong Kong Island, Hong Kong (p491)

KEREN SU

Bai woman (p660) carrying a basket on
her back, Dàlǐ, Yúnnán

Catch a concert by a traditional Naxi orchestra (p671) in Lìjiāng, Yúnnán

KRAIG LIEB

China abounds with scenic getaways and dramatic landscapes. Evade the Hong Kong crowds on **Lantau Island** (p509), size up the stupendous scenery of **Jiǔzhàigōu** (p752), set foot on the **Sichuan–Tibet Hwy** (p735), hike through tranquil **Moon Canyon** (p828), or go to **Hǎinán** (p582) for its tropical white beaches. The views of Mt Everest from **Rongphu Monastery** (p872) are a million miles from Běijīng's traffic-clogged roads, as is the Changtang plateau at **Nam-tso Lake** (p867). Sleep in a Kazakh yurt at **Tiān Chí** (p784), get a taste of the Siberian taiga at **Kanas Lake** (p800) in Xīnjiāng, or spend days hiking through Jílín's **Chángbái Shān** (p371).

MARTIN MOOS

Be hypnotised by the beauty of Yuèliàng Shān (p616) outside Yángshuò, Guǎngxī

Turn your departure from China into one great escape on the sheer Kara-koram Highway (p795), Xīnjiāng

JOHN BORTHWICK

JULIET COOMBE

Trek alongside the Yangzi River in Tiger Leaping Gorge (p675)

Getting Started

From low-cost independent exploration to comfortable tours, China can offer a sometimes bewildering choice of travel options. As the land is so vast, visitors to China need to take a long and hard look at the map, and decide exactly what it is that they want their China experience to be. Going through the Itineraries chapter (p17) will provide you with options for your visit. The only part of China you will need to carefully plan is travel to Tibet, as bureaucratic obstacles, travel restrictions and health issues will require your consideration and attention.

WHEN TO GO

Travel to China is possible year-round, as long as you're prepared for what the season can throw at you. Spring (March to May) and autumn (September to early November) can be the best time to be on the road, as you avoid the blistering heat of summer (June to August) and stinging chill of winter (November to February/March). Autumn in Běijīng, for example, is particularly pleasant, as are early spring and autumn in Hong Kong. Summer is the busiest tourist season, and getting around and finding accommodation during the peak summer crush can be draining. North China is hot and largely dry in summer, especially in the baking northwest (but Běijīng is also uncomfortable). The Yangzi River (Cháng Jiāng) region is very hot and humid, and southern China, with a coastline harassed by typhoons, also swelters. Rainfall rarely falls in quantities that can disrupt travel plans. Winter is the low season (except for Hǎinán Dǎo) and can be the quietest time of year, and good hotel discounts can be found, but while Hong Kong in winter is comfortably nippy, north China is a frozen expanse, especially in the northeast, northwest and Inner Mongolia. Wintering in clement central and southern Yúnnán province is enjoyable, but the higher altitude north of the province is frigid. Winter is inadvisable for travel to high-altitude areas in China.

See Climate Charts (p888) for more information.

Major public holidays can make travel difficult. Manoeuvring around China with 1.3 billion others at the Chinese New Year (p894) can be a nightmare, but you also get to see China at its most colourful and entertaining. Hotel rooms become very expensive during the May Day holiday (now a week long from 1 May) and National Day on 1 October (likewise a week long), and train tickets can be difficult to procure.

DON'T LEAVE HOME WITHOUT...

- Checking the visa situation (p903)
- Checking travel advisory bureaus
- Checking on your recommended vaccinations (pp926–7)
- A copy of your travel insurance policy details (p895)
- A smoke alarm – for peace of mind in budget hotels
- Good deodorant – hard to find
- Reading matter for those endless train trips
- A sense of adventure

COSTS & MONEY

China used to be incredibly cheap virtually across the board, but it has long become increasingly expensive. However, simply knowing where and how to travel according to your budget means you can live well within your means.

The most expensive destinations are Hong Kong, Macau, Běijīng, Shànghǎi, Guǎngzhōu, the eastern coastal provinces and Special Economic Zones (SEZ). Běijīng and Shànghǎi especially can be intolerably dear. You can pay criminal prices if you want: Y45 (US$5.5) for a coffee or Y50 (US$6) for a bowl of noodles at Běijīng's Capital Airport, or US$8500 a month for a plush three-bedroom apartment in the capital. Look around, learn to get savvy and get a feel for where locals shop and quickly try to get a sense of proportion; be sensible and cautious about where you shop, and what you buy. Since you're using a new currency, take your time to accurately convert prices. Even Běijīng and Shànghǎi can be cheap if you're shrewd and careful.

Staying in dormitories, travelling by bus or bicycle rather than taxi, eating from street stalls or small restaurants, and refraining from buying anything means you can live on around US$30 per day. Accommodation will take the largest chunk, but in cities where dormitory accommodation is unavailable you will have to settle for accommodation with rates from US$25 to US$35 for a double (singles are rarely available). Travelling through the booming coastal cities and much of east China for less than US$45 per day can be a challenge.

Western China and the interior remain relatively inexpensive. Popular backpacker getaways, such as Yúnnán, Sìchuān, Guǎngxī, Gānsù, Xīnjiāng, Qīnghǎi and Tibet, abound in budget accommodation and cheap eats.

Food costs remain reasonable throughout China, and the frugal can eat for as little as US$5 a day. Transport costs can be kept to a minimum by travelling by bus wherever possible or by travelling hard-seat on the train. Train travel is reasonable, and is generally about half the price of air travel. Flying in China is expensive, but those with less time may have to resort to it to cover potentially vast distances.

Mid-range hotel doubles start at around US$35 and you can eat in mid-range restaurants from around US$5. Mid-range comfort can be bought in China for around US$60 a day, making it a neither very cheap nor exorbitant way to see the land.

Top-end travel in China? For US$200 to US$250 per day, you can hit the major attractions of the country staying in five-star hotels (US$100 and up for a double), flying long distances, taking taxis to/from airports, dining on Chinese haute cuisine and enjoying a few drinks in the hotel lobby bar in the evenings. You'll find yourself well catered for, unless you venture too far from the big cities.

TRAVEL LITERATURE

River Town: Two years on the Yangtze (2001) by Peter Hessler is full of poignant and telling episodes during the author's posting as an English teacher in the town of Fúlíng on the Yangzi River. Hessler perfectly captures the experience of being a foreigner in today's China in his observations of the local people.

Revolving around the same waterway, *The River at the Centre of the World* (1998) by Simon Winchester follows the author on his journey along the river from the mouth of the Yangzi River north of Shànghǎi to its source high up on the Tibet-Qinghai plateau.

HOW MUCH?

Cigarettes: from Y3.5

International Herald Tribune from a five-star hotel: Y23

City bus ticket: Y1

Hour in an Internet café: Y2

City map: Y3-5

LONELY PLANET INDEX

Litre of petrol: Y3.5

Half a litre of bottled water: Y2

Bottle of beer from corner shop: Y3

Draught pint of local beer from a bar: Y15

Souvenir T-shirt: from Y25

Small/large lamb kebab: Y0.5/2

TOP TENS

Top Ten Movies

Some cinematic homework is a sure way to hit the ground running in China. The country's film genres sprawl from energetic Hong Kong *wŭdăpiàn* (kung fu), violence and slapstick, through the decadent excesses of the mainland fifth generation to the sombre palate of the sixth generation and beyond.

- *Raise the Red Lantern* (1991) Director: Zhang Yimou
- *Judou* (1989) Director: Zhang Yimou
- *Chungking Express* (1994) Director: Wong Karwai
- *City on Fire* (1987) Director: Ringo Lam
- *In the Mood for Love* (2000) Director: Wong Karwai
- *Drunken Master 2* (1994) Directors: Lau Karleung, Jackie Chan
- *Infernal Affairs* (2002) Directors: Lau Waikeung, Mak Siufai
- *Beijing Bicycle* (2001) Director: Wang Xiaoshuai
- *Shaolin Soccer* (2001) Director: Stephen Chow
- *Farewell My Concubine* (1993) Director: Chen Kaige

Top Ten Reads

Getting some paperwork can also gear you up for your China trip, so try some of the following penned by Chinese and non-Chinese authors.

- *God's Chinese Son*, Jonathan Spence
- *The Search for Modern China*, Jonathan Spence
- *The China Dream: The Elusive Quest for the Greatest Untapped Market on Earth*, Joe Studwell
- *Foreign Devils on the Silk Road*, Peter Hopkirk
- *The Chinese*, Jasper Becker
- *The Tiananmen Papers*, Compiled by Zhang Liang; edited by Andrew Nathan and Perry Link
- *Soul Mountain*, Gao Xingjian
- *Red Dust*, Ma Jian
- *Peking*, Juliet Bredon
- *The Republic of Wine*, Mo Yan

Top Ten Tops

- The Chinese: the world's largest population
- Ürümqi (p779): the world's furthest city from the sea
- Nam-tso Lake (p867): the highest lake in the world
- Lèshān Grand Buddha (p731): the largest seated Buddha in the world
- Central Escalator (p499), Hong Kong: the world's longest escalator
- Mt Everest (p872): the highest mountain in the world
- Guanyin statue (p174), Puning Temple, Chéngdé: the world's largest wooden statue
- The Great Wall: the longest fortification in history
- Grand Hyatt, Jinmao Tower (p283): the world's highest hotel above ground level
- Ocean Park (p503), Hong Kong: the world's largest aquarium

From Heaven Lake by Vikram Seth follows the author's journey from Xīnjiāng to Tibet and on to Delhi.

First published in hardback in 1936, *News from Tartary: A Journey from Peking to Kashmir* by Peter Fleming is a classic account of the author's journey from China to India during a chaotic chapter in China's history.

INTERNET RESOURCES

China Minority Travel (www.china-travel.nl) Offers tailor-made trips to south China and Tibet.

Human Rights in China (www.hrichina.org) Organisation set up in 1989 to promote human rights in China, with useful links.

Lonely Planet (www.lonelyplanet.com) Useful summaries on travelling China and the Thorn Tree bulletin board. Travel news and the subwwway section, with links to the most useful travel resources on the Web.

that's magazines (www.thatsmagazines.com) Full of handy tips on entertainment, dining, travel, cultural events and more in Běijīng, Shànghǎi and Guǎngzhōu.

WildChina (www.wildchina.com) Far-flung treks around China, organised within China. Monthly email newsletter.

Zhongwen: Chinese Characters and Culture (www.zhongwen.com) Includes a pinyin chat room and an online dictionary of Chinese characters.

Itineraries

CLASSIC ROUTES

SOUTHWEST TOUR   Two weeks to 18 days / Hong Kong to Yúnnán

Start by spending four days sightseeing in **Hong Kong** (p491) and **Macau**
(p529), before venturing north into China proper for one or two nights in
Guăngzhōu (p549). Take the sleeper (train or bus) to **Guìlín** (p606) for a day
of sightseeing before visiting nearby **Yángshuò** (p611). Many travellers are
seduced into spending much longer than they planned in Yángshuò, so
be prepared for a lengthy sojourn. Return to Guìlín and hop on a bus to
Lóngshèng (p617) and **Sānjiāng** (p619), not far from the Guăngxī-Guìzhōu
border, for the spectacular scenery and minority villages. Exploration
over the border into minority-rich **Guìzhōu** (p622) is also a popular option if you have an extra few days. Onward travel from Guìlín to **Kūnmíng**
(p644) can be undertaken by train or plane. Spend a few days in Kūnmíng
before flying or taking the bus northwest to **Dàlǐ** (p660) and from there
onto **Lìjiāng** (p666). Another attractive possibility is to fly or take the bus
to the **Xīshuāngbǎnnà region** (p685) south of Kūnmíng, a part of China
abundant in opportunities for hiking and exploring the southwest borders. Other possibilities include flights from Kūnmíng to Chiang Mai or
Bangkok in Thailand, or taking a train to Hanoi in Vietnam.

You'll be journey-
ing to some of
China's most allur-
ing destinations
on this 2000km
tour, taking in
key landscape
panoramas and
ethnic minority
areas. The journey
can be done in a
whistle-stop few
weeks or less, but
a month will give
you time to savour
the region.

Lìjiāng
Dàlǐ
GUÌZHŌU
Kūnmíng
Sānjiāng
Lóngshèng
Guìlín
GUĂNGXĪ
Yángshuò
YÚNNÁN
Xīshuāngbǎnnà
Region
Guăngzhōu
Macau
Hong Kong

THE HISTORY TOUR: BĚIJĪNG TO THE SILK ROAD
Three weeks / Běijīng to Xī'ān & Dūnhuáng

Four days in **Běijīng** (p93) should be enough time for visiting the sights, including the **Great Wall** (p141) and the **Forbidden City** (p110). Take the train to **Dàtóng** (p401) in Shānxī province to peruse the city's temples and the fabulous **Yungang Caves** (p403) and **Hanging Monastery** (p404) outside town. Hop on a bus from Dàtóng to the Buddhist mountain of **Wǔtái Shān** (p399) for a few days before taking a bus to **Tàiyuán** (p393) and then on for a day (or overnight) trip to the marvellous walled town of **Píngyáo** (p395). A detour east by train from Tàiyuán to **Shíjiāzhuāng** (p164) and the charming temple town of **Zhèngdìng** (p168) north of the city is also possible. From Tàiyuán take the train south to spend two days in the historic walled city of **Kāifēng** (p441), traditional home of China's Jews, before heading west by train to the former dynastic capital of **Luòyáng** (p435) and the magnificent Buddhist spectacle of the **Longmen Caves** (p438). Take the train west again from Luòyáng to **Xī'ān** (p409) to spend four days seeing the sights of the former capital of the Tang dynasty, visiting the **Army of Terracotta Warriors** (p418) and clambering up the Buddhist mountain of **Huá Shān** (p421). Xī'ān traditionally marked the start of the Silk Road and the **Mogao Caves** (p823) outside **Dūnhuáng** (p820) – reachable by plane from Xī'ān – is one of the trade route's most spectacular marvels. Return to Běijīng by plane from either Xī'ān or Dūnhuáng.

For many travellers, this tour is what coming to China is all about. Spanning around 2500km from Běijīng to Dūnhuáng, you will be visiting the major imperial monuments – including the Great Wall and the Terracotta Army – and religious sites of North China. Manageable in three weeks, a month-long tour would allow for a more relaxed expedition.

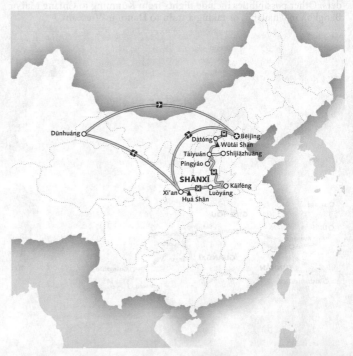

COASTAL HIGHLIGHTS & TREATY PORTS TOUR
Three to four weeks / Běijīng to Hong Kong & Macau

Having toured **Běijīng** (p93), take the train to **Tiānjīn** (p150) and spend two days wandering around its historic collection of European-style buildings. From Tiānjīn jump on the train to spend two days in breezy **Qīngdǎo** (p203), the port city in Shāndōng graced with impressive early-20th-century German architecture. **Yāntái** (p211) and its notable Yantai Hill Park is a possible day trip from Qīngdǎo. From Qīngdǎo take the overnight train through **Jǐ'nán** (p185) to booming **Shànghǎi** (p266) and its intoxicating mix of old European-style buildings and dashing modern architecture. Spend three days touring Shànghǎi's sights before using two days to visit the gardens and temples of the canal town of **Sūzhōu** (p243). Board a bus from Sūzhōu to famed **Hángzhōu** (p308) for a few days in the historic capital of Zhèjiāng province. Then board the overnight sleeper to **Xiàmén** (p335), and spend two days in the pleasant port city to admire the gorgeous, historic European architecture and charm of **Gǔlàng Yǔ** (p339). What better way to conclude this loop along the coast than with three days in **Hong Kong** (p491), perched on the south of Guǎngdōng province, with **Macau** (p529) a short boat trip away.

Voyaging down the eastern flank of China from Běijīng to Hong Kong, this tour covers over 3000km, taking in the major highlights and historic maritime towns along the coast. One of China's most fascinating journeys, this three-week journey passes through some of the must-see sights of Qīngdǎo, Sūzhōu, Shànghǎi and Hángzhōu.

ROADS LESS TRAVELLED

QĪNGHĂI TO SÌCHUĀN
One week / Xīníng to Chéngdū

Skirt the flanks of Tibet on your way from **Xīníng** (p875) to **Chéngdū** (p710) in Sìchuān. The scenery en route is magnificent and perfect for a more offbeat China experience – but do this trip only in summer (it can be dangerously cold even in spring) and take lots of food with you (you won't be able to change money or cash traveller's cheques). Wild dogs, treacherous mountain roads and bus breakdowns, and waiting a day or so for bus connections or having to hitch are all part of the adventure. Accommodation along the way will be simple but cheap, and the bus company can recommend either its own hostels or direct you to another hotel. You can jump on a sleeper bus from Xīníng to the newly opened trading town of **Yùshù** (Jyekundo; p878) in the south of Qīnghăi, which stages a marvellous annual horse festival on 25 July. The town is soon to have its own airport. Alternatively – although the landscape en route to **Măduō** is monotonous – from Măduō to **Xiēwú** (Zhiwu) and **Yùshù** through the Bayan Har Mountains, it becomes increasingly Tibetan, with picturesque mountain villages, alpine lakes and monasteries. Continue east from Xiēwú to **Sêrxu** (Shíqú) in north Sìchuān, where there are bus connections through some stunning scenery all the way to **Kāngdìng** (Dardo; p735), via **Manigango** (Yùlóng; p743) and **Gānzī** (Ganze; p742). Continue along the Sìchuān–Tibet Hwy by bus to Kāngdìng and then on to Chéngdū. Another option is to take a bus from Xīníng (p878) to Bānmǎ, where you could then get a bus to **Zöigê** (p755), then to **Sōngpān** (p749) and on to Chéngdū.

Traversing the wilds of western China, this spectacular overland 1000km+ tour takes you into Sìchuān through the mountainous back door from Qīnghăi. Manageable in one week, allow more time for unforeseen complications and prepare for rough, no-frills travel.

YÚNNÁN INTO TIBET
Eight days / Lìjiāng to Lhasa

Kick off this trip walking **Tiger Leaping Gorge** (p675), north of gorgeous **Lìjiāng** (p666), before taking the bus to **Zhōngdiàn** (p680), where your adventure proper begins. This epic, once-in-a-lifetime journey takes you from Zhōngdiàn (Tibetan name: Gyalthang) through a breathtaking landscape of valleys, mountains and Tibetan villages to **Lhasa** (p859) in Tibet. You will need a minimum of eight days for the trip and the optimum months for travel are late spring (April and May) and autumn (September and October); winter is definitely out as the route crosses half a dozen passes over 4500m. Embark on this journey only if you are in good health (medical facilities en route are basic) and ensure you read the Health chapter for information on acute mountain sickness (p932). Joining a tour (which can arrange all the necessary permits, vehicle, driver and guide for you) is probably the best and safest way as individual travel through Tibet is not permitted, but increasing numbers of travellers are hitching through with little hassle. Outfits such as China Minority Travel (www.china-travel.nl) or Khampa Caravan (www.khampacaravan.com) can arrange the entire tour for you. Your first stop after Zhōngdiàn is **Déqin** (Dechen; p684) before reaching the town of **Yánjīng** (Yandin) in southeastern Tibet's Chamdo Prefecture. Continue your journey by road to **Markam** (Mángkāng), then west to **Dzogang** (Zuǒgòng) and on to **Pasho** (Bāsù) via **Pomda** (Bāngdá; Bamda). The journey then continues to **Rawok** (Ranwu) and the gorgeous alpine lake of **Rawok-tso** and on to Lhasa via **Pomi** and **Bayi**.

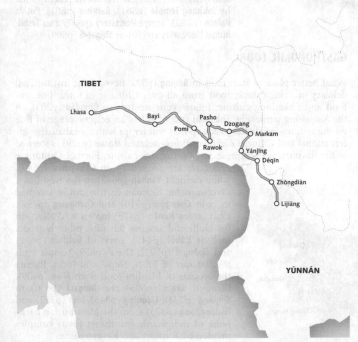

This enticing 1000km+ overland adventure takes you from southwest China into Tibet through some of China's most visually spectacular scenery. Concluding in Lhasa, the tour will involve considerable preparatory work (and flexibility time-wise), but it's second to none for those seeking a more exploratory taste of China.

TAILORED TRIPS

CHINA'S SACRED SITES

After exploring temples in **Běijīng** (p93), head to **Chéngdé** (p170) to witness the marvellous statue of Guanyin in **Puning Temple** (p174), before travelling southwest to the Buddhist mountain of **Wǔtái Shān** (p399). Then voyage south to **Zhèngdìng** (p168) for its charming legacy of pagodas and temples. East in Shāndōng province rises mighty **Tài Shān** (p190), China's most sacred Taoist peak, overlooking the magnificent **Dai Temple** (p196). The Buddhist Goddess of Compassion resides on **Pǔtuóshān** (p322), off the Zhèjiāng coast. Rising up from Hénán province is Sōng Shān, home to the renowned **Shaolin Temple** (p433) and its band of supernaturally gifted monks. Outside **Luòyáng** (p435) are the **Longmen Caves** (p438) while west again in Shaanxi province, **Xī'ān** (p409) is famed for its Tang dynasty pagodas and is the gateway to Taoist **Huá Shān** (p421). Martial arts students will appreciate the Taoist mysteries of **Wǔdāng Shān** (p456) to the southeast, while **Éméi Shān** (p725), in Sìchuān province to the southwest, is one of China's most celebrated Buddhist peaks. The world's largest Buddha sits at nearby **Lèshān** (p730). Rising up to the west is Tibet, with its unique and idiosyncratic Buddhist traditions, exemplified by **Jokhang Temple** (p861), **Barkhor** (p861), **Potala Palace** (p862), **Samye Monastery** (p867) and **Tashilhunpo Monastery** (p870) in **Shigatse** (p869).

GASTRONOMIC TOUR

What better place to start than in **Běijīng** (p93). Beyond the institutional delicacy of Peking duck, food from all over China is in town. For seafood and Shāndōng cuisine, follow your nostrils to **Qīngdǎo** (p203) on the Shāndōng peninsula. **Shànghǎi** (p266) offers an eclectic range of fine dining options, while **Hong Kong** (p491) will tempt with its exhaustive international and Chinese dining options. Relaxed **Macau** (p529) is steeped in the flavours of Cantonese and Portuguese cuisine. Further Cantonese delicacies are cooked up in **Guǎngzhōu** (p549), while clement **Yúnnán** (p642) to the west has a diverse menu. Sìchuān cuisine can be sampled in both **Chéngdū** (p710) and **Chóngqìng** (p757). Chefs from **Húnán** (p475) have a wild affection for chilli and searing flavours; other hotspots include **Húběi** (p447), parts of **Guìzhōu** (p622) and **Guǎngxī** (p593). **Lhasa** (p859) tempts with the flavours of Tibet, Nepal and India. Pursue the aromas of Muslim food from **Xī'ān** (p409), through **Gānsù** (p805) and **Níngxià** (p830) to **Xīnjiāng** (p774). **Liáoníng** (p345), **Jílín** (p362) and **Hēilóngjiāng** (p375) form the Manchurian backbone of *dōngběicài* (northeast food) complemented by Russian and Korean dishes.

CHINA'S ETHNIC MINORITIES

From **Kūnmíng** (p644), either fly or take the bus to legendary **Lìjiāng** (p666), the charming town overseen by the archetypal peak of **Yùlóng Xuěshān** (p675). Spend two days here among the famed Naxi people in the old town, enjoying the local food. Yúnnán takes on an increasingly Tibetan countenance north of Lìjiāng in **Zhōngdiàn** (p680) and **Déqin County** (p684). Catch an express bus south to **Dàlǐ** (p660) and visit the small town of **Xīzhōu** (p665), north of town, with its fine collection of Bai architecture. Make your way to **Jǐnghóng** (p687), capital of the **Xīshuāngbǎnnà region** (p685) in the south of Yúnnán for treks through villages of tribespeople around **Dàměnglóng** (p694), **Měnghǎi** (p695) and other Dai, Bulang, Lahu, Jinuo and Hani settlements. From Kūnmíng, fly or take the train to **Guìyáng** (p624) in Guizhōu and then travel by train or bus to **Kǎilǐ** (p637) and the surrounding Miao and Dong villages of **Xījiāng** (p639), **Chóng'ān** (p640) and **Zhàoxīng** (p640). Over the border in Guǎngxī you'll find Yao and Zhuang minority villages in **Lóngshèng** (p617) and the Dong villages around **Sānjiāng** (p619). Other parts of China worth visiting for their ethnic mix are **Xīnjiāng** (p774), **Inner Mongolia** (p841) and **Hēilóngjiāng** (p375).

WORLD HERITAGE SITES

China has 30 Unesco World Heritage Sites; **Běijīng** (p93) alone has the **Forbidden City** (p110) at the heart of the capital, the **Summer Palace** (p117) and the **Temple of Heaven** (p109), and outside town, the **Great Wall** (p141), the **Ming Tombs** (p145) and **Eastern Qing Tombs** (p146). En route to the Manchu **Imperial Palace** (p349) in **Shěnyáng** (p347), stop off in **Chéngdé** (p170) to admire the **Imperial Summer Villa** (p171) and the **Eight Outer Temples** (p173). The quaint walled town of **Píngyáo** (p395) in Shānxī is a charming snapshot of old China. Also in Shānxī, the **Yungang Caves** (p403) have – like the **Mogao Caves** (p823), **Longmen Caves** (p438) and the **Dàzú County grotto art** (p765) – the most important array of Buddhist carvings in China. In Shāndōng, the Taoist mountain of **Tài Shān** (p190) and the hometown of Confucius, **Qūfù** (p198), are places of national veneration. China's most picturesque peak is surely **Huáng Shān** (p259), but there are other mountains, including sacred **Éméi Shān** (p725) and **Qīngchén Shān** (p723), and the European moods and charms of **Lúshān** (p470). The classic gardens of **Sūzhōu** (p243) are a picturesque tableau but if you want raw, rugged and scenic getaways, explore **Jiǔzhàigōu** (p752), **Wǔlíngyuán** (p487), **Huánglóng** (p751) or **Wǔyí Shān** (p342), although expect tourist hordes to accompany you. While **Lìjiāng** (p666) in Yúnnán is gorgeous, the whole of Tibet to the northwest deserves to be a World Heritage Site; for now only the **Potala Palace** (p862) in Lhasa gets on the list.

The Authors

DAMIAN HARPER
Coordinating author, Běijīng, Tiānjīn, Héběi & Shāndōng

Born in London and educated at Winchester College, Damian abandoned a directionless career in bookselling to study Modern and Classical Chinese at London's School of Oriental and African Studies. This took him to Běijīng, where he developed a deep affection for the city. Damian hightailed it to Hong Kong for a year upon graduation, before chancing upon a new life as a freelance writer. To date he has contributed to eight Lonely Planet books (including *Beijing*). He lives in Shànghǎi with his Qīngdǎo-born wife, Dai Min, and his son, Timothy Benjamin (Jiafu), and daughter, Emma Rosalind (Jiale).

The Coordinating Author's Favourite Trip

After spending a week in autumnal Běijīng (p93), I'll head to nearby Chéngdé (p170) for a few days' exploration of the sights before travelling south to admire the pagodas and temple architecture of Zhèngdìng (p168). A trip to balmy Qīngdǎo (p203) is always a charming diversion, where visits are enhanced by the sale of fresh Tsingtao beer by the bag (Y1.3 per *jīn*), to accompany some of the best kebabs in China. Shànghǎi (p266) just has to be seen (but a few days is enough), and puts me within reach of the Buddhist island of Pǔtuóshān (p322). In Shànghǎi, I'll rustle up a hard-sleeper ticket for the two-day train journey to Kūnmíng (p644) in Yúnnán, from where I can explore the rest of this magic province.

STEVE FALLON
Hong Kong, Macau & Guǎngdōng

A native of Boston, Massachusetts, Steve graduated from Georgetown University with a Bachelor of Science in modern languages, including Chinese. After he had worked for several years for an American daily newspaper and earned a Master's degree in journalism, Steve's fascination with the 'new' Asia led him to Hong Kong, where he lived for over a dozen years, working for a variety of media, running a travel bookshop, and travelling frequently to Macau and the mainland. He has contributed to or written more than two dozen Lonely Planet titles, including *Hong Kong & Macau* and *Best of Hong Kong*.

KATJA GASKELL
Guìzhōu, Yúnnán, Sìchuān, Chóngqìng & Cruising Downriver

Katja's first trip to the Chinese borderlands was 10 years ago travelling overland from Nepal to Tibet. Since then she's gained an MA in Chinese from the University of Edinburgh, and worked in Běijīng as an editor and writer. She's also freelanced as a travel writer and was a contributing author of Lonely Planet's previous edition of *China*. When not on the road, she works in TV production and has helped produce several documentary series on China for major UK broadcasters. She currently moves between London and Běijīng, and is trying to decide which one to call home.

JULIE GRUNDVIG
The Culture, Food & Drink, Jiāngsū, Ānhuī, Zhèjiāng & Fújiàn

Julie has been living in Northeast Asia for the past 13 years and has done a lot of travelling there. She has worked as an editor for the *B.C. Asian Review* and is currently Associate Editor for the international journal *Yishu: Journal of Contemporary Chinese Art*. Julie now lives in Vancouver, British Columbia.

CAROLYN B HELLER
Liáoníng, Jílín, Hēilóngjiāng & Inner Mongolia

Carolyn has been fascinated with China since she first discovered egg rolls in her hometown of Bloomington, Indiana. She's an avid traveller and passionate food lover, who has eaten on the streets, in fine restaurants and everywhere in between in more than 30 countries. She has written for publications ranging from the *Boston Globe,* the *Zagat Survey* and the *Los Angeles Times,* to *FamilyFun* magazine and *Travelers' Tales Paris*. After calling Boston home for 20 years, she now lives with her husband and daughters in Vancouver, British Columbia. This is her second book for Lonely Planet.

THOMAS HUHTI
Shǎnxī, Shaanxi, Hénán, Húběi, Jiāngxī, Húnán, Hǎinán & Guǎngxī

Thomas hails from Wisconsin, USA, and still calls it home when not barrelling around the world with a backpack. A Linguistics major in university, he happily chanced upon Mandarin while fleeing the pesky grammar of Indo-European languages. A semester abroad was followed by a two-year language and research fellowship in Taiwan and the People's Republic of China. He spent five years bumming the earth as a freelance writer before joining Lonely Planet. Among other books, this is his fourth tour of duty on *China;* he also coauthored the first edition of *Southwest China*.

BRADLEY MAYHEW
Shànghǎi & Tibet

Bradley has been travelling to the remoter corners of China for much of the last decade. He's been to almost every corner of China's southwest and northwest, and has been the coordinating author of Lonely Planet's *Tibet* for the last three editions, as well as the author of Lonely Planet's *Shanghai*. A graduate of Oriental Studies from Oxford University, he speaks Chinese but would always rather try out his stumbling Tibetan or Uighur.

CHRISTOPHER PITTS

Xīngjiāng, Gānsù, Níngxià, Inner Mongolia & Qīnghǎi

Born in the year of the Tiger, Chris' first expedition to China ended in failure when he tried to dig there from Pennsylvania at the age of six. Hardened by reality but still infinitely curious about the other side of the world, he went on to study Chinese literature in Colorado, Kūnmíng and Táinán, offsetting his years abroad by working in a Chinese bookstore in San Francisco and as an editor in Berkeley. A chance meeting in a Taiwanese elevator wound up letting him off in Paris, where he currently lives with his wife Perrine.

CONTRIBUTING AUTHORS

Korina Miller lived the first 18 years of her life on Vancouver Island. Since then she hasn't stayed in any one place for very long. Along the way she picked up a degree in Communications and an MA in Migration Studies. Her first venture into China was in 1997, when she landed a job researching cooperatives and ecotourism in Shànghǎi and Lìjiāng. Her travels in China have since taken her from the Manchurian border in the north to the Tibetan Plateau in the southwest. She is coauthor of Lonely Planet's *Southwest China* and author of *Best of Beijing*. For this guide, Korina wrote the History and Environment chapters.

Dr Trish Batchelor wrote the Health chapter. She is a general practitioner and travel medicine specialist who works at the Ciwec Clinic in Kathmandu, Nepal. She is also a medical advisor to the Travel Doctor New Zealand clinics. Trish teaches travel medicine through the University of Otago, and is interested in underwater and high-altitude medicine, and in the impact of tourism on host countries. She has travelled extensively through Southeast and east Asia, and particularly loves high-altitude trekking in the Himalayas.

Snapshot

Big changes are afoot in China. The monks at the Shaolin Temple are aiming to register the Shaolin brand as a trademark in over 80 countries, while elite British private schools have decided that opening franchises in Communist China makes perfect sense. Harry Potter has weaved his magic in China, and now even Noddy is limbering up to enter the market after a Hong Kong debut. The grown-ups can wait for Aston Martin, also in the queue.

And with the authorities aiming to transform the country into a top cricketing nation within two decades, China is keeping everyone on their toes. English footballer Paul Gascoigne moved to west China in 2003 to play for second division Gansu Tianma, while Manchester United signed Chinese striker Dong Fangzhuo the following year.

China lifted a man into space for the first time in 2003 and anyone can rocket from Shànghǎi's Pudong Airport into the city at 430km/h on China's first Maglev train (although your hair can turn grey waiting for your rush hour bus to inch along Běijīng's congested streets).

In 2003 some undeveloped sections of the Great Wall were declared off-limits to tourists in a bid to preserve their disintegrating remains. Confucius would have been gobsmacked at the 2004 unveiling of China's first all-women police squad in the Chinese heartland province of Hénán.

Shànghǎi, the crown jewel of socialism with Chinese characteristics, is going places the rest of China can only dream about. First, though, the authorities have to determine how to limit the height and number of high-rises in the city after revelations that the city was subsiding faster than ever under the weight of recent construction (and over-extraction of subterranean water supplies).

With so many pundits hypnotised by China's gross domestic product (GDP) feats and statistical forecasts, it's easy to ignore the rest of the picture. According to their own analysts, Communist China has the largest disparity between urban rich and rural poor in the world. Even in these heady days, this is something this Marxist-Leninist state will have to fix, considering China's 750-million-strong peasantry. Perhaps it is no surprise that illegal immigrants from China still turn up on European shores.

China's awkward tango with the Internet took a further stumble when a fire in 2002 in an Internet café left many dead. The authorities responded by closing thousands of Internet cafés throughout the nation. At the time of writing Běijīng's population of Internet cafés was well down on just a few years ago. Internet access remains rigorously monitored, and a firewall protects China's citizens from BBC news in Chinese and other foreign pollutants.

The puritanical authorities continue to peddle their strict programme of orthodoxy: performances of Eve Ensler's play *The Vagina Monologues* were axed, and Chinese newscasters have been urged to dress modestly and avoid any Americanisms in an effort to advance China's 'spiritual civilisation'. In a surprise move, the seemingly unrevolutionary Shakespeare Association was banned in Beijing.

With the Communist Party solidly entrenched and unchallenged, China remains politically static. In 2003 China acquired a new president (Hu Jintao) and premier (Wen Jiabao), but any illusions that China's new

**FAST FACTS:
CHINA**

Population: 1.3 billion

Life expectancy male/
female: 70.4/73.7 years

GDP growth: 9.1%

GDP per capita: US$5000

Population below poverty
line: 10% (2001 estimate)

Literacy: 86%

Internet users: 59.1
million

Major exports: textiles,
clothing, footwear, toys
and machinery

Religions: Buddhism, Tao
ism, Islam, Christianity

Number of Chinese
characters: over 56,000

'For the moment, Hong Kong people power is alive'

leaders would herald a move towards political liberalisation were dashed when the National People's Congress (NPC) denied Hong Kong the hope of choosing its next leader, flying in the face of the Chinese-British deal. The sinister arrival of eight Chinese warships into Hong Kong soon afterwards underscored the message that Běijīng was calling the shots. Democrats in the ex-colony have reported a campaign of intimidation. For the moment, Hong Kong people power is alive: on the 2003 anniversary of the 1 July handover of Hong Kong to Chinese rule, an estimated 500,000 people demonstrated on the streets of the former British colony, an event replicated by an estimated 250,000 the following year.

A heavy police presence saw the 15th anniversary of the 1989 Tiananmen massacre pass with little incident, apart from the arrest of at least 16 people in and around the square. The annual candlelit vigil in Hong Kong was marked as usual. Menaced into silence, Falun Gong (an outlawed spiritual movement) rarely makes it to the newspapers. Běijīng may have successfully stamped out all dissent in the mainland, but it still has to contend with a banking system teetering on the edge of crisis and the 2004 re-election of Taiwan president and *bête noir* Chen Shuibian. People will remember 2003 as the year of SARS, which was cleverly dubbed *'tèqū bìng'* by the Chinese, or 'Special Administrative Region Disease' (SAR Disease), alluding to the illnesses' first appearance in Guǎngdōng and Hong Kong. A resurgence of the disease in 2004 thankfully failed to spread.

History Korina Miller

Littered with sieges, cults, kidnappings, indolent emperors and grand gestures like the Terracotta Warriors of the Qin dynasty and the communist's Long March, Chinese history twists its way through nearly six thousand intriguing years. Often touted as the world's oldest surviving civilisation, China has seen as many changes as the Great Wall has bricks. The territorial reach of the state, the origin of its rulers, how people speak and dress, and even what they eat have changed beyond recognition more than once. Together, the history of the many societies that have flourished on Chinese soil form the tale Chinese tell about their origins.

LEGENDS OF YORE

While China's earliest history is made up of the stuff of legends and has no contemporary written record, archaeology confirms that societies have been putting down roots in China since antiquity. Excavations at Bànpō (p419), not far from present-day Xī'ān, show that a sedentary agricultural community flourished nearly 6000 years ago. A second early culture was discovered in present-day Shāndōng. Known as Longshan culture, it shows the beginning of metallurgy and appears to have been the driving force behind the Bronze Age Shang dynasty.

DID YOU KNOW?

Bones found near Ānyáng in 1899 were oracles from the Shang dynasty. The bones were inscribed upon, heated and the resulting cracks were interpreted as responses from deceased ancestors.

TELLTALE SIGNS: THE SHANG

In 1899 peasants working near present-day Ānyáng unearthed pieces of polished bone and turtle shells. These relics were inscribed with characters and dated back to around 1500 BC, the time of the Shang dynasty. Housed in Ānyáng's museum (p440), these are the earliest examples of the elaborate writing system still used in China today.

Shang culture was spread throughout much of north China, stretching from Shāndōng to Shaanxi and Héběi to Hénán. It was headed by a sacred kingship, who was supported by officials, armies, and a peasantry that supplied labour for the building of city walls and other public works. There was also a skilled artisanry that produced the magnificent bronzeware for which this dynasty is known; visit the Henan Provincial Museum for fabulous examples (p431).

ENTER CONFUCIUS: THE ZHOU

Around three millennia ago the last Shang sovereign was defeated by the forces of Zhou who hailed from present-day Shaanxi province. The

---

PEKING MAN

In the 1920s and 1930s Chinese archaeologists unearthed skulls, stone tools and animal bones believed to be between 500,000 and 230,000 years old. Was this the birthplace of civilisation? Unfortunately, we're unlikely to ever know. Research was never carried out on Peking Man's bones because, on the eve of the Japanese invasion, the remains mysteriously disappeared – some fear to the bottom of the sea.

TIMELINE

c 4000 BC	c 3000 BC
Early settlements set up home in modern day Shaanxi and Shāndōng	Emperor Fuxi (part man, part dragon) ushers in the legendary period of 'Three Emperors and Five Sovereigns'

CHINESE DYNASTIES

Dynasty	Period	Site of Capital
Xia	2200–1700 BC	
Shang	1700–1100 BC	Ānyáng
Zhou	1100–221 BC	
Western Zhou	1100–771 BC	Hào (near Xī'ān)
Eastern Zhou	770–221 BC	Luòyáng
Qin	221–207 BC	Xiányáng
Han	206 BC–AD 220	
Western Han	206 BC–AD 9	Xī'ān
Xin	AD 9–23	Xī'ān
Eastern Han	AD 25–220	Luòyáng
Three Kingdoms	AD 220–80	
Wei	AD 220–65	Luòyáng
Shu (Shu Han)	AD 221–63	Chéngdū
Wu	AD 229–80	Nánjīng
Jin	AD 265–420	
Western Jin	AD 265–317	Luòyáng
Eastern Jin	AD 317–420	Nánjīng
Southern & Northern Dynasties	AD 420–589	
Southern Dynasties		
Song	AD 420–79	Nánjīng
Qi	AD 479–502	Nánjīng
Liang	AD 502–57	Nánjīng
Chen	AD 557–89	Nánjīng
Northern Dynasties		
Northern Wei	AD 386–534	Dàtóng, Luòyáng
Eastern Wei	AD 534–50	Linzhang
Northern Qi	AD 550–77	Linzhang
Western Wei	AD 535–56	Xī'ān
Northern Zhou	AD 557–81	Xī'ān
Sui	AD 581–618	Xī'ān
Tang	AD 618–907	Xī'ān
Five Dynasties & Ten Kingdoms	AD 907–60	
Later Liang	AD 907–23	Kāifēng
Later Tang	AD 923–36	Luòyáng
Later Jin	AD 936–47	Kāifēng
Later Han	AD 947–50	Kāifēng
Later Zhou	AD 951–60	Kāifēng
Liao	AD 907–1125	
Song	AD 960–1279	
Northern Song	AD 960–1127	Kāifēng
Southern Song	AD 1127–1279	Hángzhōu
Jin	AD 1115–1234	Kāifēng, Běijīng
Yuan	AD 1206–1368	Běijīng
Ming	AD 1368–1644	Nánjīng, Běijīng
Qing	AD 1644–1911	Běijīng
Republic of China	AD 1911–49	Běijīng, Nánjīng
People's Republic of China (PRC)	AD 1949–	Běijīng

c 1700 BC	604 BC
Members of the Shang dynasty master bronze ware production	Laotzu, the founder of Taoism, is reputedly born

Zhou went on to rule over an increasingly large territory, reaching up to Běijīng in the north and down to the lower Yangzi River (Cháng Jiāng) valley in the south. To overcome the difficulties of ruling such a vast area, the Zhou established a feudal system whereby landlords governed over principalities that were contained within walled cities.

In 771 BC the Zhou capital moved from a site near Xī'ān to one further east, leading present-day historians to divide this period into Western and Eastern Zhou. During the period of Eastern Zhou law codes were written down, iron was discovered and the fortunes of the landed aristocracy waned, while self-made men achieved places at court and merchants grew wealthy. The Zhou's control over the principalities began to fade as landlords began to fight among themselves. The Eastern Zhou was a time riddled with strife, prompting reflection and philosophising on the part of one Master Kong (Kong Fuzi), better known in the West as Confucius.

Confucius (551–479 BC) grew up in the old state of Lu, at the present-day site of Qūfù (p198) in Shāndōng province. The descendant of a minor noble family, he set off at an early age in search of an able and righteous ruler who might lead the world back to virtuous paths. In this mission he was doomed to disappointment, and his death in 479 BC was to be followed by an ever keener struggle among the states for power. Confucius did achieve enormous success as a teacher and moral exemplar, and the structure of Chinese society today remains very much rooted in his teachings. For more on Confucian beliefs, see the boxed text (p200 and p57) or head to Qūfù for a good dose of hands-on history.

CROSSING SWORDS: THE QIN

The principalities had been fighting with one another for more than 250 years, during what became known as the Warring States period. This dark era finally came to an end in 221 BC when the western state of Qin, having conquered the Zhou 35 years earlier, succeeded in subduing the remaining states to establish centralised rule.

The First Emperor of Qin (Qín Shǐ Huáng) won and reigned by the sword. His ruling philosophy focused on law and punishment, and dealt a blow to Confucius' teachings of rights and morality. His martial fanaticism was none too subtle; check out his tomb near Xī'ān, which is protected by the extraordinary Army of Terracotta Warriors (p418). He pursued campaigns as far north as Korea and south down to Vietnam while, at home, he began linking existing city walls to create the beginnings of the Great Wall. The 'First Emperor' also laid the foundations for a unified, integrated empire. He introduced a uniform currency, standardised the script, and developed infrastructure through a network of roads and canals.

Qin Shi Huang's heir to the imperial throne proved ineffectual and, shaken by rebellion, the Qin capital fell after only 15 years to an army led by the commoner Liu Bang. Liu lost no time in taking the title of emperor and establishing the Han dynasty.

WIDENING THE NET: THE HAN

The Han dynasty brought further unification of the empire as vassal states that had continued to linger on the outskirts were swept up under

DID YOU KNOW?

The conquering Zhou beheaded the Shang leader, but granted his son a state to rule, thereby hoping to diminish the wrath of the Shang ancestors.

DID YOU KNOW?

The First Emperor of Qin burned thousands of books and killed countless scholars to eliminate potential challenges to his rule.

The Emperor and the Assassin (1999) is the epic tale of the First Emperor of Qin and his lust for power. Woven with murder, love and political intrigue, this film is beautifully shot and a must see whether you're a history buff or not.

its reign. The energetic Emperor Wu, who reigned from 140 BC to 87 BC, established supremacy over neighbouring societies to the north and west, recruited able men to serve the dynasty as officials, and promoted Confucian education. An examination system was introduced and would go on to become a hallmark of government in the late imperial era; visit the Imperial College (p113) in Běijīng to learn more.

After more than a century the Han gave way to the Xin dynasty (AD 9–23), led by the radical reformer Wang Mang. This 14-year blip divides the dynasty into Former (Western) and Later (Eastern) Han periods.

Venturing Down the Silk Road

The expansion of the Han brought the Chinese into contact with the 'barbarians' that encircled their world. As a matter of course, this contact brought both military conflict and commercial gains.

To the north, the Xiongnu (a name given to various nomadic tribes of central Asia) posed the greatest threat to China. Military expeditions were sent against these tribes, initially with much success. This in turn provided the Chinese with access to central Asia, opening up the routes that carried Chinese silk as far afield as Rome.

Diplomatic links were also formed with central Asian tribes, and the great Chinese explorer Zhang Qian provided the authorities with information on the possibilities of trade and alliances in northern India. During the same period, Chinese influence percolated into areas that were later to become known as Vietnam and Korea.

UNITY & DIVISION

They say the momentum of history was ever thus: the empire, long divided, must unite; long united, must divide.

Luo Guanzhong

With these words, the storyteller of *Romance of the Three Kingdoms* (14th century) sums up the seemingly endless warring and reconstruction that followed the Han dynasty. Between the early 3rd and late 6th centuries

---

SIGNS OF THE TIMES

Dong Zhongshu (179–104 BC) was a brainy fellow with a penchant for reading omens. During the Han dynasty he took up the position of Chief Minister with the task of interpreting the will of the heavens.

At this time Liu Bang was a commoner with little claim to the throne. As founder of the Han dynasty, he seems to have had a slightly guilty conscience about being emperor and needed lots of good omens to boost his moral. Luckily, Dong came up with a cosmology that fitted Liu's needs, interpreting not only the present but the past and future, too. In Dong's 'Five Phase Cycle', earth was overcome by metal, metal by water, water by wood, wood by fire and fire by earth. Each phase was attached to a historical period, conveniently ending with the Han (earth) overcoming the Qin (fire). Therefore, the Han's legitimacy to rule was quite simply a law of nature, as natural and predictable as night and day, summer and winter.

Whether the gods really did love the Han or Dong just had a knack for reading things in a positive light is up to you to interpret.

---

214 BC	c 100 BC
Emperor Qin indentures thousands of labourers to link existing city walls into one Great Wall	Chinese traders and explorers follow the Silk Road all the way to Rome

AD north China saw a succession of rival kingdoms struggling for power. During this time of disunity a strong division formed between north and south China. The north was controlled by non-Chinese rulers and torn by warfare. Many people from the north consequently fled, carrying Chinese culture into previously non-Chinese territories. Meanwhile, the south experienced significant economic growth as Jiankang, later to become Nánjīng, served as capital for a succession of dynasties.

Culture Vultures

The most successful northern regime during this period was the Northern Wei dynasty (386–534), founded by the Tuoba, a people from the north. The Tuoba embraced Buddhism wholeheartedly and left behind some of China's top Buddhist art. Visit the cave temples near Dūnhuáng (p823) and outside Dàtóng (p403) for a glimpse. The Wei reallocation of lands to peasants and the division of the capital city into wards also outlasted the dynasty.

BRIDGING THE GAP: THE SUI

The Wei dynasty fell in 534. It was succeeded by a series of rival regimes until nobleman Yang Jian (d 604) seized all before him to establish the Sui dynasty (581–618). While the Sui was a short-lived dynasty, its accomplishments were many. Yang Jian's great achievement was to bring the south back within the pale of a northern-based empire.

Yang Jian's son, Sui Yangdi, has gone down in history as an unsavoury character who had more time for wine and women than for politics; the dynasty went into rapid decline under his rule. Nevertheless, he did contribute greatly to the unification of south and north through the construction of the Grand Canal. The canal combined earlier canals and linked the lower Yangzi River valley to Chāng'ān via the Yellow River (Huáng Hé). When Běijīng became capital of the Yuan dynasty, it was re-routed and extended northward, and remained the empire's most important communication route between south and north until the late 19th century.

After instigating three unsuccessful incursions onto Korean soil, resulting in disastrous military setbacks, Yangdi faced revolt on the streets and was assassinated in 618 by one of his high officials.

Pick up a copy of *Shi Ji* or *Records of the Grand Historian* by Sima Qian and translated by Burton Watson. Written during the Han dynasty, Sima chronicles history from antiquity to his own time, based on court records and conversations with courtiers and generals.

THE GOLDEN ERA: THE TANG

The reams of literature produced during the Tang dynasty has prompted historians to think of it as the Golden Age. The *Three Hundred Tang Poems*, compiled from over 48,000 poems preserved from this time, provides Chinese conversation with quotable quotes, much as Shakespeare does in English.

Sui Yangdi was succeeded as emperor by his own leading general, Li Yuan, who seized the capital, declared the founding of the Tang dynasty, and within 10 years had eliminated the last rival claimant to the throne. To discourage the development of regional power bases, the empire was subsequently divided into 300 prefectures (*zhōu*) and 1500 counties (*xiàn*), establishing a pattern of territorial jurisdiction that persists, with some modifications, to this day.

c 50 BC	c AD 600
One of the first documented accounts of tea-drinking in China	The Grand Canal is constructed

Li Yuan's achievements were consolidated by his son, the much admired Taizong (626–49). The relationship between Taizong, the able ruler, and his wise minister Wei Zheng (580–645) was regarded as a model one by later Confucianists. On the other hand, Taizong's concubine, Wu Zhao, was seen as a good example of what should be avoided in government.

All that Glitters...

Following Taizong's death, Wu (625–705) wielded increasing influence over the court. In 690 she managed to declare a new dynasty, the Zhou, with herself as ruler – the only woman in Chinese history to ever officially hold this position. Wu was regarded as infinitely cruel (some claim she even murdered her own son); however, it was under her leadership that the empire reached its greatest extent, spreading well north of the Great Wall and far west into inner Asia. The rich repository of texts and paintings at Dūnhuáng (p820) in Gānsù testifies to the Zhou's intense use of the Silk Road to India, Persia and on to the Mediterranean. During the 7th and 8th centuries major cities, like the capital Chāng'ān, the Yangzi port of Yángzhōu and the coastal port Guǎngzhōu, were crowded with foreign merchants. Wu later moved the capital to the more easily supplied Luòyáng.

Wu also replaced many aristocratic officials with scholars chosen through examinations. Her strong promotion of Buddhism, however, alienated her from these Confucian officials and in 705 she was forced to abdicate to Xuan Zong.

http://etext.lib.virginia
.edu/chinese/frame.htm
gives you the opportunity
to view the Golden Era
from the eyes of its poets.
This site has all 300 Tang
Poems online along with
English translations.

The Anti-Midas Touch

Emperor Xuan Zong took the reigns of power and moved the capital back to Chāng'ān. He re-established permanent armies, appointing minorities from the frontiers as generals; he believed they were so far removed from the political system and society that ideas of rebellion and coups would not enter their minds. Nevertheless, it was An Lushan, a general of Sogdian-Turkic parentage, who took advantage of his command in north China to make a bid for imperial power. The fighting, which dragged on for around eight years, overran the capital and caused massive dislocations of people and millions of deaths.

Following the failed rebellion, the aristocracy declined and a mercenary army was hired to support the imperial house. The dynasty grew increasingly dependent on the south, and began to close the door to inner and western Asia. Ideas and beliefs of the past were revived, paving the way for a comeback of Confucianism during the Song dynasty. Buddhism, on the other hand, was outlawed by Emperor Wuzong from 842 to 845. Although the ban was later modified, Buddhism never regained the power and prestige in China that it had enjoyed up until that time.

Tang power gradually weakened during the 8th and 9th centuries. In the northwest, Tibetan warriors overran Tang garrisons, while to the south the Nanzhao kingdom of Dàlǐ, Yúnnán, posed a serious threat to Sìchuān. Meanwhile, in the Chinese heartland of the Yangzi River region and Zhèjiāng, heavy taxes and a series of calamities engendered wide-ranging discontent that culminated in the Huang Chao rebellion (874–84). This reduced the empire to chaos and resulted in the fall of the capital in 907.

c 640	690–705
Buddhist pilgrim Xuan Zhuang sets out for India, returning 16 years later with countless holy texts	Wu Zhao is the first and only woman to become China's official leader

GOING SOUTH: THE SONG

Another period of disunity followed the fall of the Tang until the Northern Song dynasty (960–1127) was established. The Northern Song was a rather small empire coexisting with the non-Chinese Liao dynasty (which controlled a belt of Chinese territory south of the Great Wall) and rather less happily with the Xi Xian, another non-Chinese power that pressed hard on the northwestern provinces. In 1126 the Song lost its capital, Kāifēng, to a third non-Chinese people, the Jurchen, who had previously been their allies against the Liao. The Song was driven to its southern capital of Hángzhōu for the period of the Southern Song (1127–1279).

The Jurchen, forebears of the Manchu, established the Jin dynasty with a capital near Běijīng. A treaty was drawn up with the Southern Song that divided the empire along the boundary of Huái Hé. The Jin dynasty pulled rank over the Southern Song, demanding the payment of tribute in the form of silk, tea and silver.

Nevertheless, the Song dynasty, North and South, was a time of enormous economic and cultural vitality. Considerable advances were made in archaeology, mathematics, astronomy, geography and medicine. Philosophy, poetry, painting and calligraphy flourished. Agricultural productivity was booming, brought on by the spread of rice cultivation since the 8th century, and this left a surplus of labour that was used to develop secondary industries, like mining, ceramics, and silk manufacture. The tea-bush and lacquer trees were cultivated, and gunpowder and moveable type were invented. Paper making and print technology experienced significant advances, and a busy trade with Southeast Asia and Japan sent Song copper currency far afield.

All of these developments nurtured urbanisation and commercial classes. Kāifēng (p441) emerged as the great centre of Northern Song politics, culture and commerce. Merchants flourished, while the aristocracy more or less disappeared. Many Tang restrictions on society were abolished as the urban population became more liberated; the removal of the curfew led to a thriving nightlife. Hángzhōu (p308) prospered as capital of the Southern Song, and to this day retains its reputation as one of the most beautiful and cultured cities in the empire.

An educated class of high social standing became a distinguishing feature of Chinese society as Confucianism achieved a dominance it was to retain until the 19th century. The Song refined and expanded the examination system, selecting officials from the successful candidates.

www.confucius.org is a superb site, offering a look at the philosophy that changed the course of China. The grand sage's *Lun Yu* (Classic Sayings) is available in 21 languages, along with photos of his calligraphy, speeches and a biography.

The Wrath of Khan

While the Song literati were busy studying moral codes, Genghis Khan (1167–1227) was beginning to flex his muscles in Mongolia. The son of a chieftain, Genghis commenced his awesome rise to power by avenging his father's murder. By 1206 he was recognised as supreme ruler of the Mongols. The Mongols, despised for what was considered their ignorance and poverty, had occasionally gone to war with the Chinese but had always lost. In 1211 Genghis Khan turned his sights on China, penetrated the Great Wall two years later and took Běijīng in 1215. He fought the Jin in the east, destroyed the Xi Xia in the west and advanced on Russia. Under his descendants, a great Mongol empire was formed,

The major inventions of the pre-modern world – paper, printing, gunpowder and the compass – are all commonly used in China

Genghis Khan conquers Běijīng

stretching from the Ukraine and Persia to Korea and the northern limits of Vietnam.

The Jin fell in 1234. Hángzhōu, the Southern Song capital, was taken in 1276. The court fled and Southern Song resistance ended in 1279.

GRAND OPENING: THE YUAN

Kublai Khan, grandson of Genghis, now reigned over all of China as emperor of the Yuan dynasty. He had inherited the largest empire the world had ever known. Foreigners were easily incorporated into this ethnically complex empire as land routes were reopened. European missionaries and traders, such as Marco Polo, went to and fro across the Eurasian continent. Khan's capital, Khanbalig, was on the site of present-day Běijīng; today all that's left of his palace is a giant jade urn in Beihai Park (p112).

Under Khan, the entire population was divided into categories of Han, Mongol and foreigner, with the top administrative posts reserved for Mongols. The examination system was revived in 1315, but the Mongols and their non-Chinese allies were still strongly favoured, causing resentment among the Chinese literati.

Although they were a mighty military power, the Mongols were not masterminds at politics or economics and were soon faced with insurmountable opposition. The Mongols controlled China for less than a century; by the middle of the 14th century rebellions raged through central and north China.

Chief among the rebel groups were the Red Turbans who followed a whole gamut of religions – from Buddhism to Manichaeism, Taoism and Confucianism. By 1367 Zhu Yuanzhang, originally an orphan and Buddhist novice, had climbed to the top of the rebel leadership and in 1368 he established the Ming dynasty, restoring Chinese rule.

FORTRESS MENTALITY: THE MING

A man of no great education, Zhu Yuanzhang was a born leader and a strong if harsh ruler. Remembered for his tyranny (he had some 10,000 scholars and their families put to death in two paranoid purges of his administration), he also did much to set China back on its feet in the aftermath of the Yuan collapse.

Yuanzhang established his capital in Nánjīng, but by the early 15th century the court had begun to move back to Běijīng. A massive reconstruction project was commenced under Emperor Yongle, who reigned from 1403 to 1424, establishing the Forbidden City (p110) much as it remains today. A burgeoning commercial and residential suburbia grew up south of the walled city, and was itself enclosed by a wall in 1522. In this form the city survived through to the 1950s.

In the early Ming, relations with inner Asia were at an all-time low. Yongle had usurped power from his nephew and the civil war that this provoked left him looking overseas to establish his credentials as ruler. In 1405 he launched the first of seven great maritime expeditions. Led by the eunuch general Zheng He (1371–1433), the fleet consisted of more than 60 large vessels and 255 smaller ones, carrying nearly 28,000 men. The fourth and fifth expeditions departed in 1413 and 1417, and

www.eyewitnesstohistory.com/khan.htm has Marco Polo's eyewitness account of Kublai Khan's battle of 1287, as well as a brief history of the battle.

Kublai Khan's vast Mongol empire includes all of today's PRC

The Grand Canal is extended to Běijīng, assuming its familiar form

travelled as far as Aden, on the present Suez Canal. The great achievement of these voyages was to bring tribute missions to the capital, including two embassies from Egypt.

Retreat!

In 1439 a dramatic invasion by the Mongols resulted in the capture and year-long imprisonment of the then-emperor. The Ming reaction was to retreat into itself. The Great Wall was lengthened by 600 miles in the second half of the century, turning it into one of the great building feats of history. The coast, however, was more difficult to defend. In the middle of the 16th century the coastal provinces were harassed by pirate ships and their suppression took great effort.

Around this time, ships also arrived from Europe. The Ming allowed these foreigners to enter their domain, and in 1557 the Portuguese gained the right to establish a permanent trade base in Macau. Traders were quickly followed by missionaries and the Jesuits, led by the formidable Matteo Ricci, made their way inland and established a presence at court. There they made a great impression with their skills in astronomy and in casting canons.

DID YOU KNOW?

Emperor Jiajiang of the Ming dynasty kept over 1000 concubines. His treatment of them was notoriously cruel; over 200 died of abuse.

The Portuguese presence linked China directly to trade with the New World. New crops, such as potatoes and maize, were introduced and New World silver was used to pay for Chinese exports, like tea, porcelain and ceramics. Commerce via merchant banks became important, absentee landlordism and tenant farming became common, and urbanisation intensified.

A House of Cards

The Ming Government was undermined by the power eunuchs wielded at court and by struggles between officials. Strong emperors were needed to maintain order, but were few and far between. Zhu Houchao, ruler from 1505 to 1521, handed over matters of state to his chief eunuch so that he could devote his attention to his concubines. This was soon followed by the Tianqi reign (1621–28), a government dominated by the eunuch Wei Zhongxian (1568–1627), who purged officials and built temples in honour of himself.

Such poor leadership could not have happened at a worse time. North of the border, the Jurchen people were consolidated into a militarised state, and by the 1620s they were carrying out periodic raids, sometimes deep into Chinese territory. At the same time floods and drought devastated large areas of north China, encouraging banditry that swelled into rebellions.

The Manchu to the north had long been growing in power and looked with keen interest to the convulsions of rebellion in their huge neighbour. Taking advantage of the turmoil they saw, they launched an invasion, but were initially held back by the Great Wall. Eventually a Ming general let them pass, believing that an alliance with the Manchu was the only hope for defeating the peasant rebel armies that now threatened Běijīng itself.

In 1644 Běijīng fell, not to the Manchu but to the peasant rebel Li Zicheng, who sat on the throne for one day before fleeing from the Chinese troops who helped put a Manchu emperor in his place.

1368	1406
Chinese rule is restored with the Ming dynasty	Ming Emperor Yongle begins construction of the 800 buildings of the Forbidden City

HEAVY-HANDED: THE QING

The Manchu proclaimed their new dynasty the Qing (1644–1911), although it took them four decades to stamp out Ming loyalists in the south and pacify the entire country. This victory for the Qing came at great cost to the population with acts of severe brutality and massacre.

The Qing neutralised threats from inner Asia by incorporating their homeland of Manchuria into the empire as well as that of the Mongols, whom they had subordinated. Their cultural policy involved a careful balance of attention to the Chinese, Manchu, Mongols and Tibetans. They courted the literati via the examination system and great literary projects. Their own people were appointed to key positions in the bureaucracy, but matching positions were created for Chinese officials.

As an alien dynasty, the Qing remained keen to establish its own legitimacy. Chinese men were forced to wear their hair like the Manchustyle (shave the front and braid the back into a long tail), a look you'll quickly recognise as a sign of 'Chineseness' used in countless Western cartoons. Harsh censorship was practised during the 18th century, with a literary inquisition begun in the 1770s and cruel punishments inflicted on authors of works containing anti-Manchu sentiments. Despite such ideological control, scholarship flourished.

'the high plateau of Tibet was a cornerstone of Qing geopolitical strategy'

Women's Cultural Battleground

Women became a site of Chinese cultural resistance to Manchu rule. Chinese women continued to wear Chinese-style dress, with skirts worn over loose jackets and trousers, as opposed to the one-piece robe worn by Manchu women. Footbinding, in force from perhaps the 10th or 11th centuries, persisted despite Qing prohibitions. Chinese women remained devout to Chinese men, continuing to honour them through the practice of widow suicide. The Manchu showed considerable political skill in moving from opposition to endorsement of widow suicide, awarding honours to women who followed their husbands to the grave.

Tackling the Neighbours

Tibet was made a Chinese colony in 1751 and granted regional autonomy under the watchful eye of a Qing resident. Before this date it had many encounters with Běijīng; visit Lama Temple (p112) in Běijīng to learn more about this lopsided relationship. Although never fully integrated into the Chinese administrative system, the strategically important high plateau of Tibet was a cornerstone of Qing geopolitical strategy, particularly in the face of threats from the British and Russians.

Xīnjiāng, home to the Muslim Uighur, was also under special administrative control throughout much of the Qing dynasty. A great rebellion broke out in the 1870s, and was defeated only at enormous expense and cost to life on both sides. Regular provincial administration was established and Chinese people were settled within the Xīnjiāng borders.

Taiwan, home to a number of Austronesian peoples, had been colonised by the Dutch in the early 17th century and then occupied by the Ming loyalist Zheng Chenggong (Koxinga; 1624–62), who defeated the Dutch to make the island his base of resistance against the Manchu. The Manchu conquered Taiwan in 1683, and incorporated it into Fújiàn

1557	c 1640
The Portuguese establish a permanent trade base in Macau	The traditional *qípáo* becomes a fashionable frock for women

province. Garrison towns were constructed, evolving into walled cities that housed the Chinese officials dispatched to administer the territory. In 1872, after the island was briefly occupied by the Japanese, the Manchu made it into an independent province. In 1895 it was ceded to the Japanese as part of the settlement following the Sino-Japanese War of 1894. Nevertheless, the issue of its relationship with the mainland remains a lasting point of contention.

The population of the Qing more than doubled from the middle of the 17th century to reach around 350 million at the end of the 18th century. This may have been due to the introduction of New World crops, which could be grown in relatively harsh conditions, as well as increasingly efficient famine relief and flood control. A surge in population unsurprisingly led to increased pressure on resources, and land-hungry Han migrants headed west and south into lands of aboriginal peoples. With them went the Qing administration, which soon had ethnic conflict on its hands and, ultimately, rebellions. Suppressing these placed an enormous strain on the imperial treasury, contributing to the dynasty's downward spiral in the 19th century.

The Opium War & British Hong Kong

The early Qing emperors had shown a relatively open attitude towards Europeans in China, but this changed in the 18th century. Qianlong, ruler from 1736 to 1795, imposed strict controls on maritime trade, which from 1757 was limited to the single port of Guǎngzhōu.

Chinese exports well exceeded imports at Guǎngzhōu until Westerners hit upon the opium trade. Opium had long been a popular drug in China, but had been outlawed since the early 18th century. The Portuguese first discovered that there was profit to be made through opium, and began trading it between India and China. The British soon joined in. Stronger Chinese prohibitions against the use and sale of the drug followed, but were far from effective as many officials were opium addicts and therefore assisted in smuggling it into China. By the early 19th century the opium trade had grown to the point of shifting the balance in trade in favour of the Westerners.

In March 1839 Lin Zexiu, an official of great personal integrity, was dispatched to Guǎngzhōu to put a stop to the illegal traffic once and for all. He acted promptly, demanding and eventually getting some 20,000 chests of opium stored by the British in Guǎngzhōu. The British believed they were due compensation and, without it, had the pretext for military action. In 1840 a British naval force assembled in Macau and moved up the coast to Běi He, not far from Běijīng. The Opium War was on.

The emperor watched with mild distress and authorised a negotiation that managed to fob off the first British force with a treaty that neither side ended up recognising. This increased British frustration, leading to an attack on Chinese positions close to Guǎngzhōu.

A second treaty was drawn up, ceding Hong Kong to the British, and calling for indemnities of Y6,000,000 and the full resumption of trade. The furious Qing emperor refused to recognise the treaty, and in 1841 British forces once again headed up the coast, taking Fújiàn and eastern Zhèjiāng. In the spring of 1842 an army inflated with reinforcements moved up

1644	1751
Conquerors from Manchuria establish the Qing dynasty	Tibet is made a Chinese colony

Yangzi River. With British guns trained on Nánjīng, the Qing fighting spirit evaporated and they reluctantly signed the humiliating Treaty of Nanking. This left Hong Kong in the hands of the British 'in perpetuity'.

In 1898 the New Territories adjoining Kowloon were 'leased' to the British for 99 years and the British agreed to hand the entire colony back to China when the lease on the New Territories expired. For more details on the handover, see p493.

Christ's Kid Brother?

By the 19th century the increased presence of missionaries had fuelled hatred against 'foreign devils', leading to further rebellion throughout the provinces (see Boxed Up, opposite).

Also at this time, the Taiping Rebellion erupted in 1850 in the southern province of Guǎngxī, and commanded forces of 600,000 men and 500,000 women as it raged through central and eastern China. The Taipings owed much of their ideology to Christianity. Its leader was Hong Xiuquan, a failed examination candidate from Guǎngdōng province whose encounters with Western missionaries had led him to believe he was the younger brother of Jesus Christ. The Taipings forbade gambling, opium, tobacco and alcohol, advocated agricultural reform, and outlawed foot binding for women, prostitution and slavery. The rebellion took tens of millions of lives before being suppressed in 1864 by a coalition of Qing and Western forces – the Europeans preferring to deal with a corrupt and weak Qing government rather than a powerful, united China governed by the Taipings.

The Second Opium War

With Hong Kong in the hands of the British following the first Opium War, official trade was diverted to Shànghǎi. This left Hong Kong's economy in dire straits. With the attention of the Qing court focused on the Taiping Rebellion, the foreign powers struck again. The Anglo-French expedition of 1856 to 1860, sometimes called the Second Opium War, ended with the occupation of Běijīng and the flight of the court to Jehol in the Manchurian homeland. The final outcome was the Treaty

---

DRAGON WOMAN

Like many other Qing dynasty teenagers, at the age of 15, Cixi (1835–1908) gave up her true love to become one of Emperor Xianfeng's concubines. Her cunningness and intelligence soon made her a favourite of the emperor, particularly after she gave birth to his only son in 1856. Cixi's subsequent rise to power was largely due to the convenient deaths of her adversaries. Xianfeng died at the age of 30 and his empress followed suit a few years later. This made Cixi's five-year-old son, Tongzhi, the new emperor, and Cixi herself the ruling Dowager Empress.

Cixi held onto the government reins for over 40 years in total, galloping over anyone who got in her way – including her own son and Emperor Guangxu whom she replaced him with. Other opponents were slowly starved, thrown down wells or locked away. She spent her reign focusing on her own position rather than the country's; at the end of her life she left nine storerooms of personal treasures, a refurbished Summer Palace and the Qing dynasty in an irreparable state of decline. To see one of her more ridiculous 'achievements', take a gander at the marble boat in Běijīng's Summer Palace (p117).

1839	1842
The British hand over 20,000 chests of opium to Chinese officials, the pretext for the Opium Wars	Hong Kong is ceded to the British in perpetuity

100 DAYS REFORMS

A visionary reformer, Kang Youwei (1858–1927) became a key adviser to the Qing emperor following China's disastrous war with Japan. The result was the famous '100 Days Reforms' of 1898, which were expected to set China on the modernising path already taken by Japan. Reforms to the bureaucracy and examination system were proposed, as well as social reforms like the abolition of foot binding. Sadly, '100 Days' ended with a palace coup staged by the supposedly retired Dowager Empress Cixi, the house arrest of the Emperor Guangxu, the execution of some reformist activists and the flight of others, including Kang.

of Tianjin, which opened further Treaty ports and established a regular diplomatic corps in Běijīng. At the same time further massive rebellions were brewing: the Nian in central north China, the Panthay in Yúnnán and the Donggan in the northwest.

Bringing Home the Enemy

In the second half of the 19th century China sent embassies and students to the West. The goal was to pick up pointers from the enemy on how to strengthen Chinese military technology and industrial development. The Treaty-port cities, especially Shànghǎi, became the face of modernisation in China. Factories, banks, newspapers, new-style schools, bicycles, trains, and eventually motor cars, trade unions, chambers of commerce and political parties all made their appearance. In Shànghǎi, land conceded to Western nations quickly outgrew the old city. The unique architecture and atmosphere of the old French Concession makes it worth a wander even today (p278).

In the late 1890s China was in danger of being 'cut up like a melon, divided like a bean', as further leases of land and spheres of influence were ceded to the foreign powers. The Western powers were soon joined by the Japanese who, after a small scrap on Korean soil with Chinese forces, were ceded Taiwan in 1895. The same treaty granted the Japanese (and thereby other foreign powers) the right to construct their own factories in Shànghǎi. In 1898 Germany gained a lease in Qìngdǎo after Lutheran missionaries were murdered inland. They commenced building a railway that became the focus of protests by local people upset at the disturbance of feng shui. You'll still find a certain 'Germanness' in the air when you visit Qìngdǎo, likely to be emanating from the leftover brewery (p208).

BOXED UP

Culled from secret societies, the Boxers were a xenophobic group who erupted in rebellion at the end of the 19th century with violent attacks on missionaries and their families. Tired of the foreigners themselves, the Qing Court decided to support the Boxers. Armed with this backing and with charms and martial-arts techniques that they believed made them impervious to Western bullets, the Boxers began massacring foreigners at random and the famous 50-day siege of Běijīng's Foreign Legations began. It wasn't long before Western allies landed, handed the Qing Court a crippling foreign debt and knocked the Boxers down for the count.

1850	1908
The Taiping Rebellion erupts with unfulfilled hopes of installing a Christian ideology in China	Two-year-old Puyi ascends the throne as China's last Emperor

The Fall of the Qing

In 1908 the Dowager Empress died and two-year-old Emperor Puyi ascended to the throne. The Qing was now rudderless and teetered on the brink of collapse.

A modern classic, *The Last Emperor* (1988) is the tragic story of Puyi, China's final emperor who ascended the throne at age three. Although it's rather slow-paced, this film boasts great cinematography and is well worth it if you have a few hours to spare.

As an increasing number of new railways were financed and built by foreigners, public anger grew and gave birth to the Railway Protection Movement that spread and took on an anti-Qing nature. The movement turned increasingly violent, especially in Sìchuān, and troops were taken from Wǔhàn to quell the disturbances.

As it happened, republican revolutionaries in Wǔhàn were already planning an uprising. With troops dispensed to Sìchuān, they seized the opportunity and were able to not only take control of Wǔhàn, but to ride on the back of the large-scale Railway Protection uprisings to victory all over China.

Two months later representatives from 17 provinces throughout China gathered in Nánjīng to establish the Provisional Republican Government of China. China's long dynastic cycle had come to an end.

EARLY DAYS OF THE REPUBLIC

The Provisional Republican Government was set up on 10 October 1911 by Sun Yatsen (1866–1925). Educated in Hawaii and Hong Kong, a Christian and trained medical practitioner, Sun developed a political programme based on the 'Three Principles of the People': nationalism, popular sovereignty and livelihood. In 1895 his 'Revive China Society' initiated one of the country's first republican uprisings, after which Sun fled to Japan and on to Europe. Determined to arrest and execute him, Qing authorities hunted Sun down in London, where they kidnapped him and held him in the Chinese embassy. Sun managed to sneak out a message to one of his teachers who, in turn, alerted the British Government. The Chinese embassy was forced to release their prisoner.

Sun went on to build backing for the revolution he dreamt for China. Supporters from Chinese communities abroad, as well as among disaffected members of the Qing army, grew in number. When his revolutionist followers began their campaign for victory in Wǔhàn, Sun watched from abroad. It wasn't until the meeting in Nánjīng and the establishment of the Provisional Republic of China that Sun returned to his homeland to be named president.

Lacking the power to force a Manchu abdication, Sun had no choice but to call on the assistance of Yuan Shikai, the head of the imperial army, and the same man that the Manchu had called on to put down the republican uprisings. The republicans promised Yuan Shikai the presidency if he could negotiate the abdication of the emperor, which he achieved. The favour cost the republicans dearly. Yuan Shikai placed himself at the head of the republican movement and forced Sun Yatsen to stand down.

Yuan lost no time in dissolving the Provisional Republican Government and amending the constitution to make himself president for life. When this met with regional opposition, he took the natural next step in 1915 of pronouncing himself China's latest emperor. Yúnnán seceded, taking Guǎngxī, Guìzhōu and much of the rest of the south with it. Forces

1911–16	1927
Dynastic rule comes to an end with Sun Yatsen's Republican Government	Chiang Kaishek's Kuomintang massacre over 5000 communists in Shànghǎi

were sent to bring the breakaway provinces back into the imperial ambit, and in the midst of it all, Yuan died.

Between 1916 and 1927 the government in Běijīng lost power over the far-flung provinces and China was effectively fragmented into semi-autonomous regions governed by warlords. Nevertheless, Sun's labour had not been in vain. On 4 May 1919 large demonstrations took place outside the Gate of Heavenly Peace (p106) in Běijīng following the decision of the Allies to pass defeated Germany's rights in Shāndōng over to Japan. This surge of nationalist sentiment in China began a movement that was rooted in Sun's earlier revolution and paved the way for the changes that were to come.

KUOMINTANG & COMMUNISTS

By 1920 the Kuomintang (KMT; Nationalist Party), had emerged as the dominant political force in eastern China. Its main opposition was the Chinese Communist Party (CCP), made up of Chinese Marxist groups who had joined together in 1921. While the two groups were on far from friendly terms, it was decided that it was in their best interests to unite against the Japanese who looked poised to expand into northeastern China.

The union was short-lived. After Sun Yatsen's death in 1925 a power struggle emerged in the Kuomintang between those sympathetic to the communists and those who favoured a capitalist state supported by a military dictatorship. The latter group was headed by Chiang Kaishek (1887–1975).

In 1926 Chiang Kaishek attempted to grind the growing influence of communists to a halt by expanding his own power base. He attempted this first through a Northern Expedition that set out to wring power from the remaining warlords. The following year he took more direct action, ordering the massacre of over 5000 Shànghǎi communists and trade union representatives.

By the middle of 1928 the Northern Expedition had reached Běijīng, and a national government was established with Chiang holding both military and political leadership. Nevertheless, only about half of the country was under the direct control of the Kuomintang; the rest was still ruled by local warlords.

At this time China was heavily laden with social problems: child slave labour in factories; domestic slavery and prostitution; the destitute starving in the streets; and strikes ruthlessly suppressed by foreign and Chinese factory owners. The communists proposed solutions to these problems, namely the removal of the Kuomintang. Not surprisingly, Chiang became obsessed with stamping out the influence of the communists.

Grassroots Rebellion

After the massacre of 1927, the communists became divided in their views of where to base their rebellion – on large urban centres or in the countryside. After costly defeats in Nánchāng and Chángshā, the tide of opinion started to shift towards Mao Zedong (1893–1976, p483), who advocated rural-based revolt.

Communist-led uprisings in other parts of the country met with some success; however, the communist armies remained small and hampered by limited resources. It wasn't until 1930 that the ragged communist

The Private Life of Chairman Mao, by Li Zhisui, is a fascinating and intimate (if somewhat disturbing) look into the world of this historical giant. Li was Mao's personal physician for 22 years and tells us everything from Mao's sexual habits to his political views.

1935	1937
Mao Zedong is recognised as head of the communists in a meeting at Zūnyì	The Japanese invade China

forces had turned into an army of perhaps 40,000, which presented such a serious challenge to the Kuomintang that Chiang waged extermination campaigns against them. He was defeated each time, and the communist army continued to expand its territory.

The Long March(es)

Chiang's fifth extermination campaign began in October 1933. Many of the communist troupes had begun disregarding Mao's authority and instead took the advice of those who advocated meeting Chiang's troops in pitched battles. This strategy proved disastrous. By October 1934 the communists had suffered heavy losses and were hemmed into a small area in Jiāngxī. On the brink of defeat, the communists decided to retreat from Jiāngxī and march north to Shaanxi to join up with other communist armies in Shaanxi, Gānsù and Níngxià.

Red Star Over China, by Edgar Snow, is a journalist's first-hand perspective of China in the early days of the Communist Revolution. His portrayal of Mao may seem overly sympathetic, but Snow does consider the situation from a number of perspectives.

Rather than one long march, there were several, as various communist armies in the south made their way to Shaanxi. The most famous (and commonly referred to as *the* Long March) was from Jiāngxī province. Beginning in October 1934, it took a year to complete and covered 8000km over some of the world's most inhospitable terrain. On the way the communists confiscated the property of officials, landlords and tax-collectors, and redistributed land to the peasants whom they armed by the thousands with weapons captured from the Kuomintang. Soldiers were left behind to organise guerrilla groups to harass the enemy. Of the 90,000 people who started out in Jiāngxī, only 20,000 made it to Shaanxi. Fatigue, sickness, exposure, enemy attacks and desertion all took their toll.

The march brought together many people who held top positions after 1949, including Mao Zedong, Zhou Enlai, Zhu De, Lin Biao, Deng Xiaoping and Liu Shaoqi. It also established Mao as the paramount leader of the Chinese communist movement. En route, the posse took a breather in Zūnyì (p628), Guìzhōu; if you're in the neighbourhood, you can take in some of the sights. Serious Long March history buffs might also check out Lúdìng (p738) in Sìchuān.

Japanese Invasion

All the internal upheaval going on in China gave the Japanese the moment they'd been waiting for. In September 1931 they invaded and occupied Manchuria, setting up a puppet state with Puyi, the last Manchu emperor. (Check out his digs and one of the settings for Bertolucci's film *The Last Emperor* in Chángchūn, p365.) Chiang, still obsessed with the threat of the communists, did nothing to resist Japan's invasion and instead focused on his fifth extermination drive. The Kuomintang was bitterly criticised for not defending against the Japanese.

In particular, Manchurian General Zhang Xueliang (1898–2001) was not impressed. In 1936 he kidnapped President Chiang Kaishek and forced him to agree to a Second United Front with the CCP to resist Japan. Zhang, hero of the hour, later surrendered to the Kuomintang and spent the next half-century under house arrest in China and then in Taiwan. He was eventually released after Chiang Kaishek's death in 1975.

The rest of China was invaded by Japan in the middle of 1937. The Nánjīng massacre of 1937 (p225), human experiments in biological

1949	1957
The communist PRC is established	Mao weeds out 'rightist' intellects through the 100 Flowers Campaign

warfare factories in Hāěrbīn (p381) and 'burn all, loot all, kill all' campaigns quickly made it one of the most brutal occupations of the 20th century. China experienced massive internal migrations, and was subjected to a process of divide and rule through the establishment of puppet governments.

The Kuomintang was forced into retreat by the Japanese occupation. Its wartime capital was Chóngqìng (p757), a higgledy-piggledy town piled up on mountains in the upper reaches of Yangzi River. The city was subjected to heavy Japanese bombardments, but logistical difficulties prevented it from being approached by land.

Civil War

Following Japan's defeat and the end of WWII, the USA attempted unsuccessfully to negotiate a settlement between the CCP and the Kuomintang. The CCP had expanded enormously during the war years, filling a vacuum in local government in vast areas behind and beyond Japanese lines, and creating a base from which it would successfully challenge the Kuomintang's claims to legitimacy.

Civil war broke out in 1946. While their base at Yán'ān (p423) was destroyed by the Nationalists, Communist forces managed to outmanoeuvre the Kuomintang on the battle ground of Manchuria. Three great battles were fought in 1948 and 1949 in which the Kuomintang were not only defeated, but thousands of Kuomintang troops defected to the communists. The USA, which had lost its wartime hero status and become an object of popular vilification in China, was dismayed by the failure of the Kuomintang and refused it further support. Meanwhile, the Soviet Union played a two-faced game of alliances in the early post-war period, recognising the Nationalist government, but eventually facilitating CCP ambitions.

In Běijīng on 1 October 1949 Mao Zedong proclaimed the foundation of the People's Republic of China (PRC, Zhōnghuá Rénmín Gònghéguó). Chiang Kaishek fled to the island of Formosa (Taiwan), taking with him the entire gold reserves of the country, and what was left of his air force and navy. To prevent an attack from the mainland, President Truman ordered a protective US naval blockade.

www.chinaknowledge.de/History/history.htm has in-depth coverage of China's various dynasties and eras, with links to more specific information on everything from the religion to the technology to the economy of each period.

THE PEOPLE'S REPUBLIC OF CHINA

The PRC began its days as a bankrupt nation. Unbridled inflation and a Kuomintang legacy of economic mismanagement left the economy in chaos. The country had just 19,200km of railways and 76,800km of useable roads – all in bad condition. Irrigation works had broken down, and livestock and animal populations were dwindling. Agricultural output plummeted and industrial production was half that of the prewar period.

With the communist takeover, China seemed to become a different country. Unified by the elation of victory and the immensity of the task before them, and further bonded by the Korean War and the necessity to defend the new regime from possible US invasion, the communists made the 1950s a dynamic period. They embarked upon land reform, recognised the role of women and attempted to restore the economy.

1958–60	1966
The Great Leap Forward causes mass starvation	The birth of the Red Guards and the Cultural Revolution

By 1953 inflation had been halted, industrial production was back to prewar levels, and land had been confiscated from landlords and redistributed to the peasants. On the basis of earlier Soviet models, the Chinese embarked on a massive five-year plan that was fairly successful in lifting production.

At the same time the CCP increased its social control by organising the people according to their work units *(dānwèi)*, and dividing the country into 21 provinces, five autonomous regions and two municipalities (Běijīng and Shànghǎi). Around 2200 county governments held jurisdiction over nearly one million party sub-branches.

A Hundred Flowers

Behind the PRC's rapid economic development lingered immense social problems. Many Kuomintang intellectuals had stayed on rather than flee to Taiwan, and still more overseas Chinese, many of them highly qualified, returned to China soon after its 'liberation' to help in the enormous task of reconstruction. Returning Chinese and those of suspect backgrounds were given extensive re-education courses in special universities. Meanwhile, writers, artists and film-makers were subject to strict ideological controls guided by Mao's writings on art.

In the upper levels of the party, opinions were divided as to how to deal with these intellectuals and artists. Mao proposed 'letting a hundred flowers bloom' in the arts and 'a hundred schools of thought contend' in the sciences by welcoming open criticism.

In 1957 intellectuals around the country responded with glee. Complaints poured in on everything from party corruption to control of artistic expression, from the unavailability of foreign literature to low standards of living; but most of all, criticisms focused on the CCP monopoly on power and the abuses that went with it.

Either the party had second thoughts about the critique or, as many now believe, the campaign was a trap to 'weed out' rightists. An anti-rightist campaign was launched and within six months 300,000 intellectuals had been branded rightists, removed from their jobs and, in many cases, incarcerated or sent to labour camps for thought reform. Some would stay in these camps for up to 20 years.

To Live (1994) follows one family through the Communist Revolution, the Great Leap Forward and the Cultural Revolution, depicting how these monumental upheavals affected the average Chinese citizen. Made in China, but later banned, this film is interesting for its Chinese perspective on historical events.

The Great Leap Forward

China's agricultural output continued to lag and, as urban populations burgeoned around industrialised areas, the question of how to feed the people grew increasingly urgent.

China embarked on the Great Leap Forward (1958–60), one of the greatest failed economic experiments in human history. A radical programme was initiated to create massive agricultural communes, drawing large numbers of people from the country and urban areas into enormous water control and irrigation projects. In Mao's view, revolutionary zeal and mass cooperative effort could overcome any obstacle and transform the Chinese landscape into a productive paradise.

The communists tried to abolish money and all private property, and told everyone to build backyard blast furnaces to increase steel production. Lacking iron ore, peasants had to melt down farm tools, pots and

1971	1976
The US Ping-Pong team becomes the first American delegation to set foot in China in 49 years; Nixon soon follows	Mao Zedong dies, aged 83

doorknobs to meet their quota of steel 'production'. The villages later discovered that the steel produced was basically worthless.

Despite the enthusiastic forecasts for agricultural production, there remained little incentive to work in the fields. Large numbers of rural workers engaged in the worthless blast furnace projects, resulting in a massive slump in grain output. Bad weather in 1959 and the withdrawal of Soviet aid in 1960 made matters worse.

All effort was made to cover up the ensuing disaster and so no foreign assistance was sought. China plunged into a famine of staggering proportions – an estimated 30 million Chinese starved to death (some put the figure at 60 million). The enormous failure of the Great Leap Forward led Mao to resign as head of state, although he remained Chairman of the Communist Party.

Sino-Soviet Split

Mao watched in horror as the USSR developed a policy of peaceful co-existence with the USA. Khrushchev's de-Stalinisation speech and what Mao saw as growing moderation in the Soviet leadership did nothing to mend Mao's increasingly frosty view of his neighbours. When Khrushchev refused to provide China with the promised prototype atomic bomb and sided with the Indians in a Sino-Indian border dispute, Sino-Soviet relations hit a low. In 1960 the Soviets brought their foreign experts home from China.

The Cultural Revolution

Mao's extreme views, his recent disastrous policy decisions and his opposition to bureaucratisation led to his increasing isolation within the party. To get back into the limelight of leadership, he set about cultivating a personality cult. His right-hand man was Lin Biao, the minister of defence and head of the People's Liberation Army (PLA). He was also supported by Yao Wenyuan, Wang Hongwen, Zhang Chunqiao and Jiang Qing (Mao's wife). Together they became known as 'the Gang of Four'.

In the early 1960s Lin compiled a collection of Mao's selected thoughts into the 'little red book'. Studied by PLA troops and introduced into the general education system, this was to become one of the symbols of the era; you can still find well-used copies for sale in markets throughout the country.

In 1966 a play was released that criticised Mao. The purge of the arts that followed was the springboard for the Cultural Revolution (Wénhuà Dàgémìng; 1966–70). Sanctioned by Mao, wall posters went up at Beijing University attacking the university administration and criticising Mao's opposition within the CCP. Before long students were being issued red armbands and taking to the streets. The Red Guards (Hóngwèibīng) had been born. By August 1966 Mao was reviewing mass parades of the Red Guards in Tiananmen Square (p104), chanting and waving copies of his little red book.

Nothing was sacred in the brutal onslaught of the Red Guards as they went on a rampage through the country. Schools were shut down; intellectuals, writers and artists were dismissed, killed, persecuted or sent to labour in the countryside; scientific, artistic, literary and cultural publications

Wild Swans by Jung Chang offers a backdoor view into Chinese history, following three generations of women from the final days of Imperialism to post–Cultural Revolution China.

1980	1987
The one-child policy is enforced	*The Last Emperor*, filmed in the Forbidden City, takes the Oscar for Best Picture

ceased; and temples were ransacked and monasteries disbanded. Physical reminders of China's 'feudal', 'exploitative' or 'capitalist' past – everything from monuments to musical instruments – were destroyed.

Sometimes for fear of being accused themselves, neighbours and even family members began to turn on one another in search of 'capitalist roaders'. Millions of people are estimated to have died in these years through beatings, executions, suicide or denial of medical care. Violence, social disorder and economic upheaval were rife. The 'four olds' – old customs, old habits, old culture and old thinking – were all to be eliminated. Gender equality was promoted, but there was little room for personal life. Families were split up; sex and romance were frowned upon. Dress codes were as strict as under the most rigid religious regime with the blue 'Mao suit'.

For Mao, the Cultural Revolution succeeded in establishing his power and in supplanting President Liu Shaoqi and party Secretary-General Deng Xiaoping. Liu Shaoqi died in prison in 1969, a fact concealed from the public till 1979. Lin Biao plotted a coup in 1971, was exposed, and died in a mysterious plane crash over Mongolia.

Much of China's present population are survivors of the Cultural Revolution; be mindful if discussing this period of China's history with them as few went untouched by the difficulties and horrors of the time.

Stephen Haw squeezes a very concise and readable account of China's past into 300 pages in *A Traveller's History of China*.

Post-Cultural Revolution Years

Some measure of political stability returned during the years immediately following the Cultural Revolution. Zhou Enlai, who had supported Mao from the sidelines, exercised the most influence in the day-to-day governing of China. Among other things, he worked towards restoring China's trade and diplomatic contacts with the outside world. In the 1970s China was admitted into the UN, re-establishing formal diplomatic relations with the USA in 1979.

In 1973 Deng Xiaoping, vilified as China's 'No 2 Capitalist Roader' during the Cultural Revolution, returned to power as Deputy Premier. Nevertheless, Běijīng politics remained factional and divided. On the one side was Zhou, Deng and a faction of 'moderates' or 'pragmatists', and on the other were the 'radicals', 'leftists' or 'Maoists' led by Jiang Qing. As Zhou's health declined, the radicals gradually gained the upper hand.

During this period Mao was watching from the wings. He'd been sick for many years and was diagnosed with Lou Gehrig's disease, an extremely rare motor-neuron disorder that left him dead by September 1976. The official line soon surfaced that Mao was 70% right and just 30% wrong in his leadership of the country.

Premier Zhou Enlai died in January 1976, and in April a crowd of mourners in Tiananmen Square erupted into a demonstration that was violently suppressed. Deng fell under attack again from Madame Mao and disappeared from public view as Hua Guofeng, Mao's chosen and groomed protégé, was made acting premier. When the Gang of Four announced their opposition to Hua, he had them arrested. Celebrations took place throughout China. When the Gang finally came to trial in 1980, the blame for the entire Cultural Revolution fell on their shoulders. Jiang Qing's death sentence was commuted and she lived under house arrest until 1991, when she committed suicide by hanging.

1989	1997
Hundreds of pro-democracy protesters are killed by Chinese troops in Tiananmen Square	Britain hands Hong Kong over to the PRC

POST-MAO CHINA

The final two decades of the 20th century saw the totalitarian practices of the communist government significantly modified. In the middle of 1977 Deng Xiaoping returned to power for the third time as vice-premier, vice-chairman of the party and chief of staff. Through his 'Four Modernisations' programme (agriculture, industry, science and defence), China increased its contact with the capitalist economies of the West.

In 1980 the one-child policy was embraced; while the Chinese Government claims that it has slowed the population growth, its success has been hotly debated outside the country. Also during this period Special Economic Zones were established along China's coast, while in rural China the 'Responsibility System' allowed people to sell their agricultural surpluses on the open market.

Tiananmen Square

As China began to open up to the West, the party began to lose its ideological grip. By 1978 demands were heard for a 'fifth modernisation': democracy. In 1986 demonstrations took place in a number of major cities with further demands for political reforms and press freedoms.

Party Secretary-General Hu Yaobang was sidelined within the party for his support for some of these demands. The mass memorial following his death in 1989 turned into a popular, peaceful rebellion. Workers and hundreds of thousands of students gathered in Tiananmen Square

---

PICKLED MAO

On the eve of 8 September 1976 the ruling Politburo had an important decision to make. Mao Zedong had passed away and something had to be done with his body. While pickling doesn't immediately come to mind, China's leaders looked to Russia and Vietnam where Lenin and Ho Chi Minh's bodies laid well preserved. Mao's personal doctor, Li Zhisui, was somewhat anxious with his task at hand. Unsure as to how well his first attempt at 'preservation in perpetuity' would go, he had a wax replica of Mao constructed as backup.

Mao in all of his formaldehyde glory went on display in Tiananmen Square one year later. His mausoleum was built by workers and with supplies from each of the provinces, a symbolic show of the spread of Mao's supremacy throughout the country. Inside, Mao's glass-topped casket lies upon a black stone from Tài Shān as a reminder of an infamous Chinese quote from Sima Qian, 'One's life can be weightier than Mt Tai or lighter than a goose feather'. Each evening the casket is lowered into a refrigerator where it rests alongside the wax version, leaving many visitors to wonder which Mao they are actually viewing.

In February 2004, six Chinese scholars drafted a proposal asking authorities to remove the corpse from display and bury it in Mao's hometown of Sháoshān in Húnán. They claimed that to worship the corpse of a ruler is a display of a 'slave-based society' and that a body returning to dust in the ground is part of Chinese tradition. Their main concern, however, seems to be the world gaze that will be falling upon Běijīng with the 2008 Olympics. They want the ghoulish exhibition gone in order for the city to appear 'civilised' and 'worthy of hosting the games'. Others claim that the mausoleum ruins the feng shui of Tiananmen Square.

Mao himself wanted to be cremated. But whether the wishes of the Chairman himself will be honoured or whether he'll retain his symbolic place of pickled reverence is in the hands of the Politburo gods.

---

to press ever-escalating demands for political reform on the beleaguered party leadership. To the horror of the Western world, Deng Xiaoping sanctioned the forcible dispersal of the demonstrators. Hundreds were killed as the tanks of crack troops rolled into the square.

This was the death knell of socialist ideology in China. Since then the party has relied mainly on patriotism or nationalism for ideology. There has been a flowering of new cults, which the party eyes suspiciously – most notably Falun Gong. In 1999 Tiananmen Square was in world headlines again when thousands of Falun Gong practitioners gathered in solidarity. Freedom of religion and the fate of Falun Gong prisoners in China are among the many human-rights issues regularly raised by international rights organisations.

While China's official doctrine is communist, its leaders continue on in a totalitarian manner, all the while pushing modernisation through capitalism. In 1993 Deng Xiaoping frankly proclaimed that 'to get rich is glorious' as the government began to trim down state-owned industries, leading to mass unemployment.

THE 21ST CENTURY

With the dawning of the 21st century, President Jiang Zemin claimed popular success in playing the world stage. He presided over the return of Hong Kong and Macau to the motherland, spoke up to US president Bill Clinton on national TV, guided Běijīng to success in the Olympics bid for 2008 and oversaw the admission of China into the World Trade Organization (WTO). Nevertheless, China's economic picture remained at best hazy as Jiang pinned all of his hopes on the WTO. Critics believe that Jiang's hesitancy to reform state enterprises at a faster rate and unwillingness to nurture the private sector has sent China speeding towards a crisis point. Protests involving more than 10,000 people became increasingly widespread throughout the country and high taxes, levied by corrupt officials, led to a number of officials being killed.

In 2003 Hu Jintao took over presidency. Groomed to take the seat of power since the early 1990s, Hu is China's first modern leader to come into the communist fold post-1949. While some have high hopes that Hu is a reformer, others are quick to point out his strong party loyalty, particularly his belief in unbending controls over political opposition.

Externally, the government has had to contend with international critiques of China's human-rights record, rivalry with Japan for Asian leadership, and rejection of its claims to sovereignty over Taiwan and Tibet. The democratisation of Taiwan has created particular anxiety. In 1996 the Chinese conducted missile tests across the Taiwan Strait just before the first full elections on the island.

The turbulent story of China continues full steam ahead…

2003	2008
Běijīng introduces an anti-spitting law	Běijīng to host the 2008 Summer Olympic Games

The Culture

THE NATIONAL PSYCHE

Many travellers are surprised when they visit China at the energy and optimism of a people that has experienced tremendous social and economic upheaval over the past century. Despite political and economic uncertainties, most Chinese are excited about the rapid modernisation taking place in their country and look forward to the future. With Běijīng set to host the Olympics in 2008, the Chinese are eager to introduce their long-standing cultural traditions to the world and be accepted as a modern, progressive nation.

Chinese society, generally speaking, is based on the concept of *guānxì*. To get through difficult times, the Chinese rely on a tight network of family and friends for assistance and support. To get something done, it's often easier to 'go through a back door' *(zǒu hòu mén),* rather than through official channels. If a favour is offered, the receiver is obligated to return the favour sometime in the future. This keeps the *guānxì* system running smoothly.

Another concern of visitors is the concept of 'face', which is intimidating to many foreigners. In reality, the idea of face is very simple. All it means is not behaving in a way that would embarrass someone and cause them to lose status in front of their peers. One sure way for foreigners to make someone lose face in China is to lose their temper in public. Not only will the person targeted lose face, the foreigner loses face as well for being weak and unable to control their emotions. The Chinese pride themselves on self-control and when flustered or embarrassed will often giggle or give an evasive response, rather than deal with the situation directly. Of course, this does not mean the Chinese don't get angry, but the general rule is that self-control in dealing with people goes a long way.

Despite language barriers, most foreigners will find themselves regularly meeting locals who are eager to strike up a conversation and, for many, practise their English. Once the initial ice has been broken, many foreigners will be faced with a barrage of questions regarding their age, marital status and career. This is mere friendliness on the part of the interlocutor and not meant to be nosy. It's a good idea to travel with some pictures of your family or some postcards from your hometown. These make great items for conversation and will probably win you a few friends.

In some rural areas, foreigners remain an exotic curiosity and will be greeted with stares, giggles and a chorus of 'hellos' that can irritate even the most tough-skinned of travellers. Generally, this behaviour is not mean-spirited but it can be very unsettling, especially if you are travelling alone. Some travellers respond with a simple wave and smile, others ignore the behaviour. Most definitely, getting angry doesn't help – it's likely your Chinese audience will have no idea why you are getting angry and fits of temper will inevitably create more excitement and draw larger crowds.

The lack of privacy is perhaps one of the most disconcerting things about a visit to China. Most Chinese grow up in small apartments in crowded conditions and are not accustomed to Western standards of privacy. This applies to trains, buses, tourist sites and even toilets. Old-style Chinese toilets rarely have doors and are often separated by low partitions, making it easy to strike up a conversation with the person

DID YOU KNOW?

A Chinese man holds the world record for the heaviest weight (49.5kg) lifted with an ear.

squatting next to you. In major cities, many of these types of toilets have been replaced with private stalls (with doors), though they are still common in less developed places as well as bus and train stations.

China is a vast country with many regional differences and you'll find that the behaviour of the Chinese may differ from place to place, according to custom and exposure to the outside world. This is especially true in the countryside, which can offer a remarkably different view of China than that which can be seen in the cities. Travellers will come away amazed at the diversity of people and places they have encountered.

LIFESTYLE

Chinese culture is traditionally centred on the family, which was once considered a microcosm of society as a whole. In past Chinese society, the family provided support for every family member, including livelihood and long-term security. Extended family remains exceedingly important, with grandparents commonly acting as caretakers for grandchildren with adult children working and financially supporting their ageing parents.

The end of cradle-to-grave welfare (the 'iron rice bowl') has brought increasing pressure on families who struggle to meet the rising costs of health care and education. Economic pressures have had an impact on many young Chinese who are putting off marriage or having children until they've acquired enough money to ensure their financial security. It's estimated that today 14% of Chinese urban households consist of a single adult or childless couple who both work.

The rapid development of the 1990s has raised the standard of living for many Chinese, who now face a dazzling array of choices in consumer items and experience a lifestyle very different from earlier generations. Unfortunately, recent educational and economic opportunities are only available to a small segment of the population. The majority of Chinese live in the countryside, shut off from the benefits of China's economic reforms.

The growing gap between China's rich and poor is one of the worst in the world. City dwellers earn 2.8% more than those living in rural areas and receive subsidised health care and welfare while rural residents do not. The rural communities in inland China are the most poverty stricken, but those on the investment-laden east coast fare better. In the interior provinces, farmers eke out a meagre living growing just enough vegetables and rice to feed their own families but little to sell on the market. To make things worse, epidemics such as AIDS have hit inland

> 'City dwellers earn 2.8% more than those living in rural areas'

ETIQUETTE DO'S & DON'TS

- When beckoning to someone, wave them over to you with your palm down, motioning to yourself.
- If someone gives a gift, put it aside to open later to avoid appearing greedy.
- Never write anything in red ink unless you're correcting an exam. Red ink is used for letters of protest.
- Don't give clocks as gifts. The phrase 'to give a clock' in Mandarin sounds too much like 'attend a funeral'.
- Always take your shoes off when entering a Chinese home.
- When meeting a Chinese family, greet the eldest person first as a sign of respect.
- Always present things to people with both hands, showing that what you are offering is the fullest extent of yourself.

provinces especially hard. Many farmers have sold their blood to unscrupulous 'blood brokers', who collect the blood using unsanitary methods and pass the AIDS virus to donors and recipients.

There are few government programmes in place to help rural towns and villages, where farmers are expected to pay for their own health care and the education of their children. This unequal treatment has spurred many rural families to move to the cities to try and find work, where they often find low-paying jobs in unsafe conditions. The government has promised to address these devastating trends, but few incentives have been put in place.

While all of this sounds pretty bleak, development has also had some positive effects. With an increasingly open society, and with more exposure to the outside world, the Chinese are finding new forms of self-expression that were previously frowned upon by the communist authorities. Artists and writers are freeing themselves from earlier political restraints, contributing to a burgeoning literary and art scene that has been stifled for many years. Censorship is still common, though what defines something as 'taboo' or 'off limits' can be arbitrary.

Though Chinese women suffer from low political representation and strict family policies (see China's One-Child Policy, p54), the women's movement has made considerable progress. The Marriage Law of 2001 gives victims of spousal abuse official protection and orders that abusers be punished to the fullest extent of the law. Victims can also sue for damages. In education, women make up 44% of students in colleges and universities and their average life expectancy is 73.7, 3.3 years more than men.

China's gay and lesbian community is also taking steps to ensure its rights as citizens. Homosexuality in China is technically illegal and any official discussion of the matter is taboo. Gays and lesbians can face harassment by police and, at times, criminal punishment. Regardless, the

---

THE CHINESE ZODIAC

Astrology has a long history in China and is integrated with religious beliefs. If you want to know your sign in the Chinese zodiac, look up your year of birth in the chart but remember that Chinese astrology goes by the lunar calendar. The Chinese Lunar New Year usually falls in late January or early February, so the first month will be included in the year before. Future years are included here so you'll know what's coming:

- Rat: generous, social, insecure, prone to laziness; 1936, 1948, 1960, 1972, 1984, 1996, 2008

- Ox/Cow: stubborn, conservative, patient; 1937, 1949, 1961, 1973, 1985, 1997, 2009

- Tiger: creative, brave, overbearing; 1938, 1950, 1962, 1974, 1986, 1998, 2010

- Rabbit: timid, amicable, affectionate; 1939, 1951, 1963, 1975, 1987, 1999, 2011

- Dragon: egotistical, strong, intelligent; 1940, 1952, 1964, 1976, 1988, 2000, 2012

- Snake: luxury seeking, secretive, friendly; 1941, 1953, 1965, 1977, 1989, 2001, 2013

- Horse: emotional, clever, quick thinker; 1942, 1954, 1966, 1978, 1990, 2002, 2014

- Goat: charming, good with money, indecisive; 1943, 1955, 1967, 1979, 1991, 2003, 2015

- Monkey: confident, humorous, fickle; 1944, 1956, 1968, 1980, 1992, 2004, 2016

- Rooster: diligent, imaginative, needs attention; 1945, 1957, 1969, 1981, 1993, 2005, 2017

- Dog: humble, responsible, patient; 1946, 1958, 1970, 1982, 1994, 2006, 2018

- Pig: materialistic, loyal, honest; 1947, 1959, 1971, 1983, 1995, 2007, 2019

gay community has begun to organise social-service programmes and promote education about gay and lesbian issues on a grass-roots level. One well-established organisation is the Hong Kong–based Chi Heng Foundation which promotes gay rights through public education and media campaigns. This foundation has expanded into mainland China, focusing on AIDS prevention and the gay community. It is especially active in Hénán province, working with students whose parents are dying or who have died of AIDS.

POPULATION

China is home to 56 ethnic groups, with Han Chinese making up 92% of the population. Because Han Chinese are the majority, China's other ethnic groups are usually referred to as 'national minorities'. Han live throughout the country but are mainly concentrated along the Yellow River, Yangzi River and Pearl River basins.

China's minority groups are also found throughout the country but their main distributions are along the border regions of northwest and southwest China and from the north to the northeast. Yúnnán is home to more than 20 ethnic groups and is one of the most ethnically diverse provinces in the country. The largest minority groups in China include the Zhuang, Manchu, Miao, Uighur, Yi, Tujia, Tibetan, Mongolian, Buoyei, Dong, Yao, Korean, Bai, Hani, Li, Kazak and Dai.

Maintaining amicable relations with the minorities has been a continuous problem for the Han Chinese. Tibet and Xīnjiāng are heavily garrisoned by Chinese troops, partly to protect China's borders and partly to prevent rebellion among the local population. The Chinese government has also set up special training centres, such as the National Minorities Institute in Běijīng, to train minority cadres for these regions.

China faces enormous population pressures, despite comprehensive programmes to curb its growth. Over 40.5% of China's population live in urban centres, putting great pressure on land and water resources. It's

---

CHINA'S ONE-CHILD POLICY

The prospect of an ever-growing population, with an ever-shrinking capacity to feed itself, prompted a limited birth control programme in the 1950s, but this was abandoned during the Cultural Revolution.

The one-child policy was railroaded into effect in 1979 without a careful analysis of its logic or feasibility. The original goal was to keep China's population to one billion by the year 2000 and then massaged down to an ideal of 700 million by 2050.

The cost and difficulty of enforcing the policy has been massive, and its implementation an unprecedented intrusion by the state into the reproductive rights of its citizens. The policy was originally harshly implemented but rural revolt led to a softer stance; nonetheless, it has generated much bad feeling between local officials and the rural population.

Rural families are now allowed to have two children, but some have upwards of three or four kids, who are unreported and consequently receive no education. Families who do abide by the one-child policy will often go to great lengths to make sure their child is male. In parts of China, this is creating a serious imbalance of the sexes.

Psychologists also argue that the experiment has created a generation of spoiled children ill-prepared to deal with adult life. Growing up as the centre of attention and treated as 'little emperors' (xiǎo huángdì) has made the sharp edges of the outside world that much sharper.

Supporters of the policy argue that without it China would be dealing with runaway population growth. Others note that alternative, less coercive strategies, such as a national family planning programme and improved health care could have afforded better results.

estimated that China's total population will continue to grow at a speed of eight to 10 million each year and even with population programmes such as the one-child policy (opposite) in place, experts claim that China needs at least 30 more years to achieve zero population growth. An unbalanced gender ratio (117 boys to 100 girls) and a rapidly ageing population are very serious problems authorities are trying to address. In 2003, over 10% of China's population was over 60. This is expected to increase to 15.6% by 2020.

SPORT

China has over 3000 years of sports history. Archaeologists have found evidence of an advanced sports culture from the discovery of murals and pottery that show people playing games resembling modern-day archery, acrobatics, martial arts, wrestling and various types of ball games. Most of these games were enjoyed by the well-to-do, who had time to invest in recreational activities.

http://en.beijing-2008 .org is the official site for the Běijīng 2008 Olympics. The site gives profiles of athletes and background on China's involvement in the Olympic Games.

During the Tang dynasty, equestrian polo was at the height of fashion for aristocrats and officials. There are numerous paintings, ceramics and mirrors from this period that depict men and women engaging in the sport. Board games also became popular around this time and people enjoyed playing a game similar to contemporary mah jong.

During the Song dynasty, one of the most popular sports was kicking around a leather ball stuffed with hair. This sport, similar to football, was enjoyed by both officials and ordinary people. In 2003, the international football association FIFA officially recognised China as the birthplace of football, which is believed to have originated in present-day Shāndōng province. Golf is another sport with a long history – as far back as the Yuan dynasty the Chinese were hitting balls into holes in the ground with sticks.

It was during the Qing dynasty that modern sports such as basketball, gymnastics, volleyball and swimming came to China and Chinese athletes began participating in international sports events such as the Olympics and the Asian Games. Some Chinese athletes have achieved worldwide recognition, such as the basketball player Yao Ming, who now plays for the Houston Rockets.

Some sports China excels in today are table tennis, volleyball, gymnastics and women's wrestling, with many athletes bringing home international awards for their efforts. The first Chinese to win an Olympic gold medal was pistol-shooting champion Xu Haifeng at the 1984 Olympic Games. Deng Yaping is China's most celebrated table-tennis player, winning four gold medals in the 1992 and 1994 Olympic Games. With China set to host the 2008 summer Olympics in Běijīng, Chinese athletes are already being primed for the spotlight. The government is pouring money into the building of ultramodern sporting facilities in an effort to show off Běijīng as a world-class city on par with Olympic host cities of the past.

In the 2004 Olympic Games held in Athens, Greece, the Chinese took home 32 gold medals, 17 silver and 14 bronze, ranking second after the USA. Liu Xiang, of Shànghǎi, became the first Chinese gold medallist in track-and-field, beating his European, African and American rivals in the 110m hurdles.

RELIGION

Chinese religion has been influenced by three streams of human thought: Taoism, Confucianism and Buddhism. All three have been inextricably entwined in popular Chinese religion along with ancient animist beliefs.

The founders of Taoism, Confucianism and Buddhism have been deified. The Chinese worship them and their disciples as fervently as they worship their own ancestors and a pantheon of gods and spirits.

Muslims are believed to be the largest identifiable religious group still active in China today, numbering perhaps 2% to 3% of the nation's population. The government has not published official figures of the number of Buddhists. There are around three million Catholics and four million

CHINESE MARTIAL ARTS

Many martial arts of the East have their foundations deeply entwined with the philosophies, doctrines, concepts and religious beliefs of Confucianism, Buddhism, Taoism and Zen. It is certainly true that most of the martial art systems in existence today owe their development and ultimate dissemination to the monks and priests who taught and transferred such knowledge over much of Asia throughout history.

In China today the various martial art styles that exist number into the hundreds; many still not known to the Western world, and each style reflecting its own fighting philosophy and spirit. The following is a thumbnail sketch of two of the arts that you may see while travelling in China.

Shaolin Boxing

Shaolin boxing is one of the major branches of Chinese martial arts. The art is said to have originated at Shaolin Temple on Song Mountain in Hénán province (p433). Shàolín monk fighters were trained to help protect the temple's assets. The martial art routines of Shaolin Temple were not organised into a complete system until some 30 to 40 years later when Indian monk Bodhidharma visited the site.

Bodhidharma taught the monks various kinds of physical exercises to limber up the joints and build a good physique. These movements were expanded over time and a complicated series of Chinese boxing (or forms) evolved. By the Sui and Tang dynasties, Shaolin boxing was widely known.

The fighting styles originating from Shaolin Temple are based on five animals: dragon, snake, tiger, leopard and crane. Each animal represents a different style, each of which is used to develop different skills.

The temple's famous forms have had a profound influence on many of today's martial arts, and the temple is still being utilised today.

Taichi (Shadow Boxing)

Taichi or *tàijíquán* is a centuries-old Chinese discipline promoting flexibility, circulation, strength, balance, relaxation and meditation. While the art is seen by many outside China as a slow-motion form of gentle exercise, it is traditionally practised as a form of self-defence. Taichi aims to dispel the opponent without the use of force and with minimal effort. It is based on the Taoist idea that the principle of softness will ultimately overcome hardness. According to legend, it is derived from the movements of animals.

A major part of studying taichi is the development of chi *(qì)*, or life energy that can be directed to all parts of the body with the help of mental training. Chi must flow and circulate freely in the body.

There is no single founder of taichi as the art has been developed over many centuries by countless people. Due to different needs and environments, various styles of taichi evolved. The most popular form of taichi is the Yang style, which is not too difficult to learn in its simplified form (though the full form has 108 postures) and is not strenuous. Other styles, such as the Chen style, call for a wider array of skills as the postures are painfully low and the kicks high, so endurance and flexibility are important. Chen style is popular with younger exponents and clearly has its roots in Shaolin, mixing slow movements with fast, snappy punches. Other styles include the Sun and Wu styles.

Protestants. It's impossible to determine the number of Taoists, but the number of Taoist priests is very small.

Taoism

It is said that Taoism (Dàojiào) is the only true 'home-grown' Chinese religion – Buddhism was imported from India and Confucianism is mainly a philosophy. According to tradition, the founder of Taoism was a man known as Laotzu, variously spelled in Western literature as 'Laotse', 'Laotze' and the pinyin variant 'Lǎozǐ'. He is said to have been born around the year 604 BC, but there is some doubt that he ever lived at all. Almost nothing is known about him, not even his real name.

At the end of his life, Laotzu is said to have climbed on a water buffalo and ridden west towards what is now Tibet, in search of solitude for his last few years. On the way, he was asked by a gatekeeper to leave behind a record of his beliefs. The product was a slim volume of only 5000 characters: the *Dao De Jing* or *The Way and Its Power*. He then rode off on his buffalo. It's doubtful that Laotzu ever intended his philosophy to become a religion.

Zhuangzi (399–295 BC) picked up where Laotzu left off. Zhuangzi (also called Chuangtzu) is regarded as the greatest of all Taoist writers and his collection of stories, *The Book of Zhuangzi*, is still required reading for anyone trying to make sense of Taoism. However, like Laotzu, Zhuangzi was a philosopher and was not actually trying to establish a religion.

At the centre of Taoism is the concept of Tao (*dào*). Tao cannot be perceived because it exceeds senses, thoughts and imagination; it can be known only through mystical insight and cannot be expressed with words. The opening lines of Laotzu's *The Way and Its Power* advise that the Tao that can be expressed is not the real Tao. Tao is the way of the universe, the driving power in nature, the order behind all life and the spirit that cannot be exhausted. Tao is the way people should order their lives to keep in harmony with the natural order of the universe.

Taoism today has been much embraced in the West by many who offer their own various interpretations of what Laotzu and Zhuangzi were really trying to tell us.

Confucianism

Although more a philosophy than a religion, Confucianism (Rújiā Sīxiǎng) has become intertwined with Chinese religious beliefs.

Confucius was born of a poor family around 551 BC in the state of Lu in modern-day Shāndōng. His ambition was to hold a high government office and to reorder society through the administrative apparatus. At most he seems to have had several insignificant government posts, a few followers and a permanently blocked career.

At the age of 50 he perceived his divine mission, and for the next 13 years tramped from state to state offering unsolicited advice to rulers on how to improve their governing, while looking for an opportunity to put his own ideas into practice. That opportunity never came, and he returned to his own state to spend the last five years of his life teaching and editing classical literature. He died in 479 BC, aged 72.

The glorification of Confucius began after his death. Mencius (372–289 BC), or Mengzi, helped raise Confucian ideals into the national consciousness with the publication of *The Book of Mencius*.

Eventually, Confucian philosophy permeated every level of Chinese society. To hold government office presupposed knowledge of the Confucian classics, and his words trickled down to the illiterate masses.

Confucianism defines codes of conduct and patterns of obedience. Women obey and defer to men, younger brothers to elder brothers, and sons to fathers. Respect flows upwards, from young to old, from subject to ruler. Certainly, any reigning Chinese emperor would quickly see the merits of encouraging such a system.

All people paid homage to the emperor, who was regarded as the embodiment of Confucian wisdom and virtue – the head of the great family-nation. For centuries administration under the emperor lay in the hands of a small Confucian scholar class. In theory anyone who passed the examinations qualified, but in practice the monopoly of power was held by the educated upper classes.

In its early years, Confucianism was regarded as a radical philosophy, but over the centuries it has come to be seen as conservative and reactionary. Confucius was strongly denounced by the Communists as yet another incorrigible link to the bourgeois past. During the Cultural Revolution, Confucian temples, statues and Confucianists themselves took quite a beating at the hands of rampaging Red Guards. Confucian temples, particularly the ones at Qūfù in Shāndōng province (p198), have been restored.

DID YOU KNOW?

The oldest surviving printed book in the world is a Chinese Buddhist text printed in AD 868.

Buddhism

Buddhism (Fó Jiào) was founded in India by Siddhartha Gautama (563–483 BC), a prince brought up in luxury who became disillusioned by the world around him. At the age of 30 he sought 'enlightenment' by following various yogic disciplines. After several failed attempts he devoted the final phase of his search to intensive contemplation. One evening he slipped into deep meditation and emerged having achieved enlightenment. His title 'Buddha' means 'the awakened' or 'the enlightened one'.

The cornerstone of Buddhist philosophy is the view that all life is suffering. Everyone is subject to the traumas of birth, sickness, decrepitude and death, and to separation from what they love.

The cause of suffering is desire – specifically the desires of the body and the desire for personal fulfilment. Happiness can only be achieved if these desires are overcome, and this requires following the 'eightfold path'. By following this path the Buddhist aims to attain nirvana: a state of complete freedom from greed, anger, ignorance and the various other fetters of existence.

When Buddhism entered China from India, its exotic nature, with chanting, strange coloured robes, incense and foreign images was an attraction for many Chinese disillusioned with the uptight formalism of Confucianism. Buddhism offered answers to the afterlife that neither Taoism nor Confucianism could address, with its elaborate explanations of karma and how to find relief from suffering.

Slowly, the religion drew more followers, gathering firm support in northern China and gradually moving south. However, Buddhism had its share of critics, and many Chinese were afraid that the foreign religion was a threat to the Chinese identity, which was firmly grounded in Confucianism. The growth of Buddhism was slowed by persecutions and outright abolishment by various emperors.

The Buddhist writings that have come down to us date from about 150 years after the Buddha's death. By the time these texts came out, divisions had already appeared within Buddhism. Some writers tried to emphasise the Buddha's break with Hinduism, while others tried to minimise it. At some stage Buddhism split into two major schools: Theravada and Mahayana.

The Theravada or 'doctrine of the elders' school (also called Hinayana or 'little vehicle' by non-Theravadins) holds that the path to nirvana is an individual pursuit. It centres on monks and nuns who make the search for nirvana a full-time profession. This school maintains that people are alone in the world and must tread the path to nirvana on their own; buddhas can only show the way. Theravada is the main school of Buddhism in Sri Lanka, Myanmar, Thailand, Laos and Cambodia.

The Mahayana, or 'big vehicle', school holds that since all existence is one, the fate of the individual is linked to the fate of others. The Buddha did not just point the way and float off into his own nirvana, but continues to offer spiritual help to others seeking nirvana. Mahayana is the main school of Buddhism in Vietnam, Japan, Tibet, Korea, Mongolia and China.

Mahayana Buddhism is replete with innumerable heavens, hells and descriptions of nirvana. Prayers are addressed to the Buddha and combined with elaborate ritual. There are deities and bodhisattvas – a rank of supernatural beings in their last incarnation before nirvana. Temples are filled with images such as the future buddha, Maitreya (often portrayed as fat and happy over his coming promotion) and Amitabha (a saviour who rewards the faithful with admission to a Christian-like paradise). The ritual, tradition and superstition that Buddha rejected came tumbling back in with a vengeance.

The largest number of strokes in a Chinese character is 84.

In Tibet and areas of Gānsù, Sìchuān and Yúnnán, a unique form of the Mahayana school is practised: Tantric or Lamaist Buddhism (Lǎma Jiào). Tantric Buddhism, often called Vajrayana or 'thunderbolt vehicle' by its followers, has been practised since the early 7th century AD and is heavily influenced by Tibet's pre-Buddhist Bon religion, which relied on priests or shamans to placate spirits, gods and demons.

Generally speaking, it is much more mystical than other forms of Buddhism, relying heavily on *mudras* (ritual postures), mantras (sacred speech), *yantras* (sacred art) and secret initiation rites. Priests called lamas are believed to be reincarnations of highly evolved beings; the Dalai Lama is the supreme patriarch of Tibetan Buddhism.

Islam

The founder of Islam (Yīsīlán Jiào) was the Arab prophet Mohammed. Strictly speaking, Muslims believe it was not Mohammed who shaped the religion but God, and Mohammed merely transmitted it from God to his people. The proper name of the religion is Islam, derived from the word *salam,* which primarily means 'peace', and in a secondary sense 'surrender' or 'submission'. The full connotation is something like 'the peace that comes by surrendering to God'. The corresponding adjective is 'Muslim'.

The Prophet was born around AD 570 and came to be called Mohammed, meaning 'highly praised'. His ancestry is traditionally traced back to Abraham, who had two wives, Hagar and Sarah. Hagar gave birth to Ishmael, and Sarah had a son named Isaac. Sarah demanded that Hagar and Ishmael be banished. According to Islam's holy book, the Koran, Ishmael went to Mecca, where his line of descendants can be traced down to Mohammed. There have been other true prophets before Mohammed, but he is regarded as the culmination of them and the last.

Mohammed said that there is only one God, Allah. The name derives from joining al, which means 'the', with Llah, which means 'God'. His uncompromising monotheism conflicted with the pantheism and idolatry of the Arabs. His moral teachings and vision of a universal brotherhood conflicted with what he believed was a corrupt social order based on class divisions.

The initial reaction to his teachings was hostile. He and his followers were forced to flee from Mecca to Medina in 622, where Mohammed built a political base and an army that eventually defeated Mecca and brought all of Arabia under his control. He died in 632, two years after taking Mecca. By the time a century had passed the Arab Muslims had built a huge empire that stretched all the way from Persia to Spain. Although the Arabs were eventually supplanted by the Turks, the strength of Islam has continued to the present day.

Islam was brought to China peacefully. Arab traders who landed on the southern coast of China established their mosques in great maritime cities like Guǎngzhōu and Quánzhōu, and Muslim merchants travelling the Silk Road to China won converts among the Han Chinese in the north of the country. There are also large populations of Muslim Uighur people (of Turkic descent), whose ancestors first moved into China's Xīnjiāng region during the Tang dynasty.

Christianity

The earliest record of Christianity (Jīdū Jiào) in China dates back to the Nestorians, a Syrian Christian sect. They first appeared in China in the 7th century when a Syrian named Raban presented Christian scriptures to the imperial court at Chāng'ān (present-day Xī'ān). This event and the construction of a Nestorian monastery in Chāng'ān are recorded on a large stone stele made in AD 781, now displayed in the Shaanxi History Museum (p413) in Xī'ān.

The next major Christian group to arrive in China were the Jesuits. The priests Matteo Ricci and Michael Ruggieri were permitted to set up base at Zhàoqìng in Guǎngdōng in the 1580s, and eventually made it to the imperial court in Běijīng. Large numbers of Catholic and Protestant missionaries established themselves in China following the intrusion into China by the Western powers in the 19th century. Christians are estimated to comprise about 1% of China's population.

Judaism

Kāifēng (p441) in Hénán province has been the home of the largest community of Chinese Jews. Their religious beliefs of Judaism (Yóutài Jiào) and almost all the customs associated with them have died out, yet the descendants of the original Jews still consider themselves Jewish. Just how the Jews got to China is unknown. They may have come as traders and merchants along the Silk Road when Kāifēng was the capital of China, or they may have emigrated from India.

RELIGION & COMMUNISM IN TODAY'S CHINA

Today the Chinese communist government professes atheism. It considers religion to be base superstition, a remnant of old China used by the ruling classes to keep power. This is in line with the Marxist belief that religion is the 'opiate of the people'.

Nevertheless, in an effort to improve relations with the Muslim, Buddhist and Lamaist minorities, in 1982 the Chinese government amended its constitution to allow freedom of religion. However, only atheists are permitted to be members of the Chinese Communist Party (CCP). Since almost all of China's 55 minority groups adhere to one religion or another, this rule precludes most of them from becoming party members.

Traditional Chinese religious beliefs took a battering during the Cultural Revolution when monasteries were disbanded, temples were destroyed and the monks were sometimes killed or sent to the fields to

'In 1982 the Chinese government amended its constitution to allow freedom of religion'

labour. While traditional Chinese religion is strong in places like Macau, Hong Kong and Taiwan, in mainland China the temples and monasteries are pale shadows of their former selves.

Since the death of Mao, the Chinese government allowed many temples (sometimes with their own contingent of monks and novices) to reopen as active places of worship. All religious activity is firmly under state control and many of the monks are caretakers within renovated shells of monasteries, which serve principally as tourist attractions.

Of all people in China, the Tibetan Buddhists felt the brunt of Mao's Cultural Revolution. The Dalai Lama and his entourage fled to India in 1959 when the Tibetan rebellion was put down by Chinese troops. During the Cultural Revolution the monasteries were disbanded (some were levelled to the ground) and the theocracy, which had governed Tibet for centuries, was wiped out overnight. Some Tibetan temples and monasteries have been reopened and the Tibetan religion is still a very powerful force among the people.

In spring 1999, the CCP was caught off-guard by a congregation of thousands of practitioners of a quasi-Buddhist health system, Falun Gong (Art of the Wheel of the Law) outside the political headquarters of Zhongnanhai in Běijīng. Falun Gong was branded a cult (xiéjiào) and outlawed.

The tussle between the party and Falun Gong quickly relocated to Tiananmen Square, where followers routinely appeared with banners, only to be pounced upon by patrolling plainclothes police. Thousands of Falun Gong believers have been sent to prison where human-rights watchdogs say many are badly treated or killed.

ARTS

With such a long, unbroken history and culture, China has made one of the greatest artistic contributions to mankind. Sadly, much of China's ancient art treasures have been destroyed in times of civil war or dispersed by invasion or natural calamity. Many of China's remaining great paintings, ceramics, jade and other works of art were rescued by exile beyond the mainland – in Taiwan, Singapore, Hong Kong and elsewhere.

The West has also been guilty of ransacking China's heritage, making off with religious art and scriptures from such grottoes as Dūnhuáng. Fortunately since the early 1970s a great deal of work has been done to restore what was destroyed in the Cultural Revolution.

http://chinococulture .about.com is a good resource on culture and society in China with links to a variety of topics including food, holidays and martial arts.

China today has a flourishing contemporary art scene, with private galleries competing with government-run museums and exhibition halls. Chinese artists are increasingly catching the attention of the international art world and joint exhibitions with European or American artists are now common. The Beijing Biennale, held in the autumn of 2003, was the first international exhibit of its kind to showcase artworks from over 40 countries and serve as a representative platform for some of China's top artists.

Visual Arts

CALLIGRAPHY

Calligraphy has been traditionally regarded in China as the highest form of artistic expression. The basic tools, commonly referred to as 'the four treasures of the scholar's study', are paper, ink, ink-stone (on which the ink is mixed) and brush. These materials, which are shared by Chinese painters, reflect the close relationship between Chinese painting and calligraphy.

Calligraphy is still an extremely popular pastime in China and a major area of study. It can be seen all over China – on documents, artworks, in temples, adorning the walls of caves, and on the sides of mountains and monuments. There is an annual calligraphy festival (p318) held every year outside Shàoxīng in Zhèjiāng province.

PAINTING

Chinese painting is the art of brush and ink applied onto *xuān* (paper), or silk. The basic tools are those of calligraphy, which has influenced painting in both its style and theory. The brush line, which varies in thickness and tone, is the important feature of a Chinese painting, along with calligraphy itself, which is usually incorporated in the form of an inscription or poem along with the artist's seal. Shading and colour play only a minor symbolic and decorative role.

From the Han dynasty until the end of the Tang dynasty, the human figure occupied the dominant position in Chinese painting. The practice of seeking places of natural beauty and communing with nature first became popular among Taoist poets and painters, and landscape painting for its own sake started in the 4th and 5th centuries.

From the 11th century onwards, landscape was to dominate Chinese painting. Towards the end of the Ming dynasty, a group of painters known as the Individualists diverged from traditional techniques with unusual compositions and brushwork; however it was not until the 20th century that there was any real departure from native traditions.

CONTEMPORARY ART IN BĚIJĪNG, POST-TIANANMEN

The tragic events that followed the Tiananmen uprising of June 1989 caused many artists to become disillusioned with the current political situation in China and their artwork reflects this cynicism. This attitude continues through today and artworks are permeated with feelings of loss, loneliness and social isolation. Two of the most important Běijīng artists to characterise this period of Cynical Realism are Fang Lijun and Yue Minjun. Both created grotesque portraits of themselves and friends that convey a sense of boredom and mock joviality.

Experiments with American-style pop art were another reaction to the events of 1989. Inspired by Warhol, some artists took symbols of Socialist Realism and transformed them into kitschy visual commentary. Images of Mao appeared against floral backgrounds and paintings of rosy cheeked peasants and soldiers were interspersed with ads for Canon cameras and Coca Cola. Artists were not only responding to the tragedies of the Tiananmen massacre but also to the rampant consumerism that was sweeping through the country.

In the early 1990s, many Běijīng artists found escape from political scrutiny on the grounds of the Old Summer Palace, where they could rent cheap houses and work more freely. Because of increasing recognition of some of the artists who lived there, police raids became more common and the artistic community was broken up. Forced to move out of their haunts around the Old Summer Palace, many found less bureaucratic control in the suburbs.

Dashanzi, a factory zone on the northeastern edge of Běijīng, in the Chaoyang District, became the favourite spot of many. Over the past several years, this quiet enclave has transformed into a thriving neighbourhood of lofts, galleries, bookshops, design studios, cafés and bars, all tucked into a small section of Dashanzi called 798, named after Factory 798, a disused electronics factory complex built in the 1950s by East German architects. Here, Mao's ideals are reinterpreted through the artistic works of China's new visionaries, resulting in a lively, enigmatic and sometimes controversial community that is increasingly catching the attention of the international art world. Unfortunately, the Dashanzi art community is currently facing an uncertain future. Despite its growing reputation as China's 'new Soho', the entire area is scheduled for demolition in 2005 to make way for more of the luxury high-rise apartment buildings that dot the Běijīng landscape.

When the communists came to power, much of the country's artistic talent was turned to glorifying the revolution and bombarding the masses with political slogans. Colourful billboards of Mao waving to cheering crowds holding up the little red book were popular, as were giant Mao statues standing above smaller statues of enthusiastic workers and soldiers.

Since the late 1970s, the Chinese art scene has gradually recovered. The work of traditionally influenced painters can be seen for sale in shops and galleries all over China, while in the major cities a flourishing avant-garde scene has emerged. The work of Chinese painters has been arguably more innovative and dissident than that of writers, possibly because the political implications are harder to interpret by the authorities. For those interested in purchasing art, it's a good idea to head to the smaller independent galleries and inquire there.

CERAMICS

The Chinese began making pottery over 8000 years ago. The first vessels were hand-crafted earthenware, primarily used for religious purposes. The invention of the pottery wheel during the late Neolithic period led to the establishment of foundries and workshops and the eventual development of a ceramics industry.

Over the centuries, Chinese potters perfected their craft, introducing many new exciting styles and techniques. Art thrived under the Tang dynasty and the ceramic arts were no exception. One of the most famous styles from this period is 'three-coloured ware', named because of the liberal use of bright yellow, green and white glaze. Blue-green celadons were another popular item and demand for them grew in countries as far away as Egypt and Persia.

'The Chinese began making pottery over 8000 years ago'

The Yuan dynasty saw the first production of China's most famous type of porcelain, often referred to simply as 'blue-and-white'. Cobalt blue paint, obtained from Persia, was applied as an underglaze directly to white porcelain with a brush and then the vessel was covered with another transparent glaze and fired. This technique was perfected under the Ming dynasty and ceramics made in this style became hugely popular all over the world, eventually acquiring the name 'Chinaware', whether produced in China or not. Jingdézhèn (p466) in Jiāngxī province was established during the Yuan dynasty as the centre of the ceramics industry and still retains that importance today.

TOP CONTEMPORARY ART GALLERIES

These galleries are the most well known in China and show work by some of China's top internationally recognised artists.

- The Courtyard, Běijīng (p127)
- Red Gate Gallery, Běijīng (p109)
- China Academy of Art, Hángzhōu (p312)
- Plum Blossoms, Hong Kong (p499)
- Para/Site Art Space, Hong Kong (p499)
- Shanghai Gallery of Art, Shànghǎi (p277)
- ShanghART, Shànghǎi (p284)
- Art Scene, Shànghǎi (p284)

During the Qing dynasty, porcelain techniques were further refined and developed, showing superb craftsmanship and ingenuity. British and European consumers dominated the export market, having an insatiable appetite for Chinese vases and bowls decorated with flowers and landscapes. The Qing is also known for its stunning monochromatic ware, especially the ox-blood vases, and enamel decorated porcelain.

Jǐngdézhèn remains an excellent place to visit ceramic workshops and purchase various types of ceramic wares, from Mao statues to traditional glazed urns. Another place to pick up pottery is at Dīngshān (p242) in Jiāngsū province, which is famous for ceramic teapots.

SCULPTURE

Chinese sculpture dates back to the Zhou and Shang dynasties, when small clay and wooden figures were commonly placed in tombs to protect the dead and guide them on their way to heaven. Often these figures were in the shape of animals – dragons, lions and chimeras, all creatures with magical powers that could quell lurking evil spirits. Sculptures of humans became more common in succeeding dynasties – perhaps the best example is the amazing army of Terracotta Warriors (p418) found in the tomb of Qin Shi Huang outside present-day Xī'ān.

'Small clay and wooden figures were commonly placed in tombs to protect the dead'

It wasn't until the introduction of Buddhism in China that sculpture moved beyond tomb figurines to other realms of figurative art. The Buddhist caves of Dàtóng (p403) in Shānxi province date back to the 4th century and are an excellent example of the type of art that was introduced to China from India. The enormous figures of the Buddhas, carved directly into the rock, are stiff and formal, their garments embellished with Indian patterns and flourishes. The 4th-century Longmen Caves (p438), in Hénán province, are similar in style to those at Dàtóng, with great profusions of sculptures and Indian iconography. The later cave sculptures at Lóngmén, primarily those completed during the Tang dynasty, take on a more Chinese feel, with elongated features and less stiffness in form.

The best place to see early Buddhist sculpture is at the marvellous caves of Dūnhuáng (p823), in Gānsù province. Here, Indian and Central Asian style sculptures, particularly of the Tang dynasty, carry overtly Chinese characteristics – many statues feature long, fluid bodies and have warmer, more refined facial features. It's also common to see traditional Chinese dragons and lions mingling with the demons and gods of Indian iconography.

The caves in Dàzú County (p765), built during the Song dynasty, are another fascinating place to see cave art. The caves feature a wild assortment of sculpture, including Buddhist statues, animals and people. Many of the sculptures are more colourful and lively than those of Dūnhuáng and remarkably well preserved.

BRONZE VESSELS

Bronze is an alloy whose chief elements are copper, tin and lead. Tradition ascribes the first casting of bronze to the legendary Xia dynasty of 5000 years ago.

Shang dynasty bronzes are marvellous specimens, often fabulously patterned with *tāotiè*, a type of fierce animal design. Zhou dynasty bronze vessels tend to have long messages in ideographic characters; they describe wars, rewards, ceremonial events and the appointment of officials.

Bronze mirrors had already developed into an artistic form by the Warring States period. Ceramics gradually replaced bronze utensils by

Han times, but bronze mirrors were not displaced by glass mirrors until the Qing dynasty. The backs of bronze mirrors were inscribed with wishes for good fortune and protection from evil influence.

JADE

The jade stone has been revered in China since Neolithic times. Jade (yù) was firstly utilised for tools because of its hardness and strength, but later appeared on ornaments and ceremonial vessels for its decorative value. During the Qin and Han dynasties, it was believed that jade was empowered with magical and life-giving properties, and the dead were buried with jadeware. Opulent jade suits, meant to prevent decomposition, have been found in Han tombs, while Taoist alchemists, striving for immortality, ate elixirs of powdered jade.

Jade's value lies not just in its scarcity, but depends also on its colour, hardness and the skill with which it has been carved. While the pure white form is the most highly valued, the stone varies in translucency and colour, including many shades of green, brown and black. China's most famous jade comes from Hotan (p798) in Xīnjiāng province; much of what is sold in Hong Kong is fake.

FUNERARY OBJECTS

As early as Neolithic times (9000–6000 BC), offerings of pottery vessels and stone tools or weapons were placed in graves to accompany the departed.

During the Shang dynasty, precious objects such as bronze ritual vessels, weapons and jade were buried with the dead. Dogs, horses and even human beings were sacrificed for burial in the tombs of great rulers, later replaced by replicas (usually in pottery).

The cosmopolitan life of Tang China was illustrated by its funerary wares; western and Central Asians flocked to the capital at Chāng'ān and were portrayed in figurines of merchants, attendants, warriors, grooms, musicians and dancers.

Guardian spirits are some of the strangest funerary objects. A common one has bird wings, elephant ears, a human face, the body of a lion and the legs and hooves of a deer or horse, all rolled into one.

Literature

China has a rich literary tradition. Unfortunately – barring many years of intensive study – much of it is inaccessible to Western readers. Many of the most important Chinese classics are available in translation, but much of the Chinese literary heritage (particularly its poetry) is untranslatable, although scholars persevere.

PREMODERN LITERATURE

Prior to the 20th century there were two literary traditions in China: the classical and the vernacular. The classical canon, largely Confucian in nature, consisted of a core of texts written in ancient Chinese that had to be mastered thoroughly by all aspirants to the Chinese civil service, and was the backbone of the Chinese education system – it was nearly indecipherable to the masses.

The vernacular tradition arose in the Ming dynasty and consisted largely of prose epics written for entertainment. For Western readers it is the vernacular texts, precursors of the contemporary Chinese novel, that are probably of more interest. Most of them are available in translation and provide a fascinating insight into life in China centuries past.

Strange Tales from Make-Do Studio by Pu Songling and translated by Denis C and Victor Mair (Foreign Languages Press, 1989) is an imaginative Qing dynasty collection of supernatural stories.

Classical

Book of Songs (Shījīng) is the earliest collection of Chinese poetry including over 300 works that date back to the Zhou dynasty. Originally meant to be sung, the poems were compiled during the Han dynasty. This book belongs to the five Confucian classics *(Wǔjīng)* which includes the *I Ching (Yìjīng), Book of History (Shūjīng), Analects (Lúnyǔ), Book of Rites (Lǐjīng)* and the *Spring and Autumn Annals (Chūn Qiū).*

I Ching, or *Book of Changes,* is a divinatory system involving 64 hexagrams that dates back to antiquity. The hexagrams are symbols composed of broken and continuous lines, representing the transitory nature of heaven and earth. If interpreted correctly, the hexagrams can advise on moral conduct and foretell the future.

Analects is a collection of sayings attributed to Confucius that were remembered by his followers and compiled over a period of years. The *Analects* contain all the essential tenets of Confucianism, including filial piety, respect to ancestors and adherence to ritual. Many still consider Arthur Waley's 1938 translation to be the best.

Vernacular

Water Margin/Outlaws of the Marsh (Shuǐhǔ Zhuàn) by Shi Nai'an and Luo Guanzhong is a rollicking tale of a group of outlaws (with good hearts) who fight against corruption and evil during the Northern Song dynasty. This book is considered one of the great historical epics of China, along with *Romance of the Three Kingdoms.*

Romance of the Three Kingdoms (Sān Guó) by Luo Guanzhong is a swashbuckling historical novel about the legendary battles that took place during the latter half of the Han dynasty, when the country was divided into three kingdoms. The novel remains as popular today in China as it was when it first appeared in the Ming dynasty. The best translation is by Moss Roberts (University of California Press, 1999), whose English version of the novel is highly readable and entertaining.

Dream of the Red Chamber (Hónglóu Mèng) by Cao Xueqin, also translated as *The Dream of Red Mansions* and *The Story of the Stone,* is a novel of manners about the decline of a genteel family in 18th-century China. The preferred translation is by David Hawkes (Penguin, 1973), who provides a captivating rendition of the original.

Journey to the West (Xīyóu Jì) by Wu Cheng'en is a delightful novel about the Buddhist monk Xuanzhang's pilgrimage to India, accompanied by the rebellious 'Monkey King' Sun Wukong. The monkey's rebellious nature causes a wild assortment of misadventures. Two of the best translations of *Journey to the West* are by Arthur Waley (John Day, 1943) and Anthony Yu (University of Chicago Press, 1990).

MODERN & CONTEMPORARY LITERATURE

By the early 20th century, Western novels had begun to appear in Chinese translations in increasing numbers. Chinese intellectuals began to look at their own literary traditions more critically, in particular the classical one, which was markedly different in form from the Chinese that was spoken by modern Chinese.

After China came under the control of the communists, most writing in 20th-century China tended to echo the CCP line, with formulaic language and predictable plotlines. Writing was rigid and unimaginative, with little allowance for creative embellishment.

Things changed after Mao's death in 1976, when Chinese artists and writers were finally able to throw off political constraints and write

Red Azalea by Anchee Min (Pantheon Books, 1994) is a moving story of a young woman caught up in the horrors of the Cultural Revolution.

more freely. Writers for the first time dared to explore the traumatic events of the 20th century that had reshaped the Chinese landscape. China's economic progress and the excessive materialism of the 1990s have spawned a new generation of authors, many of whom remember little about the Cultural Revolution and instead are most affected by the day-to-day realities of growing up in the city. Growing up without war or poverty, young writers are instead writing about the loneliness and decadence of urban life.

The True Story of Ah Q by Lu Xun (Chinese University Press, 2002), and translated by Gladys Yang and Yang Xianyi, was first published in 1921 by an author who is regarded by many as the father of modern Chinese literature. Lu Xun was the first of the major Chinese writers to write in colloquial Chinese. Ah Q is a moving tale of a simple-minded man caught up in the turmoil of the 1911 revolution.

Blades of Grass: The Stories of Lao She (University of Hawaii Press, 1999), translated by William Lyell, is a collection of 14 stories by Lao She, one of China's most famous 20th-century writers. The stories contain poignant descriptions of people living through times of political upheaval and uncertainty. Lao She faced severe persecution during the Cultural Revolution and committed suicide.

Family by Ba Jin (Anchor Books, 1972) is the first in a trilogy that also includes Autumn and Spring. Influenced by the May 4th Movement, the novel offers a scathing view of Chinese feudalism.

Wild Swans by Jung Chang (Touchstone Books, 2003) is a gripping saga about three generations of Chinese women struggling to survive the tumultuous events of 20th-century China. This book has been banned in China for its frank depictions of modern Chinese life.

Half of Man Is Woman by Zhang Xianliang (WW Norton & Co, 1998), and translated into English by Martha Avery, is a candid exploration of sexuality and marriage in contemporary China and considered one of the most controversial novels to appear in the 1980s.

Love Must Not Be Forgotten (Panda Books, 1986) by Zhang Jie and translated by Gladys Yang is a novel by one of China's most famous female authors. This novel challenged the traditional structure of marriage with its intimate portrayal of a middle-aged woman and her love of a married man.

Please Don't Call Me Human by Wang Shuo (Hyperion East, 2000) and translated by Howard Goldblatt is a mocking look at the failures of China's state security system. Wang Shuo has been dubbed China's 'hooligan author' for his criticism of government policies. Wang's works appeal to a broad spectrum of Chinese society, despite being banned.

Film

Cinema in China can be traced back to 1896, when a Spanish entrepreneur by the name of Galen Bocca showed a series of one-reel films to astonished crowds at an entertainment plaza in Shànghǎi. Bocca's films drew large audiences, who packed the plaza nightly to witness the marvellous new medium. Soon after, permanent film-only theatres were being built in Běijīng and Shànghǎi and the Chinese film craze had officially begun.

The first films shown in China were largely Western, with shots of European cities and Westerners picnicking and frolicking on the beach. As film took hold in China, there grew a demand for films that echoed Chinese tastes. By the 1920s three of the most important genres in Chinese cinema were established: historical dramas, costume dramas set in

Beijing Doll by Chun Shu and translated by Howard Goldblatt (Riverhead Books, 2002) is a provocative novel about an 18 year-old who lives a life of sex, drugs and alcohol, rejecting the traditional Chinese values she was versed in.

The Miraculous Pigtail by Feng Jicai (Panda Books, 1987) is a collection of short stories which have a satirical magic realist touch to them. The stories are often humorous, some with strong moral overtones.

classical China and most importantly, 'swordsmen films' which would evolve into the modern martial arts film.

In 1931, the Nationalist Party in Nánjīng placed restrictions on film that were seen as promoting dissent or immorality. The Lianhua Film Company had close connections with the Nationalist Party, and with funding and government support created some of the most important films and film stars of what has been dubbed China's 'Golden Age of Cinema'. This age came to a standstill with the invasion of Shànghǎi by Japan in 1937, when many filmmakers fled to Hong Kong or went into hiding.

Civil war and the establishment of the People's Republic of China in 1949 was a setback for the film industry which was forced to follow rigid political guidelines. Heroic tales of the revolutionary struggle (gémìng piàn) made filmmaking into a kind of communist comic strip of beatific peasants and peerless harvests. The Cultural Revolution added its own extremist vision to this surreal cinematography.

After the death of Mao, Chinese filmmakers began to break free from years of political repression. The major turning point took place with the graduation of the first intake of students since the end of the Cultural Revolution from the Beijing Film Academy in 1982. This group of directors, the best known being Zhang Yimou, Chen Kaige and Tian Zhuangzhuang, became known collectively as the 'Fifth Generation'.

The first film to create an international stir was Chen Kaige's *Yellow Earth* (1984), a beautifully shot film about a communist cadre who visits a remote village to collect folk songs and inspires a young woman to flee the village and join the communists. The film held little interest to Chinese audiences and the government disparaged the film as too pessimistic. However, Western audiences loved the film and it spurred a taste in the West for Chinese cinema. Chen's later film *Farewell My Concubine* (1993) also received critical acclaim in Western countries.

Zhang Yimou followed Chen's success with *Red Sorghum* (1987), set in a northern Chinese village during the Japanese invasion. *Red Sorghum* won the Golden Bear at the Berlin Film Festival and also introduced to the Western world the actress Gong Li, who became the poster-girl of Chinese cinema in the 1990s. She also appeared in Zhang Yimou's *To Live* (1994), *Ju Dou* (1990), *The Story of Qiu Ju* (1991), *Raise the Red Lantern* (1991) and *Shanghai Triad* (1995), all popular in the West. These films generated a great deal of criticism in China, particularly for their candid approach to politically sensitive issues. Tian Zhuangzhuang's *The Blue Kite* (1993), a brilliant but heartbreaking movie that chronicles the events of the Cultural Revolution, was considered so controversial the filmmaker was banned from filmmaking for years.

In the 1990s, China's 'Sixth Generation' of Chinese filmmakers began to create films that were a reaction against the Fifth Generation's need to please Western audiences. In 1990, Beijing Film graduate Zhang Yuan created *Mama,* a beautiful but disturbing film about a mother and her autistic child. This small film, created without government sponsorship, started a trend in independent films that continues today. Some of these indie filmmakers include Wang Xiaoshuai, *Beijing Bicycle* (2000), Jia Zhangke, *Unknown Pleasure* (2002), Jiang Wen, *Devils on the Doorstep* (1999) and Lu Xuechang, *The Making of Steel* (1996). Their films are far grittier, more urban observations than their Fifth Generation precursors. As a result, many Sixth-Generation directors are blacklisted by the authorities and are not allowed to travel outside of China to attend film festivals.

China's contemporary film industry faces great challenges. Filmmakers are continually dealing with a shortage of funds, small audiences and high

In the Mood for Love by Wong Kar Wai (Hong Kong, 2000) is a beautifully shot film about a man and woman living in a crowded housing block who realise their spouses are having an affair.

The Orphan of Anyang by Wang Chao (Mainland China, 2001) is an emotional film about an unemployed factory worker who is hired by a prostitute to care for her baby.

ticket prices. Except for a few directors who are able to attract domestic and overseas investments, such as Chen Kaige and Zhang Yimou, most directors have very small budgets and because of limited box-office appeal, see few profits. Many Chinese prefer Hollywood blockbusters to local movies, with the exception of Hong Kong martial arts movies. Rises in ticket prices, putting many movies out of reach for the average Chinese, also contribute to dwindling audiences. Still, the movie industry carries on, producing often surprisingly high-quality movies on tiny budgets that few Westerners, or even Chinese, get to see.

HONG KONG & BEYOND

Hong Kong cinema has always been uniquely Chinese – a ramshackle, violent, slapstick, chaotic, vivid and superstitious world. Money, vendettas, ghosts, gambling and romance are endlessly recycled themes. John Woo's gun-toting films are probably the most celebrated of the action films *(dòngzuò piān)*. The master of slow motion and ultra violence *(Hard Boiled; City On Fire)* has been seduced by Hollywood and now works on gargantuan budget spectaculars *(Face/Off; Mission Impossible 2)*.

Taiwan director Ang Lee's Oscar-winning epic tale *Crouching Tiger, Hidden Dragon* (2000) caused quite a stir among Western audiences. The Chinese, a public with loftier expectations of cinematic kung fu and death-defying stunts, panned it. Northern Chinese viewers squirmed in their seats at fellow southerners Chow Yun-fat's and Michelle Yeoh's spoken Mandarin. The Western taste was enticed by the film's combination of epic story telling and novel fighting moves but Chinese suspicions were that Ang Lee had shrewdly milked the Western market.

Black Cannon Incident by Huang Jianxin (Mainland China, 1985) is a black comedy about an engineer who sends an innocent telegram referring to a 'black cannon' and comes under investigation by authorities.

Music

TRADITIONAL MUSIC

Musical instruments have been unearthed from tombs dating back to the Shang dynasty and Chinese folk songs can be traced back at least this far. Traditional Chinese instruments are often based on ancient Chinese poetry, making them very symbolic in form. Two books of the Confucian canon, the *Book of Songs* (p66) and the *Book of Rites* both dwell on music, the first actually being a collection of songs and poems, formerly set to music.

The traditional Chinese music scale differs from its Western equivalent. Unlike Western music, tone is considered more important than melody. Music to the Chinese was once believed to have cosmological significance and in early times, if a musician played in the wrong tone, it could indicate the fall of a dynasty.

Traditional Chinese musical instruments include the two-stringed fiddle *(èrhú)*, four-stringed banjo *(yuè qín)*, two-stringed viola *(húqín)*, vertical flute *(dòngxiāo)*, horizontal flute *(dízi)*, piccolo *(bāngdí)*, four-stringed lute *(pípa)*, zither *(gǔzhēng)* and ceremonial trumpet *(suǒnà)*. Traditional music places a lot of emphasis on percussion, which is what you'll most likely hear at funerals, temples and weddings.

China's ethnic minorities have preserved their own folk song traditions; a trip to Lìjiāng in Yúnnán gives you the chance to appreciate the ancient sounds of the local Naxi orchestra (p671). The communist anthem 'The East is Red' developed from a folk song popular in northern China and later became a defining element of the Cultural Revolution. Chen Kaige's *Yellow Earth* (opposite) contains many beautiful folk songs of this region.

Many department stores in China sell traditional Chinese instruments like flutes and piccolos and most music stores sell recordings of opera and instrumental music.

CHINESE OPERA

Chinese opera has been formally in existence since the northern Song dynasty, developing out of China's long balladic tradition. Performances were put on by travelling entertainers, often families, in teahouses frequented by China's working classes. Performances were drawn from popular legends and folklore. Běijīng opera became officially recognised in 1790, when performances were staged for the imperial family.

There are over 300 types of opera in China, Běijīng opera being the most familiar to Westerners. Other types include Yue opera and Kunqu opera, among others. Yue opera is commonly performed in Guǎngdōng, Hong Kong and Macau. Its singing and dialogue are all in Cantonese dialect. In addition to Chinese traditional instruments, Western instruments such as the violin, saxophone, cello and double bass are also used. Kunqu opera, originating in Jiāngsū, is notable for its soft melodies and the use of the flute.

Chinese opera is fascinating for its use of make-up, acrobatics and elaborate costumes. Face painting derives from the early use of masks worn by players and each colour suggests the personality and attributes that define a character. Chinese audiences can tell instantly the personality of characters by their painted faces. In addition, the status of a character is suggested by the size of headdress worn – the more elaborate, the more significant the character. The four major roles in Chinese opera are the female role, the male role, the 'painted-face' role (for gods and warriors), and the clown.

POPULAR MUSIC

China's thriving music industry came about in the 1980s, a time when many younger Chinese were becoming more exposed to international music trends. The energetic Hong Kong song industry had for years been popular in China, with its twinkle-eyed and pretty emissaries (Aaron Kwok, Faye Wong, Andy Lau, Kelly Chen, Jackie Cheung et al) warbling their catchy, saccharine melodies. Further north, however, their harmless songs of love and loss impacted with a growing rock scene. Cui Jian, the singer and guitarist whose politically subversive lyrics provoked authorities, led the way for a slew of gritty bands who hacked away at the edifice of rock and metal (Tang Dynasty) and punk (Underground Baby, Brain Failure). Nowadays, major cities such as Běijīng and Shànghǎi have a thriving underground music scene and plenty of places to hear live music.

'China's architectural history stretches back more than 3000 years, making it one of the longest of any civilisation'

Architecture

China's architectural history stretches back more than 3000 years, making it one of the longest of any civilisation. Many different materials and finishes can be seen throughout Chinese architecture – wood, rammed earth, masonry, stone, thatch, tiles, plaster and paint. Its use depended on function, cost, availability and aesthetics.

HISTORY

Few structures survive from before the 8th century AD. Many early buildings were constructed in wood, which has long since disappeared, with more durable buildings often destroyed by war. Much of what is known has been gathered from references to building in literature, song and artwork.

Until Qin Shi Huang became first emperor around 220 BC and unified China under a centralised system, there was no such thing as a Chinese national architecture. Under Qin Shi Huang's rule large and impressively decorated structures were built. This period saw the beginnings of what would later become the Great Wall.

It is from the Tang and Song dynasties that the first surviving structures appear. Buildings were painted in bright colours, with great attention to detail. When the Mongols ousted the Song in the late 13th century, they contributed little of their own culture to architecture, instead choosing to imitate and rebuild the style of the Chinese.

Běijīng was the long-standing capital during the Ming and Qing dynasties. The Forbidden City (p110) showcases the architecture of the time. In it we can see the epitome of traditional Chinese architectural ideas of monumentality and symmetry, with strong use of colour and decoration.

WESTERN INFLUENCE & MODERN ARCHITECTURE

China had early contact with foreign traders along the Silk Road, but it was not until the establishment of Western trading headquarters and banks in the late 18th century that a colonial influence in architecture made its presence felt. The Portuguese, Germans, British, Dutch, Spanish and Russians, among others, established communities and constructed buildings using foreign architects and Chinese craftsmen.

It was not until the 20th century that Chinese architects designed Western-style buildings themselves. Buildings with sleek, clean lines, flat roofs and materials such as steel and glass had appeared in Shànghǎi by the 1940s. There was for some time a push to revive the traditional Chinese style, but this proved uneconomical and was eventually abandoned.

The 1990s especially saw China drawing up an increasingly ambitious building agenda. Běijīng, in particular, is being transformed for the 2008 Olympics and losing much of its traditional architecture. With so many construction projects currently under way, it's uncertain what China will look like in the not so distant future. Some cities, such as Lìjiāng (p666) and Zhōuzhuāng (p250), have been designated Unesco World Heritage sites and are good places to see China's few remaining traditional buildings.

'It's uncertain what China will look like in the not-so-distant future'

RELIGIOUS ARCHITECTURE

All Buddhist, Taoist and Confucian temples are built on a north–south axis, with the main door of each hall facing south. Běijīng's *hútòng* courtyards were traditionally also constructed on this axis. Most temples tend to follow a strict schematic pattern, depending on the faith. The shape of the roof, the placement of the beams and columns and the location of deities are all carefully placed following the use of feng shui (meaning wind and water), a complex cosmological system designed to create harmonious surroundings in accordance with the natural laws of the universe.

The exteriors of many temples in China look similar. However, Taoist, Buddhist and Confucian temples are all fairly easy to distinguish, once you know what to look for. Buddhist temples have fewer images, except for statues of the Buddha, seated in the middle of the temple on an altar. Guanyin is the next most common deity you'll see, sometimes accompanied by other bodhisattvas. Pagodas are common features of Buddhist temples, built to house Sanskrit sutras, religious artefacts and documents or to store the ashes of the deceased. A number of pagodas stand alone in China, their adjacent temples gone.

Taoist and folk temples are much gaudier inside, with brightly painted statues of deities and colourful murals of scenes from Chinese mythology. On the main altar is the principle deity of the temple, often flanked by some lesser-ranked gods. Fierce-looking temple guardians are often painted on the doors to the entrance of the temple to scare away evil spirits. Large furnaces also stand in the courtyard; these are for burning 'ghost money', paper money meant to keep the ancestors happy in heaven.

Wǔtái Shān (p399), Tài Shān (p190), Qīngchéng Shān (p723), Wǔdāng Shān (p456) and Pǔtuóshān (p322) are China's famous sacred mountains and are excellent places to visit Buddhist and Taoist temples.

Confucian temples are the most sedate and lack the colour and noise of Taoist or Buddhist temples. Not nearly as active or as colourful as their Taoist or Buddhist cousins, they often have a faded and musty feel. Their courtyards are a forest of stelae celebrating local scholars, some supported on the backs of *bìxì* (mythical tortoise-like animals). The Confucius Temples in Qūfù (p198), Shāndōng province, and Běijīng (p113) are very famous.

In addition to Buddhist, Taoist and Confucian buildings, Islamic architecture may also be found across China, most of it dating after the 14th century and influenced by Central Asian styles and often combined with local Chinese style.

www.linktrip.com /gardens is a very comprehensive website with pictures and historical background on gardens around China.

Gardens

Chinese garden design reached its fullest development during the late Ming dynasty, where gardens were commonly found in homes of the elite. Gardens were particularly prevalent in southeastern China south of the Yangzi, especially in Hángzhōu (p308), Yángzhōu (p233) and Sūzhōu (p243).

Rather than lawn and flowers, the three principle elements of Chinese gardens are rock, water and stone, arranged in formations that mimic well-known mountains or paintings. Gardening was considered an intellectual pursuit and calligraphy, poetic names, references to literary classics and other complementary art forms are featured in many Chinese gardens.

Although many are park-like in scale, historically Chinese gardens were nothing like the public parks of today. They were compounds to which only a tiny portion of the population ever had access. The larger and grander of these were imperial, existing to please and entertain the emperor. In prosperous regions, private gardens also proliferated in certain periods. At its peak Sūzhōu had hundreds of gardens, and the city was registered as a Unesco World Heritage site in 1997 in recognition of those that remain. The numerous pavilions dotted around the gardens were used for everything from meditating and playing chess to musical performances and banqueting.

CHINA'S TOP 10 GARDENS

- Beihai Park, Běijīng (p112)
- Summer Palace, Běijīng (p117)
- Yuyuan Gardens, Shànghǎi (p279)
- Garden of the Master of the Nets, Sūzhōu, Jiāngsū (p244)
- Humble Administrator's Garden, Sūzhōu, Jiāngsū (p246)
- Slender West Lake, Yángzhōu, Jiāngsū (p235)
- Cuihu Park, Kūnmíng, Yúnnán (p648)
- Wuhou Temple, Chéngdū, Sìchuān (p716)
- Shuzhuang Garden, Gǔlàng Yǔ, Fújiàn (p339)
- Du Fu's Cottage, Chéngdū, Sìchuān (p716)

Environment   Korina Miller

From within the cement sea of a Chinese city, you may begin to wonder if the urban sprawl has swallowed up all that nature had to offer. Fear not. As long as you're willing to share with other visitors drawn to the great outdoors, there are still some natural wonders to behold. Spelunkers will be awed by Guìzhōu's Zhijin Cave (p634), one of the world's largest underground labyrinths. Geologists will be perplexed by Guǎngxī's bizarre karst landscape at Guìlín (p606). Hikers after a challenge with views will find it at the holy Éméi Shān (p725), and photographers (and everyone else) will be gobsmacked by the gorgeous alpine scenery of Jiǔzhàigōu (p752). From deserts to lush subtropical forests, from the elusive panda to marauding monkeys, China still has a touch of the exotic for nature lovers.

Nevertheless, China is also faced with serious environmental problems. Be prepared to encounter heavy pollution, piles of litter and dirty waterways.

THE LAND

China is the third-largest country in the world with an area of 9.5 million sq km. The land surface is like a staircase descending from west to east. At the top of the stairs, in the southwest, are the inhospitable plateaus of Tibet and Qīnghǎi averaging 4500m above sea level. At the southern rim of these plateaus is the towering Himalayan mountain range with peaks averaging 6000m high (40 peaks rise 7000m or more). Mt Everest (p872), known to the Chinese as Zhūmǔlángmǎfēng, lies on the Tibet-Nepal border.

Melting snow and ice from these and other highlands of western China provide the headwaters for many of the country's largest rivers: Yellow River (Huáng Hé), Mekong River (Láncāng Jiāng), Salween River (Nù Jiāng) and Yangzi River (Cháng Jiāng). At 6300km, Yangzi River is China's longest, and home to the Three Gorges (p772) and the controversial Three Gorges Dam Project (p766). Its watershed of almost 2 million sq km – 20% of China's land mass – supports 400 million people. Used throughout China's history for trade and navigation, the Yangzi River's advantages have been offset by flooding, which periodically inundates millions of hectares and destroys hundreds of thousands of lives.

Yellow River, about 5460km long and the second-longest river in China, is the birthplace of Chinese civilisation. The third great waterway of China, the Grand Canal, is the longest artificial canal in the world. It once stretched for 1800km from Hángzhōu in south China to Běijīng in the north. Today, however, most of the Grand Canal is silted over and no longer navigable.

Heading north and down a step from the plateaus of Tibet and Qīnghǎi lies Xīnjiāng's Tarim Basin, the largest inland basin in the world. Here you'll find the Taklamakan Desert (p796), China's largest, as well as the country's biggest shifting salt lake, Lop Nur in Xīnjiāng. (Lop Nur was also the site of China's nuclear bomb testing.) The Tarim Basin is bordered to the north by the lofty Tiān Shān (p784). Also in Xīnjiāng is China's hot spot, the low-lying Turpan Basin (p784), known as the 'Oasis of Fire'.

East from here, the third step drops to less than 1000m above sea level. These are the largely featureless plains of the Yangzi River valley

Spectacular China will whet your appetite with gorgeous pictures of China's more photogenic side. Unfortunately, readers say the binding isn't all that sturdy.

and northern and eastern China. These plains are the most important agricultural areas of the country and the most heavily populated. Keep in mind that two-thirds of China is mountain, desert or otherwise unfit for cultivation.

The exact extents of China's territory is contestable. Taiwan is considered by the People's Republic of China (PRC) government to be a province of China. The remote Spratly Islands (Nánshā) in the South China Sea are claimed by China and other countries, including the Philippines, Vietnam, Taiwan, Brunei and Malaysia. China fought and won a border war with India in the 1960s, but the boundary issue remains unresolved and a potential source of further conflict between these two nuclear states. In 1989 the Chinese forcefully took the Paracel Islands (Xīshā) from Vietnam.

WILDLIFE

China is endowed with an extremely diverse range of natural vegetation and animal life. Unfortunately, humans have had a considerable impact and much of China's rich natural heritage is rare, endangered or extinct. Many animals are officially protected, though illegal hunting and trapping continues. A bigger challenge is habitat destruction, caused by encroaching agriculture, urbanisation and industrial pollution.

While catching sight of China's rare wildlife in its natural habitat requires a great deal of time, patience and luck, many visitors do include visits to protected parks and research bases for a more guaranteed look at China's elusive residents and blooms. Bird-watching is the exception to the rule; if you're willing to rough it in China's outback, you have a good chance of seeing some rare winged friends.

Animals

China's wealth of vegetation and variety of landscapes has fostered the development of a great diversity of animals. Throughout the Chinese mountains, takin (or goat antelope), wild yaks, argali sheep, numerous species of pheasants and a variety of laughing thrushes may be found. The extreme northeastern part of China is also inhabited by some interesting mammals, such as reindeer, moose, musk deer, bears, sables and Manchurian tigers.

China has some great bird-watching opportunities, particularly in spring. Head to the strategically located Zhalong Nature Reserve (p386) in Hēilóngjiāng to take in a well-used migratory route; visit Qīnghǎi Hú (p879) in Qīnghǎi for the breeding grounds of wild geese, sandpipers and countless other birds; or head to Mai Po Marsh (p509) in Hong Kong or Cǎohǎi Hú (p635) in Guìzhōu.

For sheer diversity of wildlife, the tropical south of Yúnnán province, particularly the area around Xīshuāngbǎnnà (p685), is one of the richest in China. Here, you may have chance encounters with the parrot, hornbill, slender loris, gibbon, snub-nosed monkey, the Indochina tiger and herds of wild Indian elephants.

ENDANGERED SPECIES

China's list of endangered animals is depressingly long. In spite of the odds against them, a number of rare animals continue to survive in the wild in small and remote areas. Notable among them are the small species of alligator in Ānhuī, the giant salamander in the fast-running waters of the Yangzi and Yellow Rivers, the Yangzi River dolphin in the lower and middle reaches of the river, and the pink dolphin of the Hong

www.wwfchina.org has details of the WWF's projects for endangered and protected animals in China. You'll also find a kids' page for the budding biologists in the family.

At www.cnbirds.com China Birding can fill you in on overwinter sites, migration routes and the geographical distribution of your feathered friends in China. It also has lots of excellent photos.

DID YOU KNOW?

The fabled Chinese dragon is based on the Chinese alligator. Today there are fewer than 150 of these real-life dragons left in the wild.

KILL OR CURE?

Before you swallow that time-honoured remedy, ask for the ingredients. Despite laws banning their capture, protected and endangered animals continue to be led to the chemist counters of China.

As traditional Chinese medicine (TCM) makes it big globally, international laws prohibiting the trade of many species have forced practitioners to seek out alternative ingredients. Tiger bones, for instance, are being replaced with the bones of rodents. The difficulty lies in getting Chinese consumers to accept such alternatives. Rodent bones just don't come close to tiger bones in prestige.

Chinese Taoists and Buddhists also believe in removing protected animals from TCM. They maintain that TCM is traditionally based on achieving a balance in nature. What is bad for the environment is therefore bad for the soul.

These days poachers trading in protected species can find themselves behind bars for up to 15 years, while those found smuggling the internationally revered panda face death. Even consumers can be punished, a law that has been around for some time but only recently enforced. Ingredients to watch for include bear bile, rhinoceros horns, dried seahorse, musk deer, antelope horns, leopard bones, sea lions, macaques, alligators, anteaters, pangolins, green sea turtles, freshwater turtles, rat snakes and giant clams.

Kong islands of Sha Chau and Lung Kwu Chau. The famed giant panda is confined to the fauna-rich valleys and ranges of Sìchuān; your best chances for sighting one is in Chéngdū's Giant Panda Breeding Research Base (p714). (For more on these infamous creatures, see p715.) You can see the Siberian tiger in Hēilóngjiāng's rather disheartening Siberian Tiger Park (p381), and may be lucky enough to chance upon a golden monkey in the mountains of Sìchuān, Yúnnán and Guìzhōu. Other animals to make the endangered list include the snow leopard, South China tiger, chiru antelope, crested ibis, Asian elephant, red-crowned crane and black-crowned crane.

Intensive farmland cultivation, the reclaiming of wetlands, river damming, industrial and rural waste, and desertification are reducing unprotected forest areas and making the survival of many of these species increasingly precarious. Although there are laws against killing or capturing these rare creatures, their struggle for survival is further complicated as many remain on the most-wanted lists for traditional Chinese medicine and dinner delicacies.

Plants

China is home to around 30,000 species of seed plants and 2500 species of forest trees. The most famous of these is bamboo, which covers about 3% of the total forest area in China. Most of this bamboo is located in the subtropical areas south of Yangzi River, and the best place to surround yourself by it is in Sìchuān. Bamboo is the favourite nosh of the giant panda, and cultivated by the Chinese for building material and food. Many other well-known plants are indigenous to China, including the rhododendron, lotus flower, magnolia, ginkgo, maple, birch, poplar and spruce. Rare azaleas bring tourists to Sìchuān's Wolong Nature Reserve (p724) in summer, while the white and red Lady Slipper Orchid and rare, white-flowered Grantham's Camellia tree dazzle botanists in Hong Kong. For a good look at plants from China's north, visit Beijing Botanical Gardens (p120) in Běijīng.

China's diverse ecosystem supports a huge range of plant life: the tropical forests of the south; the desert and grasslands of the northwest; the

DID YOU KNOW?

China is one of the earth's main centres of origin for plants and has more than 17,300 species of endemic seed plants.

coniferous forests along the Russian border; and the mangrove swamps along the shores of the South China Sea. The variety of plants in China is best appreciated by comparing the vegetation of Jílín province in the semifrigid north and Hǎinán province in the tropical south. It would be difficult to find one common plant species shared by the two provinces, with the exception of a few weeds.

NATURE RESERVES

China has an incredibly diverse range of natural escapes scattered across the country. Since the first nature reserve was established in 1956, around 2000 more parks have joined the ranks, protecting about 14% of China's land area, and offering the traveller an incredible variety of landscapes and diversity of wildlife. Many of the parks are intended for the preservation of endangered animals, while others protect sacred mountains.

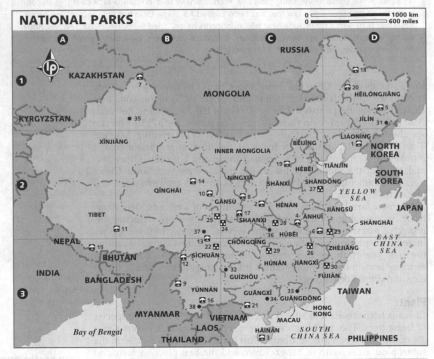

TOP NATIONAL PARKS

Reserves	Features	Activities	When to Visit	Page
Chángbái Shān	China's largest reserve: cranes, deer, tigers and some 300 medicinal plants	hiking	Jun–early Sep	p371
Éméi Shān	luxuriant scenery along a steep, ancient pilgrim route; monkeys; Buddhist sights	hiking, monasterys stays	May–Oct	p725
Jiǔzhàigōu	stunning alpine scenery and gem-coloured lakes; takins, golden monkeys, pandas	hiking, Tibetan village stays	Jun–Oct	p752
Tài Shān	holy mountain with gobsmacking views; Taoist sights	hiking	May–Oct	p190
Wulingyuan Scenic Area	craggy peaks, waterfalls, caves, subtropical forest	rafting, hiking	Jun–Oct	p487

But before you pack your hiking gear and binoculars, be prepared to share many of the more popular reserves with expanding commercial development. Tourism is generally welcomed into these reserves with open arms, meaning pricey hotels, more roads, gondolas, hawkers and busloads of tourists. With a little effort, you can often find a less beaten path to escape down, but don't expect utter tranquillity.

ENVIRONMENTAL ISSUES

As a developing country with rapid industrialisation, it's not surprising that China has some hefty environmental issues to contend with. Unfortunately, China's huge population make its environmental plights infinitely bigger than those of other nations. Air pollution, deforestation, endangered species, and rural and industrial waste are all taking their toll.

With its entry into the World Trade Organization (WTO) and the Olympics on their way, China seems to have changed its policy of 'industrial catch-up first, environmental clean-up later' to one of tidying up its environmental act now. Nevertheless, analysts continue to point to an impending environmental catastrophe, fearing that the efforts could well be too little, too late.

The impact of China's environmental problems doesn't stop at the country's borders – acid rain, desert sand storms, and silted and polluted rivers are all too familiar to China's neighbours. Across the north of China, rampaging natural fires are believed to consume more than 200 million tonnes of coal a year, further exacerbating China's contribution to global warming.

In *The River Runs Black*, Elizabeth Economy gives a fascinating account of China's environmental crisis. Her perspective is neither melodramatic nor dull, and very readable.

Energy Use & Air Pollution

Seven of the world's 10 most polluted cities are in China, with most of the country's major cities lying smothered under great canopies of smog.

The biggest source of this pollution is coal. It provides some 70% of China's energy needs and around 900 million tonnes of it go up in smoke yearly. The result is immense damage to air and water quality, agriculture and human health, with acid rain falling on about 30% of the country. Even Korea and Japan complain about damage to their forests from acid rain that is believed to have come from China.

As demand quickly outstrips domestic resources of coal, the government has made some effort to seek out alternative sources of energy. Plans to construct natural gas pipelines are underway and taxes have been introduced on high-sulphur coals.

Water & Wetlands

It is estimated that China annually dumps three billion tonnes of untreated water into the ocean via its rivers, a statement that won't likely shock you if you take a look at some of the water flowing under the bridges as you journey across the country.

China's rivers and wetlands face great pressure from draining and reclamation, as well as pollution from untreated industrial and domestic waste. This poor-quality water, coupled with often acute water shortages, is creating significant environmental health hazards. Some reports indicate that half the population is supplied with polluted water.

Drought often hits north and west China while northeast and central China are flooded: waste, silting up of riverbeds, overextraction of water and the general abuse of the environment worsen the situation. The communists' cure-all to China's water problems is the damming of the Yangzi River. For more on this monumental project, see p766.

Environmental Awareness

China has a long tradition of celebrating nature within its frontiers, from landscape paintings to poems dwelling on mountain peaks shrouded in mist. Like many nations of the world, the contradictory China of today eulogises its landscape while simultaneously destroying it.

There is legislation to curb the worst excesses of industry, but these laws are rarely enforced. Corrupt officials are partly to blame, but the drag on economic expansion is also cited as a factor.

Compelling economic pressure to exploit the environment has been exacerbated by a lack of knowledge on the part of China's citizens who have been given no education or information on ecology. Waking up to

http://china.org.cn is a Chinese government site with a link to a page covering environmental issues. While some may consider the information overly optimistic, it offers regularly updated stories and links.

THE GREEN WALL OF CHINA

If you visit Běijīng in spring and experience the sand storms that send residents rushing around with plastic bags over their heads, you may not be so surprised to hear that the city may one day be swallowed up by the Gobi Desert. Only 150km away, the winds are blowing the sands towards the capital at a rate of 2km a year, with 30m dunes closing in. In their wake, these massive dust storms have left entire towns abandoned and environmental refugees numbering in the millions. They've also brought about bizarre weather effects, like 'black winds' and 'mud rains'. Experts blame the problem on overgrazing and deforestation; every month 200 sq km of arable land in China becomes a desert.

In a rather late attempt to fend off the desert, China's government has pledged US$6.8 billion to build a green wall between Běijīng and the sands; at 5700km long, it will be longer than the Great Wall of China. Unfortunately, the work so far doesn't appear to be doing the trick. Few of the millions of planted trees are surviving, while overirrigation, air pollution, erosion and corruption – all of which are playing a role in the desertification – remain unaddressed. As researchers, bureaucrats and villagers try to hammer out a solution, the sands are beginning to find their way across the Pacific, dropping grit on Vancouver and bringing unreal sunsets to San Francisco.

this, the government now bombards viewers with green directives on TV, from saving water to planting trees and litter disposal. In the dour 1970s, such environmental concerns were more likely to be dismissed as a bourgeois conspiracy. These days a growing middle class finds itself wooed by adverts for environmentally friendly washing powders and detergents.

There has been an increase in the severity of penalties for violating China's conservation laws, with the death penalty and life sentences not uncommon. However, there remains little room for debating the issues with gusto in the media.

Food & Drink

China has one of the finest cuisines in the world, and from back-alley dumpling shops to four-star banquet halls, travellers surely won't leave disappointed. The country boasts a mind-boggling array of regional delicacies and it could take years to sample all that China has to offer.

The Chinese obsession with food is rooted in thousands of years of food scarcity. In 200 BC, an official stated, 'To ordinary people, food is tantamount to heaven'. To save cooking fuel, meat and vegetables were chopped into tiny pieces to ensure faster cooking and dishes were served communally to make sure everyone got something to eat.

The question 'Nǐ chī fànle ma?' ('Have you eaten yet?') is a common greeting among Chinese people and is taken to show the significance of food in Chinese culture. Fàn may be more loosely translated as 'grain' – as opposed to cài, which literally means 'vegetable' and, by extension, any accompaniment to grain in a meal. The principle that a proper meal is based around a staple grain dates back at least to the Shang dynasty (1700–1100 BC) and remains fundamental to Chinese cuisine wherever it is found.

> 'The question "Have you eaten yet?" is a common greeting among Chinese people'

The dichotomy between fàn and cài also shows how the principles of balance and harmony, Yin and Yang, are applied in everyday life. To be more specific, most vegetables and fruits are Yin foods, generally moist or soft, and are meant to have a cooling effect, nurturing the feminine aspect of our nature. Yang foods – fried, spicy or with red meat – are warming and nourish the masculine side of our nature. Any meal should not only harmonise a variety of tastes, but also provide a balance between cooling and warming foods.

Cooking in China is divided into four schools: the Northern, Eastern, Western and Southern. The differences among them arose not only from geographical and climatic differences, but also from historical and cultural circumstances. Ironically, it was not until China was under threat from the Jurchen Mongols in the 12th century, when the Song court fled south of the Yangzi River, that these regional cuisines were codified and developed. Widespread urbanisation, made possible by the commercialisation of agriculture and food distribution, gave rise to the restaurant industry, which in turn facilitated the development of the regional cuisines.

The Mongol conquest of the north, China's wheat bowl, also precipitated the shift to rice as the main staple. This was a significant change, as rice is the best source of nutritionally balanced calories and can therefore support more people from a given area than any other crop. Improved communications, notably the building of the Grand Canal to link many of China's innumerable waterways, allowed food to be brought from and supplied to any part of the kingdom.

During the Ming dynasty (1368–1644), the restaurant industry continued to flourish. At this time, the court kitchens in the Forbidden City alone are reputed to have employed 5000 people. Refrigeration – blocks of ice cut from northern rivers and lakes in winter and stored in deep caves for use in summer – allowed further diversification and use of products out of season.

The last significant development in Chinese cuisine, however, took place in the Qing dynasty (1644–1911), when crops were introduced from the New World. Maize, sweet potatoes and peanuts – which flourished in climates where rice, wheat and millet wouldn't grow – made life possible in formerly uninhabitable areas. The other significant import from the New World was red chillies, which are not only a spice, but also a concentrated source of vitamins A and C.

STAPLES & SPECIALITIES

Traditional breakfast in China usually consists of rice porridge (zhōu or congee) often accompanied by pickles and yóutiáo (deep-fried dough sticks), along with steamed buns, served plain or with fillings. This is usually washed down with hot soybean milk, sweetened or plain. Other dishes can include rice-noodle soups, boiled eggs, fried peanuts and dumplings.

Most hotels have breakfast buffets, often included in the room price. These can be very simple affairs, serving just peanuts and congee, to fancy spreads with Western 'highlights' such as toast, jam, boxed cereal and coffee.

The Chinese generally eat lunch between 11.30am and 2pm, many taking their midday meal from any number of small eateries on the streets. For Chinese on the run, lunch and dinner generally consist of rice or noodles, topped with a vegetable and/or some meat. For more formal affairs with family and friends, lunch and dinner usually consist of several meat and vegetable dishes and a soup. Banquets can be overwhelming affairs, with 20- to 30-course dinners being common.

The Chinese do not generally eat dessert, but fruit is considered to be an appropriate end to a good meal. Western influence has added ice cream to the menu in some upmarket establishments, but in general sweet stuff is consumed as snacks and is seldom available in restaurants. One exception to the rule is caramelised fruits, including apples (bāsī píngguǒ) and bananas (bāsī xiāngjiāo) which you can find in a few restaurants. Other sweeties include shaved ice and syrup (bīngshā), a sweet, sticky rice pudding known as eight-treasures rice (bābǎo fàn), and various types of steamed buns filled with sweet bean paste.

Rice

There's a saying in Chinese that 'precious things are not pearls or jade but the five grains'. An old legend about the origin of rice claims that rice is actually a gift from the animals. The story goes that centuries ago, China was overswept by floods which destroyed all the crops and caused massive starvation. One day, some villagers saw a dog running towards them. On the dog's tail were bunches of long yellow seeds. When the villagers planted the seeds, the rice grew and hunger disappeared.

TRAVEL YOUR TASTEBUDS

Eating in China can be an overwhelming experience, especially with the vast variety of delicious foods to try. With so many regional delicacies, it's truly a gourmand's paradise. In the north, fill up on a tasty dish of wontons (húndún), filled with leeks and minced pork or Mongolian hotpot (ménggǔ huǒguō), a savoury brew of mutton, onions and cabbage.

In the south, enjoy morning dim sum in Guǎngzhōu or a bowl of Cantonese snake soup (shé gēng) in one of the city's boisterous night markets. While in Macau, taste the Macanese dish porco à alentejana, a delicious casserole of pork and clams that is not to be missed.

When travelling through China's arid northwest, consider trying a bowl of noodles topped with sliced donkey meat (lǘròu huáng miàn) or hearty roasted mutton (kǎo yángròu).

And don't forget delectable stinky tofu (chòu dòufu) – some say it's the equivalent to European stinky cheese.

The Chinese revere rice not only as their staff of life but also for its aesthetic value. Its mellow aroma is not unlike bread. Its texture when properly done – soft yet offering some resistance, the grains detached – sets off the textures of the foods that surround it. Flavours are brought into better focus by its simplicity. Rice is the unifier of the table, bringing all the dishes into harmony.

Noodles

Noodles are a staple in the north and eaten more than rice, which is more commonly eaten in southern China. Noodles can be made by hand or by machine but many people agree that hand-pulled noodles *(lāmiàn)* are the tastiest. Watching the noodles being made is almost as much a treat as eating them. First the cook stretches the dough in their hands, shakes it gently up and down and swings it so the dough twists around itself many times until it becomes firm. The dough is pulled and stretched until it becomes very fine. Often the noodles are served in a spicy broth.

Regional Cuisines

NORTHERN SCHOOL

In the north, traditionally wheat or millet are eaten rather than rice. The most famous Chinese dish of all, Peking duck, is served with typical northern ingredients: wheat pancakes, spring onions and fermented bean paste. There is a heavy reliance on freshwater fish and chicken in the north; cabbage is ubiquitous and seems to fill any available space on trains, buses and lorries in the winter.

Not surprisingly, the influence of the Mongols is felt most strongly in the north, and two of the region's most famous culinary exports – Mongolian barbecue and Mongolian hotpot – are adaptations from Mongol field kitchens. Animals that were hunted on horseback could be dismembered and cooked with wild vegetables and onions using soldiers' iron shields on top of hot coals as primitive barbecues. Alternatively, each soldier could use their helmet as a pot, filling it with water, meat, condiments and vegetables to taste. Mutton is now the main ingredient in Mongolian hotpot.

Roasting was once considered rather barbaric in other parts of China, and is still more common in the north. The main methods of cooking in the northern style, though, are steaming, baking and 'explode-frying' (dropping items into a wok of hot oil and having them sizzle or 'explode', like deep-frying). This way, the food cooks very quickly. The last of these is the most common, historically because of the scarcity of fuel and, more recently, due to the introduction of the peanut, which thrives in the north and produces an abundance of oil. Although northern-style food has a reputation for being unsophisticated and bland, it has the benefit of being filling and therefore well suited to the cold climate.

EASTERN SCHOOL

The eastern region – blessed with the bounty of the Yangzi River and its tributaries, a subtropical climate, fertile soil and a coastline – has long been a mecca for gastronomes. The Southern Song capital of Hángzhōu, on the banks of West Lake with its abundant fish, including the highly esteemed silver carp, is the birthplace of the restaurant industry. At least one restaurant, the Lóuwàilóu Càiguǎn (p313), has been around since 1848. Sūzhōu (p243) is equally famous for its cuisine, which has been eulogised by generations of poets.

A vast variety of ingredients and condiments is available, which has led to a wide diversity of cuisine within the region. Explode-frying is used here, too, but not as much as the form of frying known as archetypally Chinese throughout the world: stir-frying in a wok. Another eastern style of cooking that has been exported to the rest of the world (from Fújiàn via Taiwan) is the red-stew, in which meat is simmered slowly in dark soy sauce, sugar and spices. Indeed, many Fújiàn dishes rely on a heavy, meaty stock for their distinctive flavour. Nonetheless, it is in this region that Chinese vegetarian cuisine reached its apex, partly thanks to the availability of fresh ingredients and partly to the specialisation of generations of chefs. As might be expected, seasoning is light to allow the natural flavours of the fresh ingredients to be fully appreciated.

WESTERN SCHOOL

The Western School is renowned most for its use of the red chilli, introduced by Spanish traders in the early Qing dynasty. While northern foods evolved to provide lasting satisfaction in a cold climate, Sìchuān dishes tend to dry out the body through perspiration, which helps it adjust to the intense humidity.

Pork, poultry, legumes and soya beans are the most commonly used items, supplemented by a variety of wild condiments and mountain products, such as mushrooms and other fungi, as well as bamboo shoots. Seasonings are heavy: the red chilli is often used in conjunction with Sìchuān peppercorns, garlic, ginger and onions. Meat, particularly in Húnán, is marinated, pickled or otherwise processed before cooking, which is generally by stir- or explode-frying.

The cuisine of the Western School has a reputation of being down-to-earth, rather like the inhabitants of the region. Mao Zedong hailed from Húnán and remained fond of the hot foods from his native province throughout his life. However, it was due to the Nationalists in the civil war that Sìchuān cuisine gained international recognition. Fleeing the Japanese in 1937, the Nationalist government took refuge in Chóngqìng until the end of the war in Asia. On its return to Nánjīng and Shànghǎi, thousands of Sìchuān chefs were brought along. Most of them continued on to Taiwan when the Nationalist government was forced to flee once more, and from there spread out across the globe.

'The southerners' gourmandising and exotic tastes have earned them a reputation around China'

SOUTHERN SCHOOL

The food from this region is easily the most common form of Chinese food found in the Western world since most overseas Chinese have their roots in the Guǎngdōng region. The humid climate and heavy rainfall mean that rice has been a staple here since the Chinese first came to the region in the Han era (206 BC–AD 220). As does the Eastern School, the Southern benefits from a cornucopia of ingredients to choose from, yet in the south the choice is even more exotic. Stir-frying is by far the most favoured method of cooking, closely followed by steaming. Dim sum, now a worldwide Sunday institution, originated in this region; to go *yám cha* (Cantonese for 'drink tea') still provides most overseas Chinese communities with the opportunity to get together at the weekend.

Not only are the ingredients more varied than elsewhere in China, methods of preparation also reach their peak of sophistication in the south, where the appearance and texture of foods are prized alongside their freshness. Such refinement is a far cry from the austere cuisine of the north and the earthy fare of the west. Consequently, the southerners' gourmandising and exotic tastes – for dogs, cats, raccoons, monkeys, lizards and rats – have earned them a long-established reputation around China.

DRINKS
Nonalcoholic Drinks

Tea is a fundamental part of Chinese life. In fact, an old Chinese saying identifies tea as one of the seven basic necessities of life, along with fuel, oil, rice, salt, soy sauce and vinegar. The Chinese were the first to cultivate tea, and the art of brewing and drinking tea has been popular since the Tang dynasty (AD 618–907).

Cheaper restaurants serve on-the-house pots of weak jasmine or green tea. Higher quality brands of tea are available in tea shops or in supermarkets. China has three main types of tea: green tea *(lǜ chá)*, black tea *(hóng chá)* and *wūlóng* (a semifermented tea, halfway between black and green tea). In addition, there are other variations, including jasmine *(cháshuǐ)* and chrysanthemum *(júhuā chá)*. Some famous regional teas of China are Fújiàn's *tiě guānyīn*, *pú'ěr* from Yúnnán and Zhèjiāng's *lóngjǐng* tea. Eight-treasures tea *(bābǎo chá)* consists of rock sugar, dates, nuts and tea combined in a cup and makes a delicious treat.

Traditionally, Chinese would never put milk or sugar in their tea but things are changing. Now 'milk tea' *(nǎi chá)* is available everywhere in China, often served cold with a whopping amount of sugar. Teahouses are everywhere in China and a great place to relax with friends.

Coffee house chic has hit China in a big way and Western-style coffee houses have sprouted up all over the country. The coffee chain Starbucks has become fashionable for trendy urban youth with money to burn. A cup of semidecent coffee should set you back around Y20, depending upon the establishment.

Soft drinks such as Sprite and Coca-Cola are easily found, as are local fizzy drinks such as Jianlibao, a honey-sweetened drink, along with ice teas and fruit drinks. Bottled water is on sale all over the place but check the cap before buying to see if it's sealed.

Milk is available fresh or powdered from supermarkets and convenience stores. Popular are sweet yogurt drinks in bottles sold in stores or fresh yogurt sold at some street stalls.

Alcoholic Drinks

If tea is the most popular drink in China, then beer must be number two. By any standards the top brands are good. The best known is Tsingtao, made with a mineral water that gives it a sparkling quality. It's essentially a German beer since the town of Qingdao (formerly spelled 'Tsingtao'), where it's made, was once a German concession and the Chinese inherited the brewery (p208). Experts claim that draft Tsingtao tastes much better than the bottled stuff. A bottle will normally cost Y1.5 to Y2 in street shops, around Y15 to Y20 in a bar.

'If tea is the most popular drink in China, then beer must be number two'

China has cultivated vines and produced wine for an estimated 4000 years. The word 'wine' gets rather loosely translated – many Chinese 'wines' are in fact spirits. Rice wine is intended mainly for cooking rather than drinking. Chinese wine-producing techniques differ from those of the West. Western producers try to prevent oxidation in their wines, but oxidation produces a flavour that Chinese tipplers find desirable and go to great lengths to achieve. Chinese diners are also keen on wines with different herbs and other materials soaked in them, which they drink for their health and for restorative or aphrodisiac qualities.

Wine with dead bees, pickled snakes or lizards is desirable for its alleged tonic properties – in general, the more poisonous the creature, the more potent the tonic effects. Maotai, a favourite of Chinese drinkers, is a spirit made from sorghum (a type of millet) and used for toasts at banquets.

CELEBRATIONS
Holidays

Food plays a major role in Chinese holidays. For many Chinese, the appearance of a food is symbolic. Chinese like to eat noodles on birthdays and on the New Year (p894) because their long thin shape symbolises longevity. That's why it's bad luck to break the noodles before cooking them. During the Chinese New Year, it's common to serve a whole chicken because it resembles family unity. Clams and spring rolls are also served during New Year festivities because their shapes represent wealth: clams resemble bullion and spring rolls are shaped like bars of gold.

Fish also plays an important role during New Year celebrations. The word for fish, *yú*, sounds similar to the word for abundance. It's custom to serve a fish at the end of the evening meal, symbolising a wish for prosperity in the coming year.

Certain holiday foods stem from legends. For example, the tradition of eating moon cakes (*yuè bing*), a sweet cake filled with sesame seeds, lotus seeds, dates and other fillings during China's Mid-Autumn Festival (p894), is based on a story from the 14th century. Supposedly, when China was battling the Mongol invasions, a certain general had a plan to take back Mongol-held territory. He dressed up as a Taoist priest, entered the city and distributed moon cakes to the populace. Hidden within the cakes were notes instructing the people to revolt and overthrow the Mongols to retake their city. The people did as instructed and threw the Mongols out.

Zòngzi (dumplings made of glutinous rice wrapped in bamboo or reed leaves) are eaten during the Dragon Boat festival (p894) and have a very long history in China. According to legend, such dumplings were thrown into the river as fish food to keep them from eating the body of Qu Yuan, a poet who committed suicide during the Warring States period (475–221 BC). Now the dumplings are eaten throughout China as well as Southeast Asia.

> 'It's bad luck to break noodles before cooking them'

Banquets

The banquet is the apex of the Chinese dining experience. Virtually all significant business deals in China are clinched at the banquet table.

Dishes are served in sequence, beginning with cold appetisers and continuing through 10 or more courses. Soup, usually a thin broth to aid digestion, is generally served after the main course.

The idea is to serve or order far more than everyone can eat. Empty bowls imply a stingy host. Rice is considered a cheap filler and rarely appears at a banquet – don't ask for it, as this would imply that the snacks and main courses are insufficient, causing embarrassment to the host.

It's best to wait for some signal from the host before digging in. You will most likely be invited to take the first taste. Often your host will serve it to you, placing a piece of meat, chicken or fish in your bowl. If a whole fish is served, you might be offered the head, the cheeks of which are considered to be the tastiest part. Try to take at least a taste of what is given to you.

Never drink alone. Imbibing is conducted via toasts, which will usually commence with a general toast by the host, followed by the main guest reply toast, and then settle down to frequent toasts to individuals. A toast is conducted by raising your glass in both hands in the direction of the toastee and crying out *gānbēi*, literally 'dry the glass'. Chinese do not clink glasses. Drain your glass in one hit. It is not unusual for everyone to end up very drunk, though at very formal banquets this is frowned upon.

Don't be late for a formal banquet; it's considered extremely rude. The banquet ends when the food and toasts end – the Chinese don't linger after the meal. You may find yourself being applauded when you enter a large banquet. It is polite to applaud back.

WHERE TO EAT & DRINK

It's hard to go hungry in China as just about everywhere you go there will be a myriad of food options to suit most budgets. The word *fàngdiàn* usually refers to a large-scale restaurant that may or may not offer lodging. A *cānguǎn* is generally a smaller restaurant that specialises in one particular type of food. The most informal type of restaurant is the *cāntīng*, which has low-end prices, though the quality of the food can be quite high.

Breakfast is served early in China, mainly between 6am and 9am. In larger cities most restaurants serving lunch and dinner open from 11am to 2pm, reopen around 5pm and close at 9pm. In smaller cities, restaurants may close as early as 8pm. Some street stalls stay open 24 hours.

Tourist-friendly restaurants can be found around tourist sights and often have English signs and menus. Sometimes food can be quite overpriced and geared towards foreign tastes. It's easy to find restaurants that cater to Chinese clientele – just look for noisy, crowded places; the noisier the better. These restaurants may not have English menus but it's OK to look at what other people are having and indicate to the wait staff what you want by pointing. You can also use the Menu Decoder (p89).

Eating solo in China can be a lonely experience, since Chinese food is meant to be shared by groups of people. Larger restaurants cater to groups of people and portions may be too large for someone dining solo. Smaller restaurants off the main streets are more welcoming, though the menus can be repetitious. For variety, solo travellers can try eating at any number of the growing number of cafés and family-style restaurants that offer set meals, usually a main course served with salad and soup, at very reasonable prices. Self-serve cafeterias (*zìzhù cān*) are another option and offer plenty of meat and vegetable dishes to choose from.

Hotels in larger cities often serve high-end regional dishes and international food, serving everything from Indian to French cuisine.

Quick Eats

Eating in China's bustling night markets is an experience not to be missed. Some of the country's best treats can be sampled in the markets, making them a gourmet's paradise. Hygiene is always a question, so make sure to eat only at the busiest of places to avoid getting sick.

Dumplings (*shuǐjiǎo*) are a popular snack item in China and a delicious, inexpensive way to fill up. They're best described as Chinese ravioli, stuffed with meat, spring onion and greens. They are sometimes served by the bowl in a soup, sometimes dry by weight (250g or half a *jīn* is normally enough). Locals mix chilli (*làjiāo*), vinegar (*cù*) and soy sauce (*jiàngyóu*) in a little bowl according to taste and dip the dumpling in. Dumplings are often created by family minifactories – one stretches the pastry, another makes the filling and a third spoons the filling into the pastry, finishing with a little twist.

Other street snacks include fried tofu, tea eggs (soaked in soy sauce), tofu soaked in soy sauce, and baked sweet potatoes, which can be bought by weight.

In addition to the markets, there are innumerable snack stalls set up around markets, train stations and bus stations. These are the places to grab something on the run, including *bāozi*, steamed buns stuffed with meat or vegetables, as well as grilled corn, mutton kebabs, noodles and plenty of regional specialities.

'Eating in China's bustling night markets is an experience not to be missed'

VEGETARIANS & VEGANS

Vegetarianism in China can be traced back over 1000 years. The Tang dynasty physician Sun Simiao extolled the virtues of vegetarianism in his 60-volume classic, *Prescriptions Worth More Than Gold*. Legend has it that Sun lived to the ripe old age of 101.

Because of China's history of poverty and famine, eating meat is a status symbol, symbolic of health and wealth. Many Chinese remember all too well the famines of the 1950s and 1960s when having anything to eat at all was a luxury. Eating meat (as well as milk and eggs) is a sign of progress and material abundance. Even vegetables are often fried in animal-based oils, and soups are most commonly made with chicken or beef stock.

In larger cities such as Běijīng, Shànghǎi, Guǎngzhōu and Hong Kong, vegetarianism is slowly catching on and there are new chic vegetarian eateries appearing in fashionable restaurant districts. These are often pricey establishments and you pay for ambience as well as the food.

Chinese vegetarian food often consists of 'mock meat' dishes made from tofu, wheat gluten and vegetables. Some of the dishes are quite fantastic to look at, with vegetarian ingredients sculpted to look like spare ribs or fried chicken. Sometimes the chefs go to great lengths to even create 'bones' from carrots and lotus roots. Some of the more famous vegetarian dishes include vegetarian 'ham', braised vegetarian 'shrimp' and sweet and sour 'fish'.

DID YOU KNOW?

Chopsticks originated in China almost 4000 years ago.

WHINING & DINING

Eating out with children in China can be a challenge. Budget eateries won't have special menus for children nor will they supply booster seats. Higher-end restaurants may be able to offer these things but it's best to check in advance. On the up side, in larger cities there are now more family-style restaurants that offer set meals and cater to families. Some of these places have special meals for children, usually consisting of fried chicken or fish. Fast-food restaurants are another option, for their kid-friendly atmosphere.

Supermarkets in China sell Western baby formula and baby foods, as well as infant cereals. For more information on children see p888.

HABITS & CUSTOMS

To the Chinese, eating is a way to socialise and friendships are made at the dinner table. Restaurants are noisy, crowded places where people get together with family and friends to unwind and enjoy themselves. Eating is a time of relaxation, away from the pressures of work and school. While friends in the West go out for a beer, the Chinese will opt for a 'hot and noisy' meal punctuated with increasingly vociferous shots of rice wine.

Typically, the Chinese sit at a round table and order dishes from which everyone partakes; ordering a dish just for yourself would be unthinkable. It's not unusual for one person at the table to order on everyone's behalf. Usually among friends only several dishes will be ordered but if guests are present, the host will order at least one dish per person, possibly more. At formal dinners, be prepared for a staggering amount of food, far more than anyone could eat.

Epicureans will tell you that the key to ordering is to get a balance of textures, tastes, smells, colours and even temperatures. Most Chinese meals start with some snacks, perhaps some peanuts or pickles. Following the little tidbits are the main courses, usually some meat and vegetable dishes. Soup is often served at the end of the meal as well as noodles or rice.

Traditionally, the Chinese had a number of taboos regarding table etiquette. Nowadays, these rules are much more relaxed and foreigners are given special allowances for social gaffes. However, there are some basic rules to follow when eating with Chinese friends or colleagues that will make things at the table go more smoothly.

Everyone gets an individual bowl and a small plate and tea cup. It's quite acceptable to hold the bowl close to your lips and shovel the contents into your mouth with chopsticks. If the food contains bones or seeds, just put them out on the tablecloth or in a dish reserved for this purpose. Restaurants are prepared for the mess and staff change the tablecloth after each customer leaves.

Chopstick skills are a necessary means of survival when eating out in China. Don't despair if at first much of the food lands on the table or in your lap and not in your bowl. Eating this way takes practice and most Chinese are understanding when it comes to foreigners and chopstick problems.

When eating from communal dishes, don't use your chopsticks to root around in a dish for a piece of food. Find a piece by sight and go directly for it without touching anything else. And remember that while dropping food is OK, never drop your chopsticks as this is considered bad luck.

Most Chinese think little of sticking their own chopsticks into a communal dish, though this attitude is changing because of SARS. Many higher-end restaurants now provide separate serving spoons or chopsticks to be used with communal dishes. If these are provided, make sure to use them. Never use a personal spoon to serve from a communal plate or bowl.

Don't be surprised if your Chinese host uses their chopsticks to place food in your bowl or plate. This is a sign of friendship and the polite thing to do is to smile and eat whatever has been given you. If for some reason you can't eat it, leave it in your bowl or hide it with rice.

Remember to fill your neighbours' tea cups when they are empty, as yours will be filled by them. You can thank the pourer by tapping two fingers on the table gently. On no account serve yourself tea without serving others first. When your teapot needs a refill, signal this to the waiter by taking the lid off the pot.

Probably the most important piece of etiquette comes with the bill: the person who extended the dinner invitation is presumed to pay, though everyone at the table will put up a fight. Don't argue too hard; it's expected that at a certain point in the future the meal will be reciprocated.

COOKING COURSES

Some Western tour operators offer 'culinary tours' of China which give visitors the opportunity to try their hand at Chinese cooking.

EATING DO'S & DON'TS

- Don't wave your chopsticks around or point them at people. This is considered rude.
- Don't drum your chopsticks on the sides of your bowl – only beggars do this.
- Never commit the terrible faux pas of sticking your chopsticks into your rice. Two chopsticks stuck vertically into a rice bowl resembles incense sticks in a bowl of ashes and is considered an omen of death.
- Don't discuss business or unpleasant topics at dinner.
- Don't let the spout of a teapot face towards anyone. Make sure it is directed outward from the table or to where nobody is sitting.
- Never flip a fish over to get to the flesh underneath. If you do so, the next boat you pass will capsize.

Some even offer a certificate of completion at the end of the course. A good agency to try is the Inspirasians Cooking School, based in Hong Kong, which offers four- to seven-day cooking classes in Guǎngdōng province. Its website www.inspirasians.com gives detailed information on courses offered.

EAT YOUR WORDS
See the Language chapter (p936) for pronunciation guidelines.

http://chinesefood.about .com has links to a wide body of topics on Chinese food and cooking. There are also pictures of commonly used ingredients and guides to etiquette and dining out in China.

Useful Phrases

I don't want MSG.	*wǒ bú yào wèijīng*	我不要味精
I'm vegetarian.	*wǒ chī sù*	我吃素
not too spicy	*bù yào tài là*	不要太辣
menu	*càidān*	菜单
bill (cheque)	*mǎidān/jiézhàng*	买单/结帐
set meal (no menu)	*tàocān*	套餐
let's eat	*chī fàn*	吃饭
cheers!	*gānbēi*	干杯
chopsticks	*kuàizi*	筷子
knife	*dàozi*	刀子
fork	*chāzi*	叉子
spoon	*tiáogēng/tāngchí*	调羹/汤匙
hot	*rède*	热的
ice cold	*bīngde*	冰的

Menu Decoder
NORTHERN SCHOOL

Běijīng kǎoyā	北京烤鸭	Peking duck
jiāo zhá yángròu	焦炸羊肉	deep-fried mutton
jiǔ zhuǎn dàcháng	九转大肠	spicy braised pig's intestine
qīng xiāng shāo jī	清香烧鸡	chicken wrapped in lotus leaf
sān měi dòufu	三美豆腐	sliced bean curd with Chinese cabbage
shuàn yángròu	涮羊肉	lamb hotpot
sì xǐ wánzi	四喜丸子	steamed and fried pork, shrimp and bamboo shoot balls
yuán bào lǐ jǐ	芫爆里脊	stir-fried pork tenderloin with coriander
zào liū sān bái	糟溜三白	stir-fried chicken, fish and bamboo shoots

EASTERN SCHOOL

jiāng cōng chǎo xiè	姜葱炒蟹	stir-fried crab with ginger and scallions
mìzhī xūnyú	蜜汁熏鱼	honey-smoked carp
níng shì shànyú	宁式鳝鱼	stir-fried eel with onion
qiézhī yúkuài	茄汁鱼块	fish fillet in tomato sauce
qīng zhēng guìyú	清蒸鳜鱼	steamed Mandarin fish
sōngzǐ guìyú	松子鳜鱼	Mandarin fish with pine nuts
suānlà yóuyú	酸辣鱿鱼	hot and sour squid
yóubào xiārén	油爆虾仁	fried shrimp
zhá hēi lǐyú	炸黑鲤鱼	fried black carp
zhá yúwán	炸鱼丸	fish balls

WESTERN SCHOOL

bàngbàng jī	棒棒鸡	shredded chicken in a hot pepper and sesame sauce
dàsuàn shàn duàn	大蒜鳝段	stewed eel with garlic
gānshāo yán lǐ	干烧岩鲤	stewed carp with ham and hot and sweet sauce
gōngbào jīdīng	宫爆鸡丁	spicy chicken with peanuts

huíguō ròu	回锅肉	boiled and stir-fried pork with salty and hot sauce
málà dòufu	麻辣豆腐	spicy tofu
shuǐ zhǔ niúròu	水煮牛肉	fried and boiled beef, garlic sprouts and celery
yúxiāng ròusī	鱼香肉丝	'fish-resembling' meat
zhàcài ròusī	榨菜肉丝	stir-fried pork or beef tenderloin with tuber mustard
zhāngchá yā	樟茶鸭	camphor tea duck

SOUTHERN SCHOOL

bái zhuó xiā	白灼虾	blanched prawns with shredded scallions
dōngjiāng yánjú jī	东江盐焗鸡	salt-baked chicken
gālí jī	咖喱鸡	curried chicken
háoyóu niúròu	蚝油牛肉	beef with oyster sauce
kǎo rǔzhū	烤乳猪	crispy suckling pig
mì zhī chāshāo	密汁叉烧	roast pork with honey
shé ròu	蛇肉	snake
tángcù lǐjí/	糖醋里脊/	sweet and sour
gǔlǎo ròu	咕老肉	pork fillets
tángcù páigǔ	糖醋排骨	sweet and sour spare ribs

Food Glossary
COOKING TERMS

chǎo	炒	fry
hóngshāo	红烧	red-cooked (stewed in soy sauce)
kǎo	烤	roast
yóujiān	油煎	deep-fry
zhēng	蒸	steam
zhǔ	煮	boil

RICE DISHES

jīchǎofàn	鸡炒饭	fried rice with chicken
jīdàn chǎofàn	鸡蛋炒饭	fried rice with egg
jīdàn mǐfàn	米饭	steamed white rice
shūcài chǎofàn	蔬菜炒饭	fried rice with vegetables
xīfàn; zhōu	稀饭; 粥	watery rice porridge *(congee)*

NOODLE DISHES

húntún miàn	馄饨面	wontons and noodles
jīsī chǎomiàn	鸡丝炒面	fried noodles with chicken
jīsī tāngmiàn	鸡丝汤面	soupy noodles with chicken
májiàng miàn	麻酱面	sesame paste noodles
niúròu chǎomiàn	牛肉炒面	fried noodles with beef
niúròu miàn	牛肉汤面	soupy beef noodles
ròusī chǎomiàn	肉丝炒面	fried noodles with pork
shūcài chǎomiàn	蔬菜炒面	fried noodles with vegetables
tāngmiàn	汤面	noodles in soup
xiārén chǎomiàn	虾仁炒面	fried noodles with shrimp
zhájiàng miàn	炸酱面	bean and meat noodles

BREAD, BUNS & DUMPLINGS

cōngyóu bǐng	葱油饼	spring onion pancakes
guōtiē	锅贴	pot stickers/pan-grilled dumplings
mántóu	馒头	steamed buns
ròu bāozi	肉包子	steamed meat buns
shāo bǐng	烧饼	clay-oven rolls

DID YOU KNOW?

The monkey, anteater, cranes and other protected animals are considered delicacies in some areas of China.

shuǐjiān bāo	水煎包	pan-grilled buns
shuǐjiǎo	水饺	boiled dumplings
sùcài bāozǐ	素菜包子	steamed vegetable buns

SOUP

húntún tāng	馄饨汤	wonton soup
sān xiān tāng	三鲜汤	three kinds of seafood soup
suānlà tāng	酸辣汤	hot and sour soup

BEEF DISHES

gānbiān niúròu sī	干煸牛肉丝	stir-fried beef and chilli
háoyóu niúròu	蚝油牛肉	beef with oyster sauce
hóngshāo niúròu	红烧牛肉	beef braised in soy sauce
niúròu fàn	牛肉饭	beef with rice
tiěbǎn niúròu	铁板牛肉	sizzling beef platter

CHICKEN & DUCK DISHES

háoyóu jīkuài	蚝油鸡块	diced chicken in oyster sauce
hóngshāo jīkuài	红烧鸡块	chicken braised in soy sauce
jītuǐ fàn	鸡腿饭	chicken leg with rice
níngméng jī	柠檬鸡	lemon chicken
tángcù jīdīng	糖醋鸡丁	sweet and sour chicken
yāoguǒ jīdīng	腰果鸡丁	chicken and cashews
yāròu fàn	鸭肉饭	duck with rice

DID YOU KNOW?

In China, the average person eats over 20kg of seafood each year.

PORK DISHES

biǎndòu ròusī	扁豆肉丝	shredded pork and green beans
gūlǔ ròu	咕噜肉	sweet and sour pork
guōbā ròupiàn	锅巴肉片	pork and sizzling rice crust
háoyóu ròusī	耗油肉丝	pork with oyster sauce
jiàngbào ròudīng	酱爆肉丁	diced pork with soy sauce
jīngjiàng ròusī	京酱肉丝	pork cooked with soy sauce
mùěr ròu	木耳肉	wood-ear mushrooms and pork
páigǔ fàn	排骨饭	pork chop with rice
qīngjiāo ròu piàn	青椒肉片	pork and green peppers
yángcōng chǎo ròupiàn	洋葱炒肉片	pork and fried onions

SEAFOOD DISHES

gélì	蛤蜊	clams
gōngbào xiārén	宫爆虾仁	diced shrimp with peanuts
háo	蚝	oysters
hóngshāo yú	红烧鱼	fish braised in soy sauce
lóngxiā	龙虾	lobster
pángxiè	螃蟹	crab
yóuyú	鱿鱼	squid
zhāngyú	章鱼	octopus

VEGETABLE & BEAN CURD DISHES

báicài xiān shuānggū	白菜鲜双菇	bok choy and mushrooms
cuìpí dòufu	脆皮豆腐	crispy skin bean curd
hēimù'ěr mèn dòufu	黑木耳焖豆腐	bean curd with wood-ear mushrooms
hóngshāo qiézi	红烧茄子	red cooked aubergine
jiācháng dòufu	家常豆腐	'home-style' tofu
jiāngzhī qīngdòu	姜汁青豆	string beans with ginger
lúshuǐ dòufu	卤水豆腐	smoked bean curd
shāguō dòufu	砂锅豆腐	clay pot bean curd

CHINA'S TOP 10

- Xiao Wang's Home Restaurant, Běijīng (p127)
- Che's Cantonese Restaurant, Hong Kong (p517)
- O Café Estalagem, Macau (p541)
- Lujiang Hotel, Xiàmén, Fújiàn (p338)
- Kuiyuan Restaurant, Hángzhōu, Zhèjiāng (p314)
- Tiān Tiān Yú Gǎng, Dàlián, Liáoníng (p357)
- Kraman, Ürümqi, Xīnjiāng (p783)
- Bǎoluó Jiǔlóu, Shànghǎi (p292)
- Yǒnghé Dàjiǔdiàn & Yǒnghé Hóngqí Měishíchéng, Dàtóng, Shānxī (p403)
- Monkey Bar, Lìjiāng, Yúnnán (p671)

sùchǎo biǎndòu	素炒扁豆	garlic beans
sùchǎo sùcài	素炒素菜	fried vegetables
tángcù ǒubǐng	糖醋藕饼	sweet and sour lotus root cakes
yúxiāng qiézi	鱼香茄子	'fish-resembling' aubergine

FRUIT

bālè	芭乐	guava
fènglí	凤梨	pineapple
gānzhè	甘蔗	sugar cane
lí	梨	pear
lìzhī	荔枝	lychee
lóngyǎn	龙眼	'dragon eyes'
mángguǒ	芒果	mango
píngguǒ	苹果	apple
pútáo	葡萄	grape
xiāngjiāo	香蕉	banana
xīguā	西瓜	watermelon

DRINKS

bái pútáo jiǔ	白葡萄酒	white wine
báijiǔ	白酒	Chinese spirits
chá	茶	tea
dòujiāng	豆浆	soya bean milk
hóng pútáo jiǔ	红葡萄酒	red wine
kāfēi	咖啡	coffee
kāi shuǐ	开水	water (boiled)
kěkǒu kělè	可口可乐	Coca-Cola
kuàngquán shuǐ	矿泉水	mineral water
mǐjiǔ	米酒	rice wine
nǎijīng	奶精	coffee creamer
niúnǎi	牛奶	milk
píjiǔ	啤酒	beer
qìshuǐ	汽水	soft drink (soda)
suānnǎi	酸奶	yogurt
yézi zhī	椰子汁	coconut juice

Běijīng 北京

HIGHLIGHTS

- Peruse the arcane secrets of the **Forbidden City** (p110), China's centre of power for over 500 years
- Spend half a day roving through Běijīng's ragged **hútòng** (p114), the city's traditional alleyways
- Survey the spectacular achievement of the **Great Wall** (p141) outside town
- Spend a sedate morning admiring the cosmic harmonies of the **Temple of Heaven** (p109)
- Play a part in the colourful Tibetan Buddhist pageant of the **Lama Temple** (p112)

Great Wall

Lama Temple

Forbidden City

Běijīng's hútòng

Temple of Heaven

■ AREA CODE: ☎ 010　　　■ POP: 13.8 MIL　　　■ www.thatsbeijing.com

京北 Běijīng

Capital of the most populous nation on earth and first city of a land that has fired the global imagination, Běijīng is the striking metropolitan core of a country with one of the world's oldest civilisations. For decades at the fringes of world events, Běijīng now finds itself positioned in the spotlight as the dynamic nucleus of a country generating staggering gross domestic product (GDP) figures. Pundits talk of the 21st century as belonging to China, and China itself – as everyone knows – belongs to Běijīng.

The city may have left the money-making to Shànghǎi and Shēnzhèn, and the music-making to Hong Kong and Taiwan, but as the dynastic capital since the 13th century, Běijīng has an indisputable pedigree. Annihilated by Genghis Khan, esteemed by Marco Polo, reshaped by the Ming, courted by the West and plunged into chaos by Mao Zedong – Běijīng has had a dramatic and turbulent past, but its authority has rarely been in question.

But exactly where this city is now heading, no one quite knows for sure. The forest of cranes, thump of jackhammers, crackle of welding torches and sweep of the wrecking ball suggests a vigorous, yet incomplete, revolution. What is certain is that Běijīng, for centuries a vast and introspective walled bastion, has long been stirring and is now moving forward in gigantic leaps. With the 2008 Olympics – the Holy Grail of Běijīng city planners – in the bag, the transformation has received new vigour.

Běijīng still stumps first-time visitors who arrive expecting a ragged tableau of communist China. New arrivals are struck by both the city's modernity and its immensity. But in this headlong rush into the future, history – an increasingly precious commodity – has not been totally condemned. Within Běijīng's environs you will find some of China's most stunning sights: the Forbidden City, the Summer Palace, Temple of Heaven Park, the Lama Temple and the Great Wall, to name just a few.

HISTORY

Běijīng – affectionately called Peking by diplomats, nostalgic journalists and wistful academics – seems to have ruled over China since time immemorial. In fact, Běijīng (Northern Capital) – positioned outside the central heartland of Chinese civilisation – emerged as a cultural and political force that would shape the destiny of China only with the 13th-century Mongol occupation of China.

Located on a vast plain that extends south as far as the distant Yellow River, Běijīng benefits from neither proximity to a major river nor the sea. Without its strategic location on the edge of the North China Plain, it would hardly be an ideal place to locate a major city, let alone a national capital.

Although the area southwest of Běijīng was inhabited by early humans some 500,000 years ago, the earliest recorded settlements in Chinese historical sources date from 1045 BC. Ancient Chinese chronicles refer to a state called Yōuzhōu (Secluded State) existing during the reign of the mythical Yellow Emperor, one of nine states that existed at the time.

Běijīng was successively occupied by foreign forces, promoting its development as a major political centre. Before the Mongol invasion, the city was established as an auxiliary capital under the Khitan Liao and later as the capital under the Jurchen Jin, when it underwent significant transformation into a key political and military city. The city was enclosed within fortified walls for the first time, accessed by eight gates.

In AD 1215 the great Mongol warrior Genghis Khan and his formidable army razed Běijīng, an event which was paradoxically to mark Běijīng's transformation into a powerful national capital; a status it enjoys to the present day, bar 21 years of Nationalist rule in the 20th century.

The city came to be called Dàdū (Great Capital), also assuming the Mongol name Khanbalik (the Khan's town). By 1279 Kublai Khan, grandson of Genghis Khan, had made himself ruler of the largest empire the world has ever known, with Dàdū its capital. Surrounded by a vast rectangular wall punctured by three gates on each of its sides, the city was centred on the Drum and Bell Towers (p114; located near to their surviving Ming dynasty counterparts), its regular layout a paragon of urban design and a form that survives in today's Běijīng.

After seizing Běijīng, the first Ming emperor Hongwu (r 1368–98) renamed the city Běipíng (Northern Peace) and established his capital in Nánjīng in present-day Jiāngsū province to the south. It wasn't until the reign of Emperor Yongle (r 1403–24) that the court moved back to Běijīng. Seeking to rid the city of all traces of 'Yuán Qì' (literally 'breath of the Yuan dynasty'), the Ming levelled the fabulous palaces of the Mongols along with the Imperial City, while preserving much of the regular plan of the Mongol capital. The Ming was the only pure Chinese dynasty to rule from Běijīng.

During Ming rule, the huge city walls were repaired and redesigned. Yongle is credited with being the true architect of the

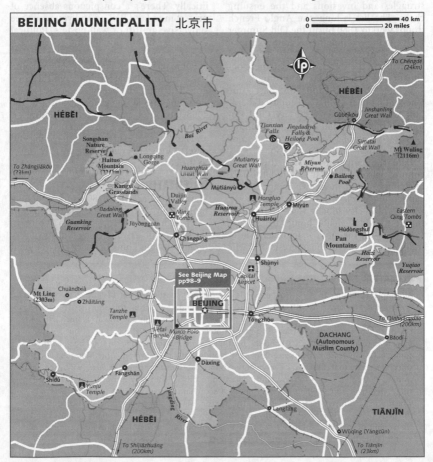

BĚIJĪNG

modern city, and much of Běijīng's hallmark architecture, such as the Forbidden City and the Temple of Heaven, date from his reign. The countenance of Ming dynasty Běijīng was flat and low-lying – a feature that would remain until the 20th century – as law forbade the construction of any building higher than the Forbidden City's Hall of Supreme Harmony. The basic grid of present-day Běijīng had been laid and the city had adopted a guise that would survive until the Communists era.

A change of government came with the Manchus, who invaded China and established the Qing dynasty. In the last 120 years of the Qing dynasty, Běijīng, and subsequently China, was subjected to power struggles and invasions and the ensuing chaos. The list is long: the Anglo-French troops who in 1860 burnt the Old Summer Palace to the ground; the corrupt regime of Empress Dowager Cixi; the Boxers; General Yuan Shikai; the warlords; the Japanese occupation of 1937; and the Kuomintang.

Běijīng changed hands one last time when, in January 1949, the People's Liberation Army (PLA) entered the city. On 1 October of that year Mao Zedong proclaimed a 'People's Republic' to an audience of some 500,000 citizens in Tiananmen Sq.

Like the emperors before them, the communists significantly altered the face of Běijīng to suit their own image. Down came the *páilou* (decorative archways), while whole city blocks were reduced to rubble to widen major boulevards. From 1950 to 1952, the city's magnificent outer walls were levelled in the interests of traffic circulation. Soviet experts and technicians poured in, leaving their own Stalinesque touches.

The capitalist-style reforms of the past quarter of a century have transformed Běijīng into a modern city, with skyscrapers, slick shopping malls and heaving flyovers. The once flat skyline is now crenellated with vast apartment blocks and office buildings. Recent years have also seen a convincing beautification of Běijīng: from a toneless and unkempt city to a greener, cleaner and more pleasant place.

The mood in today's Běijīng seems very different from the Tiananmen Sq demonstrations of spring 1989. China has decided to embrace modernity without evolving politically. There's a conspicuous absence of protest in today's Běijīng and you won't see subversive graffiti or wall posters. Political dissent exists, but unrelenting government coercion forces it into the shadows.

Some of Běijīng's largest problems could be environmental rather than political, however. The need for speedy economic expansion, magnified by preparations for the 2008 Olympics, has put extra pressure on an already degraded environment. Water and land resources are rapidly depleting and desert sands are crawling inexorably closer to the city.

ORIENTATION

With a total area of 16,800 sq km, Běijīng municipality is roughly the size of Belgium.

Though it may not appear so to a visitor in the turmoil of arrival, Běijīng is a city of very orderly design. Think of the city as one giant

---

CLIMATE

Autumn (September to early November) is the optimal season to visit Běijīng as the weather is gorgeous and fewer tourists are in town. Local Beijingers describe this short season of clear skies and breezy days as *tiāngāo qìshuǎng* (literally 'the sky is high and the air is fresh'). In winter, there are few tourists in town and many hotels offer substantial discounts – but it's glacial outside (dipping as low as -20°C) and the northern winds cut like a knife through bean curd. Arid spring is OK, apart from the (worsening) sand clouds that sweep in from Inner Mongolia and the static electricity that discharges everywhere. Spring also sees the snow-like *liǔxù* (willow catkins) wafting through the air like snow and collecting in drifts. From May onwards the mercury can surge well over 30°C. Běijīng simmers under a scorching sun in summer (reaching over 40°C), which also sees heavy rainstorms late in the season. Maybe surprisingly, this is also considered the peak season, when hotels typically raise their rates and the Great Wall nearly collapses under the weight of marching tourists. Note that air pollution can be very harsh in both summer and winter (although Běijīng is obliged to clean up its act for the 2008 Olympics)

grid, with the Forbidden City at its centre. As for the street names: Chongwenmenwai Dajie means 'the avenue (dajie) outside (wai) Chongwen Gate (Chongwenmen)' – that is, outside the old wall – whereas Chongwenmennei Dajie means 'the avenue inside Chongwen Gate'. It's an academic exercise since the gate and the wall in question no longer exist.

A major boulevard can change names six or even seven times along its length. Streets and avenues can also be split along compass points: Dong Dajie (East Ave), Xi Dajie (West Ave), Bei Dajie (North Ave) and Nan Dajie (South Ave). All these streets head off from an intersection, usually where a gate once stood.

Five ring roads circle the city centre in concentric rings.

Bus and taxi are the main methods of transport to the city centre from Běijīng's Capital Airport, 27km away. See p139 for more information.

Maps

Běijīng is huge and it's essential to score a map of town. Lonely Planet publishes a colour, waterproof, fold-out map designed for the traveller and complete with Chinese script. English-language maps of Běijīng can also be bought at the airport and train station newspaper kiosks, the Friendship Store (p137) and the Foreign Languages Bookstore (right). They can also be picked up for free at most big hotels and branches of the Běijīng Tourist Information Center (p101).

Pushy street vendors hawk cheap Chinese character maps near subway stations around Tiananmen Sq and Wangfujing Dajie – check they have English labelling before you purchase. Look out for the Beijing Tourist Map (Y8), labelled in both English and Chinese. For those who can read Chinese, look out for the handy, highly detailed Běijīng Shíyòng Dìtúcè (Y12), an A–Z of Běijīng with grids, which you can find at the Wangfujing Bookstore (north of Oriental Plaza). For the moment, it's only available in Chinese but the bookstore has a large range of alternative maps of the city.

INFORMATION
Bookshops

Cathay Bookshop (Zhōngguó Shūdiàn; Map pp102-3; ☎ 6303 2104; 34 Liulichang Xijie) There are several branches of the Cathay Bookshop on Liulichang. This one has art books, antiquarian books and stone rubbings.

China Cultural Heritage Bookshop (Cathay Bookshop; Wénhuà Yíchǎn Shūdiàn; Map pp102-3; ☎ 6303 1602; 57 Liulichang Xijie) This branch of the Cathay Bookshop is on the northern side of Liulichang Xijie. It has a marvellous museum on the ground floor containing a fascinating collection of literature and maps relating to Běijīng, some accompanied by English captions. There is also an extensive collection of calligraphy at the rear, along with displays of antiquarian books.

Foreign Languages Bookstore (Wàiwén Shūdiàn; Map pp102-3; ☎ 6512 6911; 235 Wangfujing Dajie)

BĚIJĪNG IN...

Two Days
Běijīng's top sight is undeniably the **Forbidden City**; you will need at least a morning to cover the palace and some of the nearby sights of **Tiananmen Sq**. Take the subway from Tiananmen Xi to Wangfujing and lunch at **Quanjude Roast Duck Restaurant** or **Wangfujing Snack St**. Jump in a taxi to the **Temple of Heaven** or spend the afternoon on our **bicycle tour**.

Rise early the next day for a trip to the **Great Wall** and the **Ming Tombs**, and spend the evening enjoying a performance of **Chinese acrobatics** before rounding off the day wining and dining in **Sanlitun**, at Hidden Tree or Lǎo Hànzi.

Three Days
Follow the two-day itinerary, and on your third day make an early morning visit to the **Lama Temple** before browsing among the stalls and bric-a-brac shops of **Liulichang**. In the afternoon, walk along the restored **Ming City Wall** from Chongwenmen to the Southeast Corner Watchtower or make an expedition to the **Summer Palace**. In the evening, dine at **Xiao Wang's Home Restaurant** or the **Courtyard**, snack at **Donghuamen Night Market** or spend the evening enjoying **Beijing opera** at one of the city's numerous theatres.

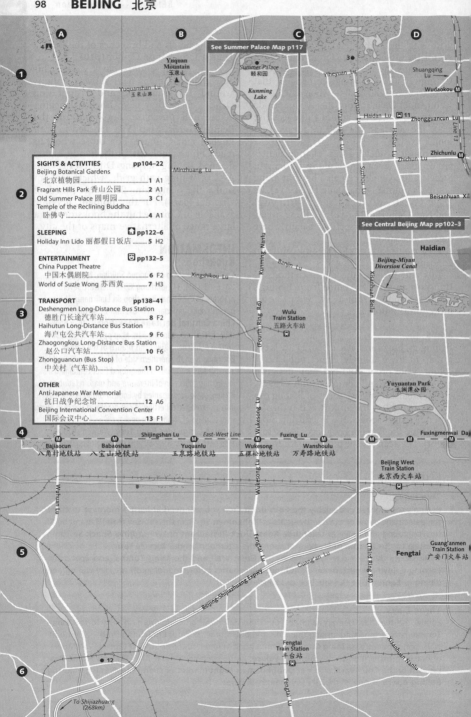

See Summer Palace Map p117

SIGHTS & ACTIVITIES   pp104–22
Beijing Botanical Gardens
  北京植物园.....................................1 A1
Fragrant Hills Park 香山公园.................2 A1
Old Summer Palace 圆明园....................3 C1
Temple of the Reclining Buddha
  卧佛寺.......................................4 A1

SLEEPING   pp122–6
Holiday Inn Lido 丽都假日饭店...............5 H2

ENTERTAINMENT   pp132–5
China Puppet Theatre
  中国木偶剧院.................................6 F2
World of Suzie Wong 苏西黄.................7 H3

TRANSPORT   pp138–41
Deshengmen Long-Distance Bus Station
  德胜门长途汽车站............................8 F2
Haihutun Long-Distance Bus Station
  海户屯公共汽车站............................9 F6
Zhaogongkou Long-Distance Bus Station
  赵公口汽车站................................10 F6
Zhongguancun (Bus Stop)
  中关村 (气车站).............................11 D1

OTHER
Anti-Japanese War Memorial
  抗日战争纪念馆.............................12 A6
Beijing International Convention Center
  国际会议中心...............................13 F1

See Central Beijing Map pp102–3

0   3 km
0   2 miles

E   F   G   H

Qinghuadong Lu

Xueyuan Lu

Badaling Expwy

Zhengfu Lu

M Datun

Beisihuan Zhonglu
(Fourth Ring Rd)

13

Beichen Lu

M Ganyangshu

Beiluchengdonglu

Beijing-Chengde Expwy

Wangjingxi M

To Capital
Airport (17km)

Narihuu Lu

Beisihuan Donglu

Airport Expwy

Qingzhan Bridge

1

Athlete's
Village

8

M Dazhongsi

Beisanhuan Zhonglu

(Third Ring Rd)

6

Line 5 (Under Construction)

Beituchengdonglu

Hepingxiqiao

M Taiyanggong

M Hepingli

2

Hepingli
Train Station
和平里火车站

Beisanhuan Donglu

Liangma River
亮马河

5

Beijing North
Train Station
北京北火车站

Circle Line

(Second Ring Rd)

Chaoyang

M

Dongsanhuan Beilu

Chaoyang
Amusement
Park
朝阳公园

3

7

Xicheng

M

(Second Ring Rd)

Circle Line

Dongcheng

Line 5 (Under Construction)

(Second Ring Rd)

Circle Line

Forbidden
City
紫禁城

Xidan

Xichang'an Jie

East-West Line

M M M M M M M

Jianguomenwai Dajie

East-West Line

M

Jingtong
Expwy

4

Beijing East
Train Station

Guang'anmen Nanbinhe Lu

Tiananmen
Square
天安门广场

Circle Line

M M M

M

Beijing
Train Station
北京火车站

Chaoyang

Dongsanhuan Nanlu

Chongwen

Grand View
Garden
大观园

Xuanwu

Taoranting
Park
陶然亭公园

Temple of
Heaven Park
天坛公园

Longtan
Park
龙潭公园

5

You'anmen Xibinhe Lu

Beijing South
Train Station
北京南站火车站

Yongdingmen Dongbinhe Lu

Guangqumen Nanbinhe Lu

Zuo'anmen Xibinhe Lu

Dongsanhuan Nanlu

Nansanhuan Xilu

Maju Qiao Lu

Nanyang Lu

Nansanhuan Zhonglu

9

Nansanhuan Donglu

10

Liujiyao

M Songjiazhuang

Beijing-Tianjin Expwy

Dayang Lu

6

This bookshop has a reasonable selection of English-language novels, as well as a plentiful children's section. There's a good range of travel books, including Lonely Planet titles, on the third floor.

Xidan Bookshop (Xīdàn Túshū Dàsha; Map pp102-3; ☎ 6607 8477; 17 Xichang'an Jie) This vast bookshop has an extensive range of English-language titles in a newly renovated floor in the basement.

Yansha Bookstore (Túshū Tiāndì; Map pp102-3; ☎ 6465 1188; 4th fl, Lufthansa Center Youyi Shopping City, 50 Liangmaqiao Lu) This bookstore has a small selection of English-language travel guides and novels.

Internet Access

Defying the trend everywhere else in the world, Internet cafés have become harder to find in Běijīng over the past few years. Many cheaper hotels (eg the Fangyuan Hotel, p124) and youth hostels provide Internet access at around Y10 per hour.

Dayusu Internet Café (Dáyǔsù Wǎngbā; Map pp102-3; 2 Hufang Lu; per hr Y3; ☺ 8am-midnight) No English sign, but it's around three shops north of Bank of China on Hufang Lu.

Moko Coffee Bar (Mòkè Wǎngbā; Map pp102-3; ☎ 6525 3712, 6559 8464; 57 Dongsi Nandajie; per hr with coffee upstairs/downstairs Y4/12) No English sign, but it's next to a chemist.

Qian Yi Internet Café (Map pp102-3; ☎ 6705 1722; 3rd fl, Old Station Bldg; per hr Y20; ☺ 9am-midnight) Very expensive, but well located.

Yongning Internet Café (Yǒngníng Wǎngbā; Map pp102-3; 71 Chaoyangmen Nanxiaojie; per hr Y2) No English sign, look for the Chinese characters for *wǎngbā* (网吧).

Medical Services

As the national capital, Běijīng has some of the best medical facilities and services in China. Ask your embassy for a list of English-speaking doctors and dentists, and hospitals that accept foreigners. Note that it is much cheaper just to ask what medicines you need and then buy them at a pharmacy on the street rather than purchasing them on-site at the international clinics listed below.

Beijing International Medical Centre (Map pp102-3; ☎ 6465 1561/2/3; emergencies ☎ 6465 1560; Suite 106-7, 1st fl, Lufthansa Center Youyi Shopping City, 50 Liangmaqiao Lu; ☺ 24hr) Medical, pharmacy, dental and counselling services; English-speaking staff.

Beijing Union Medical Hospital (Běijīng Xiéhé Yīyuàn; Map pp102-3; ☎ 6529 6114; emergencies ☎ 6529 5284; 53 Dongdan Beidajie; ☺ 24hr) Foreigners' and VIP wing in the back building.

Hong Kong International Medical Clinic (Map pp102-3; ☎ 6501 4260, 6553 2288; www.hkclinic.com; 9th fl, Office Tower, Hong Kong Macau Center, Swissôtel, 2 Chaoyangmen Beidajie; ☺ 9am-9pm) Medical and dental clinic.

International SOS (Map pp102-3; clinic appointments ☎ 6462 9112; dental appointments ☎ 6462 0333; emergencies ☎ 6462 9100; www.internationalsos.com, Bldg C, BITIC Ying Yi Bldg, 1 Xingfu Sancun Beijie; ☺ 9am-6pm Mon-Fri) Expensive, high-quality clinic with English-speaking staff.

PHARMACIES

There are several pharmacies on Wangfujing Dajie stocking both Chinese (*zhōngyào*) and Western medicine (*xīyào*), so you should be able to find any medicines you may need. Note that in Běijīng you do not necessarily need a prescription for the drug you are seeking, so ask at the pharmacy first. In other parts of China, however, you will probably find that you need a prescription. Branches of **Watson's** (Qūchénshì; Map pp102-3; Chaoyangmenwai Dajie 1st fl, Full Link Plaza, 19 Chaoyangmenwai Dajie; Dongchan'an Jie CC17, 19, CC21, 23, Oriental Plaza, 1 Dongchan'an Jie) also purvey medicines, but are more geared towards selling cosmetics, sunscreens and the likes.

Quanxin Pharmacy (Quánxīn Dàyàofáng; Map pp102-3; ☎ 652 4123; 153 Wangfujing Dajie; ☺ 8.30am-10pm) Large pharmacy opposite St Joseph's Church.

Wangfujing Medicine Shop (Wángfǔjīng Yīyào Shāngdiàn; Map pp102-3; ☎ 6524 0122; 267 Wangfujing Dajie; ☺ 8.30am-9pm) Large range of both Western and Chinese drugs.

Money

Foreign currency and travellers cheques can be changed at large branches of the Bank of China, CITIC Industrial Bank, the airport and hotel money-changing counters, and at several department stores (including the Friendship Store), as long as you have your passport. Hotels usually give the official rate, but some will add a small commission. Some upmarket hotels will only change money for their own guests. Useful branches of the Bank of China with foreign exchange counters include a branch next to Oriental Plaza on Wangfujing Dajie, in the Lufthansa Center Youyi Shopping City, and in the China World Trade Center.

It's possible to get a cash advance on credit cards at the following places but there is a steep (4%) commission.

Bank of China (Zhōngguó Yínháng; Map pp102-3; Sundongan Plaza, Wangfujing Dajie)
CITIC Industrial Bank (Map pp102-3; 19 Jianguomen-wai Dajie)

If you have an Amex card, you can also cash personal cheques at CITIC Industrial Bank and large branches of the Bank of China.

More and more ATMs now accept foreign credit cards and are linked to international bank settlement systems such as Cirrus and Plus. The network is not, however, citywide and you are more likely to find an ATM you can use in and around the main shopping areas (such as Wangfujing Dajie) and international hotels and their associated shopping arcades; some of the large department stores also have useful ATMs. For your nearest ATM, consult www.visa.com/pd/atm or www.mastercard.com/atmlocator/index.jsp; both have comprehensive listings.

There's a Bank of China ATM in the Capital Airport arrivals hall. Other useful ATMs include:
Bank of China ATM (Map pp102-3) Oriental Plaza (Oriental Plaza, cnr Wangfujing Dajie & Dongchang'an Jie); Sundongan Plaza (next to main entrance of Sundongan Plaza on Wangfujing Dajie); Peninsula Palace (2nd basement level, Peninsula Palace, 8 Jinyu Hutong); Novotel Peace Hotel (foyer, Novotel Peace Hotel); Swissôtel (2nd fl, Swissôtel); Lufthansa Center Youyi Shopping City (1st fl, Lufthansa Center Youyi Shopping City)
Citibank ATM (east of International Hotel on Jianguomennei Dajie)
Hong Kong & Shanghai Banking Corporation (HSBC; ☎ 6526 0668, 800-820 8878; www.hsbc.com.cn) Jianguomen Dajie (Ground fl, Block A, COFCO Plaza, 8 Jianguomen Dajie); Jichang Lu (1st fl, Lido Shopping Arcade, Lido Place, Jichang Lu) Both have 24-hour ATMs where you can draw money from your overseas HSBC account.
Industrial & Commercial Bank of China ATM (opposite Bank of China ATM at entrance to Sundongan Plaza, Wangfujing Dajie)

Post
There are convenient post offices in the CITIC building next to the Friendship Store; in the basement of the China World Trade Center; east of Wangfujing Dajie on Dongdan Ertiao; on the south side of Xichang'an Jie west of the Běijīng Concert Hall; and just east of the Qianmen Jianguo Hotel, on Yong'an Lu. You can also post letters via your hotel reception desk, which may be the most convenient option, or at green post boxes around town. The **International Post Office** (Guójì Yóudiànjú; Map pp102-3; Jianguomen Beidajie; 🕐 8am-7pm Mon-Sat) is 200m north of Jianguomen subway station. Large post offices are generally open daily 9am to 5pm.

Several private couriers in Běijīng offer international express posting of documents and parcels, and have reliable pick-up service as well as drop-off centres:
DHL (☎ 6466 2211, 800-810 8000; www.dhl.com; 45 Xinyuan Jie) Further branches in the Kempinski Hotel, the China World Trade Center & COFCO Plaza.
Federal Express (FedEx; ☎ 6561 2003, 800-810 2338; Hanwei Bldg, 7 Guanghua Lu) Also in Room 107, No 1 Office Bldg, Oriental Plaza.
United Parcel Service (UPS; ☎ 6593 2932; Unit A, 2nd fl, Tower B, Beijing Kelun Bldg, 12A Guanghua Lu)

Tourist Information
Beijing Tourism Hotline (☎ 6513 0828; 🕐 24hr) English-speaking operators available to answer questions and hear complaints.

Beijing Tourist Information Center (Běijīng Lǚyóu Zīxún Fúwù Zhōngxīn; 🕐 9.30am-5.30pm) Capital Airport (☎ 6459 8148; jichang@bjta.gov.cn); Chaoyang (Map pp102-3; ☎ 6417 6627, 6417 6656; chaoyang@bjta.gov.cn; 27 Sanlitun Beilu); Dongcheng (Map pp102-3; ☎ 6512 3043, 6512 2991; dongcheng@bjta.gov.cn; 10 Dengshikou Xijie); Fengtai (☎ 6332 3983; fengtai@bjta.gov.cn; Zhongyan Hotel lobby, Guangwai Dajie); Haidian (☎ 8262 2895; haidian@bjta.gov.cn; 40 Zhongguancun Dajie); Xicheng (☎ 6616 0108, 6612 0110; xicheng@bjta.gov.cn; 1st fl, Keji Guangchang, Xidan Beidajie); Xuanwu (☎ 6351 0018; xuanwu@bjta.gov.cn; 3 Hufang Lu) The Chinese state never quite got the hang of tourist offices, but a tentative step in the right direction has been made with a chain of offices (called Service Stations) with turquoise façades dotted around town. You can grab a free tourist map of Běijīng along with other material, but the operation is not very competent and English-language skills are limited. The Chaoyang Service Station west of the Sanlitun Yashou Clothing Market (p137) probably deals with more foreign travellers than any other branch, but you may interrupt the employees playing computer games.

Visas
Public Security Bureau (PSB; Gōngānjú; 2 Andingmen Dongdajie; ☎ 8402 0101; 🕐 8.30am-4.30pm Mon-Sat) The Foreign Affairs Branch of the local PSB – the police force – handles visa extensions. The visa office is on the 2nd floor on the east side of the building – take the escalator up. You can also apply for a residence permit here. Expect to wait up to five days

A   B   C   D

1

Wegongcun Lu

Xueyuan Nanlu 学院南路

Xinde Jie

Deshengmenwai Dajie

Xueyuan Nanlu

Dahuisi Lu

North Jiaotong University
北方交通大学

Caolangqiao Lu 草桥路

Wenhuiyuan Jie

Wenhuiyuan Jie

Line 13

Sidou Lu

Zhongguancun Nandajie

Dahuisi Lu

Minzuxueyuan Nanlu

Beijing-Miyun
Diversion Canal

Xizhimen Beidajie

Jixikoumen Dajie

Hucheng River (City Moat)

Deshengmen Dongdajie

Deshengmen

Jishuitan
积水潭地铁站 Jishuitan

Xihai
Lake
西海

Houhai
Lake
后海

Yangfang

2

Xisanhuan Beilu 西三环北路 (Third Ring Rd)

99

Zizhuyuan
Park
紫竹院公园 186

Haidian

Zizhuyuan Lu

Xizhimenwai Dajie

44

42

Beijing North
Train Station
北京北火车站 184

Deshengmen Xidajie 德胜门西大街 (Second Ring Rd)

Xinjiekou Beidajie

Xinjiekou Beidajie

Xizhimen
西直门地铁站 Xizhimen

Zhizhimennei Dajie

Dianmen Xidajie

Huguosi Jie 护国寺街

Xisi Beidajie

Huguosi Jie

66

Chegongzhuang

Xizhimen
Nandajie

Xicheng

Batasi Lu

Shishahai

3

Chegongzhuang Xilu 车公庄西路

Chegongzhuang Donglu 车公庄东路

Ping'an Xidajie

Xisi Nandajie

Xinjiekou Beidajie

Xinwai Dajie

Dianmen Xidajie

Chegongzhuang
车公庄地铁站 M

Fuchengmen Beidajie 阜成门北大街

61

Xisi Beidajie

Xinjiekou Nandajie

Zhuanghuangchang Beijie

Baiwanzhuang Xilu

Sanlihe Lu

Baiwanzhuang Dajie 百万庄西路

Fuchengmennei Dajie 阜成门内大街

Xi'anmen Dajie

79

Fucheng Lu 阜成路

Fuchengmenwai Dajie

Fuchengmen
阜城门地铁站 M

Fuxingmen Beidajie 复兴门北大街

Xisi Nandajie

Zhongnanhai

Yuyuantan Park
玉渊潭公园

Xisanhuan Zhonglu 西三环中路 (Third Ring Rd)

Sanlihe Donglu

Yuetan Beijie

Circle Line

Yuetan
Park
月坛公园

Xidan Beidajie

Xidan

Yongding River 永定河

Sanlihe Lu

Yuyuan Tan
玉渊潭

Yuetan Nandajie

Nanlishi Lu

Fuxingmen
复兴门地铁站 M

Xidan Beidajie

Fuxing Lu 复兴路 East-West Line

4

Gongzhufen
公主坟地铁站 M

Junshibowuguan
军事博物馆地铁站

Yangfangdian Lu

Muxidi
木樨地地铁站 M

Baifangwo Lu

Fuxingmenwai Dajie 复兴门外大街

Sanlihe Dong Lu

Nanlishilu
南礼士路地铁站 M

Xibiahemennei Dajie

Fuxingmennei Dajie

153

176

178

Xichang'an Jie

Xidan
西单地铁站 M

30

138

Xirongxian Hutong

91

80

73

Hepingmen

166

161

Liulichang
Xijie
琉璃厂西街

Yinshui Qu 河水区

71

Guang'anmen Beibinhe Lu

Guang'anmen Nanbinhe Jie

Hucheng River (City Moat) 护城河

Xuanwumen
宣武门地铁站 M

Xuanwumen Xidajie

Changchunjie
长椿街地铁站 M 77

Xuanwumen

Xuanwumennei Dajie

Xuanwumenwai Dajie

5

Beijing West
Train Station
北京西火车站

Xisanhuan Zhonglu 西三环中路

Lianhuachi Park
莲花池公园

Lianhuachi
Pond

Lianhuachi Donglu

Nanfengwo Lu

Fengtai

Shouti Nanlu

Baiyun Lu

Guang'anmennei Dajie 广安门内大街

Guang'anmenwai Dajie 广安门外大街

Xuanwu
Art Garden
宣武艺园

Guang'anmen Nanbinhe Lu

Caishikou Dajie

Nie Jie

49

52

Nanheng Xijie

Nanheng Dongjie 南横东街

Luomashi Dajie

147

76

Mishi Hutong

Xuanwu

6

Chaoyang Area

97

Xingfucun Lu

Xin Donglu

125

Sanlitun Lu

117

100

160

108

135

2

Hongtu Lu

Yizhao Lu

Wanshou
Park
万寿公园

Baizhifang Xijie

Baizhifang Jie 白纸坊街

Xuanwu

0   300 m
0   0.2 miles

114

174

150

Guang'anmen
Train Station
广安门火车站

Guang'anmen Nanbinhe Lu

Guang'anmen Nanshuncheng Jie

Nancaiyuan Jie

Youanmennei Dajie

Liren Jie

Taoranting
Park
陶然亭公园

130

Gongrentiyuchang Beilu

155

109

110

Gongrentiyuchang Donglu

148

136

Gongrentiyuchang Xilu

Workers
Stadium
工人体育场

78

46

Tiyuguan Lu

Sanluju Lu

Baijiazhuang Lu

Fengtai Beilu

Baizhifang Jie

Nanheng Xijie

Youanmen Xibinhe Lu 右安门西滨河路

Hucheng River (City Moat) 护城河

You'anmen Xibinhe Lu

Beijing Sout
Train Station
北京南火车站

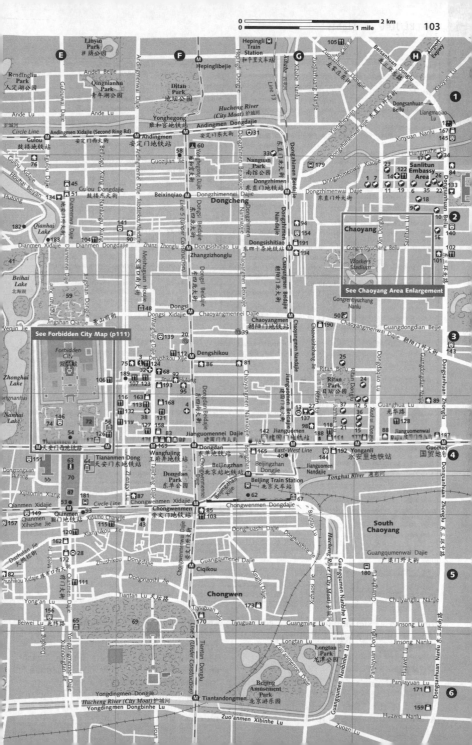

0 _____ 2 km
0 _____ 1 mile

BĚIJĪNG

for your visa extension to be processed. You can also obtain passport photographs here (Y30 for five).

SIGHTS

Most of Běijīng's sights lie within the city proper. Notable exceptions are the Great Wall and the Ming Tombs, listed in the Around Běijīng section (p141).

Chongwen & South Chaoyang
崇文区、朝阳南区   **Map pp102-3**

TIANANMEN SQUARE 天安门广场
The world's largest public square, **Tiananmen Sq** (Tiānānmén Guǎngchǎng; subway Tiananmen Xi, Tiananmen Dong or Qianmen) is a vast desert of paving stones at the heart of Běijīng and a poignant epitaph to China's hapless democracy movement. It may be a grandiose,

Maoist tourist trap, but there's more than enough space to stretch your legs and the view can be breathtaking, especially on a clear day and at nightfall. Kites flit through the sky, children stamp around on the paving slabs and Chinese out-of-towners huddle together for the obligatory photo opportunity with the great helmsman's portrait.

The square is laid out on a north–south axis. Threading through Front Gate (p107) to the south, the square's meridian line is straddled by the Chairman Mao Mausoleum (p107), cuts through the Gate of Heavenly Peace (p106) to the north and cleaves through the Forbidden City (p110) behind.

In the square, you stand in the symbolic centre of the Chinese universe. The rectangular arrangement, flanked by halls to the east and west, echoes the layout of the Forbidden City. As such, the square employs a conventional plan that pays obeisance to traditional Chinese culture, while its ornaments and buildings are largely Soviet inspired.

Tiananmen Sq as we see it today is a modern creation. During Ming and Qing times, part of the Imperial City Wall (Huáng Chéng) called the Thousand Foot Corridor (Qiānbù Láng) poked deep into the space today occupied by the square, enclosing a section of the imperial domain. The wall took the shape of a 'T', emerging from the two huge, and now absent, gates – Cháng'ān Zuǒ Mén and Cháng'ān Yòu Mén – that rose up south of the Gate of Heavenly Peace before running south to the vanished Daming Gate (Dàmíng Mén). East and west of the Thousand Foot Corridor stood official departments and temples, including the Ministry of Rites, the Ministry of Revenue, Honglu Temple and Taichang Temple.

Mao conceived the square to project the enormity of the Communist Party, so it's all a bit Kim Il Sung-ish. During the Cultural Revolution the chairman, wearing a Red Guard armband, reviewed parades of up to a million people here. In 1976 another million people jammed the square to pay their last respects to Mao. In 1989 army tanks and soldiers forced pro-democracy demonstrators out of the square. Although it seems likely that no-one was actually killed within the square itself, possibly thousands were slaughtered outside the square. Despite being a public place, the square remains more in the hands of the government than the people; it is monitored by closed-circuit TV cameras and plain-clothes police are primed to paralyse the first twitch of dissent.

West of the Great Hall of the People (opposite), the future **National Grand Theatre** is nearing completion, to compete with Shànghǎi's fine example.

If you get up early you can watch the flag-raising ceremony at sunrise, performed by a troop of PLA soldiers drilled to march at precisely 108 paces per minute, 75cm per pace. The same ceremony in reverse is performed at sunset, but you can hardly see the soldiers for the throngs gathered to watch. The square is illuminated at night.

Bicycles cannot be ridden across Tiananmen Sq – apparently tanks are OK – but you can walk your bike. Two subway stations, Tiananmen Xi (west of the square) and Tiananmen Dong (east of the square), serve the square or you can approach from the south via Qianmen stop.

GATE OF HEAVENLY PEACE 天安门

Hung with a vast likeness of Mao, the **Gate of Heavenly Peace** (Tiānānmén; ☎ 6309 9386; admission Y15, bag storage Y2; ☯ 8.30am-4.30pm; subway Tiananmen Xi or Tiananmen Dong) is a potent national symbol. Built in the 15th century and restored in the 17th century, the double-eaved gate was formerly the largest of the four gates of the Imperial Wall enclosing the imperial grounds.

Of the pair that guard the gate, legend records that the westerly stone lion blocked Li Chuangwang when he invaded Běijīng at the end of the Ming dynasty. Li fended the lion off by stabbing its belly with his spear while on horseback, leaving a mark that remains. Other locals dispute this, attesting that it is a bullet hole – the work of allied-force guns after troops entered Běijīng to quell the Boxer Rebellion in 1900. For more on the Boxer Rebellion see p41.

There are five doors to the gate, fronted by seven bridges spanning a stream. Each of these bridges was restricted in its use and only the emperor could use the central door and bridge.

Today's political coterie review mass troop parades from here and it was from this gate that Mao proclaimed the People's Republic on 1 October 1949. The dominating feature is the gigantic portrait of the ex-chairman, to the left of which runs the poetic slogan 'Long Live the People's Republic of China' and to the right 'Long Live the Unity of the Peoples of the World'. The portrait was famously pelted with paint-filled eggs during the 1989 demonstrations in the square; the iconoclasts were workers from Mao's home province of Húnán. A number of spares of the portrait exist and a fresh one was speedily requisitioned.

Climb up to great views of Tiananmen Sq and peek inside at the impressive beams and overdone paintwork. Other diversions include video presentations and paintings of the flag-raising ceremony, featuring jubilant representatives of China's ethnic minorities.

There is no fee for walking through the gate, but if you climb it you will have to buy an admission ticket and pay to store your bag at the baggage-storage kiosk, inconveniently located about 30m away from the ticket office. Security is intense with metal detectors and frisking awaiting visitors.

FRONT GATE 前门

The **Front Gate** (Qián Mén; ☎ 6525 3176; admission Y10; ⊙ 8.30am-4pm; subway Qianmen) actually consists of two gates. The northerly gate, 40m-high Zhèngyáng Mén dates from the Ming dynasty and was the largest of the nine impressive gates of the inner city wall separating the Inner or Tartar (Manchu) City from the Outer or Chinese City. Partially destroyed during the Boxer Rebellion of 1900, the gate was once flanked by two temples that have since vanished. With the disappearance of the city walls, the gate sits out of context, but you can climb it for views over the square, and the interior houses models and photos of old Běijīng. Similarly torched during the Boxer Rebellion, the Arrow Tower (Jiàn Lóu) to the south also dates from Ming times and was originally connected to Zhèngyáng Mén by a semicircular enceinte, which was demolished in the 20th century. To the east is the former British-built **Qian Men Railway Station** (Lǎo Chēzhàn), now housing shops, an Internet café and the Old Station Theater (p133), where you can watch performances of Beijing opera.

GREAT HALL OF THE PEOPLE 人民大会堂

On a site previously occupied by Taichang Temple, the Jinyiwei (the Ming dynasty secret service) and the Ministry of Justice, the **Great Hall of the People** (Rénmín Dàhuìtáng; ☎ 6309 6668; western side of Tiananmen Sq; admission Y20, bag storage Y2; ⊙ 9am-3pm; subway Tiananmen Xi) is where the National People's Congress convenes. The 1959 architecture is monolithic and intimidating; the tour parades visitors past a choice of 29 of its lifeless rooms, named after the provinces that make up the Chinese universe. Also on the billing is the 5000-seat banquet room where US President Richard Nixon dined in 1972, and the 10,000-seat auditorium with the familiar red star embedded in a galaxy of lights in the ceiling. The Great Hall is closed to the public when the People's Congress is in session.

CHAIRMAN MAO MAUSOLEUM 毛主席纪念堂

Chairman Mao died in September 1976 and his **mausoleum** (Máo Zhǔxí Jìniàntáng; ☎ 6513 2277; southern side of Tiananmen Sq; admission free, bag storage Y10; ⊙ 8.30-11.30am Mon-Sat, 2-4pm Mon, Wed & Fri; subway Tiananmen Xi, Tiananmen Dong or Qianmen) was constructed shortly thereafter on the former site of the Daming Gate (see Tiananmen Sq, p106).

However history judges Mao, his impact was enormous. Easy as it now is to vilify his deeds and excesses, many Chinese show deep respect when confronted with the physical presence of the man. China International Travel Service (CITS; Zhōngguó Guójì Lǚxíngshè) guides freely quote the old 7:3 ratio on Mao that first surfaced in 1976: Mao was 70% right and 30% wrong (it makes you wonder what the figures are for CITS itself!) and this is now the official Party line.

Join the enormous queue of Chinese sightseers, but don't expect more than a quick glimpse of the body as you file past the sarcophagus. At certain times of the year the body requires maintenance and is not on view.

MONUMENT TO THE PEOPLE'S HEROES 人民英雄纪念碑

North of Mao's mausoleum, the **Monument to the People's Heroes** (Rénmín Yingxióng Jìniànbēi; subway Tiananmen Xi, Tiananmen Dong or Qianmen) was completed in 1958. The 37.9m-high obelisk, made of Qīngdǎo granite, bears bas-relief carvings of key patriotic and revolutionary events (such as Lin Zexu destroying opium at Hǔmén in the 19th century, and Tàipíng rebels), as well as appropriate calligraphy from communist bigwigs Mao Zedong and Zhou Enlai (p48). Mao's eight-character flourish proclaims 'Eternal Glory to the People's Heroes'. The monument is illuminated at night.

MUSEUM OF CHINESE HISTORY & MUSEUM OF THE CHINESE REVOLUTION 中国历史博物馆、中国革命历史博物馆

The **Museum of Chinese History** and the **Museum of the Chinese Revolution** (Zhōngguó Lìshǐ Bówùguǎn & Zhōngguó Gémìng Lìshǐ Bówùguǎn; ☎ 6512 8986; eastern side of Tiananmen Sq; admission Y10-20; ⊙ 8.30am-4.30pm Tue-Sat; subway Tiananmen Dong) are clumped together in a sombre building, but served by individual ticket offices. From 1966 to 1978 the museums were closed so that history could be revised in the light of recent events, and the tradition continues today with frequent closures. Several halls of the Museum of Chinese History stage temporary art and culture exhibitions.

ZHONGSHAN PARK 中山公园

This lovely little **park** (Zhōngshān Gōngyuán; ☎ 6605 4594; west of the Gate of Heavenly Peace; admission Y3; ☯ 6am-9pm; subway Tiananmen Xi) has a section hedging up against the Forbidden City moat. Formerly the sacred Ming-style Altar to the God of the Land and the God of Grain (Shèjìtán) where the emperor offered sacrifices, this park is clean, tranquil and tidy, and a refreshing prologue or conclusion to the magnificence of the adjacent imperial residence.

WORKERS CULTURAL PALACE 劳动人民文化宫

On the Forbidden City's southeastern flank, the **Workers Cultural Palace** (Láodòng Rénmín Wénhuà Gōng; ☎ 6525 2189; northeast of the Gate of Heavenly Peace; admission Y2; ☯ 6.30am-7.30pm; subway Tiananmen Dong) was the site of the emperor's premier place of worship, the Supreme Temple (Tài Miào). The huge halls of the temple remain, their roofs enveloped in imperial yellow tiles. Take the northwestern exit from the park and find yourself just by the Forbidden City's Meridian Gate and point of entry to the palace.

IMPERIAL CITY MUSEUM 皇城艺术馆

This important **museum** (Huáng Chéng Yìshùguǎn; ☎ 8511 5104/114; 9 Changpu Heyan; adult/student Y20/10, audio tour Y50; ☯ 9am-4.30pm; subway Tiananmen Dong) is devoted to the Imperial City Wall (Huáng Chéng), which – apart from a few brief stretches – no longer exists. The recently opened museum is the centrepiece of a surviving section of the Imperial City wall, southeast of the Forbidden City, that has been dolled up and converted into a park. The park is decorated with a graceful marble bridge, rock features, paths, a stream, willows, magnolias, scholar trees and walnut trees.

Within the museum, a diorama reveals the full extent of the yellow-tiled wall, which encompassed a vast chunk of Běijīng virtually seven times the size of the Forbidden City. In its heyday, 28 large temples could be found in the Imperial City alone, along with many smaller shrines. Further galleries have exhibits of imperial ornaments such as *ruyi* (sceptres), porcelain and enamelware and the weapons and armour of the guards who defended the Imperial City.

IMPERIAL ARCHIVES 皇史宬

Tucked quietly away to the east of the Forbidden City are the old **Imperial Archives** (Huángshǐ Chéng; 136 Nanchizi Dajie; admission free; ☯ 9am-7pm; subway Tiananmen Dong), the former repository for the imperial records, decrees, the 'Jade Book' (the imperial genealogical record) and huge encyclopaedic works, including the *Yongle Dadian* and the *Daqing Huidian*. You can peer through the closed door and make out the chests in which the archives were stored. With strong echoes of the splendid imperial palace, the courtyard contains well-preserved halls and the **Wan Fung Art Gallery** (Yúnfēng Huàyuàn; www.wanfung.com .cn; ☯ noon-6pm Mon & 10am-6pm Tue-Sun).

ANCIENT OBSERVATORY 古观象台

Mounted on the battlements of a watchtower, Běijīng's ancient **observatory** (Gǔ Guānxiàngtái; ☎ 6524 2202; admission Y15; ☯ 9.30-11.30am & 1-4.30pm Wed-Sun; subway Jianguomen) forlornly overlooks the shuddering flyovers of the Second Ring Rd.

The observatory dates back to Kublai Khan's days, when it lay north of the present site.

Navigational equipment used by Chinese ships is displayed downstairs, and on the roof is an array of Jesuit-designed astronomical instruments. The Jesuits, scholars as well as proselytisers, came to town in 1601 when Matteo Ricci and his associates were permitted to work with Chinese scientists. Outdoing the resident Muslim calendar-setters, they were given control of the observatory, becoming the Chinese court's official advisers.

Of the eight bronze instruments on display, six were designed and constructed under the supervision of the Belgian priest Ferdinand Verbiest, who came to China in 1659 as a special employee of the Qing court.

During the Boxer Rebellion, the instruments disappeared into the hands of the French and Germans. Some were returned

Great Hall of the People (p107) in
Tiananmen Square, Běijīng

Decorative doors at the Forbidden City
(p111), Běijīng

Detail of the Nine Dragon Screen in Beihai Park (p112), Běijīng

BEIJING TRANSPORT NETWORK

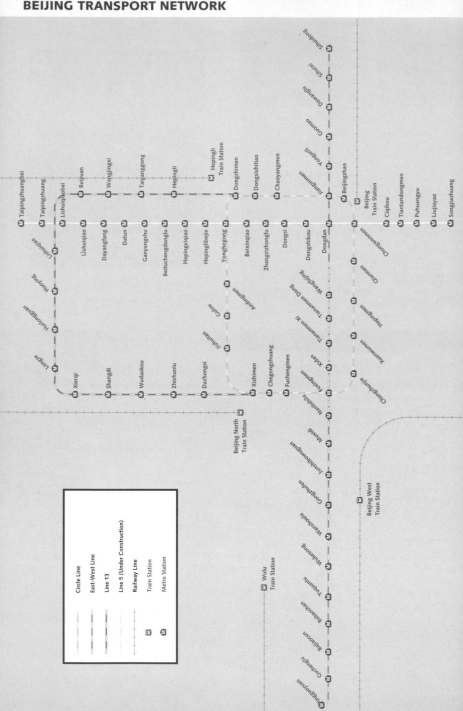

in 1902 and others were returned after WWI, under the provisions of the Treaty of Versailles (1919).

MING CITY WALL RUINS PARK
明城墙遗址公园

Running the entire length of the northern flank of Chongwenmen Dongdajie is this slender new **park** (Míng Chéngqiáng Yízhǐ Gōngyuán; Chongwenmen Dongdajie; admission free; ⏱ 24hr; subway Chongwenmen) alongside a section of the Ming inner city wall.

The wall, restored in 2002, runs for around 2km, rising up to a height of around 15m and interrupted every 80m with buttresses *(dūn tái)*, which extend south from the wall to a maximum depth of 39m.

The park runs from the former site of Chongwen Men (one of the nine gates of the inner city wall), to the **Southeast Corner Watchtower** (Dōngnán Jiǎolóu; ☎ 8512 1554; Dongbianmen; admission Y10; ⏱ 9am-5pm; subway Jianguomen or Chongwenmen). Its green-tiled, twin-eaved roof rising up imperiously, this splendid Ming dynasty fortification is punctured with 144 archer's windows. Inside the highly impressive interior is some staggering carpentry: huge red pillars surge upwards, topped with solid beams. The 1st floor is the site of the **Red Gate Gallery** (Hóngmén Huàláng; ☎ 6525 1005; www.redgategallery.com; admission free; ⏱ 10am-5pm). You can hunt down a further section of original, collapsing Ming wall if you follow Jianguomen Nandajie around to the north.

BEIJING UNDERGROUND CITY
北京地下城

By 1969, as the USA landed men on the moon, Mao had decided the future for Běijīng's people lay underground. Alarmist predictions of nuclear war with Russia dispatched an army of Chinese beneath the streets of Běijīng to burrow a huge warren of bombproof tunnels. The task was completed Cultural Revolution–style – by hand – and was finished in 1979, just as Russia decided to bog down in Afghanistan instead.

A section of the **tunnels** (Běijīng Dìxiàchéng; btwn 64 & 62 Xidamo Changjie; admission Y20; ⏱ 8am-5.30pm; subway Chongwenmen) can be visited. There's not much to see, but you'll pass chambers labelled their original function (cinema, hospital, arsenal etc) as well as flood-proof gates. You can also make out signposts to major landmarks accessed by the tunnels (Tiananmen Sq, the Forbidden City), but these routes are inaccessible.

TEMPLE OF HEAVEN PARK 天坛公园

The most perfect example of Ming architecture, the **Temple of Heaven** (Tiāntán Gōngyuán; ☎ 6702 8866; Tiantan Donglu; admission low season Y10-30, high season Y15-35; ⏱ park 6am-9pm, sights 8am-6pm; subway Chongwenmen or Qianmen) has come to symbolise Běijīng. It is set in a 267-hectare park, with a gate at each point of the compass, and bounded by walls to the north and east. It originally functioned as a vast stage for solemn rites performed by the Son of Heaven, who came here to pray for good harvests, seek divine clearance and atone for the sins of the people.

The temple halls, seen from above, are round and the bases are square, deriving from the ancient Chinese belief that heaven is round and the earth is square. Thus the northern end of the park is semicircular and the southern end is square.

The 5m-high **Round Altar** (圜丘; Yuánqiū) was constructed in 1530 and rebuilt in 1740. It is composed of white marble arrayed in three tiers, and its geometry revolves around the imperial number nine. Odd numbers were considered heavenly, and nine is the largest single-digit odd number. The top tier, thought to symbolise heaven, has nine rings of stones, each composed of multiples of nine stones, so that the ninth ring has 81 stones. The number of stairs and balustrades are also multiples of nine. If you stand in the centre of the upper terrace and say something, the sound waves are bounced off the marble balustrades, amplifying your voice.

Just north of the altar, surrounding the entrance to the Imperial Vault of Heaven, is the **Echo Wall** (回音壁; Huíyīnbì), 65m in diameter. A whisper can travel clearly from one end to your friend's ear at the other – that is, if there's not a tour group in the middle.

The octagonal **Imperial Vault of Heaven** (皇穹宇; Huáng Qióngyǔ) was built at the same time as the Round Altar, and is structured along the lines of the older Hall of Prayer for Good Harvests. It used to contain tablets of the emperor's ancestors, which were used in the winter solstice ceremony.

The dominant feature of the whole complex is the **Hall of Prayer for Good Harvests**

(祈年殿; Qínián Diàn), a magnificent piece mounted on a three-tiered marble terrace. Amazingly, the wooden pillars support the ceiling without nails or cement – for a building 38m high and 30m in diameter, that's quite an accomplishment. Built in 1420, the hall was hit by a lightning bolt during the reign of Guangxu in 1889 and a faithful reproduction based on Ming architectural methods was erected the following year.

NATURAL HISTORY MUSEUM 自然博物馆

The main entrance hall to the overblown, creeper-laden 1950s building housing the **Natural History Museum** (Zìrán Bówùguǎn; ☎ 6702 4431; 126 Tianqiao Nandajie; admission Y15; 🕒 8.30am-5pm, no tickets sold after 4pm; subway Qianmen) is hung with portraits of great natural historians, including Darwin and Linnaeus. Outside, a grove of fossilised trees has been erected.

Some exhibits, such as the spliced human cadavers and genitalia, are best seen on an empty stomach, or not at all. Otherwise check out the dinosaurs that used to roam China before party officials replaced them. There's the possibly beer-drinking *Tsingtaosaurus (Qingdaolong)*, named after the beach resort, and its cousin the *Shantongosaurus*, also from Shāndōng. The dinosaur exhibits are on the ground floor and downstairs.

Other exhibition halls offer a ghastly menagerie of creatures suspended in formaldehyde, but the pickled fish are no different from the many you see floating belly up in restaurant aquariums throughout China.

Coming at you in the human evolution chamber upstairs is a posse of apemen in Socialist Realist pose. There are limited English captions.

Dongcheng 东城

FORBIDDEN CITY 紫禁城

The **Forbidden City** (Zǐjìn Chéng; Map p111; ☎ 6513 2255; admission Y40, for all halls Y60; 🕒 8.30am-4pm May-Sep, 8.30am-3.30pm Oct-Apr; subway Tiananmen Xi or Tiananmen Dong), so called because it was off limits for 500 years, is the largest and best-preserved cluster of ancient buildings in China. It was home to two dynasties of emperors, the Ming and the Qing, who didn't stray from this pleasure dome unless they absolutely had to.

Allow yourself a full day for exploration, or perhaps several separate trips if you're an enthusiast. The palace's ceremonial buildings lie on the north–south axis of the Forbidden City, from the **Gate of Heavenly Peace** in the south to the **Divine Military Genius Gate** (Shénwǔmén) to the north.

Restored in the 17th century, **Meridian Gate** (Wǔ Mén) is a massive portal that in former times was reserved for the use of the emperor. Across the Golden Stream, which is shaped to resemble a Tartar bow and is spanned by five marble bridges, is **Supreme Harmony Gate** (Tàihé Mén). It overlooks a massive courtyard that could hold an imperial audience of up to 100,000 people.

Raised on a marble terrace with balustrades are the Three Great Halls (Sān Dàdiàn), the heart of the Forbidden City. The **Hall of Supreme Harmony** (Tàihé Diàn) is the most important and the largest structure in the Forbidden City. Built in the 15th century, and restored in the 17th century, it was used for ceremonial occasions, such as the emperor's birthday, the nomination of military leaders and coronations.

Inside the Hall of Supreme Harmony is a richly decorated Dragon Throne (Lóngyǐ) where the emperor would preside (decisions final, no correspondence entered into) over his trembling officials.

SIGHTS & ACTIVITIES		pp104–22
Divine Military Genius Gate 神武门	1	B1
Gate of Heavenly Peace 天安门	2	C6
Hall of Middle Harmony 中和殿	3	B3
Hall of Preserving Harmony 保和殿	4	B2
Hall of Supreme Harmony 太和殿	5	C3
Hall of Union 交泰殿	6	B2
Imperial Garden 御花园	7	B1
Meridian Gate 午门	8	C4
Palace of Heavenly Purity 乾清宫	9	B2
Supreme Harmony Gate 太和门	10	C4
OTHER		
Arts & Crafts Exhibit 明清工艺美术馆	11	C1
Bronzes Exhibition 青铜器馆	12	C2
Ceramics Exhibition 陶瓷馆	13	C2
Character Cultivation Hall 养性殿	14	D2
Earthly Tranquillity Palace 坤宁宫	15	B2
Eternal Spring Palace 长春宫	16	B2
Forbidden City Concert Hall 音乐堂	17	B5
Front Hall 太庙	18	C5
Hall of Military Prowess 武英殿	19	B3
Heavenly Purity Gate 乾清门	20	B2
Imperial Peace Hall 钦安殿	21	B1
Imperial Supremacy Hall (Painting Exhibit) 绘画馆	22	C2
Jewellery Exhibition 珍宝馆	23	C1
Literary Glory Hall 文渊阁	24	C3
Mental Cultivation Hall 养心殿	25	B2
Middle Hall 中殿	26	C5
Nine Dragon Screen 九龙壁	27	C2
Rear Hall 后殿	28	C5
Square Altar 五色土	29	B5
Thousand Autumns Pavilion 千秋亭	30	B1
Western Palaces 宫廷史迹陈列	31	B2

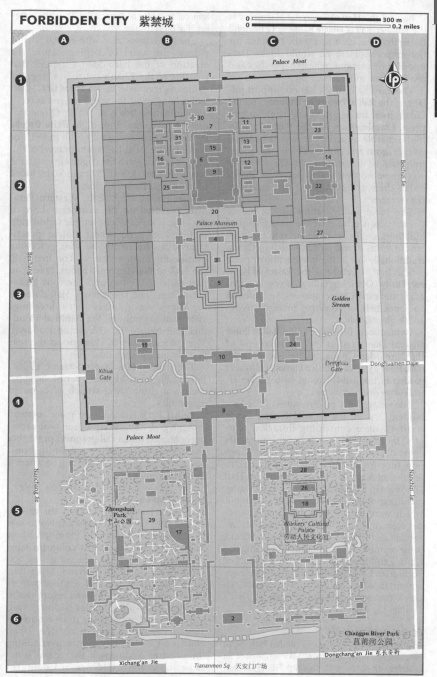

FORBIDDEN CITY 紫禁城

0 | 300 m
0 | 0.2 miles

Palace Moat

Beichizi Jie

Beichang Jie

Palace Museum

Golden Stream

Xihua Gate

Donghua Gate

Donghuamen Dajie

Palace Moat

Nanchang Jie

Nanchizi Jie

Zhongshan Park 中山公园

Workers' Cultural Palace 劳动人民文化宫

Changpu River Park 菖蒲河公园

Xichang'an Jie

Tiananmen Sq 天安门广场

Dongchang'an Jie 东长安街

Behind the Hall of Supreme Harmony is the smaller **Hall of Middle Harmony** (Zhōnghé Diàn) that was used as a transit lounge for the emperor. Here he would make last-minute preparations, rehearse speeches and receive close ministers.

The third hall, which has no support pillars, is the **Hall of Preserving Harmony** (Bǎohé Diàn), used for banquets and later for imperial examinations. To the rear is a 250-tonne marble imperial carriageway carved with dragons and clouds, which was moved into Bĕijīng on an ice path. The emperor was conveyed over the carriageway in his sedan chair as he ascended or descended the terrace.

The basic configuration of the Three Great Halls is echoed by the next group of buildings, smaller in scale but more important in terms of real power, which in China traditionally lies in the northernmost part.

The first structure is the **Palace of Heavenly Purity** (Qiánqīng Gōng), a residence of Ming and early Qing emperors, and later an audience hall for receiving foreign envoys and high officials.

Immediately behind it is the **Hall of Union** (Jiāotài Diàn) and at the northern end of the Forbidden City is the 7000-sq-m **Imperial Garden** (Yùhuā Yuán), a classical Chinese garden of fine landscaping, with rockeries, walkways and pavilions.

The western and eastern sides of the Forbidden City are the palatial former living quarters, once containing libraries, temples, theatres, gardens and even the tennis court of the last emperor. These buildings now function as museums requiring extra admission fees. The Clock Exhibition Hall (Zhōngbiǎo Guǎn) contains a fascinating collection of elaborate timepieces, many of which were presents to the Qing emperors from overseas. Opening hours are irregular and no photos are allowed without prior permission. At the time of writing the Clock Exhibition Hall was in the east part of Forbidden City. Special exhibits sometimes appear in other palace museum halls, so check the expat magazines, such as *That's Beijing*, for details.

BEIHAI PARK 北海公园

Approached via four gates, **Beihai Park** (Běihǎi Gōngyuán; Map pp102-3; ☎ 6407 1415; northwest of the Forbidden City; admission Y5, Jade Islet Y10; ❂ 6.30am-8pm, buildings open till 4pm; subway Tiananmen Xi, then bus 5) is largely lake.

The site is associated with Kublai Khan's palace, the navel of Bĕijīng before the creation of the Forbidden City. All that remains of the Khan's court is a large jar made of green jade, in the **Round City** (团城; Tuánchéng) near the southern entrance.

Dominating **Jade Islet** (琼岛; Qióngdǎo) on the lake, the 36m-high **White Dagoba** (白塔; Báitǎ) was originally built in 1651 for a visit by the Dalai Lama, and was rebuilt in 1741. You can reach the dagoba through the **Yong'an Temple** (永安寺, Yǒngān Sì) included in the Beihai Park Y10 ticket).

Xitian Fànjìng (西天梵境; Western Paradise), situated on the northern shore of the lake, is an excellent temple (admission included in park ticket). Taichi practitioners can frequently be seen practising outside the main entrance. The first hall, the Hall of the Heavenly Kings, takes you past Milefo, Weituo and the four Heavenly Kings. The Dacizhenru Hall dates to the Ming dynasty and contains three huge statues of Sakyamuni, the Amithaba Buddha and Yaoshi Fo (Medicine Buddha). The golden statue of Guanyin at the rear is sadly unapproachable.

The nearby **Nine Dragon Screen** (九龙壁; Jiǔlóng Bì), a 5m-high and 27m-long spirit wall, is a glimmering stretch of coloured glazed tiles.

Beihai Park is a relaxing place to stroll around, grab a snack, sip a beer, rent a rowing boat, and watch calligraphers practising characters on the paving slabs with brush and water, and couples cuddling on a bench in the evening.

LAMA TEMPLE 雍和宫

The **Lama Temple** (Yōnghé Gōng; Map pp102-3; ☎ 6404 4499, ext 252; 28 Yonghegong Dajie; admission Y25, English audio guide Y20; ❂ 9am-4pm; subway Yonghegong) is Bĕijīng's most colourful temple: beautiful rooftops, stunning frescoes, magnificent decorative arches, tapestries, incredible carpentry and a great pair of Chinese lions. Get to this one before you're 'templed out' – the complex is simply vast.

The Lama Temple is the most renowned Tibetan Buddhist temple outside Tibet. Northwest of the city centre overlooking the street of Andingmen Dongdajie, it became the official residence of Count Yin

Zhen after extensive renovation. There was nothing unusual in that, but in 1723 he was promoted to emperor and took up residence in the Forbidden City. His name was changed to Yong Zheng, and his former residence became Yonghe Palace. In 1744 it was converted into a lamasery (a monastery of lamas) and became a residence for large numbers of monks from Mongolia and Tibet.

The temple's most prized possession is its 55-foot high sandalwood statue of the Maitreya Buddha in the Wanfu Pavilion. An absorbing exhibition at the rear displays numerous Tibetan items and chronicles the lineage of the Dalai Lamas.

CONFUCIUS TEMPLE & IMPERIAL COLLEGE 孔庙、国子监

Forlorn and untended (someone should really take a feather duster to it), the **Confucius Temple** (Kǒng Miào; Map pp102-3; ☎ 8401 1977; 13 Guozijian Jie; admission Y10; ⊗ 8.30am-5pm; subway Yonghegong) is a quiet sanctuary from Běijīng's congested, smoggy streets and snarling traffic. It's also the second-largest Confucian temple in China after the venerable example at Qūfù in Shāndōng province (p198). Some of Běijīng's last remaining *páilou* bravely survive in the *hútòng* (narrow alleyway) outside (Guozijian Jie), braced for a possible denouement with future road-widening schemes.

The grounds are home to hundreds of stelae that record the names of successful candidates of the highest level of the official Confucian examination system. Many of the stelae pavilions are bricked up alongside gnarled cypresses that claw at the sky.

Inside the main hall, called the **Dàchéng Diàn** (Hall of Great Achievement) sits a statue of Kongzi (Confucius). A small museum of musical instruments can be also be visited in a side hall, and at the rear is a forest of 190 stelae recording the 13 Confucian classics, consisting of 630,000 Chinese characters.

West of the Confucius Temple is the **Imperial College** (Guózijiàn; Map pp102-3), where the emperor expounded the Confucian classics to an audience of thousands of kneeling students, professors and court officials – an annual rite. Built by the grandson of Kublai Khan in 1306, the former college was the supreme academy during the Yuan, Ming

and Qing dynasties and was the only institution of its kind in China. On the site is a marvellous glazed, three-gate, single-eaved decorative archway, called a *liúli páifāng* (glazed archway). The Biyong Hall beyond is a twin-roofed structure with yellow tiles surrounded by a moat and topped with a gold knob. Pop inside and take in the huge and impressive ceiling.

In the vicinity of the Lama Temple and Guozijian Jie are numerous religious artefact and souvenir shops where you can pick up effigies of Buddhist deities and Bodhisattvas (one worthy of nirvana but who remains on earth to help others attain enlightenment) along with Buddhist keepsakes and talismans *(hùshēnfú)*.

JINGSHAN PARK 景山公园

With its priceless views, **Jingshan Park** (Jǐngshān Gōngyuán; Map pp102-3; ☎ 6403 3225; north of Forbidden City; admission Y2; ⊗ 6am-9.30pm; subway Tiananmen Xi, then bus 5) was shaped from the earth excavated to create the palace moat. The hill supposedly protects the palace from the evil spirits – or dust storms – from the north (the billowing dust clouds in the spring have to be seen to be believed).

During legation days – in the late 19th and early 20th centuries, when the foreign powers had a presence in Běijīng – the mound was called Coal Hill. It was Běijīng's highest point during the Ming dynasty. Clamber to the top of this regal pleasure garden for a magnificent panorama of the capital and an unparalleled overview of the russet roofing of the Forbidden City. On the eastern side of the park a locust tree stands in the place where the last of the Ming emperors, Chongzhen, hung himself as rebels swarmed at the city walls.

ST JOSEPH'S CHURCH 东堂

One of the four principal churches in Běijīng, **St Joseph's Church** (Dōng Táng; Map pp102-3; 74 Wangfujing Dajie; ⊗ 6.30-7am Mon-Sat, 6.30-8am Sun; subway Wangfujing) is also called the East Cathedral. Originally built during the reign of Shunzhi in 1655, it was damaged by an earthquake in 1720 and rebuilt. The luckless church also caught fire in 1807, was destroyed again in 1900 during the Boxer Rebellion, and restored in 1904, only to be shut in 1966. The church has been fully repaired and is now a more sublime feature of

Wangfujing's commercial face-lift. A large square in front swarms with children playing and Chinese models in bridal outfits posing for magazine covers. You can take in the church through the steam of a cappuccino or latte at the Starbucks opposite.

DRUM TOWER & BELL TOWER
鼓楼、钟楼

Repeatedly destroyed and restored, the **Drum Tower** (Gǔlóu; Map pp102-3; ☎ 6401 2674; Gulou Dongdajie; admission Y20; ☉ 9am-4.30pm) was originally built in 1273 and marked the centre of the old Mongol capital. The drums of this later Ming dynasty version were beaten to mark the hours of the day. Stagger up the incredibly steep steps for long views over Běijīng's rooftops. On display is a large array of drums, including the large and dilapidated **Night Watchman's Drum** (gēnggǔ; gēng being one of the five two-hour divisions of the night) and a large array of reproduction drums.

Fronted by a Qing dynasty stele (a stone or slab decorated with figures or inscriptions), the **Bell Tower** (Zhōnglóu; Map pp102-3; ☎ 6401 2674; admission Y15; ☉ 9am-4.30pm) sits behind the Drum Tower and was originally built at the same time, but later burnt down. The present structure dates from the 18th century. Most Buddhist temples in China have their own drum and bell towers, as do a number of other cities (such as Xī'ān).

Both the Drum and Bell Towers can be reached on bus No 5, 58 or 107; get off at the namesake Gu Lou stop.

CHINA ART GALLERY 中国美术馆
Back in the old days, one of the safest hobbies for an artist was to retouch classical-type landscapes with red flags, belching factory chimneys or bright red tractors. The

---

BĚIJĪNG'S HÚTÒNG

If you want to plumb Běijīng's homely interior, and move beyond the must-see sights and shopping-mall glitz of town, voyage into the city's *hútòng* (narrow alleyways). Many of these charming alleyways remain, crisscrossing east–west across the city and linking to create a huge, enchanting warren of one-storey, ramshackle dwellings and historic courtyard homes.

Hútòng may still be the stamping ground of a quarter of Běijīng's residents, but many are sadly being swept aside in Beijing's race to manufacture a modern city of white tile high-rises. Marked with white plaques, historic homes are protected, but for many others a way of life is being ruthlessly bulldozed, at a rate of over 10,000 dwellings a year (the successful 2008 Olympic bid was the kiss of death).

History

After Genghis Khan's army reduced the city of Běijīng to rubble, the city was redesigned with *hútòng*. By the Qing dynasty there were over 2000 such passageways riddling the city, leaping to around 6000 by the 1950s; now the figure has dwindled again to around 2000.

Hútòng land is a hodgepodge of the old and the new, with Qing dynasty courtyards riddled with modern brick outhouses and socialist-era conversions, and cruelly overlooked by grim apartment blocks.

Sìhéyuàn

Old walled courtyards (*sìhéyuàn*) are the building blocks of this delightful world. Many are still lived in and hum with activity. From spring to autumn, men collect outside their gates, drinking beer, playing chess, smoking and chewing the fat. Inside, trees soar aloft, providing shade and a nesting ground for birds.

More venerable courtyards are fronted by large, thick, red doors, outside of which perch either a pair of Chinese lions or drum stones (*bǎogǔshí*; two circular stones resembling drums, each on a small plinth and occasionally topped by a miniature lion or a small dragon head).

Foreigners have cottoned on to the charm of courtyards and have breached this very conservative bastion; however, many have been repelled by poor heating, no hot water, no cable TV, dodgy sanitation and no place to park the 4WD. Many *hútòng* homes still lack toilets and

China Art Gallery (Zhōngguó Měishùguǎn; Map pp102-3; ☎ 6401 7076/2252; 1 Wusi Dajie; admission Y4; ☽ 9am-5pm Tue-Sun, last entry 4pm) has a more progressive range of paintings and hosts occasional photographic exhibitions. The museum – housed in a largely traditional-style building with upturned eaves – underwent a revamp in 2003. The absence of a permanent collection means that all exhibits are temporary. There are no English captions, but it's still a first-rate place to see modern Chinese art and, maybe just as importantly, to watch the Chinese looking at art. Take trolley bus No 103, 104, 106 or 108 to Meishu Guan bus stop (on Wusi Dajie).

Chaoyang 朝阳区   pp102-3
DONGYUE TEMPLE 东岳庙
The Taoist **Dongyue Temple** (Dōngyuè Miào; ☎ 6553 2184; 141 Chaoyangmenwai Dajie; admission Y10; ☽ 9am-4.30pm Tue-Sun; subway Chaoyangmen) is an unset-tling, albeit fascinating experience. The temple is an active place of worship where Taoist monks attend to a world entirely at odds with the surrounding glass and steel high-rises. Note the temples' huge *páifāng* (memorial archway) lying to the south, divorced from its shrine by the intervention of Chaoyangmenwai Dajie.

Stepping through the entrance pops you into a Taoist Hades, alongside tormented spirits reflecting on their wrongdoing and atonement beyond reach. Take your pick: you can muse on life's finalities in the **Life and Death Department** or the **Final Indictment Department**. Otherwise, get spooked at the **Department for Wandering Ghosts** or the **Department for Implementing 15 Kinds of Violent Death**. Alternatively, get roasted for bad grammar at the **Department of the Hell**. English explanations detail each department's function.

---

this explains the multitude of malodorous public loos strung out along the alleyways. Other homes have been thoroughly modernized and sport varnished wood floors, fully fitted kitchens, a Jacuzzi and air-con.

Wind-water Lanes
Hútòng nearly all run east–west to ensure that the main gate faces south, satisfying feng shui requirements. This south-facing aspect guarantees a lot of sunshine and protection from more negative forces from the north. This positioning also mirrors the layout of all Chinese temples, nourishing the *yáng* (the male and light aspect), while checking the *yīn* (the female and dark aspect).

Little connecting alleyways that run north–south link the main alleys. The resulting rectangular waffle-grid pattern stamps the points of the compass on the Beijing psyche. You may hear a local saying, for example, 'wǒ gāoxìng de wǒ bù zhī běi le', meaning 'I was so happy, I didn't know which way was north' (an extremely disorientating state of joy).

Names
Some *hútòng* are christened after families, such as Zhaotangzi Hutong (Alley of the Zhao Family). Others simply take their name from historical figures or features, while some have more mysterious associations, such as Dragon Whiskers Ditch Alley. Others reflect the merchandise plied at local markets, such as Ganmian Hutong (Dry Flour Alley) or Chrysanthemum Lane.

Hútòng Tour
The best way to see *hútòng* is just to wander around the centre of Běijīng as the alleyways riddle the town within the Second Ring Rd. Otherwise, limit yourself to historic areas, such as around the Drum Tower (opposite) or the area around the Lusongyuan Hotel (p123). Alternatively, jump on a bike (see the Bicycle Tour on p120). Otherwise do the pedicab tourist trip with the **Beijing Hutong Tour Co Ltd** (☎ 6615 9097, 6400 2787; ☽ day tours 8.50am & 1.50pm, evening tours 6.50pm May-Oct): their acolytes depart from a point 200m to the west of the north entrance of Beihai Park (p112). Any number of other pedicab tours infest the roads around the Shichahai Lakes – they will circle you like hyenas, baying 'hútòng, hútòng'.

Other halls are no less fascinating. The **Hall of Taishan Fujun** is dedicated to a Taoist god in charge of the souls of the departed who flee to the holy mountain of Tài Shān. **Divinity Mao Hall** is where a likeness of Mao Ying, founding master of the mysterious Maoshan Taoist School, resides.

A good time to visit the temple is during festival time, especially during the Chinese New Year and the Mid-Autumn festival; see p894 for more about these festivals.

POLY ART MUSEUM 保利艺术博物馆

Up the escalator on the 2nd floor of the Poly Plaza is this excellent new-generation **museum** (Bǎolì Yìshù Bówùguǎn; ☎ 6500 8117; Poly Plaza, 14 Dongzhimen Nandajie; admission Y15; ⊙ 9am-4.30pm; subway Dongsishitiao). It may be small, but it ranks as one of China's best collections. The well-lit displays consist of bronzes and carved stone Buddhist effigies sculpted between the Northern Wei and Tang dynasties, although at the time of writing the latter were on tour in the USA. The bronzes, dating from the Shang dynasty (1700–1100 BC) and passing through the Zhou period (1100-221 BC), include an impressive range of patina-coloured *ding, jue, gui, xu* (ancient Chinese vessels) and other vessels and bells *(zhong)*. Also on view are early bells with animal faces, a rare, small *zun* vessel in the shape of a rabbit and a marvellous gilt dragon head ornament from a canopy frame. A couple of Bodhisattva effigies are in the foyer downstairs, and if the rest of the stone effigies are back from abroad, you will be able to view a beautiful collection of contemplative Bodhisattvas and seated and standing Buddha statues.

Fengtai & Xuanwu
丰台区、宣武区   **Map pp102–3**
WHITE CLOUD TEMPLE 白云观
White Cloud Temple (Báiyún Guàn; ☎ 6346 3531; Baiyun Lu; admission Y10; ⊙ 8.30am-4.30pm May-Sep, 8.30am-4pm Oct-Apr) was founded in AD 739. It's a lively, huge and fascinating temple complex of numerous shrines and courtyards, tended by distinctive Taoist monks with their hair twisted into topknots. As with many of China's temples, the White Cloud Temple has been repeatedly destroyed and today's temple halls principally date from the Ming and Qing dynasties.

Drop by White Cloud Temple during Chinese New Year and be rewarded with the spectacle of a magnificent temple fair *(miàohuì)*. Worshippers funnel into the streets around the temple in their thousands, lured by artisans, street performers, *wǔshù* (martial arts) acts, craftsmen, traders and a swarm of snack merchants. Near the temple entrance, a vast, patient queue of people (a rare occurrence indeed in China) snakes slowly through the gate for a chance to rub a polished stone carving for good fortune. Beyond, throngs of worshippers further fortify their luck by tossing metal discs (Y10 for 50) at bell-adorned outsize coins suspended from a bridge.

To find the temple, walk south on Baiyun Lu and cross the moat. Continue south along Baiyun Lu and turn into a curving street on the left; follow it for 250m to the temple entrance.

COW STREET MOSQUE 牛街礼拜寺
This fascinating **mosque** (Niújiē Lǐbài Sì; ☎ 6353 2564; 88 Niu Jie; admission Y10, free for Muslims; ⊙ 8am-sunset) was designed in a Chinese temple style. With a history dating back to the 10th century, the mosque is the largest in town, and is also the burial site for a number of Islamic clerics. The temple is given over to a profusion of greenery as well as flourishes of Arabic. There is a main prayer hall (which you can enter only if you are Muslim), women's quarters and the Building for Observing the Moon (Wàngyuèlóu), from where the lunar calendar was calculated. Dress appropriately (no shorts or short skirts). To get here take bus No 6 to Niu Jie or bus No 10 to Libaisi stop.

FAYUAN TEMPLE 法源寺
In a lane just east of Cow St Mosque is this bustling **temple** (Fǎyuán Sì; ☎ 6353 3966/4171; 7 Fayuansi Qianjie; admission Y5; ⊙ 8.30-11.30am & 1.30-3.30pm Thu-Tue), originally constructed in the 7th century and still a hive of activity. Now the China Buddhism College, the temple was originally built to honour Tang soldiers who had fallen during combat against the northern tribes. Don't miss the hall at the very back of the temple, which houses an unusual copper-cast Buddha seated upon a thousand-petal lotus flower. From the entrance of Cow St Mosque, walk left 100m then turn left into the first *hútòng*. Follow the *hútòng* for about 10 minutes and you'll arrive at Fayuan Temple.

Haidian & Xicheng 海淀区、西城区
SUMMER PALACE 颐和园
One of Běijīng's most visited sights, the immense park of the **Summer Palace** (Yíhé Yuán; Map p117; ☎ 6288 1144; 19 Xinjian Gongmen; admission Y40-Y50, audio guides Y30; ☺ 8:30am-5pm) requires at least half a day of your time.

Nowadays teeming with tour groups from all over China and beyond, this dominion of palace temples, gardens, pavilions, lake and corridors was once a playground for the imperial court. Royalty came here to elude the insufferable summer heat that roasted the Forbidden City. The site had long been a royal garden and was considerably enlarged and embellished by Emperor Qianlong in the 18th century. He deepened and expanded

Kunming Lake (Kūnmíng Hú) with the help of 100,000 labourers, and reputedly surveyed imperial navy drills from a hill-top perch.

Anglo-French troops damaged the buildings during the Second Opium War (1860). Empress Dowager Cixi began a refit in 1888 with money earmarked for a modern navy; the marble boat at the northern edge of the lake was her only nautical concession.

Foreign troops, incensed by the Boxer Rebellion, had another go at roasting the Summer Palace in 1900, prompting more restoration work. By 1949 the palace had once more fallen into disrepair and a major overhaul was undertaken.

Three-quarters of the park is occupied by Kunming Lake and the most notable

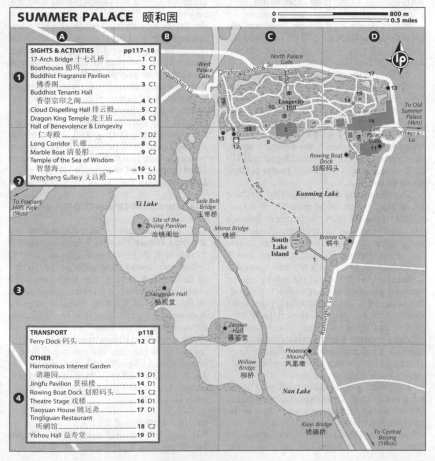

SUMMER PALACE 颐和园

0 ——— 800 m
0 ——— 0.5 miles

SIGHTS & ACTIVITIES	pp117–18
17-Arch Bridge 十七孔桥 1 C3	
Boathouses 船坞 2 C1	
Buddhist Fragrance Pavilion 佛香阁 3 C1	
Buddhist Tenants Hall 香崇宗印之阁 4 C1	
Cloud Dispelling Hall 排云殿 5 C2	
Dragon King Temple 龙王庙 6 C3	
Hall of Benevolence & Longevity 仁寿殿 7 D2	
Long Corridor 长廊 8 C2	
Marble Boat 清晏舫 9 C2	
Temple of the Sea of Wisdom 智慧海 10 C1	
Wenchang Gallery 文昌殿 11 D2	

TRANSPORT	p118
Ferry Dock 码头 12 C2	

OTHER	
Harmonious Interest Garden 谐趣园 13 D1	
Jingfu Pavilion 景福楼 14 D1	
Rowing Boat Dock 划船码头 15 C2	
Theatre Stage 戏楼 16 D1	
Tiaoyuan House 眺远斋 17 D1	
Tingliguan Restaurant 听鹂馆 18 C2	
Yishou Hall 益寿堂 19 D1	

To Fragrant Hills Park (9km)

North Palace Gate
West Palace Gate
Qinglongqiaodong Jie
Yuquanshan Lu
Longevity Hill
To Old Summer Palace (4km)
Yiheyuan Lu
East Palace Gate
Rowing Boat Dock 划船码头
Kunming Lake
Ferry
Xi Lake
Jade Belt Bridge 玉带桥
Mirror Bridge 镜桥
Site of the Zhijing Pavilion 冶镜阁址
South Lake Island
Bronze Ox 铜牛
Changguan Hall 畅观堂
Zaojian Hall 藻鉴堂
Kunminghu Lu
Willow Bridge 柳桥
Phoenix Mound 凤凰墩
Nan Lake
Xiuyi Bridge 绣漪桥
To Central Beijing (18km)

structures reside near the east gates or overlook from Longevity Hill (Wànshòu Shān). The main building is the **Hall of Benevolence and Longevity** (仁寿殿; Rénshòu Diàn), by the east gate, which houses a hardwood throne and is fronted by a courtyard decorated with bronze animals, including the mythical *qílín* (a hybrid animal that only appeared on earth at times of harmony). Unfortunately, the hall is barricaded off so you will have to peer in.

Along the northern shore, the **Long Corridor** (长廊; Cháng Láng) is trimmed with a plethora of paintings, while the slopes and crest of Longevity Hill behind are decorated with several temples. Slung out uphill on a north–south axis are **Buddhist Fragrance Pavilion** (佛香阁 Fóxiāng Gé) and **Cloud Dispelling Hall** (排云殿; Páiyún Diàn), which are connected by corridors. At the crest sits the Buddhist **Temple of the Sea of Wisdom** (智慧海; Zhì Huìhǎi), with glazed tiles depicting Buddha; many, sadly, have had their heads obliterated.

On the northern shore you can see Cixi's marble boat, north of which survive some fine Qing boathouses. You can traverse Kunming Lake by ferry to **South Lake Island** (南湖岛; Nánhú Dǎo). Cixi visited the island's **Dragon King Temple** (龙王庙; Lóngwáng Miào) to beseech the temple's statue for rain in times of drought. A graceful 17-arch bridge spans the 150m to the eastern shore of the lake.

The **Wenchang Gallery** (文昌阁; Wénchāng Gé; ☎ 6288 1144, ext 224; admission Y20; ☒ 8.30am-4.30pm) to the south of the Summer Palace's entrance is a quiet escape from the hordes rampaging through the palace. The galleries, set in a clean and engaging pocket of reproduction Qing architecture, comprise a porcelain exhibition, a jade gallery and an unusual selection of Qing artefacts (including some of Cixi's calligraphy), plus some decent bronzes; some of the artefacts were looted during the Opium War and only recently returned from private collections abroad. Towards the North Palace Gate (Sūzhōu Jiē) is a fun diversion of riverside walkways, shops and eateries.

The park is about 12km northwest of the centre of Běijīng. You can get there by taking the subway to Xīzhímén station (close to the zoo), then a minibus or bus No 375; or else get off at the Wudaokou subway station. A number of other buses can get you to the Summer Palace, including bus Nos 303, 330, 332, 333, 346, 362, 801, 808 (from the Qiánmén area) and 817. You can also get here by bicycle; it takes about 1½ to two hours from the centre of town. Cycling along the road following the Beijing-Miyun Diversion Canal is pleasant, and in summer there's the option of taking a **boat** (☎ 6823 2179, 6821 3366; one way/return incl Summer Palace admission Y45/75) from behind the Exhibition Center near the zoo; the boat voyages via locks along the canal.

PRINCE GONG'S RESIDENCE 恭王府
Reputed to be the model for the mansion in Cao Xueqin's 18th-century classic, *Dream of the Red Mansions*, this **residence** (Gōngwáng Fǔ; Map pp102-3; ☎ 6616 8149, 6601 6132; 14 Liuyin Jie; admission Y20; ☒ 8.30am-4.30pm; subway Gulou, then bus 60) is one of Běijīng's largest private residential compounds. Despite skulking ice-cream sellers and pantomime costume hire, it can be a quiet and introspective place, especially if you visit in the morning and avoid the tour groups. This remains one of Běijīng's more attractive retreats, decorated with rockeries, plants, pools, pavilions, corridors and elaborately carved gateways. Guided tours are available (Y60 including tour guide, tea-tasting and a sample of Beijing opera) and performances of Beijing opera are held regularly in the Qing dynasty **Grand Opera House** (☎ 6618 6628; Y80-120; ☒ 7.30-8.40pm Mar-Oct) in the east of the grounds.

MIAOYING TEMPLE WHITE DAGOBA 妙应寺白塔
The Yuan dynasty white dagoba of the **Miaoying Temple** (Miàoyīng Sì Báitǎ; Map pp102-3; ☎ 6616 0211; 171 Fuchengmennei Dajie; admission Y10; ☒ 9am-4pm; subway Fuchengmen) is similar to that in Beihai Park (p112). The high point of a visit here, however, is its riveting collection of thousands of Tibetan Buddhist statues. A population of bronze *luóhàn* (Buddhist, especially a monk who has achieved enlightenment and passes to nirvana at death) figures also inhabits the temple. There is liberal use of English captions. Take bus No 13, 101, 102 or 103 to Báitǎ Sì bus stop (near Baitasi Lu) or take the subway to Fuchengmen and walk east.

BEIJING ZOO 北京动物园
All zoos are animal prisons, but **Beijing Zoo** (Běijīng Dòngwùyuán; Map pp102-3; ☎ 6831 4411;

137 Xizhimenwai Dajie; admission Y10, pandas extra Y5; 7.30am-5.30pm) seems like death row. Most design features date from the 1950s – concrete and glass cells – but the pandas have plusher living quarters for good behaviour.

The polar bears pin all their hopes on graduating from their concrete hell to the **Beijing Aquarium** (Map pp102-3; ☎ 6833 8742; adult/child Y100/50; 9am-5.30pm low season, 9am-6pm high season) in the northeastern corner of the zoo. On view is an imaginative Amazon rainforest area (complete with piranha), coral reefs, a shark aquarium (where you can dive with the flesh eaters), whales, dolphins and a marine mammal pavilion. The latter hosts lively aquatic animal displays.

Getting to the zoo is easy enough; take the subway to Xizhimen station. From here, it's a 15-minute walk heading west or a short ride on any of the trolley buses.

OLD SUMMER PALACE 圆明园

Located northwest of the city centre, the original **Summer Palace** (Yuánmíng Yuán; Map pp98-9; ☎ 6262 8501; northeast of the Summer Palace; admission Y10, palace ruins Y15; 7am-7pm) was laid out in the 12th century. Resourceful Jesuits were later employed by Emperor Qianlong to fashion European-style palaces for the gardens, incorporating elaborate fountains and baroque statuary. During the Second Opium War (1856–60), British and French troops destroyed the palace and sent the booty abroad. Much went up in flames, but a melancholic array of broken columns and marble chunks remain.

Trot through the southern stretch of hawkers and arcade games to the more subdued ruins of the European Palace in the **Eternal Spring Garden** (长春园; Chángchūn Yuán) to the northeast. Alternatively, enter by the east gate, which leads to the palace vestiges. The mournful composition of tumbledown palace remains lies strewn in a long strip; alongside are black-and-white photos displaying before and after images of the residence. It's here that you can find the **Great Fountain Ruins** (大水法遗址; Dàshuǐfǎ Yízhǐ) considered the best-preserved relic in the palace.

West of the ruins you can lose your way in an artful reproduction of a former maze called the **Garden of Yellow Flowers**.

The gardens cover a huge area – some 2.5km from east to west – so be prepared to do some walking. Besides the ruins, there's the western section, the **Perfection and Brightness Garden** (Yuánmíng Yuán) and the southern compound, the **10,000 Spring Garden** (Wànchūn Yuán).

To get to the Old Summer Palace, take minibus No 375 from the Xīzhímén subway station, or get off at the Wudaokou subway station. Minibuses also connect the new Summer Palace with the old one, or a taxi will take you for Y10.

FRAGRANT HILLS PARK 香山公园

Easily within striking distance of the Summer Palace is the Western Hills (Xī Shān), another former villa-resort of the emperors. The part of the Western Hills closest to Běijīng is known as **Fragrant Hills Park** (Xiāngshān Gōngyuán; Map pp98-9; ☎ 6259 1283; admission Y5; 7am-6pm).

You can either scramble up the slopes to the top of **Incense-Burner Peak** (Xiānglú Fēng) or take the **chairlift** (one way/return Y30/50; 8.30am to 5pm). From the peak you get an all-embracing view of the countryside. Beijingers love to flock here in autumn when the maple leaves saturate the hillsides in great splashes of red.

Near the north gate of Fragrant Hills Park is **Azure Clouds Temple** (Bìyún Sì; ☎ 6259 1155, ext 470; admission Y10; 8am-5pm), which dates back to the Yuan dynasty. It took a hammering during the Cultural Revolution and reopened in 1979. The Mountain Gate Hall contains two vast protective deities: 'Heng' and 'Ha'. Next is a small courtyard containing the drum and bell towers, leading to a hall with a wonderful statue of Milefo: it's bronze, but coal black with age. Only his big toe shines from numerous inquisitive fingers.

The next hall contains statues of Sakyamuni and Bodhisattvas Manjushri, Samantabhadra and Avalokiteshvara (Guanyin), plus 18 *luóhàn*; a marvellous golden carved dragon soars above Sakyamuni. A statue of Guanyin stands at the rear, atop a fish.

The Hall of Bodhisattvas contains Wenshu, Guanyin, Dashizhi, Puxian and Dizang, plus further immortals. The Sun Yatsen Memorial Hall contains a statue and a glass coffin donated by the USSR on the death of Mr Sun (see p42).

At the very back is the marble Vajra Throne Pagoda where Sun Yatsen was interred after he died and before his body was moved to its final resting place in Nánjīng. The Hall of Arhats contains 500 *luóhàn* statues.

There are a few ways to get to Fragrant Hills Park by public transport: you can take bus No 333 from the Summer Palace, bus No 360 from the zoo or bus No 318 from Pingguoyuan (the very last stop west on the subway).

BEIJING BOTANICAL GARDENS 北京植物园

The well-tended and clean **Botanical Gardens** (Běijīng Zhíwùyuán; Map pp98-9; ☎ 6259 1283; admission Y5; ❧ 6am-8pm), set against the backdrop of the Western Hills, make for a pleasant outing among bamboo fronds, pines and lilacs. The **Běijīng Botanical Gardens Conservatory** (admission Y40), built in 1999, contains 3000 different types of plants and a rainforest house. The gardens are located 2km east of Fragrant Hills Park.

Within the grounds and about a 15-minute walk from the front gate (follow the signs) is the **Temple of the Reclining Buddha** (Wòfó Sì; Map pp98-9; ☎ 6259 1561; admission Y5; ❧ 8am-5pm). First built in the Tang dynasty, the temple's centrepiece is a huge reclining effigy of Sakyamuni weighing 54 tonnes, which apparently 'enslaved 7000 people' in its casting.

On each side of Buddha are sets of gargantuan shoes, gifts to Sakyamuni from various emperors in case he went for a stroll. Above him are the apt characters '*zìzài dàdé*', meaning 'great accomplishment comes from being at ease'. Other halls include effigies of Milefo and Weituo, the Four Heavenly Kings, Golden Buddhas and Guanyin. The temple is located near the Magnolia Garden, which flowers profusely in spring.

To get here take the subway to Pingguoyuan then bus No 318, bus No 333 from the Summer Palace or bus No 360 from Beijing Zoo.

BICYCLE TOUR

Běijīng's sprawling distances and scattered sights can make for blistering sightseeing on foot, but voyaging around the city's streets and alleyways by bike allows you to take it all in at just the right speed. Hop on a pair of wheels, get that bell jangling and join us on this eye-opening tour past some

of the city's finest monuments and through rarely visited reaches off the beaten track.

Our tour starts on Dongchang'an Jie, northeast of Tiananmen Sq. Cycle through the purple-red archway of Nanchizi Dajie and north along the tree-lined street; you'll pass the **Imperial Archives** (**1**; p108) to your right, a quiet courtyard reminiscent of

---

BIKE TOUR FACTS

Start: Dongchang'an Jie, northeast of Tiananmen Sq

Finish: Wen Tianxiang Temple

Distance: 7km

Duration: 1½ hours

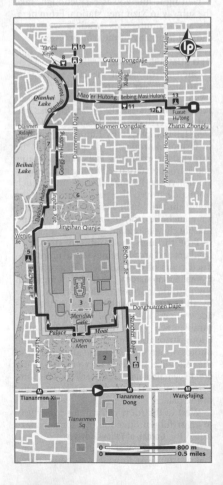

the Forbidden City and site of the Wan Fung Art Gallery. Further up to your left you'll see the eastern entrance to the **Workers Cultural Palace** (2; p108), from where you can see the imperial yellow roof of the Supreme Temple. Further up Nanchizi Dajie, the halls and towers of the Forbidden City become visible to the west; hang a left at the intersection with Donghuamen Dajie, pass the Courtyard (p127) restaurant to your right, then head left again and follow the road between the moat and the walls of the palace.

Note in particular the southeast corner tower of the wall of the **Forbidden City** (3; p110). The walls around the palace, 10m high and containing 12 million bricks, are adorned at each corner with one such tower (jiǎolóu). Each tower is of highly elaborate construction with exceptional roof arrangements, supporting three eaves.

The trip around the moat is a spectacular route with unique views of historic Běijīng. Cycle through the large gate of Quezuo Men and past the face of the Meridian Gate – imposing entrance to the Forbidden City. Cycle through the gate of Queyou Men opposite, south of which is **Zhongshan Park** (4; p108), to continue around the moat. To the west are the eastern gates of Zhōngnánhǎi (中南海), the out-of-bounds nerve centre of political power in Běijīng.

Head north onto Beichang Jie, west of the Forbidden City, and note the bright red doors and brass knockers of several sihéyuàn (courtyard homes) strung out along the road. You'll pass Fuyou Temple (Fúyòu Sì) to your right – sadly locked away behind closed gates and the palace wall.

On your left are the crumbling remains of **Wanshouxinglong Temple** (5; 万寿兴隆寺; Wànshòuxīnglóng Sì; 39 Beichang Jie); its band of monks long gone and now stripped of its holiness and occupied by Běijīng residents. The temple once served as a residence for surviving imperial eunuchs after the fall of the Qing dynasty.

Reaching the T-junction with Jingshan Qianjie and Wenjin Jie, bear right onto Jingshan Qianjie. The vast and now demolished Taoist Dagaoxuan Temple (大高玄殿; Dàgāoxuán Diàn) once occupied this portion of Jingshan Qianjie, its eastern wall hedging up against Jingshan Xijie, opposite the northwest palace corner watchtower,

and its western wall enclosed by Dashizuo Hutong.

Take Dashizuo Hutong, the first small hútòng on the left just to the east of a restaurant and the orange shells of some public phones; the alley bends to the right, then left. This hútòng, where the stone for the Forbidden City was carved, is like many in Běijīng – a mix of tumbledown dwellings and charmless modern blocks. Follow the hútòng to the end, and exit opposite the west gate of **Jingshan Park** (6; p113); park your bike if you want and clamber up the hill for unparalleled views over the Forbidden City.

Cycle north along Jingshan Xijie and at the northern tip of the street head up Gongjian Hutong; its entrance is virtually straight ahead but slightly to the west. You will exit the alley on Dianmen Xidajie; if you want to visit **Beihai Park** (7; p112) to your west, push your bike along the southern side of Dianmen Xidajie and you'll soon arrive at the park's north gate.

Continuing north, push your bike over the pedestrian crossing then cycle along Qianhai Nanyan, which runs along the eastern shore of Qianhai Lake. On the western side of the lake is Lotus Lane, a strip of cafés and restaurants. You will see the small, restored white marble Jinding Bridge (Jīndìng Qiáo) and to its east, Wanning Bridge (Wànníng Qiáo), much of which dates from the Yuan dynasty. Look over the sides of the bridge and note the timeworn statues of water dragons on either bank.

Continue north to Yinding Bridge (Silver Ingot Bridge) and turn east to head along Yandai Xiejie (Chinese Pipe Cross-Street) with its shops, bars and cafés, which are quickly dislodging the dilapidated businesses that operated here. The ancient and diminutive Guangfuguan Taoist Temple has been converted into a café now called the **Guangfuguan Greenhouse** (8; p132), run by an artist.

Exiting Yanndai Xiejie onto bustling Dianmenwai Dajie, you will see the **Drum Tower** (9; p114) rising massively to the north and obscuring the **Bell Tower** (10; p114) behind; both are worth a visit. Then head south and turn east onto Mao'er Hutong, which despite being quite modern in its earlier section, gradually emerges into something more traditional. Ahead, you'll pass a wall-mounted brass plaque, which gives you a rundown of the history of the *hútòng*. At the first main junction along Mao'er Hutong, the alley changes its name to Beibing Masi Hutong, the two alleys divided by the north–south-running Nanluogu Xiang, one of Bĕijīng's most famous alleyways. Cycle down Nanluogu Xiang and if you want to rest, take in a coffee in relaxed, snug courtyard surrounds of the **Passby Bar** (11; Guòkè; ☎ 8403 8004; 108 Nanluogu Xiang; ◷ 7pm-2am) on the corner of the second *hútòng* turning on your left as you cycle south.

Take the second turning on your left just beyond the Passby Bar at the street sign that says 'Police Station'. You are now cycling down Banchang Hutong, a charming stretch of old *sìhéyuàn*, a number of which are adorned with plaques attesting to their historic significance. You'll pass the old **Lusongyuan Hotel** (12; Lùsōngyuán Bīnguǎn; ☎ 6404 0436; 1syhotel@263.net; 22 Banchang Hutong) on the right-hand side of the road, an old courtyard house now serving as a hotel.

As Banchang Hutong meets Jiaodaokou Nandajie, cycle north into the first *hútòng* entrance on your right – Fuxue Hutong. A very short way along the alley on the left-hand side is the **Wen Tianxiang Temple** (13; Wén Tiānxiáng Cí; ☎ 6401 4968; 63 Fuxue Hutong; adult Y5; ◷ 9am-5pm Tue-Sun).

BĔIJĪNG FOR CHILDREN

Baby food and milk powder are widely available in supermarkets, as are basics like nappies, baby wipes, bottles, creams, medicine, clothing, dummies (pacifiers) and other paraphernalia. Virtually no cheap restaurants, however, have high chairs and finding baby-changing rooms is next to impossible.

Current and forthcoming events and attractions (from plays to arts and crafts events and seasonal parties) for children in Bĕijīng are listed in the monthly English language-culture magazine **That's Beijing** (www.thatsbeijing.com). Note that many museums and attractions have a cheaper rate for children, usually applying to children under 1.3m, so ask.

Many kids will dig their heels in when confronted with the measureless museum-style torpor of the Forbidden City and the Ming Tombs. Thanks to China's one-child policy, however, Bĕijīng's poor siblingless

tykes are spoiled rotten by their parents and the city is bursting with activities to keep all those demanding little egos occupied:

Beijing Aquarium (p119) Piranha, sharks, whales and dolphins.

Blue Zoo Beijing (Fùguó Hǎidǐ Shìjiè; Map pp102-3; ☎ 6591 3397; Workers Stadium south gate; adult/child under 12/tots Y75/50/free; ◷ 8am-10pm) Another aquatic option for a rainy day. There's live shark feeding (10am and 2.30pm), and the marine tunnel is quite an eye-opener. Diving lessons are also available for adults (Y380), but instruction is in Chinese only.

China Puppet Theatre (p135) In the evenings, the theatre regularly casts a spell over its audience of little (and not-so-little) ones.

ExploraScience (Suǒní Tànmèng; Map pp102-3; ☎ 8518 2255; 1st fl, Oriental Plaza, Wangfujing Dajie; adult/child Y30/20; ◷ 9.30am-5.30pm Mon-Fri, 10am-7pm Sat & Sun, closed second Mon & Tue every month) A hands-on foray into the world of science. It's full of gadgets and is perfect for inquisitive children and little Einsteins.

Le Cool Ice Rink (Map pp102-3; ☎ 6505 5776; Basement 2, China World Trade Center, 1 Jianguomenwai Dajie; per 90 min Y30-50; ◷ 10am-10pm) This is probably the best and most accessible indoor ice rink in town. It's easy to reach, surrounded by the shops of the China World Trade Center and perfect for the kids. Charges vary depending on time of day you skate; skate hire is extra.

Natural History Museum (p110) The dinosaurs should go down well, but steer the little ones away from the more grisly displays.

New China Children's Toy World (Xīn Zhōngguó Értóng Yòngpǐn Shāngdiàn; Map pp102-3; Wangfujing Dajie) If your children are fed up with window-shopping, take them to this huge and extravagant emporium of toys.

Simitai Great Wall (p144) If your kids think the Great Wall is a colossal bore, you can always plonk them on the 3km downhill toboggan ride at the Sīmǎtái section.

SLEEPING

Bĕijīng has a reasonably wide range of accommodation options, from youth hostels to two- and three-star mid-range options and four- and five-star hotels. Downtown hotels located not too far from Wangfujing Dajie and the Forbidden City and Tiananmen Square are relatively easy to find in all budget groups.

Chongwen & South Chaoyang
Map pp102–3

BUDGET

Eastern Morning Sun Youth Hostel (Bĕijīng Dōngfāng Chénguāng Qīngnián Lûguǎn; ☎ 6528 4347; fl B4, Oriental Plaza, 8-16 Dongdansantiao; s/d/tr Y80/120/180; 🖳)

Despite the sign outside, this is not a bona fide Hostelling International member. Memorise where the fire escape is as the hostel is a subterranean four floors below ground level. Single rooms are simple and small with tiled floors, without phone or TV; the better doubles have TV (no phone). Showers and phones are all communal. There is a tourist information office, a ticketing office, lockers and Internet Phone (IP) cards on sale. Internet access is Y10 per hour.

MID-RANGE

Hademen Hotel (Hādémén Fàndiàn; ☎ 6711 2244; hademen@public.gb.com.cn; 2a Chongwenmenwai Dajie; s Y420, d Y480-580; ☒) The three-star Hademen may be unexceptional, but it benefits from a decent location (near Chongwenmen subway station and Beijing Train Station) and the restored Ming City Wall Ruins Park, and rooms are good value (ask for a discount). Standard doubles are reasonably decorated and comfy, with small shower rooms. Bike

---

THE AUTHOR'S CHOICE

St Regis (Běijīng Guójì Jùlèbù Fàndiàn; Map pp102-3; ☎ 6460 6688; fax 6460 3299; 21 Jianguomenwai Dajie; d US$340, ste US$500-5300; ☒) First-rate, top-notch elegance complemented by professionalism and a superb location, the St Regis is a marvellous choice and probably Běijīng's best hotel. The absolutely splendid foyer and an enticing complement of restaurants compound this hotel's undeniable allure. In the Club Wing you can find a bowling centre, squash courts, cigar and wine lounges and the Astor Grill.

    Lusongyuan Hotel (Lūsōngyuán Bīnguǎn; Map pp102-3; ☎ 6404 0436; 1syhotel@263.net; 22 Banchang Hutong; dm/s/d/ste Y10/35/60/110; ☒ 🖳) Built by a Mongolian general during the Qing dynasty, this courtyard hotel's location among the historic *hútòng* makes it an excellent base for exploring the city. For a double bedroom, book ahead as the hotel only has two (the other rooms have two single beds). Pocket-sized singles come with pea-sized baths (albeit quite cute); dorms have three beds (with TV) and there is just one suite. All rooms facing onto the courtyard are slightly more expensive. There's also bike rental.

    Haoyuan Guesthouse (Hǎoyuán Bīnguǎn; Map pp102-3; ☎ 6512 5557; www.haoyuanhotel.com; 53 Shijia Hutong; d incl breakfast Y468-572; ☒ 🖳) This delightful and quiet Qing courtyard hotel has pleasant staff and a handful of tastefully finished rooms. Laid out with trees, the courtyard at the rear is gorgeous. At the time of writing the buildings opposite had been razed for a development project, robbing the *hútòng* of some charm. There is a restaurant as well as bike rental. Internet access is Y10 per hour. Rooms have shower rooms.

    Far East International Youth Hostel (Yuǎndōng Guójì Qīngnián Lǚshè; Map pp102-3; ☎ 6301 8811, ext 3118; courtyard@elong.com; 113 Tieshuxie Jie; dm high/low season Y60/45; ☒ 🖳) This hostel is in a pretty old courtyard opposite the hotel of the same name. Very pleasant and with loads of character, there's bike rental (Y20 per day, Y200 deposit), kitchen, washing facilities and a fine café-bar. There's also a table tennis room, a shop (selling Internet Phone cards), a tourist office (7.30am to 11.30pm) and pricey DVD rental (old/new disc Y2/5). Rooms come without TV, phone or shower. Internet access is Y10 per hour. The **Far East Hotel** (s/d/tr Y238/398/378, q per bed Y75) opposite is an unremarkable two-star hotel but the quads downstairs are clean with wood flooring strips and well-kept bunk beds. There is also a decent café-bar with sports TV downstairs (noon to midnight) in the hotel, plus a kitchen with two washing machines and a fridge. To get here head south on Nanxinhua Jie. About 200m after you pass Liulichang you'll see a sign (in English) on the right-hand side of the street saying 'Far East Hotel'. Follow the *hútòng* for about 50m.

    Beijing Gongti International Youth Hostel (Běijīng Gōngtǐ Qīngnián Lǚshè; Map pp102-3; ☎ 6552 4800; bih-yh@sohu.com or gongti@hotmail.com; East Gate, Worker's Stadium; 2-/4-bed dm Y70/50, s Y100; 🖳) This clean and appealing hostel offers both excellent value and excellent positioning. The dorm rooms (Y10 extra for non-members) are bright, clean and spacious, and come equipped with phone (incoming only), TV and radiator. Communal showers are clean and a self-service washing machine is provided. Internet access costs Y10 per hour. Non HI-members pay an extra Y20 for single rooms. A camping area is planned outside for the summer months, so enquire at reception. The hostel also has a bar and Chinese restaurant, lockers are available on the ground floor and there's a useful notice board used by travellers. However, there's no lift.

rental is available (Y50 per day, Y200 deposit). Adjacent to the hotel is the Bianyifang roast duck restaurant (see p128).

Huafeng Hotel (Huáfēng Bīnguǎn; ☎ 6524 7311; fax 6524 7495; 5 Qianmen Dongdajie; d/ste Y420/780; ☒) Situated on the site of the more illustrious Grand Hotel des Wagon-Lits (Liùguó Fàndiàn) but now rather a more dismal Chinese-style outfit, the three-star Huafeng is nevertheless well located in the former Legation Quarter, with both Tiananmen Sq and Wangfujing Dajie a stroll away. There's a Chinese restaurant and a billiard room.

TOP END

Grand Hyatt Beijing (Běijīng Dōngfāng Jūnyuè Dàjiǔdiàn; ☎ 8518 1234; www.hyatt.com; 1 Dongchang'an Jie; d US$320; ☒ ☒) This is a stunning hotel at an exclusive address, right in the shopping district of Wangfujing, with everything you could need in the shopping complex of the attached Oriental Plaza. This hotel is blessed with top-notch design, a splendid interior, exemplary service and undeniable opulence. The Forbidden City is just 10 minutes' walk away. The Hyatt also features four restaurants, including the smart Cantonese restaurant Noble Court, northern cuisine at Made in China, as well as several bars including the smart Red Moon Bar (p132).

China World Hotel (Zhōngguó Dàfàndiàn; ☎ 6505 2266; www.shangri-la.com; 1 Jianguomenwai Dajie; d US$300-410, ste US$410-3500; ☒) This excellent five-star hotel has all the hallmarks of the Shangri-La chain (reliability and style), plus all your shopping and dining needs met at the China Word Trade Center. Well-suited for the executive traveller, the hotel has a sumptuous foyer with pronounced Chinese motifs, along with glittering chandeliers, robust columns and smooth acres of marble. As with all Shangri-La hotels, an extra degree of luxury awaits on Horizon Club floors. Full tariff rate includes free airport transfer, laundry, dry cleaning, breakfast and local phone calls.

Kerry Center Hotel (Jiālǐ Zhōngxīn Fàndiàn; ☎ 6561 8833; fax 6561 2626; hbkc@shangri-la.com; 1 Guanghua Lu; d US$240-320, ste US$360-2000; ☒) Another hotel from the Shangri-La chain, this modern, slick and stylish hotel aims at the business traveller market, with trendy décor and smart dining options. Rooms are spacious and neat, with broadband Internet connection, minibar,

shower and bath, iron and ironing board. The foyer is clutter free, spacious and sleek. It may not be that graceful, but the hotel is snazzy, with smooth sounds at Centro (p131) to chill out to and the adjacent Kerry Mall has all you might need.

Dongcheng   Map pp102–3
BUDGET

Beijing Saga International Youth Hostel (Běijīng Shíjiā Guójì Qīngnián Lǚshè; ☎ 6527 2773, 8607 7516; sagayangguang@yahoo.com; 9 Shijia Hutong; member/nonmember dm Y40/50, d Y160/180, tr Y180/210; ☐) Operating over three floors, this recently opened youth hostel sits on the famous Shijia Hutong east off Chaoyangmen Nanxiaojie (look for the signpost). All of the clean and well-kept rooms above dorm level have TV. There's communal phone, laundry service (Y10 per load) and bike rental (Y20 per day), and there's a small array of essentials at reception (biscuits, washing powder etc). Great Wall trips can be arranged, plus outings to watch acrobats. Internet access is Y8 per hour.

Fangyuan Hotel (Fāngyuán Bīnguǎn; ☎ 6525 6331; www.cbw.com/hotel/fangyuan; 36 Dengshikou Xijie; d Y198-280, ste Y422; ☒ ☐) This good-value two-star hotel – its front door guarded by a pair of stone cats – could do with a refit, but it is handily located just west of Wangfujing Dajie. The cheapest rooms are the shower-room equipped junior rooms downstairs (clean and toasty in winter), which is also where you can find the suites; the standard doubles upstairs are larger. All rooms come with air-con, TV and phone. A simple breakfast (boiled eggs, rice porridge etc) is included (7.30am to 9.30am). The staff is friendly and well used to dealing with Westerners and the place is well run, with a restaurant, ticketing service and bicycle rental. Internet access is Y10 per hour.

MID-RANGE

Bamboo Garden Hotel (Zhúyuán Bīnguǎn; ☎ 6403 2229; fax 6401 2633; 24 Xiaoshiqiao Hutong; s/d/ste Y380/530/680; ☒) This cosy, intimate and tranquil courtyard hotel is situated in a *hútòng* not far from the Drum and Bell Towers. The buildings date back to the late Qing dynasty, while the gardens belonged to a eunuch from Empress Cixi's entourage. The hotel gets good reviews, but the staff may be unhelpful. Rooms are tastefully decorated with reproduction Ming furniture and the abundant foliage is pleasant. Reception is through the gates on your left.

Novotel Peace Hotel (Běijīng Nuòfútè Hépíng Bīnguǎn; ☎ 6512 8833; fax 6512 6863; 3 Jinyu Hutong; d US$80-110, ste US$100-130; 🛜) This efficient and inviting refurbished four-star hotel has a fresh and cosmopolitan touch and a fantastic central location. Eschewing the gaudiness of some top-league hotels, it delivers a straightforward elegance. There's a useful travel service and bookshop (for newspapers) and the location is fantastic, with Wangfujing Dajie just around the corner. The cheaper rooms – not huge but perfectly serviceable – are in the older and more scuffed West Wing. Ask for promotional rates.

Cui Ming Zhuang Hotel (Cuìmíng Zhuāng Bīnguǎn; ☎ 6513 6622; www.cuimingzhuanghotel.com.cn; 1 Nanheyan Dajie; d/ste Y600/1200; 🛜) Fronted by a reproduction Chinese roof with green tiles, this pleasant and quiet three-star hotel dates from the 1930s. During the 1940s, the building was an office of the Chinese Communist Party that helped agree the ceasefire between the Kuomintang and the communists. It largely caters to Chinese guests, but it's excellently located for the Forbidden City and Wangfujing Dajie and facilities include a billiard room, ticketing services, the Sunshine café and shuffleboard.

TOP END

Peninsula Palace (Wángfǔ Fàndiàn; ☎ 8516 2888; fax 6510 6311; tph@peninsula.com; www.peninsula.com; 8 Jinyu Hutong; d/ste $320/360; 🛜) Owned by the Peninsula Group, this recently renovated five-star hotel is an elegant composition, making for a consummate residence while in the capital. It boasts two excellent restaurants, including the elegant and popular Huang Ting (p130), a sparkling multitiered, exclusive shopping mall, a fine location off Wangfujing Dajie, a fitness centre and luxurious styling all round. Promotional prices frequently take the sting out of the tariff, so ask.

Chaoyang   Map pp102–3
BUDGET
You Yi Youth Hostel (Yǒuyì Qīngnián Jiǔdiàn; ☎ 6417 2632; fax 6415 6866; 43 Beisanlitun Lu; dm/tw incl breakfast Y70/180; 🛜 🖥) This hostel has a peerless location in the Sanlitun bar ghetto district, next door to the thunderously loud Poach-

ers Inn (p131). Note that the hostel is not an IYHF member, however. Twins (with phone, TV, air-con and radiator) are bright and spacious with large beds but doors only have one lock, so if you have valuables, plonk them in a hotel locker. Rooms are comfortable enough and there's the free laundry service – dump your dirty rags in the cart for washing and drying – which is a hospitable gesture (although the facility can be erratic). Internet service is Y10 per hour. Breakfast is between 7.30am and 9am and includes toast, coffee, eggs and sausage. Signs say 'Gambling, prostitution and drunkenness are strictly forbidden'.

Zhaolong International Youth Hostel (Zhàolóng Qīngnián Lǚshè; ☎ 6597 2299; outdoor@etang.com; 2 Gongrentiyuchang Beilu; 2-/4-/6-bed dm Y70/60/50; 🛜 🖥) A six-floor block tucked away off Dongsanhuan Beilu behind the Zhalong Hotel, this is a good choice with clean rooms, laundry (Y10/20, small/big load), shop, selling IP and Integrated Circuit cards, kitchen, reading room, air-con, safe, bike rental (Y20 per day) and 24-hour hot water. Internet access is Y10 per hour. Nonmembers pay an extra Y10 for all room types. There's also a recreation room with table football and a coffee machine. It is well positioned for the nearby bars at Sanlitun, but the doors shut at 1am.

MID-RANGE
Oriental Garden Hotel (Dōngfāng Huāyuán Fàndiàn; ☎ 6416 8866; fax 6415 0638; 6 Dongzhimen Nandajie; s/d/ste US$80/120/160; 🛜 🖥) This four-star Chinese-run business hotel has comfortable and attractive guest rooms, Cantonese and Shànghǎi restaurants and a coffee shop. A short walk north of Dongsishitiao subway station, the hotel is also a short distance from the nightlife on Sanlitun. Facilities include a health club, and a superior standard of service can be found on executive floors.

Red House Hotel (Ruìxiù Bīnguǎn; ☎ 6416 7500; www.redhouse.com.cn; 10 Chunxiu Lu; dm Y70, ste solo/shared Y400/200; 🛜 🖥) Dorm rooms come with attached shower room. All recently refurbished apartments come with living room, cable TV, shower rooms and kitchen, while the shared suites have two separate bedrooms. There are lockers, laundry facilities and breakfast is free. Internet access is Y10 per hour. The location near Sanlitun is good and the hotel is also home to the Club Football Center (p132). The hotel takes all major credit cards (apart from Visa).

Fengtai & Xuanwu   Map pp102–3

BUDGET

Beijing Feiying International Youth Hostel (Běijīng Fēiyíng Qīngnián Lǚshè; ☎ 6315 1165; iyhfy@yahoo.com .cn; No 10 Bldg, Changchun Jie Hou Jie, Xuanwumen Xidajie; 10-/5-bed dm Y30/50, d 180; ☒ ☒) All rooms have shower rooms and air-con at this newly opened Youth Hostel. To reach it, take the subway to Changchunjie, exit the station (exit C) and head east pass the McDonalds, walking for around 150m. At hand are bicycle hire, washing machine, kitchen and tourist info. Internet access is Y10 per hour. The hostel does not have a lift.

MID-RANGE

Qianmen Jianguo Hotel (Qiánmén Jiànguó Fàndiàn; ☎ 6301 6688; fax 6301 3883; 175 Yong'an Lu; s/d/tr/ste incl breakfast Y620/760/910/1100; ☒) Very well situated for Tiananmen Sq, Temple of Heaven Park and the shopping district of Liulichang, this hotel has an attractive interior and sees a lot of tour groups. Rooms are spacious, clean and attractively carpeted, with broadband Internet access as standard. Housed in a red brick and white shell, the hotel has gift shops and numerous restaurants serving roast duck, Chaozhou cuisine and Western food. The Liyuan Theatre (p133) is here, to the right of the domed atrium at the rear.

Beijing Ningbo Hotel (Běijīng Níngbō Bīnguǎn; ☎ 6605 2226; fax 6607 7320; 25 Xizhong Hutong; s/d/ste Y280/360/720; ☒) This clean, small, value-for-money and central two-star modern hotel is set in a historic *hútòng* district west of Tiananmen Sq. The hotel has a restaurant and is within walking distance of Hepingmen subway station.

TOP END

Marco Polo (Běijīng Mǎgē Bóluó Jiǔdiàn; ☎ 6603 6688; www.marcopolohotels.com; 6 Xuanwumennei Dajie; d/ste US$170/280; ☒ ☒) This new four-star hotel is the best in this part of town. Shopping is easy at the nearby Capital Times Sq shopping complex, the Xidan subway station is just to the north and the Xuanwumen subway station a short hop south. The hotel has a fitness centre and a decent selection of bars and restaurants, including Cantonese cuisine at Heichinrou.

Haidian & Xicheng

TOP END

Beijing Marriott West (Běijīng Jīnyù Wànháo Jiǔdiàn; Map pp102–3; 98 Xisanhuan Beilu; ☎ 6872 6699; www .marriotthotels.com; d US$260; ☒ ☒) The Marriott is a fine hotel, with vast, fully equipped and very comfortable rooms, but the location, near the intersection of Fucheng Lu and the Third Ring Rd, is a big drawback. Amenities include tennis courts, a bowling centre and a health club.

Shangri-La Hotel (Xiānggé Lǐlā Fàndiàn; ☎ 6841 2211; slb@shangri-la.com; 29 Zizhuyuan Lu; d US$130; ☒) Located in west Běijīng and well positioned for trips to the Summer Palace, the Shangri-La has a top-notch selection of restaurants, bars and shops as well as a fine spread of rooms.

Further Afield

Holiday Inn Lido (Lìdū Jiàrì Fàndiàn; Map pp98–9; ☎ 6437 6688; fax 6437 6237; cnr Jichang Lu & Jiangtai Lu; d US$76; ☒) This hotel is a bit stranded on the road to the airport, but it's a highly popular and first-rate establishment with excellent amenities and a resourceful shopping mall.

EATING

Běijīng cuisine (*jīngcài*) is one of the four major Chinese styles of cooking, so trying home-town specialities should be obligatory for all visitors. But just about any fickle fancy meets its match, so plunge in and start twiddling those chopsticks – some of your best Běijīng memories could well be table-top ones.

Eating in Běijīng is generally inexpensive; listed below are restaurants catering to all budgets. At cheap eateries, meals (for one) will cost less than Y30 to Y40; midrange dining options will cost between Y40 and Y100, and top-end choices over Y100.

Chongwen & South Chaoyang   Map pp102–3

BUDGET

Food Court (basement, Oriental Plaza, 1 Dongchang'an Jie; dishes from Y10) This hygienic fast-food emporium puts yummy Cantonese, Yúnnán, Sìchuān, teppanyaki, clay pot, Korean and porridge (*zhōu*) outlets all under one roof. Look out for the following outlets: Hokkien Delights, Lanzhou Noodles, Hotplate Specials, Indian Roti Prata, and Shànghǎi and

Chinese Dumplings; the latter puts together some great dumplings (*jiǎozi*; pork, lamb and other fillings) and buns (*bāozi*). Go to the Spicy Chafting outlet for *málà tàng* – you choose the ingredients by the skewer (broccoli Y2, fish balls Y3) to be plunged into the scalding broth (but make sure they cook them well) – adding up to a filling dish for around Y15. Sichuan Delights serves up a fine chilli-oil red *dàndanmiàn* (Sìchuān noodles in peppery sauce; Y9). The layout is both intelligent and spacious, and the food generous and good value – you can eat very well for around Y20. Don't pay in cash for your dish; buy a card (Y5 deposit; cards come in denominations of Y30, 50, 100, 200, 500 and 1000 units) at the kiosk at the entrance; credits are deducted with each dish ordered so you can pick and mix your plates from different outlets (check the expiry date of your card, however). Don't get timid at the sight of half of Běijīng eating here, it's very easy to order. Food is either cooked in front of you canteen-style or arrayed uncooked on plates – it's simply a case of pointing at what you want.

Wangfujing Snack St (Wángfǔjǐng Xiǎochījiē; west off Wangfujing Dajie; kebabs from Y3, dishes from Y5; (ꎙ lunch & dinner) Fronted by an ornate archway, the quadrant is a bright and cheery corner of restaurants and stalls overhung with colourful banners and bursting with character and flavour. This is a good place to pick up Xīnjiāng or Muslim Uighur cuisine such as lamb kebabs and flat bread. Also on offer are regional dishes from all over China,

---

THE AUTHOR'S CHOICE

Xiao Wang's Home Restaurant (Xiǎowáng Fǔ; Map pp102–3; ☎ 6594 3602, 6591 3255; 2 Guanghua Dongli; meals Y70; (ꎙ lunch & dinner) Treat yourself to home-style Běijīng cuisine from this excellent restaurant and go for one of Xiao Wang's specials. The deep-fried spareribs with pepper salt (*piāoxiāng páigǔ*; Y38) are simply delectable – dry, fleshy, crispy chops with a small pile of fiery pepper salt. Xiao Wang's fried hot and spicy Xīnjiāng-style chicken wings (*zīran jīchì*; Y35) is deservedly famous and the Peking duck is crispy and lean (Y88 per duck, Y5 for sauce, scallion and pancakes). Also try the deep-fried crispy beancurd with mild chilli sauce (Y18) or the barbecue mutton slices with coriander (*zīran yángròu*; Y28), which are very tasty. There's outside seating and a further, more sedate, branch can be found in the Sanlitun area (see p130).

   Tiāndì Yìjiā (Map pp102–3; ☎ 6511 5556; tiandicanyin@163.com; 140 Nanchizi Dajie; meals around Y300; (ꎙ lunch & dinner) This refined traditional Chinese courtyard-style restaurant is decked out with traditional furniture, water features and side rooms (*bāofáng*) for snug hotpot dinners. Further rooms upstairs include a banqueting room and a balcony overlooking the Imperial Archives. The expensive dishes – from Běijīng, Shāndōng, Zhèjiāng and beyond – include shark's fin and abalone, and Cantonese dim sum is also served (from 11am to 2pm and 5pm to 9.30pm).

   Courtyard (Sìhéyuàn; Map pp102–3; ☎ 6526 8883; cyrest@95777.com; 95 Donghuamen Dajie; meals from Y200; (ꎙ lunch & dinner) The Courtyard enjoys a peerless location overlooking the Forbidden City. The minimalist **art gallery** (☎ 6526 8882) in the basement provides cerebral nutrition and the cigar divan upstairs is the perfect conclusion to a meal, but it's the view and the menu that hog the limelight. Try the New Zealand mussel soup (Y65), steamed Shāndōng sea bass (Y165) or the grilled US Kobe beef (Y245). Sunday lunch is an affordable option at Y150 per person.

   Frank's Place (Wànlóng Jiǔbā; Map pp102–3; ☎ 6507 2617; Gongti Donglu; dishes from Y30; (ꎙ lunch & dinner) It may be simple and getting a bit hoary in its old age (it first opened in 1989), but Yankee-styled Frank's is an old original and the menu a trusted favourite of regulars who seem to have nowhere else to go. The burgers (Y40) really do the job (Y5 extra for bacon, cheese and other toppings), as do the jumbo-sized hot dogs (Y30); otherwise there is the chicken and chips (Y55) or steak. The Cuban cigars at the bar go down a treat and the huge screen for live football matches is popular with the wall of punters at the bar.

   Bāguó Bùyī (Map pp102–3; ☎ 6400 8888; 89-3 Dianmen Dongdajie; dishes from Y8; (ꎙ lunch & dinner) This popular Sìchuān restaurant has a marvellous Chinese inn-style restaurant setting with balconies and a central stairway, and dolled-up waiting staff in attendance. The ambience bursts with both character and theatre, and there's a range of good-value dishes for Y8, including *Chóngqìng lāzi jī* (Chongqing hot pepper chicken) and *xiānjiāo yúpiàn* (chilli fish slices).

including *málà tàng, zhájiàngmiàn* (noodles in fried bean sauce) and noodles in peppery sauce, *Lánzhōu lāmiàn* (Lanzhou noodles), *Shāndōng jiānbing* (Shandong pancake), *Yúnnán guòqiáo mixiàn* (Yúnnán across-the-bridge noodles) and oodles of spicy Sìchuān food.

Gongdelin Vegetarian Restaurant (Gōngdélín Sùcàiguǎn; ☎ 6511 2542; 158 Qianmen Dajie; meals Y25-40; ❧ lunch & dinner) One of Běijīng's premier bloodless dining experiences, restore your karma with dishes of mock meat that taste better than the real thing. A poet has been to work on the menu ('the fire is singeing the snow-capped mountains') even though service is pedestrian and the décor strictly no-frills. The food is not to be missed, and being a card-holding carnivore is simply no excuse.

Niúgē Jiǎozi (☎ 6525 7472; 85 Dong'anmen Nanjie; meals Y15) This pocket-sized and homely restaurant dishes up dozens of varieties of Chinese dumplings (*jiǎozi*). All *jiǎozi* are listed on red plaques on the walls; sadly, there is no English menu. Go for *yángròu* (lamb; Y5 per *liǎng* or 37.5g), *zhūròu* (pork; Y3 per *liǎng*), *niúròu* (beef; Y4 per *liǎng*), *lǘròu* (donkey; Y8 per *liǎng*) and *xiāngsū báicài* (mushroom and cabbage; Y4), among other fillings. The restaurant has no English sign, but it is opposite the building with the sign on the roof saying 'Hualong Street'.

Gǒubùlì (12 Dayuanfu Hutong; set meals Y10; ❧ lunch & dinner) The renowned Tiānjīn *bāozi* (filled bun) outlet has set up several branches in Běijīng. This branch is just south of the Beijing Department Store and serves up good-value, fine meat-filled buns (Y10 for nine pork or mushroom and vegetable *bāozi*). There are further branches opposite Quanjude in **Shuaifuyuan Hutong** (☎ 6525 7314) east of Wangfujing Dajie and a huge branch in **Dàshílàr** (☎ 6315 2389; 31 Dazhalan Jie).

MID-RANGE
Biànyìfáng Kǎoyādiàn (☎ 6712 0505; 2a Chongwenmenwai Dajie; economy/standard half duck Y44/69; ❧ lunch & dinner) Dating back to the reign of the Qing emperor Xianfeng, Bianyifang offers mid-range comfort reminiscent of a faded Chinese three-star hotel. The duck is excellent, however, roasted in the *menlu* style and costing just Y44 to Y69 for half a standard duck (plus Y2 for pancakes, scallions and sauce). Be warned that waiting

staff will steer you towards the ducks prepared in the pricier Huaxiangsu style (half/whole Y84/168). It's next to the Hademen Hotel.

Liqun Roast Duck Restaurant (Lìqún Kǎoyādiàn; ☎ 6702 5681; 11 Beixiangfeng Hutong; roast duck Y68; ❧ lunch & dinner) Buried away in a maze of *hútòng* in east Qianmen is this tiny eatery. It's well known and very busy – chefs scamper about as waiters scurry by with sacks of garlic and crates of locally distilled Erguotou; no medals for service. Stroll past the flaming ovens (fruit tree wood is exclusively used, piled up outside) to reach your table, which may be next to a frame of ducks hanging from hooks. Waiting staff insist you phone first to reserve a table. The *hútòng* is near Zhengyi Lu; the small restaurant is well signposted once you find the general area.

Liújiā Guō (☎ 6524 1487; 19 Nanheyan Dajie; meals Y80; ❧ lunch & dinner) Eye-poppingly hot Húnán (Xiāngcài) cuisine is a cauldron of flaming flavour, marked by rampant use of chilli and other spices. Liújiā Guō, however, goes easy on the seasoning, serving up medium-hot dishes that won't have you gagging. The grilled beef (Y28) is sizzlingly excellent and the 'Mao family fashion braised pork' (Y28) is fantastic: rich chunks of fatty pork steeped in a strong sauce. There are also a few vegetarian dishes such as mock mutton (Y20) and 'peasant family fashion eggplants' (Y16).

Makye Ame (Mǎjí Āmǐ; ☎ 6506 9616; 2nd fl, A11 Xiushui Nanjie; dishes from Y20; ❧ lunch & dinner) Behind the Friendship Store, this is one of Běijīng's few Tibetan restaurants. There's a comfy upper room with atmosphere, an excellent menu and a generous crop of Tibetan ornaments. Go all out for the lamb ribs (Y40), boiled yak with chilli (Y40), the *tsampa* (roasted barley meal) and yoghurt, butter tea and cooling salads (from Y20).

Qianmen Quanjude Roast Duck Restaurant (Qiánmén Quànjùdé Kǎoyādiàn; ☎ 6511 2418; 32 Qianmen Dajie; half duck Y58, scallions & sauce Y2; ❧ lunch & dinner) As fundamental to a Běijīng trip as a visit to the Great Wall, to miss out on Peking duck you'd have to be completely quackers. This place is geared mainly to the tourists: enter to photos of George Bush poking a duck with his finger and Fidel Castro sizing up an imaginary duck with his hands. Another **branch** (☎ 6301 8833; 14 Qianmen

Xidajie) is nearby and off Wangfujing Dajie (see Quanjude Roast Duck Restaurant following). There is an English menu.

Be There Or Be Square (Bú Jiàn Bú Sàn; ☎ 8518 6518; BB71 Oriental Plaza, 1 Dongchang'an Jie; ☺ 24hr; meals Y40) This funky chain is a slick yet affordable pit stop for Cantonese favourites, including *cha siu* (barbecue pork slices), *siu ngap* (barbecue duck), *cha siu bao* (sweet pork-filled buns), *chun kuen* (spring rolls) and noodles. Other branches include the **Henderson Center** (☎ 6518 6515; Level 2, 18 Jianguomennei Dajie; ☺ 24hr) and the **Landmark Tower** (☎ 6590 6999; 1st fl, 8 Dongsanhuan Beilu).

Quanjude Roast Duck Restaurant (Quànjùdé Kǎoyādiàn; ☎ 6525 3310; 9 Shuaifuyuan Hutong; ordinary/special duck Y108/168; ☺ lunch & dinner) This huge and well-presented restaurant is less famous than its Qianmen sibling, but more convenient if shopping along Wangfujing Dajie and less touristy. Examine the English menu under the light of the glittering chandeliers and go for a half duck (Y54, minus pancakes, scallions and sauce) or a range of other duck dishes including ducks webbed feet with mustard sauce (Y32), salted duck's liver (Y24) or deep-fried duck heart (Y80).

Dongcheng
Map pp102–3
BUDGET
Donghuamen Night Market (Dōnghuámén Yèshì; Dong'anman Dajie; ☺ 3-10pm, closed Chinese New Year) A sight in itself, the bustling night market near Wangfujing Dajie is a food zoo: lamb kebabs, beef and chicken skewers, corn on the cob, *chōu dòufu* (smelly tofu), cicadas, grasshoppers, kidneys, quail's eggs, squid, fruit, porridge, fried pancakes, strawberry kebabs, bananas, Inner Mongolian cheese, stuffed aubergines, chicken hearts, pitta bread stuffed with meat, shrimps – and that's just for starters. It's for tourists, not locals, so expect to pay around Y5 for a lamb kebab (much more than you would from a *hútòng* vendor).

MID-RANGE
Green Tianshi Vegetarian Restaurant (Lǜsè Tiānshí Sùcàiguǎn; ☎ 6524 2349/2476; 57 Dengshikou Dajie; meals from Y50; ☺ lunch & dinner) This is one of Běijīng's longest-serving vegetarian dining experiences. The Green Tianshi cooks up simulated meat dishes, entirely fashioned from vegetables and presented in a relaxed and attractive environment. There is no alcohol

---

STREET FOOD BEIJING STYLE

Off the main roads and in Běijīng's alleys is a world teeming with steaming food stalls and eateries buzzing with activity. Be adventurous and eat this way, and you will be dining as most Beijingers do.

Breakfast can be easily catered for with a *yóutiáo* (deep-fried dough stick), a sip of *dòuzhī* (bean curd drink) or a bowl of *zhōu* (porridge). Other snacks include the crunchy, pancake-like and filling *jiānbing*; *jiānbing* vendors are easily spotted as they cook from tricycle-mounted, white-painted wooden stalls where the pancakes are fried on a large circular griddle. The heavy meat-filled *ròubing* (cooked bread filled with finely chopped pork) are lifesavers and very cheap. A handy vegetarian option is *jiǔcài bǐng* (bread stuffed with cabbage, chives, leek or fennel and egg). *Dàbǐng* (a chunk of round, unleavened bread sprinkled with sesame seeds) can be found everywhere and of course there's *mántóu* (steamed bread). *Málà tàng* is a spicy noodle soup (very warming in winter) in which bob chunks of *dòufu* (tofu), cabbage and other veggies; choose your own ingredients from the trays. Also look out for *ròu jiāmò*, a scrumptious open-your-mouth-wide bun filled with diced lamb, chilli and garlic shoots. Another must are *kǎo yángròu chuàn* (lamb kebabs), which make for a scrumptious and cheap snack or meal. You can find kebab outlets in several places around town; try the more expensive Donghuamen Night Market (above), Wangfujing Snack St (p127) or cheaper options that are hidden away down *hútòng* (look for the billowing plumes of smoke), where you can pick up a skewer for around Y0.50. If you want your kebabs spicy ask for *là*; if you don't, ask for *búlà*. Vendors usually belong to either the Muslim Hui or Uighur minority.

Hóngshǔ (baked sweet potatoes) are cheap filling snacks (Y2) sold at street stalls throughout the city during winter. Vendors attach oil drums to their bikes, which have been converted into mobile ovens. Choose a nice soft sweet potato and the vendor will weigh it and tell you how much it costs.

served on the premises; a handy picture menu helps steer you to the right dish.

Sichuan Restaurant (Sìchuān Fàndiàn; ☎ 6513 7591/3; 37a Donganmen Jie; meal Y50; ⊗ lunch & dinner) This spacious restaurant is rather worn and the manager's office is still forlornly hung with a portrait of Mao, but the dishes are well worth your time and portions are generous. Try the filling *zhǐbāo yángròu* (crispy tinfoil-wrapped mutton; Y22), while the *yúxiāng qiézi* (deep fried eggplant with garlic and chilli sauce; Y26) is tender and swimming in a sea of hot red chilli oil.

TOP END

Huáng Tíng (☎ 8516 2888, ext 6707; Peninsula Palace, 8 Jinyu Hutong; meal for one Y150; ⊗ lunch & dinner) Faux old Peking is taken to an extreme in the courtyard setting of Huáng Tíng. Despite its artificiality and location (in a five-star hotel), the ambience is impressive. Local dishes include whole Peking duck (Y220), roast suckling pig (Y100), braised spareribs in tangy brown sauce (Y70) and braised Běijīng-style meatball with cabbage (Y40).

Chaoyang   Map pp102–30
MID-RANGE

Xiao Wang's Home Restaurant (Xiǎowáng Fǔ; ☎ 6594 3602, 6591 3255; 4 Gonrentiyuchang Beilu; meals Y70; ⊗ lunch & dinner) This branch of Xiao Wang's has a classier ambience than the Guanghua

Dongli branch, with its cavernous interior and train carriage/office-style seating (the no-smoking section is housed in an old train carriage). The food is again excellent, with the same menu; the sizzling beef slices with pepper and onion in black bean sauce (Y38) is a scorching and peppery delight. Tucked away, the restaurant is up the steps inside the Success Club, opposite the Sanlitun Yashou Clothing Market.

Beijing Dadong Roast Duck Restaurant (Běijīng Dàdǒng Kǎoyā Diàn; ☎ 6582 2892/4003; 3 Tuanjiehu Beikou; duck Y98; ⊗ lunch & dinner) A long-term favourite of the Peking duck scene, this restaurant has a tempting variety of fowl. The hallmark bird is a crispy, lean duck without the usual high fat content (trimmed down from 42.38% to 15.22% for its 'Superneat' roast duck, the brochure says), plus plum (or garlic) sauce, scallions and pancakes. Also carved up is the skin of the duck with sugar, an old imperial predilection.

Downtown Café (☎ 6415 2100; 26 Sanlitun Lu; meals Y70; ⊗ lunch & dinner) This popular Western café seems to hog the lion's share of hungry expats on Sanlitun Lu. The menu delivers dependable European dishes from salads, pasta, pizza and sandwiches to burgers. Try the crispy Croque Monsieur (Y35), the tuna sandwich (Y40) or sample its large range of vegetarian dishes, including the vegetarian lasagne (Y40).

SELF-CATERING

Supermarkets are plentiful and most visitors will find what they need, but delis stock wider selections of foreign cheeses, cured meats and wines. Note that some supermarkets annoyingly insist you hand in your other shopping bags before you browse or purchase goods.

Yansha Supermarket (Yànshā Chāoshì; Map pp102-3) The supermarket in the **Henderson Center** (basement; ⊗ 10am-8pm), opposite the Beijing International Hotel, is well stocked. There is also a 24-hour Yansha convenience store by the Henderson Center's south entrance (facing Beijing Train Station). Just north of the Great Wall Sheraton is the enormous **Lufthansa Center Youyi Shopping City**, a multistorey shopping mall. The supermarket is in the basement, chock-a-block with imported goods.

Carrefour (Jiālèfú; ⊗ 8am-9.30pm) Chaoyang (Map pp102-3; ☎ 8460 1030; 6b Beisanhuan Donglu); Fengtai (☎ 6760 9911; 15 No 2 district Fangchengyuan Fangzhuang); Haidian (☎ 8836 2729; 54a Zhongguancun Nandajie); Xuanwu (☎ 8636 2155; 11 Malian Dao) Stocks virtually everything you may need, takes credit cards, provides ATMs and a home-delivery service. There is also a branch in Zhongguancun.

There's a well-stocked supermarket in the basement of Scitech Plaza, a department store on the southern side of Jianguomenwai Dajie, where you can find an extensive range of coffee. Other useful supermarkets include:

Jingkelong (Map pp102-3; Sanlitun)

Park N Shop (Map pp102-3; basement, Full Link Plaza, 18 Chaoyangmenwai Dajie)

Super 24 (Map pp102-3; Sanlitun Lu; ⊗ 24hr)

Lǎo Hànzi (Old Character Restaurant; ☎ 6415 3376; Sanlitun Beijie; meal Y40; ☺ lunch & dinner) Kejia (Hakka) cuisine may not be one of China's main food groups (the Hakka live principally in Fújiàn and Guǎngdōng), but the dishes at the Lǎo Hànzi are deservedly popular (frequently packed) and the ambience is superb.

Four Seasons Restaurant (Měiwèi Sìjì Cāntīng; ☎ 6508 5823; east gate of the Workers Stadium; meals Y50; ☺ lunch & dinner) This clean, efficient, stylish and good-value restaurant has a large and tempting range of Cantonese seafood as well as Sìchuān and hotpot dishes. Try the fizzing and spitting *niúròu tiěbǎn* (sizzling beef platter; Y28), the *chuānlà hǎixiān bāo* (a spicy seafood pot; Y48) or the more standard but stomach-filling *yúxiāng qiézi bāo* (a scorching claypot of tender aubergines, laced with garlic and pork mince; Y22). It's next to the Workers Stadium Sports Hotel.

Serve the People (Wèi Rénmín Fúwù; ☎ 8454 4580; 1 Sanlitun Xiwujie; meals Y50; ☺ lunch & dinner) Widely acknowledged as Běijīng's trendiest Thai restaurant; its warm décor, *tom yam* (spicy, lemongrass-flavoured soup) and other Thai dishes are deservedly popular.

Xīnjiāng Red Rose Restaurant (☎ 6415 5741; Xinqfuyicun Qixiang, opposite Workers Stadium north gate, meals Y40; ☺ lunch & dinner) The southern entrance to this place leads to a small and unassuming restaurant with good value and tasty Xīnjiāng dishes. It's just a front, however, for the sheer maelstrom of table-top dancing, live Uighur music (7.30pm to 9pm) and belly dancers in the building behind. You can pass on the whole roast lamb (Y800) unless you're a crowd, but the roast leg of lamb (Y30 per *jīn*) is filling and the chunky lamb kebabs (Y3 each) are good value.

DRINKING

Sanlitun in the Chaoyang district forms the hub of expat drinking life in town. This is where about 75% of expat cafés-bars are amassed. Drawn mothlike by the lights, droves of drinkers populate the two main bar streets in Sanlitun: the main one that runs between Gongrentiyuchang Beilu and Dongzhimenwai (Sanlitun Lu), and a smaller alleyway (known as Sanlitun Nanlu, although its official name is Dongdaqiao Xijie) that runs south from Gongrentiyuchang Beilu. While the bars here are

going strong, rumours of major redevelopment darken the horizon and a relocation of bartenders and punters could take place if these pubs disappear. Taking a leaf from Sanlitun's page, other parts of town are trying to recreate the Sanlitun experience. After a few bars around Qianhai and Houhai Lakes struck gold a few years back, a swarm of prospectors has followed suit. The lakeside street running south of Houhai Lake (Houhai Nanyan) is now a long strip of bars and Yandai Xiejie – a small street just east of Silver Ingot Bridge – has recruited a new population of cafés, bars and souvenir shops, many of which are particularly samey.

Poachers Inn (Map pp102-3; ☎ 6417 2632, ext 8506; 43 Beisanlitun Lu) Cavernous Poachers literally heaves with exuberant throngs and a thumping, hammering bass at the weekend, when it's party central and the volume reaches unusual levels. If you want a conversation, take turns with a loud-hailer and if you want a beer, grease yourself down to get to the besieged bar. With the floor a writhing knot of *liúxuéshēng* (foreign students) and partygoers, this is probably the most popular bar in Běijīng, with prices to match and occasional live acts.

Centro (Xuànkù; Map pp102-3; ☎ 6561 8833, ext 6388; Kerry Center Hotel, 1 Guanghua Lu; ☺ 24hr) Swish and stylish, Centro is a highly seductive and impressive lounge bar with low mood lighting, illuminated table tops, a black glossy bar and discreet, quiet corners caressed by relaxing chill-out tunes and ambient sounds. It's an excellent place to seek refuge at the conclusion of a hectic day and offers a respite from the frantic clutter of contemporary Běijīng. There's live music (including jazz) at night and a DJ spins sounds at weekends.

Hidden Tree (Yǐnbì de Shù; Map pp102-3; ☎ 6509 3642; 12 Dongdaqiao Xiejie, Sanlitun Nanlu) Looking for a Trappist monastery-brewed Chimay, Leffe or Duvel to flush away that sour flavour of the local beer? Look no further, the deep-rooted (it's been in business for years) Hidden Tree has a cellar of Belgian brews. There's a beer garden that opens from late spring, a Mediterranean menu (pizzas around Y70), a cosy interior, soft candlelight in the evening and occasional live music of the Filipino band variety (after 10pm Tuesday, Thursday and Sunday).

Red Moon Bar (Dōngfāng Liàng; Map pp102-3; ☎ 8518 1234, ext 6366; Grand Hyatt Beijing, 1 Dongchang'an Jie) Arriving at the Red Moon, customers are met by a svelte female attendant and ushered through a looking-glass door to a gorgeous lounge bar blessed with a huge selection of wines. The lighting is subdued and soporific; jazz wafts over a very chilled-out clientele; the evening live music goes down well with those who are not in a rush to go anywhere else.

Club Football Center (Map pp102-3; ☎ 6417 0497; Red House Hotel, 10b Chunxiu Jie; ☯ 11am-2am) Probably the most genuine British pub in town, with its wall-to-wall football trophies, scarves, Liverpool FC memorabilia, live English premiership action and big sports screen, this is a must for anyone obsessed with the beautiful game and/or beer and/or pool and/or rugby (not necessarily in that order).

Guangfuguan Greenhouse (Guǎngfúguàn De Wēnshì; Map pp102-3; ☎ 6400 3234; 36 Yandai Xiejie) This laid-back place on the bar-cluttered Yandai Xiejie gets full marks for novelty. Formerly the Guanfu Taoist Temple (that's what the characters carved on the lintel above the arched doorway say), the shrine has been requisitioned for the city's exploding bar scene and simply decked out with art posters, including one of Allen Ginsberg. The temple's roof guardians are still intact and the presence of religious statuary reminds visitors that they are on sacred turf.

Durty Nellie's (Dūbǎilín Jiǔbā; Map pp102-3; ☎ 6502 2808; 11a Dongdaqiao Xiejie, Sanlitun Nanlu) This cavernous Irish pub serves Guinness (Y50), unless the Eire shipment is stranded somewhere, as well as Kilkenny's (Y50). The tavern seems to go on forever once you get past the main bar, and there's pool, table football, darts and acres of stone-flagged space behind. Adding to the atmosphere are snugs and wobbly tables straight from Dublin, as well as regular bands cranking out ballads and covers from the Emerald Isle.

Half & Half (Hǎitóng Jiǔjiā; Map pp102-3; ☎ 6416 6919; off Gongrentiyuchang Beilu; ☯ to 2am) Perhaps Bĕijīng's most famous and longstanding gay and lesbian bar, Half & Half lies in an alley to the east of the Sanlitun Yashou Clothing Market. Its interior dark and low key, the bar is secretively tucked away on the right-hand side of the road as you head

north; look for the sign saying 'Half' on the road outside.

John Bull Pub (Zūnbó Yīngshì Jiǔbā; Map pp102-3; ☎ 6532 5905; 44 Guanghua Lu) Servicing legions of Brit expats in the embassy district, this English-style pub has particularly tasty steak-and-kidney pie and other pub grub, plus a snug weeknight atmosphere (often as quiet as a library), comfy furniture, pool table, sports TV, English breakfasts and pleasant staff who speak good English.

ENTERTAINMENT

Today's Bĕijīng has seen a revolution in leisure and the entertainment industry is in full throttle. Some pastimes, such as Beijing opera (jīngjù) or acrobatics, are fixtures on the tourist circuit and draw regular crowds. Others are more upcoming events, with concerts and modern theatre receiving an enthusiastic welcome. On the live music and nightclub front, there should be something up your street most nights of the week.

Beijing Opera & Traditional Chinese Music

Beijing opera is the most famous of the many forms of the art, but its history is short. The year 1790 is the key date: in that year a provincial troupe performed before Emperor Qianlong on his 80th birthday. The form was popularised in the West by the actor Mei Lanfang (1894–1961) who is said to have influenced Charlie Chaplin.

Beijing opera bears little resemblance to its European counterpart. The mixture of singing, dancing, speaking, mime, acrobatics and dancing can go on for five or six hours, but two hours is more usual.

There are four types of actors' roles: the shēng, dàn, jìng and chǒu. The shēng are the leading male actors and they play scholars, officials, warriors and the like. The dàn are the female roles, but are usually played by men (Mei Lanfang always played a dàn role). The jìng are the painted-face roles, and they represent warriors, heroes, statesmen, adventurers and demons. The chǒu is basically the clown.

Language is often archaic Chinese and the screeching music is searing to Western ears, but the costumes and make-up are magnificent. The action that really catches the Western eye is a swift battle sequence;

trained acrobats leap, twirl, twist and somersault into attack – it's not unlike boarding a Bĕijīng bus during rush hour.

Catching at least one Beijing opera is almost mandatory for visitors to the capital. At most well-known Beijing opera venues, shows last around 90 minutes and are generally performed by major opera troupes such as the China Peking Opera House. English translations can be a bit off the wall. Westerners tend to see versions that are noisy and strong on acrobatics and *wŭshù* routines, rather than the more sedate traditional style.

Zhengyici Theatre (Zhèngyǐcí Jùchǎng; Map pp102-3; ☎ 6303 3104; 220 Xiheyan Dajie; tickets from Y50; ☺ performances 7.30-9pm) Originally an ancient temple, this ornately decorated building is the oldest wooden theatre in the country and the best place in the city to experience Beijing opera and other operatic disciplines like Kunqu. The theatre was restored by a private businessman with an interest in reviving the dying art, and reopened in 1995 after a long period of disrepair. Opera can be appreciated over a dinner of Peking duck.

Huguang Guild Hall (Húguǎng Huìguǎn; Map pp102-3; ☎ 6351 8284; 3 Hufang Lu; tickets Y100-380; ☺ performances 7.15-9pm) Decorated in a similar fashion to the Zhengyici Theatre, with balconies surrounding the canopied stage, this theatre dates back to 1807. The interior is magnificent, coloured in red, green and gold and decked out with tables and a stone floor. There's also a very small opera museum (Y10) opposite the theatre, displaying operatic scores, old catalogues and further paraphernalia, including colour illustrations of the *liǎnpǔ* (the different types of Beijing opera facial makeup).

Chang'an Grand Theatre (Cháng'ān Dàjùchǎng; Map pp102-3; ☎ 6510 1309; Chang'an Bldg, 7 Jianguomennei Dajie; tickets Y40-150; ☺ performances 7.15pm) This theatre offers a genuine experience of Beijing opera, with an erudite audience chattering knowledgably among themselves during weekend matinee classics and evening performances.

Lao She Teahouse (Lǎo Shě Cháguǎn; Map pp102-3; ☎ 6303 6830, 6304 6334; www.laosheteahouse.com; 3rd fl, 3 Qianmen Xidajie; evening tickets Y60-130; ☺ performances 7.30pm) Lao She Teahouse (west of the large KFC on Qianmen Xidajie) has nightly shows of Beijing opera, cross-talk and ac-

robatics. Enter the teahouse past statues of Weituo, Sakyamuni and Guanyin on your left and an effigy of former US president George Bush on your right. There are several halls: in the small hall there is folk music (2.30pm to 5pm Monday to Friday), in the large hall there are folk music and tea ceremony performances (3pm to 4.30pm Friday), theatrical performances (2pm to 4.30pm Wednesday and Friday), and matinee Beijing opera performances (3pm to 4.30pm Sunday). Evening performances of Beijing opera, folk art and music performances, acrobatics and magic are the most popular. Phone ahead or check online for the schedule.

Old Station Theater (Lǎo Chēzhàn Jùshè; Map pp102-3; ☎ 8284 3316; 3rd fl, Old Station Bldg; tickets Y30-180, discounts for students & seniors; ☺ performances 7.15pm Sat, 2pm Sun) On the top floor of the Old Station Building, to the east of the Qianmen Arrow Tower and southeast of Front Gate, is this new theatre with weekend performances (matinee on Sundays) of Beijing opera. The theatre itself is not old, but the railway building dates from 1901.

Sanwei Bookstore (Sānwèi Shūdiàn; Map pp102-3; ☎ 6601 3204; 60 Fuxingmennei Dajie; cover charge Y30; ☺ performances from 8pm) Opposite the Minzu Hotel, this place has a small bookshop on the ground floor and a teahouse on the second. It features music with traditional Chinese instruments on Saturday night.

Liyuan Theatre (Líyuán Jùchǎng; Map pp102-3; ☎ 8315 7297; Qianmen Jianguo Hotel, 175 Yong'an Lu; tickets Y30-200; ☺ performances 7.30pm) This touristy theatre, across the lobby of the Qianmen Jianguo Hotel (p126) and past the mannequins outside, has regular performances for Beijing opera greenhorns, performed over servings of Peking duck and other local delicacies. The setting isn't traditional and it resembles a cinema auditorium (the stage façade is the only authentic touch), but there are also matinee shows of *gōngfu* (kung fu) performed by Shaolin monks.

A good place to enjoy Beijing opera is within the Qing dynasty Grand Opera House in the setting of Prince Gong's Residence (p118), one of Bĕijīng's landmark historic courtyards. Phone ahead (☎ 6618 6628) to check on performance times (note that performances are only held March to October); tickets are Y80 to Y120.

Acrobatics & Martial Arts

Two thousand years old, Chinese acrobatics is one of the best deals in town. As well as the following listings, acrobatic performances are also held at the Dongyue Temple (p115) at 8am (Y60), while performances of Shaolin boxing are held at 12.30pm at the Liyuan Theatre (p133).

Chaoyang Theatre (Cháoyáng Jùchǎng; Map pp102-3; ☎ 6507 2421; 36 Dongsanhuan Beilu; tickets Y80; ☺ performances 7.30pm) Probably the most accessible place for foreign visitors and often bookable through your hotel, this theatre is the venue for visiting acrobatic troupes filling the stage with plate-spinning and hoop-jumping.

Universal Theatre (Heaven & Earth Theatre; Tiāndì Jùchǎng; Map pp102-3; ☎ 6416 0757/9893; 10 Dongzhimen Nandajie; tickets Y60-200; ☺ performances 7.15pm) Around 100m north of Poly Plaza, young performers from the China Acrobatic Circus and the China National Acrobatic Troupe perform mind-bending and joint-popping contortions. This is a favourite with tour groups, so book ahead; tickets are pricier the further from the stage you sit. You can also visit the circus school to see the performers training (☎ 6502 3984). Look for the awful white tower that seems like it should be in an airport – that's where you buy your tickets (credit cards not accepted).

Wan Sheng Theatre (Wànshèng Jùchǎng; Map pp102-3; ☎ 6303 7449; Tianqiao; tickets Y100-150; ☺ performances 7.15pm) West of the Temple of Heaven, the Wan Sheng Theatre offers one of Běijīng's best acrobatic displays, performed by the Beijing Acrobatics Troupe. The entrance is down the eastern side of the building.

Nightclubs

Běijīng's discos may not be cutting edge, but they pack in loyal, sweaty patrons and should wow Westerners who thought the city was still stuck in the past. Most budgets meet their match, from student dives to sharper Sanlitun venues and top-end clubs. See also Poachers Inn, p131.

Vics (Wēikèsī; Map pp102-3; ☎ 6593 6215; Workers Stadium north gate; tickets Fri/Sat Y35/50; ☺ 7pm-late) South of the Outback Steakhouse, Vics is decked out with couches, a pool table and a sweaty dance floor. This is perhaps Běijīng's most popular place, with a selection of hip-hop, R&B, pop and soul attracting solid crowds. Wednesday is ladies night, and Friday and Saturday nights see things thumping and jumping till 7am.

Loft (Cángkù Jiǔbā; Map pp102-3; ☎ 6501 7501; 4 Gongrentiyuchang Beilu; ☺ 11am-2am) The Loft delivers a fresh world of live jazz, techno and house, along with funky TV screens and an art space. There is a European-fusion menu and regular DJs, dance and live music. It's tucked away behind the huge Pacific Century Place office and apartment complex.

World of Suzie Wong (Sūxī Huáng; Map pp98-9; ☎ 6593 7889; 1a Nongzhanguan Lu, Chaoyang Amusement Park west gate, through Q bar entrance; beers Y15+; ☺ 7pm-3.30am) This elegant lounge bar attracts glamorous types who recline on traditional wooden beds piled up with silk cushions and sip daiquiris. There's attentive service, fine cocktails and beer, and the music is varied, from house, through chill-out, to techno, pop and rock.

Club Banana (Bānànà; Map pp102-3; ☎ 6526 3939; Scitech Hotel, 22 Jianguomenwai Dajie; tickets Y20-50; ☺ 8.30pm-4am Sun-Thu, 8.30pm-5am Fri & Sat) Mainstay of Běijīng club land, Banana is loud and to the point. Select from the techno, acid jazz and chill-out sections according to your energy levels or the waning of the night.

Contemporary Music

There may be an instinctive Chinese fondness for the syrupy musical genre of Canto pop, but some of Běijīng's residents have grittier tastes that need something with more bite and imagination. Nodding its head to a growing medley of sounds, China's increasingly brazen capital has found an exciting language with which to articulate the new *Zeitgeist*. On the downside, international pop and rock acts of any worth rarely make it to Běijīng, but there are several places around town where you can take in Běijīng's homegrown music scene. Taking up the rear are the usual Filipino cover bands, who perform at American-style burger bars.

CD Café (Sēndì; Map pp102-3; ☎ 6586 5532; C16 Dongsanhuan Beilu; ☺ 8pm-2.30am) This popular two-floor outfit is tilted heavily towards jazz, but rock, blues and techno (every Friday and Saturday) also get airplay. The café also hosts an international jazz festival every November. You can find it hidden away south of the Agricultural Exhibition Center, a ramshackle-looking outfit tucked away behind a passenger overhead walkway vaulting over Dongsanhuan Beilu.

CD Jazz Café (Sēndì Juéshì Jùlèbù; Map pp102-3; ☎ 6506 8288; main gate of the Agricultural Exhibition Center, Dongsanhuan Beilu; ☺ 2.30pm-2.30am) Rocker Cui Jian's saxophonist owns this small but popular club that has live jazz performances from Wednesday to Sunday. Dance events are also held, including swing lessons.

Jam House (Jièmófáng Jiǔbā; Map pp102-3; ☎ 6506 3845; Dongdaqiao Xiejie, Sanlitun Nanlu; ☺ 7.30pm-2.30am) One of the oldest fixtures on Sanlitun Nanlu, this old-timer has live music (rock, flamenco) on weekends, and free-for-all jam sessions. If you need a musical interlude, head up to the rooftop terrace.

Red Bar (Zhúchàng; Map pp102-3; Dongdaqiao Xiejie, Sanlitun Nanlu; ☺ 6.30pm-2am) On the west side of Sanlitun Nanlu, this bar (formerly the River bar) has regular rock and folk music on its small stage.

Classical Music

As China's capital and the nation's cultural centre, Běijīng has several venues around town where the city's increasingly cosmopolitan residents can satisfy their highbrow needs. The annual 30 day Beijing Music Festival takes place between October and November, and is an excellent time to catch international and home-grown classical music performances. By the time you read this, the National Grand Theatre to the west of Tiananmen Sq should be completed.

Beijing Concert Hall (Běijīng Yīnyuè Tīng; Map pp102-3; ☎ 6605 5812; 1 Beixinhua Jie; tickets Y50-500; ☺ performances 7.30pm) The 2000-seat Beijing Concert Hall showcases evening performances of classical Chinese music as well as international repertoires of Western classical music.

Forbidden City Concert Hall (Zhōngshān Gōngyuán Yīnyuè Táng; Map pp102-3; ☎ 6559 8285; Zhongshan Park; tickets Y50-500; ☺ performances 7.30pm) Located on the eastern side of Zhongshan Park, this is the venue for performances of classical and traditional Chinese music.

Poly Plaza International Theatre (Bǎolì Dàshà Guójì Jùyuàn; Map pp102-3; ☎ 6500 1188, ext 5682; Poly Plaza, 14 Dongzhimen Nandajie; tickets Y100-680; ☺ performances usually at 7.30pm) Located in the Poly Plaza right by Dongsishitiao subway station, this venue hosts a wide range of performances, including classical music, ballet and traditional Chinese folk music. Operatic works

from the good old bad old days, such as *Red Detachment of Women* have resurfaced here in recent years.

Theatre

Huàjù (theatre) never commanded much of a following in China. It only appeared in here in the 20th century. As a literary art, creative drama is still unable to fully express itself and remains sadly gagged and sidelined. But if you want to know what's walking the floorboards in Běijīng, try some of the following.

Capital Theatre (Shǒudū Jùyuàn; Map pp102-3; ☎ 6524 9847/6512; 22 Wangfujing Dajie; ☺ performances 7pm Tue-Sun) Located in the heart of the city on Wangfujing Dajie, this central theatre has regular performances of contemporary Chinese productions from several theatre companies. Classic plays in the Chinese language often feature, and there's a bookshop within the theatre.

China Puppet Theatre (Zhōngguó Mùǒu Jùyuàn; Map pp98-9; ☎ 6422 9487; 1a Anhua Xili, Beisanhuan Lu) This popular theatre has regular events, including shadow play, puppetry, music and dance.

The huge Chang'an Grand Theatre (p133), centrally located to the east of the Beijing International Hotel, largely stages productions of Beijing opera but classical Chinese theatre productions also appear.

Cinemas

The following are Běijīng's two most central multiscreen cinemas.

Star Cinema City (Xīnshìjì Yīngchéng; Map pp102-3; ☎ 8518 5399; shop BB65, basement, Oriental Plaza, 1 Dongchang'an Jie; Wed-Mon Y50, Tue Y35) This six-screen cinema might be centrally located and plush (with leather reclining sofa chairs), but you pay hefty prices for the location.

Sundongan Cinema City (Xīndōngān Yīngchéng; Map pp102-3; ☎ 6528 1988; 5th fl, Sundongan Plaza, Wangfujing Dajie; tickets Y40). Don't expect a huge selection, but you can usually find a Hollywood feature plus other English-language movies among the Hong Kong dross.

SHOPPING

There are several notable Chinese shopping districts offering abundant goods and reasonable prices: Wangfujing Dajie, Xidan and Qianmen (including Dashilar). Dashilar is a

BĚIJĪNG

hútòng running southwest from the northern end of the Front Gate, near Tiananmen Sq. It's a great jumble of silk shops, department stores, theatres, herbal medicine shops, food and clothing specialists and some unusual architecture.

More luxurious shopping areas can be found in the embassy areas of Jianguomenwai and Sanlitun; also check out five-star hotel shopping malls. Shopping at open-air markets is an experience not to be missed. Beijing's most popular markets are the Xiushui Silk Market, Panjiayuan and Pearl Market. There are also specialised shopping districts such as Liulichang.

Běijīng's premier antique street, Liulichang, is not far west of Dashilar. Worth delving into for its quaint, albeit dressed up, age-old village atmosphere, Liulichang's shops trade in (largely fake) antiques. Alongside ersatz Qing monochrome bowls and Cultural Revolution kitsch, you can also rummage through old Chinese books, paintings, brushes, ink and paper. Prepare yourself for pushy sales staff and stratospheric prices; wander round and compare price tags. If you want a chop (carved seal) made, you can do it here. At the western end of Liulichang Xijie, a collection of ramshackle stalls flog bric-a-brac, Buddhist statuary, Cultural Revolution pamphlets and posters, fake Tang dynasty three-colour porcelain (*sāncǎi*), shoes for bound feet, silks, handicrafts, Chinese kites, swords, walking sticks, door knockers etc.

Arts & Crafts

Tongli Studio Lifestyle & Arts (Tónglì; Map pp102-3; Sanlitun ☻ 11am-9pm) This impressive lifestyle and arts shopping market in Sanlitun has four floors of excellent outlets, selling ceramics, clothing, jewellery, jade and arts and crafts, among other decorative quality items. You can find Casa Bella (right) and Gēge Qípáo (right) here among loads of other outlets. Bar Blue on the 3rd floor is a smooth and stylish tavern where you can recuperate after shopping.

Beijing Curio City (Běijīng Gǔwán Chéng; Map pp102-3; ☎ 6774 7711; 21 Dongsanhuan Nanlu; ☻ 9.30am-6.30pm) South of Panjiayuan, Curio City is four floors of gifts, scrolls, ceramics, carpets, duty-free shopping and furniture. An excellent place to turn up knick-knacks and souvenirs, especially on Sundays.

Beijing Arts & Crafts Central Store (Gōngyì Měishù Fúwùbù; Map pp102-3; ☎ 6523 8747; 200 Wangfujing Dajie) Centrally located store (with a sign outside saying Artistic Mansion) well known for its good selection of jade (plus certificates of authenticity), jadeite, cloisonné vases, carpets and other Chinese arts and crafts. Jewellery (gold, silver, jade and pearl) is on the ground floor, on the 2nd floor are glass, paintings, calligraphy and fans. You can find woodcarvings, cloisonné, lacquer ware and silks on the 3rd floor and jade carvings up on the 4th floor.

Carpets

Gangchen Carpets (Kāngchén; Map pp102-3; ☎ 6465 3388; Kempinski Hotel; Lufthansa Center Youyi Shopping City, 50 Liangmaqiao Lu) You may pay more for your carpets here (ranging from around Y2000 to Y16,000), but you can be assured that what you are buying are genuine, handmade carpets from Tibet. All carpets are made from Changphel sheep wool (a wool type characterised by durable fibres) and decorated with traditional Tibetan motifs.

Qianmen Carpet Company (Qiánmén Dìtǎnchǎng; Map pp102-3; ☎ 6715 1687; 59 Xingfu Dajie) This carpet store, just north of the Tiantan Hotel, stocks a good selection of handmade carpets and prayer rugs with natural dyes from Tibet, Xīnjiāng and Mongolia. Prices start at around Y2000.

Ceramics

Casa Bella (Map pp102-3; Tongli Studio Lifestyle & Arts, Sanlitun) This marvellous porcelain emporium at the funky Tongli displays a splendid range of reproduction ceramics, many of which are flawlessly modelled on exquisite pieces that have passed through auction houses. It's worth just coming here to wander round the well-illuminated pieces on display – including celadon, *fencai* (famille rose), *doucai* (multicoloured glaze), *qinghua* (blue and white) and monochromes – which are much superior to the usual junk.

Clothing

Gēge Qípáo (Map pp102-3; ☎ 6747 1917/2811; Tongli Studio Lifestyle & Arts, Sanlitun) This retail outlet upstairs in the Tongli Studio Lifestyle & Arts in Sanlitun has a splendid range of silk *qípáo* (cheongsam) in various designs and colours, some embroidered and others hand-painted. Prices range from around Y700 to Y1800.

Sanlitun Yashou Clothing Market (Sānlǐtún Yǎxiù Fúzhuāng Shìchǎng; Map pp102-3; 58 Gongrentiyuchang Beilu) Five floors of all the clothing you may need. Basement: shoes, boots, handbags and suitcases. First floor: outdoor jackets. Second floor: hiking clothes, suits and ladies wear. Third floor: silk ties, scarves, handkerchiefs, traditional Chinese clothes, silk cloth from Sūzhōu and Hángzhōu, silk jackets (Y400+), a branch of Ruifuxiang (a silk outlet), silk carpets, batik, lace and children's jackets. Fourth floor: jade, pearls, souvenirs, ethnic jewellery, cloisonné, Buddhist statues, silver, toys, army surplus and toy cars. Fifth floor: a clean and well-organised food stall.

Department Stores

Oriental Plaza (Dōngfāng Guǎngchǎng; Map pp102-3; 1 Dongchang'an Jie) You could spend a day in this staggeringly large shopping mega-complex at the foot of Wangfujing Dajie. Prices may not be cheap, but window-shoppers will be overjoyed. There's a great range of shops and restaurants and the Food Court (p126) in the basement is a popular and eclectic Asian eatery. Many top names are here, including Rolls Royce, Swarovski, Valentino and others. It's kid-friendly, with nappy-changing rooms and a play room downstairs.

Lufthansa Center Youyi Shopping City (Yànshā Yǒuyì Shāngchǎng; Map pp102-3; 50 Liangmaqiao Lu) The gigantic Lufthansa Center is a smart, well-stocked and long-established multi-level shopping mall. You can find most of what you need here, including several restaurants (Korean, German and Italian), and there are international access ATMs on the ground floor.

Friendship Store (Yǒuyì Shāngdiàn; Map pp102-3; ☎ 6500 3311; 17 Jianguomenwai Dajie) Could be worth a perusal for its upstairs touristy junk and its ground-floor books and magazine hide-out (excellent for coffee table titles and travel books on China), supermarket and deli.

Kites

Zhāoyuángé (Map pp102-3; ☎ 6512 1937; 41 Nanheyan Dajie) If you love Chinese kites, you will love this minute shop on the western side of Nanheyan Dajie, south of the Liújiā Guō restaurant (p128). There's a range of traditional Chinese paper kites here, starting from Y10 for a simple kite, up to around Y300 for a dragon; you can also pick up Beijing opera masks. The owner does not speak much English, but you can browse and make a selection.

Markets

Pānjiāyuán (Map pp102-3; off Dongsanhuan Nanlu; ☸ dawn-around 3pm Sat & Sun) Hands down the best place to shop for *yìshù* (arts), *gōngyì* (crafts) and *gǔwán* (antiques) in Běijīng is Panjiayuan (aka the Dirt Market or the Sunday Market). The market only takes place on weekends and has everything from calligraphy, Cultural Revolution memorabilia and cigarette ad posters to Buddha heads, ceramics and Tibetan carpets.

The market sees up to 50,000 visitors daily scoping for treasures. Serious collectors are the early birds, swooping here at dawn to snare that precious relic unwittingly sold for Y10. If you want to join them, early Sunday morning is apparently the best time. You may not find that rare Qianlong *doucai* stem cup or late-Yuan-dynasty *qinghua* vase that will ease you into early retirement, but what's on view is no less than a compendium of Chinese curios and an A–Z of Middle Kingdom knick-knacks. Bear in mind that this market is chaos – especially if you find crowds or hard bargaining intimidating. Also, ignore the 'don't pay more than half' rule here – some vendors here may start at 10 times the real price. Make a few rounds at Panjiayuan before forking out for anything, to compare prices and weigh it all up. It's off Dongsanhuan Nanlu (Third Ring Rd); take the subway to Guomao, then bus No 28.

Xiushui Silk Market (Xiùshuǐ Shìchǎng; Map pp102-3; off Jianguomenwai Dajie) This market, on the northern side of Jianguomenwai Dajie between the Friendship Store and the Jianguo Hotel, is awash with the silkworm's finest, as well as top brand and designer labels such as Gucci, Burberry and North Face (much of it fake). Bargaining is imperative, although it's often a struggle because of all the foreign tourists willing to throw money around like water. At the time of writing, the market was due to be demolished and relocated indoors, although there was no set date for this. Be extra vigilant against pickpockets in the crowded quadrants; your wallet could well be taking a walk as you haggle hard.

Pearl Market (Hóngqiáo Shìchǎng; Map pp102-3; ☎ 6711 7429; 16 Hongqiao Lu; ❀ 8.30am-7pm) Besides a cosmos of clutter (shoes, clothing, electronics and much more), you'll also find Chinese arts, crafts and antiques on the 3rd floor, flanking the vendors that sell pearls. A huge range of pearls is available – freshwater and seawater, white pearls and black pearls – and prices vary incredibly with quality. Pop down to the basement for a selection of scorpions, snake meat, snails and more. Pearl Market is across from the east gate of the Temple of Heaven Park.

GETTING THERE & AWAY

As the nation's capital, getting to Běijīng is straightforward. Rail and air connections link the capital to virtually every point in China, and fleets of buses head to abundant destinations from Běijīng. Using Běijīng as a starting point to explore the rest of the land makes perfect sense.

Air

Běijīng has direct air connections to most major cities in the world. For more information about international flights to Běijīng, see p906.

You can purchase tickets for Chinese carriers flying from Běijīng at the **Aviation Building** (Mínháng Yíngyè Dàshà; Map pp102-3; domestic ☎ 6601 3336, international ☎ 6601 6667). The same tickets can be bought from numerous other ticket outlets and service counters around Běijīng, and through most mid-range and above hotels. Chinese speakers can call the ticket reservation hotline on ☎ 962581. Discounts are generally available, so it is important to ask.

You can make inquiries for all airlines at Běijīng's **Capital Airport** (Map p95; from Běijīng only ☎ 962580). Call ☎ 6459 9567 for information on international arrivals and departures and ☎ 1689 6969 for information on domestic flights.

Daily flights connect Běijīng to every major city in China. There should be at least one flight a week to smaller cities throughout China. The prices listed in this book are approximate only and represent the non-discounted air fare.

Bus

No international buses serve Běijīng, but there are plenty of long-distance domestic routes. Sleeper buses are widely available and recommended for overnight journeys. Twelve national highways radiate from Běijīng to major cities nationwide, including Shěnyáng, Tiānjīn, Hāěrbīn, Guǎngzhōu, Nánjīng, Fúzhōu and Kūnmíng.

Běijīng has a total of 12 long-distance bus stations (chángtú qìchēzhàn), so figuring out which bus station to depart from can be pretty confusing. The rule of thumb is that long-distance bus stations are on the city perimeter in the direction of the city you want to go to. The major stations are at **Xizhimen** (Map pp102-3; ☎ 6218 3454, 6217 6767) in the west and **Dongzhimen** (Map pp102-3; ☎ 6467 1346) in the northeast. Other important stations are at **Zhaogongkou** (Map pp98-9; ☎ 6722 9491/6723 7328) in the south (useful for buses to Tiānjīn), **Deshengmen** (Map pp98-9) and **Beijing South Train Station** (☎ 6303 4307).

Buses range in both type and quality, from simple minibuses (xiǎobā) to air-conditioned Volvo (Wòěrwò) buses, equipped with TV sets, reclining seats and hostesses.

DOMESTIC AIR FARES FROM BĚIJĪNG

Domestic flights from Běijīng include the following destinations (fares are for one-way flights): Chángchūn (Y960, 80 minutes), Chéngdū (Y1440, two hours and 20 minutes), Dàlián (Y710, 70 minutes), Fúzhōu (Y1530, 2½ hours), Guǎngzhōu (Y1700, two hours and 50 minutes), Guìlín (Y1590, 4½ hours), Hāěrbīn (Y1000, 1½ hours), Hǎikǒu (Y2190, three hours and 40 minutes), Hángzhōu (Y1050, 50 minutes), Héféi (Y990, one hour and 40 minutes), Hohhot (Y500, one hour), Hong Kong (Y2800, three hours), Jílín (Y960, 80 minutes), Kūnmíng (Y1810, four hours), Lánzhōu (Y1100, two hours), Lhasa (Y2040, 4½ hours), Nánjīng (Y930, one hours and 35 minutes), Nánníng (Y1870, three hours and 25 minutes), Qīngdǎo (Y660, 50 minutes), Shànghǎi (Y1030, two hours), Tàiyuán (Y510, 50 minutes), Ürümqi (Y2410, 3½ hours), Wǔhàn (Y990, two hours), Xī'ān (Y1050, 1½ hours), Xīníng (Y1450, two hours) and Zhèngzhōu (Y690, 70 minutes).

Train

Travellers arrive and depart by train at **Beijing Train Station** (Běijīng Huǒchēzhàn; Map pp102-3; ☎ 6563 3262/3242), southeast of the Forbidden City, or **Beijing West Train Station** (Běijīng Xīzhàn; Map pp102-3; ☎ 6321 6253), near Lianhuachi Park. Beijing Train Station is served by its own underground station, making access simple. International trains to Moscow, Pyongyang (North Korea) and Ulaanbaatar arrive at and leave Beijing Train Station; trains for Hong Kong and Vietnam leave from Beijing West Train Station.

There are also two other stations of significance in the city, **Beijing South Train Station** (Yǒngdìngmén Huǒchēzhàn; ☎ 6563 5222) and **Beijing North Train Station** (Běijīng Běizhàn; ☎ 6563 6122/6223) on the Second Ring Rd.

Avoid buying tickets in the main ticket hall at Beijing Train Station, as the crowds can be overwhelming. A **ticketing office for foreigners** (⏱ 5.30-7.30am, 8am-6.30pm & 7-11pm) exists in the northwestern corner of the 1st floor, accessed through the soft seat waiting room (*guìbīn hòuchēshì*). This is an excellent place to sit down and take a breather in the comfy armchairs provided. There is also a foreigners ticketing office on the 2nd floor of **Beijing West Train Station** (⏱ 24hr).

Typical train fares and approximate travel times for hard-sleeper tickets to destinations from Běijīng include: Chángchūn (Y239, eight hours), Chéngdū (Y418, 26 hours), Dàlián (Y257, 12 hours), Dàtóng (Y70, 5½ hours), Guǎngzhōu (Y458, 22 hours), Hángzhōu (Y363, 15 hours), Hànkǒu (Y281, 10 hours), Hāěrbīn (Y281, 11½ hours), Jǐ'nán (Y137, 4½ hours), Kūnmíng (Y578, 40 hours), Nánjīng (Y274, 11 hours), Nánníng (Y499, 28 hours), Qīngdǎo (Y215, 10 hours), Shànghǎi (Y327, 13½ hours), Sūzhōu (Y309, 11 hours), Tiānjīn (Y30, 80 minutes), Ürümqi (Y652, 44 hours) and Xī'ān (Y274, 12 hours).

GETTING AROUND
To/From the Airport

Běijīng's Capital Airport is 27km from the centre of town or about 20 minutes by car (bar traffic jams).

Several bus companies run services to and from the airport. Inside the airport terminal there's a service desk where tickets are sold and a further desk can be found outside, alongside a bus timetable. All buses into town cost Y16. Almost any bus that gets you into town will probably do; then you can hop in a taxi and speed to a hotel.

Express bus routes (☎ 6459 4375/4376) run to Běijīng every 15 minutes between 5.30am and 7pm daily, although some run longer hours. Route A runs 24 hours, with less frequent services between 10pm and 5.30am, and is probably the most popular with travellers. From the airport it goes to Sanyuanqiao, passes the Kunlun Hotel, Dongzhimen, Dongsishitiao and terminates at the International Hotel (Guójì Fàndiàn), just north of Beijing Train Station. Route B runs along the north Third Ring Rd and then south past the Friendship Hotel to the metro stop at Gongzhufen. Both of these buses can drop you at a subway station. Route C goes to Xinyuanli, Gongrentiyuchang, Dongdaqiao and the China Art Gallery (Zhōngguó Měishù Guǎn) north of Wangfujing Dajie.

Going in the opposite direction from the city to the airport, the most useful place to catch the bus is at the west door of the International Hotel, where buses leave every half-hour between 6.30am and 7.30pm (Y16). You can also pick up the shuttle bus (☎ 6601 7755; Y16) that leaves every 30 minutes from the eastern end of the Aviation Building (the CAAC ticket office) on Xichang'an Jie in Xidan District, between 6am and 7.30pm.

Many top-end hotels runs shuttle buses from the airport to their hotels.

A light-rail link from Capital Airport to Běijīng is under construction, but is not due for completion until 2007.

A taxi (using its meter) should cost about Y85 from the airport to the centre, including the Y15 airport expressway toll. A well-established illegal taxi operation at the airport attempts to lure weary travellers into a Y300-plus ride to the city, so be on your guard.

Bicycle

Getting around Běijīng by bike is an excellent idea. The city is as flat as a chessboard and there are ample bicycle lanes. The increase in traffic in recent years has made biking along major thoroughfares more dangerous and nerve-racking, however. Cycling through Běijīng's *hútòng* is far safer and an experience not to be missed (see the Bicycle Tour, p120).

If you have the option of buying your own bike, good-quality bikes can be bought from the **Qianmen Bicycle Shop** (Qiánmén Zìxíngchē Shāngdiàn; Map pp102-3; 97 Qianmen Dajie), opposite the post office, or you can try the bike shop next to the Beijing Gongti International Youth Hostel (p123). See p918 for more information about buying a bicycle.

Budget hotels are good places to rent bicycles, which cost around Y10 per day (plus a deposit); rental at upmarket hotels is far more expensive. A few tourist-oriented rental outfits have set up, including the expensive **Universal Bicycle Rental Outlet** (Map pp102-3; single/tandem bike per hr Y10/20, deposit Y500), which has two outlets in the vicinity of Qianhai Lake.

Car

If you are willing to endure the appalling driving standards on Běijīng's roads, you can hire a car. You will need an International Driving Licence or a Chinese driving licence (for residents) and will be limited to driving within Běijīng proper (you will not be allowed to drift off to, say, Shànghǎi). The current absence of car-hire outlets at Běijīng's Capital Airport signals a reluctant industry. Hertz used to have an office opposite the arrivals hall, but when last inspected, the sign remained even though the staff had long moved out; **Hertz** (☎ 800-810 8833; 5 Jianguomenwai Dajie; ☒ 9am-5pm) have another branch outside the Jianguo Hotel. Taxis are cheap and hiring a driver is a better proposition, which can be arranged at major hotels, CITS (☎ 6515 8566) or other travel agencies.

Public Transport

BUS

Relying on buses (gōnggòng qìchē) to get swiftly from A to B can be frustrating unless it's a short hop; thick congestion often slows things to an infuriating crawl. Getting a seat can also be impossible. Fares are typically Y1 or under depending on distance, although plusher, air-conditioned buses are more expensive. You generally pay the conductor once aboard the bus, rather than the driver.

Buses run 5am to 11pm daily or thereabouts, and stops are few and far between. It's important to work out how many stops you need to go before boarding. If you can read Chinese, a useful publication (Y5) listing all the Běijīng bus lines is available from kiosks; alternatively, tourist maps of Běijīng illustrate some of the bus routes.

One- and two-digit bus numbers cover the city-core; 100-series buses are trolleys; 200-series are night buses (yèbān gōnggòng qìchē) and 300-series are suburban lines. Useful standard bus routes include:

No 1 Runs along Chang'an Jie, Jianguomenwai Dajie and Jianguomennei Dajie, passing Sihuizhan, Bawangfen, Yonganli, Dongdan, Xidan, Muxidi, Junshi Bowuguan, Gongzhufen and Maguanying along the way

No 4 Runs along Chang'an Jie, Jianguomenwai Dajie and Jianguomennei Dajie: Gongzhufen, Junshi Bowuguan, Muxidi, Xidan, Tiananmen, Dongdan, Yonganli, Bawangfen and Sihuizhan

No 5 Deshengmen, Dianmen, Beihai Park, Xihuamen, Zhongshan Park and Qianmen

No 15 Beijing Zoo, Fuxingmen, Xidan, Hepingmen, Liulichang and Tianqiao

No 20 Beijing South Train Station, Tianqiao, Qianmen, Wangfujing, Dongdan and Beijing Train Station

No 44 (outer ring) Xinjiekou, Xizhimen Train Station, Fuchengmen, Fuxingmen, Changchunjie, Xuanwumen, Qianmen, Taijichang, Chongwenmen, Dongbianmen, Chaoyangmen, Dongzhimen, Andingmen, Deshengmen and Xinjiekou

No 54 Beijing Train Station, Dongbianmen, Chongwenmen, Zhengyi Lu, Qianmen, Dashilar, Temple of Heaven, Yongdimen and Haihutun

No 103 Beijing Train Station, Dengshikou, China Art Gallery, Forbidden City (north entrance), Beihai Park, Fuchengmen and Beijing Zoo

No 332 Beijing Zoo, Weigongcun, Renmin Daxue, Zhongguancun, Haidian, Beijing University and Summer Palace

Minibuses follow many of the main bus routes and are slightly more expensive, costing from around Y2. If you work out how to combine bus and subway connections, the subway will speed up much of the trip.

Special double-decker buses run in a circle around the city centre and are slightly more expensive but spare you the traumas of normal public buses and you should get a seat.

SUBWAY & LIGHT RAILWAY

The subway (dìtiě) is probably the best way to travel around. The system is modest and trains are showing their age, but five new subway lines are being constructed to take the strain off the roads before the 2008

Bicycle-cart rider in a *hútòng* (p114),
Dongcheng district, Běijīng

PHIL M WEYMOUTH

GLENN BEANLAND

Gate of Heavenly Peace entrance (p106)
to the Forbidden City, Běijīng

Lama Temple (p112) in Běijīng

DAMIEN SIMONIS

PHIL M WEYMOUTH

Man standing in front of Běijīng's Forbidden City (p110)

DAMIEN SIMONIS

The Forbidden City (p110) from one of the bridges over the Golden Stream, Běijīng

PHIL M WEYMOUTH

White Cloud Temple (p116), Běijīng

The Great Wall at Bādálíng (p143) outside Běijīng

NICHOLAS PAVLO

Olympics. Three lines currently exist: the Circle Line (Huánxiàn), the East–West Line (Yīxiàn) and Line 13. The fare is a flat Y3 on all lines, regardless of distance. Only a few platforms have seats, and none have toilets. Trains run at a frequency of one every few minutes during peak times and operate from 5am to 11pm daily.

To recognise a subway station (dì tiě zhàn), look for the subway symbol, which is a blue English capital 'D' with a circle around it.

In addition to the lines described below, Line 5 is currently under construction and is due for completion in 2007. When it opens, it will run north–south, intersecting with the Circle Line at Yonghegong and Chongwenmen, and intersecting with the East–West line at Dongdan.

Circle Line

This 16km line has 18 stations: Běijīng Zhan (Beijing Train Station), Jianguomen, Chaoyangmen, Dongsishitiao, Dongzhimen, Yonghegong, Andingmen, Gulou, Jishuitan, Xizhimen (Beijing North Train Station), Chegongzhuang, Fuchengmen, Fuxingmen, Changchunjie, Xuanwumen, Hepingmen, Qianmen and Chongwenmen. The Circle Line intersects with the East–West line at Fuxingmen and Jianguomen.

East–West Line

This line has 23 stations and runs from Sihuidong to Pingguoyuan, a western suburb of Běijīng. The stops are: Sihuidong, Sihuixi, Dawanglu, Guomao, Yonganli, Jianguomen, Dongdan, Wangfujing, Tiananmen Dong, Tiananmen Xi, Xidan, Fuxingmen, Nanilishilu, Muxidi, Junshibowuguan, Gongzhufen, Wanshoulu, Wukesong, Yuquanlu, Babaoshan, Bajiaocun, Guchenglu and Pingguoyuan.

Line 13

Classified as part of the subway system but actually a light-rail link (operating between 6am and 9pm), Line 13 runs in a northern loop from Xizhimen to Dongzhimen, stopping at 14 stations (approximately three minutes per station) in between. As with the subway, tickets to anywhere on Line 13 are Y3, while Y5 gets you a ticket to any station on the other lines of the underground system. The line is not of great use for tourist sights, apart from the Wudaokou stop for

the Old Summer Palace and Summer Palace. An extension to the line is currently being built which will link Dongzhimen to Běijīng's Capital Airport (due for completion in 2007).

Taxi

Běijīng taxis come in different classes. All taxis sport a red sticker on the side rear window declaring the rate per kilometre. Red Xiali (a car brand) taxis are the most economical (Y10 for the first 4km; Y1.20 per kilometre thereafter). Next are the larger Y1.60 taxis (Y10 for the first 3km; Y1.60 per kilometre thereafter); many of these are red Citroens and it pays to take these if you are going a long distance as there's more leg room and they're cleaner. Volkswagen Santana 2000 taxis cost Y12 for the first 4km and Y2 for each kilometre thereafter. Taxis are required to switch on the meter for all journeys. Between 11pm and 6am there is a 20% surcharge added to the flag fall metered fare. Always insist that the meter is used, unless taking a long trip out of town.

Běijīng taxi drivers speak little, if any English. If you don't speak Chinese, bring a map or have your destination written down in characters. It helps if you know the way to your destination; sit in the front with a map.

Cabs can be hired for distance, by the hour, or by the day (a minimum of Y350 for the day). Taxis can be hailed in the street, summoned by phone or you can wait at one of the designated taxi zones. Call ☎ 6835 1150 to register a complaint. Remember to collect a receipt (ask the driver to fāpiào); if you accidentally leave anything in the taxi, the driver's number appears on the receipt so he or she can be located.

AROUND BĚIJĪNG

THE GREAT WALL 长城

He who has not climbed the Great Wall is not a true man.

Mao Zedong

Also known to the Chinese as the '10,000 Li Wall' (one lǐ is roughly 500m), the Great Wall (Chángchéng) stretches from its scattered remains in Liáoníng province to Jiāyùguān in the Gobi Desert.

Standard histories emphasise the unity of the wall. The 'original' wall was begun over 2000 years ago during the Qin dynasty (221–207 BC), when China was unified under Emperor Qin Shi Huang. Separate walls that had been constructed by independent kingdoms to keep out marauding nomads, were linked together. The effort required hundreds of thousands of workers – many of whom were political prisoners – and 10 years of hard labour under General Meng Tian. An estimated 180 million cubic metres of rammed earth was used to form the core of the original wall, and legend has it that one of the building materials used was the bones of deceased workers.

The wall never really did perform its function as an impenetrable line of defence. As Genghis Khan supposedly said, 'The strength of a wall depends on the courage of those who defend it'. Sentries could be bribed. However, it did work very well as a kind of elevated highway, transporting people and equipment across mountainous terrain. Its beacon tower system, using smoke signals generated by burning wolves' dung, quickly transmitted news of enemy movements back to the capital. To the west was Jiāyùguān, an important link on the Silk Rd, where there was a customs post of sorts and where unwanted Chinese were ejected through the gates to face the terrifying wild west.

During the Ming dynasty a determined effort was made to rehash the bastion, this time facing it with bricks and stone slabs – some 60 million cubic metres of these. This project took over 100 years, and the costs in human effort and resources were phenomenal.

The wall was largely forgotten after that. Lengthy sections of it have returned to dust and the wall might have disappeared totally had it not been rescued by the tourist industry. Several important sections have been rebuilt, kitted out with souvenir shops, restaurants and amusement-park rides, and formally opened to the public. Not impressed with the tourist-oriented sections, explorative travellers have sought out unrestored sections of the wall for their more genuine appeal. The Chinese government has, however, begun periodically slapping fines on visitors to

such sections. The authorities argue that they are seeking to prevent damage to the unrestored wall by traipsing visitors, but they are also very keen to keep the tourist revenue flowing to restored parts of the wall. Furthermore, the wall has suffered more from farmers pillaging its earthen core for use on the fields. The wall also provided a useful supply of stone, which was stripped from the rampart for use on road and building construction.

The myth that the Great Wall is visible with the naked eye from the moon was finally laid to rest in 2003, when China's first astronaut Yang Liwei observed that he could not see the barrier from space. The Great Wall is certainly not visible from the moon, where even individual continents are barely perceptible. The myth is to be edited from Chinese textbooks, where it has cast its spell over generations of Chinese.

The most touristed area of the Great Wall is at Bādálǐng. Also renovated but ess touristed are Sīmǎtái and Jīnshānlǐng. Other travellers swear by seeing the wall au naturel, such as at Huánghuā (p145), although the authorities are starting to clamp down on this.

GREAT WALL TOURS

When choosing a tour, it is essential to check that the tour goes to where you want to go. Great Wall tours are often combined with trips to the Ming Tombs (p145), so ask beforehand; if you don't want to visit the Ming Tombs, choose another tour. Far more worrying, other tours make painful and expensive diversions to jade factories, gem exhibition halls and Chinese medicine centres. At the latter, tourists are herded off the bus and analysed by white-coated doctors, who diagnose ailments that can only be cured with high-priced Chinese remedies (supplied there and then). The tour organisers receive a commission from the jade showroom/medicine centre for every person they manage to funnel through, so you are simply lining other people's pockets. When booking a tour, it is essential to check that such scams and unnecessary diversions are not on the itinerary. As with most popular destinations in China, try and avoid going on the weekend.

Bǎdálǐng 八达岭

Most visitors see the Great Wall at **Bǎdá- lǐng** (Bādálǐng Chángchéng; Map p95; ☎ 6912 1338/1423/1520; admission Y45; ❄ 6am-10pm summer, 7am-6pm winter), 70km northwest of Bĕijīng, at an elevation of 1000m. The section of masonry at Bǎdálǐng was first built during the Ming dynasty (1368–1644), and was heavily restored in both the 1950s and the 1980s. Punctuated with *dílóu* (watchtowers), the 6m-wide wall is clad in brick, typical of the stonework employed by the Ming when they restored and expanded the fortification.

The surrounding scenery is raw and impressive and this is the place to come to see the wall snaking off into the distance over the undulating hills. Also come here for guard rails, souvenir stalls, a fairground feel and the companionship of squads of tourists surging over the ramparts. If you time your visit to coincide with a summer weekend, you won't be able to move against the wall of humanity on the battlements. Come during the week instead, and if possible, during the colder months when it's covered in snow.

Cable cars exist for the weary (Y50 round trip), but don't take the slide (*huádào*; Y30) as it's a colossal waste of money.

There are two sections of wall, trailing off to the left and right of the main entrance. The restored sections crawl for a distance before nobly disintegrating into ruins; unfortunately you cannot realistically explore these more authentic fragments.

Apart from the pristine battlements, you can be conveyed back into history via 15-minute films about the Great Wall at the **Great Wall Circle Vision Theatre** (admission Y25; ❄ 9am-9.45pm), a 360-degree amphitheatre. The admission fee also gets you into the **China Great Wall Museum** (❄ 9am-4pm).

GETTING THERE & AWAY

CITS (☎ 6515 8566), the **Beijing Tourist Information Center** (p101), **Panda Tours** (☎ 6525 8372; www.pandatourchina.com), big hotels and everyone else in the tourist business does a tour to Bǎdálǐng. Hotel tours can be convenient (and they should avoid rip-off diversions), but watch out for high-price hotel tours (up to Y300 per person).

The cheapest and easiest way to get to Bǎdálǐng is to take bus No 919 from just

north of the old gate of Deshengmen, about 500m east of the Jishuitan subway stop. Buses leave regularly from 5.30am. Ordinary buses take two hours and cost Y5, while the faster, nonstop luxury air-con buses take one hour and cost Y10. The last bus leaves Bǎdálǐng for Bĕijīng at 6.30pm.

Several tour buses run to Bǎdálǐng, taking around 90 minutes to two hours. Many visit the Ming Tombs on the way back. **Tour bus No 1** (☎ 6303 5066; Y50) runs to Bǎdálǐng, departing from the tour-bus station east of Front Gate, between 6.30am and 11.30am. **Tour bus No 2** (☎ 6764 3687; standard/luxury bus Y45/50) runs to Bǎdálǐng and the Ming Tombs from the same location as Tour Bus No 1. **Tour bus No 2** (☎ 6601 8285; Y50) also departs from the South Cathedral at Xuanwumen between 6.30am and 8.30am. **Tour bus No 5** (Y50) also departs in the morning from the western side of Qianmen for both Bǎdálǐng and the Ming Tombs. **Tour bus No 4** will get you to Bǎdálǐng from the Zhanlanguan Lu tour-bus station, near the zoo, south of the Beijing Exhibition Center. Plan about nine hours for the whole trip.

A taxi to the wall and back will cost a minimum of Y400 for an eight-hour hire with a maximum of four passengers.

Mùtiányù 慕田峪

The 2250m-long granite section of wall at **Mùtiányù** (Map p95; ☎ 6162 6873/6022; admission Y35; ❄ 6.30am-5.30pm), 90km northeast of Bĕijīng in Huáiróu County, dates from Ming dynasty remains, built upon an earlier Northern Qi dynasty conception. It was developed as a decoy alternative to Bǎdálǐng and is, on the whole, a less commercial experience. Despite some motivated hawking and tourist clutter, the stretch of wall is notable for its numerous Ming dynasty guard towers and stirring views. The wall is also equipped with a **cable car** (Y50 round trip; ❄ 8.30am-4.30pm). October is the best month to visit, for the autumn colours of the trees that envelop the surrounding countryside.

GETTING THERE & AWAY

From **Dongzhimen long-distance bus station** (Dōngzhímén Chángtú Qìchēzhàn; ☎ 6467 4995) you can take either bus No 916 (Y8, one hour) or No 936 (Y5) to Huáiróu then change for a minibus to Mùtiányù (Y25). Alternatively, the less frequent 916 branch line (zhīxiàn) goes all the way from Dongzhimen to Mùtiányù (Y15).

Tour bus No 6 (☎ 6601 8285; Y50) runs to Mùtiányù from outside the South Cathedral at Xuanwumen, operating between 6.30am and 8.30am on Saturday, Sunday and public holidays from April to October. The bus also visits the Hongluo Temple (Hóngluó Sì).

Jūyōngguān 居庸关

Originally constructed in the 5th century and rebuilt by the Ming, **Jūyōngguān** (Juyong Pass; Map p95; ☎ 6977 1665; admission Y40; ☺ 6am-4pm) was considered one of the most strategically important sections of the Great Wall because of its position as a link to Běijīng. However, this section 50km northwest of Běijīng has been thoroughly renovated to the point where you don't feel as if you're walking on a part of history. Still, if you're in a hurry, it's the closest section of the wall to Běijīng and is usually quiet. You can do the steep and somewhat strenuous circuit in under two hours.

GETTING THERE & AWAY

Jūyōngguān is on the road to Bādálǐng, so any of the buses for Bādálǐng listed earlier will get you there (but tell the bus driver you want to be dropped off at Jūyōngguān Chángchéng).

Sīmǎtái 司马台

In Mìyún County 110km northeast of Běijīng, the stirring remains at **Sīmǎtái** (Map p95; ☎ 6903 5025/5030; admission Y30; ☺ 8am-5pm) make for a more exhilarating Great Wall experience. Built during the reign of Ming dynasty emperor Hongwu, the 19km stretch is marked by watchtowers, steep plunges and scrambling ascents.

It's not for the faint-hearted: this rough section of the wall is very steep. The eastern section of wall at Sīmǎtái sports 16 watchtowers and from around the 12th watchtower, the climb gets precarious. A few slopes have a 70-degree incline and you need both hands free, so bring a day-pack to hold your camera and other essentials. The **cable car** (round trip Y50) could be an alternative to a sprained ankle. Take strong shoes with a good grip.

Sīmǎtái has some unusual features, such as 'obstacle-walls'. These are walls-within-walls used for defending against enemies who had already scaled the Great Wall. Small cannons have been discovered in this area, as well as evidence of rocket-type weapons, such as flying knives and flying swords. Another peculiar feature of Sīmǎtái is the **toboggan ride** (Y30) and unfazed by the dizzying terrain, hawkers make an unavoidable appearance. But you won't be short-changed by what are some exhilarating views.

GETTING THERE & AWAY

Early morning direct minibuses leave **Dongzhimen long-distance bus station** (☎ 6467 4995; Y20) from 6am. Otherwise take a minibus from Dongzhimen to Mìyún (Y8, 1¼ hours) and change to a minibus to Sīmǎtái, or a taxi (round trip Y120).

Weekend tour bus No 12 (☎ 6601 8285; Y50) leaves from outside the South Cathedral at Xuanwumen for Sīmǎtái between 6.30am and 8.30am Saturday, Sunday and public holidays. Backpacker hotels often run morning trips by **minibus** (Y60, not incl ticket; ☺ 8.30am). Hiring a taxi from Běijīng for the day costs about Y400.

Jīnshānlǐng 金山岭

Though not as steep (and therefore not as impressive) as Sīmǎtái, the Great Wall at **Jīnshānlǐng** (Jīnshānlǐng Chángchéng; Map p95; admission Y40), near the town of Gǔběikǒu, has 24 watchtowers and is considerably less developed than any of the sites previously mentioned, despite undergoing some restoration work.

Perhaps the most interesting thing about Jīnshānlǐng is that it's the starting point for a hike to Sīmǎtái. The distance between Jīnshānlǐng and Sīmǎtái is only about 10km, but it takes nearly four hours because the trail is steep and stony. Parts of the wall between Jīnshānlǐng and Sīmǎtái have collapsed and much is in a state of ruin, but it can be traversed without too much difficulty. Arriving at Sīmǎtái, however, you may have to buy another ticket.

You can do the walk in the opposite direction, but getting a ride back to Běijīng from Sīmǎtái is easier than from Jīnshānlǐng. Of course, getting a ride should be no problem if you've made arrangements with your driver to pick you up (and didn't pay in advance).

GETTING THERE & AWAY

From **Dongzhimen long-distance bus station** (☎ 6467 4995), take a minibus to Mìyún (Y8, 1¼ hours), change to a minibus to Gǔběikǒu, and get off at Bākèshíyíng (Y7). If you are heading to Chéngdé (in Héběi province), you will pass Jīnshānlíng en route.

Huánghuā 黄花

For a genuine wall experience close to Běijīng, the **Huánghuā** (Huánghuā Chángchéng; Yellow Flower Fortress; Map p95) section is ideal. The Great Wall at Huánghuā lies in two sections clinging to hillsides adjacent to a reservoir. Around 60km north of Běijīng, Huánghuā is a classic and well-preserved example of Ming defence with high and wide ramparts, intact parapets and sturdy beacon towers. The wall here has not benefited from restoration which makes the experience that much more genuine. Anxious to preserve the wall, the authorities are planning to put Huánghuā off limits to hikers, so check with your hotel before you set out.

It is said that Lord Cai masterminded this section, employing meticulous quality control. Each *cùn* (inch) of the masonry represented one labourer's whole day's work. When the Ministry of War got wind of the extravagance, Cai was beheaded for his efforts. In spite of the trauma, his decapitated body stood erect for three days before toppling. Years later, a general judged Lord Cai's wall to be exemplary and he was posthumously rehabilitated.

The section to the east, accessed across the dam and via a ticket collector (Y1) rises abruptly from a solitary watchtower. Be warned that it's both steep and crumbling – there are no guard rails here and the wall has not been restored. There may be further tickets ahead, depending on how far you venture. It's possible to make it all the way to the Mùtiányù section of the wall, but it'll take you a few days and some hard clambering (pack a sleeping bag). Local hawkers have got wind of foreigners in the vicinity, but they won't follow you up the wall.

The section of wall immediately to the west is in bad shape, so you'll have to clamber up the hillside from the south. Alternatively (and for ticket-free access and a great walk), walk south and take the first turning (about 500m down) on the right,

walk through the village, keep going until the river bends to the right and take the right fork following the river. Keep bearing right all the way (you'll pass fading Cultural Revolution Chinese characters on a corner that proclaim 'Long Live Chairman Mao' and just around the corner 'The Red Heart Faces the Communist Party'). Soon you'll see a watchtower ahead – the path leads up to it. The whole jaunt should take 45 minutes, and you can continue along the wall. Be warned that the wall here can be quite narrow and perilous, so don't carry on unless you feel confident.

Several places have sprung up offering beds. The shack at the entrance to the eastern section of the wall, **Xiaohong's Shop** (☎ 6165 1393/2350; damatthewall@hotmail.com) can get you a simple bed for Y50 or less and you can get something to eat here as well. **Jīntáng Shānzhuāng** (☎ 6499 4812/4813; d/tr 258/288) is a more upmarket, resort-style establishment overlooking the reservoir, north of Xiaohong's Shop.

GETTING THERE & AWAY

From the **Dongzhimen long-distance bus station** (☎ 6467 4995) take bus No 961 (Y8, two hours, two morning and afternoon departures) to Huánghuā. The last bus back to Běijīng is at 2.30pm. Ask for Huánghuāchéng and don't get off at the smaller Huánghuāzhèn by mistake. Bus Nos 916 (Y8, one hour; aircon) and 936 (Y6, one hour) also run from Dōngzhímén long-distance bus station to Huáiróu; they leave frequently from 5.30am to 6.30pm. Same-number minibuses run the same route a little quicker for Y5. From Huáiróu you can take a minibus directly to Huánghuā (Y4, 40 minutes) or hire a minicab from Huáiróu to Huánghuā (Y60 round trip).

MING TOMBS 十三陵

The **Ming Tombs** (Shísān Líng; Map p95; ☎ 6076 1156/1334/1435; admission per tomb Y20; ⊙ 8am-5.30pm), about 50km northwest of Běijīng, are the final resting place of 13 of the 16 Ming emperors. The Confucian layout and design may intoxicate more erudite visitors, but some find the necropolis lifeless and ho-hum. Confucian shrines lack the vibrancy and colour of Buddhist or Taoist temples, and their motifs can be bewilderingly inscrutable.

The Ming Tombs follow a standard layout for imperial tomb design. The plan typically consists of a main gate (líng mén), leading to the first of a series of courtyards and the main hall, the **Hall of Eminent Favours** (棱恩殿; Língēn Diàn). Beyond lie further gates or archways, leading to the **Soul Tower** (明楼; Míng Lóu), behind which rises the burial mound.

Three tombs have been opened up to the public: Cháng Líng, Dìng Líng and Zhāo Líng.

Cháng Líng (长陵), burial place of the emperor Yongle, is the most impressive, with its series of magnificent halls lying beyond its yellow-tiled gate. Seated upon a three-tiered marble terrace, the most notable structure is the Hall of Eminent Favours, containing a recent statue of Yongle and a breathtaking interior with vast *nanmu* (cedarwood) columns. The pine-covered burial mound at the rear of the complex is yet to be excavated and is not open to the public.

Dìng Líng (定陵), the burial place of the emperor Wanli, contains a series of subterranean interlocking vaults and the remains of the various gates and halls of the complex. Excavated in the late 1950s, this tomb is of more interest to some visitors as you are allowed to descend into the underground vault. Accessing the vault down the steps, visitors are confronted by the simply vast marble self-locking doors that sealed the chamber after it was vacated. Note the depression in the floor where the stone prop clicked into place once the door was finally closed.

Zhāo Líng (昭陵), the resting place of the 13th Ming emperor Longqing, follows an orthodox layout and is a tranquil alternative if you find the other tombs too busy.

` The road leading up to the tombs is a 7km stretch called the **Spirit Way** (神道; Shéndào). Commencing with a triumphal arch, the path enters the Great Palace Gate, where officials once had to dismount, and passes a giant *bìxì* (a mythical tortoise-dragon-like animal), which bears the largest stele in China. A guard of 12 sets of stone animals and officials follows this. Your tour-bus driver may well speed past them (preferring to spend half an hour at the routine Shisanling Reservoir instead), so be insistent if you want to see them.

GETTING THERE & AWAY

Tour buses usually combine a visit to the Ming Tombs with a visit to the Great Wall at Bādálǐng (see p143 for information about buses to and from Bādálǐng).

To go independently, take bus No 345 (branch line, *zhīxiàn*) from Deshengmen (500m east of Jishuitan subway station) to Chāngpíng (Y6, one hour). Get off at the Chāngpíng Dōngguān stop and change to bus No 314 for the tombs. Alternatively, take the standard bus No 345 to Chāngpíng and then take a taxi (Y20, 10 minutes) to the tombs. You can also reach the Chāngpíng Dōngguān stop on bus No 845 (Y10) from Xizhimen long-distance bus station, just outside the Xizhimen subway stop.

EASTERN QING TOMBS 清东陵

The area of the **Eastern Qing Tombs** (Qīng Dōng Líng; Map p95; admission Y55; 🕑 8am-5pm), 125km northeast of Běijīng, could be called Death Valley, housing as it does five emperors, 14 empresses and 136 imperial consorts. In the mountains ringing the valley are buried princes, dukes, imperial nurses and others.

A spirit way is a principle feature here, as at the Ming tombs. The emperors buried here are: Qianlong (裕陵; Yù Líng), Kangxi (景陵; Jǐng Líng), Shunzhi (孝陵; Xiào Líng), Xianfeng (定陵; Dìng Líng) and Tongzhi (Huì Líng). Emperor Qianlong (1711–99) started preparations when he was 30, and by the time he was 88 he had used up 90 tonnes of his silver. His resting place covers half a square kilometre. Some of the beamless stone chambers are decorated with Tibetan and Sanskrit sutras, and the doors bear bas-relief Bodhisattvas. All the emperors' tombs are open to visitors apart from Huì Líng.

Empress Dowager Cixi also got a head start. Her tomb, Dìng Dōng Líng (定东陵), was completed some three decades before her death and also underwent considerable restoration before she was finally laid to rest. It lies alongside the tomb of Empress Cian. The phoenix (symbol of the empress) appears above that of the dragon (the emperor's symbol) in the artwork at the front of Cixi's tomb – not side by side as on other tombs. Cixi's and Qianlong's tombs were plundered in the 1920s.

GETTING THERE & AWAY
Located in Zūnhuǎ County, Héběi province, the Eastern Qing Tombs are blessed with a more dramatic setting than the Ming Tombs, although getting there is an expedition and getting around is difficult without a vehicle.

A special **tour bus** (☎ 6601 8285; with/without air-con Y80/60) goes to the Eastern Qing Tombs from outside the South Cathedral at Xuanwumen; it departs when full between 6.30am and 8.30am. Pedicabs (Y15) can convey you around the tombs upon arrival. You can also take a morning bus from the Majuan long-distance bus station in Běijīng to Zūnhuǎ (Y20, four hours, first bus 7am), followed by a minibus to the tombs. A taxi from Běijīng should cost around Y350 for the day trip to the tombs.

TANZHE TEMPLE 潭柘寺
Just 45km west of Běijīng, **Tanzhe Temple** (Tánzhè Sì; Map p95; admission Y30; ☻ 8.30am-6pm) is the largest of all the Beijing temples. The Buddhist complex has a very long history, dating as far back as the 3rd century, with structural modifications dating from the Tang, Liao, Ming and Qing dynasties.

The temple is attractively set amid trees in the mountains, but most of the statuary is, sadly, very new. The ascending temple grounds are covered with towering cypress and pine trees, many so old that their gangly limbs have to be supported by metal props. The highlight of a trip to the temple is the small **Talin Temple** (Tǎlín Sì), by the forecourt where you disembark the bus, with its collection of stupas (reliquaries for the cremated remains of important lamas) reminiscent of the Shaolin Temple. You can tour them while waiting for the return bus. An excellent time to visit Tanzhe Temple is around mid-April, when the magnolias are in bloom.

GETTING THERE & AWAY
Take the subway to the Pingguoyuan stop and then take bus No 931 (Y3) to the temple, which is at the namesake final stop (don't take the bus No 931 branch line, zhīxiàn, however). This bus will also stop near Jietai Temple. Alternatively, take **tour bus No 7** (☎ 6779 7546; Y40) from the tour bus station east of Front Gate which runs between 7am and 8.30am on Saturday and Sunday between mid-April and mid-October, and also stops at Jietai Temple.

JIETAI TEMPLE 戒台寺
About 10km southeast of Tanzhe Temple is this smaller, but more engaging **temple** (Jiètái Sì; Map p95; admission Y20; ☻ 8am-6pm). Jietai (Ordination Terrace) Temple was built around AD 622 during the Tang dynasty, with major improvements made during the Ming dynasty. The main complex is dotted with ancient pine trees, which have been given names. One of these, **Nine Dragon Pine**, is claimed to be over 1300 years old, while the **Embracing Pagoda Pine** does just what it says.

GETTING THERE & AWAY
You can visit the temple on bus No 931 on the way back from, or en route to, Tanzhe Temple. It's a 10-minute walk uphill from the bus stop. Alternatively, take **tour bus No 7** (see previous entry) which visits both Tanzhe Temple and Jietai Temple.

MARCO POLO BRIDGE 卢沟桥
Described by the great traveller himself, this 266m-long grey marble **bridge** (Lúgōu Qiáo; Map p95; ☎ 8389 3919; 88 Lugouqiaochengnei Xijie; admission Y15; ☻ 8am-5pm) is host to 485 carved stone lions. Each animal is different, with the smallest only a few centimetres high, and legend maintains that they move around during the night.

Dating from 1189, the stone bridge is Běijīng's oldest (but is a composite of different eras; it was widened in 1969), and spans the Yongding River near the little walled town of Wǎnpíng.

Despite the praises of Marco Polo and Emperor Qianlong, the bridge wouldn't have rated more than a footnote in Chinese history were it not for the famed Marco Polo Bridge Incident, which ignited a full-scale war with Japan. On 7 July 1937 Japanese troops illegally occupied a railway junction outside Wǎnpíng. Japanese and Chinese soldiers started shooting, and that gave Japan enough of an excuse to attack and occupy Běijīng.

The **Memorial Hall of the War of Resistance Against Japan** is a gory look back at Japan's occupation of China, but the lack of English captions renders much of its information meaningless. Also on the site are the Wanping Castle, Daiwang Temple and a hotel.

GETTING THERE & AWAY

Take bus No 6 from the north gate of Temple of Heaven Park to the last stop at Liuli Bridge (Liúlí Qiáo) and then either bus No 339 or 309 to Lúgōu Xīnqiáo; the bridge is just ahead.

CHUĀNDǏXIÀ 川底下

Nestled in a valley 90km west of Běijīng and overlooked by towering peaks is the village time forgot: **Chuāndǐxià** (Map p95; admission Y20), a gorgeous cluster of historic courtyard homes and old-world charm. The bucolic backdrop is divine: terraced orchards and fields, with ancient houses and alleyways rising up the hillside, all the while swept by winds funnelling through the valley.

Apart from the rural beauty of the village, Chuāndǐxià is also a museum of **Maoist graffiti and slogans**, especially up the incline among the better-preserved houses. Some choice poetry daubing the walls includes 'Proletariats of the world unite!', 'Long live Mao Zedong', 'Courageously advance holding high the mighty red flag of Mao Zedong Thought' and 'Arm our minds with Mao Zedong Thought'.

Despite their impressive revolutionary credentials, Chuāndǐxià's residents have sensed the unmistakable whiff of the tourist dollar on the north-China breeze, and have flung open the doors of their antique homesteads. The village is a hamlet of rustic simplicity – despite some obvious restoration work.

Two hours is more than enough to wander around the village as it's not big, although it's possible to ascend the path rising up through the terraces above the village. Some homesteads are derelict and a few walls look dangerous and in a state of collapse, so be careful when wandering about.

If you want to stay the night, residents will find you a bed for a further Y15 or so and cook you food (many of the courtyard houses offer food and lodging). A number of houses also sell local produce, including *fēngmì* (honey) and *hétao* (walnuts).

GETTING THERE & AWAY

It's not easy to get to Chuāndǐxià; if travelling by public transport, bank on taking well over three hours from central Běijīng. Take bus No 929 (make sure it's the branch line, or *zhīxiàn*, not the regular bus) from the bus stop at the right of Pingguoyuan subway station to Zhāitáng (Y7, two hours), then hire a taxi van (Y10). If going in the off season, arrange with the taxi van to return to pick you up. The last bus returns from Zhāitáng to Pingguoyuan at 4.20pm. If you miss the last bus, a Xiali taxi will cost around Y80 to Pingguoyuan, but look out for stray minibuses piling travellers in for around Y30.

Tiānjīn 天津

BĚIJĪNG TO SHÀNGHǍI

HIGHLIGHTS

■ Take a stroll around Tiānjīn's stately **treaty port architecture** (p152), a grand blast from the past

■ Delve into Tiānjīn's **antique market** (p153) for trinkets and collectibles

■ Explore the Buddhist mysteries of Tiānjīn's premier shrine, the **Monastery of Deep Compassion** (p155)

■ Make a trip to the attractive and historic **Shi Family Courtyard** (p161) outside town

■ Sift through the busy clutter on **Ancient Culture Street** (p155) and pop into Tianhou Temple

Shi Family
Courtyard
★   ★ Tiānjīn

■ AREA CODE: ☎ 022   ■ POP: 9.6 MIL   ■ AREA: 11,632 SQ KM

Like Běijīng, Shànghăi and Chóngqìng, Tiānjīn belongs to no province – it's a special municipality, which gives it a degree of autonomy, but it's also closely administered by the central government. The city is nicknamed 'Shànghăi of the North', a reference to its history as a foreign concession, its heavy industrial output, its large port and its European architecture.

Tiānjīn is often overlooked by travellers in their rush to get to Běijīng. However, Tiānjīn has developed an intriguing individual style and laissez-faire attitude that makes it a rewarding stopping point for a few days. The city is proud of its concession-era architecture, which lends this otherwise shabby city a touch of nobility and refinement while some notable temples, mosques and churches make Tiānjīn all the more worth exploring.

Not to be upstaged by Běijīng, vast swathes of the city have been levelled in recent years to make way for new developments and to widen roads. The character 'chai' (拆) has been liberally daubed onto condemned buildings citywide earmarking them for demolition, even appearing on buildings lining the historic road of Jiefang Beilu.

The city has modern pockets, but (like the rest of China) it's also ragged and backward in parts, with smart office complexes overlooking dilapidated courtyards from which spill chickens and geese. This, however, is what China is all about.

The notorious Tángshān earthquake of 28 July 1976 registered 8.2 on the Richter scale and killed nearly 24,000 people in the Tiānjīn area in the same year that Mao also shook China by dying (a synchronicity of events hardly lost on the Chinese). The city was badly rocked, but escaped the devastation that virtually obliterated nearby Tángshān, where an estimated 240,000 residents died.

Accommodation in Tiānjīn tends to be expensive, but you can travel down from Běijīng for a day trip in less than 1½ hours.

HISTORY

The city's fortunes are, and always have been, linked to those of Běijīng. When the Mongols established Běijīng as the capital in the 13th century, Tiānjīn rose to prominence as a grain-storage point. Pending remodelling of the Grand Canal by Kublai Khan, the grain was shipped along Yangzi River (Cháng Jiāng), out into the open sea, up to Tiānjīn, and then through to Běijīng. With the Grand Canal fully functional as far as Běijīng, Tiānjīn was at the intersection of both inland and port navigation routes. By the 15th century, the town was a walled garrison.

For the seafaring Western nations, Tiānjīn was a trading post too good to be passed up. In 1856 Chinese soldiers boarded the *Arrow*, a boat flying the British flag, ostensibly in search of pirates. This was just the excuse the British and the French needed. Their gunboats attacked the forts outside Tiānjīn, forcing the Chinese to sign the Treaty of Tianjin (1858), which opened the port up to foreign trade and also legalised the sale of opium.

The English and French settled in, and were joined by the Japanese, Germans, Austro-Hungarians, Italians and Belgians between 1895 and 1900. Each of these concessions was a self-contained world with its own prison, school, barracks and hospital, occupying a much larger area than the original walled Chinese city.

This life was disrupted only in 1870 when locals attacked a French-run orphanage and killed, among others, 10 nuns – apparently the Chinese thought the children were being kidnapped. Thirty years later, during the Boxer Rebellion, the foreign powers levelled the walls of the old Chinese city.

Meanwhile, the European presence stimulated trade and industry, including salt, textiles and glass manufacture. Heavy silting of Hai River (Hǎi Hé, or Sea River) led to the construction of a new harbour 50km downstream at Tánggū. The opening of this new harbour meant that Tiānjīn lost its bustling port character.

Since 1949 Tiānjīn has been a centre for major industrialisation and it produces a wide variety of consumer goods. Brand-name products from Tiānjīn – such as Flying Pigeon bicycles and Seagull watches – are favoured within China for their good quality.

ORIENTATION

Like Běijīng, Tiānjīn is a large municipality, most of which is rural. Tiānjīn has a reasonably scattered selection of sights and hotels, which can make getting about tiring, although the central district is compact. The main train station is north of the Hai River which divides the city. To the south of the station were the foreign concessions, over the concession-era Jiefang Bridge along and around Jiefang Lu.

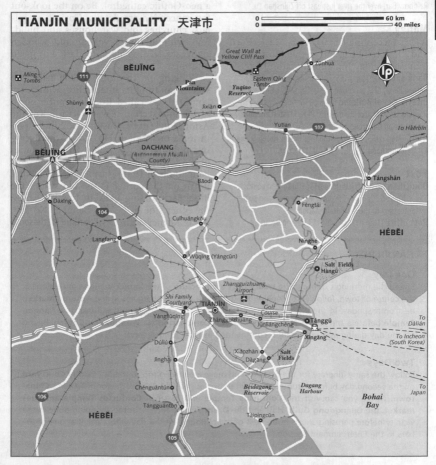

Maps

Maps of Tiānjīn can be bought from map sellers around the train station or at the Xinhua Bookstore.

INFORMATION
Bookshops

Xinhua Bookstore (Map p156; Xīnhuá Shūdiàn; cnr Xingan Lu & Binjiang Dao; ☯ 8.30am-9pm)

Emergency & Visas

Public Security Bureau (Map p156; PSB; Gōngānjú; ☎ 2311 8951; 30 Tangshan Dao)

Internet Access

Yadu Internet Café (Map p154; Yàdū Wǎngbā; per hr Y2; Yanhe Lu; ☯ 8am-midnight) 30m north of the Rainbow Bar, over the river just east off Zijinshan Lu.

Money

ATMs (accepting Cirrus, Visa, MasterCard and Plus) can be found in the Astor Hotel, Tianjin Holiday Inn and Sheraton Hotel.
Bank of China (Map p156; Zhōngguó Yínháng; 80-82 Jiefang Beilu) ATM accepting MasterCard, Visa, Cirrus & Plus.
International Building (Map p156; Guójì Dàshà; 75 Nanjing Lu) ATM accepting Cirrus, Plus, MasterCard and Visa cards on the ground floor.
HSBC (Map p156; Huìfēng Yínháng; Ocean Hotel, 5 Yuan-yang Guangchang)

Post

Dongzhan post office (Map p156; Dōngzhàn yóujú; ☯ 8.30am-6.30pm) Has Express Mail Service and poste restante; next to the main train station.
Post office (Map p156; yóujú; 153 Jiefang Beilu)

Tourist Information & Travel Agencies

China International Travel Service (CITS; Map p154; ☎ 2835 8309; fax 2835 2619; 22 Youyi Lu; ☯ 8.30am-5pm Mon-Fri)
Tianjin Tourism Bureau (Map p154; ☎ 2835 4860; fax 2835 2324; 22 Youyi Lu; ☯ 8.30am-5pm) Next door to the CITS.

SIGHTS
Treaty Port Architecture

公约港建筑   **Map p156**

Tiānjīn itself is a museum of European architecture from the turn of the 20th century. One minute you're in little Vienna, turn a corner and you could be in a London street, hop off a bus and you're looking at some vintage French wrought-iron gates or a neo-Gothic cathedral. Be on the look-out for concession-era details: Corinthian pillars, churches, old warehouses and buildings with lobbies revealing old wooden staircases leading up into dark European interiors.

Walking north along **Jiefang Beilu** (the section south of its intersection with Yingkou Dao was called Rue de France; north of the intersection it was Victoria Rd) the Astor Hotel (itself a historic building – pop in for a browse), at No 108, is the decaying nobility and wrought-iron balconies of the former **Kincheng Bank** (Jīnchéng Yínháng; built in 1937). Just a little bit further north on the corner is the old site of the **Huabi Bank**, dating back to the 1920s. On the other side of Jiefang Beilu, at No 157, is the former address of **Jardine Matheson &**

TIĀNJĪN IN...

One Day
Spend the morning exploring the **treaty port architecture** of the former foreign concessions in the centre of town, followed by looking for gems and spotting bargains at the **Antique Market**; best on a Sunday. In the afternoon, stroll along **Ancient Culture Street** and visit the **Tianhou Temple** before a trip to the **Monastery of Deep Compassion** via **Wanghailou Church**. Round off the day dining at a restaurant recommended in the Eating section.

Two Days
Follow the same itinerary for the first day and make a morning trip to the **Shi Family Courtyard** on the second day before returning to town to explore the old Chinese sector of Tiānjīn's **Chinatown**, where you can visit the **Confucius Temple** and its small **Confucius Temple antiques market**, the **Guangdong Guild Hall** and the **Drum Tower**, and get some shopping done in the vicinity before perusing shops in the rest of town. Round off the day with a drink at one of the bars in the Entertainment section.

Co Building (Yíhé Yángháng), decorated with huge pillars. North on the next corner at No 153 is the former **Chartered Bank of India, Australia and China** (Màijiālì Yínháng), a colossal and overblown edifice with vast pillars now serving as a post office. The grandiose and huge former **Citibank Building** (First National City Bank of New York; Huāqí Yínháng) across the road at No 90 dates from 1918; now it's the Agricultural Bank of China. Pop in and have a peek at the interior during banking hours. The former **Hong Kong & Shanghai Bank Building** (Huìfēng Yínháng), a pompous creation further along at No 82 is now the Bank of China, opposite the old address of the **Sino-Russian Bank** (Huáè Dàoshèng Yínháng) dating from 1895. Next door to No 82, is the former **Yokohama Specie Bank Ltd** (Héngbīn Zhèngjīn Yínháng) dating from 1926 and now also a Bank of China. Across the way on the corner is the old address of the monumental **Sino-French Industrial and Commercial Bank** (Zhōngfǎ Gōngshāng Yínháng), dating from 1932. The **former Tientsin (Tianjin) Post Office** can be found across the way, while around the corner on Chengde Dao is the **Tianjin Fine Art Museum** (p157), housed in the former French Municipal Administration Council Building (built in 1924).

Also explore the roads leading off from Jiefang Lu. At No 9 Tai'an Dao is a small **Anglican Church** (Ānlǐgān Jiàotáng). Just along the road from Kiessling's Bakery (p158) on Zhejiang Lu, the Number 3 Guesthouse (Disan Zhaodaisuo) on Zhejiang Lu was the **Former Dakuo Hotel** (Dàkuò Fàndiàn), built in 1931. Around **Zhongxin Park** (Zhōngxīn Gōngyuán) are more European-style mansions.

Another excellent district for travellers to wander around is the area known as **Wǔdàdaò** (五大道; Five Large Roads; Map p154), an area rich in European-style villas and the former residences of the well-to-do of the early 20th century. Consisting of five roads in the south of the city – Machang Dao, Changde Dao, Munan Dao, Dali Dao and Chengdu Dao – the streets are wide and particularly reminiscent of Europe, lined with charming houses dating from the 1930s. Many villas here are brick with red tiles, such as those at No 117 Kunming Lu (dating from 1934), No 141 Munan Dao and No 66 Dali Dao. Many have plaques outside identifying former inhabitants.

Of Tiānjīn's other churches, **Wanghailou Church** (Wànghǎilóu Jiàotáng; Map p154; cnr Haihe Donglu & Shizilin Dajie) was built in 1869. Burnt to the ground by locals in 1870, killing 10 nuns in the process, it was rebuilt by the Qing government in 1897, only to be trashed three years later during the Boxer Rebellion. Restored again in 1904, it was further damaged by the 1976 Tángshān earthquake. The church is closed but can be appreciated from the outside. On Gold Steel Bridge (Jīngāng Qiáo) north of the church, look out for itinerant walnut, bread and cake-sellers, sorcerers, palm readers and necromancers.

The **Catholic Church** (Xīkāi Tiānzhǔ Jiàotáng; southern end of Binjiang Dao) is the largest church in Tiānjīn and was built by the French in 1917. Serious damage during the Cultural Revolution caused it to close for a number of years. Services are permitted again and are held daily at 6am and 7.30am, when you can look around inside. The church is easy to find: you will spot the twin onion domes a mile off.

Built by the Germans, Tiānjīn's west train station (Xīzhàn; p160) is a marvellous red-brick and red-tile building. Perhaps not worth going out of your way for a visit, you can see it if departing from or arriving at the station.

Antique Market 古玩市场

The **Antique Market** (Map p156; Gǔwán Shìchǎng; cnr Jinzhou Dao & Shandong Lu; 7.30am-3pm Sat & Sun) is one of the best sights in Tiānjīn. In every direction, vendors spread blankets along the *hútòng* (narrow alleyways) making it a fascinating place to stroll around. Among the many items on sale are stamps, silverware, porcelain, clocks, Mao iconography and Cultural Revolution memorabilia.

According to the locals, much of what is on display was seized during the Cultural Revolution and warehoused; the government is now slowly selling the stuff off to vendors who, in turn, resell it in Tiānjīn. These goods supposedly come from all over China. Many of the items carry stickers on the back indicating when, where and from whom the goods were seized.

Just why everything wasn't immediately destroyed is subject to speculation – possibly it was to be used as evidence at political trials, or maybe some official was a closet

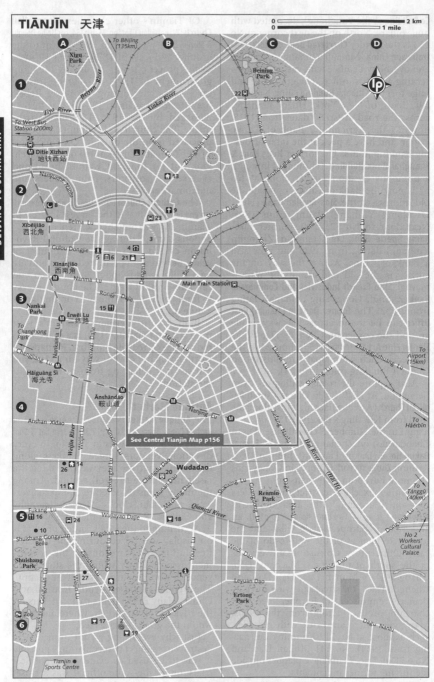

TIĀNJĪN 天津

0 _____ 2 km
0 _____ 1 mile

To Běijīng
(135km)

Xigu
Park

Běiníng
Park

Zhongshan Beilu

22

Zhongshan Beilu

Tiyo River

Xinkai River

Beijing River

To West Bus
Station (200m)

25

Ditie Xizhan
地铁西站

7

Nanyunhe Nanlu

13

Zhongshan Lu

Jinzhonghe Dajie

Haihe Lu

Zhenli Dao

Honggiao Lu

8

Xibĕijiǎo
西北角

Belma Lu

9

23

Shizilin Dajie

Xinkai Lu

Gulou Dongjie

3

Beian Dao

5   6

4

21

Dongma Lu

Xīnánjiǎo
西南角

Nanma Lu

Main Train Station

Nankai
Park

Rongji Dajie

15

Èrwĕi Lu
二纬路

Heping Lu

Huwei Lu

Zhangguzhuang Lu

To Airport
(15km)

To
Changhong
Park

Nankama Lu

Nanmenwai Dajie

Changjiang Lu

Hǎiguāng Sì
海光寺

Weijin River

Ānshāndào
鞍山道

Anshan Xidao

Nanjing Lu

Shijing Lu

Jiefang Nanlu

Hai River

To
Hǎ'ĕrbīn

See Central Tiānjīn Map p156

26   14

11

Xinxing Lu

Xiqing Dao

Wudadao

Chengdu Dao

Munan Dao

20

Machang Dao

Qiangzi River

Shaoxing Lu

Renmín
Park

Guangdong Lu

Dagu Nanlu

To
Tánggū
(40km)

Fukang Lu

16

24

Wujiayao Dajie

18

Dongling Lu

No 2
Workers'
Cultural
Palace

10

Shuishang Gongyuan
Beilu

Pingshan Dao

Youyi Lu

Weidi Dao

Shuishang
Park

Shuishang Gonglu

Jinzhan Lu

27

Qingnianxi Dao

12

Binshui Dao

Xinweidi Dao

Leyuan Dao

Ertong
Park

Dagu Nanlu

Zoo

17

2

19

Tiānjīn
Sports Centre

antique buff. Of course, not all that you see is real – there are fake antiques, fake stickers and so on.

The market is best on Sunday. A few die-hard vendors set up shop during the week for real antique enthusiasts. Get there early for the best selection.

Ancient Culture Street 古文化街

This street (Gǔwénhuà Jiē, Map p154) is a re-creation of an ancient Chinese street. Besides the traditional buildings, the road is lined with vendors plugging every imaginable type of cultural goody including Chinese calligraphy, paintings, tea sets, paper cuts, clay figurines and *chops* (name seals).

On the western side of the street is the fascinating **Tianhou Temple** (Tiānhòu Gōng; admission Y3; 🕃 8.30am-4.30pm). Tianhou (Heaven Queen), goddess of the sea, is also known as Mazu and Niangniang. Enter into a hall and pass the overbearing four great Taoist door gods. The temple was seriously desecrated in 1966, the Drum Tower being completely destroyed; now restored, you can throw a coin at the drum within for good luck. In the Bell Tower, you can also strike the bell for more good fortune (Y5).

You can also skirt a small spring called the Mazu Spring that bubbles up within the temple. The main hall is the Niang-niang Palace, with its effigy of Tianhou in a glass case, flanked by ferocious-looking weapons with attendant monsters alongside. The large fresco depicts scenes from Tianhou's life. There is a small exhibition of traditional marriage clothing and customs in one of the side halls.

Monastery of Deep Compassion 大悲禅院

The **Monastery of Deep Compassion** (Map p154; Dàbēichán Yuàn; ☎ 2626 1769; 40 Tianwei Lu; admission Y4; 🕃 9am-4.30pm) is Tianjin's most important Buddhist temple. Pass the beggars at the door, then enter through the Hall of Heavenly Kings to find a figure of Milefo (the future Buddha) flanked by the four Heavenly Kings. Worshippers congregate outside the **Shijiabao Hall** (Shìjiābǎo Diàn), which houses a large, central statue of Sakyamuni (Buddha) flanked by 18 *luóhàn* (Buddhist monks). At the rear of the hall is a large, modern, golden effigy of the Goddess of Mercy, Guanyin. The next large hall contains a huge and golden multiarmed statue of Guanyin holding an array of Buddhist instruments and surrounded by a panoply of further effigies of the goddess. The eyes of the main statue follow you around the hall. The hall to the rear was, at the time of writing, off limits. The temple is in the northern part of the city, a short walk from the Tianjin Holiday Inn and is busiest with worshippers on the 1st and 15th of each month. The road leading up to the temple is an extraordinary market of religious paraphernalia, including prayer mats, books, Buddhist rosaries, talismans, statues, incense and gifts for Buddha.

Chinatown 老城区   Map p154

Sorry, but we couldn't resist this misnomer. The old Chinese sector can easily be identified on the bus map as a rectangle with buses running around the perimeter. Roughly, the boundary roads are: Beima Lu (North Horse), Nanma Lu (South Horse), Xima Lu (West Horse) and Dongma Lu (East Horse). Originally there was one main north–south street, crossing an east–west one within that walled rectangle. Explore the lanes and side streets where traditional architecture remains, and perhaps stumble upon a dilapidated temple or two. At the centre is the restored **Drum Tower** (Gŭ Lóu; Chengxiang Zhonglu) which contains an exhibition of old domiciles within the Chinese quarter and the small *hútòng* that used to exist here. Decorated with *páilou* (decorative archways), the pedestrianised shopping street north of the Drum Tower is good for jade, pearls, souvenirs and reproduction furniture. You can

get a name chop here or have your name penned in calligraphy. From Chengxiang Donglu to the Drum Tower is a restored section of traditional Chinese houses, in the middle of which on the north side of the road stands a small and dilapidated brickwork church. Near the Drum Tower is the **Guangdong Guild Hall** (Guǎngdōng Hùi Guǎn; ☎ 2727 3443; 31 Nanmenli Dajie; ☾ 9am-4pm Tue-Sun), also known as the Museum of Opera, which was built in 1907 and was the last traditional opera house to be constructed in China before the modern opera house took over. It is also of historical relevance because Dr Sun Yatsen, known as the father of modern China, gave an important speech here in 1912. The **Confucius Temple**

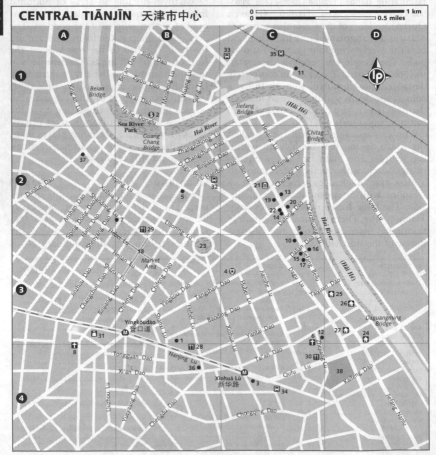

CENTRAL TIÃNJÏN 天津市中心

BĚIJĪNG TO SHÀNGHĂI

(Wén Miào; ☎ 2727 2812; 1 Dongmennei Dajie; admission Y4; ⏱ 9am-4.30pm Tue-Sun) was built in 1436 during the Ming dynasty. There are some decorative archways of interest, otherwise it's worth coming here for the **Confucius Temple antiques market** (Wénmiào gǔwán chéng) that sets up here daily, although it's busiest at the weekends. There's a large selection of Chinese literature, as well as books, propaganda posters and pamphlets from the Cultural Revolution (genuine posters cost between Y30 and Y100).

Mosque 清真寺
Although distinctly Chinese in style, this large mosque (Map p154; Qīngzhēnsì; 6 Dasi Qian) is an active place of worship for the Muslim community. It's not officially open to the public and unless you're Muslim, you are unlikely to be allowed in. If you want to try, make sure you're suitably attired. The area surrounding the mosque is an intriguing maze of *hútòng* that are well worth exploring.

Tianjin Fine Art Museum 天津艺术博物馆
The museum (Map p156; Tiānjīn Yìshù Bówùguǎn; 12 Chengde Dao; admission Y5; ⏱ 8.30am-noon & 1.30-5pm Tue-Sun) suffers from appalling lighting, but you can just about make out the prints and dreamy mist-infused silk landscape paintings on the 3rd floor.

Zhou Enlai Memorial Hall 周恩来纪念馆
Former Chinese premier Zhou Enlai grew up in Shàoxìng, Zhèjiāng province, but he attended school in Tiānjīn, so his classroom desk and schoolbooks are enshrined. The **memorial hall** (Map p154; Zhōu Ēnlái Jìniànguǎn; ☎ 2352 9257, 1 Shuishang Gongyuan Beilu; admission Y10; ⏱ 8.30am-5pm) charts the life of Zhou and his wife Deng Yingchao through photos and memorabilia. The memorial hall is next to Shuishang Park (Shuǐshàng Gōngyuán). Take bus No 8 to Bālǐ Tái from the main train station, and then bus No 54 to the Memorial Hall.

SLEEPING
Budget
Tianjin University School of International Education (Guójì Jiàoyù Xuéyuàn Yǒuyuán Gōngyù; Map p154; ☎ 2740 4372; iso@tju.edu.cn; 92 Weijin Lu; s/ste Y80/160) This is an excellent place with clean, well-kept rooms with TV, phone (incoming only), air-con, kettle, shower, safe and spacious wardrobe (plus your own key). It's a few minutes' walk to the left and south after entering Tianjin University's main gate.

Tianjin University Experts' Building (Tiānjīn Dàxué Zhuānjiā Zhāodàisuǒ; Map p154; ☎ 2740 7508; fax 2335 8714; Beiyang Dao; d/q Y196/420) Smart university accommodation can be found at this decent option. It's a metallic building at the corner of the lake near the Tianjin University west gate (xī mén).

Mid-Range

All rooms are subject to an additional 15% service charge. Discounts are common in most hotels.

Nankai University Foreigner Guesthouse (Nánkāi Dàxué Zhuānjiālóu; Map p154; Nankai University, 91 Weijin Lu; ☎ 2350 1504; d/ste Y400/600) This is an excellent place, with newly redecorated rooms and spacious doubles coming with drawing room, kitchen, bathroom and large bedroom. All rooms, arranged over four floors, are well kept and of good quality. The staff are very used to dealing with foreigners.

Míngzhūyuán (Map p154; Nankai University, 91 Weijin Lu; ☎ 2350 8028/8022; tw Y200, ste without/with balcony Y420/480) Next to the Nankai University Foreigner Guesthouse, this place has huge but rather grubby suites. Twins are spacious with large TVs, but they are nothing special. Complimentary breakfast is provided.

Tianjin First Hotel (Tiānjīn Dìyī Fàndiàn; Map p156; ☎ 2330 9988; fax 2312 3000; 158 Jiefang Beilu; rooms/ste Y664/913) Decked out with an original lift dating to concession days, this historic hotel boasts considerable Old-World charm (despite the newish wood panelling in the foyer), enormous bright rooms and even bigger bathrooms (but the carpets need replacing). Considerable discounts are often available (doubles down to Y412), so ask. Home of the brick-styled Feeling Bar. All major credit cards are accepted.

Imperial Palace Hotel (Tiānjīn Huánggōng Fàndiàn; Map p156; ☎ 2319 0888; fax 2319 0222; 177 Jiefang Beilu; s/d 360/420) Housed in a cosy building built by a British merchant in 1923, this old place has a sense of history but distinctly average, albeit inexpensive, rooms; the staff try hard and the bellboy does his best in his pantomime-quality red coat, but investment is needed.

Top End

All rooms are subject to an additional 15% service charge.

Hyatt Regency (Kǎiyuè Fàndiàn; Map p156; ☎ 2331 8888; www.hyatt.com; 219 Jiefang Beilu; d/ste US$138/250) The four-star Hyatt is set in an elegant building (its interior is showing slight signs of wear) on Jiefang Beilu and comes with some fine restaurants (including Xiang Wei Zhai, right), although rooms fall short of the Hyatt's usual high standard.

New World Astor Hotel (Lìshùndé Dàfàndiàn; Map p156; ☎ 2331 1688; astorbc@mail.zlnet.com.cn; 33 Tai'erzhuang Lu; tw/ste from Y1105/1700) This hotel retains the feel of foreign concession days. The ground floor has some interesting memorabilia on display including Emperor Puyi's gramophone.

Tianjin Holiday Inn (Jiàrì Fàndiàn; Map p154; ☎ 2628 8888; fax 2628 6666; 288 Zhongshan Lu; standard/deluxe d US$130/150) With a modern and marbled interior, and a steel and glass exterior, the Holiday Inn offers efficient service, quality and decent dining options (see following); there is also a small deli (☯ 8am-10pm) at the entrance to the Orchid Café. Regular promotions and a swimming pool are further incentives to stay.

Sheraton Hotel (Xǐláidēng Dàjiǔdiàn; Map p154; ☎ 2334 3388; www.sheraton.com; Zijinshan Lu; d/ste from US$108/160) The Sheraton is an excellent hotel with monthly promotions that make a stay here affordable even to those on a modest budget. Rates include a buffet breakfast.

EATING

Shípǐn Jiē (Food Street; Map p154; couple of blocks south of Nanma Lu) This covered alley has two levels of restaurants; you can choose from up to 50 restaurants. Prices vary (with some outlets being particularly expensive) and this is the place to come for a taste of exotica. You can try snake (expensive), dog meat (cheap) and eels (mid-range). Tiānjīn's sweet specialities such as 18th Street Dough Twists can be found here and you will also discover a branch of Donglaishun, the famous hotpot restaurant. Just one block north of Shípǐn Jiē is Rongji Dajie, an alley that boasts its fair share of restaurants.

Xiāng Wèi Zhāi (Map p156; ☎ 2331 8888; 2nd fl, Hyatt Hotel, 219 Jiefang Beilu; meals Y75) This is a well-presented, uncluttered and appealing corner restaurant that overlooks the Hai River. The *jiǎozi* (dumplings) are not cheap, but they are excellent. Enjoy a bowl of 10 lamb (*yángròu*) or pork (*zhūròu*) *jiǎozi* (Y25) while watching the bicycles surge over the bridge below. The spicy lamb soup (*málà yángròutāng*) is a must (Y25).

Kiessling's Bakery (Qǐshílín Xǐshì Cāntīng; Map p156; 33 Zhejiang Lu; cakes from Y5, milkshakes Y12) Mr Kiessling, the former chef for the German Emperor William II, established this bakery in 1918. The original structure is still standing. The bakery has grown to include an ice-cream parlour, a coffee shop and a self-service restaurant. The cakes are distributed across the city at various shops and restaurants.

Gǒubùlǐ (Map p156; ☎ 2730 2540; 77 Shandong Lu; set menu Y13-18; ◔ breakfast, lunch & dinner) Located between Changchun Dao and Binjiang Dao, this is the king of dumpling shops with a century-old history. The house speciality is *bāozi* (steamed dough bun), filled with high-grade pork, spices and gravy. You can also get *bāozi* with special fillings including chicken, shrimp or their delicious veggie version *shūcài bāozi*. What's more, Gǒubùlǐ's *bāozi* aren't greasy (a rarity in these parts). There are further branches around town, including the ground floor of Shipin Jie and opposite Kiessling's Bakery, now a kind of jazzy fast food McDonalds-style affair.

Orchid Café (Map p154; ☎ 2628 6666 ext 510; Tianjin Holiday Inn; 288 Zhongshan Lu; lunch/dinner buffet Y48/68; ◔ lunch noon-2pm & dinner 6-9.30pm) The Orchid Café has very good and filling buffet food, including stews, risottos, duck, salads and cakes. Although it's self- service, add 15% for the surcharge.

Eardrum Fried Cake Shop (Érduǒyǎn Zhágāodiàn; Map p156; 96 Nanjing Lu; cakes Y1) Getting its name from its proximity to Eardrum Lane when it first opened over 80 years ago, this place specialises in cakes made from rice powder, sugar and bean paste, all fried in sesame oil. Other specialities include the wonderfully named *kāikǒu xiàobǐng* (open your mouth and laugh cakes). There are branches all over town.

T.G.I. Friday's (Xīngqīwǔ Cāntīng; Map p154; ☎ 2300 5555/5656; Tàidá Guójì Huìguǎn bldg, 7 Fukang Lu; meals Y100+) This place has all the usual T.G.I. Friday props and salads, burgers, pasta, steaks, chicken and seafood dishes etc. All major credit cards are accepted. You can find it south across the way from Nankai University.

ENTERTAINMENT

Besides the following recommendations, try to get hold of a copy of the expat magazine *Jin* (www.expatriate-jin.com) which has listings of restaurants, bars and cultural events in town.

Cosy Café & Bar (Kèsītè Xīcān Jiǔbā; Map p154; ☎ 2312 6616; 68 Changde Dao; meal Y60-100; live music 8.30pm Wed-Mon) In the heart of the Wudadao district (see p152), this downstairs bar has table football, pool, a stage for live music (rock and Latin) and a dance floor. You can also watch MTV.

Mojo Bar & Café (Mózhōu Xīcān Jiǔbā; Map p154; ☎ 2352 4510; 7 Huanhu Zhongdao; burgers Y30-40) This fine restaurant-cum-bar delivers some very good American food (burgers, fishfingers, nachos etc) alongside live music, sports TV, darts and pool. Overseen by professional, youngsters who speak better English than at T.G.I. Friday's, it's a great place for an evening.

New York Music Kitchen (Nǐuyuē Yīnyuè Chúfáng; Map p154; ☎ 2353 9598; 212 Weidi Dao; ◔ 11.30am-1am Tue-Sun) This large upstairs place serves food in a setting that rings around the dance floor and bar. It also has regular live acts.

SHOPPING

Shopping at the Antique Market (p153), Ancient Culture Street (p155) and the Confucius Temple Antiques Market (see p157) is a must if you're on the hunt for souvenirs and curios. The area around the Drum Tower is another good shopping district for jade and souvenirs.

Binjiang Dao and Heping Lu (Map p156) are major shopping streets. Including alleyways and other commercial streets in the area, there is something like eight blocks of concentrated shopping to be found here. At the southern end of Binjiang Dao, running parallel to the street, is a clothing market with more than 100 stalls. Also at the southern end is **Isetan** (Map p156; ☎ 2722-1111; Jili Bldg, Nanjing Lu, ◔ 10am-8.30pm).

One of the more unusual shopping areas is Xiǎobǎi Lóu, a market area off Qufu Lu. In addition to the brand-name shops and market stalls housed along the lanes, there is the **Foreign Goods Market** (Bǎihuò Shìchǎng; Map p156). This is a fantastic (and very unusual for China) market selling second-hand clothes imported from Europe, Japan and Korea. The enormous selection includes leather aviator jackets, 1970s-style suits and retro dresses that can be picked up for as little as Y10. Running parallel to the Foreign Goods Market is a well-stocked, inexpensive fabric market.

The French hypermarket chain, Carrefour, has five branches in town including shops in the New World Shopping Centre (Map p154; ☎ 2726 9696; 138 Dongma Lu; ◔ 8.30am-10pm) and a second outlet on Baita Lu (☎ 2741 6464; 168 Baita Lu; ◔ 8.30am-10.30pm).

Brightly coloured clay figurines are a local speciality. They originated in the 19th century with the work of Zhang Mingshan and today, his fifth-generation descendants continue to train new craftspeople.

Zhang Caisu Clay Figure Workshop (Nírén Zhāng Căisù Gōngzuòshì; ☎ 2337 4085; 270 Machang Dao) is where the statues are made today. The small figures take themes from human or deity sources and the emphasis is on realistic emotional expressions.

GETTING THERE & AWAY

Air   Map p156

Tiānjīn's Binhai International Airport (Map p151; Tiānjīn Bīnhăi Guójì Jīchăng; ☎ 2490 2950) is 15km east from the city centre.

There are flights with Korean Air to Seoul and Civil Aviation Administration of China (CAAC; Zhōngguó Mínháng) offers daily direct flights between Hong Kong and Tiānjīn. Japan Airlines (JAL, Rìběn Hángkōng) flies to Osaka and Nagoya, but for flights to Tokyo you must fly from Běijīng. You can fly to most major cities in China from Tiānjīn, including Qīngdǎo (Y530, daily) and Shànghǎi (Y840, three per day).

Tickets can be bought from CITS and at the following:

All Nippon Airways (Quánrì Kōng; ☎ 2339 6688; 1st fl, Hyatt Regency, 219 Jiefang Beilu)

CAAC (☎ 2330 1543; 103 Nanjing Lu)

JAL (☎ 2313 9766; International Bldg; 75 Nanjing Lu)

Korean Air (Dàhán Hángkōng; ☎ 2399 0088; International Bldg, 75 Nanjing Lu)

Tianjin Air-Sales Agency (☎ 2330 1098; International Bldg, 75 Nanjing Lu) Can book flights on most airlines.

Boat

Tiānjīn's harbour is Tánggū, 50km (30 minutes by train or one hour by bus) from Tiānjīn. See p162 for details of arriving and departing by boat.

Bus

Express buses to Běijīng (Y25, 1½ hours, 7.30am to 6.30pm) depart hourly from the front of Tiānjīn's main train station and from near the Xiǎobǎi Lóu market on Qufu Lu. Regular buses to Běijīng (Y30, 6.30am to 5pm) run from the **Liuyisan Lu bus station** (Map p156; Liùyīsān Lù Qìchēzhàn) off Nanjing Lu east of the International Building. You can also catch bus No 613 to Tánggū from here (Y5, one hour). In Běijīng, catch Tiānjīn-bound buses (Y25, every 30 minutes) from the Zhaogongkou bus station (p138) on the southern side of town, but make sure they head to Tiānjīn's main train station (Tiānjīn huǒchē zhàn), if that is where you are headed. Express buses also leave from outside Běijīng train station (p139; Y25, 1½ hours).

There are four long-distance bus stations in Tiānjīn. Bus No 815 leaves from **bus station No 1** (yīlù qìchēzhàn; Map p156; cnr Haerbin Dao & Dagu Beilu) for Tánggū (Y5, one hour). Other bus stations are located at intervals along the direction of travel. The **south bus station** (bālǐtái qìchēzhàn; Map p154), southwest of the city centre, is where you catch buses going south. The **west bus station** (xī qìchēzhàn; 2 Xiqing Dao) is near Tiānjīn's west train station.

The **northeast bus station** (dōngběijiǎo qìchēzhàn; Map p154) serves the most destinations. From here buses leave to Jìxiàn and Wǔqīng. The bus station is very close to Ancient Culture Street. Bus No 24 from the city centre will drop you nearby.

Train

Tiānjīn is a major north–south train junction with frequent trains to Běijīng, extensive links with the northeastern provinces, and lines southwards to Guǎngzhōu (hard seat/hard sleeper Y266/465), Jǐ'nán (Y52), Nánjīng (hard seat/hard sleeper Y137/242), Shànghǎi (hard seat/hard sleeper Y165/291), Sūzhōu (hard seat/hard sleeper Y154/272) and Shíjiāzhuāng (hard seat/hard sleeper Y63/115). There are two fast overnight trains daily to Qingdao (Y80, 11 hours); trains leave from the West Train Station.

There are three train stations in Tiānjīn: main, north and west. Most trains leave from the **main train station** (Tiānjīn Zhàn; ☎ 2430 6444). If you have to alight at the **west train station** (Map p154; ☎ 2618 2662), bus No 24 (runs 24 hours) will take you to the main train station.

Eleven daily express air-con double-decker trains depart Běijīng train station for Tiānjīn (soft seat Y40, 1½ hours, first/last train 8.05am/7.46pm). Purchase your tickets in Běijīng up the escalator in the departure hall at one of the kiosks or at the automatic machines. In the return direction, tickets for express trains to Běijīng (soft seat Y40, 11/2 hours, first/last train 6.09am/6.08pm) can be bought at the ticket office through the Tiānjīn main train station entrance (not the main ticket office) on the right-hand side.

GETTING AROUND
To/From the Airport

Taxis ask for Y40 or more to take you to the airport from the city centre. Buses run from the CAAC ticket office. Minibuses for Běijīng's airport leave from the CAAC every 30 minutes between 5am and 6pm (Y70, 2½hours).

Bus

Key local transport junctions are the areas around the three train stations. The main train station has the biggest collection: bus Nos 24, 27 and 13, and further out towards the river are Nos 2, 5, 25, 28 and 96. At the west train station are Nos 24, 10 and 31 (Nos 11 and 37 run past the west train station); and at the north train station are Nos 1, 7 and 12.

Another major bus station point is around Zhongxin Park, at the edge of the central shopping district. From here you can get bus Nos 11 and 94, and nearby are bus Nos 9, 20 and 37. To the north of Zhongxin Park are bus Nos 1, 91, 92 and 93.

A useful bus to know is the No 24, which runs between the main and west stations 24 hours a day. Also noteworthy is bus No 8 – it starts at the main train station then zig zags down to the southwest of town. With the exception of bus No 24, buses run from 5am to 11pm.

Subway

Closed at the time of writing for refurbishment and extension, the subway (dìtiě) runs all the way from Nanjing Lu to the west train station.

Taxi

The cheapest taxis are the yellow minivans (Y5 for the first 5km and then Y1 per km up to 10km). For standard taxis, flag fall is Y5 for the first 3km, then Y1.5 per kilometre thereafter.

AROUND TIĀNJĪN

Tiānjīn can be used as a starting point for trips directly north to Jìxiàn and to the Great Wall at Yellow Cliff Pass, as well as Běidàihé in Héběi and on into the northeast (Manchuria).

SHI FAMILY COURTYARD 石家大院

In Yángliǔqīng in the western suburbs of Tiānjīn is this marvellous **Shi Family residence** (Shí Jiā Dàyuàn; admission Y10; ⏰ 9am-4.30pm), composed of numerous courtyards and similar to the more famous Qiao Family Courtyard House (p396), which is not far from Píngyáo. Belonging to a prosperous merchant family, the residence contains a theatre and 278 rooms, some of which are furnished. From Tiānjīn, take bus No 153 from the west train station or bus No 672 from the Tianjin Department Store to Yángliǔqīng. A taxi will cost you Y70 return.

TÁNGGŪ 塘沽

About 50km from Tiānjīn, Tánggū is one of China's major international seaports. There is little of interest in Tánggū and most travellers visit to catch ferries to Dàlián (northeast China), Kōbe (Japan) or Incheon (South Korea).

Chaoyin Temple (潮音寺; Cháoyīn Sì; ☎ 2531 1882; 1 Chaoyinsi Dajie; admission Y2; ⏰ 8am-5pm) Built in 1404 by fishermen to pray to Guanyin for safe passages at sea, this lovely temple features a number of interesting goddesses, including Songzi Guanyin to whom women pray if they have trouble getting pregnant. In the hall to your right as you enter the temple sits Wangsan Grandmother (Wángsān Nǎinai), a figure from local folklore who it is believed can cure ailments. Bus No 110 or 617 will get you here.

Dagu Fort (大沽炮台; Dàgū Pàotái; ☎ 2588 8544; Paotai Lu; admission Y5; ⏰ 8am-6pm) This fort on the southern bank of Hai River dates from the 16th century. There is a small museum chronicling the various invasions by foreign imperialists and a collection of large iron cannons. Bus No 110 from Tanggu train station drops you at the end of the road; from there it's a five or 10 minute walk to the fort.

Sleeping

Kangda Hotel (康大饭店; Kāngdà Fàndiàn; ☎ 2579 5941; Xingang Erhao Lu; d Y100) This is the only budget option within the vicinity of the ferry pier – it's the red-brick building across the train tracks. Rooms are fairly grotty, but tolerable; try for a room facing onto the courtyard.

TEDA Hotel International (泰达国际酒店; Tàidà Guójì Jiǔdiàn; ☎ 2532 6000; fax 2532 6216; 8 Dier

Dàjiē; d US$100) This bizarre, castle-like building is an upmarket option. Its amenities include a golf simulator, an ice-skating rink and a swimming pool. There is a 15% service charge.

Getting There & Away

From Tiānjīn, frequent minibuses and buses to Tánggū (Y5) leave from the main train station, from bus station No 1 and from the Liuyisan Lu bus station. In Tánggū, minibuses to Tiānjīn run from outside the train station. Occasional buses to Tiānjīn leave from outside the passenger ferry terminal.

From Tánggū, there are regular trains to Tiānjīn (Y3.5 to Y10, 30 minutes to one hour), and to Běidàihé (Y38, three hours).

If travelling by sea, there are daily boats to Dàlián (Y167-Y697, 13-16 hours), a weekly ferry to Kōbe (from Y1875, 48 hours) and twice-weekly boats to Incheon (from Y1000, 28 hours). Check in two hours before departure for international sailings.

Tickets can be purchased at the **passenger ferry terminal** (Tiānjīngǎng Kèyùnzhàn; ☎ 2570 6728), but if you're in Tiānjīn it's safer to buy in advance from CITS or at the **ticket office** (shòupiàochù; ☎ 2339 4290/9573; 1 Pukou Dao), south of the Hyatt and west off Tai'erzhuang Lu.

Héběi 河北

BĚIJĪNG TO SHÀNGHǍI

HIGHLIGHTS

- Get up close to the awesome multi-armed statue of **Guanyin** (p174) in Chéngdé's Puning Temple

- Amble around the ancient walled town of **Zhèngdìng** (p168) and its magnificent temple collection

- Take an expedition to the walled Ming garrison town of Shānhǎiguān to size up the Great Wall at **Jiāo Shān** (p178)

- Flee the summer heat of North China to lick ice creams in breezy **Běidàihé** (p179)

- Wander around the splendid collection at the **Hebei Provincial Museum** (p166) in Shíjiāzhuāng

Chéngdé ★

Shānhǎiguān ★
Běidàihé ★

★ Zhèngdìng
★ Shíjiāzhuāng

■ POP: 67.4 MIL   ■ AREA: 190,000 SQ KM

Wrapping itself around the centrally administered municipalities of prospering Běijīng and the manufacturing hub of Tiānjīn is the province of Héběi. The province – located north of the Yellow River (Huáng Hé), hence its name, 'North of the River' – is often seen as an extension of Běijīng and Tiānjīn, which is not far off the mark since, geographically speaking, the two municipalities take up a fair piece of the pie. But Héběi is more than a runtish sideshow or adjunct and comes up trumps with some first-rate sights.

Topographically, Héběi is divided into the mountainous tableland to the north, dramatically traversed by fragments of the Great Wall, and the monotonous dark brown earth of the southern plain. The region's agriculture, which is mainly wheat and cotton, is hampered by dust storms, droughts and flooding.

The Chinese claim that the human race possibly originated in Héběi may stir debate, but proximity to Běijīng guarantees the province a regular windfall of travellers (and the occasional anthropologist). The imperial retreat and temples of Chéngdé – together a Unesco World Heritage site – are stand-alone destinations that should not be missed. North of Shíjiāzhuāng, the provincial capital, historic Zhèngdìng is custodian to some of China's most important pagodas and constitutes a rewarding day trip. Along the northern coastline, near the Liáoníng province border, the walled town of Shānhǎiguān is a ragged snapshot of traditional north China: crisscrossed with small hútòng (alleyways), peopled by hospitable folk and overlooked by the Great Wall, which continues on to its terminus with the sea south of town.

Climate

Considerable temperature differences exist between the mountainous north and the south of the province, as well as between coastal and inland regions, but generally speaking Héběi gets very hot in summer (with an average temperature of 20°C to 27°C in July) and freezing cold in winter (average temperature in January -3°C) with dust fallout in spring and heavy rains in July and August. Autumn is the best season to visit.

Getting There & Away

Airports exist at Shíjiāzhuāng and Qínhuángdǎo, with flight connections to domestic destinations. Běijīng and Tiānjīn, with their transport facilities and infrastructure, can be used as a starting point for exploration of the province and for international connections. Héběi is linked to neighbouring and more distant provinces by both bus and rail. See p916 for more information.

Getting Around

The provincial rail hub is at Shíjiāzhuāng, with rail links to all major towns and cities in Héběi. Travel to Chéngdé, Běidàihé and Shānhǎiguān is best done from Běijīng or Tiānjīn. Bus connections cover the entire province (see the Getting There & Away sections under each destination for detailed information).

SHÍJIĀZHUĀNG 石家庄
☎ 0311 / pop 684,000

Besides Shíjiāzhuāng's splendid provincial museum, the railway junction city about 250km southwest of Běijīng has little to offer the visitor. For some travellers Shíjiāzhuāng is a useful transit point, while for most the real treat is the old walled town of Zhèngdìng (p168) to the north.

Shíjiāzhuāng has the biggest People's Liberation Army (PLA) officer training school in China, about 2km west of the city. For an industrial city known chiefly for its smokestacks, Shíjiāzhuāng also attracts hordes of itinerant beggars who swarm around the railway station district. Travellers looking for symbols of the current modernisation drive can view the large meter outside the Xinhua Bookstore on Zhongshan Donglu recording the decibel level of Shíjiāzhuāng's sonorous traffic and sulphur dioxide levels.

History

Shíjiāzhuāng is a city born of the railway age. For centuries little more than a modest-sized town, Shíjiāzhuāng was eclipsed by flourishing Zhèngdìng (p168) to the north until the railway network – constructed in the early 20th century – brought the town prosperity and a consequent population explosion.

Orientation

Most of the city's hotels and sights can be found along the east–west running Zhong-shan Lu, which divides into Zhongshan Xilu and Zhongshang Donglu, and the area around the train station.

MAPS

Maps of town (all in Chinese) can be purchased from map sellers around the train station and at Xinhua Bookstores.

Information

BOOKSHOPS

Xinhua Bookstore (199 Zhongshan Donglu; 9am-6.30pm) Next to the Yanchun Garden Hotel. A further branch is next to the Huiwen Hotel.

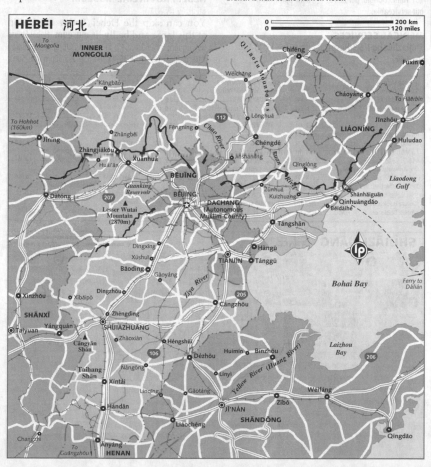

HÉBĚI 河北

0   200 km
0   120 miles

EMERGENCY & VISAS

PSB (83 Minzu Lu)

Visa office (☎ 702 4274; 8 Liming Jie; ⏰ 8am-noon & 1-5pm) Around the corner from PSB.

INTERNET ACCESS

Feiyue Internet Bar (Fēiyué Wǎngbā; 16 Dong Dajie; per hr Y2; ⏰ 8am-midnight) Head upstairs to this modern, new and slick outlet southeast of Hebei Provincial Museum.

Hongxing Internet Café (Hóngxīng Wǎngbā; 81 Yuhua Donglu; per hr Y2; ⏰ 8am-midnight)

Inhere Internet Café (Yínhé Wǎngbā; 260 Zhongshan Donglu; per hr Y2; ⏰ 8am-midnight)

Liliang Internet Café (Lìliàng Wǎngbā; 53 Yuhua Donglu; Y2 per hr; ⏰ 8am-midnight)

Xinbada (Sinbad) Internet Café (Xīnbādá Wǎngbā; 261 Yuhua Donglu; per hr Y2; ⏰ 8am-8pm) Grim but serviceable.

MEDICAL SERVICES

Shijiazhuang No 3 Hospital (☎ 604 5915; 15 Tiyu Nandajie)

MONEY

ATM (97 Zhongshan Xilu) On the west corner of Dongfang City Plaza Shopping Center. Takes Visa and MasterCard.

Bank of China (⏰ 8.30am-noon & 2-6pm) Through the west door of Dongfang City Plaza Shopping Center.

POST

Post office (cnr Gongli Jie & Zhongshan Xilu; ⏰ 24hr)

TOURIST INFORMATION & TRAVEL AGENCIES

China International Travel Service (CITS; Zhōngguó Guójì Lǚxíngshè) At the time of writing, CITS was in the process of moving.

Sights

HEBEI PROVINCIAL MUSEUM
河北省博物馆

You can skip the Hebei Today exhibition at this large and badly lit **museum** (Héběi Shěng Bówùguǎn; ☎ 604 5642, Zhongshan Donglu; admission Y10, guide Y50; ⏰ 8.30-11.30am & 2-5.30pm Tue-Sun),

SHÍJIĀZHUĀNG 石家庄

but there are some marvellous exhibits that warrant a visit. Upstairs are exhibitions on primitive settlements, early pottery, bronzes (including a bronze knocker with hydra with phoenix designs from the Warring States period), headless Bodhisattvas, marble effigies of Sakyamuni, gilt bronze Guanyin figurines and a constellation of pottery figures from the Northern Qi plus other artefacts from the Héběi region. A separate exhibition hall upstairs at the rear (shower caps are issued to cover your shoes) displays excavations from the Mancheng Western Han tombs, including two jade Han burial suits (belonging to Liusheng, emperor of Zhōngshān, and his wife Douwan), one of which is sewn with 1.1kg of gold thread. Also displayed is a resplendent reproduction Han chariot, plus funerary ornaments, including a huge array of pottery vessels.

REVOLUTIONARY MARTYRS' MAUSOLEUM
烈士陵园

This **mausoleum** (Lièshì Língyuán; ☎ 702 2904; 343 Zhongshan Xilu; admission Y3; ☉ 7.30am-6pm) is a pleasant tree-shaded park featuring an obelisk graced with calligraphy from Mao Zedong, Deng Xiaoping, Jiang Zemin and others. Among the shrines to communist martyrs is the tomb of the Canadian guerrilla doctor Norman Bethune (1890–1939). Bethune served as a surgeon with the Eighth Route Army in the war against Japan, and is eulogised in a Mao Zedong Thought – 'We must all learn the spirit of absolute selflessness from Dr Norman Bethune' (inscribed in Chinese on his tomb).

Sleeping
BUDGET
Bailin Hotel (Bǎilín Dàshà; ☎ 702 1398; fax 702 1887; 24 Chezhan Jie; s Y126-160, d Y140-300, tr Y280-420, ste Y420; 🈂) The Y160 singles have huge beds and the pricier doubles at this three-star hotel are of good quality. The TV video channel shows films of varying quality, but the staff are generally courteous, there are telephones in the bathrooms and the location opposite the train station is fine. The business doubles are large, but not worth the money.

MID-RANGE
Huiwen Hotel (Huìwén Dàjiǔdiàn; ☎ 787 9988; fax 701 5463; 6 Zhanqian Jie; s/d/ste Y268/348/490; 🈂) This

clean, fresh and newish hotel is modern and has some style, as well as an excellent location. Doubles are spacious with bathroom. You have to wait an eternity for the lift, however, as it grinds between the hotel's 27 floors.

Yanchun Garden Hotel (Yànchūn Huāyuán Jiǔdiàn; ☎ 667 1188; www.newyc.com.cn/en_gardenhotel/index .htm; 195 Zhongshan Donglu; s/d/ste incl breakfast Y350/550/750; 🈂) This modern, tower-like four-star hotel has very big rooms with vast TV sets, drinking water on tap, and smart and spacious shower rooms. Service is good, decent English is spoken but there are some odd touches, such as the tree at the rear of the foyer.

TOP END
Crowne Plaza (Shìmào Huángguān Jiǔdiàn; ☎ 667 8888; www.crowneplaza.com; 303 Zhongshan Donglu; d/ studios/ste Y818/988/1318; 🈂) This is the city's finest and most elegant hotel, a splendid five-star affair with huge and luxurious standard doubles (with bath and shower) that come with broadband Internet access, drinking water on tap and TV with HBO, CNN and ESPN. The studios are large and the suites come with bay windows. There's also a deli (open 9am to 9pm), Italian restaurant Pontini (live band nightly from 8.30pm to 1am), Chinese restaurant, café and bar.

Hebei Century Hotel (Héběi Shìjì Dàfandiàn; ☎ 703 6699; www.hebei-centuryhotel.com; 145 Zhongshan Xilu; d Y590-900, ste Y1100-8800; 🈂) Claiming to be five star, this silver tower in the west of town has reasonably smart, smallish and OK rooms with modestly sized bathrooms and minute baths. Facilities include tennis court, swimming pool, gym, underground parking, the Gem Bar on the 3rd floor (open 1pm to 2am) and a jazz restaurant. The staff speak reasonable English.

Eating
South of the Bailin Hotel is a long commercial street called **Yong'an Market** (Yǒng'ān Shìchǎng) where you can snack on cheap eats from Sìchuān, Lánzhōu, Wēnzhōu, Hui and Qīngzhēn street stalls and restaurants. Fast food is pretty widespread in Shíjiāzhuāng, with Pizza Hut, McDonalds, KFC and even Quick Burger adding its own Gallic touch (complete with piped French elevator music).

BĚIJĪNG TO SHANGHAI

Greenery Café (Lǜyīngé Kāfēitīng; ☎ 667 1188 ext 6666; Yanchun Garden Hotel, 195 Zhongshan Donglu; meals Y100; ☯ 7am-12.30am) In an enjoyable setting decorated with a Russian airplane fuselage (with seating) and undercarriage, this fun, Western restaurant serves up a range of international dishes, including steaks (Y38 to Y88), pizza and grilled meats, and there's a small wine list.

Qiánqīnggé Zhōupù (☎ 701 7757; 18 Zhanqian Jie; meals from Y20) As well as dozens of different types of *zhōu* (porridge) in steaming buckets, this highly popular and busy restaurant serves up exceedingly tasty Chinese staples such as the crispy and spicy *yúxiāng qiézi bāo* (spicy aubergine in a cooking pot; Y12) and *hóngshāo páigǔ* (braised spareribs; Y18). Filling porridge comes in all flavours, including *bābǎo* ('eight treasure' – a sweet concoction including berries and nuts; Y2), *shuǐguǒ* (fruit; Y2), *yángròu* (lamb; Y4) and *dìguā* (sweet potato; Y2).

Shopping
Dongfang City Plaza Shopping Center (Dōngfāng Dàshà; 97 Zhongshan Xilu; ☯ 9am-9pm) This shopping centre is located not far west of the train station.

Getting There & Away
AIR
Shíjiāzhuāng is connected by air to most provincial capitals as well as destinations such as Chóngqìng, Qínhuángdǎo, Shànghǎi, Shēnzhèn, Wēnzhōu and Xiàmén. There are daily flights to Běijīng.

BUS
From the central long-distance bus station (*chángtú qìchēzhàn*) there are regular services to Běijīng (Y45, five buses depart between 7.20am and 5pm) and numerous destinations including Hohhot (Y82, 3.30pm), Jǐnán (Y55, two per day), Níngbō (Y305, 10am), Shěnyáng (Y162, one per day), Qínhuángdǎo (Y105, 4.30pm), Tiānjīn (Y42, regular departures from 6am to 2pm), Yāntái (Y129, 1pm), Zhèngzhōu (Y45, six per day). Alternatively, head to the ticket office to the right of the main ticket hall for superior, luxury buses to Běijīng (Y70, every half hour); Jǐnán (Y82, nine per day), Nánjīng (Y240, sleeper at 4pm), Qīngdǎo (Y150, 11.30am), Shànghǎi (Y290, 4.30pm), Tiānjīn (Y85) and other destinations.

TRAIN
Shíjiāzhuāng is a major rail hub with comprehensive connections, including regular trains to/from Běijīng (express Y50, 2½ hours). Other destinations include Běidàihé (Y38 to Y94), Chéngdé (Y32 to Y38), Dàlián (Y76 to Y90), Dàtóng (Y38 to Y92), Jǐnán (Y63), Kowloon (hard sleeper Y596 to Y622; soft sleeper Y965), Nánjīng (Y59 to Y126) and Shànghǎi (Y72 to Y154).

Getting Around
Shíjiāzhuāng's airport is 40km northeast of town. **Civil Aviation Administration of China buses** (CAAC; Zhōngguó Mínháng; ☎ 505 4084; Y15) to the airport depart from the CAAC office at 471 Zhongshan Donglu; the office can be reached on bus No 5. There are two or three buses per day, with the first leaving at around 5.40am and the last leaving at around 5pm. A taxi to the airport will take about an hour and costs Y100. Taxis are Y5 at flag fall and Y1.40 per kilometre thereafter. Motor tricycles (*sānlún mótuōchē*) swarm around the train station and charge virtually the same as taxis.

AROUND SHÍJIĀZHUĀNG
Zhèngdìng 正定
☎ 0311
This prettified old wall town, 18km north of Shíjiāzhuāng, is the highlight of the area. The Chinese nicknamed Zhèngdìng the town of 'nine towers, four pagodas, eight great temples and 24 golden archways'. It still retains many of its temples and pagodas, and some of its archways (*páilou*) have been colourfully restored. Its once imposing city wall has sadly crumbled away, but the grand main gate in the south has been restored and the north gate is undergoing restoration. The through ticket (*tōngpiào*; Y60) gets you access to Dafo Temple, Tianning Temple, Kaiyuan Temple, the Liang Family Ancestral Temple, Guanghui Temple and Hua Pagoda, Changle Gate and the Confucius Temple; access to Linji Temple is not included.

SIGHTS
Of Zhèngdìng's many monasteries, the most famous is Longxing Temple (隆兴寺), more popularly known as **Dafo Temple** (大佛寺; Dàfó Sì; ☎ 878 6560; Zhongshan Donglu; admission Y30; ☯ 8am-5pm), or Big Buddha Temple,

located in the east of town. Tape guides are available, but only in Chinese. A useful map of Zhèngdìng is attached to the wall outside the ticket office (which calls the Confucius Temple the Confusion Temple).

Dating from AD 586, much of the temple has been restored. You are met in the first hall by the corpulent Milefo, or Laughing Buddha, here called the 'Monk with a Bag'. The four Heavenly Kings flanking him in pairs are typically vast and disconcerting. Beyond is a terrace, upon which the **Dajue Liushi Hall** (大觉六师殿) is undergoing reconstruction, funded by charitable contributions. Inside the Manichaean Hall is a huge gilded statue of Sakyamuni and some magnificent faded wall frescoes. At the rear of the hall is a distinctly male statue of the goddess **Guanyin** (see the boxed text on p174), seated in a lithe pose with one foot resting on her/his thigh (a posture known as *lalitásana*) and surrounded by *luóhàn* (those freed from the cycle of rebirth).

The **Buddhist Altar** (戒坛) behind houses an unusual bronze two-faced Buddha that was cast during the Ming dynasty, gazing north and south. There are two halls behind the Buddhist Altar. On the left is the Zhuanlunzang Pavilion, which contains remarkable revolving octagonal wooden bookcase. The hall to the right holds a magnificent painted and gilded Buddha.

Beyond these halls lie two stele pavilions that you pass on the way to the vast **Pavilion of Great Mercy** (大悲阁; Dàbēi Gé), which houses a bronze colossus of Guanyin, the Goddess of Mercy. At 21.3m high, cast in AD 971 and sporting a third eye, the effigy may lack the beauty and artistry of her sibling in Chéngdé's Puning Temple (p174), but she is still impressive. You can climb all the way up into the galleries surrounding Guanyin for free. The wooden hall in which the goddess is housed was rebuilt in 1999 after consulting Song dynasty architecture manuals.

Within the hall at the rear is a four-faced Buddha (the Buddha of four directions), crowned with another four-faced Buddha, upon which is supported a further set.

Enter **Tianning Temple** (天宁寺; Tiānníng Sì; admission Y5; ◷ 8am-6pm), around 650m west of Dafo Temple in an alleyway north off Zhongshan Donglu, and cross the remains of a now vanished temple hall. The 41m-high Tang-dynasty **Lofty Pagoda** (凌霄塔; Língxiāo Tǎ) – also called Mùtǎ or 'Wooden Pagoda' – dates from AD 779. The octagonal, nine-eaved and spire-topped pagoda is in fine condition and typical of Tang brickwork pagodas. If you wish to clamber up inside, torches are provided, but mind your head and the steep stairs. The views from the top are not great as the windows are small.

South of the crossroads between Zhongshan Donglu and Yanzhao Nandajie, **Kaiyuan Temple** (开元寺; Kāiyuán Sì; Yanzhao Nandajie; admission Y10) originally dates from AD 540. Little remains of the temple itself (the main temple hall was destroyed in 1966) and the Hall of Heavenly Kings now serves as the ticket office. The **Bell Tower** (钟楼) has survived, but the drawcard is the dirt-brown **Xumi Pagoda** (须弥塔), a well-preserved and unfussy early–Tang dynasty brickwork, nine-eaved structure, topped with a spire. Its round, arched doors are particularly attractive, as are the carved figures on the base; at the time of writing, the pagoda was cordoned off for fear of falling bricks.

Also displayed is a colossal stone *bìxì* (mythical, tortoise-like dragon) near the entrance with a vast chunk of its left flank missing and its head propped up on a plinth. Dating from the late Tang era, the creature was excavated in 2000 from a street in Zhèngdìng.

About 200m south of Kaiyuan Temple on the other side of the road is the **Liang Family Ancestral Temple** (梁氏宗祠; Liángshì Zōngcí; admission Y5), a Ming dynasty, five-bay wide single hall topped with dark tiles.

The active monastery of **Linji Temple** (临济寺; Línjì Sì; Linji Lu; admission Y8), around 700m southeast of Kaiyuan Temple, is notable for its tall, elegant, carved brick **Chengling Pagoda** (topped with an elaborate lotus plinth plus ball and spire) and the main hall behind, with a large gilt effigy of Sakyamuni and 18 golden *luóhàn*. At the rear of the hall is Puxian on elephant back, Wenshu on lion back and a figure of Guanyin.

Nothing remains of **Guanghui Temple** (广惠寺; Guānghuì Sì; admission Y10) further south, except for its unusual Indian-style pagoda decorated with lions, elephants, sea creatures, *púsa* (Bodhisattva) and other figures (some missing). With a brick base and four doors, the pagoda has stone-carved upper stories and a brickwork cap. You can climb the pagoda, but some of the lights don't work on the way up.

There is little to see at Zhèngdìng's **Confucius Temple** (文庙; Wén Miào), northwest of Kaiyuan Temple and north off Zhongshan Xilu. Part of Zhèngdìng's main street (Yanzhao Dajie) has been restored and gentrified and is now a pleasant stretch of traditional Chinese roofing and brickwork called the **Zhengding Historical Culture Street** (正定历史文化街; Zhèngdìng Lìshǐ Wénhuà Jiē). At the southern end of the street is **Changle Gate** (长乐门; Chánglè Mén; admission Y10; 🕒 8am-6pm), also known as Nanchengmen. The original wall (which dates back to the Northern Zhou) was made up of an outer wall (yuèchéng) and an inner wall (nèichéng), with enceintes (wèngchéng), and had a total length of 24km. You can climb onto Changle Gate where there is a small exhibition on damage to the wall and its restoration. Extending away from the gate to the east and west are the dilapidated remains of the wall, sprouting grass and trees.

GETTING THERE & AWAY
From Shíjiāzhuāng, minibus No 201 (Y3) runs regularly to Zhèngdìng from Daocha Jie, the road north of the central long-distance bus station (south of Shíjiāzhuāng train station). The minibus goes to Zhèngdìng bus station, from where you can take minibus No 1 to Dafo Temple (Y1). Regular train services also run through Zhèngdìng from Shíjiāzhuāng.

GETTING AROUND
Zhèngdìng is not huge and walking is relatively easy as the sights are largely clustered together. Taxis within Zhèngdìng are around Y10; three-wheel motorcycles cost Y4 for anywhere in town. Bus No 1 runs from the local bus station to Dafo Temple and bus No 3 runs to the train station.

Zhaozhou Bridge 赵州桥
This **bridge** (Zhàozhōu Qiáo; admission Y20) in Zhàoxiàn County, about 40km southeast of Shíjiāzhuāng and 2km south of Zhàoxiàn town, has spanned Jiao River (Jiǎo Hé) for 1400 years and is China's oldest-standing bridge. The world's first segmental bridge (ie its arch is a segment of a circle, as opposed to a complete semi-circle), it predates other bridges of this kind throughout the world by 800 years. In fine condition, it is 50m long and 9.6m wide, with a span of 37m. Twenty-two stone posts are topped with carvings of dragons and mythical creatures, with the centre slab featuring a magnificent tāotiè (an offspring of a dragon).

To get to the bridge from Shíjiāzhuāng's central long-distance bus station, take bus No 3 to the Huáxià long-distance bus station. Then take a minibus to Zhàoxiàn town (Y6, one hour). There are no public buses from Zhàoxiàn to the bridge, but you can hop on a sānlúnchē (three-wheeled motor scooter) for Y3.

Cāngyán Shān 苍岩山
About 60km southwest of Shíjiāzhuāng, Cāngyán Shān (admission Y30) is a scenic area of woods, valleys and steep cliffs dotted with pagodas and temples. The novelty here is a bizarre, double-roofed hall sitting on a stone-arch bridge spanning a precipitous gorge. It is known as the **Hanging Palace**, and is reached by a 300-step stairway. The palace dates from the Sui dynasty. On the surrounding slopes are other ancient halls. Morning buses (Y25) leave for Cāngyán Shān from Shíjiāzhuāng's Dongfang bus station (Dōngfāng zhàn) near the intersection of Xinhua Lu and Youyi Beidajie.

CHÉNGDÉ 承德
☎ 0314
Chéngdé is an 18th-century imperial resort area 255km northeast of Běijīng. Once known as Jehol, it boasts the remnants of the largest regal gardens in China.

The town of Chéngdé is unexciting, but the park and temples are fine and if you catch a bit of fair weather during your visit the place can be fantastic, with some inspiring views. Grab a bike, pedal through the enchanting countryside and make sure you take in the jaw-dropping statue of Guanyin at Puning Temple – one of Buddhist China's most incredible accomplishments.

History
Chéngdé was an obscure town until 1703 when Emperor Kangxi began building a summer palace with a throne room and the full range of court trappings. Chéngdé became a sort of government seat, since

wherever the emperor went his seat went too. Kangxi called his summer creation the Imperial Summer Villa or Fleeing-the-Heat Mountain Villa (Bìshǔ Shānzhuāng).

By 1790, during the reign of Kangxi's grandson Qianlong, it had grown to the size of Běijīng's Summer Palace and the Forbidden City combined. Qianlong extended an idea started by Kangxi, to build replicas of minority architecture in order to make envoys feel comfortable. In particular he was keen on promoting Tibetan and Mongolian Lamaism and this explains the Tibetan and Mongolian features of the monasteries north of the Imperial Summer Villa.

In 1793 British emissary Lord Macartney arrived and sought to open trade with China. Qianlong dismissed him with the statement that China possessed all things and had no need for trade. During the Cultural Revolution, the priceless remnants of Qing dynasty culture were allowed to go to seed. It is all now being slowly restored, in some cases from the base up, in the interests of promoting tourism. Chéngdé is on Unesco's World Heritage list, but this sadly does not guarantee a program of full restoration and some features are gone for good.

Orientation
Located in a pleasant river valley and bordered by hills, the town of Chéngdé spreads out south of the Imperial Summer Villa and the Eight Outer Temples. The train station is in the southeast of town on the east side of the Wulie River (Wǔliè Hé), with most hotels and restaurants of note on the west side of the river.

Information
EMERGENCY & VISAS
PSB (☎ 202 2352; ☼ 8.30am-5pm Mon-Fri for visa extensions) At the rear of a compound off Wulie Lu.

INTERNET ACCESS
Chaosu Internet Café (Chāosù Wǎngbā; Chezhan Lu; per hr Y2; ☼ 24hr) West of train station.
Xiandai Internet Café (Xiàndài Wǎngbā; Chezhan Lu; per hr Y2; ☼ 24hr) West of train station.

LEFT LUGGAGE
Left luggage can be found in both the long-distance bus station ticket hall and the train station ticket hall.

MONEY
Bank of China (Nanyingzi Dajie) Has an ATM that takes MasterCard and Visa. It can be found outside the Wankelong Supermarket just south of the Chengde Theatre (Chéngdé Jùchǎng).
Bank of China (3 Dong Dajie) Another branch lies east of the Mountain Villa Hotel.

POST
Post office (Nanyingzi Dajie; ☼ 8am-6pm) In the south of town. Another, small post office can be found just east of the main gate (Lizheng Gate) of the Imperial Summer Villa.

TOURIST INFORMATION
CITS (☎ 202 6418; fax 202 7484; 1st fl, 11 Zhonghua Lu) Housed in a dreadful looking compound (a dishevelled courtyard on the west side of Wulie Lu), but someone should be able to speak some English.
Tourist Appeal (☎ 202 4548/9; ☼ 8.30am-5pm) May be able to help if you have a tourism-related problem.

Sights
IMPERIAL SUMMER VILLA 避暑山庄
This fanciful **park** (Bìshǔ Shānzhuāng; ☎ 216 3761, 202 5918; admission Y50; ☼ 5.30am-6.30pm) covers a huge 590 hectares and is bound by a splendid 10km wall. Emperor Kangxi decreed that there would be 36 'beauty spots' in Jehol (the old name for Chéngdé); Qianlong decreed 36 more. Rampaging warlords and Japanese subsequently took their toll on the park, and even the forests have suffered cutbacks. Even so, the park is a great place to stroll in the shade of the trees and slowly take in the scale of the place.

With some imagination you can perhaps detect traces of the original scheme of things, with landscaping borrowed from the southern gardens of Sūzhōu, Hángzhōu and Jiāxīng, and from the Mongolian grasslands.

Passing through **Lizheng Gate** (丽正门; Lìzhèng Mén), the main gate, you arrive at the **Front Palace** (正宫; Zhèng Gōng), containing the main throne hall and the refreshingly cool Hall of Simplicity and Sincerity, built of an aromatic hardwood called *nánmù*, and displaying a carved throne; a gorgeous fragrance emanates from the wood. The emperor's bedrooms are fully furnished. Around to the side is a door without an exterior handle (to ensure privacy and security for the emperor),

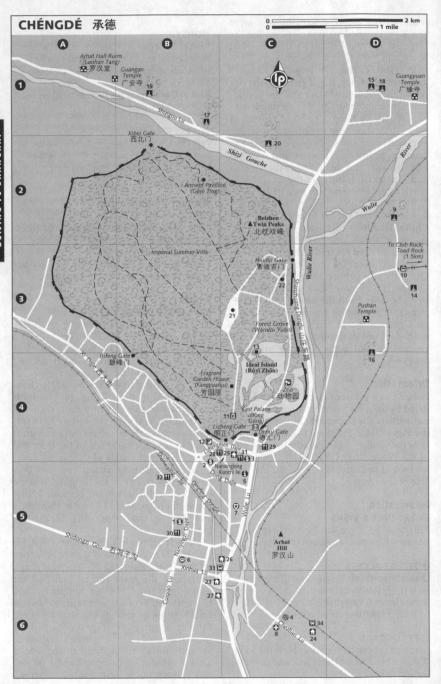

CHÉNGDÉ 承德

0 — 2 km
0 — 1 mile

- Arhat Hall Ruins (Luohan Tang) 罗汉堂
- Guangan Temple 广安寺
- Guangyuan Temple 广缘寺
- 15 18
- 19
- Shizigou Lu
- 17
- 20
- Shizi Gouche
- Xibei Gate 西北门
- Wulie River
- Ancient Pavilion (Gŭjù Tíng)
- Beizhen Twin Peaks 北枕双峰
- 9
- To Club Rock; Toad Rock (1.5km)
- Imperial Summer Villa
- Huidiji Gate 惠迪吉门
- 22
- 10
- 14
- 21
- Forest Grove (Wànshù Yuán)
- Pushan Temple
- 16
- Bifeng Gate 碧峰门
- 13
- Ideal Island (Rúyì Zhōu)
- Xī Dàjiē 西大街
- Fragrant Garden House (Fāngyuánju) 芳园居
- Zoo 动物园
- East Palace (Dōng Gōng)
- 11
- Lizheng Gate 丽正门
- Dehui Gate 德汇门
- 12
- Lihekemen Dajie
- 28 25
- 31
- 3
- 29
- 2
- Nanxinglong Xiaochi Jie
- 5
- 32
- Dong Dajie
- Qianlong Donglu
- 7
- Shanyanglu Jie
- Shidongzi Gou 石洞子沟
- 1
- 30
- Wulie Lu
- Arhat Hill 罗汉山
- 6
- 33
- 26
- Xinhua Lu
- Nanyingzi Dajie
- 23
- 27
- Cangiao Lu
- @ 4
- 8
- Chezhan Lu
- 34
- 24

through which the lucky bed partner for the night was ushered before being stripped and searched by eunuchs. Other halls display exhibitions of ceramics, drum stones and calligraphy.

The double storey **Misty Rain Tower** (雨楼; Yǔ Lóu), on the northwestern side of the main lake, was an imperial study. Further north is the **Wenjin Chamber** (文津阁; Wénjīn Gé), built in 1773 to house a copy of the Sikuquanshu, a major anthology of classics, history, philosophy and literature commissioned by Qianlong. The anthology took 10 years to put together. Four copies were made, but three have disappeared; the fourth is in Běijīng.

In the east, tall **Yongyousi Pagoda** (永佑寺塔; Yǒngyòusì Tǎ) soars above the fragments of its vanished temple, levelled by the Japanese. Wander around the pagoda and inspect the temple layout.

About 90% of the compound is taken up by lakes, hills, miniforests and plains (where visitors now play football), with the odd vantage-point pavilion. At the northern part of the park the emperors reviewed displays of archery, equestrian skills and fireworks. Horses were also chosen and tested here before hunting sorties.

Just beyond the Front Palace is a **ticket office** (☎ 203 7720) for tourist buggies that whiz around the grounds (Y40).

GUANDI TEMPLE 关帝庙
Requisitioned years ago by the local government to house generations of Chéngdé residents, the restored **Guandi Temple** (Guāndì Miào; admission Y10), west of the main gate of the Imperial Summer Villa, is a welcome addition to Chéngdé's temple population. Also called the Wumiao, the Guandi Temple is a Taoist temple first built during the reign of Yongzheng, in 1732. Enter the temple past the protective guardians of the Green Dragon (also called the Blue Dragon) on your right and the White Tiger (also called the White Lion) on your left in the **Shanmen Hall** (山门殿; Shānmén Diàn). The Chongwen Hall on the right contains modern frescoes of Confucius while in the **Shengmu Hall** (圣母殿) on the left is a statue of the Princess of Azure Clouds, the patron deity of Tài Shān (a mountain in Shāndōng), holding a baby. The hall ahead contains a statue of Guandi himself, the Taoist God of War and patron guardian of business. In the courtyard at the rear are two **stelae**, supported on the backs of a pair of disintegrating *bìxì*. The right-hand hall here is dedicated to the God of Wealth (Cáishén), the left-hand hall to the God of Medicine and his co-practitioners. The **Hall of the Three Clear Ones** (三清殿) stands at the rear to the left, while the central rear hall contains a further statue of Guandi. The former inhabitants of the temple grounds (the citizens of Chéngdé) have been moved on and the temple is now home to a band of Taoist monks, garbed in distinctive jackets and trousers, their long hair twisted into topknots.

EIGHT OUTER TEMPLES 外八庙
Some fine examples of religious architecture can be found in the foothills outside the northern and northeastern walls of the Imperial Summer Villa. The number of temples is down on its original complement and some remain closed, but there are enough to keep you busy. The surviving temples and monasteries were all built between 1750 and 1780 and are from 3km

to 5km from the Summer Villa's front gate; bus No 6 taken to the northeastern corner will drop you in the vicinity – going by bike is an excellent idea.

Puning Temple 普宁寺
Puning Temple (Pǔníng Sì; Puningsi Lu; admission Y40; ☻ 8am-5.30pm) has Chinese-style *(hànshì)* features at the front and Tibetan-style *(zàngshì)* elements at the rear. It was built to commemorate Qianlong's victory over the Mongol tribes.

Enter the temple grounds to a stele pavilion with inscriptions by the Qianlong emperor in Chinese, Manchu, Mongol and Tibetan. Behind are arranged halls in a typical Buddhist temple layout, with the **Hall of Heavenly Kings** (天王殿; Tiānwáng Diàn) and beyond, the **Mahavira Hall** (大雄宝殿; Dàxióngbǎo Diàn). The hall contains three images of the Buddhas of the three generations. Behind lie some very steep steps (the temple is arranged on a mountainside) leading to a gate tower, which you can climb.

On the terrace at the top of the steps is the huge **Mahayana Hall**. To the right and left are stupas and square, block-like Tibetan-style buildings, decorated with attractive water spouts. Some buildings on the terrace have been converted to shops, while others appear to be solid, serving a purely decorative purpose.

The highlight of any trip here is the heart-arresting golden statue of **Guanyin** (the Buddhist Goddess of Mercy) in the Mahayana Hall. The effigy is astounding: over 22m high, it's the highest of its kind in the world and radiates a powerful sense of divinity. Mesmerising in its scale, this labour of love is hewn from five different kinds of wood (pine, cypress, fir, elm and linden). Guanyin has 42 arms, with each palm bearing an eye, and each hand holds instruments, skulls, lotuses and other Buddhist devices. Tibetan features include the pair of hands in front of the goddess, below the two clasped in prayer, the right one of which holds a sceptre-like *dorje* (*vajra* in Sanskrit), a masculine symbol, and the left a *dril bu* (bell), a female symbol. On Guanyin's head sits the Teacher Longevity Buddha (Shizunwuliangshoufo). To her right stands a colossal male guardian and disciple called Shancai, opposite his female equivalent, Longnü (Dragon Girl). Unlike Guanyin, they are both painted, although their paintwork is in poor condition. On

GUANYIN
The boundlessly compassionate countenance of Guanyin, the Buddhist Goddess of Mercy, can be encountered in temples all over China. The Goddess (more strictly a Bodhisattva or a Buddha-to-be) goes under a variety of aliases: Guanshiyin, literally meaning 'Observing the Cries of the World', is her formal name, but she is also called Guanzizai, Guanyin Dashi and Guanyin Pusa or, in Sanskrit, Avalokiteshvara. In Japan she is known as Kannon and in Cantonese as Guanyam. Guanyin shoulders the grief of the world and dispenses mercy and compassion. Christians will note a semblance to the Virgin Mary in the aura surrounding the Goddess.

In Tibetan Buddhism, her earthly presence manifests itself in the Dalai Lama, and her home is the Potala Palace (p862) in Lhasa. In China, her abode is the island mount of Pǔtuóshān (p322) in Zhèjiāng province, whose first two syllables derive from the name of her palace in Lhasa.

In temples throughout China, Guanyin is often found at the very rear of the main hall, facing north (most of the other divinities, apart from Weituo, face south). She typically has her own little shrine and stands on the head of a big fish, holding a lotus in her hand. On other occasions, she has her own hall, which is generally towards the rear of the temple.

The goddess (who in earlier dynasties appears to be male rather than female) is often surrounded by little effigies of the *luóhàn* (or *arhat*, those freed from the cycle of rebirth), who scamper about; the Guanyin Pavilion outside Dàlǐ (p666) is a good example of this. Guanyin also appears in a variety of forms, often with just two arms, but sometimes also in a multi-armed form (as at the Puning Temple in Chéngdé, above). The 11-faced Guanyin, the horse head Guanyin, the Songzi Guanyin (literally 'Offering Son Guanyin') and the Dripping Water Guanyin are all manifestations, and there are many more. She was also a favourite subject for *déhuà* (white-glazed porcelain) figures, which are typically very elegant.

the wall on either side are hundreds of small effigies of Buddha.

You can clamber up to the first gallery (Y10) for a closer inspection of Guanyin; torches are provided to cut through the gloom so you can pick out the uneven stairs (take care). Sadly, the higher galleries are often out of bounds, so an eye-to-eye with the goddess may be impossible. If you want to climb the gallery, try and come in the morning, as it is often impossible to get a ticket in the afternoon (especially outside of summer).

Puning Temple has a number of friendly Lamas who manage their domain, so be quiet and respectful at all times. You can catch bus No 6 from in front of the Mountain Villa Hotel to Puning Temple.

Putuozongcheng Temple 普陀宗乘之庙
The largest of the Chéngdé temples, **Putuozongcheng Temple** (Pǔtuózōngchéng Zhīmiào; Shizigou Lu; admission Y30; ☺ 8am-6pm) is a minifacsimile of Lhasa's Potala Palace and houses the nebulous presence of Avalokiteshvara (Guanyin). The temple is a marvellous sight on a clear day, its red walls standing out against its mountain backdrop. Enter to a huge stele pavilion, followed by a large triple archway topped with five small stupas in red, green, yellow, white and black. In between the two gates, note the two large stone elephants whose knees bend impossibly. The scale of the place comes into relief when you get up to the White Palace and look up – it's an astonishing sight, especially when framed against a blue sky. Note that most of the windows are phoney and painted in. Fronted by a collection of prayer wheels and flags, the **Red Palace** (also called the Great Red Terrace) contains most of the main shrines and halls. Continue up and past an exhibition of *thangka* (Tibetan sacred art) in a restored courtyard and look out for the marvellous sandalwood pagodas further up. Both are 19m tall and contain 2160 effigies of the Amitabha Buddha. Among the many exhibits on view in the pagodas (all captions are in Chinese) are displays of Tibetan Buddhist objects and instruments, including a *kapala* bowl, made from the skull of a young girl. The main hall is located at the very top, surrounded by several small pavilions (most of which now house souvenir stalls); the

climb to the top is worth it for the views. In the uppermost hexagonal pavilion in the northwest part of the roof is a small statue of Guanyin. The temple's sacred aura is sadly spoiled by graffiti, but the faithful can buy a bust of Chairman Mao from the Buddhist Statue Shop.

Other Temples and Sights
The **Temple of Sumeru, Happiness and Longevity** (Xūmífúshòu Zhīmiào; Shizigou Lu; admission Y20; ☺ 8am-5.30pm) is another huge temple, around 1km to the east of the Putuozongcheng Temple. It was built in honour of the sixth Panchen Lama, who stayed here in 1781 and it incorporates elements of Tibetan and Han architecture, being an imitation of a temple in Shigatse, Tibet. Note the eight huge, glinting dragons (each said to weigh over 1000kg) that adorn the roof of the main hall.

Pule Temple (Pǔlè Sì; admission Y20; ☺ 8am-6pm) was built in 1776 for the visits of minority envoys (Kazaks among them). At the rear of the temple is the unusual Round Pavilion, reminiscent of the Hall of Prayer for Good Harvests at Běijīng's Temple of Heaven (p109). It's a 30-minute hike to **Club Rock** (Bàngchuí Fēng) from Pule Temple – the rock is said to resemble a club used for beating laundry dry. Nearby is **Toad Rock** (Hámá Shí). There is pleasant hiking, good scenery and commanding views of the area. You can save yourself a steep climb to the base of Club Rock (admission Y20) and Toad Rock by taking the chairlift (Y40 return), but it's more fun to walk if you're reasonably fit. Bus No 10 will take you to Pule Temple. East of Puning Temple is **Puyou Temple** (Pǔyòu Sì; admission Y10; ☺ 8am-6pm). While dilapidated, there is a plentiful contingent of merry gilded *luóhàn* in the side wings.

Anyuan Temple (Ānyuǎn Miào; admission Y10; ☺ 8am-5.30pm summer) is a copy of the Gurza Temple in Xīnjiāng. Only the main hall remains and it contains deteriorating Buddhist frescoes. **Puren Temple** (Pǔrén Sì) is not open to the public. Surrounded by a low red wall, **Shuxiang Temple** (Shūxiàng Sì) also appears to be closed, although it may open in the summer months (unless it is being restored). You can try your luck, or at least look at the pair of huge stone lions sitting outside. Just to the west of Shuxiang Temple is a military sensitive zone where foreigners are not allowed access, so don't go wandering around.

Tours

The only practical way to see all sights in one day is to take a tour by minibus, most of which start out at 8am. The cheapest bus tours cost around Y30 (check at the Mountain Villa Hotel), but are Chinese-speaking only. Most hotels (and CITS) run group tours from around Y50 per day (excluding admission prices).

Sleeping

For such an important tourist destination, Chéngdé has a particularly unremarkable range of hotels. As in other parts of China, hoteliers can be lazy and incompetent (perhaps even more so here than elsewhere). It's worth making basic checks when you look around – look for smoke alarms and unlocked emergency exits. The hotel should also provide a floor plan on your door so you know where the fire escape is in the event of fire.

BUDGET

Dianli Hotel (Diànlì Bīnguǎn; ☎ 217 3735; Daqiaotou; d/q/tr/ste Y120/150/280/260; ✿) This large, blue-glass and white-tile block hotel is opposite the bus station and offers clean, simple and functional tile-floor rooms. The cheapest doubles have no showers, there are grim carpets up the stairs and a large restaurant.

Jingcheng Hotel (Jīngchéng Fàndiàn; ☎ 208 2027; d Y200, q per bed Y30; ✿) This is a so-so place next to the train station. The quad rooms have a shared bathroom, but be warned there are no smoke alarms.

MID-RANGE

Mountain Villa Hotel (Shānzhuāng Bīnguǎn; ☎ 202 3501; fax 202 2457; 127 Xiaonanmen Lu; d Y140, tw Y240-480; ✿) The hotel has clean, cheap rooms off dark, carpeted corridors and offers pole positioning for a trip inside the Imperial Summer Villa. Take bus No 7 from the train station and from there it's a short walk. All major credit cards are accepted. The hotel has a useful east gate on Wulie Lu.

TOP END

Shenghua Hotel (Shènghuá Dàjiǔdiàn; ☎ 227 1000; 22 Wulie Lu; s/d/ste Y600/680/1200; ✿) This glossy, three-star hotel has a modern exterior of glass and steel and a voluminous marble foyer and is well located for the long-distance bus station and the train station. All major credit cards are accepted, and there's a small bar/café and restaurant.

Yunshan Hotel (Yúnshān Dàjiǔdiàn; ☎ 205 5888; 6 Nanyuan Donglu; d/ste Y680/1600) Despite the ghastly exterior (white tiles, office block-style), the rooms at this four-star hotel are clean, elegant and spacious and have benefited from recent redecoration (in 2003). They have minibars, bathrooms and Internet access, and on request DVDs. The hotel has a business center, a western restaurant, a sauna and lobby bar.

Eating

For street food, try **Shaanxiying Jie** (northern end of Nanyingzi Dajie), with its barbecue (shāokǎo) restaurants (and dog meat outlets). **Qingfeng Dongjie**, just north of the railway line and south of Dong Dajie, has a brightly lit and colourful spread of restaurants – you can't miss the lights at night. Also try **Nanxinglong Xiaochijie** (across from the Lizheng Gate), where you can get all kinds of local dishes. Chéngdé's local speciality is wild game – deer (lùròu) and pheasant (shānjī) – which you can find all over town.

Beijing Roast Duck Restaurant (Běijīng Kǎoyādiàn; ☎ 202 2979; 22 Wumiao Lu; duck Y50) This central restaurant just across the way from the Guandi Temple offers tasty duck roasted over fruit-tree wood.

Dongpo Restaurant (Dōngpō Fànzhuāng; ☎ 210 6315; Shanzhuang Donglu; meals from Y30) With red lanterns outside, steaming shāguō (claypot) at the door and a large aquarium, this lively and popular restaurant has no English menu, but a large choice of Sìchuān dishes. The warming huíguōròu (Y18) is excellent: crispy, fatty pork steeped in a hot sauce with ginger and garlic. Also try the làzijī (Y28) – spicy chunks of chicken with chilli. The mápó dòufu (tofu, Y12) is blisteringly hot. Otherwise settle for pigeon claypot (Y58). There are two further branches in town.

Saiwai Roast Duck Restaurant (Sàiwài Kǎoyādiàn; ☎ 213 9791; Shaanxiying Jie; meal Y30-40) Corner restaurant with checked tablecloths, upstairs seating, cheap duck (half duck Y25) and traditional dishes including claypot, dòufu and spareribs. The restaurant is a white, rounded building with pillars around 300m west down Shaanxiying Jie on a street corner. There's no English menu.

Henghexiang Roast Duck Restaurant (Hénghéxiáng Kǎoyādiàn; ☎ 207 5568; 2 Wenjiagou; roast duck Y60;

deer Y30) This small, clean and well-decorated place is on the right-hand side of a small alley to the west of Nanyingzi Dajie. The crisply battered, slightly spicy deer *(gānpēng lùròu)* is tasty and filling; deep-fried pheasant *(qīngzhá shānjī)* is also good. There's no English sign; look for the duck-adorned billboard above the restaurant around 50m along Wenjiagou from Nanyinzi Dajie.

Maihamu Fast Food (Màihāmǔ Kuàicān; Lizhengmen Dajie; meal Y15) Hamburgers, chicken burgers and chips are on offer here, just east of Mountain Villa Hotel.

Getting There & Away

Buses for Chéngdé leave from Běijīng's Dōngzhímén long-distance bus station (Y45; four hours). Buses from Chéngdé leave every 20 minutes for Běijīng (Y45) from the **long-distance bus station** (☎ 202 3476) on Wulie Lu, where buses also go to Qínhuángdǎo (Y64, close to Shānhǎiguān) and Shíjiāzhuāng (sleeper Y60, 9pm). Buses for Běijīng (Y45) regularly leave from outside the Yunshan Hotel and Běijīng minibuses (Y45) leave every 20 minutes from outside the train station. Regular trains run between Běijīng and Chéngdé, with the first and most convenient departing at 7.20am (arriving at 11.18am and returning to Běijīng at 2.40pm). The fastest trains take four hours (Y41 hard seat, Y61 soft seat); slower trains, although cheaper, take around seven hours. There are also connections to Shěnyáng, Dāndōng (17 hours, 6.46pm) and Tiānjīn.

Getting Around

Taxis and motor-tricycles are widely available – bargaining is necessary, especially with the tricycles. Taxis are Y5 at flag fall, which should get you to most destinations in town. There are several minibus lines, but the only one you'll probably need is No 6 (Y1) to the Eight Outer Temples (Wàibā Miào) grouped at the northeastern end of town. You can rent bicycles at many hotels (it may just be a case of staff renting theirs to you), which is an excellent way to get about.

SHĀNHǍIGUĀN 山海关

☎ 0335

Shānhǎiguān is where the Great Wall meets the sea and sits on a strategic pass that leads to northeast China. In the 1980s this part of the wall had nearly returned to dust, but it has been rebuilt and is now a first-rate tourist drawcard. Its proximity to Běidàihé guarantees it a summer tourist bonanza. The town is poor and a reminder that the benefits of economic reform remain unevenly spread. Facilities for Western visitors are basic at best. Considerable charm remains within the old walled enclosure despite its dilapidation and part of Shānhǎiguān's appeal lies in its manageable size, grid-like streets and tenacious sense of history.

History

The area was originally part of the state of Guzhu during the Shang and Zhou dynasties, but came into its own in 1381, when its was developed under General Xuda, who converted it into a garrison town with a square fortress, four gates at the compass points and two major avenues running between the gates. In 1644, the town was overrun by the invading Manchu army who pierced the defences and proceeded to enslave China for over 250 years.

Information

Bank of China (🕒 8.30am-noon & 1.30-5.30pm; no international ATM) Housed in a building with a splendid roof south of the Great Wall Museum on Diyiquan Lu.

PSB (☎ 505 1163) Opposite the entrance to First Pass Under Heaven on the corner of a small alleyway.

Shiji Internet Cafe (Shìjì Wǎngbā; 85 Nan Dajie; per hr Y2) Across the way from the People's Hospital. No English sign, but look for the big red sign that says 'Shiji Wangba'.

21st Century Internet Cafe (21st Shìjì Wǎngbā; 24 Nan Dajie; per hr Y2) Just south of the post office on the east side of Nan Dajie, in between Wutiao and Liutiao Hutong. There's no English sign, but look for the large white placard.

Yimei Internet Cafe (Yīmèi Wǎngbā; Xinglong Jie; per hr Y2; 🕒 24hr) South of the South Gate.

People's Hospital (Rénmín Yīyuàn; 46 Nan Dajie) On the east side of Nan Dajie.

Post office (🕒 8am-5.30pm) On the east side of Nan Dajie, south of the hospital.

Sights

FIRST PASS UNDER HEAVEN 天下第一关

The **First Pass Under Heaven** (Tiānxià Dìyī Guān; cnr Dong Dajie & Diyiguan Lu; admission Y40; 🕒 7.30am-5.30pm, open longer in summer) is also known as East Gate (Dōng Mén). Shredded by the wind, tattered flags flap along a restored section of Wall, itself studded with watchtowers, dummy soldiers and tourist paraphernalia. Long views of factories stretch off to the east as decayed sections of battlements trail off into the hills. The wall here is 12m high and the principle watchtower – two storeys with double eaves and 68 arrow slit windows – is a towering 13.7m high. The calligraphy at the top (attributed to the scholar Xiao Xian) reads 'First Pass Under Heaven'. Several other watchtowers can also be seen and there's a *wèngchéng* (enceinte) extending out east from the wall. Along the west edge of the wall south of the entrance is a pleasant grassy park where you can stretch your legs.

GREAT WALL MUSEUM 长城博物馆

Down the street this **museum** (Chángchéng Bówùguǎn; Diyiguan Lu; admission Y5; 8am-6pm) is housed in a pleasant, one-storey traditional Chinese building with upturned eaves. This is perhaps a more interesting way to explore the history of the wall, thanks to its collection of photographs and memorabilia. There are no captions in English. Admission is included in First Pass Under Heaven tickets.

OLD DRAGON HEAD 老龙头

Old Dragon Head (Lǎolóngtóu; 4km south of Shānhǎiguān; admission Y40; 8am-5.30pm) was the serpentine conclusion of the Great Wall as at the sea's edge. What you see now was reconstructed in the late 1980s – the original wall crumbled away long ago. The name derives from the legendary carved dragon head that once faced the waves.

There are beaches on either side of the Wall; avoid buying the extortionate ticket

and take the left-hand road to the sea where you can walk along the beach or ride a horse (Y2) to Old Dragon Head (don't get caught by the tide). The views are spectacular and you can join the periwinkle-pickers and cockle-hunters on the rocks. Minibuses go to Old Dragon Head from Shānhǎiguān's South Gate, as do bus Nos 13, 23 and 25.

JIĂO SHĀN 角山

A 4km walk (taxi Y10; motor tricycle Y5) from the town centre brings you to a steep section of rebuilt masonry, where the Great Wall mounts its first high peak, **Jiǎo Shān** (Horned Hill; admission Y10; 5am-sunset). It's a trying 20-minute clamber from the base, or a cable car can yank you up for Y20. The views are fantastic on a clear day. The path behind the hills to the **Qixian Monastery** (Qīxián Sì; admission Y5) can be traversed in an hour, but is thorny and it's easy to lose the trail, which often peters out; however, the tranquillity is peerless. Bus No 27 runs between Old Dragon Head and Jiǎo Shān.

MENGJIANGNÜ TEMPLE 孟姜女庙

Mengjiangnü Temple (Mèngjiāngnǚ Miào; admission Y30; 7am-5.30pm) is a Song–Ming reconstruction 6km east of Shānhǎiguān. It has coloured sculptures of Lady Meng and her maids and calligraphy on a famous Chinese story, Looking for Husband Rock. In that tale, Meng Jiang's husband was press-ganged into wall-building because his views conflicted with those of Emperor Qin Shi Huang. When

SHĀNHǍIGUĀN 山海关

0 ——— 400 m
0 ——— 0.2 miles

To Jiǎo Shān (3km)
To Mengjiangnu Temple (6km)
Lianhua Pool
To Haerbin
Train Station 火车站
To Old Dragon Head (4km)
To Tianjin (274km)
To Běidàihé

winter came Meng set off to take her husband warm clothing, only to discover that he had died from the hard labour. Meng wandered the Great Wall, thinking only of finding Wan's bones to give him a decent burial. The wall, a sensitive soul, was so upset it collapsed, revealing the skeleton entombed within. Overcome with grief, Meng hurled herself into the sea from a boulder.

Take bus No 23 from Guancheng Nanlu; a taxi should cost around Y12.

Sleeping

Shānhǎiguān does not have many hotels.

BUDGET

Jiguan Guesthouse (Jìguān Zhāodàisuǒ; ☎ 505 1938; 17 Dongsitiao Hutong; d Y100-180, ste Y320; ☒) This pleasant hotel has rooms off two courtyards. The simple doubles come without bathroom, but have clean, tiled floors and TV. The Y180 doubles have a shower room. There's no English sign but it's about 50m down Dongsitiao Hutong on the north side.

Lida Restaurant (Lìdá Hǎixiān Jiǔlóu; ☎ 505 1476; Dong Dajie; d/q Y30/40) Very simple lodgings are on offer at the rear of the Lida Restaurant (right). The rooms are behind an attractive little courtyard, but are small and frugal. No air-con (but there's heating and TV), no shower, and only a public loo.

North Street Hotel (Běijiē Zhāodàisuǒ; ☎ 505 1680; 2 Mujia Hutong; dm Y30, d from Y100; ☒) Attractive courtyard hotel in need of renovation. Doubles have no phones, Victorian baths with mismatched plugs, leaking taps, collapsing curtain rails, antique radiators, scalding hot water, minute sheets, unlit courtyards, little privacy and flimsy locks. The hotel has some charm, however, and a good setting. Walk along Mujia Hutong and look for the gate with the stone lions outside.

MID-RANGE

Friendly Cooperate Hotel (Yìhé Jiǔdiàn; ☎ 593 9069; 4 Nanhai Xilu; d/tr/q Y288/388/400; ☒) This large two-star hotel just south of the Xinghua Market has large, clean and smart double rooms with water cooler, TV, phone and bathroom. Staff are pleasant and there's a restaurant next door.

Longhua Hotel (Lónghuá Dàjiǔdiàn; ☎ 507 7698; fax 505 2130; 1 Nanguan Dajie; s Y168, d Y188-288, tr Y368; ☒) This hotel has spacious and so-so rooms with reproduction traditional furniture in the block at the rear, and smaller doubles in the main building at the front. There's no English sign, but it's just north of the Industrial and Commercial Bank of China.

Shangye Hotel (Shāngyè Bīnguǎn; ☎ 505 1684; 91 Guancheng Nanlu; q Y80, d Y120-228; ☒) This two-star hotel near the South Gate is good value, with decent doubles.

Eating

Small restaurants and food vendors congregate along Nan Dajie and several streets running east–west of it. Come sundown, gregarious kebab sellers set up barbecue ovens outside many of the shops along Nan Dajie, where you can feast on lamb kebabs (*yángròu chuàn*) and pick up cheap beers (Y2). The kebabs are very good value at around Y1 for five *chuàn*. On the west side of Nan Dajie opposite the entrance to Dongsitiao Hutong is a restaurant proudly proclaiming itself as '*Měiguó Kěndéjī Zhájī*' – literally 'Kentucky Fried Chicken' (it ain't). Larger restaurants can be found along the road south of the city wall heading towards the train station.

Lida Restaurant (Lìdá Hǎixiān Jiǔlóu; ☎ 505 1476; Dong Dajie; meal Y35) This restaurant is a cheerful eatery serving local, northern and northeastern fare, plus Sìchuān dishes. Try the *huíguōròu* (Y25), the tasty *hēimǐ* (black rice; Y2), a bowl of steaming *jiǎozi* (dumplings; Y5) or the *gānzhá hǎixiā* (dry fried shrimps; Y18). The owner speaks a little English and has cheap beds out the back (left).

Mike Hamn Fast Food (Màikè Hànmǔ Kuàicān; Guancheng Nanlu) If you want the Hébēi fast-food experience (chicken meals, chips, piped elevator music), come here. The food is actually not bad, but you'll have to wait while they fry it all up for you (Heinz Tomato sachets provided).

Shanghai Mianbao (Shanghai Bread; 123 Nan Dajie, btwn Batiao & Jiutiao Hutong) This small place is worth trying for tasty cakes, bread, buns, pastries and sandwiches.

Getting There & Around

See p181 for details on getting to and around Shānhǎiguān.

BĚIDÀIHÉ 北戴河
☎ 0335

The summer seaside resort of breezy Běidàihé was first cobbled together when English railway engineers stumbled across the beach in the 1890s. Diplomats, missionaries and business people from the Tiānjīn concessions and the Běijīng legations hastily built villas and cottages in order to indulge in the new bathing fad.

Today, the cream of China's leaders congregate at summer villas, continuing a tradition that has starred such personalities as Jiang Qing and Lin Biao. During the summer high season (May to October) Běidàihé comes alive with vacationers who crowd the beaches and eat at the numerous outdoor seafood restaurants. During the low season, the town is dead.

Information

Bank of China (near cnr of Dongjing Lu & Binhai Dadao; 8.30-noon & 1.30-5.30pm) Has foreign currency exchange but no ATM.

China Network Communications (CNC; 76 Dongjing Lu; 8am-noon & 3-6.30pm) It's just about possible to send/receive email on the one computer here.

Post office (Haining Lu)

PSB (404 1032; 78 Shitang Lu) A white building at the rear of the compound.

Sights & Activities

Wandering the streets and seafront of Běidàihé in summer is enjoyable, and hiring a bike or tandem (shuāngzuò zìxíngchē) and whizzing around the beachfront roads is fun. Otherwise, fork out for a rubber ring, inner tube and swimming trunks from one of the street vendors and plunge into the sea (after elbowing through the crowds).

Always be on the lookout for Běidàihé's peculiar revolutionary emblems and seaside kitsch, including a statue of **Gorky** (Gāoěrjī) surrounded by outsized seashells. For those in pursuit of bad taste, Běidàihé comes up trumps with its **Bìluó Tǎ** (Emerald Shell Tower) – it's quite ghastly.

Sleeping

Many foreign travellers stay in nearby Shānhǎiguān (p177) as hotels are expensive and limited in town. The resort is only fully open during the summer season (May to October), so many hotels shut up shop during the low season; all hotels are a long way from the train station. Prices quoted are

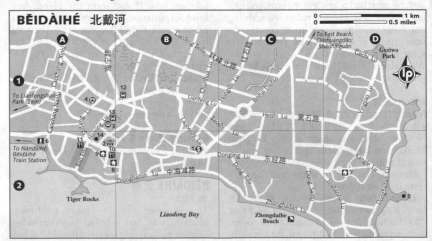

BĚIDÀIHÉ 北戴河

high season; low-season prices are cheaper, and haggling helps.

Beidaihe Friendship Hotel (Běidàihé Yǒuyì Bīnguǎn; ☎ 404 8558; fax 404 1965; 1 Yingjiao Lu; d Y300-580; ☒) Set in huge, grassy green grounds in the east of town, this hotel is a good deal with tidy doubles and singles. The cheaper doubles (also clean) are at the rear in stone terraced houses. You can exit the rear entrance, mosey down the road and get straight onto the beach.

Guesthouse for Diplomatic Missions (Wàijiāo Rényuán Bīnguǎn; ☎ 404 1287; fax 404 1807; 1 Bao Sanlu; d/tr Y650/300; ☺ Apr-Oct; ☒) This guesthouse remains an appealing place to stay and has outdoor porches, so relax in the breeze and enjoy the hotel's beach. There's also tennis and weekend barbecues.

Yuehua Hotel (Yuèhuá Bīnguǎn; ☎ 404 1575; 90 Dongjing Lu; economy r/s/d/tr Y300/400/400/400; ☒) Smack in the centre of town, this three-star hotel has a spacious lobby and ponderous cladding on the exterior. Often shut during low season, but good discounts apply when open during slack periods.

Eating

A whole string of **seafood restaurants** (*hǎixiāndiàn*) are strung out along Bao Erlu, near the beach; you can't miss them or their vocal owners. Choose your meal from the slippery knots of mysterious sea creatures kept alive in buckets on the pavement. Also look out for one of the ubiquitous **fruit sellers** wheeling their harvest around on bicycles, selling grapes, peaches, bananas, peanuts etc. Several small supermarkets can be found near the junction of Dongjing Lu and Haining Lu.

Youyi Restaurant (Yǒuyì Jiǔdiàn; ☎ 404 1613; Bao Erlu; meals Y30, seafood Y60) This popular seafood restaurant stays open off-season – choose from the bowls, buckets and pots of fresh aquatic life. Dishes include tomato and shrimps (Y38), drunken prawns (price depends on season), *suāncàiyú* (fish slices with pickled cabbage, Y35) and staple Sìchuān standards such as *huíguōròu* (Y20).

Kiessling's Restaurant (Qíshílín Cāntíng; ☎ 404 1043; Dongjing Lu; ☺ Jun-Aug) A relative of the Tiānjīn branch (p158), this place serves both Chinese and international food and has pleasant outdoor seating.

Getting There & Away

Near Shānhǎiguān, Qínhuángdǎo's little airport has flights from Dàlián, Shànghǎi, Tàiyuán, Hāěrbīn and Chángchūn.

Běidàihé, Qínhuángdǎo and Shānhǎiguān are all accessible by train. Trains are frequent, but don't always stop at all three stations or arrive at convenient hours. The fastest trains (double-deckers) take under three hours to Běidàihé from Běijīng past the flat, featureless farmed countryside; allow a bit longer for Shānhǎiguān (sleeper Y97, standing ticket Y47). More trains stop at Qínhuángdǎo (soft seat Y97) from where you can catch the No 33 bus to Shānhǎiguān (Y2) or the No 34 to Běidàihé (Y2). Hotels in Shānhǎiguān offer far better value and are within walking distance of the train station, whereas at Běidàihé the nearest hotel is at least 10km from the station. Train fares to Běidàihé's modern and bizarre-looking (steel and blue glass) train station include Tiānjīn (Y21 to Y42; five per day), Běijīng (Y90; five per day), Shānhǎiguān (Y10), Shíjiāzhuāng (Y94), Yāntái (Y70), Hāěrbīn (Y64) and Shěnyáng north (Y62 to Y70).

A convenient place to pick up a bus to Běijīng in Běidàihé is from the east side of Haining Lu, just north of the post office (Y70, three hours, departures at 6am, 12.30pm and 4pm). Comfortable buses also leave for Běijīng from Qínhuángdǎo (Y75, three hours). There are also direct buses from Qínhuángdǎo to Chéngdé (Y60, seven hours), departing at 6am, 7am and 8am.

Getting Around

Bus Nos 5 and 22 (via Nándàihé) connect Běidàihé train station to the Beidaihe bus station (Y4) or you can take a taxi (Y15). Buses connect all three towns, generally departing every 30 minutes from 6am to 6.30pm.

Cheap taxis in Běidàihé, Qínhuángdǎo and Shānhǎiguān are all Y5 flag fall and Y1.2 per km after that.

Motor tricycles cost Y2 to go anywhere in Shānhǎiguān. Shānhǎiguān and Běidàihé are good places to explore by bike. In Běidàihé bikes and tandems are available along Zhonghaitan Lu, east of Bao Erlu (Y10 per hour). In Shānhǎiguān ask at your hotel about bike rental outlets.

Shāndōng 山东

BĚIJĪNG TO SHÀNGHǍI

HIGHLIGHTS

- Stagger up sacred **Tài Shān** (p190)…and then stagger back down again

- Survey the imposing scale of the **Dai Temple** (p196) in Tài'ān

- Potter around China's premier Confucian place of pilgrimage at **Qūfù** (p198)

- Traipse around the charming streets of Teutonic **Qīngdǎo** (p203)

- Weave your way around **Yantai Hill Park** (p212) in Yāntái for flavours of yesteryear Europe

★ Yāntái
★ Tài Shān
★ Tài'ān
★ Qīngdǎo
★ Qūfù

- POP: 93.4 MIL
- AREA: 153,000 SQ KM
- www.china-sd.net

Its stumpy peninsula jutting into the Yellow Sea, Shāndōng has a history that can be traced back to the origins of the Chinese state: Confucius. China's great social philosopher was born here and lived out his days in Lǔ, one of the small states in the south of today's province. His ideas were further championed by the great Confucian philosopher Mencius, who hailed from the same region. Other local heroes include Wang Xizhi, China's most famous calligrapher, and the great military strategist of the Three Kingdoms period, Zhuge Liang. Film star Gong Li, who set new benchmarks for Chinese beauty, grew up in Jǐ'nán.

Shāndōng also has a firm foothold in China's martial arts chronicles as the home province of Wang Lang, founder of Praying Mantis Fist *(tánglángquán)*. One of the most distinctive styles of the Chinese boxing arts *(quánfǎ)*, the fighting method emulates the movements of the stick-like creepy-crawly and is famed for its ferocity and speed.

Gourmands can start sharpening their chopsticks, as Shāndōng is home to one of China's four major schools of cooking *(lǔcài)*. The province also marks the conclusion of the Yellow River (Huáng Hé), the massive waterway with an almost mythical status among the Chinese, that exits China here after its circuitous and muddy journey from the Tibet-Qīnghǎi plateau.

Shāndōng is one of China's wealthiest and most populous provinces, with drawcard sights that include the peerless Tài Shān, the phlegmatic charms of Qūfù, and the self-assured kudos of burgeoning Qīngdǎo on the coast. Beyond its mushrooming commercial districts and surprising wherewithal, Qīngdǎo has an unrivalled display of German concession-era architecture and some first-rate food. Impressive European remains have also been spruced up in Yāntái to the north, and aficionados can track down further historical remnants in Jǐ'nán and Tài'ān.

History

From the earliest record of civilisation in the province (furnished by the black pottery remains of the Lóngshān culture), Shāndōng has had a tumultuous history. It was victim to the capricious temperament of the oft-flooding Yellow River, which caused mass death, starvation and a shattered economy. In 1899 Yellow River (also aptly named 'China's Sorrow') flooded the entire Shāndōng plain; a sad irony in view of the two scorching droughts that had swept the area that same year and the year before. The flood followed a long period of economic depression, a sudden influx of demobilised troops in 1895 after China's humiliating defeat by Japan in Korea, and droves of refugees from the south moving north to escape famines, floods and drought.

To top it all off, the Europeans arrived; Qīngdǎo fell into the clutches of the Germans, and the British obtained a lease for Wēihǎi. Their activities included the building of railroads and some feverish missionary work (for a historic Jesuit map of the province from 1655, go to www.library.csuhayward.edu/atlas/xantung.htm), which the Chinese believed angered the gods and spirits. All of this created the perfect breeding ground for rebellion, and in the closing years of the 19th century the Boxers arose out of Shāndōng, armed with magical spells and broadswords.

Today Jǐ'nán, the provincial capital, plays second fiddle to Qīngdǎo's tune, a refrain picked up on by the other prospering coastal cities of Yāntái and Wēihǎi. Shengli Oilfield, inland, is China's second-largest producer of oil.

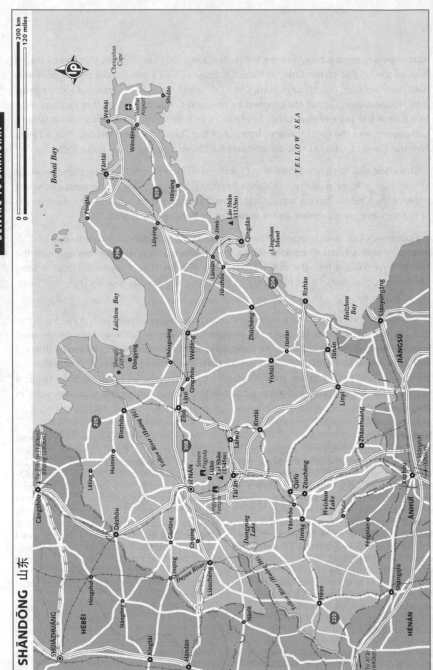

SHĀNDŌNG 山东

Climate

Summers are hot and winters are cold in Shāndōng, with an average annual temperature of 11°C to 14°C. The coastal cities of Qīngdǎo, Yāntái and Wēihǎi are cooler in summer and warmer in winter than the towns and cities of the interior.

Getting There & Away

Airports exist at Jǐ'nán, Qīngdǎo, Yāntái and Wēihǎi, with international flights to cities in Japan and South Korea from Qīngdǎo and flights to South Korea from Yāntái. Ferry connections exist between Qīngdǎo and Dàlián (p353), and destinations in South Korea and Japan. There are also boats to Dàlián and South Korea from both Yāntái and Wēihǎi. Shāndōng is also linked to neighbouring and more distant provinces by both bus and rail. See p916 for more information.

Getting Around

The provincial rail hub is Jǐ'nán, with rail connections to all major towns and cities in Shāndōng. Bus connections cover the entire province (see the Getting There & Away sections under each destination for detailed information).

JǏ'NÁN 济南

☎ 0531 / pop 1.96 million

Jǐ'nán, the capital of Shāndōng province, is for most travellers a transit point on the road to other destinations around Shāndōng. The city is not unattractive, and at night offers a pleasant selection of night markets, hole-in-the-wall restaurants and atmosphere.

Jǐ'nán is most commonly noted for its springs; however, after a visit to them you may wonder why. Downplayed in Jǐ'nán's tourist pitch, but perhaps of more interest, are the Chinese celebrities who have come from Jǐ'nán. Film idol Gong Li grew up here. Bian Que, founder of traditional Chinese medicine, Zou Yan, founder of the Yin and Yang five element school, as well as Zhou Yongnian, founder of Chinese public libraries, all herald from these parts. A number of nationally and internationally recognised writers also hail from Jǐ'nán.

At the time of writing, the city resembled an earthquake zone, road-widening schemes having levelled vast swathes of the city. Despite the devastation, Jǐ'nán has made an attempt to prettify the city with plants and grass, and even rubbish bins for recyclable litter have appeared in chic parts of town. Quancheng Lu increasingly resembles Wangfujing Dajie in Běijīng, with a pedestrianised pavement along the northern side of the road and squadrons of shoppers surging past department stores, including a Wall Mart Supercenter.

History

The area has been inhabited for at least 4000 years, and some of the earliest reminders of this are the eggshell-thin pieces of black pottery unearthed in the town of Lóngshān, 30km east of Jǐ'nán. These provide the first link in an unbroken chain of tradition and artistic endeavour that culminated in the beautifully crafted ceramics of later dynasties.

Modern development in Jǐ'nán stems from 1899, when construction of the Jǐ'nán–Qīngdǎo railway line began. When completed in 1904, the line gave the city a major communications role. The Germans had a concession near the train station after Jǐ'nán was opened to foreign trade in 1906, and old, crumbling and neglected residences from the era survive. The huge German building on Jing Yilu opposite the Shandong Hotel now houses a railway sub-office; it's made of the same stone, and in the same style, as much of the architecture in Qīngdǎo. Other notable buildings include the former People's Livelihood Bank of Shandong Province at 168 Jing Erlu, a pink and green confection dating from 1932.

Orientation

Jǐ'nán is a sprawling city, making navigation arduous for first timers. The main train station is in the west of town, to the south of which is a grid of roads with some history and charm. The east–west roads in this grid are called Jing Yilu (Longitude One Rd), Jing Erlu (Longitude Two Rd) and so on, while the north–south roads are named Wei Yilu (Latitude One Rd), Wei Erlu (Latitude Two Rd) and so forth. The major landmark in the east of town is Daming Lake (Dàmíng Hú), south of which can be found Quancheng Lu, a major shopping street.

Information

BOOKSHOPS

Xinhua Bookstore (Xīnhuá Shūdiàn; Luoyuan Dajie; ⊗ 9am-9pm) Opposite the Sofitel Silver Plaza Hotel. Xinhua Bookstore offers the usual literary fiction and translations of Chinese propaganda tomes, such as *When Serfs Stood up in Tibet*. A further branch can be found on Quancheng Lu.

EMERGENCY

Public Security Bureau (PSB; Gōngānjú; ☎ 691 5454, visa enquiries ext 2459; 145 Jing Sanlu; cnr Wei Wulu; ⊗ 8am-noon & 2-5.45pm Mon-Fri)

INTERNET ACCESS

Kuaichedao Internet Café (Kuàichēdào Wǎngbā; Xiaowei Liulu; per hr Y2; ⊗ 7am-midnight)

INFORMATION	
Bank of China 中国银行	**1** D2
CNC 中国电信	**2** C2
Kuaichedao Internet Café	
快车道网吧	**3** B2
People's Livelihood Bank of Shandong	
Province 山东省民生银行	**4** B2
Post Office 邮局	**5** D2
PSB 公安局外事科	**6** B2
Shandong Travel Service	
山东旅行社	**7** D3
Shengli Hospital 省立医院	**8** B2
Tongfu Internet Café 同福网吧	**9** B2
Xinhua Bookstore 新华书店	**10** D2
Xinhua Bookstore 新华书店	**11** D2
Yinghuochong Internet	
Café 萤火虫网吧	**12** B2

SIGHTS & ACTIVITIES	p187
Baotu Spring Park 趵突泉	**13** C2
Black Tiger Spring 黑虎泉	**14** D2
Five Dragon Pool Park	
五龙潭公园	**15** C2

Jinan Museum	
济南博物馆	**16** D3
Li Qingzhao Memorial Hall	
李清照纪念堂	**17** C2
Mosque 清真寺	**18** C2

SLEEPING	⌂ pp187-8
Crowne Plaza Jinan	
济南贵和皇冠假日酒店	**19** B2
Jinan (Tsinan) Hotel 济南饭店	**20** B2
Jinan Railway Hotel	
济南铁道大酒店	**21** B2
Shandong Hotel 山东宾馆	**22** B2
Sofitel Silver Plaza Hotel	
素菲特银座大饭店	**23** D2

EATING	⊞ p189
Café Galleria	(see 19)
Quanjude Roast Duck Restaurant	
全聚德烤鸭店	**24** D2
Yingquange Restaurant	
瀛景阁大酒店	**25** C2
Yuèdū Jiǔlóu 粤都酒楼	**26** B3

TRANSPORT	pp189-90
Bus Station	
汽车站	**27** B2
CAAC 中国民航	**28** C2
China Eastern Airlines	
东方航空公司	**29** B2
East Train Station	
火车东站	**30** D1
Long-Distance Bus Station	
长途汽车站	**31** B1
Main Train Station	
济南火车站	**32** B2
Shandong Airlines	
山东航空公司	**33** B2
Shandong China Railway International	
Travel Service	
山东中铁国路	**34** B2
Silver Plaza Shopping Centre	
银座商城	**35** D2

OTHER	
Spring City Square	
泉城广场	**36** D2

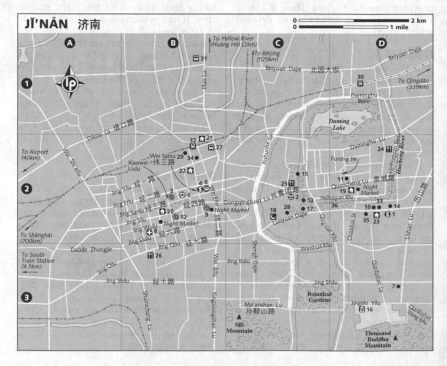

Yinghuochong Internet Café (Yínghuǒchóng Wǎngbā; Xiaowei Liulu; per hr Y2; ☿ 24hr)
Tongfu Internet Café (Tóngfú Wǎngbā; 35 Xiaowei Erlu; per hr Y2, deposit Y20; ☿ 8am-10pm)

MEDICAL SERVICES
Shengli Hospital (Shènglì Yīyuàn; ☎ 793 8911; 324 Jing Wulu)

MONEY
Two ATMs taking Cirrus, MasterCard, Visa and Amex and a foreign-exchange desk can be found in the **Bank of China** Tower (Zhōngguó Yínháng; 22 Luoyuan Dajie; ☿ 9am-5pm Mon-Fri).

POST
Post office (162 Jing Erlu, cnr Wei Erlu; ☿ 8am-6pm) A red-brick building with pillars, capped with a turret.

TELEPHONE
Telephones in the vicinity of the main train station take coins only.
China Network Communications (CNC; Zhōngguó Diànxìn; 14 Gongqingtuan Lu; ☿ 8.30am-5.30pm) Telephone office.

TRAVEL AGENCIES
Shandong Travel Service (☎ 260 0660/9; fax 260 0226; 86 Jing Shilu; ☿ 8.30am-5.30pm) South on Lishan Lu. Can arrange tours around the region and beyond.

Sights
MOSQUE 清真寺
Fronted by a spirit wall and an impressive gate tower and laid out with pines and greenery, this lovely Chinese-style **mosque** (Qīngzhēn Sì; 47 Yongchang Jie; admission free) dates from the late 13th century. The long rooftops of the mosque are clearly visible running along Luoyuan Dajie. Walk in and look around, be quiet and respectful at all times, and dress modestly (no shorts or skirts); the prayer hall is inaccessible to non-Muslims. The entrance is to the right of the main gate. The mosque is located on the left-hand side of Yongchang Jie, a street leading into the Hui (Muslim Chinese) quadrant of Jǐ'nán, where you can find stalls and restaurants cooking up Muslim food, and other, largely modern, mosques.

THOUSAND BUDDHA MOUNTAIN & JINAN MUSEUM 千佛山、济南博物馆
Many of the statues in this **park** (Qiānfó Shān; 18 Jingshi Yilu; admission Y15; ☿ 6am-7pm) to the

southeast of the city centre were disfigured or disappeared during the Cultural Revolution, but new ones are gradually being added. A cable car (one way Y15, return Y25) runs up the mountain, from where you can descend via a fantastic summer slide (Y20). Bus Nos 2 and K51 go to the park from the train station. **Jinan Museum** (Jǐ'nán Bówùguǎn; admission Y3; ☿ 8.30am-4.30pm Tue-Sun) is a short walk west on Jingshi Yilu. Galleries are devoted to painting, calligraphy, and a decent display of porcelain ware from the Sui, Song, Yuan, Ming and Qing dynasties. Also exhibited are recently excavated and sadly headless statues of Buddhist figures from the Tang dynasty. There are carved tablets, other stone pieces, bronzes and further ceramics upstairs (and a delightful miniature boat carved from a walnut shell); no English captions.

SPRINGS 泉
Jǐ'nán's 100-plus springs were once the main attraction of the city. Today however, the springs splutter rather than gush and the only time you'll see any vestige of activity is during the rainy season in August. You can see the springs at **Five Dragon Pool Park** (Wǔlóng Chí Gōngyuán; admission Y5; ☿ 7am-7pm), Black Tiger Spring (Hēihǔ Quán) and **Baotu Spring Park** (Bàotū Quán Gōngyuán; admission Y15; ☿ 7am-7pm). Within Baotu Spring Park is the **Li Qingzhao Memorial Hall** (Lǐ Qīngzhào Jìniàntáng). A native of Jǐ'nán, Li Qingzhao is seen as the most significant and most famous female poet of the Song dynasty (see The Song Poet, p188). The memorial hall is within a traditional Chinese courtyard inside Baotu Spring Park. The hall houses a statue of Li and extracts of her work engraved on tablets along the walkways.

Sleeping
BUDGET
Shandong Hotel (Shāndōng Bīnguǎn; ☎ 605 5286/7881; 92 Jing Yilu; s Y130, d Y150-180, tr Y210-240, ste Y220-260; ☒) On the corner of Jing Yilu and Wei Sanlu, this hotel has large rooms with bathroom, TV (Star Sports), water cooler/heater and phone. Staff is used to dealing with foreigners, and the location is very convenient.

MID-RANGE
Jinan Railway Hotel (Jǐ'nán Tiědào Dàjiǔdiàn; ☎ 601 2118; fax 601 2188; s/d/tr/ste Y300/368/468/800; ☒)

Next to the main train station, this three-star hotel has polite staff, a marbled interior and an upscale character at variance with most railway hotels in China. Doubles are large, bright and clean, and the smart bathrooms come with hairdryer. Push for discounts as you can regularly shave 30% off room prices.

Jinan (Tsinan) Hotel (Jǐ'nán Fàndiàn; ☎ 793 8981; fax 793 2906; 240 Jing Sanlu; Bldg No 1/2/3 d Y380/160/220, Mao Zedong Presidential ste Y1880; ❸) Rooms at this two-star hotel are average, but the setting within a small wooded garden is a blessing for those suffering from a concrete overdose. Reception is in Building No 4, and there is a north and south gate.

TOP END

Crowne Plaza Jinan (Jǐ'nán Guìhé Huángguǎn Jiàri Jiǔdiàn; ☎ 602 9999; www.crowneplaza.com; 3 Tianditan Jie; d/ste Y1245/1660; ❸) The city's finest hotel,

the elegant Crowne Plaza has stylish Art Deco touches in the foyer (including illuminated pillars) and excellent rooms, each equipped with broadband Internet connections. Facilities include a deli off the lobby selling cakes and breads, an elegant indoor swimming pool, bowling alley, basement car park, an Italian restaurant and the Tian Yuan Chinese restaurant.

Sofitel Silver Plaza Hotel (Sùfēitè Yínzuò Dàfàndiàn; ☎ 606 8888; www.accorhotels.com/asia; 66 Luoyuan Dajie; d/ste Y1079/1494; ❸) A huge five-star tower in the heart of the commercial district, this hotel has a lobby that is a kind of bizarre pastiche of European neoclassical design with an over-the-top chandelier. Rooms are luxurious and spacious, and facilities include a small deli, swimming pool, colossal banqueting hall, and European, Japanese and Chinese restaurants. Ask for discounts or promotional rates.

THE SONG POET

Li Qingzhao is famed for her elegant language, strong imagery and, perhaps most importantly, her ability to remain unpretentious in her poetry. Only 70 of Li's poems have survived, despite the fact that she wrote continuously throughout her lifetime. As the most celebrated female poet of the Song dynasty, she has a large following of literary buffs, especially in her hometown of Jǐ'nán.

Born in 1084 into the privileged world of a scholar's family, Li Qingzhao was able to cultivate her love for poetry from a young age. Her early poems are characterised by her carefree leisure and love for beauty and life.

In 1126 Li's life changed dramatically. Having fled with her family from the advancing Jin army, and with the death of her husband at the same time, Li was forced to leave her life of luxury behind. Although her writing becomes dark and melancholy, it was during this period that she created some of her most powerful work.

Alone in the Night
The warm rain and pure wind
Have just freed the willows from
The ice. As I watch the peach trees,
Spring rises from my heart and blooms on
My cheeks. My mind is unsteady,
As if I were drunk. I try
To write a poem in which
My tears will flow together
With your tears. My rouge is stale.
My hairpins are too heavy.
I throw myself across my
Gold cushions, wrapped in my lonely
Doubled quilt, and crush the phoenixes
In my headdress. Alone, deep
In bitter loneliness, without
Even a good dream, I lie,
Trimming the lamp in the passing night.

Eating

The area around the main train station is a good place to seek out cheap eats; also try the night markets for spicy lamb kebabs and other tempting *xiǎo chī* (snacks). The alley off Jing Wulu, between Wei Erlu and Wei Sanlu, is a good place to go. Marked by a *páilou* (decorative arch), Furong Jie north of Quancheng Jie has stall after stall selling noodles, kebabs, *tiěbǎn* (hot plate), squid on a stick and oodles of other snacks. Also try Nanmen Dajie off Quancheng Lu in the commercial district.

Café Galleria (Qíyún Gé; ☎ 602 9999 ext 6310; 6th fl, Crowne Plaza Jinan, 3 Tianditan Jie; buffet meal Y95) Beneath a vast atrium, this large restaurant at the distinguished Crowne Plaza serves Western and Asian dishes in a stylish setting. The Y95 lunch and dinner buffet (11.30am to 2.30pm and 5.30 to 10.30pm) is popular, and there is live music nightly.

Quanjude Roast Duck Restaurant (Quánjùdé Kǎoyādiàn; ☎ 642 8888; 61 Heihuquan Beilu; half/whole duck Y28/56) Large and spacious branch of the famous Běijīng roast duck restaurant (p128). There are Shāndōng, Běijīng and Sìchuān dishes, including *jiācháng shāo dòufu* (family-style cooked tofu, Y12) and *tiěbǎn yángtuǐ* (lamb leg hot plate, Y30), but most people come for the duck. The *zhá mógu* (fried mushrooms, Y15) are tasty, but a bit dry. Wash it all down with a bottle of Maotai (Y580), Wuliangye (Y580) or a small bottle of Erguotou (Y6). You can get here on bus No 83 from the main train station.

Yingquange Restaurant (Yíngquángé Dàjiǔdiàn; ☎ 691 9997; 3 Gongqingtuan Lu; ☸ 9am-10pm; meals from Y40) Very attractively situated alongside a fish-filled pond and bamboo fronds next to Five Dragon Pool Park (left of the south gate), this Sūzhōu-style restaurant has a large range of pricey seafood (abalone from Y38) and extravagant meals, such as Yùhuán Fótiàoqiáng (Buddha jumps over the Wall, Y88). There's also perfectly reasonable standard fare: *huíguō ròu* (pork with hot sauce, Y18), *yúxiāng ròusī* (fish-flavoured minced pork, Y18), spicy and meat-filled *shuǐzhǔ ròupiàn* (boiled spicy pork slices, Y16) and vegetable *jiǎozi* (dumplings, Y18 per *jīn*, or 600g). No English menu, no credit cards.

Yuèdū Jiǔlóu (☎ 708 8555; 588 Jing Qilu; meals Y30) Recently refitted and restyled, this popular Cantonese restaurant is smart and bright,

with dishes (prepared but uncooked) arranged on chilled shelves. Peruse the enormous selection or take a look at the huge choice of seafood in fish tanks.

Getting There & Away

AIR

Jǐ'nán is connected to most major cities: Běijīng (Y500), Dàlián (Y730), Guǎngzhōu (Y1450), Hāěrbīn (Y1030), Hángzhōu (Y780), Hong Kong (Y1940), Kūnmíng (Y1710), Shànghǎi (Y700), Xī'ān (Y870), Yāntái (Y210) and Ürümqi (Y2170).

Civil Aviation Administration of China (CAAC; Zhōngguó Mínháng; ☎ 601 0333, 24hr ticketing; 198 Luoyuan Dajie; ☸ 8am-8pm) is opposite the southern entrance to Baotu Spring Park. A **China Eastern Airlines** (☎ 693 4715/6, 24hr ticketing; 165-2 Chezhan Jie) office is located just south of the main train station. **Shandong Airlines** (☎ 691 6737) has an office on Luoyuan Jie.

BUS

Jǐ'nán has at least three bus stations. The two most useful for travellers are the long-distance bus station (*chángtú qìchē zhàn*) in the north of town and the bus station opposite the main train station.

The bus station opposite the main train station is one of the most orderly in China with buses lined up in neat rows, from Ivecos to luxury Volvos. Within Shāndōng, regular minibuses speed to Tài'ān (Y8, 1½ hours, every 30 minutes) and Qūfù (Y21, 2½ hours, every 30 minutes) until 7pm. Slow buses to Běijīng (Y72, nine hours) and Shànghǎi (Y169, 20 hours) also leave from here. There are six departures a day to Yāntái (Y66, five hours) and luxury buses every hour to Qīngdǎo (Y95, 4½ hours) until 7pm.

The long-distance bus station has frequent buses departing for Běijīng (Y96, 6½ hours), Qīngdǎo (Y50, 3½ hours, every 30 minutes), Yāntái (Y110, 4½ hours) and Wēihǎi (Y139, six hours).

TRAIN

There are two train stations in Jǐ'nán: most trains use the main train station (*Jǐ'nán huǒchē zhàn*), but a handful arrive and depart from the east train station (*huǒchē dōngzhàn*).

Jǐ'nán is a major link in the east-China rail system. From here there are direct trains to

Běijīng (Y74, four to seven hours), Shànghǎi (Y136, 9 to 14 hours) and Qīngdǎo (Y49, five hours). A night train runs to Zhèngzhōu (Y83, nine hours) and to Xī'ān (Y149, 17 hours).

Apart from at the train station, you can . buy tickets (for a service fee) from the **Shandong China Railway International Travel Service** (Shāndōng Zhōngtiě Guólù; ☎ 242 4134; 16 Chezhan Jie; ☉ 8am-5.30pm), near the train station, at the **ticket office** (huǒchē shòupiàochù; ☎ 242 8862 for sleeping tickets; ☉ 8am-6pm), just east of the CNC office on Gongqingtuan Lu, at the Shandong Travel Service (p187) or at your hotel.

Getting Around
TO/FROM THE AIRPORT

Xijiao airport is 40km west of the city and the freeway makes it possible to cover the distance in just 40 minutes. An airport bus leaves from the CAAC ticket office and from the Silver Plaza Shopping Centre (check with CAAC for times). A taxi will cost around Y150.

BUS & TAXI

Bus No 33 connects the long-distance bus station with the main train station. Bus No 51 runs from the main train station through the city centre and then south past Baotu Spring Park and on to Thousand Buddha Mountain. Taxis cost Y6 for the first 3km, then Y1.2 per km thereafter.

AROUND JǏ'NÁN
Simen Pagoda 四门塔

Near the village of Liǔbù, 33km southeast of Jǐ'nán, are some of the oldest Buddhist structures in Shāndōng. Shentong Monastery holds **Simen Pagoda** (Sìmén Tǎ; Four Gate Pagoda; ☎ 284 3051; admission Y10; ☉ 8am-6pm), which dates back to the 6th century and is possibly the oldest stone pagoda in China. The surrounding hills are old burial grounds for the monks of the monastery.

Longhu Pagoda (龙虎塔; Lónghǔ Tǎ; Pagoda of the Dragon & the Tiger) was built during the Tang dynasty. It stands close to the Shentong Monastery and is surrounded by stupas. Higher up is Thousand Buddha Cliff (千佛崖; Qiānfó Yá), with carved grottoes containing Buddhas.

To reach Simen Pagoda from Jǐ'nán, catch bus No 22 (Y4, 1½ hours) from near

the corner of Jing Silu and Wei Erlu. The Shandong Travel Service (p187) can arrange tours.

TÀI SHĀN 泰山
☎ 0538

Southern Chinese claim 'myriad mountains, rivers and geniuses' while Shāndōng citizens smugly contest they have 'one mountain, one river and one saint', implying they have the last word on each: Tài Shān, the Yellow River and Confucius. Tài Shān is not only the most revered of China's five sacred Taoist peaks, it's the most climbed mountain on earth and lends its name to a popular brand of cigarettes. Once upon a time, imperial sacrifices to heaven and earth were offered from its summit. Only five of China's emperors ever climbed Tài Shān, although Emperor Qianlong of the Qing dynasty scaled it 11 times. From its heights Confucius uttered the dictum 'The world is small'; Mao lumbered up and declared 'The East is Red'. You, too, can climb up and say 'I'm knackered'.

Tài Shān is a unique experience – its supernatural allure (see the boxed text, p193) attracts the Chinese in droves. Bixia, the Princess of the Azure Clouds, a Taoist deity whose presence permeates the temples dotted along the route, is a powerful cult figure for the rural women of Shāndōng and beyond. Tribes of wiry grandmothers trot up the steps with surprising ease, their target the cluster of temples at the summit where they burn money and incense, praying for their progeny. It's said that if you climb Tài Shān you'll live to be 100. Sun worshippers – foreign and Chinese – also muster wide-eyed on the peak, straining for the first flickers of dawn. In ancient Chinese tradition, it was believed that the sun began its westward journey from Tài Shān.

Tài Shān is 1545m above sea level, with a climbing distance of 7.5km from base to summit on the central route. The elevation change from Midway Gate to Heaven (Zhōngtiān Mén) to the summit is approximately 600m. The mountain is not a major climb, but with 6660 steps to the summit, it can be gruelling. One wonders how many backs were broken in the building of the temples and stone stairs on Tài Shān – a massive undertaking accomplished without any mechanical aids.

BEIJING TO SHANGHAI

Climate

Bear in mind that weather conditions on the mountain vary considerably compared with Tài'ān. Clouds and mist frequently envelop the mountain, particularly in summer. The best times to visit are in spring and autumn when the humidity is low, although old timers say that the clearest weather is from early October onwards. In winter the weather is often fine, but very cold. The tourist season peaks from May to October.

Due to weather changes, you're advised to carry warm clothing with you, no matter what the season. The summit can be very cold, windy and wet; army overcoats are available there for hire and you can buy waterproof coats from one of the vendors.

Climbing Tài Shān

The town of Tài'ān (p194) lies at the foot of Tài Shān and is the gateway to the mountain. Low-season tickets are Y80 (1 December to 31 January), high-season tickets are Y100 (1 February to 30 November); student and senior tickets are half-price. Voluntary insurance is available for Y2.

ON FOOT

It's possible to spend the night at Midway Gate to Heaven halfway up the mountain, or on the summit. Allow two hours for climbing between each of these points – a total of eight hours for the round trip (although

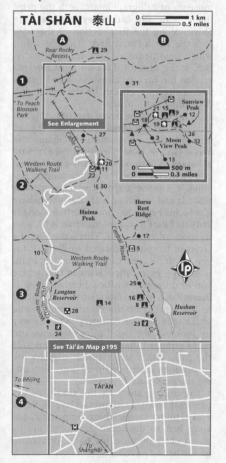

TÀI SHĀN 泰山

0 ———— 1 km
0 ———— 0.5 miles

See Tài'ān Map p195

To Běijīng

To Shànghǎi

TÀI'ĀN

you can get down to the ticket office from the Midway Gate to Heaven in an hour, at speed). Allowing several more hours would make the climb less strenuous and give you more time to look around.

If you want to see the sunrise, dump your gear at the train station or at a guesthouse in Tài'ān and time your ascent so that you'll reach the summit before sundown. Stay overnight at one of the summit guesthouses and get up early the next morning for the famed sunrise, which may or may not make its appearance. It's possible to scale the mountain at night and some Chinese do this, timing it so that they arrive before sunrise. The way is lit by lamps, but it is advisable to take a torch, as well as warm clothes, food and water.

There are two main paths up the mountain: the central route and the western route, converging midway at Midway Gate to Heaven. Most people slog up the central route (once the imperial route and littered with cultural relics) and head down (usually by bus) along the western route. Other trails run through orchards and woods.

BY MINIBUS & CABLE CAR
From the roundabout at Tianwai Village (天外村; Tiānwài Cūn), at the foot of the western route, **minibuses** (one way Y20) depart every 20 minutes (when full) to Midway Gate to Heaven, halfway up Tài Shān. The minibuses operate 4am to 8pm during high season, less regularly during low season. Bus No 3 runs to Tianwai Village from Tài'ān's train station. Frequent buses come down the mountain; however, as this is the favoured option for getting back to Tài'ān, you may have to wait several buses for a seat.

It's about a five-minute walk from Midway Gate to Heaven to the **cable car** (kōngzhōng suǒdào; ☎ 822 2606; each way Y45, children under 1.3m free; ⏲ 7am-6pm 16 Apr–15 Oct, 8am-5.30pm 16 Oct–15 Apr). The journey takes around 10 to 15 minutes to travel to **Moon View Peak** (Yùeguān Fēng), near the South Gate to Heaven (Nántiān Mén). Be warned, if you climb Tài Shān in the high season or on weekends, the queues may force you to wait for up to two hours for a cable car.

The same applies when you want to descend from the summit; fortunately, there is another **cable car** (suǒdào; Y45; ⏲ 7.30am-5.30pm 16 Apr–15 Oct, 8am-5pm 16 Oct–15 Apr) that only carries six passengers and is as regular as clockwork. It takes you from north of South Gate to Heaven down to **Peach Blossom Park** (桃花源; Taóhūa Yuán), a scenic area behind Tài Shān that is also worth exploring. From here you can take a minibus to Tài'ān (Y20, 40 minutes). You can reverse this process by first taking a minibus from Tài'ān train station to Peach Blossom Park and then ascending by cable car.

CENTRAL ROUTE
On this route you'll see a bewildering catalogue of bridges, trees, rivers, gullies, towers, inscriptions, caves, pavilions and temples. Tài Shān functions as an outdoor museum of calligraphic art, with the prize items being the **Rock Valley Scripture** (Jīng Shíyù) along the first section of the walk and the **North Prayer Rock** (Gǒngběi Shí), which commemorates an imperial sacrifice, at the summit. Lost on most foreigners are the literary allusions, word games and analogies spelt out by the calligraphy decorating the journey.

At the end of the paved part of Hongmen Lu is the **Guandi Temple** (Guāndì Miào; admission free) containing a large statue of Guandi, the Taoist God of War. Nearby is the **First Gate of Heaven** (Yītiān Mén) and the traditional commencement of the climb proper. Beyond is a stone archway overgrown with wisteria and inscribed with 'the place where Confucius began to climb. Further along is **Red Gate Palace** (Hóng Mén Gōng; admission Y5), with its wine-coloured walls. This is the first of a series of temples dedicated to Bixia (Princess of the Azure Clouds). Further again is a large gate called **Wànxiān Lóu**, where you find the ticket office. Further along is **Doumu Hall** (Dǒumŭ Gōng), first constructed in 1542 and given the more magical name of 'Dragon Spring Nunnery'. On the way up look out for small piles of stones and rocks arranged Blair Witch style, alongside the path. Other superstitious displays are invocations inscribed on ribbons, festooning the pines and cypresses.

Continuing through the tunnel of cypresses known as Cypress Cave is **Huima Peak** (Húimǎ Ling), where Emperor Zhenzong had to dismount and continue by sedan chair because his horse refused to go further.

MIDWAY GATE TO HEAVEN 中天门

This is the second celestial gate and where you can find the small and smoky **God of Wealth Temple** (Cáishén Miào). A little way on is **Five Pine Pavilion** (Wǔsōng Tíng), where, in 219 BC, Emperor Qin Shi Huang was overtaken by a violent storm and was sheltered by the pine trees. He promoted them to the 5th rank of minister.

Follow the **Path of Eighteen Bends** (十八盘) that will eventually lead to the summit. You'll pass **Opposing Pines Pavilion** (Dùisōng Tíng) and the **Welcoming Pine** (Yíngkè Sōng), with a branch extended as if to shake hands. Beyond is the **Archway to Immortality** (Shēngxiān Fáng). It was believed that those passing through the archway would become celestial beings. From here to the summit, emperors were carried in sedan chairs.

SOUTH GATE TO HEAVEN 南天门

The final stretch takes you to **South Gate to Heaven**, the third celestial gate. Walk along Tian Jie to **Azure Clouds Temple** (Bìxiá Cí; admission Y5), where elders offer money and food to the deities of Bixia, Yanguang Nainai and Taishan Songzi Niangniang (the latter helping women bear children). The iron tiling on the temple buildings is intended to prevent damage by strong winds, and on the bronze eaves are *chīwěn* (ornaments meant to protect against fire). The temple is splendid, with its location in the clouds.

Climbing higher, you will pass the Tao temple **Qingdi Palace** (青帝宫; Qīngdì Gōng), before reaching the fog- and cloud-swathed **Jade Emperor Temple** (Yùhuáng Dǐng), perched on the highest point (1545m) of the Tài Shān plateau. Within is an effigy of the

---

TÀI SHĀN

Tài Shān's place in the hearts and minds of the Chinese people is deeply rooted in their most ancient creation myth – the story of Pan Gu. In the beginning when all was chaos, and heaven and earth were swirling together, Pan Gu was born and promptly set about separating the ground and the sky. With each passing day he grew taller, the sky grew higher and the earth grew thicker, until, after 18,000 years, the two were fully separated and Pan Gu died of exhaustion. As his body disintegrated, his eyes became the sun and the moon, his blood transformed into rivers, his sweat fell as rain, and his head and limbs became the five sacred mountains of China, Tài Shān among them.

Maybe because it sprang from Pan Gu's head, or perhaps because of its location in the dominant east (which signifies birth and spring), Tài Shān is the most revered of these five sacred peaks. The throngs of modern visitors are but recipients of a tradition of pilgrimage and worship that stretches back to earliest historical times.

For nearly 3000 years emperors have paid homage, a few reaching the summit, all contributing to the rich legacy of temples, trees, pavilions and calligraphy. Originally made for sacrifices, these visits soon acquired a political significance: it was thought heaven would never allow an unworthy ruler to ascend, so a successful climb denoted divine approval.

Emperors aside, China's three most prominent schools of thought also hold Tài Shān dear. A second legend has it there once lived a she-fox on Tài Shān, who, by living a strict Taoist existence, transformed into a goddess named Bixia (Princess of the Azure Clouds). There she remained happily until the arrival of Sakyamuni, the founder of Buddhism, who fell in love with the place and asked her to leave. Bixia refused and Sakyamuni was forced to flee when he tried unsuccessfully to trick her into leaving. Today Bixia is venerated as the protectress of peasant women and as the bringer of dawn. A Taoist monk named Lang established the first temples on the mountain in 351 BC, and the most influential are still those dedicated to Bixia.

Thus Tài Shān has become a repository of Chinese culture, spanning dynasties and religions, and prompting the modern Chinese writer Guo Moruo to describe the mountain as 'a partial miniature of Chinese culture'. Indeed, it is probably best to bear this analogy in mind when you visit, as modern China is definitely leaving its mark. Even by the Qing dynasty there were several hundred thousand visitors each year, and on the Labour Day public holiday in 2001 an estimated 60,000 people crowded onto the summit. With the invasion of photographers, karaoke stands, porters and hawkers, and even an annual race to the summit, the sacred peak of Tài Shān might just become a victim of its own popularity.

Jade Emperor, an attendant statue of Tai-shan Laojun and some frescoes.

In the courtyard is a rock inscribed with the elevation of the mountain. In front of the temple is the one piece of calligraphy that you really can appreciate – the **Wordless Monument** (Wúzì Bēi). One story goes that it was set up by Emperor Wu 2100 years ago – he wasn't satisfied with what his scribes came up with, so he left it to the viewer's imagination; others attribute the monument to Qin Shi Huang (p31). Pilgrims throw coins into two urns at the exact peak (Tàishān Jǐdǐng) below a tablet upon which is written the ancient Taoist character for Tài Shān. Near the Shenqi Hotel (right) is a **Confucius Temple** (Wén Miào), with statues of Confucius (Kongzi), Mencius (Mengzi), Zengzi and other Confucian luminaries.

The main sunrise vantage point is the **North Prayer Rock** (Gǒngběi Shí); if you're lucky, visibility extends to over 200km, as far as the coast. The sunset slides over the Yellow River side. At the rear of the mountain is the **Rear Rocky Recess** (后石坞; Hòu Shíwū), one of the better-known spots for viewing pine trees; there are some ruins tangled in the foliage. It's a good place to ramble and lose the crowds for a while.

WESTERN ROUTE
The most popular way to descend the mountain is by bus via the western route. The footpath and road intercept at a number of points, and are often one and the same. Given the amount of traffic, you might prefer to hop on a bus rather than inhale its exhaust. If you do hike down, the trail is not always clearly marked. (Note that buses will not stop for you once they have left Midway Gate to Heaven.)

Either by bus or foot, the western route treats you to considerable variation in scenery, with orchards, pools and flowering plants that make traditional Chinese paintings seem incredibly realistic. The major attraction along this route is **Black Dragon Pool** (Hēilóng Tán), which is just below **Longevity Bridge** (Chángshòu Qiáo) and is fed by a small waterfall. Swimming in the waters are rare carp, which are occasionally cooked for the moneyed class. Mythical tales revolve around this pool, which is said to be the site of underground carp palaces and of magic herbs that turn people into beasts.

An enjoyable way to end the hike is with a visit to **Puzhao Temple** (Pǔzhào Sì; admission Y5). This monastery was founded 1500 years ago along the base of the mountain.

Sleeping & Eating
Accommodation prices listed here don't apply to holiday periods, such as the first week of May, when room prices can triple in price.

Shenxiu Gong Hotel (Shénxiù Gōng Bīnguǎn; 10 Dengshan Lu, Midway Gate to Heaven; 8-/4-bed dm Y20/40) By the steps opposite the God of Wealth Temple at the Midway Gate to Heaven, this place is simple, unadorned and cheap. There are other hotels in the vicinity.

Xianju Hotel (Xiánjū Fàndiàn; ☎ 823 9984; fax 822 6877; 2 Tian Jie; s/d/tr/q Y200/360/320/180) Situated just before the *páilou* marking Tian Jie beyond the South Gate to Heaven, this two-star hotel has a decent selection of rooms.

Shenqi Hotel (Shénqí Bīnguǎn; ☎ 822 3866; fax 821 5399; s Y580, d Y680-780, ste Y6800-8800; 🔀) The only three-star hotel on the summit, this reasonably smart hotel has a restaurant (serving Taoist banquets) and a bar, and is accessed up some steep steps. Rooms are reasonably clean, but nothing special (sun watchers are roused well before sunrise).

There is no food shortage on Tài Shān; the central route is dotted with teahouses, stalls, vendors and restaurants. Your pockets are likely to feel emptier than your stomach, but keep in mind that all supplies are carried up by foot and that the prices rise as you do.

TÀI'ĀN 泰安
☎ 0538 / pop 619,000
Tài'ān is the gateway town to the sacred Tài Shān. You'll probably need the better part of a day to take in the mountain and Tài'ān has a few sights, so spending the night here is advised.

Incidentally, Tài'ān is the home town of Jiang Qing, Mao's fourth wife, ex-actress and spearhead of the Gang of Four, on whom all of China's ills are sometimes blamed. She was later airbrushed out of Chinese history and committed suicide in May 1991.

Orientation
Tài'ān is not a large town, so getting about is straightforward. The most appealing part of town lies around the Dai Temple, Hongmen Lu, which leads up the mountain

itself, and the east-west running Dongyue Dajie and Shengping Jie. This area also contains a range of hotels, Internet cafés and restaurants. The train and long-distance bus stations are in the west of town.

Information

BOOKSHOPS

Xinhua Bookshop (Xīnhuá Shūdiàn; 80-82 Qingnian Lu; 8.30am-7.30pm summer, 8.30am-6pm winter) Has a selection of Tài'ān and Shāndōng maps, which you can also pick up from street vendors (non-English).

EMERGENCY & VISAS

PSB (Gōngānjú; ☎ 827 5264; cnr Dongyue Dajie & Qingnian Lu; 8.30am-noon & 1-5pm Mon-Fri) The visa office is in the eastern side of this huge new building.

INTERNET ACCESS

Billion People Internet Café (Yìzhòng Wǎngbā; 18 Hongmen Lu; per hr Y1.5; 7.30am-9.30pm)
Tangyao Internet Café (Tángyáo Wǎngbā; 22 Hongmen Lu; per hr Y1; 6am-midnight)
Wanjing Internet Café (Wànjǐng Wǎngbā; 180 Daizong Dajie; per hr Y1; 7am-10pm)

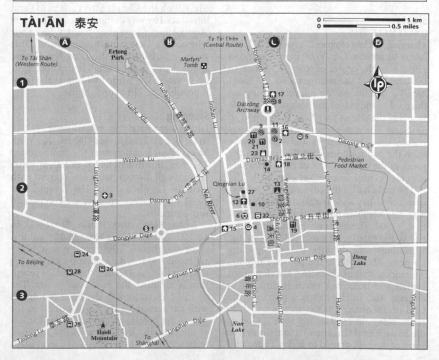

Yuan Internet Café (Yuán Wǎngbā; 206 Daizong Dajie; per hr Y1; ☯ 7am-midnight)

MEDICAL SERVICES

Central Hospital (Zhōngxīn Yīyuàn; ☎ 822 4161; 29 Longtan Lu)

Renji Pharmacy (Rénjì Yàodiàn; 131 Hushan Lu) Sells Western medicines.

MONEY

Bank of China (Zhōngguó Yínháng; 48 Dongyue Dajie; ☯ 8.30am-5pm) Has a 24-hour ATM accepting Visa, MasterCard, Cirrus, JCB and Amex.

POST

Post & Telephone Office (9 Dongyue Dajie; ☯ 8am-7pm summer, 8am-6pm winter) This main branch is across the road from McDonalds. There is also a smaller post office at 240 Daizong Dajie.

TRAVEL AGENTS

China International Travel Service (CITS; Zhōngguó Guójì Lǚxíngshè; ☎ 822 8797; fax 833 2240; 22 Hongmen Lu) At the time of writing, CITS was in the process of moving; phone for its new address. Can arrange tours, air and train tickets.

Sights

DAI TEMPLE 岱庙

This huge **temple complex** (Dài Miào; ☎ 822 3491; Daibeng Lu; admission Y20; ☯ 7.45am-6pm, last tickets 5.30pm) is in the centre of town. Entrance to the temple is at the southern end of Hongmen Lu. Traditionally a pilgrimage stop on the road to the sacred mountain, the temple was also the site of sacrifices to the god of Tài Shān. The whole complex badly requires restoration – entire trees and shrubs poke from the hall rooftops, and the lions in the south of the complex sprout flowers (where *does* the revenue from ticket sales go?).

The main hall is the colossal twin yellow-eaved, nine-bay wide **Temple of Heavenly Blessing** (天贶殿; Tiānkuàng Diàn), dating back to AD 1009. The naturally lit and dark interior is decorated with a marvellous, flaking, 62m-long Song dynasty fresco depicting Emperor Zhenzong as the god of Tài Shān. Among the cast of characters are elephants, camels and lions, but much is difficult to discern. Also in the hall is a statue of the God of Tài Shān; a tablet in front of him reads '*Dōngyuè Tàishān zhī Shén*' ('God of the Eastern Peak Tài Shān'). Note the urn in front of the hall, draped in locks. There's no

photography allowed inside, and for Y1 you get shower caps to go over your shoes.

South of the hall are several stelae supported on the backs of *bìxì* (mythical tortoise-like dragons). Look out for the scripture pillar, its etched words long lost to the Shāndōng winds and inquisitive hands.

In the Han Bai courtyard stand cypresses supposedly planted by the Han emperor Wudi. Among the trees is a stele inscribed with the characters '*Guān Hǎi*' meaning 'Look at the Sea' – a tricky feat indeed from the Dai Temple. Near the entrance to the courtyard is a vast *bìxì* with five-inch fangs.

Try and come in spring, when the trees are in bloom. To the south of the south gate (Zhèngyáng Mén) is a splendid *páilou* decorated with lion, dragon and phoenix motifs.

CHRISTIAN CHURCH 基督教堂

Hardly on a par with the Dai Temple, but it's interesting to find a German-built, possibly early-20th-century **church** (2 Dengyun Jie) tucked away in the heart of Tài'ān. Largely hidden behind a wall just west off Qingnian Lu (on a small side street called Dengyun Jie – literally 'Climb the Clouds Street'; 登云街) and introduced by way of the Chinese characters '*Àiguó Àijiào*' ('Love your country, love your religion' – a Communist intercession), this sweet little House of the Lord has Gothic arches, stone walls, a small belfry and regular services. The white building at the front is possibly the old church house.

Sleeping

Taishan Grand Hotel (Tàishān Dàjiǔdiàn; ☎ 822 7211; fax 822 6162; 210 Daizong Dajie; d Y180-380; ❀) With an excellent location near the trailhead for Tài Shān, this fine hotel has excellent-value rooms (well discounted in low season) with views of Tài Shān or the Dai Temple. The Y260 doubles are roomy, well kept and recommended.

Taishan Hotel (Tàishān Bīnguǎn; ☎ 822 5888; fax 822 1432; 26 Hongmen Lu; d Y300-420; ❀) At this three-star hotel, Y300 gets you a high-ceilinged room with a scrappy carpet. It's OK, but there is a feeling that staff at reception is awaiting the next tour group. The marbled, clean look of the foyer (equipped with flat screen TVs) fails to extend to the rest of the hotel; you can get better for less at the Taishan Grand Hotel a few minutes' walk south. The hotel shop has useful maps of Iraq and Kuwait, but only out-of-date maps of Tài Shān.

Yuzuo Hotel (Yùzuò Bīnguǎn; ☎ 822 3852; fax 822 3180; 3 Daimiao Beijie; d Y280-589, tr Y360, ste Y460-680; 🖫) There may be traditional touches, but this is a very Chinese, socialist-era hotel. It's a series of small two-floor units finely located next to the Dai Temple, with a pleasant atmosphere and polite staff. The carpeted Y480 doubles are clean and come with water cooler; the Y280 doubles are OK and have wooden floors. There's also a small pharmacy, supermarket and restaurant (cooking up Taoist dishes).

Overseas Chinese Hotel (Huáqiáo Dàshà; ☎ 822 8112; fax 822 8171; 15 Dongyue Dajie; d Y400-600, ste Y1000-1980; 🖫) With a huge golden effigy of Milefo and a bust of Beethoven in the lobby, this is a pricey and odd-looking place. You can splash out Y338 per head on set meals at the Abalone King Vigor restaurant next door if you want.

Eating

Tài'ān doesn't have a huge choice of restaurants, but there is some good food around. Remember that everything packs up around 9pm.

Ā Dōng de Shuǐjiǎo (☎ 827 3644; 178 Daizong Dajie; meals Y25-30) This handily located, simple and clean dumpling restaurant cooks a large range of tasty and filling *jiǎozi* (stuffed dumplings), including *yángròu* (lamb, Y16 per *jīn* – half a *jīn* is enough for one), *sūsānxiàn* (vegetable, Y10 per *jīn*), *xiānggūròu* (Chinese mushroom and meat, Y14 per *jīn*). Other staples include soups and *hóngshāo qiézi* (braised aubergine, Y8), sweet and laced with garlic. No English menu; look for the yellow façade with red characters.

Ā Dōng Jiāchángcài (☎ 822 0718, 823 1516; 25 Hongmen Lu; meals Y20-25) Like its sister branch, this popular and centrally located eatery serves dumplings, and a range of chicken, fish, soup and vegetable dishes. Dishes are rather hit and miss: the *suāncài yú* (fish and pickled vegetables soup) should be sharper, more watery and less oily, but you get tonnes of fish. The *gōngbào jīdīng* (spicy chicken with peanuts) is too sweet, but the *yángròu jiǎozi* (Y16 per *jīn*) are good and vegetarians can settle for *dìsānxiān* (potatoes, aubergine and green peppers, Y4).

Dàoxiāngyuán (Shengping Jie) This new-looking and brightly lit cake and bread shop not far

from the Dai Temple south gate (opposite the small Bank of China) has a large selection of tasty looking cakes, breads and tea.

Entertainment

Western films are occasionally shown at the **Tai'an Cinema** (Tài'ān Diànyǐngyuàn; Shengping Jie), diagonally opposite McDonalds.

Shopping

A lively daily market sets up at the base of Hongmen Lu, flogging all manner of items, including birds, polished and carved stones, tree roots, fake ceramics, busts of Chairman Mao, Buddhist trinkets, fish, plants and herbs.

Getting There & Away

AIR

The nearest large airport is at Jǐ'nán. If you want to organise air tickets in Tài'ān, you can purchase them from the **ticket office** (Hángkōng Dìngpiàochù; ☎ 827 0855; 111 Qingnian Lu; ⏱ 8am-6pm Mon-Sat) on the other side of Qingnian Lu from the Xinhua Bookstore.

BUS

Tài'ān can be accessed by road from either Jǐ'nán or Qūfù and is worth combining with a trip to the latter. There are several bus stations in Tài'ān. From the **Tai Shan Bus Station** (Tài Shān Qichēzhàn; Caiyuan Dajie), there are regular buses to Jǐ'nán (standard Y8.5, luxury Y12.5, every 20 to 30 minutes, 6am to 9pm) and Qūfù (luxury Y15, hourly, 7.10am to 6pm). From the **Long-Distance Bus Station** (Chángtú Qichēzhàn; ☎ 210 8606; Panhe Lu), south of the train station, are buses to Hángzhōu (Y180, 7pm), Jǐ'nán (standard Y9, luxury Y21, every 15 to 30 minutes), Kāifēng (Y43, 6.20am), Níngbō (Y220, 11.30am), Qīngdǎo (Y69, three morning buses), Qūfù (Y15, every 20 minutes, one hour), Wēihǎi (Y90, four morning buses) and Yāntái (Y83, three morning buses).

TRAIN

Exiting Tài'ān station, the first thing you see is not Tài Shān, but a huge white bust of Lei Feng, an iconic soldier of the Mao era. There are more than 20 express trains running daily through Tài'ān, including links to Běijīng (Y79, five daily), Jǐ'nán (Y9, nine daily), Shànghǎi (Y102, 10 daily), Qīngdǎo (Y60, 10 daily) and Yāntái (Y41, three daily). Some special express trains from Jǐ'nán don't stop at Tài'ān. Check schedules to avoid arriving at some unpleasant hour.

Getting Around

Getting around is easy as most destinations can be reached on foot. The long-distance bus station is just south of the train station, so all local transport is directed towards these two terminals.

There are three main bus routes. Bus No 3 runs from the Tài Shān central route trailhead to the western route trailhead via the train station. Bus Nos 1 and 2 also end up near the train station. Minibuses run on the same routes.

Taxis can be found outside the train station. Taxis start at Y5 (then Y1.5 per km thereafter).

QŪFÙ 曲阜

☎ 0537 / population 88,000

Of monumental significance to the Chinese is Qūfù, birthplace of Confucius, with its harmonies of carved stone, timber and imperial architecture. Following tradition, there are two fairs a year in Qūfù – spring and autumn – when the place comes alive with craftspeople, healers, acrobats, peddlers and peasants. It also hosts a big party on 28 September to mark Confucius' birthday.

Orientation

The old core of Qūfù is small and easy to get around, a grid of streets built around the Confucius Temple and Confucius Mansions at its heart, with the Confucius Forest north of town. Gulou Jie bisects the town from north to south, and the bus station is in the south of town.

Information

BOOKSHOPS

Xinhua Bookstore (Xīnhuá Shūdiàn; Gulou Nanjie; ☯ 8am-6.30pm summer, 8am-5.30pm winter) Opposite southeast cnr of Drum Tower.

EMERGENCY & VISAS

PSB (Gōngānjú; ☎ 449 4523; 1 Wuyuntan Lu; ☯ 8am-noon & 2.30-6pm Mon-Fri) South of town and best reached by taxi.

INTERNET ACCESS

Xiandai Internet Café (Xiàndài Wǎngbā; alley off Shendao Lu; per hr Y1.5; ☯ 8am-midnight) Head north up Shendao Lu and take first turn-off on left.

Xinchao Internet Café (Xīnchāo Wǎngbā; Dongmen Dajie; per hr Y1.5; ☯ 8am-midnight) Through gateway in courtyard to the west of the Bank of China.

Zhixin Internet Café (Zhīxīn Wǎngbā; alley east off Shendao Lu; per hr Y2; ☯ 7am-midnight) Head north up Shendao Lu and take first turn-off on left.

MEDICAL SERVICES

People's Hospital (Rénmín Yīyuàn; ☎ 441 2440; Tianguandi Jie)

People's No 2 Hospital (Rénmín Dìèr Yīyuàn; 7 Gulou Beijie)

MONEY

Bank of China (Zhōngguó Yínháng; 96 Dongmen Dajie; ☯ 8am-6pm Mon-Fri) No ATM for foreign cards, but there's a foreign-exchange desk.

POST

Post Office (8-1 Gulou Beijie; ☯ 7.30am-6.30pm summer, 8am-6pm winter) North of the Drum Tower.

TOURIST INFORMATION & TRAVEL AGENCIES

Qufu Tourist Center (Qūfù Shì Lǚyóu Zīxún Zhōngxīn; ☎ 449 0799; 4 Gulou Beijie)

Qufu Tourist Hotline (☎ 449 0799/448 6500)

Qufu Youth Travel Service (Qūfù Qīngnián Lǚxíngshè; ☎ 449 8275; cnr Queli Jie & Gulou Beijie; ☯ 8am-5pm)

Sights

CONFUCIUS TEMPLE 孔庙

The **temple** (Kǒng Miào; ☎ 449 5235; admission Y50; ☯ 8am-5pm) started out as a simple memorial hall and mushroomed into a complex one-fifth the size of the Qūfù town centre. Some visitors love the place, while others find it stale and ossified: musty, dusty and redolent of a neglected and moth-eaten tome.

The main entrance is in the south and leads through a series of triple-door gates. The first few courtyards are airy, cypress-covered and full of green grass. Magnificent gnarled, twisting pines occupy the courtyards in the temple grounds along with over 1000 steles, with inscriptions dating from Han to Qing times – the largest such collection in China. Several broken stelae (victims of the sage's episodic unpopularity perhaps) in the temple grounds have been reassembled with brackets and cement.

Roughly halfway along the north-south axis is the triple-eaved **Great Pavilion of the Constellation of Scholars** (奎文阁; Kuíwén Gé), a very tall and imposing Jin dynasty wooden

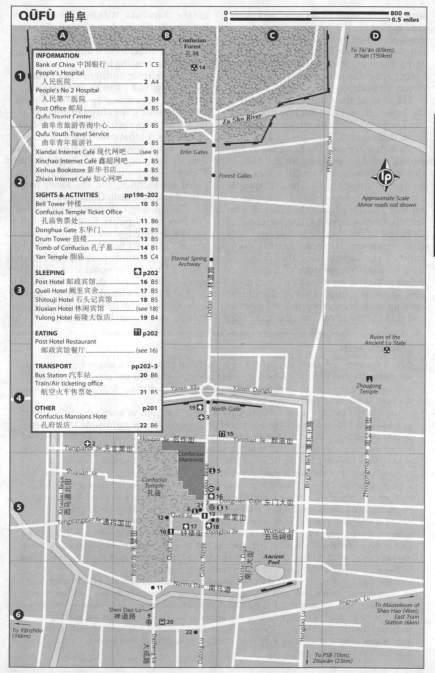

QŪFÙ 曲阜

structure containing prints detailing Confucius' exploits in the Analects. Beyond lie a series of colossal, twin-eaved stele pavilions, followed by **Dacheng Gate** (大成门; Dàchéng Mén), north of which is the **Apricot Platform** (杏坛; Xìng Tán) from where Confucius taught his students.

The core of the Confucian complex is the huge yellow-eaved **Dacheng Hall** (大成殿; Dàchéng Diàn), which, in its present form, dates from 1724; it towers 31m on a white marble terrace. The Kong family imported glazed yellow tiling for the halls in Confucius Temple, and special stones were brought in from Xīshān. The craftspeople carved the 10 dragon-coiled columns so expertly that they had to be covered with red silk when Emperor Qianlong came to Qūfù lest he felt that the Forbidden City's Hall of Supreme Harmony paled in comparison. The superb stone they're carved from is called 'fish roe stone'; the smoother pillars at the rear are also carved with dragons. Inside is a huge statue of Confucius residing on a throne, encapsulated in a red and gold burnished cabinet. Above the sage

are the characters 'Wànshì Shībiǎo', meaning 'model teacher for all ages'. The next hall, the **Chamber Hall** (寝殿; Qǐn Diàn), was built for Confucius' wife and now provides a home for roosting birds.

At the extreme northern end of the temple is **Shengji Hall** (圣迹殿; Shèngjì Diàn), a memorial hall containing a series of stones engraved with scenes from the life of Confucius and tales about him. They are copies of an older set that date back to 1592.

There are several other halls and side temples, including the **Houtu Temple**, the **Holy Kitchen** (神庖), where animals were prepared for sacrifice, and the **Family Temple**. East of Dacheng Hall, **Chongsheng Hall** (崇圣祠; Chóngshèng Cí) is also adorned with fabulous carved pillars. South of the hall is the **Lu Wall** (鲁壁), where the ninth descendant of Confucius hid the sacred texts during the book burning campaign of Emperor Qin Shi Huang. The books were discovered again during the Han dynasty (206 BC–AD 220), and led to a lengthy scholastic dispute between those who followed a reconstructed version of the last books and those who

---

CONFUCIANISM

Qūfù is the birth and death place of the sage Confucius (551–479 BC), whose impact was not felt during his own lifetime. He lived in abject poverty and hardly put pen to paper, but his teachings were recorded by dedicated followers in *The Analects of Confucius*. His descendants, the Kong family, fared considerably better.

The original Confucian temple at Qūfù (dating from 478 BC) was enlarged, remodelled, added to, taken away from and rebuilt. The majority of the present buildings are from the Ming dynasty. In 1513 armed bands sacked the temple and the Kong residence, resulting in walls being erected around the town from 1522 to 1567 to fortify it. These walls were recently removed, but vestiges of Ming town planning, like the Drum and Bell towers (Gǔlóu and Zhōnglóu), remain.

More a code that defined hierarchical relationships than a religion, Confucianism has had a great impact on Chinese culture. It teaches that son must respect father, wife must respect husband, commoner must respect official, official must respect ruler and so on. The essence of its teachings are obedience, respect, selflessness and working for the common good.

You would think that this code would have fitted nicely into the new order of communism; however, it was swept aside because of its connections with the past. Confucius was seen as a kind of misguided feudal educator, and clan ties and ancestor worship were viewed as a threat. In 1948 Confucius' direct heir, the first-born son of the 77th generation of the Kong family, fled to Taiwan, breaking a 2500-year tradition of Kong residence in Qūfù.

While the current popularity of the great sage is undeniable, it is debatable as to what extent his teachings are taking fresh root in China. The majority of devotees around Qūfù are middle-aged or elderly, suggesting that the comeback of Confucianism is more likely a re-emergence of beliefs never effectively squashed by the communists. Chinese scholars are making careful statements reaffirming the significance of Confucius' historical role and suggesting that the 'progressive' aspects of his work were even cited in the writings of Mao Zedong. Confucius, too, it seems, can be rehabilitated.

supported the teachings in the rediscovered ones. You can also hunt down **Confucius' Well**, but you may instead stumble across manhole covers inscribed with 'Qūfù Zìláishuǐ', meaning 'Qufu Tapwater'. Dotted around are ancient scholar trees (some apparently from the Tang dynasty, but virtually dead) and a Gingko from the Song. You can exit from the east gate, **Donghua Gate** (东华门; Dōnghuá Mén), if you wish.

CONFUCIUS MANSIONS 孔府

Adjacent to the Confucius Temple are the **Confucius Mansions** (Kǒng Fǔ; ☎ 441 2235; admission Y30; ☺ 8am-5pm), originally dating from the 16th century. It's a maze of 450 halls, rooms, buildings and side passages, and getting around requires a compass. The complex is not well kept, despite Unesco (World Heritage Site) patronage and copious ticket sales. Some halls, such as the **Hall of Loyalty and Forbearance** (忠恕堂; Zhōngshù Táng), are forlorn portraits of peeling paint and rotting timber. Not everything comes with English captions.

The Confucius Mansions were the most sumptuous aristocratic lodgings in China – indicative of the Kong family's former great power. From the Han to the Qing dynasties, the descendants of Confucius were ennobled and granted privileges by the emperors. They lived like kings themselves, with 180-course meals, servants and consorts. Confucius even picked up some posthumous honours.

Qūfù grew around the Confucius Mansions and was an autonomous estate administered by the Kongs, who had powers of taxation and execution. Emperors could drop in to visit – the Ceremonial Gate near the south entrance was opened only for this event. Because of this royal protection, huge quantities of furniture, ceramics, artefacts, customary and personal effects survived, and some may be viewed. The Kong family archives are a rich legacy and also survived.

The Confucius Mansions are built on an 'interrupted' north-to-south axis. Grouped by the south gate are the former administrative offices (taxes, edicts, rites, registration and examination halls).

The **Ceremonial Gate** (重光门; Chóngguāng Mén) leads to the **Great Hall** (大堂; Dà Táng). To the north is the **Neizhai Gate** (内宅门; Nèizhái Mén), a special gate that seals off the residential quarters (used for weddings, banquets and private functions). The large 'Shou' character (壽, meaning longevity) inside the single-eaved **Upper Front Chamber** (前上房; Qián Shàng Fáng) north of Neizhai Gate was a gift from empress Cixi. The **Front Chamber** (前堂楼; Qián Táng Lóu) was where the duke lived and is interestingly laid out on two floors – rare for a hall this size.

East of the Neizhai Gate is the **Tower of Refuge** (避难楼; Bìnàn Lóu), where the Kong clan could gather if the peasants turned nasty. It has an iron-lined ceiling on the ground floor, a staircase that could be yanked up into the interior, a trap and provisions for a lengthy retreat. Grouped to the west of the main axis are former recreational facilities (studies, guestrooms, libraries and small temples). To the east is the odd kitchen, ancestral temple and the family branch apartments.

One of the best aspects of the mansions is surely the garden at the rear, with greenery, foliage, flowers, blossoming trees (in spring), bamboo and a sense of space. Take a seat in one of the old pavilions and relax.

CONFUCIAN FOREST 孔林

North of town on Lindao Lu is the **Confucian Forest** (Kǒng Lín; admission Y20; ☺ 7.30am-6pm), the largest artificial park and best preserved cemetery in China.

The pine and cypress forest of over 100,000 trees (it is said that each of Confucius' students planted a tree from his birthplace) covers 200 hectares and is bounded by a wall 10km long. Confucius and his descendants have been buried here over the past 2000 years, and are still being buried here today. Flanking the approach to the **Tomb of Confucius** (孔子墓; Kǒngzi Mù) are pairs of stone panthers, griffins and larger-than-life guardians. The Confucian barrow is a simple grass mound enclosed by a low wall and faced with a Ming dynasty stele. His sons are buried nearby. Scattered through the forest are dozens of temples and pavilions. You can rent bikes at the entrance to tour the forest (Y10).

To reach the forest takes about 30 minutes by foot, 15 minutes by taxi or you can attempt to catch the infrequent bus No 1.

BEIJING TO SHANGHAI

YAN TEMPLE 颜庙

Enter this tranquil **temple** (Yán Miào; Yanmiao Jie; admission Y10; ☼ 8am-5pm) northeast of the Confucius Mansions to reach a large grassy courtyard with some vast stele pavilions sheltering dirty stelae and *bixi*. The main hall, **Fusheng Hall** (复圣殿; Fùshèng Diàn), is 17.5m high, with a hip and gable roof, and a magnificent ceiling containing the motif of a dragon head. Outside the hall are four magnificently carved pillars with coiling dragon designs and a further set of 18 octagonal pillars with gorgeous dragon and floral patterns.

MAUSOLEUM OF SHAO HAO 少昊陵

Shao Hao was one of the five legendary emperors supposed to have ruled China 4000 years ago. His pyramidal **tomb** (Shào Hào Líng; admission Y10; ☼ 8am-5pm), 4km northeast of Qūfù, dates from the Song dynasty. It is made of large blocks of stone, 25m wide at the base and 6m high, and has a small temple on top. Some Chinese historians believe that Qūfù was built on the ruins of Shao Hao's ancient capital, but evidence to support this is weak. Today the temple is deserted, but the atmosphere is serene.

Bus No 2 from the bus station will drop you 350m south of the tomb, or take a taxi (Y10) or pedicab (Y7).

Sleeping

Accommodation prices go up considerably during the high season (1 May to 8 May and 24 September to 8 October).

BUDGET

Xiuxian Hotel (Xiūxián Bīnguǎn; ☎ 441 7128; Gulou Nanjie; 6/3-bed dm Y20/60, s/d Y180/140; ❀) This small place is cheap, but there could well be problems with the English language. You can pick up good low-season discounts – the Y140 doubles (clean, well kept, with TV and tiled floor) should go for Y80. Dorms come with TV. There's an Internet café (Y1.5 per hour; 8am to midnight). The hotel has no English sign, but it's near the Drum Tower on the east side of Gulou Nanjie.

Shitouji Hotel (Shítou Jì Bīnguǎn; ☎ 448 0537; 12 Gulou Nanjie; dm/d Y10/80, q Y30-40; ❀) Next to the Xiuxian Hotel, this cheap place has OK doubles with shower room; the dorms and quads are simple, with no shower or toilet.

MID-RANGE

Queli Hotel (Quèlǐ Bīnshè; ☎ 441 2022; 15 Zhonglou Jie; s/d/ste Y298/398/988; ❀) This is perhaps the best deal in town and the location is splendid. The interior décor is passé (with a lobby resembling an early 1980s museum), but the exterior is pleasant, with water features and greenery, and traditional Chinese roofing.

Yulong Hotel (Yùlóng Da'fàndiàn; ☎ 441 3469; fax 441 3209; 1 Gulou Dajie; high season s/d Y260/380; ❀) This pleasant hotel with a traditional roof is just within the wall in the north of town. Rooms (with water cooler) are decent with fake wood flooring, although bathrooms need some work. Prices outside of the May and October holiday period are around 20% to 30% cheaper.

Post Hotel (Yóuzhèng Bīnguǎn; ☎ 448 3888; 8 Gulou Beijie; high season s/d/tr/ste Y280/260/360/1080; ❀) Rooms are so-so with dirty carpets, and come equipped with balconies, so you can get closer to Qūfù traffic. Avoid south-facing rooms, as they back onto a noisy nightclub.

Eating

Wumaci Jie, east of Gulou Nanjie, turns into a huge night market in the evenings. A string of cheap restaurants can be found on the north side of Jingxuan Lu, opposite the Confucius Mansions Hotel in the south of town.

Post Hotel Restaurant (8 Gulou Beijie) Equipped with an English menu, this clean restaurant has pricey tourist items, such as Kong Family Beancurd (Y28), but go instead for the much better-value *mápó dòufu* (Y8) or *jiǎozi – zhūròu* (pork, Y14 per jīn) and *yángròu* (lamb, Y16 per jīn) – or noodles (Y1), which are more reasonably priced.

Shopping

Being a major tourist town, Qūfù is overrun with streetside vendors hawking pocket copies of the *Analects* (Lúnyǔ), name chops, effigies, ornaments, and every name of gift and souvenir associated with the great sage. Queli Jie is a good place to hunt out souvenir stalls.

Getting There & Away

For a small surcharge you can buy train or air tickets from the **ticketing office** (Hángkōng Huǒchē Shòupiàochù; ☎ 442 2222/5122; ☼ 6am-9pm) next to the bowling alley on Gulou Beijie.

BUS

From the **bus station** (☎ 448 1554) in the south of town, buses connect with Tài'ān (Y15, every 30 minutes, one hour) and Jǐ'nán (Y21, every 20 minutes, 2½ hours) until 5.30pm. A bus leaves regularly to Qīngdǎo (Y61, hourly, seven hours) from 8am to 4.30pm.

TRAIN

When a railway project for Qūfù was first discussed, the Kong family petitioned for a change of routes, claiming that the trains would disturb Confucius' tomb. They won and the nearest tracks were routed to Yǎnzhōu, 16km west of Qūfù. Eventually another **train station** (☎ 442 1571) was constructed about 6km east of Qūfù, but only slow trains stop there, so it is more convenient to go to **Yǎnzhōu train station** (☎ 341 5239). Yǎnzhōu is on the line from Běijīng to Shànghǎi. Destinations include Běijīng (Y45 to Y81, five daily), Nánjīng (Y36, two daily), Jǐ'nán (Y12 to Y22, frequent), Qīngdao (Y38, 10 daily), Shànghǎi (Y53 to Y94) and Tiānjīn (Y36 to Y64). A taxi from Yǎnzhōu train station to Qūfù costs around Y30.

Getting Around

Minibuses to Yǎnzhōu train station (Y3.5, every 15 minutes, 5.30am to 5.30pm) leave from the bus station in the south of town. In the return direction, minibuses connect Yǎnzhōu bus station (walk straight ahead as you exit the train station, cross the parking lot and turn right; the bus station is after 50m on the left) with Qūfù (Y3.5, every 15 minutes, 5.30am to 5.30pm). A taxi from the train station to Qūfù costs around Y30.

There are only two bus lines and service is not frequent. Probably most useful for travellers is bus No 1, which travels along Gulou Beijie and Lindao Lu, connecting the bus station with the Confucian Forest. Bus No 2 travels from east to west along Jingxuan Lu.

Yellow minivans, motor tricycles and pedicabs swarm around, but expect to haggle. There are also decorated tourist horse carts (Y10 to Y15) that will take you on a 30-minute tour.

ZŌUXIÀN 邹县
☎ 0537 / pop 196,500

Zōuxiàn, the home town of Mencius (372–289 BC) – regarded as the first great Confucian philosopher – is more relaxed than Qūfù. The **Mencius Temple** (孟庙; Mèng Miào; admission Y20; ☺ 8am-6pm) and **Mencius Mansions** (孟府; Mèng Fǔ) are at the southern end of town, about a 20-minute walk from the bus station. Excellently restored, these two quiet temples are next door to each other and virtually empty.

Zōuxiàn is 23km south of Qūfù, and can be visited as a day trip by train from Yǎnzhōu or by bus from Qūfù bus station (Y3.5, every 15 minutes, 35 minutes).

QĪNGDǍO 青岛
☎ 0532 / pop 1.6 million

Perched on the southern seaboard of the Shāndōng peninsula, the picturesque town of Qīngdǎo (Green Island) is a welcome breather from the clogging conformity of socialist town planning. Its German legacy more or less intact, Qīngdǎo takes pride in its Bavarian appearance – the Chinese call the town 'China's Switzerland'. With its cool sea breezes, (relatively) clear air, balmy summer evenings and excellent seafood, this is where Chinese Communist Party (CCP) cadres come to build sand castles, lick ice cream and dream of retirement. Qīngdǎo has been selected to host the sailing events of the 2008 Olympics, prompting a further investment gale into the prosperous town.

History

Qīngdǎo was a simple fishing village until Kaiser Wilhelm II avenged himself for the killing of two German missionaries by coercing the Manchu government to cede the town to Germany in 1898 for 99 years. Under German administration, the famous Tsingtao Brewery opened in 1903, electric lighting was installed, missions and a university were established, the railway to Jǐ'nán was built, a garrison of 2000 men was deployed and a naval base was established.

In 1914 the Japanese moved into town after the successful joint Anglo-Japanese naval bombardment of the port. Japan's position in Qīngdǎo was strengthened by the Treaty of Versailles, and they held the city until 1922 when it was ceded back to the Kuomintang. The Japanese returned in 1938, after the start of the Sino-Japanese war, and occupied the town until defeated in 1945.

These days, Qīngdǎo is the fourth-largest port in China and the second-largest city in the province of Shāndōng. Booming industry and an entrepreneurial spirit have successfully carried the city into the 21st century.

Orientation

Qīngdǎo is situated on a peninsula with small bays and beaches in the south. The old part (*lǎochéng qū*) of town in the west is the

INFORMATION	
Bank of China 中国银行	1 G3
Bank of China 中国银行	2 A1
Bank of China 中国银行	(see 11)
CITS 中国国际旅行社	(see 11)
How Do Internet Café	
好读网吧	3 A1
Main Post Office 邮局	4 B2
People's Hospital 人民医院	5 B1
Post Office 邮局	6 B1
Post Office 邮局	7 B2
PSB 公安局	8 G2
South Korean Embassy	
韩国大使馆	(see 27)
Xinhua Bookstore 新华书店	9 A2

Youtiancheng Internet Café	
尤天成网吧	10 A1
Yuyuan Dasha 裕源大厦	11 F3
Zhangtingban Internet Café	
涨停板网吧	12 H3
SIGHTS & ACTIVITIES	**pp206–7**
Guanhaishan Park 观海山公园	13 C3
Huilan Pavilion 回澜阁	14 C4
Protestant Church 基督教堂	15 C3
Qingdao Hill Fort	
青岛山炮台遗址	16 D3
Qingdao Yíng Bīnguǎn	
青岛迎宾馆	17 C3
St Michael's Catholic Church	
天主教堂	18 B1

Tianhou Temple 天后宫	19 C3
Tsingtao Brewery	
青岛啤酒厂	20 D2
Xiǎo Qing Dǎo Lighthouse	
小青岛灯塔	21 C4
Zhan Bridge 栈桥	22 C3
Zhanshan Temple 湛山寺	23 F3
SLEEPING	**pp208–9**
Crowne Plaza	
青岛颐中皇冠假日酒店	24 H3
Dawei Guesthouse 大伟旅馆	25 A2
Haitian Hotel 海天大酒店	26 F4
Huiquan Dynasty Hotel	
汇泉王朝大酒店	27 D4
Jinliju Hotel 金利居宾馆	28 A2

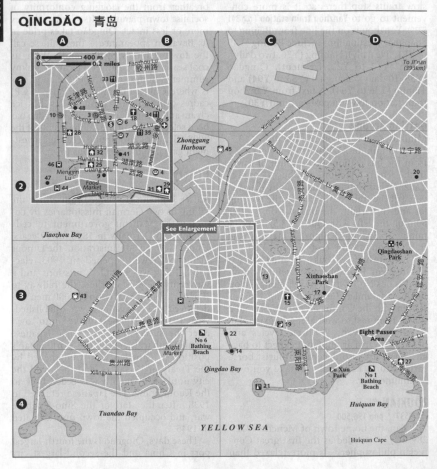

QĪNGDǍO 青岛

most charming, while the eastern districts form the commercial and industrial zones, home to high-rise towers, slick shops, departments stores, restaurants and nightlife.

Information

BOOKSHOPS

Xinhua Bookstore (Xīnhuá Shūdiàn; 10 Henan Lu) On the corner of Guangxi Lu and Henan Lu.

Oceanwide Elite Hotel	
泛海名人酒店	**29** B2
Railway Hotel	(see 46)
Shangri-La Hotel	
香格里拉大酒店	**30** G3
Zhanqiao Hotel 栈桥宾馆	**31** B2
Zhanying Hotel 栈盈宾馆	**32** A2
EATING	p209
Chūnhélóu	
春和楼饭店	**33** A1
Hóng Qīngtíng Jiǔjiā	
红蜻蜓酒家	**34** B1
Murano's	(see 24)
Xinlongyuan Restaurant	
新龙园大酒店	**35** B2

DRINKING	pp209–10
Corner Jazz Club	
街角爵士吧	**36** H3
Lennon Bar 列侬餐吧	**37** H4
Long's Café & Bar	**38** G3
SHOPPING	p210
Carrefour 家乐福	**39** G3
Jusco 佳世客	**40** H3
TRANSPORT	pp210–11
CAAC 中国民航	**41** B2
China Southern	
中国南方航空公司	(see 26)
Dragonair 港龙航空	**42** G3
Korean Air 大韩航空	(see 26)

Local Ferry 青岛轮渡站	**43** A3
Long-Distance Bus Station	
长途汽车站	**44** A2
Passenger Ferry Terminal	
青岛港客运站	**45** C2
Shandong Airlines	
山东航空公司	(see 46)
Train Station 火车站	**46** A2
Train Ticket Office	
青岛火车站便捷售票处	**47** A2
Train Ticket Office	
青岛火车航空售票处	**48** A1
OTHER	
Murphy's Irish Pub	
摩菲爱尔兰餐饮酒吧	**49** H3

BEIJING TO SHANGHAI

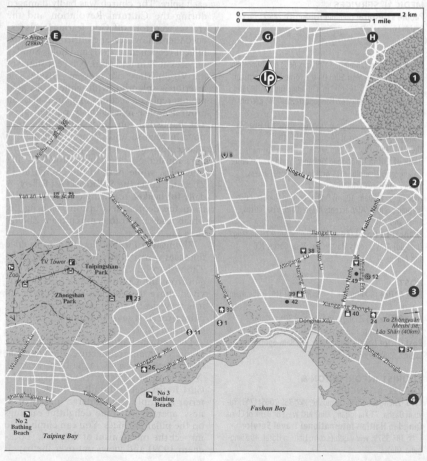

EMERGENCY & VISAS

PSB (Gōngānjú; ☎ 579 2555 ext 2860; 272 Ningxia Lu; ⏱ 9-11.30am & 1.30-4.30pm Mon-Fri) Inconveniently located in the east of town. Bus No 301 goes from the train station and stops outside the terracotta-coloured building (stop No 14). Another small branch of the PSB is at 1 Qufu Lu.

INTERNET ACCESS

How Do Internet Café (Hǎodú Wǎngbā; 2 Dagu Lu; per hr Y2; ⏱ 6am-9pm)

Youtiancheng Internet Café (Yóutiānchéng Wǎngbā; 93 Jinan Lu; per hr Y2; ⏱ 24hr) No English sign; it's the last shop on left on the roundabout with a black sign.

Zhangtingban Internet Café (Zhǎngtíngbǎn Wǎngbā; 40 Zhangzhou Yilu; per hr Y2; ⏱ 24hr) Just off Minjiang Erlu, across from Murphy's Irish Pub.

MEDICAL SERVICES

People's Hospital (Rénmín Yīyuàn; ☎ 285 2154; 17 Dexian Lu)

MONEY

Bank of China (Zhōngguó Yínháng; 66 & 68 Zhongshan Lu; ⏱ 8am-5pm Mon-Sun) On the corner of Zhongshan Lu and Feicheng Lu. Housed in a building built in 1934. Offers foreign-currency exchange; external ATM accepts foreign cards.

Bank of China (Zhōngguó Yínháng; Yuyuan Dasha, 75 Xianggang Xilu) External 24-hour ATM with international access.

Bank of China (Zhōngguó Yínháng; World Trade Centre, 6 Xianggang Zhonglu) ATM with international access; foreign-currency exchange.

Jusco (⏱ 8.30am-10pm) On the ground floor of Jusco shopping centre. ATM accepts MasterCard, Visa, Cirrus, Amex and JCB.

Shangri-La Hotel (Xiānggélǐlā Dàjiǔdiàn; 9 Xianggang Zhonglu) ATM accepts MasterCard, Visa, Cirrus, JCB and Amex.

POST

Post Office (8 Anhui Lu; ⏱ 8am-6pm) This is the main branch.

Post Office (51 Zhongshan Lu; ⏱ 8.30am-6pm) Opposite the large Parkson building.

Post Office (79 Xianggang Xilu; ⏱ 8am-6pm) With Express Mail Service (EMS)

TOURIST INFORMATION & TRAVEL AGENCIES

CITS (Zhōngguó Guójì Lǚxíngshè; ☎ 389 2065/1713; Yuyuan Dasha, 73 Xianggang Xilu) Just west of Bank of China.

Qingdao Haitian International Travel Service (☎ 386 3579; www.qdhits.com; Haitian Hotel, 48 Xianggang Xilu)

Qingdao Tourism Information and Service Station (Qīngdǎo Shì Lǚyóu Zīxún Fúwùzhàn; ☎ 582 6555) These kiosks are beginning to appear around town (eg outside the Crowne Plaza); more are planned, but at the time of writing they were of little use.

Sights

Wandering round town is the best way to appreciate Qīngdǎo's charms. The Qingdao Municipal Government has started to put up plaques identifying notable historic buildings and sites.

Completed in 1934, the twin-spired **St Michael's Catholic Church** (Tiānzhǔ Jiàotáng; ☎ 591 1400; 15 Zhejiang Lu; admission Y5; ⏱ 8am-5pm Mon-Sat, noon-5pm Sun), up a steep hill off Zhongshan Lu, is an imposing edifice with a cross on each spire. The church was badly damaged during the Cultural Revolution and the crosses were torn off. God-fearing locals rescued them, however, and buried them in the hills. It reopened in 1981, and holds Sunday services at 7am and 6pm. A recent statue of the Virgin Mary can be seen outside. The interior is splendid, with white walls, gold piping, replaced sections of stained glass all around and a marvellously painted apse. The baptismal font and statues have captions in English and Chinese, and there is a large portrait of St Teresa of Lisieux. Vendors muster outside selling crucifixes and souvenirs, while next to the church at 15 Zhejiang Lu is the **St Michael's Art Gallery**. A daily **fish market**, featuring colourful exotica from the depths, sets up on Feicheng Lu, which leads up to the church from Zhongshan Lu.

Zhongshan Lu itself has numerous **dried fish shops** worth browsing around (eg at 39 Zhongshan Lu). North of the church a slogan from the Cultural Revolution has survived above the doorway of 19 Pingdu Lu; it is very clear and no one has bothered to paint over it. It says (in Chinese) 'Long live Chairman Mao'.

Located on Jiangsu Lu, a street notable for its German architecture, the **Protestant Church** (Jīdū Jiàotáng; 15 Jiangsu Lu; admission Y3; ⏱ 8.30am-5pm, weekend services) was designed by Curt Rothkegel and built in 1908. The interior is simple and Lutheran in its sparseness, apart from some delightful carvings on the pillar cornices. You can climb up to inspect the mechanism of the clock (Bockenem 1909) and views out over the bay. It is also well worth wandering along nearby Daxue Lu for a marvellous scenic view of old German Qīngdǎo.

To the east of Xinhaoshan Park remains one of Qīngdǎo's most interesting pieces of German architecture, **Qīngdǎo Yíng Bīnguǎn** (Qingdao Ying Hotel; admission Y15; ✆ 8.30am-5pm), the former German governor's residence and a replica of a German palace (now a museum). Built in 1903, it is said to have cost 2,450,000 taels of silver. When Kaiser Wilhelm II got the bill, he immediately recalled the extravagant governor and sacked him. In 1957 Chairman Mao stayed here with his wife and kids on holiday.

The restored **Tianhou Temple** (Tiānhòu Gōng; ☎ 288 0728; 19 Taiping Lu; admission Y8; ✆ 8am-6pm) is a small temple dedicated to Tianhou (Heaven Queen), Goddess of the Sea and protector of sailors, also known as Mazu and Niangniang. The main hall contains a colourful statue of Tianhou, flanked by two figures and a pair of fearsome guardians. Other halls include the Dragon King Hall (龙王殿; Lóngwáng Diàn, where in front of the Dragon King lies a splayed pig) and a shrine to the God of Wealth. Also on display is an exhibition of Tianhou culture and photos of the temple during the years of the Cultural Revolution.

The castle-like villa of **Huāshí Lóu** (Huāshi Bldg; 18 Huanghai Lu; admission Y5; ✆ 7.30am-7pm) was originally the home of a Russian aristocrat, and later the German governor's retreat for fishing and hunting. The Chinese call it the 'Chiang Kaishek Building' as the generalissimo secretly stayed here in 1947.

For a colourful and exhaustive account of Qīngdǎo's historic architecture, turn to *Far from Home: Western Architecture in China's Northern Treaty Ports* by Tess Johnston and Deke Erh.

BEACHES 海滩

Qīngdǎo is famous for its six beaches, which are extremely popular with the Chinese. The beaches aren't bad, but don't go expecting a surfers' paradise. June to September is the main swimming season, when hordes of sun seekers fight for towel space. Shark nets, lifeguards, lifeboat patrols and medical stations provide safety.

Close to the train station is the **No 6 Bathing Beach**, neighbouring **Zhàn Qiáo** (Zhan Bridge), a pier that reaches out into the bay

and is tipped with the eight-sided **Huilan Pavilion** (Huílán Gé). The pavilion crops up on the label of Tsingtao beer. Beyond, you can see the **lighthouse** on Little Green Island (Xiǎo Qīng Dǎo). Next to the pier there are boat ticket vendors for tours around the bay and beyond (Y15, 40 minutes).

Continuing east, situated around the headland and the lighthouse, is the leafy **Lu Xun Park** (鲁迅公园; Lǔ Xùn Gōngyuán), named after the father of Chinese modern literature.

The sand of **No 1 Bathing Beach** is coarse-grained, engulfed in seaweed, and bordered by concrete beach huts and bizarre statues of dolphins. The **Eight Passes Area** (八大关; Bādàguān) is well known for its sanatoriums and exclusive guesthouses. The spas are scattered in lush wooded zones off the coast, and each street is lined with a different tree or flower, including maple, myrtle, peach, snow pine or crab apple. This is a lovely area in which to stroll.

As you head out of Eight Passes Area, Nos 2 and 3 bathing beaches are just east, and the villas lining the headlands are quite exquisite. **No 2 Bathing Beach** is cleaner, quieter and more sheltered than No 1 Bathing Beach.

About 30 minutes by boat from Qingdao and a further 30 minutes by bus is the beach of **Huáng Dǎo** (黄岛; Yellow Island), which is quieter and cleaner than Qīngdǎo's beaches. The ferry (Y10) leaves from the Qīngdǎo local ferry terminal (Qīngdǎo lúndùzhàn) to the west of the train station. The first departure is at 6.30am, with the final boat returning at 9pm. Once you reach the island, take bus No 1 to its terminus (Y2.5).

PARKS 公园

The charm of small **Guanhaishan Park** (Guānhǎishān Gōngyuán) lies in finding it – the route winds up a small hill through restful lanes; the park is at the top. Although small, the park was used as a golf course by the Germans.

Down the hill and to the east is **Xinhaoshan Park** (信号山公园; Xìnhàoshān Gōngyuán), whose summit is capped by the carbuncular towers known as the mógu lóu (mushroom buildings). Minibus No 26 can take you to the park.

Zhongshan Park (中山公园; Zhōngshān Gōngyuán) covers a vast 80 hectares, and

BĚIJĪNG TO SHÀNGHĂI

in springtime is a heavily wooded profusion of flowering shrubs and plants. Bus Nos 25 and 26 travel to the park.

The mountainous area northeast of Zhongshan Park is called **Taipingshan Park** (太平山公园; Tàipíngshān Gōngyuán), an area of walking paths, pavilions and the best spot in town for hiking. In the centre of the park is the TV Tower (Diànshì Tǎ), which has an express lift up to fabulous views of the city (Y30). You can reach the tower via cable car (Y20). Also within the park is Qīngdǎo's largest temple, **Zhanshan Temple** (Zhànshān Sì; admission Y5; ⏲ 8.30am-4.30pm). The temple has a number of dramatic sandal-wood Buddhas covered in gold foil.

Just west of Taipingshan Park is **Qingdao-shan Park** (青岛山公园; Qīngdǎoshān Gōngyuán). A notable feature of this hilly park is **Qingdao Hill Fort** (Qīngdǎoshān Pàotái Yízhǐ; admission Y8; ⏲ 8.30-11.30am & 1.30-4.30pm), built by Germans in 1899. All that remains of the fort today is the underground command post – the Germans destroyed the fort in 1914 when they lost to the Japanese. Visitors can take a look around the old living quarters, boiler room and canteen, three storeys underground.

TSINGTAO BREWERY 青岛啤酒厂

The brewery (Qīngdǎo Píjiǔchǎng) was established in 1903 by the Germans. The finest brew in China uses the mineral waters of nearby Láo Shān and Tsingtao beer has a worldwide following. Unfortunately, unless you are on a tour it's almost impossible to get into the brewery for a look. Tours can be booked through CITS (p206).

Festivals & Events

The summer months see Qīngdǎo overrun with tourists, particularly in the second and third weeks of July, when the **annual trade fair** and **ocean festival** is held. Another festival to look out for is the **beer festival** in August/September. Gardeners may be interested to note that Qīngdǎo's **radish festival** is in February, the **cherry festival** in May and the **grape festival** in September (Qīngdǎo is a major producer of wine).

Sleeping
BUDGET

If you arrive in Qīngdǎo during the summer months, be prepared to be forced into expensive accommodation. Also be warned that some of the hotels shut down during winter. All prices quoted are for the high season; bargain hard if you arrive during the low season.

Dawei Guesthouse (Dàwěi Lǚguǎn; ☎ 296 2909; 3 Mengyin Lu; s/d Y40/60) This miniature guest-house in a crumbling old house (there are only six rooms) near the train station in the old part of town has very cheap, bottom-rung rooms (some windowless, all without toilet). There's no air-con, no fans and no English sign, but it's to the north of the Agricultural Bank of China on the east side of Mengyin Lu (and south of the intersection with Hunan Lu). The owner, Mr Zhang, speaks no English, but is an affable and helpful bloke.

Zhanying Hotel (Zhànyíng Bīnguǎn; ☎ 296 1980; 11 Mengyin Lu; s/d/tw/tr Y80/100/150/165; ❄) This pleasant, family-owned hotel has OK rooms with air-con and 24-hour hot water. Singles have no shower room, but rooms are half-price during low season. There's no English sign; the hotel is on the corner of Mengyin Lu and Hubei Lu, just south of the old German building housing the PSB.

MID-RANGE

Zhanqiao Hotel (Zhànqiáo Bīnguǎn; ☎ 287 0502; fax 287 0936; 31 Taiping Lu; non-seaview d Y298-498, seaview d Y698, tr Y598; ❄) This hotel is a rather somnolent place with slow-moving staff, but seaview rooms are large, bright and quite well kept. Rooms to the side and rear of the hotel are smaller. In former ages the Prince Heinrich Hotel, Sun Yatsen stayed here in 1912 and is commemorated by a bust outside. MasterCard and Visa accepted.

Jinliju Hotel (Jīnlìjū Bīnguǎn; ☎ 288 7186; fax 288 8987; 21 Tai'an Lu; s/d/tr Y260/280/360; ❄) Close to the train station, rooms at this three-storey, friendly hotel are small and the shower rooms minute, but they are clean. Low-season discounts can be up to 50%, easing the hotel into budget territory.

Railway Hotel (Tiědào Dàshà; ☎ 606 7888; fax 286 0497; 2 Tai'an Lu; d/q/ste Y260/460/680; ❄) Located at the train station, the perfectly reasonable high-rise Railway Hotel is well located in the old part of town, with clean rooms, polite service and an external elevator. Discounts are not uncommon, even during summer months – bringing a double down to around Y160.

TOP END

Crowne Plaza (Qīngdǎo Yízhōng Huángguān Jiàrì Jiǔdiàn; ☎ 571 8888; www.sixcontinentshotels.com; 76 Xianggang Zhonglu; d/ste Y996/1411; ⊠) Situated in Qīngdǎo's dynamic commercial district to the east of Jusco shopping centre, the five-star and stylishly designed Crowne Plaza is a revamped Holiday Inn, with excellent rooms and a wide range of dining options.

Shangri-La Hotel (Xiānggélǐlā Dàjiǔdiàn; ☎ 388 3838; www.shangri-la.com; 9 Xianggang Zhonglu; s/d US$175/195, 15% service charge; ⊠) In Qīngdǎo's commercial district in the east of town is the splendid Shangri-La, delivering the high-quality hallmarks of this chain. Rooms are plush and the service is excellent.

Oceanwide Elite Hotel (Fànhǎi Míngrén Jiǔdiàn; ☎ 288 6699; 29 Taiping Lu; non-seaview d Y780-960, seaview d Y960-1160, ste Y2360; ⊠) This five-floor, low-rise, four-star hotel benefits from a superb location overlooking Qingdao Bay (as long as you opt for the pricier seaview rooms) in the old part of town.

Haitian Hotel (Hǎitiān Dàjiǔdiàn; ☎ 387 1888; www.hai-tian-hotel.com; 48 Xianggang Xilu; west Bldg s/d/tw/ste Y1229/1395/1395/2142, east Bldg s/d/tw/ste Y830/913/913/1312; ⊠) Rooms at this hotel are arranged over three buildings, with the pricier rooms in the west block and cheaper rooms in the east block (admin in the middle block). Expensive for what you get and not as impressive as the competition.

Eating

Qīngdǎo is overrun with good food. The locals are crazy about kebabs, which is understandable as these are some of the best in China. *Zhūròuchuàn* (pork kebabs) or *yángròuchuàn* (lamb kebabs) cost around Y1.5 from the ubiquitous street stalls. Ask for là (spicy) or búlà (not spicy). Don't go for the *jīxīnchuàn* (chicken hearts), unless you can stomach them.

The waterfront area is brimming with restaurants, from No 6 Bathing Beach almost all the way to No 1 Bathing Beach. For more upmarket and varied dining options, head to the commercial district in the east of town, and especially the bars and restaurants along Yunxiao Lu and Minjiang Lu. The lively street Zhongyuan Meishi Jie is packed with seafood restaurants. Entrance is off Xianggang Zhonglu, east of Carrefour.

Chūnhélóu (Chūnhélóu Fàndiàn; ☎ 282 4346; 146 Zhongshan Lu; meals from Y20) Dating back to 1891, this

unremarkable-looking restaurant remains very popular. Downstairs is a busy help-your-self-to-as-much-as-you-can-eat type diner, with a smarter option upstairs. There's a small bakery next door.

Xinlongyuan Restaurant (Xīnlóngyuán Dàjiǔdiàn; ☎ 282 9699/9799; 6 Qufu Lu; meals Y30-40) Not far from St Michael's, this pleasant and spacious restaurant presents plates of food under cling wrap so you can choose exactly what you want. Also on display are trays, buckets and aquaria of live seafood for you to take your pick. The *làzi jī* (crispy nuggets of chicken in a small mound of firecracker-red chillies, Y23) is crispy and delicious. Otherwise go for the *xiǎochuàn máxiāng yángròu* (Y26) – a scrummy plate of spicy lamb kebabs. There is another branch at 30 Rehe Lu.

Murano's (☎ 571 8888; 2nd fl, Crowne Plaza, 76 Xianggang Zhonglu; meals from Y150; ⊙ 11.30am-2pm & 5.30-10.30pm) A marvellous Italian restaurant with a gorgeous atmosphere and lovely furniture, Murano's also has an excellent menu. Choose from the range of *antipasti freddi* and *antipasti caldi*, and try some seafood, including *dentice in acqua pazza* (pan fried red snapper on cherry tomato sauce, Y98), or pasta, meats and a tempting range of around 16 pizzas. Decent wine list.

Hóng Qīngtíng Jiǔjiā (28 Anhui Lu) This simple and small hole-in-the-wall bakery sells lovely cakes (Y2 for six); ideal for snacking while on the go.

Drinking

Qīngdǎo's bars can be found in the commercial and business district in the east of town. Minjiang Lu has several recently opened bars, and there will be more by the time you visit. Score the latest copy of *Red Star* (www.myredstar.com.cn), an expat entertainment magazine (available at bars and smart hotels) for more complete listings.

Corner Jazz Club (Jiējiǎo Juéshì Bā; ☎ 575 8560; 153 Minjiang Lu; live music 6pm Tue & Thu) This popular place is spacious (with a mezzanine floor) and has lots of character. There's table football, movies, darts, jazz, blues and rock, with live music from 6pm Tuesday and Thursday. Drinks include Tsingtao (bottle Y15), draught beer (Y10) and spirits (gin and tonic, Y20). Happy hour is from 6pm to 8pm Monday to Friday.

Lennon Bar (Liènóng Cānbā; ☎ 589 3899; 20 Zhuhai Lu) Enter through the huge doors to this vast two-floor temple to Beatles culture. It has a good atmosphere and a lived-in feel, with table football, a pool table and live music on Thursday.

Long's Cafe & Bar (☎ 573 8173; 114 Minjiang Lu; 🕙 10am-2am) This relaxed and quiet Chinese-run café and bar has sports TV, table football, and blues, jazz and pop on Friday and Saturday.

Shopping

Carrefour (Jiālèfú; northwest cnr Nanjing Lu & Xianggang Zhonglu; 🕙 8.30am-10pm)

Jusco (Jiāshìkè; near southeast cnr Fuzhou Nanlu & Xianggang Zhonglu)

Getting There & Away

AIR

Flights are available to most large cities in China, including daily services to Běijīng (Y660), Hāěrbīn (Y870), Shànghǎi (Y670) and Xī'ān (Y1070). There are five flights a week to Hong Kong (Y2400). There are daily flights to Seoul with Korean Air, and four flights a week to Osaka and Fukuoka with All Nippon Airways. The Qīngdǎo airport inquiries number is ☎ 471 5139.

Tickets can be purchased at:

CAAC (Zhōngguó Mínháng) Zhongshan Lu (☎ 289 5577; 29 Zhongshan Lu); Xianggang Lu (24hr ticketing ☎ 577 5555/597 6611; 30 Xianggang Lu)

China Southern (Zhōngguó Náfāng Hángkōng Gōngsī; ☎ 389 6148; Haitian Hotel, 48 Xianggang Xilu)

Dragonair (Gǎnglóng Hángkōng ☎ 577 6110; Hotel Equatorial, 28 Xianggang Zhonglu; 🕙 9am-5pm Mon-Sat)

Korean Air (Dàhán Hángkōng; ☎ 387 0088; Haitian Hotel, 48 Xianggang Xilu).

Shandong Airlines (Shāndōng Hángkōng; ☎ 288 9160, 286 5870; train station ticket office) It also sells Yāntái to Dàlián boat tickets.

BOAT

There are four boats a week to Incheon in South Korea (Y1180) and boats to Shimonoseki (Y1160), Japan, every two weeks. Phone the **passenger ferry terminal** (Qīngdǎogǎng Kèyùnzhàn; ☎ 282 5001; 6 Xinjiang Lu) to confirm days. To reach Dàlián by boat, you will have to go from Yāntái, but tickets can be purchased from the Shandong Airlines ticket office.

BUS

Both buses and minibuses depart from the area next to the massive Hualian Building,

south of the train station. The **ticket offices** (☎ 267 6842) are in the small pastel-coloured huts.

There are buses departing for Weīhǎi (Y42.5, every 20 minutes, 6am to 6pm), Yāntái (Y31, every 15 minutes, 6.30am to 5.30pm) and Jǐ'nán (Y50, every 50 minutes, 8.50am to 4pm). There are also daily buses to Běijīng (Y219, 7.30pm), Hángzhōu (Y221, 3.50pm), Héféi (Y128, 9am and 3.30pm) and Shànghǎi (Y201, 10.30am and afternoon departures).

TRAIN

All trains from Qīngdǎo go through the provincial capital of Jǐ'nán, except for the direct Qīngdǎo to Yāntái trains. There are two trains a day to Yāntái (Y22) and regular services to Jǐ'nán (Y49). There are two express trains to Běijīng (Y102, 9.59am and 9.12pm), and trains to Shànghǎi (Y150, 1.58pm), Zhèngzhōu (Y120, 3.05pm) and Dāndōng (sleeper Y214, 6.38pm).

Apart from at the marvellous ticket office at the train station – German-built with a clock tower, red tiles and practically a sight in itself – train (and air) tickets can be bought for a service charge at several places around town, including a useful **ticket office** (Qīngdǎo Huǒchēzhàn Biànjié Shòupiàochù; Feixian Lu; 🕙 24hr) on the north side of Feixian Lu, just round the corner from the train station. A further **ticket office** (Qīngdǎo Huǒchē Hángkōng Shòupiàochù; 96 Dagu Lu) is opposite the Youtiancheng Internet Café.

Getting Around

TO/FROM THE AIRPORT

Qīngdǎo's brand-new and state-of-the-art airport is 30km north of the city. Taxi drivers should ask between Y90 and Y100 to drive into town. Buses leave hourly from the CAAC office between 6am and 6pm (Y10).

BUS

Most transport needs can be catered for by the bus No 6 route, which starts at the northern end of Zhongshan Lu, runs along it to within a few blocks of the train station and then east to the area above No 3 Bathing Beach. Bus No 26 from the train station runs along the coast and past Zhongshan Park before heading north at the end of No 3 Bathing Beach. Minibuses also follow these routes (Y2).

TAXI

Flag fall is Y7 for the first 3km and then Y1.5 per kilometre thereafter.

AROUND QĪNGDǍO

Láo Shān 崂山

This **mountain** (admission winter/summer Y30/50), 40km east of Qīngdǎo, is a famous Taoist retreat, with temples, waterfalls and secluded walking trails. Covering some 400 sq km, this is where Láo Shān mineral water starts its life. The mountain is associated with Taoist legend and myth, with the central attraction being the Song dynasty **Great Purity Palace** (太清宫; Tàiqīng Gōng; admission Y10). The first Song Emperor established the palace as a place to perform Taoist rites to save the souls of the dead. From the Great Purity Palace, there are paths leading to the summit of Láo Shān.

The cable car up the first half of the mountain costs Y30 (Y50 return) and a ride up the second half costs Y20. From Qīngdǎo, bus No 304 runs to Láo Shān (Y6.5, one to two hours). Buses can be picked up at the Zhàn Qiáo stop by No 6 Bathing Beach from around 6.30am; get off at the entrance to the first cable car up Láo Shān. Returning, the last bus leaves Láo Shān at 5pm.

Tour buses to Láo Shān (Y25 return) ply the streets of Qīngdǎo from 6am onwards, but visit at least four other 'sights' on the way to the mountain.

YĀNTÁI 烟台

☎ 0535 / pop 652,000

Yāntái is a busy ice-free port on the northern coast of the Shāndōng peninsula. One of the top three most prosperous and fast-developing cities in Shāndōng (along with Qīngdǎo and Wēihǎi), Yāntái is also quickly becoming the new summer destination for holidaying Chinese. More relaxed and less crowded than Qīngdǎo, the town sees a steady stream of visitors for its sunny beaches, friendly locals and good seafood.

History

The town started life as a defence outpost and fishing village. Yāntái means Smoke Terrace; wolf-dung fires were lit on the headland during the Ming dynasty to warn fishing fleets of approaching pirates. Its sleepy existence came to an abrupt halt in the late 19th century when the Qing government, following defeat in the Opium War, handed Yāntái over to the British who established a treaty port here, calling it Chefoo. Several nations, Japan and the USA among them, had trading establishments here and the town became something of a resort area.

Orientation

Yāntái is strung out along the north Shāndōng coastline, with the train and bus stations in the west of town near the harbour, where the cheap hotels can be found. The beaches are in the east of town, while most of the sights, treaty port buildings and restaurants are in the central districts.

Information

EMERGENCY

PSB (Gōngānjú; ☎ 653 5621; 78 Shifu Jie; 🕒 8am-5.30pm Mon-Sat) On the corner of Chaoyang Jie. The office for foreigners is on the 6th floor.

INTERNET ACCESS

There are numerous Internet cafés inside Times Square (Shídài Guǎngchǎng), west of the International Seaman's Club:

Dianjizheni Internet Café (Diànjīzhenī Wǎngbā; per hr Y2; 🕒 8am-midnight)

Jiyou Internet Café (Jíyǒu Wǎngbā; per hr Y2; 🕒 24hr)

Elsewhere you can find the following:

Chaoyang Internet Café (Cháoyáng Wǎngbā; 31 Chaoyang Jie; per hr Y2; 🕒 8am-midnight) On the corner of Shun Dajie.

Kuaile Internet Café (Kuàilè Wǎngbā; 22 Shifu Jie; per hr Y1.5; 🕒 8am-midnight)

Tiaoseban Internet Café (Tiáosèbǎn Wǎngbā; Chaoyang Jie; per hr Y2; 🕒 8am-midnight)

Yijianzhongqing Internet Café (Yījiànzhōngqíng Wǎngbā; 🕒 24hr) On the other side of the road from Kuaile Internet Café, down an alley.

MEDICAL SERVICES

Chunhehang Pharmacy (Chūnhèhéng Yàotáng; Beima Lu) Next to the International Seaman's Club.

Dongfang Hospital (Dōngfāng Yīyuàn; ☎ 620 1790; 240 Nan Dajie)

Yantaishan Hospital (Yāntáishān Yīyuàn; ☎ 622 4411; 91 Jiefang Lu)

MONEY

Bank of China (Zhōngguó Yínháng; Beima Lu) West of the International Seaman's Club. Useful for changing US dollars; no ATM.

Bank of China (Zhōngguó Yínháng; 166 Jiefang Lu) ATM accepts Visa, MasterCard, JCB and Amex.

POST

Post Office (Diànxìn Dàlóu; cnr Nan Dajie & Dahaiyang Lu)

TOURIST INFORMATION & TRAVEL AGENCIES

CITS (Zhōngguó Guójì Lǚxíngshè; ☎ 661 0661; 181B Jiefang Lu) In a building with a large blue sign. Not much use.

Yantai Tourist Information & Service Center (Yāntáishì Lǚyóu Fúwù Zhōngxīn; ☎ 663 3222; 32 Haian Jie) Next to Yantai Hill Park gate, at north end of Chaoyang Jie.

Sights

YANTAI HILL PARK 烟台山公园

This fantastic **park** (Yāntáishān Gōngyuán; admission Y20; ☯ 6.30am-7.30pm summer, 7am-5.30pm winter) is a veritable museum of well-preserved western treaty port architecture. The **Former**

American Consulate Building retains some original interior features and now houses a model ship exhibition. Nearby, the former **Yantai Union Church** dates from 1875, although it was later rebuilt. The **Yantai Museum of Peking Opera Art** can be found inside the former Chefoo Vice-Customs Commissioner's Official Residence, while within the **Former British Consulate** building is a China Fossils Exhibition. The **British Consulate Annexe** has a garden (called the English Garden) with shaped hedges and even a hedge archway, which genuinely feels like an English garden. You can walk around the veranda of the British Consulate annexe building to the rear and look in on the wooden floorboards and out over the sea and the breakwater.

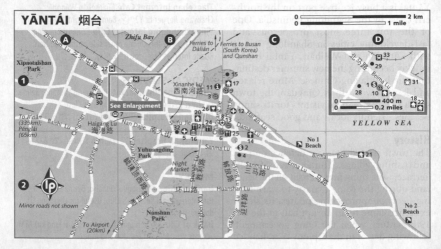

The **Former Danish Consulate**, in the north of the park, is a crenellated structure dating from 1890, decorated on the outside with 'brutalism granite', or so the blurb says. Wander in and walk around and up the staircase, perusing the period furniture, the laid-out kitchen and dining room (the latter with a lovely old fireplace), and photographs of Denmark. At the top of the hill is the Ming dynasty **Dragon King Temple**. Inside the temple, which served as a military headquarter for French troops in 1860, is a statue of the red-faced Dragon King and some murals. Above is the **smoke terrace** where the wolf-dung fires were burned, dating from the reign of Hongwu; climb up for views (binoculars Y2) out to sea and the island of Zhifu (Chefoo). In the west of the park, the 1930s-built **Japanese Consulate** is a typically austere brick lump, equipped with a 'torture inquisition room'. The **Former Japanese Consul's Official Residence** may look like a student dorm from the outside, but houses a very interesting timepiece museum, displaying a fantastic display of clocks.

YANTAI MUSEUM 烟台博物馆
The **Yantai Museum** (Yāntái Bówùguǎn; 257 Nan Dajie; admission Y5; ☉ 8.30am-12pm & 1-5pm) is definitely worth a visit, but more for the architecture than the exhibits housed within it. It can be found within the guild hall built by merchants and sailors of Fújiàn as a place of worship to Tianhou (Heaven Queen), Goddess of the Sea and protector of sailors.

The main hall of the museum is known as the **Hall of Heavenly Goddess**. It was designed and finished in Guǎngzhōu, and then shipped to Yāntái for assembly. Beyond the hall, at the centre of the courtyard, is the museum's most spectacular piece of architecture: a brightly and intricately decorated gate. Supported by 14 pillars, the gate is a collage of hundreds of carved and painted figures, flowers, beasts, phoenixes and animals. The carvings depict battle scenes and folk stories, including *The Eight Immortals Crossing the Sea*.

At the southern end of the museum is a theatrical stage that was first made in Fújiàn and then shipped to Yāntái. Apparently Tianhou wasn't particularly fond of that stage, as it was lost at sea during transportation and had to be reconstructed in Yāntái. The stage continues to be used for performances to celebrate Tianhou's birthday and anniversary of deification. On these days you can join the celebrations. The museum was closed at the time of writing as road widening was underway.

OTHER SIGHTS
There are two beaches in Yāntái, **No 1 Beach** (Dìyī Hǎishuǐ Yùchǎng) and **No 2 Beach** (Dìèr Hǎishuǐ Yùchǎng). No 1 Beach is the better of the two; a long stretch of soft sand pads a calm bay area that is ideal for swimming. No 2 beach is less crowded, but more polluted. Both beaches can be reached by bus No 17.

On Dama Lu, west of No 1 Beach, is a small, active **Catholic Church** (天主教堂; Tiānzhǔ Jiàotáng) built during treaty port days. The church has a wooden ceiling, pictures of the Stations of the Cross and a gallery. As luck would have it, this author visited the church as a baptism was taking place.

Sleeping
BUDGET
Yinpeng Hotel (Yínpéng Bīnguǎn; ☎ 626 0655; fax 626 0755; 59 Beima Lu; s/tr Y180/260, d Y196-220; ☒) This reasonably new two-star hotel next to a UBC Coffee outlet is small but well kept, with clean rooms with tiled floors. There's no lift, so rooms get cheaper the higher you climb; low-season discounts can be easy to obtain.

International Seaman's Club (Hǎiyuán Bīnguǎn; ☎ 624 3425; 68 Beima Lu; s/d/tr/ste Y120/200/260/260; ☒) Across from the train station, the Seaman is a bit tattered and battered, but he's still able-bodied with OK rooms (although rooms facing the station can be noisy) and powerful showers. Low-season discounts readily available.

Huanhai Hotel (Huánhǎi Lǚshè; ☎ 625 5668; 64 Beima Lu; s/d/q Y15/25/15) Grotty (and no aircon) but very cheap indeed, this place east of the train station and just west of Yantai City Commercial Bank is possibly the cheapest in town.

MID-RANGE
Golden Gulf Hotel (Jīnhǎiwān Jiǔdiàn; ☎ 622 4491; fax 621 6313; 34 Haian Lu; d Y520-890; ☒) This six-floor hotel contains a vast foyer, impressive décor and a massive copy of Botticelli's *Primavera*. Located near Yantai Hill Park,

this is a clean and recently renovated place offering homey rooms equipped with water cooler, Internet access and fridge. The hotel's Golden Gulf Grill serves steaks and meat grills.

TOP END

Yantai Marina Hotel (Yāntái Jiàrì Jiǔdiàn; ☎ 666 9999; marinaht@public.ytptt.sd.cn; 128 Binhai Beilu; non-seaview d/ste Y680/1380, seaview d/ste Y700/1980; 🔀) Rooms at this 25-floor Chinese-style hotel are clean, spacious and recently restored, with excellent views from the seaview rooms. A revolving restaurant is on the 25th floor and there's a 2.8 tonne stone ball and a statue of Milefo in the lobby. Take a trip in the external glass elevator for fantastic views over the bay.

Shandong Pacific Hotel (Shāndōng Tàipíngyáng Dàjiǔdiàn; ☎ 620 6888; fax 621 5204; 74 Shifu Jie; s Y660-880, tw 660-880, d Y760-980; 🔀) This central four-star hotel (white tile high-rise with an iridescent stainless-steel lobby portico) is an above average choice. Rooms have water coolers, extra large TV sets and particularly clean bathrooms. Rooms to the north have sea views, and there's a choice of Japanese, Korean and Western dining options. Facilities include a swimming pool, bowling and billiards.

Eating

In the summer months a night market sets up along Shengli Lu, good for cheap kebabs and beer.

Háojiāxiāng (☎ 662 7588; 51 Shifu Jie; set meal Y25) This lively and popular restaurant burns under bright lights. It serves some excellent steaks, ribs and grills, but there's no English menu. Sit down in the soft sofa seats and try the tasty *hēijiāo zhūpái* (black pepper pork chops, Y25) or the *yángròufàn tàocān* (lamb set meal, Y25).

For spicy food, bundle along to Taohua Jie, a street stuffed with Sìchuān restaurants directly north of Yantai Museum.

Cháotiānjiāo (☎ 623 0966; 71 Taohua Jie; meals Y25) This small eatery (there are two branches, one on either side of the road) has no English menu, but be sure to try the excellent *suāncài yú* (small Y15, big Y20), which is generous and filling. The *huíguōròu* (twice cooked pork, Y8) is scrumptious, and the *málàjī* (spicy chicken, small Y10, big Y15) hot and tasty.

Sculpting in Time (Diāokè Shíguāng; ☎ 622 1979; 17-18 Shifu Jie; meals Y30; 🕙 10.30am-midnight) This little bar/restaurant has character, with alcoves and small side rooms with saloon-style swing doors and walls hung with photos of film stars and luminaries. On the menu are pizza and steaks, and there's live music nightly. Tsingtao beer will set you back Y10.

Drinking

The section of Chaoyang Jie north of Beima Lu is full of karaoke bars, pool halls, Internet cafés, discos and other symbols of Yāntái's rapidly developing nightlife. For good coffee, try one of the branches of **UBC Coffee** (Shàngdǎo Kāfēi; Beima Lu ☎ 625 5087; 60 Beima Lu, next to Yinpeng Hotel; Jiefang Lu ☎ 620 4748; 170 Jiefang Lu, 100m south of Bank of China).

Cape of Storms Bar (Hǎijiǎo Fēngbào Jiǔbā; ☎ 606 0060; capeofstormsyt@hotmail.com; 16 Chaoyang Jie; 🕙 4pm-late) With wood panelling and a small mezzanine, this homey bar gets crowded on weekends with expat punters. English-speaking staff is at the helm and there's live music most nights. Tequila costs Y30, a bottle of local beer Y20.

Getting There & Away

AIR

Flights can be booked at the **CAAC office** (Zhōngguó Mínháng; ☎ 625 3777, 624 5596; 6 Dahaiyang Lu; 🕙 8am-6pm), the **Shandong Airlines** (Shāndōng Hángkōng; ☎ 658 4143; 236 Nan Dajie; 🕙 8am-6pm) main booking office or at **China Southwest Airlines** (Xīnán Hángkōng; ☎ 627 0919), just west of the Yantai Railway Building. Tickets can also be bought in a **ticket office** (☎ 667 7198) inside the train station.

There are flights to Hong Kong (Y2610) on Wednesday, Saturday and Sunday, and daily to Seoul (Y1260). There are four daily flights to Běijīng (Y630), three daily flights to Shànghǎi (Y720) and regular flights to Guǎngzhōu (Y1690).

BOAT

At the **passenger ferry terminal** (Yāntáigǎng Kèyùn Zhàn; ☎ 674 1774; 155 Bei Malu) or from the numerous ticket offices east of the train station you can purchase tickets for express boats to Dàlián (2nd class Y386, 3½ hours, 8.30am, 10am, 12.30pm and 2pm); tickets can only be purchased on the day of travel (although you can buy tickets in Qīngdǎo).

There are also numerous slow boats departing for Dàlián (seat/bed Y48/90, seven hours) daily from 7.30am. There are also boats to Incheon (Y881 to Y2000 and more), in South Korea, that depart from the International Passenger Ferry Terminal (5.30pm Monday, Wednesday and Friday; last tickets sold around 4pm). You will find the international terminal down a small lane off Beima Lu, not far east of the train station.

BUS

From outside the train station there are buses departing for Běijīng (sleeper Y180, 7pm and 8pm), Jǐ'nán (Y66), Nánjīng (sleeper Y165), Qīngdǎo (Y31), Shànghǎi (sleeper Y180, 2pm) and Wēihǎi (Y17.5). From Yāntái long-distance bus station (Chángtú Qìchēzhàn) on Qingnian Lu there are luxury Volvo buses to numerous destinations, including Jǐ'nán (Y110, every 50 minutes between 6am and 5.45pm), Qīngdǎo (Y50, every 50 minutes between 5am and 5.30pm) and Wēihǎi (Y21, half-hourly between 6am and 5.20pm). Sleeper buses also run to Zhèngzhōu (Y148, 1.15pm), Hángzhōu (Y223, 4pm), Shànghǎi (Y193, 7.15am) and Tiānjīn (Y112, 1.30pm).

Minibuses to Pénglái (Y10, 1½ hours, 5am to 6pm) depart every 15 minutes from the Beima Lu bus station on the corner of Beima Lu and Qingnian Lu. Luxury buses to Pénglái also depart from here every half-hour (Y14), as well as buses to Qūfù (Y91).

TRAIN

Yāntái's small train station is crying out for a refit. There are trains to Běijīng (Y111, 10.26pm), Jǐ'nán (Y38, 8.16am), Qīngdǎo (Y22, 7.36am and 1.55pm), Shànghǎi (Y137, 9.36am), Shíjiāzhuāng (Y55, 5.33pm) and Xī'ān (Y98, 4.14pm).

Getting Around

The airport is approximately 20km south of town. Airport buses (Y10, 30 minutes) leave regularly from the CAAC office; a taxi will cost around Y40 to Y50.

Bus No 3 does a loop of town, running past the train station, south down Xinanhe Lu and west on Yuhuangding Xilu. Bus No 17 runs between the two beaches. Taxi flag fall is Y5, and then Y1.3 per km thereafter.

PÉNGLÁI 蓬莱

☎ 0535

About 65km northwest of Yāntái is Pénglái with **Penglai Pavilion** (蓬莱阁; Pénglái Gé; ☎ 564 8106; admission Y55; ☀ 7am-6.30pm, no entry after 5.50pm), a place of the gods often referred to in Chinese mythology and associated with the legend of the Eight Immortals Crossing the Sea. About 1000 years old, Penglai Pavilion is perched on a cliff top overlooking the sea. You can discover a fascinating array of temples, enjoy wonderful views of fishing boat flotillas and take the cable car (Y18).

Besides the castle, Pénglái is famous for an optical illusion that the locals claim appears every few decades. The last full mirage seen from the castle was in July 2001 and lasted for 20 minutes. On 17 June 1988 this phenomenon occurred and lasted for more than five hours. Two islands appeared with roads, trees, buildings, people, bridges and vehicles, all captured on camera by Shandong TV. You can watch the video recording for Y3.

Pénglái is easily visited as a day trip from Yāntái. The last bus returning to Yāntái leaves at 6.30pm.

WĒIHǍI 威海

☎ 0631 / pop 136,000

About 60km east of Yāntái is the booming port city of Wēihǎi, which was the site of China's most humiliating naval defeat. In 1895 the entire Qing navy (armed with advanced European warships) was slaughtered by a smaller – and weaker – Japanese fleet.

The British had a concession here until 1930, though little remains to remind you of its colonial heritage.

Today visitors are drawn to Wēihǎi for its golden coastline, Liugong Island and to catch the passenger ferry to Korea.

Information

BOOKSHOPS

Xinhua Bookstore (新华书店; Xīnhuá Shūdiàn; 1 Heping Lu) On the corner with Dongcheng Lu.

EMERGENCY

PSB (公安局; Gōng'ānjú; ☎ 521 3620; 111 Chongqing Jie)

INTERNET ACCESS

Xiaole Internet Café (小乐网吧; Xiǎolè Wǎngbā; 64 Dongcheng Lu; per hr Y2; ☀ 7.30am-10pm) Upstairs, north along the road from the bus station.

MONEY

Bank of China (中国银行; Zhōngguó Yínháng; 9 Qingdao Beilu; ⊗ 8.30am-noon & 1-5pm Mon-Fri) ATM accepts MasterCard, Visa, JCB, Amex, Cirrus and Eurocard. **Bank of China** (Zhōngguó Yínháng; 38 Xinwei Lu; ⊗ 8am-6pm Mon-Fri summer, 8am-5pm Mon-Fri winter) Currency exchange.

POST

China Post (邮局; Yóujú; 40 Xinwei Lu)

TRAVEL AGENCIES

CITS (中国国际旅行社; Zhōngguó Guójì Lǚxíngshè; ☎ 581 8616; 3rd fl, 96 Guzhai Dong Lu)
CTS (中国旅行社; Zhōngguó Lǚxíngshè; ☎ 520 3477; 46 Haibin Lu)

Sights

LIUGONG ISLAND 刘公岛

Liugong Island (Liúgōng Dǎo) lies 2km off the coast in the Wēihǎi Gulf. The island was established as a stronghold during the Ming dynasty to guard against Japanese pirates. Later the Qing government made Liugong Island their naval base, and after their crushing defeat at the hands of the Japanese the island was occupied by Japanese troops for three years.

In 1898 the British wrested control of the area and governed it for 32 years. During this time they built schools, churches and even teahouses, transforming the island into a summer resort for the British Navy. In 1948 Chiang Kaishek and his troops arrived, shortly followed by the communists.

Today the island's main attraction is the well-kept and airy **Museum of the 1894–1895 Sino-Japanese War** (中国甲午战争博物馆; Zhōngguó Jiǎwǔ Zhànzhēng Bówùguǎn; admission Y25; ⊗ 7am-5.30pm). The museum is to your left as you exit the ferry terminal, housed in the old offices of the North Sea Fleet commanders. Displays include the anchor of the *Zhenyuan,* a cruiser seized by the Japanese, dioramas of the naval engagement, and shells and fragments of the warship *Jiyuan* (built in Germany), including a high-pressure water desalinisation tank. A Royal Navy torpedo is also displayed and two Krupp cannons.

The island also provides some ideal hiking trails into the hills in the north.

Regular ferry services run to Liugong Island (Y40 return, 20 minutes, price includes a boat trip around the island) between 7am

and 3.30pm from the **Liugongdao Ferry Terminal** (48 Haibin Lu), south of the passenger ferry terminal. The last ferry returning to Wēihǎi leaves at 5.30pm. There is no accommodation on the island. Buggies whizz around the island for Y10.

INTERNATIONAL BEACH 国际海水浴场

Wēihǎi's International Beach (Guójì Hǎishuǐ Yùchǎng) draws large crowds for its long stretch of golden sand, comparably clean waters and large swimming area.

Sleeping

Hailin Hotel (海林宾馆; Hǎilín Bīnguǎn; ☎ 522 4931; fax 528 2632; 146 Tongyi Lu; d/tr/ste Y130/180/380) This simple, unfussy and pleasantly designed two-star hotel, near the corner with Heping Lu, is good value. Standard rooms come with water cooler, large shower room, TV, phone and clean furniture.

Sunshine Hotel (阳光大厦; Yángguāng Dàshà; ☎ 520 8999; 88 Tongyi Lu; d/ste Y580/880) Rooms have been recently restored to a high standard. Standard doubles all have wood flooring, matching twin beds and brand-new showers. Suites are particularly spacious and clean, with inset lights, funky shower rooms and quite a bit of style. Good discounts outside of the May and October holiday periods.

Eating

Lichao Restaurant (李朝牛汤; Lǐcháo Niútāng; ☎ 523 6796; north Bldg, 73 Haigang Lu; meals Y25; ⊗ 8.30am-noon & 1-5pm) You can get into the Korean feel at this lively barbecue grill *(shāokǎo)* restaurant. For Y25 you get a platter of *yángròu* plus six vegetable dishes (including kimchee, *dòufu,* carrot, radish, fish and lettuce). Grill your lamb slices, dip them in *làjiāo* (chilli), wrap in lettuce and eat. Round it all off with some soothing and sweet *zǎochá* (jujube tea). Also on the menu are other meats, including beef and pork.

Kāixīn Cǎomào (开心草帽; ☎ 521 7978; 88-8 Tongyi Lu) Small café/bakery next to Sunshine Hotel, where you can snack up on egg tarts and sink a glass of milk.

Getting There & Around

AIR

Wēihǎi's airport is 80km away. Flights to cities include Běijīng (Y530), Guǎngzhōu (Y1460) and Shànghǎi (Y610). A taxi from the airport to town will cost around Y80.

BOAT

Ferries sail to Incheon (2nd/1st class Y750/1370, 15 hours), in South Korea, at 7pm on Tuesday, Thursday and Sunday. At the time of writing tickets were only available on the day of travel from the ticket office on Haibin Lu to the south of the passenger ferry terminal (Wēihǎi Gǎng Kèyùnzhàn).

Boats to Dàlián leave daily at 8.30am, 9.30am, 8pm and 9pm (Y90 to Y690, eight hours). Tickets should be bought from the International building adjacent to the passenger ferry terminal.

BUS

From the **long-distance bus station** (☎ 522 4591) at the southern end of Dongcheng Lu there are comfortable air-con Volvo buses departing hourly to Yāntái (Y21, 6am to 5.40pm) and Qīngdǎo (Y68, 6.30am to 5.30pm). There are also five buses to Jǐ'nán (Y139), and a bus to Shànghǎi (Y169) and Běijīng (Y142). Smaller Iveco buses also run hourly to Yāntái (Y17.5), Qīngdǎo (Y42.5) and Jǐ'nán (Y79.5) during the same hours. There is also a direct bus to Pénglái at 8am (Y24, two hours).

TRAIN

Located in the south of town, the train station has poor connections. There are trains to Běijīng (Y108, once daily), Tiānjīn (Y51, once daily) and Jǐ'nán (Y63, twice daily). Buy tickets at the train station or at the **ticket office** (☎ 520 8000; 120-1 Tongyi Lu), near the Sunshine Hotel (it also sells air tickets).

Jiāngsū 江苏

HIGHLIGHTS

- Visit the striking **Sun Yatsen Mausoleum** (p223) in Nánjīng
- Relax in **Sūzhōu**'s (p243) beautiful classical gardens
- Tour by boat around **Tài Hú** (p240), one of China's most famous manmade lakes
- Wander through the amazing pottery markets of **Dīngshān** (p242)
- Step back in time in the cobbled lanes of Zhōuzhuāng's **Old Town** (p251)

■ POP: 78.1 MIL	■ AREA: 102,600 SQ KM ·

■ www.seu.edu.cn/EC/english/js.htm

Blessed with China's most productive land, Jiāngsū is symbolic of agricultural abundance and has long been known as 'the land of fish and rice' – the original Chinese character for the province contained these two pictographs. Jiāngsū is located on the eastern coast of China with the southern regions lying within the Yangzi River delta, creating a tapestry landscape of greens, yellows and blues contrasting with whitewashed farmhouses. Together with the northern part of Zhèjiāng this region is known as Jiāngnán, a cultural and geographical entity on the southern side of the Yangzi River. The Grand Canal (Dà Yùnhé) weaves its way north–south through the province and was once an important means of trade for the region.

Being one of the longest-inhabited regions in China, the province is rich in cultural history. Nánjīng, the capital, has some excellent museums, providing insight into the background and development of the region as well as into its modern history and its position in the political landscape of 20th-century China. Chinese history buffs will not want to miss the Sun Yatsen Mausoleum on Zǐjīn Shān, the resting place of the man many consider the 'father of modern China'.

The cities of Sūzhōu and Yángzhōu are famous for their beautiful gardens and draw visitors from around the world. Despite the modern appearance of Sūzhōu, the city still retains some traditional charm and is laced with rivers and canals, a reminder of its once great importance as a trading port. Another city famous for water is Wúxī, which has one of the top tourist spots in the country, Tài Hú. The lake offers wonderful scenery, with parks, pagodas and fishing boats.

History
As far back as the 16th century, the towns on the Grand Canal set up industrial bases for silk production and grain storage, and are still ahead of the rest of the nation. While heavy industry is based in Nánjīng, the other towns concentrate more on light industry, machinery and textiles. They're major producers of electronics and computer components, and haven't been blotted out by the scourges of coal mining or steelworks.

Today, southern Jiāngsū is increasingly being drawn into the ever-expanding economy of nearby Shànghǎi, aided in part by an expressway between Nánjīng and Shànghǎi. It's one of the most rapidly developing provinces in China, evident in the fast rate of construction in the major cities.

Climate
Jiāngsū is hot and humid in summer, yet has overcoat temperatures in winter (when visibility can drop to zero because of fog). Rain or drizzle can be prevalent in winter, but it's a gentle rain that adds a misty, soft touch to the land. The natural colours can be brilliant in spring. Heavy rains fall in spring and summer, but autumn is fairly dry.

Language
The Wu dialect (Wú yǔ) is the primary language spoken in Jiāngsū and variations of it are heard throughout the province. Mandarin is also spoken, particularly in the northern regions closest to Shāndōng province.

Getting There & Away
Jiāngsū is well connected to all major cities in China. There are numerous flights daily from Nánjīng to points around the country as well as frequent bus and train connections. The recently built highway between Shànghǎi and Nánjīng has reduced travel

times considerably. In addition, there are ferries between Sūzhōu and Hángzhōu and from Nánjīng to Chóngqìng and Wǔhàn.

Getting Around

Jiāngsū has a comprehensive bus system that allows travellers to get to most destinations within the province without difficulty. Taking the train is also an option and booking tickets has become quite easy as most hotels now operate their own travel agencies.

NÁNJĪNG 南京

☎ 025 / pop 5.29 million

Nánjīng is one of China's more attractive major cities. It sports a long historical heritage and has twice served briefly as the

nation's capital, first in the early years of the Ming dynasty (1368–1644) and second as the capital of the Republic of China in the early years of the 20th century. Most of Nánjīng's major attractions are reminders of the city's former glory under the Ming.

Like many other major Chinese cities, Nánjīng is developing fast; vast construction projects are visible everywhere. Nánjīng is home to several colleges and universities and a large foreign student population. There are many international-style restaurants, a lively nightlife and access to just about any amenity from around the world.

Just east of the city is Zǐjīn Shān (p223), where it's possible to spend a pleasant day hiking around the many historical sites.

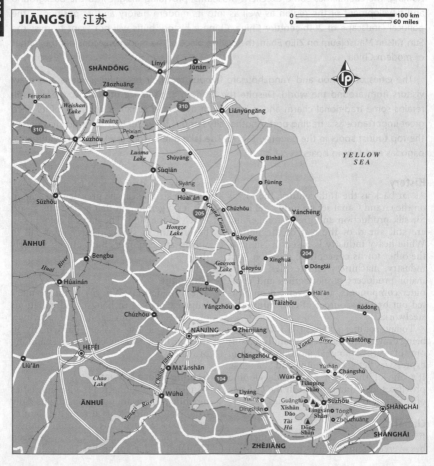

History

The Nánjīng area has been inhabited for about 5000 years, and a number of prehistoric sites have been discovered in or around the city. Recorded history, however, begins in the Warring States period (453–221 BC), when Nánjīng emerged as a strategic object of conflict. The arrival of a victorious Qin dynasty (221–207 BC) put an end to this, allowing Nánjīng to prosper as a major administrative centre.

The city's fortunes took a turn for the worse in the 6th century when it was successively rocked by floods, fires, peasant rebellions and military conquest. With the advent of the Sui dynasty (AD 589–618) and the establishment of Xī'ān as imperial capital, Nánjīng was razed and its historical heritage reduced to ruins. Although it enjoyed a period of prosperity under the long-lived Tang dynasty, it gradually slipped into obscurity.

In 1356, a peasant rebellion led by Zhu Yuanzhang against the Mongol Yuan dynasty was successful. The peasants captured Nánjīng and 12 years later claimed the Yuan capital, Běijīng. Zhu Yuanzhang took the name of Hongwu and took over as the first emperor of the Ming dynasty, with Nánjīng as capital. A massive palace was built and walls were erected around the city.

Nánjīng's glory as imperial capital was short-lived. In 1420, the third Ming emperor, Yongle, moved the capital back to Běijīng. From then on, Nánjīng's fortunes variously rose and declined as a regional centre, but it wasn't until the 19th and 20th centuries that the city again entered the centre stage of Chinese history.

In the 19th century, the Opium Wars brought the British to Nánjīng and it was here that the first of the 'unequal treaties' were signed, opening several Chinese ports to foreign trade, forcing China to pay a huge war indemnity, and officially ceding the island of Hong Kong to Britain. Just a few years later, Nánjīng became the Taiping capital during the Taiping Rebellion (1850–64), which succeeded in taking over most of southern China. In 1864, the combined forces of the Qing army, British army and various European and US mercenaries surrounded the city. They laid siege for seven months, before finally capturing it and slaughtering the Taiping defenders.

In the 20th century, Nánjīng has been the capital of the Republic of China, the site of the worst war atrocity in Japan's assault on China (see Broken as Jade, p225), and the Kuomintang capital from 1928 to 1937 and 1945 to 1949 before the communists 'liberated' the city and made China their own.

Orientation

Nánjīng lies entirely on the southern bank of the Yangzi, bounded in the east by Zíjīn Shān. The centre of town is a roundabout called Xinjiekou, which has a bronze statue of Sun Yatsen, giving the street a somewhat patrician air rarely felt in cities on the Chinese mainland. This is where some of the hotels, including Jinling Hotel, and most tourist facilities are located. Nánjīng train station and the main long-distance bus station are in the far north of the city.

The historical sights, including the Sun Yatsen Mausoleum, Linggu Temple and the Ming Xiaoling Tomb are on Zíjīn Shān.

MAPS

Several different versions of local maps are available from newspaper kiosks and street hawkers around Nánjīng. Many of these maps contain local bus routes. Some of the upscale hotels give out free English language maps of the city.

Information

EMERGENCY & VISAS

Nanjing International SOS Clinic (☎ 8480 2842, 24hr alarm centre ☎ 010-6462 9100) On the ground floor of the Hilton Hotel. Staff on duty speak English.
Public Security Bureau (PSB; Gōngānjú) On a small lane called Sanyuan Xiang down a maze of streets west off Zhongshan Nanlu.

INTERNET ACCESS

Nanjing University Foreign Students Dormitory (p228; per hr Y2; ☒ 9am-1.30am) It has an Internet bar on the ground floor. There are quite a few Internet bars around the universities.

INTERNET RESOURCES

www.mapmagazine.com.cn For current events in Nánjīng.

MEDICAL SERVICES

Jiangsu Provincial Hospital (Jiāngsū Shěng Rénmín Yīyuàn; ☎ 8503 8022; 300 Guangzhou Lu; ☒ 8am-noon & 2-5.30pm) Runs a clinic for expatriates and has English-speaking doctors available.

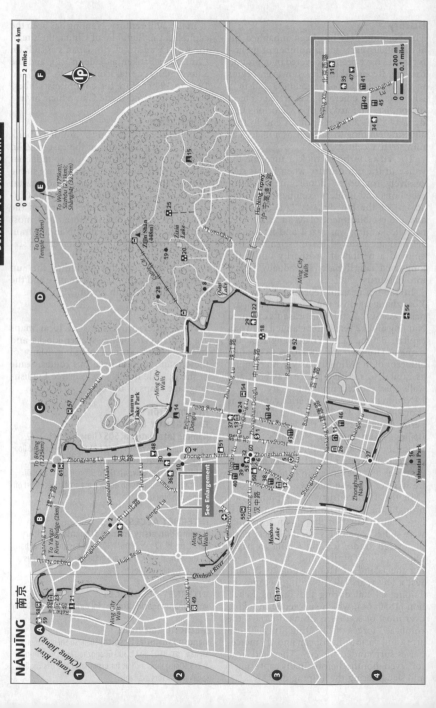

NÁNJĪNG 南京

See Enlargement

MONEY

Bank of China (Zhōngguó Yínháng; 29 Hongwu Lu; ☻ 8am-5pm Mon-Fri, 8am-12.30pm Sat) Changes major currency and travellers cheques. There's a 24-hour ATM which takes international cards. You can also change money at many top-end hotels.

POST

Post Office (Yóujú; 2 Zhongyang Lu; ☻ 8am-6.30pm) Offers postal services and international phone calls. Upmarket tourist hotels also offer postal services.

TOURIST INFORMATION & TRAVEL AGENCIES

Most hotels have their own travel agencies and can book tickets for a small service charge. They can also arrange tours around town and to neighbouring sights. There are many inexpensive travel agencies along Zhongshan Lu and around the universities. **China International Travel Service** (CITS; Zhōngguó Guójì Lǚxíngshè; ☎ 8342 1125; 202 Zhongshan Beilu; ☻ 9am-4pm) Arranges tours and books tickets.

Sights

ZĬJĪN SHĀN 紫金山

Most of Nánjīng's historical sights are scattered over the southern slopes of this forested mountain at the city's eastern fringe. The mountain is also translated in some tourist brochures as 'Purple Mountain'. A half-hour cable car ride (one-way Y15, return Y25) goes to the top of the 448m hill for a panoramic, if somewhat hazy, view of Nánjīng, or you can walk up the stone path that runs beneath the cable cars. An **observatory** (admission Y15; ☻ daylight) is located 350m up the hill, with bronze astronomical instruments from the Ming dynasty on display.

Bus No 9 or Y1 goes from the city centre to the Sun Yatsen Mausoleum at the centre of the mountain. From here, bus No 20 runs between all of the sites on the mountain, operating from 8am to 5pm, costing Y2 per ride.

SUN YATSEN MAUSOLEUM 中山陵

As the crowds of tourists indicate, for many Chinese a visit to the **Sun Yatsen Mausoleum** (Zhōngshān Líng; admission Y25; ☻ 6.30am-6.30pm) is something of a pilgrimage. Sun is recognised by the communists and Kuomintang alike as the father of modern China. He died in Běijīng in 1925, leaving behind an unstable Chinese republic. He had wished to be buried in Nánjīng, no doubt with greater simplicity than the Ming-style tomb his successors built for him. Nevertheless, less than a year after his death, construction of this immense mausoleum began.

The tomb itself lies at the top of an enormous stone stairway, 323m long and 70m wide. At the start of the path stands a stone gateway built of Fujian marble, with a roof of blue-glazed tiles. The blue and white of the mausoleum symbolise the white sun on the blue background of the Kuomintang flag.

The crypt is at the top of the steps at the rear of the memorial chamber. A tablet hanging across the threshold is inscribed with the 'Three Principles of the People', as formulated by Dr Sun: nationalism, democracy and people's livelihood. Inside is a seated statue of Dr Sun. The walls are carved with the complete text of the Outline of Principles for the Establishment of the Nation put forward by the Nationalist government. A prostrate marble statue of Sun seals his coffin.

MING XIAOLING TOMB 明孝陵

This **tomb** (Míng Xiàolíng; admission Y15; ☯ 6.30am-6.30pm) lies on the southern slope of Zǐjīn Shān. Construction began in 1381 and was finished in 1383; the emperor died at the age of 71 in 1398.

The first section of the avenue leading up to the mausoleum is lined with stone statues of lions, camels, elephants and horses. There's also a mythical animal called a *xiè zhì* – which has a mane and a single horn on its head – and a *qílín*, which has a scaly body, a cow's tail, deer's hooves and one horn.

As you enter the first courtyard, a paved pathway leads to a pavilion housing several stelae. The next gate leads to a large courtyard with the **Linghun Pagoda** (Línghún Tă), a mammoth rectangular stone structure. Behind the tower is a wall, 350m in diameter, surrounding a huge earth mound. Beneath this mound is the tomb vault of Hongwu, which has not been excavated.

The area surrounding the tomb is the **Ming Xiaoling Scenic Area** (Míng Xiàolíng Fēngjǐngqū). A tree-lined, stone pathway winds around pavilions and picnic grounds and ends at **Zixia Lake** (Zǐxiá Hú), a small lake you can swim in – a very relaxing way to spend a hot afternoon.

LINGGU TEMPLE 灵谷寺

This large **temple complex** (Línggǔ Sì; admission Y15; ☯ 6.30am-6.30pm) has one of the most interesting buildings in Nánjīng – the **Beamless Hall** (Wúliáng Diàn). In 1381, when Hongwu was

building his tomb, he had a temple on the site torn down and rebuilt a few kilometres to the east. Of this temple only the Beamless Hall (so called because it is built entirely of bricks and contains no beam supports) remains. The structure has an interesting vaulted ceiling and a large stone platform where Buddhist statues once sat. In the 1930s the hall was turned into a memorial to those who died in the 1926–28 revolution. One of the inscriptions on the inside wall is the old Kuomintang national anthem.

A road runs on both sides of the hall and up two flights of steps to the **Pine Wind Pavilion** (Sōngfēng Gè), originally dedicated to Guanyin as part of Linggu Temple. It houses a small shop and teahouse.

The temple itself and a memorial hall to Xuan Zang are close by; after you pass through the Beamless Hall, turn right and follow the pathway. Xuan Zang was the Buddhist monk who travelled to India and brought back the Buddhist scriptures. Inside the memorial hall is a 13-storey wooden pagoda model that contains part of his skull, a sacrificial table and a portrait of the monk.

Nearby is the **Linggu Pagoda** (Línggǔ Tă). This nine-storey, 60m-high, octagonal pagoda was built in the 1930s under the direction of a US architect as a memorial to Kuomintang members who died in the 1926–28 revolution.

BOTANIC GARDENS 植物园

These **gardens** (Zhíwù Yuán; admission Y15; ☯ 8.30am-4.30pm) were established in 1929. Covering over 186 hectares, more than 3000 plant species including roses, medicinal plants and bonsai gardens are on display.

TAIPING HEAVENLY KINGDOM HISTORY MUSEUM 太平天国历史博物馆

Hong Xiuquan, the leader of the Taipings, had a palace built in Nánjīng, but the building was completely destroyed when Nánjīng was taken in 1864.

The **museum** (Tàipíng Tiānguó Lìshǐ Bówùguǎn; 128 Zhanyuan Lu; admission Y10; ☯ 8am-6pm) was originally a garden complex, built in the Ming dynasty, which housed some of the Taiping officials before their downfall. There are displays of maps showing the northward progress of the Taiping army from Guǎngdōng, Hong Xiuquan's seals, Taiping coins, weapons and texts that describe the Taiping laws on agrarian reform, social law and cultural policy. Other texts describe divisions in the Taiping leadership, the attacks by the Manchus and foreigners, and the fall of Nánjīng in 1864. Most of the original literature is kept in Běijīng. This museum is one of the best in the city and well worth a visit if there is time.

Bus No Y2 goes to the museum from the Ming Palace Ruins or Taiping Nanlu.

NANJING MUSEUM 南京博物馆
Just inside the eastern city walls, the Nánjīng **museum** (Nánjīng Bówùguǎn; 321 Zhongshan Donglu; admission Y20; ☉ 9am-5.30pm) houses an array of artefacts from Neolithic times right through to the communist period. The main building was constructed in 1933 in the style of an ancient temple with yellow-glazed tiles, red-lacquered gates and columns. A brand-new complex, similar in design to the first, recently opened.

The museum houses an interesting burial suit made of small rectangles of jade sewn together with silver thread, dating from the Eastern Han dynasty (AD 25–220) and excavated from a tomb discovered in the city of Xúzhōu in northern Jiāngsū. Other exhibits include bricks with the inscriptions of their makers and overseers from the Ming city wall, drawings of old Nánjīng, an early Qing mural of Sūzhōu and relics from the Taiping Rebellion.

NANJING TREATY HISTORY MUSEUM
南京条约史料陈列馆
This **museum** (Nánjīng Tiáoyuē Shǐliào Chénlièguǎn; 116 Chao Yue Lou; admission Y4; ☉ 8.30am-5pm) houses a small collection of photographs, maps and newspaper clippings (no English captions) related to the Nanjing Treaties. It's in **Jinghai Temple** (Jìnghǎi Sì) near the west train station, off Rehe Lu. To get there catch bus No 16 from Zhongshan Lu. It's probably not worth the effort to visit unless you're keen on Chinese history.

MEMORIAL HALL OF THE NANJING MASSACRE 南京大屠杀纪念馆
The exhibits at this **memorial hall** (Nánjīng Dàtùshā Jìniànguǎn; ☎ 661 2230; 418 Shuiximen Dajie; admission

---

BROKEN AS JADE

In 1937, with the Chinese army comparatively weak and underfunded and the Japanese army on the horizon, the invasion into and occupation of Nánjīng by Japan appeared imminent. As it packed up and fled, the Chinese government encouraged the people of Nánjīng to stay, saying: 'All those who have blood and breath in them must feel that they wish to be broken as jade rather than remain whole as tile.' To reinforce this statement, the gates to the city were locked, trapping over half a million citizens inside. Nevertheless, thousands of civilians attempted to follow the retreating government by escaping through Xiaguan Gate, the only gate in the city wall that remained unlocked. Leading up to the gate was a 21m tunnel inside of which reigned panic and mayhem. In the resulting chaos and collisions, thousands of people were suffocated, burned or trampled to death.

What followed in Nánjīng was six weeks of continuous, unfathomable victimisation of civilians to an extent that had yet to be witnessed in modern warfare. During Japan's occupation of Nánjīng, between 300,000 and 400,000 Chinese civilians were killed, either in group massacres or individual murders. Within the first month, at least 20,000 women between the ages of 11 and 76 were brutally raped. Women who attempted to refuse or children who interfered were often bayoneted or shot. It has been reported by those involved that the atrocities committed in Nánjīng were condoned and encouraged by the Japanese officers in command as acceptable and expected military procedure.

The Japanese, however, underestimated the courage and strength of the Chinese people. Instead of breaking the people's will, the invasion only served to fuel a sense of identity and determination. Those who did not die – broken as jade – survived to fight back.

The Rape of Nanjing is conspicuously absent from many world history books. Despite this, it is hoped that a growing awareness of the horrific event will help to prevent such atrocities from occurring again. As the ancient Chinese proverb says, 'Past experience, if not forgotten, is a guide for the future' (Qián shì bù wàng hòu shì zhī shí).

Y10; ⊙ 8am-5.30pm) document the atrocities committed by Japanese soldiers against the civilian population during the occupation of Nánjīng in 1937 (see Broken as Jade, p225). They include pictures of actual executions – many taken by Japanese army photographers – and a gruesome viewing hall built over a mass grave of massacre victims. Captions are in English, Japanese and Chinese but the photographs, skeletons and displays tell their own haunting stories without words.

The exhibits conclude on a more optimistic note, with a final room dedicated to the post-1945 Sino-Japanese reconciliation. It's in the city's southwestern suburbs; take bus No Y4 from Zhonghua Gate or the west train station.

JIANGSU ART GALLERY 江苏美术馆
The **gallery** (Jiāngsū Měishùguǎn; ☎ 8664 1962; 266 Changjiang Lu; admission Y10; ⊙ 8-11.30am & 2-5pm) displays works of local painters in frequently changing exhibitions.

MONUMENT TO THE CROSSING OF THE YANGZI RIVER 渡江纪念碑
In the northwest of the city on Zhongshan Beilu, this **monument** (Dùjiāng Jìniànbēi), erected in April 1979, commemorates the crossing of the river on 23 April 1949 and the capture of Nánjīng from the Kuomintang by the Communist army. The characters on the monument are in the calligraphy of Deng Xiaoping. To get there catch bus No 31 from Taiping Lu.

YANGZI RIVER BRIDGE 南京长江大桥
One of the great achievements of the communists, and one of which they are justifiably proud, is the **Yangzi River Bridge** (Nánjīng Cháng Jiāng Dàqiáo) at Nánjīng. Opened on 23 December 1968, it's one of the longest bridges in China – a double-decker with a 4500m-long road on top and a train line below. There are some wonderful socialist realist sculptures on the approaches.

Apparently the bridge was designed and built entirely by the Chinese after the Russians marched out and took the designs with them in 1960. Given the immensity of the construction it's an impressive engineering feat, before which there was no direct rail link between Běijīng and Shànghǎi. Probably the easiest way to get up on the bridge is

to go through the **Bridge Park** (Dàqiáo Gōngyuán; ☎ 582 2455; admission Y9; ⊙ 7.30am-6.30pm). Catch bus No 67 from Jiangsu Lu, northwest of the Drum Tower, to its terminus opposite the park.

HEAVEN DYNASTY PALACE 朝天宫
This **palace** (Cháotiān Gōng; admission Y30; ⊙ 8am-5pm), off Mochou Lu, was originally established in the Ming dynasty as a school for educating aristocratic children in court etiquette. Most of today's buildings, including the centrepiece of the palace, a Confucian temple, date from 1866 when the whole complex was rebuilt. Today the buildings are used for a range of endeavours, including an artisan market.

To reach the palace, take bus No 4 from the Xinjiekou roundabout and get off two stops to the west.

MING CITY WALLS
Nánjīng enjoyed its golden years under the Ming dynasty and there are numerous remnants of the period. One of the most impressive is the Ming city wall measuring over 33km – the longest city wall ever built in the world. About two-thirds of it still stands. It was built between 1366 and 1386, by more than 200,000 labourers.

The layout of the wall is irregular, an exception to the usual square format of these times, as much of it is built on the foundations of earlier walls, which took advantage of strategic hills. Averaging 12m high and 7m wide at the top, the wall was built of bricks supplied from five Chinese provinces. Each brick had stamped on it the place it came from, the overseer's name and rank, the brick-maker's name and sometimes the date. This was to ensure that the bricks were well made; if they broke they had to be replaced.

MING CITY GATES
Some of the original 13 Ming city gates remain, including the **Centre Gate** (Zhōngyāng Mén) in the north and **Zhonghua Gate** (Zhōnghuá Mén; admission Y8) in the south. The city gates were heavily fortified; Zhonghua Gate has four rows of gates, making it almost impregnable, and could house a garrison of 3000 soldiers in vaults in the front gate building. Today some of these vaults are used as souvenir shops.

MING PALACE RUINS 明故宫

Built by Hongwu, the **Ming Palace Ruins** (Míng Gùgōng; Zhongshan Donglu; admission Y1; ☺ 6.30am-11pm) is said to have been a magnificent structure after which the Imperial Palace in Běijīng was modelled. Virtually all that remains of it are five marble bridges lying side by side, known as the **Five Dragon Bridges** (Wǔlóng Qiáo), the old ruined **Wu Gate** (Wú Mén) and the enormous column bases of the palace buildings.

The palace suffered two major fires in its first century and was allowed to fall into ruins after the Ming court moved to Běijīng. It was later looted by the Manchus and then, during the Taiping Rebellion, bombardments by Qing and Western troops finished it off.

You can reach the Ming Palace Ruins by catching bus No Y1 from the Nánjīng train station or Zhongyang Lu.

JIMING TEMPLE 鸡鸣寺

Close to the Ming walls and Xuanwu Lake (Xuánwǔ Hú) is the Buddhist **Jiming Temple** (Jīmíng Sì; admission Y5) which was first built in AD 527, during the Three Kingdoms period. It's been rebuilt many times since but has retained the same name (which literally translates as 'rooster crowing') since 1387. This temple is the most active temple in Nánjīng and is packed with worshippers during the Lunar New Year. The area around the temple is quite pretty and worth a look.

EARLY REMAINS

Nánjīng has been inhabited since prehistoric times. Remains of a prehistoric culture have been found at the site of the Drum Tower and in surrounding areas. About 200 sites of small clan communities, mainly represented by pottery and bronze artefacts dating back to the late Shang and Zhou dynasties, were found on both sides of the Yangzi.

In AD 212, towards the end of the Eastern Han period, the military commander in charge of the Nánjīng region built a citadel on Qíngjìng Shān (Qingjing Mountain) in the west of Nánjīng. At that time the mountain was referred to as Stone Mountain (Shítou Shān) and so the citadel became known as the Stone City (Shítou Dūshì). The wall measured over 10km in circumference. Today, some of the red sandstone foundations are still visible.

DRUM TOWER 鼓楼

Built in 1382, the **Drum Tower** (Gǔ Lóu; ☎ 442 1495; 6 Zhongyang Lu; admission free; ☺ 8am-midnight) lies roughly in the centre of Nánjīng, on a roundabout. Drums were usually beaten to give directions for the change of the night watches and, in rare instances, to warn the populace of impending danger. Only one large drum remains today.

BELL TOWER 大钟亭

East of the Drum Tower, the **Bell Tower** (Zhōng Lóu; Beijing Donglu; admission free; ☺ 8.30am-5.30pm) houses an enormous bell, cast in 1388 and originally situated in a pavilion on the western side of the Drum Tower. The present tower dates from 1889 and is a small two-storey pavilion with a pointed roof and upturned eaves. A garden and teahouse surround the tower and remain open late into the evening.

FUZI TEMPLE 夫子庙

This ancient Confucian **temple** (Fūzǐ Miào; Gongyuan Jie; admission Y12; ☺ 8am-9pm) is located in the south of the city in a pedestrian zone. This was a centre of Confucian study for more than 1500 years. Fuzi Temple has been damaged and rebuilt repeatedly; what you see here today are newly restored, late-Qing dynasty structures or wholly new buildings reconstructed in traditional style. The main temple is behind the small square in front of the canal.

Across from the temple complex to the east is the **Imperial Examinations History Museum** (Jiāngnán Gōngyuàn Lìshǐ Chénlièguǎn; 1 Jinling Lu; admission Y6; ☺ 8am-6pm). This is a recent reconstruction of the building where scholars once spent months – or years – in tiny cells studying Confucian classics in preparation for civil service examinations.

Today, the area surrounding Fuzi Temple has become Nánjīng's main amusement quarter and is a particularly lively and crowded place on weekends and public holidays with restaurants and rows upon rows of souvenir shops. The whole area is lit up at night, adding to the kitsch ambience.

Catch bus No 1 from Xinjiekou and get off at the last stop.

PRESIDENTIAL PALACE 总统府

After the Taiping took over Nánjīng, they built the Mansion of the Heavenly King

(Tiānwáng Fǔ) on the foundations of a former Ming dynasty palace. This magnificent place did not survive the fall of the Taipings but there is a reconstruction and a classical Ming garden, now known as the **Presidential Palace** (Zŏngtŏng Fǔ; 292 Changjiang Lu; admission Y40; ☯ 8am-5.30pm). Other buildings on the site were used briefly as presidential offices by Sun Yatsen's government in 1912 and by the Kuomintang from 1927 to 1949.

MARTYRS' CEMETERY 烈士墓地
This **cemetery** (Lièshì Mùdì; Yuhuatai Lu; admission Y10; ☯ 7am-10pm) is in the south of the city. Once the Kuomintang's execution grounds, the communists turned it into a garden dedicated to revolutionaries who had lost their lives here. Along with a large monument, there's an English-captioned **museum** (☯ 8am-5.30pm) with a history of the period before 1949 and biographies of revolutionaries.

Tours
Local tours can be arranged through hotels or any one of the inexpensive travel agencies on Zhongshan Donglu.

Festivals & Events
The **Nanjing International Plum Blossom Festival**, held every year from the last Saturday of February to 18 March, draws visitors from around China. The festival takes place on Zǐjīn Shān near the Ming Xiaoling Tomb when the mountain is covered with pink and white blossoms.

Sleeping
Most Nánjīng accommodation is mid-range to top end in price.

BUDGET
Nanjing University Foreign Students Dormitory (Nánjīng Dàxué Wàiguó Liúxuéshēng Sùshè; ☎ 8359 3589; 20 Jinyin Jie; d Y100-200) This 20-storey, white-tiled building has decent budget accommodation, though nothing fancy. Take bus No 13 from the train station or the Zhongyang Men long-distance bus station and get off at the intersection of Beijing Xilu and Shanghai Lu.

Nanjing Normal University Nanshan Hotel (Nánjīng Shīfàn Dàxué Nánshān Bīnguǎn; ☎ 8371 6440 ext 6060; 122 Ninghai Lu; s Y100, d Y80-130, tr Y105-240)

Many travellers think the rooms here are more comfortable than those at Nanjing University. To get here from the Nanjing University dorm, walk south along Shanghai Lu. Turn right into the second or third alleyway, then take the first road left to the main gate of Nanjing Normal University (next to a McDonald's). The dormitory is inside the campus compound, to the left up the hill.

MID-RANGE
Jingli Hotel (Jīnglì Jiǔdiàn; ☎ 8331 0818; fax 8663 6636; 7 Beijing Xilu; s/d Y420/545) Located on a pretty, tree-lined street close to Nanjing University, this hotel is clean, modern and comfortable. All rooms have free Internet. Discounts of 20% to 30% are available.

Jiangsu Hotel (Jiāngsū Dàjiǔdiàn; ☎ 8332 0888; fax 330 3308; 28 Zhongshan Beilu; s/d Y420/500) This hotel near the Drum Tower is in an excellent location and has upmarket rooms without the price. Discounts of 35% are available.

Zijing Hotel (Zǐjīng Dàjiǔdiàn; ☎ 8444 5999; fax 8664 5129; 37 Taiping Beilu; s & d Y340) Close to the Presidential Palace, this small hotel offers spacious, sparkling-clean rooms with free Internet. Management are courteous and helpful. Double rooms can be discounted to Y240 if booked ahead.

TOP END
Nanjing Hotel (Nánjīng Fàndiàn; ☎ 8341 1888; 259 Zhongshan Beilu; s & d Y400-800) A charming place built in 1936, this hotel is set on pleasant grounds away from the street. The more expensive rooms are newly renovated and cheaper rooms are in a separate building. Discounts of 30% make this place quite a good deal.

Jinling Hotel (Jīnlíng Fàndiàn; ☎ 8471 1888; fax 8471 1666; Xinjiekou; d Y1535) This 36-storey establishment is one of the most upmarket hotels in the city. Ignore the posted prices – the hotel discounts rooms up to 40%.

Hilton Hotel (Xī'érdùn Fàndiàn; ☎ 8480 8888; 319 Zhongshan Donglu; s/d US$180/200) Don't be too alarmed by these prices – doubles are often discounted to Y599. The Hilton is close to Zǐjīn Shān and the Nanjing Museum.

Ramada Plaza (Huáměidá Qiàhuá Jiǔdiàn; ☎ 8330 8888; fax 8330 8999; 45 Zhongshan Beilu; d US$120-140) This place is very good value when discounts of 50% are offered. It has a great location near the Drum Tower.

Eating

Some of Nánjīng's livelier eating houses are in the Fuzi Temple quarter. A number of teahouses above the shops in the area across the river offer excellent night views of Fuzi Temple. There's still lots of variety in traditional Chinese fare from the many food stalls and restaurants in the area.

Wǎnqíng Lóu (Dashiba Jie; mains Y30-60; ☺ breakfast, lunch & dinner) This restaurant is on the opposite side of the river from Fuzi Temple's main square. Here you can try delicious Nánjīng snacks and local specialities.

Sìchuān Jiǔjiā (171 Taiping Nanlu; mains Y25-50; ☺ breakfast, lunch & dinner) Despite the name, this is also a good place to sample local specialities. Here, Nánjīng pressed duck (*yánshuǐ yā*) is slathered with roasted salt, steeped in clear brine, baked dry and then kept under cover for some time; the finished product should have a creamy-coloured skin and red, tender flesh. The Sìchuān-style dishes are also good and spicy. A **snack place** occupies the ground floor and the main restaurant is on the 2nd floor. There's no English sign or menu; look for the large red lanterns beside KFC.

Luliuju Vegetarian Restaurant (Lùliǔjú Càiguǎn; 248 Taiping Nanlu; mains Y2-8; ☺ breakfast, lunch & dinner) This unassuming little eatery is just down the road from Sìchuān Jiǔjiā and serves excellent mock-meat dishes made with tofu, among other things.

Anleyuan Muslim Restaurant (Qīngzhèn Ānlèyuán Càiguǎn; 138 Wangfu Dajie; mains Y30-50; ☺ breakfast, lunch & dinner) This is the largest Muslim restaurant in town and very popular with locals. The spicy hand-pulled noodles (*lā miàn*) are especially good here.

Many small restaurants are found in the streets around the two universities. If you want to forget all about local delicacies, head over to one of the cluster of restaurants around Nanjing University catering to adventurous locals and foreign students.

Jack's Place (Jiékè Dìfāng; 160 Shanghai Lu; mains Y20-40; ☺ breakfast, lunch & dinner) Jack's now has three branches in Nánjīng, including one opposite Nanjing Normal University. Food (pizzas, pastas and salads as well as other Western items) is rather uninspired but cheap.

Kèjiāfú Kǎodiàn (38 Yinyang Ying; mains Y10-50; ☺ breakfast, lunch & dinner) A spotlessly clean and popular place, this Korean restaurant

serves huge bowls of cold noodle dishes. There's an English menu.

Skyways Bakery & Deli (Yúnzhōng Shípǐndiàn; 3-6 Hankou Xilu; mains Y15-30; ☺ breakfast, lunch & dinner) The sandwiches are really tasty in this small deli and it's a good place to meet foreign teachers and students who crowd in here during lunch time. The bulletin board is a good place to learn what's going on around town.

Henry's Home Cafe (Hēnglì Zhījiā; 33 Huaqiao Lu; mains Y40-80; ☺ breakfast, lunch & dinner) Henry's Home Cafe serves pasta, pizza, fajitas and steak dishes and has very friendly service.

City Garden Coffee Shop (Chéngshì Huāyuán Kāfēidiàn; 87 Guanjia Qiao; mains Y30-70; ☺ breakfast, lunch & dinner) This is a large, clean place serving set meals of rice and meat dishes (Y35) and sandwiches (Y30). The menu is in English and Chinese.

Drinking

Nánjīng's nightlife is not as active as Shànghǎi's but there is a range of bars, pubs and discos to choose from. The best place to ask about entertainment is at the foreign student dormitories where you'll find advertisements and posters.

Blowing in the Wind (Dǎ'àn Jiǔbā; 13 Jinyin Jie; beer from Y15; ☺ 7pm 2am) This unpretentious place has live music and a relaxed atmosphere.

Castle Bar (Gúbáo Shénqū; Zhongyang Lu; beer Y16; ☺ 7pm 2am) Inside the Drum Tower complex, this is another good place to go for live and house music. The dance floor can get pretty crowded once the DJs get going.

Scarlet Bar (Luànshì Jiārén Jiǔbā; 29 Gulou Chezhan Dongxiang; beer Y10; ☺ 6pm-3am) This small place is on a lane off Zhongyang Lu and is popular with a younger, local crowd. The dancing starts around 10pm.

Entertainment

Jiangsu Kunju Theatre (Jiāngsū Shěng Kūnjùyuàn; 2 Chao-tian Gong; tickets Y30) Excellent opera performances are held here. The theatre is next to the eastern entrance of the Heaven Dynasty Palace. *Kūnjù* or *kūnqǔ* is a regional form of classical Chinese opera that developed in the Sūzhōu-Hángzhōu-Nánjīng triangle. It's similar to (but slower than) Beijing opera and is performed with colourful and elaborate costumes. To reach the theatre, take bus No 4 from the Xinjiekou roundabout and get off two stops to the west.

Nanjing Shenying Warner Cinema (Nánjīng Shàngyǐng Huánàyǐng Chéng; 3rd fl, New City Shopping Centre, 98 Caochangmen Dajie; tickets Y30) English-language movies are shown here.

Shopping

There's little you can't buy in Nánjīng – from designer clothing to trinket souvenirs. Hunan Lu has a late-night market and is lined with shops and stalls. It's good for clothes shopping during the day. The area surrounding Fuzi Temple is a pedestrian zone with souvenirs and antiques for sale. Around Hanzhong Lu and Zhongshan Lu you'll find a number of major department stores.

Zhongshan Department Store (Zhōngshān Dàshà; 200 Zhongshan Lu) This older establishment is a good place to head to for a whole range of products.

GE International Shopping Centre (Jīnyíng Guójì Gòuwù Zhōngxīn; 89 Hanzhong Lu) A little more up-market, this shopping centre is aimed at a younger crowd with a more disposable income.

Getting There & Away

AIR

Nánjīng has regular air connections to all major Chinese cities, including daily flights to and from Hong Kong (Y2080).

The main office for the **Civil Aviation Administration of China** (CAAC; Zhōngguó Mínháng; ☎ 8448 5131; 50 Ruijin Lu) is near the terminus of bus route No 37, but you can also buy tickets at most top-end hotels. **Dragonair** (Gǎnglóng Hángkōng; ☎ 8471 0181; Room 751-53, World Trade Centre, 2 Hanzhong Lu) has daily flights to Hong Kong.

BOAT

Several ferries depart daily from Nánjīng's Yangzi port downriver (eastward) to Shànghǎi (about 10 hours) and upriver (westward) to Wǔhàn (two days); a few boats also go to Chóngqìng (five days). The passenger dock is in the northwest of the city at **No 6 dock** (Liù Hào Mǎtóu). Tickets can be booked at the dock in the terminal building. For full details on Yangzi cruises, see p768.

BUS

There are many long-distance bus stations in Nánjīng. In the north, Zhongyang Men long-distance bus station is southeast of the wide-bridged intersection with Zhongyang Lu. Buses from here go to Shànghǎi (Y88, four hours), Héféi (Y42, 2½ hours) and Sūzhōu (Y64, 2½ hours). Another useful station is on Hanzhong Lu, where buses go to Zhènjiāng (Y22, 1½ hours) and Yángzhōu (Y26, two hours). The Hanfu Jie bus station on Changjiang Lu has buses to Hángzhōu (Y98, five hours). All three stations cover most other major destinations.

From the train station, take bus No 13 north to Zhōngyāng Mén bus station or south to the Hanzhong Lu station. Bus No Y1 from the train station via Zhongyang Lu goes near the Hanfu Jie station.

TRAIN

Nánjīng is a major stop on the Běijīng–Shànghǎi train line, and the station is mayhem. There are several trains a day in both directions. Heading eastward from Nánjīng, the line to Shànghǎi connects with Zhènjiāng, Wúxī and Sūzhōu.

Four daily express trains run between Nánjīng and Shànghǎi (Y47, three hours). Other trains to Shànghǎi take four hours, stopping in Zhènjiāng (Y11, one hour) and Sūzhōu (Y26, 2½ hours). Some of the express trains also stop in Zhènjiāng and Sūzhōu.

There are trains to Hángzhōu (Y73, five hours) and a slow train to Guǎngzhōu (Y401, 32 hours) via Shànghǎi. There's a train from Shànghǎi to Huáng Shān in Ānhuī province that passes through Nánjīng (Y94, seven hours) and also a train to the port of Wúhú on the Yangzi River which continues on to Huáng Shān (Y54, seven hours). There is a local train to Huáng Shān from Nánjīng (no air-con, Y23, nine hours) which is hard seat and recommended only for the brave.

You can buy train tickets at most hotels for a Y5 to Y10 service charge.

Getting Around

TO/FROM THE AIRPORT

Nánjīng airport is approximately one hour south of the city. Most hotels have hourly shuttle buses to and from the airport. A taxi will cost around Y150.

LOCAL TRANSPORT

Taxis cruise the streets of Nánjīng and are very cheap – most destinations in the city are Y7, but make sure the meter is switched on. Motor-tricycles are also common; be sure to agree on a price beforehand.

You can get to Xinjiekou, in the heart of town, by jumping on bus No 13 from the train station or the Centre Gate. There are also tourist bus routes that visit many of the sites. Bus No Y1 goes from the train and bus station through the city to the Sun Yatsen Mausoleum. Bus No Y2 starts in the south at the Martyrs' Cemetery, passes Fuzi Temple and terminates halfway up Zǐjīn Shān.

Many local maps contain bus routes. Normal buses cost Y1 and tourist buses cost Y2.

AROUND NÁNJĪNG
Qixia Temple 栖霞寺

This **temple** (Qīxiá Sì; Morning of the Birds Temple; admission Y10; ☼ 7am-5.30pm) on Qixia Mountain 22km northeast of Nánjīng, was founded by the Buddhist monk Ming Sengshao during the Southern Qi dynasty, and is still an active place of worship. This temple has long been one of China's most important monasteries, and even today is one of the largest Buddhist seminaries in the country. There are two main temple halls: the Maitreya Hall, with a statue of the Maitreya Buddha sitting cross-legged at the entrance, and behind this the Vairocana Hall, housing a 5m-tall statue of Vairocana.

Behind the temple is the **Thousand Buddha Cliff** (Qiānfó Yá). Several small caves housing stone statues are carved into the hillside, the earliest of which dates from the Qi dynasty (AD 479–502), although there are others from succeeding dynasties through to the Ming. There is also a small stone pagoda, **Sheli Pagoda** (Shělì Tǎ), built in AD 601, and rebuilt during the late Tang period. The upper part has engraved sutras and carvings of Buddha; around the base, each of the pagoda's eight sides depicts Sakyamuni.

You can reach this temple from Nánjīng by a public bus (marked Qīxiá Sì; Y3, one hour) that departs from opposite the train station.

ZHÈNJIĀNG 镇江
☎ 0511 / pop 2.65 million

Just an hour from Nánjīng, Zhènjiāng is known for its production of vinegar, a lingering aroma of which floats over the streets, especially near the train station. The city's main attraction is Jinshan Park (Jīnshān Gōngyuán), where an active Buddhist temple attracts large crowds of worshippers.

Orientation & Information

The oldest part of the city is found around Daxi Lu, which is an interesting area to wander around, especially beyond the western end of the street. A new promenade along the shores of the Yangzi is also a pleasant place for a stroll.

Bank of China (Zhōngguó Yínháng; ☼ 9am-5.30pm) Located on Zhongshan Lu, just east of the intersection with Jiefang Lu. It has an ATM that takes international cards. There's another branch near the bus station by the train station.

Internet Café (per hr Y4) Beside the Shàngyè Dàshà department store on Zhongshan Donglu, near the intersection of Jiefang Lu.

Post and Telephone Office (Zhōngguó Diànxìn) Is on Dianli Lu, on the corner of Xinma Lu.

PSB (Gōngānjú; 24 Shizheng Lu) Can help in case of emergencies. For visa extensions, it's best to go to Nánjīng.

Sights
JINSHAN PARK 金山公园

This **park** (Jīnshān Gōngyuán; Gold Hill Park, 62 Jīnshān Xilu; admission Y25) packs in the crowds who fill the flights of stairs leading up through Buddhist **Jinshan Temple** (Jīnshān Sì), to the seven-storey, octagonal **Cishou Pagoda** (Císhòu Tǎ; admission Y3).

The temple gains its name from a Zen master who is said to have come into copious amounts of gold (jīn) after opening the gates at the entrance of the park. There are four caves at the mount; of these **Buddhist Sea** (Fáhǎi) and **White Dragon** (Báilóng) feature in the Chinese legend *The Story of the White Snake*. To get to Jinshan Park take bus No 2 (p233) to the last stop.

JIĀO SHĀN 焦山

The green foliage on this **island** (admission Y25), east of Zhènjiāng, is said to give it the impression of a piece of jade floating in the river. There's good hiking here with a number of pavilions along the way to the top of the 150m-high mountain, from where **Xijiang Tower** (Xījiāng Lóu) gives good views over the river. At the base of the mountain is an active monastery.

To get to Jiāo Shān take bus No 4 from Zhongshan Xilu or Jiefang Lu to the terminal. From there it's a short walk and a boat ride (included in the ticket), or you can take a cable car (just north of the boat dock) to the top of the hill (Y15).

NORTH HILL PARK 北固山公园

North Hill Park (Běigù Shān Gōngyuán; 3 Dongwu Lu; admission Y15; ⏱ 7am-7pm) is home to **Ganlu Temple** (Gānlù Sì), which features an iron pagoda first built in the Tang dynasty. Once 13m high, the pagoda has since suffered damage from fire, lightning and overzealous Red Guards during the Cultural Revolution. It's on the No 4 bus route.

SOUTH HILL SCENIC PARK 南山风景区

At the southern end of town, **South Hill Scenic Park** (Nánshān Fēngjǐngqū; Zhulin Lu; admission Y15; ⏱ 7.30am-5.30pm) contains the **Bamboo Forest Temple** (Zhúlín Sì; admission Y2). As temples go, it won't qualify as the biggest or best in China, but its setting among the trees and hills makes it a relaxing spot. To get there take bus No 15 from Zhongshan Lu.

ZHENJIANG MUSEUM 镇江博物馆

Between Jinshan Park and the centre of town is the old British consulate, built in 1890 and now converted into a **museum** (Zhènjiāng Bówùguǎn; 85 Boxian Lu; adult/child Y10/5; ⏱ 9am-noon & 2-5.30pm). It houses pottery, bronzes, gold and silver found in excavations around Zhènjiāng. There are English captions and the building has been nicely restored. To get there catch bus No 2 from Zhongshan Lu.

SONG JIE AREA

It's well worth taking time to explore the old area surrounding the museum. Winding cobblestone alleys pass through an

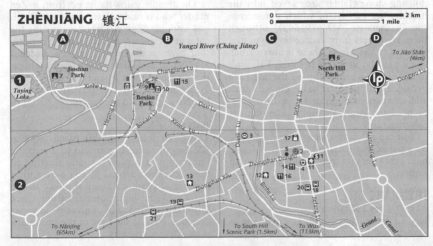

ancient neighbourhood and meander down to boat docks on the Yangzi.

The staircase to the east of the museum leads around to a narrow street known as Song Jie. A small stone pagoda, **Zhaoguang Pagoda** (Zhāoguǎng Tǎ), sits above an archway and is said to date from the Yuan dynasty. There are a few antique stores and stalls here and if you keep following the street all the way down and past the train tracks, you'll hit Xinhe Lu. On the north side the **Revolutionary History Museum** (Gémìng Lìshǐ Bówùguǎn; 60 Xinhe Lu; admission Y3; ⊙ 9-11.30am & 2-5pm Mon-Fri) is set up in a former temple from the Qing dynasty. It's full of photographs from the Sino-Japanese war and civil war fought in the region, but no English captions. Not many visitors come here but you will be welcomed with warm if somewhat puzzled smiles.

Sleeping
Jingkou Hotel (Jīngkǒu Fàndiàn; ☎ 522 4866; fax 523 0056; 407 Zhongshan Donglu; d Y120-480, tr Y180-320) There are a variety of rooms to choose from here, though the older, cheaper rooms are a bit on the tattered side. A 50% discount is available for the Y480 doubles.

Zhenjiang Hotel (Zhènjiāng Bīnguǎn; ☎ 523 3888; 92 Zhongshan Xilu; d Y300-580) Close to the train station, this hotel has newer rooms in the front building with slight discounts available.

International Hotel (Guójì Fàndiàn; ☎ 502 1888; fax 502 1777; 218 Jiefang Lu; d Y560-730) This four-star hotel looks incredibly ugly from the outside, but has the most upmarket standard rooms in town and caters to international tourists and business people.

Eating
The best places to look for restaurants are on the streets off Zhongshan Donglu, west of the intersection with Jiefang Lu.

Zuìxiānlóu Jiǔjiā (50 Jiankang Lu; mains Y20-30; ⊙ breakfast, lunch & dinner) This restaurant serves tasty home-style meals at reasonable prices.

Yànchūn Jiǔlóu (17 Renmin Lu; mains Y25-40; ⊙ breakfast, lunch & dinner) This is another unassuming restaurant that offers very good noodle and rice dishes.

For cheap eats in a lively atmosphere head to the **night market** (yè shìchǎng) parallel and south of Zhongshan Donglu. Things generally get lively around 6pm and last until 2am.

Shopping
Zhenjiang Antique Shop (Zhènjiāng Wénwù Shāngdiàn; 191 Jiefang Lu) This large shop is a good place to purchase souvenirs. You'll find silk, embroidery, porcelain, jade and other crafts as well as antiques.

Getting There & Away
BUS
Most buses from the **South Gate Long-distance Bus Station** (Nánmén Qìchēzhàn) are slow buses. Express buses leave from the **Express Bus Station** (Kuàikè Qìchēzhàn) across the street. Buses leave for Nánjīng (Y22, 1½ hours), Shànghǎi (Y64, 3½ hours), Wúxī (Y28, two hours) and Sūzhōu (Y37, two hours). Buses for major destinations also leave from the **Long-distance Bus Station** (Chángtōng Qìchēzhàn) near the train station. Frequent buses leave here for Yángzhōu (Y12.5, one hour), which includes a short ferry ride.

TRAIN
Zhènjiāng is on the main Nánjīng–Shànghǎi train line. It's a little over three hours to Shànghǎi (Y38) and an hour to Nánjīng (Y13). Although some of the special express trains don't stop at Zhènjiāng, there's still a grand choice of schedules. Most hotels offer a train booking service. The business centre at the International Hotel will book sleepers for a Y30 service charge but it's fairly easy to book sleepers in advance at the train station.

Getting Around
Almost all transport (local buses, pedicabs and motor-tricycles) is close to the train station. Taxis start at Y6.

Bus No 2 is a convenient tour bus. It travels east from the train station along Zhongshan Lu to Jiefang Lu. It then swings west to the museums and continues on to the terminus at Jinshan Park. Bus No 4, which crosses the No 2 route in the city centre on Jiefang Lu, runs past North Hill Park and terminates at Jiāo Shān in the east.

YÁNGZHŌU 扬州
☎ 0514 / pop 4.46 million
Today Yángzhōu is a pleasant, small city with broad, tree-lined boulevards dotted with canals, bridges and gardens. It's more attractive and cleaner than Zhènjiāng and

is a worthwhile break from Jiāngsù's bigger centres of Nánjīng and Sūzhōu. The main tourist sight, Slender West Lake (Shòu Xī Hú), tends to get swamped with tour groups on the weekends but the other places remain quiet enough. Yángzhōu has enough to keep you busy for a couple of days or can be visited on a day trip from Nánjīng.

History

Yángzhōu, near the junction of the Grand Canal and the Yangzi, was once an economic and cultural centre of southern China. It was home to scholars, painters, storytellers, poets and merchants in the Sui and Tang dynasties.

Orientation

Yángzhōu sights are concentrated around the Grand Canal in the north and northwest parts of the city and this is where you'll find Slender West Lake and Daming Temple. It's easy to get around by foot in Yángzhōu and walking along the river that winds its way through town is quite pleasant.

Information

EMERGENCY & MEDICAL SERVICES

No 1 People's Hospital (Yángzhōu Shì Dìyī Rénmín Yīyuàn; 45 Taizhou Lu) For medical treatment go to this modern hospital.

PSB (Gōngānjú; 1 Huaihai Lu) Can help with nonmedical problems, such as visa extensions.

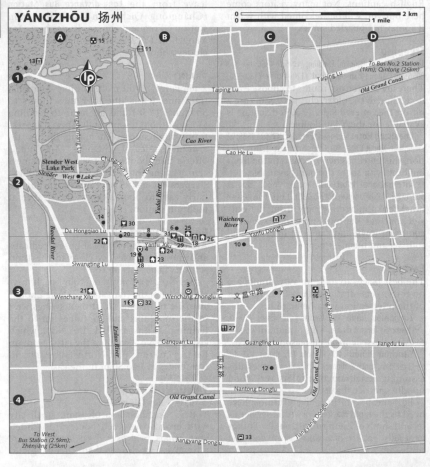

INTERNET ACCESS

The best place to look for Internet access is around the university. Most places charge Y4 an hour.

INTERNET RESOURCES

www.travelchinaguide.com/cityguides/jiangsu /yangzhou/ Provides a look at Yángzhōu in history and the present day.

MONEY

Bank of China (Zhōngguó Yínháng; 279 Wenchang Zhonglu) Will change travellers cheques and cash. The ATM takes international cards.

POST

Post Office (Yóujú; 162 Wenchang Zhonglu) Conveniently located in the town centre.

TOURIST INFORMATION & TRAVEL AGENCIES

Yangzhou International Travel Agency (Yángzhōu Guójì Lǚxíngshè; 10 Fengle Shangjie; 9am-5pm) For train and air tickets. Most hotels have their own booking service but they may tack on a surcharge of Y10 to Y20.

Sights

SLENDER WEST LAKE PARK 瘦西湖公园

The top scenic spot in Yángzhōu stretches north from Da Hongqiao Lu up towards Daming Temple. **Slender West Lake** (Shòu Xī Hú; 28 Da Hongqiao Lu; admission Y40; 6.30am-6pm) is a slim version of West Lake in Hángzhōu. Mass local tourism has helped restore this garden and it's a worthwhile trip if you're lucky enough to visit on a quiet day. The highlight is the triple-arched **Five Pavilion Bridge** (Wǔtíng Qiáo), built in 1757.

Emperor Qianlong's fishing platform is also in the park. Supposedly, local divers used to put fish on the emperor's hook so he'd think it was good luck and provide more funding for the town.

There's an entrance on Da Hongqiao Lu and another entrance at the Five Pavilion Bridge on bus route No 5 from Wenhe Lu. A Y70 admission ticket includes admission to the Ge and He Gardens.

GE GARDEN 个园

This **garden** (Gè Yuán; 10 Yanfu Donglu; admission Y30; 8am-6pm) was built by a salt merchant as his garden residence during the Qing dynasty and highlights the use of bamboo and the convoluted rockeries typical of classical Chinese gardens. Its design features four separate components to represent the four seasons.

HE GARDEN 何园

This **garden** (Hé Yuán; 77 Xuningmen Jie; admission Y25; 7.30am-6pm) was built in 1883. It contains rockeries, ponds, pavilions and walls inscribed with classical poetry. It's a little out of the way, but worth visiting if you're interested in Chinese gardens. Bus No 1 from Yanfan Xilu stops nearby on Nantong Donglu.

YANGZHOU POTTED PLANT GARDEN 扬州盆景园

Don't be put off by the name. This **garden** (Yángzhōu Pénjíng Yuán; 12 Youyi Lu; admission Y30; 7am-6pm) offers a quiet escape along a small canal dotted with birds and blossoms, archways, bridges, pavilions and a marble boat. There are hundreds of bonsai-style potted plants on display as well as a **bonsai museum**. The entrance fee is a bit steep, but is well worth the price and a must for garden-lovers.

CANALS

Yángzhōu once had 24 stone bridges spanning its network of canals. Although the modern bridges are concrete, they still offer good vantage points to view canal life.

As the Grand Canal actually passes a little to the east of Yángzhōu, you might like to investigate the environs a short way out of town. The bus No 2 station in the northeast is a boat dock on the river. Bus Nos 4 and 9 run over a bridge on the canal. There are also two ship locks to the south of Yángzhōu.

DAMING TEMPLE 大明寺

This **temple** (Dàmíng Sì; 1 Pingshantang Lu; admission Y12; ☯ 7.30am-5pm) has been an important centre for Buddhism since ancient times. Founded more than 1000 years ago, the complex was subsequently destroyed and rebuilt. Then it was destroyed right down to its foundations during the Taiping Rebellion; what you see today is a 1934 reconstruction. The nine-storey **Qiling Pagoda** (Qīlíng Tǎ) nearby was completed in 1996.

The original temple is credited to the Tang dynasty monk Jianzhen, who studied sculpture, architecture, fine arts and medicine, as well as Buddhism. In AD 742 two Japanese monks invited him to Japan for missionary work, which turned out to be mission impossible – Jianzhen made five attempts to get there, failing due to storms. On the fifth attempt he ended up in Hǎinán. On the sixth trip, aged 66, he finally arrived. He stayed in Japan for 10 years and died there in AD 763. Later, the Japanese made a lacquer statue of Jianzhen, which was sent to Yángzhōu in 1980.

Near the temple is **Pingshan Hall** (Píngshān Táng), the former residence of the Song dynasty writer Ouyang Xiu. A **Martyrs' Shrine** (Lièshì Língyuán) is also nearby. To the east of Daming Temple you'll find some **Tang dynasty ruins** (Táng Chéng Yízhǐ) and the **Han Dynasty Tomb Museum** (Hànmù Bówùguǎn; 16 Xiangbie Lu; admission Y15; ☯ 8.30am-4.30pm).

You can reach Daming Temple by taking bus No 5 along Wenhe Lu to the last stop. The temple is a short walk north of here.

TOMB OF PUHADDIN 普哈丁墓园

This **tomb** (Pǔhādīng Mùyuán; 17 Jiefang Nanlu) contains documentation of China's contact with the Muslims. It's on the eastern bank of a canal on the bus No 2 route. Puhaddin came to China during the Yuan dynasty (1271–1368) to spread the Muslim faith. There's also a mosque but casual visitors are only allowed to enter the grounds from 6am to noon and you need special permission to visit the tomb.

YANGZHOU CITY MUSEUM 扬州市博物馆

This **museum** (Yángzhōu Shì Bówùguǎn; 2 Fengle Shanglu; admission free; ☯ 8am-5pm) is in a temple originally dedicated to Shi Kefa, a Ming dynasty official who refused to succumb to his new Qing masters and was executed.

Large wooden coffins dating to the Han and Northern Song dynasties, a 1000-year-old wooden boat and a Han dynasty jade funeral suit are on display. Inside the grounds, the museum is surrounded by an antique market.

YANGZHOU ARTS & CRAFTS MUSEUM 扬州工艺美术馆

This **museum** (Yángzhōu Gōngyì Měishùguǎn; 50 Yanfu Donglu; admission free) is a great place to see some local crafts of the region. On display are paper cuts, embroidery and lacquerware as well as other folk arts and crafts.

YANGZHOU EIGHT ECCENTRICS MEMORIAL 扬州八怪纪念馆

This **memorial** (Yángzhōu Bāguài Jìniànguǎn; Huaihai Lu; admission free) is dedicated to a group of painters who lived in Yángzhōu during the Qing dynasty (1644–1911). They were deemed 'eccentric' because they used bold and uncontrolled brush strokes in their paintings.

Tours

Tour buses Nos 1 and 5 leave from the West Bus Station and circle all the sights.

Festivals & Events

The **Qintong Boat Festival** is held from 4 to 6 April every year in Qīntóng (溱潼), which is a small town outside of Yángzhōu. Folk dances are staged on boats 'borrowed' from surrounding fishing villages. The boat races attract both Chinese and international tourists.

Sleeping

Hongqiao Foreign Experts Building (Hóngqiáo Zhuānjiālóu; ☎ 797 5275; 8 Liuhu Lu; s Y180, d Y160-260, tr Y180) The rooms here are gloomy but very close to Slender West Lake. Take bus No 20 from west bus station to the intersection of Liuhu Lu and Siwangting Lu and walk north up Liuhu Lu.

Xiyuan Hotel (Xīyuán Fàndiàn; ☎ 734 4888; fax 723 3870; 1 Fengle Shanglu; d Y280-600, tw/tr Y240/260) This huge place is said to have been constructed on the site of Qianlong's imperial villa, and the surrounding grounds are certainly appealing. There is a choice of rooms, from basic to very plush.

Yangzhou Hotel (Yángzhōu Bīnguǎn; ☎ 734 2611; fax 734 3599; 5 Fengle Shanglu; s/d Y480/580) Next door to the Xiyuan, this hotel also offers upmarket accommodation of similar value with 40% discounts.

Tiandi Hotel (Tiāndì Dàjiǔdiàn; 79 Wenhe Beilu; ☎ 731 1222; fax 732 0963; s/d/tr Y300/360/400) This hotel is not as nice as the Xiyuan or Yangzhou and rooms are a bit shabby but it makes a good budget option. Rooms are discounted up to 30%.

Lantian Hotel (Lántiān Dàshà; ☎ 736 0000; fax 731 4101; 159 Wenhe Beilu; d Y320-480, tr Y460-560) Very centrally located, this place is clean, friendly and offers lots of diversions, such as a bowling alley.

Grand Metropole Hotel (Yángzhōu Jīnghuá Dàjiǔdiàn; ☎ 732 3888; 1 Wenchang Xilu; d Y805) This hotel is a little out of the way but offers very upmarket rooms with five-star amenities.

Eating

One of Yángzhōu's most famous culinary exports is Yángzhōu fried rice (Yángzhōu *chǎofàn*) and, as most travellers who have tried it will confirm, it tastes just like fried rice. There are lots of restaurants in Yángzhōu so competition is keen and the prices are reasonable.

Yěchūn Huāyuán (8 Fengle Xialu; mains Y10-30; ☯ breakfast, lunch & dinner) This is another place that's good for early morning dim sum as well as dinner. The location is pleasant, down near the small canal just below the museum.

Fùchūn Cháshè (35 Desheng Qiao; mains Y10-30; ☯ breakfast, lunch & dinner) One of Yángzhōu's oldest teahouses, this place is on a lane just off Guoqing Lu, in an older section of town.

Laoma Rice Noodles Hotpot (Lǎomā Mǐfén Huǒguō; 48 Siwangting Lu; hotpot Y30; ☯ 9am-2am) This restaurant features a wide variety of hotpot and noodle dishes at reasonable prices. The seafood hotpots are especially good.

Drinking

Gobi Cafe & Gallery (26 Da Hongqiao Lu; drinks Y12-30; ☯ 2pm-12.30am) For more sedate entertainment, try this café. Paintings and sculptures from local artists hang on the walls and there's a delicious variety of snacks, tea, coffee and other drinks. It also has board games, magazines, jazz and a mellow crowd and is a wonderful place to while away a couple of hours.

July 5 Bar (Qī Yuè Wǔ Hào BAR; 8 Fengle Xiajie; drinks Y30; ☯ until late) Another place with a mellow atmosphere, this bar is a good place to relax and unwind after a long day sightseeing.

Entertainment

Century Cinema (Shìjì Diànyǐng Chéng; 269 Wenchang Zhonglu, 4th fl Times Square; admission Y30) This is the place to go to see English-language movies in Yángzhōu.

Shopping

Cheap clothing stores line both sides of Guoqing Lu. A number of stalls sell cooking knives down the alley towards Fùchūn Cháshè restaurant.

True to its image as a city of gardens, Yángzhōu also has a lively **bird and flower market**. If you feel the need to stock up on plants, vases and bird cages, this is the place to do it. It's full of people from early morning until dusk.

Getting There & Away

The nearest airport is in Nánjīng. Shuttle buses make the trip from larger hotels. There are trains to Guǎngzhōu (Y224, 27 hours) which pass through Nánjīng, and Huángshān. Trains to Shànghǎi (Y47, six hours) pass through Nánjīng, Zhènjiāng, Wúxī and Sūzhōu.

From the Yángzhōu long-distance bus station south of the city centre there are buses to different points in Shànghǎi (Y69 to Y84, 4½ hours) and Hángzhōu (Y90, five hours). Buses to Nánjīng (Y26, two hours) and Zhènjiāng (Y12.5, one hour) depart from the west bus station, southwest of the city. Buses cross over the Yangzi by ferry.

BĚIJĪNG TO SHÀNGHǍI

Getting Around

Most of the main sights are at the edge of town. Taxis are cheap and start at Y6, the smaller ones are Y5. The area from the southern entrance of Slender West Lake Park on Da Hongqiao Lu to the City Museum can easily be covered on foot and it's a pleasant walk.

Bus No 8 runs from the west bus station to the long-distance bus station, and then makes its way up Guoqing Lu to the north of the city. Bus No 5 takes you from the long-distance bus station to Huaihai Lu, Youyi Lu then terminates near Daming Temple.

Renting a bike is another option. There are **bike hires** scattered around town. Most will cost Y15 an hour or Y60 a day.

WÚXĪ 无锡

☎ 0510 / pop 4.3 million

Wúxī is a possible stopover between Sūzhōu and Nánjīng. Wúxī itself has little to recommend it, but nearby Tài Hú (p240) continues to be an extremely popular destination for tourists.

Orientation

The city centre of Wúxī is ringed by Jiefang Lu. The train station and the long-distance bus station are only about a 10-minute walk north of Jiefang Beilu. A network of canals, including the Grand Canal, cuts through the city. Tài Hú is about 5km from the city centre.

Information

EMERGENCY

PSB (☎ 270 5678 ext 2215; 54 Chongning Lu) Takes care of emergencies and visa problems.

INTERNET ACCESS

China Telecom (per hr Y4; ☽ 7.30am-11.30pm) At the western end of the post office.

INTERNET RESOURCES

Wúxī Provincial Government (www.wuxi.gov.cn) Information on Wúxī.

MEDICAL SERVICES

Wuxi Nanzhan Hospital (Wúxī Nánzhàn Yīyuàn; 97 Tangnan Lu) This hospital has good facilities and is centrally located.

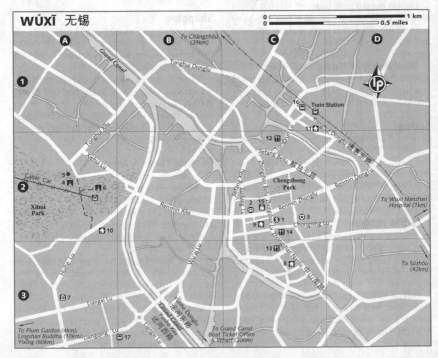

MONEY
Bank of China (Zhōngguó Yínháng; 258 Zhongshan Nanlu; ☺ 9am-5.30pm) Changes travellers cheques and major currency. The ATM here takes international cards.

POST
Post Office (Yóujú; Renmin Zhonglu) Close to the Bank of China.

TOURIST INFORMATION & TRAVEL AGENCIES
CTS (Zhōngguó Lǚxíngshè; 88 Chezhan Lu) In the basement of the Zhonglu Hotel. The office beside the hotel entrance sells train and air tickets and transport to Shànghǎi's Hongqiao Airport. English maps (Y5) are available at the hotel's business centre.

Sights
The city of Wúxī has very few tourist attractions though some of its parks are pleasant places to visit. The nicest by far is **Xihui Park** (Xīhuì Gōngyuán; Huihe Lu; admission Y10). The highest point in the park is West Hill (Xī Shān), 75m above sea level. If you climb **Longguang Pagoda** (Lóngguāng Tǎ), the seven-storey octagonal structure at the top of the hill, you'll be able

to take in a panorama of Wúxī and Tài Hú. The brick and wood pagoda was built during the Ming dynasty, burned down during the Qing dynasty and rebuilt years later. For an even greater view, take the cable car (Y22), which is 1km into Hui Hill (Huì Shān).

There's a total of 18 historical and cultural sights within the park, including the **Hui Hill Temple** (Huì Shān Sì), once a Buddhist monastery, an azalea garden with over 300 different species, and the famous Ming-style **Jichang Garden** (Jìcháng Yuán).

Another very pretty park is **Plum Garden** (Méi Yuán; Huyi Gonglu; admission Y25; ☺ 6am-6pm), once a small peach garden built during the Qing dynasty. It's renowned for its thousands of plum trees that blossom in spring. Plum Pagoda (Méi Tǎ) offers views of Tài Hú. The garden is opposite the bus No 2 terminus on the highway to Yíxīng.

If parks get tiring, the **Wuxi Museum** (Wúxī Bówùguǎn; 2nd fl, 71 Huihe Lu; admission Y5; ☺ 8-11am & 1.30-4.30pm) makes a good diversion. This museum contains over 200 historical articles and craft works from the past 6000 years, which look at the development of the local culture and its interaction with neighbouring counties. The best part is what's lying around outside. There's some old British textile machinery from the 1920s on display – reminders of Wúxī's development as a major textile centre.

Southwest of Wúxī is the **Lingshan Buddha** (Língshān Dàfó; Lingshan Lu; adult/child Y50/25; ☺ 6.30am-6pm), an 88m-high bronze Buddha that local tourism officials are marketing as Wúxī's star tourist attraction. Take bus No 88 from the train station.

Sleeping
Wúxī's hotels mainly fall into the mid-range category though there are a few budget options. Many hotels around the train station will charge foreigners double for rooms so be careful. The city itself is not very attractive and it's much more pleasant to stay around Tài Hú (p241).

Qinggongye University Foreign Experts Hotel (Qīnggōngyè Dàxué Zhuānjiālóu; ☎ 586 1034; 170 Huihe Lu; s/d Y100/110) The rooms here are quite dreary but cheap. From the train station take bus No 2 and get off at the second stop over the Grand Canal. The hotel is 200m further down, on the opposite side of the street.

Liangxi Hotel (Liángxī Fàndiàn; ☎ 272 3798; 63 Zhongshan Nanlu; d Y200-680) This place has a whole range of rooms and very pleasant grounds, while still situated close to the city centre. Cheaper doubles have 20% discounts and more expensive rooms are up to 50% off. Take bus No 201 from the train station.

Zhonglu Hotel (Zhōnglǚ Dàjiǔdiàn; ☎ 230 0888; 88 Chezhan Lu; d Y480-628) Run by the CTS, this hotel is convenient, though nothing to get excited about. Inspect the cheaper doubles before handing over your cash.

New World Courtyard Marriott Hotel (Xīn Shìjiè Wànyí Jiǔdiàn; ☎ 276 2888; www.courtyard.com; 335 Zhongshan Lu; d US$70-80) Right in the city centre, this hotel offers all the amenities expected in an international hotel. Standard rooms are often discounted to Y438.

Eating

Wúxī has no shortage of restaurants.

Lóushànglóu Miànguǎn (61 Tongyun Lu; mains Y5-10; ☯ breakfast, lunch & dinner) On the ground floor of this large, attractive place, cheap noodle and fried rice dishes are available. More substantial meals are upstairs.

Wángxìngjì (221 Zhongshan Nanlu; mains Y10-20; ☯ breakfast, lunch & dinner) Close to the city centre, this is a long-established Wúxī restaurant, though you wouldn't know it from the plastic décor. It's famous for *húntun* (wonton soup) and delicious *xiǎolóngbāo* (steamed dumplings filled with meat or seafood), for Y8.

Wúxī Kǎoyāguǎn (222 Zhongshan Lu; mains Y20-60; ☯ lunch & dinner) This place has delicious *kǎoyā* (Peking duck) for Y45 (Y30 for half a duck). Although a bit expensive, it's a comfortable and popular place with a wide variety of dishes.

A number of hole-in-the-wall restaurants are clustered around the entrance to the Qinggongye University Foreign Experts Hotel, popular with students for their cheap meals. There's also a string of restaurants and bars on Liangxi Lu near the intersection with Liangqing Lu.

Shopping

Silk products and embroidery are good buys. Also look out for the clay figurines known as Huì Shān Nírén. A local folk art, the figurines take many forms and shapes, but are most commonly modelled after famous opera stars. The models of obese infants are symbols of fortune and happiness. You can find these along with other souvenirs at the **Wúxī Shàngyè Dàshà** (343 Zhongshan Lu), a large department store in the central part of town.

Getting There & Away

Most long-distance buses depart from the long-distance bus station next to the train station. The west bus station is on Liangqing Lu but has fewer services. Frequent buses to Yíxīng (Y10, 1½ hours) leave from both the long-distance and west bus stations. For Dīngshān change buses in Yíxīng.

From the long-distance bus station, direct buses go to Shànghǎi (Y36, two hours), Sūzhōu (Y18, 45 minutes) and Nánjīng (Y52, 2½ hours).

Wúxī is on the Běijīng–Shànghǎi train line and has frequent services. There are trains to Sūzhōu (Y10, 30 minutes), Shànghǎi (Y20, 1½ hours) and Nánjīng (Y26, two hours) every two hours or so.

CTS books sleepers for a Y30 service charge but there are numerous ticket agents around the long-distance bus station that book train tickets.

Overnight passenger boats travel between Wúxī and Hángzhōu on the Grand Canal. Departure is at 5.30pm from the wharf off Hubin Lu. You can book tickets at the wharf. Two-person cabins are Y130 per person and four-person cabins are Y88 per person. The trip takes 13 hours.

Getting Around

It's fairly easy getting around Wúxī by bus. Bus No 2 runs from the train station, along Jiefang Lu, across two bridges to Xihui Park, then out to Plum Garden. Bus No 201 heads from the train station down Zhongshan Lu to the city centre. The Wúxī sightseeing bus is very useful, stopping at all major sights. It has no number, but it's in the first row of buses to the right as you exit the train station. Tickets are Y3 or Y2 depending on the distance.

Taxis start at Y8.

TÀI HÚ 太湖

Tài Hú is a freshwater lake with a total area of 2200 sq km and an average depth of 2m. There are some 90 islands, large and small, and more than 30 varieties of fish. Despite some major water pollution problems, the fishing industry here is still active. Tài Hú's sights are more than a little overrun. For banks, Internet cafés etc, go to Wúxī.

For information on the eastern side of the lake, see p250.

Sights & Activities

Turtle Head Isle (Yuán Tóuzhǔ; admission Y65; 🕒 6.30am-6pm) is not actually an island, but a peninsula. This is a scenic strolling area where you can walk a circuit of the park and take in the views of Tài Hú. A monorail (Y10) does the circuit if you don't feel like walking.

The entrance at the southern end of the park is just north of the **Baojie Bridge** (Bǎojiè Qiáo). This end of the park is peaceful with a lovely narrow road leading up to the **Brightness Pavilion** (Guāngmíng Tíng), the highest point of Turtle Head Isle, offering all-round vistas. The northern end of the park has souvenir stalls and a pier with ferries to Sānshān. From here, the **Perpetual Spring Bridge** (Chángchūn Qiáo) leads across a small pond to a rocky vantage point on the lake.

Also on Turtle Head Isle are three amusement parks, **Tang Dynasty World** (Táng Cháo Jǐngqū; admission Y30), **Three Kingdoms World** (Sān Guó Jǐngqū; admission Y35) and **Water Margin World** (Shuǐhǔ Jǐngqū; admission Y35), set up by Wuxi Film Studios. These replica cities were built to film TV dramas based on famous historical novels. A visit to one of these parks offers some good tacky fun.

Southwest of Turtle Head Isle is the island park of **Sānshān** (Three Hills Isle). Vantage points at the top look back towards Turtle Head Isle, so you can work out if it really does look like a turtle head. The islands have a number of pavilions and temples as well as three large Buddha statues, the smallest measuring over 16m high. Watch out for the monkeys here. Ferries to the islands are included in the entry ticket to Turtle Head Isle.

Sleeping

Several hotels by Tài Hú offer clean comfortable rooms in peaceful surroundings.

Taihu Hotel (Tàihú Fàndiàn; ☎ 551 7888; Yonggu Lu; d Y438-890) Located on the shores of the lake, this is a very relaxed place to stay and an excellent escape from the noise and dust of Wúxī.

Yuquan Hill Hotel (Yúquán Shān Zhuāng; ☎ 555 9999; 7 Dafuqitang Lu; d Y300) With bright, airy rooms and friendly management, this unpretentious hotel is popular with both foreign and local tourists.

Lakeview Park Resort Hotel (Tàihú Huāyuán Dùjiàcùn; ☎ 555 5888; 8 Qitang Lu; US$72) This hotel is the most luxurious of the three and service is top-notch. Rooms are spacious and modern, some with views of the lake.

Eating

There are restaurants at the northern end of the park. At the teahouse **Clear Ripples Hall** (Chénglán Táng) you can enjoy some tea while viewing the lake.

Getting There & Away

Bus No 820 goes to Baojie Bridge from the train station in Wúxī. The Wúxī sightseeing bus goes to the northern entrance from the

TÀI HÚ 无锡、

To Lingshan Buddha (2km); Yíxìng (60km)

Plum Gardens

Jiangxi Lu

Fish Ponds

Perpetual Spring Bridge

Fish Ponds

Toll Gate

Sānshān

Ferry

Turtle Head Isle

Toll Gate

Tài Hú

train station. Speedboats take people out on the lake from the pier at the northern entrance for Y20.

YÍXĪNG COUNTY 宜兴县

Yíxīng County (Yíxīng Xiàn) is famous for its tea utensils, particularly pots. Delicious tea can be made in an aged Yíxīng teapot simply by adding hot water, or so they say. The potteries of Yíxīng, especially in Dīngshān, are a popular excursion for Chinese tourists but see few foreign visitors.

Dīngshān 丁山
☎ 0510

Dīngshān is the pottery centre of Yíxīng County and has enjoyed that reputation since the Qin and Han dynasties; some of the scenes here, especially at the loading dock that leads into Tài Hú, are timeless.

Almost every local family is engaged in the manufacture of ceramics and at least half of the houses are made of the stuff. It's extremely dusty (and probably not recommended for people with respiratory problems). Everywhere you look vehicles are hauling rocks from the mountains outside of town.

Dīngshān, about 15km south of Yíxīng town, has two dozen ceramics factories producing more than 2000 varieties of pottery – quite an output for a population of 100,000. Among the products are the ceramic tables and garbage bins you find around China, jars used to store oil and grain, the famed Yíxīng teapots, and glazed tiling and ceramic frescoes that are desperately needed as spare parts for tourist attractions – the Forbidden City in Běijīng is a customer. The ornamental rocks you see in Chinese gardens are also made here.

Outside of Dīngshān the **Ceramics Museum** (宜兴陶瓷博物馆; Yíxīng Táocí Bówùguǎn; 150 Dingshan Beilu; admission Y15; ❍ 7.30am-5pm) displays examples of Yíxīng pottery from 6000 years ago to the present day. Nearby workshops have ceramic artisans at work.

SLEEPING

It's easy to visit this area on a day trip from Wúxī but you can also stay overnight.

Yixing Shanghai Hotel (宜兴上海宾馆; Yíxīng Shànghǎi Bīnguǎn; ☎ 740 1811; Gongyuan Lu; d Y300-360) This is a nice enough hotel and 30% discounts make it a reasonable deal.

SHOPPING

If you've taken the trouble to get here, don't leave without buying some pottery. There's a lot of variety, not just the standard Yíxīng style, and it's very cheap. The best place to go is a huge **pottery market** (lóngxī táocí shìchǎng; ❍ 7.30am-7pm), across the highway from the Ceramics Museum. There's a number of stores and small stalls with literally tonnes of pottery. Mid-size teapots range in price from Y20 to Y300 and they also have wonderful goldfish bowls on elongated stems for Y150 that would make great bird baths if you could get them home.

JUDGING A YÍXĪNG TEAPOT

Buying a teapot in Dīngshān or the surrounding area can be a memorable experience. To help convince you of the high quality of their teapots, shopkeepers can be extremely animated. You'll encounter shopkeepers standing on the pot, blowing through its spout, striking a match on it, showing you that the inside is the same colour as the outside or rubbing their hand against the side and showing you their palm. Unfortunately, none of these antics give you much of an indication of whether a pot is good quality.

So what should you look for? First, make sure the teapot is stable – the body, spout, handle, lid and knob should all be balanced. Also, the lid should be deep-seated and firm (it shouldn't rattle or jam). The clay should be naturally shiny and slightly rough rather than glazed smooth. Finally (and this is the most important thing), ask if you can put water in the pot – the water should shoot out straight from the spout instead of dribbling.

Prices can range wildly, from just a few yuán to US$20,000 for a pot made by a renowned artist. Some say that unless you are buying a teapot made by a well-known artist, don't pay more than Y30. You may want to visit the Ceramics Museum, located between Yíxīng and Dīngshān, to view high-quality teapots before venturing to the market across the street where a dizzying variety of generally low-quality teapots are for sale.

GETTING THERE & AWAY
Frequent buses go from Wúxī to Yíxīng (Y10, 1½ hours). From Yíxīng minibuses go back and forth to Dīngshān (Y3, 20 minutes).

SŪZHŌU 苏州
☎ 0512 / pop 5.71 million
Sūzhōu is Jiāngsū's most well-known attraction, famous for its classical gardens, silk and lovely women. Located only a one-hour train ride from Shànghǎi, along the Grand Canal, the city offers visitors a glimpse into Chinese classical history.

New developments and construction have changed the face of Sūzhōu over the past few years but there are still opportunities to wander through the city's gardens and remaining cobbled alleys, well-preserved despite the ravages of time. Sūzhōu's gardens are looked upon as works of art – a fusion of nature, poetry and painting designed to ease, move or assist the mind.

History
Dating back some 2500 years, Sūzhōu is one of the oldest towns in the Yangzi basin. With the completion of the Grand Canal in the Sui dynasty, Sūzhōu found itself strategically located on a major trading route, and the city's fortunes and size grew rapidly.

Sūzhōu flourished as a centre of shipping and grain storage, bustling with merchants and artisans. By the 12th century it had attained its present dimensions and layout.

The city walls, a rectangle enclosed by moats, were pierced by six gates (north, south, two in the east and two in the west). Crisscrossing the city were six north–south canals and 14 east–west canals. Although the walls have largely disappeared and a fair proportion of the canals have been plugged, central Sūzhōu retains some of its 'Renaissance' character. The Waicheng River moat still encircles the city.

A legend was spun about Sūzhōu through tales of beautiful women with mellifluous voices, and through the famous proverb 'In heaven there is paradise, on earth Sūzhōu and Hángzhōu'. The story picks up when Marco Polo arrived in 1276. He added the adjectives 'great' and 'noble', although he reserved his finer epithets for Hángzhōu.

By the 14th century Sūzhōu had established itself as China's leading silk producer, and aristocrats, pleasure-seekers, famous scholars, actors and painters were attracted to the city, constructing villas and garden retreats for themselves.

At the height of Sūzhōu's development in the 16th century, the gardens, large and small, numbered over 100. If we mark time here, we arrive at the town's current tourist formula, 'Garden City, Venice of the East', a medieval mix of woodblock guilds and embroidery societies, whitewashed housing, cobbled streets, tree-lined avenues and canals.

The wretched workers of the silk sweatshops, protesting against paltry wages and the injustices of the contract hire system, were staging violent strikes back in the 15th century, and the landlords shifted as a result. In 1860 Taiping troops took the town without a blow. In 1896 Sūzhōu was opened to foreign trade, with Japanese and international concessions. During WWII, it was occupied by the Japanese and later by the Kuomintang. Somehow it managed to slip through the worst ravages of the Cultural Revolution relatively unscathed. These days Sūzhōu is a popular alternative to Shànghǎi for foreign companies coming to China to invest in hi-tech and light industrial manufacturing.

Orientation
Besides the numerous small canals, Sūzhōu is surrounded by a large, rectangular outer canal (Waicheng River, or Wàichéng Hé). The main thoroughfare, Renmin Lu, bisects the city into western and eastern halves, while a large canal cuts across the middle. The train and main bus stations are at the northern end of town, on the north side of the outer canal. A large boat dock and another long-distance bus station are at the southern end.

MAPS
The **Foreign Language Bookshop** (Wàiwén Shūdiàn; 44 Renmin Lu) sells maps of Sūzhōu in English and Chinese.

Information
EMERGENCY
PSB (Gōngānjú; ☎ 522 5661 ext 20593; 201 Renmin Lu) Can help with emergencies and visa problems. Look for the lane called Dashitou Xiang by the main gate. The visa office is about 200m down the lane.

INTERNET ACCESS
China Telecom Internet Café (Wǎngyǒu Kōngjiān; 333 Renmin Lu; per hr Y4; ☺ 9.30am-9pm) Fast connections.

INTERNET RESOURCES
www.echinaromance.com/destinations/suzhou .htm This is one of many websites about Sūzhōu. Visit it for basic information on places to see around town.

MEDICAL SERVICES
No. 1 Hospital (Sūlìfù Yīyuàn; 96 Shizi Jie) One of many hospitals around town if you need medical assistance.

MONEY
Bank of China (Zhōngguó Yínháng; 490 Renmin Lu) Changes travellers cheques and foreign cash. Major tourist hotels also have foreign-exchange counters. There are ATMs that take international cards at most larger branches of the Bank of China.

POST
Post Office (Yóujú) Located on the corner of Renmin Lu and Jingde Lu.

TOURIST INFORMATION & TRAVEL AGENCIES
CITS (Zhōngguó Guójì Lǚxíngshè) Next to the train ticket office, beside the Lexiang Hotel and inside the Suzhou Hotel.

Sights & Activities
GARDEN OF THE MASTER OF THE NETS
网师园

Off Shiquan Jie, this is the smallest **garden** (Wǎngshī Yuán; admission Y10; ☺ 8am-5pm) in Sūzhōu –

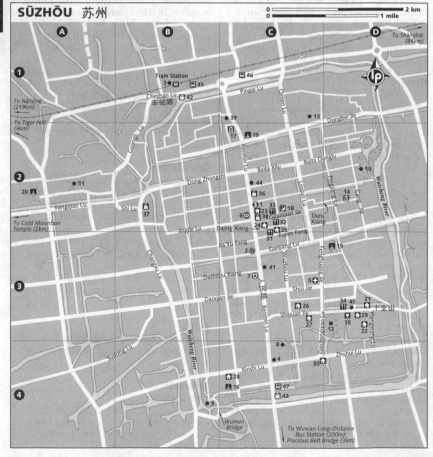

half the size of the Blue Wave Pavilion and one-tenth the size of the Humble Administrator's Garden. It's well worth a visit as it's better than all the others combined.

The garden was laid out in the 12th century, abandoned, then restored in the 18th century as part of the residence of a retired official. According to one story, he announced that he'd had enough of bureaucracy and would rather be a fisherman. Another explanation of the name is that it was simply near Wangshi Lu. The eastern part of the garden is the residential area – originally with side rooms for sedan-chair lackeys, guest reception and living quarters. The central section is the main garden. The western section is an inner garden where a courtyard contains the **Spring Rear Cottage** (Diànchūn Yì), the master's study. This section, including the study with its Ming-style furniture and palace lanterns, was duplicated and unveiled at the Metropolitan Museum of Art in New York in 1981.

The most striking feature of this garden is its use of space. Despite its size, the scale of the buildings is large, but nothing appears cramped. A section of the buildings is used by a co-operative of woodblock artists.

There are two entrances to the entry gate, with English signs and souvenir stalls marking the way. You can enter the alley on Shiquan Jie or an alley off Daichengqiao Lu. There are also music performances in the evening (p249).

GARDEN FOR LINGERING IN 留园

Extending over an area of three hectares, the **Garden for Lingering In** (Liú Yuán; 79 Liuyuan Lu; adult/child Y16/8; ⏰ 7.30am-5pm) is one of the largest gardens in Sūzhōu, noted for its adroit partitioning with building complexes. The garden dates from the Ming dynasty and managed to escape destruction during the Taiping Rebellion.

A 700m covered walkway connects the major scenic spots, and the windows have carefully selected perspectives. The walkway is inlaid with calligraphy from celebrated masters and the garden has a wealth of potted plants. In the northeast section of the garden, there's a particularly large example of a sculptured rock from Tài Hú; at 6.5m high you couldn't miss it if you tried.

The garden is about 3km west of the city centre. Tourist bus No Y2 goes there from the train station or Renmin Lu.

BLUE WAVE PAVILION 沧浪亭

A bit on the wild side with winding creeks and luxuriant trees, this one-hectare **garden** (Cānglàng Tíng; admission Y8; ⏰ 8am-4.30pm), off Renmin Lu, is one of the oldest in Sūzhōu. The buildings date from the 11th century, although they have been rebuilt on numerous occasions since.

Originally the home of a prince, the property passed into the hands of the poet and scholar Su Shunqin (Su Zimei), who gave it its name. The designers have tried to create optical illusions with the scenery both outside and inside – you look from the pool immediately outside to the distant hills. **Enlightenment Hall** (Míngdào Táng), the largest building, is said to have been a site for delivery of lectures during the Ming dynasty. Close by, on the other side of Renmin Lu, is the former Confucian Temple.

The entrance is signposted as 'Surging Wave' Pavilion.

HUMBLE ADMINISTRATOR'S GARDEN
拙政园

Many consider the **Humble Administrator's Garden** (Zhuōzhèng Yuán; 178 Dongbei Jie; adult/child Y32/16; ⏰ 7.30am-5.30pm) to be one of Sūzhōu's best, second only to the Garden of the Master of the Nets.

Dating back to the early 1500s, this garden's five hectares feature streams, ponds, bridges and islands of bamboo. There's also a teahouse and a small museum that explains Chinese landscape gardening concepts.

SUZHOU SILK MUSEUM 丝绸博物馆

Highly recommended, this **museum** (Sūzhōu Sīchóu Bówùguǎn; 661 Renmin Lu; admission Y7; ⏰ 9am-5.30pm) houses a number of fascinating exhibitions that give a thorough history of Sūzhōu's silk industry over the past 4000 years. Many of the captions are in English.

NORTH TEMPLE PAGODA 北寺塔

This is the tallest **pagoda** (Běisì Tǎ; 652 Renmin Lu; adult/child Y10/5; ⏰ 7.30am-6pm) south of the Yangzi – at nine storeys it dominates the area. Climb it for fine views of the town and the farmland beyond, where tea, rice and wheat are grown. The factory chimneys (the new pagodas of Sūzhōu) loom on the outskirts, hovering in the haze and smoke they create.

The temple complex goes back 1700 years and was originally a residence. The pagoda has been burnt, built and rebuilt. Off to the side is **Nanmu Guanyin Hall** (Nánmù Guānyīn Diàn), which was rebuilt in the Ming dynasty with some of its features imported from elsewhere. There's a teahouse with a small garden out the back.

MUSEUM OF OPERA & THEATRE
戏曲博物馆

In the old city of Sūzhōu, this small **museum** (Xìqǔ Bówùguǎn; 14 Zhongzhangjia Xiang; admission Y3; ⏰ 8.30am-4pm) is worth going to for the surrounding small cobblestone lanes lined with stalls selling vegetables and inexpensive snacks. The museum features the history of *kūnqǔ*, the opera style of this region, and the singing and storytelling art form sung in Sūzhōu dialect known as *píngtán*. It houses a moveable stage, old musical instruments, costumes and photos of famous performers. They also put on occasional performances of *kūnqǔ* and *píngtán*.

COUPLE'S GARDEN 耦园

This secluded **garden** (Ǒu Yuán; admission Y15; ⏰ 8am-4.30pm) sees fewer tourists than the others, though the gardens, pond and courtyards are quite beautiful. Surrounding the garden are the few remaining examples of traditional Sūzhōu architecture, bridges and canals. The garden can be found off a small maze of alleys near the Museum of Opera and Theatre.

TWIN PAGODAS 双塔

These seven-storey **pagodas** (Shuāng Tǎ; admission Y10; ⏰ 7am-4.30pm) were built during the Northern Song dynasty by candidates for the imperial examination who wanted to pay tribute to their teachers. The pagodas

---

SŪZHŌU'S GARDENS

The key elements of these famous gardens are rocks and water. Just like the Zen gardens of Japan, there are surprisingly few flowers, and no fountains. Although the gardens were designed to perfection, they were intended to give the illusion of a natural scene consisting of only moss, sand and rock. These microcosms were laid out by master craftspeople and have changed hands many times over the centuries.

The gardens suffered a setback during the Taiping Rebellion in the 1860s and under subsequent foreign domination of Sūzhōu. Efforts were made to restore them in the 1950s, but during the so-called Horticultural Revolution gardeners downed tools, as flowers were frowned upon.

In 1979 the Suzhou Garden Society was formed, and an export company was set up to promote Sūzhōu-designed gardens. A number of the gardens have been renovated and opened to the public.

stand in the centre of a lovely garden filled with stone sculptures and a teahouse at the far end.

WEST GARDEN TEMPLE 西园寺
A short distance west of the Garden for Lingering In, this garden was built on the site of a garden laid out at the same time as the Garden for Lingering In, and then donated to the Buddhist community. The **temple** (Xīyuán Sì; Xiyuan Lu; admission Y10; 7.30am-5.30pm) was destroyed in the 19th century and entirely rebuilt; it contains some expressive Buddhist statues.

COLD MOUNTAIN TEMPLE 寒山寺
About 2km west of the Garden for Lingering In, this **temple** (Hánshān Sì; 24 Hanshansi Long; admission Y10; 7.30am-5pm) was named after the poet-monk Han Shan, who lived in the 7th century. It was repeatedly burnt down and rebuilt, and was once the site of local trading in silk, wood and grain. Not far from its saffron walls lies the Grand Canal. Today, the temple holds little of interest except for a stele by poet Zhang Ji immortalising both the nearby Maple Bridge and the temple bell (since removed to Japan). However, the fine walls and the humpback bridge are worth seeing.

Tourist bus No Y3 takes you from the train station to the temple.

COILED GATE 盘门
In the southwest corner of the city, straddling the outer moat, this stretch of the city wall has Sūzhōu's only remaining original **city gate** (Pán Mén; 1 Dongda Jie; admission Y15; 8am-5pm). It's one of the nicest areas of the city to visit. The exquisite, arched Wumen Bridge (Wúmén Qiáo) crosses the canal just to the east. From the top of the gate there are good views of the moat, surrounding houses and **Ruiguang Pagoda** (Ruìguāng Tǎ), the oldest pagoda in Jiāngsū, dating from the 3rd century AD. You can climb the pagoda (Y6) for a view of Sūzhōu.

To get there, take tourist bus No Y5 from the train station or Changxu Lu.

TIGER HILL 虎丘山
In the far northwest of town, **Tiger Hill** (Hǔqiū Shān; Huqiu Lu; adult/child Y20/10; 7.30am-6pm) is extremely popular with local tourists. The hill itself is artificial and is the final resting

place of He Lu, founding father of Sūzhōu. He Lu died in the 6th century BC and myths have coalesced around him – he is said to have been buried with a collection of 3000 swords and to be guarded by a white tiger.

Built in the 10th century, the leaning **Cloud Rock Pagoda** (Yúnyán Tǎ) stands atop Tiger Hill. The octagonal seven-storey pagoda, also known as Huqiu Pagoda, is built entirely of brick, an innovation in Chinese architecture at the time. The pagoda began tilting over 400 years ago, and today the highest point is displaced more than 2m from its original position.

Tourist buses Nos Y1 and Y2 from the train station go to Tiger Hill.

TEMPLE OF MYSTERY 玄妙观
This Taoist **temple** (Xuánmiào Guàn; Guanqian Jie; admission Y10; 7.30am-5.30pm) seems almost an anomaly, plunked in the middle of the rampant commercialism that is Guanqian Jie.

The temple was founded and laid out during the Jin dynasty in the 3rd century AD, with additions in the Song dynasty. From the Qing dynasty on, the bazaar fanned out from the temple with tradespeople and travelling performers using the grounds.

The enormous temple hall, **Sānqīng Diàn**, is supported by 60 pillars and capped by a double roof with upturned eaves. It dates from 1181 and was burnt and seriously damaged in the 19th century.

Tours
By the canal south of the train station, boat tours go north to Tiger Hill or west to Cold Mountain. Either trip takes about an hour. Solo travellers will find it difficult to get on a boat without joining a tour. At the time of writing, for two people a tour cost Y200. This can be negotiated if there are more of you. Boats depart from the **Foreign Travellers Transportation Company Pier** (Waishi Lǚyóu Chēchuán Gōngsī Mǎtóu; 753 9985) on Chezhan Lu.

Festivals & Events
Every September, Sūzhōu hosts the **Suzhou Silk Festival**. There are exhibitions devoted to silk history and production and silk merchants get to show off their wares to crowds of thousands. If you're interested in purchasing high-quality silk at bargain prices, this is a great festival to attend.

Sleeping

Sūzhōu has little to offer in the way of cheap accommodation. It's often possible to bargain room prices down, however, so don't be immediately deterred by the posted rates.

BUDGET

Dongwu Hotel (Dōngwú Fàndiàn; ☎ 6519 4437; fax 6519 4590; 24 Wuyachang; d without bathroom Y100, with bathroom Y180-280) This clean place, off Shiquan Jie, is run by the Suzhou University International Cultural Exchange Institute.

Home Inn (Rújiā Jiǔdiàn; ☎ 6523 8770; 246 Guanqian Jie; s/d Y148/198) This newish hotel offers spanking-clean rooms at very cheap (for Sūzhōu) prices. The location off Guanqian Jie is central, though it can be a little noisy at night. Ask for a room on one of the upper floors to avoid this.

MID-RANGE

Youyi Hotel (Yǒuyì Bīnguǎn; ☎ 6529 1601; 243 Zhuhui Lu; s Y380, d Y240-400) This hotel offers good midrange accommodation. The more expensive rooms are in the newer west building and 10% discounts are sometimes available.

Nanlin Hotel (Nánlín Fàndiàn; ☎ 6519 6333; 20 Gunxiufang; d Y270-600) Nanlin Hotel, just off Shiquan Jie, has pleasant gardens and caters to foreign tour groups. Doubles are in a new building and the suites are upmarket.

Lexiang Hotel (Lèxiāng Fàndiàn; ☎ 6522 2815; fax 6524 4165; 18 Dajing Xiang; s Y380, d Y480-580) Close to the city centre, this hotel has been recommended by readers.

TOP END

Longfeng Hotel (Lóngfēng Bīnguǎn; ☎ 6515 4800; fax 6515 7878; 9 Dajing Xiang; d/tr Y460/480) If you really want to be in the centre of everything, this hotel is a good choice. Located in the busy Guanqian Jie shopping area, the Longfeng has reasonable rooms, although they are a bit overpriced.

Gusu Hotel (Gūsū Fàndiàn; ☎ 6520 0566; fax 6519 9727; 5 Xiangwang Lu; d Y480-560) The prices at this hotel put it in the upmarket range but the rooms have certainly seen better days. The Gusu is close to Shiquan Jie and offers 35% discounts.

Suzhou Hotel (Sūzhōu Fàndiàn; ☎ 6520 4646; fax 6520 5191; 115 Shiquan Jie; d Y500-600) This is a sprawling place that does a brisk trade in tour groups. Discounts bring the prices

down slightly but both the Nanlin and Nanyuan have nicer grounds.

Nanyuan Guesthouse (Nányuán Bīnguǎn; ☎ 6519 7661; fax 6519 8806; 249 Shiquan Jie; d Y436-600) This place is inside an exquisite, large, walled garden compound with many different buildings to stay in. Discounts of 30% make it very good value.

Sheraton Suzhou Hotel & Towers (Sūzhōu Xǐláidēng Dàjiǔdiàn; ☎ 6510 3388; www.sheraton-suzhou.com; 388 Xinshi Lu; d US$180) The Sheraton is one of Sūzhōu's fanciest hotels and caters to well-heeled tour groups. The enormous hotel complex is surrounded by lovely gardens and the rooms are, to be expected, quite plush and comfortable.

Eating

Sūzhōu is a tourist town and consequently there's no shortage of places dishing up local and tourist cuisine. Shiquan Jie, between Daichengqiao Lu and Xiangwang Lu, is lined with bars, restaurants and bakeries.

Yángyáng Shuǐjiǎoguǎn (144 Shiquan Jie; mains Y5-25; ☯ 7am-3am) This very popular restaurant has fresh dumplings, snails and veggie dishes for very reasonable prices – a dozen *shuǐjiǎo* (boiled dumplings) are Y5. This place also calls itself the 'Authentic Chinese Dumpling House'.

Sōnghé Lóu (141 Guanqian Jie; mains Y20-40; ☯ dinner) If money is no object, try this restaurant, rated as the most famous in Sūzhōu; Emperor Qianlong is said to have eaten here. Among the large variety of dishes is *sōngshǔ guìyú* (squirrel fish) – fish cooked in sweet and sour sauce. The entrance is around the corner on Taijian Lu. Travellers give the restaurant mixed reviews.

Wangsi Restaurant (Wángsì Jiǔjiā; 23 Taijian Xiang; meals Y20-50; ☯ dinner) This restaurant is across from the Sōnghé and well known for its chicken dishes. Like the Sōnghé, it gets mixed reviews and the staff can be a little surly.

Sicily Pub & Restaurant (Xīxīlì Cāntīng; 1 Shaomozhen Xiang; mains Y15-30; ☯ 11am-2am) This is a nice, intimate place to go if you feel like a beer and some Western food in pleasant surroundings. Sandwiches are Y12 and a meal of baked chicken is Y25.

Drinking

West Street Bar (Xījiē Jiǔláng; 181 Shiquan Jie; drinks Y25-30; ☯ 6pm-late) This uniquely furnished three-storey bar is crammed full of Chinese and European antiques. With its homey ambience, eclectic crowd and friendly management, it's a great place to unwind with a beer.

Entertainment

The **music shows** (tickets Y60; ⏱ 7.30-9.30pm) at the Garden of the Master of the Nets (p244), where the audience moves from pavilion to pavilion to watch a variety of traditional Chinese performing arts, are quite popular with tour groups.

Shopping

Sūzhōu-style embroidery, calligraphy, paintings, sandalwood fans, writing brushes and silk underclothes are for sale nearly everywhere. For good-quality items at competitive rates, shop along Shiquan Jie, east off Renmin Lu. The street is lined with shops and markets selling souvenirs.

Suzhou Antique & Curio Store (Sūzhōu Wénwù Shāngdiàn; 328 Renmin Lu; ⏱ 10am-5.30pm) Offers a wide variety of embroidery, ceramic and figurines for sale along with other traditional crafts.

These items can also be found in the lively **night market** (⏱ 6.30-9.30pm) near Shi Lu which also sells food, clothing and all kinds of stuff.

The northern part of Renmin Lu has a number of large silk stores.

Dōngwú Sīchóu Shāngdiàn (540 Renmin Lu; ⏱ 8am-10pm) Is attached to a silk factory and has clothes, material and bedding. Wonderful silk duvets go for Y320.

Suzhou Food Centre (Sūzhōu Shípín Dàshà; 246 Renmin Lu; ⏱ 8.30am-9pm) Sells all kinds of local, traditional specialities and teas in bulk.

Getting There & Away

AIR

Sūzhōu does not have an airport, but **China Eastern Airlines** (Dōngfāng Hángkōng Gōngsī; ☎ 6522 2788; 192 Renmin Lu) can help with booking flights out of Shànghǎi. For international tickets, you can also try the CITS beside the Lexiang Hotel. Buses leave frequently for Hóngqiáo Airport in Shànghǎi. Tickets are Y45.

BOAT

Overnight passenger boats travel along the Grand Canal to Hángzhōu and many travellers enjoy this experience. The boat departs daily at 5.30pm and arrives the next morning at 7am. You can purchase tickets at the dock at the southern end of Renmin Lu or at the **Lianhe Ticket Centre** (Liánhé Shòupiàochù; 556 Renmin Lu; ⏱ 8.30am-5pm). Tickets in a four-person cabin cost Y70 or Y98 per person. A two-person cabin costs Y86 to Y150 per person.

BUS

Sūzhōu has three long-distance bus stations. The main one is at the northern end of Renmin Lu, next to the train station, and a second is at the southern end of Renmin Lu. Both have connections to just about every major place in the region, including Shànghǎi (Y30, 1½ hours), Hángzhōu (Y75, three hours), Wúxī (Y18, 30 minutes), Nánjīng (Y64, 2½ hours) and Zhōuzhuāng (Y15, 1½ hours).

A third station, the Wuxian long-distance bus station (Wúxiàn chēzhàn), further south on Renmin Lu, has similar connections with other buses that are slightly cheaper, but run less frequently than from the other two stations.

Travelling by bus on the Nánjīng–Shànghǎi freeway takes about the same amount of time as the train, but tickets are generally slightly more expensive.

TRAIN

Sūzhōu is on the Nánjīng–Shànghǎi train line. The fastest train to Shànghǎi (Y15) takes about 45 minutes; more frequent trains take one hour. There are also trains to Wúxī (Y10, 30 minutes) and Nánjīng (Y28, 2½ hours). CITS will book sleepers for a Y30 service charge or you can book train tickets on the 2nd floor of the **Lianhe Ticket Centre** (Liánhé Shòupiàochù; 556 Renmin Lu; ⏱ 8.30am-5pm).

Getting Around

BICYCLE

Riding a bike is a good way to tour Sūzhōu, though increased traffic makes it not as pleasurable as in earlier years. Search out the quieter streets and travel along the canals to get the most of what this city has to offer.

There are a couple of bicycle rental shops near the Silk Museum and on Shiquan Jie near the entrance to Suzhou Hotel. The rate is Y30 per day (this can be bargained) and a deposit is required. Check out the seat and brakes carefully before you pedal off.

BUS
Sūzhōu has some convenient tourist buses that visit all sights and cost Y2. They all pass by the train station. Bus No Y5 goes around the western and eastern sides of the city. Bus No Y2 travels from Tiger Hill, Coiled Gate and along Shiquan Jie. Bus Nos Y1 and Y4 run the length of Renmin Lu. Bus Nos Y3 and Y4 also pass by Cold Mountain.

TAXI
There are plenty of taxis in Sūzhōu. They start at Y10 and drivers generally use their meters. Pedicabs hover around the tourist areas and, like elsewhere in China, can be fairly aggressive. Expect to bargain hard.

AROUND SŪZHŌU
Head 44km northeast to **Chángshú** (常熟), known for its lace making and **Yúshān** (虞山) with its nine-storey Song Pagoda.

Grand Canal 大运河
The Grand Canal (Dà Yùnhé) proper cuts to the west and south of Sūzhōu, within a 10km range of the town. Suburban bus Nos 13, 14, 15 and 16 will get you there. In the northwest, bus No 11 follows the canal for a fair distance, taking you on a tour of the enchanting countryside. Hop off the bus once you find yourself a nice bridge on which you can perch and watch the world of the canal float by. Parking yourself for too long could make you the main attraction.

PRECIOUS BELT BRIDGE 宝带桥
With 53 arches, this is considered one of China's best bridges (Bǎodài Qiáo). It straddles the Grand Canal and is a popular spot with fisherfolk. The three central humpbacks of the bridge are larger to allow boats through. It recently had some extensive maintenance done and is no longer used for traffic – a modern one has been built alongside it.

Precious Belt Bridge is thought to be a Tang dynasty construction named after Wang Zhongshu, a local prefect who sold his precious belt to pay for the bridge's construction for the benefit of his people.

The bridge is 4km southeast of Sūzhōu. You can get there by taxi or a 30-minute bike

ride. Head south on Renmin Lu, over Waicheng River. Turn left on Nanhuan Donglu after you pass the Wuxian long-distance bus station. Head east until you hit the canal on Dongqing Lu then south to the bridge.

Tài Hú Area
The towns surrounding Sūzhōu provide ample opportunity for a visit to Tài Hú and the countryside beyond the lake.

The following destinations can be reached by long-distance bus from Sūzhōu's southern or Wuxian long-distance bus station.

Língyán Shān (灵岩山; Lingtian Lu; admission Y11; ☷ 6.30am-4.30pm), 11km southwest of Sūzhōu, is home to an active Buddhist monastery; **Tiānpíng Shān** (天平山; Lingtian Lu; admission Y6; ☷ 8am-5.30pm), 13km west of Sūzhōu, is famous for its medicinal spring waters; and **Guāngfú** (光福), 22km west of Sūzhōu, borders the lake with an ancient seven-storey pagoda.

Tourist bus No Y4 goes to Língyán Shān and Tiānpíng Shān.

Dōng Shān (东山; admission Y15; ☷ 7.30am-5pm), 37km southwest of Sūzhōu, is surrounded by the lake on three sides and is noted for its gardens and the Purple Gold Nunnery (紫金庵; Zǐjīn'ān), containing 16 coloured clay icons. To see eroded Tài Hú rocks 'harvested' for landscaping, visit **Xīshān Dǎo** (西山岛), 33km southwest of Sūzhōu.

ZHŌUZHUĀNG 周庄
☎ 0512
Set in the countryside 32km southeast of Sūzhōu, Zhōuzhuāng offers a step back in time into what is known as a water town, bisected by canals and stone bridges. Established over 900 years ago, Zhōuzhuāng has 14 bridges and over 60% of its buildings are from the Yuan, Ming and Qing dynasties.

Zhōuzhuāng also has a huge tourism industry and is extremely popular with Chinese tourists. Despite the crowds and souvenir stalls, a day walking through Zhōuzhuāng is definitely worthwhile. The bridges and cobbled lanes of the Old Town are picturesque and it's long been a favourite place for art students who sit alongside the canals with their easels.

Orientation
Zhōuzhuāng's Old Town is quite small and it's possible to walk around the whole area in

less than two hours. Maps are sold through-out the town and have English names for the sights and more famous bridges.

Information
Zhōuzhuāng is not a convenient town to change money; to be on the safe side, have enough cash before arriving.

Sights & Activities
The entrance to Zhōuzhuāng's **Old Town** (Quangong Lu; admission Y60; ⏲ 7.30am-6pm) is at the western end of Quangong Lu. The admission includes the entry fee for all the exhibits inside.

Quanfu Pagoda (Quánfú Tǎ; Quanfu Lu) was built in 1987 to hide the water tower in preparation for the tourism boom promoted by the provincial government. The campaign seems to have been an enormous success, with Zhōuzhuāng declared a World Heritage Site by the UN in 1998.

From the pagoda it's a short walk south to the **Ancient Memorial Arch** (Gǔbēi Lóu; Quanfu Lu).

There are daily performances of classical Chinese music at **Zhōuzhuāng Gǔxìtái** (Beishi

Jie), one of the first set of buildings you'll see on entering the Old Town.

The **Hall of Zhang's Residence** (Zhāng Tíng; Nanshi Jie) dates from the Ming dynasty and has six courtyards and over 70 rooms. Running through the back of the residence is a small waterway that allowed access to the house by boat.

South of here, the **Hall of Shen's Residence** (Shěn Tíng; Nanshi Jie) is considered the best residence in Zhōuzhuāng, containing seven courtyards and over 100 rooms, each connected to a main hall.

At the southern end of town, **Quanfu Temple** (Quánfú Sì) contains 21 gold Buddhas plus one large bronze Buddha measuring over 5m in height. The temple is surrounded by pagodas and courtyard buildings, extending into **South Lake Garden** (Nán Hú Yuán). The garden was built for Zhang Jiying, a literary man of the Jin dynasty, and consists of bridges crisscrossing over the water.

The **Zhouzhuang Museum** (Zhōuzhuāng Bówùguǎn) is home to nearly 1000 artefacts including items from the local fishing and artisan industries.

South of the museum is the **Chengxu Temple** (Chéngxū Dàoyuàn; Zhongshi Jie), a Taoist temple built during the Song dynasty.

It's fun to take a **boat tour** through the canals. The ticket office and wharf are just south of Fu'an Bridge (Fú'ān Qiáo) across Tiyun Bridge (Tíyún Qiáo). You can't miss the cluster of boats. Half-hour trips in an eight-seater cost Y60 per boat. Speedboats

ZHŌUZHUĀNG 周庄

are available for hire to another nearby water town, **Tónglǐ**. Tickets are Y250 return.

Wooden sailboats tour around **South Lake** (Nán Hú) for Y120. Speedboats go around the lake for Y80. Tickets are sold at an office at the southern end of Nanshi Jie. The trip lasts about 30 minutes.

Sleeping

Zhōuzhuāng can easily be visited on a day trip from either Sūzhōu or Shànghǎi or as a stopover between the two.

Fengdan Double Bridge Resort (Fēngdān Shuāngqiáo Dùjiàcūn; ☎ 721 1549; Daqiao Lu; d Y258-280) This hotel has 20% discounts on weekdays but you need to ask for it. The rooms are very shabby but the location in the Old Town with a view of the water more than makes up for it. To find the hotel, head south on Nanshi Jie and take the first alley left after the Hall of Shen's Residence.

Eating

The central area of the Old Town has many nondescript restaurants catering to tour groups at astronomical prices. For more reasonable prices try the north end of town along the main canal on Xianjiang Jie. Unfortunately, overcharging is the norm here. Make sure you agree on a price beforehand and don't accept any 'freebies' (even tea) without asking the price first.

Páilóu Càiguǎn (23 Xianjiang Jie; mains Y20-50; ☯ breakfast, lunch & dinner) This small courtyard restaurant gets you out of the pedestrian traffic, though there are other restaurants across the lane that look over the canal if you prefer a view. Zhōuzhuāng's local speciality is *wànsāntí*, a large, fatty dish of stewed pork knuckle. Expect to pay Y40.

The southwest part of the Old Town is quieter and Zhongshi Jie has some nice teahouses along the canal.

Shopping

A number of local specialities are available in Zhōuzhuāng, including woven goods, carved wooden buckets and utensils, sweets, lace and Yíxīng teapots. Locally harvested freshwater pearls are available at reasonable prices in every form from traditional jewellery to animal and pagoda shapes and even face powder.

Shuixiang Pearl Mill (Shuǐxiāng Zhēnzhūfáng; Zhongshi Jie; ☯ 8.30am-5.30pm) The souvenir stalls sell pearls, but this is a reputable shop with fixed prices. Pearl necklaces range from Y120 to Y650.

Getting There & Away

Public buses let you off at the new bus station northwest of town and it's a bit of a hike across the Zhouzhuang Bridge and down to the entrance of the Old Town. Some buses cross the bridge and drive right up to the entry gate. The tourist sightseeing bus from Shànghǎi parks in a lot on the east end of Quangong Lu.

Frequent buses run between Sūzhōu's north long-distance bus station and Zhōuzhuāng (Y15, 1½ hours). The first leaves Sūzhōu at 7.10am with the last bus returning to Sūzhōu at 4.40pm.

The easiest way to get to Zhōuzhuāng from Shànghǎi, especially for a day trip, is the tourist bus from Shanghai Sightseeing Bus Centre. Tickets are Y110 and include the entry ticket and return trip. From Shànghǎi, three buses depart daily from the Northern Bus Station (p302; 80 Gongxing Lu).

Ānhuī 安徽

ĀNHUĪ

HIGHLIGHTS

- Travel to far northwest **Bózhōu** (p258), an ancient trading centre for Chinese medicine
- Climb the misty peaks of **Huáng Shān** (p259), an inspiring place for Chinese poets and painters
- Sleep in a monastery in **Jiǔhuá Shān** (p264), one of China's sacred Buddhist mountains
- Sample the fragrant **teas** (p259) of the Huáng Shān region, known for their delicate flavours and health-enhancing properties
- Bargain for antiques in Túnxī's bustling **Lao Jie** (p263)

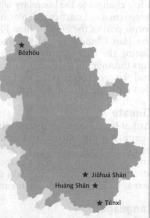

■ POP: 61.5 MIL	■ AREA: 139,000 SQ KM

■ www.travelchinaguide.com/cityguides/anhui

Ānhuī is one of the least-developed provinces in eastern China, largely due to its unfriendly terrain. The province's southern regions, covered with rugged mountains, are impossible to cultivate and the arid northern plains are largely infertile. Only small pockets of land, mainly in the warmer south, provide a means for growing food. The Yangzi River (Cháng Jiāng) cuts through the province and is prone to flooding the low plains, contributing to poverty and the lack of development. Infrastructure in Ānhuī lags behind other parts of China, and there is little of the hustle and bustle that characterises other provinces in the east. Provincial authorities have made significant efforts to improve highways and rail lines, but progress is slow.

Ānhuī's lack of development can be a bonus for travellers looking for an out-of-the-way adventure. Héféi, the capital, is a pleasant city and most people use it as a jumping-off point for trips to spectacular Huáng Shān in the south. While Huáng Shān has been deservedly drawing tourists for years to goggle at its misty peaks and cloud-filled vistas, there are other, less-explored regions in Ānhuī to discover. Less-developed mountain areas include the Buddhist mountains of Jiǔhuá Shān, near Huáng Shān, which provide wonderful opportunities for hiking and sleeping in monasteries. The ancient trading town of Túnxī is an interesting place to explore, with its winding streets and vibrant Lao Jie area.

For those who really want to escape to somewhere remote, the far northwest town of Bózhōu shouldn't be missed. For hundreds of years it has served as a central marketplace for traditional Chinese medicine, something that still continues to this day.

History
The provincial borders of Ānhuī were defined by the Qing government and, except for a few changes to the boundary with Jiāngsū, have remained unchanged. Northern Ānhuī forms part of the North China Plain, where the Han Chinese settled in large numbers during the Han dynasty. The Yangzi River cuts through the southern quarter of Ānhuī, and the area south of the river was not settled until the 7th and 8th centuries.

Climate
Ānhuī has a warm-temperate climate, with heavy rain in spring and summer that brings plenty of flooding. Winters are damp and cold. When travelling through Ānhuī at any time of year, bring rain gear and a warm jacket for the mountain areas.

Language
Anhui residents largely speak Mandarin. In the southern parts of the province some people speak the Hui dialect (Huí Yǔ), the language of China's Muslim Hui minority.

Getting There & Away
The historical and tourist sights of Ānhuī are concentrated in the south, and are more accessible from Hángzhōu or Shànghǎi than from the provincial capital, Héféi.

Getting Around
Travelling around Ānhuī is not as easy as other provinces in the southern regions, such as Jiāngsū and Zhèjiāng. Ānhuī is not a wealthy province and road conditions reflect this. If travelling by bus, visitors should be aware that roads are often flooded in the summer and the wet muddy conditions can make getting around dangerous. The train is a safer option. Rail lines connect Héféi to Túnxī and the northwest city of Bózhōu.

HÉFÉI 合肥
☎ 0551 / pop 4.2 million
Prior to 1949 Héféi was a quiet market town, but has since boomed into an industrial centre. It's a pleasant, friendly city with lively markets. While there are few cultural or historical attractions, the parks

ĀNHUĪ 安徽

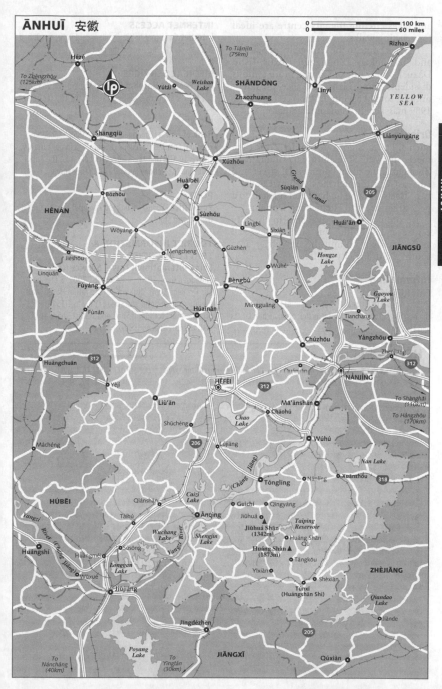

| | 100 km |
| | 60 miles |

To Tiānjīn (75km)

Hézé

To Zhèngzhōu (125km)

Yútái

Weishan Lake

SHĀNDŌNG

Zhaozhuang

Línyí

Rizhao

YELLOW SEA

Shāngqiū

Liányúngǎng

Xúzhōu

Huáiběi

Bózhōu

HÉNÁN

Sùqián

Grand Canal

205

Sùzhōu

Língbì

Sìxiàn

Huái'ān

JIĀNGSŪ

Wǒyáng

Mengcheng

Gùzhèn

Wúhé

Hongze Lake

Jiēshǒu

Linquán

Fúyáng

Běngbù

Mingguāng

Gaoyou Lake

Fúnán

Húainán

Tiancháng

Yángzhōu

Chúzhōu

Zhēnjiāng

Huángchuān

312

Quánjiāo

NÁNJĪNG

312

Yèjí

HÉFÉI

312

To Shànghǎi (110km)

Liù'ān

Mǎ'ānshān

Cháohú

To Hángzhōu (170km)

Shūchéng

Chao Lake

Wúhú

Máchéng

206

Lújiāng

Nan Lake

HÚBĚI

Qiánshān

Caizi Lake

(Cháng Jiāng)

Tóngling

Nánling

Xuānzhōu

318

Tàihú

Ānqìng

Guìchí

Qīngyáng

Jiǔhuá

Jiǔhuá Shān (1342m)

Taiping Reservoir

Yangzi River (Chang Jiang)

Wuchang Lake

Shengjiu Lake

Huáng Shān Qū

Huángshí

Huángméi

Susōng

Longgan Lake

Huáng Shān (1873m)

Tāngkǒu

ZHÈJIĀNG

Wúxué

Yìxiàn

Shèxiàn

Jiǔjiāng

Túnxī (Huangshan Shi)

Qiandao Lake

Jiànde

Jingdézhèn

205

Poyang Lake

To Nánchāng (40km)

To Yīngtán (30km)

JIĀNGXĪ

Qūxiàn

and lakes circling the city centre are ideal for relaxing walks.

Héféi is home to the University of Science and Technology (Zhōngguó Kēxué Jìshù Dàxué), where one of China's more famous dissidents, Fang Lizhi, was vice president until he sought asylum in the West after the 1989 massacre in Tiananmen Square.

Orientation

Shengli Lu leads down to Nanfei River then meets up with Shouchun Lu. Changjiang Zhonglu is the main commercial street and cuts east-west through the city. Between these two streets, Huaihe Lu has been made into a pedestrian street to Huancheng Donglu.

Accommodation is available in the city centre and near the bus stations, as well as on Meishan Lu and the university area southwest of the city centre.

Information

EMERGENCY
Public Security Bureau (PSB; Gōngānjú) Located on the northwest corner of the intersection of Shouchun Lu and Liu'an Lu.

INTERNET ACCESS
Internet Café (per hr Y2; ⏰ 8am-midnight) You'll find this café on the 2nd floor of the post office.

MEDICAL SERVICES
No 1 People's Hospital (Rénmín Yīyuàn; ☎ 265 2893; 322 Huaihe Lu) Conveniently located in the city centre.

MONEY
Bank of China (Zhōngguó Yínháng; 155 Changjiang Zhonglu) Changes traveller's cheques and major currency. There's an ATM that takes international cards. The Anhui Hotel and the Holiday Inn will also change money.

POST
Post Office (Yóujú; Changjiang Zhonglu) Next to the City Department Store.

TOURIST INFORMATION & TRAVEL AGENCIES
China International Travel Service (CITS; Zhōngguó Guójì Lǚxíngshè; ☎ 281 1909; 8 Meishan Lu; ⏰ 8am-5pm) Situated next to Anhui Hotel. Staff members are helpful and speak English. CITS can arrange tours to Huáng Shān and Jiǔhuá Shān, as well as tours around Héféi.

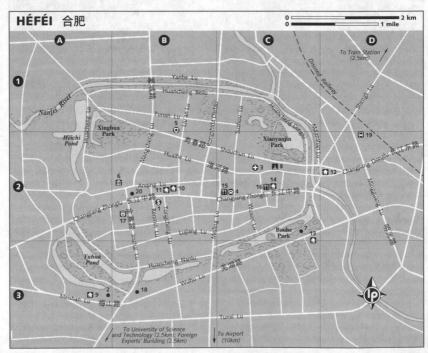

Sights

Héféi has some pleasant parks. In the northeast, **Xiaoyaojin Park** (Xiāoyáojīn Gōngyuán; Shouchun Lu; admission Y5; 6am-7pm) is the largest and has a small, rather depressing zoo. **Baohe Park** (Bāohé Gōngyuán) is nicer and contains the splendid **Lord Bao's Tomb** (Bāo Gōng Mùyuán; 58 Wuhu Lu; admission Y15; 8am-6pm). Lord Bao was (that rare thing in government) an upright and conscientious official during the Northern Song dynasty, and died in 1062. The tomb was excavated in 1973 and restored at this site in 1987.

Small **Mingjiao Temple** (Míngjiào Sì; Huaihe Lu; admission Y5; 7am-6pm) sits 5m above ground. Built in early AD 500, the temple saw military skirmishes a few centuries later when troops from the Wu and Wei kingdoms fought in the area.

Finally, the **Anhui Provincial Museum** (Ānhuī Shěng Bówùguǎn; 268 Anqing Lu; admission Y10; 8.30am-11.30am & 2.30-5pm Tue-Sun) chronicles the history of Ānhuī, with some good displays of bronzes, Han dynasty tomb rubbings and some fine examples of the wooden architectural style found around Huáng Shān.

Sleeping

Chang Jiang Guibin Hotel (Cháng Jiāng Guìbīn Dàjiǔdiàn; ☎ 266 1108; 268 Anqing Lu; d Y198) Located in a small courtyard behind the Chang Jiang Hotel. Rooms are small, but tolerable and cleaner than those of its neighbour.

Foreign Experts' Building (Zhuānjiālóu; ☎ 360 2881; 96 Jinzhai Lu; s Y150, d Y180-240) Comfortable and clean rooms are available in the park-like campus setting of the University of Science and Technology. Take bus No 1 from the train station to the university bus stop, which is opposite the north gate of the university entrance. Enter here, turning left at the first road past the pond. Reception is in the large building on the north side of the pond.

Overseas Chinese Hotel (Huáqiáo Fàndiàn; ☎ 265 2221; 68 Changjiang Zhonglu; s Y260-440, d Y300-440) This hotel is centrally located, with 50% discounts for the more expensive rooms.

Anhui Hotel (Ānhuī Fàndiàn; ☎ 281 1818; 18 Meishan Lu; d Y660-930) This is an elegant four-star establishment that has a health centre and bowling alley. Prices are subject to a 15% service charge, though 40% discounts are available.

Fuhao Hotel (Fùhào Dàjiǔdiàn; ☎ 281 8888; 18 Meishan Lu; s/d Y138/188) This hotel is within the grounds of the Anhui Hotel and has clean simple rooms. Rates include buffet breakfast.

Holiday Inn (☎ 429 1188; 1104 Changjiang Donglu; d Y920) This has all you would expect from an international hotel, complete with swimming pool and health club. Half-price discounts are often available.

Novotel Hotel (Nuòfùtè Héféi Qíyún Shānzhuāng; ☎ 288 7777; 199 Wuhu Lu; d Y488) This four-star hotel is across the street from Lord Bao's tomb and within walking distance to the city centre. Amenities are first-rate and service is very professional.

Chang Jiang Hotel (Cháng Jiāng Fàndiàn; ☎ 265 6441; 262 Changjiang Zhonglu; d Y100-160) This hotel offers very tattered doubles and its only redeeming quality is that it's centrally located. Look at the rooms before deciding to stay here. Bus No 1 goes right by here.

Eating

Huáishàng Jiǔjiā (104 Changjiang Zhonglu; mains Y20-30; lunch & dinner) A clean, lively place on the 2nd floor overlooking Changjiang Zhonglu, it serves has standard dishes found throughout east China, but spiced up a bit, Ānhuī style.

Outdoor restaurants abound near the long-distance bus station and on Changjiang Donglu near the Holiday Inn. Choose from the ingredients on display – fish, meat, vegetables etc. Depending on your choice, meals cost Y20 to Y60. There are also plenty of places to eat in the lanes next to the Guangming Cinema.

The **City Department Store** (Shì Bǎihuò Dàlóu; Changjiang Donglu; ⊙ 9am-9pm) has a supermarket, which is good for self-catering or stocking up for Huáng Shān.

Entertainment
Guangming Cinema (Guāngmíng Yīngbù; 445 Jinzhai Lu; tickets Y15) Shows English-language movies in a large complex.

Getting There & Away
AIR
Daily flights go to Běijīng (Y990), Shànghǎi (Y490), Guǎngzhōu (Y1040), Hángzhōu (Y460) and Xī'ān (Y1060). Less-frequent services go to Chéngdū (Y1210), Xiàmén (Y860) and Kūnmíng (Y1660). At the time of writing there were no flights to Túnxī.

Bookings can be made at **China Eastern Airlines** (Dōngfāng Hángkōng Shòupiàochù; ☎ 282 2357; 246 Jinzhai Lu), or through CITS and at the train-ticket booking office.

BUS
Several long-distance bus stations are located north of the Changjiang Donglu and Mingguang Lu intersection in the city's east, which is a bit confusing. Your best bet is to go to the Héféi **long-distance bus station** (Héféi Qìchē Zhàn; 168 Mingguang Lu). There are daily services to Hángzhōu (Y150, eight hours), Bózhōu (Y50, five hours) Wúhàn (Y140, 10 hours) and Túnxī (Y28, seven hours).

The freeway to Nánjīng has shortened travel times considerably; air-con buses take 2½ hours to Nánjīng (Y53) and six hours to Shànghǎi (Y145). The freeway connection south to Jiǔjiāng (Y70), in Jiāngxī, allows for an eight-hour journey. Frequent minibuses also depart for Wúhú (Y27, 2½ hours).

TRAIN
The train station is 4km northeast of the city centre. Trains go to Shànghǎi (Y198,

8½ hours), Běijīng (Y230, 12 hours), Zhèngzhōu (Y97, 9½ hours), via Kāifēng, and Bózhōu (Y25, 4½ hours). The train to Túnxī (Y96, seven hours) is more comfortable than the bus.

Tickets are available at the train station, but it's much better to get them at the **train ticket booking office** (216 Changjiang Zhonglu; ⊙ 24hr) on the northeast side at the intersection with Jinzhai Lu. You can book sleepers five days in advance.

Getting Around
Héféi is easy to get around. Bus No 1 runs from the train station down Shengli Lu to the city centre on Changjiang Zhonglu, then south along Jinzhai Lu towards the university. Taxis are cheap, starting at Y5. Taking a taxi (Y20, 30 minutes) is the best way to the airport, which is about 11km south of the city centre.

BÓZHŌU 亳州
☎ 0558 / pop 5.2 million
Bózhōu lies in Ānhuī's far northwest, near Hénán. It's known as one of the most important trading centres for traditional medicine in central China, attracting merchants and Chinese herbalists from a wide area. It's also the birthplace of China's legendary woman-warrior Hua Mulan and the Han general Cao Cao, the villain of the Three Kingdoms, something Bózhōu locals are extremely proud of.

Orientation & Information
Most travellers will arrive at the train station 4km southeast of the city centre. There are two bus stations on Qiaoling Lu that have buses to Héféi. Renmin Zhonglu is Bózhōu's 'high street', where many of the main sites are located. The **Bank of China** (中国银行; Zhōngguó Yínháng) and the **post office** (邮局; Yóujú) are at the intersection of Renmin Lu and Qiaoling Lu. The Medicinal Market is 4km southeast of the city centre near the train station.

Sights
Bózhōu's main attraction is its **Medicinal Market** (中药市场; Zhōngyào Shìchǎng; Mulan Lu). You'll see mounds of pressed herbs, roots, rocks, minerals, wasp nests, animal skins, tortoise shells, dried insects and snakes here. The market is in a large, white-tiled

exhibition hall, near the train station. Things slow down in the afternoon, so it's best to visit before noon.

The **Underground Tunnel** (地下运兵道; Dìxià Yùnbīng Dào; 49 Renmin Zhonglu; admission Y12; 8am-6pm) is a 600m-long subterranean passageway parallel to Renmin Zhonglu. General Cao Cao built it as a secret route for soldiers to surprise the enemy.

The **Flower Theatre** (花戏楼; Huā Xìlóu; 1 Xian ning Jie) features an ornate tiled gate built in the Qing dynasty. In the theatre is a small **museum** (admission Y12; 8am-6pm) featuring a Han dynasty burial suit made from pieces of jade sewn together with silver thread.

It's worthwhile walking from the Flower Theatre south towards Renmin Zhonglu through the old part of the city, with its narrow stone-flagged streets and ancient buildings.

Sleeping & Eating

There's a cluster of hotels around the bus stations and most places seem willing to accept foreigners. Some hotels are downright filthy (despite having clean lobbies), so check the rooms first before paying.

Lidū Dàshà (丽都大厦; 552 3008; 50 Xinhua Lu; d Y100) Rooms are clean and cheap, and management are quite friendly.

Zhonghua Hotel (中华大酒店; Zhōnghuá Dàjiǔdiàn; 552 1766; 7 Qiaoling Lu; s/d Y88/168) This newish hotel is one of the better places to stay and has a good restaurant.

There are restaurants along the pavement at the intersection of Heping Lu and Qiaoling Lu, beside the Zhonghua Hotel. A steaming bowl of delicious *jiǎozi* (stuffed dumplings) and a bottle of beer will set you back Y10.

Getting There & Away

Daily buses depart for Zhèngzhōu (Y50, five hours), Kāifēng (Y35, four hours), Héféi (Y50, five hours) and Xúzhōu (Y30, five hours).

Bózhōu is on the Zhèngzhōu–Héféi train line, though most trains stop here either very early in the morning or around midnight. One useful train leaving at a reasonable time and going south is to Wēnzhōu (Y317, 22 hours), passing through Nánjīng, Shànghǎi and Hángzhōu.

There's a daily train service to Héféi (Y25, 4½ hours).

HUÁNG SHĀN 黄山

0559

In good weather Huáng Shān (Yellow Mountains) is truly spectacular, and the surrounding countryside, with its traditional villages and patchwork paddy fields, is among the most beautiful in China. Huáng Shān has a 1200-year history as a tourist attraction. Countless painters and poets have trudged around the range, seeking inspiration and bestowing the peaks with fanciful names, such as Nine Dragons, Taoist Priest, Ox Nose, Fairy Capital and Hunchback.

Today the reclusive artists seeking an inspirational retreat from the hustle and bustle of the temporal world have been replaced by crowds of tourists, who bring the hustle and bustle with them. Still, with a little effort, you might be rewarded with a small moment of tranquillity, and the views are quite breathtaking.

Orientation & Information

Buses from Túnxī drop you off in Tāngkǒu, the main village at the mountain's foot, or at the terminal near **Yellow Mountain Gate**

THE TEA OF HUÁNG SHĀN

The people living in the vicinity of Huáng Shān are serious tea drinkers, and nowhere is this more reflected than in the small towns and villages surrounding Túnxī and Huáng Shān. This region has been cultivating tea for over 1200 years and over 30 varieties are produced. Qihong Black Tea is one of the most famous of the Huáng Shān teas and is sold around the world. Other kinds include Songluo tea, claimed to have medicinal values and reduce blood pressure, and Shimo tea, which is reputed to prevent diseases and increase longevity.

Tea making here differs from other regions of China. Often the tea is infused right in the cup and hot water is added during the course of drinking. Tea is meant to be lingered over, not gulped, to experience the full flavour.

One of the best places to sample and buy tea is in Túnxī's Lao Jie area. There are numerous shops here selling their goods, all claiming to have the best tea in Huáng Shān. It's recommended that you insist on sampling the tea first, and then bargain hard.

(Huángshān Mén) in upper Tāngkǒu. Maps, raincoats, food and accommodation are available here.

There's also accommodation 4km further up the valley in the hot springs area. The lovely bamboo forests and fresh air make this a much more pleasant place to stay than Tāngkǒu. Don't let the Tāngkǒu hotel touts try and talk you out of staying here by claiming the area is 'inconvenient', as it's regularly served by taxis and buses. Unfortunately, the **hot springs** (Huángshān Wénquán; communal/private bath Y30/80; ☾ 8am-11pm) have been piped into a rather slimy bathhouse next to the Huangshan Hotel.

The road from Tāngkǒu continues beyond the hot springs area and ends halfway up the mountain at the Cloud Valley Temple cable-car station, 890m above sea level, where the eastern steps begin. Hotels are scattered on trails around the summit area.

Another cable car goes from the **Jade Screen Peak** (Yùpíng Fēng) area to just above the hot springs resort. A third cable car, which at 3709m claims to be the longest in Asia, approaches Huáng Shān from the northwest going to **Pine Forest Peak** (Sōnglín Fēng), and is accessible from the southern side of Taiping Lake.

There's a **Bank of China** (Zhōngguó Yínháng; ☾ 9am-5pm) next to Huangshan Hotel in the hot springs area. Another branch is across from the Beihai hotel, with an ATM that accepts international cards. The Taoyuan Hotel can also change money.

Guides

Guides are unnecessary because the mountain paths are easy to follow, with plenty of English signs. The truly decadent might make their ascent in a sedan chair strung between bamboo poles and bounced (literally) along by two porters. The price? Around Y400 one way or Y1000 for the day, depending on your bargaining skills.

Routes to the Summit

There are three basic routes to the top: the short, hard way (eastern steps); the longer,

HUÁNG SHĀN 黄山

0 ——— 2 km
0 ——— 1 mile

harder way (western steps); and the very short, easy way (cable car). The eastern steps lead up below the Cloud Valley Temple cable-car line, and the western steps lead up from the parking lot near **Ciguang Temple** (Cíguāng Gé), about 3km above the hot springs. The Jade Screen Peak cable car also goes from here to the Jade Screen Peak area, bringing you about halfway up the mountain.

Regardless of how you ascend Huáng Shān, you'll have to pay a steep Y130 entrance fee. Pay at the eastern steps near the Cloud Valley Temple cable-car station or where the western steps begin. Minibuses run to both places from Tāngkŏu for Y10. Be careful about being overcharged.

Make sure to pack enough water, food and appropriate clothing before you take your first step towards the summit. Bottled water and food prices increase the higher you go. The market under the stone bridge in Tāngkŏu has a good selection of food at affordable prices.

EASTERN STEPS

The 7.5km eastern steps route can be climbed comfortably in about three hours. It's a killer if you push yourself too hard, but it's definitely easier than the western steps.

Purists can extend the eastern steps climb by several hours by starting at Yellow Mountain Gate, where a stepped path crosses the road at several points before connecting with the main eastern steps trail at the Cloud Valley Temple cable-car station.

If you have time, the recommended route is a 10-hour circuit hike taking the eastern steps to the top and descending to the hot springs resort via the western steps. Don't underestimate the hardship involved. While cut-stone stairways make climbing a little easier, the extremely steep gradients can wreak havoc on your knees.

WESTERN STEPS

The 15km western steps route has some stellar scenery, following a precarious route hewn out of the sheer rock cliffs. But it's twice as long and strenuous as the eastern steps, and much easier to enjoy if you're clambering down rather than gasping your way up.

The western steps descent begins at the **Flying Rock** (Fēilái Shí), a rectangular boulder perched on an outcrop half an hour from

Beihai Hotel, and goes over **Bright Summit Peak** (Guāngmíng Dǐng), where there is an odd-shaped weather station and a hotel.

Highlights on the western steps include the ascent to the highest summit, **Lotus Flower Peak** (Liánhuā Fēng), which is located above Yupinglou Hotel, and the exhilaratingly steep and exposed stairway leading to the **Heavenly Capital Peak** (Tiāndū Fēng). Young lovers bring locks engraved with their names up here and fix them to the chain railings. This symbolises that they are 'locked' together. It can get quite crowded on this narrow stairway, however, and if you're afraid of heights it might be better to skip this one. The sheer amount of human traffic on Huáng Shān has resulted in restricting access to Heavenly Capital Peak for maintenance and repair, but it should be open by the time you read this. It is possible that Lotus Flower Peak may be closed for maintenance.

The western path continues past **Banshan Temple** (Bànshān Sì) and back to the hot springs area. Halfway between the temple and the hot springs resort is a parking lot with minibuses. For Y10, you can skip the last 1½ hours of walking and get a lift to the hot springs area.

CABLE CAR

The least painful way up is by taking the **Cloud Valley Temple Cable Car** (Yúngǔsì Suǒdào; adult/child Y80/40; ◷ 6.30am-4pm). For Y10, minibuses take you from the Yellow Mountain Gate to the cable-car station. Either arrive very early or late (if you're staying overnight). Queues of more than one hour are the norm. In the high season, many people wait up to three hours for a ride – you may as well walk.

The **Jade Screen Peak Cable Car** (Yùpíng Fēng Suǒdào; adult/child Y80/40; ◷ 6.30am-5pm) goes from just below Yupinglou Hotel to the parking lot above the hot springs area.

Accessing Huáng Shān from the north via the **Taiping Cable Car** (Tàipíng Suǒdào; adult/child Y80/40; ◷ 6.30am-5pm) is also an option. Minibuses (Y15, 30 minutes) run from Huáng Shān Qū (an additional access point to Huáng Shān) to the cable-car station. The cable car runs to the Pine Forest Peak area.

On the Summit

Many people find that the highlight of Huáng Shān is the Běihǎi sunrise: a 'sea' of low clouds blanketing the valley to the north with 'island' peaks hazily reaching for the heavens. **Refreshing Terrace** (Qīngliáng Tái) is located five minutes from Beihai Hotel and attracts sunrise crowds (hotels supply thick padded jackets for the occasion). If you're seeking some solitude, head for the area around **Purple Cloud Peak** (Dānxiá Fēng).

Sleeping & Eating

Huáng Shān has five locations where hotels and restaurants can be found. Prices and bed availability vary according to season.

TĀNGKŌU

There are affordable hotels here, though Tāngkǒu itself quite gloomy and nothing to get excited about.

Tangkou Hotel (Tāngkǒu Bīnguǎn; ☎ 556 2400; fax 556 2687; q per bed without bathroom Y35, d Y200) This place is marginally better than the Xiaoyao Hotel and staff are friendlier. It's up the hill about 300m, to your left as you leave the Xiaoyao.

Xiaoyao Hotel (Xiāoyáo Bīnguǎn; 556 2571; fax 556 1679; dm Y35, tr per bed with/without bathroom Y60/40, d Y300/220) This hotel is really only for the desperate. Dumpy doubles and pushy management make this place a last resort.

There's plenty of food in Tāngkǒu, many eateries specialising in expensive local treats, such as frogs and preserved meats. Watch out for overcharging – simple dishes should cost Y15 to Y20 – and for overzealous touts. For cheap eats, try the makeshift restaurants under the main bridge.

HOT SPRINGS AREA

The hot springs area, 4km further uphill, is an attractive place to stay, but more expensive than Tāngkǒu.

Taoyuan Hotel (Táoyuán Bīnguǎn; Peach Blossom Hotel; ☎ 556 2666; fax 556 2666; d Y486-580) This is the nicest hotel in the hot springs area, with clean, modern rooms, some with views. The hotel restaurant has good food.

Yiyuan Hotel (Yíyuán Shānzhuāng; ☎ 558 5666; fax 558 5377; d Y280-340) This small hotel has large, so-so rooms with discounts of 35%. It's popular with Chinese tour groups.

Huangshan Hotel (Huángshān Bīnguǎn; ☎ 558 5808; fax 558 5818; d Y340-420) The tiny rooms have seen better days and are a bit on the tattered side. Look over the rooms carefully (especially the sheets) before agreeing to stay.

All the hotels have restaurants and, as in Tāngkǒu, restaurant touts look for hungry travellers. Watch out for overcharging.

CLOUD VALLEY TEMPLE CABLE CAR STATION

This is a secluded, if somewhat inconvenient, setting within the pine and bamboo forest.

Yungu Hotel (Yúngǔ Shānzhuāng; ☎ 556 2444; 556 2466; d Y580) This is probably the best place to stay if you have the money. Government officials stay here when they're visiting Huáng Shān. It's down the steps from the car park in front of the cable-car station.

SUMMIT AREA

Ideally, a Huáng Shān visit should include a stay on the summit.

Beihai Hotel (Běihǎi Bīnguǎn; ☎ 558 2555; fax 558 1996; dm Y150-180, d Y700-850) This hotel is overpriced but comfortable, and provides the best location for seeing the sunrise.

Xihai Hotel (Xīhǎi Bīnguǎn; ☎ 558 8888; fax 558 8988; d Y960-1280) This is a real 'mountain hotel' designed by Swedish architects. All rooms have heating and 24-hour hot water. It caters to international tour groups.

Paiyunlou Hotel (Páiyúnlóu Bīnguǎn; ☎ 558 3208; fax 558 3999; dm/d/tr Y150/800/880) This hotel is up from Tiānhǎi Hú (Heavenly Sea Lake). It's a little out of the way, but the dorms are good value.

Shilin Hotel (Shílín Fàndiàn; ☎ 558 4040; dm Y150, d Y850) This is a good place near the summit, and the dorms are adequate.

Xihai and Beihai Hotels have bars and restaurants serving international and Chinese food, but as they tend to cater to tour groups, it's sometimes difficult to get service outside meal times. There are cheaper restaurants nearby.

WESTERN STEPS

There are a few accommodation options on this route.

Baiyunlou Hotel (Báiyúnlóu Bīnguǎn; ☎ 556 1708; fax 556 1602; dm/d Y150/800) This peaceful hotel offers reasonable accommodation in beautiful surroundings. It's secluded and set on the mountain's edge.

Yupinglou Hotel (Yùpínglóu Bīnguǎn; ☎ 556 2317; fax 556 2258; s/d Y150/180) Further down the mountain, this hotel is perched on a spectacular 1660m-high lookout with a view of Heavenly Capital Peak. The rates and conditions reflect its relative inaccessibility. Washing arrangements are basic and be prepared for water shortages.

There are few eating options on this route. Yupinglou Hotel has a cheap dining hall beside its courtyard, and a better restaurant upstairs.

Getting There & Away

Buses from Túnxī (aka Huángshān Shì) take around 1½ hours to reach Yellow Mountain Gate. Minibuses to Túnxī leave from the bridge area in Tāngkǒu; tickets are Y13.

In summer, direct buses to Tāngkǒu come from Héféi (Y63, six hours), Nánjīng (Y75, six hours) and Shànghǎi (Y153, 11 hours). Other buses go to Jiǔhuá Shān (Y40, four hours), and the Yangzi ports of Wúhú (Y50, four hours) and Guìchí (Y50, five hours). Most buses leave Tāngkǒu very early in the morning. The long-distance bus station is just below the Yellow Mountain Gate, but closes early. Try booking bus tickets at your hotel or at Lianhua Hotel (Liánhuā Fàndiàn) in Tāngkǒu, where you can also book train and airline tickets. It's on the highway leading to the Yellow Mountain Gate across from the main bridge area.

Getting Around

Minibuses are the easiest and cheapest way to get around Huáng Shan, though they usually don't budge until enough people are on board. In the morning they ferry people to the eastern and western steps. You can usually find minibuses on Tāngkǒu's streets or on the highway across the bridge. Likewise, minibuses wait at the bottom of mountain routes in the afternoon. Minivan taxis abound; you'll have to bargain.

TÚNXĪ 屯溪
☎ 0559 / pop 1.5 million

The old trading town of Túnxī (Huángshān Shì) is roughly 70km southeast of Huáng Shān. As its other name implies (meaning Huángshān City), Túnxī is the main springboard for Huáng Shān. It's also a pleasant town to explore for a day.

Orientation & Information

Túnxī is located at the junction of the Xin'an River (Xīn'ān Jiāng) and Heng River (Héng Jiāng). The older (and most inter-

esting) part of town is in the southwest, around Huangshan Lu and Xin'an Lu. The newer part of town is in the northeast, near the bus and train stations.

Bank of China (中国银行; Zhōngguó Yínháng; 9 Xin'an Lu; ⏰ 9am-5pm) Changes traveller's cheques and major currencies.

CITS (中国国际旅行社; Zhōngguó Guójì Lǚxíngshè; ☎ 252 6184; 6 Xizhen Jie) Arranges English-speaking guides for tours of Huáng Shān and the surrounding area.

PSB (公安局; Gōngānjú; ☎ 231 5429; 108 Chang'an Lu) Located in the eastern section of Túnxī.

Sleeping & Eating

Several Túnxī hotels, especially the cheaper ones, don't accept foreigners.

Jiangnan Hotel (江南大酒店; Jiāngnán Dàjiǔdiàn; ☎ 251 1067; 25-27 Qianyuan Beilu; s Y150, d Y280-400) The cheaper rooms are very small and cramped, but convenient for the train and bus stations. It's located on the corner of the first intersection you meet coming out of the train station. The prices can be bargained.

Huaxi Hotel (花溪饭店; Huāxī Fàndiàn; ☎ 251 4312; fax 251 4990; 1 Xizhen Jie; d Y210-680) Located to the west of town, directly across the bridge where the Heng and Xin'an Rivers meet. This huge hotel has clean rooms and friendly staff; the main attraction is its proximity to the old part of town.

Měishí Rénjiā (美食人家; 1 Lao Jie; dishes Y2-15; ⏰ lunch & dinner) This restaurant stands at the entrance to Lao Jie and is one of the most popular places to eat in town. You can choose from a variety of inexpensive meat and veggie dishes on display, and have them cooked fresh to order.

There are numerous cheap restaurants and food stalls around the train station and down Qianyuan Beilu.

Shopping

Running a block in from the river, **Lao Jie** (老街; Old Street; ⏰ 7.30am-10.30pm) is a souvenir street lined with wooden shops and Ming-style buildings. Besides the usual trinkets, you can also buy goods similar to those in the Shànghǎi antique markets – prices may be lower here, especially for antique furniture.

Getting There & Away
AIR

There are flights from Túnxī to Běijīng (Y990, twice weekly), Guǎngzhōu (Y880, daily), Shànghǎi (Y460, daily), Hong Kong (Y1880, twice weekly) and less frequent flights to other cities. Flights to Héféi have been temporarily suspended.

CAAC (中国民航; Zhōngguó Mínháng; ☎ 953 4111) is on Huangshan Lu beside the Huangshan International Hotel. You can book airline tickets at outlets near the train station.

BUS
The long-distance bus station is 400m east of the train station. Buses run between Túnxī and Tāngkǒu (Y13, 1½ hours). Buses also go to Shànghǎi (Y83, nine hours), Hángzhōu (Y55, six hours), Héféi (Y65, six hours) and Jǐngdézhèn (Y28, four hours).

TRAIN
Trains from Běijīng (Y323, 21 hours), Shànghǎi (Y97, 11½ hours) and Nánjīng (Y54, seven hours) stop at Túnxī. Some trains heading south also stop here, such as to Xiàmén (Y217, 32 hours) and Jǐngdézhèn (Y25, 3½ hours). For better connections to southern destinations, first go to Yīngtán (Y51, five hours) in Jiāngxī and change trains there. Hotels will usually book train tickets for a service charge.

Getting Around
The 5km taxi ride to the airport will cost about Y25. To get around, it's cheapest to catch a pedicab but make sure to negotiate the price first.

JIŬHUÁ SHĀN 九华山
☎ 0566
With 99 peaks, Jiǔhuá Shān (Nine Brilliant Mountains) is one of China's four sacred Buddhist mountains (the others are Pǔtuóshān in Zhèjiāng, Éméi Shān in Sìchuān and Wǔtái Shān in Shānxī). Third-century Taoist monks built thatched temples at Jiǔhuá Shān, but with the rise of Buddhism, stone monasteries gradually replaced them.

Jiǔhuá Shān owes its importance to Kim Kiao Kak (Jīn Qiáojué), a Korean Buddhist disciple who arrived in China in AD 720 and founded a worshipping place for Ksitigarbha, the guardian of the earth. Pilgrims flock to Jiǔhuá Shān for the annual festivities held on the anniversary of Kim's death, which falls on the 30th day of the seventh lunar month. The mountain apparently received its name after the poet Li Bai was so moved by seeing nine peaks that he wrote that they help hold the world and heaven together.

In its heyday, during the Tang dynasty, as many as 3000 monks and nuns, living in more than 150 monasteries, worshipped at Jiǔhuá Shān. Today only 70 temples and monasteries remain, but a palpable feeling of spirituality still permeates the place. Jiǔhuá Shān is also an important place for believers to come and bless the souls of the recently deceased to ensure them a passage to Buddhist heaven.

Orientation & Information
Jiǔhuá is a village that lies 600m above sea level, about halfway up the mountain (or, as the locals say, at roughly navel height in a giant Buddha's potbelly). The bus stops below the main gate where you pay an entrance fee for the mountains (Y70 between March and November; Y60 the rest of the year).

From here the narrow main street heads south up past restaurants, souvenir stalls and hotels, then turns east towards temples.

Located near a school field, **China Travel Service** (CTS; 中国旅行社; Zhōngguó Lǚxíngshè; ☎ 501 1588; 135 Beimai Xintun Lu) offers tours for Y200 per day, though guides are not really necessary. The **Bank of China** (中国银行; Zhōngguó Yínháng; 65 Huachen Lu) changes traveller's cheques.

Sights & Activities
Hiking up the ridge behind **Zhiyuan Temple** (祇园寺; Zhíyuán Sì), at the bottom of Jiuhua Jie, leads you to the **Longevity Palace** (百岁宫; Bǎisuì Gōng; admission Y5). This is an active temple built in 1630 to consecrate the Buddhist monk Wu Xia, whose shrunken, embalmed body is on display. If you don't feel like hiking, take the funicular tram (up Y28, down Y18) to the ridge.

From the top, walk south along the ridge until you reach two paths; a western one that leads to town, or an eastern one that dips into a pleasant valley and continues to **Tiantai Zheng Peak** (天台正顶; Tiāntái Zhèng Dǐng). The walk to the peak takes about four hours, and small temples, nunneries and restaurants line the path along the way.

From the valley, a cable car (up Y30, down Y20) whisks passengers to the peak.

Shuttle buses take people back to Jiǔhuá village from here for Y5. Chinese-language maps that outline the mountain paths are available. Exploring the village, talking to the monks and listening to their soothing chanting can be very relaxing.

Sleeping & Eating

Zhiyuan Temple (执园寺; Zhíyuán Sì; ☎ 501 1281; dm Y10-20) This beautiful palace-style monastery sits at the bottom of the village. Its beds range from basic to more comfortable. You may have difficulty staying here if you don't speak Chinese.

Nányuàn Lǚguǎn (南院陆旅馆; ☎ 501 1122; 26 Furong Lu; r with/without bathroom Y150/50) This friendly, family-run hotel is a great place to stay if it's not full. Meals are also served. It's up a small trail at the south end of the main street.

On the path to Tiantai Zheng Peak it's possible to stay in the small village at the bottom of the valley near the cable car.

Fènghuángsōng Mǐnyuán Shānzhuāng (凤凰松山庄; ☎ 501 1146; d without bathroom Y80, d & tr with bathroom Y200) This very small, clean, family-run hotel is the most luxurious accommodation available.

Jiǔhuá village has numerous restaurants.

Gōngxiāo Dàjiǔdiàn (公销大酒店; 24 Furong Lu; mains Y10-40; ☺ breakfast, lunch & dinner) Located away from the main street, this unpretentious place serves good meals. It also has more expensive 'speciality' dishes, like *tiāntái shuāngdōng* (bamboo shoots and mushrooms, Y35). It's about 50m west down the first lane off the main street south of Nanyuan Luguan.

Getting There & Away

Two buses a day go to Jiǔhuá Shān from Tāngkǒu via Qīngyáng (Y40, four hours) following the road along Taiping Lake. Buses also depart for Shànghǎi (Y80, eight hours), Nánjīng (Y54, four hours), Wúhú (Y35, three hours) and Guìchí (Y9, one hour).

Shànghǎi 上海

SHANGHAI

HIGHLIGHTS

■ Recapture the past on the **Bund** (p273), the single most evocative symbol of the 'Paris of the East'

■ Get lost on the leafy, villa-lined backstreets of the historic former **French concession** (p278)

■ Admire the gardens and savour snack food at **Yuyuan Bazaar** (p279), tacky but fun

■ Shop for bargain-priced silk at **Dongjiadu Cloth Market**, clothes at **Xiangyang Lu market** (p299) and antiques at **Dongtai Lu market** (p300)

■ Savour world-class food and then hit the dance floor at some of Asia's most stylish and cutting-edge **restaurants** (p291) and **clubs** (p297)

The French Concession ★   ★ The Bund
Dongtai Lu ★   ★ Yuyuan Bazaar
Market   ★ Dongjiadu Cloth
   Market

■ AREA CODE: ☎ 021   ■ POP: 13.2 MIL   ■ www.thatsshanghai.com

Whore of the Orient, Paris of the East; city of quick riches, ill-gotten gains and fortunes lost on the tumble of dice; the domain of adventurers, swindlers, gamblers, drug runners, tycoons, missionaries, gangsters and backstreet pimps; the city that plots revolution and dances as the revolution shoots its way into town – Shànghǎi was a dark memory during the long years of forgetting that the Communists visited upon their new China, when the city put away its dancing shoes and the masses shuffled instead to the dour strains of Marxist-Leninism and the wail of the factory siren.

Today China's largest city has reawakened and is busy snapping the dust off its cummerbund. Shànghǎi typifies the huge disparities of modern China – monumental building projects push skywards, glinting department stores swing open their doors to the stylish elite; while child beggars, prostitutes and the impoverished congregate among the champagne corks and burst balloons of the night before. History is returning to haunt Shànghǎi and, at the same time, put it squarely back on the map.

For the visitor, Shànghǎi can't match the epic history of Běijīng or Xī'ān's grander sights but there's no better place to catch the pace and contradictions of modern China.

As the pulse of this metropolis quickens, its steps are firmer, and at this point we make an apology. A lot of what you read in this guide will have changed by the time you have the book in your hands. The booming metropolis of Shànghǎi is evolving at a pace so unmatched by any other Chinese city that even the morning ritual of flinging open one's hotel curtains reveals new facets to the skyline and new sounds on the streets

The best times to visit Shànghǎi are spring and autumn. In winter, temperatures can drop well below freezing and there is often a blanket of drizzle. Summers are hot and humid with temperatures as high as 40°C.

HISTORY

As anyone who wanders along the Bund or through the backstreets of the former French concession can see, Shànghǎi (the name means 'by the sea') is a Western invention. As the gateway to the Yangzi River (Cháng Jiāng), it was an ideal trading port. When the British opened their first concession in 1842, after the first Opium War, it was little more than a small town supported by fishing and weaving. The British changed all that.

The French followed in 1847, an International Settlement was established in 1863 and the Japanese arrived in 1895 – the city was parcelled up into autonomous settlements, immune from Chinese law. By 1853 Shànghǎi had overtaken all other Chinese ports. By the 1930s the city had 60,000 for-

eign residents and was the busiest international port in Asia.

Built on the trade of opium, silk and tea, the city also lured the world's great houses of finance, who erected grand palaces of plenty. One of the most famous traders was Jardine Matheson & Company. In 1848 Jardine's purchased the first land offered for sale to foreigners in Shànghǎi and grew into one of the great *hongs* (literally a business firm); today it owns just about half of Hong Kong.

Shànghǎi also became a byword for exploitation and vice; its countless opium dens, gambling joints and brothels managed by gangs were at the heart of Shànghǎi life. Guarding it all were the American, French and Italian marines, British Tommies and Japanese bluejackets.

After Chiang Kaishek's coup against the Communists in 1927, the Kuomintang cooperated with the foreign police and the Shànghăi gangs, and with Chinese and foreign factory owners, to suppress labour unrest. Exploited in workhouse conditions, crippled by hunger and poverty, sold into slavery, excluded from the high life and the parks created by the foreigners, the poor of Shànghăi had a voracious appetite for radical opinion. The Chinese Communist Party (CCP) was formed here in 1921 and, after numerous setbacks, 'liberated' the city in 1949.

The communists eradicated the slums, rehabilitated the city's hundreds of thousands of opium addicts, and eliminated child and slave labour. These were staggering achievements. Later, during the Cultural Revolution, the city was the power base of the so-called Gang of Four (see p47).

Shànghăi's long malaise came to an abrupt end in 1990, with the announcement of plans to develop Pǔdōng, on the eastern side of the Huangpu River. Shànghăi's goal is to become a major financial centre along with its emerging economic strength. Lùjiāzǔi, the area that faces off the Bund on the Pǔdōng side of the Huangpu, has blossomed as a modern high-rise counterpoint to the austere, old-world structures on the Bund.

The city's political influence now ripples through the whole of the party apparatus to the top: former president Jiang Zemin is Shànghăi's ex-party chief and premier Zhu Rongji and minister Wu Bangguo also hail from the municipality. Furthermore, Hong Kong's chief executive, Tung Chee-hwa, is a Shànghăi man.

Shànghăi's burgeoning economy, its leadership and its intrinsic self-confidence have put it miles ahead of other cities in China. Nothing would satisfy the central government more than for Shànghăi to replace Hong Kong as China's frontier on the future, swinging the spotlight of attention from the ex-colony onto a home-grown success story.

Until recently, Shànghăi was a vast architectural museum, housing an inheritance of foreign trophies. While state-protected

---

SHÀNGHĂI IN...

Two Days

Give yourself a couple of hours to stroll the **Bund**, preferably at night or early morning. For more of a perspective, get sweeping views of the Bund from the Pǔdōng side (take the tourist tunnel or the metro) and then visit the **Jinmao Tower**. For something special, eat at **M on the Bund** if on the Bund, or the **Grand Hyatt** if in Pǔdōng (reservations advised at both).

To fill out the first day take the metro to the **Shanghai Museum**, one of China's finest, which deserves the best part of half a day.

The other great attraction of Shànghăi is the old town, incorporating **Yuyuan Gardens** and the surrounding teahouses and bazaar, so take a taxi here for your second day. If you don't like crowds then give this a miss at the weekends. After a visit to Yuyuan Gardens add on a walk to **Dongtai Lu Antique Market** for some shopping and then take lunch (or dinner) at one of **Xīntiāndì**'s trendy restaurants.

Try to save time for one big night out in Shànghăi to experience the modern side of the city. Take in the **acrobats** or a performance at the **Grand Theatre**, try one of the excellent restaurants and then take your pick of the bars and clubs.

Four Days

With more time, savour a slower-paced Shànghăi and fit in a walk through the faded 1930s architecture of the **French concession** backstreets, where Shànghăi still shows its old magic.

You'll also have time to hop aboard a **boat cruise** for views of the Bund. From the Bund, stroll down China's most famous shopping street, **Nanjing Donglu**, which links the Bund with the Shanghai Museum.

Finally, if you have time after all the shopping, take a half-day trip out to Shēshān, or a day trip to **Zhōuzhuāng** or **Tónglǐ** in neighbouring Jiāngsū province.

The Bund (p273) with Pudong New Area
(p283) in the background (Shànghǎi)

Yuyuan Bazaar (p300),
Shànghǎi

The personality cult surrounding Chairman Mao (p45) is still thriving in China

The lights of Nanjing Lu (p277), Shànghǎi

SHANGHAI TRANSPORT NETWORK

Legend:
- Metro Lines 1 & 2
- Light Rail/Pearl Line
- Railway Line
- Planned Metro Lines

- Ⓜ Metro Station
- Lightrail Station
- Train Station

Under Construction

To Pudong International Airport

Zhangjiang High-Tech Zone 张江高科站
Maglev Terminal 上海磁浮列车站
Longyang Rd 龙阳路站
Century Park 世纪公园站
Shanghai Science and Technology Museum 上海科技馆站
Dongchang Rd 东昌路站
Dongfang Rd 东方路站
Lujiazui 陆家嘴站
Dongchang Rd 东昌路站
Renmin Square 人民广场站
Middle Henan Rd 河南中路站
Henan Rd 河南中路站

Jiangwan Town 江湾镇站
East Wenshui Rd 汶水东路站
Chifeng Rd 赤峰路站
Hongkou Stadium 虹口足球场站
East Baoxing Rd 东宝兴路站
Baoshan Rd 宝山路站

Wenshui Rd 汶水路站
Shanghai Circus World 上海马戏城站
Yanchang Rd 延长路站
North Zhongshan Rd 中山北路站
Zhongtan Rd 中潭路站
Shanghai Train Station 上海火车站
Hanzhong Rd 汉中路站
Xinzha Rd 新闸路站
Shimen No1 Rd 石门一路站
South Shaanxi Rd 陕西南路站
South Huangpi Rd 黄陂南路站

Zhenping Rd 镇坪路站
Caoyang Rd 曹杨路站
Jinshajiang Rd 金沙江路站
Jiangsu Rd 江苏路站
Jing'an Temple 静安寺站
Changshu Rd 常熟路站
Hengshan Rd 衡山路站
Xujiahui 徐家汇站
Shanghai Stadium 上海体育馆站
Longcao Rd 龙漕路站

Shanghai West Train Station

Zhongshan Park 中山公园站
West Yan'an Rd 延安西路站
Yishan Rd 宜山路站
Caoxi Rd 漕溪路站
Shilong Rd 石龙路站

Gubei Rd 古北路站
Shuicheng Rd 水城路站
Hongqiao Rd 虹桥路站
Caobao Rd 漕宝路站
Shanghai South Train Station 上海南站
Jinjiang Amusement Park 锦江乐园站
Lianhua Rd 莲花路站
Waihuan Rd 外环路站
Xinzhuang 莘庄站

Beixinjing 北新泾站
Xiehe Rd 协和路站
Hongqiao Airport 虹桥机场站

Huangpu River
Suzhou Creek (Wusong River)

landmark buildings on the Bund and else-where are safe from the ball-and-chain, in other parts of town huge chunks of history have given way to department stores and office blocks.

Shànghăi is shackled to a past it is both suspicious and proud of, and nobody can predict what the city will look like two decades from now. But as the Chinese saying goes, *jiùde bùqù, xīnde bùlái* (if the old doesn't go, the new won't come).

ORIENTATION

Shànghăi municipality covers a substantial area, but the city proper is a more modest size. Broadly, central Shànghăi is divided into two areas: Pŭdōng (east of the Huangpu River) and Pŭxī (west of the Huangpu River). The First Ring Rd does a long elliptical loop around the city centre proper.

For visitors, the historical attractions of Shànghăi are in Pŭxī. Here you will find the Bund, the shopping streets, the former foreign concessions, hotels, restaurants, sights and nightclubs.

The area around the Bund is the historical heart of the former International Settlement. From here Nanjing Donglu, China's busiest shopping street, runs west to Renmín Square, the cultural centre of town, home to the Shanghai Museum and Grand Theatre.

South of Yan'an Lu, and squeezed north of the Chinese city, is the former French concession. The Chinese old town, to the southeast, is a maze of narrow lanes, lined with closely packed houses and drying laundry. The Yuyuan Gardens are in this part of town.

On the northern border of the French concession is Nanjing Xilu, one of Shànghăi's glitziest streets, lined with top-end shopping centres, hotels and foreign offices.

In the central district (around Nanjing Lu) the provincial names run north–south, and the city names run east–west. Some roads use compass points, such as Sichuan Nanlu (Sichuan South Rd) and Sichuan Beilu (Sichuan North Rd). Encircling Shànghăi proper, Zhongshan Lu is split by sectors, such as Zhongshan Dong Erlu and Zhongshan Dong Yilu, which mean Zhongshan East 2nd Rd and Zhongshan East 1st Rd.

Maps

English maps of Shànghăi are available at the Foreign Languages Bookstore (see below), major hotel bookshops and occasionally from street hawkers (most of the latter are Chinese-only).

The bilingual *Shanghai Tourist Map*, produced by the Shanghai Municipal Tourism Administration, is free at hotels and Tourist Information Centres (p273).

INFORMATION
Bookshops

Most hotels, including the Peace Hotel, sell English-language books on Shànghăi. Fuzhou Lu has traditionally been the bookshop street of Shànghăi and is worth a stroll.

Foreign Languages Bookstore (Wàiyŭ Shūdiàn; Map pp274–5; ☎ 6322 3200; 390 Fuzhou Lu; metro Henan Zhonglu; ⏰ 9.30am-6pm, until 7pm Fri & Sat) The 1st floor has a good range of postcards, maps and English-language books on Shànghăi. The 4th floor (Shanghai Book Traders) has a wide range of imported books and novels, including Lonely Planet guides.

Old China Hand Reading Room (Hànyuán Shūwū; Map pp280–1; ☎ 6473 2526; 27 Shaoxing Lu) Run by local photographer Deke Erh. Besides his and Tess Johnston's excellent series of books on Western architecture in Shànghăi, the bookshop-cum-café has a whole range of books on art, architecture and culture.

TOP FIVE BOOKS ON SHÀNGHĂI

- *Shanghai* by Harriet Sergeant. A recommended reconstruction of Shànghăi's swinging history.

- *Shanghai: The Rise and Fall of a Decadent City* by Stella Dong. Another well-researched history of the good-old bad-old days.

- *In Search of Old Shanghai* by Pan Ling. An easy read into the characters of Shànghăi's murky past.

- *New Shanghai: The Rocky Rebirth of China's Legendary City* by Pamela Yatsko. Bring yourself up to date with this portrait of the new Shànghăi.

- *Candy* by Mian Mian. Hip modern novel from a darling of the city's social set, proving that sex, suicide and drug addiction aren't just limited to Shànghăi's past.

SHANGHAI

0 |——————| 2 km
0 |——————| 1 mile

To Jiangwan Zhen (Terminal) (1km)

Fudan University

Wenshui Donglu 汶水东路

Chifeng Lu 赤峰路站

Jiangwan Lu

Tongji University 同济大学

Dalian Xilu

Hongkou Stadium 虹口足球场站

Lu Xun Park

Hongkou

Zhabei

Yangpu

Planned Metro Line 8

East Baoxing Lu 东宝兴路站

Heping Park

Planned Metro Line 4

16

Yangpu Bridge

Luoshan Lu

See Huangpu & Jing'an Map pp274–6

18

12

17

Yangshupu Lu

5 33

34

Huangpu River

Pearl Park 浦东公园

Liujiazui Park 陆家嘴公园

Pudong Dadao

Yangpu

6   13

9   22

Huangpu

28

8

Dongchang Lu

Liujiazui Lu 陆家嘴

19

Lujiazui Lu

Century Ave

Dongfang Lu 东方路

Century Square

Riverside Park

Pudong New Area

36

32

Dongfang Lu (Shiji Dadao)

25

Shanghai Science and Technology Museum

Century Park 世纪公园

Luwan

Tianlin Lu

Dongjiadu Lu

31

Nanshi

27

Pujian Lu

Century Park 世纪公园

Nanpu Bridge

Zhongshan Nanlu

Longyang Lu 龙阳路

Longyang Lu

Maglev Terminal 上海磁浮列车

Lupu Bridge

Proposed Site of Expo 2010

Planned Hua Qiao (Flower Bridge)

Huangpu River

ENTERTAINMENT   pp297–8
Er Ding Mu Bar 二丁目酒吧   24   E2
Oriental Arts Centre 东方艺术中心   25   H3

SHOPPING   pp298–300
Carrefour 家乐福   26   B5
Dongjiadu Cloth Market
董家渡轻纺面料市场   27   F4
Superbrand Mall 正大广场   28   F3

TRANSPORT   pp302–4
Asiana   29   B4
Bus to Pudong Airport
至浦东飞机场的公共汽车   30   D5
Buses to the Bund   31   F4
Ferry Dock 轮渡站   32   F3
Ferry Offices   33   F2
International Passenger Terminal
国际客运码头   34   F2
Shanghai Sightseeing Bus Centre
上海旅游集散中心   35   D5
Shiliupu Wharf 十六铺   36   F3
Xujiahui Bus Station
徐家汇客运站   37   C5

SLEEPING   pp287–91
Changyang Hotel 长阳饭店   16   G2
Daming Fountain Garden Hotel
大名星苑酒店
E-Best Hotel 上海一百假日酒店   18   F2
Grand Hyatt
上海金茂凯悦大酒店   19   F3
Huating Gesthouse 华亭宾馆   20   C5
Huating Hotel 华亭宾馆   (see 20)

EATING   pp291–5
1221   21   C4
Lulu Restaurant 鹭鹭酒家   22   F3
Zentral 膳趣   23   E4

DRINKING   pp295–7
Cloud 9   (see 19)

Shanghai Book City (Shànghǎi Shūchéng; Map pp274-5; 465 Fuzhou Lu; 🕙 9.30am-6.30pm Mon-Thu, until 9pm Fri-Sun) Massive local bookshop with foreign-language books on the 7th floor.

Shanghai Museum (Shànghǎi Bówùguǎn; Map pp274-5; 201 Renmin Dadao; metro Renmin Square) Excellent range of books on Chinese art, architecture, ceramics and calligraphy, plus a wide selection of cards and slides.

Cultural Centres

Alliance Française (Fǎyǔ Péixùn Zhōngxīn; Map pp274-5; 🕾 6357 5388; www.alliancefrancaise.org.cn; 5th fl, 297 Wusong Lu) French films every Friday at 6.30pm, plus TV5, a large French library and the occasional exhibition.

British Council (Yīngguó Wénhuà Jiāoyǔchù; Map pp274-5; 🕾 6391 2626; www.britishcouncil.org.cn; Pidemco Tower, 318 Fuzhou Lu; metro Henan Zhonglu; 🕙 8.30am-noon & 1.30-5pm Mon-Fri) Recent British newspapers and music magazines like *Q* and *NME*.

Emergency & Visas

English-speaking police (🕾 6357 6666)

Public Security Bureau (PSB; Gōngānjú; Map pp274-5; 🕾 6357 7925; 333 Wusong Lu, near cnr Kunshan Lu; 🕙 9-11.30am & 1.30-4.30pm Mon-Sat) Handles visas and registrations; 30-day visa extensions cost around Y160.

Internet Access

Shànghǎi has many Internet cafés but there's a frequent turnover of locales. You'll need your passport for ID in most places.

China Telecom (Zhōngguó Diànxìn; Map pp274-5; 30 Nanjing Donglu; per min/hr Y0.3/10; 🕙 7am-10.30pm)

E100 Internet Bar (Map pp274-5; 9th fl, No 1 Department Store, 830 Nanjing Donglu; per hr Y3; 🕙 9.30am-midnight)

Shanghai Library (Shànghǎi Túshūguǎn; Map pp280-1; 🕾 6445 5555; 1555 Huaihai Zhonglu; ground-fl terminals per hr Y4; 🕙 9am-8.30pm)

Internet Resources

http://shanghai.asiaxpat.com Aimed at expats; ask an expert if you have a specific query.

www.8days.sh The latest player on the city scene, brought to you by veterans of *That's Shanghai*

www.cityweekend.com.cn Another good listings website with searchable database of articles.

www.expatsh.com A must-see if you are thinking of relocating to Shànghǎi, though some links don't work.

www.sh.com Guide to tourist attractions but dated on entertainment.

www.shanghai-ed.com Everything from what's on to historical essays, though parts are a bit outdated.

www.shanghaiguide.com Good guide to living in Shànghǎi, with a strong focus on tourism.

www.talesofoldchina.com Lots of reading on Old Shanghai, with the text of hard-to-find books online.

www.thatsshanghai.com Always on top of what's happening in Shànghǎi entertainment.

www.shanghaiexpat.com Another sight aimed at foreign residents.

Media

The first thing to do when you land in town is to head to a top-end hotel and swipe a free copy of the monthly *That's Shanghai*, followed swiftly by a copy of *City Weekend*, *Shanghai Talk*, or the new weekly magazine *8days*. These offer an instant plug into what's on in town, from art exhibitions and club nights to restaurant openings. The *That's Shanghai* team also produce separate guides (Y50 each) to the city's restaurants, bars, fitness and shopping scenes.

A small range of foreign newspapers and magazines is available from the larger tourist hotels and the Foreign Languages Bookstore (p269). You can read foreign magazines and newspapers at the Shanghai Library (bring your passport; left).

The two local government-produced English newspapers are the *Shanghai Star* and *Shanghai Daily*, which offer some local and international news.

Medical Services

Shànghǎi is credited with the best medical facilities and most advanced medical knowledge in China.

Huashan Hospital (Huáshān Yīyuàn; Map pp280-1; 🕾 6248 9999 ext 1921; 12 Wulumuqi Zhonglu) Hospital treatment and out-patient consultations are available at the 19th-floor foreigners' clinic, which has a Hong Kong joint-venture section.

New Pioneer International Medical Centre (NPIMC; Xīnfēng Yīliáo Zhōngxīn; Map pp280-1; 🕾 6469 3898; fax 6469 3897; 2nd fl, Geru Bldg, 910 Hengshan Lu, just north of Xújiāhuì; 🕙 24hr) Comprehensive private medical care.

Shanghai First People's Hospital (Dìyī Rénmín Yīyuàn; Map pp274-5; 🕾 6306 9480; 585 Jiulong Lu, northeast Shànghǎi) Also known as the International Medical Care Centre (IMCC).

World Link (Ruìxīn Guójì Yīliáo Zhōngxīn; Map pp274-5; 🕾 6279 7688; www.worldlink-shanghai.com; Suite 203, Shanghai Centre, 1376 Nanjing Xilu; 🕙 9am-7pm Mon-Fri, 9am-4pm Sat, 9am-3pm Sun) Private medical care by expat doctors and dentists and specialists. For nonmembers, expect a doctor's consultation fee of US$70 and an ambulance charge of US$100.

World Link Hongqiao clinic (Map pp270-1; ☎ 6405 5788; fax 6405 3587; Unit 30, Mandarine City, 788 Hongxu Lu; ☻ 9am-5pm Mon-Fri) Offers dental work.

Money
Almost every hotel has money-changing counters. Most tourist hotels, restaurants, banks and Friendship Stores accept major credit cards. ATMs at various branches of the Bank of China and the Industrial and Commercial Bank of China (ICBC) accept most major cards.

Bank of China (Zhōngguó Yínháng; Map pp274-5; The Bund; ☻ 9am-noon & 1.30-4.30pm Mon-Fri, 9am-noon Sat) Right next to the Peace Hotel. Tends to get crowded, but is better organised than Chinese banks elsewhere around the country (it's worth a peek for its grand interior). Take a ticket and wait for your number. For credit card advances head to the furthest hall (counter No 2).

Citibank (Huāqí Yínháng; Map pp274-5; The Bund) Useful ATM open 24 hours.

Hong Kong & Shanghai Bank (HSBC; Huìfēng Yínháng) Has ATMs in the Shanghai Centre on Nanjing Xilu (Map pp274-5), at Pudong Airport arrivals hall and at 15 Zhongshan Dong Yilu on the Bund (Map pp274-5).

Post
Larger tourist hotels have post offices where you can mail letters and small packages, and this is by far the most convenient option.

DHL (☎ 6536 2900, 800-810 8000) Shanghai Central Plaza (Map pp280-1; 381 Huaihai Zhonglu) Shanghai Centre (Map pp274-5; 1376 Nanjing Xilu)

FedEx (☎ 6237 5134)

International Post Office (Guójì Yóujú; Map pp274-5; cnr Sichuan Beilu & Suzhou Beilu, 2nd fl; ☻ 8.30am-11am & 1-4.30pm) The section for international parcels is in the same building around the corner; poste restante is at counter No 7.

UPS (Map pp280-1; ☎ 6391 5555; room 1318-38, Shanghai Central Plaza, 381 Huaihai Zhonglu)

Telephone
IP cards are the cheapest way to call internationally (Y2.4 to the US) but may not work with hotel phones.

China Mobile (Zhōngguó Yídòng Tōngxìn; Map pp274-5; 21 Yuanmingyuan Lu) Head here for cell phone queries.

China Telecom (Zhōngguó Diànxìn; Map pp274-5; ☻ 7am-10.30pm) Branch office next to the Peace Hotel on Nanjing Donglu.

Tourist Information
Shànghăi operates several Tourist Information and Service Centres located near major tourist sights, the most useful of which is

at 561 Nanjing Donglu (Map pp274-5; ☎ 5353 1117). The level of service and language ability among the staff here tends to vary, but maps and metro maps are available in a wide array of languages, including English, Japanese, German and French. There's another **branch** (Map pp274-5; ☎ 6355 5032; 149 Jiujiaochang Lu) near the Temple of the Town Gods.

The international arrivals hall of Hongqiao Airport has a tourist information booth with staff who give out maps and are very helpful. There was no comprehensive tourist information booth at Pudong International Airport at the time of writing but plans were afoot to install one.

Tourist Hotline (☎ 6252 0000, 6426 5555) Useful English-language service.

Travel Agencies
See p300 for details on train and ferry ticket agencies and airline offices.

China International Travel Service (CITS; Zhōngguó Guójì Lǚxíngshè; Map pp274-5; ☎ 6323 8770; 1st fl, Guangming Bldg, 2 Jinling Donglu) Can book air and train tickets if the staff can be bothered. There's another CITS office on Nanjing Donglu (Map pp274-5) near the Peace Hotel, primarily for booking airline tickets.

Spring International Travel Service (Chūnqiū Guójì Lǚxíngshè; Map pp274-5; ☎ 6351 6666; www.china-sss .com; 347 Xizang Zhonglu) Centrally located, IATA-bonded and good for air tickets.

STA (Map pp280-1; ☎ 6445 5396; www.statravel.com .cn; 2 Hengshan Lu; ☻ 9am-5pm Mon-Sat) Branch of the student travel organisation, operated by Shanghai China Youth Travel Service (SCYTS). Sells train and air tickets, and can issue ISIC cards.

SIGHTS
The Bund & Nanjing Donglu
Map pp274-5

The area around the Bund is the tourist centre of Shànghăi and the city's most famous mile. Head here first.

THE BUND 外滩
The Bund (Wàitān) is an Anglo-Indian term for the embankment of a muddy waterfront. The term is apt: mud bedevils Shànghăi. Between 1920 (when the problem was first noticed) and 1965, the city sank several metres. Water was pumped back into the ground, but the Venetian threat remains. Concrete rafts are used as foundations for high-rises in this spongy mass.

0 _____ 1 km
0 _____ 0.5 miles

E **F** **G** **H** 18

Hurren Lu
Chongqing Lu
102
Baoshan Lu 宝山路站
Baoshan Lu 天目路
Haining Lu
Wujing Lu
Wusong Lu 吴淞路
Jiulong Lu

Tianmu Donglu 天目东路
Shanxi Beilu
Anqing Lu
Hailing Lu
Sichuan Beilu 四川北路
Zhapu Lu
Kunshan Lu 昆山路
14

1

Huaxing Lu
Zhijiang Beilu
新建路
Kangle Lu
Fujian Beilu
Tangqu Lu
Henan Beilu 河南北路
Wuchang Lu
71

Xinjiang Lu 新疆路
Tiantong Lu
46
Changzhi Lu
35
51
2

Xizang Beilu 西藏北路
Qufu Lu
Tiantong Lu
13
16
Garden Bridge

Jinyuan Lu
Suzhou Beilu
Yuanmingyuan Lu
26
23
Huangpu Park 黄浦公园

Xiamen Lu
Suzhou Nanlu
Zhou Creek
(Wusong River)
105
84
96 Pedestrian Tunnel

Xinzha Lu 新闸路
Beijing Donglu 北京东路
Shanxi Nanlu
Tianjin Lu
6 Dianchi Lu 3
7 48
92
Huangpu River

Xinzha Lu 新闸路
Fujian Zhonglu 福建中路
Ningbo Lu
Henan Zhonglu
Henan Zhonglu 河南中路
86
72
49
Zhongshan
12
27
Tai'an Donglu Tunnel

Beijing Xilu 北京西路
Fengyang Lu
Guizhou Lu
Zhejiang Zhonglu
Hankou Lu
89
60
44
36
69
64
33

Tangyang Lu
95
47
Nanjing 南京西路
Donglu
19
52
37
87
20
31
40
10 5
17
4
Fuzhou Lu
Jiujiang Lu
Henan Zhonglu 福州路
91
Guangdong Lu
55
8
61
99
24
100

Renmin Park 人民公园
Renmin Square
77
80
M
Renmin Square 人民广场
Renmin (People's) Square 人民广场
42
Yan'an Donglu 延安东路
Yunnan Lu
Ninghai Lu
Jinling Donglu
Renmin Lu 人民路

43
28
79
Huangpi Beilu
29
31
75
70
107
78
Fuyou Lu
34
66
73
32

Sanjiao Park
Wusheng Lu
Jinling Zhonglu
Huaihai Donglu 淮海东路
Dajing Lu
21
Zhonglu
85
Zhoujin Lu
65

98
81
Shouning Lu
Qinglian Jie
Old Town
5

Huangpi Lu 黄陂南路
68 Huaihai Park 淮海公园
67
83
Dongtai Lu
Jinjia Fang
6

Xing'an Lu
Taicang Lu
Chongde Lu
Hubin Lu
Henan Nanlu 河南南路
Renmin Lu 人民路
Waigaoqiao Lu

SHÀNGHÃI

Its muddy predicament aside, the Bund is symbolic of Shànghăi. To the Europeans, it was Shànghăi's Wall Street, a place of feverish trading, of fortunes made and lost. Constant throngs of Chinese and foreign tourists pad past the porticoes of the Bund's grand edifices with maps in hand. The buildings themselves loom serenely; a vagabond assortment of neoclassical 1930s downtown New York styles and monumental antiquity thrown in for good measure.

There are plenty of things to see and do around the Bund: take a boat trip on the Huangpu (see p284), enjoy the views of Pŭdōng, visit the Bund Historical Museum (p285) or shop at the Friendship Store (p299). These delights are easily combined with an up-close visit to Pŭdōng via the Bund Sightseeing Tunnel (p283) or metro from Nanjing Donglu.

The best thing to do is simply stroll and admire the bones of the past. See the walking tour (p285) for a rundown of the buildings on the Bund. The Bund is particularly beautiful at night.

The Bund today is undergoing yet another transformation. The ambitious North Bund Development project is set to revamp the area north of Dianchi Lu to Suzhou Creek (Wusong River) over the next few years.

On the south end of the Bund, **Three on the Bund** (Wàitān Sānhào; www.threeonthebund.com) is a new upscale retail centre that mixes Armani and Evian with the Shanghai Gallery of Art (admission free), plus an impressive 3rd-floor gallery space, and several top-end bars and restaurants (see p294). Expect more of the same in 2005 at No 18 the Bund, which was under renovation at the time of writing.

NANJING DONGLU 南京东路

Nanjing Donglu, from the Peace to the Park Hotels, has long been China's golden mile, though its glamour has slipped a few notches in the last 15 years. Hoping to regain its former glory, the city began a massive renovation project in 1999, turning Nanjing Lu into a pedestrian-only shopping extravaganza from Xizang Lu to Henan Lu. Today it's a favourite of Chinese shoppers (foreigners generally prefer Huaihai Lu) and is worth a stroll to or from the Bund.

Two of the most famous department stores are **No 1 Provisions Store** (Dìyī Shípǐn Shāngdiàn;

720 Nanjing Donglu), built as the Sun Sun store in 1926, and **No 1 Department Store** (Dìyī Bǎihuò Shāngdiàn; 800 Nanjing Donglu), which opened in 1936 as the Sun Company and was for decades China's largest and most famous department store (see also p299).

At the east end of Renmin Park the **Park Hotel** is worth checking out for its brooding Art-Deco design. It was built as a bank in 1934 and was the tallest building in the Far East at the time.

Renmin Square 人民广场   Map pp274–5

Nanjing Donglu becomes Nanjing Xilu at **Renmin Park** (Rénmín Gōngyuán; admission Y2). The park and the adjacent Renmin (People's) Square were once the site of the Shanghai Racecourse, now occupied by the Shanghai Museum, the Shanghai Grand Theatre, the Shanghai Urban Planning Exhibition Hall and the drab municipal government building. If Shànghăi has a city centre, this is it.

SHANGHAI MUSEUM 上海博物馆

The stunning **Shanghai Museum** (Shànghăi Bówùguǎn; ☎ 6372 3500; 201 Renmin Dadao; adult/child or student Y20/5; ☑ 9am-5pm Sun-Fri, 9am-8pm Sat) was built in 1994 at a cost of Y570 million and is symbolic of the many changes that are afoot in China. Gone are those airy corridors, dry exhibits, yawning security guards and stale air, replaced by state-of-the-art lighting and spacious halls. Designed to recall the shape of an ancient Chinese *dǐng* vessel, this architectural statement is home to one of the most impressive collections of art in China, making it a must-see.

Take your pick from the galleries that house some fantastic specimens – from the archaic green patina of the Ancient Chinese Bronze Gallery through to the silent solemnity of the Chinese Sculpture Gallery,

---

NO DOGS OR CHINESE

Famously, a sign at the entrance to Huangpu Park announced 'No Dogs or Chinese Allowed'. Or that's how posterity remembers it. In actual fact the restrictions on Chinese and dogs were listed in separate clauses of a whole bevy of restrictions. The regulation was finally rescinded in 1928 but has since become a powerful symbol of Shànghăi's semicolonial rule.

SHANGHAI

from the exquisite beauty of the ceramics in the Zande Lou Gallery to the measured and timeless flourishes captured in the Chinese Calligraphy Gallery. Chinese painting, seals, jade, Ming and Qing furniture, coins and ethnic costumes are also on offer, intelligently displayed in well-lit galleries.

While guiding you through the craft of millennia, the museum simultaneously takes you through the pages of Chinese history. Expect to spend half a day here.

Photos are allowed in some galleries. The English-language audio guide (Y40) is worth investing in.

SHANGHAI ART MUSEUM 上海美术馆

This **museum** (Shànghăi Měishùguǎn; ☎ 6327 2829; 325 Nanjing Xilu; admission adult/student Y20/5; ☷ 9am-5pm) is the city's premier art gallery, with an interesting collection of Chinese art, from traditional landscapes to pop art. It's worth visiting for the building (the former Shanghai Race Club) alone.

SHANGHAI URBAN PLANNING EXHIBITION HALL 上海城市规划展示馆

This **government exhibition** (Chéngshì Guīhuà Zhǎnshìguǎn; ☎ 6372 2077; 100 Renmin Dadao; adult/student/child Y25/23/12; ☷ 9am-5pm Mon-Thu, 9am-6pm Fri-Sun, last ticket sold 1hr before closing) paints a picture of how Shànghăi will develop in the next 20 years and the highlight is definitely the absorbing scale plan of the Shànghăi of the future. There are also some interesting photos of 1930s Shànghăi, a few interactive displays, lots on the World Expo (due to hit town in 2010) and a top-floor café.

French Concession
法国租界   Map pp280–1

The core of the former French concession is the area around Huaihai Lu and the Jinjiang Hotel. Huaihai Lu is the shopper's Pǔdōng, a glittering alternative to worn Nanjing Lu,

offering a line of department stores such as Isetan, Printemps and Parkson.

On side streets off Huaihai Lu, from Sinan Lu west to Huashan Lu, is some of the best old architecture, from old Art-Deco apartment complexes to neoclassical mansions and villas with quaint balconies and doorways. This part of town is one of the best for random exploration, on foot or bike. Despite the name, there were never all that many French people in the concession – 90% of the residents were Chinese, and the most numerous foreigners were Russians. Nevertheless, it remains one of the most interesting parts of Shànghăi.

SITE OF THE 1ST NATIONAL CONGRESS OF THE CCP 中共一大会址

The CCP was founded in July 1921 in this French concession building which is now a **museum** (Zhōnggòng Yídàhuìzhǐ; ☎ 5383 2171; 374 Huangpi Nanlu; admission Y3; ☷ 9am-5pm) with photographs and reconstructions of the historic meeting with English captions. The site is now part of stylish Xīntiāndì – a brilliant if ironic juxtaposition for this historical site.

XĪNTIĀNDÌ 新天地

The ambitious new business, entertainment and cultural complex of **Xīntiāndì** (www.xintiandi.com; cnr Taicang Lu & Madang Lu) has quickly become the city's most stylish collection of restaurants, bars and designer shops. The heart of the complex, just off Huangpi Nanlu, consists of several blocks of renovated (largely rebuilt) traditional *shíkūmén* (stone-framed doorways) houses, low-rise tenement buildings built in the early 1900s, brought bang up to date with a stylish modern twist.

SUN YATSEN'S FORMER RESIDENCE
孙中山故居

China is simply brimming with Sun Yatsen memorabilia, and here is one of his **former residences** (Sūn Zhōngshān Gùjū; ☎ 6437 2954; 7 Xianshan Lu; admission Y8; ☷ 9am-4.30pm) on what was formerly the rue Molière. He lived here for six years, supported by overseas Chinese funds. After Sun's death, his wife, Song Qingling (1893–1981), continued to live here until 1937, constantly watched by plainclothes Kuomintang and French police. The two-storey house is set back from the street and furnished as it was back in Sun's days,

---

TIP

If visiting more than one site in Renmin Square investigate the various combination tickets, as you'll save yourself Y10 or so on admissions. The Y60 (Y30 student) ticket, for example, gives you admission to Shanghai Museum, Shanghai Art Museum and the Urban Planning Exhibition Hall.

even though it was looted by the Japanese. The admission price gets you a brief tour of the house.

TAIKANG LU ART CENTRE 泰康路艺术中心

Shànghǎi is light on artistic focus, which makes this new **art centre** (Tàikāng Lù Yìshù Zhōngxīn; Lane 210, Taikang Lu) doubly welcome. It's a collection, 'community' even, of art galleries, cafés and shops hidden down an alley, while an adjacent multistorey warehouse hides a handful of design studios, media companies and trendy boutiques, many of which front the small alley on the east side of the building.

Highlights here include the **Pottery Workshop** (Lètiān Táoshè; ☎ 6445 0902; www.ceramics.com.hk), which exhibits and sells designer pottery and, further down the alley, the **Deke Erh Art Centre** (Ěrdōngqiáng Yìshù Zhōngxīn; ☎ 6415 0675; www.han-yuan.com; No 2, Lane 210 Taikang Lu), an impressive warehouse space with ground-floor exhibits and 1st-floor photos. The **Taikang Art Museum** is a gallery/showroom with changing exhibits in a barn-like space.

Old Town 老城市 — Map pp274–5

YUYUAN GARDENS & BAZAAR 豫园

At the northeastern end of the old Chinese city, **Yùyuàn** (☎ 6326 0830; 218 Anren Jie; adult/child Y25/10; ☀ 8.30am-5pm) is one of Shànghǎi's premier sights. Try not to visit on the weekend, though, as the crowds are pressing to say the least. See p292 for details on the surrounding bazaar's justifiably famous and delicious snacks.

The Pan family, rich Ming dynasty officials, founded the gardens, which took 18 years (1559–77) to be nurtured into existence and were snuffed out by a bombardment during the Opium War in 1842. The gardens took another trashing during French reprisals for attacks on their nearby concession by Taiping rebels. Now restored, they are a fine example of Ming garden design.

Enveloping the gardens is a glorified shopping centre, jammed with **antique** and **souvenir shops**, which spills over into Fangbang Zhonglu. The street, the nearby **Temple of the Town Gods** (Chénghuáng Miào; admission Y5) and the Yuyuan Bazaar present a rather Disneyfied version of historical China but it's a fun place to grab lunch and polish off some souvenir shopping.

Nanjing Xilu & Jing'an

南京西路、静安 — Map pp274–5

Nanjing Xilu is where Shànghǎi's streets are paved with gold, or at least Prada and Gucci. There aren't many sights in this part of town but Nanjing Xilu is an interesting street for experiencing modern Shànghǎi. It's lined with top-end shopping malls – glittering cathedrals to consumerism – and anchored by the Shanghai Centre, home to the Portman Ritz-Carlton Hotel and the city's densest collection of embassies and foreign offices.

For a view into Shànghǎi's past look across the road to the Shanghai Exhibition Centre, where architectural buffs will appreciate the monumentality and unsubtle Bolshevik strokes – there was a time when Pǔdōng was set to look like this.

JADE BUDDHA TEMPLE 玉佛寺

This **temple** (Yùfó Sì; ☎ 6266 2668; 170 Anyuan Lu; admission Y20; ☀ 8.30am-5pm) is one of Shànghǎi's few active Buddhist temples. It attracts large numbers of local and overseas Chinese tourists.

Built between 1911 and 1918, the centrepiece is a 2m-high white jade Buddha around which the temple was built. The story goes that a monk from Pǔtuóshān travelled to Myanmar (Burma) via Tibet, lugged the Buddha back to its present site and then went off in search of alms to build a temple for it. During the Spring Festival in January or February, some 20,000 Chinese Buddhists come to worship.

The seated Buddha, encrusted with jewels, is said to weigh 1000kg. A smaller Buddha from the same shipment reclines on a mahogany couch. There's an extra Y5 admission to view the Buddha. No photography is permitted.

A **vegetarian restaurant** (meals Y20-30) on the premises serves cheap lunches.

The best way to get to Jade Buddha Temple is to take a taxi from Nanjing Xilu (Y10). Bus No 19 runs along Tiantong Lu near Broadway Mansions and eventually on past the temple.

Northeast Shànghǎi — Map pp270–1

The gritty northeast districts of Zhabei and Hongkou are little visited but offer some interesting backstreets and a couple of minor sights.

SHÀNGHǍI

Wuding Xilu 武定西路

Wanghangdu Lu 万航渡路

Bejing Xilu 北京西路

Changde Lu 常德路

Tongren Lu

A

B

C

D

1

4

77

47

75

38

Jing'an Temple
30 静安寺

Jing'an Park
静安公园

Yan'an Zhonglu

Yuyuan Lu 愚园路

Zhenning Lu 镇宁路

Jiangsu Lu
江苏路
M

Nanjing Xilu 南京西路

76

Wulumuqi Beilu

Fumin Lu
41

2

Dong Zhu'anbang

21

60

40 29

27

Jiangsu Lu 江苏路

Yan'an Xilu 延安西路

Huashan Lu 华山路

66

74

5

Changle Lu

Changshu Lu

Huaihai Lu

Lixi Lu

Anfu Lu

65

Wuyuan Lu

3

Changshu Lu
常熟路
M

Ding Xiang Garden
丁香花园

7

68

Fuxing Xilu 复兴西路

56

Baoqing Lu

12

52 Taojiang

50

53

24

Yongfu Lu

11

26

10

Lu

Dongping Lu

42

4

Pingwu Lu

Huashan Lu 华山路

Wukang Lu

Yongjia Lu

31

Yueyang Lu

Niuqiao Bang

69

9

37
46

Wulumuqi Nanlu

Panyu Lu

Huaihai Zhonglu 淮海中路

Wukang Lu

63

35

Yongjia Lu

5

Fahuazhen Lu

57

Hengshan Lu
衡山路
M

17

Wanping Lu

Xinhua Lu

Huaihai Xilu 淮海西路

Hengshan Lu 衡山路

Gao'an Lu

Yuqing Lu

Kangping Lu

36

Dingan Lu

20

Guangyuan Lu

6

Jiaotong University

Tianping Lu

28

Huashan Lu

Hengshan Lu 衡山路

51

6

0 — 500 m
0 — 0.3 miles

E **F** **G** **H**

1

Jinling Zhonglu

Huangpi Nanlu 黄陂南路

Shaanxi Lu

3

M

64

71

Xing'an Lu

Chengdu Nanlu

72

45

Danshui Lu

Taicang Lu

Jinxian Lu

32 62

2

13

16

67

Ruijin Yilu

Xiangyang Beilu

23

19

Shaanxi Lu

2

43

Yandang Lu

Nanchang Lu

Zizhong Lu

Xinle Lu

22 33

Huaihai Zhonglu

34

Xiangyang Park

54

Fuxing Park 复兴公园

Chongqing Nanlu

Fuxing Zhonglu 复兴中路

70

M Shaanxi Nanlu 陕西南路

58

Gaolan Lu

14

Xianshan Lu

Donghu Lu

39

Hefei Lu

73

48

Maoming Nanlu

3

1

55

18

Fenyang Lu

Fuxing Zhonglu 复兴中路

59

Ruijin Erlu

25

Sinan Lu

Luwan

61 49

Jianguo Donglu

Xiangyang Nanlu

Xinjiaping Nanlu

Yongjia Lu

Taiyuan Lu

8

Shaoxing Lu

Jianguo Zhonglu

建国中路

Xujiahui Lu 徐家汇路

4

15

44

Taikang Lu

Mengzi Lu

Libhan Lu

Liyuan Lu

Xujiahui Lu 徐家汇路

Xiexu Lu

5

Jianguo Xilu 建国西路

Dapu Lu

Xietu Lu

Zhaojiabang Lu

Panglang Lu

Yixueyuan Lu

Fenglin Lu

Xiaomuqiao Lu

Qingzhen Lu

Damuqiao Lu

Xietu Lu

Branch

Rihui

Quxi Lu

6

Xietu Lu

DUOLUN LU CULTURAL STREET
多伦文化名人街

Formerly known as Doulean Rd, this recently restored **cultural street** (Duōlún Wénhuà Míngrén Jiē; light rail station East Baoxing Lu) of fine old houses, just off Sichuan Beilu, was home in the 1930s to several of China's most famous writers, such as Lu Xun and Mao Dun (as well as several Kuomintang generals). Today it is lined with art supply stores, curio shops, galleries and teahouses (see p300). Check out Wang Zaoshi's fabulous collection of 10,000 Chairman Mao badges at No 183 (Y2).

Look for the 'Hongde Temple' (No 59), built in 1928 in a Chinese style as the Great Virtue Church, and also the **Shanghai Duolun Museum of Modern Art** (Duōlún Xiàndài Měishùguǎn; ☎ 6587 2530; www.duolunart.com; 27 Duolun Lu; admission Y10; ☯ 10am-6pm), which has some interesting exhibits.

If you need a break try the **Old Film Café** (Lǎo Diànyǐng Kāfēibā; ☎ 5696 4763; 123 Duolun Lu; ☯ 10am-midnight; coffee Y22-30). Film buffs come here to catch screenings of old Chinese films from the 1920s, '30s and '40s. The café is decorated with film posters, old film magazines, books and mementos.

Bus No 21 runs to the street from Suzhou Creek, or take the light railway and walk 10 minutes.

OHEL MOISHE SYNAGOGUE 摩西会堂

This gutted **synagogue** (Móxī Huìtáng; ☎ 6541 5008; 62 Changyang Lu; admission Y50; ☯ 9am-4.30pm Mon-Fri) was built by the Russian Ashkenazi Jewish community in 1927. The synagogue lies in the heart of the Jewish ghetto, which was created in the 1940s when most of Shànghǎi's 30,000 Jews were forced into the area by the Japanese after fleeing Nazi Germany.

There's not much to see in the building except for a few black-and-white pictures. The real reason to come is to take a tour of the surrounding streets from the excellent resident guide Mr Wang.

For a mini walking tour of the surrounding streets turn right outside the synagogue then right again past the former Jewish tenements of Zhoushan Lu, once the commercial heart of the district. Head back southwest along Huoshan Lu (former Wayside Rd) past the Art- Deco façade of the former Broadway Theatre (No 49; now the Bailaohui Restaurant), with its rooftop Vienna Café, to the Ocean Hotel. Turn right up Haimen Lu (Muirhead Rd), past Changyang Lu, to what was once a row of Jewish shops and a kosher delicatessen on Haimen Lu, which still has the faded, original painted sign from the 1940s proclaiming 'Horn's Imbiss Stube' and 'Café Atlantis'.

At the top of the road (crossing with Kunming Lu) you'll see the large renovated Xiàhăi Miào Buddhist monastery; take a right turn, then another right, down Zhoushan Lu once again, past a small fish and bird market on the right and on the left the Ward Rd Jail, once Shànghăi's biggest, to complete the circle back to the synagogue.

To get to the synagogue, take bus No 97 or 934 from the Bund.

Pǔdōng New Area 浦东新区

Larger than the city of Shànghăi itself, the **Pudong New Area** (Pǔdōng Xīnqū; Map pp270-1) is on the eastern bank of the Huangpu River. Before 1990, when development plans were first announced, Pǔdōng constituted 350 sq km of boggy farmland supplying vegetables to Shànghăi's markets. Since then Pǔdōng has become China's financial heartbeat and the Liujiazui District has sprouted a forest of skyscrapers. For a rare look into Pǔdōng's past admire the external architecture of the **Liujiazui Development Exhibition Hall** (Liùjiāzuǐ Mínsúguǎn; Shiji Dadao; Map pp270-1; admission Y5), once a merchant's house and now an uninteresting museum.

There are many ways to get across the river to Pǔdōng but if you're craving a psychedelic experience take the **Bund Sightseeing Tunnel** (Wàitān Guānguāng Suìdào; Maps pp270-1 & pp274-5; ☎ 5888 6000; 300 Zhongshan Dong Yilu;

one-way/return Y30/40; ☼ 8am-10pm). Futuristic train modules carry passengers through a tunnel of garish lights between the Bund and the opposite shore. The ticket office is in the underpass directly across from the Peace Hotel. If you are headed to one of the sights in Pǔdōng you can save money on a combined ticket.

Riverside Park (Bīnjiāng Gōngyuán; admission free) offers good river-level views of the Bund, along with several coffee bars and a rare opportunity to sit and rest.

ORIENTAL PEARL TOWER 东方明珠电视塔

The inverted hypodermic of this gaudy **TV tower** (Dōngfāng Míngzhū Diànshì Tǎ; Map pp270-1; ☎ 5879 8888; 1 Shiji Dadao; adult/child Y50/25; ☼ 8am-9.30pm) is a uniquely uninspiring piece of architecture, although the views of Shànghăi from its lookout halfway up (263m) are sensational.

The tower has a complex ticket system. You can go to the second bauble and outdoor viewing platform (Y50); the second bauble and the Municipal Historical Museum (Y70); or the lower two baubles and the museum (Y85). For Y100 you can get to all three baubles.

SHANGHAI MUNICIPAL HISTORY MUSEUM 上海城市历史发展陈列馆

This modern new **museum** (Shànghăi Chéngshì Lìshǐ Fāzhǎn Chénlièguǎn; Map pp270-1; ☎ 5879 8888; admission Y35, audio tour Y30; ☼ 8am-9pm) is the base of the Oriental Pearl Tower. Fun multimedia presentations and imaginative displays re-create the history of Shànghăi with emphasis on the pre-1949 era. One of the pair of bronze lions that once stood outside the Hong Kong & Shanghai Bank is now housed here. It's definitely worth a visit, for adults and kids alike.

JINMAO TOWER 金茂大厦

The stunning **Jinmao Tower** (Jīnmào Dàshà; Map pp270-1; ☎ 5047 0088; 88 Shiji Dadao; adult/child Y50/25; ☼ 8.30am-9pm) is probably Shànghăi's most beautiful piece of modern architecture. It's also the tallest building in China (420.5m) and currently the fourth-tallest building in the world. An observation deck on the 88th floor offers the kind of views you normally only get from an airplane but you may be better off putting your cash towards a drink in the coffee shop in the nearby Grand

Hyatt on the 54th floor or, even better, the Cloud 9 Bar on the 87th floor (minimum charge Y100).

Next to the Jinmao is the incomplete Shanghai World Finance Building, which when (if?) finished will total 90 storeys and 460m (1518 ft).

Southern Shànghǎi   Map pp270–1
The Xújiāhuì area, bordering the western end of Frenchtown, once had a Jesuit settlement with an observatory (which is still in use). **St Ignatius Cathedral** (Tiānzhǔjiào Táng; ☎ 6253 0959; 158 Puxi Lu; ⏰ 5.45am-5pm), whose spires were lopped off by Red Guards, was restored and has regular Catholic services. Take the metro to Xujiahui station; it's a short walk south to the church.

Southwest of here, **Longhua Pagoda** (Lónghuá Tǎ; ☎ 6457 0098; 2853 Longhua Lu; admission Y5; ⏰ 7am-4.30pm) is part of a beautifully restored temple complex said to date from the 10th century. Take the light rail to Longcao Lu station and head east along Longshui Beilu for about 1km. Bus No 44 goes there from Xújiāhuì.

Further south the **Shanghai Botanical Gardens** (Shànghǎi Zhíwùyuán; ☎ 6451 3369; 1111 Longwu Lu; admission Y15; ⏰ 7am-5pm) is a huge area with an exquisite collection of plants, including special pavilions for bonsai and orchids (extra Y7 admission). It's an ideal place to replenish your oxygen intake for an afternoon.

ACTIVITIES
Huangpu River Trip 黄浦江游览船
The Huangpu River offers some remarkable views of the Bund and the riverfront activity (Shànghǎi is one of the world's largest ports). **Tour boats** (huángpǔ jiāng yóulǎnchuán; Map pp274-5; ☎ 6374 4461; 153 Zhongshan Dong Erlu) depart from the dock on the Bund, near Yan'an Lu, and pass an enormous variety of craft – freighters, bulk carriers, roll-on roll-off ships, sculling sampans, giant prayingmantis cranes, the occasional junk and Chinese navy vessels (which aren't supposed to be photographed).

The one-hour cruise (Y25 to Y35) goes as far as Yangpu Bridge. There are also 3½-hour cruises (Y70/90 lower/upper deck, other boats Y50 to Y100), a 60km return trip northwards up Huangpu River to the junction with the Yangzi. More expensive tickets often include refreshments.

Departure times vary, but there are afternoon and evening departures for all three categories during weekdays, with the addition of morning cruises on weekends. For an idea of boats and prices see www.pjrivercruise.com.

TOP FIVE SHÀNGHǍI ART GALLERIES

■ **ShanghART** (Xiānggénà Huàláng; Map pp280-1; ☎ 6359 3923; www.shanghart.com; 2a Gaolan Lu; ⏰ 10am-10pm Tue-Sat, 10am-7pm Sun & Mon) One of the first places in Shànghǎi to display cutting-edge works by modern Chinese artists. Located near Fuxing Park, it has new shows roughly every month.

■ **Eastlink** (Dōngláng; Map pp274-5; ☎ 6276 9932; eastlink@sh163c.sta.net.cn; 5th fl, Bldg 6, 50 Moganshan Lu) You can find anything from contemporary Chinese and foreign art to video installations in this warehouse space. It's part of the fragile Suzhou Creek art scene that keeps moving around in an attempt to find a long-term space.

■ **Bizart** (Bǐyì Huàláng; Map pp274-5; www.biz-art.com; ☎ 6247 0484; 4th fl, Bldg 7, 50 Moganshan Lu) In the same complex as Eastlink, this gallery exhibits avant-garde Chinese and foreign art in all media. Viewing is by appointment only outside of exhibitions.

■ **Art Scene** (Yìshùjīng Huàláng; Map pp280-1; ☎ 7437 0631; www.artscenechina.com; No 8, Lane 37, Fuxing Xilu) Contemporary Chinese art from pop to modern in a lovely restored 1930s villa. The gallery is hidden down a quiet alley. Art Scene has a **warehouse gallery** (Map pp274-5; ☎ 6277 2499; 2nd fl, Bldg 4, 50 Moganshan Lu; ⏰ 10.30am-8pm Tue-Sun) in the Suzhou Creek art centre.

■ **Aura Gallery** (Yìàn Huàláng; Map pp270-1; ☎ 6595 0901; www.aura-art.com; 5th fl, 713 Dongdaming Lu; ⏰ noon-8pm Tue-Sun) This old warehouse space houses changing exhibits by young contemporary Chinese artists. While here, check to see what's exhibiting at the 3rd-floor **DDM Warehouse** (☎ 3501 3212; ⏰ closed Sun.)

WALKING TOUR

This walk reveals the architectural glories of the Bund, Shànghăi's most impressive mile. The walk is just as enjoyable during the day or at night, when the buildings are closed but the Bund is spectacularly lit up. To walk it in one go, cross Suzhou Creek over Garden Bridge, work your way down the east side of Zhongshan Dong Yilu and either view the buildings from a distance or cross the underpass for a closer view.

At the northern end of the Bund, on the north bank of Suzhou Creek, is **Broadway Mansions** (**1**; p289), built in 1934 as an exclusive apartment block. The Foreign Correspondents' Club occupied the 9th floor in the 1930s and used its fine views to report the Japanese bombing of the city in 1937. The building became the headquarters of the Japanese army during WWII.

Behind the **Russian consulate** (**2**; p893) is the **Pujiang Hotel** (**3**; p288), Shànghăi's backpacker favourite. The hotel opened in 1846 as Astor House, the first hotel in Shànghăi, and later became the Richard Hotel. In 1990 China's first stock exchange was set up here in the former ballroom, until the exchange moved to Pŭdōng in 1998.

Heading south over Suzhou Creek, **Huangpu Park** (**4**; Huángpú Gōngyuán), the first park in Shànghăi, was laid out by a Scottish gardener shipped out especially for that purpose. Today the park holds an uninspiring Monument to the People's Heroes, which offers some of the best photo opportunities of Pŭdōng. Underneath the monument is the **Bund Historical Museum** (**5**; Wàitān Lìshǐ Jìniànguǎn; admission free; ⏱ 9am-4.15pm), which is worth a stop for its great old photos of the Bund. Turn left at the entrance to go chronologically. The socialist sculpture at the entrance of Huangpu Park was built on the site of the old British bandstand.

Continuing south down the Bund you pass the **former British consulate** (**6**; 1873; No 33), the Bund's first building. Further down, at No 27 is the former headquarters of early opium traders **Jardine Matheson (7)**, which became one of Shànghăi's great *hongs*.

The imposing **Bank of China** (**8**; p273) building, at No 23, was built in 1937 with specific instructions that it should be higher than the adjacent Cathay Hotel. The building is a strange architectural mishmash,

WALK FACTS

A stroll of the Bund from north to south.
Duration One hour
Start Broadway Mansions
End Yan'an Donglu

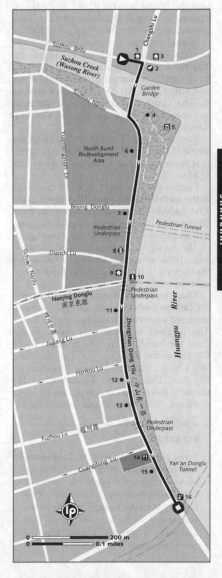

designed in a New York/Chicago style and later topped with a blue Chinese roof to make the building appear more patriotic.

Next door to the Bank of China, the famous **Peace Hotel** (9; 1926 to 1929; p289) was once the most luxurious hotel in the Far East, when it was known as the Cathay, and is still an Art Deco masterpiece (see the boxed text on p289). Even if you are not staying at the hotel you can look around the wonderful lobby (only half its original size) and if you're lucky visit the famous ballroom with its sprung floor. The main east entrance (next to the Citibank sign) is no longer in use but there are still some nice Art-Deco touches around it. The Gang of Four used the hotel as an operations base during the Cultural Revolution.

Across the road from the Peace Hotel is a statue of **Chen Yi (10)**, Shànghãi's first mayor, that bears more than a passing resemblance to Mao.

Further south, at No 17, is the former home of the **North China Daily News (11)**. Known as the 'Old Lady of the Bund' the *News* ran from 1864 to 1951 as the main English-language newspaper in China and the mouthpiece of the foreign-run municipality commission. Look above the central windows for the paper's motto. Huge Atlas figures support the roof.

Three buildings down, at No 13, stands the **Customs House (12)** built in 1925 as one of the most important buildings on the Bund. The original customs jetty stood across from the building, on the Huangpu River. On top of the building is a clock face and 'Big Ching', the bell that was modelled on Big Ben. The bell was dismantled in the Cultural Revolution and replaced by loudspeakers that blasted out revolutionary slogans and songs. The clockworks were restored in 1986 for the visit of Queen Elizabeth II.

Next door to Customs House at No 12 is the grandest building on the Bund, the former **Hong Kong & Shanghai Bank (13**; HSBC). The bank was established in Hong Kong in 1864 and in Shànghãi in 1865 to finance trade and it soon became one of the richest banks in Shànghãi, arranging the indemnity paid after the Boxer Rebellion. When the current building was constructed in 1923 it was the second-largest bank in the world and reportedly 'the finest building east of Suez'. Until 1995 the building held the offices of the municipal government before it moved to Renmin Park; it holds the Pudong Development Bank. Enter the building and marvel at the beautiful mosaic ceiling, featuring the 12 zodiac signs and the world's eight great banking centre.

At No 3 is **Three on the Bund (14**; see p277), an impressive new restaurant and retail development.

The **Shanghai Club (15**; 1911), the city's best-known bastion of British snobbery, stood at No 2 on the Bund. The club had 20 rooms for residents, but its most famous accoutrement was the bar, which at 110 feet was said to be the longest in the world. Businessmen would sit here according to rank (no Chinese or women were allowed in the club), with the taipans (company bosses) closest to the view of the Bund, sipping chilled champagne and comparing fortunes. These days the modern-day variants of the Shanghai Club's creaking leather chairs, ironed newspapers and expensive cigars are more likely to be spotted in the Portman Ritz-Carlton or the American Club.

Just across from the overpass you can see the 49m-tall **Meteorological Signal Tower (16)**, originally built in 1908 opposite the French consulate and, in 1993, moved 22m north as part of the revamping of the Bund. Today there is a small collection of old prints of the Bund and a replica 1855 map of the Bund, free of charge.

By the overpass you'll find Yan'an Donglu, once a canal and later filled in to become Ave Edward VII, the dividing line between the International Settlement and the French concession.

PIT STOP

If you need to take a break, try **Bonomi Café** (p296) inside the former HSBC building (enter through the right side entrance). For a special meal with superb views of the Bund try **M on the Bund** (p294) just off the Bund. For a simple lunch of Suzhou-style noodles try **Wùyuè Rénjiā** (p292) down the side of the Royal Thai consulate.

SHÀNGHĂI FOR CHILDREN

Shànghăi's parks can be a bit tame for kids, though several new amusement and water parks are favourites and a blessing in summer when temperatures can be uncomfortably high. The zoo and circus are other favourite stand-bys. There are several kid's stores around town, particularly along Nanjing Donglu.

In general 1.4m is the cut-off height for children's cheaper fares or entry tickets. Children under 0.8m normally get in free.

Shanghai Zoo (Shànghăi Dòngwùyuán; Map pp270-1; ☎ 6268 7775; 23 Hongqiao Lu; admission Y15-30; ☯ 6am-6pm) has pandas and South China tigers, and a few thousand other animal species. Take bus No 831 from Jingling Donglu at the Bund or bus No 911 from Huaihai Lu.

Aquaria 21 (Dàyáng Hăidĭ Shìjiè Chángfēng Hăiyáng Shìjiè; Map pp270-1; ☎ 5281 8888; 451 Daduhe Lu, Changfeng Park, Gate No 4; adult/child over 1m Y80/60) is an aquarium park, built and managed by New Zealanders, with touching tanks, rides and even an aquarium made out of a car. The neighbouring water-slide park and boating opportunities on Yinchu Lake mean that families can make a nice day of it.

At **Shanghai Aquarium** (Hăiyáng Shuĭzúguăn; Map pp270-1; ☎ 5877 9988; 158 Yincheng Beilu; adult/senior/child Y110/65/70; ☯ 9am-9pm) education meets entertainment in a slick, impressive Singaporean joint venture. The 155m-long underwater viewing tunnel is awesome. Try to time your visit with one of the fish feedings (currently 10.30am and 3.30pm).

Jinjiang Amusement Park (Jĭnjiāng Lèyuán; ☎ 6468 0844; 201 Hongmei Lu; admission Y60) has roller coasters, rides and a huge Ferris wheel in the southern suburbs, with its own metro stop.

Dino Beach (Rèdài Fēngbào; ☎ 6478 3333; 78 Xinzhen Lu; adults Tue Y30, Mon & Wed-Fri Y60, Sat & Sun Y80, children half-price; ☯ 9am-9pm Jun-Sep), way down south in Minhang District, is a popular summer place with a beach, a wave pool, water slides and tube hire to beat the summer heat, but it can be heaving at the weekends.

FESTIVALS & EVENTS

January & February
New Year Longhua Temple (Map pp270-1) has large New Year celebrations, with dragon and lion dances. At New Year the abbot strikes the bell 108 times while the monks beat on gongs and offer prayers for the forthcoming year.

Lantern Festival A colourful time to visit Yuyuan Gardens (Map pp274-5). People take the time to walk the streets at night carrying coloured paper lanterns and make *yuánxiao* or *tángyuán* (sweet dumplings of glutinous rice with sweet fillings). The festival falls on the 15th day of the first lunar month.

April
Longhua Temple Fair This fair at Longhua Temple (Map pp270-1) during the first 10 days of April is eastern China's largest and oldest folk gathering, with all kinds of snacks, stalls, jugglers and stilt walkers.

May
Shanghai International Music Festival Week-long programme of concerts and musical events.

September
Shanghai Tourism Festival Kicks off in mid-September with a parade down Huaihai Zhonglu or Nanjing Donglu and then offers a wide variety of cultural programmes.

November & December
Shanghai International Arts Festival A month-long programme of cultural events in late November and early December that is the highlight of the arts year. Events include an art fair, exhibitions of the Shanghai Biennale (2006 and 2008), and a varied programme of international music, dance, opera and acrobatics.

SLEEPING

Shànghăi has some of the highest real estate values in China, and lower-end accommodation has felt the squeeze for a while now. Apart from a couple of dormitories, the cheapest double room will cost at least Y250. Budget accommodation is worth booking in advance during the summer and on holidays.

Mid-range accommodation in Shànghăi starts at around Y400. The city is stacked with hotels in the top end (over Y500) category, though many of them have discounts that bring them into mid-range prices. Top-end hotels fall into two categories: the historic hotels of old Shànghăi and the stylish new one bursting with modern amenities.

Those with a sense of history might want to stay at one of the more urbane options, such as the Peace Hotel or Ruijin Guesthouse, where they can wrap themselves in nostalgia and fumble for the bell-pull in the middle of the night.

Most hotels offer discounts of 20% to 30% at least on their rack rates. Four- and five-star hotels add on a 10% or 15% service charge but this is again often negotiable. Note that most hotels listed here have air-conditioning and Internet access (the latter often overpriced).

If you're landing at Hongqiao Airport, try the list of discounted hotel rooms at the **Shanghai Airport Tourism Company** (☎ 6268 3683), which has booths in both the international and domestic arrival halls. If you are arriving late and leaving early, CAAC runs the good-value **Hualong Hotel** (Huálóng Fàndiàn; ☎ 6268 8500; 2 Yingbing Lu; d Y240-340), a short (free) bus ride from the terminal.

The Bund & Nanjing Donglu
BUDGET   Mappp274–5

Pujiang Hotel (Pǔjiāng Fàndiàn; ☎ 6324 6388; www .pujianghotel.com; 15 Huangpu Lu; dm Y55, d from Y300) Built on the site of the Richards Hotel, the Pujiang was originally called the Astor House Hotel, one of Shànghǎi's first grand hotels. Now it's the place for those counting their shekels – it's central, has loads of style and the rooms are vast. Although the galleries upstairs look like they belong in a Victorian asylum, there's a distinguished nobility to the rooms and halls that makes it a bargain and a half. It's recently started calling itself the Astor House Hotel again, though everyone knows it as the Pujiang. From the Bund, it's a short walk across Suzhou Creek.

Nanjing Hotel (Nánjīng Fàndiàn; ☎ 6322 2888; 200 Shanxi Nanlu; metro Henan Zhonglu; d Y330-450, discounted by 20%) Newly renovated modern doubles make this hotel quite good value, especially as it's just off Nanjing Donglu.

Jinjiang Inn (Jǐnjiāng Zhìhuáng Lǚguǎn; ☎ 6326 0505; www.jj-inn.com; 33 Fujian Nanlu; s/d Y188/228, f Y238) This friendly and modern hotel is tucked away from the fashionable districts, but still fairly close to the Bund, which makes it quite a good deal. The rooms facing Fujian Nanlu are noisy (there's a bus stop just outside the hotel). Rooms facing inwards are smaller, cheaper and quieter; the higher-floor rooms are generally best. There are a few family rooms that come with a double and single bed. The hotel is just south of the Yan'an Donglu overpass.

MID-RANGE
Yangtze Hotel (Yángzǐ Fàndiàn; ☎ 6351 7880; www .e-yangtze.com; 740 Hankou Lu; s Y450, d Y680-780, discounts of up to 30%) One of the nicest mid-range hotels around, the Yangtze is right behind the Protestant church that faces Renmin Park. Built in 1934, the exterior is largely unchanged, including the wonderful Art Nouveau balconies. 'A' rooms are bigger and better. Check to see if local construction work still means the rooms are noisy.

East Asia Hotel (Dōngyà Fàndiàn; ☎ 6322 3233; fax 6322 4598; 680 Nanjing Donglu; d Y380-580) This hotel is not as nice as the Yangtze, but is cheaper with rooms available for around Y280 when

---

AUTHOR'S CHOICE

Captain Hostel (Chuánchǎng Qīngnián Jiǔdiàn; Map pp274-5; ☎ 6325 5053; www.captainhostel.com.cn; 37 Fuzhou Lu; metro Henan Zhonglu; dm Y55, r Y400-550, discounts of up to 20% except in dm) Affiliated to YHI, this hostel is more central than the Pujiang, in an old Art-Deco building a stone's throw from the Bund. Dorms are clean and fresh, with maritime-inspired bunk beds and personal lockers. The clean communal bathrooms have 24-hour hot water. The rooms with private bathroom rank as some of the best value in Shànghǎi. Budget facilities include a useful notice board, bike hire, free use of a microwave and washing machine. A YHI card gets you a Y5 discount. You can make reservations online but note that they'll only honour them until 6pm.

Ruijin Guesthouse (Ruìjīn Bīnguǎn; Map pp280-1; ☎ 6472 5222; www.shedi.net.cn/outedi/ruijin; 118 Ruijin Erlu; s/d US$85/150, discounted to around Y500/840) This is a charmingly historic place, frequented by Zhou Enlai and Ho Chi Minh among others, which has elegant grounds and a series of old mansions converted into rooms. Some of the city's most stylish bars and restaurants are on the grounds. You can book online.

Grand Hyatt (Jīnmào Kǎiyuè Dàjiǔdiàn; Map pp270-1; ☎ 5049 1234; www.hyatt.com; 88 Shiji Dadao; d from US$260; 🏊) This is the brightest star on the Shànghǎi hotel horizon. It starts on the 54th floor of the Jinmao Building in Pǔdōng and shoots up another 33 stylish and dramatic storeys. Dramatic corner rooms cost an extra US$45, plus US$15 for a Bund view.

discounted. It's very central but some of the rooms don't have windows. The reception is on the 2nd floor through a clothing shop.

Metropole Hotel (Xīnchéng Fàndiàn; ☎ 6321 3030; metropolehotel-sh@China-dirs.com; 180 Jiangxi Nanlu; d Y450-550) Down near the Bund, this was once a grand old hotel and some of the old touches remain, like the basement bar. The rooms are a little overpriced (higher floors are better) but the location is unbeatable.

New Asia Hotel (Xīnyà Dàjiǔdiàn; ☎ 6324 2210; 422 Tiantong Lu; d Y330-400, superior Y540) Near the main post office in Hóngkǒu but also within walking distance of the Bund, is this '30s-era hotel. Extensive renovations inside have taken away some of its historical feel but it's good value with singles discounted to around Y288 and doubles for Y320.

TOP END

Peace Hotel (Hépíng Fàndiàn; ☎ 6321 6888; www .shanghaipeacehotel.com; 20 Nanjing Donglu; s US$120, d US$160-220, ste from US$350) If there's one place left in Shànghǎi that will give you a sense of the past, it's this hotel, which rises up majestically from the Bund. Previously known as the old Cathay, this 12-storey edifice has a sumptuous lobby, restaurants, shops, a bookshop, bank, barber, bar and rooftop café. Some travellers have rightly pointed out, however, that in terms of service, this hotel is way overpriced. The deluxe suites

are laid out in 1930s Art-Deco style to represent the concessions of the time – French, British, American and Japanese, not to mention Chinese.

Peace Palace Hotel (Hépíng Huìzhōng Fàndiàn; ☎ 6329 1888; fax 6329 7979; 23 Nanjing Donglu; s US$120, d US$160-220, discounts of 25-40%) An annexe of the Peace Hotel right across the street, this hotel is older and with similar rates. It's sometimes referred to as the Peace Hotel South.

Broadway Mansions (Shànghǎi Dàshà; ☎ 6324 6260; www.broadwaymansions.com; 20 Suzhou Beilu; d from Y960, discounts of up to 30%) Across Suzhou Creek from the Bund, this old hotel has great views. Formerly called the Shanghai Mansions, this was a block of apartments that housed American officers just after WWII.

Park Hotel (Guójì Fàndiàn; ☎ 6327 5225; fax 6327 6958; 170 Nanjing Xilu; metro Renmin Park; s US$80-100, d from US$150) Erected in 1934, this hotel overlooks Renmin Park and is one of Shànghǎi's best examples of Art-Deco architecture. The lobby exudes old-world charm, rooms are quite comfortable and the service is efficient. Doubles are discounted to around Y880.

Sofitel Hyland Hotel (Hǎilún Bīnguǎn; ☎ 6351 5888; www.sofitel.com; 505 Nanjing Donglu; s/d from US$185/200, discounts up to 40%) Down at the other end of town near the Bund is another good-value, centrally located place. Plus there's

---

THE CATHAY HOTEL

The Peace Hotel is a ghostly reminder of the immense wealth of Victor Sassoon. From a Baghdad Jewish family, Sassoon made millions out of the opium trade and then ploughed it back into Shànghǎi real estate and horses.

Sassoon's quote of the day was 'There is only one race greater than the Jews, and that's the Derby'. His office-cum-hotel was completed in 1930 and was known as Sassoon House, incorporating the Cathay Hotel from the 4th to 7th floors. From the top floors Sassoon commanded his real estate – he is estimated to have owned 1900 buildings in Shànghǎi.

Like the Taj in Bombay, the Stanley Raffles in Singapore and the Peninsula in Hong Kong, the Cathay was *the* place to stay in Shànghǎi. The guest list included Charlie Chaplin, George Bernard Shaw and Noel Coward, who wrote *Private Lives* here in four days in 1930 when he had the flu. Sassoon himself resided in his personal suite on the top floor, with its unsurpassed 360-degree views, just below the green pyramidal tower. He also maintained Sassoon Villa, a Tudor-style villa out near Hongqiao Airport, just west of the zoo.

After the communists took over the city, the troops were billeted in places like the Cathay and Picardie (now Héngshān Bīnguǎn on the outskirts of the city), where they spent hours experimenting with the elevators, used bidets as face-showers and washed rice in the toilets – which was all very well until someone pulled the chain.

In 1953 foreign owners tried to give the Cathay to the Chinese Communist Party in return for exit visas. The government refused at first, but finally accepted after the payment of 'back taxes'.

the advantage of German home-brewed beer on the premises.

Other top-end chain hotels near Nanjing Donglu include:

Ramada Plaza (Nán Xīnyà Huáměidá Dàjiǔdiàn; ☎ 6350 0000; www.ramadainternationalhotel.com; 700 Jiujiang Lu; d from US$150)

Howard Johnson Plaza Hotel (Gùjiā Dàjiǔdiàn; ☎ 3313 4888; www.hojochina.com; 595 Jiujiang Lu; d from US$150)

Westin Shanghai (Wēisītīng Dàfàndiàn; ☎ 6335 1888; www.westin.com; 88 Henan Zhonglu; d US$320-345, discounts of 40-50%; 🔁) Luxurious and stylish.

French Concession   Map pp280–1
BUDGET

Conservatory of Music Guest House (Yīnyuè Xuéyuàn Wàibīn Zhāodàisuǒ Liúxuéshēng Lóu; ☎ 6437 2577; 20 Fenyang Lu; metros Shaanxi Nanlu/Changshu Lu; d with shared bathroom Y100, with private bathroom Y200-300) This old budget stand-by has a great location off Huaihai Zhonglu. The pleasant strains of music practice waft around the campus courtyards, giving the surroundings a civilised air. The snag? It's often fully booked in summer so it's essential to ring ahead or come with a contingency plan. The cheapest rough-and-ready doubles come with a fan and access to a clean, shared bathroom. Nicer standard doubles with private bathroom have carpet and air-con. To find it, walk through the entrance to the conservatory, carry on around the curve to the left past a green villa.

Education Hotel (Jiàoyù Bīnguǎn; ☎ 6466 0500; fax 6466 3149; 3 Fenyang Lu; metros Shaanxi Nanlu/Changshu Lu; r Y380, discounted to around Y300 with tax & breakfast) A slightly smoky and noisy hotel frequented by Chinese businessmen, this wouldn't be a bad bet if it weren't for the noisy building site nearby. Still, it's the cheapest hotel in the district.

MID-RANGE

Jinchen Hotel (Jīnchén Dàjiǔdiàn; ☎ 6471 7000; www.jinchenhotel.com; 795-809 Huaihai Zhonglu; s/d Y680/780, discounted to around Y498/580) Readers have recommended this hotel for its clean rooms and convenient location on bustling Huaihai Zhonglu. Shopaholics can stumble out of the lobby into the heart of the shopping district for optimum efficiency.

Hengshan Hotel (Héngshān Bīnguǎn; ☎ 6437 7050; fax 6433 5732; 534 Hengshan Lu; standard d US$88, superior US$100-115) The former 1930s Picardie Apartments still hold a few hints of their original interior Art-Deco charm. The quality has been raised a bit recently, with a nice ground-floor restaurant (Planet Shanghai), particularly nice bathrooms and some classy architectural touches. The location is good, between the Hengshan Lu restaurant strip and Xujiahui shopping centre. The cheapest standard rooms are small and may require you to walk up one or two flights of stairs.

TOP END

Jinjiang Hotel (Jǐnjiāng Fàndiàn; ☎ 6258 2582; 59 Maoming Nanlu; Cathay Bldg s/d US$155/165, Jinnan Bldg d Y450, discounts of up to 30%; 🔁) This historic complex comprises three separate buildings, all of which have access to the gym and pool. The luxurious Grosvenor Villa (Guìbīn Lóu; doubles US$200) is a separate building that's been meticulously restored.

Radisson Plaza Xingguo Hotel (Xīngguó Bīnguǎn; ☎ 6212 9998, toll free reservation in China 800-3333 3333; www.radissonasiapacific.com; 78 Xingguo Lu; s/d US$220/240, discounted to around US$138/158; 🔁) The Radisson has upgraded the historic former Xingguo Hotel, adding a Clark Hatch gym and pool, a nice lounge, squash court and a restrained elegance. What hasn't changed are the lovely gardens and sense of oasis. An extra US$20 gets you a garden view.

Four of the seven villas set around the manicured grounds are rented out by the attached **Xingguo Hotel** (Xīngguó Bīnguǎn; ☎ 6212 9070; fax 6251 2145; garden villas from US$75-120, discounted to around US$68-105), which has a separate reception. Building No 1 (Room 103) was apparently one of Mao's favourite places to stay. Room décor is suitably old fashioned (you can still picture Mao briefing Zhou Enlai in the en suite meeting rooms), but rates give access to the Radisson's modern facilities.

Garden Hotel (Huāyuán Fàndiàn; ☎ 6415 1111; www.gardenhotelshanghai.com; 58 Maoming Nanlu; d from US$250, discounted to around US$170; 🔁) The elegant Japanese-run Garden Hotel has similar rates but nicer grounds than the Ritz-Carlton. It is on the site of the old French Club, across from the Jinjiang Hotel.

Other five-star options include the trusty **Hilton Hotel** (☎ 6248 0000; www.hilton.com; 250 Huashan Lu; s US$230-270, d US$250-290; 🔁).

Nanjing Xilu　　　　Map pp274–5

Shanghai Haigang Hotel (Hǎigǎng Bīnguǎn; ☎ 6255 3553; 89 Taixing Lu; metro Shimen Yilu; d Y480-580, ordinary d Y350, discounts of up to 20%) This new, clean and pleasant hotel has some stylish touches and a great location by the metro line and a street of restaurants. The cheapest rooms have interior facing windows.

　　Jingtai Hotel (Jīngtài Dàjiǔdiàn; ☎ 6272 2222; fax 6218 4778; 178 Taixing Lu; metro Shimen Yilu; d Y680-780, discounted to Y476-546) This professional hotel has well-trained staff, comfortable, clean rooms and a great location, just off Nanjing Xilu. There are also a few unadvertised economy rooms for Y580, discounted to around Y380, though they have no windows and can feel a bit claustrophobic. Rooms are slightly smaller on the Nanjing Xilu side.

　　Portman Ritz-Carlton (Bōtèmàn Lìjiā Jiǔdiàn; ☎ 6279 8888; www.ritzcarlton.com; 1376 Nanjing Xilu; d US$320; 🏊) The Ritz-Carlton is in the Shanghai Centre and is considered to be one of the best, if not the best, hotel in Shànghǎi. Walk-in discounts of up to 30% are possible.

　　New five-star hotels in the neighbourhood include:

JW Marriott Tomorrow Square (Míngtiān Guǎngchǎng JW Wànyí Jiǔdiàn; ☎ 5359 4969; www.marriotthotels .com/shajw; 399 Nanjing Xilu; d from US$320; 🏊)

Four Seasons (Sìjì Jiǔdiàn; ☎ 6256 8888; www.fourseasons.com; 500 Weihai Lu; d from US$200; 🏊)

Northern Shànghǎi

Changyang Hotel (Chángyáng Fàndiàn; Map pp270-1; ☎ 6543 4890; fax 6543 0986; 1800 Changyang Lu; d/tr Y210/270) This excellent hotel in the northeast is a little out of the way but it's cheap. Push for a discount – doubles may come down to Y150. Bus Nos 22 and 934 from the Bund run right past it.

　　E-Best Hotel (Yìbǎi Jiàrì Jiǔdiàn; Map pp270-1; ☎ 6595 1818; ebest@public6.sta.net.cn; 687 Dongdaming Lu; s Y198, d Y228-288, d with view Y408-428) This mid-range place has some budget rooms, though the cheapest singles have no windows. Superior doubles are more spacious, with river views on the 5th floor.

　　Daming Fountain Garden Hotel (Dàmíng Xīngyuàn Jiǔdiàn; Map pp270-1; ☎ 6537 3399; daming@sfc.com .cn; 1191 Dongdaming Lu; d with city/river view Y359/459, discounted to around Y268/298) This new hotel has good-value discounted rates, if you don't mind being a bit out of the action. It's next

to the large Ocean Hotel, which has some cheap rooms starting at a similar price. The top-floor Western restaurant and bar has excellent views over the Huangpu and very reasonable prices, with a happy hour (5pm to 8pm).

　　Zhao'an Hotel (Zhàoān Jiǔdiàn; Map pp274-5; ☎ 6317 2221; fax 6317 0338; 195 Hengtong Lu; metro Hanzhong Lu; d Y498-588, discounted to Y350-450) The location close to the metro stop makes for easy transport, and the helpful staff and pleasant bright rooms and clean bathrooms make this a decent choice for not silly money. Deluxe rooms are much more spacious.

　　Zhongya Hotel (Zhōngyà Fàndiàn; Map pp274-5; ☎ 6317 2317; www.zhongyahotel.com; 330 Meiyuan Lu; metro Shanghai Train Station; d from Y378, discounted to around Y286) Just across the road from the similar East China Hotel, this is a comparable but cheaper place, with a bowling alley and small fitness centre. Pricier rooms are often a good deal as they are discounted by 50%. The hotel claims to have nonsmoking and disabled rooms.

　　Other dependable options include:

Holiday Inn Downtown (Shànghǎi Guǎngchǎng Chángchéng Jiàrì Jiǔdiàn; Map pp274-5; ☎ 6353 8008; www.holiday-inn.com; 285 Tianmu Xilu & 585 Hengfeng Lu; d US$140, discounted to around Y790) Near the train station and divided into two buildings

Crowne-Plaza Shanghai (Yínxīng Huángguān Jiǔdiàn; Map pp280-1; ☎ 6280 8888; www.shanghai .crowneplaza.com; 400 Panyu Lu; s US$210-230, d US$230-250, discounts of up to 40%) Located midway between Hongqiao and the Bund.

Southern Shànghǎi　　　Map pp270–1

Huating Hotel (Huátíng Bīnguǎn; ☎ 6439 1000; www .huating-hotel.com; 1200 Caoxi Beilu; metro Shanghai Stadium; s/d US$215/235, discounted to around US$110; 🏊) This was the former Sheraton hotel and first 'modern' hotel to appear in Shànghǎi in 1987. Its five-star facilities have now been completely handed over to local management.

　　Huating Guesthouse (Huátíng Bīnguǎn; ☎ 6439 1818; fax 6439 0322; 2525 Zhongshan Xilu; d Y680) Smaller and cheaper three-star rooms are right next door in this annexe. The rooms go for Y448 at a discount. Note that both places have the same name in Chinese.

EATING

Shànghǎi's restaurant scene just keeps getting better and better. If you're on a tight

SHANGHAI

budget, however, keep to the side streets where small restaurants serve cheap, local food. Other inexpensive food options include the numerous Chinese fast-food chains and the food courts that are in the basement or top floor of almost every department store in town. You can get a wide range of Chinese food here for less than Y25. In pricier restaurants the set lunches offer the best value; dinners are often double the price.

Look out for Shànghăi's favourite dumpling, *xiǎolóngbāo*, which is copied everywhere else in China, but is only true to form here. For Y5, you should get a steamer with four of these. They are wonderful, but there's an art to eating them without getting scalded by hot oil.

Fads sweep regularly through the city's culinary scene. Plug into the current trends by reading *That's Shanghai* and its annual *Shanghai Restaurant Guide* (Y50).

The Bund & Nanjing Donglu   Map pp274–5

There's just about everything near the Bund; Chinese fast food, KFC, bars, coffee shops and a couple of elegant Western restaurants, all staking out territory along the famous skyline.

For all kinds of cheap eats try the **Zhapu Lu food street** near the Pujiang Hotel or the **Yunnan Lu food street**, not far from Renmin Square.

Croissant de France (Kěsòng; Jiangxi Zhonglu near Nanjing Donglu; cnr Sichuan Nanlu & Jinling Donglu) This chain serves up decent croissants and pastries for a DIY breakfast.

Gino Café (Jìnuò Yìdàlí Tǐxián Cāntīng; ☎ 6361 2205; 66 Nanjing Donglu; meals Y20-40; ⏰ 9am-midnight) If you're trekking through the city and need a budget lunch, Gino Café is a good-value, if unexciting, option for pasta and pizza. There are eight branches in the city and this one is down near the Peace Hotel.

Kathleen's 5 (☎ 6327 2221; www.kathleens5 .com.cn; 325 Nanjing Xilu; mains Y130-240, set lunch Y80-100) The spectacular glassed rooftop of the Shanghai Art Museum hosts this bright and buzzy restaurant, whose outside terrace has fine views over Renmin Park. The menu is full of hearty straightforward dishes such as the steak baguette and surf and turf options. There's a popular Sunday brunch.

Yuyuan Bazaar Area   Map pp274–50

If for no other reason than you are hungry, head down to the Yuyuan Bazaar for some excellent snack food that ranks among the

---

AUTHOR'S CHOICE

Wùyuè Rénjiā (Map pp280-1; ☎ 5306 5410; No 10, Lane 706, Huaihai Zhonglu) Hidden down a backstreet off Huaihai Zhonglu, and at a handful of other locations, this chain serves up cheap bowls of Suzhou-style noodles for Y10 to Y15 in a very civilised 'old Cathay' atmosphere, with Chinese opera and folk tunes in the background. Choose between *tāng* (soupy) or *bān* (dry) noodles; in either case the flavouring comes on a side plate. The excellent *xiābāo shànbèi miàn* comes with shrimp and fried eels in an oniony fish soup (Y16).

There are several other branches across town, including another hidden down a backstreet at 595 Nanjing Xilu, hidden just off the Bund between the Thai consulate and Fuzhou Lu (Map pp274–5), and on Taikang Lu (Map pp280–1).

Băoluó Jiŭlóu (Map pp280-1; ☎ 5403 7239; 271 Fumin Lu; mains Y20-50) Once you've mastered the basics of a Chinese menu, gather up a boisterous bunch of friends and join the Shanghainese night owls who queue down the street all through the night to get into this amazingly busy place. It's open 24 hours and the restaurant's labyrinthine twists and turns are always packed; it's a great place to get a feel for Shànghăi's famous buzz. Try the excellent *ruìshì niúpái* (Swiss steak), *géli shīzitóu* (lion's head with clams) or *shī tóuzi* (mandarin fish). There's no English menu.

1221 (Map pp270-1; ☎ 6213 2441; 1221 Yan'an Xilu; meat dishes Y28-38, seafood twice this) No-one has a bad thing to say about this stylish expat favourite. The crispy duck (Y48) is excellent, as are the drunken chicken and *yóutiáo niúròu* (beef with dough strips) The pan-fried sticky rice and sweet bean paste (from the dim sum menu) makes a good dessert. It's also worth ordering the eight-fragrance tea just to watch it served spectacularly out of two-foot long spouts. The service is excellent.

best in China. Dumplings and teppanyaki squid (Y2) are the perennial favourites.

Nanxiang Steamed Bun Restaurant (Nánxiáng Mántoudiàn; ☎ 6326 5265; 85 Yuyuan Lu; meals Y10-20; ☯ 7am-10pm) Join the queue in front of this place on the western side of the pond, opposite the Huxinting teahouse – you can fill yourself up with more than a dozen *xiǎolóngbāo* for Y8. Upstairs offers seating if you can find some.

Mǎntiānxīng Jiǔlóu (All Stars Restaurant; ☎ 6336 7245; 35 Sanpailou Lu; mains Y15-30; ☯ 11am-10pm) To get away from the crowds and enjoy a quiet lunch, head to this street slightly southeast of the bazaar. A delicious dish of *yángcōng chǎo niúròu* (fried beef and onions) is Y16.

French Concession
BUDGET
Yang's Kitchen (Yángjiā Chúfáng; Map pp280-1; ☎ 6445 8418; No 3, Lane 9, Hengshan Lu; metro Hengshan Lu; mains Y15-30) Though it's not quite as good as it once was, Yang's is still recommended for reasonably priced Chinese food. The *ròumò qiéguā jiābǐng* (stewed eggplant with pork mince; Y18), which you roll up in little pancakes, is out of this world. It's down a lane off Hengshan Lu and has an English menu.

Grape Restaurant (Pútáo Yuán; Map pp280-1; ☎ 5404 0486; 55 Xinle Lu; metro Shaanxi Nanlu; dishes Y15-25; ☯ 10am-2am) One of the most enduring and reliable private Chinese restaurants from the 1980s, this place still packs in the crowds in its premises beside the old Orthodox church. Try the delicious *yóutiáo chǎoniúròu* (dough sticks with beef).

Bai's Restaurant (Báijiā Cānshì; Map pp280-1; ☎ 6437 6915; No 12, Lane 189, Wanping Lu; metro Hengshan Lu; dishes Y15-25) Hidden down another backstreet off Hengshan Lu, is this small, clean, family-style restaurant with tasty Shanghainese food and an English menu. The *hǔpí jiānjiāo* (tiger skin chillies) are mild and sweet and there are plenty of affordable delicacies like the *cháozhou tóngbái xiè* (baked crab, onion and green pepper). The *suànxiāng bàngbànggǔ* (fried pork ribs in garlic) are a house speciality but a little overpriced (Y9 each).

Fēngyù Shēngjiān (Map pp280-1; 41 Ruijin Erlu, cnr Nanchang Lu; metro Shaanxi Nanlu) Don't let the Stalinist service and plastic orange seats put you off at this nondescript canteen, as it

turns out some of the best shrimp and pork *shēngjiān* (fried dumplings) in town for a bargain Y2.50, plus a range of other snacks.

Pamir Restaurant (Pàmiěr Cāntīng; Map pp280-1; Fumin Lu; kebabs Y2, mains Y15) Excellent lamb kebabs, nan bread and Central Asian noodles (try the *suoman* – fried noodle squares with tomatoes and green peppers) offer a refreshing change of tastes at this no-frills Uighur restaurant. Wash it down with a bottle of Xinjiang Black Beer or a pot of *kok chai* (green tea).

Zentral (Shànqù; Map pp270-1; ☎ 6374 5815; www.zentral.com.cn; 567 Huangpi Nanlu; set meals Y15-18) If your system is craving an alternative to oily Shanghainese fry-ups but your wallet is as empty as your stomach, Zentral is your best bet. There are cheap lunch sets, good smoothies, brown rice, sugar-free desserts and Y10 cappuccino.

Délifrance (Déyīfǎlánxī; Map pp280-1; ☎ 5382 5171; 125 Shanghai Central Plaza, 381 Huaihai Zhonglu; metro Huangpi Nanlu; set meals Y28-35; ☯ 8am-10pm) There's not a great deal of Chinese character here but the croissants and sandwiches are tasty, and the set breakfasts and lunches are good value. It's the only place in town for a chicken curry baguette.

MID RANGE
Western-style restaurants abound, especially around Hengshan Lu.

Xīnjíshí Cāntīng (Map pp280-1; ☎ 6336 4746; No 9 Xīntiāndì, Lane 181, Taicang Lu; mains Y30-40; ☯ 11am-2pm & 5-9.30pm) Shànghǎi is full of so many excellent Chinese restaurants, it's impossible to list them all. One of the latest new favourites among expats and locals alike is this place in Xīntiāndì.

Azul (Map pp280-1; ☎ 6433 1172; 18 Dongping Lu; mains Y90-120, tapas Y50, set lunch Y48-58) This trendy Latin place is currently popular for its fresh New World cuisine and hip décor. Downstairs is the cool tapas bar and lounging area, upstairs is a more formal space for dinner.

Keven Café (Kǎwén Kāfēi; Map pp280-1; ☎ 6433 5564; 525 Hengshan Lu; mains Y30-70; ☯ 7.30am-2am) For a reasonable and authentic American breakfast (Y38), as well as other Western and Asian dishes, try this café.

Badlands (Bǎigǎng; Map pp280-1; ☎ 6466 7788; 895 Julu Lu; mains Y50-70; ☯ 10am-late) This bar-cum-restaurant is an old favourite for good-value nachos, tacos and burritos, washed down by a cold Corona (Y35).

Brasil Steak House (Bāxī Shāokǎowū; Map pp280-1; lunch/dinner Y55/66; 🕙 11am-11pm) 1582 Huaihai Zhonglu (☎ 6437 7288) 1649 Nanjing Xilu (☎ 6255 9898) For carnivores, this is probably the best deal in the city for an absolutely filling Western meal. Servers come around with hunks of roasted meat on skewers, slicing off bits onto your plate. There's also a buffet salad and dessert bar. It's opposite the Shanghai Library, with another branch next to Jing'an Park.

Simply Thai (Tiāntài Cāntīng; Map pp280-1; ☎ 6445 9551; 5-C Dongping Lu; mains Y50-60) Everyone raves about this place for its delicious, reasonable dishes and comfortable décor. There's nice outdoor seating and the lunch specials are particularly good value.

Dīshuǐdòng (Map pp280-1; ☎ 6253 2689; 2nd fl, 56 Maoming Nanlu; metro Shaanxi Nanlu; mains Y28-45) Shànghǎi's favourite Hunanese restaurant is surprisingly down-home (with waitresses decked out in Hunanese blue cloth) but serves up killer cuisine. Try the *làzi jīdīng* (fried chicken with chilli) or one of the ex-

cellent claypot dishes and brace yourself for a chilli onslaught. There's an English menu, though, as ever, the Chinese version offers more range. Booking is advised.

Indian Kitchen (Yìndù Xiǎochú; Map pp280-1; ☎ 6473 1517; 572 Yongjia Lu; dishes Y20-30) Follow your nose through the French concession backstreets to track down this top-notch neighbourhood curry house, which is packed on the weekends with Brits desperate for a chicken Balti. The great-value set lunches run from Y18 to Y50 and come with a Tiger Beer. It's a five-minute walk from Hengshan Lu.

Spice Market (Dōngnányà Cāntīng; Map pp274-5; ☎ 6384 68388; 8 Jinan Lu; metro Huangpi Lu; set lunch Y35, mains Y30-60) The menu is a Who's Who of Asian dishes, from *pad thai* to *nasi goreng*, along with more interesting fare like the pomelo, chicken and chilli salad (Y35), and grilled whole fish with chilli dry shrimps and coconut stuffing (Y60); but the unbeatable-value five-course Malaysian, Thai or Indonesian set lunches are the main draw here.

Something Special

All the following restaurants require reservations, preferably several days in advance if you want a plum table with a view.

M on the Bund (Map pp274-5; ☎ 6350 9988; www.m-onthebund.com; 7th fl, 5 The Bund, cnr Guangdong Lu; mains Y100-200, set lunches Y118-138; 🕙 closed Mon lunch) For the latest trends in international cuisine, Michelle Garnaut has brought her renowned skills from Hong Kong to Shànghǎi to create this restaurant on the 7th floor of the Huaxia Bank. There's a magnificent terrace view of the Bund for which you need to reserve a day or two in advance. There's a popular weekend brunch (Y188; 11.30am to 3pm), and a very British Sunday afternoon tea (3.30pm to 5.30pm).

T8 (Map pp280-1; ☎ 6355 8999; 8 North Block, Xīntiāndì, 181 Taicang Lu; mains Y200, set lunch Mon & Wed-Fri 2/3 courses Y158/198; 🕙 dinner until 11.30pm, closed lunch Tue) Recently voted one of the best 50 restaurants in the world by *Condé Nast* magazine, T8 is giving M on the Bund a run for its money as the most lauded restaurant in Shànghǎi. The food is best described as 'modern Mediterranean fusion with Asian influences', with subtle flavours and excellent presentation (this is modern cuisine so don't expect any side dishes). The seductive interior is just as impressive as the food. Dress to impress here.

Jean Georges (Map pp274-5; ☎ 6321 7733; jgreservation@on-the-bund.com; 4th fl, Three on the Bund; mains from Y250) The *enfant terrible* of French cooking opened this, another of his world-famous restaurants, on the Bund in 2004, serving modern fusion cuisine at top-end prices. The dark, lush interior was designed by architect Michael Graves. There's a large wine selection, starting at US$50 a bottle.

Grand Hyatt (Jīnmào Kǎiyuè Dàjiǔdiàn; Map pp270-1; ☎ 5830 3338; Jinmao Tower, Zhongyang Dadao) If it's a special night out with a view you're after, the steakhouse **Grill**, Japanese **Kobachi**, Italian **Cucina** and Cantonese-style **Canton** restaurants at the Grand Hyatt really can't be beaten. The breathtaking atrium is a great place to meet. The **Grand Café** offers stunning views through its glass walls, and a good-value buffet (Y198 to Y228). If you're going to spend Y40 on a coffee in some crummy Shànghǎi café, you might as well make an afternoon of it here with the all-you-can-manage weekend high tea for Y100.

Five-course dinners cost Y88. You can save more money on a bucket of beer (five bottles) for Y135.

Vegetarian Life Style (Zǎozi Shù; Map pp274–5; ☎ 5306 8000; 77 Songshan Lu; metro Huangpi Lu; mains Y20-30) For light and healthy Chinese vegetarian food, lacking the oil that blights so many Shanghainese restaurants, try this bright place, just off the eastern end of Huaihai Zhonglu. The name translates as 'Jujube Tree' but is also a pun on the characters, roughly meaning 'hurry up and become a vegetarian'. There's an English menu.

TOP END   Map pp280–1

Xīntiāndì has one of the densest collections of top-end restaurants, with everything from Starbucks to Cuban restaurants, and is one of the nicest places to stroll on a summer evening.

Le Garçon Chinois (Shànghǎi Lè Jiàěrsōng; ☎ 6445 7970; No 3, Lane 9, Hengshan Lu; mains Y100; ⊗ dinner only) This elegant, hidden villa offers Spanish cuisine, an intimate bar (a great place for a date) and a downstairs teahouse. Try the three seafood tapas (Y98), the paella for two (Y120) and the hot chocolate soup (Y35). It's tucked down a lane on the way to Yang's Kitchen.

Ooedo (Dà Jiānghù; ☎ 5403 3332; 30 Donghu Lu; buffet Y200; ⊗ 5.30-11pm) Shànghǎi has too many Japanese restaurants to list here, but one of the best is Ooedo which offers a delicious all-you-can-eat sushi, sake and tempura buffet.

Shintori 02 (Xīdùlì; ☎ 5404 5252; 803 Julu Lu; mains Y60-80; ⊗ dinner only) Prepare for your jaw to drop when you enter this Japanese restaurant. The warehouse-industrial-chic interior resembles a set from a Peter Greenway film, from the eye-catching open kitchen that looks like it should house Hannibal Lector, to the sleek staff running around like an army of black ninja. The Japanese menu is equally witty; the cold soba noodles come in a bowl made of ice.

Nanjing Xilu   Map pp274–5

Element Fresh (Yuánsù Cāntíng; ☎ 6279 8682; Shanghai Centre, 1376 Nanjing Xilu; sandwiches Y35-75, lunch mains Y60-90, dinner Y80-180) The focus here is on fresh, healthy sandwiches and salads; vegetarians may well faint with excitement at the roasted eggplant on walnut bread

with mozzarella and olives. Then there are lots of fresh juices, imaginative smoothies and the best-value coffee around. The décor is bright and stylish, with a small bar and comfy sofas, and there's a takeaway service.

Yuányuán Fàndiàn (Map pp280–1; 195 Chengde Lu; metro Jing'an Temple; dishes Y8-20) A typical homestyle Chinese restaurant, this place is like thousands of others in the city, except that for some reason it's got an English menu. It's cheap, tasty and worth a stop if you are on the west end of Nanjing Xilu. The décor needs some serious attention, though.

Bì Fēng Táng (☎ 6279 0738; 1333 Nanjing Xilu; dim sum Y13-25) This is an incredibly popular place that serves cheap dim sum snacks like shrimp dumplings, honeyed pork and egg tarts, as well as coffee and cheap Budweiser. This Nanjing Xilu branch, across from the Shanghai Centre, has an English menu on request and plenty of fine outdoor seating when the weather is good.

Gongdelin Vegetarian Restaurant (Gōngdélín Sùshíchù; ☎ 6327 0218; 445 Nanjing Xilu; mains Y15-25) This is probably Shànghǎi's most famous vegetarian restaurant, in operation since 1922 and recently revamped. All the food is designed to resemble meat, and is convincingly prepared. The food and atmosphere are worth experiencing, even if you are not a vegetarian. The sign says 'Godly Restaurant'.

Lulu Restaurant (Lùlù Jiǔjiā; ☎ 6288 1179; 1266 Nanjing Xilu; dishes Y12-30, seafood Y70) The **Pǔdōng branch** (Map pp270–1; ☎ 5882 6679; 2nd fl, China Merchants' Bldg, 161 Lujiazui Donglu; metro Liujiazui Lu) established Lulu's reputation as one of the best bets for decent Shanghainese cuisine but the most stylish and spectacular of its branches now sits pretty on the 5th floor of the Plaza 66 shopping centre. It is the epitome of stylish, modern Shànghǎi, perfect for a trendy group meal blowout. All your Shanghainese favourites are here, including *xièfěn shīzi tóu* (crab and pork meatballs; Y15 each).

DRINKING
Bars

There are several bar strips in town, the most reliable being Maoming Nanlu, which regularly degenerates into a street party every Saturday night. Grab a Y6 beer from the nearby Lawson's convenience store and join the masses. Bar names come and go but there's always at least half a dozen to choose from. One thing stays the same, however; drinks at most of the popular bars in Shànghǎi are expensive at around Y40.

Blue Frog (Lánwā; Map pp280-1; ☎ 6445 6634; 207-223 Maoming Lu; beer Y35, shots Y30) Good bar food, classy décor and a comfy upstairs lounge raise this place a notch above the other Maoming dives. Stagger your way through all 100 shots and you'll get your name on the wall and a shot a day for life. Plus the logo's cute. There are cheap(er) drinks on Tuesdays.

O'Malley's Bar (Oūmǎlì Cāntīng; Map pp280-1; ☎ 64744533; 42 Taojiang Lu; ☽ 11am-1am) O'Malley's brought up the standards of beer drinking considerably when it introduced draught Guinness and Kilkenny beers to Shànghǎi residents. It remains one of the most popular expat hang-outs, either on the large lawn in good weather, or inside within the old-world pub atmosphere.

Kiwi Bar (Map pp280-1; ☎ 6407 3861; 88 Guangyuan Xilu; beer Y20) Cheap drinks all the time and random free rounds of tequila shots make this rowdy but friendly local a place to get buzzed without cashing a fistful of travellers cheques. Draught and bottled Steinlager and meat pies reflect the Kiwi management. As the manager (recognisable by his consistent lack of any kind of shirt) says, 'It's a privilege if you get barred from the Kiwi'.

Noah's Bar (Map pp274-5; ☎ 6323 7869; 6th fl, 37 Fuzhou Lu; beer Y15-30) The crummy lift up to the top floor of the Captain Hostel won't impress your date but the rooftop views of Pǔdōng just might make up for it. There's outdoor and indoor seating, big portions of American food (special prices for hostel guests) and a large screen for movies.

Cloud 9 Bar (Map pp270-1; minimum charge Y100; ☽ from 6pm Mon-Fri, from 11am Sat & Sun) The 88th floor of the Grand Hyatt guarantees spectacular views from this up-market hotel bar, making this a great place for a splurge, especially if you were going to pay Y50 anyway to get to the Jinmao Building's observation floor (just one storey above).

Face Bar (Map pp280-1; ☎ 6466 4328; Bldg 1, Ruijin Guesthouse, 18 Ruijin Erlu; beer Y50-55, cocktails Y50-60) Wonderfully decorated in the ground floor of a wonderful old building, this is a strong contender for most beautiful bar in Shànghǎi. Prices aren't cheap but there's nowhere better to take a date or laze in front of the manicured lawn on a summer's afternoon. Drinks of choice include draught Tetley's or Hoegaarden, plus great cocktails (try the chocolate mint martini). The excellent but pricey Thai-style Lan Na Thai and Indian-style Hazara restaurants offer top cuisine in the same building. Don't forget the hotel's 10% service charge.

Malone's American Cafe (Mǎlóng Měishì Jiǔlóu; Map pp274-5; ☎ 6247 2400; 257 Tongren Lu; set lunches Y50; ☽ 11am-2am) This place was started by Canadians, but is strictly an American-style bar. If you want to forget you're in China, turn your back on the window and focus on the TV screen. Beer is Y40.

Päulaner Bräuhaus (Bǎojiánà Cāntīng; Map pp280-1; ☎ 6474 5700; 150 Fenyang Lu; ☽ 5pm-2am) This is the grand master of the Shànghǎi microbreweries, insanely popular with Shanghainese high rollers. A pint of wheat beer will set you back about Y80 (yes, that's US$10!).

Tea & Coffee Houses

1931 (Map pp280-1; ☎ 6472 5264; 112 Maoming Nanlu; dishes Y20-60; ☽ 11am-2am) One of the nicest places is this intimate café/bar outfitted with a 1930s theme and serving coffee, tea, drinks and meals.

Huxinting Teahouse (Húxīntíng Cháguǎn; Map pp274-5; ☎ 6373 6950; Yuyuan Bazaar; pot of tea ground fl Y20-25, upstairs Y40-Y55; ☽ 6am-9.30pm) Next to the Yuyuan Gardens, this ornate spot is one of the best places to sit and look over the mob below and pretend you're part of the scene on a blue willow teacup. Make sure you stay a while, however, as the price is steep for a quick pot of tea. Get there early in the day for one of the prime window seats. Classical Chinese music (no charge) is performed upstairs Friday, Saturday and Sunday at 6.30pm and Monday from 2pm to 5pm.

Bonomi Café (Bōnuòmi Kāfēidiàn; Map pp274-5; ☎ 6329 7506; room 226, 12 Zhongshan Dongyilu; coffee Y25-32) Bonomi is an Italian chain that has cleverly set up shop in some of Shànghǎi's best locations. Our favourite is here on the Bund, hidden in the Whitehall-like corridors of the former building of the HSBC.

Donghai Café (Dōnghǎi Kāfēiguǎn; Map pp274-5; ☎ 6321 1940; 145 Nanjing Donglu; coffee Y12) At last, a place with reasonably priced coffee within reach of the Bund! Downstairs serves up decent coffee (and even beer) and there are also cheap set meals. Upstairs is more comfortable but a tad more expensive.

Harn Sheh (Hánshè Pàomò Hóngcháfǎng; Map pp280-1; ☎ 6474 6547; 10 Hengshan Lu; meals Y15-30; ✆ 9.30am-4am) One of a number of Taiwanese-style teahouses around town. There's four of these in the city, featuring a cornucopia of bizarre and delicious beverages highlighted by various kinds of bubble tea. Set meals are also served.

There were over 25 Starbucks in Shànghǎi at the time of writing and surely more will come. We'll let you find them.

ENTERTAINMENT

The last few years have seen an explosion of nightlife options, with everything from the incredibly sleazy to the painfully chic. There's pretty well something for everyone: rock, hip-hop, techno, salsa and early morning waltzes in Renmin Square. None of it comes cheap, however (except for the waltzing, which is free). A night on the town in Shànghǎi is now comparable to a night out in Hong Kong or Taipei.

Venues open and close all the time. Check out the Shànghǎi entertainment magazines for guidance.

Cinemas

Foreign movies are generally dubbed into Chinese and Chinese movies very rarely have English subtitles but there are exceptions at the following multiplexes. Tickets cost Y40 to Y60.

Peace Cinema (Héping Diànyǐngyuàn; Map pp274-5; ☎ 6322 5252; 290 Xizang Zhonglu; Y50) A useful location at Raffles Plaza by Renmin Square, with an IMAX cinema (Y80).

Studio City (Huányì Diànyǐngchéng; Map pp274-5; ☎ 6218 2173; Westgate Mall, 10th fl, 1038 Nanjing Xilu)

Ultimate Movie Experience (UME; Map pp280-1; ☎ 6373 3333; www.ume.com.cn; Xintiāndì)

Clubs & Discos

Shànghǎi pulls in some top-notch DJs from abroad and there are a lot of dance venues. There's also a high turnover, so check listings magazines. If you're looking for large, pulsating places, try these spots:

Rojam Disco (Map pp280-1; ☎ 6390 7181; 4th fl, Hong Kong Plaza, 283 Huaihai Zhonglu; admission Y40-50; ✆ 8.30pm-2am) This is a popular place for

techno on the weekends. The cover charge includes one drink.

Real Love (Zhēn'ài Jiùbā; Map pp280-1; ☎ 6474 6830; 10 Hengshan Lu; admission Sun-Thu Y30, Fri & Sat Y50; ✆ 8.30pm-2am) Real Love attracts a young, mainstream local crowd.

Judy's Too (Map pp280-1; ☎ 6473 1417; 176 Maoming Nanlu) A bar during the weekdays, this place is insanely crowded on the weekends, with more of an older crowd, both local and expat. It's a lot of fun. A whole range of music is played throughout the week and house music features on weekends.

California Club (Map pp280-1; ☎ 6318 0785; 2 Gaolan Lu; ✆ 6pm-late) Owned by the Lan Kwai Fong group and located in the Park 97 restaurant complex in Fuxing Park, this club is one of the places to be seen. Take a break from the bass in the upstairs Kasbah lounge.

Gay & Lesbian Venues

Shànghǎi has a few places catering to gay patrons, but the locales keep moving around, so check the listings. Men or women, gay or straight, are welcome at the places listed below. For the latest gay venues look for the cryptic comments in local listings magazines.

Eddy's Bar (Jiānóng Kāfēi; Map pp280-1; ☎ 6282 0521; www.eddys-bar.com; 1877 Huaihai Zhonglu; drinks Y15-20) A gay-friendly bar/café that occasionally pushes the envelope.

Home Bar (Báilíng Jiùbā; Map pp280-1; ☎ 5382 0373; 18 Gaolan Lu; ✆ 8pm-2am Wed-Sun) This is a friendly, medium-sized place with plush, red velvet couches for lounging.

Er Ding Mu Bar (Èrdīngmù; Map pp270-1; ☎ 5696 3986; 67 Siping Lu; ✆ 6.30pm-2am) This is another large place, located in Hóngkǒu. It's popular on weekends and can get quite crowded.

Live Music

Cotton Club (Map pp280-1; ☎ 6437 7110; 1428 Huaihai Zhonglu; admission free; ✆ 7.30pm-2am) One of the best bars for live music is this comfortable, unassuming place that features mostly blues bands. The music doesn't usually get going until after 9pm.

Peace Hotel Old Jazz Bar (Map pp274-5; ☎ 6321 6888 ext 6210; Peace Hotel, 20 Nanjing Donglu; admission Y50, with a reservation Y80; ✆ 8pm-1.30am) Home of the ancient jazz band that has been strumming since time immemorial, it's doubtful whether this place is worth the cover charge. If you're feeling nostalgic it's the place to go though.

Ark House (Map pp280-1; ☎ 6326 8008; 15, North Block, Xīntiāndì, Lane 181, Taicang Lu; cover charge Y30-50) This is a rare opportunity to catch underground Chinese bands with an alternative edge. Gigs get going Friday and Saturday from 9.30pm. Local bands Crystal Butterfly and The Honeys are worth looking out for.

Shanghai Grand Theatre (Shànghǎi Dà Jùyuàn; Map pp274-5; ☎ 6372 8701; www.shgtheatre.com; 300 Renmin Dadao; admission from Y120) This magnificent venue is in Renmin Square and features both national and international opera, dance, music and theatre performances.

Shanghai Concert Hall (Shànghǎi Yīnyuè Tīng; Map pp274-5; ☎ 6460 4699; 523 Yan'an Donglu) A classical music venue for smaller local and international orchestras. The entire building was picked up and moved 70m in 2003!

Oriental Arts Centre (Dōngfāng Yìshù Zhōngxīn; Map pp270-1; ☎ 6854 0322) Pǔdōng's financial and business emphasis will be given an artistic balance when this arts centre opens in 2005. The complex features a 2000-seat philharmonic orchestra hall, a 300-seat chamber music hall and a 100-seat theatre.

Conservatory of Music (Yīnyuè Xuéyuàn; Map pp280-1; ☎ 6431 0034; 20 Fenyang Lu; admission Y20) The conservatory, off Huaihai Zhonglu, has regular music performances on Sunday at 7pm in its He Luting Concert Hall.

Jing'an Hotel (Jìng'ān Bīnguǎn; Map pp280-1; ☎ 6248 1888; 370 Huashan Lu; admission Y20) Chamber music is played every Sunday evening at 8pm at the Jing'an, located next to the Hilton Hotel.

Jinjiang Hotel (Jǐnjiāng Fàndiàn; Map pp280-1; ☎ 6258 2582; 59 Maoming Nanlu) Hosts a classical music concert Sunday afternoons at 2pm (see p290). Tickets cost Y50 and include refreshments.

House of Blues & Jazz (Bùlǔsī Yǔ Juéshì Zhī Wū; Map pp280-1; ☎ 6437 5280; 158 Maoming Nanlu) Serious jazz lovers should make a beeline to this restaurant and bar, owned by a Chinese TV celebrity. The in-house band whips up live music from 10pm to 1am. Sunday night is a free-for-all jam, and Mondays are quiet. At other times, there are recorded classics.

Theatre
Majestic Theatre (Měiqí Dàxìyuàn; Map pp274-5; ☎ 6217 3311; 66 Jiangning Lu; admission Y20-300)

All kinds of performances are held in this former cinema, such as ballet, local opera and the occasional revolutionary-style opera, which can be great fun to watch, especially for reactions from the audience.

Modern plays in Chinese are staged at the **Shanghai Theatre Academy** (Shànghǎi Xìjù Xuéyuàn; Map pp280-1; ☎ 6248 2920 ext 3040; 630 Huashan Lu) and the **Shanghai Dramatic Arts Centre** (Shànghǎi Huàjù Zhōngxīn; Map pp280-1; ☎ 6473 4567; 288 Anfu Lu) with tickets ranging from Y20 to Y100, depending on the production.

Traditional Performances
Unfortunately, Beijing opera, local opera and Chinese drama (often an extravagant display of costumes, make-up and acrobatics) are almost exclusively delivered in Chinese and therefore inaccessible to most foreigners.

Yifu Theatre (Yìfǔ Wǔtái; Map pp274-5; ☎ 6351 4668; 701 Fuzhou Lu; admission Y10-40) Beijing opera is performed on Saturday and Sunday at 1.30pm. Other regional opera performances are on weekdays at 7.30pm.

Great World (Dà Shìjiè; Map pp274-5; ☎ 6326 3760; 1 Xizang Lu; admission Y30; ☉ 9.30am-6.30pm & 7.30-10pm) For cheaper, if less sophisticated shows, check out this wedding-cake building near Renmin Square. It was once the famous and salacious Great World in pre-1949 Shànghǎi. There's a potpourri of performances available on different stages: opera, acrobatics and magic, but nothing too risqué yet.

Chinese acrobatic troupes are among the best in the world, and Shànghǎi is a good place to see a performance. If you've never seen the show, it's not to be missed. In the shows listed here, the only performing animals present are humans.

Shanghai Centre (Shànghǎi Shāngchéng Jùyuàn; Map pp274-5; ☎ 6279 8600 ext 6744; 1376 Nanjing Xilu; admission Y100-200) The Shanghai Acrobatics Troupe (Shànghǎi Zájì Tuán) has performances here most nights at 7.30pm but the tickets recently doubled in price.

Lyceum Theatre (Lánxīn Dàxìyuàn; Map pp280-1; ☎ 6217 8530; 57 Maoming Nanlu; admission Y30-60) Evening acrobatic shows are held here at an old Shànghǎi theatre across from the Jinjiang Hotel.

SHOPPING
Shànghǎi has long been the most famous shopping city in China and almost all

Chinese products and souvenirs find their way here. The traditional shopping streets have always been Nanjing Lu and Huaihai Lu, but now it seems almost every side street is overflowing with boutiques and shops. The Shanghainese live to shop.

Clothing & Shoes

Tall and large people may have difficulty finding their size in Shànghăi, but it's a shopping paradise for smaller folk. The **Xiangyang Market** (Xiāngyáng Shìchăng; Map pp280–1; Huaihai Zhonglu; metro Shaanxi Nanlu; 10am-6pm), on the corner of Xiangyang Lu and Huaihai Lu, is the place for knock-off brand name fashions, North Face gear and souvenirs. It's a pale shadow of its predecessor on Huating Lu but still gets very busy at weekends.

Try Maoming Nanlu (Map pp280–1) and Shanxi Nanlu (Map pp274–5) for various **boutiques**, especially if you're shopping for a *qipao* (Chinese dresses, also known as *cheongsam*). Nanjing Lu (Map pp274–5) and Huaihai Lu (Map pp280–1) have the big-name brands. Shanxi Nanlu is packed with small **shoe shops** with good prices.

If you want to make your own clothes or choose your own cloth for a tailor, the **Dongjiadu Cloth Market** (Dōngjiādù Qīngfāng Miàn- liào Shìchăng; Map pp270–1; cnr Dongjiadu Lu & Zhongshan Dong Erlu) has the cheapest silk (from Y35 per metre), brocade cashmere and other cloth by the metre at a fraction of the cost in the West. Buses run south from the Bund to the market, or take a taxi.

You can also get slightly pricier silk (Y68 to Y88 per metre) at more convenient locations near the Bund at **Silk King** (Zhēnsī Shàngshà; Map pp274-5; 66 Nanjing Donglu) or **Laokaofook Silk and Woollen Store** (Lăojiéfú Sīchóu Níróng Shāngdiàn; Map pp274-5; 373 Nanjing Donglu).

Department Stores

Shànghăi has some of the best department stores in China, including flashy Western- and Japanese-style outlets that are probably of more interest to residents than to visitors. On the other hand, if you can find your size, there are sometimes good fashion deals in some of the department stores. Because the competition is so fierce, you can even bargain in some department stores depending on the item.

Hualian Department Store (Húalían Shāngshà; Map pp274-5; ☎ 6322 4466; 635 Nanjing Donglu; 9.30am-

10pm) Formerly called No 10, and before that the famous Wing On, this place is best for mid- and low-range prices.

No 1 Department Store (Dìyī Băihuò Shāngdiàn; Map pp274-5; ☎ 6322 3344; 830 Nanjing Donglu; 9.30am-10pm) This is another good place that caters to the masses.

Friendship Store (Yŏuyì Shāngdiàn; Map pp274-5; ☎ 5308 0600; 40 Beijing Donglu; 9.30am-9.30pm) This is a good place to pick up last-minute souvenirs at fixed prices, and the lack of crowds makes it possible to browse at your leisure. There's a money-changing facility here.

Nanjing Xilu has the most glam malls, including **Westgate Mall** (Méilóngzhèn Guăngchăng; Map pp274-5; 1038 Nanjing Xilu) with a branch of Isetan and basement supermarket, the exclusive **Plaza 66** (Map pp274-5; 1266 Nanjing Xilu) and **CITIC Square** (Zhōngxìn Tàifù Guăngchăng; Map pp274-5; 1168 Nanjing Xilu).

Over in Pŭdōng, across from the Oriental Pearl Tower, the Thai-financed **Superbrand Mall** (Zhèngdà Guăngchăng; Map pp270-1; metro Liujiazui) is currently Shànghăi's largest.

Outdoor Gear

Weald Outfitter (Kuàngyě Hùwài Lǚxíng Yòngpǐn Zŏnghuì; Map pp280-1; ☎ 6372 4180; 22 Chongqing Nanlu) has a small selection that includes tents stoves, GPS units and Gore-Tex gear.

Luo Ben (Map pp280-1; ☎ 6433 4932; 293 Fuxing Xilu) stocks the Patagonia brand of outdoor clothing.

Photographic Supplies

Major hotels often stock basic photographic supplies. Passport photos are available in most metro stations (Y20).

Guànlóng (Map pp274-5; ☎ 6323 8681; 190 Nanjing Donglu; 9am-10pm) You can get slide film, memory sticks and all kinds of camera accessories here at Shànghăi's foremost photographic supplies shop.

New Ray Photo (Xinzhíguāng Shèyíng Túpiàn Zhìzuò; Map pp280-1; ☎ 6433 0101; 1650 Huaihai Zhonglu; 8am-9pm) This is another good place to buy and develop slide film, close to the Shanghai Library.

Porcelain

Shanghai Museum (Shànghăi Bówùguăn; Map pp274-5; ☎ 6372 3500; 201 Renmin Dadao; 9am-5pm) The best place to find decent porcelain is this shop (see p277), which sells imitations

SHANGHAI

of the pieces displayed in the Zande Lou Gallery (within the museum). The imitations are fine specimens and far superior to the mediocre pieces you see in the tourist shops. However, be prepared to pay a hefty whack.

Jingdezhen Porcelain Artware (Jǐngdézhèn Cíqì Diàn; Map pp274–5; ☎ 6253 8865; 1185 Nanjing Xilu; ⏰ 10am-9pm) There's a variety of more prosaic porcelain for sale here and pricey speciality items as well.

Souvenirs, Collectibles & Antiques

Yuyuan Bazaar (Map pp274–5), in the old town, is a souvenir-hunters mecca. Shops in the bazaar and along nearby Fangbang Zhonglu flog calligraphy, pearls from nearby Tài Hú, old bank notes, woodcuts, artwork, blue cloth, teapots and pretty much everything else. Haggle hard as it's all overpriced.

Fuyou Antique Market (Fúyòu Gòngyìpǐn Shìchǎng; Map pp274–5; 459 Fangbang Zhonglu) There's a permanent antique market here on the 1st and 2nd floors, near the Yuyuan Gardens in the old town, but the place really gets humming early on Sunday mornings when local dealers crowd all four floors with ceramics, 'antique' posters, pocket watches, paintings and a host of other collectibles.

Dongtai Lu Antique Market (Dōngtái Lù Gǔshāngpǐn Shìchǎng; Map pp274–5; Dongtai Lu; ⏰ 8.30am-6pm) This market of over 100 stalls, a block west of Xizang Nanlu, is the city's most popular market for both expats and visitors alike. There's a lot of interest here, among the Mao memorabilia and carved wood, though only a fraction of the items really qualify as antique. Haggle hard here. Larger antique shops hide behind the stalls. It's a nice 15-minute walk from the old town to Dongtai Lu along Fangbang Zhonglu.

Shanghai Antique & Curio Store (Shànghǎi Wénwù Shāngdiàn; Map pp274–5; ☎ 6321 5868; 192-246 Guangdong Lu; ⏰ 9am-5pm) Designated tourist shops like this long-established place are expensive alternatives to the markets. Their range is good, but again, there's a lot of rubbish so you need a shrewd eye.

In the Hóngkǒu district, **Duolun Lu** (Map pp270–1) is lined with antique shops, art galleries, bookshops and curio stores. Dig around and you'll turn up all kinds of stuff, from revolutionary souvenirs to shadow puppets. Duolun Lu is within walk-ing distance of the East Baoxing Lu light rail station.

Supermarkets & Pharmacies

Local supermarkets are in almost every residential area and often stock many Western food items, especially the local chains **Hualian** and **Tops**.

City Supermarket (Chéngshi Chāoshì; Map pp274–5; ☎ 6279 8081; Shanghai Centre, 1376 Nanjing Xilu; ⏰ 8am-11.30pm) If you're craving obscure foods from home or need Western pharmaceutical items in a hurry, this is a convenient place in the Shanghai Centre but items are priced to the hilt. There's a good notice board with job and other miscellaneous ads. There's a branch in the basement of Times Square, 99 Huaihai Zhonglu (Map pp274–5).

Parkson (Bǎishèng Gòuwù Zhōngxīn; Map pp280–1; ☎ 6415 8818; 918 Huaihai Zhonglu; ⏰ 10am-10pm) The supermarket in the basement of the Parkson department store has a good selection.

Carrefour (Jiālèfú; Map pp270–1; ☎ 6209 8899; 268 Shuicheng Nanlu; ⏰ 8am-10pm) This French hypermarket chain has this branch in Gǔběi, plus others in Pǔdōng and the south of the city. It has very reasonable prices for food, clothes and household items and is extremely popular with locals.

Watson's (Qūchénshì; Westgate Mall, 1038 Nanjing Xilu (Map pp274–5) 787 Huaihai Zhonglu (Map pp280–1) This pharmacy has Western cosmetics, over-the-counter medicines and health products, with another convenient branch near the Jinchen Hotel and many other outlets around the city. Prices are similar to those you would pay in Hong Kong.

GETTING THERE & AWAY

Shànghǎi has rail and air connections to places all over China, ferries travelling up the Yangzi River (Cháng Jiāng), boats along the coast and buses to destinations in adjoining provinces.

Air

Shànghǎi has international flight connections to most major cities, many operated by China Eastern, which has its base here.

Daily (usually several times) domestic flights connect Shànghǎi to every major city in China. Prices include Běijīng (Y1030), Guǎngzhōu (Y1160), Chéngdū (Y1470) and Guìlín (Y1190), but travel agencies normally

KEREN SU

Night view of the Bund (p273), Shànghǎi

PHIL M WEYMOUTH

Shanghai Grand Theatre (p298)

Cafés and bicycles line Huaihai Lu in the former French concession (p278), Shànghǎi

CHRIS MELLOR

PHIL M WEYMOUTH

Shànghǎi skyline from M on the Bund (p294)

Riverfront walkway at Huangpu Park (p285), Shànghǎi

Revolutionary relief on the Customs House (p286), Shànghǎi

Old coins in the Dongtai Lu Antique Market (p300), Shànghǎi

Thousand-armed Avalokiteshvara (Guanyin) at the Jade Buddha Temple (p279) in Shànghǎi

offer discounted fares of up to 40%. Minor cities are less likely to have daily flights, but the chances are there will be at least one flight a week, probably more, to Shànghăi. The domestic departure tax is Y50.

You can buy air tickets almost anywhere, including major hotels and all travel agencies (see p273). The following airlines have offices in Shànghăi.

Aeroflot Russian Airlines (Map pp274-5; ☎ 6279 8033; 203A, Shanghai Centre, 1376 Nanjing Xilu)

Air China (Zhōngguó Mínháng; Map pp280-1; ☎ 6269 2999; www.airchina.com.cn; 600 Huashan Lu)

Air France (Map pp274-5; ☎ 6360 6688; www.airfrance .com.cn; room 1301, Novel Plaza, 128 Nanjing Xilu)

Asiana (Hanyà Hángkōng; Map pp270-1; ☎ 6219 4000; 2nd fl, Rainbow Hotel, 2000 Yan'an Xilu)

China Eastern Airlines (Zhōngguó Dōngfāng Mínháng; Map pp280-1; ☎ 6247 5953 domestic, ☎ 6247 2255 international; www.ce-air.com; 200 Yan'an Xilu; ☯ 24hr)

Dragonair (Gǎnglóng Hángkōng; Map pp274-5; ☎ 6375 6375; room 2103, Shanghai Square, 138 Huaihai Zhonglu)

Japan Airlines (JAL; Map pp274-5; ☎ 6288 3000; room 435, Plaza 66, 1266 Nanjing Xilu)

KLM (Map pp274-5; ☎ 6884 6884; room 2810, Plaza 66, 1266 Nanjing Xilu)

Malaysia Airlines (Map pp274-5; ☎ 6279 8607; 209, Shanghai Centre, 1376 Nanjing Xilu)

Northwest Airlines (Map pp274-5; ☎ 6279 8009; 204, Shanghai Centre, 1376 Nanjing Xilu)

Qantas Airways (Map pp274-5; ☎ 6279 8660; 203a, Shanghai Centre, 1376 Nanjing Xilu)

Singapore Airlines (Map pp280-1; ☎ 6289 1000; room 606, Kerry Centre, 1515 Nanjing Xilu)

Thai Airways International (Tàiguó Hángkōng; Map pp280-1; ☎ 5298 5555, 105 Kerry Centre, 1515 Nanjing Xilu)

United Airlines (Map pp280-1; ☎ 3311 4567; www .cn.united.com; 3301-17 Shanghai Central Plaza, 381 Huaihai Zhonglu)

Virgin Atlantic (Wéizhēn Hángkōng; Map pp274-5; ☎ 5353 4600; room 221-23, 12 Zhongshan Dong Yilu)

Boat

Boats are definitely one of the best ways to leave Shànghăi and they're often also the cheapest, especially for destinations inland along the Yangzi River. Many coastal routes, however, have all but dried up.

Domestic boat tickets can be bought from the **ferry booking office** (Shànghăi Gǎng Chuánpiào Dingshòuchù; Map pp274-5; 1 Jinling Donglu).

Overnight boats to Pǔtuóshān (11 hours) depart every day at 8pm. Tickets cost Y87 to

Y347, depending on the class. A rapid ferry service has buses departing daily at 8.15am and costs Y195 or Y225 deluxe. It's roughly a two-hour bus ride to the wharf and then a two-hour boat ride.

There are also boats every four days to Dàlián (36 hours) in Liáoníng province with tickets ranging from Y182 to Y662.

The main destinations of ferries up the Yangzi from Shànghăi are Nántōng, Nánjīng, Wúhú, Guìchí, Jiǔjiāng and Wǔhàn, with daily departures from Shiliupu Wharf. From Wǔhàn you can change to another ferry going to Chóngqìng. If you're only heading as far west as Nánjīng, take the train, which is much faster. (For full details on Yangzi cruises, see p768.)

Weekly ferries (every Tuesday) to Osaka and twice-monthly boats to Kōbe in Japan depart from the new **international passenger terminal** (Guójì Kèyùn Mǎtou; Map pp270-1; 100 Yangshupu Lu), by Lintong Lu. Tickets are sold by the two boat operators, **China Japan International Ferry Co** (☎ 6595 7988; 18th fl) and **Shanghai International Ferry Co** (☎ 6537 5111, www.shanghai-ferry.co.jp; 15th fl), both in the Jin'an Bldg, 908 Dongdaming Lu (Map pp270–1) in the northeast of town. Tickets to either destination (44 hours) range from Y1300 in an eight-bed dorm to Y6500 in a deluxe twin cabin. Reservations are recommended in July and August. Passengers must be at the harbour three hours before departure to get through immigration.

Bus

Shànghăi has a few long-distance bus stations but the most useful for travellers is probably the **Hengfeng Lu station** (Héngfēng Lù Kèyùnzhàn; Map pp274-5; ☎ 5663 0230), not far from Hanzhong Lu metro station. Deluxe buses leave for Běijīng (Y244, 13 hours), Hángzhōu (Y55, 2½ hours), Sūzhōu (Y30, 1½ hours), Nánjīng (Y88, four hours), Shàoxīng (Y70, three hours) and Níngbō (Y97, four hours).

Buses also leave from the **Xujiahui Bus Station** (Xújiāhuì Kèyùnzhàn; Map pp270-1; 6469 7325; 211 Hongqiao Lu), just west of the Xujiahui metro station. Besides the above destinations, buses here also go to Yángzhōu (Y81, 4½ hours) and Wúxī (Y36, two hours). Buses to Sūzhōu (Y50, 10am to 8pm), Hángzhōu (Y70, 10am to 7.30pm) and Nánjīng (Y100, 11.20pm to 7.40pm) also leave from the parking lot directly in front of the domestic arrival hall at Hongqiao Airport. There are also four or five buses a day from Shanghai Stadium to Wúxī (Y39) and Nánjīng (Y88).

There are three buses a day to Zhōuzhuāng (Y21, one hour), but you have to go to the **Northern Bus Station** (Běiqū Kèyùnzhàn; Map pp274-5; 80 Gongxing Lu), near the Baoshan Lu light rail station. Bus No 65 from the Bund passes nearby. Buses to Zhōuzhuāng also leave at 7am, 8.30am and 9am from the Shanghai Sightseeing Bus Centre (Map pp270-1; see p304) near the east entrance to the Shanghai Stadium, returning at 4.30pm. Tickets are Y110 return, which includes the entrance fee to Zhōuzhuāng. There are also daily return sightseeing buses to Tónglǐ for the same price.

Buses from the Shanghai Sightseeing Bus Centre, also run to Wūzhèn (Y120 including the entry) and Xītáng (Y110). You can also get to Wūzhèn by taking a bus from Shànghǎi to Jiāxīng (Y31, one hour) and from there take another bus to Wūzhèn (Y8, one hour).

Train
Shànghǎi is at the junction of the Běijīng–Shànghǎi and Běijīng–Hángzhōu train lines and many parts of the country can be reached by direct train from here.

Many options are available for buying train tickets in Shànghǎi. The easiest option is at the **Longmen Hotel ticket office** (Lóngmén Bīnguǎn huǒchēpiào shòupiàochù; Map pp274-5; ☎ 6317 9325; ⏰ 8-11.30am & 1-5pm), a short walk west of Shanghai train station. You can book sleepers up to nine days in advance here, with a Y5 service charge. You can also buy tickets at the much more chaotic ticket office to the southeast of the train station (no service charge).

There are also two advance **train booking outlets** (huǒchēpiào yùshòuchù; ⏰ 8am-6pm) 230 Beijing Donglu (Map pp274-5) 121 Xizang Nanlu (Map pp274-5) in the town centre. CITS at Jinling Donglu (see p273) also books train tickets (except to Hong Kong) for a Y5 service charge.

Most trains depart and arrive at the Shanghai train station (Shànghǎi zhàn; Map pp274-5). Trains to Hángzhōu (1¾ hours) also leave from the Meilong train station in the southwestern suburbs (take the metro to Jinjiang Amusement Park and walk 200m south).

Train No K99 leaves for Hong Kong's Kowloon (Jiǔlóng) district every other day at lunch time and takes 24 hours. Hard sleepers are Y559 to Y583, though they're more like the soft sleepers on standard Chinese trains. Soft sleepers cost Y908. You can get tickets at the Longmen Hotel ticket office.

The fast train from Shànghǎi to Běijīng (T110) does the journey in 14 hours. Hard sleepers are Y306 to Y327; soft sleepers cost Y499.

Other trains departing from Shànghǎi are: Fúzhōu (Y249, 21 hours), Guǎngzhōu (Y379, 25 hours), Hángzhōu (Y33 hard seat, two hours), Huángshān (Y103, 11½ hours), Kūnmíng (Y519, 46 hours), Chéngdū (Y490, 40 hours), Nánjīng (Y68 hard seat, Y86 soft seat, three hours), Xī'ān (Y333, 17 hours) and Ürümqi (Y675, 51 hours). All the above fares are hard sleeper unless otherwise noted.

Special double-decker 'tourist trains' operate between Shànghǎi and Hángzhōu, and Shànghǎi and Nánjīng (with stops at Wúxī, Sūzhōu, Hángzhōu and Zhènjiāng). They are comfortable soft-seat trains and smoking is forbidden; attendants bring around drinks and food.

GETTING AROUND
Shànghǎi is not a walker's dream. There are some fascinating areas to stroll around, but new road developments, building sites and shocking traffic conditions conspire to make walking an exhausting and often stressful experience.

The buses, too, are hard work; they're not easy to figure out, are difficult to squeeze into and out of and it's hard to know where they are going to stop. The metro system, however, is a dream.

Shànghǎi taxis are reasonably cheap and easy to flag down. Despite the improvements in roadways, Shànghǎi's traffic is turning into gridlock once again. Whichever mode of transport you use try to avoid rush hours between 8am and 9am, and 4.30pm and 6pm.

To/From the Airport
Hongqiao Airport (Hóngqiáo Fēijīchǎng; Map pp270-1; ☎ 6268 8918) is 18km from the Bund; getting there takes about 30 minutes if you're lucky, or over an hour if you're not. You can

take bus No 925 from Renmin Square to the airport. Bus No 806 goes from Xújiāhuì and Bus No 938 stops in front of the Huating Guesthouse (Map pp270–1) on Zhongshan Xilu. A CAAC bus (Y5) goes from the northeast corner of Yan'an Zhonglu and Shanxi Beilu. All these buses leave the airport from directly in front of the domestic departure hall. Taxis from the centre of town cost from Y50 to Y70, depending on the route taken, traffic conditions and the time of day.

Pudong International Airport (Pǔdōng Guójì Fēijīchǎng; ☎ 3848 4500) handles most international flights and some domestic flights. Always check your ticket to be sure which airport you're arriving at or departing from. **Airport bus No 1** (☎ 3848 4500; Y30) runs between Hongqiao and Pudong airports, bus No 2 (Y19) runs from Pudong International Airport to the **Airport City Terminal** (Jīchǎng Chéngshì Hángzhànlóu; Map pp280–1) near Jing'an Temple on Nanjing Xilu and bus No 5 (Y18) goes from Pudong International Airport to Pǔdōng and then the Shanghai train station. Buses run from 7am to 11pm. A taxi to Pudong International Airport from the city centre (one hour) costs around Y140.

The **Maglev train** (☎ 2890 7777; Y75) runs from Pudong airport to its terminal (Map pp270–1) in Pǔdōng in just eight minutes, from where you can transfer to the metro (Longyang Lu station). Trains run every 20 minutes from 8.30am to 5.30pm and hit warp speed at 430km/h.

Major hotels run an airport shuttle to both airports (generally free to Hongqiao; Y30 to Pǔdōng).

Bicycle
Captain Hostel (see p288) is one of the few places in town offering bike hire (Y10 for four hours, then Y2 per hour).

Bus
Many routes now offer deluxe air-con vehicles (Y2). Some useful bus routes are listed below, though the metro lines may be more convenient. Once on board, keep your valuables tucked away since pickpocketing is easy under such conditions.
No 11 Travels the ring road around the old Chinese city.
No 19 Links the Bund area to the Jade Buddha Temple area. Catch it at the intersection of Beijing Donglu and Sichuan Zhonglu.

No 20 Takes you to Renmin Square from the Bund.
No 42 Goes from the Bund at Guangdong Lu, passes Renmin Lu close to the Yu Gardens, heads along Huaihai Lu, up Xiangyang Lu then on to Xújiāhuì, terminating at the Shanghai Stadium.
No 61 Starts from just north of the Broadway Mansions at the intersection of Wusong Lu and Tiantong Lu, and goes past the PSB (Public Security Bureau) on its way along Siping Lu. No 55 from the Bund also goes by the PSB.
No 64 Gets you to Shanghai train station from near the Bund. Catch it on Beijing Donglu, close to the intersection with Sichuan Zhonglu. The ride takes 20 to 30 minutes.
No 65 Runs from the northeast of Shanghai train station and goes near the long-distance bus station on Gongxing Lu. It passes the Broadway Mansions, crosses Garden Bridge, and then heads directly south along the Bund to the end of Zhongshan Lu.
No 71 Takes you to the CAAC airport bus stop on Yan'an Zhonglu; catch it from Yan'an Donglu close to the Bund.
No 112 Zigzags north from the southern end of Renmin Square to Nanjing Xilu, down Shimen Erlu to Beijing Xilu then up Jiangning Lu to Jade Buddha Temple.
No 911 Leaves from Zhonghua Lu near the intersection with Fuxing Zhonglu, close to the Yuyuan Bazaar, and goes up Huaihai Lu, continuing to the zoo.

A tourist bus (Y2) shuttles exhausted shoppers up and down the pedestrian zone of Nanjing Donglu. Shanghai Sightseeing Buses (see p304) mostly runs buses to sights outside Shànghǎi, as well as two city bus routes that link up some useful sights:
No 3 Travels via Renmin Square to Pǔdōng's Pearl Tower (Y4) and Jinmao Tower (Y4); every 30 minutes from 7am to 5.30pm; pick it up from the stop just south of the Shanghai Museum on Yan'an Donglu.
No 10 Goes to Huaihai Zhonglu, Nanjing Donglu, Sichuan Beilu and Lu Xun Park (Y3); every 15 minutes from 6.30am to 7.30pm.

Ferry
Ferry boats shuttle across the Huangpu every 15 minutes between the southern Bund and Pǔdōng's Liujiazui District (Y0.5, Y2 air-con).

Metro
Shànghǎi has two metro lines and one light rail line. The No 1 line runs from Shanghai train station in the north through Renmin Square and down to the Xinzhuang metro station in the southern part of town.

The No 2 line runs from Zhongshan Park to Longyang Lu in Pǔdōng. Eventually it will extend to Hongqiao airport. The light rail doubles as the third metro line and runs on the western perimeter of the city from the southern suburbs to Shanghai train station then northeast towards Fudan University.

Tickets are between Y2 and Y6 depending on the distance. Stored value tickets are available for Y50 and Y100 but don't offer any savings.

Taxi

Taxi fares start at Y10 for the first 3km (Y13 from 11pm to 5am). Major taxi companies include:

Bashi (☎ 96840)
Dazhong (☎ 96822, 82222)
Qiansheng (☎ 6258 0000)

AROUND SHÀNGHǍI

Shànghǎi municipality includes the satellite towns of Sōngjiāng, Jiādìng, Jīnshān and Bǎoshān. The sights listed in this section can be done as day trips. Some sites can even be reached by intrepid bikers, though to really enjoy the trip you may want to transport yourself and your bike partway out of the city in a taxi first.

The most popular day trips from Shànghǎi are probably to Zhōuzhuāng (p250) and Tónglǐ (p252), outside the municipality.

The best way to get to most of the following sights is one of the punctual and convenient **Shanghai Sightseeing Buses** (Shànghǎi Lǚyóu Jísàn Zhōngxīn; Map pp270-1; ☎ 6426 5555 Chinese only) based at the eastern end of Shanghai Stadium.

SŌNGJIĀNG 松江

Sōngjiāng County, 30km southwest of Shànghǎi, was thriving when Shànghǎi was still a dream in an opium trader's eye, though you only get a sense of its antiquity in the timeless backstreets in the west and southwest of town.

The most famous monument is the **Square Pagoda** (Fāng Tǎ; admission Y5), in the southeast of the town. The 48.5m nine-storey tower was built between 1068 and 1077 as part of the Xingshengjiao Temple, which is long gone. During reconstruction in 1975 a brick vault containing a bronze Buddha and other relics was discovered under foundations. The

screen wall in front of the pagoda shows the legendary *tan*, a monster of such greed that it tried to drink the sea and ended up killing itself. The Buddhist frieze teaches that desire leads to disaster.

Next to the park is the mildly interesting **Songjiang Museum** (Sōngjiāng Bówùguǎn; admission Y2; ⊗ closed noon-1pm Tue-Sun).

Other attractions in town include the **Xilin Pagoda**, a 30-minute walk to the west of town, and the **Toroni Sutra Stela**, built in AD 859, which is Shànghǎi's oldest Buddhist structure. The tower stands rather incongruously in the Zhongshan Primary School, directly opposite the Songjiang Hotel. You can go in to look but be prepared to be shadowed by a trail of nine-year-olds following you like the Pied Piper.

The **Songjiang Mosque** (Sōngjiāng Qīngzhēnsì; admission Y5), in the west of town, is worth a visit. Built between 1341 and 1367 in the Chinese style, it's one of the oldest mosques in China. There are around 300 Muslims in Sōngjiāng and worshippers converge on the mosque every Friday lunch time. To get there, head south from the junction of Zhongshan Zhonglu and Renmin Nanlu, and follow a signposted alley leading off to the west.

South of the mosque is the **Zuibaichí** (Pool of Drunken Bai; admission Y5). The park is built around the villa of the painter Gu Dashen, who built the pool in 1659 in honour of Li Bai (or Li Bo), the famous Tang poet. Bai drowned when he fell drunk into a pond, trying to grasp a reflection of the moon.

Getting There & Away

The best way to get to Sōngjiāng is by sightseeing bus No 1A, which runs every 20 minutes for Y10. If you don't fancy the walk between sights, cycle rickshaws ferry people around town for a few kuài. It's possible to combine a visit to Sōngjiāng with Shéshān but you'd need to take a taxi to Shéshān (around Y30), before taking the sightseeing bus back to Shànghǎi.

SHÉSHĀN 佘山

The resort area of Shéshān is 30km southwest of Shànghǎi and is the only part of Shànghǎi to have anything that even remotely resembles a hill.

The main reason to come out here is to see the Catholic **Sheshan Cathedral** (Shéshān Tiānzhǔjiào Táng; admission to the hill Y8, to the church Y2), which is perched magnificently on the top of the hill. The original Holy Mother Cathedral was built here between 1863 and 1866, and the current Basilica of Notre Dame was completed in 1935. The most interesting way to climb the hill is via the south gate, which takes you up along a Via Dolorosa, past a smaller church (built 1894), a shop selling crucifixes and statues of the Virgin Mary, and several holy shrines. You can also take a cable car up to the top for Y15 return, or Y8 down.

Sunday is an interesting time to visit, as is May when many local Catholics make pilgrimages here. Photography is not allowed in the church.

Just next to the church is the **Jesuit observatory** (Tiānéntái; admission Y6), built in 1900. Its modern counterpart stands to the west. China's latest hi-tech earthquake monitoring system in the East China Sea was named after the observatory. On the east side of the hill is the 20m, seven-storey **Xiudaozhe Pagoda** (built 976–84).

Intrepid explorers can head 8km southwest of Shēshān to Tiānmăshān and the **Huzhu Pagoda** (Hùzhŭ Tă), built in AD 1079 and known as the leaning tower of China. The 19m-high tower started tilting 200 years ago and now has an inclination exceeding the tower at Pisa by 1.5°. There are occasional minibuses from Shēshān to Tiānmăshān village, which is at the foot of the hill. A better option is to take a taxi (Y20) or a motorcycle taxi (Y10).

Getting There & Away

Sightseeing bus No 1B heads to Shēshān every hour from Shànghăi, as do private minibuses (Y6). If you want to combine a visit to Shēshān with Sōngjiāng, head to Shēshān first as it's easier to catch a bus on to Sōngjiāng than vice versa. A taxi to/from Shànghăi costs around Y70 one-way.

JIĀDÌNG 嘉定

Jiādìng is a laid-back town surrounded by a canal, about 20km northwest of Shànghăi. Together with Nánxiáng, the town makes for a pleasant day excursion, especially if you pack a picnic for one of the parks.

Sightseeing bus No 6A drops passengers at the **Dragon Meeting Pond** (Huìlóng Tán; admission Y5), a peaceful garden built in 1588 and named after the five streams that feed into the central pool.

Exit out of the west gate to get to the **Confucius Temple** (Wén Miào; ☻ 8-11.30am & 1.30-4.30pm), built in 1219. On the way you'll pass 72 carved lions, representing the 72 outstanding disciples of Confucius. The temple houses the **Jiading County Museum** (Jiādìng Xiàn Bówùguăn), which exhibits the history of the county as well as some local bamboo carving.

A five-minute walk north of the temple along Nan Dajie takes you to the seven-storey **Fahua Pagoda**, and the interesting cobbled and canalled heart of the town. There are several enticing shops and places to eat around the pagoda.

Five minutes' walk northeast along the canal on Dong Dajie takes you to the enchanting **Garden of Autumn Clouds** (Qiūxiápŭ; admission Y8), one of the finest gardens around Shànghăi. Nearby, across the canal, is a huge produce market.

On the way back to Shànghăi, sightseeing bus No 6A passes through the town of Nánxiáng, where (if you are not gardened out) you can stop off at the large **Garden of Ancient Splendour** (Gŭyì Yuán), which was built between 1522 and 1566, and then rebuilt in 1746.

Getting There & Away

Sightseeing bus No 6A runs to Jiādìng (Y10) every 40 minutes from Shanghai Stadium via Nánxiáng (Y6).

Zhèjiāng 浙江

CONTENTS

HIGHLIGHTS

- Sunbathe on the tranquil Buddhist island of **Pǔtuóshān** (p322)
- Journey to spectacular **Tiāntái Shān** (p327), home of Tiantai Buddhism
- Explore the rural villages of remote **Jǐngnìng County** (p326)
- Stroll along the shores of the legendary **West Lake** (p311) in Hángzhōu
- Pay a visit to the stately home of **Lu Xun** (p317) in Shàoxīng, considered the father of modern Chinese literature

Hángzhōu ★
Pǔtuóshān ★
★ Shàoxīng
Tiāntái Shān ★
★ Jǐngning (Hèxī)

■ POP: 44.7 MIL	■ AREA: 101,800 SQ KM	■ http://english.zjol.com.cn

Zhèjiāng is one of China's smallest, and most prosperous, provinces. The region is mainly divided between the area north of Hángzhōu, which is part of the Yangzi River delta, cut with rivers and canals, and the mountainous area to the south, which continues the rugged terrain of Fújiàn. The jagged coastline of Zhèjiāng has 18,000 islands – more than any other province.

Intensely cultivated for a thousand years, northern Zhèjiāng has lost most of its natural vegetation and is now a flat, featureless plain. The Grand Canal (Dà Yùnhè) ends here – Zhèjiāng was part of the great southern granary from which food was shipped to the depleted areas of the north. The southern Jiāngsū and northern Zhèjiāng region is known as Jiāngnán, 'south of the river'.

Most of Zhèjiāng's tourist sites are in the northern parts of the province. Hángzhōu, the capital, is home to China's most famous tourist attraction, West Lake, which has a deserved reputation for its beautiful scenery. The city is also famous for its tea and has long been a centre of silk production. Not far from Hángzhōu is Shàoxīng, a pleasant town that was once the home of such notables as the Ming Painter Xu Wei, and Lu Xun, one of China's most famous 20th-century writers.

Zhèjiāng has many other natural attractions for those looking for an escape from the frenzy of city life. A major destination for travellers is the Buddhist island of Pǔtuóshān, with its sandy beaches and temples. Tiāntái Shān, the birthplace of the Tiantai sect of Buddhism, draws a steady string of pilgrims every year to its sacred temples, some of which date back over 1300 years. In the far south of the province is remote Yàndàng Shān, a mountain paradise with sheer cliffs and lush subtropical terrain.

History

The Yangzi delta was inhabited over 7000 years ago and archaeologists have found the remains of advanced agricultural communities. By the 7th and 8th centuries Hángzhōu, Níngbō and Shàoxīng had become three of the most important trading centres and ports. Their growth was accelerated when, in the 12th century, the Song dynasty moved court to Hángzhōu in the wake of an invasion from the north.

Níngbō was opened up as a treaty port in the 1840s, only to fall under the shadow of its great northern competitor, Shànghǎi. Chiang Kaishek was born near Níngbō, and in the 1920s Zhèjiāng became a centre of power for the Kuomintang.

Climate

Zhèjiāng has a humid, subtropical climate, with hot, sticky summers and chilly winters. Rain hits the province hard in May and June but slows to a drizzle throughout the rest of the year. The best times to visit are during the spring (late March–early May) when the humidity is lowest and the vegetation a brilliant green.

Language

Zhèjiāng residents speak a variation of the Wu dialect (Wú Yǔ), which is also spoken in Jiāngsū. The dialect is almost unintelligible from city to city and residents rely on standard Mandarin to communicate.

Getting There & Away

Being an important tourist destination, Zhèjiāng is very well connected, with many planes, trains and buses leaving daily. Ferries were once the traditional means of getting around the region and still in use today, though mainly for shuttling hordes of tourists around. Ferries travel from Háng-zhōu and Wēnzhōu to Nánjīng, Shànghǎi and Sūzhōu.

Getting Around

As the province is quite small, getting around is easy. For the most part, travelling by bus is safe, fast and convenient. Trains are also an option, though at times more circuitous and slower than buses. Flying is an option, especially for those with limited time and cash to spare.

HÁNGZHŌU 杭州

☎ 571 / pop 6.16 million

'In heaven there is paradise, on earth Sūz-hōu and Hángzhōu'. So runs one of China's oldest tourist blurbs. For the Chinese, Hángzhōu (along with Guìlín) is the country's most famous tourist attraction. With its greenery and parks, the city itself is quite pleasant. However, the star attraction is scenic West Lake, which has inspired poets and painters for centuries.

History

Hángzhōu's history goes back to the start of the Qin dynasty (221 BC). When Marco Polo passed through the city in the 13th century he described it as one of the most splendid in the world.

Although Hángzhōu prospered greatly after it was linked with the Grand Canal in AD 610, it really came into its own after the

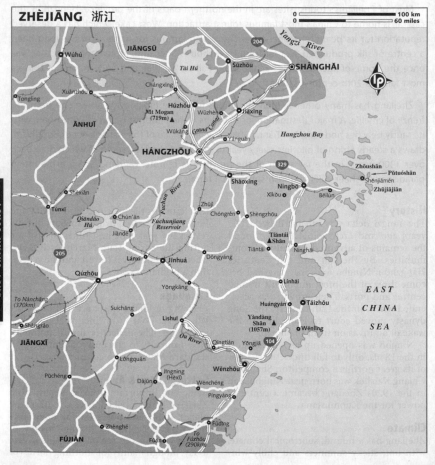

Song dynasty was overthrown by the invading Juchen, predecessors of the Manchus.

The Song capital of Kāifēng, along with the emperor and the leaders of the imperial court, was captured by the Juchen in 1126. The rest of the Song court fled south, finally settling in Hángzhōu and establishing it as the capital of the Southern Song dynasty.

When the Mongols swept into China they established their court at Běijīng. Hángzhōu, however, retained its status as a prosperous commercial city. In 1861 the Taipings laid siege to the city and captured it, but two years later the imperial armies took it back. These campaigns reduced almost the entire city to ashes, led to the deaths of over half a million of its residents through disease, starvation and warfare, and finally ended Hángzhōu's significance as a commercial and trading centre.

Few monuments survived the devastation, and most of those that did became victims of the Red Guards a century later during the Cultural Revolution. Much of what can be seen in Hángzhōu today is of fairly recent construction.

Orientation

Hángzhōu is bounded to the south by the Qiantang River and to the west by hills. Between the hills and the urban area is West Lake. The eastern shore of the lake is the developed touristy district; the western shore is quieter.

Information

BOOKSHOPS
Foreign Languages Bookshop (Zhèjiāng Wàiwén Shūdiàn; 446 Fengqi Lu) Has a good selection of maps and books about Hángzhōu in English and Chinese.

EMERGENCY
Public Security Bureau (PSB; Gōngānjú; ☎ 8706 8080; 35 Huaguang Lu) Helps in emergencies in addition to extending visas.
SOS Evacuation Services (☎ 021-6295 0099) In a medical emergency, call this English-speaking service, located in Shànghǎi.
Tourist Complaint Hotline (☎ 8796 9691)

INTERNET ACCESS
Internet cafés are plentiful around the universities and around West Lake. Most cafés charge Y2 to Y4 per hour.

INTERNET RESOURCES
www.hangzhou.com.cn or **www.gotohz.com** Both websites provide current information on events, restaurants and entertainment venues around the city.

MEDICAL SERVICES
Shengzhong Hospital (Shēngzhōng Yīyuàn; ☎ 7068 8001; 3 Qingchun Lu) Has a good reputation among expats and is close to the lake.

MONEY
Bank of China (Zhōngguó Yínháng; 320 Yan'an Lu; ⊙ 9am-5pm) Has a secure, well-lit ATM. Travellers cheques can be changed here, as well as at other branches

THE GRAND CANAL

The world's longest canal, the Grand Canal once meandered the almost 1800km from Běijīng to Hángzhōu and is a striking example of China's sophisticated engineering prowess. Today perhaps half of it remains seasonally navigable. The government claims that since liberation, large-scale dredging has made the navigable length 1100km. However, canal depths are up to 3m and canal widths can narrow to less than 9m. Putting these facts together, and taking into account some of the old stone bridges spanning the route, it's clear that it's restricted to fairly small, flat-bottomed vessels in some places.

The Grand Canal's construction spanned many centuries. The first 85km were completed in 495 BC, but the mammoth task of linking the Yellow River (Huáng Hé) and the Yangzi River (Cháng Jiāng) was undertaken during Sui times by a massive conscripted labour force between AD 605 and 609. It was developed again during the Yuan dynasty (1271–1368). The canal enabled the government to capitalise on the growing wealth of the Yellow River basin and to ship supplies from south to north.

Sections of the canal have been silted up for centuries; however, the canal comes into its own south of the Yellow River, where concern for tourism has ensured year-round navigation. The Jiāngnán section of the canal (Hángzhōu, Sūzhōu, Wúxī and Chángzhōu) is a skein of canals, rivers and branching lakes.

HÁNGZHŌU 杭州

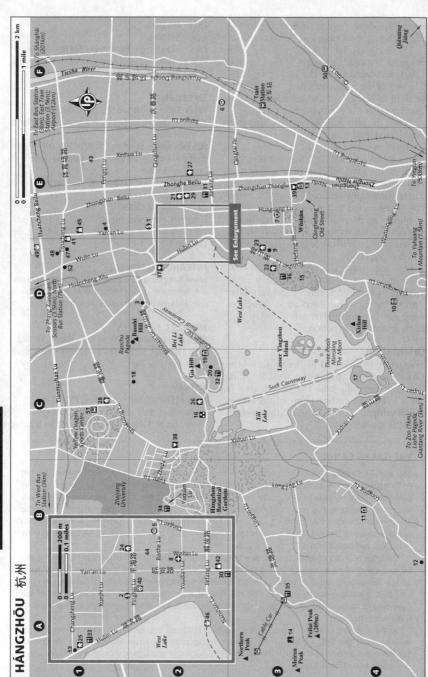

around town. It's also possible to change money at high-end hotels (guests only).

POST

Post Office (Yóujú) At the western end of Jiefang Lu. More convenient post and telephone offices can be found on Yan'an Lu.

TOURIST INFORMATION & TRAVEL AGENCIES

There's a tourist office immediately to your left as you exit the train station at the bottom level. It has maps (Y5) in English and Chinese.

China International Travel Service (CITS; Zhōngguó Guójì Lūxíngshè; ☎ 8521 5525; 1 Beishan Lu) Look for its office in the collection of buildings overlooking the north end of the Báidī Causeway.

Sights

WEST LAKE 西湖

There are 36 lakes in China called **West Lake** (Xī Hú), but this one is by far the most famous. Indeed, this West Lake is the one from which all others take their name.

West Lake was originally a lagoon adjoining the Qiantang River. In the 8th century the governor of Hángzhōu had it dredged;

later a dyke was built that cut it off from the river completely. The resulting lake is about 3km long and a bit under 3km wide. Two causeways, the Báidī and the Sūdī, split the lake into sections.

The largest island in the lake is **Gu Hill** (Gū Shān) – the location of the Zhejiang Provincial Museum, **Zhongshan Park** (Zhōngshān Gōngyuán) and the restaurant Lóuwàilóu Càiguǎn (p313). The island's buildings and garden were part of the holiday palace of Emperor Qianlong in the 18th century. The Báidī Causeway links the island to the mainland.

The smaller island in the middle of the lake is known as **Lesser Yingzhou Island** (Xiǎo Yíngzhōu), where you can look over at **Three Pools Mirroring the Moon** (Sāntán Yìnyuè), the three small towers in the water on the south side of the island. **Red Carp Pond** (Huāgǎng Guānyú; admission Y10) is a chief attraction and is home to a few thousand red carp.

Hángzhōu's **Botanical Gardens** (Zhíwùyuán) are very pleasant to wander around and even have a sequoia pine presented by Richard Nixon on his 1972 visit.

Liulang Wenying Park (Liǔlàng Wènyīng Gōngyuán; admission Y5) was once an imperial garden during the Song dynasty. Today the park is famous for its willow trees and is the site of the West Lake lantern festival, held after the spring festival.

LINGYIN TEMPLE 灵隐寺

This **temple** (Língyǐn Sì; Lingyin Lu; admission adult/child Y20/10; 🕐 7am-5pm) is another of Hángzhōu's main attractions.

It was built in AD 326 and, due to war and calamity, has been destroyed and restored no fewer than 16 times.

The present buildings are restorations of Qing dynasty structures. The Hall of the Four Heavenly Guardians at the front of the temple is inscribed with the couplet 'cloud forest Buddhist temple', penned by the Qing emperor Kangxi, a frequent visitor to Hángzhōu, who was inspired by the sight of the temple in the mist and trees.

Bus No K7 and tourist bus No 2 (both from the train station), and tourist bus No 1 from the roads circling West Lake, go to the temple. Behind Lingyin Temple is the **Northern Peak** (Běi Gāofēng), which can be scaled via cable car (Y20). From the summit there are sweeping views across the lake and city.

ZHEJIANG PROVINCIAL MUSEUM 浙江省博物馆

This is an excellent **museum** (Zhèjiāng Shěng Bówùguǎn; 25 Gushan Lu; 🕐 8.30am-4.30pm Tue-Sun; admission Y10), with exhibits on the pre-history and history of Zhèjiāng. Captions are in English and Chinese.

MAUSOLEUM OF GENERAL YUE FEI 岳飞墓

During the 12th century, when China was attacked by Juchen invaders from the north, General Yue Fei (1103–41 BC) was commander of the Song armies.

Despite his successes against the invaders, he was recalled to the Song court where he was executed after being deceived by Qin Hui, a treacherous court official. More than 20 years later, in 1163, Song emperor Gao Zong exonerated Yue Fei and had his corpse reburied at the present site.

The **mausoleum** (Yuè Fēi Mù; Beishan Lu; admission adult/child Y20/10; 🕐 7am-5.30pm) is in a compound bounded by a red-brick wall. Inside is a large statue of the general and the words, 'return the mountains and rivers to us', a reference to his patriotism and resistance to the Juchen.

LIUHE PAGODA 六和塔

Southwest of the city stands an enormous rail-and-road bridge that spans the Qiantang River. Close by is this 60m-high octagonal **pagoda** (Liùhé Tǎ; 16 Zhijiang Lu; admission Y20; 🕐 6am-6pm), which once also served as a lighthouse. Climbing the pagoda is Y10 extra.

Behind the pagoda is a charming walk through terraces dotted with shrines, bells, sculptures and inscriptions. Take bus No 308 from near the post office on Yan'an Lu.

OTHER SIGHTS

The **China Academy of Art** (Zhōngguó Měishù Xuéyuàn; ☎ 8778 8027; 218 Nanshan Lu), founded in 1928, was the first comprehensive art academy established in China. Located on the bank of the West Lake, the academy teaches traditional and modern art forms to local and international students. Departments include painting, design, sculpture and art history. There are short-term classes available to visiting foreign students who wish to learn something about traditional Chinese painting. The gallery inside the academy features exhibitions by students and well-known artists working in a variety of media.

The **Zoo** (Dòngwùyuán; Hupao Lu; admission adult/child Y10/5; 🕐 9.30am-3.30pm) is south of the lake, on the way to Liuhe Pagoda. It has Manchurian tigers, which are larger than their southern counterparts and are protected species.

Travellers have recommended the **China Silk Museum** (Zhōngguó Sīchóu Bówùguǎn; 73-1 Yuhuangshan Lu; admission Y10; 🕐 8.30am-4.30pm). There are good displays of silk samples, and exhibits explaining the history and process of silk production. English-speaking tour guides are available. Bus No 38 from Zhongshan Beilu or Nanshan Lu goes by the museum.

Tea is another one of Hángzhōu's specialties and you'll find all you need to know at the **China Tea Museum** (Zhōngguó Cháyè Bówùguǎn; Longjing Lu; admission Y10; 🕐 8am-5pm). Tourist bus No 3 or bus No 27 from Beishan Lu will take you there. Further up the road you can enjoy one of Hángzhōu's most famous teas at the **Dragon Well Tea Village** (Lóngjǐng Wènchá; admission Y35), named after the spring where the pattern in the water resembles a dragon. Tourist bus No 3, which leaves from in front of the Yellow Dragon Sports Centre, will take you there.

At the south end of Zhongshan Zhonglu, **Qinghefang Old Street** (Qīnghéfáng Gǔjiē) has undergone extensive restoration. It's the location of the **Huqing Yutang Chinese Medicine Museum** (Zhōngyào Bówùguǎn; 95 Dajing Gang; admission Y10; ☯ 8.30am-6pm), which is an actual dispensary and clinic. Originally established by the Qing dynasty merchant Hu Xueyan in 1874, the medicine shop and factory retain the typical style of the period.

Yellow Dragon Cave (Huánglóngdòng; admission Y5) is in a secluded park with steep hills, bamboo and teahouses. The cave itself is not interesting, but the surrounding park is very picturesque.

Tours

Just about every mid-range to top-end hotel offers tours to West Lake and the surrounding areas. Special tour buses leave from the front of the Yellow Dragon Sports Centre and pass by all the major tourist sights. A ride on one of these buses costs Y2.

Festivals & Events

One of the most important festivals is the **International Qiantang River Tide-Observing Festival**, which takes place every autumn in Yánguān, outside Hángzhōu (see p315).

Sleeping

Hángzhōu's hotels are mainly mid-range and top end, with only a few budget options. During the busy summer months and during Chinese New Year, hotels can be booked out, prices soar and finding accommodation can be difficult. Most mid-range and top-end hotel rooms are equipped with free broadband Internet.

BUDGET

Hangzhou International Youth Hostel (Hángzhōu Guójì Qīngnián Lǚshè; ☎ 8791 8948; 101 Nanshan Lu; dm Y40/120) Located right on the lake and across from the China Academy of Art, this hostel is in a convenient location. It offers ticket booking, Internet access, and rents bikes and camping gear.

International Art Centre Inn (Yìyàn Bīnguǎn; ☎ 8707 0100; 220 Nanshan Lu; d Y480) This hotel is across from the lake and next to the China Academy of Art. Rooms are clean and offer good value.

Tang's Ruibao Inn (Tángrén Ruìbǎo Bīnguǎn; ☎ 8788 0088; fax 8702 5007; 125 Qingyin Street; s & d Y178) This simply furnished hotel is just off the intersection of Pinghai Lu and Zhonghe Beilu in a very convenient location. All rooms come with free Internet access. Make sure to ask for a discount.

MID-RANGE & TOP END

Zhongshan Hotel (Zhōngshān Dàjiǔdiàn; ☎ 8706 8899; fax 8702 2403; 15 Pinghai Lu; d Y680) This hotel offers very modern comfortable rooms and is about a ten minute walk to the lake. Most rooms come with free Internet. Rooms are often discounted as low as Y280.

Overseas Chinese Hotel (Huáqiáo Fàndiàn; ☎ 8707 4401; fax 8707 4978; 15 Hubin Lu; d Y544-603) This hotel is in a great location on the lakeside and very popular with tour groups.

Marco Polo Hotel (Mǎkěbōluó Jiàrì Fàndiàn; ☎ 8701 8888; 38 Pinghai Lu; d Y800-1000) One of the nicest hotels within walking distance to the lake, with spacious rooms and free Internet access. The hotel restaurants (p314) are quite good and worth checking out, even if you don't stay here.

Hangzhou Continental Hotel (Wǔzhōu Dàjiǔdiàn; ☎ 8708 8088; fax 8707 7618; 2 Pinghai Lu; d Y1000) This four-star hotel is on the Pinghai Lu hotel strip, and offers superior facilities and a good location.

Shangri-La Hotel (☎ 8707 7951; www.shangri-la.com; 78 Beishan Lu; s US$180-290, d US$200-310, plus 15% service charge) The most elegant and romantic top-end hotel in Hángzhōu, surrounded by spacious forested grounds.

World Trade Centre Hotel (Shìjiè Màoyì Zhōngxīn Dàfàndiàn; ☎ 8799 0888; fax 8795 0088; 122 Shuguang Lu; d/tw Y1180) This massive plaza near the Yellow Dragon Sports Centre is very ugly on the outside, but the amenities are typical of a five-star hotel.

Eating

Across from the China Academy of Art is Xīhú Tiāndì, a collection of upscale restaurants and coffee shops in a beautiful garden setting on the shores of West Lake. At the time of writing, many of the restaurants were in the process of being built.

Luówàilóu Càiguǎn (30 Gushan Lu; mains Y30-100; ☯ breakfast, lunch & dinner) Right on West Lake, this place has been around since 1848 and is probably Hángzhōu's most famous restaurant. The local speciality is *xīhú cùyú* (poached fish in sweet vinegar sauce; Y35).

Tiānwàitiān Càiguǎn (2 Lingying Tianzhu Lu; mains Y30-90; ☺ lunch & dinner) Run by the same group who own Luówàilóu Càiguǎn, this restaurant gets mixed reviews. Dishes to look out for are *dōngpō ròu* (fatty pork slices flavoured with Shàoxīng wine; Y45), named after the Song dynasty poet Su Dongpo, and *jiàohuàzi jī* (Y85), chicken wrapped up and baked in charcoal, known in English as 'beggar's chicken'.

Shānwàishān Càiguǎn (8 Yuquan Lu; mains Y40-80; ☺ lunch & dinner) Set amid the lush vegetation of the Botanical Gardens, this sprawling place is another Hángzhōu 'famous' restaurant.

Kuiyuan Restaurant (Kuíyuán Guǎn; 124 Jiefang Lu; mains Y10; ☺ lunch & dinner) This restaurant is over 100 years old, and has garnered a reputation for its excellent noodle and seafood dishes. It serves over forty kinds of noodles, the most famous being the shrimp and fried eel.

Paradise Restaurant (36 Hubin Lu; meals Y45-120; ☺ lunch & dinner) Located right by the lake, this fashionable restaurant serves good Italian food in a comfortable atmosphere.

Top-end hotels dish out a wide range of superior cuisine. The **Marco Polo Hotel** (Mǎkēbōluó Jiàrì Fàndiàn; ☎ 8701 8888; 38 Pinghai Lu) offers a Mediterranean-style set dinner for Y48, including dessert.

The **Yintai Department Store** (Yíntài Bǎihuò Dàlóu; ☺ 9am-9pm) and the **International Department Store** (Guójì Dàshà; ☺ 9am-9pm) at the northern end of Yan'an Lu have decent food courts on the upper levels.

To self-cater, head to **Carrefour Shopping Centre** (Jiālèfú; 135 Yan'an Lu; ☺ 9am-9pm)

Drinking

Shamrock (Sān Xiě; 70 Zhongshan Zhonglu; beer Y25; ☺ until late) This pub in the Qinghefang area has a wonderful laidback atmosphere and is popular with foreign teachers.

Casablanca Country Pub (Kǎsàbùlánkǎ Xiāngcūn Jùlèbù; 23 Hubin Lu; beer Y25; ☺ 6pm-late) This cosy bar has been around for a while, still attracting locals and tourists alike.

Reggae Bar (Lígén Jiǔbā; 46 Shuguang Lu; beer Y20; ☺ 7pm-late) This rather nondescript place is popular with the foreign student crowd.

Entertainment

Hángzhōu has several cinemas that screen English-language movies. Close to the lake is the **West Lake Cinema** (Xīhú Diànyǐngyuàn; 95 Pinghai Lu; admission Y30).

Shopping

Hángzhōu is well known for its tea, in particular Longjing (Dragon Well) green tea (grown in the Lóngjǐng area, southwest of West Lake), as well as silk, fans and, of all things, scissors.

Wúshān has all sorts of touristy kitsch. Fake ceramics jostle with ancient pewter tobacco pipes, Chairman Mao memorabilia, silk shirts and pirated CDs. Get the gloves off and haggle hard if something catches your eye.

For silk, try the **market** (Xinhua Lu; ☺ 8am-6pm), a couple of blocks east of Zhonghe Beilu. The silk area starts on the north side of Fengqi Lu. Make sure you check that the silk is genuine and not a polyester clone (it should feel smooth and soft between your thumb and finger).

Jiefang Lu Department Store (Jiěfàng Lù Bǎihuò Shāngdiàn; 211 Jiefang Lu; ☺ 9am-9pm) Another good place to buy silk is on the 2nd floor of this place. A range of prints, as well as solid colours, cost Y40 to Y60 per metre.

Zhang Xiaoquan Scissors (Zhāng Xiǎoquán Jiǎndāo; 27 Daguan Lu; ☺ 8am-5pm Mon-Fri) This enterprise has been around since the beginning of the Qing dynasty. It also has a small museum (admission Y2), but phone ahead for an appointment. Take bus No 58 from Tiyuchang Lu.

Getting There & Away

AIR

For flights, Hángzhōu is serviced by **Dragonair** (Gǎnglóng Hángkōng Gōngsī; ☎ 8506 8388; 5th fl, Radisson Plaza Hotel, 333 Tiyuchang Lu), with regular connections to all major Chinese cities. There are several flights a day to Běijīng (Y1050), Guǎngzhōu (Y960) and Hong Kong (Y1840).

The best place to book air tickets is the **Hangzhou Xiaoshan International Airport Ticketing Office** (Hángzhōu Xiǎoshān Guójì Jīchǎng Shòupiàochù; ☎ 8515 4259; 309 Tiyuchang Lu) Most hotels will also book flights, generally with a Y20 to Y30 service charge.

BOAT

You can get to both Wúxī and Sūzhōu by boat up the Grand Canal from Hángzhōu. There's one boat daily for Sūzhōu, leaving at

5.30pm, and one leaving for Wúxī at 6pm. Both trips take 13 hours. Economy class in a cabin of four people costs Y70. Deluxe cabins for four people are Y98 per bed and two-person cabins cost Y86 to Y150 per bed. Buy tickets at the wharf just north of Huancheng Beilu and get on the boat at a new facility nearby at 138 Huancheng Beilu.

BUS

All three long-distance bus stations are located outside the city centre. Note that with all the new bus companies appearing, prices change rapidly. The north bus station on Moganshan Lu has buses to Nánjīng (Y113, five hours), Wǔkāng (Y10, 1½ hours) and other points in Jiāngsū.

Buses for Qiāndǎo Hú (Y30, four hours) and Huáng Shān (Y55, six hours) leave from the west bus station on Tianmushan Lu.

The east bus station is the most comprehensive, with frequent deluxe buses to Shànghǎi (Y54, 2½ hours), Shàoxīng (Y18.5, one hour) and Níngbō (Y42, two hours). Economy buses are cheaper, but slower. Buses to Tiāntái Shān (Y43, six hours) and Hǎiníng (Y20, one hour) also leave from here. The south bus station has buses to Wenzhou (Y100, nine hours).

TRAIN

Trains from Hangzhou's main train station go south to Xiàmén (Y224, 25 hours), Nánchāng (Y159, 10 hours), Wēnzhōu (Y62, eight hours) and Guǎngzhōu (Y379, 23 hours), and east to Shàoxīng (Y13, one hour) and Níngbō (Y29, 2½ hours). Most trains heading north have to go to Shànghǎi, but there's a direct train to Běijīng (Y363, 16 hours) from Hángzhōu.

Fast trains from Hángzhōu to Shànghǎi (Y17) make the trip in two hours, with some trains continuing through to Sūzhōu. Booking sleepers can be difficult at the Hángzhōu train station, especially to Běijīng. Most hotels can do this for you for a Y20 service charge. You can also buy tickets at the **train ticket booking office** (199 Wulin Lu; ✆ 8am-5pm).

Getting Around
TO/FROM THE AIRPORT

Hángzhōu's airport is 30km from the city centre; taxi drivers ask around Y120 for the trip. Shuttle buses leave from the Marco Polo Hotel.

BICYCLE

Bikes are available for hire from a couple of places and are the best way to get around. Probably the most convenient place is the outlet beside the Overseas Chinese Hotel. Rentals are Y6 per hour and a deposit of Y300 to Y400 is required.

Check out the bikes before you take off, especially the brakes.

BOAT

The boating industry on West Lake has been regulated in recent years. Boat operators are dressed in light blue uniforms and charge Y80 per hour. They are on the northern and eastern shores. Hiring a private boat is worth the splurge. Less intimate larger boats depart from the eastern shore, crossing the lake and visiting the islands en route for Y45.

BUS

Bus No K7 is very useful, as it connects the main train station to the major hotel area on the eastern side of the lake. Bus Nos 15 and K15 connect the north bus station to the northwest area of West Lake. Bus No K56 travels from the east bus station to Yan'an Lu. Bus No 27 is useful for travel between the east and west sides of the lake. Tourist bus No 1 does a circles the lake to Lingyin Temple, and tourist bus No 2 goes from the main train station, along Beishan Lu and up to Lingyin Temple. Tourist bus No 3 travels around West Lake to the China Tea Museum, Dragon Well Tea Village, the Zoo and Yuhuang Mountain. Tickets are Y2.

TAXI

Metered taxis are ubiquitous and start at Y10; figure on around Y20 to Y25 from the train station to Hubin Lu.

AROUND HÁNGZHŌU
Qiantang River Tidal Bore 钱塘江潮

A spectacular natural phenomenon occurs when the highest tides of the lunar cycle cause a wall of water to thunder up the narrow mouth of the Qiantang River from Hangzhou Bay (Hángzhōu Wān).

Although the tidal bore can be viewed from the riverbank in Hángzhōu, the best place to witness this amazing phenomenon is on either side of the river at Yánguān, a small town about 38km northeast of

Hángzhōu. Viewing the bore among the Chinese has traditionally been associated with the **Mid-Autumn Festival** around the 18th day of the 8th month of the lunar calendar, but you can see it throughout the year when the highest tides occur at the beginning and middle of each lunar month.

Hotels and travel agencies offer tours to see the bore during the Mid-Autumn Festival, but you can visit just as easily on your own. Buses to Yánguǎn leave from Hángzhōu's east bus station for Y20.

SHÀOXĪNG 绍兴
☎ 0575 / pop 4.3 million
Just 67km southeast of Hángzhōu, Shàoxīng is the centre of the waterway system on the northern Zhèjiāng plain. The waterways, with their rivers (subject to flooding), canals, boats and arched bridges, are part of the city's charm.

History
Since early times, Shàoxīng has been an administrative centre and an important agricultural market town. It was capital of the Yue kingdom from 770–211 BC.

Shàoxīng is the birthplace of many important intellectual and artistic figures in China's modern history, including the country's first great modern novelist, Lu Xun. It's also the home of Shàoxīng wine, which most travellers would agree is definitely an acquired taste.

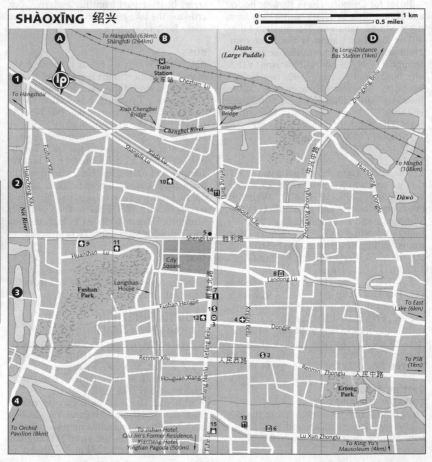

Orientation

Encircled by large bodies of water and rivers, and crossed by canals, Shàoxīng is a pleasant place to explore by bicycle or foot. The hill in Fushan Park is a good place for shady walks. A large city square was recently created that fills up the corner of Shengli Lu and Jiefang Beilu.

Information

BOOKSHOPS

Xinhua Bookshop (Xīnhuá Shūdiàn; cnr Shengli Lu & Jiefang Beilu; ☾ 9am-9pm) Sells English-language maps of the city.

EMERGENCY

PSB (Gōngānjú; ☎ 865 1333 ext 2104) Located about 2km east of the city centre on Renmin Donglu, near Huiyong Lu.

INTERNET ACCESS

China Telecom (Zhōngguó Diànxìn; per hr Y2; ☾ 24hr) It's office has an Internet café on Dongjie near Xinjian Beilu.

INTERNET RESOURCES

www.travelchinaguide.com/cityguides/zhejiang /shaoxing Provides general background information on Shàoxīng.

MEDICAL SERVICES

Shaoxing People's Hospital (Shàoxīng Rénmín Yīyuàn; 61 Dongjie) Has a central location near the post office. There are quite a few hospitals scattered around the city.

MONEY

Bank of China (Zhōngguó Yínháng; 201 Renmin Zhonglu; ☾ 8am-8pm) Changes travellers cheques and major currency. It's ATM accepts international credit cards. There's another branch at 472 Jiefang Beilu.

POST

Post Office (Yóujú; 1 Dongjie; ☾ 8am-5pm) Centrally located on the corner of Dongjie and Jiefang Beilu.

TOURIST INFORMATION & TRAVEL AGENCIES

Shaoxing Hotel (Shàoxīng Fàndiàn; ☎ 515 5858; fax 515 5565, 9 Huanshan Lu) Can arrange tours and book trips onwards.

Sights

LU XUN'S FORMER RESIDENCE 鲁迅故居

Lu Xun (1881–1936), one of China's best-known modern writers and author of such stories as *Diary of a Madman* and *Medicine*, was born in Shàoxīng and lived here until he went abroad to study. He later returned to China, teaching at Guǎngzhōu's Zhongshan University in 1927. He was forced to hide out in Shànghǎi's French Concession when the Kuomintang decided his books were too dangerous. His tomb is in Shànghǎi.

There are several sights associated with Lu Xun, grouped together in a cluster of buildings on Lu Xun Zhonglu. A combined ticket to see everything costs Y80. You can visit **Lu Xun's Former Residence** (Lǔ Xùn Gùjū; 393 Lu Xun Zhonglu; ☾ 8am-5.30pm), where his living quarters are faithfully preserved. At the same site, is the **Lu Xun Memorial Hall** (Lǔ Xùn Jìniànguǎn). Opposite is the school where he was a pupil (his desk is still there).

ANCESTRAL HOMES

Although he was born in the town of Huái'ān (now called Chǔzhōu) in Jiāngsū, **Zhou Enlai's Ancestral Home** (Zhōu Ēnlái Zǔjū; 369 Laodong Lu; admission Y18; ☾ 8am-5.30pm) is here in Shàoxīng.

The **studio** (Qīngténg Shūwū; admission Y2; ☾ 8am-4pm) of the controversial Ming painter Xu Wei (see boxed text, p318) is off Renmin Lu in a small alley. In his studio are displays of his paintbrushes, painting and calligraphy. Another interesting home to visit is **Qiu Jin's Former Residence** (Qiū Jǐn Gùjū; 35 Hechang Tang; admission adult/child Y3/1.5; ☾ 8am-5.30pm), where the pioneering woman revolutionary Qiu Jin was born. Qiu Jin studied in Japan, and was active in women's rights and the revolutionary movement against the Qing government. She was executed by Qing authorities at the age of 29. There's a memorial statue of Qiu Jin on Jiefang Beilu, near Fushan Hengjie.

YINGTIAN PAGODA 应天塔

This **pagoda** (Yìngtiān Tǎ; admission Y2) stands at the southern end of Jiefang Nanlu on a small hill in a park. The pagoda offers good views of Shàoxīng from it's top.

KING YU'S MAUSOLEUM 大禹陵

According to legend, the first Chinese dynasty held power from the 21st to the 16th century BC, and its founder was King Yu, who is credited with having engineered massive flood-control projects.

A temple and mausoleum complex to honour the great-grandfather of China was first constructed in the 6th century and was added to over the centuries that followed. The **mausoleum** (Dà Yǔ Líng; admission Y25; ⊙ 7.30am-5.30pm) is about 4km southeast of the city centre and is composed of several parts: the huge 24m-tall Main Hall, the Memorial Hall and the Meridian Gate (Wǔ Mén). A statue of Yu graces the Main Hall.

Bus No 2 will get you to King Yu's Mausoleum from the train station area or from Jiefang Beilu (get off at the last stop).

EAST LAKE 东湖

The East Lake (Dōng Hú; admission Y25; ⊙ 7am-4pm) is an attractive place of sculpted rock formations, around 6km east of the city centre. The **East Lake Temple** (Dōnghú Sì) stands by the lake. Take bus No 1 from the train station or Jiefang Beilu to the last stop.

Festivals & Events

The **Orchid Pavilion Calligraphy Festival** is held each year on the third day of the third lunar month (3 March) at the Orchid Pavilion (opposite). Calligraphy exhibitions are held as well as calligraphy contests.

Sleeping

Few budget travellers visit Shàoxīng, but it has some of the cheapest accommodation in east China.

Shaoxing Hotel (Shàoxīng Fàndiàn; ☎ 515 5858; fax 515 5565, 9 Huanshan Lu; s Y300-450, d Y350-550) This hotel offers a wide choice of rooms and is one of the nicest places to stay in the city centre. Choose from older double rooms to newer modern rooms with Internet access.

Longshan Hotel (Lóngshān Bīnguǎn; ☎ 515 5710; fax 515 5308; 500 Shengli Lu; s/tr Y250/300, d Y200-400) This place isn't as nice as the Shaoxing, though it still offers a wide variety of rooms. Discounts are the norm, but check out the room first before paying your deposit.

Xianheng Hotel (Xiánhēng Dàjiǔdiàn; ☎ 806 8688; fax 805 1028; 680 Jiefang Nanlu; d Y447) This fancy four-star hotel is located in the southern part of town and is the most upscale hotel in the area. Facilities include Internet access, a Western restaurant and a coffee shop.

XU WEI, ART & LIFE

The Ming Chinese painter and dramatist Xu Wei (1521–1593) remains one of the most controversial artists of his time. Famed for his bold, brilliant brushstrokes and innovative painting style, he still holds influence over Chinese artists today.

Born in Shàoxīng, Xu was the son of a minor official and a concubine. In his late teens he raced off to join the army to fight the Japanese pirates that repeatedly pillaged the Jiāngsū and Zhèjiāng coasts. When he was 21 he married his first wife, who died five years later. Deeply depressed, Xu retreated to a monastery where he wrote poetry and painted. Word of his talent reached far beyond the monastery, and he was eventually coaxed into serving as a personal assistant to the governor of the southeastern provinces. When the governor was killed for treason Xu spiralled into madness. Over a period of years he attempted suicide nine times, once by trying to split his skull with an axe. Later in a fit of rage he stabbed second wife to death and was sent to prison. Skilful manoeuvring on the part of his friends got him free.

In his later years Xu remained in Shàoxīng, living in the small studio Qīngténg Shūwū, now open to tourists, where he spent the remainder of his life painting and writing plays. Xu is most known for his ink and wash paintings, which set a new direction for Ming dynasty artists. Xu's paintings are highly sought after today and he is remembered as one of the most innovative artists of the Ming.

Jishan Hotel (Jishān Bīnguǎn; Toulaohekou; ☎ 806 3838; d Y188-388) This small hotel is located directly behind the Xianheng on a quiet street. Staff go out of their way to be helpful. Rooms have free Internet access.

Shàoxīng Dàjiǔdiàn (☎ 513 9666; 469 Jiefang Beilu; s/d Y280/350) If convenience is important, this hotel is right in the middle of the city. Rooms are so-so, but they're a viable option with discounts.

Overseas Chinese Hotel (Huáqiáo Fàndiàn; ☎ 513 2323; fax 513 3602; 156 Shangda Lu; d Y150-300) It's rooms are pretty grubby, though the location is quite central. This place is a last resort.

Eating
Food Junction (Wǔfú Yuán; 177 Jiefang Lu; mains Y6-12; ☺ 6am-1am) This crowded place serves very cheap noodles and standard dishes.

Zhìyù Lóu (Shaoxing Hotel, 9 Huanshan Lu; mains Y25-40; ☺ lunch & dinner) This restaurant serves great food, is a popular place for locals and has an English menu. It's in a separate building near the north entrance of the hotel off Shengli Lu.

Two restaurants set up for tourists near the Lu Xun Memorial are **A-pó Miànguǎn** and **A-Q Jiǔdiàn** (100 Lu Xun Zhonglu; meals Y30; ☺ lunch & dinner). Both serve 'traditional' Shàoxīng specialties, including Shàoxīng wine, Shàoxīng chicken and *chòu dòufu* (smelly tofu).

Shopping
Fuhe Jie is home to the Tonglian Antique Market (Tōnglián Gǔwán Shìchǎng), which consists of rows of antique stalls and shops selling ceramics and calligraphy. It's a fun place to browse.

Getting There & Away
All Hángzhōu–Níngbo trains and buses stop in Shàoxīng. Luxury buses go to Níngbō (Y38, 1½ hours), Hángzhōu (Y18.5, one hour) and Shànghǎi (Y70, three hours) from the long-distance bus station, 1km from the city centre.

Getting Around
The bus system in Shàoxīng is fairly straightforward. Bus No 1 travels from the train station down Jiefang Beilu and then east to East Lake. Bus No 8 travels south down Zhongxing Lu from the long-distance bus station. Taxis are cheap, starting at Y5.

AROUND SHÀOXĪNG
Considered one of Shàoxīng's 'must see' spots, the **Orchid Pavilion** (Lán Tíng; admission Y25; ☺ 8am-5pm) has great significance for Chinese and Japanese calligraphy enthusiasts. A **calligraphy festival** (opposite) is held yearly in March. The Orchid Pavilion is around 10km southwest of the city and is reached by bus No 3 from Shengli Lu.

NÍNGBŌ 宁波
☎ 0574 / pop 5.4 million
Like Shàoxīng, Níngbō rose to prominence in the 7th and 8th centuries as a trading port. Ships carrying Zhèjiāng's exports sailed from here to Japan, the Ryukyu islands and along the Chinese coast.

By the 16th century the Portuguese had established themselves as entrepreneurs in the trade between Japan and China, as the Chinese were forbidden to deal directly with the Japanese.

Although Níngbō was officially opened to Western traders after the first Opium War, its once-flourishing trade gradually declined as Shànghǎi boomed. By that time the Níngbō traders had taken their money to Shànghǎi and formed the basis of its wealthy Chinese business community.

Today Níngbō is a bustling city with fishing, textiles and food processing as its primary industries. Many travellers use Níngbō as a transit stop on the way to nearby Pǔtuóshān, one of Zhèjiāng's premier tourist attractions.

Information
EMERGENCY
PSB (Gōngānjú; ☎ 8706 2505; 658 Zhongxing Lu) Also takes care of visa matters.

INTERNET ACCESS
Internet cafés are plentiful along the pedestrian walkway behind the Drum Tower on Zhongsan Xilu. Most cafés charge Y2 for 30 minutes.

INTERNET RESOURCES
www.chinaats.com/ningbo For general information on Níngbō.

MEDICAL SERVICES
Li Huili Hospital (Lì Huìlì Yīyuàn; ☎ 8739 2290; 57 Xingning Lu) On the outskirts of town, but it has good facilities.

EAST CHINA COAST

MONEY

Bank of China (Zhōngguó Yínháng; 139 Yaohang Jie; ⏰ 8am-5pm) Changes travellers cheques and major currency. There's another smaller branch on Zhongshan Xilu.

POST

Post Office (Yóujú; ⏰ 7.30am-8pm) Just south of the Xinjiang Bridge (Xīnjiāng Qiáo), where the Fenghua River (Fènghuà Jiāng) forks into the Yuyao River (Yúyáo Jiāng).

TOURIST INFORMATION & TRAVEL AGENCIES

CITS (Zhōngguó Guójì Lǚxíngshè; ☎ 8731 9999; 129 Yaohang Jie) Has an office on the ground floor of the Mirage Hotel.

Sights

MOON LAKE 月湖

Moon Lake (Yuè Hú) is an open park with a wide expanse of green grass and water. Just west of the lake is the **Tianyi Pavilion** (Tiānyī Gé; 10 Tianyi Jie; admission Y20; ⏰ 8am-5.30pm), an inspired combination featuring a garden pavilion full of books. Built during the Ming dynasty, it's thought to be China's oldest existing private library.

At the northern end of Moon Lake there's a restored building known as **Fan's House** (Fàn Zhái), which has antique stalls, painting galleries and bookshops. Across Zhongshan Xilu the **Drum Tower** (Gǔ Lóu) marks the entrance to a pedestrian street full of restored buildings housing travel agencies, Internet cafés and restaurants. Near the Drum Tower is the **Tianning Pagoda** (Tiānníng Sì Tǎ).

Beyond Níngbō's modern bustling streets are plenty of small lanes and alleys that capture a charming traditional side of the city. Near the junction of Jiefang Nanlu and Kaiming Jie is the 14th-century **Tianfeng Pagoda** (Tiānfēng Tǎ), which offers great views of the city and is a worthwhile climb.

Qing'an Hall (Qìng'ān Huìguǎn; 156 Jiangdong Beilu; admission Y10) on the eastern banks of the Fenghua River was originally built by sea merchants in 1853. The temple is dedicated to Matsu, Goddess of the Sea, who watches over fishermen out at sea.

If you're near the passenger ferry terminal, the old Portuguese **Catholic Church** (Tiānzhǔ Jiàotáng; 40 Zhongma Lu; admission free) is well worth a visit. First built in 1628, it was destroyed and

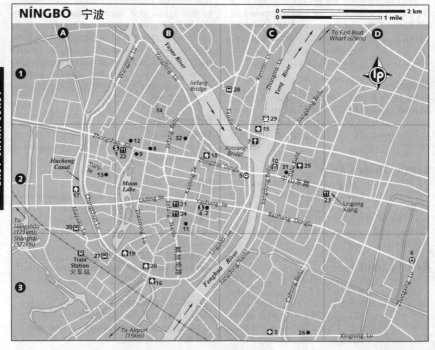

NÍNGBŌ 宁波

rebuilt in 1872. It's an active church (Mass is held daily at 6am), with a Mediterranean-style whitewashed interior displaying prints of the 14 Stations of the Cross, colourful icons and a vaulted ceiling.

Sleeping

Níngbō is not exactly a Mecca for budget travellers but the large discounts available make it good value for mid-range prices.

Dongya Hotel (Dōngyà Bīnguǎn; ☎ 8735 6224; 88 112 Zhongma Lu; d Y168-180). This place is convenient because of its location near the ferry terminal. However, it also serves as a brothel and attracts some questionable clientele. Use your best judgement.

Ningbo Hotel (Níngbō Fàndiàn; ☎ 8712 1688; 65 Mayuan Lu; s/d Y288/375) This hotel is nicely located by the Hucheng Canal. Rooms are small and drab, but come with free Internet access.

Nanyuan Hotel (Nányuàn Fàndiàn; ☎ 8709 5678; fax 8709 7788; 2 Lingqiao Lu; s/d Y780/980) This five-star hotel is one of the best places to stay. It is relatively new and offers all of the usual comforts. Discounts of up to 30% are available.

Ningbo World Hotel (Níngbō Dàjiǔdiàn; ☎ 2788 0088; fax 2788 0788; 145 Zhongshan Donglu; d Y818) This four-star hotel is located in a busy shopping area. Substantial discounts make it a very good deal for the quality.

Wanghu Hotel (Wànghú Bīnguǎn; ☎ 8732 8688 ext 7101; 38 Changchun Lu; s/d Y220/230) Close to the train and bus stations, this hotel gets a lot of traffic. Rooms are a little run-down, but the location is good for early morning bus or train connections.

Eating

Níngbō is known mainly for its seafood. The best places to look are around the ferry terminal and between Kaiming Jie and Jiefang Nanlu.

Wǔyī Dàjiǔdiàn (51 Xianxue Jie; mains from Y20; ☻ lunch & dinner) This is a good place to try out Níngbō seafood. Menu items, from clams to turtles, are on display in aquariums, so don't worry about having your order misunderstood.

Lǎo Fángzi Chuānwèiguǎn (141 Leigong Xiang; mains Y10-30; ☻ lunch & dinner) This small, family run restaurant on the east side of Fenghua River offers tasty home-style dishes and is a popular place for foreign teachers in Níngbō.

At 155 Zhongshan Xilu, very near the Drum Tower, are a collection of rather upscale restaurants, including Vietnamese, East Indian and a steakhouse.

Nanyuan Hotel has a number of restaurants to choose from, including one serving Western food.

Drinking

LBB English Bar (14-1 Dahe Gang; beer Y25; ☻ 6pm-late) This place is a favourite with foreign teachers and a good place to meet people. Head down the lane next to the Agricultural Bank of China on Zhongshan Lu.

Getting There & Away
AIR

The **CAAC** (Zhōngguó Mínháng; ☎ 742 7888; 91 Xingning Lu) sells air tickets. There are daily flights to Hong Kong (Y1680) and air connections with most major Chinese cities. Many hotels also sell tickets.

EAST CHINA COAST

BOAT

Overnight ferries leave for Shànghǎi (12 hours) from the **passenger ferry terminal** (*lúnchuán mǎtóu*) near the Xinjiang Bridge. Tickets cost Y300 for a two-person cabin to Y72 for a seat. Schedules and prices vary according to season. See p301 for more details.

Frequent fast boats to Pǔtuóshān take 2½ hours, including a 1½-hour rickety bus ride from the Níngbō passenger ferry terminal to a fast boat wharf outside the city. Tickets are Y58, including the bus ride.

The ferry terminal is poorly serviced by public buses. It's best to take a taxi, which will cost about Y8 to Y13 to most of the hotels.

BUS

Deluxe buses leave Níngbō frequently for Shànghǎi (Y96, four hours), Hángzhōu (Y42, two hours) and Shàoxīng (Y38, 1½ hours) from the south bus station. There are also buses to Wēnzhōu (Y116, 3 hours) and Tiāntái Shān (Y18.5, two hours).

Minibuses to Xīkǒu (Y8, one hour) depart from a minibus station on the small street running southeast from the train station.

TRAIN

Frequent trains run between Shànghǎi and Níngbō but it's still faster to take a deluxe bus. There are trains to Guǎngzhōu (Y353, 26 hours) and Héféi (Y130, 13 hours). It's not too difficult to book tickets at the train station. CITS will book sleepers for a Y20 service charge.

Getting Around

Níngbō's Lìshè airport is a 20-minute drive from town. Airport buses (Y8) leave from CAAC. A taxi should cost around Y45.

Taxis around town are fairly cheap, starting at Y8.

PǓTUÓSHĀN 普陀山

☎ 0580

Pǔtuóshān is the China we all dream about, the one we see on postcards and in coffee-table books – temples, pagodas, arched bridges, narrow alleys, fishing boats, artisans and monks. Here you feel miles away from the hustle and bustle that characterises modern Chinese cities.

Orientation

You pay a Y110 entrance fee to the island upon arrival, which does not include entry fees to other sights. The central part of town is about 1km north of the ferry terminal and where most of the hotels are located, as well as Puji Temple (below). The roundabout way to reach central square is to take the roads leading west, or west from the ferry terminal. Either way takes about 20 minutes. Alternatively, hop on a minibus at the ferry terminal, which will whisk you off to Puji Temple for Y5.

Information

There's a post office (*yóujú*) southwest of Puji Temple and a **Bank of China** (Zhōngguó Yínháng; ☼ 8-11am, 1-4.30pm) further west down the road.

Sights

Pǔtuóshān's temples are shrines for Guanyin, the Buddhist Goddess of Mercy, and you will see her image everywhere. A striking landmark is the **Nánhǎi Guānyīn** (admission Y6), a 33m-high golden statue of Guanyin overlooking the sea at the southernmost tip of the island.

The two large beaches, **One Hundred Step Beach** (Bǎibùshā) and **One Thousand Step Beach** (Qiānbùshā) on the east of the island are attractive and largely unspoilt, although you have to pay to get in (Y15).

Fanyin Cave (Fànyīn Dòng; admission Y5; ☼ 5.30am-6pm) on the far eastern tip of the island has a temple dedicated to Guanyin perched between two cliffs with a seagull's view of the crashing waves below. The sound of the roaring waves in **Chaoyang Cave** (Cháoyáng Dòng; admission Y5), which overlooks the sea, is said to imitate the chanting of the Buddha. Other natural wonders include the **Shancai Cave** (Shàncái Dòng; admission Y5), **Gufo Cave** (Gǔfó Dòng; admission Y5), **Xianren Cave** (Xiānrén Dòng; admission Y5) and **Xitian Cave** (Xītiān Dòng; admission Y5).

The area around **Puji Temple** (Pǔjì Chánsì; admission Y5; ☼ 5.30am-6pm) is a treat, and from here it is easy to plan an attack on the rest of the island. Most of the minibuses go from the bus stop near here.

The highest point of the island is **Foding Mountain** (Fódǐng Shān), which is also the site of the **Huiji Temple** (Huìjì Chánsì; admission Y5; ☼ 5.30am-6.30pm). A cable car goes up the back side of the mountain (Y35), and stone steps lead down to sea level and **Fayu Temple** (Fǎyǔ Chánsì; admission Y5; ⏰ 5.30am-6pm), a peaceful place surrounded by huge camphor trees. The nearby **Xiangyun Pavilion** (Xiāngyún Tíng) is a nice place to relax if you've been walking for a while.

Other sights on the island include the five-storey **Duobao Pagoda** (Duōbǎo Tǎ) near

Puji Temple, which was built in 1334. It's currently under renovation.

Sleeping

It's difficult to provide reliable details on Pǔtuóshān's accommodation as prices vary with demand. The arrival hall at the ferry terminal has a counter for booking hotels.

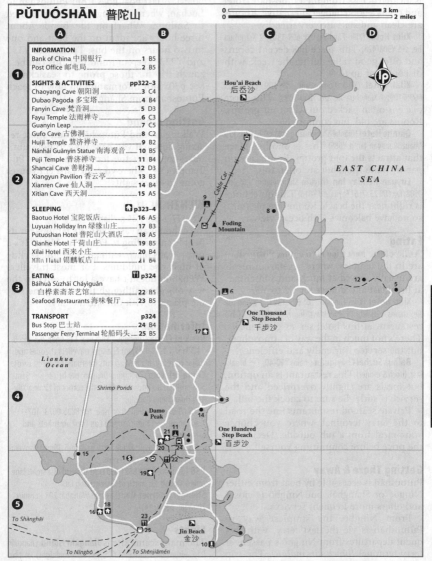

PǓTUÓSHĀN 普陀山

0 — 3 km
0 — 2 miles

INFORMATION
Bank of China 中国银行 **1** B5
Post Office 邮电局.............................**2** B5

SIGHTS & ACTIVITIES   pp322–3
Chaoyang Cave 朝阳洞 **3** C4
Dubao Pagoda 多宝塔 **4** B4
Fanyin Cave 梵音洞 **5** D3
Fayu Temple 法雨禅寺 **6** C3
Guanyin Leap.....................................**7** C5
Gufo Cave 古佛洞 **8** C2
Huiji Temple 慧济禅寺 **9** B2
Nánhǎi Guānyīn Statue 南海观音 **10** B5
Puji Temple 普济禅寺 **11** B4
Shancai Cave 善财洞 **12** D3
Xiangyun Pavilion 香云亭 **13** B3
Xianren Cave 仙人洞 **14** B4
Xitian Cave 西天洞 **15** A5

SLEEPING   p323–4
Baotuo Hotel 宝陀饭店 **16** A5
Luyuan Holiday Inn 绿缘山庄 **17** B3
Putuoshan Hotel 普陀山大酒店 **18** A5
Qianhe Hotel 千荷山庄 **19** B5
Xilai Hotel 西来小庄 **20** B4
Xilin Hotel 锡麟饭店 **21** B4

EATING   p324
Báihuà Sùzhāi Cháyìguǎn
  白桦素素茶艺馆 **22** B5
Seafood Restaurants 海味餐厅 **23** B5

TRANSPORT   p324
Bus Stop 巴士站 **24** B4
Passenger Ferry Terminal 轮船码头 **25** B5

East China Sea

Lianhua Ocean

Shrimp Ponds

Hou'ai Beach 后岙沙

Cable Car

Foding Mountain

One Thousand Step Beach 千步沙

One Hundred Step Beach 百步沙

Damo Peak

Jin Beach 金沙

To Shànghǎi
To Níngbō
To Shěnjiāmén

Putuoshan Hotel (Pǔtuóshān Dàjiǔdiàn; ☎ 609 2828; fax 609 1818; 93 Meicen Lu; tw/d Y880/988) This hotel is the nicest by far on the island, with an opulent lobby and sprawling grounds. The hotel is located on the west road leading from the ferry terminal.

Baotuo Hotel (Bǎotuó Fàndiàn; 118 Meicen Lu; ☎ 609 2090; fax 609 1148; s/d Y500/680) This modest hotel is located across from the Putuoshan Hotel and offers a good budget alternative. Rooms are clean and staff are very friendly.

Xilin Hotel (Xīlín Fàndiàn; ☎ 609 1303; 2 Xianghua Jie; s/d Y308/428) This place has decent rooms and offer good value during the week, with discounts of up to 50%.

Xilai Hotel (Xīlái Xiǎozhuāng; ☎ 609 1505; fax 609 2109; 1 Xianghua Jie; s/d Y880/1080) This large place is often packed out with tour groups. Rooms are old, but comfortable.

Qianhe Hotel (Qiánhé Shānzhuāng; ☎ 609 1630; 125 Miaozhuangyan Lu; d Y685) This is another place that attracts the tour groups. Rooms are on par with the Xilai, but are often full.

Luyuan Holiday Inn (Lǚyuán Shānzhuāng; ☎ 669 0588; fax 609 2537; 61 Fayu Lu; d Y816) This quiet hotel is right near the beach. Rooms are pleasant; some have balconies with ocean views.

Eating

Some of the best places to eat in Pǔtuóshān are in the temples, where vegetarian meals are usually served at lunch and sometimes at breakfast and dinner for Y2 to Y5.

Xilin Hotel (Xīlín Fàndiàn; ☎ 609 1303; 2 Xianghua Jie; mains Y20-60; ☯ breakfast, lunch & dinner) The restaurant at this hotel serves good meals. There's not much in the way of atmosphere, but the service is friendly and efficient.

Báihuà Sùzhái Cháyìguǎn (mains Y10-40; ☯ breakfast, lunch & dinner) This restaurant is an option, but meals are slightly overpriced and the service is surly. Be sure to check the bill.

Private seafood restaurants line the road to the ferry terminal, where you choose your meal from a tub outside. Decide on the price before committing yourself.

Getting There & Away

Pǔtuóshān is accessible by boat from either Níngbō or Shànghǎi, but Níngbō is closer and offers more frequent services.

From Níngbō, the simplest way to Pǔtuóshān is via the fast ferry, with frequent departures from Níngbō's passenger ferry terminal (lúnchuán mǎtóu). The trip takes about 2½ hours, which also includes the bus ride from the fast boat wharf outside Níngbō to the Níngbō passenger ferry terminal. Tickets are Y58.

A daily night boat (two on Sunday) leaves Pǔtuóshān at 4.40pm for the 12-hour voyage to Shànghǎi. Tickets cost Y84 to around Y340; it's easy to upgrade once you're on board. A fast boat goes from Pǔtuóshān to Lúcháo, where passengers are then bussed to Shíliùpù Wharf on the Bund. About three hours are spent on the boat and one to two hours on the bus. Tickets are Y192 and Y222. Keep in mind that this can be a rough trip for those prone to seasickness. See p301) for information on how to reach Pǔtuóshān from Shànghǎi.

Getting Around

Walking around Pǔtuóshān is the most relaxing option if you have time. If not, minibuses zip from the ferry terminal to Puji Temple (Y4), where you can transfer to buses going to other sights.

WĒNZHŌU 温州

☎ 0577 / pop 7.39 million

Wēnzhōu is an east coast city famous for its people emigrating to France and Italy. It's a prosperous place, with an emerging skyline of high-rise buildings. For most travellers Wēnzhōu doesn't have a lot to offer in the way of sights, although there are some scenic places to visit outside the city.

Information

Bank of China (Zhōngguó Yínháng; 113 Chan Jie; ☯ 8-11.30am & 1.15-4.45pm) Changes travellers cheques and major currency. It's ATM accepts international credit cards.

China Telecom (Zhōngguó Diànxìn; per hr Y4; ☯ 8am-5.30pm) Has an Internet café on the corner of Liming Xilu and Huancheng Donglu.

CITS (Zhōngguó Guójì Lǚxíngshè; ☎ 8825 0673; 107-1 Xiaonan Lu; ☯ 8am-5.30pm) Can book air tickets and arrange tours.

Post Office (Yóujú; Xinhe Jie; ☯ 8am-5.30pm) Conveniently located in the city centre.

PSB (Gōngānjú; ☎ 8821 0851) At the end of a small lane called Xigong Jie, north of Guangchang Lu.

Shengyi Internet Bar (Shèngyì Wǎngbā; 201 Renmin Zhonglu; per hr Y4)

Sights

The main scenic site is **Jiangxin Island** (Jiāngxīn Dǎo; admission adult/child Y15; ☯ 8am-midnight) in the

EAST CHINA COAST

middle of the **Ou River** (Ōu Jiāng). The island park is dotted with pagodas, a lake and footbridges. It's easily reached by ferry (Y10) from the **Mahang pier** (Máháng mǎtóu) on Wangjiang Donglu.

There are two active old churches (*jīdū jiàotáng*), one **Protestant** (Chengxi Jie) and one **Catholic** (Zhouzhaici Xiang). Both were built in the late 19th century.

Maguo Temple (Mǎguǒ Sì; admission Y3), located on Songtai Hill on Renmin Xilu, is a peaceful restored Tang dynasty temple. It makes an interesting diversion from the concrete and noise of the city.

Sleeping

Wēnzhōu is a major business centre and has many mid-range hotels, although there are a few budget options.

Shunsheng Hotel (Shùnshēng Dàjiǔdiàn; ☎ 8827 000; fax 8827 8899; 36 Lucheng Lu; s/d Y385/430) This hotel is just a short walk from the west bus station and offers clean, comfortable rooms. Discounts of 20% to 30% are available.

Dong'ou Hotel (Dōng'ōu Dàshà; ☎ 8818 7901; 1 Wangjiang Donglu; s Y178, d Y190-280) This 14-storey

EAST CHINA COAST

waterfront hotel is close to the ferry dock. Rooms are run-down and should probably only be considered as a last choice. Discounts of 20% make this a good budget option.

Chamber of Commerce Hotel (Zǒng Shānghuì Jùlèbù; ☎ 8822 5555; fax 8822 2333; 22 Canghou Jie; d Y488) This hotel is very centrally located and a quick walk to all major shopping areas. Some floors are currently getting a facelift. It's a good mid-range option, and all rooms have free Internet access.

Wenzhou International Hotel (Wēnzhōu Guójì Dàjiǔdiàn; ☎ 8825 2525; fax 8825 1100; 1 Renmin Donglu; s/d Y430/450) This four-star hotel is one of the best, with restaurants, a swimming pool, in-house movies and free Internet access. There is a choice of rooms, often discounted up to 30%.

Eating

Not surprisingly for a port, Wēnzhōu is known for its seafood, and there are numerous restaurants near the west bus station and the river.

Cafe de Champs-Elysées (Xiāngxiè Lìshè Xī Cāntīng; 2nd fl, Wǔzhōu Dàshà; mains Y20-60, set meals Y38-48; ⓨ lunch & dinner) For Western food, try this elaborately decorated restaurant with good set meals and coffee. There's an extensive English menu.

Getting There & Away

AIR

The **CAAC** (Zhōngguó Mínháng; ☎ 8833 3197) is in the southeast section of town. Wēnzhōu has reasonably good connections with other Chinese cities, but the airport is notorious for its heavy fog – pilots often end up flying at ridiculously low altitudes trying to find the runway.

BUS

Wēnzhōu has several bus stations, the west bus station, the Xincheng bus station and the south bus station near the train station. Buses to Fúzhōu (Y145, 10 hours) leave from the south bus station. For longhaul destinations, you're better off taking the train. Frequent buses to Níngbō (Y116) leave from the Xincheng bus station and take about 3½ hours.

TRAIN

The train line from Wēnzhōu connects the city to Hángzhōu (Y62, eight hours),

Shànghǎi (Y94, 9½ hours) and Běijīng (Y418, 30 hours). The train station is south of the city. Take bus No 5 or 20 from Renmin Lu. Alternatively, a taxi to the train station will cost around Y20.

CITS doesn't book train tickets, though most hotels do. There's a **train ticket booking office** near the west bus station.

Getting Around

Wēnzhōu airport is 27km southwest of the city and taxis charge between Y100 and Y120 for the trip. A bus goes from the CAAC for Y10.

Taxis around the city centre start at Y10.

AROUND WĒNZHŌU
Yàndàng Shān 雁荡山

Along the coast, about 80km northeast of Wēnzhōu, is Yàndàng Shān, a group of mountains featuring sheer cliffs and peaks similar to the geography of Wǔyí Shān in Fújiàn province (p342).

The whole area of Yàndàng Shān is huge, about 450sq km, but the most accessible sights are found in three main scenic areas. A long ribbon of water falls into **Big Dragon Pool** (大龙湫; Dàlóng Qiū; admission Y25; ⓨ 5.30am-6.30pm), reached by a winding path passing beneath rock columns towering over 200m above.

Walkways and a suspension bridge cling to the **Divine Cliffs** (灵岩; Líng Yán; admission Y25), which can also be reached by cable car (Y9). Further east, **Divine Peaks** (灵峰; Líng Fēng; admission Y25) is the largest section and is dotted with caves and more bizarre peaks. It's the best place for longer hikes.

There's lots of accommodation in Yàndàng Shān, including **Míngyàn Bīnguǎn** (明岩宾馆; 15 Buxing Jie; d Y198), which is a nice, small family-run place. It's around the corner and just north of the bus stop for services from Wēnzhōu.

Buses for Yàndàng Shān leave four times daily from Wēnzhōu's south bus station. Tickets are Y27 and the trip takes 1½ hours.

JĪNGNÌNG COUNTY 景宁县
☎ 0578

In southern Zhèjiāng, close to the border of Fújiàn province, Jǐngnìng County (Jǐngnìng Xiàn) is a mountainous, undeveloped region full of rushing rivers and old villages.

It's home to the She ethnic group and is the only autonomous national minority district in east China; the She make up about 10% of the Han-dominated population.

The lure of Jǐngníng County is the lack of tourism and the scenery and unspoiled countryside, which make it an ideal place to visit for some rural respite.

Hèxī (鹤溪), in Jǐngníng County, is a large, sprawling place with modern buildings and little charm. The best thing to do is to hop on a minibus (Y3) heading out of town to Dàjūn, 13km away along the river. From this small village it's possible to float back down the river (Xiǎo Xī) on bamboo rafts to the bridge near Hèxī. The trip takes two hours and costs Y245 per raft. Better yet, take a small boat to the other side of the river and hike around the hills. Chinese maps of the region are available at the Hèxī bus station.

It's possible to stay in Hèxī, though some hotels may not take foreigners. Try **Jǐngníng Bīnguǎn** (景宁宾馆; ☎ 508 2760; 85 Renmin Zhonglu; s/d Y280-400), which has tolerable rooms, and prices can be bargained down.

To get to Hèxī, take a train from Wēnzhōu (Y31, two hours) or Hángzhōu (Y70, six hours) to Lìshuǐ. Then take bus No 3 from the train station to Lìshuǐ's old bus station (lǎo chēzhàn), where you can catch one of the frequent minibuses to Hèxī (Y14, 2½ hours).

TIĀNTÁI SHĀN 天台山
☎ 0576

Noted for its many Buddhist monasteries, which date back to the 6th century, Tiāntái Shān (Heavenly Terrace Mountain) is the home of the Tiāntái Buddhist sect, which is heavily influenced by Taoism.

From Tiāntái it's a 3.5km hike to **Guoqing Monastery** (国清寺; Guóqīng Sì; admission Y15; ☽ 7.30am-4pm) at the foot of the mountain. A road leads from the monastery 25km to **Huading Peak** (华顶峰; Huàdǐng Fēng; admission Y25; ☽ 8am-4pm). From here continue by foot for 1km or so to **Baijing Temple** (拜经台寺, Bàijīngtái Sì) on the mountain's summit.

Public transport up to the peak and waterfall is sporadic, though you may be able to hook up with a tour bus. Expect to pay about Y20.

There's a **CITS** (中国国际旅行社; Zhōngguó Guójì Lǚxíngshè; ☎ 398 8899) in Tiāntái town at Tiāntái Bīnguǎn that can help arrange tours.

Buses link the mountain with Hángzhōu, Shàoxīng, Níngbō and Wēnzhōu.

Fújiàn 福建

HIGHLIGHTS

- Ride a bamboo raft down the wild rivers of **Wǔyí Shān** (p343)
- Explore Xiàmén's colonial heritage on **Gǔlàng Yǔ** (p339)
- Visit early **Hakka settlements** (p340) in Yǒngdìng
- Take a boat ride along Fúzhōu's **Min River** (p333)
- Stroll through the ancient streets of **Quánzhōu** (p341)

★ Wǔyí Shān
Fúzhōu ★
Quánzhōu ★
★ Yǒngdìng
★ Gǔlàng Yǔ

| ■ POP: 35 MIL | ■ AREA: 227,420 SQ KM | ■ www.taiwan.8m.net/fujian/ |

EAST CHINA COAST

Fújiàn province, in southeast China, doesn't see a lot of travellers, which is unfortunate due to the province's truly amazing coastal and mountain scenery. Along the lush subtropical coastline are the historic ports of Fúzhōu, Xiàmén and Quánzhōu, where it's possible to see the remains of old forts, mosques and colonial buildings that make up an intriguing portion of Fújiàn's eclectic history.

In recent years the modern and bustling capital of Fúzhōu has become one of the richest cities in China, with towering high-rises and innumerable construction sites. In contrast, Xiàmén retains an old-world charm, with pleasant beaches, lovely secluded parks and excellent tourist facilities. The Taiwan-claimed island of Jīnmén (Kinmen) lies only a few kilometres from the coast of Xiàmén and was once the site of ferocious battles between the mainland communists and the Nationalist Party. Nowadays, Xiàmén attracts a lot of Taiwanese investment, evidenced by fancy shopping malls and top-end restaurants. Just off the coast of Xiàmén is the tiny island of Gŭlàng Yǔ; with its tree-lined streets and colonial buildings it's a great place to explore the region's colonial heritage. Quánzhōu, considered during the Tang dynasty to be one of the most prosperous ports in the world, drew merchants to its shores from all over the world, especially Middle Eastern traders whose descendants still live there today.

The rugged interior of Fújiàn is largely unexplored and not as economically developed as the coastal regions due to its inaccessibility. Wǔyí Shān in northwest Fújiàn is a popular tourist destination and famous for its scenery, which some say rivals Guìlín for beauty. It's great fun to explore Wǔyí Shān by taking a bamboo raft down the magnificent Nine Twists River. Southwest Fújiàn, near Yŏngdìng, is the place to see the ancient settlements of the Hakka people, one of Fújiàn's many ethnic groups.

History

The coastal region of Fújiàn, known in English as Fukien or Hokkien, has been part of the Chinese empire since the Qin dynasty (221–207 BC), when it was known as Min.

Sea trade transformed the region from a frontier into one of the centres of the Chinese world. During the Song and Yuan dynasties the coastal city of Quánzhōu was one of the main ports of call on the maritime silk route, which transported not only silk, but other textiles, precious stones, porcelain and a host of other valuables. The city was home to more than 100,000 Arab merchants, missionaries and travellers.

Despite a decline in the province's fortunes after the Ming dynasty restricted maritime commerce in the 15th century, the resourcefulness of the Fújiàn people proved itself in the numbers heading for Taiwan, Singapore, the Philippines, Malaysia and Indonesia. Overseas links were forged that continue today, contributing much to the modern character of the province.

Climate

Fújiàn has a subtropical climate, with hot, humid summers and drizzly cold winters. June through August brings soaring temperatures and humidity, with torrential rains and typhoons common. In the mountainous regions, winters can be fiercely cold.

Language

Fújiàn is one of the most linguistically diverse provinces in China, due to its mountainous terrain. Locals speak variations of the Min dialect, which includes Taiwanese. Min is divided into various subgroups – you can expect to hear Southern Min (Mǐnnán Huà) in Xiàmén and Quánzhōu, and Eastern Min (Dōng Mǐn) in Fúzhōu.

Getting There & Away

Fújiàn is well connected to the neighbouring provinces of Guǎngdōng and Jiāngxī by train and coastal highway. Xiàmén and Fúzhōu have airline connections to most of the country, including Hong Kong, Taipei and Kaohsiung in Taiwan. Wǔyí Shān has flight connections to China's larger cities, including Běijīng, Shànghǎi and Hong Kong.

Getting Around

Getting around Fújiàn coastal areas is a breeze, thanks to the well-maintained coastal highway. For exploring the interior, trains are slow but more comfortable and safer than travelling by bus. Wǔyí Shān is linked to Fúzhōu, Quánzhōu and Xiàmén by train. If the train is too slow, there are daily flights between Xiàmén, Fúzhōu and Wǔyí Shān. See the Getting There & Away sections of the relevant sections of this chapter for more details.

FÚZHŌU 福州

☎ 591 / pop 5.8 million

Fúzhōu dates back to the 3rd century AD, when it was known as Yěchéng (Smelting City). Later it emerged as a major commercial port specialising in the export of tea.

Marco Polo, passing through Fúzhōu towards the end of the 13th century, described the city as being so 'well provided with every amenity' as to be a 'veritable marvel'. It is second only to Xiàmén as a centre of

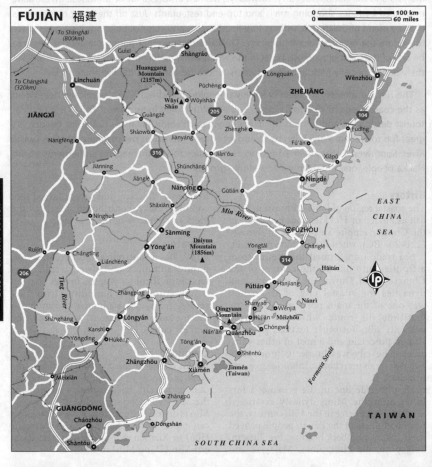

Taiwanese investment, and the money that the town has attracted is reflected in a lot of pricey new hotels and restaurants.

Orientation

Fúzhōu's city centre sprawls northward from the Min River (Mǐn Jiāng). The train station is in the northeast of the city, while most of the accommodation is on Wusi Lu, sandwiched between Hualin Lu and Dongda Lu. Travellers arriving by bus will be dropped off either at the north long-distance bus station, close to the train station, or the south long-distance bus station at the intersection of Guohuo Xilu and Wuyi Zhonglu. The airport is 50km south of the city.

Information

EMERGENCY

Public Security Bureau (PSB; Gōngānjú; 107 Beihuan Zhonglu) Opposite the Sports Centre in the northern part of town.

INTERNET ACCESS

Dong Jie has several nondescript Internet cafés. Check out those in the alley south of Dong Jie near the intersection of Wuyi Beilu.

INTERNET RESOURCES

www.lnfj.cn/travel/bifz.ntm This website by the Fujian Provincial Department of Foreign Trade & Economic Cooperation provides background on Fuzhou and surroundings.

MEDICAL SERVICES

Fujian Provincial Hospital (Shěng Èr Rénmín Yīyuàn; 134 Dong Jie) Conveniently located in the city centre.

MONEY

Bank of China (Zhōngguó Yínháng; 136 Wusi Lu; 8am-6pm) The main branch changes travellers cheques and cash, and has an ATM. Be warned that changing travellers cheques in Fúzhōu requires a photocopy of your passport and lots of patience. There is another branch on Gutian Lu.

POST

Post and telephone office (Yóudiàn Dàlóu) On the southeast corner of Dong Jie and Bayiqi Lu.

TOURIST INFORMATION & TRAVEL AGENCIES

China Travel Service (CTS; Zhōngguó Lǚxíngshè; 8753 6250; 128 Wusi Lu) Sells plane tickets and offers a number of tours to areas around Fújiàn, but it doesn't book train tickets.

Sights & Activities

Fúzhōu's sights are minor attractions and the city has few places remaining of historical interest. The areas worth seeing are scattered about the city, which makes travel between them difficult.

The **Yu Shan Scenic Area** (Yú Shān Fēngjǐngqū), which has some remains of the old city wall, is one of the most pleasant places in Fúzhōu. The Ming dynasty wall has been largely reconstructed and only a small portion of the original wall remains. The principle attraction in Yu Shan is the **White Pagoda** (Bái Tǎ), built in AD 904. The pagoda is 41m high and has a great view from the top. Next to Yu Shan is an imposing **Mao Zedong Statue** (Máo Zhǔxì Xiàng), presiding over a sea of cyclists.

Nearby is the 31m **Black Pagoda** (Wū Tǎ), which stands on the southern slope of Black Hill and faces the White Pagoda. During the Lunar New Year Festival, both pagodas are strung with lanterns and look quite festive.

The **Lin Zexu Memorial Hall** (Línzéxú Jìniànguǎn; 90 Aomen Lu; admission Y5; 8am-5pm) is an interesting place to visit if time allows. Lin Zexu (1785–1850) was a Qing dynasty official who attempted to stop the influx of opium into China by writing letters to Queen Victoria and destroying large quantities of the drug. He has been blamed for instigating the Opium War (p39) and was exiled to Xīnjiāng. The Memorial Hall has several courtyards and halls with exhibits on Lin's life.

In the northwest of Fúzhōu is **West Lake Park** (Xīhú Gōngyuán; admission Y10; 6am-10pm), which features a large artificial lake and is a popular place for locals to congregate on the weekends. The **Fujian Provincial Museum** (Fújiàn Shěng Bówùguǎn; admission Y20; 9am-4pm) in the park is an ugly futuristic-style building with lots of columns and spires. The exhibits inside are quite good, some with English captions. By far the most interesting (and creepy) exhibit is the pair of remarkably well-preserved mummies that were unearthed in 1986 and date back to AD 1235.

Less remarkable is the lakeside **zoo** (Dòngwùyuán; admission Y10; 8am-6pm), home to a

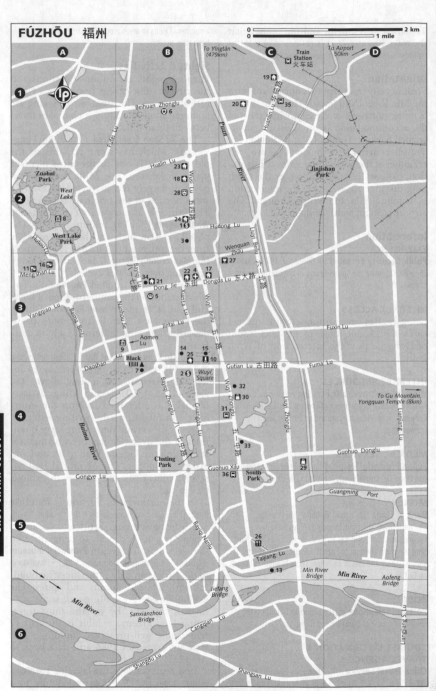

FÚZHŌU 福州

To Yíngtán (479km)

Train Station 火车站

To Airport 50km

0 —————— 2 km
0 —————— 1 mile

Beihuan Zhonglu

Fufei Lu

Pujun River

Hualin Lu

Hualin Lu

Wusi Lu 五四路

Zuohai Park

West Lake

West Lake Park

Hutou Lu

Mengshan Lu

Jinjishan Park

Luyi Beilu 六一北路

Hudong Lu

Wenquan Zhilu

Yangqiao Lu

Baima Beilu

Nanhou Jie

Bayiq Beilu 八一七路

Dong Jie

Xianta Jie

Jintai Lu

Dongda Lu 东大路

Wuyi Beilu 五一北路

Fuxin Lu

Aomen Lu

Daoshan

Black Hill

Gutian Lu 古田路

Fuma Lu

Luyi Zhonglu 六一中路

Lianjiang Lu

To Gu Mountain, Yongquan Temple (8km)

Wuyi Square

Wuyi Zhonglu 五一中路

Bayiq Zhonglu 八一七路

Guangda Lu

Guohuo Donglu

Guohuo Xilu

South Park

Guangming Port

Chating Park

Bayiq Nanlu 八一七路

Baima River

Gongye Lu

Taijiang Lu

Min River Bridge

Min River

Aofeng Bridge

Jiefang Bridge

Sanxianzhou Bridge

Min River

Cangqian Lu

Lianjiang S Lu

Shangdu Lu

Shangsan Lu

EAST CHINA COAST

sad collection of animals, and **Panda World** (Xióngmāo Shìjiè; 88 Meng Shan Gang; admission Y30; ☺ summer 7.30am-6pm, winter 8am-5.30pm), a place devoted to Giant Panda research.

About 10km east of the town, on **Gu Mountain** (Gǔ Shān), is **Yongquan Temple** (Yǒngquàn Sì; admission Y6). Gu Mountain (Drum Mountain) takes its name from a large, drum-shaped rock at the summit that apparently makes a racket when it's stormy. Yongquan Temple is a monastery that dates back 1000 years and is said to house a collection of 30,000 Buddhist scriptures, of which 657 are written in blood. You can take bus No 7 from Gutian Lu, from where it's a 15-minute minivan ride (Y10) up the hill.

To experience river life along the Min River, consider taking a boat tour from **Taijiang Harbour** (Táijiāng Mǎtou). Boats leave according to demand and prices vary depending upon the number of people who want to take the tour. Most hotels and travel agencies can arrange this trip for you.

Sleeping

Fúzhōu accommodation falls mainly in the mid-range and top end categories. Many hotels offer discounts, making them affordable even for those on tight budgets. Wusi Lu and Dongda Lu are the best places to look for places to stay. Many hotels are equipped with broadband Internet, though you must pay Y30 a day for access.

BUDGET
Jin Hui Hotel (Jīnhuī Dàjiǔdiàn; ☎ 8759 9999; fax 8757 5988; 492 Huanlin Lu; d Y395) This hotel is very conveniently located across from the train

station. Rooms are clean and comfortable, and have Internet access.

Tianfu Hotel (Tiānfú Dàjiǔdiàn; ☎ 8781 2328; fax 8781 2308; 138 Wusi Lu; s/d Y253/330) Close to the Bank of China, this hotel is currently updating its rather tattered décor. There are a variety of rooms to choose from, including standard doubles and more expensive 'special-shaped rooms'.

MID-RANGE
Jin Ye Hotel (Jīnyè Dàjiǔdiàn; ☎ 8757 5888; fax 8758 5888; 378 Huanlin Lu; d Y530) The Jin Ye is a classy hotel close to the train station, with modern rooms and professional management. Don't be frightened by the posted rates as rooms are generally discounted 30%.

Yushan Hotel (Yúshān Bīnguǎn; ☎ 8335 1668; fax 8335 7694; 10 Yushan Lu; d Y390-490) This newer hotel is one of the best deals in town. Located in the Yushan Scenic Area, rooms are immaculate and have good views of the surrounding park. Rooms are discounted up to 50%, making this place a definite bargain.

Fuzhou Hotel (Fúzhōu Dàjiǔjiā; ☎ 8755 6631; fax 8755 5795; 18 Dongda Lu; d/s/tr Y358/398/498) This hotel is centrally located and offers spacious, comfortable rooms with Internet access. Because of its location and price, it's popular with Chinese tourists and fills up fast. If arriving on a weekend, make sure to book ahead.

Oriental Hotel (Dōngfāng Dàjiǔdiàn; ☎ 8750 7088; fax 8750 2788; 96 Dong Jie; d Y498) The Oriental has reasonable rooms and is in a busy shopping area. Rooms are so-so, but large discounts on rooms make it worthwhile if other places are full.

EAST CHINA COAST

TOP END

Juchunyuan Hotel (Jùchūnyuán Dàjiǔdiàn; ☎ 8750 2328; fax 8750 2228; 2 Dong Jie; s Y438-498, d Y498) The Juchunyuan is one of the better-known hotels in town. Rooms are overpriced, but staff are helpful. The hotel restaurant (below) has an excellent reputation for serving some of the best Fujian-style cuisine in town.

Successlink International Hotel (Chénglóng Guójì Dàjiǔdiàn; ☎ 8782 2888, 2284 5716; 252 Wusi Lu; d Y396-578) This hotel has been around for quite a while. Rooms vary in quality – some are quite shabby and need an update. Have a look before agreeing to stay the night.

Hot Spring Hotel (Wēnquán Dàfàndiàn; ☎ 8785 1818; fax 8783 5150; 218 Wusi Lu; d Y988-1380, ste Y1780-5280) Near Successlink, the five-star Hot Spring Hotel has excellent facilities, including natural hot-spring water in the bathrooms, an outdoor swimming pool and a tennis court.

Eating

Because of its proximity to the Min River and the ocean, the city is deservedly famous for both freshwater fish and seafood. Fúzhōu's most famous dish is the imaginatively named 'Buddha Leaps the Wall' (Fó Tiào Qiáng), a mixture of 30 different kinds of vegetables, meats and seafood, including abalone, sea slugs, dried scallops, pigeon eggs and mushrooms, stewed for hours in an aged liquor. The story goes that the dish is so delicious, Buddha would leap a wall to get to it.

Juchunyuan Restaurant (Jùchūnyuán Dàjiǔdiàn; ☎ 8753 3604; 2 Dong Jie; Fó Tiào Qiáng Y200; ☒ lunch & dinner) Located in the Junchunyuan Hotel, this is the most famous restaurant in town and has built a reputation on Fúzhōu's spectacular dish.

For cheap noodles and dumplings in a lively nocturnal environment, locals head south to Taijiang Lu – an ancient pedestrian food street (cài bù xíngjiē) lined with Ming dynasty–style wooden buildings and lanterns. Take bus No 51 from Wusi Lu to get there.

Drinking

Yi'anju Teahouse (Yiānjù; 39 Wenquan Zhilu; tea from Y30) This teahouse is a lovely place to spend a few hours. A variety of teas and snacks are served in private rooms decorated with local arts and crafts.

Entertainment

Fuzhou Great Theatre (Fúzhōu Dàxìyuàn; 212 Wusi Lu; admission Y30) A large complex that screens English-language movies.

Shopping

Fúzhōu is famous for its lacquerware, bamboo furniture, and stone and cork carvings. The city is also famous for its 'clay people' (ní rén), small clay figurines painted in bright colours. A good place to look for souvenir items is in the **Huadu Department Store** (Huádū Shāngshà; 49 Wuyi Zhonglu), where you'll find paper parasols and jade combs, and other popular Fúzhōu mementos.

By the river is the **Flower & Bird Market** (Huā Niǎo Shìchǎng), filled with people selling birds, puppies and kittens among other things.

Getting There & Away

AIR

The **Civil Aviation Administration of China** (CAAC; Zhōngguó Mínháng; ☎ 8334 5988; Wuyi Zhonglu) has daily flights to major destinations, such as Běijīng (Y1530, 2½ hours), Guǎngzhōu (Y800, one hour), Shànghǎi (Y730, 70 minutes), Hong Kong (Y1610, 80 minutes) and Wǔyí Shān (Y480, 30 minutes). Airport buses leave from the **Apollo Hotel** (Ābóluó Dàjiǔdiàn; ☎ 8305 5555; 132 Wuyi Zhonglu) every 25 minutes beginning at 5.50am. The last bus is at 7.15pm. Tickets are Y20 a person and the 50km trip takes about an hour.

BUS

There are two long-distance bus stations in town: one in the north near the train station, and one at the southern end of town, down from the CAAC office on the corner of Guohuo Xilu and Wuyi Zhonglu. Most services are available from both bus stations.

There are economy bus services departing for Guǎngzhōu (Y180 to Y258, 18 hours), Shànghǎi (Y280, 24 hours), Wēnzhōu (Y125 to Y190, 10 hours), Quánzhōu (Y52 to Y60, 3½ hours) and Xiàmén (Y68 to Y80, six hours). Deluxe buses to Guǎngzhōu (Y258 to Y280, 16 hours) and Shēnzhèn (Y260, 13 hours) depart from the south bus station. Luxury buses travel to Xiàmén (Y80 to Y99, 4½ hours) and depart from the north bus station. Night buses leave the north bus station for Wǔyí Shān (Y86 to 90, eight hours).

TRAIN

The train line from Fúzhōu heads northwest and joins the main Shànghǎi–Guǎngzhōu line at the Yīngtán junction in Jiāngxī. There are also trains from Fúzhōu to Wǔyí Shān (Y47, seven hours). The rail route to Xiàmén has been discontinued.

There are direct trains from Fúzhōu to Běijīng and Shànghǎi. It's fairly easy to buy tickets at the train station, from a spot about 100m to the left of the main train station building, when you are facing it. Many hotels will book train tickets for a service fee, and there's also a train ticket booking office in the entrance of the **Lida building** (Lìdà Dàshà; 8am-5pm), opposite the post office.

Getting Around

Fúzhōu is a sprawling city, which makes it difficult to get around by foot. Taxi flag fall is Y10. There's a good bus network, and bus maps are available at the train station or from hotels. Bus No 51 travels from the train station along Wuyi Lu, and bus No 1 goes to West Lake Park from Bayiqi Lu.

XIÀMÉN 厦门

☎ 0592 / pop 1.24 million

With its lovely colonial-style buildings and refreshing ocean breezes, Xiàmén is one of the most pleasant cities to visit in Fújiàn. The city has been attracting foreigners for centuries and still retains a captivating old-world charm, especially around the bustling waterfront district.

Gǔlàng Yǔ, a tiny island off the coast of Xiàmén, is a wonderful maze of colonial homes and seaside gardens and is one of the highlights of a visit to Fújiàn.

History

Xiàmén, also known as Amoy, was founded around the mid-14th century in the early years of the Ming dynasty. A town had been in existence at the site since the Song dynasty, but the Ming built the city walls and established Xiàmén as a major seaport and commercial centre.

In the 17th century it became a place of refuge for the Ming rulers fleeing the Manchu invaders. Xiàmén and nearby Jīnmén were bases for the Ming armies who, under the command of the pirate-general Koxinga, had as their battle-cry, 'resist the Qing and restore the Ming'.

The Portuguese arrived in the 16th century, followed by the British in the 17th century, and later by the French and the Dutch, all of whom attempted rather unsuccessfully to establish Xiàmén as a trade port.

The port was closed to foreigners in the 1750s and it was not until the Opium War that the tide turned. In August 1841 a British naval force of 38 ships carrying artillery and soldiers sailed into Xiàmén harbour, forcing the port to open. Xiàmén then became one of the first treaty ports.

Japanese and Western powers followed soon after, establishing consulates and making the island of Gǔlàng Yǔ (p339) a foreign enclave. Xiàmén turned Japanese in 1938 and remained that way until 1945.

Orientation

Xiàmén is a bustling, metropolitan city that has a relaxing, coastal charm.

The neighbouring island of Gǔlàng Yǔ is an enchanting retreat of meandering lanes and shaded backstreets, set in an architectural twilight of colonial villas and crumbling remains. It's well worth spending a few days exploring the place.

The town of Xiàmén is on the island of the same name. It's connected to the mainland by a long causeway bearing a train line, road and footpath.

The interesting part of Xiàmén is near the western (waterfront) district, directly opposite the small island of Gǔlàng Yǔ. This is the old area of town, known for its quaint architecture, parks and winding streets.

Information
EMERGENCY

Complaints Hotline (☎ 800 8582 ext 36) For complaints about overpricing, theft, bad taxi drivers etc.
PSB (Gōngānjú; ☎ 226 2203) Opposite the main post and telephone office. The visa section is located in the northeast section, near the entrance on Gongyuan Xilu.

INTERNET ACCESS

There are Internet cafés scattered around the harbour area. The lanes surrounding Datong Lu are a good place to look. Most cafés charge Y4 per hour.
Fengyun Internet Cafe (Fēngyún Wǎngbā) Located next to the Xiamen University Hotel on the university grounds.

INTERNET RESOURCES

www.amoymagic.com One of the most comprehensive websites on Xiàmén.

MEDICAL SERVICES

Life Line Medical Clinic (Mǐfú Zhénsuǒ; 123 Xidi Villa Hubin Beilu; ☎ 532 3168; ☷ 8am-5pm Mon-Fri, 8am-12pm Sat) A clinic for expats, with English-speaking doctors. Telephone operated 24 hours.

Zhongshan Hospital (Zhōngshān Yīyuàn; Hubin Nanlu) Has a foreigner's ward.

MONEY

Bank of China (Zhōngguó Yínháng; 10 Zhongshan Lu) Near the Lujiang Hotel by the waterfront. Has an ATM.

Hong Kong Bank (HSBC; Huìfēng Yínháng; 189 Xiahe Lu) Also changes money and has an ATM.

POST

Post and telephone office (Yóudiànjú; cnr Xinhua Lu & Zhongshan Lu)

TOURIST INFORMATION & TRAVEL AGENCIES

China International Travel Services (CITS; Zhōngguó Guójì Lǚxíngshè; 335 Hexiang Xilu) There are several offices around town. This branch near Yundang Lake is recommended.

Sights

NANPUTUO TEMPLE 南普陀寺

On the southern outskirts of Xiàmén city, this attractive **temple** (Nánpǔtuó Sì; ☎ 208 6490; Siming Nanlu; admission Y3; ☷ 8am-5pm) was built more than 1000 years ago during the Tang dynasty. It was ruined during the Ming dynasty, but rebuilt during the Qing dynasty.

Entering the temple through **Heavenly King Hall** (Tiānwáng Diàn) you are met by Milefo (Laughing Buddha), with the four heavenly kings on either side. The classical Chinese inscription reads: 'When entering, regard Buddha and afterwards pay your respects to the four kings of heaven'.

Behind Milefo is Wei Tuo, a Buddhist deity who safeguards the doctrine. He holds a stick that points to the ground, indicating that the temple is rich and can provide visiting monks with board and lodging (if the stick is held horizontally it means the temple is poor and is a polite way of saying 'find somewhere else to stay').

XIÀMÉN & GǓLÀNG YǓ 厦门、鼓浪屿

In front of the courtyard is the **Great Heroic Treasure Hall** (Dà Xióngbǎo Diàn), a two-storey building containing three Buddhas that represent Buddha in his past, present and future lives.

The **Great Compassion Hall** (Dàbēi Diàn) contains four statues of Guanyin (the Goddess of Mercy). Worshippers cast divining sticks at the feet of the statues to seek heavenly guidance.

The temple has a vegetarian restaurant in a nice shady courtyard where you can dine in the company of resident monks.

Take bus No 1 from the train station or bus No 21 from Zhongshan Lu to reach the temple.

XIAMEN UNIVERSITY 厦门大学
Next to Nanputuo Temple, **Xiamen University** (Xiàmén Dàxué) was established with overseas Chinese funds. It features an attractive lake and makes for a pleasant stroll. The campus entrance is next to the stop for bus No 1. At the southern entrance to the university there's a pleasant beach, which is also the terminus for bus No 2.

Not too far from the university is the **Huli Shan Fortress** (Húlí Shān Pàotái; admission Y25), which was built in 1890 and used to deter foreigners from entering the city. It overlooks the beach, popular with locals in the sticky summertime.

OVERSEAS CHINESE MUSEUM 华侨博物官
This **museum** (Huáqiáo Bówùguǎn; 73 Siming Nanlu; admission Y10; 🕑 9am-4.30pm) has excellent photos and paintings of the history and various activities of Chinese communities abroad.

Tours
CITS (Zhōngguó Guójì Lǚxíngshè; 335 Hexiang Xilu) can arrange tours around Xiàmén and Gǔlàng Yǔ. Most hotels can also help with tours.

Festivals & Events
The **Xiamen International Marathon** is held in the spring, and draws local and international participants. Runners race around the coastal ring road that circles the island. It's quite an event – in 2003, 10,000 athletes from around the world participated.

Dragon Boat races are held in Xiàmén every June and are quite a sight.

Sleeping
By far the best area to stay is on Gǔlàng Yǔ (p339). It lacks any real budget options, but it will make your stay in Xiàmén both memorable and relaxing. In Xiàmén city the western district around the harbour, park or university area has a few decent places to stay.

Lodging becomes expensive and hard to find around the first week of September, when a large investment fair takes place in the city.

BUDGET
Overseas Student Dormitory (Càiqīngjié Lóu; ☎ 208 4528; fax 208 6774; Xiamen University; d/tr Y180/200) Rooms are adequate but nothing fancy. To reach the dormitory walk uphill for about

EAST CHINA COAST

100m from the university's south gate, then take a left and look out for a purple 10-storey building.

Singapore Hotel (Xīnjiāpō Jiǔdiàn; ☎ 202 6668; fax 202 5950; 113-121 Xian Lu; d Y328) Conveniently located next to Zhongshan Park (Zhōngshān Gōngyuán), this hotel has clean, reasonable rooms.

MID-RANGE

Most accommodation in Xiàmén is mid-range, shading top end. Many hotels in this range are equipped with broadband Internet for an extra Y30 a day if you have your own computer.

Gem Hotel (Jīnhòu Jiǔdiàn; ☎ 399 6666; fax 399 6789; 444 Zhongshan Lu; tatami-style r Y280, s/d Y400) This hotel has an outlandishly decorated lobby, but very clean, comfortable rooms. Some rooms have glass 'peek-a-boo' panels separating the bathroom from the sleeping area.

Lujiang Hotel (Lùjiāng Bīnguǎn; ☎ 202 2922; fax 202 4644; 54 Lujiang Dao; s Y410-580, d Y700-830, tw Y468) This hotel, in a 1940s Chinese-style building, has a prime location opposite the Gǔlàng Yǔ ferry terminal. It often has good deals, and some rooms have ocean views. Add a 10% service charge to your bill. The rooftop restaurant is excellent (see review, right).

Xiamen Hotel (Xiàmén Bīnguǎn; ☎ 202 2265; fax 202 1765; 16 Huyuan Lu; d Y650) This large, stately place has a certain colonial elegance, and a swimming pool.

Xiamen University Hotel (Xiàmén Dàxué Guójì Xuéshù Jiāoliú Zhōngxīn; ☎ 208 7988; fax 208 6116; Xiamen University; d Y270-410) This comfortable hotel, located on the pleasant grounds just inside Xiamen University's north gate, has bright, clean standard rooms.

TOP END

There is a wide range of top-end accommodation in Xiàmén, but much of it is badly located in the eastern part of town. Most places offer 50% discounts. Add a 15% service charge to all prices.

Holiday Inn (Jiàrì Huángguān Hǎijīng Dàjiǔdiàn; ☎ 202 3333; fax 203 6666; 12-8 Zhenhai Lu; d US$160-820) The Holiday Inn has typical four-star standards and you'll be well looked after here. It also has some of the best international and Chinese restaurants in town.

Marco Polo Hotel (Mǎgē Bōluō Dōngfāng Dàjiǔdiàn; ☎ 509 1888; www.marcopolohotels.com/xiamen; 8 Jianye Lu; r US$160-225, ste US$295-980) This posh hotel, on a small street off Hubin Beilu, has a pool, bar, and Chinese and Japanese restaurants. If booked on the Internet, prices drop dramatically.

Xiamen Miramar Hotel (Xiàmén Měilìhuá Dàjiǔdiàn; ☎ 603 1666; Xinglong Lu; d US$85-168) Although a little austere, the Miramar offers comfortable, reasonable rooms. It's popular with Chinese and Japanese business travellers.

Xiamen Plaza Hotel (Xiàmén Dōngnányà Dàjiǔdiàn; ☎ 505 8888; fax 505 8899; 908 Xiahe Lu; d Y988-1330) Beside the train station, the elegant but uncharismatic Xiamen Plaza has standard rooms.

Eating

You won't go hungry in Xiàmén. Most alleys off Zhongshan Lu harbour cheap eats. Head down Jukou Jie, near the intersection of Siming Beilu and Zhongshan Lu, which offers a plethora of Sichuan restaurants.

Huang Zehe Peanut Soup Shop (Huángzéhé Huāshēng Tāngdiàn; 20 Zhongshan Lu; snacks Y1-6; ☯ breakfast, lunch & dinner) This busy restaurant by the harbour is popular for its local snacks, including peanut soup, a regional speciality.

Near the university, good, cheap, attractive restaurants line Siming Nanlu and Yanwu Jie. Two cheap vegetarian restaurants are **Dàfāng Sùcàiguǎn** (412-4 Siming Nanlu; meals Y8; ☯ lunch & dinner) and **Gōngdé Sùcàiguǎn** (418-10 Siming Nanlu; meals Y8; ☯ lunch & dinner). Try the monks' vegetables *(luóhàn zhāifàn)*.

Venezzia Cafe (Wéiníxíyè; 3 Nanhua Lu; meals from Y28, drinks Y25; ☯ lunch & dinner) Near the university, this place is popular with the university crowd, and has pretty good pizza and Western food.

Lujiang Hotel rooftop restaurant (☎ 202 2922; meals from Y30; ☯ breakfast, lunch & dinner) Overlooking the sea, this is one of the nicest places to eat. There's an excellent Cantonese buffet as well as an English menu. Reservations for dinner are recommended, especially on the weekends.

World Trade Centre (Shìjiè Màoyì Zhōngxīn; Xiahe Lu) Next to the train station, there is an excellent food court on the 5th floor, with a variety of small fast-food restaurants to choose from.

Entertainment

For English-language movies, head to the **World Trade Centre** (Shìjiè Màoyì Zhōngxīn; Xiahe Lu), which has a cinema on the top floor.

EAST CHINA COAST

Shopping

Xiàmén has lots of hidden curio and food shops tucked away off the busy streets. There is a **night market** *(yè shìchǎng)* on Ding'an Lu, between Zhongshan Lu and Zhenhai Lu.

Getting There & Away

AIR

Xiamen Airlines is the main airline under the CAAC banner in this part of China. There are innumerable ticket offices around town, many of which are in the larger hotels, like the Holiday Inn.

CAAC has flights to Hong Kong, Kuala Lumpur, Manila, Penang and Singapore. **Silk Air** (☎ 205 3280) flies to Singapore and has an office in the Holiday Inn. **All Nippon Airways** (☎ 573 2888) flies to Osaka, and has ticketing agents at the Holiday Inn and the Lujiang Hotel. **Dragonair** (☎ 202 5433) is located in the Marco Polo Hotel.

Xiàmén airport has flights to all major domestic destinations around China, including Wǔyí Shān (Y590) four times a week. Airport departure tax is Y90.

BUS

Deluxe and economy buses leave from the long-distance bus station and the ferry terminal. Destinations include Fúzhōu (Y60 to Y99), Wǔyí Shān (Y124 to Y202, nine hours), Quánzhōu (Y18 to Y35, 1½ hours) and Shàntóu (Y100, five hours). There are also express buses to Guǎngzhōu (Y200 to Y300, 12 hours), Shēnzhèn (Y180, nine hours), Hong Kong (Y300 to Y350, 10 hours) and Shànghǎi (Y330 to Y413). Buses also make trips inland to Lóngyán (Y46, three hours) and Yǒngdìng (Y38, five hours).

TRAIN

From Xiàmén there are direct trains to destinations, including Hángzhōu (Y224, 23 hours), Shànghǎi (Y309, 25 hours), Běijīng (Y458, 39 hours) and Wǔyí Shān (Y157, 14 hours). Book tickets at the train station or through CITS, who will make bookings for a Y35 service fee.

Getting Around

Xiàmén airport is 15km from the waterfront district, about 8km from the eastern district. From the waterfront, taxis cost around Y35. Bus No 27 travels from the airport to the ferry terminal via the train station.

Frequent minibuses run between the train station and ferry terminal (Y1). Buses to Xiàmén University go from the train station (bus No 1) and from the ferry terminal (bus No 2). Taxis start at Y7.

GǓLÀNG YǓ 鼓浪屿

A five-minute boat trip from Xiàmén takes you to this sleepy island of winding paths, creeper-laden trees, Christian cemeteries and almost-Mediterranean flavours. By 1860 the foreign powers had residencies that were well established on Gǔlàng Yǔ. As the years rolled by, churches, hospitals, post and telegraph offices, libraries, hotels and consulates were built.

The best way to enjoy the island is to wander along the streets, peeking into courtyards and down alleys to catch a glimpse of colonial architecture seasoned by local life. Most sights and hotels are just a short walk from the ferry terminal.

Sights

The most prominent attraction on the island is **Sunlight Rock** (Rìguāng Yán) – the island's highest point at 93m. On a clear day you can see the island of Jīnmén.

At the foot of Sunlight Rock is a large colonial building known as the **Koxinga Memorial Hall** (Zhèngchénggōng Jìniànguǎn; ☼ 8am-11am & 2-5pm). The hall has an exhibition partly dedicated to the Dutch in Taiwan, and partly to Koxinga's throwing them out. Both sights are located in **Sunlight Rock Park** (Rìguāng Yán Gōngyuán; admission Y60; ☼ 8am-7pm).

Yingxiong Hill (Yīngxióng Shān) is near the memorial hall and has an open-air aviary (admission Y15) on the top with egrets and parrots.

Near the ferry terminal is **Xiamen Underwater World** (Xiàmén Hǎidǐ Shìjiè; 2 Longtou Lu; admission Y70; ☼ 8am-6pm), with an impressive collection of penguins, seals, dolphins, and exotic fish in cramped tanks. The immense shark tank is viewed via a tubular passageway.

Shuzhuang Garden (Shūzhuāng Huāyuán; admission Y20) is a very pleasant garden on the waterfront and close to the beach.

Sleeping & Eating

Lizhidao Hotel (Lìzhīdǎo Jiǔdiàn; ☎ 206 3309; fax 206 3311; 133 Longtou Lu; s/d Y135/210) This hotel has clean but small rooms. The cheapest rooms have no windows.

EAST CHINA COAST

Luzhou Hotel (Lúzhōu Jiǔdiàn; ☎ 206 5390; fax 206 5843; 1 Longtou Lu; d Y198-268, tr Y368) This hotel, across from the ferry terminal, has bright, airy rooms. Some rooms have ocean views.

Gulang Villa (Gǔlàng Yǔ Bièshù; ☎ 206 3280; fax 206 0165; 14 Gusheng Lu; d Y490-590) Right on the waterfront, this hotel has spacious grounds, large rooms and is a popular place for tour groups. Discounts of 30% make staying here a great deal.

Xiamen Jinquan Hotel (Xiàmén Jīnquán Bīnguǎn; ☎ 206 5621; fax 206 4273; 26 Sanmin Lu; d Y196) This hotel was formerly the American Consulate. Rooms are reasonable and the grounds are pleasant, though staff are a bit aloof.

Gǔlàng Yǔ is the place to go for seafood. Chinese travellers report that seafood here is fresher and cheaper than places like Hǎinán Dǎo. For budget eats, wander up Longtou Lu towards Lizhidao Hotel where there are many small restaurants and stalls.

Getting There & Away

Ferries to Gǔlàng Yǔ leave from the ferry terminal just west of Xiàmén's Lujiang Hotel. Tickets are Y3 going over plus Y10 for the top deck. The return trip from Gǔlàng Yǔ is free, or Y10 for the top deck.

HAKKA EARTH BUILDINGS

During the Jin dynasty (AD 265–314) the Hakka peoples of northwest China began a gradual migration south to escape persecution and famine. They eventually settled in Jiāngxī, Fújiàn and Guǎngdōng, where they began to build *tǔlóu* (earth buildings) to protect themselves from bandits and wild animals.

These early circular structures were large enough to house entire clans. The buildings were communal, with interior buildings enclosed by enormous peripheral ones that could hold hundreds of people. Nestled in the mud walls were bedrooms, wells, cooking areas and storehouses, circling a central courtyard. The walls were made of rammed earth and glutinous rice, reinforced with strips of bamboo and wood chips.

Today there are 20,000 of these buildings still in existence. Yǒngdìng in southwest Fújiàn has some truly amazing structures, many of them still in use.

YǑNGDÌNG 永定

☎ 0597 / pop 40,160

Yǒngdìng is an out-of-the-way place in southwest Fújiàn. Set in an area dominated by small mountains and farmland, it isn't worth a mention, except for its unusual architecture. Known as *tǔlóu* (earth buildings), these large, circular edifices resemble fortresses and were built by the Hakka, one of China's ethnic minorities. Some are still inhabited today. See the boxed text, left.

Coming from Hénán in northern China, the Hakka people first moved to Guǎngdōng and Fújiàn to escape severe persecution in their homelands. The name Hakka means 'guests'; today Hakka communities are scattered all over Southeast Asia.

There are no *tǔlóu* in Yǒngdìng itself. One of the main buildings sought out by visitors is the **Zhènchénglóu**, 43km northeast of Yǒngdìng, in Húkēng. Frequent minibuses travel there from the Yǒngdìng bus station (Y10, 1½ hours). Other buildings are in the villages southeast of Yǒngdìng – Hóngkēng, Xiàyáng, Gǔzhú and Dàxī – you'll have to hire a driver to get to them. Yǒngdìng is accessed by bus from Guǎngdōng, Xiàmén (Y38, five hours) or Lóngyán (with/without air-con Y15/10, one hour).

QUÁNZHŌU 泉州

☎ 0595 / pop 7.4 million

Quánzhōu was once an international port and an instrumental stop on the maritime silk route. Marco Polo, back in the 13th century, called it Zaiton and informed his readers that '…it is one of the two ports in the world with the biggest flow of merchandise'. It's slipped a few pegs since then, but Quánzhōu still has a few products of note, including the creamy-white *déhuà* (or 'blanc-de-Chine' as it is known in the West) porcelain figures, and locally crafted puppets.

Quánzhōu is prettier and cleaner than Fúzhōu and evidence of its Muslim population can still be detected among the city's residents and buildings. Quánzhōu's prime attraction is the relaxing Kaiyuan Temple.

Orientation

Because Quanzhou is so small, most of its sights can be reached on foot. The centre of town lies between Zhongshan Lu and Wenling Lu. This is where you'll find most of the tourist sights, the bank and the post office. The oldest part of town is to the west, where there are many narrow alleys and lanes to explore that still retain their traditional charm. The Jin River lies to the southwest of the city.

Information

Quánzhōu's many Internet cafés are clustered together on Wenhua Jie, and charge around Y3 per hour.

Quanzhou is very small and most tourists don't require a tour to see the sights. However, if you would like a tour, inquire at your hotel or at any of the small travel agencies along Wenling Lu.

Bank of China (Zhōngguó Yínháng; Jiuyi Jie; 🕙 9am-5pm) This branch also exchanges travellers cheques.

Post and telephone office (Yóudiànjú; Dong Jie)
PSB (Gōngānjú; ☎ 218 0308) Has an office on Dong Jie.
Quanzhou Xiehe Hospital (Quánzhōu Xiéhé Yīyuàn; Tian'an Nanlu) Located in the southern part of town.
www.fzu.edu.cn/fujian/equanz.html This website has some interesting background on Quánzhōu and other places in Fújiàn.

Sights

Kaiyuan Temple (Kāiyuán Sì; 176 Xi Jie; admission Y4; 🕙 6am-6pm) is in the northwest of the city, and can be distinguished by its pair of tall pagodas and the huge grounds in which it is set.

Originally called Lotus Temple (Liánhuā Sì), construction of the temple began in AD 686. In AD 738, during the reign of the famous Tang emperor Tang Minghuang, it's name was changed to Kāiyuán.

Within the grounds of Kaiyuan Temple, behind the eastern pagoda, is a **museum** containing the enormous hull of a Song dynasty seagoing junk, which was recently excavated near Quánzhōu. A ride to the temple by minivan taxi from the long-distance bus station will cost Y6, or take bus No 2 from Wenling Nanlu.

There are some charming little side streets off Xi Jie; take a pedicab to Kaiyuan Temple from the south of Quánzhōu and the driver will probably take you down the maze of winding streets that lead there.

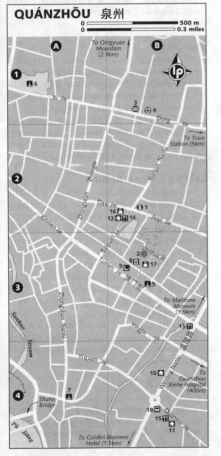

QUÁNZHŌU 泉州

0 500 m
0 0.3 miles

To Qingyuan Mountain (2.9km)

To Train Station (5km)

To Maritime Museum (1.5km)

To Quanzhou Xiehe Hospital (400m)

To Golden Business Hotel (1.5km)

Shunji Bridge

Jin Jiang

Quánzhōu is studded with small temples and can make for an interesting ramble. The pleasant **Qingjing Mosque** (Qīngjìng Sì; 113 Tumen Jie; admission Y2; ☯ 8am-6pm) is one of China's only surviving mosques from the Tang dynasty. A small museum with signs in English describes the history of Quánzhōu's once large Muslim community.

Behind the mosque is a **Puppet Museum** (Mù'ǒu Bówùguǎn; 24 Tongzheng Xiang; admission free; ☯ 9am-6pm), which has some interesting exhibits and captions (in English and Chinese) of this unique art form.

Another temple worth visiting is **Guandi Temple** (Guāndì Miào; Tumen Jie), located close to the mosque. Dedicated to Guan Yu, Three Kingdoms hero and God of War, the temple attracts a steady stream of visitors who come to light incense and pray. Inside the temple are statues of the god and panels along the walls that detail his life.

The **Mazu Temple** (Tiānhòu Gōng; admission Y5), on the southeastern end of Zhongshan Lu, is dedicated to Mazu, Goddess of the Sea, who watches over fishermen. Around the third month of the Lunar New Year (23 March), the temple is packed with worshippers celebrating Mazu's birthday.

The **Maritime Museum** (Quánzhōu Hǎiwài Jiāotōngshǐ Bówùguǎn; Donghu Lu; admission Y10; ☯ 8.30am-5.30pm Tue-Sun) on the northeast side of town is worth a visit. Exhibits explain Quanzhou's trading history and the development of Chinese shipbuilding.

Sleeping

Jianfu Hotel (Jiànfú Dàshà; ☎ 228 3511; fax 218 8850; 150 Wenling Nanlu; s/d Y200/320-370) This hotel's clean, comfortable rooms are a pretty good deal. Discounts of up to 50% are possible.

Jinzhou Hotel (Jìnzhōu Dàjiǔdiàn; ☎ 258 6788; fax 218 8850; 106 Quanxiu Jie; d Y200-260) Rooms at this hotel, also near the bus station, are a bit run-down, but adequate.

Overseas Chinese Hotel (Huáqiáo Dàshà; ☎ 228 2192; fax 228 4612; Baiyuan Lu; tw Y150-188; s & d Y228-596) This three-star property, with a choice of newer and older rooms, offers good value.

Golden Business Hotel (Jīnbǎo Shàngwù Jiǔdiàn; ☎ 253 0066; fax 253 8999; Baozhou Lu, Middle Section; s/d Y468) This hotel is a little far from the town centre, but still worth it for its excellent amenities and plush, comfortable rooms. Some rooms are fitted with computers and offer broadband Internet for Y30 a day.

Eating

There are loads of small restaurants and bakeries in the area surrounding Kaiyuan Temple. A nightly **food market** (Baiyuan Lu) sets up in front of the Overseas Chinese Hotel. For some reason, restaurants in the centre of town are hard to find outside of the hotels.

Red, Blue & White (Hóng Lán Hé Bái; 98 Quanxiu Jie; meals Y8; ☯ lunch & dinner) This chain restaurant is open late and offers cheap, simple, cafeteria-style meat and vegetable dishes.

Overseas Chinese Hotel (Huáqiáo Dàshà; Baiyuan Lu) The restaurant in this hotel offers reasonably priced Chinese dishes and traditional Fújiàn specialities, such as steamed oysters and pounded pork.

Ānjīkèwáng (Wenling Nanlu; meals Y30; ☯ lunch & dinner) Come here for traditional Hakka dishes, such as deep-fried chicken and stewed pork.

Shopping

Jǐnxiù Zhuāng (101-C Daxi Jie) A small shop selling locally made puppets and puppet heads, as well as embroidery and other handicrafts. It's a fun place to browse and the whimsical marionettes make great souvenirs.

Another place to find Fújiàn crafts and curios is at the **night market** (yè shìchǎng) near Qingjing Mosque. It generally gets going around 5pm and lasts until 2am.

Getting There & Around

The long-distance bus station is in the southern corner of town on the intersection of Wenling Nanlu and Quanxiu Jie, and serves destinations as far away as Shànghǎi and Guǎngzhōu. Deluxe buses go to Xiàmén (Y18 to Y35, two hours) and Fúzhōu (Y52 to Y60, 3½ hours).

Trains travel from Quánzhōu to Wǔyí Shān once every few days (Y148 to Y157 sleeper, 15 hours), leaving from the train station 5km east of the town centre.

Quánzhōu's most useful bus is the No 2 (Y1), which goes from the bus station to Kaiyuan Temple. Minivan taxis can take you to most places for Y6.

WǓYÍ SHĀN 武夷山

☎ 0599 / pop 22,710

In the far northwest corner of Fújiàn is Wǔyí Shān, an attractive region of rivers, crags and forests. It is a protected area and well worth a visit.

The scenic area lies on the west bank of Chongyang Stream (Chóngyáng Xī), and some of the accommodation is located along its shore. Most of the hotels are concentrated in the resort district *(dù jià qū)* on the east side of the river. The main settlement is Wǔyí Shān city, about 10km to the northeast, with the train station and airport roughly half-way between.

Information

Maps of the Wǔyí Shān area are available in bookshops in the resort district.

Bank of China (中国银行; Zhōngguó Yínháng; Wujiu Lu; ☺ 9am-5pm) Located in Wǔyí Shān city, this branch will change travellers cheques.

CITS (中国国际旅行社; Zhōngguó Guójì Lǚxíngshè; ☎ 525 0380; 35 Guanjing Lu; ☺ 9am-4pm Mon-Sat) The staff are very helpful, and can arrange train tickets and tours to surrounding ancient cities.

Sights & Activities

The main reason to visit Wǔyí Shān is to walk up to the sheer rock peaks that jut skywards, and take a trip down the **Nine Twists River** (九曲溪, Jiǔqū Xī) on bamboo rafts. The main entrance is at **Wǔyí Gōng** (武夷宫; ☎ 525 2702; admission Y111; ☺ 6.30am-6.30pm), about 200m south of the Wuyi Mountain Villa (right), near the confluence of the Chóngyáng and Nine Twists rivers.

A couple of nice walks are the 530m **Great King Peak** (大王峰, Dàwáng Fēng), accessed through the main entrance, and the 410m **Heavenly Tour Peak** (天游峰, Tiānyóu Fēng), where an entrance is reached by road up the Nine Twists River. Trails within the scenic area connect all the major sites. At the northern end of the scenic area, the **Water Curtain Cave** (水帘洞, Shuǐlián Dòng) is a cleft in the rock about one-third of the way up a 100m cliff face. In winter and autumn, water plunges over the top of the cliff creating a curtain of spray.

One of the highlights for visitors is floating down the Nine Twists River on **bamboo rafts** (Y102; ☺ 7am-5pm) fitted with rattan chairs. Departing from Xīngcūn, a short bus ride west of the resort area, the trip down the river takes over an hour.

One of the mysteries of Wǔyí Shān is the cavities carved out of the rock faces at great heights that once held boat-shaped coffins. Scientists have dated some of these artefacts back 4000 years. If you're taking a raft down the river, it's possible to see some remnants of these coffins on the west cliff face of the fourth meander or 'twist', also known as **Small Storing Place Peak** (小藏山峰, Xiǎozàngshān Fēng).

Sleeping

There's a whole range of accommodation in Wǔyí Shān, mostly concentrated on the east side of the river. Consequently, the west side is quieter. Discounts are often available mid-week.

There are a few places scattered on the west bank immediately across from the main bridge spanning Chongyang Stream that accept foreigners.

Jiāngnán Bīnguǎn (江南宾馆; ☎ 525 2268; d Y280) At the time of writing this hotel was being renovated. Hopefully by the time you visit the rooms will be updated and the dirty carpet changed. The hotel surroundings are lovely and rooms have balconies. Turn left just after you cross the river and cross the lawn on your right.

Wuyi Mountain Villa (武夷山庄; Wǔyí Shānzhuāng; ☎ 525 1888; d Y280-528, ste Y528-18,000) Beautiful Chinese fountains, secluded grounds and a pool make this one of the nicest choices for accommodation in the Wǔyí Shān region. The hotel restaurant is also very good and popular with tourists.

The east bank area is packed with many hotels.

Lántíng Fàndiàn (兰亭饭店; ☎ 525 2880; Wujiu Lu; d Y360-638) At the southern end of the district, this hotel has decent rooms with balconies and scenic views. Discounts of up to 45% are available in the off season.

International Trade Hotel (国贸大酒店; Guómào Dàjiǔdiàn; ☎ 525 2521; Wangfeng Lu; d Y480-580) This hotel is in one of the more unattractive parts of town and currently in a construction zone. However, rooms are quite comfortable and amenities are upscale.

Eating

Frogs, mushrooms and bamboo shoots are the specialities of Wǔyí Shān's cuisine. One of the best places to try out these items is at the **Bamboo Palace Restaurant** (大堂竹楼; Dàtáng Zhúlóu; meals Y20-40; ☺ lunch & dinner), where you can eat on a patio overlooking the river. The food is excellent and the service good. It's a good idea to bring mosquito repellent, unless you want to be dessert.

Getting There & Away

Wǔyí Shān has air links to Běijīng (Y1350, two hours), Shànghǎi (Y660, one hour), Fúzhōu (Y310, 35 minutes), Xiàmén (Y590, 50 minutes), Guǎngzhōu (Y890, 1½ hours) and Hong Kong (Y1300, two hours).

Frequent buses go to Xiàmén (Y159), Fúzhōu (Y90) and Shàowǔ (Y15, 1½ hours). The other long-distance bus station is in the northwest part of Wǔyí Shān city. Daily buses go south to Fúzhōu (Y86, eight hours), northeast to Wēnzhōu (Y138, 12 hours) and Nánpíng (Y37, three hours), and north to Shàngráo (Y26, two hours) in Jiāngxī.

Direct trains go to Wǔyí Shān from Fúzhōu, Quánzhōu and Xiàmén. See the Getting There & Away section of those cities for details.

Getting Around

Minivans or a public bus (Y2) shuttle between Wǔyí Shān city and the resort district, and there are minibuses between Wǔyí Shān city and Xīngcūn.

Expect to pay about Y10 for a motorised trishaw from the resort district to most of the scenic area entrances. A ride from the train station or airport to the resort district will cost between Y10 to Y20.

Liáoníng 辽宁

CONTENTS

HIGHLIGHTS

- Climb the easternmost stretch of the Great Wall, little-touristed **Tiger Mountain Great Wall** (p360), near Dāndōng

- Hang out at the beach – or explore the bustling urban centre – in dynamic **Dàlián** (p353)

- Approach the border in **Dāndōng** (p359), gateway to North Korea

- Swing, balance or sprint across the 50 suspended bridges in the **Shěnyáng Botanical Garden** (p350)

- Ogle the stalactites and stalagmites in the **Benxi Water Caves** (p353)

★ Shěnyáng

★ Benxi Water Caves

Tiger Mountain Great Wall ★

Dàndōng ★

★ Dàlián

NORTH OF THE WALL

■ POP: 43 MIL   ■ AREA: 145,700 SQ KM   ■ www.liaoning-gateway.com

Sandy beaches, dynamic cities and nuggets of Manchu history all draw visitors to Liáoníng, once the southernmost province of Manchuria. Those hoping to get a peek into North Korea – or to visit the easternmost section of the Great Wall – may also enjoy the pilgrimage to the border town of Dāndōng.

Liáoníng's most popular destination for travellers is the enticing refuge of Dàlián. Nicknamed 'Hong Kong of the North', Dàlián is a fast-developing city complemented by historic architecture, clean streets and parkland. Shopping seems to be a favourite pastime here, with megamalls springing up all over town. Several attractive beaches lure sun-and-sand seekers, and in this waterfront city, fresh seafood is a speciality. Dàlián alone makes a trip to Liáoníng worthwhile.

The province's eastern edge borders North Korea. Dāndōng, set on the river that divides the two countries, not only has a tourist industry based on glimpsing the border, but also offers a mix of Chinese and Korean culture. Just outside of Dāndōng is the easternmost stretch of the Great Wall, a restored section that still sees comparatively few tourists. If you've climbed the Great Wall near Běijīng shoulder-to-shoulder with hordes of other visitors, a visit to this section of the wall near Dāndōng will seem unexpectedly peaceful.

In contrast, Shěnyáng, the provincial capital, is a frenzied modern metropolis. Yet scattered around the city are serene temples, tombs and pagodas, as well as the Imperial Palace, which recalls Běijīng's Forbidden City. Shěnyáng is also home to a striking contemporary museum that offers an intriguing, if one-sided, view of the Japanese occupation of Manchuria in the 1930s. For a more light-hearted experience, take a swing on the suspended bridges in the Shenyang Botanical Garden.

History

The region formerly known as Manchuria, including the provinces of Liáoníng, Jílín and Hēilóngjiāng, plus parts of Inner Mongolia, is now generally called Dōngběi, which simply means 'the northeast'.

The Manchurian warlords of this northern territory established the Qing dynasty, which ruled China from the 1640s until the early 20th century. In the late 1800s and early 1900s, when the Western powers were busy carving up pieces of China for themselves, Manchuria was occupied alternately by the Russians and the Japanese. These occupations have shaped both the region's architecture and its consciousness.

To the outrage of Tsar Nicholas II, Japan gained the Liaodong Peninsula at the southeastern tip of Liáoníng province under an 1895 treaty (after defeating Chinese battleships off Port Arthur, near present-day Dàlián, in 1894). With French and German support, Nicholas II managed not only to get the Japanese to withdraw from Dàlián, but also to receive it as a Russian concession in 1898. Russia then began constructing a port as an alternative to the only partially ice-free port of Vladivostok. Russia's reign over Liáoníng province was short-lived, however, ending (at least temporarily) with the Russo-Japanese War (1904–05).

On 18 September 1931, Japanese troops marched into Shěnyáng and occupied the city. The Japanese ruled Manchuria, which became known as the puppet state of Manchukuo, until the end of WWII.

Getting There & Around

Getting around Liáoníng is easy. In addition to the rail lines that crisscross the region, a network of new highways between the major cities makes bus travel – in modern air-con vehicles – a speedy, comfortable alternative.

Shěnyáng, the province's transport hub, is a convenient starting point for exploring the northeast. Extensive rail connections link Shěnyáng with cities south and north. From Shěnyáng, rail and bus transport runs frequently to other Liáoníng cities.

If you're coming to Liáoníng from points further south, an alternative is to travel by sea or air to Dàlián, and from there head north by bus or train to Dāndōng or Shěnyáng. Boats connect Dàlián with Shànghǎi, Tiānjīn and several cities in Shāndōng province, while frequent flights link Dàlián with Běijīng, Shànghǎi and other major cities.

SHĚNYÁNG 沈阳

☎ 024 / pop 3,527,800

At first glance, Shěnyáng may be a hard city to love. While it's a convenient transport hub for travels further north, this sprawling mass of socialist town planning labours under horrendous traffic. Pedestrians share the walkways with speeding bicycles and the occasional impatient car!

Yet once you navigate through the urban sprawl, Shěnyáng – the birthplace of internationally renowned orchestra conductor Seiji Ozawa – deserves a closer look. Amid the grey buildings are well-preserved relics of the Manchu era, as well as museums that illuminate the northeast's more recent history. Pedestrian streets like Zhong Jie intriguingly

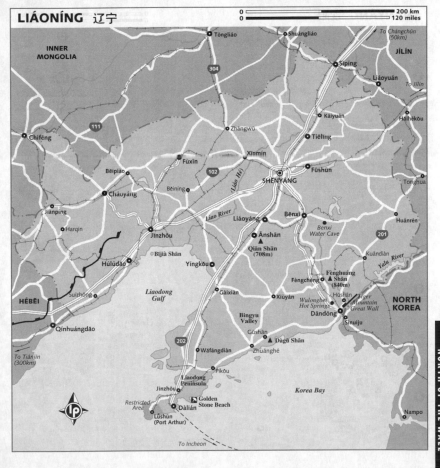

blend old and new, and urban oases – from tranquil temples to botanical gardens – offer relief from the city's hubbub.

History

Shěnyáng was a Mongol trading centre as far back as the 11th century, becoming the capital of the Manchu empire in the 17th century. With the Manchu conquest of Běijīng in 1644, Shěnyáng became a secondary capital under the Manchu name of Mukden, and a centre of the ginseng trade.

Throughout its history, Shěnyáng has rapidly changed hands, dominated by warlords, the Japanese (1931), the Russians (1945), the Kuomintang (1946; see p43) and the Chinese Communist Party (1948).

Orientation

The north train station *(běizhàn)*, south train station *(nánzhàn)*, and Government Sq (Shìfǔ Guǎngchǎng) serve as transport hubs and landmarks within the city. Accommodation and sights are scattered all over town.

Information

BOOKSHOPS

Foreign Language Bookstore (Wàiwén Shūdiàn; 48 Taiyuan Jie) Stocks a small selection of English-language books, mostly classics and 19th-century fiction.

Northern Book Town (Zhonghua Lu) Opposite the Traders Hotel, this busy bookstore has a slightly larger but similar English-language section in a less musty environment.

EMERGENCY
Public Security Bureau (PSB; Gōngānjú; ☎ 2253 4850; Zhongshan Sq)

INTERNET ACCESS
Internet bar (Wǎngbā; Lower level, North Train Station; per hr Y2)
Internet bar (Wǎngbā; Chaoyang Jie; per hr Y2) North of the Imperial Palace.
Internet bar (Wǎngbā; Huigong Jie; per hr Y2) Near Government Sq.

MONEY
ATMs accepting foreign cards can be found near the north train station, Zhongshan Sq, the Zhong Jie shopping district and Government Sq. Most large hotels change money
Bank of China (Zhōngguó Yínháng) Shifu Dalu (☎ 2285 6666; 253 Shifu Dalu; ☯ 8am-noon & 1-4pm Mon-Fri); Zhonghua Lu (Zhonghua Lu; ☯ 8am-noon & 1-4pm Mon-Fri) The Shifu Dalu branch is near Government Sq. The Zhonghua Lu branch is near the Traders Shopping Centre.

POST
Post office (Yóujú; 78 Beizhan Lu; ☯ 8am-8pm Mon-Fri) Near the north train station.

TELEPHONE
China Telecom (Zhōngguó Diànxìn; 185 Shifu Dalu) A short walk from Government Sq.

TOURIST INFORMATION
Liaoning Tourism Bureau (Liáoníng Shěng Lǚyóujú; ☎ 8680 7316; fax 8680 9415; 113 Huanghe Dajie) Near the North Tomb, this office has English-language maps and brochures of the province's attractions.

TRAVEL AGENCIES
China International Travel Service (CITS; Zhōngguó Guójì Lǚxíngshè; ☎ 8689 9383; fax 8680 8772; 113 Huanghe Dajie) In the same building as the Liaoning Tourism Bureau.

Sights

NORTH TOMB 北陵
One of Shěnyáng's most popular sights, the **North Tomb** (Běi Líng; ☎ 8689 6294; 12 Taishan Lu; admission park/tombs Y6/30; ☯ 6am-6pm) is the burial place of Huang Taiji (1592–1643), the founder of the Qing dynasty (although he didn't live to see the conquest of China). Set in Beiling Park, the tomb complex took eight years to build. The tomb's animal statues are reminiscent of the Ming tombs and lead up to the central mound known as the Luminous Tomb (Zhāo Líng).

Take bus No 220 from the south train station or bus No 217 from the north train station. Bus No 227 from the Imperial Palace (see next entry) via the east side of the north train station also travels to and from the North Tomb.

IMPERIAL PALACE 故宫
This sprawling **palace** (Gùgōng; ☎ 2282 1999; 171 Shenyang Lu; admission Y50; ☯ 8.30am-5.30pm) complex is a mini-Forbidden City in layout, with Manchu features. The main structures were started by Nurhachi (1559–1626) and completed in 1636 by his son, Huang Taiji.

Straight through the main gate, at the far end of the courtyard, is the main structure: the octagonal Dazheng Hall with its

NORTH OF THE WALL

coffered ceiling and elaborate throne. Nurhachi's grandson, Emperor Shunzhi, was crowned here, before he launched the Manchu invasion of China in 1644.

The central courtyard contains a conference hall, living quarters and some shamanist structures (one Manchu custom was to pour boiling wine into the ear of a sacrificial pig, so that its cries would attract the devotees' ancestors).

The palace is in the oldest section of the city. Take bus No 237 from the south train station, or bus No 227 from the North Tomb via the east side of the north train station.

EAST TOMB 东陵
Also known as Fú Líng, this small **tomb** (Dōng Líng; 210 Dongling Jie; admission Y10; ☯ 6am-6.30pm) is set in a forested area overlooking a river, 8km east of the city centre. It's the final resting place of Nurhachi and his mistress.

Take bus No 218 (45 minutes) from the Imperial Palace.

NORTH PAGODA 北塔
Of the four pagodas that once marked the city boundaries, **North Pagoda** (Běi Tǎ; 27 Beita Jie; admission Y5; ☯ 8.30am-4.30pm) is the best restored. The pagodas are said to symbolise the four Buddhist Heaven Kings and were constructed in the 1640s to protect the city and its people.

Within North Pagoda, the only original structures to remain are the Great Hall and Falun Temple. The other halls were added in 1984.

The Great Hall features detailed (and slightly gruesome) murals of deities and a wonderful statue of the Sky and Earth Buddha. The second hall has two magnificent panelled paintings of city life in the Qing dynasty, painted by tutors and students of Shěnyáng's art college in 1984. The final hall contains the Laughing Buddha – big, gold and jovial with a belly to match.

Bus No 611 from the south train station, No 325 from the north train station, or No 213 from the North Tomb, will drop you near the pagoda.

18 SEPTEMBER HISTORY MUSEUM 九一八历史博物馆
This striking modern **museum** (Jiǔ Yī Bā Lìshǐ Bówùguǎn; ☎ 2389 2316; 46 Wanghua Nanjie; admission Y20; ☯ 8.30am-4pm) is named after the date

when Shěnyáng was captured by the Japanese in 1931. The many exhibits, including more than 800 photographs, explore the Japanese occupation of Manchuria. Although the tone is obviously biased, this is the most elaborate and comprehensive museum dedicated to this period of Chinese history.

Gruesome examples of torture on display include a 'rolling cage' (a long metal tube lined with spikes in which prisoners were rolled to death) – not for the fainthearted.

Most of the captions are in Chinese, but enough are in English to provide a good overview.

Bus No 325 from the north train station stops in front of the museum. It's about a 10- to 15-minute walk between the museum and North Pagoda.

PAGODA OF BUDDHIST ASHES 无垢净光舍利塔
This 13-storey brick **pagoda** (Wúgòu Jìngguāng Shělì Tǎ; ☎ 8678 1651; 22 Taiwan Jie; admission Y4; ☯ 8.30am-5.30pm) dates back to AD 1044. A small museum on the grounds includes relics removed from inside the pagoda. This peaceful place is a pleasant escape from the city.

Take bus No 205 from the North Tomb or the south train station and get off at the corner of Taiwan Jie and Ningshan Lu. Walk north, cross the bridge and turn right. The pagoda is a three-minute walk north of here, down an alley on the right. Look for a red gate.

MAO ZEDONG STATUE 毛主席像
Towering over Zhongshan Sq, at the intersection of Zhongshan Lu and Nanjing Jie, Mao's **statue** (Máo Zhǔxí Xiàng) stands aloft, flanked by ecstatic intellectuals, and vociferous peasants, miners and soldiers. Cultural chronicle or common kitsch? You decide.

SHENYANG BOTANICAL GARDEN 沈阳植物园
About 20km east of the city centre, these rambling **gardens** (Shěnyáng Zhíwù Yuán; admission Y20; ☯ 8am-5pm) are home to numerous plants and flowers native to northeastern China. Special exhibitions highlight tulips (May), peonies (June) and chrysanthemums (October).

The real reason to make the trek here, though, has nothing to do with vegetation. It's the nearly 50 bridges suspended across a shallow river that visitors try to traverse.

There are narrow log bridges – like over-water balance beams – as well as rolling barrels, swinging bridges, tight wires, floating rafts and more. Cross if you dare; you'll likely end up in the water – it's great fun!

Bus No 330 from the intersection of Zhonghua Lu, Shiyi Wei Lu, and Heping Dajie, goes directly to the Botanical Garden (Y4, 45 minutes). Not all of the 330 buses go here, though, so ask before boarding.

Sleeping

BUDGET
Méishān Bīnguǎn (Main Sun Hotel; ☎ 2273 5538; fax 2272 8048; 48 Xiaoxi Lu; s Y60-100, d Y120-160) This small hotel, a short walk from the Zhong Jie shops, is one of the best values in Shěnyáng. Don't expect lots of space, but most rooms have wooden floorboards and cosy duvets.

Hépíng Bīnguǎn (Peace Hotel; ☎ 2383 3033; fax 2383 7389; 104 Shengli Beijie; d Y100-190, tr Y150, q Y160-200) A stone's throw from the south train station, this friendly budget choice is basic but clean. Fortunately, it's much quieter inside than out on the frenetic street.

MID-RANGE
Shěntiě Dàjiǔdiàn (Railway Hotel; ☎ 6223 1058; fax 6223 2888; 102 Beizhan Lu; d Y368-386 incl breakfast; 🍴 🖥) Within the north train station building, this hotel has well-kept doubles with modern furnishings and upscale amenities like hair dryers and minibars. With discounts to around Y180, it's a great deal.

Dōngfāng Dàshà (Railway New East Hotel; ☎ 2252 7388; fax 2252 4520; 112 Beizhan Lu; d Y200-368, ste Y348-528, incl breakfast; 🍴 🖥) Rooms here look more expensive than they are, especially the spacious suites. Some rooms are more recently updated than others, however, so be sure to look.

Also try **Yóuzhèng Dàshà** (Shenyang Post Hotel; ☎ 2259 3333; fax 2259 3077; 78 Beizhan Lu; d Y100-328; 🍴 🖥) with newish rooms and near-budget prices.

TOP END
New World Courtyard (Xīnshìjiè Jiǔdiàn; ☎ 2386 9888; www.courtyard.com; 2 Nanjing Nanjie; d Y500-700; 🚫 🍴 🖥 🐾) This swanky contemporary tower, run by the Marriott chain, is close

to the Taiyuan Jie shops. If they quote less than Y350, it's excellent value.

Other top-end choices include the stately and serene **Liaoning Hotel** (☎ 2383 9104; fax 2383 9104; 97 Zhongshan Sq; d Y520-580; 🍴 🖥), a 1927 dowager facing the Mao statue on Zhongshan Sq, and the coolly modern Shangri-La-owned **Traders Hotel** (Shāngmào Fàndiàn; ☎ 2341 2288; www.shangri-la.com; 68 Zhonghua Lu; d US$140-175; 🚫 🍴 🖥).

Eating
Both the north and south train stations are cheap restaurant zones. Stroll the Taiyuan Jie and Zhong Jie shopping areas for snacks, fruit and evening food stalls. Head to Xita Jie for the bright lights of Korea Town, where streetside eateries sell barbecued squid and *bulgogi* (Korean barbecue).

Lǎobiān Jiǎoziguǎn (Lao Bian Dumpling Restaurant; ☎ 2486 5369; 206 Zhong Jie; dumplings Y8-16; 🕙 lunch & dinner) The Bian family have had time to perfect their delicious dumplings – this restaurant has been steaming and frying since 1829.

Xiǎo Tǔdòu (Small Potato; ☎ 2291 5040; 37 Xiaoxi Lu; dishes Y10-15; 🕙 10am-11pm) This *dōngběi* (northeastern) eatery is packed with families, couples and groups of all ages who come for the oponymous potato dish that's anything but small; it's a hearty and delicious stew of spuds and greens in a meaty broth (Y10).

Dàjīndū Hánshì Měiwèi Shāokǎo Diàn (Dajindu Korean Korean BBQ Restaurant; ☎ 2252 5507; A4 Zhongzhan Lu; 🕙 lunch & dinner) Just west of Nanjing Beijie, between Korea Town and the north train station, this friendly local spot has table-top grills where you can cook your own pork, squid or even sweet potatoes.

Summer Christmas (Xiàrì Shèngdàn; ☎ 2347 4704; 99 Xita Jie; pizzas from Y40; 🕙 7am-2am) This bizarrely named Korea Town restaurant is known for its pizzas.

The department store inside Zhongxing Shenyang Commercial Building (see following section) has a decent supermarket. The **Happy Family Store** (160 Zhong Jie) has a well-stocked supermarket on the lower level and a bustling food court (dishes Y5 to Y15) on the 5th floor.

Shopping
Near the south train station is Taiyuan Jie, one of Shěnyáng's major shopping streets,

with a bustling night market. Below Taiyuan Jie is an underground shopping street.

Traders Shopping Centre (68 Zhonghua Lu; 9.30am-9pm) Just off Taiyuan Jie, this small shopping centre is home to international names like Dunhill and Ferragamo.

Nearby, inside the **Zhongxing Shenyang Commercial Building** (86 Taiyuan Jie), there's a large department store.

Zhong Jie, near the Imperial Palace, is another pedestrian street, with a large concentration of electronics stores. Even if you're not buying, the mix of Japanese architecture and flashy neon makes it an interesting stroll.

Getting There & Away
AIR
The **International Air Transport Association ticket office** (IATA; Guójì Hángxié Hángkōng Shòupiàochù; ☎ 2286 7029; 229 Zhonghua Lu; 8am-6pm) sells tickets to a huge number of domestic destinations, including Běijīng (Y710, one hour and 10 minutes), Shànghǎi (Y1300, two hours), and Guǎngzhōu (Y2310, 3¾ hours). Air China (p906) has daily service from Shěnyáng to Seoul (Y2900, 2½ hours).

Aeroflot (☎ 2334 1517; 208 Nanjing Beijie; 9am-5pm) has an office in the Intercontinental Hotel, but at the time of writing, there were no flights to Russia from Shěnyáng, only from Běijīng.

Larger hotels can book airline and train tickets.

BUS
The modern, long-distance express **bus station** (qìchē kuàisù kèyùnzhàn; Huigong Jie) is south of Beizhan Lu, about a five-minute walk from the north train station. See table below for information.

If you come out of the south train station, cross Shengli Jie, and bear right onto Minzu Lu, you'll be confronted with a line

of buses – this is the south long-distance bus station. There are regular departures to Ānshān (鞍山; Y20, 1½ hours) and Běnxī (本溪; Y12.50, one hour).

TRAIN
Shěnyáng's major train stations are the north station and the south station. Many trains arrive at one station, then after a short stop, travel to the next. However, when departing this is not always the case, so double check which station you need.

Buying sleepers anywhere in the northeast can be a headache, and Shěnyáng is no exception; purchase your ongoing ticket as soon as you arrive.

The south train station has services departing for Hāěrbīn (Y53 to Y76, five to seven hours), Chángchūn (Y28, four to six hours), Dāndōng (Y24, four hours), Běijīng (seat/sleeper Y110/215, eight to 10 hours) and Dàlián (Y55, four to five hours). Express trains from the north train station travel to destinations including Běijīng (seat/sleeper Y110/215, eight hours), Guǎngzhōu (seat/sleeper Y305/552, 30 hours) and Shànghǎi (seat/sleeper Y206/373, 27 hours).

Getting Around
Although Shěnyáng has lots of bus routes, getting anywhere by public transport in this sprawling city is likely to require at least one transfer. Maps of the bus routes – definitely a worthwhile Y4 to Y5 investment – are sold at the train stations.

Bus Nos 203 and 602 run between the north and south train stations. Bus No 227 runs between the North Tomb, the north train station and the Imperial Palace. Bus No 207 runs east–west across Government Sq.

Taxis cost Y7 for the first 4km.

The airport is 25km south of the city centre. Taxis to the airport will cost around Y100.

Destination	Price	Duration	Frequency	Departs
Běijīng	Y190	7½hr	6 daily	8am-10pm
Chángchūn	Y75	3½hr	hourly	7am-6pm
Dāndōng	Y65	3hr	every 30 min	6am-7pm
Hāěrbīn	Y140	6½hr	6 daily	8am-3.30pm
Jílín	Y96	4½hr	6 daily	7.30am-4.30pm
Jīnzhōu	Y53	3hr	hourly	7am-6pm

AROUND SHĚNYÁNG
Benxi Water Caves 本溪水洞

These **caves** (Běnxī Shuǐdòng; admission Y85, plus Y5 for tram from ticket office to cave entrance; ☯ 8am-5pm), 30km east of Běnxī (which is 60km southeast of Shěnyáng) feature a forest of stalactites and stalagmites. The entry ticket includes a 45-minute boat ride along the 'Milky Way', a 3km-long river that zigzags through caves of differing shapes and sizes. Pink, green and blue lights illuminate the formations, making the place feel like a movie set, but the rock shapes are dramatic despite the hokey lighting. The formations' evocative names – Seal Playing with a Pearl, Tiger's Mouth, Ginseng Baby – are entertaining too.

The caves maintain a constant temperature of 10°C. Coats are provided for the boat journey, but it gets cold so bring extra layers. Try to avoid visiting on crowded summer weekends.

A direct bus leaves Shěnyáng's south long-distance bus station at 7.30am and departs the caves at 2.30pm (Y20 each way, 2½ hours). Buses to Běnxī train station (Y12.50, one hour) depart regularly from Shěnyáng's south long-distance bus station. From Běnxī, minibuses ply the route to the caves (Y6, 1½ hours).

Qiān Shān 千山

These hills are composed of nearly 1000 lotus-shaped peaks – giving rise to the name, an abbreviation of Qiānlián Shān (Thousand Lotuses Mountain). You can hike around the hills, which have a scattering of Tang, Ming and Qing temples. Qiān Shān itself gets very crowded on Sunday and public holidays. It is steep in parts and takes about three hours to reach the summit.

At the southern foot of the mountain are the Tanggangzi Hot Springs (Tānggǎngzi Wēnquán). The last Qing emperor, Puyi, used to bathe here with his empress. Today Tānggǎngzi's hot springs are piped into ordinary baths for ordinary folk.

This area is about 80km south of Shěnyáng. From Shěnyáng's south long-distance bus station regular buses cover the 60km journey to Ānshān (Y20), where you change buses to Qiān Shān. The whole trip takes around 2½ hours.

Maps can be bought from hawkers near the gate or from the ticket office. Qiān Shān area admission is Y50.

DÀLIÁN 大连
☎ 411 / pop 1,925,200

Perched on the Liaodong Peninsula bordering the Yellow Sea, Dàlián is one of the most modern and prosperous cities in China. The city manages to feel both bustling and relaxed, as if the entire population is on holiday – or shopping. Consumer culture has arrived in a big way, with new shopping malls springing up seemingly on every block. Yet, while many flashy towers are being built, the city retains some wonderful early-20th-century architecture and refreshing acres of grass.

Several beaches surround the city, and relaxing by the sea is the main reason most travellers visit Dàlián. The city has the largest harbour in the northeast and not one but two splashy aquariums. Dàlián's extremely successful soccer team also lures many fans.

Dàlián has been known by several names: Dalny, Dairen, Lüshun and Lüda. Today, Lüshun (formerly Port Arthur) is the part further south, and Lüshun and Dàlián comprise Lüda. A military base at Lüshun is considered a 'sensitive zone' – much of the area is off limits to foreigners.

Orientation

The hub of the city is in the eastern part of town around Zhongshan Sq. The Dàlián train station is centrally located, west of Zhongshan Sq; the ferry terminal is to the northeast. Several beaches dot the coast south of town.

Information   Map p356

Dàlián recently adopted eight-digit phone numbers. To convert an old seven-digit number, precede it with an '8'.

BOOKSHOPS
Xinhua Bookshop (Xīnhuá Shūdiàn; 96 Tongxing Jie) Near Tianjin Jie.

> **WARNING**
>
> Before attempting to head southwest of Dàlián towards Lüshun (Port Arthur), check with the PSB (p354) in Dàlián. This area at the end of the Liaodong Peninsula is considered a sensitive military zone and has historically been off limits to foreigners.

NORTHERN WARLORDS

Formerly known as Manchuria, northeastern China has historically served as a springboard for conquerors.

In the late 1800s, Manchuria was a sparsely populated region, rich in untapped resources. Both the Russians and the Japanese eyed it enviously. When the Chinese were defeated in the Sino-Japanese War (1894–95), Liaodong Peninsula was ceded to Japan.

Russia's Influence

Japan's strength alarmed other foreign powers, Russia among them, and Japan was forced to hand the area back to China. As a reward for their intervention, the Russians were permitted to build a railway across Manchuria to their treaty port (a port from which foreigners were allowed by treaty to conduct trade) of Port Arthur (now Lüshun), near present-day Dàlián. The Russians moved troops in with the railway and, for the next 10 years, effectively controlled northeastern China.

Russia's reign ended with the Russo-Japanese War (1904–05). By the time the Qing dynasty fell, Zhang Zuolin, a bandit leader in charge of a large and well-organised private army, had taken full control of Manchuria. Between 1926 and 1928 Zhang ran a regional government recognised by foreign powers. The Japanese killed Zhang in a bomb attack in 1928, and his son, Zhang Xueliang, took over his role with the blessing of the Kuomintang (for more about the Kuomintang see p43).

Secret Alliances & Double Crosses

In September 1931 the Japanese invaded Manchuria and established the puppet state Manchukuo. Zhang Xueliang and his Dōngběi (Northeastern) Army were forced out of Manchuria and moved into central China to fight with the Kuomintang against the communists.

Zhang's loyalty to Chiang Kaishek had never wavered. But he came to realise that Chiang's promises to recover Manchuria from the Japanese were empty. Zhang formed a secret alliance with the communists and, when Chiang flew to Xī'ān in December 1936 to organise another anticommunist campaign, Zhang had him arrested. Chiang was released after agreeing to join

EMERGENCY

PSB (Gōngānjú; ☎ 8363 2718; 16 Yan'an Lu; ⏱ 8-11.30am & 1-4.30pm Mon-Fri)

INTERNET ACCESS

There are several Internet bars around Zhongshan Sq.
Evolution (Wǎngbā; cnr Zhongshan Lu & Youhao Lu; per hr Y3) This Internet café is on the northern side of Friendship Sq.

INTERNET RESOURCES

Daliannews (www.daliannews.com) English-language local news and tourist information.
Shide-global (www.shide-global.com/sports.htm) Background and contact information for the local football (soccer) team.

MONEY

Bank of China (Zhōngguó Yínháng; ☎ 8280 5711; 9 Zhongshan Sq; ⏱ 8.30-11.30am & 1-7pm Mon-Fri) Inside the stately green dome-roofed building on Zhongshan Sq.

China Merchants Bank (Victory Sq) ATM; opposite the train station, off Jiefang Lu.
HSBC (cnr Renmin Lu & Zhigong Jie) ATM; accepts Cirrus, Plus, MasterCard and Visa cards.

POST & TELEPHONE

Post & telephone office (Yóujú; 134 Changjiang Lu; ⏱ 8am-5pm Mon-Fri)

TRAVEL AGENCIES

CITS (Zhōngguó Guójì Lǚxíngshè; ☎ 8368 7843; 1 Changtong Jie; ⏱ 8.30am-5.30pm Mon-Fri) West of Labour Park.

Sights & Activities

ZHONGSHAN SQUARE 中山广场

Zhongshan Sq (Zhōngshān Guǎngchǎng; Map p356) is Dàlián's hub: a panorama of grand buildings encircling a huge roundabout. The square (in fact a circle) comes alive at night, when young people hang out and play badminton or hacky sack. An even larger

the communists to resist the Japanese. Chiang never forgave Zhang for his treachery and later had him arrested and taken to Taiwan, where he was detained for several decades (in 2001 Zhang died at age 100 in Hawaii).

Communists vs Kuomintang

The WWII bombings of Hiroshima and Nagaskaki in August 1945 forced the Japanese government to surrender, and Soviet armies moved into Manchuria. With American assistance, Kuomintang troops moved north to oversee the Japanese surrender and regain control of northern China. The US navy stationed 53,000 marines at Qīngdǎo to protect the railways leading to Běijīng and Tiānjīn, and the coal mines that supplied those railways.

In defiance of Chiang's orders, the communists marched to Manchuria, picking up arms from abandoned Japanese depots along the way. Other communist troops headed north by sea from Shāndōng. In November 1945 the Kuomintang attacked the communists, despite US-organised peace negotiations between the two sides. This attack put an end to all talks.

Manchurian Battlegrounds

The communists occupied the countryside, and their land-reform policies quickly built up support among the peasants. Soon the 100,000 men that had marched into Manchuria had tripled in size as peasants and ex-soldiers of the Manchurian armies eagerly joined the ranks. Within two years the Red Army had grown to 1.5 million combat troops and four million support personnel.

On the Kuomintang side, troops numbered three million, with Soviet and US support, but soldiers were disheartened. Many either deserted or joined the communists. Chiang's army was also weakened by generals he had chosen for their loyalty rather than their military competence.

In 1948, in Manchuria, the communists made their move. Three great battles led by Lin Biao decided the outcome. In the first, in August 1948, the Kuomintang lost 500,000 people. In the second battle, from November 1948 to January 1949, whole Kuomintang divisions went over to the communists. The final battle was fought in and around Běijīng and Tiānjīn. Tiānjīn fell on 23 January and another 500,000 Kuomintang troops switched sides, sealing the fate of the Kuomintang and allowing the communists to drive southwards.

crowd comes to watch the local football team Dàlián Shide (the Manchester United of China) on the giant TV screen above the Dàlián Bīnguǎn (see p357 for more about this hotel).

FRIENDSHIP SQUARE 友好广场

Just west of Zhongshan Sq, **Friendship Sq** (Yǒuhǎo Guǎngchǎng; Map p356) is a traffic circle that surrounds a Dàlián landmark – a vast spheroid that's illuminated like a giant disco ball in the evenings.

PEOPLE'S SQUARE 人民广场

Formerly known as Stalin Sq, **People's Sq** (Rénmín Guǎngchǎng; Map p358), about 2km west of Zhongshan Sq is another popular gathering spot at dusk. A small park to the east of the square is where the older folk come to chat, have a haircut or indulge in a massage. Bus No 15 travels to the People's Sq from Zhongshan Sq.

LABOUR PARK 劳动公园

At this hilly **park** (Láodòng Gōngyuán; Map p356; admission Y10; ⊙ 7am-7pm) in the city centre, the landmark is a giant football, further testimony to the sport's popularity. Take the chairlift (Y40) up to the TV Tower (Map p358) for excellent views of the city and come down via the hilarious 'land slide', a chute that winds down the hill.

POLAR AQUARIUM & TIGER BEACH PARK
老虎滩极地海洋动物馆

It's not Sea World, but this huge **aquarium complex** (Lǎohǔtān Jídì Hǎiyáng Dòngwùguǎn; Map p358; admission Y130; ⊙ 8am-6pm) displays polar marine life in a Disney-style setting. There's a whale and dolphin show, and big glass enclosures housing whales, seals, walruses, sea otters, penguins and polar bears. There's nothing especially Chinese about the place (except for the crowds), but it's worth a stop if you're travelling with kids or dolphin devotees.

Surrounding the aquarium is **Tiger Beach Park** (Lǎohǔtān Lèyuán; Map p358), which has a massive carved-marble tiger sculpture, a small beach, a honky-tonk amusement park, and a zip line (Y50) that whisks you over the bay. On either side of the park, the coastal road provides excellent views of the ragged cliffs and crashing waves.

Bus Nos 30 and 712 from Zhongshan Sq travel to Tiger Beach Park in about 20 to 30 minutes (Y1).

SUN ASIA OCEAN WORLD 圣亚欢乐港湾

At this wildly popular **aquarium** (Shèngyà Huānlè Gǎngwān; Map p358; ☎ 8467 9517; admission Y70; ☀ 8.30am-5pm), you ride a moving footpath past tanks where sharks, rays and other aquatic life swim overhead. It's fun for children, though the crowded exhibit areas aren't for the claustrophobic. Skip the adjacent **Sun Asia Polar World** (Map p358; admission Y80, combined admission with Ocean World Y120; ☀ 8.30am-5pm), where the souvenir shop is better stocked than the exhibit halls.

Ocean World is inside **Xinghai Park** (Map p358; admission Y10; ☀ 7.30am-5.30pm), a park with a rocky beach, carnival rides, a bungee jump, and a hair-raising zip line over the water.

Bus Nos 22 and 23 frequently run from the corner of Jiefang Lu and Zhongshan Lu to Xinghai Park in about 20 minutes (Y1).

OTHER BEACHES

Five kilometres southeast of the city centre is **Bàngchuídǎo Jǐngqū** (Map p358; admission Y20), which has a secluded sandy swimming beach on the grounds of Bàngchuídǎo

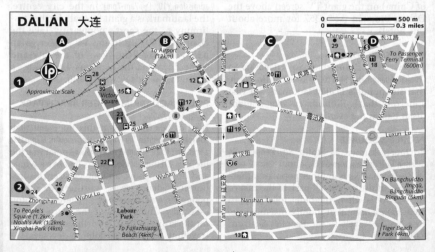

Bīnguǎn, a hotel complex that's a favourite with top-ranking Communist Party members and cadres. Unfortunately, there's no bus service to this area; a taxi from town will cost about Y20.

Another good swimming spot is **Fujiazhuang Beach** (Map p358; admission Y5; 6am-11pm), a deep bay with pebbly sand. Take bus No 401 from the northwest corner of Jiefang Lu and Zhongshan Lu.

Golden Stone Beach (Jīnshítān), situated about 60km north of Dàlián, is an attractive beach with splendid coves and rock formations. There is also a golf course, cross-country motorcycling, an amusement park and hunting grounds within a forest. Buses to Golden Stone Beach leave every 40 minutes from the square in front of the Dàlián train station (Y9).

Sleeping   Map p356

Dàlián has no end of first-class accommodation. Unfortunately that choice doesn't extend to those on a budget, and the city's building boom has claimed many cheap hotels. In summer, expect higher prices than those quoted here.

BUDGET

Dàlián Fàndiàn (8263 3171; fax 8280 4197; 6 Shanghai Lu; s/d Y198/228) This red-brick hotel, which looks like a 1930s warehouse from the outside, has simple, cosy rooms. Discounts may put doubles under Y120.

MID-RANGE

Huayu Pearl Hotel (Huáyǔ Míngzhū Dàjiǔdiàn; 8265 0888; fax 8280 4723; 8 Victory Sq; d Y380-500;) With comfortable facilities and a handy location near the train station, this tower is a solid mid-range option.

Foreign Experts Hotel (Zhuānjiā Gōngyù Bīnguǎn; 8280 1199; fax 8263 9958; 110 Nanshan Lu; d Y240-300) On the University of Foreign Languages campus south of the city centre, this hotel has pleasant rooms and a public kitchen on every floor. Take bus No 23 down Yan'an Lu to its terminus and then, heading west (the same direction the bus was travelling when it pulled into the last stop), take the second left on Qilingdong Lane. Go up the hill; the hotel is on the right, just before the street curves sharply.

Dàlián Bóhǎi Fàndiàn (8363 3671; fax 8363 2037; 124 Zhongshan Lu; d Y298-398;) At this rather chaotic behemoth, rooms range from dreary to big and bright.

TOP END

Dàlián Bīnguǎn (8263 3111; www.chinadalianhotel.com; 4 Zhongshan Sq; s/d Y450/600;) This dignified dowager appeared in the movie The Last Emperor. Its wrought iron entrance leads to a grand marbled interior.

Furama Hotel (Fùlìhuá Dàjiǔdiàn; 8263 0888; www.furama.com.cn; 60 Renmin Lu; d Y598 plus 15% service charge;) This glitzy five-star hotel has a sleek Asian-fusion style, spacious rooms with high-speed Internet connections, and surprisingly reasonable prices for the level of quality; a top choice for a splurge.

Eating   Map p356

For cheap eats, the area around Youhao Lu is popular with students. Bars and restaurants line the roads leading off Zhongshan Sq. The New-Mart Shopping Mall (p358) has a huge food court (dishes Y5 to Y8) on the 5th floor and a well-provisioned supermarket on the lower level.

Dàbáicài Gǔtou Guǎn (8263 6656; 21 Zhongyuan Jie, btwn Youhao Lu & Xiangqian Jie; dishes Y12-24; lunch & dinner) Friendly, loud and smoky, this informal eatery serves up fresh seafood and fiery northern-style fare. Don't miss the greens with hot mustard, and cool off with a local beer (Y5 to Y10).

Tiān Tiān Yú Gǎng (8280 1118; 10 Renmin Lu; dishes Y25-60; lunch & dinner) Choose your dinner from the many sea creatures swimming in the tanks at this upscale seafood restaurant with doting service. Great veggie dishes, too.

Shanyi Curry & Coffee (8282 7111; 63 Baiyu Jie; curry Y20-28, coffee Y25; breakfast, lunch & dinner) This swish little café serves the unlikely combination of, er, curry and coffee.

Pizza King Italian Restaurant (Yìdàlì Bǐsàbǐng Diàn; pizzas Y20-38, pastas Y26, steaks Y48; lunch & dinner) Renmin Lu (8282 3008; 65 Renmin Lu); Youhao Lu (8280 6888; 122 Youhao Lu) A classier restaurant than its name implies, Pizza King offers reasonable Italian food in two locations.

Drinking

The area around Friendship Sq is worth exploring for small bars and late-night coffee shops. You'll find similar places around the University of Foreign Languages, particularly around Qi'qi Jie and Yan'an Lu. A patio bar on Victory Sq (Shengli Guangchang) serves decent coffees and has Carlsberg and Heineken on tap.

Karffer Coffee (Map p356; Level 1, New-Mart Shopping Mall) At this sleek place you can ignore the frenzied shoppers while you recharge yourself with an espresso (Y12) or cappuccino (Y22).

Entertainment

Noah's Ark (Nuóyà Fāngzhōu; Map p358; ☎ 8369 2798; 32 Wusi Lu) Local bands play regularly at this cool bar. It's just south of People's Sq, on the western side of the flower market building.

Shopping   Map p356

Tianjin Jie is one of Dàlián's main shopping thoroughfares, though at the time of writing, many stores had closed due to extensive construction nearby. Try one of the following options instead.

New-Mart Shopping Mall (Youhao Jie, btwn Zhongshan Lu & Wuhan Lu) This lively place is packed with young people scoping out the latest fashions.

Friendship Shopping Centre (8 Renmin Lu) This department store, off Zhongshan Sq, stocks expensive brand-name goods.

Opposite the train station, there's an enormous underground shopping centre below Victory Sq.

Getting There & Away

AIR

Airport shuttles leave regularly from the office of the **Civil Aviation Administration of China** (CAAC; Zhōngguó Mínháng; Map p356; ☎ 8364 2136; 143 Zhongshan Lu; ⏰ 8am-6pm); check with the CAAC for times.

Domestic flights include Běijīng (Y710, one hour), Hāěrbīn (Y840, 1½ hours), Shànghǎi (Y1060, 1¾ hours), Guǎngzhōu (Y2050, 3½ hours) and Hong Kong (Y3000, 3½ hours).

Dragonair (Map p356; 15th fl, 68 Renmin Lu; ⏰ 8271 8855) has an office next door to the Furama Hotel. **Japan Airlines** (JAL; Map p356; 147 Zhongshan Lu; ⏰ 8369 2525) and **All Nippon Airways** (Map p356; 147 Zhongshan Lu; ⏰ 8360 6611) are both in the Senmao Building, near the CAAC. International destinations include Tokyo

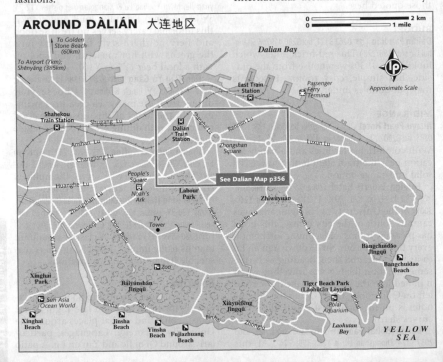

AROUND DÀLIÁN 大连地区

(Y4850, 2½ hours), Osaka (Y4150, two hours and 20 minutes), Fukuoka (Y3540, 2¼ hours), Sendai (Y5070, 2½ hours) and Seoul (Y2390, one hour).

BOAT
Boats are a sensible and enjoyable way to leave Dàlián, as trains and buses are a long haul. Buy ferry tickets at the passenger ferry terminal in the northeast of Dàlián or from a counter in front of the train station.

There is an international service to Incheon in South Korea that departs from Dàlián on Monday, Wednesday and Friday at 3.30pm (Y850 to Y1469, 16 hours). A boat to Shànghǎi (Y660, 37 hours) leaves on even-numbered days at 4pm.

Several daily boats go to Yāntái (Y60 to Y680, four to seven hours). There are two boats daily to Wēihǎi (Y150 to Y190, seven to nine hours), departing at 9:40am and 9pm. Boats to Tiānjīn depart daily at either 5pm or 6pm (Y172 to Y720, 13 to 14 hours).

Take bus No 13 from the Dàlián train station or bus No 708 from Zhongshan Sq to the passenger ferry terminal.

BUS
The **long-distance bus station** (Map p356; 20 Anshan Lu) is west of the train station, though at the time of writing, the station was being rebuilt. Buses also leave from in front of the train station.

There are regular buses to Dāndōng (Y57, six hours) and a daily fast bus to Běijīng (Y210, nine hours). Other destinations include Tōnghuà (Y73, 12 hours) and Běnxī (Y75 to Y90, five hours).

A **ticket office** (Map p356; 14 Changjiang Lu) for buses to Běijīng is behind the Furama Hotel.

TRAIN
Mayhem! Before braving the crowds at Dàlián train station, write down your destination, preferred travel dates and seat-class, then be prepared for long lines. Buy your ticket as early as possible.

Several daily trains run to Shěnyáng (Y55, four to five hours). An overnight train to Dāndōng (sleeper Y110) departs at 6.56pm and arrives at 6.25am. Other destinations include Běijīng (seat/sleeper Y140/290, 10 to 12 hours), Hāěrbīn (seat/sleeper Y125/231,

nine to 10 hours), Chángchūn (seat/sleeper Y99/171, eight to 9½ hours) and Tōnghuà (seat/sleeper Y71/143, 13 hours).

Getting Around
Dàlián's central district is not large and can generally be covered on foot.

The airport is 12km northwest of the city centre; bus Nos 701 and 710 run between Zhongshan Sq and the airport (Y1). A taxi from the city centre will cost about Y30.

Bus No 23 runs south down Yan'an Lu. Bus No 13 runs from the train station to the passenger ferry terminal. Colourful trams (Y1 to Y2) also glide around parts of the city until 11pm.

Taxis start at Y8.

DĀNDŌNG 丹东
☎ 0415 / pop 604,600
Dāndōng lies at the border of Liáoníng and North Korea, and its tourist industry thrives on the views of North Korea across Yalu River (Yālù Jiāng). Unfortunately, you get only a brief, distant peek at this otherwise closed society. More interesting, perhaps, is Dāndōng's mix of Chinese and Korean culture. Outside the city, you can also visit the easternmost stretch of the Great Wall.

Check with CITS if you want to join a tour to Pyongyang, the North Korean capital. (At the time of writing, American, Israeli and South Korean nationals were not being issued North Korean visas). However, applying for a visa at the North Korean embassy in Běijīng would probably prove quicker than attempting to make arrangements in Dāndōng.

Orientation
The river is about 500m southeast of the train station. The 'Business and Tourism District' (Shāngmào Lǚyóuqū), a good place to find riverfront restaurants, is southwest of the Yalu River bridge. The main shopping district is just east of the station.

Information
Bank of China (Zhōngguó Yínháng; ☎ 213 7721; 60 Jinshan Dajie)
CITS (Zhōngguó Guójì Lǚxíngshè; ☎ 213 5854; fax 214 1922; 20 Shiwei Lu at Jiangcheng Dajie; ☼ 8am-5pm)
Internet café (Wǎngbā; Bajing Jie, btwn Qiwei Lu & Bawei Lu; per hr Y2)
Post office (Yóujú; 78 Qiwei Lu)

NORTH OF THE WALL

PSB (Gōngānjú; ☎ 210 3138; 15 Jiangcheng Dajie; ⏰ 8am-12.30pm & 1.30pm-5.30pm Mon-Fri)

Sights

NORTH KOREAN BORDER 北朝鲜边界

For a view of the **border** (Běi Cháoxiǎn Biānjiè), head for **Yalujiang Park**, an appealing riverfront park that's a favourite with tourists posing for the standard 'I visited the Sino–Korean border' shot.

The original steel-span bridge between the two countries was 'accidentally' strafed in 1950 by the Americans, who also accidentally bombed the airstrip at Dāndōng. The Koreans dismantled this bridge as far as the mid-river boundary line – all that's left on the Korean side is a row of support columns. You can wander along the **remains of the original bridge** (admission Y15; ⏰ dawn-dusk), which still shows shrapnel pockmarks and ends abruptly mid-river. The Sino–Korean Friendship Bridge runs parallel to the remains of the old one.

Those without a North Korean visa can get pretty close to the country by taking a **boat cruise** (guānguāng chuán). Don't bother with the large boats (Y8, 20 minutes); you have to wait for them to fill up with passengers, which can take forever. Instead, board one of the speed boats (Y18, 10 minutes, from dawn to dusk) at the Tour Boat Piers and zip along the river right up along the North Korean side. Apart from some locals and the odd smokestack, there isn't much to see. Nevertheless, if you want to visit North Korea, this may be as close as you get.

MUSEUM TO COMMEMORATE US AGGRESSION 抗美援朝纪念馆

With everything from statistics to shrapnel, this **museum** (Kàngměi Yuáncháo Jiniànguǎn; ☎ 215 0510; admission Y22; ⏰ 8am-4.30pm) offers Chinese and North Korean perspectives of the war with the United States (1950–53). Most captions are in Chinese and Korean, but the visual displays are interesting. Don't miss the Chinese propaganda leaflets dropped across enemy lines. The adjacent North Korean War Memorial Column was built 53m high symbolising the year the war ended.

Bus No 3 from just north of the train station will drop you off near the stadium. Cross the train tracks and walk west towards the Memorial Column.

TIGER MOUNTAIN GREAT WALL 虎山长城

About 25km northeast of Dāndōng, this steep, restored stretch of the **Great Wall** (Hǔshān Chángchéng; admission Y30), built during the Ming dynasty, parallels the current North Korean border. Unlike other sections of the wall, this one still sees comparatively few tourists.

You can hike up the wall and view the unrestored sections. The restored wall ends at a small but worthwhile **museum** (admission Y10).

To return to the entrance, either hike back over the wall or hire a boat (Y15, 10 minutes) to row you back along the river. The river marks the border, so even if it appears unguarded, don't attempt to cross to the other side. A gun-toting soldier may suddenly appear.

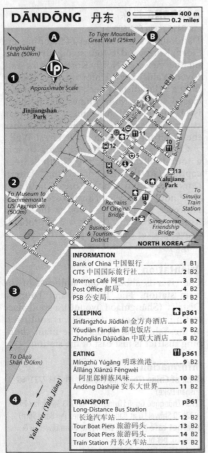

DĀNDŌNG 丹东

0 ———— 400 m
0 ———— 0.2 miles

To Tiger Mountain
Great Wall (25km)

Fènghuáng
Shān (50km)

Approximate Scale

Jinjiangshān
Park

To Museum to
Commemorate
US Aggression
(500m)

To Dàgū
Shān (90km)

Remains
Of Original
Bridge

Yalujiang
Park

To
Sinuiju
Train
Station

Business
& Tourism
District

Sino-Korean
Friendship
Bridge

NORTH KOREA

Yalu River (Yàlù Jiāng)

INFORMATION	
Bank of China 中国银行	1 B1
CITS 中国国际旅行社	2 B2
Internet Café 网吧	3 B2
Post Office 邮局	4 B2
PSB 公安局	5 B2

SLEEPING	🔒 p361
Jinfāngzhōu Jiǔdiàn 金方舟酒店	6 B2
Yóudiàn Fàndiàn 邮电饭店	7 B2
Zhōnglián Dàjiǔdiàn 中联大酒店	8 B2

EATING	🍴 p361
Míngzhū Yúgǎng 明珠渔港	9 B2
Āliláng Xiānzú Fēngwèi 阿里郎鲜族风味	10 B2
Āndōng Dàshìjiè 安东大世界	11 B2

TRANSPORT	p361
Long-Distance Bus Station 长途汽车站	12 B2
Tour Boat Piers 旅游码头	13 B2
Tour Boat Piers 旅游码头	14 B2
Train Station 丹东火车站	15 B2

Buses to the wall (Y4, 45 minutes) run about every 30 minutes from the Dāndōng long-distance bus station.

Sleeping

Yóudiàn Fàndiàn (Post & Telecommunications Hotel; ☎ 216 6888; fax 213 5988; 78 Qiwei Lu; s Y168, d Y218-368, tr Y135-288, q Y180-320, incl breakfast) The simple rooms here are comfy, and the 'economical' triples and quads are a very good deal. Just beware of the late-night karaoke hall.

Jìnfāngzhōu Jiǔdiàn (☎ 212 3068; fax 216 0076; 2 Shiwei Lu; dm Y40, d Y200-328) Choose a room on the river side at this barebones but welcoming guesthouse, where even some of the dorms have great water views.

Zhōnglián Dàjiǔdiàn (☎ 317 0666; www.zlhotel.com.cn; No 1, A2, Shangmao Luyouqu; s Y398, d Y498-658; ⚇) Opposite the old bridge, Dāndōng's most upscale hotel has an English-speaking staff, a glam lobby, and well-appointed rooms; the higher-priced ones overlook the river.

Eating

For fresh seafood and good Korean fare, explore the riverfront in Dāndōng's Business and Tourism District. Stick to the small restaurants around the train station for authentic Dāndōng *xiǎo chī* (snacks).

Āndōng Dàshìjiè (An Dong Great World Restaurant; ☎ 216 6666; 29 Liujing Jie; dishes Y8-16; ⚇ lunch & dinner) In this stylish, yet boisterous and inexpensive dining room, do as the locals do and order a selection of *dōngběi* small plates: sesame-scented cabbage, spicy tofu, or yummy crispy ribs.

Ālǐláng Xiānzú Fēngwèi (Arirang Korean Restaurant; ☎ 212 2333; Binjiang Lu; dishes Y10-20; ⚇ lunch & dinner) This restaurant opposite Yalujiang Park is a good choice for Korean food. It is popular with young people sharing soups in stone pots, garlicky greens, and fiery clams, washed down with the local Yalu River beer.

Míngzhū Yúgǎng (Pearl Bay Seafood Restaurant; ☎ 312 0442; Shangmao Luyouqu; dishes from Y10; ⚇ lunch & dinner) Facing the river, this local eatery specialises in seafood. They make tasty noodles, vegetables, and dumplings, too.

Getting There & Away

AIR

Flights from Dāndōng are limited, and service to Běijīng is not always available. Check with CITS for schedules and bookings. Other destinations include Shànghǎi (Y990,

two hours and 20 minutes) and Shēnzhèn (Y2010, five hours and 20 minutes).

BUS

The **long-distance bus station** (98 Shiwei Lu) is near the train station.

Destination	Price	Duration	Frequency	Departs
Dàlián	Y57	6hr	10 daily	5.30am-2.30pm
Hāěrbīn	Y153	12hr	daily	10am
Shěnyáng	Y65	3hr	every 30 min	6am-7pm
Tōnghuà	Y45	8hr	2 daily	6.30am & 8.50am

TRAIN

The train station is in the centre of town, north of the river.

Destination	Price	Duration
Běijīng	Y263 (sleeper)	14hr
Chángchūn	Y72/136 (seat/sleeper)	10hr
Dàlián	Y110 (sleeper)	11hr
Qīngdǎo	Y214 (sleeper)	24hr
Shěnyáng	Y24	4hr

The train from Moscow to Pyongyang stops at Dāndōng at 7.30am on Monday, Wednesday, Thursday and Saturday (Dāndōng to Pyongyang takes 11 hours). If you have the necessary visas, you can jump aboard and head for the border.

AROUND DĀNDŌNG

About 52km northwest of Dāndōng is the town of Fèngchéng. The nearby **Fènghuáng Shān** (凤凰山; Phoenix Mountain) is 840m high and dotted with temples, monasteries and pagodas from the Tang, Ming and Qing dynasties. A mountain temple fair in April attracts thousands of people. Buses to Fèngchéng leave from Dāndōng's bus station every 10 minutes between 6am and 5.30pm (Y8, one hour).

Dàgū Shān (大孤山; Lonely Mountain) is about 90km southwest of Dāndōng, en route to Dàlián, close to the town of Gūshān. Several groups of Taoist temples here date from the Tang dynasty. Buses to Dàgū Shān run every 20 minutes (Y12.50, 2½ hours) from Dāndōng's bus station, starting at 6am.

Jílín 吉林

HIGHLIGHTS

- Gaze across **Heaven Lake** (p371), a volcanic crater lake in stunning Chángbái Shān, China's largest nature reserve
- Visit **Chángbái Shān**'s (p371) waterfalls, hot springs and dense green forests
- **Ski** (p370) at Sōnghuā Hú or Běidàhú, two of China's leading winter resorts
- Explore Korean–Chinese culture in Yánjí and the **Korean Autonomous Prefecture** (p374)
- Hang out with the locals in Jílín's **city parks** (p369)

★ Jílín
★ Běidahu Ski Area
Yánjí ★
Mt Changbai Nature Reserve ★
Heaven Pool ★

■ POP: 28.5 MIL	■ AREA: 187,000 SQ KM	■ www.jl.gov.cn

Bordering Russia, North Korea and Inner Mongolia, Jílín is part of the historic territory of the Manchus, founders of the Qing dynasty (1644–1911). The province was industrialised under the Japanese who seized Manchuria and shaped it into the puppet state of Manchukuo (1931–45). In Chángchūn, the provincial capital, you can visit the elaborately re-created palace that was home to Puyi, the Qing's legendary 'Last Emperor'.

Jílín's main attraction for tourists is the Chángbái Shān nature reserve on the province's far eastern border. Within the park, Heaven Lake, a volcanic crater lake high in the mountains, is a highlight. In summer, there are plenty of opportunities to hike the reserve's varied terrain that ranges from pine-lined trails to tundra-like moonscapes, but in winter, heavy snows make the reserve virtually inaccessible.

Also in eastern Jílín province, the Korean Autonomous Prefecture offers a fascinating look at this border area's mix of Korean and Chinese cultures. Yánjí, the bilingual capital, makes a convenient base for exploring this region. Don't expect to find a well-tuned tourist infrastructure or many English speakers, although in this rapidly developing area, that may soon change.

The province's other natural attractions include Sōnghuā Hú, a lake outside of Jílín city that's popular for boating in the summer, and the surrounding hills, popular for skiing in winter. For those who brave the frigid winter months, Jílín offers an Ice Lantern Festival, as well as the spectacle of frost-laden trees that sparkle in the weak midwinter sun. Jílín's riverfront is also an appealing place to stroll in milder weather.

Chángchūn and Jílín are modern industrial cities, roaring with traffic, booming – both literally and figuratively – with new construction, and often dimmed by urban haze. Yet both have pockets of historical and contemporary interest, from temples and palaces to pleasant city parks and bustling shopping districts.

History

Jílín province's claim to recent historical fame came after the Japanese occupation of Manchuria in the early 1930s, when the province's capital, Chángchūn, became the centre of Japan's puppet government. Henry Puyi, born in Běijīng in 1906, became the 10th (and last) emperor of the Qing dynasty at the tender age of three. In 1932, the Japanese installed Puyi as their 'puppet emperor', the executive nominally in charge of the government of the Manchukuo puppet state. Puyi governed the region from a palace in Chángchūn until 1945.

After Japan's defeat in WWII, Puyi attempted to flee to Japan. He got as far as Shěnyáng, where Russian troops captured him. In 1950, he was returned to China,

where he spent 10 years in a re-education camp. Puyi died of cancer in 1967.

Getting There & Around

The main rail and road routes across Jílín province run north–south through Chángchūn, with frequent connections to and from Shěnyáng in Liáoníng province and Hāěrbīn in Hēilóngjiāng province. With relatively new highways along this corridor, bus travel is a comfortable and convenient alternative to taking the train. From Chángchūn, there are also frequent eastbound trains and buses to the city of Jílín; you can reach Jílín city directly from Shěnyáng or Hāěrbīn as well.

Travel to the eastern part of the province, particularly the area around Chángbái Shān

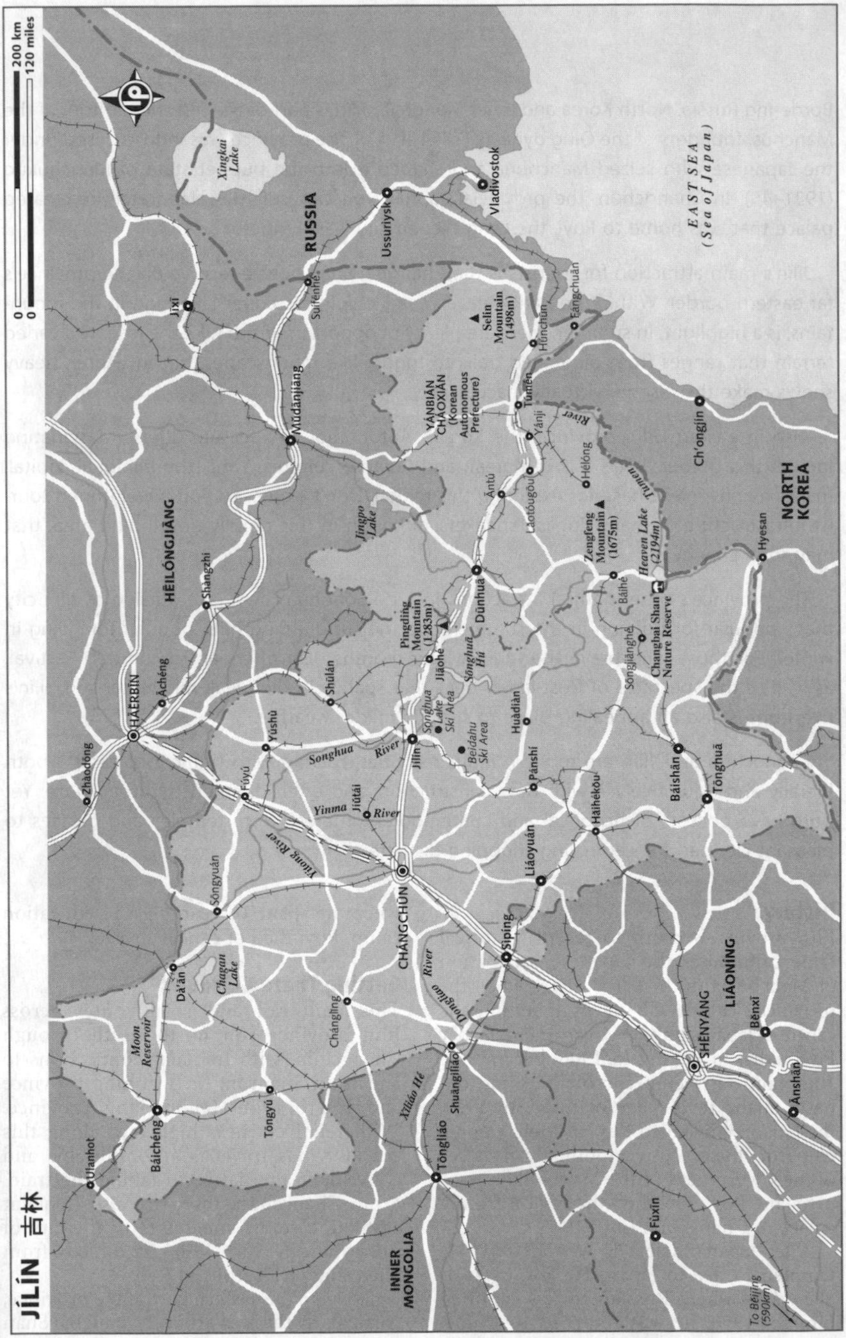
JÍLÍN 吉林
0 200 km
0 120 miles
RUSSIA
Xingkai Lake
Jíxī
Suífēnhé
Ussuriysk
Vladivostok
EAST SEA
(Sea of Japan)
Selin Mountain (1498m)
Húnchūn
Fángchuān
Mǔdānjiāng
YÁNBIĀN CHÁOXIĂN (Korean Autonomous Prefecture)
Túmen
Yánjí
Tumen River
Ch'ongjin
Hélóng
Āntú
Lǎotóugōu
NORTH KOREA
Jingpo Lake
Zengfeng Mountain (1675m)
Heaven Lake (2194m)
Hyesan
HĒILÓNGJIĀNG
Shàngzhì
Dūnhuà
Báihé
Changbai Shan Nature Reserve
Pingding Mountain (1283m)
Sōngjiānghé
Jiāohé
Sōnghuā Hú
Shūlán
Āchéng
HĀĚRBĪN
Songhua Lake Ski Area
Beidahu Ski Area
Huádiàn
Yúshù
Songhua River
Jílín
Pánshí
Báishān
Tōnghuà
Zhàodōng
Fúyú
Yinma River
Jiǔtái
Hǎihékǒu
Liáoyuán
Yitong River
CHÁNGCHŪN
Sōngyuán
Sìpíng
LIÁONÍNG
Dà'ān
Chagan Lake
Moon Reservoir
Chánglǐng
Dongliao River
Shuāngliáo
Xiliáo Hé
Tōngyú
Báichéng
Ulanhot
Tōngliáo
INNER MONGOLIA
Fùxīn
Běnxī
SHĚNYÁNG
Ānshān
To Běijīng (590km)

nature reserve, is a little more challenging. There is a regular, if slow, rail service east from Chángchūn and Jílín to Yánjí. From Yánjí, buses wind south through the hills toward Chángbái Shān; the small town of Báihé is the main transport centre for the nature reserve. It's possible to visit Chángbái Shān on a day trip from Yánjí; however, if you're coming to the reserve from Chángchūn, Jílín, or Shěnyáng, allow a full day to travel to Báihé and plan to visit the reserve the following day.

CHÁNGCHŪN 长春

☎ 0431 / pop 2,337,000

Chángchūn was the Japanese capital of Manchukuo (known as Hsin-king) between 1933 and 1945. In 1945 the Russians arrived on a year-long looting spree. When they departed, the Kuomintang moved in only to find themselves surrounded by the Communists who had assembled a formidable array of scrounged and captured weaponry – even former Japanese tanks and US jeeps. The Communists took over the city in 1948.

With Soviet assistance, China's first car-manufacturing plant was set up here in the 1950s, starting with 95-horsepower Jiefang (Liberation) trucks, and moving on to vehicles like the now-defunct Red Flag limousines. Wonder why so many Volkswagen cars plough China's streets? The company has a factory in Chángchūn (as well as one in Shànghǎi).

Chángchūn is also a film production centre. The city may lack silver screen glamour, but the Chángchūn Film Studio has produced over 600 feature films since it was established in 1946.

Orientation

Chángchūn sprawls from north to south. The long-distance bus station and the train station are in the north of the city.

Information
BOOKSHOPS
Foreign Language Bookshop (1660 Tongzhi Jie)

EMERGENCY
Public Security Bureau (PSB; Gōngānjú; 2627 Renmin Dajie) On the southwestern corner of People's Square (Rénmín Guǎngchǎng), this office is in a yellow building left over from the Japanese occupation.

INTERNET ACCESS
Internet café (wǎngbā; btwn Changbai Lu & Hankou Jie; per hr Y2) This basement room opposite the train station has fast connections.
Internet café (wǎngbā; Longli Lu; per hr Y2) Amid the Longli Lu bars in the southern part of town, just west of Lixin Jie.

MONEY
Bank of China (Zhōngguó Yínháng; 296 Xinmin Dajie) In the Yinmao building, near Nanhu Park (Nánhú Gōngyuán). There is another branch at 91 Tongzhi Jie, near the Shangri-La Hotel in the main shopping district, which has an ATM that accepts Cirrus, Plus, VISA, MasterCard and other credit cards.

POST
Post office (yóujú; Renmin Dajie; 🕙 8.30am-5pm) South of the long-distance bus station.
Post office (yóujú; Changbai Lu; 🕙 8.30am-5.30pm) This branch is near the train station.

TRAVEL AGENCIES
China International Travel Service (CITS; Zhōngguó Guójì Lǚxíngshè; ☎ 690 9076; fax 690 9456; 1296 Xinmin Dajie; 🕙 8.30am-5pm) In the Yinmao building, this office sells airline tickets and books tours of the province.

Sights
PUPPET EMPEROR'S PALACE & EXHIBITION HALL 伪皇宫
Chángchūn's main attraction, this restored palace (Wěi Huánggōng; 5 Guangfu Lu; admission Y40; 🕙 8.30am-5.20pm summer, 8.40am-4.50pm winter, last entry 1hr before closing) is the former residence of the last emperor of the Qing dynasty, Henry Puyi. His story was the basis for Bernardo Bertolucci's 1987 film, *The Last Emperor*.

At age three, Puyi became the 10th Qing emperor, though China's 1911 revolution ended his brief reign. Puyi lived in exile until 1932, when the Japanese installed Puyi at this palace as the 'puppet emperor' of Manchukuo.

Puyi's study, bedroom and temple, as well as his wife's quarters, his lover's quarters and his offices, have all been elaborately re-created, right down to his toilet (from where he reportedly approved all government decisions). Period photos of the luckless Puyi and his entourage are on view, and you can clamber through the royal bomb shelter – as long as damp dark cellars don't spook you.

From the train station, bus No 10 or 18 will drop you within walking distance of the palace.

CHANGCHUN FILM PALACE 长春电影宫

Those expecting Hollywood will be disappointed with the faded remains of Chángchūn's original **Film Studio** (Chángchūn Diànyǐng Gōng; ☎ 594 8427; cnr Hongqi Jie & Huxi Lu; admission Y35; ⏱ 8am-4.30pm). Although the photo exhibit of China's silver screen stars will interest cinema aficionados, most of what's on show – demonstrations of sound effects, dubbing and other techniques – is a bit stale (and in Chinese only).

Take bus No 25 from the train station to the corner of Gongnong Lu and Hongqi Jie.

Turn right (southwest) onto Hongqi Jie; it's about a 10-minute walk.

CHANGCHUN FILM CITY 长春电影城

The **Film City** (Chángchūn Diànyǐng Chéng; ☎ 762 8874; Zhengyang Jie; admission Y40; ⏱ 8am-4.30pm) is a comical attempt to create a Universal Studios-style theme park. Unfortunately, the facilities are forlorn and the demonstrations amateurish. If you want to visit anyway, take minibus No 262 from the train station.

Sleeping

Chūnyì Bīnguǎn (☎ 209 6888; www.chunyihotel.com; 80 Renmin Dajie; s/d/tr Y260/260/270 incl breakfast; 🖧) This excellent-value mid-range hotel was built in 1909 for high-ranking Japanese and

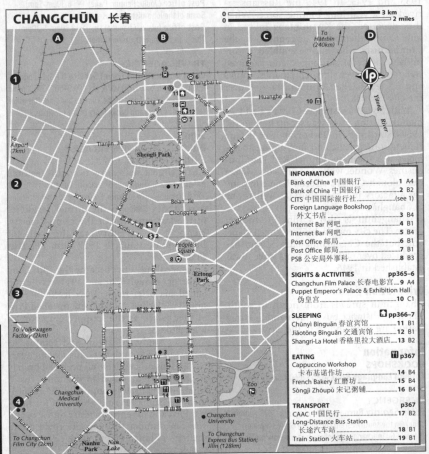

CHÁNGCHŪN 长春

INFORMATION	
Bank of China 中国银行	1 A4
Bank of China 中国银行	2 B2
CITS 中国国际旅行社	(see 1)
Foreign Language Bookshop 外文书店	3 B4
Internet Bar 网吧	4 B1
Internet Bar 网吧	5 B4
Post Office 邮局	6 B1
Post Office 邮局	7 B1
PSB 公安局外事科	8 B3

SIGHTS & ACTIVITIES	pp365-6
Changchun Film Palace 长春电影宫	9 A4
Puppet Emperor's Palace & Exhibition Hall 伪皇宫	10 C1

SLEEPING	🖩 pp366-7
Chūnyì Bīnguǎn 春谊宾馆	11 B1
Jiāotōng Bīnguǎn 交通宾馆	12 B1
Shangri-La Hotel 香格里拉大酒店	13 B2

EATING	🍴 p367
Cappuccino Workshop 卡布基诺作坊	14 B4
French Bakery 红磨坊	15 B4
Sòngjì Zhōupù 宋记粥铺	16 B4

TRANSPORT	p367
CAAC 中国民行	17 B2
Long-Distance Bus Station 长途汽车站	18 B1
Train Station 火车站	19 B1

Manchurian officials. It retains old-world charm today, with dark woodwork, stained glass and a courtly staff.

Jiāotōng Bīnguǎn (Traffic Hotel; ☎ 611 5888 ext 3008; 238 Renmin Dajie; d Y110-190) In this tall circular building behind Chūnyì Bīnguǎn, the rooms are frayed but clean. The hotel's location next to the long-distance bus station is handy.

Shangri-La Hotel (Xiānggélǐlā Dàjiǔdiàn; ☎ 898 1818; www.shangri-la.com; 9 Xi'an Dalu; d US$130-150; ⌧ ☒ ☒) From the elegant marble and gold lobby to the cordial English-speaking staff, nothing but luxury awaits those who want to splash out in Chángchūn's most upmarket hotel, just off Tongzhi Jie, a main shopping street.

Eating & Drinking

South of People's Square, between Renmin Dajie and Xinmin Dajie, explore Guilin Lu and Xikang Lu for bakeries and good *dōngběi* (northeastern) restaurants, and Longli Lu for popular bars.

Sòngjì Zhōupù (cnr Xikang Lu & Lixin Jie; dishes Y3-12; ☯ lunch & dinner) For comfort food *dōngběi* style, choose from several kinds of porridge, filled bread and vegetables at this inexpensive caféteria.

Cappuccino Workshop (Kǎbùjīnuò Zuòfáng; ☎ 564 6216; cnr Guilin Lu & Raihui Jie; coffees Y15, pizza from Y30; ☯ 9.30am-11pm) It's obvious that the chef isn't Italian, but the pizza is a welcome respite from a diet of dumplings.

French Bakery (Hóng Mò Fáng; ☎ 562 3994; 745 Guilin Lu; coffees Y15, pastries Y5; ☯ 7.30am-10pm) This bakery serves European coffee-shop treats, including get-you-going espressos and fluffy croissants.

Getting There & Away

AIR

Civil Aviation Administration of China (CAAC; Zhōngguó Mínháng; ☎ 798 8781 information, 869 0215 tickets) operates daily flights to most major domestic cities, including Běijīng (Y960, 1½ hours), Shànghǎi (Y1600, 2½ hours), Shēnzhèn (Y2490, five hours) and Dàlián (Y580, one hour). The local **CITS** (Zhōngguó Guójì Lǚxíngshè; ☎ 690 9076; fax 690 9456; 1296 Xinmin Dajie; ☯ 8.30am-5pm) office also books airline tickets.

International service includes a flight to Hong Kong every Tuesday (4½ hours) and to Tokyo every Sunday (2 hours and 40 minutes).

BUS

The **long-distance bus station** (kèyùn zhōngxīn; 226 Renmin Dajie) is behind Chūnyì Bīnguǎn (hotel).

Destination	Price	Duration	Frequency
Běijīng	Y220	7½hr	5 daily
Dàlián	Y138	8hr	several daily
Hāěrbīn	Y75	3½hr	every 30 min
Jílín	Y20	1½hr	every 15 min
Shěnyáng	Y75	3½hr	several daily

Express buses from Jílín arrive at the Chángchūn express bus station (*gāosù gōnglù kèyùn zhàn*) on Renmin Dajie in the southern part of town.

TRAIN

Regular trains run to Hāěrbīn (Y61, three to four hours), Jílín (Y10, two hours), Shěnyáng (Y28, four to five hours), Běijīng (seat/sleeper Y130/239, nine to 10 hours), Dàlián (seat/sleeper Y99/171, eight to 9½ hours) and Shànghǎi (seat/sleeper Y227/437, 22 to 28 hours).

Getting Around

Chángchūn's airport is a few kilometres west of the city centre. At the time of writing a new airport was under construction between Chángchūn and Jílín and was expected to open in 2005.

Bus No 6 follows Renmin Dajie south from the train station. Bus No 62 takes a more circuitous route, travelling between the train station and Nanhu Park, via the Tongzhi Jie shopping district. Bus No 25 also heads south from the train station but along the western edge of town.

Taxi fares start at Y5.

JÍLÍN 吉林

☎ 0432 / pop 1,625,7000

Despite its industrial nature, Jílín is noted for its winter scenery. The city also has an appealing riverfront promenade, as well as several large parks, which, in mild weather, offer respite from the urban hubbub.

Originally established as a fortress in 1673, Jílín was severely damaged during WWII and suffered wholesale looting by Russian soldiers. It may have few tourist attractions, but it's more pleasant and manageable than some of the northeast's cities.

NORTH OF THE WALL

Information

EMERGENCY
PSB (Gōngānjú; ☎ 240 9315; cnr Beijing Lu & Nanjing Jie)

INTERNET ACCESS
Internet café (wǎngbā; Nanjing Jie; per hr Y2) Centrally located in an underground arcade (p370).
Internet café (wǎngbā; Tianjin Jie; per hr Y2; ◷ 8am-midnight) South of the train station.

MONEY
Bank of China (Zhōngguó Yínháng; ☎ 467 0216; 1 Shenzhen Jie) South of the Línjiāngmén Bridge. Another branch (cnr Tianjin Jie & Chongqing Jie), near the train station, has a 24-hour ATM.

POST
Post office (yóujú; Jilin Dajie) Just north of the Jílín Bridge.

TRAVEL AGENCIES
CITS (Zhōngguó Guójì Lǚxíngshè; ☎ 243 5819; ◷ 8.30am-6.30pm Mon-Fri, 9am-5.30pm Sat & Sun) This office, between Jilin Dajie and Chongqing Jie just north of the Jilin Bridge, organises skiing trips and tours to Chángbái Shān.

Sights

ICE-RIMMED TREES 树挂
Jílín is most attractive during January and February when the branches of the pine and willow trees along Songhua River (Sōnghuā Jiāng), the river that winds through the city, are covered in needle-like hoarfrost. It's a spectacular scene that's hugely popular with Spring Festival (Chinese New Year) visitors.

The Hydroelectric Station in Fēngmǎn causes this phenomenon. Built by the Japanese, disassembled by the Russians and then reassembled by the Chinese, this station fuels three large chemical plants. Water passing from Sōnghuā Hú (Songhua Lake) through the power plant becomes a steamy current that merges with the Songhua River and prevents it from freezing. Vapour rising from the river overnight meets the -20°C air temperature, causing the display.

The best time to catch this sight is in the morning, on either side of the Jílín Bridge.

WÉN MIÀO 文庙
Temples dedicated to Confucius were built so that the great sage would bestow good

CENTRAL JÍLÍN 吉林市中心

luck on hopefuls taking *huìkǎo*, the notoriously difficult imperial examinations. The main hall of this **temple** (Confucius Temple; Wenmiao Hutong; admission Y15; ⏰ 8.30am-4pm Mon-Fri, 9am-4pm Sat & Sun) was built in 1907.

An interesting exhibition illustrates how examinees were confined to solitary cells during examinations. Also on display are ingenious cheating devices (despite the risk that the ultimate penalty for cheating was death), including undershirts covered in minuscule characters. Captions are in Chinese only.

The temple entrance is off Jiangwan Lu, next to Jiāngchéng Bīnguǎn (hotel). Bus No 13 runs near here from the train station.

BEISHAN PARK 北山公园

If you need some exercise, head for this hilly **park** (Běishān Gōngyuán; admission Y5), where the footpaths through the forest are dotted with temples and pavilions. On the park's western side, you can take a short hike up **Táoyuán Shān**. Visit on weekdays if you can; the park gets mobbed on weekends and holidays, in particular during Běishān's **temple fair** held annually on 8, 18 and 28 April.

Take bus No 7 from the train station or bus No 59 from Century Square.

CATHOLIC CHURCH 天主教堂

This stately **Catholic Church** (Tiānzhǔ Jiàotáng; 3 Songjiang Lu; ⏰ from 5am Mon-Fri, from 8am Sat & Sun), built in 1917, was completely ransacked during the Cultural Revolution, and its small library of religious works was torched. In 1980 the church reopened and now holds regular services.

CENTURY SQUARE 世纪广场

South of Songhua River is **Century Square** (Shìjì Guǎngchǎng), a popular hang-out for locals to play badminton, eat ice cream and whirl around on roller skates. Several vendors on the eastern side of the square, across Jilin Dajie, rent skates (Y5).

The large Lego-type building in the centre of the square is the **Century Boat** (admission Y10). For views of the city take the elevator to the 12th floor.

To get to the square, take bus No 3 or 103 from the train station.

METEORITE SHOWER MUSEUM
陨石雨博物馆

In March 1976 Jílín received a heavy meteor shower, and the largest meteor fragment is on view in this **museum** (Yǔnshí Yǔ Bówùguǎn; Century Square; admission Y40; ⏰ 8.30-11.30am & 1-4.30pm). Apparently it's the largest example of stone meteorite on display anywhere in the world, weighing in at a hefty 1770kg.

Festivals & Events

Jílín, like Hāěrbīn, has an **Ice Lantern Festival** (Bīngdēng Jié), held at Jiangnan Park (Jiāngnán Gōngyuán) on the southern side of the Songhua River. It runs for about 10 days in mid-January. Contact CITS for exact dates.

Sleeping

For inexpensive beds, try one of the cheap hotels along Tianjin Jie (bear left from the train station). When snowflakes start to fall, expect large increases from the rates quoted here.

Jiāotōng Bīnguǎn (Traffic Hotel; ☎ 255 6859; fax 253 8149; 6 Zhongkang Lu; s Y200, d Y240-280) If you want to be close to the train and bus stations, opt for these clean, comfy rooms. The hotel is nothing fancy, but with doubles discounted to between Y150 and Y180, it offers excellent value.

Jiāngchéng Bīnguǎn (☎ 216 2777; www.jlcta .com.cn; 4 Jiangwan Lu; d/tr Y280/300 incl breakfast; 🖫) Most of these older, well-looked-after rooms come with river views. The staff is friendly, too. Take bus No 3 or 103 from the train station, or hop in a taxi (Y5).

Century Hotel (Shìjì Dàfàndiàn; ☎ 216 8888; www .centuryhotel.com.cn; 77 Jilin Dajie; d Y880-950 plus 10% service charge; 🖫 🖭) The stocky red-brick exterior belies the luxury within this top-end hotel, where amenities include Shiatsu massages and a Turkish steam bath.

Eating

During the summer night markets spring up around the city; one of the liveliest is on Hunchan Jie.

Xīnxīngyuán Jiǎoziguǎn (☎ 202 4393; 399 Henan Jie; dishes Y5-10; 🕙 lunch & dinner) On the Henan Jie pedestrian mall, first-rate *jiǎozi* (dumplings) and *dōngběi* cold plates will fill your belly without emptying your wallet. The vegetable dumplings are particularly good.

Qīnghuāyuán Restaurant (☎ 245 8806; 53 Tianjin Jie; dishes from Y10; 🕙 lunch & dinner) Staff in traditional garb bring hearty platefuls of *dōngběi* fare at this busy eatery with an elaborate carved-wood façade. Floral-scented tea from the long-spouted pot or cheap mugs of beer are the drinks of choice.

Chuānwángfǔ Huǒguó Dà Shìjiè (Chuanwangfu Hot Pot World; ☎ 204 0055; 96 Jiefang Dalu; hot pots Y15-30; 🕙 lunch & dinner) At this multistorey hot pot palace, each tasty order comes with several side dishes – pickled garlic, sweet beans, crispy dried shrimp – that you choose from roving carts.

Entertainment

Just east of Henan Jie, there's a huge **underground arcade** (cnr Nanjing Jie & Jiefang Dalu; 🕙 till 10pm Mon-Fri, till midnight Sat & Sun), with video games, a bowling alley, pool tables, ping-pong tables, Internet access and even a small roller-skating rink. The entrance is on the north side of Jiefang Dalu, opposite the plaza.

Getting There & Away

AIR

The **CAAC** (Zhōngguó Mínháng; ☎ 245 4260; 1 Chongqing Jie) is just north of the Jílín Bridge. There

is a daily flight to Běijīng (Y960, 1½ hours). Flights to Shànghǎi (Y1460, two hours and 40 minutes) and Guǎngzhōu (Y2430, six hours) leave on Wednesday and Sunday.

BUS

Jílín has two long-distance bus stations. The bus station near the train station has several daily departures to Hāěrbīn (Y44 to Y62, five to six hours) and Shěnyáng (Y96, 4½ hours).

For Chángchūn, buses depart every half-hour between 6am and 6pm (Y20, 1½ hours) from Líjiāng bus station (Líjiāng kèyùnzhàn) on Xian Lu, just west of the Lijiangmen Bridge. To get to the Líjiāng depot take the bright yellow minibus that leaves from outside the train station.

TRAIN

The Jílín train station is in the northern part of the city. Frequent trains run to Chángchūn (Y10, two hours). There are daily services to Hāěrbīn (Y18, five hours), Yánjí (Y26, seven hours), Shěnyáng (Y32, six hours) and Dàlián (seat/sleeper Y55/181, 13 hours). Overnight trains go to Běijīng (seat/sleeper Y55/263, 11 hours), but buy your tickets in advance; if you can't nab a sleeper from Jílín, try going from Chángchūn, where there are more frequent trains to Běijīng.

Getting Around

Jílín's airport is about 10km west of the city. A taxi to or from the airport will cost around Y50. A bus to the airport leaves from the CAAC at 1.30pm on Wednesday and Sunday (Y10).

Bus Nos 3 and 103 run between the train station and Century Square. Bus No 30 runs up Jilin Dajie.

Taxi fares start at Y5.

AROUND JÍLÍN
Ski Resorts

Located 25km southeast of Jílín, the **Songhua Hu Ski Area** (松花湖滑雪场; Sōnghuā Hú Huáxuě Chǎng; ski season Dec-Feb) attracts beginner and intermediate skiers to slopes that reach an elevation of 934m. The resort has rental equipment, a restaurant and a shopping arcade, as well as a cross-country skiing area. In milder weather, you can go boating (rental Y30 to Y40 per hour) or hiking at Sōnghuā Hú (admission Y10), the lake near the ski slopes. Take bus No 9 from Jílín's train station.

Another ski area, **Beidahu Ski Area** (北大湖 滑雪场; Běidàhú Huáxuě Chǎng; ski season Dec-Feb), is 53km south of Jílín. The only way to reach Běidàhú is by taxi (Y60).

CHÁNGBÁI SHĀN 长白山
☎ 0433

China's largest nature reserve, **Chángbái Shān** (Ever White Mountains; admission Y65) covers 210,000 hectares of dense, virgin forest far from the maddening crowds. Also known as Mt Paekdu, or Paekdusan in Korean, Chángbái Shān is popular with South Korean and Chinese tourists but still sees comparatively few Westerners. Chángbái Shān's main attraction is Heaven Lake, a dramatic volcanic crater lake at the top of a mountain peak.

Because of elevation changes there is a wide variety of animal and plant life in the reserve. From 700m to 1000m above sea level there are mixed coniferous and broad-leaf trees (including white birch and Korean pines); from 1000m to 1800m there are cold-resistant coniferous trees, such as dragon spruce and fir; from 1800m to 2000m is a third forest belt; and above 2000m the landscape is alpine tundra – treeless and windy.

The temperatures, too, can plunge from steamy at the reserve entrance to downright frigid at the summit. Some shy animal spe-cies also make their homes in the mountain range; the rarer ones include protected cranes, deer and Manchurian tigers.

During summer, tour buses bring day-trippers who pose for photos in front of the waterfall, gorge on eggs boiled in the natural hot springs, stampede up the mountain to Heaven Lake (a two-hour hike or 20-minute 4WD ride) and then rush down again. Since Chángbái Shān is a long haul from anywhere, though, it's worth slowing down. You can easily spend a couple of sublime and peaceful days hiking around.

Orientation & Information

Chángbái Shān straddles the Chinese–North Korean border. From the park's northern entrance gate (běipō shānmén) to the dàozhànkōu, a parking area where you can board 4WDs for the ride up to Heaven Lake, it's about 16km. From the dàozhànkōu to the pùbù (waterfall) is about 3km further.

The nearest town, about 20km north of the reserve, is Èrdào Báihé, generally called Báihé.

A 3rd-floor **Internet café** (网吧; wǎngbā; per hr Y2) is adjacent to Báihé's market.

Sights & Activities
HEAVEN LAKE 天池

Heaven Lake (Tiān Chí), a spectacular volcanic crater lake at an elevation of 2194m, is the highlight of Chángbái Shān. The lake,

---

MYTHS AND MISTS OF HEAVEN LAKE

The enchanting scenery at Heaven Lake would not be complete without some sort of legend or mystery. Couples throw coins into the lake, pledging that their love will remain as deep and lasting as Heaven Lake, and the Chinese and Koreans both have attached many myths to the region.

One of the most intriguing is the origin of the Manchu race. According to legend, three heavenly nymphs descended to the lake in search of earthly pleasure. While they were frolicking in the water, a magic magpie appeared and dropped a red berry. When one of the nymphs picked it up to smell it, the berry flew through her lips. She became pregnant and gave birth to a handsome boy with an instant gift of the gab. He went on to foster the Manchus and their dynasty.

Korean legend says that the Lord of Heaven came down to the mountain region and formed ancient Korea. More recent North Korean folklore claims that Kim Jong Il was born here (though he's actually thought to have been born in Khabarovsk, Russia).

Dragons and other things that go bump in the night were believed to have sprung from the lake. In fact, there have been intermittent sightings of unidentified swimming objects – China's very own Loch Ness monsters. However, Heaven Lake is the deepest alpine lake in China, and it's frozen over in winter with temperatures well below zero, so it would take a pretty hardy monster to make this place home (even plankton can't). Sightings from both sides point to a black bear, oblivious to the paperwork necessary for crossing these tight borders.

13km in circumference, is surrounded by jagged rock outcrops and 16 mountainous peaks; the highest is **White Rock Peak** (Báiyán Fēng), which soars to 2749m. The lake is also said to be home to a Loch Ness-style 'monster' (see Myths and Mists of Heaven Lake, p371).

From the *dàozhànkōu*, 4WDs (Y80 per person) take groups of five passengers up to Heaven Lake.

WATERFALL & HOT SPRINGS

At the *dàozhànkōu*, the road forks, with one branch climbing steeply to Heaven Lake, and the other leading past several hotels to the **waterfall** (admission Y15) and hot springs. Erdaobai River (Èrdàobái Hé) runs off

Heaven Lake, creating this rumbling 68m waterfall that is the source of Songhua River (Sōnghuā Jiāng) and Tumen River (Túmén Hé). You can hike up to the waterfall and then continue on up to Heaven Lake.

On the path to the waterfall, vendors boil eggs in the hot springs, and there's also a **bathhouse** where you can soak in the odoriferous waters.

UNDERGROUND FOREST 地下森林

Between the park entrance and the *dàozhànkōu*, about 12km from the north gate, this verdant **forest** (Dìxià Sēnlín) is a pretty hiking spot.

BÁIHÉ 白河

If you're visiting Chángbái Shān on a day trip, Báihé makes a convenient base. Not only does it have good budget accommodation, the town is famous for being the only part of China where you can find a tall, elegant pine tree called a Měirén Sōng. Wander through Báihé's **Měirén Sōng Sēnlín** (admission Y8; ⏰ 6am-8pm), or just stroll past and look at the trees from the road.

Tours

CITS in Jílín city (p368) runs three-day/two-night trips to Chángbái Shān, generally on weekends only in May, June and September, and daily in July and August. Other travel agencies in Jílín offer similar packages; ask at any of the hotel travel desks.

A tour can greatly simplify getting to and around Chángbái Shān. Just be aware that the 'three-day' tour gives you just one day to explore the reserve – you'll be travelling most of the other two days.

Sleeping & Eating

Accommodation in Chángbái Shān is expensive. If you're staying for a couple of days, however, sleeping in a dorm here is likely to prove cheaper than returning to Báihé daily.

Camping here is a possibility, although technically against the rules to do so. Be prepared for thunderstorms and try to find a place away from curious spectators and the authorities.

Chángbái Shān Guójì Lǚyóu Bīnguǎn (Mt Changbai International Tourist Hotel; ☎ 574 6001; fax 574 6002; d Y700-800) At this well-appointed hotel, some rooms have views of the waterfall.

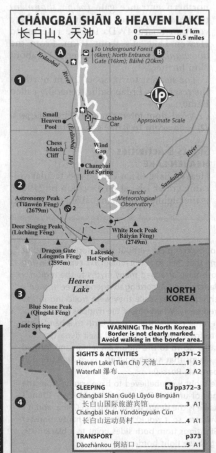

CHÁNGBÁI SHĀN & HEAVEN LAKE
长白山、天池

0 ——————— 1 km
0 ——————— 0.5 miles

To Underground Forest (6km); North Entrance Gate (16km); Báihé (20km)

Erdaobai River

Small Heaven Pool

Cable Car

Approximate Scale

Chess Match Cliff

Wind Gap

Changbai Hot Spring

Astronomy Peak (Tiānwén Fēng) (2679m)

Tianchi Meteorological Observatory

Sandaobai River

Deer Singing Peak (Lùchàng Fēng)

White Rock Peak (Báiyán Fēng) (2749m)

Dragon Gate (Lóngmén Fēng) (2595m)

Lakeside Hot Springs

Heaven Lake

NORTH KOREA

Blue Stone Peak (Qīngshí Fēng)

Jade Spring

WARNING: The North Korean Border is not clearly marked. Avoid walking in the border area.

SIGHTS & ACTIVITIES	pp371–2
Heaven Lake (Tiān Chí) 天池	1 A3
Waterfall 瀑布	2 A2

SLEEPING	🏠 pp372–3
Chángbái Shān Guójì Lǚyóu Bīnguǎn 长白山国际旅游宾馆	3 A1
Chángbái Shān Yùndòngyuán Cūn 长白山运动员村	4 A1

TRANSPORT	p373
Dàozhànkou 倒站口	5 A1

Chángbái Shān Yùndòngyuán Cūn (Mt Changbai Athletes Village; ☎ 574 6066; fax 574 6055; dm/d Y50/400) This modest place is opposite the *dàozhànkōu* on the road to the waterfall.

In Báihé, several family-run guesthouses (dorm Y15 to Y25) surround the train station. For more typical hotel accommodation, try the large pleasant rooms at **Xìndá Bīnguǎn** (信达宾馆; ☎ 572 0444; s/d Y220/320 incl breakfast; [X]) on the town's main drag, just south of Měirén Sōng Sēnlín. The hotel's restaurant serves decent Korean-influenced Chinese fare (dishes from Y8).

One block south of Xìndá Bīnguǎn, there's a small market building where you can pick up bread, fruit and drinks.

Getting There & Away

The best time to tackle Chángbái Shān is from June to early September – when the road from Báihé to the nature reserve isn't iced over. Telephone one of the hotels in the area for a weather check before you head out.

There are two routes to the Chángbái Shān area. The southern approach is from Shěnyáng to Báihé, via Tōnghuā (通化). The northern route is from Yánjí to Báihé.

Trains run from Tōnghuā to Báihé at 8.15am and 11.18pm (seat/sleeper Y21/60, seven hours), and from Báihé to Tōnghuā at 8.10am and 12.45am. From Tōnghuā, you can catch trains to Shěnyáng (seat/sleeper Y40/88, six to seven hours), Běijīng (seat/ sleeper Y115/224, 18 hours) and Dàlián (seat/sleeper Y71/143, 13 hours).

From Chángchūn or Jílín, catch a train east to Yánjí, or if you're coming from Hēilóngjiāng take a train from Mǔdānjiāng to Yánjí. In Yánjí there are several buses daily to Báihé (Y25, four hours) between 6.30am and 1pm. Between June and September, there is a direct bus to Chángbái Shān from Yánjí that leaves at 5.30am and returns at 4pm (one way/return Y55/110).

Báihé's train station is north of Měirén Sōng Sēnlín, while the rest of town is south of the forest; a taxi from the train station into town is Y5. Buses leave from the long-distance bus station on the main street or from in front of the train station.

Getting Around

Minibuses leave for Chángbái Shān from the Báihé train station from 6am to noon, although there is no fixed timetable. Prices vary, but the return trip should cost around Y50. Unfortunately, buses may not run outside the peak July/August tourist season, when your only option may be to hire a taxi (Y120 to Y150 return).

Both buses and taxis drop you off either at the *dàozhànkōu*, where you can board a 4WD for the final trek up to the lake, or at the waterfall, where you can hike to the lake. Some taxi drivers may offer to drop you at the park entrance gate for about Y40, but don't do it – you'll still be 16km from the *dàozhànkōu* with no easy transport options (other than hitchhiking).

No buses travel from Báihé when there's snow and ice, but you may find a local driver who can navigate the icy roads with tyre chains. This will probably cost a small fortune and may result in the odd broken rib, followed by the possibility of frostbite, so weigh it up carefully.

YÁNJÍ 延吉

☎ 0433 / pop 302,900

If you can't visit Korea, Yánjí may be the next best thing. The capital of China's Korean Autonomous Prefecture, Yánjí feels different from other Chinese cities. Many people are of Korean descent, signs are bilingual

---

BEWARE OF THE BORDER

Hiking at Heaven Lake is limited not only by the sharp peaks, but also because the lake overlaps the Chinese–North Korean border. Unfortunately, the border is either not clearly marked or not indicated at all.

Even worse, there are no detailed maps of the area available. Approximately one-third of the lake, the southeastern corner, is on the North Korean side and off-limits. Do not venture east of White Rock Peak or the Lakeside Hot Springs at Chángbái Shān's summit. If you think that you are nearing the border or are unsure where exactly it lies, do not proceed further!

If you're planning to hike off the beaten tourist trail, bring dried food, sunscreen and other medical supplies, and hike in a group. Be prepared, too, for fickle weather. No matter how warm it is in the morning, sudden high winds, rain and dramatic drops in temperature are entirely possible by afternoon.

(Chinese/Korean) and the food is Korean or Korean-influenced. Yánjí is also developing into a transport hub for trips to Chángbái Shān and elsewhere in the region.

Orientation

Buerhatong River (Bùěrhǎtōng Hé) bisects the city. The train and bus stations are south of the river. The north side of the river houses the commercial district, banks and the post office.

Information

EMERGENCY
PSB (公安局; Gōngānjú; 255 Guangming Jie) Located north of the river.

INTERNET ACCESS
Internet café (网吧; wǎngbā; 909-12 Zhanqian Jie; per hr Y2) Just north of the train station, this well-maintained Internet spot has fast computers and cushy chairs.

MONEY
Bank of China (中国银行; Zhōngguó Yínháng; ☎ 253 6454; 107 Renmin Lu; ☯ 8.30am-4pm Mon-Fri, 9am-4pm Sat) Opposite the post office, this branch has a 24-hour ATM.

POST & TELEPHONE
Post & telephone office (邮电大楼; yóujú dàlóu; cnr Juzi Jie & Renmin Lu; ☯ 8am-5pm Mon-Fri, 8am-4.30pm Sat) A telephone office is in the same building.

Sleeping & Eating

On the right as you exit the train station, several places advertise cheap beds (Y25 or less). It's worth asking if they'll take you.

Yánbiān Fāyín Bīnguǎn (延边发银宾馆; ☎ 290 8855; 4-4 Guanghua Lu; d/ste Y280/480) This new hotel, with sleek contemporary rooms, is about a 10-minute walk from the train station. Go north on Zhanqian Jie and turn right onto Guanghua Lu.

Dōngběiyà Dàjiǔdiàn (东北亚大酒店; Northeast Asia Hotel; ☎ 280 8111; fax 282 0970; 109 Changbai Lu; d Y228-368) Next to the long-distance bus station, this cylindrical tower has cramped doubles with quirky plumbing. Bargain for rates of Y150 to Y180. The casual restaurant serves decent lěng miàn (Y8), noodles in a cold spicy beef broth – a Yánjí spe-

cialty. From the train station, it's about a 15-minute walk; head north on Zhanqian Jie and turn right onto Changbai Lu.

Getting There & Away

AIR
There are daily flights between Yánjí and Běijīng (Y1700, one hour and 40 minutes), and four flights a week to Dàlián (Y1100, 2½ hours). The airport is about 5km west of the city centre.

BUS
Buses travelling to Chángbái Shān and Báihé leave from the long-distance bus station on Changbai Lu. Buses to Jílín, Chángchūn, Hāěrbīn and Mǔdānjiāng depart from in front of the train station.

TRAIN
There are daily trains to Jílín (Y30, seven hours), Chángchūn (nine hours) and Mǔdānjiāng (Y22, seven hours).

AROUND YÁNJÍ
Korean Autonomous Prefecture
延边朝鲜

The Korean Autonomous Prefecture (Yánbiān Cháoxiǎn) has China's greatest concentration of Korean and Hàn–Korean groups. The majority inhabit the border areas northeast of Báihé, extending up to the capital Yánjí. While the local people of Korean descent are often indistinguishable from their Chinese counterparts, many of their traditions link them to their heritage. If you visit around mid-August, you can join in the **Old People Festival**.

In the prefecture, the green mountains, virgin forests and babbling brooks provide more dramatic scenery than Jílín's flatter western areas. From Yánjí, you can head east to Túmén (图门) or even further east to Fángchuān (防川), a border outpost on a finger of land where China meets both Russia and North Korea.

Trains running east from Jílín to Túmén pass through Āntú, Lǎotóugōu and Yánjí. To get to Fángchuān, take a bus from Yánjí to Húnchūn (混春), from where you take another bus to the border town.

Hēilóngjiāng
黑龙江

HIGHLIGHTS

- Chill out at Hāěrbīn's **Ice Lantern Festival** (p382), the region's most spectacular winter event

- Hike and boat at shimmering **Jìngpò Hú** (Mirror Lake; p385)

- Stroll though Hāěrbīn's **Dàolǐqū district** (p379) to explore the city's Russian past

- Wander the peaceful wetlands of **Zhalong Nature Reserve** (p386), home to 260 species of birds

- Sample northern-style snacks, from cornmeal dumplings to pickled vegetables to Russian-style *piroshki* (turnovers) in **Hāěrbīn's** restaurants and markets (p383)

★ Zhalong Nature Reserve

★ Hāěrbīn

Jìngpò Hú ★

- POP: 38.1MIL
- AREA: 469,000 SQ KM

NORTH OF THE WALL

China's northernmost province, Hēilóngjiāng (Black Dragon River) is known for its sub-arctic climate. Come January, with its -30°C weather and howling Siberian gales, the locals sensibly huddle around their stoves, swathed in thickly padded clothing, quaffing the local firewater. Activity slows to a crunch in this snowflake-spitting weather, while hibernating animals bypass the season completely.

Welcome, believe it or not, to the tourist season. Don't be put off – if you come prepared for weather conditions similar to winter on Pluto, the city of Hāěrbīn puts on a sparkling spectacle of ice-encrusted buildings, winter sports and its famous Ice Lantern Festival. Hēilóngjiāng also offers some of China's best skiing facilities at Yàbùlì, east of Hāěrbīn.

At any time of year, Hāěrbīn is worth a visit for its Russian-influenced architecture, pleasant pedestrian streets and hearty northern-style food. A Hāěrbīn park houses (and attempts to protect) the rare Siberian tiger, and on the outskirts of the city, a haunting museum details grim wartime experiments by the Japanese.

Though much of Hāěrbīn is marred by the same bleak industrial buildings and ever-present construction that blight other parts of northern China, the city retains enough of its Russian style, particularly in the Dàolǐqū district near the tree-lined riverfront, to give it plenty of charm. And when the sun is shining, you can unwind with a walk along the river or on cobblestone-lined Zhongyang Dajie, taking time out to sample a kebab, a bun or a sausage.

The months of May to September open up the rest of the province to exploration. Attractions include relatively secluded lakes and forests – particularly the sparkling Jìngpò Hú (Mirror Lake) and the Wǔdàlián Chí volcanic area with its several lakes, caves and mineral springs; the Zhalong Nature Reserve that's home to rare wild cranes; and the remote regions along the Russian border.

History

Hēilóngjiāng forms the northernmost part of the region formerly known as Manchuria. Like the other provinces in China's Dōngběi (northeast), Hēilóngjiāng's recent history has been influenced by its neighbours, notably Russia, which wraps around the province to the north and east.

In the mid-1800s, Russia annexed parts of Hēilóngjiāng's territory, and in the late 1890s, Russia's influence in the region strengthened when Russian workers began the construction of a railway line linking Vladivostok with Hāěrbīn and with Dàlián to the south. Hēilóngjiāng also saw an influx of Russian refugees following the Russian revolution in 1917. Hāěrbīn still retains Russian-style buildings constructed during this era.

The Japanese took control of Hēilóngjiāng in the 1930s when they occupied Manchuria and retained their hold on the region until the end of WWII.

Getting There & Around

The city of Hāěrbīn is the gateway to Hēilóngjiāng province. Since trains, buses and flights connect Hāěrbīn with other cities throughout China, it's a logical starting point for exploring the far north. From Hāěrbīn, you can travel west to Qíqíhā'ěr, north to Wǔdàlián Chí and the Russian border regions, or east to Yàbùlì, Mǔdānjiāng and Jìngpò Hú. New highways make bus transport worth considering as an alternative to sometimes-slower local trains.

If you're headed for Inner Mongolia, direct trains run from Hāěrbīn to the cities of Hǎilǎěr or Mǎnzhōulǐ.

HĀĚRBĪN 哈尔滨
☎ 0451 / pop 3,129,000
If a city of more than three million people can be considered relaxing, Hāěrbīn is – at least if you join the strollers and shoppers wandering its tree-lined streets and riverfront promenade. One of the largest cities in northeastern China, Hāěrbīn is influenced by its relationship with nearby Russia and dotted with architectural gems handed down from the Russian era. Plenty of first-rate snack shops line the streets, too, and good restaurants serve rib-sticking fare to

sustain you as you explore sights ranging from Russian Orthodox churches to Buddhist temples to the grim remains of a germ warfare base.

History
In 1896 Russia negotiated a contract to build a railway line from Vladivostok to Hāěrbīn and Dàlián (in Liáoníng province to the south), which brought Russian workers to the region. In the early 1900s, large numbers of Russian refugees fled to Hāěrbīn as well. Although the Japanese gained control of the railway after Russia's defeat in the Russo–Japanese War (1904–05), the Russian imprint on Hāěrbīn remained in one way or another until the end of WWII.

HĒILÓNGJIĀNG 黑龙江

Many of the Russian émigrés were Jewish, and by the 1920s, Hāěrbīn's Jewish population topped 20,000. Little remains of this Jewish legacy today, although the local government has announced plans to establish a Museum for Jewish History and Culture in a former Hāěrbīn synagogue.

Following the Japanese invasion of Manchuria (which was made up of part of Inner Mongolia and the provinces of Hēilóngjiāng, Jílín and Liáoníng) in 1931, the Japanese occupied Hāěrbīn until 1945, when the Soviet army wrested the city back. The following year, as agreed by Chiang Kaishek and Stalin, Kuomintang troops were installed, marking the end of the Russian era.

Hāěrbīn, which derives its name from *alejin* (Manchu for 'honour' or 'fame'), is an industrial city but improved relations with Russia have resulted once more in flourishing trade and in growing cross-border tourism. Most foreign faces on the streets are Russian; the Chinese – who call them *lǎo máozi* (hairy ones) – may speak to you in Russian, whether you are Russian or not.

The fast pace of city life – with glitzy modern buildings replacing historic neighbourhoods – may slowly threaten Hāěrbīn's allure. Enjoy its charm while it lasts.

Orientation

In the north is Songhua River (Sōnghuā Jiāng), which separates the city from Sun

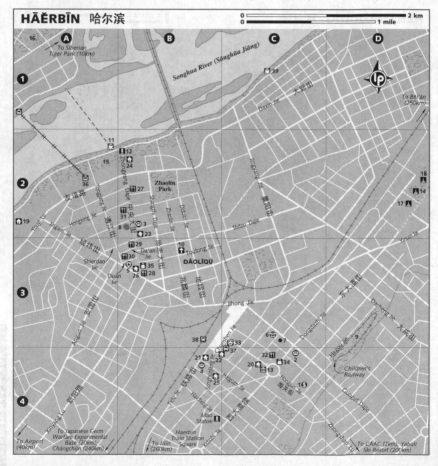

Island Park (Tàiyángdǎo Gōngyuán). The Dàolǐqū district, just south of Songhua River, houses the main shopping zone and most of the historical buildings that give the city its character.

The main train station is in the centre of town, surrounded by a cluster of hotels.

Information

BOOKSHOPS

Xinhua Bookshop (Xīnhuá Shūdiàn; Guogeli Dajie) Has a small selection of English-language books, mostly classic 19th-century novels. It's northwest of the main post office.

EMERGENCY

Public Security Bureau (PSB; Gōngānjú; 26 Duan Jie; ⏰ 8.30-11.30am & 1.30-4.30pm Mon-Fri) Located west of Zhongyang Dajie.

INTERNET ACCESS

Internet bar (per hr Y3) Conveniently located on the second level of the main train station.

Yidu Kongjian Wangba (27 Hongzhuan Jie; per hr Y2; ⏰ 24hr) Off Zhongyang Dajie, one block from Mǎdié'ěr Bīnguǎn (p382).

MONEY

Any of the large hotels will also change money.

Bank of China (Zhōngguó Yínháng; ☎ 5363 3518, 19 Hongjun Jie; ⏰ 8.30am-noon & 1-4.30pm Mon-Fri, 8.30am-4.30pm Sat & Sun) Has 24-hour ATMs. There are also many ATMs along Zhongyang Dajie in the Dàolǐqū district.

POST

Post office Dongdazhi Jie (328 Dongdazhi Jie; ⏰ 8am-7pm Mon-Fri, to 6.30pm Sat); Dàolǐqū area (111 Zhongyang Dajie; ⏰ 8.30am-7pm); train station area (Tielu Jie; ⏰ 8.30am-5.30pm Mon-Fri, to 5pm Sat) The main post office is on Dongdazhi Jie, a shopping district in the city centre. The branch in the Dàolǐqū area is between Xi Wu Jie and Xi Liu Jie. The branch in the train station area is to the right as you exit the station.

TELEPHONE

China Telecom (Guogeli Dajie) Northwest of the main post office. There's also a telephone office on the 2nd floor of the main train station.

TRAVEL AGENCIES

Most mid-range and top-end hotels have travel services that book tickets and arrange tours throughout the province.

China International Travel Service (CITS; Zhōngguó Guójì Lǚxíngshè; ☎ 8469 2168, 8854 7535; fax 8645 0605; 89 Zhongyang Dajie; ⏰ 8.30am-noon & 1.30-5.30pm Mon-Sat). On the 2nd floor of Mǎdié'ěr Bīnguǎn, this helpful office can arrange all sorts of tours and activities.

Harbin Modern Travel Company (☎ 8488 4444; 89 Zhongyang Dajie) Also at Mǎdié'ěr Bīnguǎn, this office offers ski trips to Yàbùlì.

Sights

DÀOLǏQŪ 道里区

Don't miss walking through the Dàolǐqū area, along cobblestone-lined Zhongyang Dajie and the surrounding side streets; it's like wandering through an outdoor museum. The architecture here shows a strong

NORTH OF THE WALL

Russian influence, with spires, cupolas and scalloped turrets. Thirteen preserved buildings have plaques outlining their histories.

CHURCH OF ST SOPHIA 圣索菲亚教堂
The majority of Hāěrbīn's Orthodox churches were ransacked during the Cultural Revolution and have since fallen into disrepair. However, the **Church of St Sophia** (Shèng Sùfēiyà Jiàotáng; cnr Zhaolin Jie & Toulong Jie; admission Y25; ۞ 9.30am-5.30pm), built by the Russians in 1907 in the Dàolǐqū area, has been beautifully restored. The church now houses the **Haerbin Architecture Arts Centre**, which displays black-and-white photographs of Hāěrbīn from the early 1900s.

STALIN PARK 斯大林公园
Locals and visitors alike congregate year-round in **Stalin Park** (Sīdàlín Gōngyuán). The tree-lined promenade, dotted with statues, playgrounds and cafés, is built along a 42km-long embankment that was built to curb unruly Songhua River. The odd **Flood Control Monument** (Fánghóng Shènglì Jìniàntǎ), built in 1958, celebrates the embankment's victory in holding back the river and commemorates the thousands of people who had previously died in the floods.

A resort feel holds sway in summer, with ice-cream stands, photo booths and boating trips (Y30) along the river and across to Sun Island Park.

Songhua River itself comes alive in winter with **ice-skating**, **ice hockey**, **tobogganing** and even **ice sailing** (vessels sail on the ice surface, assisted by wind power, and reach speeds of 30km/h). Equipment for each of these sports can be hired from vendors who set up shop along the riverbank. Slightly madder folk astound onlookers by swimming in gaps in the ice.

SUN ISLAND PARK 太阳岛公园
Across the river from Stalin Park is **Sun Island Park** (Tàiyángdǎo Gōngyuán), a 3800-hectare recreational zone offering gardens, forested areas and a 'water world'. In summer the area is alive with both flora and tour groups. In the winter it has its own mini snow-sculpture exhibition.

Buy a boat ticket (Y5) from one of the government-run ticket vendors (guóyíng chuánpiào), whose dock is directly north of the Flood Control Monument. Private boat operators, whose touts aggressively seek out customers, charge Y10. You can also take a cable car (one way/return Y20/30) to Sun Island Park from the end of Tongjiang Jie.

SPECIES UNDER THREAT

The Manchurian tiger is one of the rarest of all tigers. Long resident in China, these big cats, also known as the Amur, Siberian and Northeastern China tiger, today make their home in eastern Russia, North Korea and northeastern China.

The average male can grow up to four metres long, with a healthy weight of 300kg. But have no fear – it's extremely unlikely that you'll run into one of these beasts in the wilds of China. Estimates put the number of remaining Manchurian tigers somewhere between 360 and 400, with only 30 to 35 of those roaming freely in China.

Though given protection by the Chinese government and recognised as one of the most endangered species worldwide, the Manchurian tigers' situation remains perilous, due to urban encroachment on the tigers' territory and to the lucrative poaching business. Tiger bones are prized in traditional Chinese medicine, while tiger skins also fetch a hefty price on the black market. One tiger can earn up to 10 years' income for a Chinese poacher.

In response to the tigers' plight, the Chinese government set up a number of breeding centres, including the Siberian Tiger Park (opposite) outside Hāěrbīn. The purpose of these centres is ostensibly to restore the natural tiger population by breeding them and reintroducing them into the wild. However, conservationists stress the need for minimal human contact with tigers, and for the centres to emulate as much as possible the life that the tigers will face once released. China's centres, which see busloads of tourists snapping photos of big cats munching on cows and chickens, may instead produce tigers with a taste for livestock who will associate people with feeding time. Until the first captive tiger is set free, the long-term fate of China's Manchurian tigers remains unknown.

SIBERIAN TIGER PARK 东北虎林园
The mission of the **Siberian Tiger Park** (Dōngběi Hǔ Línyuán; ☎ 8808 0098; www.dongbeihu.net.cn in Chinese; 88 Songbei Jie; adult/child Y50/25; ☺ 8am-4.30pm, last tour at 4pm) is to study, breed, release and ultimately save the Manchurian tiger from extinction (see boxed text opposite). The park houses about 90 of these animals, as well as 15 African lions and a pair of rare white tigers. While you definitely get an up-close look at the cats as you drive safari-like through the fenced-off fields, those who are not too keen on zoos might want to give this supposed sanctuary a miss. The minibus drivers encourage passengers to buy chunks of meat to throw to the tigers, which makes you wonder how exactly the park is preparing these animals for the wild.

The park is located roughly 15km north of the city. From the corner of Youyi Lu and Zhongyang Dajie in Dàolǐqū, take bus No 65 westbound to its terminus, then walk one block east to pick up bus No 85, heading north on Hayao Lu. Bus No 85 doesn't go all the way to the park. The stop is a 15- to 20-minute walk or a Y10 to Y15 (return) pedicab ride away from the park entrance. Alternatively, to take a taxi from the city centre, figure around Y100 (return), but expect to bargain.

You can combine the trip with a visit to Sun Island Park. Bus No 85 stops at the western end of Sun Island Park en route between the city and the Siberian Tiger Park.

GERM WARFARE BASE
侵华日军地731部队遗址
In 1939 the Japanese army set up a top-secret, germ warfare research centre in Hāěrbīn, where medical experts performed gruesome experiments on Chinese, Soviet, Korean, Mongolian and British prisoners of war. Over 4000 people were exterminated: some were frozen or infected with bubonic plague, others were injected with syphilis and many were roasted alive in furnaces.

The history of these war horrors is on view at the **Japanese Germ Warfare Experimental Base – 731 Division** (Qīnhuá Rìjūn Dì 731 Bùduì Yízhǐ; ☎ 8680 1556; Xinjiang Dajie; admission Y20; ☺ 9am-5pm, last entry at 4pm), where grim photos and sculptures illustrate various tortures. In videotaped interviews (with English subtitles), Japanese officers describe what went on at the base with eerie detachment.

When the Soviets took back Hāěrbīn in 1945, the Japanese blew up the base. Their secret could have remained buried forever, but a tenacious Japanese journalist dragged out the truth in the 1980s.

The museum is about 20km south of the city, a 45-minute trip on bus No 343 from the train station; board the bus in front of Kūnlún Fàndiàn, a hotel to your right as you exit the station. When you get off the bus, walk in the same direction (west) until you cross the train tracks; the base is on the right.

TEMPLES
To reach these temples, take bus No 14 from the southern end of Zhongyang Dajie. Get off when the bus bears right off Dongdazhi Jie onto Yiman Jie. Dongdazhi Jie is a pedestrian plaza in front of the temples.

Temple of Bliss 吉乐寺
Inside the serene **Temple of Bliss** (Jí Lè Sì; 9 Dongdazhi Jie; admission Y2; ☺ 8.30am-4pm), the many statues include Milefo (Maitreya), the Buddha yet-to-come, whose arrival will bring paradise on earth. Though the temple can feel almost deserted, there's an active Buddhist community in residence.

Seven-tiered Buddhist Pagoda
七级浮屠塔
Next door to the Temple of Bliss is Hēilóngjiāng's largest temple, the **Seven-tiered Buddhist Pagoda** (Qījí Fútú Tǎ; 11 Dongdazhi Jie; admission Y10; ☺ 8.30am-4pm). This complex, built in 1924, has an elegant stone pagoda in the middle of the courtyard. The illustrations along the back wall tell classical stories of filial piety. In spring, the air resonates with the sound of wind chimes and makes for a peaceful retreat.

Temple of Universal Light 普照寺
The **Temple of Universal Light** (Pǔzhào Sì) is a working monastery next door to the Seven-tiered Buddhist Pagoda. It's open to the public only for worship on the 1st and 15th of every month. At other times you might find a monk who'll let you peek inside.

CHILDREN'S PARK 儿童公园
The **Children's Park** (Értóng Gōngyuán; ☎ 5367 8325; cnr Guogeli Dajie & Hegou Jie; adult/child Y2/1; ☺ 4.30am-10pm in summer, 6.30am-8pm rest of year) is a fun

place for kids and bustles with carnival rides, playgrounds, ping pong tables, and the **Children's Railway** (Értóng Tiělù; admission Y5), which was built in 1956. A miniature diesel engine, pulling seven cars, plies its 2km of track; the trip from 'Běijīng' to 'Hā͞erbīn' and back takes 20 minutes.

Take bus No 8 from the southern end of Zhongyang Dajie or bus No 109 from the train station.

HEILONGJIANG PROVINCIAL MUSEUM
黑龙江省博物馆

This **museum** (Hēilóngjiāng Shěng Bówùguǎn; ☎ 5364 4151; 48-50 Hongjun Jie; admission Y10; ☯ 9am-4pm) will appeal to dinophiles and others arch-aeologically inclined, though there are few English captions. The Historical Relics Exhibition on the 2nd floor displays finds from archaeological digs in the province, including examples of fish-skin clothing worn by the Hezhen minority (see the boxed text p388). The Nature Exhibition has huge dinosaur skeletons.

On the museum's lower level is the **Sea World** aquarium, which charges a separate admission (Y40). The museum is about a 10-minute walk from the train station; al-ternatively, take bus No 64 from Dàolǐqū.

Festivals & Events

Ice Lantern Festival (Bīngdēng Jié; ☎ 8625 0068; ☯ 8am-10pm) Hā͞erbīn's main winter attraction is this festival, held in Zhaolin Park and along Songhua River, where fanciful and elaborate ice sculptures in the shapes of animals, plants, buildings or motifs taken from legends sparkle in the frigid air. Sculptures have even included a miniature Great Wall of China and a scaled-down Forbidden City. At night the sculptures are illuminated from the inside with coloured lights, turning the area into a temporary fantasy world. Figure-skating shows, hockey tournaments and other winter events round out the calendar. Officially, the festival runs from 5 January to 15 February, although it frequently starts a week earlier and glistens into March. The main entrance is by the Flood Control Monument.

Harbin Music Festival (☎ 8469 1450; www.festival-harbin.net) In summer, this annual festival brings together traditional and modern musicians from all over China for about two weeks in July or August. Ticket prices, locations and exact dates vary from year to year, so check the website or inquire at CITS.

Sleeping

During the Ice Lantern Festival, expect hotel prices to jump at least 20% from those listed here. In the low season discounts of 30% are not uncommon.

BUDGET
Follow the train station touts if you're look-ing for a cheap dive.

Zhōngdà Dàjiǔdiàn (☎ 8463 8888; fax 8465 2888; 32-40 Zhongyang Dajie; d Y200; ☒) Good value in pricey Dàolǐqū, this excellent budget ac-commodation has spacious rooms, some overlooking Zhongyang Dajie.

Tiānzhú Bīnguǎn (☎ 8647 2109; fax 5364 3720; 6 Songhuajiang Jie; s Y238, d Y238-298, tr Y290) This tower is about two blocks south of the train station; bear right as you exit. Rooms are decent and clean, if old.

MID-RANGE
Mǎdié'ěr Bīnguǎn (Modern Hotel; ☎ 8461 5846; www.modern.com.cn in Chinese; 89 Zhongyang Dajie; s incl breakfast Y280, d incl breakfast Y348-580; ☒ ☒) Built in 1906 in the centre of Dàolǐqū, this lovely hotel is packed with character, and the solicitous staff are fantastic. Marble and carved woodwork fill the common areas, while most rooms are more contem-porary (some older rooms may dip under Y250). The bountiful breakfast buffet is first rate.

Lóngyún Bīnguǎn (☎ 8283 0102; Chunshen Jie; d/tr Y248/300; ☒) Next to the long-distance bus station, these nicely updated rooms are good value. Though prices hover near the budget range, the feel is more upscale.

Huáqiáo Fàndiàn (Overseas Chinese Hotel; ☎ 8257 1888; fax 5362 3429; 72 Hongjun Jie; d Y248-338; ☒) At this three-star hotel, which is a 10- to 15-minute walk from the train station, the pub-lic spaces are a little gloomy, but the quiet, comfortable rooms are well maintained.

TOP END
Songhuajiang Gloria Inn (Sōnghuājiāng Kǎilái Shāngwù Jiǔdiàn; ☎ 8463 8855; www.giharbin.com; 257 Zhongyang Dajie; d Y588-688; ☒) Half a block from Stalin Park, this inn offers plush rooms in a prime location.

Kūnlún Fàndiàn (☎ 5361 6688; www.hljkunlun .com in Chinese; 8 Tielu Jie; d from Y640 plus 15% service charge; ☒ ☒) To your right as you exit the train station, this first-class hotel is an oasis of calm with an indoor pool, sauna and six restaurants.

Another top-end choice is the **Haerbin Shangri-La Hotel** (Hā͞erbīn Xiānggé Lǐlā Dàjiǔdiàn;

☎ 8485 8888; www.shangri-la.com; 555 Youyi Lu; s/d US$175/195 plus 15% service charge; ⊠ ⌘ ▣), with great views of the Ice Lantern Festival.

Eating

Lanterns hang above the entrance to most restaurants in Hāěrbīn. It's a rating system – the more lanterns, the higher the standard and price. Red lanterns mean Chinese food, while blue denotes pork-free cuisine from the Muslim Hui minority (mainly lamb dishes).

Sausages are particularly popular in Hāěrbīn. This culinary art developed with the growth in Russian tourism, and now you'll find sausage vendors dotted all around town.

Zhongyang Dajie is a good place to stroll for bakeries, restaurants and bars where you can sample the local 'Hapi' beer.

Dōngfāng Jiǎozi Wáng (Kingdom of Eastern Dumplings; ☎ 8465 3920; 39 Zhongyang Dajie; dumplings Y4-8; ⏲ lunch & dinner) This always-busy restaurant serves royal helpings of *jiǎozi* (dumplings) with a large choice of fillings; try the pork with coriander or the veggie with egg. Look for the large walking dumpling out front.

Máomáo Xūnròu Dàbǐng (Maomao Meat Pancakes; ☎ 8464 3731; 56 Da'an Jie; dishes Y10-18; ⏲ lunch & dinner) Carnivores make tracks to this cosy restaurant with a warren of small rooms, where the specialities are savoury roast meats and tasty fried breads.

Míngjiē Kǎoròudiàn (Mingjie BBQ; ☎ 8468 0111; 132 Zhongyang Dajie; dishes Y6-12; ⏲ lunch & dinner) Casual, loud and cheap, this cook-your-own BBQ is packed with young people who come to stroll along Zhongyang Dajie.

Cafe Russia 1914 (☎ 8456 3207; 57 Xi Toudao Jie; dishes Y18-30; ⏲ lunch & dinner) For home-cooking Russian-style, including puffy *piroshki*, comforting cabbage rolls and succulent sausages, head for this authentic Russian tearoom, just off Zhongyang Dajie.

Outside Mǎdié'ěr Bīnguǎn, a busy snack shop serves kebabs, dumplings and ice cream (Y2 to Y5); nearby, a **food market** (Zhongyang Dajie, btwn Shierdao Jie & Da'an Jie; ⏲ 8.30am-8pm) has stalls offering buns, cookies, sausages, fruits and candies.

About a 15-minute walk from the train station – east of Hongjun Jie and north of Dongdazhi Jie – is a night market, with vendors hawking kebabs, grilled squid and other nibbles.

Entertainment

Bèibèi Hànbīng Díshìgāo (Beibei Dry Ice Disco; admission Y20; ⏲ 9am-midnight) This bar/disco/roller-skating rink is a must for anyone with a sense of humour and a high tolerance for blaring music and flashing disco lights. It's in the underground shopping centre opposite the train station; enter from the underground passage on Hongjun Jie, near Bèibèi Dàjiǔdiàn (a hotel). Admission includes skate hire.

Shopping

Zhongyang Dajie is the place to go and is lined with department stores, stylish boutiques, and souvenir shops, many of which hawk Russian-inspired goods. At the time of writing, a large shopping complex was under construction at the end of Zhongyang Dajie, near Stalin Park.

Sweet Chocolate Shop (Tiánsīsī Qiǎokèlì Diàn; ☎ 8469 3350; 45 Zhongyang Dajie) To fuel your shopping forays, stop in here, where the shelves are stacked with imported chocolate, coffee and sweets.

Dongdazhi Jie, in the city centre southeast of the train station, is another major shopping street. Below the street, the Hongbo Century Square shopping complex extends for blocks underground.

BREAKFAST OF CHAMPIONS

At many mid-range hotels throughout northeastern China, you can begin your day with a hearty breakfast buffet. Don't expect Western-style bacon and eggs, but you certainly won't go hungry either. The lavish morning spreads typically start with a variety of cold vegetable dishes: perhaps spicy cabbage, wild greens with peanuts, or pickled radish. Hot dishes might include stewed pork, tender eggplant or bean-curd noodles.

Hard-boiled eggs, often bubbling in soy sauce, are a staple, as are puffy steamed breads. Sticks of fried dough to dunk in hot soy milk make frequent appearances, and don't forget the porridge – plain rice, rice with beans, corn or millet are all cooked into comfortingly soupy hot cereals. If you're lucky, there'll be nut-filled cookies or sugary bean buns to sate the sweet tooth, and you'll be set till supper time.

Getting There & Away

AIR

Civil Aviation Administration of China (CAAC; Zhōngguó Mínháng; ☎ 8262 7070; 101 Zhongshan Lu) is in the hotel of the same name. **China Travel Service** (CTS; Zhōngguó Lǚxíngshè; 72 Hongjun Jie; ☎ 5364 0916) has a ticketing office in Huáqiáo Fàndiàn.

Both Air China and **Asiana Airlines** (www .flyasiana.com) fly non-stop to Seoul (Y3200, 2½ hours). Air China has flights to Khabarovsk (Y1450, 1½ hours) in Siberia and to Vladivostok (Y1530, one hour). China Eastern Airlines flies once a week to Los Angeles (12 hours). See p917 for airline details.

From Hāěrbīn, you can fly to a huge number of domestic destinations including Běijīng (Y960, one hour and 50 minutes), Shànghǎi (Y1780, two hours and 40 minutes), Shēnzhèn (Y2700, six hours) and Dàlián (Y840, 1½ hours).

BUS

The main long-distance bus station is directly opposite the train station. If you're going to Mǔdānjiāng, the bus, which departs at least once an hour, is a bit faster than the train (Y59, four hours). Other buses run regularly to Qíqíhā'ěr (Y61), Jílín (Y60), and Shěnyáng (Y140).

TRAIN

Hāěrbīn is a major rail transport hub with routes throughout the northeast and beyond, including daily service to the following cities:

Destination	Seat/Sleeper Price	Duration
Běijīng	Y154/281	13hr
Chángchūn	Y61	3-4hr
Dàlián	Y125/231	9-10hr
Mǔdānjiāng	Y50	5hr
Qíqíhā'ěr	Y50	3-4hr
Shěnyáng	Y76	5hr
Suífēnhé	Y76/143	9½hr

Travellers on the Trans-Siberian Railway to or from Moscow can start or finish in Hāěrbīn (six days). Contact the **Hāěrbīn Railway International Tourist Agency** (7th fl, Kūnlún Fàndiàn, 8 Tielu Jie) for information on travelling through to Russia. CITS may also be able to help.

Getting Around

TO/FROM THE AIRPORT

Hāěrbīn's airport is 46km from the city centre. Shuttle buses (Y20) to the airport from the CAAC office, leave about 2½ hours before flight departure times. A taxi will take 45 minutes to an hour (Y100).

BUS

Hāěrbīn's buses (Y1) operate between 5am and 10pm (9.30pm in winter). Some useful routes include bus Nos 101 and 103 that run along Shangzhi Dajie from Stalin Park to the train station. Bus No 109 runs from the train station to Children's Park. Bus No 64 goes from Dàolǐqū to the Provincial Museum.

AROUND HĀĚRBĪN

Yabuli Ski Resort 亚布力滑雪中心

The biggest and best-equipped ski resort in the country, **Yabuli** (Yàbùlì Huáxuě Zhōngxīn), 200km southeast of Hāěrbīn, has 11 runs and nine lifts on Daguokui Mountain (Dàguōkuī Shān). **Windmill Village** (☎ 5345 5168; fax 5345 5138; www.yabuliski.com; d Y380-780), the resort village, hosted the 1996 Asian Winter Games. Weather permitting, the ski season lasts from late November until early April. In summer the area is popular for hiking.

CITS and other travel agencies in Hāěrbīn (see p379), offer ski packages that include transport, ski passes, equipment rental and accommodation. One-day trips start at around Y380.

For lodging information, contact Windmill Village. Or try one of the small hotels in Yàbùlì village (not the ski resort) where beds can often be found for Y70.

Buses and trains to Yàbùlì depart from Hāěrbīn (Y22 to Y33, three hours) and Mǔdānjiāng (1½ hours). Minibuses in Yàbùlì village run to the ski resort.

MǓDĀNJIĀNG 牡丹江

☎ 0453 / pop 650,000

A nondescript city of more than half a million people, Mǔdānjiāng's main interest is as a transit point to nearby Jìngpò Hú (Mirror Lake) and the Underground Forest.

Information

Bank of China (☎ 692 9833; 9 Taiping Lu; ☼ 8am-4pm Mon-Fri) The main bank office is two blocks south of the train station. There's a 24-hour ATM one block further south.

China Telecom (Dongyi Tiaolu) One block east of the post office.

CITS (☎ 691 1944; www.citsmdj.com.cn in Chinese; 34 Jingfu Jie; ☯ 8am-5pm) The helpful staff at this office, two blocks east of Taiping Lu, can arrange day trips to Jìngpò Hú.

Post office (Taiping Lu; ☯ 8am-5.30pm Mon-Fri) Three blocks south of the main Bank of China office.

PSB (Guanghua Jie) Two blocks west of the train station.

Yèláng Wǎngba (Xinhua Lu; per hr Y2) Internet access. It's on the eastern side of the street, one block from Bèishān Bīnguǎn (see next section).

Sleeping & Eating

Bèishān Bīnguǎn (北山宾馆; ☎ 652 5788; fax 652 4670; 1 Xidiming Jie at Xinhua Lu; d Y398-428 incl breakfast; ✲) This stately hotel, about 1km north of the train station, has large airy doubles, including some modern, smartly outfitted ones overlooking the hotel garden. Bus No 201 from the train station stops on Xinhua Lu, about a block south of the hotel; a cab from the station will cost Y6 to Y7.

Mǔdānjiāng Fàndiàn (牡丹江饭店; ☎ 692 5833; fax 699 7779; 128 Guanghua Jie; d Y150-220) More run-of-the-mill but more convenient to transport options is this well-kept budget hotel. When you exit the train station, turn left, walk one block, and cross the street to the hotel.

Dongyibuxing Jie, southeast of the train station, is a pedestrian mall with a night market, where you can graze from the kebab sellers, noodle makers and other snack vendors.

Getting There & Away

Mǔdānjiāng has rail and bus connections to Hāěrbīn (Y50, five hours), Suífēnhé (Y27, six hours), Yánjí (Y22, seven hours), Túmén (six hours), Jiāmùsī (8 hours) and Dōngjīng (Y10, 1¼ hours). Long-distance buses arrive and depart from in front of the train station.

There's an airline ticket office at Bèishān Bīnguǎn. Flight destinations include Běijīng (Y1190, two hours), Shànghǎi (Y1830, two hours and 20 minutes) and Guǎngzhōu (Y2600, six hours). A taxi to the airport will cost about Y45.

AROUND MǓDĀNJIĀNG
Jìngpò Hú 镜泊湖

The clear reflections of the tree-lined coast and many small islands within **Jìngpò Hú** (Mirror Lake; admission Y30) leave no question about why it has been named Mirror Lake. Covering an area of 90 sq km and 45km in length, the lake was formed on the bend of the Mudan River 5000 years ago by the falling lava of five volcanic explosions. It is extremely popular with busloads of Chinese tourists who roll up during the summer months. Jìngpò Hú is about 100km southwest of Mǔdānjiāng.

Near the lake is the **Diaoshuilou Waterfall**, 20m tall and 40m wide, an attractive spectacle that swells in size during the rainy season.

Apart from cruising the lake by **ferry** (Y60) or wandering the woods that ring the lake, the main visitor pastime is **fishing**, primarily for different varieties of carp. The fishing season is from June to August; you can hire tackle and boats (prices are negotiable).

Unfortunately, the area is relinquishing its majesty to the tourist industry, which has pockmarked the surrounding greenery with hotels and other development. Visiting during low season, from October to May, provides a more peaceful getaway. Just note that many hotels and restaurants shut down outside of the summer months, and transport options are limited.

A number of hotels encircle the lake, all of which fill quickly in summer. Call ahead. Options include **Shānzhuāng Bīnguǎn** (山庄宾馆; Mountain Village Hotel; ☎ 627 0039; d from Y200), **Yóudiànjú Bīnguǎn** (邮电局宾馆; Post & Communication Hotel; ☎ 627 0096; dm/d Y60/200) and **Zhōngguó Bīnguǎn** (中国宾馆; China Hotel; ☎ 627 0030; d & tr Y300). Many small restaurants near the lake serve local fish.

The easiest way to get to Jìngpò Hú is on the direct bus from Mǔdānjiāng that leaves from opposite the train station at 7am (one way/return Y20/40, about two hours) and departs from the lake around at 3.30pm. The bus stops at the lake shore and the waterfall.

Regular trains run from Mǔdānjiāng to Dōngjīng (Y10, 1¼ hours). From there, it's one hour by minibus (Y10) to the lake, but these buses run only from June to September; at other times, you'll have to take a taxi.

If you're touring the northeast's lakes, you can take the bus from Báihé, near Chángbái Shān in Jílín province, to Yánjí and

NORTH OF THE WALL

from there take the train to Mǔdānjiāng or Dōngjīng.

At Jìngpò Hú, trams take visitors from the lake to the waterfall (Y5 per ride).

Underground Forest 地下森林

Although called the **Underground Forest** (Dìxià Sēnlín; ☺ June-Sep) by locals, the forest has actually grown within the craters of volcanoes that erupted some 10,000 years ago. There are 10 craters in total; Crater No 3 is the largest. The lush forest is home to a rich variety of plants and animals including the Purple Pine and the Dragon Spruce, and the leopard and black bear.

The forest is 50km from Jìngpò Hú. Take a bus or train from Mǔdānjiāng to Dōngjīng and from there change to a minibus for the forest. Some buses combine a trip to the forest with visits to Jìngpò Hú.

QÍQÍHĀ'ĚR 齐齐哈尔

☎ 0452 / pop 860,000

Qíqíhā'ěr, approximately 250km northwest of Hāěrbīn and one of the oldest settlements in the northeast, was established in 1684, and today this largely industrial city is a gateway to the Zhalong Nature Reserve, a bird-watching area 30km southeast. Its name comes from the Daur word for 'borderland'.

Though it's not really a tourist destination, Qíqíhā'ěr is pleasant enough, with several parks dotting the city; the largest, Longsha Park (龙沙公园; Lóngshā Gōngyuán), straddles the river and houses a small zoo, gardens and lakes.

Qíqíhā'ěr holds an ice-carving festival from January to March. Annual highest and lowest temperatures achieve a nice symmetry: 39°C in July and -39°C in January.

Orientation

The train station is east of the city centre. Longhua Lu heads west from the station to the downtown area, where you'll find the bank, post and telephone offices, lots of shops, and buses to the Zhalong Nature Reserve. Bus No 14 runs between the train station and the city centre.

Information

Bank of China (☎ 247 5674; 3 Bukui Dajie, off Longhua Lu; ☺ 8am-4.30pm Mon-Fri, 8.30am-4.30pm Sat & Sun) An ATM inside the bank accepts cards from several networks.

China Telecom (Zhonghua Lu) Next door to the post office.

CITS (☎ 240 7538; fax 247 4646) Staff here can advise you about the best times and places for bird-watching. They also run tours to the Zhalong reserve.

Internet bar (Longhua Lu; per hr Y2) Across from the train station, near Báihè Bīnguǎn (see next section).

Post office (cnr Zhonghua Lu & Bukui Dajie; ☺ 8am-5pm Mon-Fri) Diagonally across from the Bank of China.

PSB (cnr Bukui Dajie & Longsha Lu; ☺ 8-11.30am & 1.30-5pm Mon-Fri) One block north of the Bank of China.

Sleeping & Eating

Báihè Bīnguǎn (白鹤宾馆; White Crane Hotel; ☎ 292 1112; fax 212 7639; 25 Zhanqian Dajie; s/d Y160/220 incl breakfast) This comfortable, well-furnished tower is to your left as you exit the train station. There are several restaurants, and the staff is helpful, but don't expect to hear much English spoken.

Tiědào Fàndiàn (铁道饭店; Railway Hotel; ☎ 212 4579; 7 Longhua Lu; dm/s/d incl breakfast Y22/140/220) This friendly budget hotel one block from Báihè Bīnguǎn has old but clean rooms and frequent discounts.

Qīngyánglóu (清洋楼; ☎ 213 3999; hotpots Y18-24) This popular spot on the 3rd floor of Báihè Bīnguǎn specializes in tasty lamb hotpots.

To the left as you exit the train station, Zhanqian Dajie is lined with dumpling shops and other cheap eateries.

Getting There & Away

Qíqíhā'ěr is linked by rail to Běijīng (seat/sleeper Y182/333, 14½ hours), via Hāěrbīn (Y50, three to four hours). There are trains north to Běi'ān (北安; Y27) and Hēihé (Y60). A train leaves for Hēihé at 7.35am, stopping in Běi'ān at 11.30am and arriving in Hēihé at 5.58pm. A second (slower) train to Běi'ān leaves at 3.15pm and arrives at 8.20pm.

There are also buses to Hāěrbīn (Y61, 3½ hours).

There are flights between Qíqíhā'ěr and Běijīng (1¼ hours), Guǎngzhōu (five hours and 40 minutes), and Shànghǎi (two hours and 40 minutes). The **CAAC** (☎ 242 4445) ticket office is at 2 Minhang Jie; there's also an airline ticket office in Báihè Bīnguǎn.

ZHALONG NATURE RESERVE 扎龙自然保护区

If you're a bird-lover, it's worth a stop at this **nature reserve** (Zhālóng Zìrán Bǎohùqū; admission

Y20; ☻ 7am-5pm), home to some 260 species of bird, including storks, swans, geese, ducks, herons, grebes and egrets. The highlight is the rare red-crowned crane (see right).

On a bird migration path that extends from the Russian Arctic, around the Gobi desert and down into Southeast Asia, the reserve is at the northwestern tip of a giant marsh, and is made up of about 210,000 hectares of wetlands. Thousands of birds arrive from April to May, rear their young from June to August and depart from September to October. While some of the red-crowned cranes are more than 1.5m tall, the reed cover is taller. The best time to visit is in spring, before the reeds grow. Unfortunately, you may also find a significant percentage of the birds in zoo-like cages.

Even if you're not a bird fan, a trip into this peaceful countryside will be bliss to those who have been traipsing around China's cities. During the summer, you can hire a boat to explore the freshwater marshes. Be warned: in summer the mosquitoes are almost as big as and definitely more plentiful than the birds – take repellent!

The CITS office in Qíqíhā'ěr (see opposite) offers **day tours** of the reserve (approximately Y100 per person, plus Y150 to Y200 for transportation), though it's easy enough to explore on your own in a half-day trip from Qíqíhā'ěr. If you prefer to stay overnight, the somewhat run-down **Zhālóng Bīnguǎn** (扎龙宾馆; ☎ 0452-452 0024; d low/high season Y100/Y360) is the only hotel on the reserve grounds. Call ahead if you're arriving in low season to be sure the hotel is open.

Zhālóng is 30km from Qíqíhā'ěr. Minibuses travel to the reserve (Y20, one hour) from the corner of Longhua Lu and Xiongying Jie, one block west of the Bank of China. The schedule is erratic, however.

You can also hire a taxi to take you to the reserve; bargaining starts at about Y150.

WǓDÀLIÁN CHÍ 五大连池
☎ 0456

Wǔdàlián Chí is a nature reserve and health spot about 250km northwest of Hāěrbīn that has been turned into a 'volcano museum' and park. The area's malodorous, allegedly curative mineral springs draw busloads of tourists, including many Russians, who arrive in the summer to slurp the waters or slap mud onto themselves.

As for the volcanoes themselves, don't come expecting Krakatoa. The most recent volcanic eruptions occurred in 1719 and 1720, when lava blocked the nearby North River (Běi Hé) and formed a series of barrier lakes. The area has lava fields, hot springs and a little geothermal activity here and there, but not much else. It's pretty, though – at least when you get out of the dreary town and onto the hills and lava fields.

The only way to see the sights is by taxi; there are no public buses. To hire a taxi for a 20km loop taking in the lakes, volcanoes and caves, expect to pay around Y150.

A three-day 'water drinking festival', including music, dancing and unbridled drinking of the local waters, is held each year in early June by the Daur minority.

Sights & Activities
LĂOHĒI SHĀN 老黑山
Of the 14 volcanoes in the area, **Lǎohēi Shān** (Laohei Mountain; admission Y40; ☻ 7.30am-4.30pm) is the most popular. Taxis take you to a parking area partway up the volcano – from there, it's a steep one-hour (return) walk to the summit, but the reward is awesome views. From the base of the mountain, it's a short walk to **Shí Hǎi** (石海; Stone Sea), an expansive lava field that resembles an ocean of lava rocks.

RARE CRANES FIND SANCTUARY

Of the world's 15 species of cranes, eight are found in China and six can be seen at the Zhalong Nature Reserve. One of China's first nature reserves, Zhālóng was set up in 1979.

Four of the species that migrate here are on the endangered list: the red-crowned crane, the white-naped crane, the Siberian crane and the hooded crane. Both the red-crowned and white-naped cranes breed at Zhālóng (as do the common and demoiselle cranes), while hooded and Siberian cranes use Zhālóng as a stopover.

The red-crowned crane is a particularly fragile creature whose numbers worldwide are estimated at only about 1900. The near-extinct bird is, ironically, the ancient symbol of immortality and has long been a symbol of longevity and good luck in the Chinese, Korean and Japanese cultures.

CAVES

Two underground caves boast a year-round ice-lantern festival. Both the **Lava Ice Cavern** (熔岩冰洞; Róngyán Bīngdòng; admission Y20; ☻ 9am-4.30pm) and the **Lava Snow Cavern** (熔岩雪洞; Róngyán Xuědòng; admission Y20; ☻ 9am-4.30pm) have a steady temperature of -10°C, even during summer. The ice sculptures are lit from the inside by fluorescent coloured lights that create a psychedelic effect.

ZHONGLING TEMPLE 钟灵寺

High on a hill off the road to Lǎohēi Shān, this large **temple** (Zhōnglíng Sì; admission Y10) complex houses several fat golden Buddhas. A tall marble Buddha overlooks the whole place – with fine views of the area. It's about a 15- to 20-minute walk up to the temple from the road.

Sleeping & Eating

Wǔdàlián Chí might look small, but there are over 40 sanatoriums and hotels with beds ranging from Y30 to Y60, and well-priced doubles, too. During low season (October to May), many lodgings close or reduce their services.

Tiědàobù Hǎwǔfēnjú Wǔdàliánchí Liáo-yǎng-yuàn (铁道部哈武分局五大连池疗养院; ☎ 722 1962; d Y180-360) In a park-like setting west of the traffic circle, this new-ish hotel has huge, light-filled doubles, as well as cheaper, more standard rooms.

Dìshuì Wǔdàliánchí Bīnguǎn (地税五大连池宾馆; ☎ 722 3387; d Y120-180) This imposing structure next door to the Workers Sanatorium has light and airy (if basic) doubles, with run-down bathrooms. Breakfast is Y5. The hotel's modest-looking restaurant (in the adjacent building) is surprisingly good. Try the *daozi* (a local fish), or the savoury potato-tomato soup (dishes Y12 to Y22).

Gōngrén Liáoyǎngyuàn (公人疗养院; Workers Sanatorium; ☎ 722 1569; dm/d Y40/250; ☻ May-Nov) This complex east of the traffic circle is a popular summer destination for ailing Russians.

Getting There & Away

To reach Wǔdàlián Chí, take a train from Hāěrbīn (5½ hours) or Qíqíhā'ěr (Y27, four hours) to Běi'ān (北安). Fast buses also run between Hāěrbīn and Běi'ān (Y52, four hours). In Běi'ān, several buses depart daily for Wǔdàlián Chí (Y10, 1½ hours, 10.50am, 12.40pm, 3.30pm, with additional buses during the summer). Returning to Běi'ān, buses leave Wǔdàlián Chí from the traffic circle (6.30am, 7.30am, 11am).

From Běi'ān, there's a bus north to Hēihé (Y49, 3½ hours) departing at 8.30am; there are also several slow trains for Hēihé (five to six hours, 1am, 11.40am, 1.25pm).

Běi'ān's bus station is one block from the train station. If you get stuck in Běi'ān for the night, try **Tiānlóng Dàjiǔdiàn** (☎ 666 4818;

THE FISH PEOPLE

The Hezhen are a people of fish; they hunt fish, eat fish, celebrate fish and even wear fish.

One of the smallest ethnic groups in China (numbering roughly 4000), the Hezhen minority is spread across the northern plains of Hēilóngjiāng. Yet despite their landlocked homeland, they are expert fishermen. Legend has it that they can determine what kind of fish is under water by looking at the bubbles on the water's surface.

Traditionally, the Hezhen make clothes out of locally caught fish, such as salmon, carp or green pike. Buttons are made from catfish bones. Dresses, trousers, shoes, aprons and gloves can all be made, but you'd have to be a patient fisherman as it apparently takes around 250kg of fish to make one suit.

These fishy designs have recently made a splash on the international fashion stage. Clothes enthusiasts, in particular from Korea, Japan and the USA, are paying through the gills for the fish-skin costumes – one suit is reported to fetch US$660.

Fashion aside, the lifestyle of the Hezhen is rapidly changing. Although they continue to maintain their own language and traditions, just how much of Hezhen culture has remained intact is open to speculation. The official line trumpets wondrous change from a primitive, nomadic lifestyle to settled consumerism, complete with satellite TV. Some would argue that such change is not a bad thing – not least because the Hezhen can now watch their fish skin creations hit the international catwalks.

fax 666 4943; d with/without bath Y160/90) opposite the train station.

RUSSIAN BORDERLANDS

Much of the northeastern border between China and Siberia follows the Black Dragon River (Hēilóng Jiāng), known to the Russians as the Amur River. Along the border it's possible to see Siberian forests and the dwindling settlements of northern tribes, such as the Daur, Ewenki, Hezhen (see The Fish People, opposite) and Oroqen.

To visit these areas, you may need permits – international borders and ethnic minority regions are sensitive places. Check with the PSB in Hāěrbīn (p379) before undertaking the long journey north. Also take a small medical kit, insect repellent and warm clothing.

Major towns in the far north include Mòhé and Hēihé. On the eastern border, Suífēnhé is a gateway to Vladivostok.

Mòhé 漠河
Natural wonders are the attraction in Mòhé, China's northernmost town, dubbed the Arctic of China. In mid-June, the sun is visible for as long as 22 hours. The aurora borealis (northern lights) are another colourful phenomenon here.

Mòhé holds the record for China's lowest plunge of the thermometer: -52.3°C, recorded in 1956. On a normal winter day a temperature of -40°C is common.

Getting to Mòhé requires a train trip north from Jiāgédáqí, in Inner Mongolia, to Gǔlián, followed by a 34km bus ride. You can get to Jiāgédáqí by train from Qíqíhā'ěr

Hēihé 黑河
Hēihé, a small riverfront city, is enjoying a mini boom in cross-border tourism. Chinese tour groups are now able to cross the border to Blagoveshchensk, a large Russian river port opposite Hēihé.

Unfortunately it's not so easy for foreigners to visit Blagoveshchensk. A Russian tourist visa is needed, as is a re-entry visa for China. All this must be arranged in Běijīng, not in Hēihé.

The departure point for Russia and the customs and immigration facilities are on **Dà Hēihé Dǎo** (Big Black River Island) at the eastern end of Hēihé's waterfront promenade. Also on the island is **International Market City** (Dà Hēihé Guójì Shāngmào Cháng), where Chinese and Russian traders'haggle over wholesale shoes and bras.

Those without a Russian visa can console themselves with hour-long cruises of Black Dragon River (Y10), departing from various points along the riverfront.

Trains run daily to and from Hāěrbīn (sleeper Y153, 12 hours). Buses also travel to Hāěrbīn, Běi'ān, and Qíqíhā'ěr.

Suífēnhé 绥芬河
Like other borderland outposts, Suífēnhé has enjoyed a spasmodic growth in cross-border trade and tourism in recent years. If you're planning on crossing the border into Russia from here, you will need to have organised a Russian visa in Běijīng.

Suífēnhé is linked by rail to Hāěrbīn (seat/sleeper Y76/143, 9½ hours) and Mǔdānjiāng. There is a daily international passenger train for Vladivostok.

Shānxī 山西

CONTENTS

HIGHLIGHTS

- Gape in astonishment at the sublime Buddhist statuary (over 50,000 works) of the **Yungang Caves** (p403) west of Dàtóng

- Explore fragments of the **Great Wall** (p404) that few visit, an easy hike from the Yungang Caves

- Pedal a bike through time-locked **Píngyáo** (p395) along cobblestone back streets and past fetching Ming dynasty architecture

- Chat with monks in one of the innumerable temples surrounding **Táihuái** (p399)

- Do some bus-bound daydreaming along the scenic route over Wǔtái Shān and hop off en route for the astonishing **Hanging Monastery** (p404), literally carved into a cliff

■ POP: 33.8 MIL	■ AREA: 156,000 SQ KM	■ www.sxta.com.cn

To start, a caveat: Shānxī is not to be confused with its neighbour to the west, the nearly homophonic and much more touristed Shaanxi (Shǎnxī). Locals here are (rightly) a tad sensitive about this.

Shānxī translates as 'West of the Mountains', the mountains being Tàiháng Shān, the modestly high but seemingly endless range paralleling Shānxī's entire eastern border. Tàiháng Shān may dominate the ethos, but the entire province is hemmed in by other ranges; in fact, nearly 70% of the province is mountainous, with much of the population residing in an inner loessial plateau.

The mighty Yellow River (Huáng Hé) borders Shānxī to the west *and* the south, which, when added to the topographic seclusion, helps explain the province's millennia of isolation, relatively paltry population (for China) and, most troublesome for the post–Communist Revolution government, poverty.

Unsurprisingly, then, garnering more historical glory is Shānxī's less isolated neighbour Shaanxi, the terminus of the Silk Road and self-proclaimed cradle of Chinese civilisation. Shānxī, though, arguably surpasses its neighbour in its archaeological and scenic riches. This is especially true of the northern half, a virtual gold mine of temples, monasteries and cave-temples. Among these, the main attractions for travellers are the Yungang Caves at Dàtóng, the extant Ming dynasty architecture of Píngyáo and the Buddhist mountain of Wǔtái Shān. Indeed, all things totalled, Shānxī was itself also a cultural centre of China.

Touristic glimpses at a glorious past are a growing Shānxī economy. Still underpopulated and poor, Shānxī's economic linchpin today remains coal. The subterranean rivers of carbon gold here are astonishing – one-third of China's coal is extracted here.

The downside? Shānxī's environment is by any standard a toxic cocktail. Of the world's most polluted cities, the lion's share are in China, and the bulk of the worst are in northern Shānxī, where toxic watersheds, chronic bronchial diseases and rainbows refracted from airborne coal dust are among the challenges of a province proudly reclaiming its past.

History

Neighbouring, history-rich Shaǎnxī garners most tourists and press, yet Shānxī rivalled it as a contemporary centre of Chinese civilisation. Qin Shi Huang (the 'First Emperor of Qin') used northern Shānxī – buttressed to the north by the Great Wall, the north-west by the Gobi Desert, and the east by Tàiháng Shān – as the key defensive bulwark against outside 'barbarians', even after the collapse of the Tang dynasty in the 9th century and the relocation of the capital to the east.

This isolation effectively prevented any real development in the province, though this also ensured that the mountains and arid plains were left to Buddhists to create extraordinary temple complexes and grottoes.

After 1949 the communist government began to exploit Shānxī's mineral and ore deposits, and developed Dàtóng and Tàiyuán as major industrial centres. China's biggest coal mines can be found near these cities, and the province accounts for a third of China's known iron and coal deposits.

Climate

Bordering the Gobi desert, Shānxī misses out on most of the moisture deposited by summer monsoon winds; bitterly icy winter

SHĀNXĪ 山西

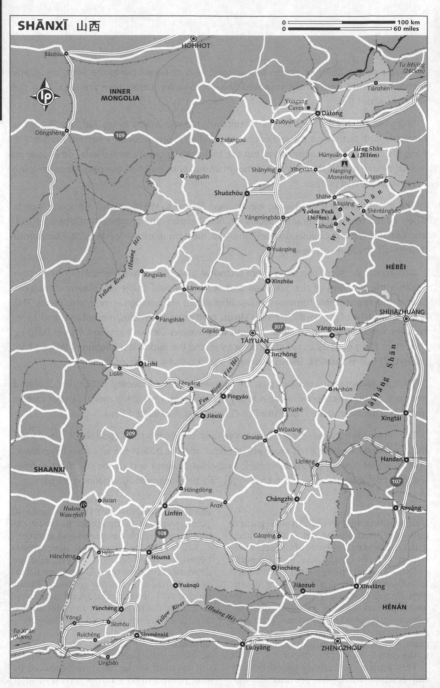

0   100 km
0   60 miles

HOHHOT

Bāotóu

INNER MONGOLIA

Tiānzhèn

Dōngshèng

109

Yungang Caves
Zuǒyùn
Dàtóng

Bailangou

Hěng Shān ▲ (2016m)
Húnyuán
Shānyǐng   Yìngxiàn
Hanging Monastery
Lìngqiū

Piánguān

Shuòzhōu

Shāhè
Báiqiáng   Shéntángbǎo
Yadou Peak (3058m) ▲
Yángmíngbǎo
Tàihuái

Wǔtái Shān

HÉBĚI

Yellow River (Huáng Hé)

Xīngxiàn
Lánxiàn
Yuánpíng

Xīnzhōu

SHÍJIĀZHUĀNG

Fāngshān
Gǔjiāo
307
Yángquán

TÀIYUÁN
Jìnzhōng

Lǐshí
Liǔlín

Fén River (Fén Hé)

Héshùn

Taiháng Shān

Fényáng
Píngyáo

Jièxiū
Yúshè

Xīngtái

209
Qínxiàn   Wǔxiāng

Lǐchéng

SHAANXI
Handan

Hóngdòng
Ānzé   Chángzhì
Jīxiàn

107

Hukou Waterfall
Línfén
Gāopíng
Ānyáng

108

Héjīn
Hánchéng
Houmǎ

Jīnchéng
Xīnxiāng

Yuánqǔ
Jiāozuò

Yùnchéng

HÉNÁN

Yǒngjì
Jièzhōu
Yellow River (Huáng Hé)

Ruìchéng
Sānménxiá

To Xī'ān (90km)
Luòyáng
ZHÈNGZHŌU

Língbǎo

To Běijīng (260km)

winds slicing from the northwest are even drier – precisely 0cm of rain in February is normal – and laden with yellow Gobi loess dust. All in, the province averages a mere 35cm of rain a year. the only time it really does rain is July, but it's usually only 12cm.

Temperature fluctuations are serious. In Tàiyuán (at just 800m above sea level) expect lows of around –8°C in January, with wind chills icing that down quite a bit; at least the summer average high is a relatively comfortable 25°C. Remember that much of the province is mountainous, so adjust temperatures accordingly. Plan to arrive in May or September for optimal conditions.

Language

Shānxī has 45 million speakers of Jin. Linguists argue whether it should be classified as a distinct language rather than a Mandarin dialect (since it has eight subgroups inside the province); if so, it is the 22nd-most spoken world language. Jin uses a final glottal stop, unlike standard Mandarin; other unique features are complex grammar-induced tone shifts and breaking monosyllabic words into two.

Getting There & Around

Modern and extensive rail lines and highways split Shānxī on a northeast–southwest line, so getting from Běijīng to Tàiyuán and thence to Xī'ān (in Shaǎnxī) is no problem. Outside of that, lots of mountain roads – often impassable in winter – await to bog you down.

TÀIYUÁN 太原

☎ 0351 / pop 2,932,800

Tàiyuán, provincial capital and industrial sprawl often shrouded in fog, is more cosmopolitan than its northern neighbour Dàtóng and a decent place to await onward connections.

The first settlements on the site of today's Tàiyuán date back 2500 years. By the 13th century it had developed into what Marco Polo referred to as 'a prosperous city, a great centre of trade and industry'. But it was also the site of constant armed conflict, sitting squarely on the path by which successive northern invaders entered China. There were once 27 temples here dedicated to the God of War.

Orientation

Yingze Dajie runs east to west through Tàiyuán. To the east is the train station, and westward several kilometres are the lion's share of accommodation, services and May 1st Sq (Wǔyī Guǎngchǎng). Most sights and eating options are north of Yingze Dajie. Jiannan Bus Station (Jiànnán Zhàn) is 4.5km south of the train station.

Information

Bank of China (Zhōngguó Yínháng; Yingze Dajie) West of Jiefang Lu. You can change travellers cheques and use credit cards.

China International Travel Service (Zhōngguó Guójì Lǚxíngshè; CITS) Pingyang Lu (☎ 723 2188; 38 Pingyang Lu); Yingze Dajie (☎ 407 4209; 282 Yingze Dajie) The Yingze Dajie branch is next door to the Bank of China, but the main branch on Pingyang Lu is inconveniently located far south just off Xinjian Lu, over 3km south of Yingze Dajie.

China Telecom (Yingze Dajie) At the western end of the street.

Internet café (wǎngbā; cnr Yingze Dajie & Jiefang Lu; per hr Y2) West of China Telecom.

Internet café (wǎngbā; Yingze Dajie; per hr Y2) The most convenient place to log on is west of the train station, nearly opposite the Changtai Fandian; it's actually inside the movie theatre (go in and turn left).

Post & telephone office Diagonally opposite the train station. The post office is open 8am to 8pm daily and the telephone office operates 24 hours a day.

Public Security Bureau (PSB; Gōngānjú; 9 Houjia Xiang; 8.30-11.30am & 3-5pm Mon-Fri) Has a foreign affairs office near May 1st Square (Wǔyī Guǎngchǎng).

Sights

CHONGSHAN TEMPLE 崇善寺

This Buddhist **monastery** (Chóngshàn Sì; Taiwan Wenmiao Xiang; admission Y4; ⏰ 8am-5pm) was built on the site of a monastery that is said to date back to the 6th or 7th century. The main hall contains three impressive statues; the central figure is Guanyin, the Goddess of Mercy with 1000 hands and eyes.

Also on display are some Buddhist scriptures of the Song, Yuan, Ming and Qing dynasties. The monastery is on a side street running east off Wuyi Lu.

TWIN PAGODA TEMPLE 双塔寺

This **temple** (Shuāngtǎ Sì; Twin Pagoda Park; admission Y6; ⏰ 8.30am-5.30pm) has two Ming dynasty pagodas, each a 13-storey octagonal structure almost 55m high. It is possible to climb one of the pagodas, but it is only recommended for those who enjoy dark, slippery spiral stairs. The pagodas are built entirely of bricks carved with brackets and cornices to imitate ancient Chinese wooden pagodas.

The best way to get to this temple is by bicycle. Ride along Chaoyang Jie for about 750m, turn right on Shuangta Beilu and then continue south for 1.5km. Otherwise, catch a taxi (Y6). Bus Nos 19 and 802 from the train station get you relatively close.

SHANXI PROVINCIAL MUSEUM
山西省博物馆

This museum is located in two separate sections. The **main museum** (Shānxī Shěng Bówùguǎn; Qifeng Jie; admission Y5; ☺ 8am-noon & 2.30-7pm summer, reduced hr rest of year) is northwest of May 1st Sq in an temple for offering sacrifices to the Tang dynasty Taoist priest Lu Dongbin. The **second section** (Taíwǎn Wénmiào Xiàng; Y10; ☺ 9am-noon & 2.30-5pm) is south of Chongshan Temple and housed in attractive Ming buildings that were once a Confucian temple. It is sometimes closed on Monday.

Sleeping

Tiělù Bīnguǎn (Railway Hotel; ☎ 404 0624; 18 Yingze Dajie; dm Y20-50, s/d with private bath Y50-290; ✷) Expect ever-cheery staff and myriad rooms (the best cheap digs around).

Chángtài Fàndiàn (☎ 223 0888; fax 403 4931; 60 Yingze Dongdajie; s/d incl breakfast Y188-300; ✷) A very recent makeover has transformed this into a reasonable lower mid-range place

to stay (great floor staff!). Many of the cheaper rooms have new hardwood floors and fixtures. There's a rail ticket office in the lobby.

Diànlì Dàshà (Electric Power Hotel; ☎ 404 1784; fax 404 0777; 39 Yingze Dajie; s & tw Y188-380; ✷) This is another place with decent value for the rooms which, though not as new as the Chángtài Fàndiàn's, are well kept.

Yíngzé Bīnguǎn (☎ 882 8888; book@shanxiyingze hotel.com; 189 Yingze Dajie; older east wing d Y280, newer east wing d from Y580; ✷ ✷) This hotel incorporates two massive buildings. The west block is a glittering four-star hotel, complete with sauna, gym, medical clinic and English-language satellite TV. The cheaper east block is usually for Chinese guests. No longer the most luxurious in town (though close), it gets a nod for its great location.

Eating

Local highlights include *zhūjiǎo* (pigs' trotters) stewed in a cauldron, and a savoury pancake called *làobǐng*. Local potato noodles called *liángpí* are often served in steaming bowls of spicy soup redolent with spring onions.

Head west along Yingze Dajie and turn north onto Luxiang Nanlu. Work your way north and west. You'll hit the mother lode of boisterous eateries at Shípǐn Jiē, a street whose name literally means 'foodstuffs'. Perhaps not a true night market – too many proper sit-down places – but it still comes alive only when the sun goes down.

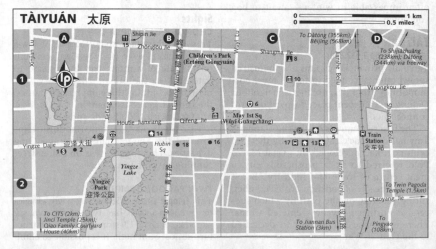

Getting There & Away

AIR

The **China Eastern Airlines booking office** (☎ 404 2903; 158 Yingze Dajie; h8am-8pm) is the main purveyor of tickets in town and is where you hop aboard the airport bus. Useful flights include Běijīng (Y510, several daily), Guǎngzhōu (Y1160, daily), and Xī'ān (Y460, several daily).

BUS

Tàiyuán's long-distance bus station is a five-minute walk west of the train station and currently still serves most destinations. However, the Jiannan Bus Station (Jiànnán Zhàn), 4.5km south of the train station, serves Píngyáo (Y18 to Y25, 1½ to three hours). A new eastern station may have buses to Wǔtái Shān soon.

Otherwise, regular buses and luxury air-conditioned superliners barrel to Dàtóng (Y55 to Y70, five hours) hourly 6.30am to roughly 4pm from the long-distance bus station. There are half-hourly buses to Wǔtái Shān (Y43, four hours) from the bus station leaving 6am to 2.30pm (the earlier, the better, so you're guaranteed a departure).

From the long distance bus station there are express buses travelling to most destinations, including Běijīng (Y120, six hours)

INFORMATION	
Bank of China 中国银行	1 A2
CITS 中国国际旅行社	2 A2
Internet Café 网吧	3 C2
Internet Café 网吧	4 A2
Post & Telephone Office 邮电大楼	5 D2
PSB 公安局	6 C1
Telephone Office 电信局	7 A2
SIGHTS & ACTIVITIES	**pp393-4**
Chongshan Temple 崇善寺	8 C1
Shanxi Provincial Museum (Section 1) 省博物馆	9 B1
Shanxi Provincial Museum (Section 2) 省博物馆	10 C1
SLEEPING	**p394**
Chángtài Fàndiàn 长泰饭店	11 C2
Diànlì Dàshà 电力大厦	12 C2
Tiělù Bīnguǎn 铁路宾馆	13 C2
Yíngzé Bīnguǎn 迎泽宾馆	14 B2
EATING	**p394**
Night Market 夜市场	15 B1
TRANSPORT	**p395**
China Eastern Airlines Booking Office 东方航空公司售票处	16 B2
Long-Distance Bus Station 长站汽车站	17 C2
Train Booking Office 火车售票处	18 B2

every half hour from 7am to 11pm; also check the train station parking lot for buses to Běijīng.

TRAIN

It's fairly easy getting sleeper tickets for trains originating from Tàiyuán, but difficult for other trains. For advance purchases go to the **train booking office** (138 Yingze Dajie; h8am-7pm), or the lobby of the Chángtài Fàndiàn. Services leaving from Tàiyuán include express trains to Běijīng (eight to ten hours), Chéngdū (30 hours), Dàtóng (six to eight hours), Luòyáng (12 hours), Zhèngzhōu (10 hours) and Shànghǎi (22 hours).

If you're headed to Xī'ān, your best bets are train Nos 1485 and 2535 as they start from Tàiyuán.

AROUND TÀIYUÁN
Jinci Temple 晋祠寺

Dating from AD 1023, this Buddhist **temple** (Jìncí Sì; admission Y40; h8am-6.30pm summer, reduced hr rest of year) is at the source of Jin River (Jìn Hé), by Xuanwang Hill, 25km southwest of Tàiyuán. Take bus No 804 from Tàiyuán's train station (Y2, one hour).

A canal cuts through the temple complex, spanned by the Huixian (Meet the Immortals) Bridge, providing access to the Terrace for Iron Statues, which displays figures cast in AD 1097.

Further back is the Goddess Mother Hall, the oldest wooden building in the city and home to 42 Song dynasty clay figures of maidservants of the sacred lady, said to be the mother of Prince Shuyu of the ancient Zhou dynasty. Adjacent is the Zhou Cypress, an unusual tree growing at an angle of about 30° for the last 900 years.

Zhenguan Baohan Pavilion houses four stone stelae (a decorated stone slab or column) inscribed with the handwriting of the Tang emperor Tai Zong. In the south of the temple grounds is the Sacred Relics Pagoda, a 7th-century seven-storey octagonal building.

PÍNGYÁO 平遥

☎ 0354 / pop 40,000
Surrounded by a completely intact 6km Ming dynasty city wall (claimed to be the last remaining in China), Píngyáo is an exceptionally well-preserved traditional Han Chinese city offering a rare glimpse into

the architectural styles and town planning of imperial China.

Píngyáo was a thriving merchant town during the Ming and Qing dynasties when China's earliest *tongs* (banks) were set up. Píngyáo rose to be the financial headquarters of all of China during the Qing dynasty. After its heyday the city fell into poverty, and without the cash to modernise, Píngyáo's streets remained unchanged.

Until the turn of the new millennium, Píngyáo saw few visitors. While the status of undiscovered jewel is long gone, the city is so well preserved that most travellers still cite this as one of their favourite Chinese experiences. So far, general over-restoration has not taken place and several hundred homes have been deemed cultural relics and are thus protected from being demolished or radically altered. In 1997 Píngyáo was listed as a Unesco World Heritage Site.

A good, though crowded, time to visit Píngyáo is during the Lantern Festival (15 days after Chinese New Year, during the full moon). Red lanterns are hung outside the doors of residences, and every year a small, country-style parade takes place. Locals flood the streets and vendors sell *yuán xiāo*, a traditional round white snack (which symbolises the moon) made of glutinous rice flour, filled with a sweet sesame and walnut paste and served in soup.

Orientation & Information

The city's main drag is Nan Dajie, also known as Ming Qing Jie, inside the walls. Inns, restaurants, museums, temples (and

---

QIAO FAMILY COURTYARD HOUSE
乔家大院

This ornately decorated **house** (Qiáo Jiā Dàyuàn, admission Y30) is the site where Zhang Yimou's film *Raise the Red Lantern*, starring Gong Li, was filmed. The courtyard house complex consists of six courtyards, containing over 300 rooms, and was built by Qiao Guifa, a small-time tea and beancurd merchant who rose to riches.

To get to the house from Tàiyuán take any Píngyáo-bound minibus. On the right-hand side of the highway you'll see red lanterns and a large gate marking the complex. It's 40km southwest of Tàiyuán.

---

antique shops) are positively ubiquitous on all streets branching from it – and more sights are just outside the walls.

Take cash with you; no bank exists. The PSB is in the southwestern part of the old town. The busy post office is near the corner of Ming Qing Jie and Xi Dajie. The one Internet café had closed but lodgings offer access.

Sights & Activities

Note that the number of museums, temples and historic structures greatly exceeds the scope of this book. Some of these are now hosting cultural or theatrical events of the Ming dynasty. Additional admission is charged for these.

A flat fee of Y85 is now charged; this gains access to (most) city attractions. Some sights are not included, and spots outside the city aren't covered at all.

In the middle of the Ming Qing Jie (and marking the centre of town) is the **Town Building/Bell Tower** (Shì Lóu; Ming Qing Jie; ☺ 9am-5pm). At a modestly imposing 18.5m, it's the tallest building in the city. You can see over the tiled roofs of the entire city from the top, but at the time of writing visitors weren't allowed to the top.

The ancient **city wall**, originally erected in the Zhou dynasty (827–728 BC), completely surrounds the city. Most of what you'll see now was actually built during the Ming dynasty; notice the stamped bricks below your feet. The outer portion of the wall has a few shell marks, remnants of the Japanese invasion in the 1930s. If you ascend the wall at the north gate, you can hire a pedicab to pedal you around the wall.

Not to be missed here is the **Rishengchang Financial House Museum** (40 Xi Dajie; ☺ 8am-7pm summer, reduced hr rest of year), one of the hundreds of financial 'houses' which operated from the city. In the late 18th century a man opened a small dye shop here. As it expanded, the proprietor introduced a system of cheques and deposits for its remote offices, eventually growing into a financial agent for other businesses, individuals and the Qing government, with 57 branches around China. The Japanese invasion and civil strife in the 1930s, along with increased competition from foreign banks, forced its eventual closure. The museum has nearly 100 rooms, including offices, living quarters and a kitchen, as well as several old cheques.

To see how the wealthy financiers lived, head down Qing Ming Jie to the south wall and turn right. After the parking area you'll arrive at the **Former Residence of Lei Lùtai** (Leílùtaí Gùjū; ☉ 8am-6.30pm). Impressive still, even after centuries; the complex's artefacts and furnishings have gone, but the extant architecture is definitely worth a look.

Exploring Píngyáo streets, you'll come across several other small museums within traditional courtyard houses, temples and even a Catholic church.

All this without even getting to the numerous Taoist temples! Inside the city are a handful – all intriguing enough for a visit. Nearby to Píngyáo is the most popular: **Shuanglin Temple** (Shuānglín Sì; admission Y18). This monastery, 7km southwest of Píngyáo (a motorcycle taxi is around Y15 return, or it's a pleasant bike ride), is well worth the effort. It contains around 2000 exquisitely painted clay figurines and statues dating from the Song, Yuan, Ming and Qing dynasties.

Sleeping & Eating

The cheapest beds are around Y30 with shared bathroom, though if you don't need a Ming-style room you can find a clean double with private bathroom for Y50. Another mid-range traditional courtyard-style hotel opens every week.

Tiānyuánkuí Kèzhàn (Tianyuankui Folk Guesthouse; ☎ 568 0069; www.pytyk.com; 73 Nan Dajie; dm Y60, d/tr from Y200/300, f & ste from Y380; ✕ 🖥) This top-notch guesthouse is a rare place catering to budget travellers and foreign ambassadors with equal verve. You can find basic shared dorm rooms, as well as spotless standard rooms in a variety of sizes and configurations, the bigger ones with nice touches like sparkling new bathtubs, hair dryers, and even Internet hook-ups. The gracious owners have even gone the extra mile, setting up their own power/water supply and hauling in a real espresso machine! The inevitable downside is that it might be booked out. There are discounts in the low season.

Jinjinglóu Kèzhàn (Golden Well Folk Guesthouse; ☎ /fax 568 3751; pyjjl@pyonline.net; 29 Nan Dajie; d with shared bathroom from Y60) This is another friendly

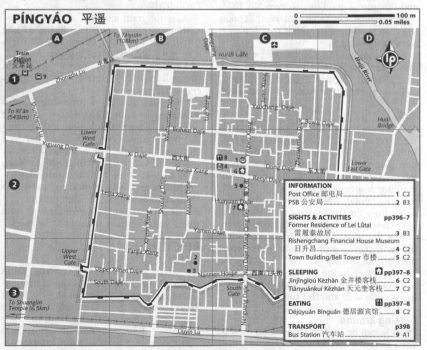

place with cheaper but good rooms; they're also amenable to friendly negotiation.

Local fare includes such treats as *shuǐ jiānbāo* (fried pork-filled bread) and *dòu miàn jiānbǐng* (fried pancake with string beans), along with local pastas made and cooked in a seemingly infinite variety. Local restaurants sport photos on large posters outside and a few have English menus.

Déjūyuán Bīnguǎn (Nan Dajie) Superb Shānxī and local cuisine in a relaxed traditional courtyard setting are the highlights at this mid-range inn and eatery. Two can savour and stuff for around Y40.

Getting There & Away
TRAIN
Most visitors arrive on a day trip from Tàiyuán, or overnight from Běijīng. Train No N203 leaves Běijīng west train station daily at 8pm and arrives in Píngyáo at 5.32am. Although several trains depart Píngyáo for Běijīng, tickets are extremely limited, so if returning to Běijīng your best bet is to take a minibus to Tàiyuán.

Loads of trains travel between Tàiyuán and Píngyáo (a good one is train No 2023, which originates in Tàiyuán at 9am). It takes less than two hours so even if you don't get a seat it's an easy ride.

From Píngyáo to Xī'ān can be problematic. Guesthouses can usually land sleepers from Píngyáo but don't count on it, especially on weekends in summer or holidays.

BUS
Taking a train from Tàiyuán is easier than the express buses, four-lane highway notwithstanding. Tàiyuán's Jiannan Bus Station (Jiànnán Zhàn), some 4.5km south of the train station, is the only departure point for Píngyáo-bound buses (Y18 to Y25, 1½ to three hours). Many buses go there (or close) from the train station area, including No 811, which terminates at the bus station.

The Píngyáo bus 'station' is really just the train station parking lot; buses depart for Tàiyuán as they fill. To get an express bus anywhere to the south, you may have to hoof it up to the expressway (Y2 in a motorcycle taxi) and flag one down.

Getting Around
Píngyáo can be easily navigated on foot, or you can rent a bike for the day (about Y10)

at one of the shops on Xi Dajie or outside the city walls. Motorcycle taxis average Y2 for local trips; Y15 to Y20 should get you around the countryside.

YÙNCHÉNG 运城
☎ 0359 / pop 188,800
Yùnchéng is in the southwestern corner of Shānxī, near where the Yellow River (Huáng Hé) completes its great sweep through far northern China and begins to flow eastwards. The small city is famed for the gutsy little orange tractors that are assembled here and often seen chugging along country roads.

At Jièzhōu, 18km south of Yùnchéng, is large **Guāndì Miào** (关帝庙; God of War Temple; admission Y25). This is the spot, legends say, where legendary general (or, more apropos, the god of war) Guan Yu was born. Martial-themed art abounds. The autumn festival here is superb; it's generally held on or around the 26th day of the 10th month of the lunar calendar, when acrobats and dancing troupes predominate. Bus No 11 (Y2, 30 minutes) from Yùnchéng train station terminates at Guāndì Miào.

Near the train and bus stations are numerous cheap, clean hotels. **Huánghé Dàshà** (黄河大厦; ☎ 202 3135; s/d from Y240; 🕸) is a well-run place east of the train station.

Yùnchéng is on the Tàiyuán–Xī'ān train line; all trains, including daily express trains, stop here.

There are direct bus connections from Yùnchéng to Luòyáng in Hénán province (Y35 to Y60, four to six hours), leaving from the bus station every half hour between 7am and 4.30pm. There are also regular buses and express air-con buses to Xī'ān (Y40 to Y60, three to four hours) departing half-hourly. All transport passes by Húa Shān in neighbouring Shaanxi province.

The bus station is a five-minute walk south from the train station on the right.

RUÌCHÉNG 芮城
☎ 0359
At utterly untouristed Ruìchéng, 93km south of Yùnchéng via the sometimes rugged mountains of Zhōngtiao Shān, is **Yongle Taoist Temple** (永乐宫; Yǒnglè Gōng; Y30), which has valuable frescoes dating from the Tang and Song dynasties. The temple is 3km directly south from the main intersection

(it was moved here from beside the Yellow River for a new dam site).

The surrounding area is quite charming, with many people continuing to live in simple cave dwellings.

East of the bus station, the solid lower mid-range **Ruìchéng Bīnguǎn** (芮城宾馆; d from Y130) is the best of the nearby bunch; cheaper options surround the station.

From Yùnchéng buses run every half hour to Ruìchéng (Y10, 2½ hours). On the way, the bus passes Jièzhōu before climbing the cool subalpine slopes of Zhōngtiáo Shān. It is also possible to hop on this bus in Jièzhōu, but you will need to catch a motor tricycle back to the main road from Guāndì Miào from where you can just wave the bus down.

WǓTÁI SHĀN & TÁIHUÁI
五台山、台怀

Travelling north from Tàiyuán, the loessial plateau gives way to a more ambitious topography of rolling hills. These quickly rise, east of all roads, into the sublime

beauty of **Wǔtái Shān** (Five-Terrace Mountains). One of China's sacred Buddhist mountain ranges, the highest of Wǔtái Shān's five peaks is the 3058m northern Yedou Peak (Yèdǒu Fēng), known as the roof of northern China.

Ensconced deep within an alpine valley here lies Táihuái, a sleepy monastic village with 15 or so old temples and monasteries (another 20 other temples and monasteries dot the surrounding mountainsides). The remoteness of the region spared it the worst of the Cultural Revolution, but don't assume this to mean modern escape – the village itself is overrun with tourists late-April to early October, but even then, wondrous solitude can still be found along trails spiderwebbing into the mountains around Táihuái.

It's now but five hours from either Dàtóng or Tàiyuán on improved roads. October to March temperatures are often below freezing (roads can be impassable), and even in summer the temperature drops rapidly at night.

INFORMATION				TRANSPORT	p401
Bank of China 中国银行	1 D2	Tayuan Temple 塔院寺	10 C2	Bus Station	
CITS 中国国际旅行社	2 D2	Wanfo Temple 万佛寺	11 C2	汽车站	18 B2
Internet Café 网吧	3 D2	Xiantong Temple 显通寺	12 C2	Local Tour Minibuses	
		Youguo Temple 佑国寺	13 B2	一日游中巴站	19 D2
SIGHTS & ACTIVITIES	p400			Public Buses to Dàtóng	
Elfu Temple 惠福寺	4 L1	SLEEPING		大同营汽车站	20 D1
Guangren Temple 广仁寺	5 C2	Fóguó Bīnguǎn 佛国宾馆	14 D1	Public Buses to Tàiyuán	
Longquan Temple 龙泉寺	6 D2	Qíxiángé Bīnguǎn 栖贤阁宾馆	15 B2	太原国营汽车站	21 D2
Luohou Temple 罗侯寺	7 C2	Xiānhé Bīnguǎn 先禾宾馆	16 C2		
Nanshan Temple 南山寺	8 B2			OTHER	
Shuxiang Temple 殊像寺	9 B1	EATING	p400	Guanyin Cave 观音洞	22 B2
		Zhèngxīnlián 净心莲	17 D2		

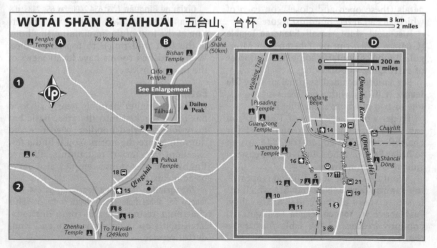

WǓTÁI SHĀN & TÁIHUÁI 五台山、台怀

Information

If you need to reach the PSB for any reason, talk to the owner of the hotel you're staying at.

The Bank of China's (Shijuliangcheng Gonglu) 'foreign exchange' means US dollars. Some of the expensive tourist hotels south of town may exchange cash but generally only for guests.

CITS (☎ 654 3218; Shijuliangcheng Gonglu) Along Qingshui River (Qīngshuǐ Hé) right in Táihuái. The staff arrange tours of the outlying temples. CITS doesn't always have English-speaking guides, so a Chinese tour from Táihuái costs much less (see right).

Internet café (Shijuliangcheng Gonglu; per hr Y3) South of the Bank of China.

Sights

You'd have to either be a devout Buddhist or utterly temple-crazed to take in every temple and monastery in the Wǔtái Shān area. Best bet: just strike off onto one of the many trails snaking into the hills! Temples vary in admission price, Y4 to Y8. All travellers – unless you're a card-carrying Tibetan pilgrim – are charged a Y90 entrance fee for the area, with an optional Y5 insurance fee levied.

Tayuan Temple (Tǎyuàn Sì) with its large, white, bottle-shaped pagoda built during the Ming dynasty is the most prominent temple in Táihuái. **Xiantong Temple** (Xiāntōng Sì) has seven rows of halls, totalling over 400 rooms. **Luohou Temple** (Luóhòu Sì) contains a large wooden lotus flower with eight petals (these open and close!), on each of which sits a carved Buddhist figure.

Just next door, small **Guangren Temple** (Guǎngrén Sì), run by Tibetan and Mongolian monks, contains some fine examples of early Qing woodcarvings.

For a more secluded, spiritual visit, try **Cifu Temple** (Cífú Sì), with a few pleasant monks, one or two of whom speak English.

To get a bird's-eye view of Táihuái, you can make the somewhat strenuous trek (or chairlift cheat, Y31 round-trip, Y16 up) up to **Dailuo Peak** (Dàiluó Dǐng), on the eastern side of Qingshui River.

About 2.5km south of Táihuái is sprawling **Nanshan Temple** (Nánshān Sì), which offers nice views of the Wǔtái Shān valley. Just above it, **Youguo Temple** (Yòuguó Sì) contains frescoes of the fable *Journey to the West*.

Other sights include the marble archway of **Longquan Temple** (Lóngquán Sì) and the 26m-high Buddha and carvings of 500 arhats in **Shuxiang Temple** (Shūxiàng Sì).

In the summer, free Shanxi opera performances are given during the evenings at 7.30pm (and some mornings around 11.30am) at **Wanfo Temple** (Wànfó Sì).

Tours

Privately operated minibuses make half-day and full-day tours (in Chinese) of the outlying temples, departing from a local minibus tour station on Shijuliangcheng Gonglu Lu. For a group of four to six people, this kind of tour costs Y50 per person, but if there is a larger number of tourists taking the same bus you may only have to pay Y40. All leave between 7am and 7.30am.

Sleeping

Lodging options are everywhere! High season (July to August and holidays) rates are given here (knock off 40% otherwise).

Fóguó Bīnguǎn (☎ 654 5962; Zhenjianfang Jie; dm Y30, d with private bath Y80) In a warren of back alleys, this isolated place has a very quiet location and clean rooms. Innumerable similar options (many cheaper) surround it.

Xiānhé Bīnguǎn (☎ 654 2531; 25 Taiping Jie; tw with bath from Y120; 🖳) Spiffy rooms (and bathrooms) and friendly staff make this a solid mid-range choice.

Wǔtái Shān's luxury hotels are several kilometres south of the village.

Qīxiángé Bīnguǎn (☎ 654 2400; fax 654 2183; d & tw from Y380, ste Y898; 🖳) With a peaceful setting at the foot of the mountains, this hotel is the best mid-range to top-end choice. Well-furnished rooms have lovely views of the mountainside.

Eating

Prices are higher here, as nearly all food has to be trucked into the area. Basic but tasty *liángpí*, fried noodles, fried rice and dumplings are the norm. You'll find a few excellent vegetarian restaurants; all have English menus. Some temples also serve basic meals.

Zhèngxīnlián (Pure Lotus Restaurant; ☎ 654 5202; Yanglin Jie; dishes from Y5; 🕑 lunch & dinner) This charming restaurant has some mistranslated items but a copious menu and wonderful service.

Getting There & Away

The nearest train station is 50km away in Shāhé, and minibuses to Wǔtái Shān from there (Y20) are infrequent.

Several early morning buses head to Wǔtái Shān from Dàtóng during summer, departing from the bus station near the train station. The trip, via Húnyuán, Shāhé and over the scenic pass near Yedou Peak, takes five to six hours (Y45). Officials claim ongoing road work will pare this down to a mere 3½ hours.

From Wǔtái Shān, these buses to Dàtóng leave from the northern part of the village three or four times daily, from 6am to 1.30pm. Drivers park in the lot of whatever hotel they've got a working deal with, so you could get on there rather than at the bus stop. Try cajoling your driver to stop off at Hanging Monastery, p404) for 30 minutes en route.

Tàiyuán's main bus station has buses to Wǔtái Shān (Y43, four hours) from 6.30am to around 1pm.

Public buses to Tàiyuán leave from the middle of the village or the bus station; many leave in the morning (Y43, four hours). The Wǔtái Shān bus 'station' some 3km south of the village centre is generally empty.

DÀTÓNG 大同

☎ 0352 / pop 2,696,800

Dàtóng's chief attraction is the magnificent Yungang Caves, carved during the town's zenith as an ancient capital. In the 5th century AD, the Tuoba, a Turkic-speaking people, succeeded in unifying all of northern China and forming the Northern Wei dynasty. Adopting Chinese ways, they saw trade, agriculture and Buddhism flourish. Their capital was Dàtóng. It remained as such until AD 494, when the court moved to Luòyáng.

On arrival, you'll note the forlorn industrial outlying sections: this is coal country. The central area, though, is turning into a pretty lively place, with rows of trying-to-be-chic shops and restaurants surrounding the city's few – but worthy – historical sights.

Orientation

The pivotal point is Red Flag Sq (Hóngqí Guǎngchǎng) at the intersection of Da Xijie and Xinjian Nanlu. The central historic sights (and shops/nightlife) lie inside the crumbling old city walls.

At Dàtóng's northern end is the train station. The main bus station (Xinnan bus station) is far to the south.

Information

Internet access is available for Y2 per hour from cafés just west of the train station along Xinjian Beilu.

Bank of China (Yingbin Xilu) This branch is the only place to change travellers cheques, unless you're staying at Yúngāng Bīnguǎn.

CITS train station (☎ 712 4882; ✦ 6:30am-6:30pm); Yúngāng Bīnguǎn (21 Yingbin Donglu; ☎ 502 1601) Staff arrange discounted hotels, can purchase train tickets and run regular tours (in English and French) of the city and the Yungang Caves. The staff at the train station branch are helpful.

Main post & telephone office (cnr Da Xijie & Xinjian Nanlu) South of Red Flag Sq. Another post office is adjacent to the train station.

PSB (Public Security Bureau; Xinjian Beilu) North of the large department store.

Sights

NINE DRAGON SCREEN 九龙壁

The **Nine Dragon Screen** (Jiǔlóng Bì; Da Dongjie; admission Y3; ✦ 8am-6pm summer, reduced hr rest of year) is one of Dàtóng's several 'dragon screens': tiled walls depicting fire-breathing dragons. It was originally part of the gate of the palace of Ming dynasty emperor Ming Taizhu's 13th son, and is 8m high, over 45m long and 2m thick. Take bus No 4 from the train station to get here.

HUAYAN TEMPLE 华严寺

This monastery/regional **museum** (Huáyán Sì; Xiasipo Xiang; admission in summer Y20, less rest of year; ✦ 8am-6pm summer, reduced hr rest of year) is west of the old city. The original monastery dates back to AD 1140 and the reign of Emperor Tian Ju'an of the Jin dynasty.

Mahavira Hall is one of the largest Buddhist halls in China. The five gilded Ming dynasty Buddhas on lotus thrones are impressive. Around them stand Bodhisattvas, soldiers and mandarins. The ceiling is decorated with restored paintings dating from the Ming and Qing dynasties.

Bojia Jiaocang Hall (Bójiā Jiàocàng Diàn, or Hall for the Conservation of Buddhist Scriptures of the Bojia Order) is smaller but more interesting than the main hall. It contains 29 coloured clay figures made during the Liao dynasty (AD 907–1125).

CENTRAL CHINA

Huayan Temple is about 500m east of the post office at the end of Xiasipo Lane, which runs south off Da Xijie. Bus No 4 from the train station also passes nearby.

SHANHUA TEMPLE 善化寺

Built during the Tang dynasty, this **temple** (Shànhuà Sì; Nansi Jie; admission in summer Y30, less rest of year; 🕑 8.30am-6pm summer, fluctuating hr rest of year) was destroyed by fire during a war at the end of the Liao dynasty.

In AD 1128 more than 80 halls and pavilions were rebuilt; further restoration was done during the Ming dynasty. The main hall contains statues of 33 divine generals and nearly 200 murals. There is a small dragon screen within the monastery grounds.

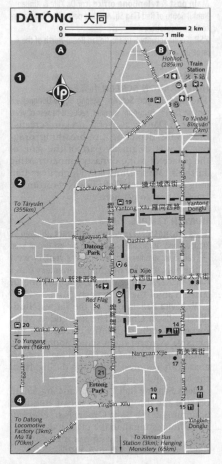

DATONG LOCOMOTIVE FACTORY
大同机车厂

This **factory** (Dàtóng Jīchē Chǎng) on the southwestern outskirts was the last in China to make the 'iron rooster' steam engines. In 2004, the factory's collection of old rail memorabilia was shipped to Beijing, but it's worth inquiring at CITS if you can arrange a group to see the diesel engines made now. Groups are the only way to see the place, if at all.

Sleeping

Booking through CITS at the train station shaves a few *yuán* off mid-range rooms.

Fēitiān Bīnguǎn (☎ 281 5117; Chezhan Qianjie; dm Y45, tw with bathroom Y180-220; 🖭) Your lowest price budget and mid-range option is this stand-by. If you book through CITS you can get a discount on a standard room – they're fine but unremarkable.

Hóngqí Dàfàndiàn (☎ 281 6813; fax 281 6671; Huochezhan Bei; tw incl breakfast from Y290; 🖭) In 2004 heavy renovation upped this hotel to three-star status. Furnishings and amenities are all very well kept (carpets shampooed daily!) and floor attendants are solicitous.

Yànběi Bīnguǎn (☎ 602 4116; fax 602 7287; 1 Yuhe Beilu; tw from Y300; ☒) This clean and modern place is about 2km southeast of the train station (a 20-minute walk). Isolated, it's quieter than the hotels near the train station. Definitely bargain.

Dàtóng Bīnguǎn (☎ 203 2476; fax 203 2288; 37 Yingbin Xilu; d & tw from Y460; ☒) A four-star leviathan after a 2003 renovation, this is the city's most well-run hotel. Rooms are fresh and small balconies overlook park-like grounds.

Eating & Drinking

Yŏnghé Dàjiǔdiàn (☎ 204 7999; Nanguan Nanjie; mains from Y15; ☽ lunch & dinner) Dàtóng's locals regard this to be the best restaurant in Shānxī (and it has an English menu!). Lunch and dinner crowds provide a glimpse of Dàtóng's upper crust.

Yŏnghé Hóngqí Měishíchéng (☎ 510 1555; 3 Yingbin Donglu; dishes from Y15; ☽ lunch & dinner) Run by the Yŏnghé Dàjiǔdiàn, this eatery also sports an English menu. The decor is glitzy and the prices are fairly stratospheric but it's a good place for a splurge.

Yúngāng Bīnguǎn (21 Yingbin Donglu; ☎ 502 1601; dishes from Y15; ☽ breakfast, lunch & dinner) This hotel's three restaurants get high praise for meticulously created fare and superb service.

Habitat (Xinjian Nanlu; meals from Y20, ☽ lunch & dinner) This expat-filled pub is a welcome place to unwind and indulge in infrequently found pub grub.

Getting There & Away

AIR

Dàtóng's airport was supposed to be ready for business as of 2004, but even CAAC (and hotel) staff were still claiming that the city had no airport. Locals will think you daft for even asking, as trains and buses are much more practical.

BUS

Dàtóng now has three bus stations: the old (or north) station, near the train station; the regional station on Yantong Xilu; and the newest, Xinnan Bus Station (Xīnnán Zhàn), about 5km south of Red Flag Sq on Xinjian Nanlu (bus No 30 runs from here to the train station along Xinjian Lu).

Basically, everything you need leaves from Xinnan Bus Station (and express buses

drop you here), though the old station does have buses to Wǔtái Shān (Y43, five hours) and a few slower ones to Tàiyuán.

Buses to Hohhot in Inner Mongolia (Y55, 3½ to four hours) leave *only* from the old station (and sometimes the train station square), not Xinnan Bus Station.

Daily regular and express buses to Tàiyuán leave Xinnan Bus Station; a few leave the old station. About a half-dozen per day depart from 6.30am to early afternoon. Slower minibuses take five to six hours (Y50); express air-con buses take four hours (Y80).

For information on how to get to Wǔtái Shān, see p401.

TRAIN

A train line northeast to Běijīng and a northern line to Inner and Outer Mongolia meet in a Y-junction at Dàtóng. Trans-Siberian trains via Ulaanbaatar in Mongolia come through here. It is possible to do Dàtóng as a day trip from Běijīng using night trains coming and going, but you can never be guaranteed of getting a berth, even going through CITS.

There are daily express trains to Běijīng (5½ to nine hours), Lánzhōu (24 hours), Hohhot (four to seven hours), and Tàiyuán (seven to eight hours). Only one train to Hohhot originates in Dàtóng, so it's possible to reserve tickets; the problem is it's an achingly slow local train and other trains are virtually always booked out.

Tickets can be hard to get for all trains not originating in Dàtóng. If you want to buy sleeper or advance tickets try the office just south of the main ticket building or the **advance booking office** (cnr Nanguan Nanjie & Nanguan Xijie). Failing that, contact the staff at CITS who might be able to get you a ticket: they charge a Y40 commission per hard-sleeper berth.

AROUND DÀTÓNG

Yungang Caves 云岗石窟

These **caves** (Cloud Ridge Caves; Yúngāng Shíkū; admission in summer Y80, less rest of year; ☽ 8.30am-5.30pm) are the main reason most people make it to Dàtóng; no one leaves unwowed. The caves are cut into the southern cliffs of Wǔzhōu Shān, 16km west of Dàtóng, next to the pass leading to Inner Mongolia. The caves contain over 50,000 Buddhist statues and stretch for about 1km east to west. Those numbers alone are enough to impress.

Atop the overlooking cliffs are the remains of a huge, mud brick 17th-century Qing dynasty fortress. Truncated pyramids were once the watchtowers. Sadly, many of the caves suffer damage from coal and other pollution, largely a result of the neighbouring coal mine (new access roads divert coal trucks now). East of the caves you can walk to a remnant of the Great Wall (see right). No guides are available, but decent English descriptions are found in most caves. For details, see Bodhisattvas, Dragons & Celestial Beings, below.

Bus No 3 (Y1.5) from the terminal at Xīnkāilǐ, on the western edge of Dàtóng, goes past the Yungang Caves. You can get to Xīnkāilǐ on bus No 4 from the train station or bus No 17 from opposite the main Bank of China (both Y1). From Xīnkāilǐ it's about a 25-minute ride to the caves.

Many travellers take a CITS tour (see p401) out to the caves, which costs Y100 per person (minimum of five people). The tour also includes the Hanging Monastery and a visit to some local cave dwellings and possibly remnants of the Great Wall.

Great Wall

Dàtóng lies between an inner and outer section of the Great Wall. The inner lies 100km east, near the Hanging Temple. The outer wall here parallels Shānxī's border with Inner Mongolia. It predates the much better-known Great Wall sites near Beijing. To get there, walk approximately 15 minutes east of the Yungang Caves entrance. You can't miss it, sitting forlornly, if still imposingly, in a field. Nobody seems to mind if you stroll about. A real treat: a solitary experience along the Great Wall.

Hanging Monastery 悬空寺

This **monastery** (Xuánkōng Sì; ☎ 832 2142; admission in summer Y36, less rest of year; ☿ 7am-7pm summer, reduced hr rest of year) is just 5km outside the town of Húnyuán, 75km southeast of

---

BODHISATTVAS, DRAGONS & CELESTIAL BEINGS

Here near Dàtóng are some of the oldest and finest examples of stone sculpture in China. Most of the Yungang Caves (p403; likely modelled on the terracotta Mogao Caves at Dūnhuáng in Gānsù) were carved into ridges of sandstone during the Northern Wei dynasty between AD 460 and 494; work continued in fits and starts during the Liao dynasty (11th and 12th centuries) and up through the Qing dynasty.

Various foreign influences can be seen in the caves: Persian and Byzantine weapons, Greek tridents, and images of the Indian Hindu gods Vishnu and Shiva. The Chinese style is reflected in the robust Bodhisattvas (one worthy of nirvana but who remains on earth to help others attain enlightenment), dragons and flying apsaras (celestial beings rather like angels).

From east to west the caves fall into three major groups, although their numbering has little to do with the order in which they were constructed. Highlights of Caves 1–4 are intricately chiselled pagodas and, in capacious Cave 3, a seated Buddha flanked by two Bodhisattvas.

Yúngāng art is at its best in Caves 5–13. Cave 5's colossal and famed seated Buddha is an astonishing work over 17m high (cave 13 later on has a 15m-high Buddha statue). In cave 6 get a gander at a two-storey pagoda-pillar about 15m high with images of the Maitreya Buddha (Future Buddha). Gautama Buddha's life story from birth to his attainment of nirvana is carved throughout Cave 6. Hindu influences appear in caves 7 and 8. Shiva, with eight arms and three heads and seated on a bull, is book-ended by a multifaced Indra, perched on a peacock. Caves 9, 10 and 12 are notable for their front pillars and figures bearing musical instruments.

The Buddha in each of caves 16–20 represents a Northern Wei emperor. In cave 18 find Emperor Taiwu, once a great patron of Buddhism, but later empathising with Taoism. After a revolt that he blamed on the Buddhists, Taiwu ordered the destruction of Buddhist statues, monasteries and temples, and the persecution of Buddhists. This lasted from AD 446 to 452, when Taiwu was murdered. His son is said to have died of a broken heart, having been unable to prevent his father's atrocities, and was posthumously awarded the title of emperor. Taiwu's grandson (and successor) Emperor Wencheng, who restored Buddhism to the dynasty, is represented by the 14m-high seated Buddha of cave 20.

Dàtóng. Built precariously on sheer cliffs above Jinlong Canyon, the monastery dates back more than 1400 years. Its halls and pavilions were built along the contours of the cliff face using the natural hollows and outcrops. The buildings are connected by corridors, bridges and boardwalks and contain bronze, iron and stone statues of gods and buddhas, most notably the Three Religions Hall where Buddha, Laotzu and Confucius sit side by side.

The CITS tour to the Yungang Caves will include the Hanging Monastery. Chinese 'tours' costing Y35 and taking four to five hours leave from opposite Dàtóng's old bus station but beware that some unscrupulous drivers may just try to drop you in Húnyuán.

You can also take a public or private bus from Dàtóng to Húnyuán. Public buses to Húnyuán leave from the old bus station around 7am, take two hours and cost Y8. When they're full, private minibuses leave from near the bus station and cost the same, or whatever the driver can get. A taxi from Húnyuán to the monastery costs Y30

return. The last bus back to Dàtóng from Húnyuán leaves at around 4pm. Another option is the bus to Wǔtái Shān, which goes directly past the monastery and may stop for half an hour (not likely). Getting back to Dàtóng is usually simple, but not as many buses run to Wǔtái Shān.

Mù Tǎ 木塔

This 11th-century **Wooden Pagoda** (admission Y36) at Yìngxiàn, 70km south of Dàtóng, is one of the planet's oldest wooden buildings. Not a single nail was used in the construction of the nine-storey, 97m-high structure. In 2001 a yet-unfinished US$1 million renovation project was undertaken to relieve damage done by earthquakes and problems from internal weight.

It's possible to travel here from the Hanging Monastery, then head to Wǔtái Shān the next morning. Yìngxiàn has a couple of decent hotels.

Tours of the Hanging Monastery sometimes include Mù Tǎ. You can also get there by taking a minibus from near the old bus station in Dàtóng (Y10 to Y14, two hours).

Shaanxi (Shǎnxī) 陕西

CONTENTS

HIGHLIGHTS

- Meander among the mysterious and imposing **Army of Terracotta Warriors** (p418), an unforgettable experience
- Visit the understated but enthralling newly discovered **Tomb of Han Jing** (p419), a Taoist-influenced emperor who lived modestly and ruled with a gentle fist
- Stroll around Xī'ān's **Muslim quarter** (p412), alleys with extant architecture, wonderful food and a beautiful mosque
- Struggle up one of China's sacred mountains **Huá Shān** (p421) in the pitch-black night to see the jaw-droppingly gorgeous sunrise
- Poke around the **caves** (p423) of Yán'ān, where Mao and cohorts planned a revolution (and possibly nap on a party official's old bed!)

Yán'ān ★

Tomb of Han Jing ★
Xī'ān ★★ ★ Huá Shān
Army of Terracotta Warriors

■ POP: 38.3 MIL	■ AREA: 205,000 SQ KM

Shaanxi *is* Chinese history, ancient and modern. Peruse any text on China and the pages for this province are laden with the words 'centre', 'nucleus' and 'heart', not to mention the ubiquitous 'cradle'.

Wei River (Wèi Hé), a branch of the Yellow River, lazily slices through central Shaanxi, paralleling the Qinling Mountains (the biggest mountain range in the province). This fertile belt became the 'centre' of Chinese civilisation. Sloping away from the mountains to the north is the magnificent (if arid) Loess Plateau, riven with gullies and preternatural stone formations. One of the oldest settled regions of China, northern Shaanxi has revealed human habitation – unearthed from the desiccated, windblown loess soil bit by bit – dating back to prehistoric times.

History pushed and pulled here as eastern China was slowly and forcibly cobbled together into the country's first great dynastic entity, the Qin (one of many dynasties to call the province home), and the country literally touched the world.

For travellers, what matters most is that the Shaanxi province is absolutely loaded with extraordinary archaeological sights – mostly near the city of Xī'ān, one of the top tourist destinations in the country. (A mind-staggering 35,000-plus – not a misprint – historical sites pockmark the province!) Yet keep in mind that history didn't stop with ancient dynasties. In Yán'ān in 1937 Mao wrested control of the Chinese Communist Party, and for a decade this new haven in the hills became the broadcast centre for revolutionary thought. For those less historically inclined, Huá Shān – with its temperate climate and breathtaking sunrises – is one of China's most sacred mountains.

Some 38 million people live in Shaanxi, mostly in the central and southern regions. Like so much of China, this province is rich in natural resources, particularly coal and oil.

History

Who lies beneath the sands of Shaanxi time? The Zhou people, spreading from their Shaanxi homeland, conquered the Shang and established their dominion over much of northern China. Later, the Qin held sway here, ruling from their capital of Xiányáng near modern-day Xī'ān and forming the first dynasty to rule over all of eastern China. The great Sui and Tang capital of Chāng'ān (Xī'ān) was built there and the province was a crossroads on the trading routes from eastern China to central Asia.

Shaanxi remained the political heart of China until the 9th century. With the migration of the imperial court to pastures further east, Shaanxi's fortunes declined. Rebellions afflicted the territory from 1340 to 1368,

again from 1620 to 1644, and finally in the mid-19th century, when the great Muslim rebellion left tens of thousands of the province's Muslims dead.

Famines have regularly decimated peasant populations, and it was these dismal conditions that provided the communists such willing support in the province (especially in Yán'ān, their base) in the late 1920s and during the subsequent civil war.

Climate

This province can get bloody hot, particularly in the central and western regions; in winter, bitter northwesterly winds laden with microscopic loess soil blow in from the Gobi and cause temperatures to plummet. Only in the province's southwestern and eastern pockets does topography allow for

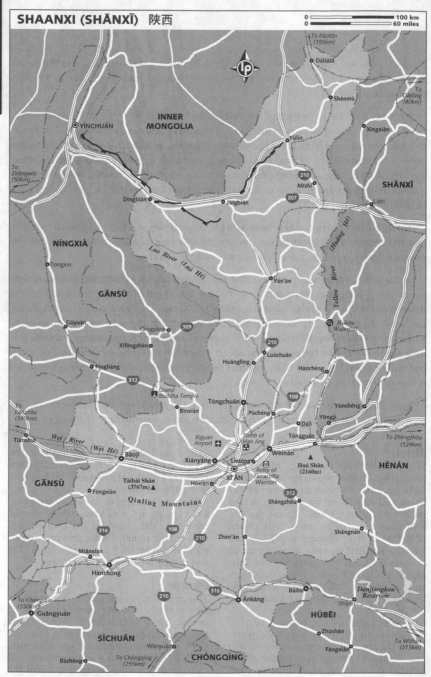

SHAANXI (SHĂNXĪ) 陕西

0 _____ 100 km
0 _____ 60 miles

a rise in elevation and fall in temperatures; the Wei River valleys (around Xī'ān) also keep things a bit variable. Summer monsoon winds deposit most moisture in provinces further southeast, leaving the majority of the province extremely arid (which has helped protect its archaeological treasures). Annual rainfall is a sparse 50cm, most of it falling June through August (deforestation means summer downpours can wreak ecological havoc). Spring and autumn are the best times to come.

Language

You'll not likely notice it, but northeastern Shaanxi has some speakers of Lüliang, a dialect of Jinyu, itself a northern Mandarin dialect (though some call it a separate language), distinctive by its more numerous consonant sounds, particularly at the end of syllables.

Getting There & Around

Xī'ān has one of China's most well-served airports (see p415); a new train station currently being planned for the city will be among the most modern (and, hopefully, efficient) in China. East and west from Xī'ān rail and road connections are quite good (particularly into Shaanxi); however travelling north or south is more problematic.

XĪ'ĀN 西安

☎ 029 / pop 6,620,600

Shaanxi was the centre of Chinese civilisation, and Xī'ān is a magnificent window through which to view it. For more than two millennia, over a dozen dynasties rose and fell in Shaanxi, but always in proximity to this splendid living museum. Two centuries before Homer penned the *Iliad* and the *Odyssey* (and Rome was founded), five centuries prior to the Buddha's enlightenment, Xī'ān was already a classic world city.

Indeed, Xī'ān – the eastern terminus for the epic caravans of the Silk Road(s) – did influence the world outside the Middle Kingdom. Opening China to Central Asia and the Occident, here arrived camels laden with exotic trade goods. Invited Buddhist monks and Islamic emissaries influenced cultural, political and scientific thought. Xī'ān, in short, effected a blossoming of China.

Today Xī'ān is understandably one of China's major tourist attractions. The city's big drawcard is the nearby Army of Terracotta Warriors, and there are countless other sights scattered in and around town. An Islamic element is found throughout the city, with mosques and marketplaces tucked away in back alleys. Consistent with its history, the city's extraordinary ability to change with the times is apparent; travellers cannot help but notice its efficient infrastructure and lack of grit and pollution. In short, past and present are beautifully realised.

Orientation

Xī'ān retains the same rectangular shape that once characterised Chāng'ān, with streets and avenues forming in a neat grid pattern.

The central block of the modern city is bound by the city walls. The centre of town is the enormous Bell Tower, and from here run Xī'ān's four major streets: Bei, Nan, Dong and Xi Dajie. The train station stands at the northeastern edge of the central city block. Jiefang Lu runs south from the station to intersect with Dong Dajie.

Most of the tourist facilities can be found either along or in the vicinity of Jiefang Lu or along Xi Dajie and Dong Dajie. However, many of the city's sights, such as the Shaanxi History Museum, Dàyàn Tǎ and Xiǎoyàn Tǎ, and Banpo Neolithic Village are outside the central block.

Further afield on the plains surrounding Xī'ān are sights such as the Xianying City Museum, Famen Temple, the Tomb of Qin Shi Huang and the Army of Terracotta Warriors near Líntóng.

MAPS

Pick up a copy of the widely available *Xi'an Traffic & Tourist Map*. This bilingual publication has exhaustive listings and is regularly updated – even the bus routes are correct.

Information

EMERGENCY & VISAS

Public Security Bureau (PSB; Gōngānjú; ☎ 8723 4500, ext 51810; 138 Xi Dajie; ☒ 8am-noon & 2-6pm Mon-Fri) A five-minute walk west of the Bell Tower. Visa extensions generally take three days.

INTERNET RESOURCES

www.toureasy.net

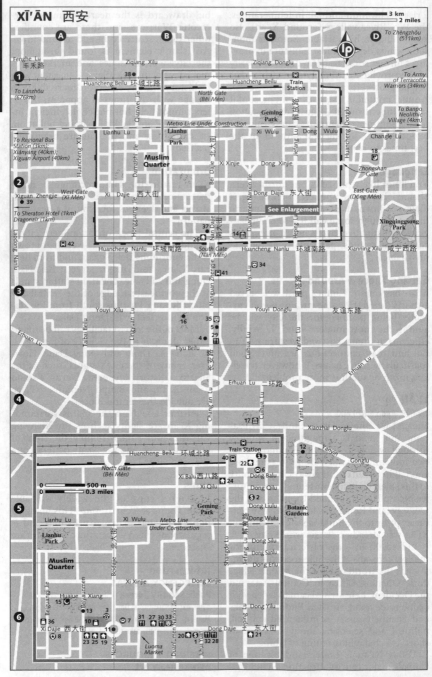

XĪ'ĀN 西安

0 — 3 km
0 — 2 miles

To Zhèngzhōu (511km)

Fenghe Lu 手禾路
Ziqiang Xilu
Ziqiang Donglu

To Lánzhōu (676km)
Huancheng Beilu 环城北路
Huancheng Beilu
Train Station

To Army of Terracotta Warriors (34km)

North Gate (Běi Mén)

Gening Park

To Banpo Neolithic Village (4km)

Metro Line Under Construction

Lianhu Lu
Lianhu Park

Xi Wulu
Dong Wulu

Changle Lu

18

Zhongshan Gate

To Regional Bus Station (3km); Xiányáng (40km); Xiguan Airport (40km)

Muslim Quarter

Bei Dajie 北大街

Xi Xinjie
Dong Xinjie

West Gate (Xī Mén)
Xi Dajie 西大街

Dong Dajie 东大街

East Gate (Dōng Mén)

Xiguan Zhengjie
39

Xingqingsong Park

To Sheraton Hotel (1km)
Dragonair (1km)

See Enlargement

42

37
26
14

Huancheng Nanlu 环城南路
South Gate (Nán Mén)
Huancheng Nanlu 环城南路
Xianning Xilu 咸宁西路

41

34

Youyi Xilu
Youyi Donglu
友谊东路

16
35
5
29

4

Tiyu Beilu

Erhuan Lu

Erhuan Lu 一环路

17

Xiaozhai Donglu

Yanyin

12

Gonglu

Train Station
40
22
9
6

North Gate (Běi Mén)

Xi Balu 西八路
Xi Qilu

24

Dong Balu
Dong Qilu

0 — 500 m
0 — 0.3 miles

2

Dong Liulu

Botanic Gardens

Lianhu Lu
Lianhu Park

Xi Wulu
Metro Line Under Construction

Gening Park

Dong Wulu

Dong Silu
Dong Sanlu
Dong Erlu

Muslim Quarter

Xi Xinjie
Dong Xinjie

Huajue
15
13

3

31 27 30 33
7

Dong Yilu

36
10
11

Xi Dajie 西大街
8
23 25 19

Nandajie

Luoma Market

20
1
32 28

Dong Dajie 东大街

21

MONEY

Bank of China (Zhōngguó Yínháng; 223 Jiefang Lu; 8.30am-noon & 2-5pm Mon-Fri, 9am-3pm Sat & Sun); branch office (Dong Dajie; 8.30am-noon & 2-5pm Mon-Fri, 9am-3pm Sat & Sun) At the branch office, foreigners can change cash and travellers cheques as well as use foreign credit/debit cards in the ATMs.

POST & COMMUNICATIONS

There are a host of Internet bars (around Y3 per hour) along Dong Dajie just east of the YMCA Hotel.

China Telecom (Zhōnglóu Guǎngchǎng) Next to the Bell Tower Square and opposite the post office.

Post office (Beidajie; 8.30am-8pm) Another post and telephone office (Dong Balu) is opposite the train station.

TOURIST INFORMATION

Xi'an Tourist Information Services Centre (8745 5043; Jiefang Lu; 7.30am-8pm) In front of the train station; this centre offers advice on bus routes and accommodation, and also runs daily Eastern and Western tours (see p417).

TRAVEL AGENCIES

China International Travel Service (CITS; Zhōngguó Guójì Lǚxíngshè; 8524 1864, 8539 9999; www.citsxa .com in Chinese) main office (Chang'an Lu); branch office (2nd fl, Bell Tower Hotel, Xi Dajie); branch office (8742 2227; Jiěfàng Fàndiàn, 321 Jiefang Lu) All branches mainly organise tours.

China Travel Service (CTS; Zhōngguó Lǚxíngshè) main office (8526 1760, 8322 3522; 63 Chang'an Lu); branch office (8725 9693; YMCA Hotel, 339 Dong Dajie) An ever-helpful travel company. Any of the lodging options

listed (p413) also have travel information and services. The Lǚdǎo Bīnguǎn is hard to beat.

Golden Bridge Travel (8725 7975, fax 8725 8863; 2nd fl, Bell Tower Hotel) This is a popular choice. The staff work very hard and get good reviews; keep in mind it is a private business and not a city information office.

Sights

BELL TOWER 钟楼

This **tower** (Zhōng Lóu; admission Y15; 7.30am-7pm summer, hrs vary other seasons) is a huge building in the centre of Xī'ān that is entered through an underpass on its north side. Dating from the 14th century, it was rebuilt by the Qing at the present location in 1739. Musical performances are held inside the tower every afternoon and most mornings.

DRUM TOWER 鼓楼

This **tower** (Gǔ Lóu; Beiyuanmen; admission Y12; 8am-7pm) is a smaller building to the west of the Bell Tower, and marks the Muslim quarter of Xī'ān. Beiyuanmen is an interesting restored street of traders and craftspeople that runs directly north from the Drum Tower. It's a good spot to see traditional artists and musicians at work.

CITY WALLS 城墙

Xī'ān is one of the few cities in China where old **city walls** (Chéngqiáng; admission Y12; 8am-10pm) are still visible. The walls were built on the foundations of the walls of the Tang Forbidden City during the reign of Hongwu, first emperor of the Ming dynasty.

The walls form a rectangle with a circumference of 14km. On each side is a gateway, and over each gateway stand three towers. At each of the four corners is a watchtower, and the top of each wall is punctuated with defensive towers. The walls are 12m high, with a width at the top of 12m to 14m and at the base of 15m to 18m.

Most sections have been restored or rebuilt, but others have disappeared completely (although they're still shown on the maps) after centuries of use as air-raid shelters or warehouses, so unfortunately you can't walk right around Xī'ān along the city walls.

There are a number of access ramps up to the walls, some of which are located just east of the train station, near Heping Lu, and at the South Gate (Nán Mén) beside the Forest of Stelae Museum. Note that as of 2004, the city government was working out an intriguing plan to reconstruct segments and connect all the walls, allowing for a circumnavigation of the downtown area.

BIG GOOSE PAGODA 大雁塔

This **pagoda** (Dàyàn Tǎ; ☎ 8521 5014, Yanta Lu; admission Y21, plus Y5 to climb the pagoda; ☷ 8.30am-7pm summer, hrs vary other seasons) stands in the former Temple of Great Maternal Grace in the south of Xī'ān. The temple was built by Emperor Gaozong (Tang dynasty) around AD 648, when he was still crown prince in memory of his deceased mother. The Ming-style buildings that stand today date from the Qing dynasty.

The original pagoda was built in AD 652 with only five storeys, but it has been renovated, restored and added to many times – now rising 64 climbable metres. It was built to house the Buddhist scriptures brought back from India by the travelling monk Xuan Zang, who then set about translating them into 1335 Chinese volumes.

Take bus No 41 or 610 from the train station; bus No 609 goes there from the South Gate.

The **Tang Dynasty Arts Museum** (Tángdài Yìshù Bówùguǎn; ☎ 8524 2894; admission Y15; ☷ 8.30am-5.30pm), on the eastern side of the temple, has a collection specifically devoted to the Tang period in Xī'ān.

LITTLE GOOSE PAGODA 小雁塔

This **pagoda** (Xiǎoyàn Tǎ; Youyi Xilu; admission Y10; ☷ 8.30am-5pm) is in the pleasant grounds of Jianfu Temple (Jiànfú Sì). The top of the pagoda was shaken off by an earthquake in the middle of the 16th century, but the rest of the 43m-high structure is intact.

Jiànfú Sì was originally built in AD 684 as a site to hold prayers to bless the afterlife of the late Emperor Gaozong. The pagoda, a rather delicate building of 15 progressively smaller tiers, was built from AD 707 to 709 and housed Buddhist scriptures brought back from India by another pilgrim. You can climb to the top of the pagoda for a worthy panorama of Xī'ān.

Bus No 610 runs from the train station to the Bell Tower then down Nanguang Zhengjie; bus No 203 goes there from the South Gate.

GREAT MOSQUE 大清真寺

This **mosque** (Dàqīngzhēn Sì; ☎ 8727 2541; Huajue Xiang; admission Y15; ☷ 8am-8.30pm summer, hrs vary other seasons) is one of the largest in China. The present buildings only date back to the mid-18th century, though the mosque might have been established several hundred years earlier.

The mosque is built in a Chinese architectural style with most of the grounds taken up by gardens. Still an active place of worship, it holds several prayer services each day.

The courtyard of the mosque can be visited, but only Muslims may enter the prayer hall.

The mosque is a five-minute walk from the Drum Tower: go under the arch, then take the second tiny lane leading left to a small side street. From here the mosque is a few steps to the right past a gauntlet of souvenir shops.

MUSLIM QUARTER

The backstreets to the north and west of the Great Mosque have been home to the city's Hui community for centuries.

Walking through the narrow laneways lined with old mud brick houses, you pass butcher shops, sesame oil factories, smaller mosques hidden behind enormous wooden doors and proud, stringy-bearded men wearing white skullcaps. Good streets to explore are Nanyuan Men, Huajue Xiang and Damaishi Jie, which runs north off Xi Dajie through an interesting Islamic food market (p415).

SHAANXI HISTORY MUSEUM
陕西历史博物馆

Built in huge (70,000 sq m), classical Tang style, this **museum** (Shǎnxī Lìshǐ Bówùguǎn; ☎ 8525 4727; 90 Xiaozhai Donglu; adult/student Y35/15; ⏱ 8.30am-5.30pm) is one of the best museums in China. The collection – some 400,000 pieces in holdings and displays – is chronologically arranged and includes many objects that have never been on permanent display before. (Do take walking shoes!)

The ground floor deals with China's prehistory and the early dynastic period. Particularly impressive are several enormous Shang and Western Zhou dynasty bronze cooking tripods, Qin burial objects, bronze arrows and crossbows, and four original terracotta warrior statues taken from near the Tomb of Qin Shi Huang.

Upstairs, the second section is devoted to Han, Western Wei and Northern Zhou dynasty relics.

The third section has mainly artefacts from the Sui, Tang, Ming and Qing dynasties. The major advances in ceramic-making techniques during this period are most evident, with intricately crafted terracotta horses and camels, fine pale-green glazed misi pottery and Buddhist-inspired Tang dynasty statues.

Photography is allowed but you must deposit (free of charge) any hand luggage in the lockers provided. English guided tours are available for Y60 (or free in winter), although most exhibits include labels and explanations in English. Take bus Nos 5, 610 or 14 from the train station to get here or bus No 701 from the South Gate.

FOREST OF STELES MUSEUM 碑林博物馆

Once the Temple of Confucius, this **museum** (Bēilín Bówùguǎn; ☎ 8721 3868, Shuyuanmen; admission Y30; ⏱ 8am-6pm) houses a fine collection devoted largely to the history of the Silk Road.

One of the more extraordinary exhibits is the **Forest of Steles** (Bēilín), the heaviest collection of books in the world. The earliest of these 2300 large engraved stone tablets dates from the Han dynasty.

Most interesting is the popular Stele of Daiqin Nestorianism, which can be recognised by the small cross at the top, engraved in AD 781 to mark the opening of a Nestorian church. The Nestorians were an early Christian sect who differed from orthodox Christianity in their belief that Christ's human and divine natures were quite distinct.

Other tablets include the Ming De Shou Ji Stele, which records the peasant uprising led by Li Zhicheng against the Ming, and the 114 Stone Classics of Kaichen, from the Tang dynasty, inscribed with 13 ancient classics and historical records.

All of the museum's important exhibits have labels in English, or you can pay Y100 for an English guide. The museum entrance is on a side street that runs west off Baishulin Lu, close to the South Gate of the old city wall.

TEMPLE OF THE EIGHT IMMORTALS
八仙庵

This is Xī'ān's largest Taoist **establishment** (Bāxiān Ān; Yongle Lu; admission Y3; ⏱ 8am-5pm) and an active place of worship, purportedly on the site of an ancient wine shop. The temple was later constructed to protect against subterranean divine thunder. Scenes from Taoist mythology are painted around the temple courtyard; artisans were touching up many on a recent visit.

To get there take bus Nos 10, 11, 28 or 42 east along Changle Lu and get off two stops past the city walls, then continue 100m on foot and turn right (south) under a green-painted iron gateway into a market lane. Follow this, turning briefly right then left again into another small street leading past the temple. You can also reach the temple by following the street running directly east from Zhōngshān Gate (Zhōngshān Mén). Bus No 502 runs to the temple from the South Gate.

Sleeping
BUDGET

In one edition, Xī'ān has gone from a sad dearth of budget lodging to a major surplus of fine choices. Hurrah!

Lüdaǒ Bīnguǎn (☎ 8742 0308, ☎ /fax 8210 1222; 80 Xi Balu; dm Y20-35, d/tw Y138-188; ❄ 🖳) This super hotel, five minutes from the train/bus stations is the new budget lodging of choice, managed by the irrepressibly cheery manager, coincidentally named Jim Beam. The rooms – dorms with two to six beds, singles/doubles/triples with private bathroom and powerful air-con (and hot/cold drinking water units) – are well-kept. Travellers with kids have two 'family rooms' to choose from. Extras like self-service laundry are nice; Internet hook-up and bicycle rentals should be ready by the time you read this. Pickup from the train station (free) and airport (Y25) are guaranteed. Ticket booking is a major plus; expect dirt-cheap plane tickets (but not miracles with next-day train tickets). Highlight: Jim Beam can arrange Tibet visas and tours quickly. He's even got an in with the visa office of the PSB!

Shuyuan Youth Hostel (Shūyuàn Qīngnián Lüvshè; ☎ 8728 7720, 8728 7721; tm4wd@163.net; Xi Nanmen; dm Y25-50; d with private bathroom Y160; ✖ 🖳) This HI hostel is also well-located just 20m west of the South Gate. Built around the courtyard of the old county government buildings, it has cramped but clean dorm rooms (the rooms with private bathroom are not worth the money) and iffy plumbing, but is a great place to hang with other travellers. Myriad tours and travel services are offered. To get here, take bus No 603 from opposite the train station on Jiefang Lu.

MID-RANGE
Jiēfàng Fàndiàn (☎ 8769 8881 or 8769 8882; www .jiefanghotel.com; 321 Jiefang Lu; d & tw Y220-320, tr Y280; ✖) Diagonally across the wide square to your left as you leave the train station, this hotel is conveniently located and well-run. Take a look at a few rooms – some of the most inexpensive doubles are actually quite spacious and in pretty good shape, considering the huge guest turnover. Discounts are generally possible and travel offices here have been good.

YMCA Hotel (Qīngniánhuì Bīnguǎn; ☎ 8767 3002; 339 Dong Dajie; tw/ste Y298/488; ✖) Down a lane off Dong Dajie, the YMCA has generally solicitous staff and rooms are well maintained but its best drawcard is its central but quiet location. Rates include breakfast. Some unadvertised dirt-cheap singles/doubles are very clean but tiny and windowless.

Lìjīng Jiǔdiàn (☎ /fax 8728 8731; 6 Xi Dajie; s/tw US$48; ✖) Opposite the Bell Tower Square, this hotel is also very central. Singles are small and twins are comfy if a tad worn. If you need a place to unwind from the noise and pollution, it has a very pleasant tea garden on the 4th floor.

Melody Hotel (Měilún Jiǔdiàn; ☎ 8728 8888; fax 8727 3601; 86 Xi Dajie; s & d & tw Y400-600; ✖) Opened in 2001, this great mid-range choice remains fresh and service has yet to show any signs of losing its initial exuberance! An exercise room, restaurant and bar are also on site.

TOP END
This is the category most Xī'ān hotels aim for, and there are dozens of choices. Following are some that stand out from the crowd.

Bell Tower Hotel (Zhōnglóu Fàndiàn; ☎ 8727 9200; bthotel@pub.xaonline.com; Xi Dajie; d/tw Y748, ste Y1190; ✖) The prize for best position among Xī'ān's hotels has to go to the Bell Tower. Managed by the Holiday Inn group, this hotel is among the more reasonably priced top-end choices. The service and amenities don't match the Hyatt or other luxury hotels, but the entire complex was exhaustively redone in 2003 and facilities sparkle.

Hyatt Regency Xi'an (Kǎiyuè Fàndiàn; ☎ 8723 1234; www.hyatt.com; 156 Dong Dajie; standard/luxury tw Y1320/2320, plus 15% service charge; ✖ 🖳) For location *and* luxury you can't beat the Hyatt Regency. Its services and facilities – an exhaustive laundry list of amenities – have garnered it a five-star rating, and it's just a few minutes' walk to Xī'ān's restaurant and nightlife scene. The regency club rooms are better equipped for business travellers.

Hotel Royal Xi'an (Xī'ān Huángchéng Bīnguǎn; ☎ 8723 5311; www.royalxa.com; 334 Dong Dajie; tw/ste US$100/210; ✖ 🖳) Enjoying a fine location, and a bit cheaper than the Hyatt, is the four-star Hotel Royal, which is a member of Japan's Nikko Hotels group. Room prices are usually discounted, even in summer.

Eating
Hit the streets for fine eating in Xī'ān. Most local street food is of Islamic origin, and some common dishes are *fěnrèròu* (made by frying chopped mutton in a wok with ground wheat), *héletiáo* (dark brown sorghum or buckwheat noodles) and *ròujiāmó* (fried pork or beef in pita bread, sometimes with green peppers and cumin).

Another dish worth tasting is *yángròu pàomó*, a soup dish that involves breaking (or grating) a flat loaf of bread into a bowl and adding a delicious mutton stock. You will first be served a bowl and one or two pieces of flat bread: try and break the bread into tiny chunks, the better to absorb the broth.

Hike around the Bell Tower square and then east along Dong Dajie and you'll find a half-dozen of the city's (and province's) most famed restaurants.

Wǔyī Fàndiàn (☎ 8721 2212; 351 Dong Dajie; dishes Y1-10) This cheap ground-floor restaurant is good for staple northern Chinese food like pork dumplings and hearty bowls of noodles. It's popular with locals and always frenetic and noisy; there's some English on the menu here.

Wāngfǔ Cānyǐn (☎ 8725 0133; 333 Dong Dajie; dishes from Y2) Just to the east, this place is similar to Wǔyī Fàndiàn with its point-and-eat canteen-style food. Head upstairs to the 2nd floor and try some of the specials – mid-range pricing here. The *wāngfǔ zhásūpái* (home-style ribs), *xiāngjiān yínxuěyú* (fish) and *měiwèi páigǔbāo* (rib soup) are all very tasty.

Xī'ān Fànzhuàng (Dong Dajie; dishes from Y5) Four floors of trans-provincial fare are here, with some cheap and tasty options prepared before your eyes, but the sit-down meals are very pricey indeed. Still, another thriving example of *rènaò* (hot and noisy), the way Chinese like it!

Lǎosūnjiā (Dong Dajie; dishes from Y5) This ageing wonder – over a century old – is the best place to sample local lamb dishes. It's one of three branches in town; another one is further east, outside the East Gate. Sit-down meals are pricey, but point-and-choose stations are there for snacking.

Mīmī Jiǎoziguǎn (61 Chang'an Lu; dishes from Y6) Just across the road from CITS, this friendly restaurant serves a good range of tasty dumplings. Two people can eat on Y10 worth of dumplings.

Entertainment

Xī'ān has an increasingly lively nightlife scene. Virtually every month along Dong Dajie, east of the Bell Tower, a new bar or club opens. Remember that these places are never cheap.

1+1 Nightclub (Yījiāyī; 285 Dong Dajie) A very popular nightclub and a long-standing fave that draws large crowds at the weekend.

Tang Dynasty (Táng Yuègōng; ☎ 8526 1633; 75 Chang'an Lu; performance with cocktail Y200, with dinner Y400) One of a few dinner theatre choices in town, this one is an over-the-top spectacle of Broadway-esque costumes, traditional dance, music and singing. Tourists abound

(it's dubbed into English), but it's unforgettable, even at the stiff price.

Shaanxi Song and Dance Theatre (Shǎnxī Gēwǔ Jùyuán; ☎ 8785 3293; 165 Wenyi Lu; dinner & performance Y200, performance only Y125) Much less touristy but no less impressive are the provincial performances by this group.

Shopping

Huajue Xiang is a narrow alley running beside the Great Mosque with many small souvenir and 'antique' shops that are great for browsing. This is one of the best places to pick up souvenirs like name chops or a pair of chiming steel balls. Bargaining is the order of the day.

The **City of God's Temple** (Chénghuáng Miào; Damaishi Jie) is an old-style wooden structure that possibly dates from the early Qing period. It's no longer a temple, but a small wares market that looks like the China of the early 1980s: lots of older consumer goods, some interesting porcelain ware, Chinese musical instruments and calligraphy implements. The temple is a 10-minute walk west of the Drum Tower at the end of a long covered market running north off Xi Dajie. There's no English sign, so look for the large red Chinese characters above the entrance.

Around town you'll also find worthy conversation pieces like carved-stone ink trays used in Chinese calligraphy, and a wide range of jade products from earrings to cigarette holders. There are plenty of silks too, but you're probably better off buying these closer to their source (Sūzhōu, Shànghǎi etc). Most travellers (and not few locals) find a pleasant variety of shops along the small streets between the South Gate and the Forest of Steles Museum.

If you're interested in Chinese and Buddhist classical music, there's a good selection at Little Goose Pagoda (p412). The main streets of central Xī'ān are now home to ultra-chic fashion boutiques (and the inevitable mobile phone dealers); not exactly culturally relevant, but intense competition makes for some great sale prices.

Getting There & Away
AIR
Xī'ān's Xiguan airport is one of China's best-connected – you can fly to almost any major Chinese destination from here, as well as several international ones.

China Northwest Airlines (☎ 8870 2299; Xiguan Zhengjie & Laodong Nanlu; ☑ 8am-9pm) runs most flights to and from Xī'ān. It is also somewhat inconveniently located, 1.5km from the West Gate (Xī Mén). Daily flights include Běijīng (Y1050), Chéngdū (Y630), Guǎngzhōu (Y1490) and Shànghǎi (Y1260).

There are numerous other outlets around town, as well as at most hotels, which normally sell plane tickets and are more centrally located. Shop around, as travel agents almost always have good deals going.

On the international front, there are flights to Hong Kong for around HK$2170 with both China Northwest and **Dragonair** (☎ 8426 9288; Sheraton Hotel, 262 Fenghao Donglu). China Northwest Airlines also has flights to Macau, Seoul, Bangkok, and to Nagoya, Fukuoka, Niigata and Hiroshima in Japan. New international destinations are being added all the time.

BUS

The most central long-distance bus station is opposite Xī'ān's train station. From here you can get buses to Huá Shān and Yán'ān (Y42 to Y120, six to nine hours, six departures daily), as well as sleeper buses to more distant destinations such as Zhèngzhōu (Y98, 12 hours), Luòyáng (Y69, eight to 10 hours), Tàiyuán (Y128, 12 hours), and Yínchuān (Y110, 15 hours). For these destinations, the ticket sellers may encourage you to try the train station, as even with expressways and air-con buses, it's a long haul.

Local authorities are slowly trying to wean buses to stations on the fringes of the downtown area; you may get referred to these. Xī'ān's west bus station is on Huancheng Nanlu, west of the South Gate; the south bus station is, naturally, south of the South Gate along Nanguan Zhengjie.

For more regional destinations like the Grand Buddha Temple (Dàfó Sì; see p420), there is a regional bus station (chéngxī kèyùnzhàn) several kilometres west of downtown just off Daqing Lu. Bus No 103 from the train station stops a block away, or bus Nos 223, 301 and 210 go right past.

TRAIN

Plans have apparently been finalised for a new train station (not far from the current one); it'll be a long time until it's completed, but construction may start within the life of this edition. Currently, among a zillion other places, there are direct trains from Xī'ān to Běijīng (14 to 18 hours), Chéngdū (16 to 27 hours), Guǎngzhōu (24 hours), Lánzhōu (10 to 13 hours), Qīngdǎo and Shànghǎi (18 to 24 hours), Tàiyuán (nine to 12 hours), Ürümqi (56 hours) and Wǔhàn (15 to 16 hours), Chóngqìng (14 hours) and Nánníng (36 hours), and Kūnmíng (53 hours).

For travellers to Luòyáng and Zhèngzhōu, there is a daytime air-con tourist train that only takes 8½ hours to reach Zhèngzhōu.

Help is hard to find in the ticket hall chaos. Staff insist an English speaker is on duty at most times, but good luck finding them. While you can sometimes get same-day tickets here, you'll likely get hard-seat, if anything at all. Luckily, most lodging operations (budget too) can help, but remember that nobody can work miracles on next-day sleeper tickets to major destinations.

There's an **advance rail booking office** (ICBC Bank, Nandajie) near the South Gate, but it can only guarantee tickets for trains starting from Xī'ān; other ICBC banks also sell tickets but some have refused to serve foreigners for some reason.

Of the two dozen other local ticket outlets, locals recommend the **advance rail ticket office** (187 Huancheng Beilu), on the ground floor of the Dongli Building (Dōnglì Dàshà), ten minutes by foot west of the train station.

CITS and other travel agents can organise tickets with a minimum of fuss, providing you give two or three days' notice. Some travellers have complained about service (and especially price) from travel agencies.

Getting Around

Xī'ān's Xiguan Airport is around 40km northwest of Xī'ān. China Northwest Airlines runs shuttle buses hourly from 5am to 6pm between the airport and its Xī'ān booking centre (Y25, 50 minutes). Thankfully it now offers two additional departure points inside the city walls, one in front of the Melody Hotel and one in front of the Jiěfàng Fàndiàn, opposite the train station. Both run approximately hourly from 6am to 6pm and cost Y25.

Taxis into town charge over Y100 on the meter!

Xī'ān's packed public buses are a pickpocket's paradise, so watch your wallet when you ride them. More comfortable minibuses run on the same routes and charge around Y1 or Y2 for most central destinations.

Local buses go to all the major sights in and around the city, such as Banpo Neolithic Village and the Army of Terracotta Warriors.

Taxis are abundant and reasonably cheap: flag fall is around Y6, although short trips around town are a set Y5.

Bicycle hire is available at most budget lodging options (and a few mid-range ones as well) for around Y1 to Y2 per hour.

AROUND XĪ'ĀN
Tours

One-day tours allow you to see all the sights around Xī'ān more quickly and conveniently than if you arranged one yourself. Itineraries differ somewhat, but there are two basic tours: a Western Tour and an Eastern Tour. There are also Chinese tours that leave from the square in front of the Xī'ān train station, but see advice following.

EASTERN TOUR

The Eastern Tour (Dōngxiàn Yóulǎn) is the most popular as it includes the Army of Terracotta Warriors as well as the Tomb of Qin Shi Huang, Banpo Neolithic Village and Huaqing Pool. See Travel Agencies (p411) for details; asking around can also have good results. Most travel agencies charge Y300 to Y350 for an all-day, all-in

excursion. Many travellers use tours from their hotels or hostels.

CITS offers an Eastern Tour, including lunch, all entry tickets and a visit to Big Goose Pagoda (Dàyàn Tǎ). The coach leaves Xī'ān around 9am and returns by 5pm. An English-speaking guide is provided and you usually get two hours at the terracotta warriors and the Tomb of Qin Shi Huang.

The Xi'an Tourist Information Services Centre has daily Eastern Tours with 10 stops (Y44) that depart from the office at the train station between 7.30am and 8.30am. For a little extra the staff may provide you with an English-speaking guide.

Riskier are local Chinese tours (Y35 to Y40), leaving from kiosks in front of the train station. Travellers have mixed reports about these tours – some have griped mightily about spending just a few minutes at the best spots while being 'forced' to stop at souvenir shops for 'rest breaks'. Others find it an amusing glimpse at local tourist practices.

WESTERN TOUR

The longer Western Tour (Xīxiàn Yóulǎn) includes the Xianyang City Museum, some of the imperial tombs, the Qian Tomb and sometimes also Famen Temple.

It's far less popular than the Eastern Tour and consequently you may have to wait a couple of days for CITS (or any other travel agency or hotel) to organise enough people. Otherwise contact the tourist bureau's office

AROUND XĪ'ĀN 西安地区

at the station, which seems to run the most frequent tours. Its Western Tour visits seven locations and costs Y54. Private minibuses lurking at the train station also offer tours for around Y45, but remember: this can be an extremely long, hot experience if you don't ascertain prices and the itinerary clearly before you get on the bus.

Most of the really interesting sights are outside the city. The two biggest drawcards are the Army of Terracotta Warriors (see the boxed text, below) near the Tomb of Qin Shi Huang, and the Banpo Neolithic Village; a newer attraction is the Tomb of Han Jing, a fascinating contrast to that of Qin Shi Huang.

Tomb of Qin Shi Huang 秦始皇陵

In its time this **tomb** (Qín Shǐhuáng Líng; ☎ 391 2369; admission Y26; ☺ 7am-6pm), guarded by the

---

ARMY OF TERRACOTTA WARRIORS 兵马俑

Ranking up there with the Great Wall and the Forbidden City as one of China's top historical sights, the 2000-year-old **Army of Terracotta Warriors** (Bīngmǎyǒng; ☎ 8391 1961; admission Y85; ☺ 8am-5pm) remains stunningly well preserved: a perpetually vigilant force standing guard over an ancient imperial necropolis. In 1974 peasants digging a well uncovered what turned out to be perhaps the most major archaeological discovery of the 20th century: an underground vault of earth and timber that eventually yielded thousands of life-size terracotta soldiers and their horses in battle formation.

The first underground vault measures about 210m east to west and 60m from north to south. The pit varies in depth from 5m to 7m. Walls were built running east to west at intervals of 3m, forming corridors. In these corridors, on floors laid with grey brick, are arranged the terracotta figures. Pillars and beams once supported a roof.

The 6000 terracotta figures of warriors and horses face east in a rectangular battle array. The vanguard appears to be three rows of 210 crossbow and longbow bearers who stand at the easternmost end of the army. Close behind is the main force of armoured soldiers holding spears, dagger-axes and other long-shaft weapons, accompanied by 35 horse-drawn chariots (the latter, made of wood, have long-since disintegrated). Every figure differs in facial features and expressions.

The archers have bodies and limbs positioned in strict accordance with an ancient book on the art of war. Some speculate that the sculptors used fellow workers, or even themselves, as models for the warriors' faces.

Many of the figures originally held real weapons of the day, and over 10,000 pieces have been sorted to date. Surface treatment made the swords resistant to rust and corrosion, so that after being buried for more than 2000 years they were still sharp. The weapons are now kept in storage, out of public view.

A second vault, excavated in 1976, contained about 1000 figures and a third contained only 68 warriors and one war chariot. Archaeologists believe the warriors discovered so far may be part of an even larger terracotta army still buried around the Tomb of Qin Shi Huang. Excavation of the entire complex and the tomb itself could take decades.

Almost as impressive is a pair of bronze chariots and horses unearthed in 1980 just 20m west of the Tomb of Qin Shi Huang and now housed in the small **Qínyǒng Museum** (Qínyǒng Bówùguǎn), which is within the enclosure of the warriors' site.

Visitors are now permitted to take photos at the site. The admission price includes entry to the vaults and museum, and a documentary on the warriors and excavation. The last admission is around 4.30pm.

You also can't help but experience the world-famous frenetic sales pitches of the souvenir hawkers here; their, er, passionate pursuit of tourist yuán leaves many folks breathless.

You can see the site as part of a tour from Xī'ān (see Tours p417), or it is possible to do it yourself by public bus. From the parking lot just east of the train station take bus No 306 (one way/return Y5/8), which travels via Huaqing Pool. Be wary of private minibuses lurking near these buses; they'll tell you they're going to the warriors but you'll likely get overcharged and spend most of your time at tourist traps along the way.

Terracotta Warriors, must have been one of the grandest mausoleums the world had ever seen.

In the year 246 BC, at the age of 13, Ying Zheng ascended the throne of the state of Qin and assumed the title 'Shi Huang', or First Emperor. One by one he defeated his enemies, until in 221 BC the last of them fell. Qin Shi Huang united the country, and standardised the currency and written script.

On the down side, he acquired a reputation for purges, mass book-burning parties, enforced labour in massive construction projects, and other tyrannical behaviour. His rule lasted until his death in 210 BC. His son and successor was quickly overthrown by the revolt that established the Han dynasty.

Historical accounts describe Qin's tomb as containing palaces filled with precious stones and ingenious defences against intruders. It is said that the artisans who brought it all into being were buried alive within, taking its secrets with them.

Yet basically all there is to see nowadays is a mound. If you are interested, the tomb is about 1.5km west of the Army of Terracotta Warriors. Take bus No 306 from Xī'ān train station.

Tomb of Han Jing 汉阳陵

In the early 1990s, road workers discovered unusual dirt formations while excavating for a new highway 40km west of the Tomb of Qin Shi Huang. What lay underneath stunned archaeologists: the **Tomb of Han Jing** (Hàn Yánglíng; ☎ 371 5373; Y45; ☯ 8.30am-5.30pm). Only recently opened and barely excavated, the tomb is a great contrast to the grandiosity and ferocity of Qin Shi Huang's reign.

Han Jing could not have been more opposite to Qin Shi Huang. He was a pragmatic ruler who preferred to use the Taoist idea of *wuwei* (non-action) to rule; his subjects no doubt adored him for a much less tight-fisted rule – and much lower taxes. His tomb, only partially explored to await more sophisticated excavation methods, also displays a rather strong sense of humility – the terracotta figurines are much smaller and less imposing (but no less grand) than those in the Army of Terracotta Warriors and reveal more about daily life than martial preoccupations.

To get there, take Tour Line 4 buses (Y6) from near the buses to the Terracotta Warriors (in the parking lot just east of the train station); they leave for the tomb at 9am and 2pm, and return at noon and 4.30pm. Take food with you – there's nothing but history there.

Huaqing Pool 华清池

This **pool** (Huáqīng Chí; admission Y30; ☯ 8am-7pm) is 30km east of Xī'ān, at the foot of Lí Shān (Black Horse Mountain). Water from hot springs is funnelled into public bathhouses, which have 60 pools accommodating 400 people.

During the Tang dynasty these natural hot baths were a favoured retreat of emperors and their concubines. Try the museum up the road or take a walk along one of the paths leading up through the forest behind the complex.

A Taoist temple on Lí Shān is dedicated to the 'Old Mother' Nüwa, who created the human race and also patched up cracks in the sky after a catastrophe. To get to Huaqing Pool take bus No 306 from the Xī'ān train station.

Banpo Neolithic Village 半坡博物馆

Officially rated as Xī'ān's number two attraction, surpassed only by the Army of Terracotta Warriors, the **Banpo Neolithic Village** (Bànpō Bówùguǎn; ☎ 353 2482; Y20; ☯ 8am-6.30pm) gets mixed reports.

The best advice is to limit your visit to the Neolithic Village and avoid the adjacent Matriarchal Clan Village, where matriarchs in Neolithic garb, high heels and stockings merely reinforce the feeling that you're in modern, not ancient, China.

Banpo is the earliest example of 'Yangshao culture', named after the village where this culture was first discovered. It appears to have been occupied from 4500 BC until around 3750 BC. As less than a quarter of the site has been excavated, little is really known of the early agrarians; however, of interest is the circumstantial evidence that the culture was strongly matriarchal.

The Banpo ruins are divided into three parts: a pottery-manufacturing area, a residential area and a cemetery. These include the remains of 45 houses or other buildings, over 200 storage cellars, six pottery kilns and 250 graves.

The Eastern Tour (see Tours p417) to the Army of Terracotta Warriors usually includes Banpo Neolithic Village. Otherwise, some buses from town (electric trolley No 105 from the train station, No 15 from the Bell Tower, among others) run past, but you have to ask when to get off.

Grand Buddha Temple 大佛寺

This large **temple** (Dàfó Sì; admission Y8) is quite a distance from Xī'ān, about 115km to the northwest outside Bīnxiàn. However, it is easy to reach on public transport and better still, it opens up a route to the excellent Taoist temples of Kōngdòng Shān in Píngliáng, Gānsù. The main Buddha is 30m high and 34m wide; the grotto's exterior is framed by an impressive three-storey fortress tower. Two other caves house nearly 2000 arhat sculptures, shrines and stelae.

Buses to Bīnxiàn (Y15, three hours) leave from the west bus station in Xī'ān. From Bīnxiàn it's around 7km north to the temple complex; a motorcycle taxi will cost Y10. From the temple it's easy to flag down buses back.

Xiányáng 咸阳

☎ 0910 / pop 976,200

Half an hour's bus ride from Xī'ān is Xiányáng. Its chief attraction is the **Xianyang City Museum** (咸阳市博物馆; Xiányáng Shì Bówùguǎn; ☎ 321 3015; Zhongshan Jie; admission Y20; ❂ 8.30am-5.30pm), which houses a remarkable collection of 3000 half-metre-tall terracotta soldiers and horses, excavated from a Han dynasty tomb in 1965.

To get to the Xianyang City Museum from Xī'ān, take bus No 611 from the train station to the regional bus stop and then jump on any bus to Xiányáng; or, from the regional bus stop, walk south to Daqing Lu to get bus No 59 to Xiányáng. From the bus station, ahead on the left-hand side of the road, you'll see a clock tower; turn right at this intersection and then left at Xining Jie.

The museum is 20 minutes by foot from the bus station on Zhongshan Jie, a continuation of Xining Jie.

Imperial Tombs 皇陵

A large number of lesser-known imperial **tombs** (huáng líng) dot the Guānzhōng plain around Xī'ān. The easiest way to get there is by tour from Xī'ān (see Tours p417).

In these tombs are buried the emperors of numerous dynasties, as well as empresses, concubines, government officials and high-ranking military leaders. Admission to the tombs varies from Y15 to Y35. Most are open 8.30am to 5pm daily (closing later in summer).

ZHAO TOMB 昭陵

This tomb (Zhāo Líng) set the custom of building imperial tombs on mountains, breaking the tradition of building them on the plains with an artificial hill over them. This tomb on Jiǔzong Shān, 70km northwest of Xī'ān, belongs to the second Tang emperor, Taizong, who died in AD 649.

Of the 18 imperial mausoleums on the Guānzhōng plain, this is probably the most representative. With the mountain at the centre, the tomb fans out to the southeast and southwest and contains 167 lesser tombs of the emperor's relatives and high-ranking officials.

Buried in the sacrificial altar of the tomb were six statues known as the 'Six Steeds of Zhaoling', representing the horses that the emperor used during his wars of conquest.

QIAN TOMB 乾陵

This tomb (Qián Líng) is one of the most impressive, 85km northwest of Xī'ān, in Liáng Shān. It's the joint resting place of Tang Emperor Gaozong and his wife, Empress Wu Zetian.

Gaozong died in AD 683, and the following year Empress Wu (once a concubine of Gaozong's father) dethroned her husband's successor, Emperor Zhongzong. She reigned as an all-powerful monarch until her death around AD 705.

The grounds of the imperial tomb boast a number of large stone sculptures of animals and officers of the imperial guard. There are 61 (now headless) statues of the leaders of minority peoples of China and of the representatives of friendly nations who attended the emperor's funeral. The two stelae on the ground each stand more than 6m high. The Wordless Stele (Wúzì Bēi) is a blank tablet; one story goes that it symbolises Empress Wu's absolute power, which she considered inexpressible in words.

Tour Line bus 2 from in front of the Xī'ān train station (Y18, three hours) stops here and at Famen Temple.

PRINCESS YONG TAI'S TOMB 永泰墓

This tomb (Yǒng Tài Mù) features tomb paintings and graceful line engravings on the stone outer coffins.

Yong Tai was a granddaughter of Tang Emperor Gaozong, and the seventh daughter of Emperor Zhongzong. Put to death by Empress Wu in AD 701, she was rehabilitated posthumously by Emperor Zhongzong after he regained power.

PRINCE ZHANG HUAI'S TOMB 章怀墓

Near Princess Yong Tai's Tomb is the tomb of Zhang (Zhāng Huái Mù), the second son of Emperor Gaozong and Empress Wu. For some reason the prince was exiled to Sìchuān in AD 683 and died the following year, aged only 31.

Empress Wu posthumously rehabilitated him. His remains were brought to Xī'ān after Emperor Zhongzong regained power after Empress Wu died. Tomb paintings show horsemen playing polo, but these and other paintings are in a terrible state.

MAO TOMB 茂陵

This tomb (Mào Líng), 40km northwest of Xī'ān, is the resting place of Emperor Wu (who died in 87 BC), the most powerful ruler of the Han dynasty. The cone-shaped mound of rammed earth is almost 47m high, and is the largest of the Han imperial tombs.

It is recorded that the emperor was entombed clad in jade clothes sewn with gold thread and with a jade cicada in his mouth. Apparently buried with him were live animals and an abundance of jewels.

Famen Temple 法门寺

This **temple** (Fǎmén Sì; temple & crypt/museum Y28/32; 🕑 8am-6pm), 115km northwest of Xī'ān, was built during the Eastern Han dynasty in about AD 200. By far this is the highlight west of Xī'ān for many travellers.

In 1981, after torrential rains had weakened the temple's ancient brick structure, the entire western side of the 12-storey pagoda collapsed. The subsequent restoration of the temple produced a sensational discovery. Below the pagoda in a sealed crypt (built during the Tang dynasty to contain four sacred finger bones of Buddha, known as *sarira*) were over 1000 sacrificial objects and royal offerings, including stone-tablet Buddhist scriptures, gold and silver items and some 27,000 coins – all forgotten for over 1000 years.

The best way to visit Famen Temple is to take a Western Tour from Xī'ān (see p417). Some tours don't include the temple so check before you book. Note that the pagoda itself is not open to the public. Tour Line 2 from Xī'ān train station (Y18, three hours) does include the temple, as well as the Qian Tomb.

HUÁ SHĀN 华山

The 2160m-high granite peaks of Huá Shān, 120km east of Xī'ān, tower above the plains to the north, forming one of China's sacred Taoist mountain areas. The tough climb to the top rewards you with stunning views, particularly of the sunrise.

Choose from three ways up the mountain to the **North Peak** (Běi Fēng), the first of five summit peaks. Two of these options start from the eastern base of the mountain, at the cable car terminus. If your legs aren't feeling up to the task, an Austrianbuilt cable car is the easiest route. It can get you to the North Peak in 10 scenic minutes (one way/return Y60/110).

The second option is to work your way to the North Peak under the cable car route. This takes a sweaty two hours; note that two sections of 50m or so are quite literally vertical with nothing but a steel chain to grab onto and tiny chinks cut into the rock for footing.

The third option is the most popular and the one that will leave the most memories, both physically and psychologically. A 6km path leads to the North Peak from the village of Huáshān, at the base of the mountain. It usually takes between three to five hours to reach the North Peak, and another hour or so to get to any one of the others. The first 4km up are pretty easy going, but after that it's all steep stairs, and from the North Peak on to the other summits it's also fairly strenuous. Several narrow and almost vertical 'bottleneck' sections can be dangerous when the route is crowded, particularly under wet or icy conditions.

Then again, the scenery is often sublime; along **Green Dragon Ridge** (Cānglóng Fēng), which connects the North Peak with the **East Peak** (Dōng Fēng), **South Peak** (Nán Fēng) and **West Peak** (Xī Fēng), the way has been cut along a narrow rock ridge with impressive sheer cliffs on either side.

The South Peak is the highest at 2160m, but all three rear peaks afford great views when the weather cooperates.

There is accommodation on the mountain, most of it quite basic and overpriced, but it does allow you to start in the after-

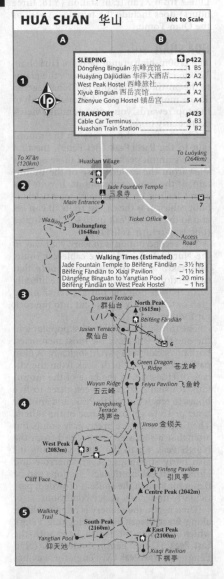

HUÁ SHĀN 华山 Not to Scale

SLEEPING	📖 p422
Dōngfēng Bīnguǎn 东峰宾馆	1 B5
Huáyáng Dàjiǔdiàn 华洋大酒店	2 A2
West Peak Hostel 西峰旅社	3 A4
Xīyuè Bīnguǎn 西岳宾馆	4 A2
Zhenyue Gong Hostel 镇岳宫	5 A4

TRANSPORT	p423
Cable Car Terminus	6 B3
Huashan Train Station	7 B2

To Xī'ān (120km)
Huashan Village
To Luòyáng (264km)
Jade Fountain Temple 三泉寺
Main Entrance
Walking Trail
Dashangfang (1648m)
Ticket Office
Access Road

Walking Times (Estimated)
Jade Fountain Temple to Běifēng Fàndiàn – 3½ hrs
Běifēng Fàndiàn to Xiaqi Pavilion – 1½ hrs
Dāngfēng Bīnguǎn to Yangtian Pool – 20 mins
Běifēng Fàndiàn to West Peak Hostel – 1 hrs

Qunxian Terrace 群仙台
North Peak (1615m)
Běifēng Fàndiàn
Juxian Terrace 聚仙台
Green Dragon Ridge 苍龙峰
Wuyun Ridge 五云峰
Feiyu Pavilion 飞鱼岭
Hongsheng Terrace 鸿声台
Jinsuo 金锁关
West Peak (2083m)
Yinfeng Pavilion 引凤亭
Cliff Face
Centre Peak (2042m)
Walking Trail
South Peak (2160m)
East Peak (2100m)
Yangtian Pool 仰天池
Xiaqi Pavilion 下棋亭

noon, spend the night, and catch the sunrise from either the East Peak or South Peak. Many tourists actually make the climb at night, aided by torches (flashlights) and countless tea and refreshment stands. The idea is to start off at around 11pm to midnight, which should get you to the East Peak at sunrise. In summer this is certainly a much cooler option, but you do miss the scenery on the way up.

The gate ticket price starts at around Y70. **Jade Fountain Temple** (Yùquán Sì; admission Y8) is the first thing you'll pass if you go through the main entrance. This is the first of many spots with separate entrance fees and is the cheapest one!

Sleeping & Eating

Take your own food or eat well before ascending or you're left with instant noodles and processed meat at the top – a proper meal can be eye-poppingly expensive. Don't forget a torch and enough warm clothes. Most hotels on the mountain offer dorms as well as private rooms, but none have their own bathrooms and expect nothing remotely luxurious.

There are also plenty of places to stay – budget and mid-range – in Huáshān village along the road leading up to the trailhead and Jade Fountain Temple.

Zhenyue Gong Hostel (dm Y30-50, tw Y200) This hostel sits in the valley between the rear peaks. It receives the morning sun and is centrally located. Expect to be offered only the private rooms.

West Peak Hostel (Xīfēng Lǚshè; dm/tw Y40/120) This place atop West Peak nearly sparkles. A lack of washing facilities hurts but it was set for renovation at the time of writing. The mid-range hotel above it at the peak is overly pricey but has creature comforts.

Dōngfēng Bīnguǎn (dm/tw Y60/480). Anything near the East Peak – given the sunrise – is going to cost you. Dorms are not good but twins, though expensive, are at least comfy.

Huáyáng Dàjiǔdiàn (☎ 0913-436 6178; q Y20, d with private bathroom Y90; ⚡) This fairly clean place is 100m from the main intersection heading towards the Huá Shān trailhead. The manager speaks some English.

Xīyuè Bīnguǎn (☎ 0913-436 4741; fax 0913-436 4559; tw/tr with air-con & bathroom Y220/320; ⚡) This place is at the main intersection and has more creature comforts than any other place in town.

Getting There & Away

The nearest train station is at Mèngyuán, on the Xī'ān-Luòyáng line, about 15km east of Huáshān. This station is also referred to as Huáshān, and is served by nearly a dozen trains a day in either direction. Trains to and from Xī'ān take two to three hours (hard seat Y31). Infrequent minibuses run between the train station and Huáshān village (Y3, 30 minutes).

There are minibuses (Y10) and motorcycle taxis (Y5) that go directly to the cable car from a separate ticket entrance just east of Huáshān village. It's a lovely hour's walk from the cable car to the ticket entrance; it's all downhill and follows the gurgling river.

From Xī'ān to Huáshān, Tour Line 1 buses (Y20, two hours) depart from just southeast of the train station throughout the day. These don't stop along the way, unlike the private minibuses (2½ hours, at best) that also troll in front of the train station. Tell them if you want to disembark in Huáshān village.

Minibuses to Xī'ān leave when full from around the main intersection or the eastern ticket entrance from 7am to around 5.30pm.

If you are heading east, there are regular buses that pass through Huáshān going to Luòyáng, Ruìchéng and Tàiyuán. The bus station is a few hundred metres west of the main intersection.

YÁN'ĀN 延安

☎ 0911 / pop 117,200

Yán'ān, 350km from Xī'ān in northern Shaanxi, is a small city, but together with Mao's birthplace at Sháoshān it has special significance as a major communist pilgrimage spot.

Between 1936 and 1947 Yán'ān was the headquarters of the fledgling Chinese Communist Party. The Long March from Jiāngxī ended in 1936 when the communists reached the northern Shaanxi town of Wúqí. The following year they moved their base to Yán'ān.

Apart from being home to some of the revolution's historical sites, Yán'ān is a low-key place – not necessarily unattractive but definitely understated. On the way there

from the more heavily populated south, buses or trains roll through variegated, at times challenging, terrain, with crags and ridges rising from the parched loess soil.

Orientation

Yán'ān is intriguingly spread out along a Y-shaped valley formed where the east and west branches of Yan River (Yán Hé) meet. The town centre is clustered around this junction, while the old communist army headquarters is at Yángjiālǐng on the northwestern outskirts of Yán'ān. The train station is at the far southern end of the town, 4.5km from the centre.

Information

Bank of China (Zhōngguó Yínháng, Beiguan Jie; ⊕ 9am-noon & 2.30-5pm) Inconveniently located in the north of town.

Internet bar (Wǎngbā; Zhongxin Jie) Inside the post and telephone office.

Internet café (Wǎngbā; Zhongxin Jie) Next to the Yán'ān Bīnguǎn.

Post and telephone office (Zhongxin Jie)

PSB (Gōngānjú; Zhongxin Jie) This can be found inside Yán'ān Bīnguǎn.

Sights

During their extended stay, the communist leadership moved house quite a bit within Yán'ān. As a result there are numerous former headquarters sites.

One of the most interesting sites is the **Yangjialing Revolution Headquarters Site** (Yángjiālǐng Gémìng Jiùzhǐ; ☎ 211 2671; Zaoyuan Lu; admission Y11; ⊕ 7am-8pm summer, hrs vary other seasons), 3km northwest of the town centre. Here you can see the assembly hall where the first central committee meetings were held, including the 7th national plenum, which formally confirmed Mao as the leader of the party and the revolution.

Nearby are simple **dugouts** built into the loess earth where Mao, Zhu De, Zhou Enlai and other senior communist leaders lived, worked and wrote. Further uphill are **caves** that used to house the secretariat, propaganda and personnel offices.

About 1km southeast is the **Yan'an Revolution Museum** (Yán'ān Gémìng Jiniànguǎn; ☎ 238 2161; Zaoyuan Lu; admission Y15; ⊕ 8am-6pm summer, hrs vary other seasons), which has old uniforms, weaponry, and many photographs and illustrations of the old communist days – even a stuffed white horse which Mao purportedly rode during the Long March. But there are no English signs.

Just a few minutes' walk south is the last site occupied by the communist leadership in Yán'ān, the **Wangjiaping Revolution Headquarters Site** (Wángjiāpíng Gémìng Jiùzhǐ; ☎ 238 2161; Zaoyuan Lu; admission Y12; ◷ 8am-6pm). Of note primarily is the improvement in living standards enjoyed by Mao and top-ranking comrades.

All these sights can be reached by taking bus No 1, which runs from the train station along the road east of the river and then heads up Zaoyuan Lu. Bus No 3 runs along the other side of the river along Zhongxin Jie; get off when it crosses north over the river. Both of these start at the train station. Bus No 8 also passes by all these places and can be caught from Da Bridge.

More accessible from the city is the **Fenghuangshan Revolution Headquarters Site** (Fènghuángshān Gémìng Jiùzhǐ; admission Y9; ◷ 8am-6pm summer, hrs vary other seasons), about 100m north of the post office. This was the first site occupied by the communists after their move to Yán'ān, as reflected by the relatively primitive lodgings of the leading cadres. Someone is often around until 8pm.

Treasure Pagoda (Bǎo Tǎ; admission Y20, plus Y5 to climb pagoda; ◷ 8am-7.30pm), built during the Song dynasty, stands on a prominent hillside southeast of the river junction.

Qīngliáng Shān (☎ 211 2236; admission Y10; ◷ 7am-8pm) is a pleasant hillside park with

some nice trails and a few sights, including **Ten Thousand Buddha Cave** (Wànfó Dòng) dug into the sandstone cliff beside the river. The cave has relatively intact Buddhist statues.

Sleeping & Eating

Technically, only the priciest option below is supposed to take foreigners, yet not many places had qualms about letting us sleep – only the cheapest ones, naturally. Nothing budget is to be found centrally.

Jiālíng Bīnguǎn (☎ 231 5470; Baimi Dadao; dm/tw with private bathroom Y40/158; ⊗) This place has unofficially accepted foreigners forever, yet they did hesitate a bit on last check. If accepted, you can get dorm beds or slightly dingy but comfortable twins.

Yàshèng Dàjiǔdiàn (☎ 213 2778; fax 213 2779; Erdao Jie Zhongduan; tw & d Y225-400; mains from Y20; ⊗) Located in the centre of town, the once-stylish rooms here are clean but less than luxurious. The best food experience in town (both Chinese and Western) is found in the rotating restaurant on the top floor of the hotel.

Yán'ān Bīnguǎn (☎ 211 3122; fax 211 4297; 56 Zhongxin Jie; s/d from Y380/480; ⊗) It will tout that world leaders lodge here, yet the clean but unimpressive rooms – and indifferent service – aren't really worth the money unless it offers its usual 20% discount. Then again,

the better Yàshèng Dàjiǔdiàn is usually full. The restaurants are quite good.

Zhōngyuàn Dàjiǔdiàn (Beiguan Jie; dishes from Y5) If you have to do any banking, then drop into this popular place next to the Bank of China, which serves a tasty bowl of *niúròu shāozi* (a kind of spaghetti bolognese).

Markets set up on both sides of the Da Bridge during the day and in the evening with lots of tea tables. The locals while away the day here, chewing pumpkin seeds and playing chess.

Getting There & Away

AIR

There are daily flights to Xī'ān (Y380) and Běijīng (Y800) five times a week.

The airline booking office **Civil Aviation Administration of China** (CAAC; Zhōngguó Mínháng; ☎ 211 3854; ◷ 8am-noon & 2.30-5.30pm) is located on Jichang Lu (also known as Baimi Dadao), diagonally opposite Jiālíng Bīnguǎn. A bus service (Y5) connects the office with the airport, 7km northeast of the city.

BUS

Heading to Xī'ān, a large variety of buses run every half-hour to hour from 6am to late afternoon. The ride takes anywhere from six to nine hours and costs Y42 all the way up to Y120 (for an express air-con luxury bus). Iveco vans take seven hours and run every 30 minutes; the express buses leave a handful of times between 9am and 2.30pm.

From Yán'ān there are Iveco vans and express buses departing for Yúlín (Y33 to Y55, five to seven hours) roughly hourly 6am to 1pm. Heading west, there are three daily departures to Yínchuān in Níngxià (Y57, 12 hours). You can also get into Shānxī and Hénán.

TRAIN

A train line links Yán'ān with Xī'ān via an interesting route along Luo River (Luò Hé). There are two daily overnight trains in either direction (7½ hours) that are the most convenient. A day train from Yúlín to Xī'ān passes through Yán'ān at 1.20pm; it departs from Xī'ān at 8am.

Getting sleeper tickets north to Yán'ān from Xī'ān is usually no problem (No 4762 departs Xī'ān at 10pm), but since the train to Xī'ān starts in Yúlín, getting them back

can be quite difficult: either get down to the station by 3pm to line up for the overnight train, or try the foyer of the large hotel opposite the bus station at 9am. No advance tickets are sold. A taxi from the train station into town costs Y10.

YÚLÍN 榆林

☎ 0912 / pop 93,700

Yúlín lies on the fringe of Inner Mongolia's Mu Us Desert in far northern Shaanxi. During the Ming dynasty, Yúlín was a fortified garrison town and patrol post serving the Great Wall.

Yúlín's remoteness and relative poverty have kept the old town somewhat insulated from the 'white-tile' trend in Chinese architecture, which is rapidly destroying what remains of the country's older buildings. Along the narrow brick and cobblestone lanes near the unrestored Bell Tower (Zhōng Lóu) are traditional family houses with tiny courtyards hidden behind low enclosure walls and old stone gates. (From the tower, remnants of the Great Wall can be espied.) The city's old Ming walls are mainly still standing, although in places their original outer brick layer has been removed.

A large three-tiered **fortress** and **Beacon Tower** (正北台; Zhèngběi Tái) lie 7.5km north of town, nearby is a lovely riverine park with caves and modest craggy cliffs.

Sleeping & Eating

Yúxī Dàjiǔdiàn (榆西大酒店; ☎ 328 0492; 64 Renmin Xilu; tw/tr with bathroom from Y80/105; ⌘) Friendly service here, but upkeep varies by floor, so look at several rooms if the first one doesn't strike your fancy. The management has always been friendly.

Yúlín Bīnguǎn (榆林宾馆; ☎ 328 3971; fax 328 3970; Xinjian Lu; tw/tr with bathroom from Y100/120; ⌘) Just north of the city walls, this mid-range option is the official tour group and hotel. The hotel's dining hall is not bad and quite cheap.

There's a depressing dearth of anything culinarily special. Your best bet is to walk along Xinjian Lu, where a number of modest restaurants – clean and with good food – are found.

Getting There & Away

There are daily flights to Xī'ān (Y590) and possibly seasonal flights to Běijīng and

Bāotóu (which are generally cancelled) from the airport, 10km east of town.

The city has two bus stations. If you get off the bus inside the city walls, you're at the south station (the main one); the other is next to Yúxī Dàjiǔdiàn downtown and though it has mostly regional buses it's got express buses to Xī'ān too. From the main station there are buses roughly every 90 minutes between Xī'ān and Yúlín (Y70 to Y128, 10 to 15 hours), but it's more convenient and less tiring to stop in Yán'ān. There are also six express buses each day between Yán'ān and Yúlín (Y45,

six to seven hours), and several morning expresses to Tàiyuán.

There are daily buses departing in the early morning to Yínchuān (Y55 to Y90, eight to 12 hours) following a route close to the Great Wall. Express buses take the new expressway, but some slower local buses putter along old roads. Half-hourly buses also depart for Dàliùtǎ (Y7, 1½ hours), from where you can travel on by train to Dōngshèng and Bāotóu in Inner Mongolia.

Trains to Xī'ān (13 hours) via Yán'ān depart at 8am and 4.12pm, but sleepers aren't easy to get.

Hénán 河南

HIGHLIGHTS

- Wander kilometres of preternatural Buddhist grottoes in a splendid riverine setting at the **Longmen Caves** (p438) near Luòyáng

- Take a Jackie Chan kung fu retreat at Shaolin Temple (Shàolín Sì) before striking off into the lovely temple-dotted hills of **Sōng Shān** (p433)

- Scramble about the cave tomb complexes of **Gongyi City** (p432) to see how emperors were interred, followed by a visit to a modern family's cave home in the region

- Get a jolting historical lesson in Chinese-Jewish culture in **Kāifēng** (p441), and then gorge yourself at the phenomenal night market

- Set out for a rest-and-relaxation retreat in the splendid alpine areas (and ersatz English country village) of **Jīgōng Shān** (Rooster Mountain; p441)

Gōngyì City
Kāifēng
Longmen Caves
Sōng Shān
Jīgōng Shān

■ POP: 95.5 MIL	■ AREA: 167,000 SQ KM	■ www.hnly.com.cn

Modestly, Hénán lets its western provincial neighbours take the credit as 'cradles' of Chinese civilisation, yet here, Henanese could argue, is where it truly all began.

Nascent Chinese civilisation can be traced back about 3500 years (human habitation dates back nearly 7000 years), when primitive settlements here began to coalesce into a true urban sprawl. The landscape certainly beckoned these early settlers, forever trailing the fickle course of the Yellow River (Huáng Hé) and settling into the fertile plains of its basin. Telling is the province's name itself, which means 'South of the River'. Neighbouring Shaanxi (Shǎnxī) garners acclaim as the 'cradle of Chinese history', yet Hénán, smack in the middle of China's nine original regions, was originally dubbed 'Central Region' – culturally as well as geographically. Ancient capitals rose and fell and northern Hénán (particularly time-warped Kāifēng and overlooked Ānyáng) is an east-to-west melange of Chinese dynastic antiquity.

Spirituality blossomed within the dynastic centres. The province witnessed the initial blooming of Buddhism in China; Luòyáng's White Horse Temple is likely the oldest Buddhist temple in the country. Later, Muslim traders and pilgrims intermarried with Han Chinese and established an Islamic presence. So welcoming were the early emperors that Hénán even found itself the site of China's only settlement of Jews.

Geography is trumped by history here (only some 40% of the province features hills or mountains), but intrepid travellers will find picturesque mountains amid the history in central Hénán. These modest rises slope gradually from west (flanked by the Qinling Mountains of Shānxī and Shaanxi) to east; the nucleus of Sōng Shān is home to one of the most legendary of China's temples, Shaolin Temple, the birthplace of kung fu. Better still, those venturing to the little-visited south will find precipitous rises and cooler temperatures near one of Central China's most pleasant – if isolated – mountain retreats.

History

First, a history primer. It was long thought that tribes who migrated from western Asia founded the Shang dynasty (1700–1100 BC). Shang dynasty settlement excavations in Hénán, however, have shown these towns to be built on the sites of even more ancient – prehistoric even – settlements. The first archaeological evidence of the Shang period was discovered near Ānyáng in northern Hénán. Yet it is now believed that the first Shang capital, perhaps dating back 3800 years, was at Yǎnshī, west of modern-day Zhèngzhōu. Around the mid-14th century BC, the capital is thought to have moved to Zhèngzhōu, where its ancient city walls are still visible.

Hénán again occupied centre stage during the Song dynasty (AD 960–1279),

but political power deserted it when the government fled south from its capital at Kāifēng following the 12th-century Juchen invasion from the north. Nevertheless, with a large population on the fertile (although periodically flood-ravaged) plains of the unruly Yellow River, Hénán remained an important agricultural area.

Not until communist victory was the province able to begin keeping up with the neighbours in progress. Nice-enough Zhèngzhōu hardly resembles a living history book, but the remaining cities are excellent slices of history.

Climate

Think warm-temperate climate: dry, windy and cold (average temperature of -2°C in January) in winter, hot (average temperature

28°C) and humid in summer. Rainfall increases from north to south and ranges from 60cm to 120 cm annually; most of it falls July through September.

Language
The lion's share of Hénán's nearly 96 million inhabitants speak one of nearly 20 subdialects of Zhōngyuán Huà, itself a dialect of Northern Mandarin. Two of 15 dialects of Jin, a distinct language or a simply a dialect of Mandarin (linguists wrangle), are found in northern Hénán.

Getting There & Around
Hénán is that rarity in China: a province in which travellers can get from point A

to point B (inside or outside the province) with relative ease. Zhèngzhōu is a major regional rail hub, with myriad trains originating or whizzing through the city leading in all directions. Spanking new expressways laden with comfy express buses parallel rail lines and, as of 2003, finally stretched into southern parts of the province.

Zhèngzhōu is the main hub for flying to/from Hénán (see p432); Luòyáng also has a smaller airport (p437) but it's recommended that you use Zhèngzhōu.

ZHÈNGZHŌU 郑州
☎ 0371 / pop 6,210,000
The provincial capital of Hénán since 1949, Zhèngzhōu is a sprawling mini-metropolis

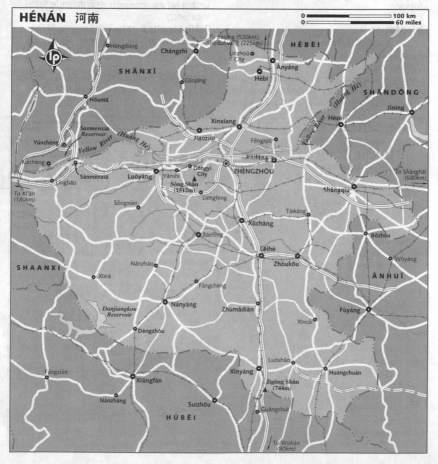

that, despite its ancient history, retains fewer historical anachronisms than some of its neighbouring cities. The quickly modernising town is not unattractive – with clean, wide boulevards lined with numerous upmarket boutiques and shops branching off around the train station – but its role as a major rail transport junction in the region is the real reason it's the capital city.

You will likely at least pass through Zhèngzhōu. Ignore the naysayers who grouse about it not being as cool as Kāifēng. Other provincial cities grab the touristic glory, but a few decent sights are here and the friendly folks busying down the gentrifying streets help make it a pleasant stopover.

Orientation

All places of interest to travellers lie east of the railway line.

Northeast of the train station, five roads converge at the prominent modern landmark 7 February Pagoda (Èrqī Tǎ) to form the messy traffic circle 7 February Square (Èrqī Guǎngchǎng) that marks Zhèngzhōu's not unattractive commercial centre. Erqi Lu runs northward from the traffic circle to intersect with Jinshui Lu near Renmin Park.

Information

Bank of China (Zhōngguó Yínháng; 16 Huayuankou Lu); branch office (8 Jinshui Lu) The main bank is in the northern part of the city. The branch will exchange travellers cheques and cash; credit cards are iffy.

Post office (yóujú; 8am-8pm) Located to your right as you exit the train station.

China International Travel Service (CITS; Zhōngguó Guójì Lǚxíngshè; ☎ 392 7758; fax 381 1753; 8th fl, Hǎitōng Dàshà Bldg, 50 Jingqi Lu; 8.30-noon & 2-6pm Mon-Fri) Inconveniently located in Zhèngzhōu's north. It has also representatives in the pricier Sofitel Hotel (p432).

Public Security Bureau (PSB; Gōngānjú; 70 Erqi Lu; 8.30am-noon & 3-6.30pm summer, 2pm-5.30pm Mon-Fri other seasons) Situated not far from Renmin Park.

Internet café (wǎngbā; 2nd fl, train station ticket office; per hr Y3) Above the far end of the train station ticket office.

ZHÈNGZHŌU 郑州

Sights

SHANG DYNASTY RUINS 商代遗址

Out on Zhèngzhōu's eastern outskirts long, high mounds of earth indicate the erstwhile city walls, one of the earliest relics of Chinese urban life. Of two **ruins** (Shāngdài Yízhǐ) sites, the portion that still has some of the old city wall standing is in the city's southeastern section at the junction of Chengdong Lu and Chengnan Lu. Bus No 64 from the train station stops nearby. Bus No 3 runs near the old Shang city. The other ruins can be found in **Zijingshan Park**.

HENAN PROVINCIAL MUSEUM 河南省博物馆

This fantastic provincial **museum** (Hénán Shěng Bówùguǎn; ☎ 351 1237; 8 Nongye Lu; admission Y20; ⏰ 8.30am-6pm) is housed in a pyramid-shaped building north of the city. The impressive collection includes relics of the Shang and Zhou dynasties, as well as examples of pottery, porcelain, bronze and jade craftsmanship. The 4th floor has a small display of dinosaur-egg fossils discovered

in the region. Captions are in Chinese and English.

Take bus No 39 from the train station; it should be the seventh stop.

YELLOW RIVER 黄河

This **river** (Huáng Hé; admission Y25; ⏰ 6.30am-sunset) is 25km north of Zhèngzhōu. The road passes near Huāyuánkǒu village, where in April 1938 Kuomintang general Chiang Kaishek blew a dyke to flood Japanese troops. This desperate, ruthless tactic drowned about one million Chinese people and left another 11 million homeless and starving.

The US helped repair the dyke in 1947 and Mao's instruction 'Control the Huáng Hé' is etched into the embankment. Dubbed 'China's sorrow' for its propensity to flood, the river carries masses of silt from the loess plains and deposits them on the riverbed, causing the water to overflow the banks. Peasants have built the dykes higher and higher over the centuries and, as a result, parts of the river flow along an elevated channel that is sometimes more than 15m in height. Tourists can can explore the Yellow River by hopping aboard a tourist hydrofoil (Y65).

Bus No 16 goes to the river from Erma Lu, north of the train station.

Sleeping

Tiān'è Bīnguǎn (☎ 676 8690; q without bathroom Y30, s/d with bathroom Y90-220; ❄) This clean budget place is in the cavernous white complex opposite the train station. It's one of a half-dozen hotels within the towers.

Jīnyángguāng Dàjiǔdiàn (Golden Sunshine Hotel; ☎ 696 9999; fax 699 9534; 86 Erma Lu; s/d economy from Y108, s/d standard Y298-398; ❄) This hotel's lower-end rooms are definitely a bargain – despite rock-hard beds; *fairly* recent renovations in the remaining rooms are holding up well.

Yǒuyì Bīnguǎn (Friendship Hotel; ☎ 622 8807; fax 622 4728; 97 Jinshui Lu; d/tr Y160/270; ❄) Tranquilly located, this friendly mid-range hotel's ambitious renovation hasn't nudged prices up! An odd layout means myriad choices, so snoop about.

Hóngshānhú Jiǔdiàn (Red Coral Hotel; ☎ 698 6688; fax 699 3222; 20 Erma Lu; s/d Y360/388; ❄ ▣) The marble lobby of this hotel outshines its not-quite-great rooms; a discount would make it a deal.

Holiday Inn Crowne Plaza (Huángguān Jiàrì Bīnguǎn; ☎ 595 0055; www.sixcontinentshotels.com; 115 Jinshui Lu; s/d from US$140; ☒ ☒ ☐ ☒) A 1950s-era Russian hotel is now a three-hotel (three to five stars) complex with superb facilities and service. Guests in lower mid-range wings share the same facilities as the five-star folks in the Crowne Plaza – hint, hint.

Hotel Sofitel (Sùfēitè Guójì Fàndiàn; ☎ 595 0088; www.accorhotels.com; 289 Chengdong Lu; s/d from Y990; ☒ ☒ ☐ ☒) The Sofitel is another top-end hotel in this area and is pretty much perfect, particularly the service.

Eating & Drinking

Háoxiǎnglái Zhōngxī Cāntīng (☎ 662 6038; 221 Minggong Lu; set meals from Y24) Solid Chinese-Western food here; a second **branch** (79 Erqi Lu) is near the PSB. Best of all – they never close.

Cola Planet (Kělè Xīngqiú Cāntīng; ☎ 397 7155, ext 7777; 159 Jiankang Lu; dishes Y15-50) This hip bar/restaurant with Asian/Western dishes is filled with expats and seen-on-the-scene young locals dancing to DJs.

Target Pub (Mùbiāo Jiǔba; Jingliu Lu) This laid-back bar that plays jazz, blues and hip-hop is also run by Lao Wang of Cola Planet fame.

Getting There & Away

AIR

Civil Aviation Administration of China (CAAC; Zhōngguó Mínháng; ☎ 599 1111; 3 Jinshui Lu) sells tickets. The airport is about 30km south of the city centre. An airport shuttle bus (Y15,

40 minutes, hourly) leaves from the CAAC office. A taxi to the airport costs from Y80 to Y100.

There are flights to more than 20 domestic destinations. Daily flights serve Běijīng (Y690), Shànghǎi (Y790), Guìlín (Y1130) and Hong Kong (Y2200). Less frequent services fly to Wǔhàn (Y500) and Xī'ān (Y510).

BUS

The city has eight bus stations; all you need is the long-distance one opposite the train station.

Fast buses run every 15 to 20 minutes to Luòyáng (Y26 to Y43, two hours) via the expressway. Slow buses (Y18 to Y23, two to three hours) take the old road and pass through Gongyi City (see the boxed text below).

Air-con expresses and regular buses leave four times daily to Ānyáng (Y33 to Y60, two to four hours). To Kāifēng, slow buses (Y12, one hour) and expresses (Y17 to Y24) leave constantly.

Express coaches go to Běijīng (Y170 to Y190, eight hours) leaving every 40 minutes between 8.30am and 10pm daily. For other destinations outside the province, far fewer departures are to be found.

A new highway connecting Zhèngzhōu and Dēngfēng has cut the travelling time dramatically between the two; another highway is being built from Dēngfēng to Luòyáng. Buses services departing for Shaolin Temple (Y20 to Y28, 1½ to 2½ hours) or Dēngfēng (Y15 to Y22, 45 minutes to 2½ hours) leave every 20 to 30 minutes.

GONGYI CITY

Gongyi City (Gǒngyì Shì), formerly called Gongxian County, is between Zhèngzhōu and Luòyáng and is home to a fascinating series of Buddhist caves and tombs built by the Northern Song emperors (c AD 517). More than 7700 Buddhist figures populate 256 shrines.

Song Tombs (Sòng Líng; admission Y5) are scattered over an area of 30 sq km, and within them repose seven of the nine Northern Song emperors (the other two were carted off by the Juchen armies who overthrew the Northern Song in the 12th century). Some 800 years later all that remain of the tombs are ruins, burial mounds and the statues which, amid fields of wheat, line the sacred avenues leading up to the ruins. About 700 stone statues are still standing, and together they comprise the main attraction of the tombs.

Buses running on the old highway (not the freeway) from Luòyáng to Gǒngyì pass by one of these Song Tomb sites. You can get off the bus there and visit the tombs, or you can continue on into Gǒngyì and hire a taxi to visit both the tombs and **Buddhist Caves** (Shíkūsì; admission Y5). It's possible to do this in half a day; expect to pay about Y80 for the taxi. If you're coming from the direction of Zhèngzhōu, get off at Gǒngyì.

TRAIN

Nearly 100 trains pass through or depart from Zhèngzhōu daily for *everywhere*. The train station ticket office is often crowded and tickets are easier to buy at the **advance booking office** (☎ 697 1920; 134 Erqi Lu; ⊗ 8.30am-noon & 2.30-5pm). Another office is at the corner of Zhengxing Jie and Fushou Jie, with similar hours. Most hotels also book tickets.

Popular routes include: Běijīng (Y178, six to seven hours), Luòyáng (Y16, two hours), Wǔhàn (Y83, six hours) and Tàiyuán (Y147, 12 hours). The Běijīng–Kowloon express train also stops in Zhèngzhōu.

For Xī'ān take the faster, two-tiered 'tourist train' (Y78 hard seat, 7½ hours) that leaves Zhèngzhōu at 9am and arrives in Xī'ān around 4.30pm.

Getting Around

Bus No 64 runs from the train station to Zijingshan Park, and bus No 3 runs near the Shang dynasty ruins. Bus No 39 runs from the train station to the Henan Provincial Museum and bus No 26 runs from the train station past 7 February Square and along Jinshui Lu to the high-end hotels and CAAC office.

Taxis and minivan cabs start at Y7.

SŌNG SHĀN 嵩山
☎ 0371

Three main peaks and two areas – Shaolin Temple (Shàolín Sì) and Dēngfēng – comprise Sòng Shān, which rises to 1512m and sits about 80km west of Zhèngzhōu.

In Taoism, Sòng Shān is considered the central mountain, symbolising earth in the religion's belief that five elements make up the world. Legend says that Taoists searched China for mountains to match these crucial elements. Sòng Shān occupies the axis – directly under heaven.

While kung fu's popularity draws crowds to Shaolin Temple during the high season, it's possible to eke out an alternative visit by trekking the area for some peace and quiet.

Shaolin Temple 少林寺

An international melange of tourists, Bruce Lee wannabes and Hong Kong movie buffs journey to this **temple** (Shàolín Sì; ☎ 274 9204; admission Y60; ⊗ 6am-6.30pm), some 80km southwest of Zhèngzhōu, to see where China's most famous martial art was born.

Hop off the bus and see chiselled acolytes, many as young as five, outside a school ramming a javelin through their imaginary opponent's body or gracefully kicking into a sparring dummy with enough force to wind an elephant. You can also catch regular performances (Y40) that wow even black belts.

Despite fires and vandalism, many of the monastery buildings are still standing, although much of their original charm has been restored out of them. Must-see sights are **Pagoda Forest** (少林塔林; Shàolín Tǎlín), a cemetery of 246 pagodas including the

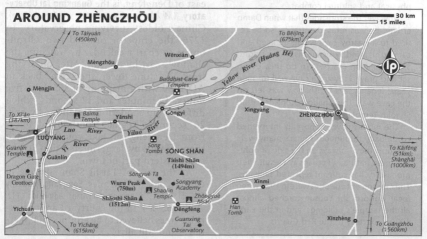

AROUND ZHÈNGZHŌU

0 — 30 km
0 — 15 miles

To Tàiyuán (450km)
To Běijīng (675km)
Wènxiàn
Mèngzhōu
Mèngjīn
Buddhist Cave Temples
Yellow River (Huáng Hé)
To Xī'ān (387km)
Báima Temple
Yánshī
Gŏngyì
Xingyáng
ZHÈNGZHŌU
Luo River
Yiluo River
LUÒYÁNG
Guànlín Temple
Guànlín
Sòng Tombs
SŌNG SHĀN
Tàishì Shān (1494m)
To Kāifēng (51km); Shànghǎi (1000km)
Dragon Gate Grottoes
Sòngyuè Tǎ
Wuru Peak (750m)
Shàoshi Shān (1512m)
Shaolin Temple
Songyang Academy
Zhōngyuè Miào
Xinmi
Han Tomb
Yíchuān
Dēngfēng
Guanxing Tai Observatory
To Yíchāng (615km)
Xinzhèng
To Guǎngzhōu (1560km)

ashes of an eminent monk, and a small grouping of stelae respectfully offered by foreign martial arts schools.

Your admission ticket gives access to all buildings and an educational video.

Flee the din of touristdom by heading into the hills and seeing the cave where Damo meditated for nine years. As you face Shaolin Temple, paths on your left lead up **Wuru Peak** (五乳峰; Wǔrǔ Fēng).

At 1512m above sea level, **Shǎoshì Shān** (少室山) is the area's tallest peak and has a more scenic trek beside craggy rock formations along a path that often hugs the cliff. The trek takes about six hours return, covers 15km and takes you to the 782-step **Rope Bridge** (索桥; Suǒ Qiáo).

For safety reasons, monks recommend trekking with a friend. The path starts to the east of the Shàolín cable car (Y20), which takes you to part of Shǎoshì Shān. Maps in Chinese are available at souvenir stalls.

The **Shaolin Monastery Wushu Institute at Tagou** (塔沟武术学校; ☎ 274 9627) is sup-

---

MIND AND BODY

Legend says Shaolin Temple (Shàolín Sì) was founded in the 5th century by an Indian monk. Several decades later another monk called Bodhidharma (Damo in Chinese) arrived. Apparently, for relief between long periods of meditation, Bodhidharma's disciples imitated the natural motions of birds and animals, evolving over centuries into physical and spiritual combat.

However the story goes that when Damo arrived he was refused entrance, so he retired to a nearby cave where he lived and calmed his mind by resting his brain 'upright' as the religion teaches. To do this, Damo sat and prayed toward a cave wall for nine years; legend says his shadow was left on the cave wall. This 'Shadow Stone' is within Shaolin Temple.

The monks have supposedly intervened continually throughout China's many wars and uprisings – always on the side of righteousness, naturally. Perhaps as a result, their monastery has suffered repeated sackings. The most recent episodes were in 1928 when local warlord Shi Yousan torched almost all the temple's buildings, and in the early 1970s, courtesy of the Red Guards.

---

posedly Shàolín's oldest and largest school with around 7000 students. It offers one-day classes (US$24); the price includes accommodation. Ask at the school's hotel for more information. Smaller schools in the hills (dozens of them) are generally cheaper; foreigners are not uncommon anywhere.

Sōngshān Bīnguǎn (嵩山宾馆; ☎ 274 9050; d Y120; 🛏), beside the Tagou school, is the best of nearby mediocre hotels. Alternatively, all schools have dormitories and cheap restaurants.

Dēngfēng 登封
☎ 0371

About 15 minutes by minibus east of Shaolin Temple, at the foot of Tàishì Shān, lies the peaceful town of Dēngfēng, home to some noteworthy trekking and historical attractions. Many travellers base themselves here and make a day trip to the temple.

CITS (中国国际旅行社; Zhōngguó Guójì Lǚxíngshè; ☎ 288 3442; Beihuan Lu Xiduan) has helpful, English-speaking staff.

The Qing dynasty **Zhōngyuè Miào** (中岳庙; admission Y15; 🕐 8am-6.30pm) is modelled after the Forbidden City in Běijīng. Originally a place to worship the God of the central mountain Sōng Shān, its significance eventually meshed with Taoism, whose adherents dubbed Sōng Shān the earth's centre. The temple is 4km east of the city centre. Take the green bus No 2 along Zhongyue Dajie.

In the town of Gàochéng, 15km southeast of Dēngfēng, is the **Guanxing Tai Observatory** (观星台; admission Y10; 🕐 8am-6.30pm), China's oldest surviving observatory. In 1276, the emperor ordered two astronomers to chart a calendar by watching the shadows cast by the sun. After observing from the stone tower, they came back in AD 1280 with a mapping of 365 days, five hours, 49 minutes and 12 seconds, which differs from modern calculations by only 26 seconds. Regular southbound buses from Dēngfēng can take you there; catch them from any large intersection in the southeastern part of town.

At the foot of Tàishì Shān sits one of China's oldest academies, **Songyang Academy** (嵩阳书院; Sōngyáng Shūyuàn; admission Y12; 🕐 8am-6.30pm). In the courtyard are two cypress trees believed to be around 4500 years old – and still alive!

Nearby is **Central High Mountain Pagoda** (嵩岳塔; Sōngyuè Tǎ; admission Y4; ⏱ 8am-6.30pm). Built in AD 509, during the Northern Wei dynasty, it's China's oldest brick pagoda.

Take bus No 2 (the green one that runs along Zhongyue Dajie) to the last stop and then a motor-rickshaw to the pagoda; the ride should cost Y10 to Y15. A return trip to the academy and pagoda by motor-rickshaw is Y20.

North of Dēngfēng the 1494m-high **Tàishì Shān** (太室山) provides ample trekking opportunities. Area maps show trails leading to the summit. There is a Y10 fee to enter the Tàishì Shān scenic area.

Shàolín Guójì Dàjiǔdiàn (少林国际大酒店; ☎ 286 6188; fax 287 1448; 16 Shaolin Lu; d from Y258; ❸), in the eastern part of Dēngfēng, is a mid-range standby with decent rooms and good views of Tàishì Shān. Definitely bargain.

Getting There & Away

A new expressway has been completed between Dēngfēng and Zhèngzhōu, the latter half to Luòyáng is still unfinished. Buses to/from Zhèngzhōu (Y15 to Y22, 45 minutes to 2½ hours) and Luòyáng (Y16, roughly one hour) run every 20 to 30 minutes.

Hotels in Zhèngzhōu and Luòyáng often arrange day tours (Y40, excluding entrance fees) that include sites along the way.

In Shàolín, return buses leave from opposite the Pagoda Forest and at the town's major intersection. The last bus leaves at around 8pm.

The Dēngfēng bus station is on western Zhongyue Dajie. Direct minibuses between Shàolín and Dēngfēng also run regularly.

LUÒYÁNG 洛阳

☎ 0379 / pop 6,230,000

Founded during the Xia dynasty, Luòyáng was the capital of 13 dynasties until the Northern Song dynasty moved its capital to Kāifēng in the 10th century. In the 12th century Juchen invaders from the north of China stormed and sacked Luòyáng, which never quite recovered.

For centuries the city languished with only memories of greatness. By the 1920s it had just 20,000 inhabitants. The communists brought life back to Luòyáng, constructing an industrial city that now houses more than six million people.

Today, it's hard to imagine that Luòyáng was once the centre of the Chinese world and home to more than 1300 Buddhist temples. Reminders of the city's historical greatness are scattered about town but the main attractions are the splendid Longmen Caves 13km out of town.

Orientation

Luòyáng is spread across the northern bank of the Luo River (Luò Hé). The train station (and long-distance bus station) is located in the northern part of the city. Luòyáng's chief thoroughfare is Zhongzhou Zhonglu, which meets Jinguyuan Lu leading down from the train station at a central T-junction.

The old city is in the town's eastern part, beyond the West Gate (Xī Guǎn) where sections of the original city walls can still be seen. Throughout Luòyáng's maze of narrow streets and winding laneways stand many older houses. Using Wen Feng Pagoda (Wén Fēng Tǎ) as a landmark, it's a great area to explore on foot or by bicycle.

Information

Bank of China (Zhōngguó Yínháng; 439 Zhongzhou Zhonglu); branch office (Zhongzhou Xilu) Exchanges travellers cheques but winces at credit cards.

CITS (Zhōngguó Guójì Lǚxíngshè; ☎ 432 3212, 433 1337; Changjiang Lu); Peony Hotel (Mǔdān Dàjiǔdiàn; 15 Zhongzhou Xilu)

Internet café (wǎngbā; Jinguyuan Lu; per hr Y2) This small café is just south of the bus station on the opposite side of the street.

Post & China Telecom (Yóudiànjú; cnr Zhongzhou Zhonglu & Jinguyuan Lu)

PSB (Gōngānjú; ☎ 393 8397; cnr Kaixuan Lu & Tiyuchang Lu; ⏱ 8am-noon & 3-6pm Mon-Fri) Look for the large modern building right out of a science fiction novel.

Sights & Activities

WHITE HORSE TEMPLE 白马寺

Founded in the 1st century AD, this **temple** (Báimǎ Sì; admission Y30; ⏱ 7am-7pm Apr-Oct, hrs vary rest of the year) was the first Buddhist temple built on Chinese soil, though the original structures are long gone.

Two Han dynasty court emissaries went in search of Buddhist scriptures. In Afghanistan, they met two Indian monks and together they returned to Luòyáng carrying Buddhist scriptures and statues on the backs of two white horses. The impressed emperor built the temple to house the monks; it is also their resting place. Of note are wonderful arhats.

The temple is located 13km east of Luòyáng. To get there, hop aboard bus No 56 from the train station.

KING CITY PARK 王城公园
The **Peony Festival** (admission Y20) is centred in King City Park (Wángchéng Gōngyuán). The festival is held annually from 15 to 25 April, when thousands of tourists descend on Luòyáng to view the peony flowers. Trolleys No 102 or 103 run here from the train station.

LUOYANG MUSEUM 洛阳博物馆
This **museum** (Luòyáng Bówùguǎn; ☎ 393 7107; 298 Zhongzhou Zhonglu; admission Y10; ☻ 8am-6.30pm) displays early bronzes, Tang figurines and implements dating back to the Stone Age. There are some eye-catching pieces, look out for those in jade. To get here, take trolleys No 102 or 103 which depart from the train station.

LUOYANG MUSEUM OF ANCIENT TOMBS 洛阳古墓博物馆
The thousands of tombs unearthed by archaeologists in and around Luòyáng form the basis of this fascinating **museum** (Luòyáng Gǔmù Bówùguǎn; admission Y15; ☻ 8.30am-6pm). There are 25 restored tombs on view, dating from the Han to the Song dynasties and belonging to different social strata. Burial items and murals showing the exorcising of demons and mortals ascending to heaven are also on display. Captions are in Chinese and English.

The museum is on the road to the airport, north of the city. Bus No 83 departs from opposite the long-distance bus station – ask the driver to let you off at the turn-off to the museum. A motor-rickshaw costs around Y10.

Sleeping
Prices here are expensive for the quality but not much competition exists. Opposite the bus station are a few cheap hotels.

Míngyuán Bīnguǎn (☎ 390 1377; lymingyuan@yahoo .com.cn; 20 Jiefang Lu; dm Y80, s/d/tr Y165/175/260; ☒)

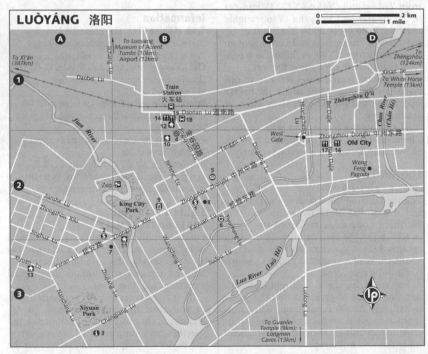

LUÒYÁNG 洛阳

Affiliated with Hostelling International, this generally efficient hotel is just south of the train station. The rooms are large and clean (almost new furnishings and amenities) and the staff is friendly. Rates include breakfast.

Xīn Yǒuyì Bīnguǎn (New Friendship Hotel; ☎ 468 6666; fax 491 2328; 6 Xiyuan Lu; d with bathroom Y358-458; ❌) The fresh-looking rooms here are small but renovated fairly recently, and the staff seem happy to get the odd foreign guest. No buses run directly here from the train station, but bus No 103 runs just to the north.

Peony Hotel (Mǔdān Dàjiǔdiàn; ☎ 468 0000; peonysmdept@yahoo.com.cn; 15 Zhongzhou Xilu; d with bathroom Y480-550 plus 5% tax; ❌ ❐) This high-rise hotel is more economical than its four-star cousin on Nancang Lu. Rooms are tastefully decorated and well maintained – it also gets kudos for the bathroom renovations. The restaurants come recommended.

Eating

No visitor should miss sampling the famous Water Banquet. The main dishes of this 24-course meal are soups and are served up with the speed of 'flowing water' – hence the name.

Zhēn Bù Tóng Fàndiàn (Une of a Kind Restaurant; ☎ 399 5787; Zhongzhou Donglu; dishes Y15-45, water banquet from Y60) This is the place to come for a water banquet experience – one half is

for the hoi polloi, one section is upmarket. If 24 courses seem a little excessive, you can opt to pick individual dishes from the menu. So overwhelmingly crowded is this place you may get lost in the service shuffle – harried staff tend to ignore nervous travellers.

Night market (Nándàjiē yèshì; cnr Nan Dajie & Zhongzhou Donglu) This lively market in the old city is a great place for dinner. Barbequed beef and squid, cold dishes and an assortment of bugs can be had for as little as Y2 per dish. Other tasty roadside snacks include *jiǎnpào* (fried pastries filled with chopped herbs and garlic) and *dòushā gāo* (a sweet 'cake' made from yellow peas and Chinese dates).

Luòyáng Dàshà (Daonan Lu) Opposite the train station, this friendly little Sìchuān canteen has a fractured-English menu and excellent inexpensive fare.

Getting There & Away

AIR

You would do better to fly into or out of Zhèngzhōu; the **CAAC** (Zhōngguó Mínháng; ☎ 393 1120; Jichang Lu) is in town, north of the train station, though hotels sell tickets more quickly.

There are daily flights operating to Běijīng (Y660) and Shànghǎi. Flights to Chéngdū (Y800), Xī'ān and a few other places leave less regularly.

BUS

Fast buses to Zhèngzhōu run every 15 to 20 minutes (Y26 to Y43, two hours) via the expressway. Slow buses (Y18 to Y23, two to three hours) take the old road and pass through Gongyi City (see the boxed text p432).

Fast buses to Shàolín (Y16, one to 1½ hours) depart every half hour until 4.30pm; slow buses (Y14, two hours) run until 6pm and pass through Dēngfēng. Travel time will speed up when the expressway to Dēngfēng is completed.

There are frequent buses to Ānyáng (Y50, four to five hours) and Kāifēng (Y35, 2½ hours).

Sleeper and express buses travelling to extra-provincial destinations seem to rumble past the outside of the train/bus stations continually. Their destinations include Běijīng (seat/sleeper Y148/188, nine hours), Xī'ān (Y65 to Y79, eight to 10 hours) and Tàiyuán (Y89 to Y96, 10 to 11 hours).

TRAIN
Direct trains go to Běijīng (eight to 10 hours), Shànghǎi (14 to 15 hours) and Xī'ān (six hours). A two-tiered tourist train runs between Zhèngzhōu and Xī'ān daily – it stops in Luòyáng en route at 12.25pm (arriving in Xī'ān around 7pm the same day).

There are some direct trains heading north to Tàiyuán (Y198, 13 hours) and some going south to Yíchāng (10 hours). Yíchāng is a port on Yangzi River (Cháng Jiāng), where you can catch the ferry for Chóngqìng.

CAVE DWELLINGS

The road between Zhèngzhōu and Luòyáng features some of China's cave dwellings. Over 100 million Chinese people live in cave houses cut into dry embankments, or in houses where the hillside makes up one or more walls. These cave dwellings are not peculiar to the Hénán province: a third of these dwellings are found in the dry loess plain.

Some communities use both caves and normal houses; the former are warmer in winter and cooler in summer, but also tend to be darker and less ventilated than ordinary houses. Sometimes a large square pit is dug first and then caves are hollowed into the four sides of the pit. A well is sunk in the middle of the yard to prevent flooding during heavy rains. Other caves, such as those in Yán'ān (p423), are dug into the side of a cliff face.

The floors, walls and ceilings of these cave dwellings are made of loess, a fine yellowish-brown soil, which is soft and thick and makes good building material. The front wall may be made of loess, mud-brick, concrete, brick or wood, depending on the availability of materials. Ceilings are shaped according to the quality of the loess. If the loess is hard then the ceiling is constructed to be arched; if not, the ceiling may rise to a point. Besides the doors and windows in the front wall, there may additional vents may let in light and air.

Getting Around
The airport is 12km north of the city; bus No 83 runs from opposite the long-distance bus station and takes 30 minutes. A taxi from the train station will cost about Y25.

Bicycles can be hired across the street from the train station (Y5 per day, Y100 deposit), but check your bike carefully before setting off.

The bus system runs until 8pm or 9pm, although bus No 5 operates until 11pm. Bus Nos 5 and 41 run to the old city from the train station. Bus Nos 102 and 103 run in a westerly direction from the train station past King City Park to the Peony Hotel.

Taxis and yellow minivan cabs start at Y6. Motor-rickshaws are a good way to get around and start at Y2.

LONGMEN CAVES 龙门石窟
In AD 494 the Northern Wei dynasty relocated its capital here from Dàtóng and followed up the impressive Yungang Caves (Yúngāng Shíkū) with initial work on the equally amazing **Longmen Caves** (Dragon Gate Grottoes; Lóngmén Shíkū; Map p433; admission Y80; ⊙ 6am-8pm summer, 6.30am-7pm winter). Over the next 200 years or so, more than 100,000 images and statues of Buddha and his disciples were carved into the cliff walls for over a kilometre along both banks of the Yi River (Yī Hé), 16km south of the city. The displays in the caves of Luòyáng, Dūnhuáng and Dàtóng represent the peak of Buddhist cave art.

In the 19th and 20th centuries, Western souvenir hunters beheaded almost every figure they could lay their saws on. These heads now grace the museums and private paperweight collections in Europe and North America. Also removed were two murals that today hang in the Metropolitan Museum of Art in New York and the Atkinson Museum in Kansas City. The Cultural Revolution also took its toll on the caves and the Ten Thousand Buddha Cave was particularly damaged during this period.

Three Binyang Caves 宾阳三洞
Construction began on the Three Binyang Caves (Bīnyáng Sān Dòng) during the Northern Wei dynasty. Despite the fact that two of the caves were completed

during the Sui and Tang dynasties, the statues here all display the benevolent expressions that characterised the Northern Wei style.

Ten Thousand Buddha Cave 万佛洞
South of Three Binyang Caves is the Tang dynasty era Ten Thousand Buddha Cave (Wànfó Dòng), built in 680. In addition to the incredible legions of tiny bas-relief Buddhas that give the cave its name, there is a fine, big Buddha and images of celestial dancers.

Lotus Flower Cave 莲花洞
The Lotus Flower Cave (Liánhuā Dòng) was carved in 527 during the Northern Wei dynasty and has a large standing Buddha, now faceless. On the cave's ceiling are wispy apsaras (celestial nymphs) drifting around a central lotus flower. A commonly used symbol in Buddhist art, the lotus flower represents purity and serenity and can be seen on many of the cave ceilings.

Ancestor Worshipping Temple 奉先寺
Carved in the Tang dynasty between 672 and 675, this temple (Fèngxiān Sì) is the largest structure at Lóngmén and contains the best works of art, though climatic ravaging is evident.

Tang figures tend to be more three-dimensional than the Northern Wei figures. Their expressions and poses also appear to be more natural, but unlike the other-worldly figures of the Northern Wei, the Tang figures add a fearsome ferocity to their human forms.

The seated central Buddha is 17m high and said to be Losana. Allegedly, the face was modelled on Empress Wu Zetian of the Tang dynasty who funded the carving of the statue.

Medical Prescription Cave 药方洞
Located south of Ancestor Worshipping Temple is the tiny Medical Prescription Cave (Yàofāng Dòng). The entrance to this cave is filled with 6th-century stone stelae inscribed with remedies for a range of common ailments.

Earliest Cave 古阳洞
Adjacent to the Medical Prescription Cave is the much larger Earliest Cave (Gǔyáng

Dòng), carved between 495 and 575. It's a narrow, high-roofed cave featuring a Buddha statue and a profusion of sculptures, particularly of flying apsaras.

Carved Cave 石窟洞
The Carved Cave (Shíkū Dòng) is the last major cave in the Lóngmén complex and features intricate carvings depicting religious processions of the Northern Wei dynasty.

Getting There & Away
The Longmen Caves are 13km south of town. Bus No 81 runs from the east side of Luòyáng's train station and No 60 runs from opposite Yǒuyì Bīnguǎn. Bus No 53 runs from the east end, near the old town. Figure around Y30 for a taxi.

GUANLIN TEMPLE 关林寺
North of the Longmen Caves is this **temple** (Guānlín Sì; admission Y20; ☉ 8.30am-6pm), the burial place of the legendary general Guan Yu of the Three Kingdoms period (220 to 265). Legend has it that Guan Yu was executed by King Sunquan of the Wu Kingdom who then tried to put the blame on Cao Cao of the Wei Kingdom. Cao Cao saw straight through Sunquan's trickery, and respectfully buried Guan Yu's head in a grave south of Luòyáng.

The temple buildings were built during the Ming dynasty and Guan Yu was issued the posthumous title 'Lord of War' in the early Qing dynasty. Bus No 81 runs past Guānlín from the train station in Luòyáng.

ĀNYÁNG 安阳
☎ 0372 / pop 5,170,000
Ānyáng, north of the Yellow River near the border for Hénán–Héběi, is now believed to be the site of Yīn, the last capital of the ancient Shang dynasty and one of the first centres of an urban-based Chinese civilisation.

Peasants in the late 19th century unearthed pieces of polished bone inscribed with an ancient form of Chinese writing: divining bones with questions addressed to the spirits and ancestors. Other etchings were found on tortoise shells and on bronze objects, suggesting that the late Shang capital once stood here in the 14th century BC.

These are the earliest examples of Chinese characters in all of China.

Not until the late 1920s, however, did excavations uncover tombs, the ruins of a royal palace, and workshops and houses – proof that the legendary Shang dynasty had indeed existed.

CITS (中国国际旅行社; Zhōngguó Guójì Lǚxíngshè; ☎ 592 5650; 1 Youyi Lu) has an office located on the 2nd floor of Ānyáng Bīnguǎn (on Youyi Lu).

Sights

MUSEUM OF YIN RUINS 殷墟博物馆
This constantly expanding **museum** (Yīnxū Bówùguǎn; ☎ 393 2171; admission Y21; ☯ 8am-6.30pm) at Yīn's site has enough English captions to make it worthy of a trip. The museum's exhibits include reassembled pottery, oracle bone fragments and jade and bronze artefacts. Reconstructions of tombs holding wheeled vehicles with horses and drivers are the highlight.

The museum is located a fair way out of town. Bus No 1 from the train station travels past the museum turn-off. From there you will need to walk across the railway tracks and head along the river for about 10 minutes until you come to the museum.

TOMB OF YUAN SHIKAI 袁世凯墓
A more recent remnant of Chinese history is this **tomb** (Yuán Shìkǎi Mù; ☎ 291 0473; Shengli Lu; admission Y20; ☯ 8am-6pm). Yuan Shikai had it constructed in the style of the tomb of the American Civil War general and president, Ulysses S Grant, with a few Chinese touches. A bit of a Napoleonic Qing military official, he wrested the presidency from Sun Yatsen and attempted a restoration of the imperial system (quite short-lived), crowning himself emperor in 1916!

The tomb is 3km east of the Yin museum; you can take bus No 2 from the train station. Get off at the bridge and walk in a northerly direction to the site.

Activities
It's worth walking around the town's old section, a few blocks east of the train station and south of Jiefang Lu. For a view of the city climb **Wén Fēng Tǎ** (文峰塔), an ancient Buddhist pagoda.

Sleeping & Eating
Huáxià Bīnguǎn (华夏宾馆; ☎ 328 0726; Jiefang Dadao; s & d without bathroom from Y30, with bathroom from Y80) Ten minutes straight ahead from the train station on the right-hand side of the road is this fading but friendly (if a bit musty) hotel.

Yángguāng Bīnguǎn (阳光宾馆; ☎ 591 0669; 9 Xingxing Jie; s & d Y98-168; ✖) From the train station, walk straight ahead a block to Xinxing Jie, then turn right; it's on the left about 50m from the corner. The pricier rooms here are large and have wooden floorboards, along with new furnishings – definitely a bargain, considering the prices at other local hotels.

Ānyáng Bīnguǎn (安阳宾馆; ☎ 592 2219; fax 592 2244; 1 Youyi Lu; s & d from Y508; ✖) Recently upgraded to four stars, this place is the most sybaritic place in town; it also has a decent restaurant.

The old town is a good place to head to for restaurants, in particular along Hongqi Lu near the restored gate tower. The area surrounding Ānyáng Bīnguǎn is busy with roadside restaurants serving Muslim food.

Getting There & Away
BUS
Ānyáng's long-distance bus station has connections to Zhèngzhōu (Y33 to Y60, two to four hours) and Kāifēng (Y36, 3½ hours) every 20 to 30 minutes until noon and every hour thereafter. Frequent buses serve Linzhou City (Y7, two hours) and Luòyáng (Y50, four to five hours). A new road to Tàiyuán (in Shānxī) should reduce the journey time to five hours (Y90) but at the time of writing it was still seven or eight; consider going via Shíjiāzhuāng (in Héběi).

The long-distance bus station is close to the train station. Turn right after exiting the train station and then take the first left.

TRAIN
Ānyáng is on the main Běijīng–Zhèngzhōu railway line and it is easy to get connections to Wǔhàn, Guǎngzhōu and Běijīng, as most express trains stop here.

AROUND ĀNYÁNG
About 50km to the west of Ānyáng, in the Tàiháng Shān foothills, lies Línxiàn

County, although the name of the main town has been changed to **Linzhou City** (Lìnzhōu Shì).

Línxiàn is a rural area that ranks as one of the 'holy' places of Maoism because of the famous **Red Flag Canal** (Hóngqí Qú). To irrigate the district, a river was rerouted through a tunnel beneath a mountain and then along a new bed built on the side of steep cliffs.

The Red Flag Canal statistics are impressive: 1500km of canal dug, hills levelled, 134 tunnels pierced, 150 aqueducts constructed and enough earth displaced to build a road 1m high, 6m wide and 4000km long. The communists insist that this colossal job, carried out during the Cultural Revolution, was done entirely by the toiling masses without the help of engineers and machines.

Buses running from Ānyáng to Chángzhì in Shānxī go past the canal site. Alternatively, take a bus to Linzhou City and then transfer to another bus for the canal.

JĪGŌNG SHĀN 鸡公山
☎ 0376 / **elevation 744m**

Jīgōng Shān (Rooster Mountain; ☎ 691 2044; admission Y40), on the Hénán–Húběi border, was developed as a hill station resort by American missionaries in the early 20th century and became popular with Westerners living in Hànkǒu and Wǔhàn as a relief from the sweltering summers.

The name of the main peak, **Dawn Heralding Peak** (报晓峰; Bàoxiǎo Fēng), a large stone outcrop closely resembling a crowing rooster, pretty much says it all for views to be had here.

Over 200 European-style stone villas are spread around this breezy mountain retreat. Sites include the well-preserved former **American School** (美国事大; Měiguóshì Dàlóu), near the resort's main entrance. To the south, near the cable car, **Chiang Kaishek's Air Raid Shelter** (蒋介石防空洞; Jiǎng Jièshí Fángkōng Dòng) is part of his former residence and is open to visitors. On the path to the air raid shelter is the **Meiling Dance Hall** (美龄舞厅; Měilíng Wǔtīng), named after Chiang Kaishek's wife. The area also provides travellers with some good hiking opportunities. The main village in Jīgōng Shān, known as **Nánjiē**, is on the western flank of the mountain.

Sleeping & Eating
Some hotels here close during the winter months, so call before heading out. There are a handful of small, cheap guesthouses off the main road.

Yúnzhōng Bīnguǎn (云中宾馆; ☎ 691 2025; d/ste Y200/480; ✖) This stone castle is ideally located if you plan to catch the sunrise from Dawn Heralding Peak. The suites have fantastic views over the valley.

Friendship Hotel (友谊宾馆; Yǒuyì Bīnguǎn; ☎ 691 2091; tr/tw Y210/220; ✖) This large hotel is near the air raid shelter. All rooms have a private balcony.

Both these hotels have restaurants, but there are places to eat throughout the village – try the family-run teahouse next to the cable car.

Getting There & Away
The train station for Jīgōng Shān (with the same name) is on the railway line from Běijīng to Guǎngzhōu. However, almost nothing stops here.

The nearest main train station is located in Xìnyáng (信阳), one hour away; *lots* of trains stop here. Frequent minibuses depart for Xìnyáng (Y5) from the foot of Jīgōng Shān and also from the main gate (Y10).

From Xìnyáng you'll find minibuses to Jīgōng Shān's main gate (Y10) leave from in front of the train station. If you get dropped off at the foot of the mountain, you can catch a cab to the main gate for Y20.

A new expressway linking Zhèngzhōu with Húběi province was just being finished at the time of research, so express buses should be winging here from Wǔhàn and Zhèngzhōu.

KĀIFĒNG 开封
☎ 0378 / **pop 4,630,000**

Ubiquitous architectural anachronisms and thriving markets line the funky back streets of Kāifēng, the erstwhile prosperous capital of the Northern Song dynasty (960 to 1126).

Established south of the Yellow River but not far enough to avoid the river's occasional wrath, after centuries of flooding, the city of the Northern Song lies buried 8m to 9m below ground. Between 1194 and 1938 the city was flooded 368 times, an average of once every two years.

Damaging, yes, but travellers love the city for how it has deftly sidestepped the loss of aesthetic and cultural gems. The result? A thoroughly charming city. (Although locals do tut with embarrassment about being left behind in China's modernisation drive). One of the reasons you won't see soaring skyscrapers here is because civic planners and engineers are prohibited from constructing buildings requiring deep foundations for fear of destroying the city below.

Dynasties aside, Kāifēng was also the first city in China where Jewish people settled when they arrived, via India along the Silk Road, during the Song dynasty. A

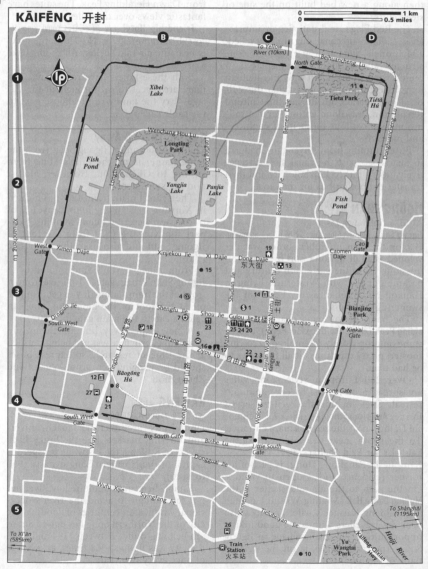

KĀIFĒNG 开封

small Christian community also lives in Kāifēng alongside a much larger local Muslim community.

Orientation

The southern long-distance bus station and the train station are both outside the old city walls (about 1km south); the rest of Kāifēng is mostly within the walled area. The city's pivotal point is the Sihou Jie and Madao Jie intersection; the famed street market here is particularly lively at night. Many of the wooden restaurants, shops and houses in this area were constructed during the Qing dynasty in the traditional Chinese style.

Information

Bank of China (Zhōngguó Yínháng; 64 Gulou Jie)
China Travel Service (CTS; Zhōngguó Lǚxíngshè; ☎ 595 5743; 98 Dayuan Kengyan Jie)
CITS (Zhōngguó Guójì Lǚxíngshè; ☎ 595 3698) Just east of the Kāifēng Bīnguǎn.
Internet café (wǎngbā; 2nd fl, Zhongshan Lu) A good surfing spot north of the PSB.

INFORMATION	
Bank of China 中国银行	1 C3
CITS 中国国际旅行社	2 C4
CTS 中国旅行社	3 C4
Internet Café 网吧	4 B3
Post Office 邮电局	5 B7
Post Office 邮电局	6 C3
PSB 公安局	7 B3
SIGHTS & ACTIVITIES	pp443–5
Bicycle Rental	8 B4
Dragon Pavilion 龙亭	9 B2
Fan Pagoda 繁塔	10 C5
Iron Pagoda 铁塔	11 D1
Kaifeng Museum 开封博物馆	12 A4
Kaifeng Synagogue 开封犹太教堂遗址	13 C3
Memorial to Liu Shaoqi 刘少奇陈列馆	14 C3
Shanshangan Guild Hall 陕山甘会馆	15 B3
Temple of the Chief Minister Market 大相国寺市场	16 B4
Temple of the Chief Minister 大相国寺	17 C4
Yanqing Temple 延庆观	18 B3
SLEEPING	◘ p445
Biànjīng Fàndiàn 汴京饭店	19 C3
Dàjīntái Bīnguǎn 大金台宾馆	20 C3
Dōngjīng Dàfàndiàn 东京大饭店	21 A4
Kāifēng Bīnguǎn 开封宾馆	22 C4
EATING	◘ p445
Dìyīlóu Bāozi Guǎn 第一楼包子馆	23 B3
Jiǎozi Guǎn 饺子馆	24 C3
Night Market 鼓楼夜市	25 C3
TRANSPORT	pp445–6
Southern Long-Distance Bus Station 长途汽车南站	26 C5
Western Long-Distance Bus Station 长途汽车西站	27 A4

Post and China Telecom (yóudiànjú; cnr Zhongshan Lu & Ziyou Lu); branch office (cnr Mujiaqiao Jie & Wushengjiao Jie)
PSB (Gōngānjú; ☎ 532 2242; 86 Zhongshan Lu; ✆ 8.30am-noon & 3-6pm) Gets fairly good reviews on visa renewals.

Sights

TEMPLE OF THE CHIEF MINISTER 大相国寺

This **temple** (Dà Xiàngguó Sì; ☎ 566 5878; Ziyou Lu; admission Y20; ✆ 8am-6.30pm) was founded in AD 555, but frequently rebuilt over the following 1000 years. The temple and the city were completely destroyed in the early 1640s when rebels opened the Yellow River's dikes.

Within the temple is a Qing dynasty statue of the 1000 Eye and 1000 Arm Guanyin. This beautiful sculpture, 6m tall, was carved entirely from one gingko tree. The temple is next door to an enormous market, **Temple of the Chief Minister Market** (Dà Xiàngguó Sì Shìchǎng), that sells all manners of goods.

SHANSHANGAN GUILD HALL 陕山甘会馆

Likely the most impressive of the city's extant edifices is this **guild hall** (Shǎnshān Gānhuì Guǎn; ☎ 598 5607; 85 Xufu Jie; admission Y15; ✆ 8.30am-6.30pm), built as a lodging and meeting place during the Qing dynasty by an association of merchants from other provinces. Wing-like eaves, fabulous carvings and ornate murals all smack of a temple. Restored (well) only recently, it's definitely worth a visit for a look-see at the life of the itinerant well-to-do. It's just east of Zhongshan Lu along a narrow side street.

IRON PAGODA 铁塔

The 55m-tall 11th-century **pagoda** (Tiě Tǎ; ☎ 286 2279; 210 Beimen Dajie; admission Y20; ✆ 7am-7pm) is made of brick covered in glazed chocolate-coloured tiles that look like you-know-what). Climb (warily and breathlessly) to the top of this impressive structure for a further Y10.

Take bus No 3 from the train station via Jiefang Lu to the route terminus, not far from the Iron Pagoda; it's a short walk east to the park's entrance from here.

FAN PAGODA 繁塔

This unusual **pagoda** (Fán Tǎ; admission Y5; ✆ 7am-7pm) is the oldest Buddhist structure in Kāifēng. The original was a nine-storey hexagonal building, typical of the Northern Song style. The pagoda is covered in tiles decorated with 108 different Buddha images.

You'll find the pagoda hidden among the alleyways in the southeastern part of the city. To get here cross southward over the railway tracks from Tielubeiyan Jie and take the first alleyway on your left. From here follow the red arrows spray-painted on the walls. Bus No 15 gets relatively close; ask the driver to let you off at the right stop.

MEMORIAL TO LIU SHAOQI 刘少奇陈列馆

This **memorial/museum** (Liú Shàoqí Chénlièguǎn; ☎ 596 5306; 10 Beitu Jie; admission Y10; ☼ 8am-6.30pm), filled with the most quotidian paraphernalia of daily life, is in the house where Liu spent the last month of his life. Liu Shaoqi (1898–1969) was Mao's intended successor until he was purged during the Cultural Revolution.

KAIFENG MUSEUM 开封博物馆

This **museum** (Kāifēng Bówùguǎn; ☎ 393 2178; 26 Yingbin Lu; admission Y10; ☼ 8.30am-11.30am & 3-6pm Tue-Sun), situated southwest of Bǎogōng Hú

(Baohong Lake), is a rather forlorn affair but for two Jewish stelae and some other artefacts from early settlers, but these are not open to the public without permits (Y50). This is also the location for the **Kaifeng Institute for Research on the History of Chinese Jews** (☎ 393 2178, ext 8010), which has detailed information about history of Jewish people in the region. Bus No 4 travels past here.

LONGTING PARK 龙亭公园

This **park** (Lóngtíng Gōngyuán; ☎ 566 0316; Zhongshan Lu; admission Y25; ☼ 6.30am-7pm) is largely covered by lakes and was the site of earlier dynastic palaces. On its drier northern rim near **Dragon Pavilion** (Lóng Tíng) there is a small children's fun park. A new theme park is slated to recreate the Kāifēng of its heyday, complete with cultural performances, folk art and music demonstrations; a new Jewish cultural center will also have displays.

YANQING TEMPLE 延庆观

Small Taoist **Yanqing Temple** (Yánqíng Guàn; ☎ 393 1800; Dazhifang Jie; admission Y25; ☼ 6.30am-7pm) was built in commemoration of Wang Zhe, founder of the True Unity Sect of

---

KĀIFĒNG'S ISRAELITES

Father Nicola Trigault translated and published the diaries of the Jesuit priest Matteo Ricci in 1615, and based on these diaries he gives an account of a meeting between Ricci and a Jew from Kāifēng. The Jew was on his way to Běijīng to take part in the imperial examinations, and Trigault writes:

When he (Ricci) brought the visitor back to the house and began to question him as to his identity, it gradually dawned upon him that he was talking with a believer in the ancient Jewish law. The man admitted that he was an Israelite, but he knew no such word as 'Jew'.

Ricci found out from the visitor that there were 10 or 12 families of Israelites in Kāifēng. A 'magnificent' synagogue had been built there and the five books of Moses had been preserved in the synagogue in scroll form for more than 500 years.

The visitor was familiar with the stories of the Old Testament, and some of the followers, he said, were expert in the Hebrew language. He also told Ricci that in a province which Trigault refers to as 'Cequian' at the capital of 'Hamcheu', there was a far greater number of Israelite families than in Kāifēng. Ricci sent one of his Chinese converts to Kāifēng, where he confirmed the visitor's story.

Today several hundred descendants of the original Jews live in Kāifēng, and though they still consider themselves Jewish, the religious beliefs and customs associated with Judaism have almost completely died out. The original synagogue was destroyed in a Yellow River (Huáng Hé) flood in 1642. It was rebuilt but destroyed by floods again in the 1850s. This time there was no money to rebuild it. Christian missionaries 'rescued' the temple's scrolls and prayer books in the late 19th century and these are now in libraries in Israel, Canada and the USA.

Taoism. The yurt-shaped Tower of the Jade Emperor was repeatedly buried during the floods but was excavated and repaired in 1985.

KAIFENG SYNAGOGUE 开封犹太教堂遗址
Unfortunately there is almost nothing left of the **synagogue** (kāifēng yóutài jiàotáng yízhǐ; 59 Beitu Jie), now the boiler room of the No 4 People's Hospital (on the bus No 3 route). You can see the remains of an iron cover over an old well, which still has water. The staff at the hospital have seen so many visitors coming through, they'll know what you're looking for. See the boxed text opposite for more details.

YELLOW RIVER 黄河
You can visit Yellow River (Huáng Hé), about 10km north of the city, although there isn't much to see because the water level is so low these days. Bus No 6 runs from near the Iron Pagoda to Yellow River twice daily. A taxi will cost Y50 to Y60 for the return trip.

Sleeping
Kāifēng is a place where independent travellers get a wider range of accommodation than those with lots of money to throw around.

Dàjīntái Bīnguǎn (☎ 595 6677, 255 2888; 17 Gulou Jie; dm Y50, d Y180; ❄) The Dàjīntái has fantastic, recently renovated rooms and is located next to the night market. The only downside – rooms are a bit small. Staff are friendly and seem willing to deal. Bus No 4 runs past.

Biànjīng Fàndiàn (☎ 288 6699; fax 288 2449; 109 Dong Dajie; dm Y50, d/tr from Y120/180; ❄) The cheaper rooms here are comfortable and quite clean – the downside is that they face the street. Take bus No 3 from the train station or the western long-distance bus station.

Dōngjīng Dàfàndiàn (☎ 398 9388; fax 595 6661; 99 Yingbin Lu; d from Y288; ❄ ❄) The grimness of this hotel's location belies its rather nice rooms – well, the recently redecorated ones, anyway. Once a jewel, it's well faded but is still a pretty good mid-range choice.

Kāifēng Bīnguǎn (☎ 595 5589; www.kfhotel.com; 66 Ziyou Lu; d/tr/q from Y200/270/320; ❄) This ornate Russian-built hotel, constructed in the style of traditional Chinese architecture, is in the centre of town. Set well off the road within an attractive back courtyard, the lodging wings offer travellers a very quiet night's sleep. No one will mistake this for a sybaritic international luxury hotel; still, the service and rooms make this competitive, *yuán* for *yuán* with four-star hotels in town. Bus No 5 runs here from the train station.

Eating
Kāifēng offers the traveller some gastronomic delights, especially at the famed **night market** (cnr Gulou Jie & Madao Jie). Worth sampling here is *ròuhé* (a local snack of fried vegetables and pork, or mutton, stuffed into a 'pocket' of flat bread); there is also a good veggie version. Another speciality are *chòu gānzǐ* (smelly dried things), which taste as bad as they sound! With a big bottle of beer costing Y2, this is the place to table-hop and try the different *xiǎo chī* (small eats), such as hand-pulled and shaved noodles, won ton soup and kebabs.

Jiǎozi Guǎn (Gulou Jie; dishes from Y2) Adjacent to the Dàjīntái Bīnguǎn, this three-storey Chinese building is straight out of a Qing dynasty novel. What's more, the dumplings are tasty and inexpensive.

Dìyīlóu Bāozi Guǎn (☎ 565 0780; 8 Sihou Jie; dumplings Y5) The *xiǎolóng bāo* (small buns filled with pork) served here are so tasty, the restaurant is always packed.

Getting There & Away
BUS
To Zhèngzhōu slowpoke buses (Y12, one hour) and expresses (Y17 to Y24) leave from both the western long-distance bus station and the southern long-distance bus station (opposite the train station) – more from the former, but the latter has more expresses.

To Luòyáng (Y35, 2½ hours), express buses leave every twenty minutes; it's hard to get a regular bus now.

From the southern long-distance bus station there are half-hourly buses to Ānyáng (Y36, 3½ hours) from 7am until 5pm. These buses do not use the expressway, and at times it takes over four hours.

A new expressway east into Ānhuī has finally been completed.

TRAIN

Kāifēng is on the railway line between Xī'ān and Shànghǎi and trains are frequent. Tickets (especially for sleepers) can be hard to obtain, so consider leaving from Zhèngzhōu instead. Express trains to Zhèngzhōu take about one hour (Y12); to Shànghǎi 12 hours; and to Xī'ān 10 hours. Slow trains heading to Bózhōu and Héféi in Ānhuī run from here but departure times are inconvenient.

Getting Around

Buses departing from both of Kāifēng's bus stations travel to all the major tourist areas. Gulou Jie, Sihou Jie and Shudian Jie are all good for catching buses. Pedicabs and taxis are also available and can be found congregating around the bus and train stations. Budget hotels can generally help you find a bicycle to rent, generally for around Y10 per day.

Húběi 湖北

CONTENTS

HIGHLIGHTS

- Contemplate Yangzi River history and modernisation aboard a **river ferry** (p459)
- Putt across the Yangzi River on classic **river ferries** (p456) in Wǔhàn
- Get to the roots of *tàijíquán* in the temples (and now schools) where it was born in **Wǔdāng Shān** (p456)
- Hop on a bus from Yíchāng to gape at the leviathan **Three Gorges Dam** (p458)
- Explore the forests of **Shénnóngjià** (p457), and perhaps stumble across the region's legendary ape-man

★ Wǔdāng Shān

★ Shénnóngjià

Three Gorges
★ Dam

★ Wǔhàn

★ Yangzi River

■ POP: 64.2 MIL   ■ AREA: 187,400 SQ KM   ■ www.hubei.gov.cn

Site of the great industrial city and river port of Wǔhàn, dissected by the Yangzi River (Cháng Jiāng) and its many tributaries, and supporting over 60 million people, Húběi is one of China's most important provinces. Eminently fertile, it has for millennia been economically and strategically important. Indeed, it is the self-touted 'Gateway to Nine Provinces'.

Travellers have long known the province for lazy ferry cruises down Cháng Jiāng from Chóngqìng. Today ferry traffic stops in Yíchāng due to the construction of the Three Gorges Dam. This massive dam is itself arguably one of the modern wonders of China. Eons of history will sink below the waterline, but the government hopes to finally arrest the wrath of the mighty river during flood periods.

And now that the leviathan dam has slowed boats, travellers also have a chance to experience Húběi's variegated and oft-overlooked regions.

The province comprises two quite different areas. The eastern two-thirds is a low-lying plain drained by the Yangzi River and its main northern tributary, Han River (Hàn Jiāng). Don't let the word 'plain' fool you: much of this area is carpeted by undulating hills. These gumdrop ranges rise steeply into a more rugged area of highlands channelled with small cultivated valleys and basins dividing Húběi from Sìchuān. Eventually, the province tops out in the wilder mountainous and forested third of the province. In total, more than 70% of the province is hill or mountain – and chock-full of lakes. (A perfect escape from the Yangzi River region's notorious summer swelter!)

Some 95% of the province is populated by ethnic Han Chinese, but pockets of Tujia, Miao, Hui, and Mongol minority groups can also be found.

History

The plain was settled by the Han Chinese in 1000 BC. Following the demise of the Eastern Han dynasty in AD 220, warlords skirmished for control from the Yellow River (Huáng Hé) basin all the way through to the southwest regions. Initially weak, the warlords along the Yangzi River finally united and defeated military groups in what is modern-day Húběi. The resultant political manoeuvrings and continued armed struggle ultimately gave rise to the Three Kingdoms Period (AD 220–60). Around the 7th century the region was intensively settled and cultivated, and by the 11th century it was producing a rice surplus, an extraordinary agricultural output that still continues today. In the late 19th century Húběi was the first area in the Chinese interior to undergo considerable industrialisation.

Climate

Wǔhàn, the capital, is aptly dubbed a 'Furnace of China'; in July and August, it's abysmally hot and humid (above 40°C commonly) and no prevailing monsoon winds from the southeast make it this far. The eastern plains aren't much better; however, the western mountains are far more temperate.

Rainfall is heavy in the southeast (averaging 160cm annually), and decreasing north and west (a mere 80cm per annum average). Expect most of it April through July.

Language

Húběi officially has two dialects of Northern Mandarin – South-West Mandarin and Lower-Mid Yangzi Mandarin – but these are broken into innumerable local variants. 'Wuhanese' is a catch phrase for the capital's peculiar speech; this varies, literally, from neighbourhood to neighbourhood. Most

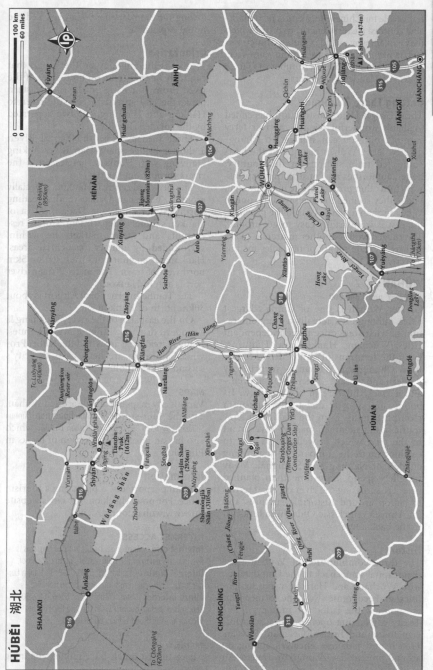

HÚBĚI 湖北

SHAANXI

To Beijing (850km)

HÉNÁN

ÁNHUĪ

Fùyáng

Fúnán

Huángchuān

Máchéng

106

Jieong Mountain (820m)

Guǎngshuǐ

Dàwù

107

Xīnyáng

WŬHÀN

Huánggāng

Xiàogǎn

Yangtzi Lake

Qíchūn

Huángshí

Wùxué

Yángxīn

Huángméi

Lú Shān (1474m)

Jiǔjiāng

Gūshān

105

316

NÁNCHĀNG

JIĀNGXĪ

Xúshuǐ

Fùtóu Lake

Xiánníng

Jiāyú

Chángjiāng (Yangzi)

107

Yuèyáng

To Chángshā (170km)

Yangtzi River

Dòngtíng Lake

Ānlù

Yúnmèng

Xiāntáo

Hong Lake

318

Chang Lake

Jīngzhōu

Suízhōu

Nányáng

Zǎoyáng

Dèngzhōu

316

Xiāngfán

Han River (Hàn Jiāng)

Nánzhāng

Jīngmén

Yàquèlíng

Zhǐjiāng

Sōngzī

Lǐ lan

Chángdé

HÚNÁN

Zhāngjiājiè

To Lùōyáng (240cm)

Dānjiāngkǒu Reser-oir

Dānjiāngkǒu

Wǔdāngshān

Wǔdāng Shān

Tiānzhù Peak (1612m)

Fángxiàn

Dàmáng

Xīngshān

Xiàngxī

Zǐguī

Wǔfēng

Sandoúpíng (Three Gorges Dam Construction Site)

Yídū

Yíchāng

Shíyàn

Lǜpǐng

Yúnxiàn

316

Bāhé

Zhúshān

Sōngbǎi

Mùyúpíng

209

Láojūn Shān (2936m)

Shénnóngjià

Shénnóngjià Shān (3105m)

Bādōng

Qīng River (Qīng Jiāng)

Fēngjié

Chánt Jiāng

Qīng River (Qīng Jiāng)

Lǐchuān

Ēnshī

209

Xiānfēng

Zhāngjiājiè

318

SHAANXI

Ānkāng

Yángxī

Wànxiàn

CHÓNGQÌNG

To Chóngqìng (420km)

100 km
60 miles
0
0

noticeable for Chinese speakers is its remarkable contrast (read: strength) in pitch, which may explain why outside Chinese sometimes feel denizens of Húběi are a bit in-your-face. Southeastern Húběi has a number of Gàn (a dialect of Mandarin) speakers.

Getting There & Around

Three Gorges Dam construction has ended Wǔhàn's wonderful reign as a river ferry stop-off, but you can still get to Chóng-qìng by ferry. Wǔhàn has one of the best-connected train stations in the country; better, authorities are constructing express-ways into other provinces like mad (though, oddly, they seemed to have saved the one to Wǔdāng Shān for last). Within the province, the east is wonderfully easy to get around. The rugged west is another matter, as peaks and trees create plenty of obstacles for bus drivers.

WǓHÀN 武汉

☎ 027 / pop 8,340,000

Greater Wǔhàn is one of China's largest cities, although it's actually a conglomeration of what were once three independent cities: Wǔchāng, Hànkǒu and Hànyáng. Long the terminus of Yangzi River ferries from Chóngqìng, Wǔhàn is surprisingly modern and vibrant – cosmopolitan even – and a lovely mixture of old and new. Its boom came mostly due to its long-term river port status. Even the decline in ferry traffic hasn't stemmed massive investment in the city, which is well on its way to catching up to the comparatively sparkling citadels of Nánjīng and Shànghǎi. Many travellers spend more time than planned here, crisscrossing the river on local ferries to snoop around historic structures and museums; even classic Old China lurks yet in the back alleys.

History

The three communities of Wǔhàn trace their capital status back to the Han dynasty, with Wǔchāng and Hànkǒu vying for po-litical and economic sway (the former wins for politics, the latter for industry). The Treaty of Nanjing opened the city to for-eign trade, and British, German, Russian, French and Japanese enclaves sprang up around present-day Zhongshan Dadao. An industrialisation effort started in 1895, fol-

lowing the Sino-Japanese War, sparked the initial expansion.

Orientation

Wǔhàn is the only city on the Yangzi that can truly be said to lie on both sides of the river. From Wǔchāng on the southeastern bank, the city spreads across the river to Hànkǒu and Hànyáng, the two separated by the smaller Han River.

Three bridges cross the Yangzi River; a shorter bridge spans Han River linking Hànyáng with Hànkǒu. Ferries cross the rivers throughout the day.

The city's real centre is Hànkǒu, especially around Zhongshan Dadao (and spreading northwest across Jiefang Dadao). Most of Hànkǒu's hotels, department stores, res-taurants and street markets lie within, surrounded by quieter residential areas. Hànkǒu has an enormous train station 5km northwest of town. The main Wǔhàn river port is also in Hànkǒu.

The Tianhe International Airport is about 30km north of Hànkǒu.

On the east side of the river, Wǔchāng is a modern district with long, wide avenues. Many recreational areas and the Hubei Pro-vincial Museum are here, as is the city's second train station.

MAPS

Various city maps are on sale around Wǔhàn. Try the four-storey **Xinhua Bookshop** (Xīnhuá Shūdiàn; ☎ 8378 3952; 896 Zhongshan Dadao), which also has an impressive selection of books in English.

Information

Wǔhàn purportedly is preparing a tourism office. For now, check out the city's website on www.wuhantour.gov.cn.

INTERNET ACCESS

Internet café (wǎngbā; per hr Y2) In Wǔchāng, this is five minutes north of the train station, on the 2nd floor.
Internet World (wǎngbā; ☎ 8221 0189; 38 Tianjin Lu; per hr Y2) China Telecom's Internet café, in Hànkǒu.
Mínzú Internet (Mínzú Wǎngbā; ☎ 8566 2089; 608 Zhongshan Dadao; per hr Y3) On the 2nd floor of the Wǔhàn Xīn Mínzhòng Lèyuán building.

MONEY

Major tourist hotels have money-changing services.

Bank of China (Zhōngguó Yínháng; cnr Zhongshan Dadao & Jianghan Lu) Credit card advances (ATMs soon) are straightforward at this main branch in Hànkǒu.

POST & COMMUNICATIONS
Long-distance telephone calls can be made from China Telecom phones throughout the city.

Phone office (Zhōngguó Diànxìn; 2nd fl, Wǔhàn Xīn Mínzhòng Lèyuán, 608 Zhongshan Dadao) This convenient office is in a popular shopping centre in a yellow concession-era building.

Post office (yóujú; Zhongshan Dadao) Opposite the Bank of China. Another is opposite Wǔhàn's train station.

TRAVEL AGENCIES
China International Travel Service (CITS; Zhōngguó Guójì Lǚxíngshè; ☎ 8578 4125; 26 Taibei Yilu) Helpful; it's in Hànkǒu opposite the Swiss-belhotel on the Park (the building entrance has a CITS sign). Take the lift to the 7th floor. Bus No 9 stops near the western end of Taibei Yilu on Xinhua Lu; from there it's a five-minute walk.

China Travel Service (CTS; Zhōngguó Lǚxíngshè; ☎ 8285 5259; 142 Yanjiang Dadao) Offers the usual services and has staff members who speak English. Across from the Wǔhàn ferry terminal.

VISAS
Public Security Bureau (PSB; Gōngānjú; ☎ 8271 2355; 306 Shengli Jie; ☽ 9-11.30am & 2-5pm) A 20-minute walk northeast of Jiang Han Fàndiàn (p454). Visas generally take three days.

Sights & Activities
Many European-style buildings from the concession era remain – Russian buildings along Yanjiang Dadao on the northwestern bank of the Yangzi, and British, French and German structures on Zhongshan Dadao.

WUHAN YANGZI RIVER BIG BRIDGE
武汉长江大桥
Wǔchāng and Hànyáng are linked by this enormous 110m-long and 80m-high **bridge** (Wǔhàn Chángjiāng Dàqiáo). The completion of the bridge in 1957 marked one of Communist China's first great engineering feats. Until then all traffic had to be laboriously ferried across the river. Forty years passed before another rose to the north.

HUBEI PROVINCIAL MUSEUM
湖北省博物馆
This **museum** (Húběi Shěng Bówùguǎn; ☎ 8679 4127; 1856 Donghu Lu; admission Y30; ☽ 8.30-11.30am &

1.30-4.30pm summer, 11am-4pm rest of year) is well worth your time, highlighted by a large collection of artefacts from the Zenghouyi Tomb, unearthed in 1978 on the outskirts of the city of Suízhōu, between Xiāngfán and Wǔhàn.

The Zenghouyi Tomb dates from around 433 BC, when the male internee, surnamed Yi, was buried with about 7000 of his favourite artefacts – informative photographs and English captions help explain all of it. Spectacular is a two-tone, seven-note scale of 64 bronze bells that are played using hammer-like objects and poles. The entire bell set has intricate carvings and has warrior figures serving as bases. The set also shows that a musical scale existed in ancient China.

Throughout the day wonderful musical performances on duplicate bells are introduced in English.

The museum is beside Dōng Hú (East Lake) in Wǔchāng, one of the most pleasant areas in Wǔhàn. Tourist bus No 402 passes by. Alternatively, take bus No 14 from the Zhonghua Lu pier to the last stop, then walk back along the road for about 10 minutes, turning down a road that's signposted for Mao Zedong Villa.

MAO ZEDONG VILLA 毛泽东别墅
This bucolic hideaway **villa** (Máo Zédōng Biéshù; ☎ 8679 6109; Donghu Lu; admission Y10; ☽ 8am-6pm) was one of the Chairman's faves. Mao stayed here more than 20 times between 1960 and 1974, including nearly 18 months between 1966 and 1969. The villa's pleasant tree-filled grounds have become a haven for a variety of birds.

There is plenty to see, even if you feel over-Maoed. To get there, take bus No 14 from the Zhonghua Lu pier to the last stop and walk about 10 minutes further. Tourist Bus No 402 also passes by.

WUHAN UNIVERSITY 武汉大学
Wuhan University (Wǔhàn Dàxué), beside Luòjiā Shān in Wǔchāng, was founded in 1913, and many of the charming campus buildings originate from that period.

The university was the site of the 1967 'Wuhan Incident' – a protracted battle during the Cultural Revolution, where machine gun nests were built on top of the library and supply tunnels were dug through the

CENTRAL CHINA

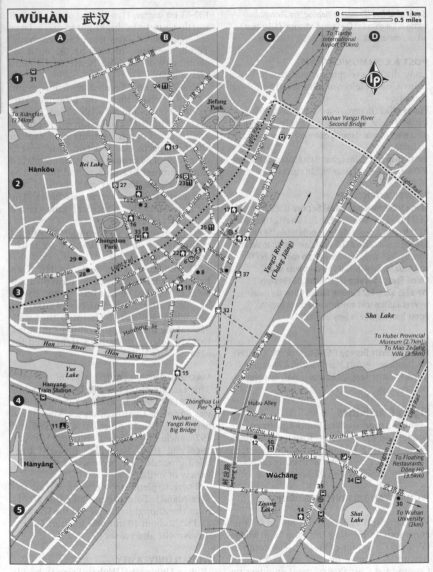

WǓHÀN 武汉

0 _____ 1 km
0 _____ 0.5 miles

To Tianhe
International
Airport (30km)

To Xiángfán
(334km)

Fazhan Dadao 发展大道

Huangpuzhe Lu

Sanyan-qiao Lu

Jiefang
Park

Wuhan Yangzi River
Second Bridge

Light Rail

Zhongshan Dadao

Hànkǒu

Bei Lake

Xinhua Xialu

Qingshan Lu

19

Jianghan Beilu

Hangkong Lu

27

20

Taibei Lu

Taibei Lu

2

Jiefang Dadao

Jianghan Dadao

26
23

7

Linjiang Dadao

Light Rail

Jianghan Lu
16
33
18

Zhongshan
Park

17

Shengli

Jianghan Dadao
25

5
21

Jiefang Dadao

29

28

Light Rail

Shundao Jie

Qiaokou Lu

22
1

Nanjing Lu

Yanjiang Dadao 沿江大道

Yangzi River
(Chang Jiang)

Zhongshan Dadao

8

3

37

Biohua Jie

13

Minsheng Lu

Zhongshan Dadao

Hanzheng Jie

32

Han River
(Hàn Jiāng)

Yue
Lake

Hanyang
Train Station

11

Zhongjia Lu

Lanjiang Lu

Yaolu Di

Hànyáng

Qintai Lu

15

Linjiang Dadao

Sha Lake

To Hubei Provincial
Museum (2.7km);
To Mao Zedong
Villa (3.5km)

Zhonghua Lu
Pier

Wuhan
Yangzi River
Big Bridge

Hubu Alley

Zhonghua Lu

Minzhu Lu 民主路

Zhongshan Lu

Minzhu Lu

12

10

To Floating
Restaurants;
Dōng Hú
(3.5km)

Wuluo Lu

9

34

Ziyang Lu

Wǔchāng

Ziyang
Lake

Zhongshan Lu

14

35
4

36

30

Shai
Lake

To Wuhan
University
(2km)

Vingwu Dadao

---

hill. For a bit of Cultural Revolution nostalgia take bus No 12 from Zhonghua Lu pier to the terminus.

HISTORIC BUILDINGS

Doubling as a curiosity shop and active Buddhist temple, **Guiyuan Temple** (☎ 8484 1434; 20 Cuiweiheng Lu; admission Y10; ☯ 8am-4.30pm)

in Hànyáng has buildings dating from the late-Ming and early Qing dynasties. The main attractions are statues of Buddha's disciples in an array of comical poses. To get there, Tourist Bus No 401 passes by; public bus No 6 also comes close.

Once serving as a military observation post, the five-level **Yellow Crane Tower**

INFORMATION		TRANSPORT	pp455-6
Bank of China 中国银行................1 B3	Holiday Inn Riverside	CAAC	
CITS 中国国际旅行社.............2 B2	晴川假日酒店.............15 B4	中国民航售票处........28 A3	
CTS 中国旅行社............3 C3	Huáxià Dàjiǔdiàn 华夏大酒店.........16 B2	China Southern Airlines (Hànkǒu)	
Internet Café 网吧..........4 C5	Jiāng Hàn Fàndiàn 江汉饭店.........17 C2	中国南方航空公司........29 A3	
Internet World 网吧.........5 C2	Mèngtiān Hú Bīnguǎn 梦天湖宾馆..18 B2	China Southern Airlines (Wǔchāng)	
Post Office 邮局..........6 B3	Shangri-La Hotel	中国南方航空公站........30 D5	
PSB 公安局...........7 C2	香格里拉大酒店.........19 B2	Hankou Train Station	
Telephone Office 中国电信..........(see 5)	Swiss-belhotel on the Park	汉口新火车站..........31 A1	
Xinhua Bookshop 新华书店.........8 B3	瑞雅国际酒店.........20 B2	Hankou-Wuchang Ferries	
	Xiélì Bīnguǎn 协力宾馆.........21 C3	汉口武昌渡船........32 B3	
SIGHTS & ACTIVITIES	pp451-3	Xuángōng Fàndiàn 璇宫饭店.........22 B3	Long-Distance Bus Station (Hànkǒu)	
Changchun Temple 长春观.........9 D5		长途汽车站........33 B3	
Former Headquarters of the Wuchang	EATING	pp454-5	Long-Distance Bus Station (Wǔchāng)	
Uprising 武昌起义纪念馆......10 C4	Fantasy Land of Oz	武昌长途汽车........34 D5	
Guiyuan Temple 归园寺.........11 A4	野仙踪素食店.........23 B2	Long-Distance Bus Station (Wǔchāng)	
Yellow Crane Tower 黄鹤楼........12 C4	Kaiwei Beer House 凯威啤酒室.........24 B1	武昌长途汽车........35 C5	
	Lǎotōngchéng Jiǔlóu 老通城酒楼........25 B2	Wuchang Train Station	
SLEEPING	pp453-4		武昌火车站........36 C5	
Dàhuá Fàndiàn 大华饭店........13 B3	ENTERTAINMENT	p455	Wuhan Ferry Terminal	
Hánghǎi Bīnguǎn 航海宾馆........14 C5	Mèimèi Jiǔbā 美美酒吧.........26 B2	武汉港客运站........37 C3	
	Red Passion Club..........27 B2		

(Huánghè Lóu; ☎ 8887 5179; Wuluo Lu; admission Y35; ⏱ 7.30am-6pm) sits at the southern end of the Wuhan Chang Jiang Big Bridge and is one of Wǔhàn's noted landmarks. Constructed during the Warring States period, the 51m tower was a site of inspiration for poets like Li Bai. The double-decker bus No 64 loops the city and stops near the tower; alternatively, take bus No 1, 4 or 10.

At the beginning of Wuluo Lu, below the Yellow Crane Tower, is a small square with a statue of Sun Yatsen. Behind is a colonial-style red brick building that is the **Former Headquarters of the Wuchang Uprising** (Xīnhàigémìng Wǔchāng Qǐyì Jìnianguǎn) of 10 October 1911, which marked the end of the Qing dynasty. Sun Yatsen wasn't in China at that time, but he returned as president of the new republic.

Further east on Wuluo Lu is the lovely Ming dynasty-style **Changchun Temple** (Chángchūn Guān; ☎ 8280 1399; admission Y5; ⏱ 7.30am-5pm), a Taoist temple dating from the Han dynasty. In the middle of the courtyard is a statue of a very sagely looking Laotzu, the founder of Taoism. There is also a vegetarian restaurant on site.

Sleeping
BUDGET
Wuhan University Foreign Student Dormitory (Liúxuéshēnglóu; ☎ 8768 2813; dm Y40; ✖) In eastern Wǔchāng, via bus No 12 from Zhonghua Lu pier and then a 30-minute walk uphill via Xuefu Lu and Wenti Lu, this is the cheapest place in town (phone first). This dormitory also has clean, basic doubles. About 200m from here is a **guesthouse** (☎ 8768 2930; tw with bathroom & air-con Y180)

for visiting scholars and students and which you'll probably be referred to.

Hánghǎi Bīnguǎn (Marine Hotel; ☎ 8874 0122; fax 8807 8717; 452 Zhongshan Lu; s/d from Y128/138; ✖) Diagonally opposite the Wǔchāng train station is this homey place with an exceedingly helpful staff. Nice pluses are the solid restaurant, ticket booking, and even satellite TV. Bus No 507 from the Wǔchāng train station chugs to the ferry terminal in Hànkǒu.

Mèngtiān Hú Bīnguǎn (Mengtian Lake Hotel; ☎ 8579 6368 ext 8188; fax 8575 070; 1305 Jiefang Dadao; s/d from Y78/108; ✖) Next to the Hànkǒu long-distance bus station, this hotel has a variety of rooms, ranging from simple to comfy; the more you pay, the better the room.

MID-RANGE
Mid-range is where most travellers can find the best bargains.

Xiélì Bīnguǎn (☎ 8280 3903; 2 Tianjin Lu; s/tw Y158/208; ✖) Just north of the Wǔhàn ferry terminal, this place has decent twins, though something of a dark interior and atmosphere – but an unbeatable location.

Huáxià Dàjiǔdiàn (☎ 6230 0787; fax 8579 5688; 294 Xinhua Lu; s & d Y188-348; ✖) An oft-overlooked hotel, it's about 500m northwest of the Hànkǒu long-distance bus station. Deluxe rooms set around a courtyard on the top floor can go much lower than listed.

Dàhuá Fàndiàn (☎ 8566 3454; fax 8566 5076; 708 Zhongshan Dadao; s/d/ste Y320/620/1080; ✖) Fantastically central, this sophisticated hotel has gorgeous rooms – some with balconies. Much cheaper rooms (from Y158) are available, though these generally have seen little renovation.

DAY TRIP

A lovely day trip includes the enormous East Lake Park (Dōnghú Gōngyuán), which the Hubei Provincial Museum sits adjacent to. Over a dozen scenic spots are found along (and in the middle of) the lake and you could easily spend a day tracing its shoreline on buses. Take a ferry from Hànkǒu to the Zhonghua Lu pier in Wǔchāng, then board bus No 36 to Mó Shān. Take another ferry across the lake to East Lake Park, walk to the museum, then get bus No 14 to the Yellow Crane Tower (Huánghè Lóu), and finally catch a ferry back to Hànkǒu. Or cheat via tourist buses 401 and 402 (see p456).

Swiss-belhotel on the Park (Ruìyǎ Guójì Jiǔdiàn; ☎ 6885 1888; www.swiss-belhotel.com; 9 Taibei Yilu; s/d from Y330/410; ☒ ☒ ☐) The paint was drying on this spotless Swiss-run operation when we visited – it's a good deal, considering the amenities and level of service. Excellent business apartments and family suites are available. All rooms have high-speed Internet access. Rates include buffet breakfast.

Xuángōng Fàndiàn (☎ 6882 2588; www.xuangong hotel.com; 57 Jianghan Lu; s/d with balcony Y380/480; ☒) Superbly located on a pedestrian-only shopping street in Hànkǒu's city centre, this hotel has a variety of rooms (some triples), so peruse a few and definitely bargain.

TOP END

Most of the top-end places have an additional 15% service charge.

Jiāng Hàn Fàndiàn (☎ 8281 1600; www.jhhotel .com; 245 Shengli Jie; d US$80, ste US$200-280; ☒ ☒) This is *the* place to stay if you can afford it. The erstwhile French embassy, it is one of the best examples of colonial architecture in this part of China with a smashing interior. The hotel has its own post office, shops and an excellent restaurant.

Holiday Inn Riverside (Qíngchuān Jiàrì Jiǔdiàn; ☎ 8471 6688; www.sixcontinentshotels.com; 88 Xima Chang Jie; d with river view Y449-899; ☒ ☒ ☐ ☒) Accessible only by taxi, this branch of the Holiday Inn in Hànyáng is near an old city gate, on the edge of the river, north of the Wuhan Chang Jiang Big Bridge – not a convenient location but very quiet. The

hotel attendants and bellboys wear traditional Chinese dress. Steep discounts are also given here.

Shangri-La Hotel (Xiānggélǐlā Dàjiǔdiàn; ☎ 8580 6868; www.shangri-la.com; 700 Jianshe Lu; d US$167-215; ☒ ☒ ☐ ☒) Although a bit far from central Hànkǒu, the well-equipped Shangri-La is still unbeatable in terms of service and facilities. Its Western café serves excellent cuisine.

Eating & Drinking

Popular local snacks worth trying include fresh catfish from Dōng Hú in the east of the city, and charcoal-grilled whole pigeons served with a sprinkling of chilli. You can try some of these dishes on the **floating restaurants** at the end of Bayi Lu on the shore of Dōng Hú.

Night markets (*yèshìchǎng*) spring up east and west of the Jianghan Lu pedestrian zone in Hànkǒu, particularly Minsheng Lu to the west and Dazhi Jie, between Jiefang Dadao and Zhongshan Dadao.

No city in China breakfasts like Wǔhàn (no exaggeration – poets have celebrated it for centuries). Head directly to Wǔchāng's **Hùbù Xiàng** (Hubu Alley), a few minutes from the Zhonghua Lu pier and packed with cubbyhole purveyors of local wake-up sustenance, many over a century old. Mrs Xu's fish mush is appetising, but Granny Shi's *règàn miàn* (hot/dry noodles) are quite simply a reason for living (Wǔhàn's hot/dry noodles are one of China's five famous noodle dishes).

Lǎotóngchéng Jiǔlóu (☎ 8285 9036; 1 Dazhi Lu; dishes Y4-52) This bustling canteen on the corner of Dazhi Lu and Zhongshan Dadao is a great place to do a bit of people watching. It serves a tasty snack called *dòupí*, made with a bean curd base – its name translates as 'bean skin' – rolled around a filling of rice and diced meat, vegetables (*shuāngdōng dòupí*) or egg (*dànguāng dòupí*). *Dòupí* is no great delicacy, but at Y4 a serving you can't go wrong. There is also a restaurant upstairs.

Fantasy Land of Oz (Lǜyè Xiānzōngsù Shídiàn; ☎ 8573 4226; 83 Xianggang Lu; dishes from Y15) Strange name but a phenomenal vegetarian restaurant, with dishes so resembling meat-based dishes in form and taste that you can hardly tell the difference. The at-attention staff and devotion to presentation belie its semi-casual atmosphere. Trendy mid-range eateries are found nearby.

Kaiwei Beer House (Kǎiwēi Píjiǔwū; ☎ 8260 5679; 71 Huangxiaohe Lu) Which is better, the spicy, all-you-can-eat Sichuanese hotpot (Y28) or rich, German-brewed beer? You be the judge!

Entertainment
Discos and nightclubs are opening all over Hànkǒu; currently, Jianshe Dadao and off-streets is the most popular area.

Red Passion Club (Jianshe Dadao) This is the most central of many white-hot dance clubs in this zone; just follow the crowds to the others nearby.

Měiměi Jiǔbā (Meimei Bar; 100 Xianggang Lu) This longtime fave has dancing most nights. From the Xianggang Lu and Jiefang Dadao intersection, walk north for about 10 minutes. The club is on the left.

Getting There & Away
The best way to get to eastern destinations such as Nánjīng and Shànghǎi is by air, rather than the circuitous rail route.

AIR
More than 120 flights a day serve almost everywhere. The **Civil Aviation Administration of China ticket office** (CAAC; Zhōngguó Mínháng; 1089 Jiefang Dadao) is in Hànkǒu, but it's better to go to **China Southern Airlines** (Zhōngguó Nánfāng Hángkōng Gōngsī; ☎ 8361 1/56; 1 Hankong Lu). In Wǔchāng there is a **China Southern Airlines office** (☎ 8764 5121; 586 Wuluo Lu). Major daily flights include Běijīng (Y1080), Guǎngzhōu (Y910), Shànghǎi (Y810) and Xī'ān (Y690). Daily international flights go to Hong Kong (Y1850), and less regular ones to Bangkok, Fukuoka and Macau.

BOAT
You have to take a bus to Yíchāng, from where boats travel upriver to Chóngqìng. If you're looking to travel downstream on the Yangzi River toward Nánjīng or Shànghǎi, be aware that at the time of writing bottom-end passenger ferry traffic was dwindling and may not even be available within the life of this edition. (You should also keep in mind that most travellers find the waters downstream from Wǔhàn to Shànghǎi the least impressive in any event.)

You can, however, still find myriad mid-to high-end cruises – sybaritic foreigner-filled behemoths along with some much cheaper Chinese tour boats – operating between Chóngqìng and Shànghǎi, with a stop in Wǔhàn.

BUS
It's most convenient (but not always necessary) to use Hànkǒu for northern routes and Wǔchāng for southern routes (and Yíchāng).

The main **long-distance bus station** (Chángtú Qìchēzhàn; Jiefang Dadao) is in Hànkǒu, between Xinhua Lu and Jianghan Beilu. From Hànkǒu there are daily departures to Chángshā (Y92, 4½ hours), Nánchāng (Y85 to Y116, seven hours) and Shànghǎi (Y310, 15 hours), among others. For services to Zhèngzhōu (Y96, 12 hours) staff were pointing to the train station, but with a new expressway, this should change.

An expressway to Wǔdāng Shān is *gradually* being built, and some day will result in a smooth ride of five or six hours. Currently, buses to Xiāngfán (Y65 to Y86, five to six hours), en route to Wǔdāng Shān, leave from the Hànkǒu and Wǔchāng long-distance bus stations; sometimes the latter has direct express buses to Wǔdāng Shān, though these are generally sleeper buses that travel through the night. You can also get buses to Yíchāng (Y85 to Y116, three to four hours), Shànghǎi and other destinations from Wǔchāng. One bus station is on Wuluo Lu; the other one is a five-minute walk north of the train station.

TRAIN
Wǔhàn is on the main line running between Běijīng and Guǎngzhōu; express trains to Kūnmíng, Xī'ān, Hong Kong (Kowloon) and Lánzhōu run via the city. Trains going to major destinations such as these depart from both the Hànkǒu and Wǔchāng train stations. Trains to Shànghǎi, however, leave from the Wǔchāng station. Most trains going to Shíyàn (Y150, 12 hours) and Liùlǐpíng – cities near Wǔdāng Shān – leave from the Wǔchāng station. At Hànkǒu station, hard and soft sleepers must be booked in the small ticket office between the waiting hall and the main ticket office.

There is also a train ticket office in Hànkǒu adjacent to the long-distance bus station. You can book sleepers three days in advance.

Tickets for trains originating from Wǔchāng must be purchased at the Wǔchāng station rather than the Hànkǒu station. You can also book tickets at the Wǔchāng bus stations.

Destinations include Běijīng (Y248 to Y347, 12 to 13 hours), Guǎngzhōu (Y257 to Y315, 15 to 17 hours), Guìlín (Y220 to Y245, 11 to 12 hours), Shànghǎi (Y262 to Y281, 17 hours) and Xī'ān (Y215 to Y235, 15 to 16 hours). Prices are for hard-sleepers.

Getting Around

A light rail line has been under construction forever; its projected 2004 christening ride didn't happen.

TO/FROM THE AIRPORT

Buses to Tianhe International Airport (Tiānhé Fēijīchǎng, Y20, 40 minutes) leave 11 times a day from the China Southern Airlines office on Hangkong Lu and five times daily from the office on Wuluo Lu in Wǔchāng (see p455; free for China Southern Airlines ticket-holders). Another bus departs from the Hànkǒu train station.

Flag fall for taxis is Y8. A taxi to the airport should cost about Y80 and take 30 minutes.

BUS & FERRY

Bus routes crisscross the city, but getting where you want to go may mean changing at least once. Take a book, given the legendary traffic jams.

All most tourists really need are Tourist Bus Lines Nos 401 and 402 (each Y5), which run to the major attractions in the city. Both terminate at the lovely Dōnghú Lake area and both run along the riverfront in Hànkǒu.

A useful bus is the No 603, which passes Jiāng Hàn Fàndiàn to and from the Hànkǒu train station. Bus No 9 runs from the train station down Xinhua Lu to the Wǔhàn ferry terminal. Bus No 10 connects both train stations.

In Wǔchāng, bus No 12 runs from Wuhan University to the Zhonghua Lu pier.

The Hànkǒu–Wǔchāng ferries are a much faster way of crossing the river during the day. The large boats (Y1) take 15 minutes, while smaller speedboats (Y5) carry around 15 people and do it in five minutes.

WǓDĀNG SHĀN 五当山
☎ 0719

The mountains of **Wǔdāng Shān** (entrance gate ☎ 566 7415; admission Y51) stretch for 400km across northwestern Húběi and are particularly sacred to Taoists, with inspirational vistas. The highest summit is the 1612m **Tianzhu Peak** (天柱峰; Tiānzhú Fēng), or 'Heavenly Pillar Peak'. The peaks spread widely, but the climbs aren't exceedingly difficult.

The Wǔdāng Shān style of martial arts was developed here and traditionally practised by Taoist priests; this is the 'internal' form as opposed to Sōng Shān's 'external'. There are numerous schools in and around the town and you can expect to meet eager foreign students on personal pilgrimages.

Ming emperors Chengzu and Zhenwu duelled to construct the most temples. The most notable is the **Golden Hall** (金殿; Jīn Diàn; admission Y10; ☯ 8.30am-5pm) on Tianzhu Peak. Built entirely of gilded copper in 1416, the hall contains a bronze statue of Zhenwu, who became a Taoist deity.

Below, on Soaring Flag Peak (Zhǎnqí Fēng), are two temples. The attractive **Purple Cloud Temple** (紫霄宫; Zǐxiāo Gōng; admission Y10; ☯ 7am-6pm) originates from the Song dynasty. The less remarkable **Nanyan Temple** (南岩宫; Nányán Gōng) is at the beginning of the trail used to ascend Tianzhu Peak.

These temples are about 10km from the **entrance gate** to the mountain, which is about 1km from town. Most skip the initial kilometre by taking a minivan taxi up to the parking lot for Y10. From there it's another two-hour hike up to the Golden Hall; a cable car (Y45) can help.

Sleeping & Eating

Wǔdāngshān Bīnguǎn (五当山宾馆; ☎ 566 5548; 33 Yongle Lu; tw Y130-200; ☒) This hotel is the town's best, but even so, it's not exactly luxurious.

Stay on the mountain for superb views; you can expect a clean(ish) room and shared facilities.

Jīndǐng Lǚguǎn (金丁旅馆; ☎ 695 0718; bed in d&tr Y44, s with shared bathroom Y88) On Tianzhu

ZHANG SAN FENG

Zhang San Feng was a Wǔdāng Shān monk in the 13th or 14th century, and is reputed to be the founder of the martial-art tàijíquán, or taichi. A master of the Shaolin martial arts, Zhang disliked the 'hard' techniques of the Shaolin style and was searching for something 'softer'. As he was sitting on his porch one day, he was inspired by a battle between a huge bird and a snake. The sinuous snake used flowing movement to evade the bird's attacks. The bird, exhausted, eventually gave up and flew away. There is a close association between taichi and Taoism, and virtually all of the Taoist priests on Wǔdāng Shān practice some form of the art.

Peak, just below the temple (where they also accept foreigners), bathroom and eating facilities are basic, but there are fantastic views and chances to meet local monks.

Báihuì Shānzhuāng (百汇山庄; ☎ 568 9191; fax 568 9088; tw Y88-120; 🅿) Near Nanyan Temple, this is the best place to stay on the mountain.

In town, there are a couple of good **private restaurants** on Yongle Lu near its intersection with the main road.

Getting There & Away

The train station is called Wǔdāngshān, but the town used to go by the name of Laǒyīng. Wǔdāngshān is on the railway line from Wǔhàn to Chóngqìng. Few trains stop and you may have to take a minibus to/from either Shíyàn (Y5, one hour) or Liùlǐpíng (one hour); the former station has trains to Yíchāng and north into Shaanxi. There are daily trains from Xiāngfán (Y35, two hours).

A new expressway to Xiāngfán was completed in early 2004; officials seem to not even want to finish the expressway from there to Wǔhàn. Agonizingly slow sleeper and regular buses serve Wǔhàn (12 hours) leaving from the bus station.

SHÉNNÓNGJIÀ 神农架
☎ 0719
The Shénnóngjià district in remote northwestern Húběi has the wildest scenery in the province. Old-growth stands of fir, pine and hemlock are a treasure trove of more than 1300 species of medicinal plants. Indeed, the name commemorates a legendary emperor, Shennong, believed to be the founder of herbal medicine and agriculture.

A more modern legend pertains to local wild, ape-like creatures – a Chinese equivalent of the Himalayan yeti or the North American bigfoot. Curiously, the creatures seem to be able to distinguish between peasants and scientists – molesting the former and evading the latter. A small base station set up in the reserve has displays of 'evidence' of sightings. More real, but just as elusive, are leopards, bears, wild boars and monkeys (including the endangered golden snub-nosed monkey).

Foreign travellers are allowed into the area of the Shénnóngjià district near the town of **Mùyúpíng** (木鱼平), 200km northwest of Yíchāng. Two grand peaks, Shénnóngjià Shān at 3105m and Lǎojūn Shān at 2936m, dominate. It's an eight-hour bus ride to Mùyúpíng from Yíchāng (Y80), or you can take a boat to Xiāngxī (five hours) on the Three Gorges (Sānxiá) and from there it's a 90km ride to Mùyúpíng. From Mùyúpíng you will have to hire a car to get into the reserve.

CITS in Yíchāng (see p458) arranges a three-day tour that includes visits to botanical sites, rafting and Shénnóngjià Shān, but be prepared to pay up to Y1400 per person. The tour includes accommodation, although much of the time is taken up with transportation. Other local travel agencies are unaccustomed to travel restrictions for foreigners, leading to adventures with the police.

It is now possible to visit **Sōngbǎi** (松柏), an area in the Shénnóngjià reserve that has been off limits to foreigners. Yíchāng CITS reports foreigners were allowed to visit the area, but only when accompanied by tour guides.

A caveat: the PSB in Yíchāng doesn't seem to know whether independent travel is possible or not. Some travellers claim to have been told by the PSB here that it was OK, then found themselves detained and fined Y1000 (with an ignoble ejection from the region). Politely asking Yíchāng's PSB to ring their comrades in the area *and* write down what they told you might be a good idea.

YÍCHĀNG 宜昌

☎ 0717 / pop 3,996,700

Situated just below the famous Three Gorges, Yíchāng is the gateway to the upper Yangzi and was a walled town as long ago as the Sui dynasty. The city was opened to foreign trade in 1877 by a treaty between Britain and China. Major battles during the Period of Three Kingdoms were fought here.

Today Yíchāng is best known as the gateway city to the massive and controversial Three Gorges hydroelectric project being built at Sāndòupíng, about 40km upstream.

Bargain bucket passenger ferry traffic downstream is drying up as water levels continue to fluctuate (and will quite possibly not even be running when you read this), though you can still hop aboard a cruise ship (starting at mid-range and moving up through to absolute luxury monsters). Upstream is a different matter, as this is the eastern terminus to or from Chóngqìng. Aside from the dam site/sight, Yíchāng is a pleasant enough town (with a few attractive back alleys to explore) and is a useful jumping-off point for travel to wilder places north.

Orientation

Yíchāng spreads along a bend of the Yangzi River. Ferry terminals are located at the far east and west ends of town, and are connected via Yanjiang Dadao, the main thoroughfare. To the north, Dongshan Dadao has the bus stations, while one block north, Dongshan Dadao lies just below the train station.

Information

Bank of China (Zhōngguó Yínháng; Shengli Silu) Near Longkang Lu.

CITS (Zhōngguó Guójì Lǚxíngshè; ☎ 624 1875; www.yc cits.com; 18 Longkang Lu) This friendly bunch offers tours of the Three Gorges that include rafting trips (Y280 per person), but you will need at least four people for a tour. Note that residents still call this street by its old name, Kangzhuang Lu.

Internet cafés (wǎngbā; per hr Y2) There are a number near the corner of Fusui Lu and Erma Lu.

Post office (yóujú; cnr Yunji Lu & Yiling Dadao)

PSB (Gōngānjú; ☎ 674-4861; Huancheng Dongu) Generally open weekday mornings and afternoons. Not famous for knowing what's what.

Sights

THREE GORGES DAM 三峡大坝

The construction site of the **Three Gorges Dam** (Sānxiá Shuǐlì Shūniǔ Gōngchéng), to be completed in 2009, perhaps epitomises China's leap into modernity (see the boxed text 'The Damned Yangzi', p766).

Take yellow minibus No 4 (Y1) from the train station to the bus No 8 terminus. Bus No 8 (Y18 return) takes 40 minutes and drops you off at the dam's southwestern end. Minibuses (Y20 return) and motorcycle taxis (Y10 return) take you to the top. Easier still: along western Dongshan Dadao is the Hǎotōng Kèyùnzhàn, a regional bus station; wander in and say *sānxiá dàbà* ('Sanxia big dam', the local moniker).

Sleeping

Tiělù Dàjiǔdiàn (Railway Hotel; ☎ /fax 646 3073; beds in common s/d Y40, standard s & d Y168-188; ❷) Next to the train station is this popular budget option, one of a few nearby offering cheap, clean beds. Discounts of up to 30% are sometimes available.

Yángguāng Dàjiǔdiàn (Sunshine Hotel; ☎ 644 6075; fax 644 6086; 1 Yunji Lu; s & d Y198-328; ❷) Ten minutes from the train station is this good deal with clean rooms and helpful staff. Splurge for the Y216 rooms (trust us).

Táohuālíng Fàndiàn (☎ 623 6666; fax 623 8888; 29 Yunji Lu; tw Y398 plus 10%, common tw Y140; ❷ ▣) This central luxury option has lush landscaping and nice twins with wooden floors in the main building – many renovated fairly recently.

Yichang International Hotel (Yíchāng Guójì Dàjiǔdiàn; ☎ 622 2888; www.ycinthotel.com; 127 Yanjiang Dadao; d Y428-989; ❷ ▣) Towering over the Yangzi, this place is the city's newest and poshest palace. The revolving restaurant perched on top is outstanding for river watching (and good food).

Eating & Drinking

Neptune Coffee (Hǎiwángxīng Kāfēi; ☎ 622 9934; 40 Fusui Lu; mains Y8-45) Great coffee, pizza and salads here, which brings a slice of Paris to Yíchāng. A number of imitators are found along nearby streets.

Běijīng Jiǎoziguǎn (☎ 624 1691; 28 Longkang Lu; mains Y8-40) This bustling place serves an array of northern-style cold dishes.

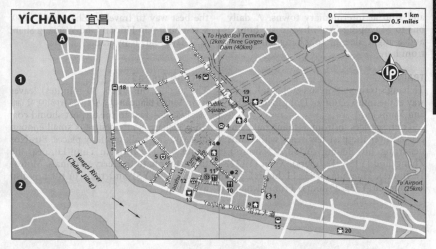

There is a lively **night market** (yèshìchǎng; Taozhu Lu) for dining.

Herd People in the West (Erma Lu) How can you pass up a music bar with this name? Best place to quaff a cold one and watch live music.

Getting There & Away
AIR
Yíchāng's airport is 25km southeast of the city centre and has flights to Běijīng (Y1250), Shànghǎi (Y990) and other cities. There are several ticket offices around

town, especially near the train station and ferry terminals. There's a helpful **China Southern Airlines office** (Zhōngguó Nánfāng Hángkōng Gōngsī; ☎ 625 1538; 21 Yunji Lu).

BOAT
River ferries stop at either the Yíchāng ferry terminal or the Dàgōngqiáo bus and ferry terminal. Typical 1st-/2nd-/3rd-class fares are Y942/582/261.

There is also a hydrofoil service that goes to Wànxiàn in Chóngqìng at the western end of the Three Gorges (Y205, six hours), as well as to Chóngqìng (Y428, 11 hours). Tickets can be purchased at either of the ferry terminals but services arrive/depart to the west of town at the hydrofoil terminal. There is access to the city centre from the hydrofoil terminal via by bus No 3.

For full details on Yangzi River cruises, see Cruising Downriver (p768).

BUS
Yíchāng's main **long-distance bus station** (chángtú qìchēʼzhàn; Dongshan Dadao) is located south of the train station. There are also long-distance services departing from the two ferry terminals on Yanjiang Dadao. Air-con express buses to Wǔhàn (Y90 to Y116, 3½ to four hours) leave from all bus stations every hour constantly and make stops in Wǔchāng and Hànkǒu. Regular buses (Y60 to Y80, four to five hours) run from the long-distance station

and stop at intermediary towns. A daily bus to Mùyúpíng (Y60, five to six hours) and a night sleeper to Zhāngjiājiè leave from here.

TRAIN

Yíchāng's train station sits atop a tall stairway at the intersection of Dongshan Dadao and Yunji Lu.

Train services to/from Yíchāng have improved over the past few years with trains departing for Běijīng (Y330, 22 hours), Zhèngzhōu (Y156, 12 hours), Xī'ān (Y132, 12 hours), Huáihuà (Y83, 11 hours) and Guǎngzhōu (Y335, 25 hours). From Yíchāng,

the best way to travel to Zhāngjiājiè (Y60, seven hours) in Húnán (and Wǔdāng Shān; Y29 hard seat) is by train.

Getting Around

The airport bus (Y20, 30 minutes) leaves from **Sānxiá Bīnguǎn** (☎ 673 9888 ext 8100; 42 Yanjiang Dadao). A taxi to the airport should cost Y60. Yíchāng's city centre is small enough that you can walk to many places. Bus Nos 3 and 4 (Y1) run from Yunji Lu, near the train station, to the ferry terminals. Motorcycle taxis (Y5) and taxis (Y10) are also available.

Jiāngxī 江西

HIGHLIGHTS

- Shop (or rather, bargain) till you drop in **Jǐngdézhèn** (p466), the funky city that changed 'ceramics' into 'china'

- Retreat into the misty mountains of **Lúshān** (p470), an inspiration to artists for centuries

- Trek lovely **Jǐnggāng Shān** (p473), the 'Cradle of the Chinese Revolution', peppered with over 100 Red Army historical sites

- Snoop about the funky backstreets of **Nánchāng** (p464), site of the first gathering of Communist forces into an army in 1927

- Boat on **Póyáng Hú** (p466), one of China's largest lakes and a crucial waterfowl flyway

- POP: 42.3 MIL
- AREA: 166,600 SQ KM
- www.jcn.cn

Tucked between wealthier (and more conveniently located, transport-wise) cities and provinces, Jiāngxī sees few foreign visitors, an alluring fact for many intrepid travellers.

Denizens of Jiangxi boast – rightfully – of the extraordinary natural world found here, a landscape that has inspired China's civilisation. Over 60% of the province remains covered by forest – the highest rate in China – and some mountain ranges. This natural isolation allowed literati and philosophers to ponder uninterrupted until well into the 20th century. In Jiāngxī's mountains Taoism was purportedly born, Lúshān's grandeur has impelled some of China's most epic verse. The clay and kilns of Jǐngdézhèn were used to create porcelain that changed the world's concept of beauty. And the rugged mountains of the province were the place where communist thought was fully translated into active engagement.

Yet it is the waters that dominate the ethos here. Stretching along the middle and lower reaches of the Yangzi River, Jiāngxī lies in one of the most crucial watersheds in China. More than 2400 rivers and ecologically crucial lakes spiderweb throughout the province. Jiāngxī is the source of much of the drinking water of southeast China and Hong Kong. Indeed, locals claim that so bountiful and pristine are the waterways that Chinese culture has sprung from them.

For the modern traveller, what lies within? For starters, Jǐngdézhèn continues to churn out massive amounts of its famed porcelain, with techniques unchanged for centuries The province's population centres spread around Póyáng Hú; that massive pool, and the rivers feeding it around the province account for some of the most crucial waterfowl habitat in the world, particularly for prized white cranes. Jiāngxī also has Jǐnggāng Shān, one of the most famous communist guerrilla bases that travellers can visit. It was only after several years of war that the Kuomintang were able to drive the communists out of here onto their Long March to Shaanxi.

History

The Grand Canal (linking major waterways) was built from the 7th century onwards, opening up the southeastern regions and making Jiāngxī an important point on the trade route from Guǎngdōng. Industries such as silver mining and tea growing later allowed the formation of a wealthy Jiāngxī merchant class. By the 19th century, however, the province's role as a transport route from Guǎngzhōu was reduced by the opening of coastal ports to foreign ships, which forced the Chinese junk trade to decline.

Climate

North-central and central Jiāngxī lie in the Gàn Jiāng river plain and experience a four-season, subtropical climate. Mountains encircle the plain in each direction, and to these locals flock to escape the summer heat, which averages around 30°C in July. (Temperatures average 3°C to 9°C north to south in January.) Rainfall averages 120cm to 190cm annually and is usually heaviest in the northeast; half falls between April and June.

Language

Most Jiāngxī natives speak one of innumerable local variants of Gàn, a dialect of Mandarin whose name in fact comes from the Chinese abbreviation for Jiāngxi (赣). Similar to Hakka, which is also spoken in the province, some linguists have in fact

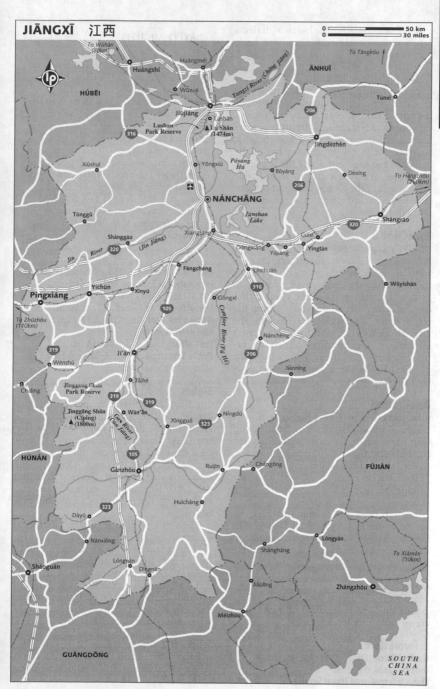

0 _____ 50 km
0 _____ 30 miles

To Wǔhàn
(80km)

Huángméi

Huángshí

To Tángkǒu

ĀNHUĪ

Wúxué

Yangzi River (Cháng Jiāng)

HÚBĚI

Túnxī

Jiǔjiāng

Lúshān

Lushan
Park Reserve

Lú Shān
(1474m)

Jǐngdézhèn

Xiūshuǐ

Yǒngxiū

Póyáng
Hú

Bōyáng

Déxìng

To Hángzhōu
(260km)

206

Tónggǔ

NÁNCHĀNG

Junshan
Lake

206

Shàngráo

Shànggāo

320

(Jǐn Jiāng)

Xiāngtáng

Guìxī

320

Jǐn   River

Dōngxiāng

Yújiāng

Yīngtán

Fēngchéng

Línchuān

Pingxiáng

Yíchūn

Xīnyú

Gòngxī

316

Wǔyíshān

105

To Zhūzhōu
(110km)

Comfort River (Fǔ Hé)

Nánchéng

319

Wénzhú

Jǐ'ān

206

Jiànníng

Cháling

Jinggang Shan
Park Reserve

Tàihé

319

319

Jǐnggāng Shān
(Cíping)
(1800m)

Wàn'ān

Gàn River (Gàn Jiāng)

Xìngguó

323

Níngdū

HÚNÁN

105

Gànzhōu

Ruìjīn

Chángtīng

FÚJIÀN

323

Huìchāng

Dàyú

Nánxióng

Lóngyán

To Xiàmén
(10km)

Sháoguān

Lóngnán

Dīngnán

Shànghàng

Jiāolíng

Zhāngzhōu

Méizhōu

GUĂNGDŌNG

SOUTH
CHINA
SEA

insisted on classifying the two dialects much more closely than they have been traditionally.

Getting There & Around

Jiāngxī's transport infrastructure is not as extensive as neighbouring provinces, though all major sites are linked via efficient expressways. Nánchāng's airport is underserved; it has a decent, but not frenetic, train service. A new expressway has finally breached the southern tier of the province. Otherwise, it's a slow-go province. Inside Jiāngxī, one of the coolest transport options is hopping aboard a ferry boat across massive Póyáng Hú.

NÁNCHĀNG 南昌

☎ 0791 / pop 4,078,900

Nánchāng's Chinese characters literally translate as 'southern prosperity', yet for the traveller, the light-speed growth so evident in other parts of the country has only recently begun to show along the city's main thoroughfares. Though the city strives to hum with the rhythm of a boomtown, for travellers Nánchāng remains a laid-back, friendly place boasting pleasant strolls along ungentrified, sleepy backstreets.

Orientation

Gàn Jiāng lies to Nánchāng's north, and Fǔ Hé (Comfort River), which branches off Gàn Jiāng, sits to the city's west. Zhanqian Lu leads directly west from the train station to the Fushan roundabout.

Bayi Dadao heads northwest from the roundabout and is the main north–south artery.

Most tourist sights and facilities are on or in the vicinity of Bayi Dadao. The People's Square sits at the town's centre, at the intersection of Bayi Dadao and Beijing Xilu.

MAPS

Maps (Y5) are available from the Xinhua Bookshop (Xīnhuá Shūdiàn), on Bayi Dadao across from People's Square.

Information

Bank of China (Zhōngguó Yínháng; Zhanqian Xilu) Opposite Nánchāng Bīnguǎn.

China International Travel Service (CITS; Zhōngguó

BĀYĪ (1 AUGUST)

On 1 August (bāyī in Chinese, now a common street name) 1927, 30,000 troops led by Zhou Enlai and Zhu De seized Nánchāng and held it for several days. The revolt, staged in retribution for a spring massacre of communists by Chiang Kaishek's forces, was largely a fiasco, but the gathering of soldiers marked the beginning of the Chinese Communist army. The army retreated south from Nánchāng to Guǎngdōng, but Zhu De led some soldiers and circled back to Jiāngxī to join forces with the ragtag army that Mao Zedong had organised in Húnán. From there, the soldiers sought refuge in Jīnggāng Shān (Well-Shaped Ridge Mountains).

Guójì Lǚxíngshè; ☎ 626 3437) and the helpful **Jiangxi International Tour and Aviation Corporation** (☎ 621 5891) share a building at 169 Fuzhou Lu, just in front of Qīngshānhú Bīnguǎn. CITS is on the 2nd floor.

Daitian Internet (Dàitián Wǎngbā; 211 Sipu Lu; per hr Y2) Just off Minde Lu.

Post office (yóujú; cnr Bayi Dadao & Ruzi Lu)

Public Security Bureau (PSB; Gōngānjú; Shengli Lu) About 100m north of Minde Lu.

Sights

On Bayi Dadao is Nánchāng's nucleus, **People's Square** (Rénmín Guǎngchǎng). Here you will find the **Monument to the Martyrs** (Bāyī Jìniàn Tǎ), a sculpture of red-tiled flags and a stone column topped with a rifle and fixed bayonet. Opposite the square is the immense, Stalinist **Exhibition Hall** (Zhǎnlǎnguǎn), its erstwhile red star replaced by the red of Coca Cola and billboards.

The city's pride is nine-storey **Téngwáng Gé** (Jumping King Pavilion; 7 Yanjiang Beilu; admission Y30; ☾ 8am-6pm) overlooking Fǔ Hé and around a lotus pond. Built by the Tang dynasty, the latest of 28 reconstructions was in 1989. Art exhibitions, teahouses, the terraced grounds, and a traditional Chinese music and dance theatre with performances most weekends, make it worthwhile.

North of Dōng Hú (East Lake), **Youmin Temple** (177 Minde Lu; admission Y2; ☾ 8am-5.30pm) is an attractive Liang dynasty temple. It was destroyed during the Cultural Revolution and rebuilt in 1995.

NÁNCHĀNG 南昌

The **Memorial Hall to the Martyrs of the Revolution** (Géming Lièshì Jiniànguǎn; 399 Bayi Dadao; admission Y15; ☺ 8-11.30am & 2.30-6pm Mon-Thu) is north of People's Square. Exhibits are in Chinese, but the archival photos from the 1920s to 1940s are fascinating.

The **Former Headquarters of the Nanchang Uprising** (Bāyī Nánchāng Qǐyì Jiniànguǎn; 380 Zhongshan Lu; admission Y15; ☺ 8.30am-5.30pm), housed in an old hotel, sports wartime paraphernalia and Party history, mostly in Chinese.

Sleeping

Budget places near the bus/train stations offer sub-Y100 rooms but require polite badgering.

Nánchāng Bīnguǎn (☎ 885 5800; fax 622 3193; 16 Bayi Dadao; s & d Y100-298, tr Y270; ⊠) At this leviathan stand-by near the Fushan roundabout the Y100 doubles are the teensiest bit worn and musty; higher prices garner comfort.

Jiāngxī Fàndiàn (☎ 885 8888; www.jx8858888.com; 356 Bayi Dadao; s & d Y120-200, tr Y180; ⊠) This reasonable three-star hotel has cosy rooms,

a restaurant and a business centre. Cheaper rooms seem to be ever occupied.

Póyánghú Dàjiǔdiàn (☎ 885 6588; www.poyanghu.com.cn; 1128 Jinggang Shan Dadao; s & d Y218-325; ⊠ ⊠) This mid-range hotel, on the roundabout's southwestern side, is quite a bit plusher for the money, with marble floors and an exercise room.

Qīngshānhú Bīnguǎn (☎ 636 3888; fax 622 1447; 169 Fuzhou Lu; s & d Y298-722; ⊠ ⊠) This trusty four-star hotel features a bar, sauna, shops and solid restaurants. It's across from People's Park, ensuring tranquillity (and park views).

Eating

Central parks and the Fushan roundabout come alive with pseudo-night markets; try *xiànbǐng* (fried pancakes stuffed with vegetables).

Several Western-style restaurants and bars congregate on Bayi Dadao, just south of the Martyrs of the Revolution memorial. Zhongshan Lu (and north along Shengli Lu) has other trendy (and not always pricey) 'ethnic' eateries (most have photo menus).

Zìzài Xuāngān Sīlóu (☎ 625 5537; 147 Supu Lu; dishes Y5-40) Chinese dishes are served in the ground-floor cafeteria, the 2nd-floor restaurant, and on the top floor, where there's casual, open-air dining.

Shíshén Fànzhuāng (☎ 629 7799; 191 Ruzi Lu; dishes Y15-40) This rustic Jiāngxī restaurant (near a couple of knock-offs) serves spicy specialities like *kèjiājiǔ zāoyú* (fish stewed in white wine) and *cōngyóuluòbǐng* (fried green onion pancake).

Getting There & Away

AIR

The main office of the **Civil Aviation Administration of China** (CAAC; Zhōngguó Mínháng; ☎ 627 8246; 37 Beijing Xilu) is near People's Square, but the bus/train station area has travel agencies.

Chāngběi airport is 28km north of the city. Popular flights go to Běijīng (Y1310), Guǎngzhōu (Y710), Hong Kong (Y1490, four times weekly), Shànghǎi (Y710) and Xī'ān (Y1000).

BOAT

The small **Nanchang Ferry Terminal** (Nánchāng Gǎngkèyùnzhàn; ☎ 681 2251) is found south of the two Bayi Bridges. An alternative route to Jǐngdézhèn is to catch a boat across Póyáng Hú to Bōyáng (Y20 to Y65, three to seven hours), from where you have another two hours on a bus (Y10). However, given the beaverish completion of expressways looping around the lake, these trips are dwindling. Most boats now are the summertime tourist cruise boats.

BUS

Nánchāng's **long-distance bus station** (kèyùn zhōngxīn; Bayi Dadao) is between People's Square and the Fushan roundabout. Air-con buses go three times a day to Chángshā (Y85 to Y110, six to seven hours); highway upgrades are ongoing. Buses run constantly to Jiǔjiāng (Y35 to Y43, 1½ hours) and Lúshān (Y37 to Y41, 1½ hours) to the north and east to Jǐngdézhèn (Y32 to Y65, three to five hours); for the latter, slower buses generally do not take the expressway. There are also buses to Jǐnggāng Shān (Y65 to Y90, six to nine hours) in Jiāngxī's southwestern mountains.

TRAIN

Nánchāng lies off the main Guǎngzhōu–Shànghǎi railway line, but many trains make the detour north via the city. Direct trains operate to Fúzhōu (Y100, 10 to 12 hours), Shànghǎi and Wǔhàn. Heading west to Chángshā in neighbouring Húnán almost always necessitates a stop in Zhūzhōu. Express trains run daily to Jiǔjiāng (Y22, 2½ hours) and Jǐngdézhèn (Y30, four hours), although the freeway makes it far quicker to do the trip by bus. An **advance rail ticket office** (tiělù shòupiàochù; 🕑 8am-8pm) is just south of the Memorial Hall to the Martyrs of the Revolution.

Getting Around

Airport buses (Y15, 40 minutes) leave from the main CAAC office (see left). A taxi will cost about Y100.

From the train station, bus No 2 goes up Bayi Dadao past the long-distance bus station, and bus No 5 heads north along Xiangshan Beilu. Meter taxis (Y6 flag fall) are available.

AROUND NÁNCHĀNG

Póyáng Hú 鄱阳湖

China's largest freshwater lake at 3583 sq km, Póyáng Hú (www.poyanglake.net) has been feted by poets for centuries for its tranquil atmosphere and scenery. A few historical temple/pavilion odds and ends are dotted along the shoreline, but aficionados of avian life are simply agog at the seeming millions of migrating birds that pass through here, arguably the planet's largest migratory habitat. Over 300 species pass through the area in winter, highlighted by over 5000 white cranes of a variety of species; Póyáng Hú is home to 95% of the world's population of some of these species.

Getting there is tricky. Few buses rattle to villages on the banks. The best bet is to catch a semi-regular ferry across Póyáng Hú to Bōyáng (Y20 to Y65, three to seven hours). In summer, and usually during periods of migration, some tour boats circumnavigate the lake.

JǏNGDÉZHÈN 景德镇

☎ 0798 / pop 1,404,700

An ancient town with many narrow streets and wooden buildings, Jǐngdézhèn manufactures the country's much-coveted porcelain. The city continues to be one of the country's major ceramics producers, and the industry employs nearly half of Jǐngdézhèn's residents.

Chimney stacks belching out coal from firing kilns dominate the city skyline, so be prepared for some grim vistas on the way in. Fear not! This funky town has some charming, leafy backstreets and a noticeably relaxed populace.

Orientation

Most of Jǐngdézhèn lies on the eastern bank of the Yangzi River. Main arteries are Zhongshan Lu and Zhushan Lu. Maps are available at the Xinhua Bookshop (Xīnhuá Shūdiàn, Lianshe Beilu) and the bus/train stations.

Information

Bank of China (Zhōngguó Yínháng; Maanshan Lu) Towards the train station. Travellers cheques are exchanged at the main branch at 448 Cidu Dadao.
CITS (Zhōngguó Guójì Lǚxíngshè; ☎ 851 5888; Zhushan Lu) Lies west of the river.
Internet cafés (wǎngbā; per hr Y2) There are a couple along Zhonghua Beilu.
Internet resources (www.jdz.gov.cn)
Post offices (yóujú; Zhushan Lu) One is centrally located, another is west of the river.

Sights & Activities

The tiny older side streets between Zhongshan Lu and the river are a lovely place for wandering.

Exquisite bowls, vases and sculptures are on display at the centrally located **Museum of Porcelain** (Táocí Guǎn; ☎ 822 9784; 21 Lianshe Beilu; admission Y5; ⏰ 8-11am & 2.30-5pm). The collection includes pieces from the Song, Ming and Qing dynasties and the post-1949 era.

The **Museum of Ceramic History** (Táocí Lìshí Bówùguǎn; ☎ 852 1594; admission Y15; ⏰ 8am-5pm) is situated on the city's western edge. Its stone-and-wood structures display pieces taken from ancient kiln sites. Next door, the **Ancient Pottery Factory** (Gǔyáo Cíchǎng; ☎ 851 6124; admission Y15; ⏰ 8am-5pm) is a workshop where craftsmen demonstrate the traditional Qing and Ming porcelain-making technology of moulding and baking. With potters tinkering away in ancient workshops amid bamboo groves, it's a special place.

To get there take bus No 3 past the old long-distance bus station to the terminus near Cidu Dadao. Walk under the stone gate and follow the road through forest and tea groves for about 800m to the museum entrance. From the city centre, a taxi will cost about Y10.

Pottery factories otherwise dot the city, some of which used to be government run. One small factory known for good-quality

CHINA'S 'CHINA'

In 2004 Jǐngdézhèn celebrated its millennium as the country's imperial-decreed ceramics-producing heart, though the region has produced it since the Eastern Han dynasty. In the Jingde period of the Song dynasty, Emperor Zhen Zong decreed that only porcelain from the erstwhile Changnanzhen could grace dynastic tables. This lasted through to the Qing dynasty. Ancient Yuan dynasty kilns excavated since October 2002 have yielded over 3000 nearly priceless pieces (out of 10 tonnes of detritus).

Why here? A plethora of folk artisans and rivers (for transport), but mostly for nearby Gāolǐng village's durable (but oddly textured) eponymous clay. Jǐngdézhèn is home to nine of the 26 Masters of Art and Craft of China, the supreme national honour; the city has the nation's only college of ceramics. Then again, modern mass production may be compromising quality so purchasing good items depends on which factory made the porcelain and how much money you want to spend. Growing illegal use of the 'Jingdezhen' trademark at overseas fairs and import shops has made finding real-deal wares somewhat dicey.

duplicates from the Yuan, Ming and Qing dynasties is **Jingdezhen Jiayang Ceramics** (Jiāyáng Táocí Yǒuxiàn Gōngsī; ☎ 844 1200; 356 Chaoyang Lu; admission free; ☼ 8am-6pm), in the city's eastern suburbs. You'll need to take a taxi (Y10) to get there.

To help you better understand porcelain, CITS (p467) offers tours with helpful English-speaking guides. A half-day tour costs Y100. Tours may include the city's museums, the Art Porcelain Factory (Yìshù Táochǎng), the Porcelain Sculpture Factory (Měidiāo Táochǎng) or the modern Wèimín Porcelain Factory (Wèimín Táochǎng). Confirm with the CITS staff as to where you'll go because you may not see workers at all the factories.

Sleeping

Cheap but unmemorable rooms are found at a few hotels near the train station.

Jǐngdézhèn Jīnshèng Dàjiǔdiàn (☎ 820 7818; 29 Zhushan Lu; tw Y108-190; ☒) This is a reasonable, central hotel with clean rooms and service with a smile from the cheery staff. Bus No 1 runs from the train station.

Liángyǒu Bīnguǎn (☎ 820 0188; 8 Zhushan Lu; tw Y190-288; ☒) This relatively new hotel popular with business travellers has larger, bright rooms and a quiet location tucked off the street. You'll note that some 'basic' singles/doubles cost half the standard twins, but none ever seems available.

Jǐngdézhèn Bīnguǎn (☎ 822 5015; www.jdzhzbg .com; 60 Fengjin Lu; tw with refrigerator Y320-540; ☒) This three-star guesthouse is near a quiet lake park, about 15 minutes' walk from the town centre and has restaurants, a post office and a money-changing counter. It's a better deal than pricier hotels.

Eating

Tasty are thick rice noodles known as *liáng-bàn mǐfěn*. At night there's a lively **market area** (*yèshíchǎng*) with restaurants near the Xinhua Bookshop.

Xiǎomáquè Jiǔdiàn (☎ 822 3615; 67 Shengli Lu; ☎ 823 6777; 5 Lianshe Beilu; dishes Y8-32) This restaurant has two branches; the one on Lianshe Lu specialises in Beijing duck and seafood.

Shopping

Porcelain is sold everywhere, piled on pavements, lined up on street stalls and tucked away in antique shops, particularly those on Lianshe Beilu, towards the Museum of Porcelain.

Porcelain Friendship Store (Yǒuyì Shāngdiàn; 13 Zhushan Lu) The selection of vases, teapots and ceramic figures is great, but prices are more expensive.

The **market** (Táocí Shìchǎng) on the same road as Jǐngdézhèn Jīnshèng Dàjiǔdiàn is a good alternative. Huge blue and white summer teapots sell for Y15 or you can purchase a 2m-high mega-vase for Y1000 and up. Also worth checking out are the hand-painted *cíbǎn* (tiles) that come in a variety of sizes and prices. Dinner sets are also a bargain, ranging from Y60 to Y90.

Getting There & Away

Jǐngdézhèn is a bit of a transport bottle-neck, but the situation has improved with the Luójiā airport and expanded bus service.

AIR
Luójiā airport is 10km northwest of the city. The CAAC ticket office was in the process of relocating to Zhushan Lu, just east of the river. Flights only go to Shànghǎi (Y430), Shēnzhèn (Y730), Xiàmén (Y650) and Běijīng (Y1080).

BUS
In the north of town, the **long-distance bus station** (*kèyùn zhōngxīn*) has hourly services to Yīngtán (Y25, four hours), Jiǔjiāng (Y30 to Y40, two hours) and Nánchāng (Y32 to Y65, three to five hours), as well as less frequent departures to Túnxī (for Huángshān Shì; Y40 to Y50, four hours). Another long-distance bus station near the train station has fewer routes.

TRAIN
Though the Jǐngdézhèn train station is like a deserted crypt, tickets other than hard seat don't exist.

It may be worth calling **CITS** (Zhōngguó Guójì Lǚxíngshè; ☎ 851 5888), where you can organise hard-sleeper and soft-sleeper tickets by booking a few days in advance.

Heading north are trains to Shànghǎi (Y122, 17 hours) and Nánjīng (Y86, seven hours) via Túnxī, the gateway to legendary Huáng Shān (Y13, four hours) and Wúhú (Y31, five hours).

There is train service to Nánchāng (Y22, 5½ hours), but for better connections go to the railway junction at Yīngtán (Y12, three hours).

Getting Around
A taxi to the airport should cost Y30; no bus runs there. From the newer bus station, yellow bus 35 departs to the town centre along Zhushan Lu. Bus No 3 crawls at a snail's pace from the south long-distance bus station to the town centre, also along Zhushan Lu. Taxis are reasonable, but you probably have to bargain. A taxi to the new bus station should be Y5.

JIŬJIĀNG 九江
☎ 0792 / pop 4,376,900
For most travellers, Jiǔjiāng is a stopover on the road to Lúshān. If you're travelling from Nánchāng, you can safely miss the city by taking a bus that goes directly to Lúshān.

Situated close to Póyáng Hú, which drains into the Yangzi, the city has been a port and tea/rice market town serving nearby Húběi and Ānhuī since ancient times. Its status took a serious hit in 2004 when work on the Three Gorges Dam project halted long-distance Yangzi ferry traffic. The dam should at least alleviate floods, which have for centuries devastated the city.

Orientation
Jiǔjiāng stretches along the southern bank of the Yangzi. Two interconnected lakes divide the older northeastern part of the city from the southern industrial sprawl. The long-distance bus station is located on the city's eastern side and the train station is on the city's southern edge.

Information
Bank of China (Zhōngguó Yínháng; 52 Xunyang Lu) East of Nánmén Hú (South Gate Lake) at the intersection of Nanhu Lu.
CITS (Zhōngguó Guójì Lǚxíngshè; ☎ 821 5793; Xunyang Lu) Centrally located at the intersection with Huancheng Lu. It has details on tours of the area, particularly Lúshān.
Hong Internet (Hóng Wǎngbā; 1 Huancheng Lu; per hr Y2) On the 3rd floor; has relatively quick Internet access.
Internet resources (www.jj.jx.cn)
Post office (yóujú) Close to the intersection of Jiantong Lu and Xunyang Lu.

Sights & Activities
Small **Nengren Temple** (Benevolent Temple; Yuliang Nanlu; admission Y2) has a disused five-storey Yuan dynasty pagoda (and smiling monks); one hall contains a largish Buddha figure.

On a tiny island in Gāntáng Hú (linked to the shore by a footbridge), the monk-built **Misty Water Pavilion** (Yānshuǐ Tíng; ☎ 822 2168; admission Y5; ⊙ 8am-10pm) has a small museum containing some interesting photographs of Jiǔjiāng taken during its treaty port days.

Sleeping
No more ferry service means hotels (budget and mid-range) positively clamour for your business.
Xúnyáng Bīnguǎn (☎ 812 3888; 82 Xunyang Lu; s & d Y100-190; ✖) This has spruced-up rooms with new floors and amenities. Staff are unused to foreigners but quite friendly.
Báilù Bīnguǎn (White Deer Hotel; ☎ 822 2818; fax 822 1915; 133 Xunyang Lu; tw Y295-380; ✖) Diagonally

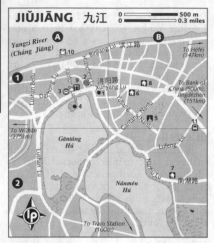

JIŬJIĀNG 九江

INFORMATION
CITS 中国国际旅行社 1 A1
Hong Internet 红网吧 2 A1
Post Office 邮电局 3 A1

SIGHTS & ACTIVITIES   p469
Misty Water Pavilion 烟水亭 4 A1
Museum 博物馆.................................(see 4)
Nengren Temple 能仁寺 5 B1

SLEEPING   pp469-70
Báilù Bīnguǎn 白鹿宾馆 6 B1
Jiǔjiāng Bīnguǎn 九江宾馆 7 B2
Xúnyáng Bīnguǎn 浔阳宾 8 B1

EATING   🍴 p470
Chuānwáng Fēngwèi Xiǎochīdiàn
川王风味小吃店 9 A1

TRANSPORT   p470
Chang Jiang Ferry Terminal 轮船客运码头 10 A1
Long-Distance Bus Station 长途汽车站 11 B1

opposite is this perfectly comfortable three-star luxury hotel. It has many tours to Lúshān.

Jiǔjiāng Bīnguǎn (☎ 856 0018; fax 856 6677; 30 Nanhu Lu; tw Y380, ste Y500-1300; 🅿) On the southeastern shore of Nánmén Hú, this hotel has modest luxury rooms bettering those of Báilù Bīnguǎn; it sports a nicer location.

Eating
The eastern perimeter of Jiǔjiāng's two central lakes see **street food stalls** spring up at night. Upscale hotel restaurant menus carry the occasional oddities like white sturgeon and Jiāngxī herring. Simple yet solid Sichuanese fare is found at **Chuānwáng Fēngwèi Xiǎochīdiàn** (Jiatong Lu; dishes Y5-Y20), near the corner of Xunyang Lu.

Getting There & Away

AIR
Nánchāng's Chāngběi airport serves the city and you'll have to head there first (see Bus, below).

BOAT
Boats no longer make the long Yangzi cruises, but shorter hops may become an option. Expect tour boats to begin plying nearby waters from the Chang Jiang ferry terminal.

BUS
Buses to Lúshān leave from the long-distance bus station between 7.30am and 4.30pm. The fare is Y10 to Y15. It's a short hop but may take up to two hours given the serpentine, hilly roads.

Buses – virtually all expresses – depart for Jingdézhèn (Y30 to Y40, two hours) every half-hour from the long-distance bus station. Frequent buses run to Nánchāng (Y35 to Y45, 1½ hours) and Wǔhàn (Y65 to Y75, three to four hours), among other places.

Buses to Nánchāng sometimes also leave from the train station.

TRAIN
There are several Jiǔjiāng–Nánchāng express trains each day (Y22, 2½ hours). Heading towards Wǔhàn, options are not as plentiful as one might expect.

The train to Héféi in Ānhuī province takes four hours.

Getting Around
Bus No 1 and minibuses (Y1) whip between Xunyang Lu, the long-distance bus station, the Bank of China and the train station. Motor-tricycles (a negotiable Y3) are at the bus and train stations.

LÚSHĀN 庐山
☎ 0792
Lúshān's mountain jaw-dropping vistas have been the subject of poems and paintings, and it has seen some historical, epoch-making events. Travellers find welcome temperature reprieve from the lowland furnace of the Yangzi River basin, peaks thrusting through carpets of verdant green, and preternaturally lovely mists shrouding everything. Summer crowds and winter chills (those picturesque fog banks can

cut through you) notwithstanding, there's something special, an understated charm, about Lúshān.

History

Late-19th-century Westerners established Lúshān, or Kuling as English-speakers called it, as a refreshing summer retreat. Gǔlǐng village was plotted after an English countryside village and its hotchpotch of stone cottages reminiscent of southern Germany, small French-style churches, and more grandiose hotels built in classical Victorian style remain today.

In 1959 the Central Committee of the Communist Party here held a fateful meeting, which eventually ended in Peng Dehuai's dismissal, sent Mao almost into a political wilderness and provided the seeds for the rise and fall of Liu Shaoqi and Deng Xiaoping.

In 1970 another meeting was held in Lúshān, this time of the Politburo. Exactly what happened here is shrouded in as much mist as the mountains, but it seems that Lin Biao clashed with Mao, opposed his policies of rapprochement with the USA and probably proposed continuing the Cultural Revolution's xenophobic policies. Whatever happened, Lin was dead by the following year.

Orientation & Information

The arrival point in Lúshān is the charming resort village of Gǔlǐng, perched 1167m high at the range's northern end. Two kilometres before Gǔlǐng is the entrance gate (☎ 828 3627), where pay a Y85 fee.

Detailed maps showing roads and walking tracks are available from shops and hawkers in Gǔlǐng.

Gǔlǐng village has shops and restaurants, a post office, bank, Internet cafés and the long-distance bus station. Scores of tourist hotels, sanatoriums and factory work-units' holiday hostels sit in the surrounding hills.

CITS (Zhōngguó Guójì Lǚxíngshè; ☎ 828 2497), uphill from Lúshān Bīnguǎn, is well organised and helpful.

Sights & Activities

While it costs Y10 to visit most (of the uncountable) tourist attractions, an alternative is to skip these and explore the mountain roads and paths on your own. No matter

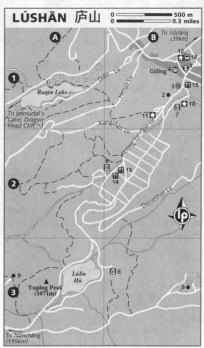

LÚSHĀN 庐山

0 ————— 500 m
0 ————— 0.3 miles

INFORMATION
Bank 银行 .... (see 4)
Bank of China 中国银行 1 B1
CITS 中国国际旅行社 2 B1
Internet Café 网吧 3 B1
Post Office 邮局 4 B1

SIGHTS & ACTIVITIES pp471–2
Botanical Gardens 植物园 5 B3
Lushan Museum 博物馆 6 B3
Meilu Villa 美庐别墅 7 B1
People's Hall 人民剧院 8 B2
Three Ancient Trees 三宝树 9 A3

SLEEPING 🛏 p472
Lúshān Biéshù Cūn 庐山别墅村 10 B1
Lúshān Bīnguǎn 庐山宾馆 11 B1
Lúshān Fàndiàn 庐山饭店 12 B1

EATING 🍴 p472
Lúshān Fēngwèi Shānzhuāng
  庐山风味山庄 13 B2
Zhēngfǔ Fàndiàn 14 B2
Zuìshí Dàjiǔdiàn 醉石酒家 15 B1

TRANSPORT pp472–3
Long-Distance Bus Station 长途汽车站 16 B1

the season or the mad swells of tourists, plenty of solitude can be found.

Built by Chiang Kaishek in the 1930s, **Meilu Villa** (Měilú Biéshù; 180 Hedong Lu; admission Y15; �'s 8am-6pm) was named after the general's wife, Song Meiling. The villa has enough historical flotsam to interest anyone; it warrants a look-see anyway since 'sights' of Chiang Kaishek are few and far between in the PRC.

The **People's Hall** (Rénmín Jùyuàn; 504 Hexi Lu; admission Y10; ⏱ 8am-5pm), the venue for the Communist Party's historic 1959 and 1970 get-togethers, is now a museum. On display are photos (barely display quality), but it's worth the admission to imagine oneself sitting in the conference theatre as Mao gave his fiery Great Leap Forward speeches.

At Lúshān's northwestern rim, the land falls away abruptly to give some spectacular views across Jiāngxī's densely settled plains. A long walking track south around these precipitous slopes passes the **Immortal's Cave** (Xiānrén Dòng) and continues to **Dragon Head Cliff** (Lóngshŏu Yá), a natural rock platform tilted above an eye-popping vertical drop.

The sombre **Three Ancient Trees** (Sānbǎoshù) are not far by foot from Lúlín Hú. Ancient indeed: the gingko and two cedar trees were planted five centuries ago by Buddhist monks.

The **Lushan Museum** (Lúshān Bówùguǎn; ☎ 828 2341; 1 Lulin Lu; admission Y10; ⏱ 8am-5.30pm) was once Mao's former residence, beside Lúlín Hú. A photo collection commemorates the historic 1970 Communist Party meeting. Scrolls and inscribed stelae displaying Li Bai's calligraphy are also visible. Unfortunately, the English explanations are limited.

The **Botanical Gardens** (Zhíwù Yuán; ☎ 707 9828; admission Y10; ⏱ 7.30am-5.30pm) is mainly devoted to subalpine tropical plants that thrive in the cooler highland climate. In the open gardens are spreads of rhododendrons, camellias and conifers.

Tours
From Jiŭjiāng, return day trips cost Y100 and give you about five hours in Lúshān. Báilù Bīnguǎn (see p469) in Jiŭjiāng runs tours which normally include pavilions, a nature hike and the museum.

Sleeping
During the low season (from October to May, excluding the 1 May and 1 October holidays), when it's chilly and drizzly, few people stay overnight and there are better deals. In summer, particularly the stratospherically priced weekends, and on holidays, budget travellers can positively forget about Lúshān – it's cheaper to do a day trip from Jiŭjiāng (or visit travel agents there for lodging deals, especially villas).

Getting accepted by local budget places depends on the mood of the PSB that day. Prices here are average in high season; double everything during holidays.

Lúshān Fēngwèi Shānzhuāng (☎ 828 5348; s & d Y30-100) This restaurant/hotel has basic rooms with squat toilets, a great deal if the PSB doesn't interfere.

Lúshān Fàndiàn (☎ 828 2861; 1044 Zhengjie; tw & d Y200-400) Here you'll find the best mid-range deals. Rooms are nice but the bathrooms don't match them. A face-lift was imminent, so prices may have risen.

Lúshān Bīnguǎn (☎ 828 2060; fax 828 2843; 446 Hexi Lu; tw & d in main bldg Y350-900, villas Y290-600; ❄) This large three-star colonial-era hotel has villa and main building rooms. Quite a variety exists, so look at a few. Steep discounts aren't unheard of.

Lúshān Biéshù Cūn (☎ 828 2927; fax 828 8946; 182 Hedong Lu; ste Y550-3000) This place has cottages scattered throughout a lovely old pine forest – unbeatable for location. Discounts of up to 20% are available.

Eating
Check the prices before digging in. The restaurants listed all serve Chinese dishes (Y15 to Y45) and *shíjī* (Lúshān cave frog; Y60).

Zuìshí Dàjiŭdiàn (☎ 828 1531; 102 Hedong Lu; dishes Y12-30) The name means 'drunk stone' and probably alludes to the future state of the many Chinese patrons feasting and *gānbēi'*ing (draining liquor shots) inside.

Zhēngfŭ Fàndiàn (☎ 828 9938; dishes Y10-30) On the road to the People's Hall, this hotel is housed in a quaint stone building. It's pricey but dependable.

Lúshān Fēngwèi Shānzhuāng (☎ 828 5348; dishes Y8-30) With a friendly owner, it serves delicious lemon chicken.

Getting There & Around
Daily buses go regularly in summer to Nánchāng (Y37 to Y41, 1½ hours), Jiŭjiāng (Y10 to Y15, one to two hours) and Wŭhàn (Y65, four hours); from November to late March direct buses to places other than Jiŭjiāng are less common. In summer, it may be a good idea to book your return seat upon arrival, particularly for day-trippers.

Minibuses to Jiǔjiāng also congregate opposite the long-distance bus station on the road heading towards Jiǔjiāng.

Lúshān's myriad footpaths make explorations on foot outstanding. Consider hiring a taxi to visit sights and walking back; it's usually Y10 per sight. Most opine that the southern sections of the mountain offer the best scenery. Lúshān furthermore has more cable cars and tramways (Y50 to Y60 return) than any other Chinese mountain.

YĪNGTÁN 鹰潭
☎ 0792 / pop 1,025,800

Although most trains make the detour to Nánchāng (north of the Shànghǎi–Guǎngzhōu railway line), you may have to catch some at Yīngtán. If you're here, the river area near the old town is worth exploring – locals may offer to ferry you about.

Huáqiáo Fàndiàn (华桥饭店; Overseas Chinese Hotel; ☎ 622 1344; fax 622 1149; 21 Zhanjiang Lu; tw Y300; ☒) This adequate hotel is a large 15-storey building on the main street down from the station. Cheaper hotels on the same street may or may not accept foreign visitors (at the time of writing they did).

The long-distance bus station is opposite the train station. There are buses to Jǐngdézhèn (Y38, four bumpy hours) and Nánchāng (Y36, three equally rough hours).

Yīngtán is a railway junction, so trains run everywhere: Nánchāng (two hours), Fúzhōu (9½ hours) and Shànghǎi (11½ hours) among others. The line to Jǐngdézhèn (2½ hours) rolls via Guìxī.

JǏNGGĀNG SHĀN 井冈山
☎ 0796

Few foreigners venture to this 500-peak region in Luóxiāo Shān (Clouds on Display Mountains) along the Húnán–Jiāngxī border. Yet with its tree-lined streets and misty mountain ranges Jǐnggāng Shān provides a welcome respite from China's congested, noisy cities. June to October are optimal travel months.

Oh, and it's the 'Cradle of the Chinese Revolution'. After repeated defeats attempting an urban-based revolution, Mao led 900 men here in 1927, joined later by Zhu De's battered forces. From these hills Mao launched the Long March into Shaanxi. Over 100 sites lie within these peaks.

Orientation & Information
The main township, Cípíng (茨坪; also called Jǐnggāng Shān), is nestled around a small lake in the mountains, 820m above the sea.

For an English-language tourist brochure (Y3) or a map showing hiking trails in the hills (Y2), try the Xinhua Bookshop (Xīnhuá Shūdiàn) in the Cuihu Hotel on Hongjun Nanlu. Your hotel may be able to help you hire a van for about Y100 to tour major sites, but be careful of overcharging. CTS provides tours for Y300.

Emergency phone numbers, including the **PSB** (Gōng'ānjú; ☎ 655 2360) and **medical help** (☎ 655 2595), are listed on roadside signs.
Bank of China (Zhōngguó Yínháng; 6 Nanshan Lu) On the lake's southeastern end.
China Travel Service (CTS; Zhōngguó Lǚxíngshè; ☎ 655 6788 or 655 2504; 2 Tianjie Lu) Across from Jǐnggāngshān Bīnguǎn. Some English is spoken here.

Sights & Activities
Jǐnggāng Shān's natural highland forest is unrivalled, particularly its square-stemmed bamboo and some 26 kinds of alpine azaleas that bloom from late April (when the mountain has a boisterous festival feting these lovely plants). Adventurous trekkers can venture into the surrounding mountains for **self-guided walks** on dirt trails. Local maps from the Xinhua Bookshop show trails but are mediocre. You'll have to ask locals where they start.

At **Five Dragon Pools** (五龙潭; Wǔlóng Tán; ☎ 655 6937; admission Y30; ☒ 6am-6pm), about 7km northwest of town, five cascading waterfalls and gorgeous views reward a long but sweatless trek (with English signs). The total hike can take six hours (three hours each way). Cheat with a cable car (Y60 return). CITS can help hire a van, and a few sporadic minibuses (Y3) leave from the bus station.

The watching post, **Huángyángjiè** (黄洋界; admission Y7; ☒ 7am-6pm), sits to the west. At 1300m above sea level, this spot saw the outnumbered Red Army battle nationalist forces. (You can enjoy the magnificent views.)

Standing 1438m above sea level, **Five Fingers Peak** (五指峰; Wǔzhǐ Fēng; admission Y20; ☒ 7am-6pm) is to the south and is featured on the back of the old Y100 banknote. Five Dragon Pool has better hiking paths though.

The **Revolutionary Museum** (革命博物馆; Gémìng Bówùguǎn; ☎ 655 2248; 12 Hongjun Nanlu; admission Y8; ☼ 8am-5.30pm) is devoted to the Kuomintang and Communists' struggle for control of the Húnán–Jiāngxī area in the late 1920s.

The **Former Revolutionary Quarters** (革命 旧居群; Gémìng Jiùzhǐqún; Tongmu Linglu; admission Y5; ☼ 8am-6pm) is a reconstruction of the mud-brick building that served as a Communist command centre between 1927 and 1928, and where Mao lived temporarily.

Sleeping & Eating

Same old thing: pricey hotels love you, budget hotels require some convincing.

Tongmu Linglu has heaps of hotels, from Y45 dorm beds to an average of around Y250 for a double room. Prices rise like a rocket on peak weekends.

Túshūguǎn Zhaòdaísuǒ (图书馆招待所; ☎ 655 2276; 22 Hongjun Beilu; s & tw from Y80) Modest rooms with bathroom are decent (and cheap); staff are good at sign language! It's a 10-minute walk from the bus station, just past the lake. Look for a white sign with red lettering.

Jǐnggāngshān Bīnguǎn (井冈山宾馆; ☎ 655 2272; fax 655 2551; 10 Hongjun Beilu; tw Y320-680; ☒) Stay where all PRC chairmen have lain their heads. A mind-boggling variety of rooms and villas are here – not cheap but staying where Mao did is worth a splurge, no? There's no English sign.

Jǐnggāngshān Dàshà (井冈山大厦; Jinggang-shan Plaza; ☎ 655 2251; fax 655 2428; 31 Hongjun Beilu;

tw & tr Y260-390; ☒) Further down the road from Jǐnggāngshān Bīnguǎn is this monolithic stone villa with stately rooms. A sign refers to the hotel as the Jinggangshan Grand Hotel. Tour groups often book out rooms.

The **restaurant** in Yuándǐng Bīnguǎn (10 Tongmu Linglu) is cheap and serves tasty food. For something a bit more romantic, try the place on the island in the middle of the lake.

Shopping

Ubiquitous shops advertise bamboo wares. Some are tacky, but nice summer mats (Y90) and comfortable rocking chairs (Y15 to Y70) are a good buy here.

Getting There & Away

From Nánchāng there are several direct buses to Jǐnggāng Shān (Y65 to Y90, six to nine hours). With the completion of the new expressway as far south as Tàihé, air-con buses (more expensive but faster) will soon ply the route (but you lose the wonderful vistas of water buffalo and bamboo forests).

Sporadic buses run from Jǐnggāng Shān to Chángshā (Y70, 12 hours) and Héngyáng (Y50, 10 hours) in Húnán, though it may be quicker to head to Jí'ān in Jiāngxī (Y23 to Y31, three hours) and transfer.

Don't be confused with the Jǐnggāng Shān train station, which is in Tàihé, a town south of Jí'ān. From the Tàihé station, you'll have to take a bus or taxi to the town centre and then catch a long-distance bus to Jǐnggāng Shān.

Húnán 湖南

CONTENTS

HIGHLIGHTS

- Visit Chairman Mao's birthplace, childhood home, and ancestral burial ground (and buy a Mao watch) in **Sháoshān** (p482), the obligatory Communist history pilgrimage
- Collect peaks and spot wildlife in **Wulingyuan Scenic Area** (p487) in Húnán's rugged northwest
- Contemplate under a Song dynasty pavilion at Yuelu Academy in **Chángshā** (p480), the point of beginnings for the Chinese civil examinations
- Contrast the classical education of the Yuelu Academy with the radical socialism discovered by Mao during his time at the Hunan No 1 Teachers' Training School, also in **Chángshā** (p479)
- Take a boat to Yuèyáng's **Jūnshān Dǎo** (p484) to sip precious silver needle tea, a drink worthy of emperors

- POP: 70.3 MIL
- AREA: 210,000 SQ KM
- www.hunan-china.org

Húnán 湖南

Húnán, province of chilli peppers and birthplace (quite literally) of the Party. This cash-poor but land-rich region reveals its fecundity (fifth-most production in China) with streets of farmers hawking the rich red spicy vegetable.

Land that is not used for a cornucopia of food beckons the intrepid traveller with a spectacular topography. Spreading east, west and south from the province's Yangzi River basin plain (and the capital Chángshā) are rough, isolated mountain ranges. Strike out to the south for a pilgrimage to Héng Shān, one of China's most sacred mountains.

Ventures westward have always been inspiring, if a bit off the path of less resistance! Wǔlíngyuán, north and west of the capital, is one of China's most spectacular mountain reserves. Surrounding this amazing area are heretofore inaccessible – to the average traveller – regions of the western frontier. In 2004, Herculean work was begun on transportation infrastructure in these relatively impoverished highlands.

The northern pocket is for hydrophiles, home to Dòngtíng Hú, one of China's largest lakes, and the legendary Yangzi River. So rewarding are the forests and waters of the province that many people overlook the remarkable history here. In no small way, Húnán helped to shape the nation. A small village west of Chángshā produced Mao Zedong, and he received his education in the province's capital. Liu Shaoqi, Peng Dehuai and Hu Yaobang, prominent communist leaders, also hail from Húnán. This ubiquity of revolutionary thinkers is merely a modern version of the province's prowess in producing top-notch leaders. Húnán's fame as an agricultural gold mine was matched by its reputation as a crucible for testing and moulding leaders. Its famed academies have produced noted poets, philosophers and officials dating from the Song dynasty.

Most of Húnán's residents are Han Chinese, but hill-dwelling minorities occupying the border regions include the Miao, Tujia, Dong (a people related to the Thais and Lao) and Yao. In Húnán's far north, there's a pocket of Uighurs.

History

Between the 8th and the 11th centuries the population of Húnán increased fivefold, spurred on by a prosperous agricultural industry and southerly migration. Under the Ming and Qing dynasties the region was one of the empire's granaries, and vast quantities of rice were shipped to the depleted north.

By the 19th century, Húnán began to suffer from the pressure of its big population. Land shortage and landlordism caused widespread unrest among Chinese farmers and hill-dwelling minorities. This increasingly desperate economic situation led to the massive Taiping Rebellion of the mid-19th century and the commu-

nist movement of the 1920s. The communists later found strong support among Húnán's peasants and established a refuge on the mountainous Húnán–Jiāngxī border in 1927.

Climate

Subtropical Húnán has more temperate forested elevations in the east, west and south. The northern half's climate is more fickle, with plunging winter temperatures and snow; the orange-growing south is more bearable. From April to June expect lead-grey skies and most of the province's annual 125cm to 175 cm of rain; thereafter, July and August are pressure-cooking months of heat and humidity.

Language

Hunanese *(xiāng)*, the language of Mao, is a Northern Mandarin dialect and has six to eight 'dialects'. Fewer consonants means confusion – l, n, f and h sounds, for example, are famously pesky. 'Fronting' (eg 'zh' sounds like 'z') is also noticeable.

Gàn, another Northern Mandarin dialect, is spoken in the west and south. Border regions are home to a mosaic of local dialects and minority languages that defy family group classification.

Getting There & Around

Yuèyáng's Yangzi River ferry port of call status is at the moment quite up in the air; at the time of writing ferries had been suspended, and even cruise lines were removing the city from their schedules. This, naturally, could change. Frustratingly, the capital Chángshā is not the main rail conduit: Zhūzhōu to the south is. Expressways are finally being finished in the province, which has literally gone from backwater to the 21st century since the late 1990s. Intra-provincially, the rugged north and west are rife with rivers and Dòngtíng Hú is the country's second-largest lake; funky ferries here are a fun way to get about.

CHÁNGSHĀ 长沙

☎ 0731 / pop 5,830,000

On the fertile plains of the Xiang River (Xiāng Jiāng), Chángshā has been inhabited

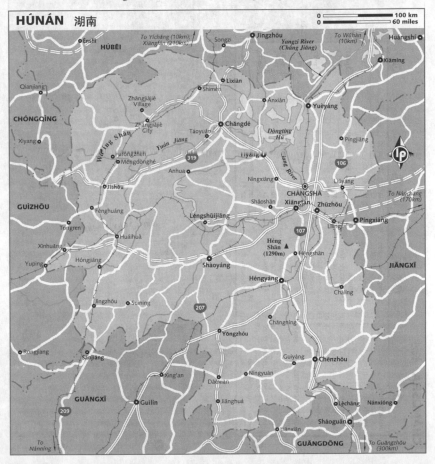

CHÁNGSHĀ 长沙

Xiāng River (Xiāng Jiāng)

for 3000 years, with a large complex here by the Warring States period. Then, as now, the city was a major agricultural trading centre.

In 1904, after the signing of the 1903 Treaty of Shanghai between Japan and China, Chángshā opened to foreign trade. The 'most-favoured nation' principle allowed foreigners to establish themselves in Chángshā, and large numbers of Europeans and Americans arrived to build factories, churches and schools. Yale University started a college here, which eventually became a medical centre.

Orientation

Most of Chángshā lies on the eastern bank of Xiang River. The train station is in the city's far east. From the station, Wuyi Lu leads to the river.

From Wuyi Lu, you cross the Xiang River bridge to the western bank, passing over Long Island (Júzi Zhōu) in the middle of the river. City maps are on sale at kiosks around the train station and in hotel shops.

Information

EMERGENCY
Public Security Bureau (PSB; Gōngānjú; Huangxing Lu) The PSB is situated in a cream-tiled building at the western end of town just south of Jiefang Xilu. Chic boutiques were inching this way, so relocation may be in the offing. Ask at your hotel before visiting.

INTERNET ACCESS
Internet café (wǎngbā; per hr Y2) This reliable outlet is opposite the Chángdǎo Fàndiàn on Wuyi Donglu.

MONEY
Bank of China (Zhōngguó Yínháng; 8.30am–noon & 2.30-5.30pm) The bank is next to the Civil Aviation Administration of China (CAAC; Zhōngguó Mínháng) office on Wuyi Donglu. There is an ATM in front of Xiāngjiāng Bīnguǎn.

POST & COMMUNICATIONS
Post Office & China Telecom (yóudiànjú; Wuyi Zhonglu) Near the intersection of Yingbin Lu. Another post office is to the right of the train station exit.

TRAVEL AGENCIES
China International Travel Service (CITS; Zhōngguó Guójì Lǚxíngshè; ☎ 228 0184; 46 Wuyi Donglu) Inside Xiàoyuán Dàshà. Its **Foreign Department** (☎ 228 0439; citsamer@public.cs.hn.cn) has (generally) multi-lingual staff. Another CITS **office** (☎ 486 5885) next

to Fúróng Huátiān Bīnguǎn assists with plane (not train) bookings.

Sights

HUNAN PROVINCIAL MUSEUM
湖南省博物馆

This **museum** (Húnán Shěng Bówùguǎn; ☎ 222 4385; Dongfeng Lu; admission Y20; 8am–noon & 2.30-5pm Tue-Fri, 8.30am-5pm Sat & Sun) chronicles revolutionary history and the 2100-year-old Western Han tombs of Mǎwángduī, some 5km east of the city.

Not to be missed are the mummified remains of a Han dynasty woman. Her preserved body, which was discovered wrapped in more than 20 layers of silk and linen, is displayed along with the removed organs. Another building houses the enormous solid outer timber casks.

To get here, take bus No 113 from the train station.

MAOIST PILGRIMAGE SPOTS
Hunan No 1 Teachers' Training School (Dìyī Shīfàn Xuéxiào; 324 Shuyuan Lu; admission Y6; 8am-5.30pm) is where Mao attended classes between 1913 and 1918; he returned as a teacher and principal from 1920 to 1922. A fun self-guided tour takes in Mao's dormitory, study areas, halls where he held some of his first political meetings and an open-air well where he enjoyed taking cold baths. A quote from him above the well states that this was a good way to 'exercise fearlessness'. The school is still in use. Take bus No 1 from the train station.

The **Former Office of the Hunan Communist Party Committee** (Zhōng Gòng Xiāngqū Wěiyuánhuì Jiùzhǐ; 480 Bayi Lu; admission Y10; 8am–noon & 2-5.30pm) includes Mao's living quarters, photos, and historical items from the 1920s along with a wall of Mao's poems, showing his characteristic expansive brushstrokes. Take bus No 1 from the train station.

LEI FENG MEMORIAL MUSEUM 雷锋纪念馆
Devotees of Communist propaganda simply must visit this **museum** (Léi Fēng Jìniànguǎn; ☎ 810 5014; admission Y5; 8am-6pm), an hour's bus ride west of Chángshā.

Lei Feng, model worker, party member and all-round communist citizen, was a 22-year-old soldier whom the communists lionised in 1963 following his death in a car accident. Posters of him selflessly assisting citizens, with his ever-smiling face, adorned homes, inculcating a sense of selfless duty to the nation's comrades.

The museum exhibits a group of photos featuring Lei smiling over a washtub of dirty socks and cartoon-like renderings of him and his parents facing down evil landlords and Japanese invaders.

Bus No 12 from the train station runs to its terminus at Róngwānzhèn. Then take bus No 315, whose final stop is just south of the museum.

YUELU PARK 岳麓公园

This **park** (Yuèlù Gōngyuán; Bottom of the High Mountain Park) and Hunan University (Húnán Dàxué) are pleasant places to visit on the western bank of Xiang River. The university evolved from the site of the **Yuelu Academy** (Yuèlù Shūyuàn; Lushan Lu; summer Y30, other times Y18; ☺ 7.30am-5.30pm), which was established during the Song dynasty for scholars to prepare for civil examinations. In 1903 the Confucian classics were replaced by more practical subjects as the Qing government attempted to reform education to foster modernisation. There's a teahouse inside and a good Chinese bookshop in the back.

The hike to **Loving Dusk Pavilion** (Àiwǎn Tíng) offers lovely views.

To get to the university, take bus No 202 from Wuyi Xilu or the train station and get off three stops before the end. Continue downhill and turn right (the bus goes left); walk straight for the Mao statue.

OLD CITY WALLS

The only remaining part of the old city walls is **Tiānxīn Gé** (Heart of Heaven Pavilion; park Y2, pavilion Y5), off Chengnan Xilu, which is an interesting area to explore.

Sleeping

Foreign-friendly budget lodging is PSB-induced scarce. Cheaper university digs suffer from location and price (not budget).

Húnán Shīfàn Dàxué Zhuānjiālóu (Hunan Normal University Foreign Experts' Bldg; ☎ 887 2211; Lushan Lu; beds in d Y30, tw with bathroom Y120-180; 🖭) It's in the west, so phone first. Take bus No 202 from the train station and disembark at the *shīfàn dàxué* stop. Nearly opposite the stop is a dorm and housing complex with budget rooms. Travellers usually have to slog about

750m uphill to a white building with the rates given here.

Hunan Agricultural University Guesthouse (Húnán Nóngyè Dàxué Wàibīnlóu; ☎ 461 8060; d Y120; 🖭) On the eastern outskirts of town, past the eastern bus station, this is the other budget option. Take bus or minibus No 110 from the south car park beside the train station. The university is the last stop, about a 40-minute ride.

Chēzhàn Dàshà (☎ 229 3366; 1 Wuyi Donglu; tw/tr Y168/198; 🖭) On the northern side of the train station, this lower mid-range hotel is mobbed with clients but still holds up – though look at a few rooms – and the staff can book train tickets.

Nánhǎi Bīnguǎn (☎ 229 7888; fax 229 6771; 1 Rongyuan Lu; s & tw Y180-235, tr Y218-288; 🖭) This convenient hotel is in the city centre (eminently quieter than the train station) with comfy (though not plush) rooms and solicitous staff.

Chángdǎo Fàndiàn (☎ 446 5133; fax 446 5157; 90 Wuyi Donglu; tw/tr Y268/338; 🖭) This hotel's relatively new rooms feature nearly sparkling bathrooms and wood floors; for the money, it's a good lower mid-range option. Discounts aren't unheard of.

Fúróng Huátiān Bīnguǎn (Lotus Huatian Hotel; ☎ 440 1888; fax 440 1889; 128 Wuyi Donglu; s/tw Y398/458; 🖭) This fancy hotel offers a 30% discount on its new, clean rooms. It's a definite step up for service, especially if you're doing business on a budget.

Dolton Hotel (Tōngchéng Guójì Dàjiǔdiàn; ☎ 416 8888; www.dolton-hotel.com; 149 Shaoshan Beilu; d & tw Y888-1288; 🗙 🖭 💻 🌊) One of the two best hotels in the city, the rooms and service here rarely fail to impress. An excellent all-round hotel.

Huá Tiān Dàjiǔdiàn (☎ 4442888; www.huatian-hotel .com; 380 Jiefang Donglu; tw/ste US$88/318 plus 15% service charge; 🗙 🖭 🌊) Constant renovations at this five-star hotel explain the fabulous rooms; its laundry list of international awards certainly backs up its reputation for service. The Palace Restaurant is without question one of the most fabulously designed and decorated eateries in central China. In short, one of the best hotels in central China.

Eating & Drinking

Hunanese food equals spicy. Plenty of **street-side stalls** pop up at night on Chaoyang Lu.

Xīnhuá Lóu (Wuyi Dadao; dishes Y4-25) This local institution, not far west of the train station, is a can't-miss option for local food like *málà zǐjì* (spicy diced chicken). Harried staff wheel around trolleys; patrons pick and choose (show some restraint, as the bills add up!). There are actually two locations opposite each other.

On Jiefang Lu, Western-style establishments (none cheap) compete for attention for city yuppies trying to be seen on the scene.

Oasis (Ōuxiāng Wū; ☎ 411 0532; 378 Jiefang Donglu) This Taiwan-style coffee house offers set meals with tea or coffee for Y35.

Life is Beautiful Bar (Měilíshēng; ☎ 416 0716; 328 Jiefang Donglu; meals Y30-50) This dark and sultry place has steak, chips, ice cream and Guinness beer.

Entertainment

Within kilometres of where Mao contemplated the plight of the rich and poor you can groove at a flash disco or bend the elbow at a hip bar.

Top One (☎ 413 0452; 137 Jiefang Donglu) This is the trendiest disco on the hippest street. Another is on Wuyi Donglu opposite the Fúróng Huátiān Bīnguǎn. There's no cover charge, but you have to purchase Y30 worth of drinks.

Shopping

Hunan Embroidery Research Institute (Húnánshěng Xiāngxiù Yánjiūsuǒ; ☎ 229 1821; 1 Chezhan Lu) Exquisite embroidered items (from Y20) are here; it's geared for tour groups but still a fascinating peek at Húnán folk art.

Getting There & Away

AIR

Civil Aviation Administration of China (CAAC; Zhōngguó Mínháng; ☎ 411 9821) is one block west of the train station.

From Chángshā, there are flights almost daily to many major cities such as Běijīng (Y1140), Chéngdū (Y830), Guǎngzhōu (Y630), Shànghǎi (Y810) and Xī'ān (Y810). Flights to Zhāngjiājiè (Y460) are officially (but occasionally optimistically) daily. Flights (daily except Wednesday and Sunday) go to Hong Kong (Y1600).

The airport is 26km from the city centre. CAAC shuttle buses (Y15) leave about two hours before scheduled flights.

BUS

A **bus station** (61 Chezhan Lu) across from the train station has buses to *some* major locations including Zhāngjiājiè (Y90 to Y105, seven to 12 hours) and Zhūzhōu (Y15, 1½ hours). Three other bus stations are all outside the city centre. From the train station, bus No 126 goes to the eastern bus station (*dōngzhàn*), bus No 12 followed by bus No 315 goes to the western bus station (*xīzhàn*) and bus No 107 goes to the southern bus station (*nánzhàn*). Bus No 502 links the east and south stations.

Buses for Yuèyáng (Y24 to Y35, 1½ to 2½ hours) and Nánchāng (Y85 to Y110, six to seven hours) leave from the eastern bus station. Buses for Huáihuà (Y99, 11 hours) and Zhāngjiājiè leave from the western bus station.

Buses for Sháoshān (Y22, 2½ hours) and Héng Shān (Y24 to Y32, two to three hours) leave from the southern bus station.

TRAIN

There are two Guǎngzhōu–Chángshā–Běijīng express trains daily in each direction and a daily train to Shànghǎi (Y300, 20 hours). Other important routes via Chángshā are Běijīng–Guìlín–Kūnmíng and Guǎngzhōu–Xī'ān–Lánzhōu. Not all trains to Shànghǎi, Kūnmíng and Guìlín stop in Chángshā, so it may be necessary to go to Zhūzhōu first and change there. Trains run to Zhāngjiājiè, but only N375 leaves at a good time (6.30am); the trip takes 12 hours. To Wǔhàn (Y50, three to four hours), it's no problem.

If you're heading to Hong Kong, you can take one of a few overnight Chángshā–Shēnzhèn air-conditioned express trains that get into Shēnzhèn early in the morning. The Běijīng–Kowloon express train also passes through Chángshā. A daily train to Sháoshān (Y11, three hours) leaves at 6.45am. Counter No 7 at the Chángshā train station is supposedly for foreigners.

SHÁOSHĀN 韶山
☎ 0732

Flyspeck-sized Sháoshān, about 130km southwest of Chángshā, looms large as Mao Zedong's birthplace. Three million pilgrims once came here each year, and a railway line and paved road from Chángshā were built. Mao's death and Cultural Revolution excesses slowed things, but of late Shàoshān has basked in the glory of China's rediscovered Maomania.

The countryside hasn't lost its charm. Traditional adobe houses dot this landscape of mountains and lush rice paddies.

Orientation

Shàoshān has two distinct parts: the new town clustered around the train and bus stations, and the original Shàoshān village about 5km away.

From the train station minibuses (Y1.50) and motorcycle taxis head to village sites. Some minibuses will take you to all the key sites for Y10.

Sights & Activities

MAO'S CHILDHOOD HOUSE 毛泽东故居

This **mud-brick house** (Máo Zédōng Gùjū; admission Y6; 7am-6pm, closes 5pm outside summer) with a thatched roof and stable is the village's shrine. Mao was born here in 1893 and returned to live here briefly in 1927. Exhibits include kitchen utensils, original furnishings, bedding and photos of Mao's parents, and a newer attraction – the tiny school (admission Y6) where he began his education.

MUSEUM OF COMRADE MAO
毛泽东纪念馆

This **museum** (Máo Zédōng Jìniànguǎn; 568 4957; admission Y7; 8am-5pm) has no English captions, but the exhibits of Mao's belongings and photos with communist leaders are graphic enough. Only those with serious Chinese skills could grapple with the Mao family genealogy in an adjacent annexe (admission Y6).

OTHER SIGHTS

Some 3km up from Shàoshān village is the **Dripping Water Cave** (滴水洞; Dī Shuǐ Dòng; 568 4957; admission Y25). In June 1966, Mao lived in this retreat (no, it's not a cave, but his villa was quite bunker-like), for 11 days. The Mao clan are entombed nearby. Buses to the cave leave from the car park opposite Shàoshān Bīnguǎn.

Shao Peak (韶峰; Sháo Fēng) is the conical-shaped mountain visible from the village. The summit has a lookout pavilion, and the 'forest of stelae' on the lower slopes has stone tablets engraved with Mao's poems.

The area has pleasant paths that will take you through pine forests and stands of bamboo.

From Shàoshān village you can take a minibus or motorcycle taxi (Y5) south to the end of the road at the cable car station. Hiking to the top of the mountain takes about an hour.

Sleeping & Eating

Shàoshān Bīnguǎn (韶山宾馆; 568 5080; d/tr Y240/280;) Mid-range options are the rule here; this place is on the main street into town. A hotel extension (568 5064) is around the corner to the right, up a small hill, and has nice grounds and decent rooms.

In the village itself you might get asked to stay with a local family; no-one seems to mind.

Meals are pricey in Shàoshān. **Restaurants** on the road across from Shàoshān Bīnguǎn are typically good.

Shopping

Fancy a Chinese fan that unfolds to reveal a jolly profile of none other than Mao himself? Drop your cash at your choice of the three **tourist markets**. All should satiate any craving for Maoist kitsch. Must-have Maobilia includes a Mao portrait good-luck charm – ubiquitous on Chinese rear-view car mirrors – and Mao-festooned cigarette lighters.

Getting There & Away

BUS

Chángshā's southern bus station has several buses a day to Shàoshān (Y22, 2½ hours) that run from 8am onwards. During the summertime, travel group kiosks sprout up around the train station. The Shàoshān **long-distance bus station** (长途汽车站; chángtú qìchēzhàn; Yingbin Lu), just north of the train station, has daily buses to Chángshā. There are also frequent minibuses to Xiāngtán (Y6, 1½ hours). From there you can catch a train or bus to Chángshā or Huáihuà. Buses also go to Héng Shān.

TRAIN

There is one train daily (Y11, three hours) to Shàoshān from Chángshā. It departs from Chángshā at 6.45am and returns from Shàoshān at 5.35pm, so you can visit the town as a day trip.

MAO ZEDONG

Mao was born in Sháoshān, not far from Chángshā, in 1893. Once poor, his father served in the military to make money. Ultimately, their new surpluses raised their status to 'rich' peasants.

A famine in Húnán and a subsequent uprising of starving people in Chángshā ended in the execution of the leaders by the Manchu governor, an injustice that deeply affected Mao. At the age of 16 he left Sháoshān to enter middle school in Chángshā. Though not yet anti-monarchist, he felt that the country was in desperate need of reform.

In Chángshā, Mao was first exposed to the ideas of revolutionaries active in China, most notably Sun Yatsen's revolutionary secret society. Later that year an army uprising in Wǔhàn quickly spread and the Qing dynasty collapsed. Mao joined the regular army, but resigned six months later, thinking the revolution was over when Sun handed the presidency to Yuan Shikai and the war between the north and south of China did not take place.

Voraciously reading newspapers, Mao was introduced to socialism. While at the Hunan No 1 Teachers' Training School (p479), he inserted an advertisement in a Chángshā newspaper 'inviting young men interested in patriotic work to make contact with me…'. Among them was Liu Shaoqi, who later became president of the People's Republic of China (PRC); Xiao Chen, who became a founding member of the Chinese Communist Party (CCP); and Li Lisan.

Mao graduated in 1918 and went to Běijīng, where he worked as an assistant librarian at Beijing University. In Běijīng he met future co-founders of the Chinese Communist Party: the student leader Zhang Guodao, Professor Chen Duxiu and university librarian Li Dazhao. Chen and Li are regarded as the founders of Chinese communism.

On returning to Chángshā, Mao became increasingly active in communist politics. He became editor of the *Xiang River Review*, a radical Húnán students' newspaper, and began teaching. In 1920 he organised workers and truly felt himself a Marxist. In Shànghǎi in 1921 Mao attended the founding meeting of the CCP and helped organise Húnán's provincial branch. Differing from orthodox Marxism, Mao saw the peasants as the lifeblood of the revolution and from 1922 to 1925, the CCP organised its first unions of peasants, workers, and students. Vengeful warlords impelled Mao's flight to Guǎngzhōu (Canton).

In April 1927, following Chiang Kaishek's massacre of communists, Mao was dispatched to Chángshā to organise what became known as the 'Autumn Harvest Uprising'. Mao's army scaled Jǐnggāng Shān's peaks to embark on a guerrilla war – step one towards the 1949 Communist takeover.

Mao became the new chairman of the PRC (till his death in 1976) and embarked on radical campaigns to repair his war-ravaged yet jubilant country. In the mid-1950s he became more disillusioned with the Soviets and began to implement peasant-based and decentralised socialist development. The outcome was the ill-fated Great Leap Forward and, later, the Cultural Revolution (for details, see p45).

The current regime officially says Mao was 70% correct and 30% wrong. Torturous experiences are remembered, but he is revered like a god who united his people and returned China to the status of world power. 'Great Leader', 'Great Teacher', 'supremely beloved Chairman' are oft-used monikers; his ubiquitous images reveal a saint who will protect them (or make them rich).

Biographies of Mao Zedong include Ross Terrill's *Mao*, Jerome Ch'en's *Mao and the Chinese Revolution* and Stuart R Schram's *Mao Tse-tung*. An interesting account of Mao's earlier years is recorded in Edgar Snow's *Red Star Over China*. The five-volume *Selected Works of Mao Tse-tung* provide abundant insight into his thoughts.

ZHŪZHŌU 株州

☎ 0733 / pop 3,656,500

Formerly a small market town, Zhūzhōu underwent a rapid industrialisation following the completion of the Guǎngzhōu–Wǔhàn railway line in 1937, developing into an important coal and freight reload-ing point and manufacturing centre. Most travellers only stop here long enough to change trains, but the city has some pleasant areas.

Qìngyún Bīnguǎn (☎ 822 4851; fax 822 5356; 1 Chezhan Lu; tw Y180-288, tr Y165; 🛇) This impressive, reasonable three-star hotel is opposite the train station and is generally better value than higher-priced hotels further from the station.

Zhūzhōu is at the junction of the Běijīng–Guǎngzhōu and the Shànghǎi–Kūnmíng railway lines. From Chángshā it's one hour by express train.

The **bus station** (xinhua xilu) has buses to Xiāngtán, which has buses to Sháoshān. It's a 15-minute walk to the train station: turn right and cross the railway bridge, then turn left again at the next intersection.

YUÈYÁNG 岳阳

☎ 0730 / pop 5,103,500

Yuèyáng, long a port of call for ferries plying the Yangzi River (Cháng Jiāng) between Chóngqìng and Wǔhàn prior to the Three Gorges Dam, is legendary for its pagoda. Perched on enormous Dòngtíng Hú (Dongting Lake), hydrophiles can get their fix puttering in local boats on the way to Jūnshān Dǎo, home to a tea so sublime emperors demanded it as a gift of respect.

Orientation & Information

Yuèyáng is situated south of the Yangzi on the northeastern shore of Dòngtíng Hú, where the lake flows into the river. Yuèyáng proper is in the southern section of the city; it's where you'll find the train and bus stations, and many hotels and sights. Some 17km away to the north at Chénglíngjī, the city's main port (and two smaller local docks in the city centre) is rather dormant with the decline of Yangzi ferry traffic.

CITS (Zhōngguó Guójì Lǚxíngshè; ☎ 823 2010; 25 Chengdong Lu) is in the courtyard of Yúnmèng Bīnguǎn and can help you book train tickets.

An **Internet café** (wǎngbā) can be found to the west of town, near Dongting Beilu.

Sights & Activities

Yuèyáng has a working-class atmosphere, and its narrow, old backstreets are a colourful contrast to China's modernisation drive.

The local landmark is the **Yueyang Tower** (Yuèyáng Lóu; Dongting Beilu; admission Y46; ⏰ 7.30am-4.30pm), a temple complex constructed during the Tang dynasty. Housed within is a sublime gold replica of the complex. Splendid vistas of the lake can be had by climbing to the top.

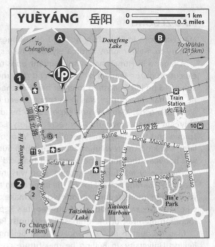

For a foray into the past, **Cí Shì Tǎ** (Loving Clan Pagoda) is a crumbling brick tower dating back to 1242. Walk or take any bus south on Dongting Nanlu to Baling Lu. Continue south on Dongting Nanlu, keeping to the left. After about seven minutes, you'll see the pagoda, up a lane to the right in a residential courtyard.

Dongting Nanlu and the old railway area also have some of Yuèyáng's oldest and most interesting streets, with vegetable markets, brown brick buildings and fish drying on poles.

Yuèyáng borders the 3900 sq km **Dòngtíng Hú**, China's second-largest body of fresh water. There are several islands in the lake; the most famous is **Jūnshān Dǎo** (admission Y30), where the legendary yínzhēn chá (silver needle tea) is grown. Added to hot water, the tea supposed to remain on the surface, sticking up like tiny needles. Silver needle tea remains a popular souvenir to amaze friends back home. It's not cheap – the best quality goes for Y120 for 50g – but you can buy the same amount of a lesser quality for Y48.

The island is also known for its late-spring or early summer dragon boat races, held since ancient times. Trails lined with pavilions cover the island.

Boats leave approximately every two hours for Jūnshān Dǎo (Y40 return, 45 minutes) from the Yueyang Tower Ferry Dock (Yuèyáng Lóu Lúnchuán Kèyùnzhàn) on Dongting Beilu. The earliest boats leave around 7.30am, and the last boat returns at 4.30pm.

Sleeping

Xuělián Bīnguǎn (☎ 832 1633; Dongting Beilu; d/tr Y70/90, with bathroom Y100-180; 🏠) In a funky riverfront neighbourhood, the building is of traditional Chinese architecture, with hexagonal windows and wooden balconies. Rooms vary from spartan to quite comfy. From the train station, take bus No 22 to the Yueyang Tower.

Yuèyáng Lóu Bīnguǎn (☎ 832 1288; 57 Dongting Beilu; tw/u Y100/190, 🏠) Just off Dongting Beilu, this friendly place has somewhat tattered rooms; look at a few, as housekeeping varies by floor. Bus No 22 will get you there.

Yúnmèng Bīnguǎn (☎ 822 1115; 25 Chengdong Lu; tw/tr Y288/328; 🏠) This three-star hotel has good service and generally well-kept rooms (bargaining is the key). It is oft-recommended by Chinese foodies as a good spot to indulge in local flavours.

Highsun Hotel (Hànsēn Bīnguǎn; ☎ 831 8888; fax 832 2666; 1 Bailing Lu; tw from Y390; 🏠) This hotel is the best top-end place in town and is pretty much packed out with tour groups from spring through autumn.

Eating

Yuèyáng cuisine is recognisable for its liberal usage of starch and oil in many dishes. There are good fish and **seafood restaurants**, particularly on Dongting Beilu, which also has a choice of cheap places where you can buy dumplings, noodles and breakfast; **food stalls** and small **restaurants** are near the Nanyuepo Dock.

Getting There & Away

Yuèyáng is on the main Guǎngzhōu–Běijīng railway line. There are trains to Wǔhàn (Y35, four hours), Chángshā (Y20 to Y28, 1½ to two hours) and Guǎngzhōu (Y200 to Y250, 12 hours). You can book train tickets at the Yuèyáng Lóu Bīnguǎn ticket counter and at CITS.

There are also daily buses to Chángshā (Y24 to Y35, 1½ to 2½ hours), and Wǔhàn (Y50 to Y60, three to four hours) from the long-distance bus station.

Yuèyáng's once-busy port for Yangzi River ferries has been in serious decline and was not a scheduled stop at the time of writing; as things are constantly in flux, expect things to change.

HÉNGYÁNG 衡阳

☎ 0734 / pop 6,924,200

Húnán's second-largest city, Héngyáng is no beauty, but it is on the junction of the Guìlín–Chángshā and Běijīng–Guǎngzhōu lines and relatively close to Héng Shān.

Héngyáng has important lead and zinc mining industries, but was badly damaged during WWII. Despite post-1949 reconstruction, it still lags noticeably behind its northern neighbour, Zhūzhōu.

CITS (Zhōngguó Guójì Lǚxíngshè; ☎ 825 4160; 206 Huancheng Lu) has some obliging English speakers and is around the corner from Yànchéng Bīnguǎn. It can book train tickets and arrange guided visits to Héng Shān.

Héngyáng is strict about where foreigners can stay.

Nányuè Dàjiǔdiàn (南岳大酒店; ☎ 833 6999; 5 Guangdong Lu; tw Y70-120; 🏠) Inexpensive rooms at this hotel near the train station are basic but clean.

Jìngyuán Bīnguǎn (静园宾馆; ☎ 822 2971; fax 822 8814; cnr Jiefang Lu & Zhengxiang Lu; tw Y168; 🏠) Close to the bus station, this three-star hotel is quite nice with an equally good restaurant.

Trains to Chángshā take 2½ hours and hard seats cost Y28.

From the bus station, hourly buses depart for Chángshā (Y40, 2½ hours) and Nányuè (for Héng Shān; Y12, one hour); a bus to Jǐnggāng Shān (Y60, eight hours) in Jiāngxī leaves around 6am. To get to the long-distance bus station, take bus No 1 from the train station to the last stop on Jiefang Lu.

HÉNG SHĀN 衡山
☎ 0734

Héng Shān (☎ 566 2571; admission Y40) is one of China's holy mountains, shooting up 1290m above sea level and covering 400km. About 100km south of Chángshā, it is also known as Nányuè Shān (Southern High Mountain), and is where kings and emperors once hunted and made sacrifices to heaven and earth.

Today Buddhists and Taoists live peacefully on the mountain and Chinese tourists flock here, especially during the summer, to pray before the gods. This mountain perhaps get overlooked a bit by travellers, particularly foreigners, keen on other better-known spiritually cleansing climbs; that alone may intrigue intrepid walkers.

Orientation
Héng Shān's main streets are Zhurong Lu, running north to south, and Xi Jie, running west to east, just in front of the Nányuè Temple. Dengshan Lu is north of the temple.

English-language maps (Y2) can be purchased at the Xinhua Bookshop (Xīnhuá Shūdiàn), near the south end of the temple's entrance on Bei Jie.

Information
Bank of China (中国行; Zhōngguó Yínháng; 37 Hengshan Lu) As you leave the archway at the foot of Bei Jie, the bank is on your left.
CITS (中国国际旅行社; Zhōngguó Guójì Lǚxíngshè; ☎ 825 4160) English is spoken, and staff can help arrange a guide (not necessary).
Post office (邮局; yóujú) As you enter the archway, this is about a block down on your left.
PSB (公安局; Gōngānjú; Xi Jie) About a block south of Dengshan Lu.

Sights & Activities
To get to Héng Shān, follow Dengshan Lu until it curves to your right. Hiking on the paved road or marked paths to **Wishing**

SHĀN: HILL, MOUNTAIN

This character can be seen either as a mountain range with three peaks or as a mountain in its own right, with its peak in the middle. Either way, it is one of the simplest to remember!

Harmony Peak (祝融峰; Zhùróng Fēng), the mountain's highest point, takes four hours and another four hours to descend. The time excludes visiting the monasteries, temples, villas and gardens on the mountain. A motorcycle taxi (Y30 to Y50) from the bottom or a cable car (Y30 one-way) that starts midway on the mountain and goes nearly to the top can help you reduce the walk.

Wishing Harmony Palace (祝融殿; Zhùróng Diàn), built during the Ming dynasty, is the resting place of Zhu Rong, an official 'in charge of' fire during one of China's early periods. Zhu Rong used to hunt on Héng Shān, and so Taoists selected the mountain to represent fire.

The large and attractive **Nanyue Temple** (南岳大庙; Nányuè Dàmiào; ☎ 566 2353; admission Y20; ⊗ 7am-7pm), dating from the Tang dynasty, was rebuilt during the Qing dynasty. Note the column supports, one for each of the mountains in the range, purportedly.

Sleeping & Eating
The cheapest option is to sleep in an extra room over a restaurant (expect to be asked) at the base of the mountain or in the Taoist monastery **Xuandu Temple** (玄都寺; Xuándū Sì) halfway up the mountain.

Jiāchéng Jiǔlóu (家城酒楼; 10 Dengshan Lu; dm Y35) This inexpensive restaurant also has basic but clean rooms (no heating or private bathrooms).

Nóngyè Bīnguǎn (农业宾馆; Agricultural Bank of China Hotel; ☎ 566 6492; fax 566 6491; 19 Zhurong Lu; tr Y90, tw with bathroom Y138; ⊗) This hotel has surprisingly good rooms for the money; you can thumb your nose at the pricier options across the street.

Zizhúlín Bīnguǎn (紫竹林宾馆; ☎ 566 1400; dm Y20-35, tw Y145; ⊗) Midway up Héng Shān, this place offers basic twins with stunning vistas – which makes the plank dorm beds hurt a bit less. A motorcycle taxi is probably the best way to get there, and it's best to call about vacancies. A number of other options are nearby.

Fúróng Shānzhuāng (扶蓉山庄; ☎ 566 3013; tw Y120-200; ⊗) At the summit, you can't beat the views here; the rooms are pretty good for a mountain hotel.

For food, there are plenty of street-side **restaurants** on Dengshan Lu; **Xuandu Temple** on the mountain also has a vegetarian restaurant.

Getting There & Away

From the archway on Bei Jie, turn right and the long-distance bus station is a few minutes' walk across the street on your left. It's the gateway to Héng Shān and also has buses to Chángshā (Y24 to Y32, two to three hours) and Héngyáng (Y12, one hour). Arriving buses may drop you at Dengshan Lu. Trains from Chángshā are an option, but they're slower than buses on the new expressways and require switching to a minibus for a half-hour ride from the railhead.

HUÁIHUÀ 怀化

☎ 0745 / pop 4,766,200

Huáihuà is a town built around a railway junction in western Húnán. Most people use the town as a transit point to or from Zhāngjiājiè or Liǔzhōu. Note that southwestern Húnán between here and Sānjiāng (in Guǎngxī province) is off limits to foreigners; Shàoyáng's PSB may issue travel permits to closed areas (then again, you may get in hot water just trying to get there). One place that should be OK (though it's a good idea to check) is **Fènghuáng** (凤凰), a predominantly Miao village straight out of the past; it's 50km northwest of Huáihuà. Flagstone streets, traditional gabled houses built on stilts, towers and pagodas everywhere, funky boats poled down the river – a time warp and not yet too touristy. You can also disembark at Jíshǒu, one train stop north, and arrange transport.

Places to stay in Huáihuà include **Tiānfù Fàndiàn** (天副饭店; ☎ 226 4792; 30 Huochezhan Kou; tw Y120-260; ⊠). A short hop from the train station, this place has a variety of rooms, so look around; you'll likely find a better bargain here than in pricier places nearby.

Getting There & Away

Běijīng–Kūnmíng, Chéngdū–Guǎngzhōu and Shànghǎi–Chóngqìng express trains run via Huáihuà. There are also slower trains from Guìyáng, Guǎngzhōu, Zhèngzhōu and Liǔzhōu, terminating in Huáihuà. Chángshā is about the only place for which there are plenty of departures.

There are several daily trains to Zhāngjiājiè (four to 5½ hours). You can also catch a train to Sānjiāng (5½ hours) in northern Guǎngxī, though departure and arrival times are awful.

WǓLÍNGYUÁN & ZHĀNGJIĀJIÈ 武陵源、张家界

☎ 0744 / pop 1,537,700

Parts of Wǔlíng Shān in northwestern Húnán were set aside in 1982 as nature reserves collectively known as the **Wulingyuan Scenic Area** (Wǔlíngyuán Fēngjǐngqū; www.zhangjiajie.com.cn), encompassing the localities of Zhāngjiājiè, Tiānzǐshān and Suǒxīyù. Zhāngjiājiè is the best known, and many Chinese refer to this area by that name.

The first area of its kind in China, and recognised by Unesco in 1990 as a World Heritage Site, Wǔlíngyuán is home to three minority peoples – Tujia, Miao and Bai – who maintain their cultures.

Rising from the misty subtropical forest are 243 – count 'em – majestic peaks surrounded by over 3000 karst upthrusts, an assemblage not seen elsewhere in the world. Not to mention waterfalls, limestone caves (including Asia's largest chamber), and rivers suitable for organised rafting trips. Nearly two dozen rare species of flora and fauna call the region home; botanists delight in the 3000-odd plant species within the park. Even amateur wildlife spotters may get a gander at a clouded leopard or a pangolin.

Several towns serve as access points to Wǔlíngyuán, but the most popular ones are Zhāngjiājiè city (Zhāngjiājiè *shì*) and Zhāngjiājiè village (Zhāngjiājiè *cūn*). The city is near the railway line, while the village is situated nearly 600m above sea level in the Wǔlíng foothills, surrounded by sheer cliffs and vertical rock outcrops.

A fee of Y158, good for two days with extension, must be paid at the Zhāngjiājiè forest reserve's main entrance just past the village. Chinese maps showing walking trails, only some of them have sites marked in English, are on sale in Zhāngjiājiè city and village.

Sights & Activities

The highest area closest to Zhāngjiājiè village is **Huángshízhài** (黄石寨) and, at 1048m, it's a two-hour hike up 3878 stone steps (or a few minutes in a cable car for Y50).

In the northern section of the reserve, **Tiānzǐ Fēng** (天子峰; Tianzi Peak) is another good hike. Every rock, crag and gully has been given an elaborate name.

Organised tours to the park and **Jiutian Cave** (九天洞; Jiǔtiān Dòng) often include a **rafting trip** (*piāolǚ*), or you can join a tour

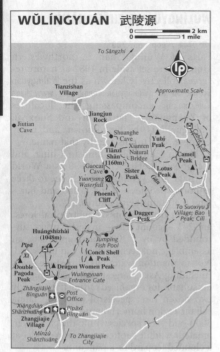

WŬLÍNGYUÁN 武陵源

0 ——— 2 km
0 ——— 1 mile

To Sāngzhí

Tiānzishān
Village

Jiǔtian
Cave

Jiāngjūn
Rock

Approximate Scale

Shuānghe
Cave

Yubi
Peak

Tiānzǐ
Shān
(1260m)

Xiānrén
Natural
Bridge

Camel
Peak

Gaocai
Cave

Sister
Peak

Lotus
Peak

Gǔtn Xī

Yuanyang
Waterfall

Phoenix
Cliff

To Suòxīyù
Village; Bao
Peak; Cili

Dagger
Peak

Huángshízhài
(1048m)

Pípā
Xī

Jumping
Fish Pool

Conch Shell
Peak

Double
Pagoda
Peak

Dragon Women Peak

Wulingyuan
Entrance Gate

Zhāngjiājiè
Bīnguǎn

Post
Office

Xiāngdiàn
Shānzhuāng

Pípāxī
Bīnguǎn

Zhangjiajie
Village

Mínzú
Shānzhuāng

To Zhangjiajie
City

and just do the rafting trip. While there are good white water rafting possibilities northwest of Zhāngjiājiè near the Húběi border, you'll have to make special arrangements for the equipment and transport.

Most rivers are pretty tame, so don't expect great thrills; still, the scenery inspires. The actual rafting usually lasts about two hours with about the same amount of time taken up in travel to the launch area.

You can join tours or arrange your own through hotels in Zhāngjiājiè or at a travel agency in Zhāngjiājiè city. The **Dongsheng Travel Agency** (Dōngshēng Lǚxíngshè; ☎ 828 6258; 36 Jiefang Lu) offers good rates for group tours (Y180 to Y250 per person). **CITS** (中国国际旅行社; Zhōngguó Guójì Lǚxíngshè; ☎ 822 7111; 37 Jiefang Lu) has English speakers and offers rafting tours (Y300 per person).

Sleeping

It's more convenient and interesting (and at times cheaper) to stay in Zhāngjiājiè village. A few budget-range places are near the bus station. Note that these prices generally rise on weekends.

Wǔlíng Guójì Jiǔdiàn (武陵国际酒店; ☎ 822 2630; fax 822 2165; 1 Jiefang Lu; tw & tr Y228; 💥) This hotel, past Puguang Temple, has nice twin rooms in the city.

Xiánglóng Guójì Jiǔdiàn (祥龙国际酒店; Dragon International Hotel; ☎ 822 6888; fax 822 2935; 46 Jiefang Lu; tw in older/newer wing Y488/775, plus 15% service charge; 💥) This glittering marble and chrome establishment masquerading as a four-star hotel is the region's top hotel.

In Zhāngjiājiè village most places accept foreigners; some travellers have also stayed with local families within the park, but don't expect it. All of the following hotels are on the main road.

Zhāngjiājiè Bīnguǎn (张家界宾馆; ☎ 571 2388; fax 571 2816; dm Y75, tw Y260-500; 💥) There's a three-star addition next door that offers upmarket air-con twins; tough-to-get dorm beds are adjacent in a wing of so-so twins. The hotel can also book train tickets three days in advance.

Xiāngdiàn Shānzhuāng (香殿山庄; Xiangdian Mountain Inn; ☎ 571 2266; fax 571 2172; tw Y400; 💥) This nice place, just 50m off the main road, is good value, even after a rate hike with a four-star makeover. The hotel is nicely laid out amid picturesque gardens, and some rooms have balconies with super mountain vistas.

Mínzú Shānzhuāng (民族山庄; ☎ 571 9288; fax 571 2516; s/d Y220, tr Y260; 💥) This thatched, Tujia-run establishment is by far the best in town. The beautiful, Tujia-style wood rooms even have balconies with more lovely views. The restaurant features Tujia folk music performances in its restaurant.

For those hiking overnight in Wǔlíngyuán, there are places to stay inside the park along the popular trail routes. Local visitors often do a two- to three-day circuit hike, going in at Zhāngjiājiè village and hiking or bussing it to villages within the park boundaries such as Tiānzǐshān and Suòxīyù, both of which have a bewildering choice of hotels and hostels. If you're just interested in day hiking, a stay in Zhāngjiājiè will suffice.

Eating

There are simple **eating houses** scattered around the village, and the better hotels, such as Mínzú Shānzhuāng, also have **restaurants**. None are memorable. Adventurous foodies can sample roast/fried/steamed beasts of many varieties – amphibians to avian species to unclassifiable mammals.

Just be absolutely certain it isn't endangered (if possible) and that the price has been established before the cooking begins.

Taiwan Barbecue Village (Bābǐ Q Taíwāncūn Cāntīng; ☎ 823 5595; 13 Tianmen Lu; dishes Y10-40) At the corner of Jiaochang Lu, this 2nd-floor bar/restaurant has a great atmosphere and good meals featuring barbecued chicken. Beer is available in the afternoon and evening. Mr Ding, who is Tujia (by way of Taiwan), started the restaurant.

Shopping

A good buy in Zhāngjiājiè are the tightly woven baskets with a simple black line pattern; Tujia women often carry the baskets on their backs. You can find the baskets at markets in Zhāngjiājiè city and on Huilong Lu. These aren't the coloured baskets sold to tourists but the real thing, and cost about Y20. Also available are other items such as wooden buckets and bamboo cradles.

Getting There & Away
AIR
The airport is 4km southwest of Zhāngjiājiè city and 24km from the park entrance; a taxi should cost around Y75 to the park. More and more flights link Zhāngjiājiè city with the rest of China; thankfully, the once frequent cancellations are now leaving more regularly. Major destinations with daily flights include Běijīng (Y1310), Chángshā (Y460), Chóngqìng (Y560), Guǎngzhōu (Y730), Shànghǎi (Y1070), Wǔhàn (Y500) and Shēnzhèn (Y760); seasonal flights also go direct to/from Hong Kong twice weekly.

BUS & MINIBUS
Buses leave the Zhāngjiājiè city bus station for Chángshā in the early morning. Herculean work on an expressway from Chángshā should be finished by the time you read this. The once 12-hour bump fest should be cut to a more endurable seven. The trip costs Y85, or Y105 for cosier buses.

Minibuses to Zhāngjiājiè village (Y10, one hour) pick up incoming passengers at the car park in front of the train station but sometimes you have to wait over an hour. If so, hop on a bus to the bus station in Zhāngjiājiè city, which lies across the river, 14km from the train station. At the Zhāngjiājiè city bus station, you can also get buses to Tiānzǐshān and Suǒxīyù (Y5).

TRAIN
The train station is 8km southeast of the city. Direct trains run from Zhāngjiājiè city to Chángshā (Y98 to Y250, five to eight hours) and other points east. A fast train leaves Chángshā around 9am and arrives at Zhāngjiājiè city at 2pm. You can also get trains from the Yangzi River port of Yíchāng that pass through Zhāngjiājiè on their way to Huáihuà, including the daily train from Xiāngfán in Húběi that passes through Sānjiāng and terminates at Liǔzhōu in Guǎngxī. Another train to Guǎngxī leaves Zhāngjiājiè at 5.33pm and terminates at Guilín's north station (but skips Sānjiāng).

China Travel Service (CTS; Zhōngguó Lǚxíngshè; ☎ 822 7718; Jiefang Lu) in Zhāngjiājiè city is opposite Xiánglóng Guójì Jiǔdiàn. The staff can book hard and soft sleepers, as well as air tickets. The travel service adjacent to the Mínzú Shānzhuāng has also received good reviews.

MĚNGDÒNGHÉ 猛洞河
☎ 0743
An hour and a half south of Zhāngjiājiè by train, Měngdònghé is nestled between the hills and rivers of western Húnán.

From here you can take a 45-minute boat ride to Wáng Cūn, better known as **Fúróngzhèn** (扶蓉镇; Hibiscus Town). It was the location for Xie Jin's 1986 film of the same name. The film, adapted from Gu Hua's novel *A Town Called Hibiscus*, portrayed how the political turbulence of the 1950s and 1960s unsettled the lives of ordinary villagers. The film turned the town into a tourist destination. Wandering up the twisting stone streets and looking at the dilapidated wooden buildings just up from the pier is a trip into the past. On the main street, there's a worthwhile private **museum** (博物馆; bówùguǎn; ☎ 585 3363; 60 Hepan Jie; admission Y5; ☑ 8am-6pm) of Tujia culture in an old house.

One reason to visit Fúróngzhèn is for **rafting**. Trips here are better organised than in Zhāngjiājiè and you can buy tickets at the rafting ticket office at the dock. The cost is around Y125 and includes transport to the launch site. Be prepared to get drenched, as water warfare between passing rafts, using ladles and bamboo squirt guns, is highly encouraged. There are also swimming opportunities. Flimsy ponchos are sold by vendors and around town.

Sleeping & Eating

Tiānxià Dìyī Jiǔlóu (天下第一酒楼; First Snail Under Heaven Restaurant; ☎ 585 3418; fax 585 3898; 19 Hepan Lu; s & d Y80-328; 🕄) About 150m up the stone steps from the pier and to your right, this quaintly named hotel/restaurant has nice, airy rooms overlooking the river. There's no English sign, but look out for a white and blue sign with red characters across from a wide stairway. The staff can also arrange tickets for rafting trips, and throw in a free hat as well.

It's obvious where you should go if you enjoy eating snails. Other **restaurants** line the main street.

In the film *Hibiscus Town* the protagonist is renowned for making *mǐdòufu*, a tasty snack that looks like cubes of tofu, but is actually milled rice flour topped with pickles and chilli sauce. The stalls down by the dock sell it for about Y2.

Getting There & Away

Trains coming from Zhāngjiājiè, Huáihuà and Liǔzhōu all stop in Měngdònghé. From the train station, walk down the steps towards the ferry boat dock. Bus or boat tickets to Fúróngzhèn are Y4, but beware of overcharging. Boats depart infrequently, so it's probably easier to take a minibus.

Hong Kong

HIGHLIGHTS

- Ride the historic **Peak Tram** (p498) and enjoy the view from Victoria Peak
- Cross the harbour the original way: on the **Star Ferry** (p526)
- Enjoy the hubbub that is the **Temple St night market** (p508)
- Climb the colossal **Tian Tan Buddha statue** (p509) on Lantau
- Bar-hop in **Lan Kwai Fong** and **Soho** (p521)

Temple St Night Market
Lan Kwai Fong; Soho
Tian Tan Buddha Statue
Star Ferry
Peak Tram

■ AREA CODE: ☎ 852   ■ POP: 6.8 MIL   ■ www.discoverhongkong.com

Hong Kong, a pulsating fusion of two cultures, is like no other city in the world. The long-anticipated handover of the territory from Britain to China in 1997 brought an end to Hong Kong's century and a half as a 'borrowed place on borrowed time'. The meeting of East and West, however, continues to shake and stir the city into an invigorating cocktail of colour and aroma, taste and sensation.

Hong Kong has something for everyone: shopping malls with bargains galore; romantic vistas across Victoria Harbour or down from the Peak; museums with rich collections devoted to local history and culture; stunning modern architecture; and a seemingly endless choice of restaurants and cuisines.

Despite its size and rapid urbanisation, Hong Kong has a surprising number of accessible beaches and natural retreats for lovers of the great outdoors. Much of Lantau Island, for example, is designated country park and boasts two of the territory's highest peaks. The New Territories cuts a huge swath to the north and, while it is becoming increasingly built up, still offers dramatic scenery, bracing hikes and one of the region's most important wetlands.

Even after its return to the so-called motherland, Hong Kong's political and economic systems are still significantly different from those of mainland China. Thus, much of the general information you've read elsewhere in this book concerning visas, currency, accommodation, international phone calls and so on does not apply to Hong Kong.

Most visitors will have very few problems getting around Hong Kong; English is widely spoken and street signs are bilingual. The vast majority of the population – in fact, some 94% – is Cantonese-speaking Chinese, though Mandarin is increasingly used since the handover and the arrival of mass tourism from the mainland.

HISTORY

European trade with China began in earnest in the late 16th century when Portuguese navigators were granted permission to set up a base within a walled enclave in Macau. Trade mushroomed during the 18th century as European demand for Chinese tea and silk grew. However, as the Chinese were largely self-sufficient, the balance of trade was unfavourable to the Europeans – until they began running opium into the country.

While the drug had long been used medicinally in Asia as well as in Europe, addiction to the drug soon became widespread. The British, with a virtually inexhaustible supply of the drug from the poppy fields of Bengal, developed the trade aggressively and by the start of the 19th century this

'foreign mud' formed the basis of most of their transactions with China.

China's attempts to stamp out the trade, including confiscating and destroying a huge shipment of the drug, gave the British the pretext they needed for military action against China. Two British gunboats were sent in and managed to demolish a Chinese fleet of 29 ships. A British naval landing party hoisted the Union flag on Hong Kong Island in 1841, and the Treaty of Nanking, which brought an end to the so-called First Opium War, ceded the island to the British crown 'in perpetuity'.

At the end of the Second Opium War in 1860, Britain took possession of the Kowloon Peninsula; in July 1898 a 99-year lease was granted for the New Territories. What would happen after the lease ended on

RICHARD I'ANSON

Detail of a golden Buddha in the Ten Thousand Buddhas Monastery (p509), Hong Kong

CHRIS MELLOR

The Hong Kong Convention & Exhibition Centre (p499), Hong Kong Island

View of the harbour and city at night from Victoria Peak (p498), Hong Kong

CHRIS MELLOR

地鐵路綫圖 MTR system map

www.mtr.com.hk

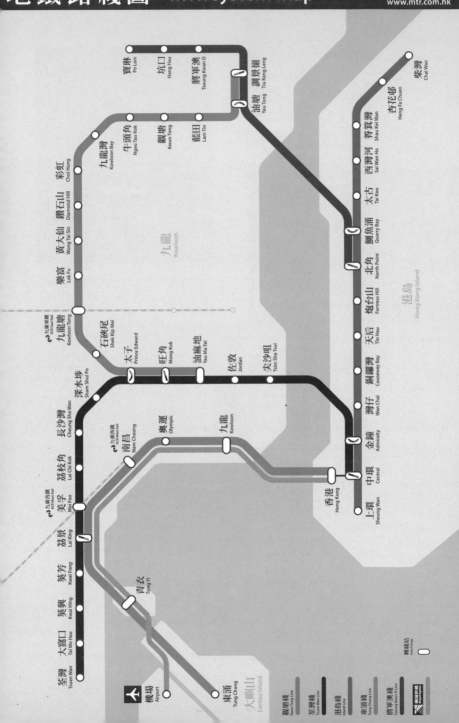

30 June 1997 was the subject of considerable speculation.

In late 1984 an agreement was reached: China would take over the entire territory in 1997, but what would become the Special Administrative Region (SAR) of Hong Kong would retain its free-market economy as well as its social and legal systems for 50 years. The Chinese catch phrase for this was, 'One country, two systems'.

Nervousness grew as the handover date drew near, especially after 1989 when Chinese troops mowed down prodemocracy demonstrators in the streets around Běijīng's Tiananmen Sq, and both people and capital moved to safe havens overseas.

A belated attempt by Britain to increase the number of democratically elected members of Hong Kong's Legislative Council spurred China to set up a pro-Beijing Provisional Legislative Council across the border in Shēnzhèn. On 1 July 1997 this body took office in Hong Kong, and Shànghǎi-born shipping magnate, Tung Chee Hwa (1937–) was named as the council's chief executive.

Hong Kong has weathered a lot of storms since the British handover: from the economic downturn affecting all of the Southeast Asia region to the outbreak of Severe Acute Respiratory Syndrome (SARS), which led to the deaths of almost 300 people in the territory and all but destroyed tourism. But perhaps the greatest damage to the credibility of the SAR administration came in 1999 when the government, with Běijīng's help, overturned a high court ruling allowing residency rights for the China-born offspring of parents who became Hong Kong citizens after 1997. Tung was returned for a second five-year term in March 2002.

ORIENTATION

Hong Kong's ever-growing 1102 sq km of territory is divided into four main areas: Hong Kong Island, Kowloon, the New Territories and the Outlying Islands.

Hong Kong Island, particularly Central on the northern side, is the economic heart of the colony but comprises just over 7% of the total land mass. Kowloon is the densely populated peninsula to the north, the southern tip of which is Tsim Sha Tsui, with lots of hotels, guesthouses and tourist-

---

A SYMBOL FOR HONG KONG

When the British packed their bags and left town in 1997, they took with them the Union Jack – leaving Hong Kong without a flag. Finding itself grafted onto China, the new Special Administrative Region (SAR) made a fitting choice for its new symbol: the *Bauhinia blakeana*, a sterile tree unique to the territory.

Priests from the French Mission (now the Court of Final Appeal) in Central apparently discovered the tree near the seashore in the late 19th century. As no identical one had been found anywhere else in the world, it was declared a new species of bauhinia (of which there are 250 to 300) and named after Sir Henry Blake, governor of Hong Kong from 1898 to 1904.

The *Bauhinia blakeana*, also known as the Hong Kong Orchid Tree, has spreading branches and broad, heart-shaped leaves. Its delicately scented flowers have five magenta-coloured petals and white stamens; it blossoms from early November to March. The tree does not produce seeds and can only be propagated by air-layering, cutting or grafting. Thus all *Bauhinia blakeana* today are direct descendants of that single tree discovered by the missionaries.

---

oriented shops. The New Territories, which officially encompass the 234 outlying islands, occupy more than 88% of Hong Kong's land area.

Hong Kong International Airport, located about 20km northwest of Central, is easily reached by the Airport Express rail line (p526). The main train station is at Hung Hom and is the terminus of the KCR East rail line (p528). There are several important bus stations; Central's is below the Exchange Sq complex on Connaught Rd Central.

Maps

Most travellers won't need much more than the *Hong Kong Map*, distributed by the Hong Kong Tourist Board (HKTB). It covers the northern coast of Hong Kong Island from Sheung Wan to Causeway Bay as well as part of the Kowloon Peninsula and has inset maps of Aberdeen, Stanley, Hung Hom, Sha Tin and Tsuen Wan.

INFORMATION

The **Hong Kong Museums Pass** (7 days $30; 6 months adult $50, student & senior $25; 1 year adult $100, student & senior $50) allows multiple entries to a half-dozen of Hong Kong's museums and is available from HKTB outlets (p498).

Bookshops

Hong Kong has more bookshops than ever before, although English-language books are relatively few. The widest selection of shops is on Hong Kong Island.

Bookazine (Map pp500-2; ☎ 2521 1649; ground fl, Pacific House, 20 Queen's Rd Central; ☯ 9.30am-7.30pm Mon-Sat, 10am-6.30pm)

Cosmos Books (Map pp504-5; ☎ 2866 1677; basement & 1st fl, 30 Johnston Rd, Wan Chai; ☯ 10am-8pm)

Dymocks Booksellers (Map pp500-2; ☎ 2117 0360; shop 2007-2011, 2nd fl, IFC Mall, 1 Harbour View St, Central; ☯ 8.30am-9.30pm Mon-Sat, 9am-9pm Sun)

Hong Kong Book Centre (Map pp500-2; ☎ 2522 7064; basement, On Lok Yuen Bldg, 25 Des Voeux Rd Central; ☯ 9am-6.30pm Mon-Fri & 9am-5.30pm Sat year-round, 1-5pm Sun summer)

Kelly & Walsh (Map pp500-2; ☎ 2522 5743; shop 236, 2nd fl, Pacific Place, 88 Queensway, Admiralty; ☯ 10.30am-8pm Sun-Thu, 10.30am-8.30pm Fri & Sat)

Emergency

In the event of an emergency, you should ring ☎ 999 for the fire services, police or an ambulance.

Internet Access

Most hotels and many guesthouses have Internet access. You'll also be able to log on for free at major Mass Transit Railway (MTR) stations (eg Central and Tsim Sha Tsui) and many public libraries, including the following Causeway Bay branch of the Central Library.

Central Library (Map pp504-5; ☎ 2921 0503; www.hkpl.gov.hk; 66 Causeway Rd, Causeway Bay; ☯ 10am-9pm Thu-Tue, 1-9pm Wed)

Cyber Clan (Map pp506-7; ☎ 2523 2821; south basement, Golden Crown Court, 66-70 Nathan Rd, Tsim Sha Tsui; membership $5, per hr $10 midnight-noon Mon-Fri, $13 noon-midnight Mon-Fri, all day Sat & Sun; ☯ 24hr)

IT.Fans (Map pp500-2; ☎ 2542 1868; ground fl, Man On Commercial Bldg, 12-13 Jubilee St, Central; membership $10, per hr members/nonmembers $16/20 Mon-Thu, $18/22 Fri-Sun; ☯ 8am-5am)

Pacific Coffee Company (Map pp500-2; ☎ 2868 5100; www.pacificcoffee.com; shop 1022, 1st fl, IFC Mall, 1 Harbour View St, Central; ☯ 7am-11pm) All it takes to log on to one of up to a half-dozen terminals at the Pacific Coffee Company is the purchase of a coffee or a piece of cake ($10 to $35).

Media

Hong Kong has two local English-language daily newspapers, the *South China Morning Post* and the *Hong Kong Standard*, published Monday to Friday and at the weekend. Asian editions of *USA Today*, the *International Herald Tribune*, the *Financial*

HONG KONG IN ...

One day

Catch a tram up to **Victoria Peak** for a good view of the city and stretch your legs on a summit circuit. Back down at sea level, you could have lunch at the **Tan Ta Wan Thai Restaurant**, do some shopping at the **Pacific Place** shopping mall in Admiralty and watch the sun go down from the 7th floor of the **Hong Kong Convention & Exhibition Centre**.

Two days

In addition to the above, you could take the **Star Ferry** to Tsim Sha Tsui and visit the **Art**, **Space** or **History Museums**, have dim sum at **Wan Loong Court** in the Kowloon Hotel, then browse along **Nathan Rd** until you're hungry enough for afternoon tea at the **Peninsula Hong Kong** hotel. After dark, wander up Temple St to the **night market**.

One week

With this amount of time you can see many of the sights, such as **Victoria Peak**, **Man Mo Temple**, **Kowloon Park** and **Temple St night market**, visit an outlying island (eg **Lantau** for the big Buddha, the fabulous walks and the beaches), jump aboard a bus or the Kowloon-Canton Railway (KCR) for the **New Territories**, and take a day trip to Macau.

Times and the *Asian Wall Street Journal* are printed in Hong Kong.

Hong Kong has two English-language terrestrial TV stations: TVB Pearl and ATV World. There's also a variety of English-language government and commercial radio stations.

Medical Services

Medical care is generally of a high standard in Hong Kong, though public hospital facilities are stretched and private hospital care quite expensive.

The general inquiry number for hospitals is ☎ 2300 6555. The Hong Kong Medical Association (HKMA) maintains a **MediLink hotline** (☎ 90000 223 322) with recorded information.

Hospitals with 24-hour emergency services include:

Queen Elizabeth (Map pp506-7; ☎ 2958 8888; 30 Gascoigne Rd, Yau Ma Tei)

Matilda International (Map pp496-7; ☎ 2849 0700, 24hr hotline ☎ 2849 0111; 41 Mt Kellett Rd, Peak)

Money
ATMS

ATMs are scattered throughout Hong Kong, including at the airport. They are almost all linked to international money systems such as Cirrus, Maestro, Plus and Visa Electron.

CHANGING MONEY

The Hong Kong dollar is pegged to the US dollar at a rate of US$1 to $7.80, though it is allowed to fluctuate a little.

Banks give the best exchange rates, but three of the biggest – HSBC, Standard Chartered and the Hang Seng Bank – levy a HK$50 commission for each transaction.

Licensed moneychangers are abundant in tourist districts. One that we've been using since the ink was still wet in the Treaty of Nanking is **Wing Hoi Money Exchange** (Map pp506-7; ☎ 2723 5948, ground fl, shop No 9B, Mirador Arcade, 58 Nathan Rd, Tsim Sha Tsui; ✆ 8.30am-8.30pm Mon-Sat, 8.30am-7pm Sun). They'll change just about any currency as well as travellers cheques. Avoid the exchange counters at the airport; they offer some of the worst rates in Hong Kong.

International credit cards are readily accepted everywhere. Some shops may try to add a surcharge to offset the commission

charged by credit companies, which can range from 2.5% to 7%. In theory, this is prohibited by the credit companies, but to get around this many shops will offer a 5% discount if you pay cash.

COSTS

Hong Kong has become an extremely pricey destination, but if you stay in dormitories and eat budget meals, you can survive – just – on around $250 per day.

In general, tipping is not done in Hong Kong; taxi drivers only expect you to round up to the nearest dollar. However, most up-market restaurants and hotels add a 10% service charge to their bills.

Bargaining, on the other hand is *de rigueur* in Hong Kong, except in department stores and clothing chain stores.

CURRENCY

The unit of currency is the Hong Kong dollar ($), which is divided into 100 cents. Bills are issued in denominations of $10, $20, $50, $100, $500 and $1000. Copper coins are worth 50c, 20c and 10c, while silver ones are issued in denominations of $10, $5, $2 and $1. Prices in this chapter are in HK$.

Post

General post office (Map pp500-2; 2 Connaught Pl, Central; ✆ 8am-6pm Mon-Sat, 9am-2pm Sun) Pick up poste restante from counter No 29 Monday to Saturday only.

Kowloon post office (Map pp506-7; ground fl, Hermes House, 10 Middle Rd, Tsim Sha Tsui; ✆ 8am-6pm Mon-Sat, 9am-2pm Sun)

Telephone

Local calls in Hong Kong are free on private phones and cost $1 for five minutes on pay phones. All landline numbers in the territory have eight digits (except ☎ 800 toll-free numbers) and there are no area codes.

Hong Kong's country code is ☎ 852. To call abroad from Hong Kong, dial ☎ 001, then the country code, area code and number. Phone rates are cheaper from 9pm to 8am on weekdays and throughout the weekend. You can make international direct-dial calls to almost anywhere in the world from public phones with a phonecard. These are available in two forms. Stored-value cards ($100) allow you to call from any phone – public or private – by punching in a PIN code. Hello Smartcards

HONG KONG & MACAU

HONG KONG

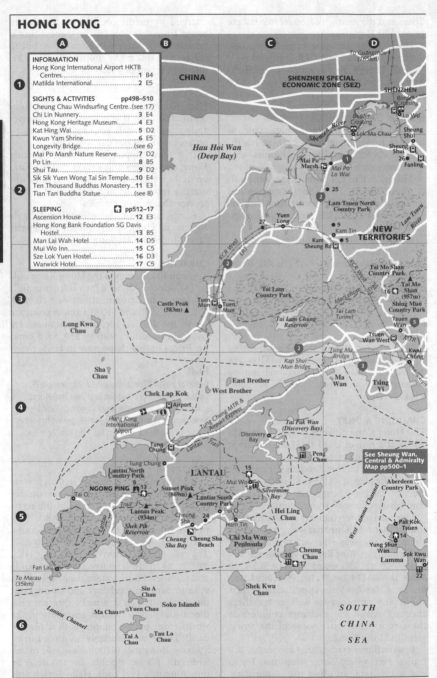

INFORMATION
Hong Kong International Airport HKTB
 Centres...1 B4
Matilda International...............................2 E5

SIGHTS & ACTIVITIES   pp498–510
Cheung Chau Windsurfing Centre..(see 17)
Chi Lin Nunnery......................................3 E4
Hong Kong Heritage Museum............4 E3
Kat Hing Wai...5 D2
Kwun Yam Shrine...................................6 E5
Longevity Bridge.............................(see 6)
Mai Po Marsh Nature Reserve...........7 D2
Po Lin...8 B5
Shui Tau..9 D2
Sik Sik Yuen Wong Tai Sin Temple...10 E4
Ten Thousand Buddhas Monastery...11 E3
Tian Tan Buddha Statue..................(see 8)

SLEEPING   pp512–17
Ascension House....................................12 E3
Hong Kong Bank Foundation SG Davis
 Hostel...13 B5
Man Lai Wah Hotel..............................14 D5
Mui Wo Inn...15 C5
Sze Lok Yuen Hostel............................16 D3
Warwick Hotel.......................................17 C5

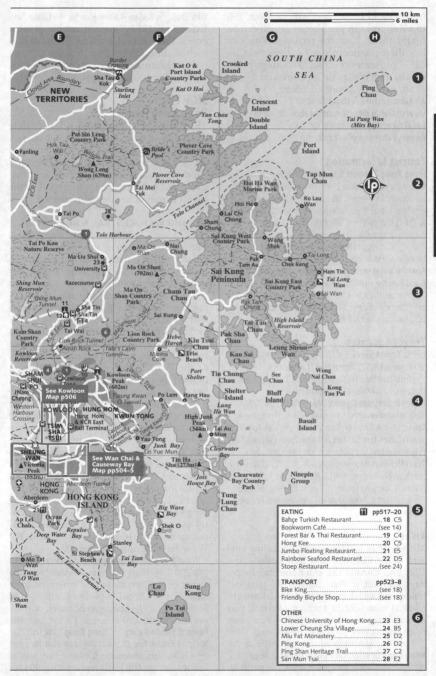

SOUTH CHINA
SEA

NEW TERRITORIES

Border Crossing

Closed Area Boundary

Sha Tau Kok

Starling Inlet

Kat O & Port Island Country Parks

Kat O Hoi

Crooked Island

Crescent Island

Ping Chau

Yan Chau Tong

Double Island

Tai Pang Wan (Mirs Bay)

Fanling

Hok Tau Wai

Pat Sin Leng Country Park

Wilson Trail

Bride's Pool

Plover Cove Country Park

Port Island

KCR East

Wong Leng Shan (639m)

Plover Cove Reservoir

Tai Mei Tuk

Hoi Ha Wan Marine Park

Tap Mun Chau

Hoi Ha

Ko Lau Wan

Tai Po

28

Tolo Channel

Lai Chi Chong

Sham Chung

Tai Po Kau Nature Reserve

Tolo Harbour

Ma Liu Shui

23

University

Ma On Chung

Nai Chung

Sai Kung West Country Park

Wong Shek

Pak Tam Au

Tai Long

Chek Keng

Ham Tin

Racecourse

Shing Mun Reservoir

Shing Mun Tunnel

Ma On Shan (702m)

Ma On Shan Country Park

Sai Kung Peninsula

High Island Reservoir

Ham Tin

Tai Long Wan

Sai Wan

Sha Tin

11
12

Sha Tin

4

Tai Wai

Cham Tau Chau

Sai Kung

Sai Kung East Country Park

Kam Shan Country Park

Kowloon Reservoir

Lion Rock Tunnel

Lion Rock Country Park

Madehose Trail

Hebe Haven

Pak Sha Chau

Pak Tam Chung

Tai Tan Chau

Amah Rock

Tate's Cairn Tunnel

Marina Cove

Trio Beach

Kiu Tsui Chau

Leung Shuen Wan

SHAM SHUI PO

4

5

10

Kowloon Tong

Kowloon Peak (602m)

Wilson Trail

Kau Sai Chau

See Chau

Wong Nai Chau

Nam Cheong

Western Harbour Crossing

KOWLOON

HUNG HOM

Tseung Kwan O Tunnel

Po Lam

Hang Hau

Port Shelter

Tiu Chung Chau

Shelter Island

Kong Tau Pai

Hung Hom & KCR East Rail Terminal

KWUN TONG

Tseung Kwan O

High Junk Peak (344m)

Lung Ha Wan

Bluff Island

Basalt Island

TSIM SHA TSUI

Eastern Harbour Crossing

Yau Tong

Lei Yue Mun

Junk Bay

Tai Au Mun

Clearwater Bay

SHEUNG WAN

See Wan Chai & Causeway Bay Map pp504–5

Victoria Peak (552m)

Tin Ha Sha (273m)

Joss House Bay

Clearwater Bay Country Park

Ninepin Group

HONG KONG

Aberdeen Tunnel

HONG KONG ISLAND

Aberdeen

21

Ocean Park

Big Wave Bay

Tung Lung Chau

Ap Lei Chau

6

Repulse Bay

Deep Water Bay

Shek O

East Lamma Channel

Mo Tat Wan

Stanley

St Stephen's Beach

Tai Tam Bay

Tung O Wan

Lo Chau

Sung Kong

Sham Wan

Po Toi Island

0 ———— 10 km
0 ———— 6 miles

EATING 🍴 pp517–20
Bahçe Turkish Restaurant...............**18** C5
Bookworm Café............................(see 14)
Forest Bar & Thai Restaurant.........**19** C4
Hong Kee...................................**20** C5
Jumbo Floating Restaurant............**21** E5
Rainbow Seafood Restaurant..........**22** D5
Stoep Restaurant.........................(see 24)

TRANSPORT pp523–8
Bike King...................................(see 18)
Friendly Bicycle Shop....................(see 18)

OTHER
Chinese University of Hong Kong....**23** E3
Lower Cheung Sha Village..............**24** B5
Miu Fat Monastery.......................**25** D2
Ping Kong..................................**26** D2
Ping Shan Heritage Trail................**27** C2
San Mun Tsai.............................**28** E2

(available in five denominations from $50 to $500) work in pay phones, which can be found throughout the territory. You can buy these phonecards at 7-Eleven and Circle K convenience stores, Mannings pharmacies and Wellcome supermarkets.

Some handy phone numbers:

Air temperature & time ☎ 18501
International directory assistance ☎ 10013
Local directory assistance ☎ 1081
Reverse charge/collect calls ☎ 10010

Tourist Information

Hong Kong Tourism Board (HKTB; www.discoverhong kong.com; visitor hotline 2508 1234 8am-6pm) Hong Kong International Airport (Map pp496-7; Chek Lap Kok; 🕙 7am-11pm); Hong Kong Island (Map pp500-2; ground fl, The Center, 99 Queen's Rd Central; 🕙 8am-6pm); Kowloon (Map pp506-7; Star Ferry Concourse, Tsim Sha Tsui; 🕙 8am-6pm) The enterprising HKTB maintains Visitor Information & Service Centres on Hong Kong Island, in Kowloon and at Hong Kong International Airport (in Halls A and B on the arrivals level and E2 transfer area) as well as an immensely useful Visitor Hotline. Staff at the centres are extremely efficient, helpful and have reams of information, most of which is free.

Travel Agencies

China Travel Service (CTS; Map pp500-2; ☎ 2853 5333; ground fl, CTS House, 78-83 Connaught Rd Central; 🕙 9am-7pm Mon-Fri, 9am-5pm Sat, 9.30am-5pm Sun) China visas available at CTS head office.

Phoenix Services Agency (Map pp506-7; ☎ 2722 7378; info@phoenixtrvl.com; room 1404-5, 14th fl, Austin Tower, 22-26A Austin Av, Tsim Sha Tsui; 🕙 9am-6pm Mon-Fri, 9am-1pm Sat) One of the best places in Hong Kong to buy air tickets, get China visas and seek travel advice.

Traveller Services (Map pp506-7; ☎ 2375 2222; www .taketraveller.com; room 1012, 10th fl, Tower 1, Silvercord Towers & Shopping Centre, 30 Canton Rd, Tsim Sha Tsui; 🕙 9am-1pm & 2-6pm Mon-Fri, 9am-1pm Sat) Reliable for tickets.

Visas

Most visitors to Hong Kong, including citizens of the EU, Australia, New Zealand, the USA and Canada can enter and stay for 90 days without a visa. British EU passport holders get 180 days while South Africans are allowed to stay 30 days without a visa. If you do require a visa, apply at a Chinese embassy or consulate (see p891) before arriving.

For tourist visa extensions, inquire at the **Hong Kong Immigration Department** (Map pp504-5; ☎ 2852 3047; 5th fl, Immigration Tower, 7 Gloucester Rd,

Wan Chai; 🕙 8.45am-4.30pm Mon-Fri, 9-11.30am Sat). Extensions ($135) are not readily granted unless there are extenuating circumstances such as illness.

For information on obtaining a China visa in Hong Kong, see p904.

SIGHTS
Hong Kong Island

The northern and southern sides of Hong Kong Island have totally different characters. The northern side is a mostly urban jungle. Much of the south, on the other hand, remains surprisingly green and relatively undeveloped. The central part of the island is mountainous and protected.

SHEUNG WAN, CENTRAL & ADMIRALTY
Map pp500–2

The northern part of the island is dominated by the Central business district, with more traditional Sheung Wan to the west and Admiralty to the east.

One of Hong Kong's highlights is riding the **Peak Tram** (☎ 2522 0922; one way/return adult $20/30, 3-11 yrs $6/9, senior over 65 $7/14; 🕙 7am-midnight), a funicular running every 10 to 15 minutes from the lower terminus behind St John's Building at 33 Garden Rd, Central, to the Peak Tower on top of **Victoria Peak** (552m). Night-time views are spectacular, but check the weather before you ascend.

From the upper tram terminus, wander 500m west up Mt Austin Rd, then follow the path to **Victoria Peak Garden** or take the more leisurely stroll around Lugard and Harlech Rds that makes a 3.5km circular **walking trail** around the summit. You can walk right down to Central by following Old Peak Rd north for a few kilometres. The more energetic, however, will brave the 50km-long **Hong Kong Trail**, which traverses four country parks along the top of the mountainous spine of the island from the Peak to Big Wave Bay just north of Shek O.

The **Hong Kong Zoological & Botanical Gardens** (☎ 2530 0154; Albany Rd, Central; admission free; terrace gardens 🕙 6am-10pm, zoo & aviaries 🕙 6am-7pm, greenhouses 🕙 9am-4.30pm) is a pleasant collection of fountains, sculptures, greenhouses, a playground, a zoo and aviaries. To the east, the **Edward Youde Aviary** in **Hong Kong Park** (☎ 2521 5041; 19 Cotton Tree Dr, Admiralty; admission free; park 🕙 6.30am-11pm, conservatory & aviary 🕙 9am-5pm) is home to some 600 birds representing 90 spe-

DEITIES OF SOUTH CHINA

Chinese religion (see p55) is polytheistic, meaning it worships many deities. In Hong Kong and most of the rest of southern China, virtually every household has its house, kitchen and/or door god; trades and businesses have their own deities too. Pawnshop owners pray to Kwan Yu (or Kwan Tai), for example, while students worship Man Cheung. Some of the most important divinities to which temples and shrines are frequently dedicated in Hong Kong, Macau and Guǎngdōng include:

Kwan Yu A real-life Han dynasty soldier born in the 2nd century AD, Kwan Yu (Guānyǔ in Mandarin) is the red-cheeked god of war worshipped not just for his prowess in battle but for his righteousness, integrity and loyalty. In addition to soldiers, he is the patron of restaurateurs, the police force and members of secret societies, including the Triads. There's a temple dedicated to Kwan Yu in Tai O on Lantau Island, and he shares the Man Mo Temple (below) on Hollywood Rd in Sheung Wan with Man Cheung (see below).

Kwun Yam Kwun Yam (Guānyīn) is the Buddhist equivalent of Tin Hau (see below). As the goddess of mercy, she radiates tenderness and compassion for the unhappy lot of mortals. You'll find Kwun Yam shrines or temples at Sheung Wan (p511) on Hong Kong Island and in Macau (where her name is spelled Kun Iam).

Man Cheung This civil deity (Wénchāng) was a Chinese statesman and scholar of the 3rd century BC. Today he is worshipped as the god of literature and shares the Man Mo Temple on Hollywood Rd in Sheung Wan with Kwan Yu.

Tin Hau The queen of heaven, whose duties include protecting seafarers, Tin Hau (Tiānhòu) is one of the most popular gods in coastal South China, where she also goes under the name A-Ma. There are almost 60 temples dedicated to her in Hong Kong alone, including ones in Yau Ma Tei (p508) in Kowloon and in Causeway Bay (p503) on Hong Kong Island.

Tou Tei Tou Tei (Tǔdì) is the earth god who rules over anything and everything from a one-room flat or shop to a section of a village or town. Shrines to Tou Tei, which are everywhere, are usually small and inconspicuous but always a delight.

cies. The park also contains the rich **Flagstaff House Museum of Tea Ware** (☎ 2869 0690; 10 Cotton Tree Dr, Admiralty; admission free, ☒ 10am-5pm Wed-Mon) in a colonial structure built in 1846.

Just north of Hong Kong Park is **St John's Cathedral** (☎ 2523 4157; 4-8 Garden Rd; ☒ 7.15am-6.30pm Mon-Tue, Fri & Sat, 9.30am-5.15pm Wed, 8.30am-1.15pm Thu, 8am-6.30pm Sun), built in 1847 and one of the very few colonial structures extant in Central; enter from Battery Path.

Northwest of the cathedral, linking Des Voeux Rd Central with Queen's Rd Central, **Li Yuen St East** and **Li Yuen St West**, known as 'the lanes' here, are narrow alleys closed to motorised traffic and crammed with shops selling cheap clothing, handbags and jewellery. For exotic produce – from frogs' legs and cows' heads to durian and mangosteens, head uphill to the **Graham St market**. Running parallel to it is the 800m-long **Central Escalator** (☒ down 6-10am, up 10.20am-midnight), the longest in the world, which transports pedestrians from Des Voeux Rd Central up to Conduit Rd in the Mid-Levels in 20 minutes.

To the west of Central is **Man Mo Temple** (☎ 2540 0350; 124-126 Hollywood Rd, Sheung Wan; admission free; ☒ 8am-6pm), built in 1847 and one of the oldest in Hong Kong. For more

about the deities in this temple see above. Further north is the restored **Western Market** (☎ 2815 3586; 323 Des Voeux Rd Central; ☒ 10am-7pm), built in 1906 and filled with shops selling textiles, knick-knacks and souvenirs.

This area has some good art galleries. **Para/Site Art Space** (☎ 2517 4620; www.para-site .org.hk; 4 Po Yan St, Sheung Wan; ☒ noon-7pm Wed-Sun) is an adventurous, artist-run art space that knows no boundaries when it comes to mixing media. **Plum Blossoms** (☎ 2521 2189; www .plumblossoms.com; ground fl, Chinachem Hollywood Centre, 1-19 Hollywood Rd, Central; ☒ 10am-6.30pm Mon-Sat), though very much a commercial concern, is one of the most exquisite and well-established art galleries in Hong Kong.

WAN CHAI & CAUSEWAY BAY Map pp504–5

Just east of Admiralty is Wan Chai, known for its raucous nightlife but by day just an ordinary district of shops and offices. One place worth visiting is the **Hong Kong Arts Centre** (☎ 2582 0200; 2 Harbour Rd, Wan Chai), which contains the **Pao Galleries** (☎ 2824 5330; admission free; ☒ 10am-8pm) on the 4th and 5th floors, with exhibitions of contemporary art.

The **Hong Kong Convention & Exhibition Centre** (☎ 2582 8888; 1 Expo Dr, Wan Chai) is an huge

A   B   C   D

To Macau
63

Victoria
Harbour

1

Western Harbour Crossing

West Fire service St

Connaught Rd West

To Western (1km);
Kennedy Town (3.5km);
Aberdeen (10km)

Des Voeux Rd West

Kong Chung St

64
9

New Market St
22

SHEUNG WAN

Government
Pier

SAI YANG PUN

Tramway

Queen St

Sutherland St

Ko Shing St

Wing Lok St

Bonham Strand West

Sheung
Wan M

58

Connaught Rd Central

Des Voeux Rd Central

3
MTR

Hospital Rd

New St

Hollywood
Road
Park

Possession St

Queen's Rd West

Bonham Strand

Wing Lok St

Hillier St

Morrison St

Cleverly St

Bonham Rd

High St

Centre St

Eastern St

King George V
Memorial Park

Po Yan St

Hollywood Park

Pound Lane

Upper Station St

Shin Hing St

Ladder St

Upper Lascar Row (Cat St)

Lok Ku Rd

Hollywood Rd

73

Queen's Rd Central

Jervois St

Myrtle St

Gough St

U Fong

62

Wing Wo St

Wing Kut St

Gilman's Bazaar

Tramway

Man Yee La

Queen's Rd Central

7
The Center

8 @

Jubilee St

Pottinger

2

Park Rd

Bonham Rd

Lyttelton Rd

Kotewall Rd

Breezy Path

Po Hing Fong

Tai Ping Shan St

Blake
Garden

Ku Lam

Tank Lane

Cane La

18

Bridges St

Wing Lee

Shing Wong St

Staunton St

Hollywood Rd

Gage St

Cochrane St

Food
Market

37

SOHO

31
49

17

51

Wyndham St

Stanley St

53

3

Conduit Rd

Castle Rd

Seymour Rd

Robinson Rd

MID-LEVELS

Po Shan Rd

Aberdeen St

Peel St

Graham St

Elgin St

Shelley St

Central Escalator

46
30

20

88

Lyndhurst Tce

42

43

47
38
41
32
39
35
50

33

Shelley St

Peel St

Mosque St

Prince's Tce

Caine Rd

Leung Fai Tce

Old Bailey St

Chancery Lane

Wyndham St

D'Aguilar St

45

44

LAN
KWAI
FONG

34

Clenelly

48
34

4

Hong Kong Trail

Mosque Jct

Conduit Rd

24

Clenelly

▲ Victoria Peak
(552m)

Lugard Rd

Pok Fu Lam
Country Park

Homsey Rd

Old Peak Rd

Robinson Rd

25

5

Mt Austin Rd

Mt Austin Rd

Victoria
Peak Garden

The Governor's Walk

Old Peak Rd

Treginter Path

May Rd

Brewin

Treginter Path

Albany Rd

6

Harlech Rd

Mt Austin Rd

Old Peak Rd

Finlay Rd

19

Pok Fu Lam
Country Park

Peak Tramway

Baker Rd

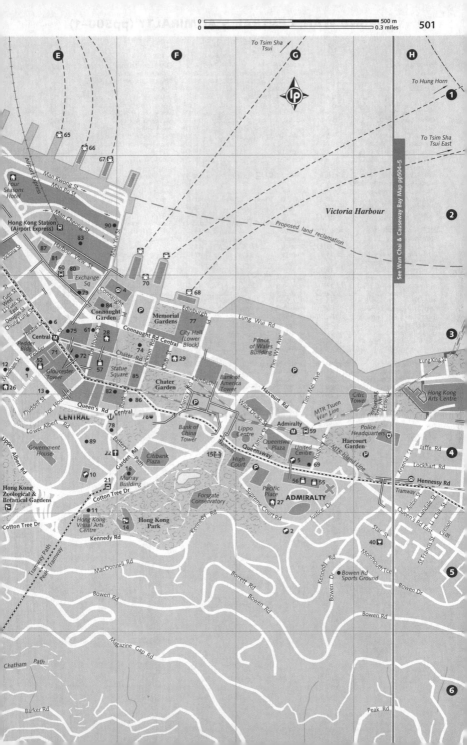

0 — 500 m
0 — 0.3 miles

To Tsim Sha
Tsui

To Hung Horn

To Tsim Sha
Tsui East

Victoria Harbour

Proposed land reclamation

Four
Seasons
Hotel

Man Kwong St
Man Po St

Airport Express

Hong Kong Station
(Airport Express)

Man Cheung St

Harbour View St

Exchange
Sq

Connaught
Garden

Connaught
Garden

Memorial
Gardens

Edinburgh

City Hall
(Lower
Block)

Connaught Rd Central

Lung Wui Rd

Prince
of Wales
Building

Tim Wa Ave

Central

Pedder
Bldg

Gloucester
Tower

Chater Rd

Statue
Square

Chater
Garden

Lambeth

Bank of
America
Tower

Harcourt Rd

Citic
Tower

Lung King St

Hong Kong
Arts Centre

Queen's Rd Central

CENTRAL

Lower Albert Rd

Bank of
China
Tower

Lippo
Centre

Queensway
Plaza

Admiralty

United
Centre

Police
Headquarters

Harcourt
Garden

Jaffe Rd

Lockhart Rd

MTR Tsuen Wan Line

MTR Island Line

Upper Albert Rd

Government
House

Garden
Path

Citibank
Plaza

Murray
Building

High
Court

Queensway

Pacific
Place

ADMIRALTY

Hennessy Rd

Tramway

Queen's Rd East

Hong Kong
Zoological &
Botanical Gardens

Cotton Tree Dr

Cotton Tree Dr

Hong Kong
Visual Arts
Centre

Hong Kong
Park

Kennedy Rd

Forsgate
Conservatory

Supreme Court Rd

Justice Dr

Star St

St Francis St

MacDonnell Rd

Borrett Rd

Kennedy Rd

Bowen Rd
Sports Ground

Monmouth Tce

Bowen Dr

Bowen Rd

Bowen Rd

Bowen Rd

Bowen Dr

Magazine Gap Rd

Chatham Path

Barker Rd

Peak Rd

Peak Tramway

Tramway Path

See Wan Chai & Causeway Bay Map pp504–5

building on the harbour boasting the world's largest 'glass curtain' – a window seven storeys high. Ride the escalator to the 7th floor for a superb harbour view. The centre's waterfront wing, with its distinctive 'fly-away' roof, is where the handover to China took place at midnight on 30 June 1997. The **Golden Bauhinia**, a 6m-tall statue of Hong Kong's symbol (see p493) commemorating the event, stands on the promenade facing the harbour just in front of the centre.

East of Wan Chai is Causeway Bay, one of Hong Kong Island's top shopping areas. It is dominated by 17-hectare **Victoria Park**, best visited on weekday mornings when it becomes a slow-motion forest of taichi practitioners. East of the park is Hong Kong's most famous **Tin Hau Temple** (☎ 2721 2326; 101 Tin Hau Temple Rd, Causeway Bay; ☼ 7am-5pm) and a place of worship for at least three centuries. For more about the deities in this temple see p499.

ISLAND SOUTH   Map pp496–7

The south coast of Hong Kong Island is dotted with decent beaches and other recreational facilities. If you're anxious to reach the beach, hop on bus No 6 (or the express No 260) to **Stanley** from the Central bus terminus in Exchange Sq. You can rent windsurfing boards and kayaks at **St Stephen's Beach** about 400m south of Stanley Village. Busy **Stanley Market** (Stanley Village Rd; ☼ 10am-6pm), a covered market filled with cheap clothing and bric-a-brac, is best visited during the week.

The same buses also go to beautiful **Repulse Bay**; if heading here from Stanley hop on bus No 73, which takes you along the coast. At the southeastern end of the bay is the unusual **Kwun Yam shrine**, filled with likenesses of the goddess of mercy and other deities (see p499). Crossing **Longevity Bridge** just in front of the shrine is supposed to add three days to your life.

Northwest of Repulse Bay (and accessible on bus No 73) is **Deep Water Bay**, a quiet inlet with a sandy beach flanked by shade trees, and **Aberdeen**. The big attraction at the latter is the busy harbour. Sampans will take you on a half-hour tour of the harbour for $40 per person (less if there's a group of you). For a free 10-minute trip, hop on one of the shuttle boats heading out to the har-

bour's **floating restaurants** (see p517). From Aberdeen, bus No 70 will take you back to Central.

If you're feeling vigorous, the entrance to **Aberdeen Country Park** and **Pok Fu Lam Country Park** is about a 15-minute walk north (and uphill) along Aberdeen Reservoir Rd. From there you can walk up to Victoria Peak and catch the Peak Tram to Central.

To the southeast of Aberdeen, the impressive **Ocean Park** (☎ 2552 0291; www.oceanpark .com.hk; Ocean Park Rd; adult/child $185/93; ☼ 10am-6pm) is a huge amusement park and educational theme park, complete with requisite roller coasters and other rides, the **world's largest aquarium** and an impressive **atoll reef**. You can reach Ocean Park on bus Nos 6A and 6X from the Central bus terminus in Exchange Sq or on green minibus No 6 from Star Ferry. Otherwise, there are package tickets (adult/child $209/105) available that include transportation and admission to the park from Central and Admiralty (bus No 629).

Kowloon

Kowloon, the peninsula pointing southward towards Hong Kong Island whose name means 'nine dragons', is a riot of commerce and tourism set against a backdrop of crumbling tenement blocks. Its main drag, **Nathan Rd**, is packed with shops, hotels, bars, restaurants, nightclubs, touts and tourists.

TSIM SHA TSUI   Map pp506–7

Start your exploration from Tsim Sha Tsui, the touristed area at Kowloon's southern tip. Adjacent to the Star Ferry terminal is the **Hong Kong Cultural Centre** (☎ 2734 2009; 10 Salisbury Rd; ☼ 9am-11pm) with its controversial windowless façade facing one of the most spectacular views in the world. Behind the cultural centre to the southeast, the **Hong Kong Museum of Art** (☎ 2721 0116; adult/child or senior $10/5, admission free Wed; ☼ 10am-6pm Fri-Wed) has six floors filled with Chinese antiquities, historical paintings and contemporary art.

The **Hong Kong Space Museum** (☎ 2721 0226; exhibition halls adult $10, child or senior $5, admission free Wed; planetarium adult $24-32, child or senior $12-16; ☼ 1-9pm Mon, Wed-Fri, 10am-9pm Sat & Sun) has several exhibition halls and a Space Theatre (planetarium) showing between seven and nine Omnimax films daily. To the southeast

Victoria Harbour

Proposed land reclamation

To Tsim
Sha Tsui

To Hung
Hom

Expo Dr

Hong Kong
Convention &
Exhibition Centre

Expo Dr Central

Atrium

Lung King St

Convention Ave

Great Eagle
Centre

Harbour
Centre

Wan Chai
Sports
Ground

Flemming Rd

Harbour Rd

China
Resources
Building

Causeway
Centre

Sun Hung
Kai Centre

Hung Hing Rd

Marsh Rd

Tonnochy Rd

Hong Kong
Arts Centre

Shui on
Centre

Wan Chai
Tower

Central
Plaza

Exhibition
Centre

Harbour Rd

Harbour Dr

Jaffe Rd

Lockhart Rd

Revenue
Tower

Immigration
Tower

Gloucester Rd

Wan Chai
Police Station

Stewart Rd

Tonnochy Rd

MTR Island Line

Tramway

Jaffe Rd

Luard Rd

Jaffe Rd

O'Brien Rd

Lockhart Rd

Fleming Rd

Lockhart Rd

Marsh Rd

Hennessy Rd

Hennessy Rd

Wan Chai Rd

Tin Lok

Arsenal St

MTR Island Line

Fenwick St

WAN CHAI

Sharp St
West

Tai Yuen St

Johnston Rd

Morrison
Hill

Sung Tak

Wong Nai Chung Rd

Southern
Playground

Thomson Rd

Johnston Rd

Li Chit St

Thomson Rd

Tramway

Gresson St

Queen's Rd East

Ship St

Wan Chai Rd

Cross La

Wood Rd

Swatow St

Amoy St

Lee Tung St

Spring Garden La

Stone Nullah La

Tai Wo St

Wan Chai Rd

Burrows St

Heard St

Stewart Rd

Ruttonjee
Hospital

St Francis St

St Patrick St

Tai Wong St East

Queen's Rd East

Cross St

Morrison
Hill Rd

Wan Chai
Park

Salvation
Army St

Oi Kwan Rd

Bowen Rd

Kennedy Rd

Fung Wong Tce

Queen's Rd East

MORRISON
HILL

Ching Fung La

Wan Chai Gap Rd

Kennedy Rd

Queen's Rd East

Stubbs Rd

Hau Tak La

Muslim Cemetery

Catholic
Cemetery

St Margaret's
College

Hong Kong
Cemetery

To Aberdeen
Tunnel (400m),
Aberdeen (6km)

Aberdeen
Tunnel

Olympic City

To Mong Kok (500m); Hotel Concourse Hong Kong (650m); Yuen Po St Bird & Flower Markets (1.5km);

To CTS Mong Kok Branch (150m); Flying Ball Bicycle Co (650m)

Hoi Fu Court

Kwong Wah Hospital

Wah Yan College

HO MAN TIN

King's Park

Meteorological Station

PROSPEROUS GARDEN

YAU MA TEI

King's Park Sports Ground

King's Park Sports Ground

Wylie Path

Jordan Rd

Gascoigne Rd

Chatham Rd South

Jordan

Austin Rd

Hong Kong Polytechnic University

Hung Hom & KCR East Rail Terminal

Austin Rd

Hillwood Rd

Observatory Rd

Miramar Shopping Centre

Knutsford Tce

Chinese Garden

TSIM SHA TSUI

Kowloon Park

Kimberley St

Granville Rd

TSIM SHA TSUI EAST

Chinatchem Plaza

Energy Plaza

Peninsula Centre

Auto Plaza

Empire Centre

Hong Kong International Mail Centre

Centenary Gardens

Houston Centre

Mirror Tower

Wing On Plaza

HARBOUR CITY

Ocean Centre

Humphreys Ave

Hanoi Rd

Hart Ave

Prat Ave

Mody Rd

Minden Ave

Salisbury Rd

Tsim Sha Tsui East Promenade

Tsim Sha Tsui East Ferry Pier

Peking Rd

Middle Rd

Signal Hill Garden

Ocean Terminal

Harbour Sightseeing Cruises Pier

Star Ferry Pier

Star Ferry Terminal

Clock Tower

Salisbury Gardens

Ave of the Stars

Victoria Harbour

To Central

To Wan Chai

To Central (1km)

Victoria Harbour

Cross-Harbour Tunnel

Hung Hom Bypass

along Tsim Sha Tsui Promenade, the new **Ave of the Stars** pays homage to the Hong Kong film industry and its stars, with handprints, sculptures and a light show at 8pm.

The lower end of Nathan Rd is known as the **Golden Mile**, a reference to both the price of its real estate and its ability to make money out of tourism. Halfway up the thoroughfare is **Kowloon Park** (Nathan & Austin Rds; ☺ 6am-midnight), an oasis of greenery after the hustle and bustle of Tsim Sha Tsui. Here you'll find an **aviary** (☺ 6.30am-6.45pm Mar-Oct, 6.30am-5.45pm Nov-Feb), **Sculpture Walk**, with work by local and international sculptors, and a **swimming pool complex** (☎ 2724 3577; adult $19, child 3-13 yrs & senior $9; ☺ outdoor 6.30am-noon, 1-6pm & 7-10pm Apr-Oct, indoor 6.30am-noon, 1-6pm & 7-9.30pm Nov-Mar), complete with waterfalls.

The **Kowloon Mosque & Islamic Centre** (☎ 2724 0095; 105 Nathan Rd; ☺ 5am-10pm) was opened in 1984 on the site of an earlier mosque constructed in 1896. Non-Muslims should seek permission to enter. It's usually given but make sure you are dressed modestly and have removed your shoes or sandals.

The **Hong Kong Museum of History** (☎ 2724 9042; 100 Chatham Rd South; adult $10, child or senior over 60 $5, admission free Wed; ☺ 10am-6pm Mon & Wed-Sat, 10am-7pm Sun), in the reclaimed area known as Tsim Sha Tsui East, takes visitors on a fascinating wander through Hong Kong's past from prehistoric times to the 1997 handover.

The **Hong Kong Science Museum** (☎ 2732 3232; 2 Science Museum Rd; adult $25, child, student or senior over 60 $12.50, admission free Wed; ☺ 1-9pm Mon-Wed & Fri, 10am-9pm Sat & Sun), in the same complex as the science museum, is a multilevel complex housing more than 500 exhibits, some of which are looking a bit dated.

YAU MA TEI & MONG KOK   Map pp506-7

Just north of Tsim Sha Tsui, in the district known as Yau Ma Tei, the **Jade Market** (Kansu, Canton & Battery Sts, Yau Ma Tei; ☺ 9am-6pm), where some 450 stalls sell all varieties and grades of jade. Unless you really know your nephrite from your jadeite, it's wise not to buy expensive pieces here. From here's it's a short walk to the **Tin Hau Temple** (☎ 2332 9240; cnr Public Sq St & Nathan Rd; ☺ 8am-5pm) and to the **Temple St night market** (Temple St, Yau Ma Tei; ☺ 4pm-midnight), the liveliest place in town to bargain for cheap clothes, fake name-brand goods and knockoff DVDs.

To the east of the Prince Edward MTR station in Mong Kok is the delightful **Yuen Po St Bird Market** (Flower Market Rd, Mong Kok; ☺ 7am-8pm), a place where birds are 'aired', preened, bought and sold. En route you'll pass the fragrant **flower market**, which keeps the same hours but only gets busy after 10am.

NEW KOWLOON   Map pp496-7

The southernmost 31 sq km of the New Territories is officially called New Kowloon since Boundary St just above Mong Kok technically marks the division between Kowloon and the New Territories. But what's in a name?

Sik Sik Yuen Wong Tai Sin Temple (☎ 2854 4333; Lung Cheung Rd; admission by $2 donation; ☺ 7am-5.30pm) is a large and very active Taoist temple complex built in 1973 and dedicated to the god worshipped both by the sick and those trying to avoid illness. It's right next to the Wong Tai Sin MTR station just north of Kowloon. Just below and to the left of the temple is an arcade of fortune tellers, some of whom speak English.

East of Wong Tai Sin in the Diamond Hill district is the much more serene **Chi Lin Nunnery** (☎ 2354 1604; 5 Chin Lin Dr; admission free; nunnery ☺ 9am-4pm Thu-Tue, garden ☺ 6.30am-7pm), a large Buddhist complex with lotus ponds, immaculate bonsai and silent nuns delivering offerings of fruit and rice to Buddha and his disciples. To reach it, take the MTR to Diamond Hill.

New Territories

The New Territories are so called because they were leased to Britain in 1898, almost half a century after Hong Kong Island and four decades after Kowloon were ceded to the crown. Despite rapid urbanisation, temples, museums, fabulous mountain walks and sandy beaches abound in the New Territories and all are easily reached by bus, minibus, Kowloon-Canton Railway (KCR) and/or MTR.

TAI MO SHAN   Map pp496-7

The easiest way to reach **Tai Mo Shan**, Hong Kong's tallest mountain at 957m, in the central New Territories is on bus No 51 from Tsuen Wan, which is itself on the MTR's Tsuen Wan line. The climb to the summit isn't too gruelling and the way up is part of the 100km-long **MacLehose Trail** that runs from Tuen Mun in the west to the Sai Kung Peninsula in the east. If you want to hike anywhere along this trail, the 1:25,000 *MacLehose Trail* map, available from the Map Publications Centre (see p510) is essential.

KAM TIN & MAI PO MARSH
Yuen Long, which is on both the KCR West Rail and the Light Rail transit (LRT) rail lines (see p528), is the springboard for Hong Kong's most important grouping of walled villages as well as a nature reserve.

The area around Kam Tin is home to two 16th-century walled villages. Their fortifications serve as reminders of the marauding pirates, bandits and imperial soldiers that Hong Kong's early residents faced. Just off the main road and easily accessible, tiny **Kat Hing Wai** (Map pp496–7) is the more popular of the two. Drop $1 in the donation box at the village's entrance and wander the narrow little lanes. The old Hakka women in traditional clothing will let you take their photograph for the right price (about $10). **Shui Tau** (Map pp496–7), a 17th-century village about a 15-minute walk north of Kam Tin Rd, is famous for its prow-shaped roofs decorated along the ridges with dragons and fish. To reach Kam Tin, take bus No 64K, 77K or 54 from Yuen Long.

The 270-hectare **Mai Po Marsh Nature Reserve** (Map pp496–7; ☎ 2526 4473; San Tin, Yuen Long; admission $100 plus $100 deposit; ☒ 9am-6pm), a protected wetland near the mouth of the Shenzhen River at Deep Bay in the northwestern New Territories, is home to up to 300 species of migratory and resident birds. You can visit on your own (bus No 76K from Yuen Long) or join a guided visit organised by the **World Wide Fund for Nature Hong Kong** (WWFHK; Map pp500–2; ☎ 2526 4473; www.wwf .org.hk; 1 Tramway Path, Central; ☒ 9am-5pm Mon-Fri). Three-hour tours ($70) leave the marsh's visitor centre six times between 9am and 3pm on Saturday and Sunday.

SHA TIN   Map pp496–7
Sha Tin is popular not just for its racecourse but also for its **Ten Thousand Buddhas Monastery** (☎ 2691 1067; admission free; ☒ 9am-5pm), about 500m northwest of Sha Tin KCR station, which actually has some 12,800 miniature statues lining the walls of its main temple. To reach it, take exit B at Sha Tin

KCR station and walk down the ramp, turning left onto Pai Tau St. After a short distance turn right onto Sheung Wo Che St; at the end of this road, a series of signs in English will direct you to the left along a concrete path and through bamboo groves to the first of some 400 steps leading up to the monastery.

While in Sha Tin do not miss the opportunity of visiting the **Hong Kong Heritage Museum** (☎ 2180 8188; 1 Man Lam Rd, Tai Wai; adult $10, student or senior over 60 $5, admission free Wed; ☒ 10am-6pm Mon & Wed-Sat, 10am-7pm Sun), an exceptional museum in Tai Wai, south of Sha Tin KCR station, with both rich permanent collections (Chinese opera, fine art, ceramics) and extremely innovative temporary exhibits in a dozen different galleries.

SAI KUNG   Map pp496–7
The **Sai Kung Peninsula** is the garden spot of the New Territories and great for all sorts of outdoor activities, notably hiking and sailing. The best beaches in the New Territories are around this area, including **Clearwater Bay Peninsula** further south. To get here from Sha Tin, take bus No 299. To explore the eastern side of the Sai Kung Peninsula, take bus No 94 from Sai Kung to Wong Shek.

Outlying Islands   Map pp496–7
In addition to Hong Kong Island, there are 234 islands dotting the waters around Hong Kong but only four have substantial residential communities and are easily accessible by ferry.

LANTAU
Twice the size of Hong Kong Island, Lantau has only 45,000 residents, and you could easily spend a couple of days exploring its hilly walking trails and enjoying its uncrowded beaches.

From **Mui Wo**, the main settlement and arrival point for ferries, most visitors board bus No 2 to **Ngong Ping**, a plateau 500m above sea level in the western part of the island where you'll find **Po Lin** (admission free; ☒ 9am-6pm), an enormous monastery and temple complex that contains the **Tian Tan Buddha statue** (☒ 10am-6pm), the world's largest outdoor seated bronze Buddha statue, which can be climbed (260 steps).

En route to Ngong Ping you'll pass 3km-long **Cheung Sha Bay** (South Lantau Rd), boasting

Hong Kong's longest beach. Another place to visit is **Tai O**, a picturesque village at the western end of Lantau famous for its pungent shrimp paste, **rope-tow ferry** across a narrow channel of water and temple dedicated to Kwan Yu (also known as Kwan Tai).

The 12-stage **Lantau Trail** (70km) is a superb footpath stretching the length of the island and passing over both **Lantau Peak** (934m) and **Sunset Peak** (869m).

OTHER ISLANDS

Other islands include **Lamma**, the closest to Hong Kong Island, with decent beaches, excellent walks and a plethora of restaurants in **Yung Shue Wan** and **Sok Kwu Wan**, the two main settlements to the north and south respectively; dumbbell-shaped **Cheung Chau**, with a harbour filled with sampans and fishing boats, a windsurfing centre (see right) and several fine temples; and **Peng Chau**, the smallest and most traditionally Chinese of the easily accessible islands.

ACTIVITIES

Sporting buffs should contact the **South China Athletic Association** (Map pp504-5; ☎ 2577 6932; www.scaa.org.hk in Chinese; 5th fl, Sports Complex, 88 Caroline Hill Rd, Causeway Bay; visitor memberships $50), which has facilities for any number of sports. Another excellent place to contact is the **Hong Kong Amateur Athletic Association** (Map pp504-5; ☎ 2504 8215; www.hkaaa.com; rm 2015, Sports House, 1 Stadium Path, Causeway Bay).

Running

Good places to run on Hong Kong Island include Harlech and Lugard Rds on the Peak (p498) and the running track in Victoria Park (p503) in Causeway Bay. A popular place to run in Kowloon is the Tsim Sha Tsui East Promenade, just northeast of the Ave of the Stars (p508).

Fitness Clubs

A number of fitness clubs in Hong Kong allow short-term memberships, including **California Fitness** (Map pp500-2; ☎ 2522 5229; www.californiafitness.com; 1 Wellington St, Central; ☺ 6am-midnight Mon-Sat, 8am-10pm Sun; $150 daily), with six outlets in Hong Kong, and **Pure Fitness** (Map pp500-2; ☎ 2970 3366; www.pure-fit.com; 1st-3rd floors, Kinwick Centre, 32 Hollywood Rd, Central; per day $200; ☺ 6am-midnight Mon-Sat, 8am-10pm Sun), with an entrance on Shelley St.

Windsurfing

Some popular places for windsurfing – the only sport in which Hong Kong has won an Olympic gold medal (Atlanta, 1996) to date – are Stanley (p503), Shek O and Cheung Chau, where you'll find the **Cheung Chau Windsurfing Centre** (Map pp496-7; ☎ 2981 8316, 2981 2772; 1 Hak Pai Rd, Tung Wan Beach, ☺ 10am-7pm). Board rental is $60 to $120 per hour while single kayaks are $50 and double kayaks $80. Windsurfing courses start at $550. The best months for windsurfing in Hong Kong are October, November and December.

Taichi

The HKTB (p498) offers free taichi lessons from 8am to 9am on Monday and Wednesday to Friday along the Ave of the Stars, Tsim Sha Tsui Promenade (see p508).

Wildlife-Watching

Hong Kong usually doesn't spring to mind when you think of wildlife, but birders visiting the SAR should consider a trip to the **Mai Po Marsh** (see p509). Visitors can also cruise the waters around Lantau to observe endangered Chinese white dolphins with **Hong Kong Dolphinwatch** (Map pp506-7; ☎ 2984 1414; www.hkdolphinwatch.com; 1528A Star House, 3 Salisbury Rd, Tsim Sha Tsui; adult/child under 12 $280/140). Four-hour tours depart from the Mandarin Oriental (p513) in Central at 8.30am and the Kowloon Hotel Hong Kong (p515) in Tsim Sha Tsui at 9am on Wednesday, Friday and Sunday.

Hiking

Hong Kong is an excellent place to go hiking and there are numerous trails to enjoy on Hong Kong Island, the New Territories and the Outlying Islands. There are four main ones: the MacLehose Trail (p508), the longest at 100km; the 78km-long Wilson Trail, which runs on both sides of the harbour; the 70km-long Lantau Trail (left); and the Hong Kong Trail (p498), which is 50km long. Both the **Map Publications Centre** (Map pp506-7; ☎ 2780 0981; 382 Nathan Rd, Yau Ma Tei; ☺ 9am-5pm Mon-Fri, 9am-noon Sat) and the **Government Publications Office** (Map pp500-2; ☎ 2537 1910; rm 402, 4th fl, Murray Bldg, 22 Garden Rd, Central; ☺ 9am-6pm Mon-Fri, 9am-noon Sat) sell maps for hiking in the hills and country parks.

WALKING TOUR

A one-hour walk through Sheung Wan is a wonderful (and easy) step back into Hong Kong's past. Begin the tour at the Sutherland St stop of the Kennedy Town tram. Have a look at (and sniff of) Des Voeux Rd West's **dried seafood and shrimp paste shops (1)** then turn up Ko Shing St, where there are **herbal medicine wholesalers (2)**. At the end of the street, walk northeast along Des Voeux Rd West and turn right onto Connaught Rd West, where you'll find **Western Market (3**; p499) at the corner of Morrison St. Walk south along this street past Bonham Strand, which is lined with **ginseng root sellers (4)** and turn right on Queen's Rd West. To the right you'll pass **traditional shops (5)** selling bird's nests (for soup) and paper funeral offerings for the dead.

Cross Queen's Rd Central and turn left onto **Possession St (6)**, where the British flag was first planted in 1841 (see p492). Climbing Pound Lane to where it meets Tai Ping Shan St, look to the right to spot **Pak Sing Ancestral Hall (7**; ⏱ 8am-6pm), originally a storeroom for bodies awaiting burial in China

and, to the left, to find two small temples dedicated to **Kwun Yam** and **Sui Tsing Pak (8)**.

Descend Upper Station St to the start of Hollywood Rd's **antique shops (9)**. Walking east on Hollywood Rd brings you to **Man Mo Temple (10**; p499). Take a short hop down Ladder St to Upper Lascar Row, home of the **Cat St market (11**; ⏱ 9am-6pm), with Chinese bric-a-brac, curios and souvenirs. Ladder St brings you to Queen's Rd Central. Cross the road and follow Hillier St to Bonham Strand. From there head east to **Man Wa Lane (12)** where you'll find traditional carved chops (or seals), an excellent gift or memento. The Sheung Wan MTR station is a short distance to the northwest.

> **WALK FACTS**
>
> Distance: 2km
> Duration: 1 hour
> Start: Kennedy Town tram (Sutherland St stop)
> End: Sheung Wan MTR station

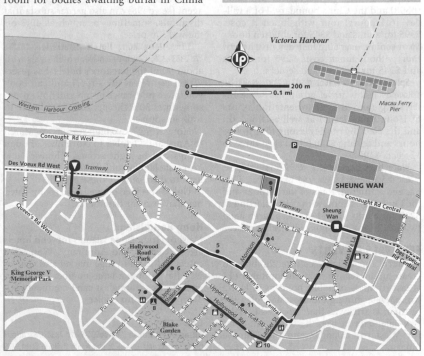

HONG KONG FOR CHILDREN

Hong Kong is a great travel destination for children, although the crowds, traffic and pollution might be off-putting to some parents.

Hong Kong Space Museum (p503) In Tsim Sha Tsui.
Hong Kong Zoological & Botanical Gardens (p498) In Central.
Ocean Park (p503) In Aberdeen.

Kids also love Hong Kong's more retro forms of transport, including the Star Ferry (p526) and the trams (p528).

Most hotels can recommend babysitters if you've got daytime appointments or want a night out without the kids. Otherwise call **Rent-A-Mum** (Map pp500-2; ☎ 2523 4868; rentamum@netvigator.com; 12A Amber Lodge, 21-25 Hollywood Rd, Central; per hr HKS$110-160).

TOURS

HKTB (p498) Some of the most popular surface tours of the New Territories are offered by the HKTB, including the ever-popular Land Between Tour, which takes in temple complexes, fishing villages, Tai Mo Shan (p508) and the China boundary. For a full-day (6½ hours) tour with lunch it costs $395 for adults and $345 for children under 16 or seniors over 60; a half-day (five hours) tour without lunch costs $295 for adults and $245 for children and seniors.

Splendid Tours & Travel (☎ 2316 2151; www.splendidtours.com) This travel group has some interesting (and useful) 'orientation' tours of Hong Kong Island as well as Kowloon and the New Territories lasting four to five hours and costing $280 (child aged three to 12 years $190).

Watertours (Map pp506-7; ☎ 2926 3868; shop 5C, ground fl, Star House, 3 Salisbury Rd, Tsim Sha Tsui) This has eight different tours of the harbour and the Outlying Islands, with prices starting at $220 for adults and $130 for children aged two to 12 for a two-hour morning cruise.

FESTIVALS & EVENTS

Western and Chinese culture combine to create an interesting mix – and number (17 at last count) – of public holidays in Hong Kong. Determining the exact date of some of them is tricky as there are traditionally two calendars in use: the Gregorian solar (or Western) calendar and the Chinese lunar one.

The HKTB's website (www.discoverhongkong.com) has the latest schedule of upcoming events, but key annual happenings include:

Hong Kong Arts Festival February and March
Hong Kong International Film Festival April
International Dragon Boat Races June or early July
Invitational Seven-a-Side Rugby Tournament late March or early April

SLEEPING

Accommodation in Hong Kong is more expensive than in other cities in China but cheaper than in Europe and the USA.

Budget accommodation in Hong Kong amounts to guesthouses, many of which offer dormitory accommodation for those on very tight budgets, and official hostels, most of which are located in very remote areas of the New Territories.

The rates at many of Hong Kong's mid-range and even some top-end hotels have dropped substantially in recent years and big discounts are available on their posted rates (those listed here) during the shoulder and low seasons. Booking through a travel agent (see p498) can also garner substantial discounts, sometimes as much as 40% off the walk-in price.

The **Hong Kong Hotels Association** (HKHA; ☎ 2383 8380; www.hkha.com.hk), which deals with about 90 of the territory's hotels, has reservation centres at the airport and can book you into a mid-range or top-end hotel room sometimes 50% cheaper than if you were to walk in yourself.

Hong Kong's two high seasons are March to April and October to November, though things can be tight around Chinese New Year (late January or February) as well. Rates tend to drop outside these periods.

Unless specified otherwise, all rooms listed here have private bathrooms.

Hong Kong Island

Most of Hong Kong Island's top-end hotels are in Central and Admiralty. Wan Chai caters to the mid-range market and Causeway Bay counts a large number of budget guesthouses (though it can't compete with Tsim Sha Tsui for choice).

BUDGET

Alisan Guest House (Map pp504-5; ☎ 2838 0762; http://home.hkstar.com/~alisangh; Flat A, 5th fl, Hoito Court, 275

THE AUTHOR'S CHOICE

Hong Kong Hostel (Map pp504-5; ☎ 2895 1015, ☎ 9353 0514; Flat A2, 3rd fl, Paterson Bldg, 47 Paterson St, Causeway Bay; s/d/tr with bathroom $220/260/350, without bathroom $180/240/290, dm $120; 🖳) This excellent 105-room series of hostels and guesthouses, incorporating the long-established **Wang Fat Hostel** (www.wangfathostel.com.hk) on the same floor and the Asia Hostel on the 6th floor, is just about the best deal on Hong Kong Island. It's quiet and clean and most of the rooms have private phones, TVs and fridges. There's also cooking and laundry facilities and a computer room with 10 terminals offering free Internet access.

Ice House (Map pp500-2; ☎ 2836 7333; www.icehouse.com.hk; 38 Ice House St, Central; s & d $700-900) In terms of location, this place offers one of the coolest deals in Central. Spread over 13 floors, the hotel has 64 standard and superior open-plan 'suites', each with a kitchenette, work desk and Internet access. Weekly/monthly rates start at $4500/12,000.

Mandarin Oriental (Map pp500-2; ☎ 2522 0111; www.mandarinoriental.com; 5 Connaught Rd Central; s & d $2950-4200, ste from $5500) The Mandarin, Hong Kong Island's counterpart to the Peninsula (p516), is not as architecturally impressive but has a healthy dose of old-world charm. Styling is subdued, and the décor in some of its 486 rooms may even be a bit outdated, but the service, food and atmosphere are stellar. Rooms are 40% cheaper May to September.

Rent-A-Room (Map pp506-7; ☎ 2366 3011, ☎ 9023 8022; www.rentaroomhk.com; Flat A, 2nd fl, Knight Garden, 7-8 Tak Hing St, Yau Ma Tei; s/d/tr $300/400/$510; 🖳) This fabulous place has 50 positively immaculate rooms in a block around the corner from the Jordan MTR station. Each room has shower, TV, telephone (no charge for local calls), Internet access and a fridge.

Stanford Hillview Hotel (Map pp506-7; ☎ 2722 7822, 2313 7031; www.stanfordhillview.com; 13-17 Observatory Rd, Tsim Sha Tsui; s & d $880-1580, ste from $2380) This 170-room hotel is a great place, set back from Nathan Rd in a quiet, leafy little corner of Tsim Sha Tsui but close to the food, fun and frolicking of Knutsford Tce, from where you enter the lobby.

Gloucester Rd, Causeway Bay; s/d/tr $280/320/390) This is an excellent and spotlessly clean, family-run guesthouse. You will find the entrance at 23 Cannon St.

Noble Hostel (Map pp504-5; ☎ 2576 6148; www.noblehostel.com.hk; Flat A3, 17th fl, Great George Bldg, 27 Paterson St, Causeway Bay; s/d $220/320) Each one of the 26 rooms is squeaky-clean and equipped with a private phone.

Causeway Bay Guest House (Map pp504-5; ☎ 2895 2013; www.cbgh.net; Flat B, 1st fl, Lai Yee Bldg, 44A-D Leighton Rd, Causeway Bay; s/d/tr $250/350/400) On the south side of Causeway Bay and wedged between a pub and a church, this comfortable, seven-room guesthouse, entered from Leighton Lane, can get booked up quickly so phone ahead.

MID-RANGE

Garden View International House (Map pp500-2; ☎ 2877 3737; www.ywca.org.hk; 1 MacDonnell Rd, Central; s & d $1250, ste $2300) Straddling the border of Central and the Mid-Levels, the YWCA-run Garden View (133 rooms) overlooks the Zoological & Botanical Gardens. Daily rates drop substantially in the low and shoulder seasons, typically in to $660 to $770

for a single or double and from $1210 for a suite. There are biweekly/monthly packages from $6930/9900.

Wesley Hotel (Map pp504-5; ☎ 2866 6688; www.hanglung.com; 22 Hennessy Rd, Wan Chai; s & d $700-1800) This central, 22-storey property with 251 rooms offers some of the best deals on the island, but there are very few facilities and the service is cavalier at best. Rates depend on the size of the room; there are monthly packages from $7800.

Bishop Lei International House (Map pp500-2; ☎ 2868 0828; www.bishopleihtl.com.hk; 4 Robinson Rd, Mid-Levels; s $1080-1280, d $158-1680, ste from $1880) This 203-room hotel is not luxurious but is central and has its own swimming pool. From mid-May to mid-September standard singles and doubles are available by the week/month from $3080/9000.

Wharney Hotel Hong Kong (Map pp504-5; ☎ 2861 1000; www.wharney.com; 57-73 Lockhart Rd, Wan Chai; s & d $1000-1600, ste from $2400) Noteworthy for its rooftop swimming pool and outdoor whirlpool, the 358-room Wharney is a mid-range option in the heart of Wan Chai with good long-stay packages (weekly/monthly from $3290/10,800).

Charterhouse Hotel (Map pp504-5; ☎ 2833 5566; www.charterhouse.com; 209-219 Wan Chai Rd, Wan Chai; s $950-1600, d $1500-1700, ste from $2000) This 277-room property on the leafy side of Wan Chai is a pretty good deal. You're almost getting top-end accommodation for mid-range rates.

Empire Hotel Hong Kong (Map pp504-5; ☎ 2866 9111; www.asiastandard.com; 33 Hennessy Rd, Wan Chai; s & d $1400-2000, ste from $2200) With its sunny staff, pleasant rooms, outdoor swimming pool and fitness centre on the 21st floor terrace, the 345-room Empire (enter from Fenwick St) is a good option. Weekly/bi-weekly/monthly rates are $3850/7000/13,500 during low season.

TOP END

Grand Hyatt Hong Kong (Map pp504-5; ☎ 2588 1234; www.hongkong.hyatt.com; 1 Harbour Rd, Wan Chai; s $3600-4000, d $3850-4250, ste from $4400) This 556-room hotel is among the most sumptuous in town but as up to date and technologically charged as any. Its gourmet Chinese restaurant, One Harbour Road (p518) is celebrated and with good reason.

Island Shangri-La Hong Kong (Map pp500-2; ☎ 2877 3838; www.shangri-la.com; Supreme Court Rd, Admiralty; s & d $2400-3700, ste from $5800) The 56-storey Shangri-La's sterile exterior conceals its swish sophistication; its 565 guestrooms are among the loveliest in Hong Kong. Bubble lifts link the 39th and 56th floors; take a quick ride up to glimpse the hotel's 60m-high Chinese landscape painting. Among its fabulous outlets is the French restaurant Petrus (p518).

Ritz-Carlton Hong Kong (Map pp500-2; ☎ 2877 6666; www.ritzcarlton.com; 3 Connaught Rd Central; s & d $3200-4200, ste from $6800) This 216-room hotel manages to be cosy and incredibly distinguished at the same time. Views from the outdoor pool are breathtaking.

Kowloon   Map pp506–7

Kowloon has an incredible array of accommodation choices for travellers: from the waterfront Peninsula, Hong Kong's poshest hotel, to its infamous neighbour, Chungking Mansions, a crumbling block stacked with dirt-cheap hostels and guesthouses. Of course, a huge range of other hotels and guesthouses catering to all budgets can be found between these two extremes.

BUDGET

Cosmic Guest House (☎ 2739 4952; info@cosmic guesthouse.com; Flat A1-A2 & F1-F4, 12th fl, Mirador Mansion, 58-62 Nathan Rd, Tsim Sha Tsui; dm/s $60/150, d $200-240) This is a very clean, recently upgraded and very quiet guesthouse with big and bright rooms and a very helpful owner.

Welcome Guest House (☎ 2721 7793, ☎ 9838 8375; guesthousehk@hotmail.com; Flat A5, 7th fl, A Block, Chungking Mansions, 36-44 Nathan Rd, Tsim Sha Tsui; s 120-150, d $180-200, s without shower $100) This place is a cut above the rest in Chungking Mansions and its friendly owner, John Wah, speaks excellent English. What's more, it has laundry service.

Caritas Bianchi Lodge (☎ 2388 1111; cblresv@ bianchi-lodge.com; 4 Cliff Rd, Yau Ma Tei; s/tr $360/510, d & tw $410-600) This 90-room hotel-cum-guesthouse is run by a Catholic social welfare organisation. Though it's just off Nathan Rd, the rear rooms are very quiet and some have views onto King's Park.

Garden Guesthouse (☎ 2368 0981; Flat C5, 16th fl, C Block, Chungking Mansions, 36-44 Nathan Rd, Tsim Sha Tsui; s & d $150-180) This is a clean place favoured by backpackers. They have a **7th floor branch** (☎ 2366 0169; Flat C5, 7th fl) in the same block.

Hakkas Guest House (☎ 2771 3656; fax 2770 1470; Flat L, 3rd fl, New Lucky House, 300 Nathan Rd, Yau Ma Tei; s/d/tr $200/250/300) Each of the nine ultraclean rooms in this guesthouse has a phone and TV. The affable and helpful owner, Kevin Koo, is a keen hiker and often invites guests out along with him for country walks on Sunday.

With a total of 40 rooms, the excellent **Star Guesthouse** (☎ 2723 8951; www.starguesthouse .com; Flat B, 6th fl, 21 Cameron Rd, Tsim Sha Tsui; s/d/tr with bathroom $250/300/350, s/d without bathroom $180/200) and its sister property just up the road, the **Lee Garden Guest House** (☎ 2367 2284; charliechan@iname.com; 8th fl, D Block, 36 Cameron Rd, Tsim Sha Tsui), are owned and run by the charismatic Charlie Chan, who can arrange most things for you, including China visas.

Travellers Hostel (☎ 2368 7710; mrspau⊙yahoo .com.hk; Flat A1-A4, 16th fl, A Block, Chungking Mansions, 36-44 Nathan Rd, Tsim Sha Tsui; dm $60-65, d $130 with bathroom, s/d without bathroom $90/120) This popular hostel is a landmark in this building, and cooking facilities, cable TV and student discounts are available.

Man Hing Lung Hotel (☎ 2722 0678; http://home .hkstar.com/~mhlhotel; Flat F2, 14th fl, Mirador Mansion, 58-62 Nathan Rd, Tsim Sha Tsui; s $120-150, d $150-200, tr $210-240; ⌨) This decent place has clean rooms, a good atmosphere and Internet access. If you need a roommate, the very friendly manager, Mr Chan, will put you in with another traveller for $80.

Park Guesthouse (☎ 2368 1689; fax 2367 7889; Flat A1, 15th fl, A Block, Chungking Mansions, 36-44 Nathan Rd, Tsim Sha Tsui; s/d with bathroom $150/200, without bathroom $120/150) This clean and friendly guesthouse comes recommended by readers.

MID-RANGE

Booth Lodge (☎ 2771 9266; http://boothlodge.salvation .org.hk; 11 Wing Sing Lane, Yau Ma Tei; s & d incl breakfast $620-1500) Run by the Salvation Army, this 54-room place is spartan and clean but comfortable too. Promotional rates for standard singles and doubles are $420 to $540. Reception is on the 7th floor.

Kimberley Hotel (☎ 2723 3888; www.kimberley hotel.com.hk; 28 Kimberley Rd, Tsim Sha Tsui; s $1100-1750, d $1200-1850, ste from $2150) The 546-room Kimberley is one of the better mid-range hotels in Tsim Sha Tsui, with assured staff and good rooms and facilities. Summer rates are half the quoted ones. The pond and palm-filled lobby are on the 2nd floor.

Salisbury (☎ 2268 7888; www.ymcahk.org.hk; 41 Salisbury Rd, Tsim Sha Tsui; dm $210, s $630, d $700-890, ste from $1100) The 365 rooms and suites are comfortable but simple at this YMCA-run hotel. The four-bed dormitory rooms on the 9th floor are a bonus, but there are restrictions: check-in is at 2pm; no one can stay more than seven consecutive nights; and walk-in guests for the dorms aren't accepted if they've been in Hong Kong for more than 10 days.

Kowloon Hotel Hong Kong (☎ 2929 2888; www .thekowloonhotel.com; 19-21 Nathan Rd, Tsim Sha Tsui; s $1300-2550, d $1400-2650, ste from $3600) Part of the Peninsula Hotel group, the 736-room Kowloon Hotel has an 'also ran' feel about it, but is popular for its unflappable service, decent rooms and wonderful Wan Loong Court restaurant (p519) in the basement. Rates drop dramatically off season.

Holiday Inn Golden Mile (☎ 2369 3111; www .goldenmile-hk.holiday-inn.com; 50 Nathan Rd, Tsim Sha Tsui; s $1000-1500, d $1050-1600, ste from H$3500) The 600 guestrooms at this place are Holiday Inn–reliable and you've got the Delicatessen Corner (p520) in the basement for all your picnic needs.

Miramar Hotel (☎ 2368 1111; www.miramarhk.com; 118-130 Nathan Rd, Tsim Sha Tsui; s & d $1200-2000, ste from $3800) This 525-room landmark is very central and convenient to the Miramar Shopping Centre just across Kimberley Rd.

BP International House (☎ 2378 7611; www.bpih .com.hk; 8 Austin Rd; Tsim Sha Tsui; s $990-1450, d $1100-1500, ste from $2950) This recently renovated 535-room hotel owned by the Scout Association of Hong Kong overlooks Kowloon Park from its northwestern corner. Haggle before you book; depending on the season and day of the week, prices are often reduced by 50%.

Nathan Hotel (☎ 2388 5141; www.nathanhotel.com; 378 Nathan Rd, Yau Ma Tei; s $500-950, d $600-1300, tr $780-1450, ste from $1200) The Nathan Hotel is surprisingly quiet and pleasant; even the cheapest of its 185 rooms are spacious, clean and serene. It's near the Jordan MTR station and Temple St; enter from Pak Hoi St.

Park Hotel (☎ 2366 1371; www.parkhotel.com.hk; 61-65 Chatham Rd South, Tsim Sha Tsui; s $1100-$1900, d $1200-2000, ste from $2600) Ongoing renovation at this 430-room hotel has seen standards (and prices) go up.

YMCA International House (☎ 2771 9111; www .ymcaintlhousehk.org; 23 Waterloo Rd, Yau Ma Tei; dm $220, s & d $680-1180, ste from $1600) Though a bit out of the way, this 427-room hotel with all the mod cons is a steal for what it offers. It is open to men and women. There are weekly/ monthly packages from $2730/8100.

Shamrock Hotel (☎ 2735 2271; www.shamrock hotel.com.hk; 223 Nathan Rd, Yau Ma Tei; s $550-1250, d $750-1450, ste from $1500) The Shamrock offers fantastic value for its category and location, with 158 well-sized, clean and airy guestrooms. Jordan MTR is right outside the door.

Dorsett Seaview Hotel (☎ 2782 0882; www .dorsettseaview.com.hk; 268 Shanghai St, Yau Ma Tei; s $880-1280, d $1280-1580, ste from $2400) The 257 guestrooms in this tall, thin building are fine, and the Temple St and Jade Markets and Nathan Rd are just around the corner.

Royal Pacific Hotel & Towers (☎ 2736 1188; www .royalpacific.com.hk; China Hong Kong City, 33 Canton Rd, Tsim Sha Tsui; s & d $1080-2100, ste from $2200) Rooms – some 675 in total – are more expensive in the harbour-facing tower. There's a walkway to Kowloon Park, leading onto Nathan Rd and the MTR station, and the hotel is connected to the ferry terminal from where boats sail to Macau and China.

TOP END

Hotel Inter-Continental Hong Kong (☎ 2721 1211; www.hongkong-ic.intercontinental.com; 18 Salisbury Rd, Tsim Sha Tsui; s & d $3100-3700, ste from $5500) This 514-room hotel, which can boast the finest waterfront position in the territory, tilts at modernity while bowing to colonial traditions, such as a fleet of Rolls Royces, uniformed doormen and incessant brass polishing.

Marco Polo Hong Kong Hotel (☎ 2113 0888; www .marcopolohotels.com; Harbour City, 3 Canton Rd, Tsim Sha Tsui; s $2300-3530, d $2400-3630, ste from $4660) This 665-room property is the linchpin in the Marco Polo Hotel group's Canton Rd trio, which includes the Marco Polo Gateway and the Marco Polo Prince – both of which are also in the Harbour City complex. This one is closest to the Star Ferry and has plenty of shopping in the attached mall.

Peninsula Hong Kong (☎ 2920 2888; www.penin sula.com; Salisbury Rd, Tsim Sha Tsui; s & d $3000-4900, ste from $5600; 🖳) Lording it over the southern tip of Kowloon, Hong Kong's finest hotel evokes colonial elegance but its 300 guestrooms are as up to date as any other hotel, with Internet access, fax machines and CD and DVD players.

Royal Garden Hotel (☎ 2721 5215; www.rghk.com .hk; 69 Mody Rd, Tsim Sha Tsui East; s $2100-2600, d $2250-2750, ste from $3700) This often-overlooked 442-room property is one of the best-equipped hotels on this side of the harbour and one of the territory's most attractive options overall. Its Chinese restaurant (p519) deserves its fine reputation.

New Territories   Map pp496–7

The New Territories does not offer travellers a tremendous choice in terms of accommodation, but there are both official and independent hostels here, usually in the more remote parts of the region. At the same time, the **Country & Marine Parks Authority** (☎ 2420 0529; http://parks.afcd.gov.hk/newparks/chi /recreation/campsite/eindex.htm) maintains 28 no-frills camp sites in the New Territories and 11 in the Outlying Islands for hikers and trekkers. They are all free and are clearly labelled on the four trail maps (see p510).

Ascension House (☎ 2691 4196; www.achouse.com; 33 Tao Fong Shan Rd, Sha Tin; dm $125) This 11-bed place affiliated with the Lutheran Church is one of the best deals in Hong Kong as the price of a bed includes free laundry service

and three meals. To get there, take the KCR East Rail to Sha Tin station, leave via exit B and walk down the ramp, passing a series of traditional village houses on the left. Between them is a set of steps. Go up these steps, follow the path and when you come to a roundabout, go along the uphill road – Pak Lok Path – to your right. After about 150m you'll come to a small staircase and a sign pointing the way to Ascension House on the right. When you reach the fork in the path and the Tao Fong Shan Christian Centre, bear to the right and you'll soon come to more steps leading up to Ascension House. The walk should take between 15 and 20 minutes. A taxi from the station in Sha Tin will cost around $20.

Sze Lok Yuen Hostel (☎ 2488 8188; www.yha.org .hk; Tai Mo Shan; dm under/over 18 yrs $30/45) This 92-bed hostel, usually open Saturday and on the eve of public holidays only (telephone the Hong Kong Youth Hostel Association in advance on ☎ 2788 1638), sits in the shadow of Hong Kong's highest peak, Tai Mo Shan (p508). There are cooking facilities, but you should bring your own food and drink. To get here take bus No 51 from the Tsuen Wan MTR station and alight at Tai Mo Shan Rd. Follow Tai Mo Shan Rd for about 45 minutes (3km), pass the car park and turn on to a small concrete path on the right-hand side. This leads directly to the hostel.

Outlying Islands

Lantau, Lamma and Cheung Chau all have accommodation options and are excellent places in which to escape from the hustle and bustle of urban Hong Kong. The **Country & Marine Parks Authority** (left) maintains nine camp sites on Lantau. Camping is strictly prohibited on Hong Kong beaches.

Man Lai Wah Hotel (☎ 2982 0220; hotel@my.net vigator.com; 2 Po Wah Garden, Yung Shue Wan, Lamma; s & d Mon-Fri $300-350, Sat & Sun $500) This eight-room guesthouse faces you as you get off the ferry and begin to walk up Main St. Some of the rooms have little balconies.

Mui Wo Inn (☎ 2984 7225; fax 2984 1916; Tung Wan Tau Rd, Silvermine Bay Beach, Lantau; s & d incl breakfast Sun-Fri $350, Sat $520) This is the last hotel on Silvermine Bay Beach and can be identified by the ring of faux-classical statues in front. It's a bit ragged around the edges but a friendly place to stay.

Hongkong Bank Foundation SG Davis Hostel (☎ 2985 5610; www.yha.org.hk; Ngong Ping, Lantau; dm under/over 18 yrs $30/45, d $150) This 46-bed hostel is a 10-minute walk from the bus stop near the Tian Tan Buddha statue (see p509) in Ngong Ping and is the ideal place to stay if you want to watch the sunrise at nearby Lantau Peak. From the bus stop, take the paved path to your left as you face the Tian Tan Buddha, pass the public toilets on your right and the Lantau Tea Garden on your left and follow the signs to the maze-like steps going up to the hostel.

Warwick Hotel (☎ 2981 0081; www.warwickhotel .com.hk; Cheung Chau Sports Rd, Tung Wan Beach, Cheung Chau; d with mountain/sea view Mon-Fri $690/790, Sat & Sun $990/1190, ste from $1490/2190) This massive, 71-room hotel is an eyesore but has wonderful views across the sea to Lamma and Hong Kong Island. There are weekly/ monthly packages from $3500/12,000.

EATING

Chinese food – whether it be Cantonese, Chiu Chow (a regional cuisine of southern China), Northern, Shanghainese or Sichuan – is not the only cuisine local people and travellers enjoy here. The territory also counts some of the world's top international eateries, ranging from trendy Italian and Asian fusion to basic Thai and fiery Indian curries.

While in Hong Kong, you should try dim sum, uniquely Cantonese dishes served for breakfast, brunch or lunch. Dim sum delicacies are normally steamed and you pay by the number of baskets or dishes you order. These are usually stacked up on trolleys and wheeled around the dining room. Just point at whatever catches your eye as it (the trolley) rolls by.

In Cantonese restaurants, tea is often served free of charge or at nominal cost and refilled indefinitely. When the teapot is empty and you want a refill of hot water, signal the waiter by taking the lid off the pot and resting it on the handle.

Hong Kong Island

Eateries on Hong Kong Island range from silver-service restaurants in five-star hotels to Chinese fried noodles enjoyed at pavement cafés. In between is an embarrassment of ethnic cuisines, from Indian and Mexican to Chiu Chow and Vietnamese. The place to go for reasonably priced eats and late-night revelry is the neighbourhood known as Lan Kwai Fong, where you'll find a plethora of pubs and bars.

CHINESE

Jumbo Floating Restaurant (Map pp496-7; ☎ 2553 9111; Shum Wan Pier Dr, Wong Chuk Hang, Aberdeen; meals from $250 per person; ☻ 10.30am-11.30pm Mon-Sat,

---

THE AUTHOR'S CHOICE

Beijing Shui Jiao Wong (Map pp504-5; ☎ 2527 0289; 118 Jaffe Rd, Wan Chai; dishes $25-40; ☻ 7am-11pm Mon-Sat, noon-11pm Sun) The 'Dumpling King' serves the best (and cheapest) northern-style dumplings, *guo tie* (pot stickers) and soup noodles in Hong Kong.

Che's Cantonese Restaurant (Map pp504-5; ☎ 2528 1123; 4th fl, the Broadway, 54-62 Lockhart Rd, Wan Chai; meals from $300 per person; ☻ 11am-3pm & 6-11.30pm) This excellent Cantonese restaurant serves a variety of home-style delicacies and offers a special seasonal menu with a dozen additional dishes.

Rughetta (Map pp500-2; ☎ 2537 7922; basement, Carfield Commercial Bldg, 75-77 Wyndham St, Central; starters $78-138, pasta $145-155, mains $178-228; ☻ noon-3pm & 7pm-midnight Mon-Sat, 7pm-midnight Sun) This new kid on the block with a branch in New York city serves faultless 'Roman' (read earthy Italian) cuisine.

Busan Korean Restaurant (Map pp506-7; ☎ 2376 3385; ground fl, Kowloon Centre, 29 Ashley Rd, Tsim Sha Tsui; rice & noodle dishes $90-150, barbecue $100-130; ☻ 11.30am-3pm, 6-11.30pm) This authentic place in the bustling hub of touristed Tsim Sha Tsui manages to stay on, despite nearby competition. The barbecue is particularly good.

Rainbow Seafood Restaurant (Map pp496-7; ☎ 2982 8100; shops 1A-1B & 23-24 First St, Sok Kwu Wan, Lamma; meals per person $200; ☻ 11am-11pm) This place, with several waterfront locations, specialises in seafood, especially steamed groper, lobster and abalone. Book a table in advance and you'll be transported by small ferry from Queen's Pier in Central.

7.30am-11.30pm Sun) The larger of two floating restaurants moored in Aberdeen Harbour and specialising in seafood, the Jumbo is touristy in the extreme and the food is just so-so. Think of it more as a spectacle – a show – and you'll have fun. There's free transport for diners from the pier on Aberdeen Promenade (see p503). Dim sum is served from 7.30am to 4.30pm on Sunday.

Luk Yu Tea House (Map pp500-2; ☎ 2523 5464; 24-26 Stanley St, Central; rice & noodle dishes $65-160, mains $100-350; ☺ 7am-10pm) This old-style teahouse is a museum piece. Service is cavalier at best but the surrounds are stunning and the dim sum (served from 7am to 6pm) is very good.

Mak's Noodle (Map pp500-2; ☎ 2854 3810; 77 Wellington St, Central; dishes $25-50; ☺ 11am-8pm) The wonton soup noodles (a major hangover cure) and beef brisket noodles here are highly recommended.

One Harbour Road (Map pp504-5; ☎ 2588 1234; 7th & 8th fl, Grand Hyatt Hong Kong, 1 Harbour Rd, Wan Chai; dim sum $36-60, starters $90-165, mains $150-390; ☺ noon-2.30pm & 6-10.30pm) In addition to the beautiful design and fabulous harbour views at what is Hong Kong's classiest Chinese restaurant, six pages of gourmet dishes await your perusal. There's a set lunch/dinner for $330/650.

Yung Kee (Map pp500-2; ☎ 2522 1624; 32-40 Wellington St, Central; dishes HK60-120; ☺ 11am-11.30pm) This culinary institution is probably the most famous Cantonese restaurant in Central. The roast goose here has been the talk of the town since 1942, and its dim sum (served from 2pm to 5pm daily) is excellent.

OTHER ASIAN
Blowfish (Map pp500-2; ☎ 2815 7868; 20-26 Peel St, Central; sushi & sashimi $30-160, yakitori $28-50, set lunches $55-88; ☺ noon-2.30pm & 6-10.30pm Mon-Thu, noon-2.30pm & 6-11.30pm Fri & Sat) This classy Japanese eatery, with its long sushi bar and enviable selection of sake, is a colourful and cool place.

Bon Appetit (Map pp500-2; ☎ 2525 3553; 14B Wing Wah Lane, Central; dishes $16-33; ☺ 10am-midnight) Cheap but tasty dishes for those on a budget are available at this little Vietnamese nook at the bottom of Lan Kwai Fong.

Good Luck Thai (Map pp500-2; ☎ 2877 2971; 13 Wing Wah Lane, Central; dishes $35-120; ☺ 11am-2am Mon-Sat, 4pm-midnight Sun) After sinking a few beers in Lan Kwai Fong (p521), make your

way over to this chaotic but friendly place for a cheap fix of late-night Thai food.

Saigon Beach (Map pp504-5; ☎ 2529 7823; 66 Lockhart Rd, Wan Chai; noodles & rice dishes $28-35, mains $60-75; ☺ 11.30am-4pm & 6-10.30pm) This popular little hole in the wall may not impress at first sight, but the affable service and good food makes it well worth sharing a table with strangers.

Tan Ta Wan Thai Restaurant (Map pp504-5; ☎ 2865 1178; shop 9, Rialto Bldg, 2 Landale St, Wan Chai; starters $40-78, rice & noodle dishes $35-38; curries & mains $40-128; ☺ 11am-11pm Mon-Fri, noon-10.30pm Sat & Sun) This smallish restaurant on the border between Admiralty and Wan Chai serves some of the most authentic Thai food in Hong Kong.

WESTERN
Archie B's Delicatessen (Map pp500-2; ☎ 2522 1262; lower ground fl, 7-9 Staunton St, Soho; sandwiches & burgers $40-110, salads $50; ☺ 10am-10pm) This little place just off the Central Escalator serves as authentic New York deli food as you'll find west of the US of A.

Petrus (Map pp500-2; ☎ 2820 8590; 56th fl, Island Shangri-La Hong Kong, Supreme Court Rd, Admiralty; 2/3-course set lunches $278/328, 5/6-course set dinners $750/900; ☺ noon-2.30pm & 6.30-11pm Mon-Sat, 6.30-11pm Sun) With its head (and prices) in the clouds, Petrus is one of the finest restaurants in Hong Kong. Expect traditional (not *nouvelle*) French cuisine and stunning views.

VEGETARIAN
Fringe Club (Map pp500-2; ☎ 2521 7251; 2nd fl, Dairy Farm Bldg, 2 Lower Albert Rd, Central; set lunches $65; ☺ noon-2pm Mon-Fri) Vegetarians weighing their options in Central at lunchtime during the week might try the Western vegetarian buffet; it's available upstairs in the Volkswagen Fotogalerie at the Fringe Club. There's seating on the roof terrace in fine weather.

Kung Tak Lam (Map pp504-5; ☎ 2881 9966; ground fl, Lok Sing Centre, 31 Yee Wo St, Causeway Bay; meals from $150; ☺ 11am-11pm) This long-established place, which serves Shanghai-style meatless dishes, is more modern-feeling than most Chinese vegetarian eateries and is usually packed out. All the vegetables are 100% organic and dishes are free of MSG.

QUICK EATS & SELF-CATERING
Chicken on the Run (Map pp500-2; ☎ 2537 8285; shop A, lower ground fl, 1 Prince's Tce; dishes $25-60;

11.30am-9.30pm) This brightly lit and pristine place is where to go if you fancy take-away chicken in all its guises, with salads and prepared vegetables.

city'super (Map pp500-2; ☎ 2234 7128; shop 1041-1049, 1st fl, IFC Mall, 1 Harbour View St, Central; 10.30am-9.30pm) This enormous gourmet supermarket, with five additional branches elsewhere in Hong Kong, has ready-to-eat food like sushi and salads and lots of fresh produce.

Kowloon   Map pp506-7

Kowloon is not able to boast the same range of restaurants that Hong Kong Island can, but you will still find an amazing assortment of ethnic eateries here, especially in Tsim Sha Tsui.

CHINESE

Dai Pai Dong (☎ 2317 7728; ground fl, Hanley House, 70 Canton Rd, Tsim Sha Tsui; breakfast $15-30, rice & noodle dishes $28-68, set meals from $44; 7.30am-midnight Mon-Sat, 9am-midnight Sun) This modern version of a *cha chan tang*, a uniquely Hong Kong café with local dishes, serves meals throughout the day, but it's best to come at afternoon tea (2.30pm to 5.30pm) for such oddities as *yuan yang* (equal parts coffee and black tea with milk), boiled cola with lemon and ginger, and toast smeared with condensed milk.

Happy Garden Noodle & Congee Kitchen (☎ 2377 2604; 76 Canton Rd, Tsim Sha Tsui; rice & noodle dishes $20-110, congee $13-100; 7am-2am) This is a budget option, with a choice of some 200 rice, noodle and *congee* dishes on the menu, including shrimp wonton noodles ($28). There's also main dishes like beef in oyster sauce ($55) and roasted duck ($45).

Royal Garden Chinese Restaurant (☎ 2724 2666; lower basement, Royal Garden Hotel, 69 Mody Rd, Tsim Sha Tsui East; meals per person from $250; 11.30am-3pm & 6-11pm Mon-Sat, 10am-3pm & 6-11pm Sun) This splendid hotel restaurant is one of the best places in Tsim Sha Tsui for dim sum.

Spring Deer (☎ 2366 4012; 1st fl, 42 Mody Rd, Tsim Sha Tsui; meals per person from $150; noon-3pm & 6pm-11pm) This is probably Hong Kong's most famous Peking restaurant and serves some of the crispiest Peking duck ($280 for the whole bird) in town.

Wan Loong Court (☎ 2734 3722; lower level 2, Kowloon Hotel Hong Kong, 19-21 Nathan Rd, Tsim Sha Tsui; meals per person from $300; 11am-3pm & 6-11.30pm Mon-

Fri, 11am-11pm Sat & Sun) Wonderful Cantonese food with modern touches is served here. Unusually, they are particularly known for their Chinese desserts.

Wu Kong Shanghai Restaurant (☎ 2366 7244; basement, Alpha House, 27-33 Nathan Rd, Tsim Sha Tsui; dim sum $26-48; rice & noodle dishes $32-78, meat mains $60-140, seafood mains $110-280; 11.30am-midnight) This place and its signature dishes (cold pigeon in wine sauce and crispy fried eels) are excellent.

INDIAN

Gaylord (☎ 2376 1001; 1st fl, Ashley Centre, 23-25 Ashley Rd; Tsim Sha Tsui; veg dishes $56-68, meat mains & tandoori dishes $66-136, lunch buffets Mon-Sat $88; noon-3pm & 6-11pm) Dim lighting and live Indian music set the scene for enjoying the excellent rogan josh, dhal and other favourite dishes at Hong Kong's oldest Indian restaurant.

You'll find the greatest concentration of cheap Indian and Pakistani restaurants (called messes) in Kowloon at Chunking Mansions, a rabbit warren of hostels and guesthouses. Lunch or dinner will cost from about $50; for $100 you'll get a blow-out. Only one of the places is licensed, but you are usually allowed to BYO.

Delhi Club (☎ 2368 1682; Flat C3, 3rd fl, C Block, Chunking Mansions, 36-44 Nathan Rd, Tsim Sha Tsui; noon-3.30pm & 6pm-11.30pm) Good-value Indian and Nepalese food, especially chicken tandoori ($20).

Islamabad Club (☎ 2721 5362; Flat C4, 4th fl, C Block, Chunking Mansions, 36-44 Nathan Rd, Tsim Sha Tsui; noon-3.30pm & 6-10.30pm) Serves Indian and Pakistani halal food.

Swagat Restaurant (☎ 2722 5350; Flat C3-4, 1st fl, C Block, Chunking Mansions, 36-44 Nathan Rd, Tsim Sha Tsui; noon-3pm & 6-11pm) This place has the only liquor license held by a mess in Chunking Mansions.

OTHER ASIAN

Banana Leaf Curry House (☎ 2721 4821; 3rd fl, Golden Crown Court, 68 Nathan Rd, Tsim Sha Tsui; starters $32-78, mains $54-128; 11.30am-3pm & 6pm-midnight Mon-Fri, 11.30am-midnight Sat & Sun) This centrally located branch of a chain of Malaysian/Singaporean restaurants is convenient to the guesthouses on the southern end of Nathan Rd.

Genki Sushi (☎ 2722 6689; shop G7-G9, ground fl, East Ocean Centre, 98 Granville Rd, Tsim Sha Tsui East; sushi per pair $9-35, sushi sets $40-235; 11.30am-11.30pm) This is a branch of the popular (and inexpensive) sushi chain with a 'meany face' logo.

WESTERN

Dan Ryan's Chicago Grill (☎ 2735 6111, shop 315, level 3, Ocean Terminal, Harbour City, Canton Rd, Tsim Sha Tsui; starters $52-98, salads $98-145, pasta $98-130, mains $95-240; ☯ 11am-midnight Mon-Fri, 10am-midnight Sat & Sun) The theme here is 'Chicago', including a model elevated rail system overhead and jazz and big-band music on the sound system. It is the place for burgers and ribs (half/full rack $132/198) in Hong Kong.

Fat Angelo's (☎ 2730 4788; 35 Ashley Rd, Tsim Sha Tsui; salads $45, pasta $88-175; mains $125-215; ☯ noon-midnight) Huge portions, free side salads, un-limited bread and relatively low prices are the keys to success at this chain of Italian-American restaurants.

Orphée (☎ 2730 1128; 18A Austin Ave, Tsim Sha Tsui; starters $53-88, mains $110-210, set lunches $78-98, set dinners $165; ☯ noon-2.30pm & 6.45-10.15pm) If you feel like a fix of foie gras, this small Parisian oasis in deepest Tsim Sha Tsui is the spot.

VEGETARIAN

Branto Pure Vegetarian Indian Food (☎ 2366 8171; 1st fl, 9 Lock Rd; dishes $28-57; ☯ 11am-3pm & 6-11pm) This cheap but excellent place is where to go if you want to try south Indian dishes.

Joyful Vegetarian (☎ 2780 2230, 530 Nathan Rd, Yau Ma Tei; dishes $40-60; ☯ 11am-11pm) The vegetable country-style hotpot is made with a wide range of fungi at this Buddhist place, and there's a snack counter facing the street.

QUICK EATS & SELF-CATERING

Delicatessen Corner (☎ 2315 1020; Basement 1, Holiday Inn Golden Mile, 50 Nathan Rd, Tsim Sha Tsui; shop ☯ 9am-9.30pm, café-restaurant ☯ 11am-11pm) This is an excellent place to shop for a picnic or just to pause for a pastry and coffee.

Wellcome (☎ 2369 6451; 28 Hankow Rd, Tsim Sha Tsui; ☯ 8am-10pm) This branch of the large supermarket chain is much better stocked and maintained than others in the area.

Outlying Islands   Map pp496–7

The restaurant scene varies from island to island. While Lamma can boast the lion's share in Yung Shue Wan (café-restaurants) and Sok Kwu Wan (Chinese seafood restaurants), there are also some decent choices on Lantau, Cheung Chau and Peng Chau.

Bahçe Turkish Restaurant (☎ 2984 0222; shop 19, ground fl, Mui Wo Centre, 3 Ngan Wan Rd, Mui Wo, Lan-tau; kebabs & falafel $40-48, meze $28-45, mains $45-80; ☯ 11.30am-11pm Mon-Fri, 10.30am-11pm Sat & Sun)

The 'Garden' might be a somewhat ambi-tious name for this small eatery but it has all our Turkish favourites, including *sigara böreği* (filo parcels filled with cheese) and *yaparak dolmasi* (stuffed vine leaves).

Bookworm Café (☎ 2982 4838; 79 Main St, Yung Shue Wan, Lamma; breakfasts $25-60, dishes $40-80; ☯ 10am-9pm Mon-Fri, 9am-10pm Sat, 9am-9pm Sun) This place is not just a great vegetarian café-restaurant with fruit juices and organic wine ($35 per glass, from $198 a bottle) but a second-hand bookshop and an Internet café (50c per minute) as well.

Forest Bar & Thai Restaurant (☎ 2983 8837; 38C Wing Hing St, Peng Chau; snacks $35-50, rice & noodle dishes $35-68, mains $62-100; ☯ 11am-11pm Tue-Sun) This cosy bar-restaurant has a large outside seating area and a pub with snooker. The kitchen whips up fairly authentic Thai food six days a week.

Hong Kee (☎ 2981 9916; 11A Pak She Praya Rd, Cheung Chau; dishes $45-145; ☯ 10.30am-10.30pm) This is ar-guably the top spot along the Cheung Chau waterfront and serves excellent fish dishes.

Stoep Restaurant (☎ 2980 2699; 32 Lower Che-ung Sha Village, Lantau; mains $45-85; ☯ 11am-10pm Tue-Sun) This Mediterranean-style restaurant with a huge terrace right on Lower Cheung Sha Beach has acceptable meat and fish dishes and a South African *braai* (barbecue; $80 to $150).

DRINKING
Cafés & Teahouses

The last few years have seen a miniature explosion of cafés – both local and inter-national – that serve a wide range of coffees. Tea and teahouses (see p84), of course, have been a major component of Chinese culture since time immemorial.

First Cup Coffee (Map pp506-7; ☎ 2316 7793; 12 Hankow Rd, Tsim Sha Tsui; coffees $10-58; ☯ 7am-1am) This hole in the wall of a shop serves some excellent gourmet coffees and sweet treats.

Moon Garden Tea House (Map pp504-5; ☎ 2882 6878; 5 Hoi Ping Rd, Causeway Bay; tea & snacks $120; ☯ noon-midnight) Choose from many brews, then lose an afternoon perusing tea books, admiring antiques (all for sale) and taking refills from the heated pot beside your table.

TW Café (Map pp500-2; ☎ 2544 2237, shop 2, ground fl, Capitol Plaza, 2-10 Lyndhurst Tce, Central; afternoon tea/coffee $35; ☯ 8am-8pm) This tiny café offers more than 20 types of coffee as well as light snacks ($20 to $35).

Pubs & Bars

Lan Kwai Fong, a narrow pedestrian alleyway in Central, is the best – and most expensive – area for bars, though it's the stomping grounds of expat and Chinese suits and professionals. **Soho**, another area for bars and restaurants, can be found south of Hollywood Rd and is easily accessed by the Central Escalator. In general, the pubs and bars in **Wan Chai** are cheaper and more relaxed; those in **Tsim Sha Tsui** in Kowloon attract more locals.

Most pubs, bars and some clubs give discounts on drinks (usually one-third to one-half off) or offer two-for-one specials. Happy hour is usually in the late afternoon or early evening – 4pm to 8pm, say – but the times vary widely from place to place.

HONG KONG ISLAND

1/5 (Map pp500–2; ☎ 2520 2515; 1st fl, Starcrest Bldg, 9 Star St, Wan Chai; ☯ 6pm-1am Mon-Wed, 6pm-2am Thu, 6pm-3am Fri, 8pm-3am Sat; happy hour 6-9pm Mon-Fri) This sophisticated lounge bar has a broad bar backed by a two-storey drinks selection, from which bar staff concoct some of Hong Kong's best cocktails. It gets packed at the weekend.

Club 64 (Map pp500–2; ☎ 2523 2801; 12-14 Wing Wah Lane, Central; ☯ 3pm-2am Mon-Thu, 3pm-3am Fri & Sat, 6pm-1am Sun; happy hour 3-9pm) This laid-back place with a memory – its name recalls the date of the 1989 massacre around Tiananmen Sq in Běijīng (4 June) – is one of the best drinking spots for nonposeurs and those looking for some simple, unfussy fun.

Groovy Mule (Map pp504–5; ☎ 2527 2077; 37-39 Lockhart Rd, Wan Chai; ☯ 4pm-3am or 5am) This pulsating Aussie bar – staff in cork hats, no less – attracts punters with its never-ending happy hour.

Staunton's Wine Bar & Cafe (Map pp500–2; ☎ 2973 6611, 10-12 Staunton St, Soho; ☯ 8am-2am; happy hour 5-9pm) Staunton's is a swish venue with decent wines, a Central Escalator–watching scene and lovely terrace.

KOWLOON   Map pp506–7

Chemical Suzy (☎ 2736 0087; ground fl, AWT Centre, 2A-B Austin Ave, Tsim Sha Tsui; ☯ 6pm-4am, happy hour 6-9pm) This is a popular hide-out with DJs, snacks and a mixed crowd.

Delaney's (☎ 2301 3980; basement, Mary Bldg, 71-77 Peking Rd, Tsim Sha Tsui; ☯ 9am-2.30am; happy hour 5-9pm) This immensely popular Irish pub has

lots of dark wood, green felt and a long bar that you can really settle into.

Sky Lounge (☎ 2369 1111; 18th fl, Sheraton Hong Kong Hotel & Towers, 20 Nathan Rd, Tsim Sha Tsui; ☯ 4pm-1am Mon-Fri, 2pm-2am Sat & Sun) It may at first glance look like a departure lounge but, well, the view… Don't take flight: sit down in a scoop chair and sip a drink.

ENTERTAINMENT

To find out what's on in Hong Kong, pick up a copy of **HK Magazine** (asiacity@asia-city.com.hk), a comprehensive entertainment listings magazine. It's free, appears on Friday and can be picked up at restaurants, bars, shops and hotels throughout the territory. Also worth checking out is the freebie **bc magazine** (www.bcmagazine.net), a biweekly guide to Hong Kong's entertainment and party scene.

Bookings for most cultural events can also be made by telephoning **Urbtix** (☎ 2734 9009; www.urbtix.gov.hk; ☯ 10am-8pm). You can also book tickets for many films and concerts and a great variety of cultural events through **Cityline** (☎ 2317 6666; www.cityline.com.hk).

Live Music

Wanch (Map pp504–5; ☎ 2861 1621; 54 Jaffe Rd; ☯ 11am-2am Sun-Thu, 11am-4am Fri & Sat; happy hour 11am 10pm Mon Thu, 11am 9pm Fri Sun) This small venue has live music (mostly rock and folk) seven nights a week from 9pm (10pm on Friday and Saturday), with the occasional solo guitarist thrown in.

Ned Kelly's Last Stand (Map pp506–7; ☎ 2376 0562; 11A Ashley Rd, Tsim Sha Tsui; ☯ 11.30am-2am; happy hour 11.30am-9pm) This Aussie pub features Ned Kelly's Big Band playing jazz from 9.30pm till 1am. Food (eg meat pies) is available and there's never a cover charge.

Nightclubs

Bahama Mama's Caribbean Bar (Map pp506–7; ☎ 2368 2121; 4-5 Knutsford Terrace, Tsim Sha Tsui; ☯ 5pm-3am Mon-Thu, 5pm-4am Fri & Sat, 6pm-2am Sun; happy hour 5-9pm & midnight-closing Mon-Sat, all day Sun) Bahama Mama's, with palm trees and surfboards to create an 'island' feel, has DJs at the weekend and folks bopping on the shrimp-sized dance floor.

Club 97 (Map pp500–2; ☎ 2186 1897; ground fl, Cosmos Bldg, 9-11 Lan Kwai Fong; ☯ 6pm-2am Mon-Thu, 6pm-4am Fri, 8pm-4am Sat & Sun; happy hour 6-9pm Mon-Fri, 8pm-10pm Sun) This schmooze lounge bar has a selectively enforced 'members only' policy to turn away the badly dressed – so make an effort. Happy hour on Friday is a gay event.

Drop (Map pp500-2; ☎ 2543 8856; basement, On Lok Mansion, 39-43 Hollywood Rd; ⏰ 7pm-2am Mon & Tue, 7pm-3am Wed, 7pm-4am Thu, 7pm-5am Fri, 10pm-5am Sat; happy hour 7pm-10pm Mon-Fri) Deluxe lounge action, excellent tunes and potent cocktails keep Drop strong on the scene. The entrance is on Cochrane St.

Dusk till Dawn (Map pp504-5; ☎ 2528 4689; ground fl, 76-84 Jaffe Rd, Wan Chai; ⏰ noon-6am Mon-Thu, noon-7am Fri & Sat, 3pm-5am Sun; happy hour 5pm-11pm) This fun place has live music nightly from 10.30pm. The dance floor can be packed but the atmosphere is usually more friendly than sleazy.

Gay & Lesbian Venues

Along with the gay and lesbian clubs and bars listed below, a few straight and mixed clubs, such as Club 97 (p521), have gay happy hours or evenings.

Curve (Map pp500-2; ☎ 2523 0998; ground & lower ground floors, 2 Arbuthnot Rd; cover $60; ⏰ 8pm-3am Mon-Thu, 8pm-late Fri & Sat; happy hour 8pm-3am Mon & Tue, 8pm-10pm Wed-Sat) Glitzy, innovative club with award-winning modern décor.

Propaganda (Map pp500-2; ☎ 2868 1316; lower ground fl, 1 Hollywood Rd; weekend cover $100; ⏰ 9pm-4am Tue-Thu, 9pm-6am Fri & Sat; happy hour 9pm-1.30am Tue-Thu) Propaganda is still Hong Kong's premier gay dance club. The weekend cover charge gets you into Works on Friday. Enter from Ezra's Lane, which runs between Pottinger and Cochrane Sts.

Works (Map pp500-2; ☎ 2868 6102; 1st fl, 30-32 Wyndham St; weekend cover $60-100; ⏰ 7pm-2am; happy hour 7-9pm) Propaganda's sister club, Works is where most people start an evening on the town.

SHOPPING

Central (Map pp500-2) and **Causeway Bay** (Map pp504-5) are the main shopping districts on Hong Kong Island. If you're shopping for clothes, the two alleyways called **Li Yuen St East** and **Li Yuen St West** (p499) in Central have some bargains. For antiques and curios, head for **Hollywood Rd** (Map pp500-2). Hong Kong Island's glitziest shopping mall is **Pacific Place** (Map pp500-2; ☎ 2844 3888; 88 Queensway, Admiralty).

Shopping in Kowloon is a bizarre mixture of the down at heel and the glamorous;

you can find just about anything – especially in **Tsim Sha Tsui** (Map pp506-7) – and you don't even have to look very hard. If you prefer everything under one roof, head for **Harbour City** (Map pp506-7; ☎ 2118 8668; Canton Rd, Tsim Sha Tsui), an enormous shopping centre comprising Ocean Terminal and Ocean Centre with 700 shops in four zones.

The HKTB (p498) advises visitors only to shop where they see the HKTB logo of a twin-sailed red junk on display, though this is no guarantee. Their free *Guide to Quality Shops and Restaurants* might be useful if you're looking for a specific item.

Antiques & Curios

Arch Angel Antiques (Map pp500-2; ☎ 2851 6848, 53-55 Hollywood Rd, Central; ⏰ 9.30am-6.30pm) This shop has a good selection of affordable antiques and curios and helpful, knowledgeable staff.

Curio Alley (Map pp506-7; lane btwn Lock & Hankow Rd; ⏰ 10am-8pm) This is a fun place to shop for chops, soapstone carvings, fans and other Chinese bric-a-brac.

Mountain Folkcraft (Map pp500-2; ☎ 2523 2817, 12 Wo On Lane, Central; ⏰ 9.30am-6.30pm Mon-Sat) This is one of the nicest shops in Central for folk craft and is piled with bolts of batik and sarongs, clothing, wood carvings and lacquerware made by ethnic minorities in China and Southeast Asia.

Clothing

On Hong Kong Island, **Jardine's Bazaar** (Map pp504-5) in Causeway Bay has low-cost garments, though it may take some hunting to find anything decent. There are several sample shops and places to pick up cheap jeans in nearby **Lee Garden Rd** (Map pp504-5), three streets to the west. It's also worth taking a stroll down **Johnston Rd** (Map pp504-5), where the tram runs, in Wan Chai, which has lots of mid-priced and budget clothing outlets.

The **Temple St night market** (p508) has the cheapest clothes. For mid-priced items, check out the eastern end of **Granville Rd, Austin Ave** and **Chatham Rd South** (Map pp506-7), in Tsim Sha Tsui.

For bespoke clothing, **Pacific Custom Tailors** (Map pp500-2; ☎ 2845 5377; shop 110, 1st fl, Pacific Place, 88 Queensway, Admiralty; ⏰ 9.30am-8pm Mon-Sat) is one of the best choices in the entire territory.

If you prefer to shop where the stars do, head for **Sam's Tailor** (Map pp506-7; ☎ 2367 9423; shop K, Burlington Arcade, 92-94 Nathan Rd, Tsim Sha Tsui; ◷ 10am-7.30pm Mon-Sat, 10am-midnight Sun).

Department Stores & Emporiums

Chinese Arts & Crafts (CAC; Map pp506-7; ☎ 2735 4061; 1st fl, Star House, 3 Salisbury Rd, Tsim Sha Tsui; ◷ 10am-9.30pm) Mainland-owned CAC is probably the best place to buy quality bric-a-brac and other Chinese knick-knacks.

Lane Crawford (Map pp500-2; ☎ 2118 3388; 70 Queen's Rd Central; ◷ 10am-7.30pm) This posh, four-floor emporium is Hong Kong's original Western-style department store – it dates back to the 1840s.

Wing On (Map pp500-2; ☎ 2852 1888; 211 Des Voeux Rd Central; ◷ 10am-7.30pm) 'Forever Peaceful' is notable for being locally owned and carries a full range of goods.

Yue Hwa Chinese Products Emporium (Map pp506-7; ☎ 2384 0084; 301-309 Nathan Rd, Yau Ma Tei; ◷ 10am-10pm) This enormous place has seven floors of ceramics, furniture, souvenirs and clothing.

Music

The **Temple St night market** (see p508) is the place to pick up cheap CDs, DVDs and videos. Otherwise try either of the following.

HMV (Map pp500-2; ☎ 2739 0268; 1st fl, Central Bldg, 1-3 Pedder St, Central; ◷ 9am-10pm) Hong Kong's largest choice of (legitimate) CDs, DVDs and cassettes.

Hong Kong Records (Map pp500-2; ☎ 2845 7088; shop 252, 2nd fl, Pacific Place, 88 Queensway, Admiralty; ◷ 10am-8.30pm Mon-Thu, 10am-9pm Fri-Sun) Local outlet with good selection of music, including Chinese traditional, jazz and classical.

Photographic Equipment

When shopping for camera equipment, keep in mind that you should never buy anything that doesn't have a price tag (to avoid rip-off prices). This will basically preclude 99% of the shops in Tsim Sha Tsui. One of the best spots in Hong Kong for buying photographic equipment is Stanley St in Central; everything carries price tags, though some low-level bargaining might be possible. Tsim Sha Tsui has a couple of reliable shops on Kimberley Rd dealing in new and used cameras.

Everbest Photo (Map pp500-2; ☎ 2522 1985; 28B Stanley St, Central; ◷ 9am-7pm Mon-Sat) This reliable

shop is where many of Hong Kong's professional photographers buy their equipment.

Hing Lee Camera Company (Map pp500-2; ☎ 2544 7593; 25 Lyndhurst Tce, Central; ◷ 9.30am-7pm Mon-Sat, 11am-5pm Sun) Come here for new and second-hand 35mm camera bodies and lenses and mid-range compact SLR and digital cameras.

Onestop Photo Company (Map pp506-7; ☎ 2723 4668; shop 2, ground fl, Champagne Ct, 16 Kimberley Rd, Tsim Sha Tsui; ◷ 11am-9pm) This retail outlet has price tags on its equipment – a rare find in Tsim Sha Tsui – but it won't hurt to bargain a bit.

Sporting Goods

Chamonix Alpine Equipment (Map pp506-7; ☎ 2770 6746; 1st fl, On Yip Bldg, 395 Shanghai St, Mong Kok; ◷ 11am-8pm Mon-Sat, noon-7pm Sun) Far-flung but worth the trip, this Mong Kok shop run by an avid mountaineer has a wide range of camping, hiking and climbing equipment.

Giga Sports (Map pp500-2; ☎ 2524 6992; shop 125, 1st fl, Pacific Place, 88 Queensway, Admiralty; ◷ 10.30am-9.30pm) This gigantic store has a wide range of sports equipment, backpacks, clothing and footwear.

KS Ahluwalia & Sons (Map pp506-7; ☎ 2368 8334; 8C Hankow Rd, Tsim Sha Tsui; ◷ 10am-7.30pm Mon-Sat, 10am-5pm Sun) This long-established store is well stocked with golf gear, tennis racquets, cricket bats, shirts and balls. No prices are marked, so haggle away.

Ocean Sky Divers (Map pp506-7; ☎ 2366 3738; 1st fl, 17-19 Lock Rd, Tsim Sha Tsui; ◷ 10.30am-9pm) This speciality shop has the whole range of diving and snorkelling gear in stock.

GETTING THERE & AWAY
Air

A total of 70 airlines operate between Hong Kong International Airport and 130 destinations worldwide. Competition keeps fares relatively low, and it's a great place to hunt down discounted tickets.

You can generally get a good idea of what fares are available at the moment by looking in the classified section of the *South China Morning Post*.

Some budget return fares available in Hong Kong follow, but please note that these are discounted fares and certain restrictions (eg validity, routing) will apply.

There are few bargain airfares between Hong Kong and China as the government regulates the prices. Depending on the season, seats can be difficult to book due to the enormous volume of business travellers and Chinese tourists, so book well in advance. Some normal return fares valid for a year from Hong Kong are: Běijīng $2500; Chéngdū $2800; Guǎngzhōu $800; Kūnmíng $2300; and Shànghǎi $2000. One-way fares are half the return price.

You should be able to do better than that, however, on both scheduled flights and charters, especially in summer. To Běijīng, China Southern Airlines has a fixed return ticket for as low as $1600. An open ticket valid for 30 days on the same airline is $2200 and a 90-day one on Dragonair costs $3200. Group (just a few friends can make up a 'group') flights are available to Chéngdū for $2600. A direct flight to Lhasa in summer is $3500.

You can save at least 30% on those fares by flying from Guǎngzhōu or Shēnzhèn, in nearby Guǎngdōng province, rather than Hong Kong.

AIRLINES

Air New Zealand (NZ; Map pp500-2; ☎ 2862 8988; suite 1701, 17th fl, Jardine House, 1 Connaught Pl, Central)
British Airways (BA; Map pp500-2; ☎ 2822 9000; 24th fl, Jardine House, 1 Connaught Place, Central)
China Airlines (CI; Map pp500-2; ☎ 2868 2299; 3rd fl, St George's Bldg, 2 Ice House St, Central)
China Southern/China Eastern Airlines (CZ/MU; Map pp500-2; ☎ 2861 0322; 4th fl, CNAC Group Bldg, 10 Queen's Rd Central)
Dragonair (KA; Map pp500-2; ☎ 3193 3888; Room 4611, 4th fl; Cosco Tower, 183 Queen's Rd Central)
Northwest Airlines (NW; Map pp500-2; ☎ 2810 4288; room 1908, 19th fl, Cosco Tower, 183 Queen's Rd Central)

AIRFARES TO/FROM HONG KONG

Destination	Price
Bangkok	$1100-1600
Johannesburg	$6000
London	$4500
Los Angeles	$4500
Moscow	$4050
Seoul	$2300-2800
Singapore	$1300-2100
Sydney	$4000
Taipei	$1500-1700
Tokyo	$3000
Vancouver	$4000

WARNING

Rip-offs with flight tickets are not unknown here; be sure to use reputable travel agents (see p498) only.

Tickets are normally issued the day after booking, but you usually pick up the really cheap tickets (actually group fares) at the airport from the 'tour leader' just before the flight. Check these tickets carefully as there may be errors (eg the return portion of the ticket being valid for only 60 days when you paid – or thought you paid – for a ticket good for six months).

Qantas Airways (QF; Map pp500-2; ☎ 2822 9000; 24th fl, Jardine House, 1 Connaught Pl, Central)
Singapore Airlines (SQ; Map pp500-2; ☎ 2520 2233; 17th fl, United Centre, 95 Queensway, Admiralty)
United Airlines (UA; Map pp500-2; ☎ 2810 4888; 29th fl, Gloucester Tower, the Landmark, 11 Pedder St, Central)
Virgin Atlantic Airways (VS; Map pp500-2; ☎ 2532 6060; 8th fl, Alexandra House, 16-20 Chater Rd, Central)

DEPARTURE TAX

Hong Kong's airport departure tax – $120 for everyone over the age of 12 – is always included in the price of the ticket. Those travelling to Macau by helicopter (see p544) must pay the same amount.

Boat

Due to competition with road, rail and air transportation, boats between Hong Kong and other coastal cities in China have largely been phased out. However, regularly scheduled ferries link the **China ferry terminal** (Map pp506-7; Canton Rd, Tsim Sha Tsui) in Kowloon and/or the **Macau ferry pier** (Map pp500-2; 200 Connaught Rd Central) on Hong Kong Island with towns and cities on the Pearl River delta – but not central Guǎngzhōu or Shēnzhèn. For sea transport to/from Macau, see p544.

High-speed ferries run by **TurboJet** (☎ 2921 6688; www.turbojet.com.hk; $189; 1hr) leave the China ferry terminal for Fúyǒng ferry terminal (Shēnzhèn airport) six to eight times a day between 7.30am and 5.30pm. There are five or six return sailings from Fúyǒng ($171) starting at 9am with the last at 5pm. One boat a day leaves the Macau ferry pier at 8am. Return sailings are at 5.50pm, 7pm and 8.30pm.

CHRIS MELLOR

Although no longer in use in Hong Kong, rickshaws still make good photo subjects

MARTIN MOOS

JOHN HAY

Hong Kong Zoological & Botanical Gardens (p498)

The Bank of China skyscraper, towering over a colonial building on Hong Kong Island (p498)

The Star Ferry (p527) crossing Victoria Harbour

CHRIS MELLOR

Interior of Man Mo Temple (p499), with incense cones suspended from the ceiling, Hong Kong

Lanterns outside a restaurant in Soho (p521), Hong Kong

Ten Thousand Buddhas Monastery (p509) in Hong Kong

A junk on Victoria Harbour (p526), Hong Kong

Some 13 Jetcats run by **CMSE Passenger Transport** (☎ 2858 0909; day/night sailing $105/125; 1 hr) link Hong Kong daily with Shékǒu, 20km west of Shēnzhèn town. Seven of these leave from the China ferry terminal (between 7.45am and 7pm), while the rest go from the Macau ferry pier (9am to 9pm). Sailings from Shékǒu (day/night $90/110) are between 7.45am and 9.30pm.

Zhūhǎi can also be reached from Hong Kong on seven ferries a day from the China ferry terminal (from 7.30am to 5.30pm) and on the same number from the Macau ferry pier (8.40am to 9.30pm) on ferries operated by the **Chu Kong Passenger Transportation Co** (☎ 2858 3876; www.cksp.com.hk; $148; 70 min). The dozen return sailings from Zhūhǎi run between 8am and 9.30pm.

Chu Kong also has ferries from the China ferry terminal to a number of other ports in southern Guangdong province, including: Hǔmén (Tàipíng; $150, 90 minutes, three a day at 8am, 1.45pm and 5.30pm); Kāipíng ($170, four hours, 8.30am); Nánhǎi in Píngzhōu ($168, 2¾ hours, 8.05am and 2pm); Shùndé ($158, 110 minutes, six sailings between 7.30am and 6pm); Zhōngshān ($189, 90 minutes, eight or nine sailings from 8am to 8pm); and Zhàoqìng ($190, 3¾ hours, daily at 8.15am).

The $19 departure tax levied when leaving Hong Kong by sea is almost always included in the ticket price.

Bus

You can reach virtually any major destination in Guǎngdōng province by bus from Hong Kong. With KCR East Rail services so fast and cheap, however, few buses call on Shēnzhèn proper, though most of the big hotels run minivans to and from that destination for $100 one way. One-way fares from Hong Kong include: Chángshā ($280); Dōngguǎn ($100); Fóshān ($100); Guǎngzhōu ($100); Shàntóu ($200); Shēnzhèn airport ($110); Xiàmén ($350) and Zhōngshān ($130).

Buses in Hong Kong are run by a multitude of transport companies and depart from various locations around the territory; the list that follows is only a sampling of routes. Schedules vary enormously according to carrier and place, but buses leave throughout the day and departures are frequent.

CTS Express Coach (☎ 2365 0118; http://cts bus.hkcts.com) buses depart from locations throughout Hong Kong, including the CTS on Hong Kong Island (p498) and from Nelson St opposite the **CTS Mong Kok branch** (Map pp506-7; ☎ 2789 5882; 62-74 Sai Yee St) in Kowloon.

Eternal East Cross Border Coach (Map pp506-7; ☎ 2723 2923, 3412 6688; www.eebus.com; 13th fl, Kaiseng Commercial Centre, 4-6 Hankow Rd, Tsim Sha Tsui; ☾ 7am-8pm) buses leave from outside the Hang Lung Bank next door.

Motor Transport Company of Guangdong & Hong Kong (☎ 2317 7900; www.gdhkmtc.com) buses bound for destinations throughout Guangdong leave from the **Cross-Border Coach Terminus** (Map pp506-7; ☎ 2317 7900; ground fl, Hong Kong Scout Centre, 8 Austin Rd, Tsim Sha Tsui; ☾ 6.30am-7pm). The entrance is on Scout Path.

Trans-Island Limousine Service (☎ 3193 9333; www.trans-island.com.hk) cars and minivans leave from in front of the **Hotel Concourse Hong Kong** (Map pp506-7; ☎ 2397 6683; 22 Lai Chi Kok Rd, Mong Kok).

Train

Reaching Shēnzhèn by train is a breeze. Board the KCR East Rail train at Hung Hom in Kowloon (1st/2nd class $66/33, 35 minutes) or any KCR East Rail station along the way, and ride it to the China border crossing at Lo Wu. From Shēnzhèn you can take a local train or bus to Guǎngzhōu and beyond.

The most comfortable way to reach Guǎngzhōu by surface is via the Kowloon–Guǎngzhōu express train (usually via Dōngguǎn), which covers the 182km route in approximately 1¾ hours. They leave Hung Hom station for Guangzhou East train station 12 times a day between 7.30am and 7.15pm, returning from Guangzhou East the same number of times from 8.35am to 9.23pm. One-way tickets cost $230/190 in 1st/2nd class for adults and $115/95 for children under nine.

There are also direct rail links between Hung Hom and both Shànghǎi and Běijīng. Trains to Beijing (hard/soft sleeper $574/934, 24 hours) depart on alternate days at 3pm and travel via Guangzhou East, Chángshā and Wǔhàn, arriving at 3.18pm the next day. Trains to Shànghǎi (hard/soft sleeper $508/825, 23 hours) also depart on alternate days at 3pm and pass through

Guangzhou East and Hangzhou East stations, arriving at 1.38pm the next day.

There is one daily departure to Zhàoqìng (adult/child $235/117.50) via Dōngguǎn, Guangzhou East and Fóshān at 2.20pm, arriving in Zhàoqìng at 6.30pm. The train departs Zhàoqìng at 9.37am, reaching Hung Hom at 1.38pm.

Immigration formalities at Hung Hom are completed before boarding; you won't get on the train without a visa for China. Passengers are required to arrive at the station 45 minutes before departure. One-way and return tickets can be booked in advance from CTS (p498) and KCR East Rail stations in Hung Hom, Mong Kok, Kowloon Tong and Sha Tin. Tickets booked with a credit card by phone (☎ 2947 7888) must be collected at least one hour before departure.

GETTING AROUND
To/From the Airport
The Airport Express line of the MTR is the fastest – and most expensive – way to get to/from **Hong Kong International Airport** (☎ 2181 0000; www.hkairport.com) at Chek Lap Kok off the northern coast of Lantau; a gaggle of much cheaper buses connect it with Lantau, the New Territories, Kowloon and even Hong Kong Island.

Trains run by **Airport Express** (☎ 2881 8888; www.mtr.com.hk) depart from Hong Kong station (Map pp500–2) in Central every 10 minutes from 5.50am to 12.48am daily, calling at Kowloon station in Jordan and at Tsing Yi Island en route. The journey from Central/Kowloon/Tsing Yi takes 23/20/12 minutes and costs $100/90/60, with children three to 11 and seniors over 65 half price. Adult return fares, valid for a month, are $180/160/110. A same-day return is equivalent to a one-way fare.

Most areas of Hong Kong are linked to the airport by bus, of which there is an enormous choice. The most useful for travellers are the A11 ($40) and A12 ($45), which go past major hotel and guesthouse areas on Hong Kong Island, and the A21 ($33), which serves similar areas in Kowloon. These buses run from about 6am to midnight; the 'N' series of buses follows the same route after midnight.

Cheaper buses from the airport include the E11 ($21) to Hong Kong Island or the S1 ($3.50) to Tung Chung and then the MTR to Kowloon or Central.

A taxi from the airport to Central will cost about $335.

Bicycle
Cycling in built-up Kowloon or Central would be suicidal, but in quiet areas of the Outlying Islands or the New Territories, a bike can be a lovely way of getting around.

Flying Ball Bicycle Co (Map pp506-7; ☎ 2381 3661; 201 Tung Choi St, Mong Kok; ☿ 10am-8pm Mon-Sat, 10.30am-8pm Sun) is where serious cyclists will find a great selection of bicycles and cycling accessories.

At Silvermine Bay on Lantau Island, bicycles are available for hire ($10 per hour, $25/35 weekdays/weekend and overnight) at two central locations a short distance from the ferry pier: **Friendly Bicycle Shop** (Map pp496-7; ☎ 2984 2278; shop 12, Mui Wo Centre, 1 Ngan Wan Rd; ☿ 10am-8pm Wed-Mon), just opposite Wellcome supermarket, and **Bike King** (Map pp496-7; ☎ 2984 9761; shop B, ground fl, Silver Centre, 10 Mui Wo Ferry Pier Rd; 10am-9pm).

In the New Territories, bicycles can be rented in season from a kiosk within Sha Tin Park, as well as from several stalls around Tai Po Market KCR station and in Tai Mei Tuk.

Boat
With such a wide variety of ferries in Victoria Harbour, commuting by ferry is the most enjoyable (and surprisingly the cheapest) way of getting around.

CROSS-HARBOUR FERRIES
First launched in 1888 (see boxed text, opposite), the **Star Ferry** (☎ 2366 2576; www.starferry .com.hk) is as much a tourist attraction as a mode of transport. It operates on four routes, but the most popular one by far is the seven-minute run between Tsim Sha Tsui and Central.

Central–Hung Hom $5.50, 15 minutes, from Star Ferry Pier every 15 to 20 minutes 7.20am to 7.20pm Monday to Friday, every 20 minutes 7am to 7pm Saturday and Sunday.

Central–Tsim Sha Tsui $1.70/2.20 lower/upper deck, seven minutes, from Star Ferry Pier every four to 10 minutes 6.30am to 11.30pm.

Wan Chai–Hung Hom $5.30, 10 minutes, from Wan Chai Ferry Pier every 15 to 20 minutes 7.08am to 7.17pm Monday to Friday, 7.08am-7pm Saturday, every 20 to 22 minutes 7.08am to 7.10pm Sunday.

A STAR IS BORN

Star Ferry service between Pedder's Wharf (now reclaimed land) and Tsim Sha Tsui began in 1888 when boats sailed 'every 40 minutes to one hour during all hours of the day' except on Monday and Friday, when they were seconded for coal delivery. Service has continued ever since, with the only major suspension occurring during WWII.

The old workhorse has figured prominently during several periods of history. During the Japanese invasion in 1941 boats were used to evacuate refugees and Allied troops from the Kowloon Peninsula. And in 1966, when Communist China was locked in the grip of the so-called Cultural Revolution, agitators used the ferry company's proposed fare increase of 5c as a pretext for fomenting violent demonstrations.

Until the Cross-Harbour Tunnel opened in 1978 and the first line of the MTR two years later, the Star Ferry was the only way to cross the harbour by public transport.

Wan Chai–Tsim Sha Tsui $2.20, eight minutes, from Wan Chai Ferry Pier every eight to 20 minutes 7.30am to 11pm Monday to Saturday, every 12 to 20 minutes 7.40am to 11pm Sunday.

Three other companies run cross-harbour routes but about the only one of interest to travellers is the boat from Queen's Pier (Map pp500–2) in Central to Tsim Sha Tsui East, which runs every 20 minutes from 7.40am (from 8am Sunday) to 8.20pm and costs $4.50. It is run by the **Discovery Bay Transportation Service** (☎ 2987 7351; www.discoverybay.com.hk).

OUTLYING ISLANDS FERRIES

The main company serving the islands is **New World First Ferry** (☎ 2131 8181; www.nwff.com .hk), which runs services to Lantau, Cheung Chau and Peng Chau, and the **Hong Kong & Kowloon Ferry Co** (☎ 2815 6063; www.hkkf.com .hk), which serves destinations on Lamma only. Schedules are posted at all ferry piers and the ferry companies' websites. Fares are higher on so-called fast ferries and on Sunday and public holidays. Most ferries depart from the Outlying Islands ferry piers just west of the Star Ferry pier in Central, though there are some services at the weekend and on holidays from the Star Ferry pier in Tsim Sha Tsui to Lantau and Cheung Chau.

Car & Motorcycle

For a neophyte to consider driving in Hong Kong would be sheer madness. Traffic is heavy, the roads can get hopelessly clogged and the new system of highways and bridges is complicated in the extreme. But if you're hellbent on ruining your holiday, **Avis** (Map pp504–5; ☎ 2890 6988; fax 2895 0371; ground fl, Bright Star Mansion, 93 Leighton Rd, Causeway Bay; ☼ 8am-6pm Mon, 9am-6pm Tue-Fri, 9am-4pm Sat) will rent you a Toyota Corolla for the weekend (from 2pm on Friday to 10.30am Monday) for $1500; the same car costs $720/3200 for a day/week with unlimited kilometres.

Public Transport

TRAVEL & TRANSPORT PASSES

The **Octopus card** (☎ 2266 2266; www.octopuscards .com), a 'smart card' valid on most forms of public transport in Hong Kong, costs $150/100/70 for adults/students aged 12 to 25/children aged three to 11 and seniors over 65. The card includes a refundable deposit of $50. To add more money to your card, just go to one of the add-value machines or the ticket offices located at every MTR station. Octopus fares are between 5% and 10% cheaper than ordinary fares on the MTR, KCR, LRT and certain green minibuses.

The Airport Express Tourist Octopus card costs $220 (including $50 deposit) and allows one trip on the Airport Express, three days' unlimited travel on the MTR and $20 usable on other forms of transport. For $300 you get two trips on the Airport Express and the same benefits. For shorter stays there's the new Tourist MTR 1-Day Pass ($50), valid only on the MTR for 24 hours.

BUS

Hong Kong's extensive bus system will take you just about anywhere. The HKTB (p498) has useful leaflets on the major bus routes or try the **Yellow Pages Map website** (www.ypmap .com). Most buses run from about 5.30am or 6am until midnight or 12.30am, though there are a handful of night buses including the N121 (running from the Macau ferry pier bus terminus (Map pp500–2) on Hong Kong Island to Chatham Rd in Tsim Sha Tsui East and on to eastern Kowloon), the N122 (running from North Point on Hong

Kong Island to Nathan Rd and on to Lai Chi Kok in Kowloon) and the N112 (running from Percival St in Causeway Bay to the Prince Edward MTR station in Kowloon).

Fares range from $1.20 to $45, depending on the destination, with night buses costing from $12.80 to $23. You need to have exact change.

PUBLIC LIGHT BUSES

'Public light buses' (an official term that no one ever uses) are vans with no more than 16 seats. Small red 'minibuses' supplement the regular bus services and cost $2.50 to $20. They generally don't run regular routes, but you can get on or off almost anywhere – provided you can get the driver to stop. Pay as you exit.

Green 'maxicabs' are like minibuses except that they operate on some 325 set routes and make designated stops. Two popular routes are the No 6 from Hankow Rd in Tsim Sha Tsui to Tsim Sha Tsui East and Hung Hom station in Kowloon and the No 1 from east of the Star Ferry pier in Central for Victoria Peak on Hong Kong Island.

MASS TRANSIT RAILWAY (MTR)

The **Mass Transit Railway** (MTR; ☎ 2881 8888; www .mtr.com.hk) operates on six lines, including the Airport Express, on Hong Kong Island, Kowloon and the New Territories. It is fast and convenient, but fairly pricey and not great value for short journeys. Ticket prices range from $4 to $26 ($3.80 and $23.10 with an Octopus card). The ticket machines give change and single-journey tickets are valid only for the day they are purchased. Once you go past the turnstile, you must complete the journey within 90 minutes. The MTR operates from 6am to sometime between 12.30am and 1am.

KOWLOON-CANTON RAILWAY (KCR)

The **Kowloon-Canton Railway** (KCR; ☎ 2602 7799; www.kcrc.com) consists of two lines. KCR East Rail runs from Hung Hom station in Kowloon to Lo Wu, gateway to Shēnzhèn and the mainland. KCR West Rail, which opened in

late 2003, links Nam Cheong station in Sham Shui Po with Tuen Mun via Yuen Long. Eventually it will be linked to the station at Hung Hom via an extension of the KCR East Rail. The KCR offers excellent transport to the New Territories and some nice vistas. Trains run every five to eight minutes or every three minutes during rush hour. KCR fares are cheap, starting at $3.50, with a half-hour ride to Sheung Shui/Tuen Mun costing just $9/13 though the 40-minute trip to the border at Lo Wu is $33.

LIGHT RAIL TRANSIT (LRT)

The **Light Rail Transit** (LRT; ☎ 2468 7788; www.kcrc .com) operates on eight routes in the western part of the New Territories between Tuen Mun and Yuen Long and is now an important feeder service for the KCR West Rail. Fares are $4 to $5.80.

TRAM

Hong Kong's century-old trams, operated by **Hongkong Tramways Ltd** (☎ 2548 7102; www .info.gov.hk/td/eng/transport/tram.html), are tall and narrow double-decker streetcars, the only all double-deck wooden-sided tram fleet in the world. They operate on six overlapping routes on 16km of track running east–west along the northern side of Hong Kong Island. The tram is fun to travel on and a bargain at $2 for any distance travelled. You pay as you get off.

Taxi

On Hong Kong Island and Kowloon, the flag fall is $15 for the first 2km then $1.40 for every additional 200m. In the New Territories, flag fall is $12.50 and $1.20 for every subsequent 200m. On Lantau the equivalent charges are $12 and $1.20. There is a luggage fee of $5 per bag but, depending on the size, not all drivers insist on this. It also costs an extra $5 to book a taxi by telephone.

If you go through the Cross-Harbour Tunnel ($10) or the Eastern or Western Harbour Crossing ($15), you'll be charged double the toll unless you manage to find a cab heading back to its base.

Macau

HONG KONG & MACAU

HIGHLIGHTS

- Climb the majestic ruins of the **Church of St Paul** (p537), the very symbol of Macau

- Visit the incomparable **Macau Museum** (p536) at Monte Forte, a fascinating introduction to the territory

- Enjoy Portuguese or Macanese soul food with a bottle of *vinho verde* in **Taipa Village** (p541)

■ AREA CODE: ☎ 852   ■ POP: 448,500 MIL   ■ AREA: 27.3 SQ KM

Lying 65km west of Hong Kong, on the opposite side of the mouth of the Pearl River, tiny Macau, measuring just 27.3 sq km, was the oldest European settlement in Asia when it reverted to Chinese sovereignty in December 1999. With about 2% of its residents Portuguese, some 95% of them Chinese and the rest Macanese (people with mixed Portuguese, Chinese and/or African blood), Macau is a fascinating fusion of Mediterranean and Asian peoples, lifestyles, temperaments, architecture and food.

Portuguese galleons visited Macau in the early 16th century. In 1557, as a reward for clearing out pirates endemic to the area, China allowed the Portuguese to establish a tiny enclave here, and for centuries Macau was the principal meeting point for trade with China. However, after the Opium War between the Chinese and the British and the establishment of Hong Kong, Macau went into decline.

China's Cultural Revolution spilled over into the territory in 1966–67. The government reportedly proposed that Portugal should leave Macau forever but, fearing the loss of foreign trade, the Chinese refused the offer.

In 1999, under the Sino-Portuguese Pact, Macau was returned to China and designated a Special Administrative Region (SAR). Like Hong Kong, Macau is to continue to enjoy a 'high degree of autonomy' in all matters except defence and foreign affairs for 50 years.

While Macau is a popular destination for Hong Kong residents lured by the city's many casinos (particularly the new Las Vegas-style ones), it has much more to offer than just gambling. Macau is a colourful palette of pastels and ordered greenery – a city of cobbled back streets, baroque churches, ancient stone fortresses and restful parks and gardens. You will also find many world-class museums, as well as some excellent hotels and restaurants.

While both Cantonese and Portuguese are official languages, Cantonese is by far the more widely spoken.

ORIENTATION

Most of Macau's sights are on the peninsula jutting down from Zhūhǎi on the mainland. Avenida de Almeida Ribeiro (San Ma Lo, or 'New St', in Cantonese), running from Avenida da Praia Grande to the Inner Harbour, is Macau's main street. Its extension, Avenida do Infante Dom Henrique, runs south to the Outer Harbour.

South of here are the islands of Taipa and Coloane, joined together by an ever-widening causeway and connected to the mainland by bridges.

Maps

The Macau Government Tourist Office (MGTO) distributes the excellent (and free) *Macau Tourist Map*, with all the major tourist sights and streets labelled in Portuguese and also in Chinese characters. Small inset maps also highlight the Taipa and Coloane areas and show details of Macau's bus routes.

INFORMATION

The **Macau Museums Pass** (adult/child under 18 & senior MOP$25/12) allows entry to a half-dozen of Macau's most important museums over a five-day period.

Emergency

In the event of an emergency, dial ☎ 999. You can also reach the police on ☎ 573 333 and the fire services on ☎ 572 222.

Internet Access
Team Spirit (Map p535; ☎ 355 859; 102a Rua dos Mercadores; per hr MOP$10; ☻ 24hr)
Unesco Internet Café (Map pp532-3; ☎ 727 066; Alameda Doutor Carlos d'Assumpção; per 30/60 min MOP$5/10; ☻ noon-8pm Wed-Mon)

Medical Services
Macau's two hospitals both have 24-hour emergency services.
Centro Hospitalar Conde São Januário (Map pp532-3; ☎ 313 731; Estrada do Visconde de São Januário) Southwest of the Guia Fort.
Hospital Kiang Wu (Map pp532-3; ☎ 371 333; Rua de Coelho do Amaral) Northeast of the ruins of the Church of St Paul.

Money
ATMS
You will find ATMs everywhere, especially just outside the Lisboa Hotel, where you'll find half a dozen. Most allow you to choose between patacas and Hong Kong dollars.

CURRENCY
Macau's currency is the pataca (MOP$), which is divided into 100 avos. Bills are issued in denominations of MOP$10, MOP$20, MOP$50, MOP$100, MOP$500 and MOP$1000. There are little copper coins worth 10, 20 and 30 avos and silver-coloured MOP$1, MOP$2, MOP$5 and MOP$10.

CHANGING MONEY
The pataca is pegged to the Hong Kong dollar (see p495) and exchange rates are virtually the same.

Hong Kong dollars, including coins, are readily accepted throughout Macau and, in big hotels, restaurants and department stores, your change will be returned in that currency. Try to use up all your patacas before departing Macau.

You can change cash and travellers cheques at the banks lining Avenida da Praia Grande and Avenida de Almeida Ribeiro as well as at all major hotels.

Major credit cards are readily accepted at Macau's hotels, larger restaurants and casinos.

COSTS
Macau is generally much cheaper than Hong Kong. If possible, avoid visiting at the weekend when hotel prices increase substantially and ferries cost more.

As in China, tipping is not expected, though a gratuity offered will not be refused. Top-end hotels add a 10% service charge and a 5% tourism tax to their room rates.

Most stores have fixed prices, but clothing, trinkets and curios from the street markets offer some scope for bargaining.

Post
Main post office (Map p535; ☎ 323 666; Avenida de Almeida Ribeiro; ☻ 9am-6pm Mon-Fri, 9am-1pm Sat); ferry terminal branch (Map pp532-3; ☎ 396 8526; ☻ 10am-7pm Mon-Sat). Little red vending machines dispense stamps throughout Macau. *Poste restante* service is available at counter Nos 1 and 2 of the main post office.

Telephone
Companhia de Telecomunicações de Macau (CTM; Map p535; inquiry hotline ☎ 1000; www.ctm.net; Kam Loi Bldg, 22 Rua do Doutor Pedro José Lobo; ☻ 10.30am-7.30pm), with a branch north of the Lisboa Hotel, is Macau's main telephone company.

Local calls are free from private phones and most hotel telephones, while at a public pay phones they cost MOP$1 for five minutes. All pay phones permit International Direct Dialling (IDD) using a phonecard available from CTM for between MOP$50 and MOP$200. Rates are cheaper from 9pm to 8am during the week and all day Saturday and Sunday.

The international access code is ☎ 00. For Hong Kong, dial ☎ 01 then the number; you do not have to dial Hong Kong's country code (☎ 852). To call Macau from abroad – including from Hong Kong – the country code is ☎ 853.

Some useful phone numbers in Macau include:
Local directory assistance ☎ 185
International directory assistance ☎ 101
Time (in English) ☎ 140

Tourist Information
Macau Government Tourist Office (MGTO; Map p535; ☎ 315 566, ☎ 397 1120, tourist hotline ☎ 333 000; www.macautourism.gov.mo; 9 Largo do Senado; ☻ 9am-6pm); ferry terminal branch (Map pp532-3; ☎ 726 416; ☻ 9am-10pm) Knowledgeable, helpful staff dispense themed leaflets on Macau's sights and bilingual maps with a list of public bus routes. The MGTO also maintains tourist offices in **Hong Kong** (☎ 2857 2287; rm 336-337 Shun Tak Centre, 200 Connaught Rd, Sheung Wan;

HONG KONG & MACAU

MACAU PENINSULA

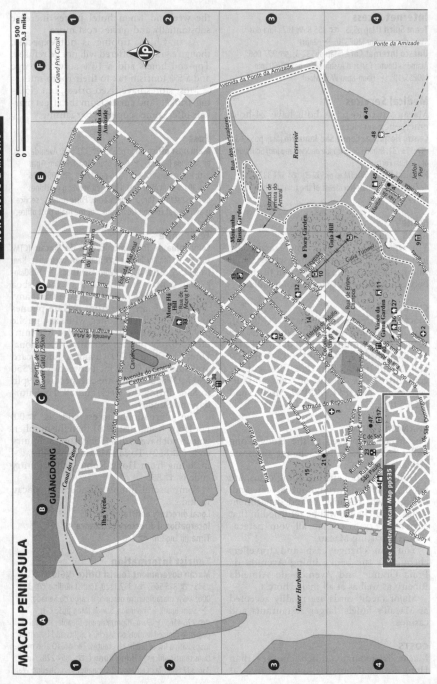

Grand Prix Circuit

See Central Macau Map pp535

HONG KONG & MACAU

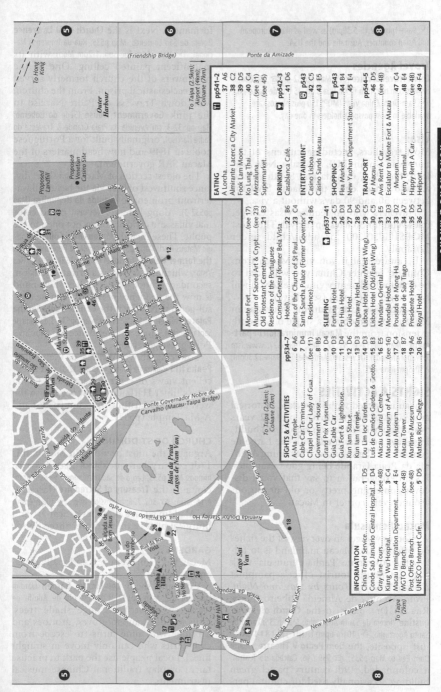

(Friendship Bridge)

Ponte da Amizade

To Taipa (2.5km);
Airport (4km);
Coloane (7km)

Outer
Harbour

To Hong
Kong

Proposed
Venetian
Casino Site

Proposed
Landfill

Ponte Governador Nobre de
Carvalho (Macau-Taipa Bridge)

To Taipa (2.5km);
Coloane (7km)

Baía da Praia
(Lagos de Van Van)

Lago Sai
Van

New Macau - Taipa Bridge

To Taipa
(2km)

EATING pp541–2
A Lorcha............................37 A6
Almirante Lacerca City Market...38 C2
Fook Lam Moon....................39 D5
Ko Lung Thai......................40 C4
Mezzaluna........................(see 31)
Supermarket.....................(see 45)

DRINKING p543
Casablanca Café...................41 D6

ENTERTAINMENT p543
Casino Lisboa.....................42 C5
Casino Sands Macau...............43 E5

SHOPPING p543
Flea Market.......................44 B4
Fu Hua Market....................45 E4
New Yaohan Department Store....(see 48)

TRANSPORT pp544–5
Air Macau.........................46 D5
Avis Rent A Car..................(see 48)
Escalator to Monte Fort & Macau
Museum..........................47 C4
Ferry Terminal....................48 E4
Happy Rent A Car.................(see 48)
Heliport.........................49 F4

Monte Fort.......................(see 17)
Museum of Sacred Art & Crypt....(see 23)
Old Protestant Cemetery...........21 B3
Residence of the Portuguese
Consul-General (former Bela Vista
Hotel)...........................22 B6
Ruins of the Church of St Paul.....23 C4
Santa Sancha Palace (Former Governor's
Residence).......................24 B6

SLEEPING pp537–41
Fortuna Hotel.....................25 C5
Guia Hotel........................27 D4
Hou Hua Hotel....................26 D3
Kingsway Hotel....................28 D5
Lisboa Hotel (New/West Wing).....29 C5
Lisboa Hotel (Old/East Wing)......30 C5
Mandarin Oriental.................31 E5
Mondial Hotel.....................32 D3
Pousada de Mong Há...............33 D2
Pousada de Saõ Tiago.............34 A7
Presidente Hotel..................35 A6
Royal Hotel.......................36 D4

SIGHTS & ACTIVITIES pp534–7
A-Ma Temple......................6 A6
Cable Car Terminus................7 D4
Chapel of Our Lady of Gua.........8 B5
Government House.................9 D4
Grand Prix Museum................10 D3
Guia Cable Car...................11 D4
Guia Fort & Lighthouse............12 D6
Kun Iam Statue...................13 D3
Kun Iam Temple...................14 D3
Lou Lim Ioc Garden...............15 B3
Luís de Camões Garden & Grotto...16 E5
Macau Cultural Centre............(see 16)
Macau Museum of Art..............17 C4
Macau Museum....................18 B7
Macau Tower......................19 A6
Maritime Museum.................(see 48)
Mateus Ricci College..............20 B6

INFORMATION
China Travel Service................1 D5
Conde Saõ Januário Central Hospital..2 D4
Gray Line Tours...................(see 48)
Kiang Wu Hospital.................3 C4
Macau Immigration Department......4 C4
MCTO Branch......................5 D5
Post Office Branch................(see 48)
UNESCO Internet Cafe

Ⓨ 9am-1pm & 2.15-5.30pm) as well as many European and Asian countries, Australia and the USA.

Travel Agencies

China Travel Service (CTS; Map pp532-3; ☎ 700 888; cts@cts.com.mo; 10th fl, Xin Hua Bldg, 35 Rua de Nagasaki; Ⓨ 9am-5pm) China visas (MOP$150 plus photos) are available to most passport-holders in one day.

Visas

Most travellers, including citizens of the European Union (EU), Australia, New Zealand, the USA, Canada and South Africa, are allowed to enter the Macau SAR for between 30 and 90 days without a visa.

Travellers who do require visas can get ones valid for 30 days on arrival. They cost MOP$100/50/200 for adult/child under 12/family.

Be aware that if you visit Macau from China to re-enter China you will need to be on a multiple-entry visa, or else you will have to get a new visa (see above).

If your visa expires during your stay in Macau, you can obtain a single one-month extension from the **Macau Immigration Department** (Map pp532-3; ☎ 725 488, 798 5327; www.fsm .gov.mo; ground fl, Travessa da Amizade; Ⓨ 9am-12.30pm, 2.30-5pm Mon-Fri).

SIGHTS & ACTIVITIES

Macau is packed with important historical and cultural sights. In the past 12 years more than half of Macau's significant buildings have been restored, with the Largo de Senado and the splendid villas lining Avenida da Praia Grande being good examples. It's no exaggeration to say that you'll discover something pretty or old or curious around every corner in Macau.

Macau Peninsula

A good way to get an overview of the riches on offer on the Macau mainland is to follow the 90-minute 'Penha Peninsula' walk outlined in the tourist office's pamphlet *Macau Walking Tours by Day and Night*. From Avenida de Almeida Ribeiro follow Rua do Dr Soares to the **Church of St Augustine** (Igreja de Santo Agostinho; Map p535; Largo de Santo Agostinho; Ⓨ 10am-6pm) built in 1814 and, just opposite, the **Dom Pedro V Theatre** (Teatro Dom Pedro; Map p535; ☎ 939 646; Calçada do Teatro), a colonnaded, 19th-century pastel green building occasionally used for cultural per-

formances. Next is the **Church of St Lawrence** (Igreja de São Lourenço; Map p535; Rua da Imprensa Nacional; Ⓨ 10am-6pm Tue-Sun, 1-2pm Mon) with its magnificent painted ceiling. One of the two towers of the church formerly served as an ecclesiastical prison. From the church, walk down Travessa do Padre Narciso to the pink **Government House** (Sede do Goberno; Map pp532-3; cnr Avenida da Praia Grande & Travessa do Padré Narciso), originally built for a Portuguese noble in 1849 and now headquarters of the Macau SAR government.

The oldest section of Macau is a short distance southwest of here via the beautiful waterfront promenade **Avenida da República** (Map pp532-3). Along here are several grand colonial villas and civic buildings not open to the public. These include **Mateus Ricci College** (Colégio Mateus Ricci; Map pp532-3; Avenida da República) and the **former Bela Vista Hotel** (Map pp532-3; Rua do Boa Vista), which has served as a private mansion, secondary school, WWII refugee shelter and is now the residence of the Portuguese consul-general. Nearby is the ornate **Santa Sancha Palace** (Palacete de Santa Sancha; Map pp532-3; Estrada de Santa Sancha), once the residence of Macau's Portuguese governors.

Towering above Avenida da República, **Penha Hill** (Colina da Penha; Map pp532-3) offers excellent views of central Macau and China across Inner Harbour. Below the hill to the west are the Maritime Museum (p536) and A-Ma Temple (p537).

CHURCH OF ST DOMINIC

Arguably the most beautiful in Macau, this 17th-century baroque **church** (Igreja de São Domingos; Map p535; Largo de São Domingos; Ⓨ 8am-5pm) contains the **Treasury of Sacred Art** (Tesouro de Arte Sacra; ☎ 367 706; admission free; Ⓨ 10am-6pm), an Aladdin's Cave of ecclesiastical art and liturgical plates exhibited over three floors.

GARDENS

Macau has a number of exceptionally pleasant gardens.

Cool and shady **Lou Lim Ioc Garden** (Jardim Lou Lim Ioc; Map pp532-3; 10 Estrada de Adolfo de Loureiro; Ⓨ 6am-9pm) has huge shade trees, lotus ponds, bamboo groves, grottoes and a bridge with nine turns (to escape from evil spirits who can only move in straight lines). Local people use the park to practise taichi or play traditional Chinese musical instruments.

CENTRAL MACAU

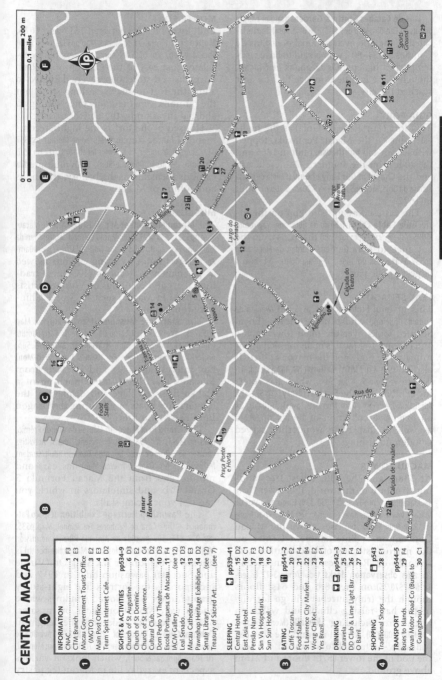

INFORMATION	
CNAC	1 F3
CTM Branch	2 E3
Macau Government Tourist Office (MGTO)	3 E2
Main Post Office	4 E3
Team Spirit Internet Cafe	5 D2

SIGHTS & ACTIVITIES	pp534–9
Church of St Augustine	6 D3
Church of St Dominic	7 E2
Church of St Lawrence	8 C4
Cultural Club	9 D2
Dom Pedro V Theatre	10 D3
Escola Portuguesa de Macau	11 F4
IACM Gallery	(see 12)
Leal Senado	12 D3
Macau Cathedral	13 E3
Pawnshop Heritage Exhibition	14 D2
Senate Library	(see 12)
Treasury of Sacred Art	(see 7)

SLEEPING	pp539–41
Central Hotel	15 D2
East Asia Hotel	16 C1
Pensão Nam In	17 F3
San Va Hospedaria	18 C2
Sun Sun Hotel	19 C2

EATING	pp541–2
Caffé Toscana	20 F2
Food Stalls	21 F4
St Lawrence City Market	22 B4
Wong Chi Kei	23 E2
Yes Brazil	24 E1

DRINKING	pp542–3
Caravela	25 F4
DD Club & Lime Light Bar	26 F4
O Barril	27 F4

SHOPPING	p43
Traditional Shops	28 E1

TRANSPORT	pp544–5
Buses to Islands	29 F4
Kwan Motor Road Co (Buses to Guangzhou)	30 C1

Luís de Camões Grotto & Gardens (Jardim e Gruta de Luís de Camões; Map pp532-3; ☉ 6am-9pm) is dedicated to the one-eyed national poet Luís de Camões (1524-80), who is said to have written part of his epic *Os Lusiadas* in Macau, though there is little evidence that he ever reached the city.

GUIA FORT

This fort (Fortaleza de Guía) is the highest point on the Macau Peninsula, topped with a 15m-tall **lighthouse**, built in 1865 and the oldest on the southern Chinese coast, and the **Chapel of Our Lady of Guia** (Capela de Nossa Señora da Guia; Map pp532-3; ☉ 9.30am-5.30pm), built in 1622.

The easiest way up is to hop on the little **Guia Cable Car** (Teleférico da Guia; one way/return MOP$2/3; ☉ 9am-6pm Tue-Sun) that runs from the entrance to **Flora Gardens** (Jardim da Flora; Map pp532-3; Travessa do Túnel; ☉ 9am-6pm), Macau's largest public park.

LEAL SENADO

This **graceful building** (Map p535; 163 Avenida de Almeida Ribeiro), whose name means 'Loyal Senate', looks over the main town square and is home to Macau's main municipal administrative body and the mayor's office. It also houses the **IACM Gallery** (☎ 387 333; admission free; ☉ 9am-9pm Tue-Sun), which has rotating exhibits, and the **Senate Library** (☎ 572 233; admission free; ☉ 1-7pm Mon-Sat), which houses an extensive collection of books on Asia as well as displaying wonderful, carved wooden furnishings.

MACAU TOWER

At 338m and the 10th tallest freestanding structure in the world, this **tower** (Torre de Macau; Map pp532-3; ☎ 933 339; Largo da Torre de Macau; www.macautower.com.mo; ☉ 10am-9pm Mon-Fri, 9am-9pm Sat & Sun) rises above the Macau Convention & Entertainment Centre on the narrow isthmus of land southeast of Avenida da República. You can ascend to the **observation decks** (adult/child 3-12 & senior MOP$70/35) on the 58th and 61st floors though the truly intrepid will go for any of the hair-raising climbs and walks on offer here, including **Skywalk** (Mon-Fri/Sat & Sun MOP$100/120), a twirl around the covered walkway – attached to a lanyard – under the pod of the tower (57th floor) and 216m above ground.

MONTE FORT

Built by the Jesuits between 1617 and 1626, **Monte Fort** (Fortaleza do Monte; Map pp532-3; ☉ 6am-7pm May-Sep, 7am-6pm Oct-Apr) is accessible by escalator just east of the Church of St Paul. Barracks and storehouses were designed to allow the fort to survive a long siege, but the cannons were fired only once: during an aborted invasion by the Dutch in 1622.

Housed in the fort is the highly recommended **Macau Museum** (Museu de Macau; ☎ 357 911; adult/child under 11 & senior MOP$15/8, free on 15th of month; ☉ 10am-6pm Tue-Sun), with multimedia exhibits focusing on the history, traditions and culture of Macau.

MUSEUMS

The **Macau Museum of Art** (Museu de Arte de Macau; Map pp532-3; ☎ 791 9800; Macau Cultural Centre, Avenida Xian Xing Hai; adult/child/senior MOP$5/3/free; ☉ 10am-7pm Tue-Sun) houses visiting exhibits as well as permanent collections of Chinese traditional art and paintings by Western artists who lived in Macau, such as George Chinnery (opposite).

The **Maritime Museum** (Museu Marítimo; Map pp532-3; ☎ 595 481; 1 Largo do Pagode da Barra; adult/child 10-17 MOP$10/5 Mon & Wed-Sat, MOP$5/3 Sun, under 10 & over 65 free; ☉ 10am-5.30pm Wed-Mon) has interesting boats and artefacts from Macau's seafaring past, a mock-up of a Hakka fishing village and displays of the long narrow boats raced during the Dragon Boat Festival in June.

The **Grand Prix Museum** (Museu do Grande Prémio; Map pp532-3; ☎ 798 4130; basement, Tourist Activities Centre, 431 Rua de Luís Gonzaga Gomes; adult/student MOP$10/5; ☉ 10am-6pm Wed-Mon) has cars and motorcycles from the Macau Formula 3 Grand Prix and simulators in which you can test your racing skills.

The **Pawnshop Heritage Exhibition** (Espaço Patrimonial – Uma Casa de Penhores Tradicional; Map p535; ☎ 921 811; 396 Avenida de Almeida Ribeiro; admission MOP$5; ☉ 10.30am-7pm, closed 1st Mon of the month) is housed in the former Tak Seng On (Virtue and Success) pawnshop built in 1917 and incorporates the fortress-like eight-storey granite tower with slotted windows where goods were stored on racks or in safes. Sharing the same building is the delightful **Cultural Club** (Clube Cultural; ☎ 921 811; 390 Avenida de Almeida Ribeiro; admission free; ☉ 10.30am-7pm Mon-Fri, 10.30am-8pm Sat & Sun), which looks at various aspects of everyday life in Macau (eg pastry making) on three floors. There's also an exhibition gallery and a lovely teahouse.

OLD PROTESTANT CEMETERY

As church law forbade the burial of non-Catholics on hallowed ground, this **cemetery** (Antigo Cemitério Protestante; Map pp532-3; 15 Praça de Luís de Camões; ☉ 8.30am-5.30pm) was established in 1821 as the last resting place of (mostly Anglophone) Protestants. Among those interred here are the Irish-born artist George Chinnery (1774–1852), who spent most of his adult life in Macau painting, Robert Morrison (1782–1834), the first Protestant missionary to China and author of the first Chinese-English dictionary, and Lord John Spencer Churchill (1797–1840), great-great uncle of Winston.

RUINS OF THE CHURCH OF ST PAUL

The façade and majestic stairway are all that remain of the **Church of St Paul** (Ruinas de Igreja de São Paulo; Map pp532-3; Rua de São Paulo), built in the early 17th century. However, with its wonderful statues, portals and engravings that effectively make up a 'sermon in stone', some consider it to be the greatest monument to Christianity in Asia.

The church was designed by an Italian Jesuit and built in 1602 by Japanese refugees who had fled anti-Christian persecution in Nagasaki. After the expulsion of the Jesuits from Macau in 1762, a military battalion was stationed here. In 1835 a fire erupted in the kitchen of the barracks, destroying everything except what you see today.

The small **Museum of Sacred Art** (Museu de Arte Sacra; Rua de São Paulo; admission free; ☉ 9am-6pm) behind the ruins contains polychrome carved wooden statues, silver chalices, monstrances and oil paintings. The adjoining **crypt** *(cripta)* contains the remains of Vietnamese and Japanese Christians martyred in the 17th century.

TEMPLES

A-Ma Temple (Templo de A-Ma; Map pp532-3; Rue de São Tiago da Barra; ☉ 10am-6pm), almost opposite the Maritime Museum and facing the Inner Harbour, was probably already standing when the Portuguese arrived, although the present one may only date back to the 16th century. The temple is dedicated to A-Ma, better known as Tin Hau (see right). The boat people of Macau come here on a pilgrimage each year in late April or early May.

Dating back four centuries, **Kun Iam Temple** (Templo de Kun Iam; Map pp532-3; Avenida do Coronel Mesquita; ☉ 7am-6pm) is Macau's oldest and most interesting temple. The likeness of Kun Iam, the goddess of mercy, is in the main hall; to the left of the altar and behind glass is a bearded statue believed to represent Marco Polo. The first treaty of trade and friendship between the USA and China was signed in the temple's terraced gardens in the east wing in 1844.

The Islands   Map p538

Connected to the Macau mainland by two (soon to be three) bridges and joined together by an area of reclaimed land called Cotai, Coloane and, to a lesser extent, Taipa are oases of calm and greenery, with striking, pastel-coloured colonial villas, quiet lanes and some decent beaches. There's ample opportunity for walking and cycling, and the Portuguese and Macanese restaurants of Taipa Village are worth the trip alone.

TAIPA

Traditionally an island of duck farms and boat yards, Taipa (Tam Chai in Cantonese)

WHAT'S IN A NAME?

The name 'Macau' is derived from the name of the goddess A-Ma, better known as Tin Hau. At the southwestern tip of Macau Peninsula stands the A-Ma Temple; many people believe that when the Portuguese first arrived on this spot and asked the name of the place, they were told 'A-Ma Gau' (bay of A-Ma).

According to legend, A-Ma, a poor girl looking for passage to Canton (now Guǎngzhōu), was turned away by wealthy junk owners. Instead, a poor fisherman took her on board; shortly afterward a storm blew up, wrecking all the junks but leaving the fishing boat unscathed. When it returned to the Inner Harbour, A-Ma walked to the top of nearby Barra Hill and, in a glowing aura of light, ascended to heaven. In her honour, the fisherman built a temple on the spot where they had landed.

In modern Cantonese, 'Macau' is Ou Mun, meaning 'gateway of the bay'.

HONG KONG & MACAU

THE ISLANDS – TAIPA & COLOANE

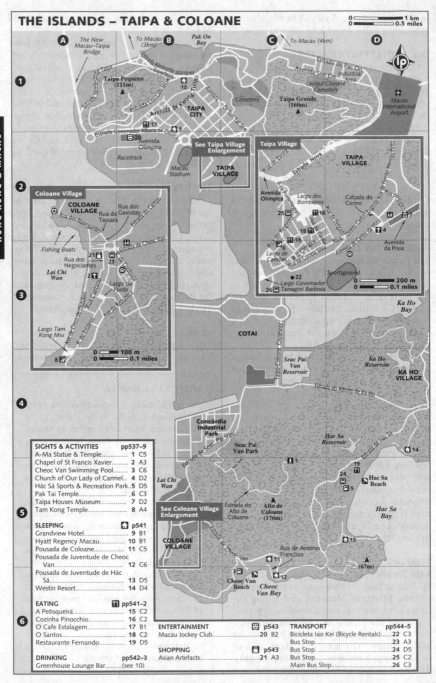

SIGHTS & ACTIVITIES	pp537–9
A-Ma Statue & Temple	1 C5
Chapel of St Francis Xavier	2 A3
Cheoc Van Swimming Pool	3 C6
Church of Our Lady of Carmel	4 D2
Hác Sá Sports & Recreation Park	5 D5
Pak Tai Temple	6 C3
Taipa Houses Museum	7 D2
Tam Kong Temple	8 A4

SLEEPING	p541
Grandview Hotel	9 B1
Hyatt Regency Macau	10 B1
Pousada de Coloane	11 C5
Pousada de Juventude de Cheoc Van	12 C6
Pousada de Juventude de Hác Sá	13 D5
Westin Resort	14 D4

EATING	pp541–2
A Petisqueira	15 C2
Cozinha Pinocchio	16 C2
O Cafe Estalagem	17 B1
O Santos	18 C2
Restaurante Fernando	19 D5

DRINKING	pp542–3
Greenhouse Lounge Bar	(see 10)

ENTERTAINMENT	p543
Macau Jockey Club	20 B2

SHOPPING	p543
Asian Artefacts	21 A3

TRANSPORT	pp544–5
Bicicleta Iao Kei (Bicycle Rentals)	22 C3
Bus Stop	23 A3
Bus Stop	24 D5
Bus Stop	25 C2
Main Bus Stop	26 C3

is rapidly becoming urbanised and now boasts major hotels, a university, a racecourse and stadium, high-rise apartments and an airport. But a parade of baroque churches and buildings, Taoist and Buddhist temples, overgrown esplanades and lethargic settlements mean it's still possible to experience the traditional charms of the island.

Taipa Village, in the south-central part of the island, is a window to the island's past. Here you'll find the stately **Taipa Houses Museum** (Casas – Museu da Taipa; ☎ 825 314, 827 103; Avenida da Praia; adult/child under 10 & senior MOP$5/free, free on Sun; ☯ 10am-6pm Tue-Sun) housed in five lime-green waterfront villas, which gives a good sense of how the Macanese middle class lived in the early 20th century. Also in the village is the **Church of Our Lady of Carmel** (Igreja de Nossa Senhora de Carmo; Rue da Restauração; ☯ 10am-8pm), built in 1885, and three small temples, including **Pak Tai Temple** (Templo Pak Tai; Rua do Regedor). The village **market** is at the end of Rua do Regedor.

You can rent bicycles in Taipa Village from **Bicicleta Iao Kei** (☎ 827 975; 36 Largo Governador Tamagini Barbosa; MOP$12-18 per hr).

COLOANE
A haven for pirates until the start of the 20th century, Coloane (Lo Wan in Cantonese) now attracts large numbers of tourists eager to explore its sleepy main fishing village and enjoy its sandy coastline. In **Coloane Village** you'll find the main attraction, the **Chapel of St Francis Xavier** (Capela de São Francisco Xavier; Avenida de Cinco de Outubro; ☯ 10am-8pm) built in 1928. In front of the chapel is a monument surrounded by four cannonballs commemorating the successful – and final – routing of pirates in 1910. There are three interesting temples in the village, including the **Tam Kong Temple** (Templo Tam Kong; Largo Tam Kong Miu) dedicated to the Taoist god of seafarers.

About 1.5km southeast of the Coloane Village is **Cheoc Van Beach**, where you can swim in the ocean or in the **outdoor pool** (☎ 870 277; adult/child MOP$15/5; ☯ 10am-9pm Mon, 8am-9pm Tue-Fri & Sun, 8am-11pm Sat). Larger and more popular is **Hac Sa Beach** to the northeast. The **Hac Sa Sports & Recreation Park** (☎ 882 296; ☯ 8am-9pm Sun-Fri, 8am-11pm Sat) offers everything from a swimming pool to tennis courts and mini-golf.

TOURS
Quality Tours, coach trips organised by the MGTO and tendered to such agents as **Gray Line** (Map pp532-3; ☎ 336 611; ground fl, rm 1015, Macau ferry terminal; adult/child 2-9 MOP$98/78), depart in both the morning and the afternoon and take four to five hours.

The Tour Machine, run by **Avis Rent A Car** (Map pp532-3; ☎ 336 789; ground fl, rm 1022, Macau ferry terminal; adult/child under 12 MOP$150/80), is a replica 1920s-style English bus that seats nine people and runs on fixed routes lasting about two hours and taking in some of Macau's most important sights. There are departures at 11am and 3pm from the Macau ferry terminal.

FESTIVALS & EVENTS
The mixing of two very different cultures and religious traditions for over 400 years has left Macau with a unique collection of holidays, festivals and cultural events.

Key annual events include the **Macau Arts Festival** in March, the **International Fireworks Display Contest** in September, the **International Music Festival** in October and November and the **Macau Marathon** in early December. But the biggest event of the year is the **Macau Formula 3 Grand Prix** on the third weekend in November, when the city's streets become a racetrack for 30 national championship drivers.

Some of the highlights of Chinese and Portuguese religious festivals and holidays are:
Lunar New Year As elsewhere in China, the lunar New Year (or Spring Festival) is a three-day public holiday in late January or early February.
Procession of the Passion of Our Lord A colourful procession in February bears a statue of Jesus Christ from the Church of St Augustine Church through the streets to Macau Cathedral.
Feast of the Drunken Dragon In mid-May, people who make their living by fishing close up shop and take a break to enjoy three days of drinking and feasting. Watch for dancing dragons in the streets.
Dragon Boat Festival As in Hong Kong, this is a major public holiday held in June.

SLEEPING
Be advised that on Saturday night and the eve of a public holiday hotels are often fully booked and room rates can be double or even treble weekday rates.

Discounts of 30% or more are available if you book through a travel agency, but this usually only applies to hotels of three stars and above. In Hong Kong you'll find a lot of these agents at the **Shun Tak Centre** (200 Connaught Rd, Sheung Wan) from where the ferries to Macau depart. There are also hotel desks in the arrivals hall of the Macau ferry terminal.

Macau Peninsula

Hotels on the mainland are generally split geographically into price constituencies, with many cheap guesthouses and hotels occupying the southwestern part of the peninsula, around Rua das Lorchas and Avenida de Almeida Ribeiro, and top end hotels generally in the east and centre of town.

BUDGET

East Asia Hotel (Map p535; ☎ 922 433; fax 922 430; 1a Rua da Madeira; s MOP$260-340, d MOP$400-500, tr MOP$500) This 98-room hotel is housed in a classic colonial-style building and, though it's been remodelled, it has not lost all of its charm.

Mondial Hotel (Map pp532-3; ☎ 566 866; fax 514 083; 8-10 Rua de António Basto; s & d Sun-Fri HK$380, Sat HK$450-600). This hotel is on the eastern side of peaceful Lou Lim Ioc Garden.

San Va Hospedaria (Map p535; ☎ 573 701; info@sanvahotel.com; 67 Rua de Felicidade; s MOP$60-85, d MOP$70-150) On the 'Street of Happiness' that was once the hub of the red-light district, this traditional-style place has character, though the rooms are like cupboards and separated by flimsy cardboard partitions.

Central Hotel (Map p535; ☎ 373 888; fax 332 275; 264 Avenida de Almeida Ribeiro; s Sun-Fri MOP$150-188, Sat MOP$173-210, d Sun-Fri MOP$160-198, Sat MOP$210-232) This tired old place has seen better days, but it is just what its name suggests.

Pensão Nam In (Map p535; ☎ 710 024; fax 711 127; 3 Travessa da Praia Grande; s/d MOP$150/200) In a little alley south of the Avenida da Praia Grande, this tiny pension has singles with shared bath and pleasant doubles with private bath.

MID-RANGE

Royal Hotel (Map pp532-3; ☎ 552 222; www.hotel royal.com.mo; 2-4 Estrada da Vitória; s & d MOP$750-1100, ste from MOP$2200) This large hotel is a bit removed from the action but has great week-day packages.

Guia Hotel (Map pp532-3; ☎ 513 888; guia@macau .ctm.net; 1-5 Estrada do Engenheiro Trigo; s & d MOP$520-720, tr MOP$750, ste from MOP$850) If you are after something smaller and a bit more 'isolated', choose this place at the foot of Guia Hill.

Pousada de Mong Há (Map pp532-3; ☎ 561 252; www.ift.edu.mo; s/d/ste Mon-Fri MOP$400/500/900, s/d/ste Sat & Sun MOP$500/700/1000). This traditional-style Portuguese inn with 20 rooms near the ruins of a hilltop fort is run by tourism students. Rates include breakfast.

Kingsway Hotel (Map pp532-3; ☎ 702 888; rsvn kwh@macau.ctm.net; 230 Rua de Luís Gonzaga Gomes; s & d MOP$780-980, ste from MOP$1180) Consider this 410-room hotel, which has its own casino, if you want to be close to the ferry terminal.

Fortuna Hotel (Map pp532-3; ☎ 786 333; www .hotelfortuna.com.mo; 63 Rua da Cantão; s & d Sun-Thu MOP$720, Fri & Sat MOP$980-1120, ste from MOP$1888) This smart hotel is in a useful position if you want to frequent the casino in the Lisboa Hotel but don't actually want to stay there.

Presidente Hotel (Map pp532-3; ☎ 553 888; www .hotelpresident.com.mo; 355 Avenida da Amizade; s & d MOP$660-920, ste from MOP$2280) The Presidente is a 312-room hotel on a busy road with all the mod-cons and within easy walking distance of the NAPE nightlife area.

Sun Sun Hotel (Map p535; ☎ 939 393; sunsun@yp .com.mo; 14-16 Praça Ponte e Horta; s & d MOP$600-980, ste from MOP$1680) This modern, 178-room Best Western property usually offers big discounts during the week. Upper floor rooms have views of the Inner Harbour.

Fu Hua Hotel (Map pp532-3; ☎ 553 838; fax 527 575; 98-102 Rua de Francisco Xavier Pereira; s/d MOP$730/830, ste from MOP$1380) If you want to stay in the northern part of the peninsula, choose this modern and bright 142-room hotel a stone's throw from the Kun Iam Temple.

TOP END

Pousada de São Tiago (Map pp532-3; ☎ 378 111; www.saotiago.com.mo, Fortaleza de São Tiago da Barra, Avenida de República; s & d MOP$1620-1960, ste from MOP$2300) The 'St James Inn', built into the ruins of a 17th-century fort, commands a splendid view of the harbour and is worth visiting for a drink on the terrace even if you don't stay. It only has 24 rooms so book well in advance.

Mandarin Oriental (Map pp532-3; ☎ 567 888; www.mandarinoriental.com/macau; 956-1110 Avenida da Amizade; s & d MOP$1900-3000, ste from MOP$5100). This superb five-star hotel has a huge swimming pool, lovely gardens and a couple of stunning restaurants.

Lisboa Hotel (Map pp532-3; ☎ 377 666; lisboa@ macau.ctm.net; 2-4 Avenida de Lisboa; s & d MOP$1480-2800, ste from MOP$3800) This is Macau's most famous (and unsightly) landmark, with an old (east) and a new (west or tower) wing, and close to 1000 rooms. For many punters the casino here is still the only game in town.

The Islands

Taipa and Coloane have several excellent mid-range and top end hotels, a couple of which are more like resorts than hotels. Macau's two HI-affiliated hostels are both on Coloane Island.

BUDGET

Pousada de Juventude de Cheoc Van (Map p538; ☎ 882 024; Rua de António Francisco, Coloane; bed in dm/d Sun-Fri MOP$40/70, Sat MOP$50/100) This very clean hostel is on the eastern side of Cheoc Van Bay, below (and not to be confused with) the Pousada de Coloane (below). It has a small kitchen and garden. Book through the **Education & Youth Services Department** (☎ 555 533; www .dsej.gov.mo). You must have a Hostelling International card or equivalent and there are separate quarters for men and women.

Pousada de Juventude de Hac Sa (Map p538; ☎ 882 701; Estrada Nova de Hac Sa, Coloane) The sister hostel of Pousada de Juventude de Cheoc Van, this place is at the southern end of Hac Sa Beach and is usually reserved for groups.

MID-RANGE

Grandview Hotel (Map p538; ☎ 837 788; www.grand view-hotel.com; 142 Estrada Governador Albano de Oliveira, Taipa; s & d MOP$980-1280, ste from MOP$2180) This rather tasteful 406-room hotel is a short gallop northeast of the Macau Jockey Club and close to Taipa Village.

Pousada de Coloane (Map p538; ☎ 882 143; www .hotelpcoloane.com.mo; Estrada de Cheoc Van, Coloane; s & d MOP$680-750) This cosy hotel overlooks Cheoc Van Beach. With a relaxed atmosphere, its own swimming pool and a fantastic Sunday lunch buffet, it's an excellent choice. Renovations in the near future will add another eight rooms.

TOP END

Westin Resort (Map p538; ☎ 871 111; macau@westin .com; 1918 Estrada de Hac Sa, Coloane; s & d MOP$2100-2450, ste from MOP$5500) This five-star 'island resort' is on the eastern side of Hac Sa Beach. Each of the rooms has a large terrace and facilities include an 18-hole golf course, tennis and squash courts, swimming pools, outdoor spa, sauna and gym.

Hyatt Regency Macau (Map p538; ☎ 831 234; www .macau.hyatt.com; 2 Estrada Almirante Marques Esparteiro, Taipa; s & d MOP$600-1750, ste from MOP$2800) More of a resort than a hotel, this 326-room place has tennis and squash courts, a fitness centre, spas for men and women, a huge heated swimming pool and a casino. There's an excellent delicatessen and bakery off the lobby if you want to make yourself a picnic.

EATING

While Macau is renowned for its Chinese cuisine (especially dim sum), most people come here to sample Portuguese and Macanese food.

Portuguese cuisine is meat-based and uses a lot of olive oil, garlic and *bacalhau* (dried salted cod). Popular dishes include *caldo verde*, a soup of green cabbage or kale thickened with potatoes; *pasteis de bacalhau* (codfish croquettes); *sardinhas grelhadas* (grilled sardines); and *feijoada*, a casserole of beans, pork, spicy sausages, potatoes and cabbage that is actually Brazilian in origin.

Macanese food borrows from Chinese and other Asian cuisines, as well as from those of former Portuguese colonies in Africa and Indian. It is redolent of coconut, tamarind, chilli, jaggery (palm sugar) and shrimp paste. The most famous Macanese speciality is *galinha africana* (African chicken) made with coconut, garlic and chillies. Apart from cod, there's plenty of other fish and seafood: shrimp, crab, squid and white fish. Sole is a Macanese delicacy. The contribution from the former Portuguese enclave of Goa on the west coast of India is spicy prawns.

Portuguese & Macanese

O Café Estalagem (Map p538; ☎ 821 041; 410 Estrada Governador Albano de Oliveira, Taipa; starters MOP$30-70, mains MOP$62-120; ❍ noon-3.30pm & 7-10.30pm Tue-Sun) This small place is fast becoming the yardstick by which Macau measures its fine-quality (yet affordable) Portuguese eateries. Absolutely sublime prawn & crab dishes.

Restaurante Fernando (Map p538; ☎ 882 531; 9 Praia de Hac Sa, Coloane; soups MOP$22-26, mains MOP$50-148, rice dishes MOP$60-66; ❍ noon-9.30pm) Famed for its seafood, Fernando has a devoted clientele and a pleasantly relaxed atmosphere – though it can get pretty crowded in the evening.

A Lorcha (Map pp532-3; ☎ 313 193; 289a Rua do Almirante Sérgio; starters MOP$24-30, mains MOP$58-128; ❍ 12.30-3pm & 6.30-11pm) Among the fine dishes at this much loved Portuguese restaurant facing the Inner Harbour are chicken with onion and tomato, *feijoada* and raw codfish salad.

Cozinha Pinocchio (Map p538; ☎ 827 128; 4 Rua do Sol, Taipa; starters MOP$25-58, mains MOP$48-128; ⏰ 11.45am-11.45pm) This is the Macanese place that launched the Taipa Village restaurant phenomenon. Recommended dishes include grilled fresh sardines and roast lamb.

A Petisqueira (Map p538; ☎ 825 354; 15a-b Rua de São João, Taipa; starters MOP$22-38, mains MOP$75-135; ⏰ noon-3pm & 7-11.30pm) This excellent place has some of Taipa Village's best Portuguese food. Try the spicy prawns (MOP$135), the *acorda de marisco* (seafood cooked with mashed bread; MOP$75) or the *bife à portuguesa* (beef cooked in a clay pot; MOP$90).

O Santos (Map p538; ☎ 827 508; 20 Rua da Cunha, Taipa; mains MOP$62-120; ⏰ noon-3pm & 6.30-10.30pm) This tiny place is famous for its stuffed pork loin and its codfish dishes, especially *bacalhau à zé do pipo* (dried cod baked with mashed potatoes; MOP$72) and, at the weekend, *sapateira recheada* (MOP$150 for two), a type of crab flown fresh from Portugal.

Chinese & Other Asian

Fook Lam Mun (Map pp532-3; ☎ 786 622; 259 Avenida da Amizade; meals from MOP$250; ⏰ 11am-3pm & 5.30pm-11pm Mon-Fri, 8.30am-3pm & 5.30pm-11pm Sat & Sun) This place serves some of the best Cantonese food in Macau and is noted for its seafood dishes.

Ko Lung Thai (Map pp532-3; ☎ 334 067; 23 Rua de Ferreira do Amaral; dishes MOP$25-90; ⏰ 11am-7am) This place that almost never sleeps is one of the most authentic Thai restaurants north of Bangkok. The picture menu will help the uninitiated.

Wong Chi Kei (Map p535; ☎ 331 313; 17 Largo do Senado; noodle & rice dishes MOP$15-24; ⏰ 8am-midnight) Visit this centrally located Chinese eatery for a fix of late-night cheap noodles.

Western

Caffè Toscana (Map p535; ☎ 370 354; 11 Travessa de São Domingos; pizza MOP$47-62, pasta MOP$45-68, mains MOP$50-68; ⏰ noon-9pm Wed-Mon) You can enjoy a full-blown Italian meal at this pleasant café-restaurant, but it's especially recommended for focaccia (MOP$16 to MOP$38) and its excellent desserts (MOP$18 to MOP$26).

Mezzaluna (Map pp532-3; ☎ 793 3861; 2nd fl, Mandarin Oriental Hotel, 956-1110 Avenida da Amizade; starters MOP$65-100, pizzas MOP$90-110, pasta MOP$80-110, mains MOP$150-245; ⏰ 12.30-3pm & 6.30-11pm Tue-Sun) This restaurant serves *la cucina italiana* in classy (and recently renovated) surroundings. The pasta is fresh and the pizzas piping hot from wood-fired ovens. Try the lobster ravioli or the gnocchi made with spinach and ricotta.

Yes Brazil (Map p535; ☎ 358 097; 6a Travessa Fortuna; mains MOP$38-70; ⏰ 11.30am-7pm Mon-Fri, 11.30am-9pm Sat) This always welcoming hole-in-the-wall serves an excellent *feijoada* (MOP$70) and other Brazilian dishes. Come here too for a late breakfast (MOP$7 to MOP$25).

Markets & Self-Catering

Peninsular Macau's **food stalls** sell excellent stir-fried dishes; try any of the *dai pai dong* along Rua do Almirante Sérgio near the Inner Harbour. There are a few food stalls in Rua da Escola Commercial, a tiny lane one block west of the Lisboa Hotel and next to a sports field.

Yuk gon (dried sweet strips of pork and other meats) are a Macau speciality, as are *hung yan bang* (almond-flavoured biscuits sprinkled with powdery white sugar). Look for both around Rua da Caldeira and Travessa do Matadouro at the northern end of Avenida de Almeida Ribeiro.

Two of the largest markets are the **Almirante Lacerda City Market** (Mercado Municipal Almirante Lacerda; Map pp532-3; 130 Avenida do Almirante Lacerda; ⏰ 6am-8pm), also called the Red Market, in northern Macau and the **St Lawrence City Market** (Mercado Municipal de São Lourenço; Map p535; Rua de João Lecaros; ⏰ 6am-8pm) in the south.

Opposite the Macau ferry terminal, **New Yaohan Department Store** (Map pp532-3; ☎ 725 338; Avenida da Amizade; ⏰ 11am-10.30pm) has the largest supermarket in Macau on the 2nd floor.

DRINKING

There's a fine line between cafés, most of which serve food as well, and pubs and bars in Macau. Here we've listed our favourite places for a warm beverage under 'Cafés' and those where we seek something colder (and stronger) under 'Pubs & Bars'. The main place for a pub crawl is the reclaimed Dochas (Docks) area (Map pp532-3), where attractive bars line the waterfront area to the southeast and opposite the Kum Iam statue.

Cafés

Caravela (Map p535; ☎ 712 080; ground fl, Kam Loi Bldg, 7 Pátio do Comandante Mata e Oliveira; cakes MOP$10-25; ☺ 8am-10.30pm) This excellent *pastelaria* (pastry shop) just north of Avenida de Dom João IV serves excellent coffee as well as delectable pastries and snacks.

O Barril (Map p535; ☎ 370 533; 14a-b Travessa de São Domingos; small dishes MOP$18-40, main dishes MOP$53-90; ☺ 8am-10pm Mon-Fri, 9am-10pm Sat & Sun) This little place is where to head if you want something fast and savoury *à portuguesa*. It also has a good range of Portuguese and Macanese pastries, cakes and aromatic coffees.

Pubs & Bars

Casablanca Café (Map pp532-3; ☎ 751 281; ground fl, Vista Magnifica Court Bldg, Avenida Doutor Sun Yat Sen; ☺ 6pm-4am, happy hour 6-8pm) One of several watering holes in the Dochas, this somewhat elegant place has photos of Hollywood and Hong Kong film icons decorating the walls, cool jazz in the background and pool tables.

DD Club (Map p535; ☎ 711 800; cnr Avenida do Infante Dom Henrique & Avenida de Dom João IV; ☺ 11pm-7am, happy hour 11pm-2am) This popular bar and dance club disco opposite the landmark Escola Portuguesa de Macau has a small hall with live music, a main hall with a big dance floor and the **Lime Light Bar**, with live music every night except Wednesday from 11pm.

Greenhouse Lounge Bar (Map p538; ☎ 831 234; Hyatt Regency Macau, 2 Estrada Almirante Marques Esparteiro; ☺ noon-1am Sun-Fri, noon-2am Sat, happy hour 5-7pm) This hotel bar attracts academics from the nearby University of Macau, jockeys from the racecourse and workers from the airport. Martinis here are excellent.

ENTERTAINMENT

While modern-day Macau has any number of cultural performances on offer each week throughout the year – consult the territory's premier venue, the **Macau Cultural Centre** (Centro Cultural de Macau; Map pp532-3; ☎ 797 7215; www.ccm .gov.mo; Avenida Xian Xing Hai) for details – the vast majority of visitors are in search of an assignation with Lady Luck.

Gambling

At present Macau has 15 casinos, with many more on the way. All of them operate 24 hours a day, and punters must be 18 years old and properly dressed. None of the casinos in Macau offer the atmosphere or service considered minimal elsewhere, but with the end of the casino monopoly in 2002 and the arrival of the two consortia from Las Vegas, that's changing. The following two offer a unique comparison of how gambling was and is now being enjoyed in Macau:

Casino Lisboa (Map pp532-3; ☎ 375 111; 2-4 Avenida de Lisboa) Some 107 slot machines and 146 games tables over four floors.

Casino Sands Macao (Map pp532-3; ☎ 883 388; Avenida de Amizade) Some 405 state-of-the-art slot and poker machines and 277 gaming tables.

Macau Jockey Club (☎ 821 188, racing information hotline ☎ 820 868; www.macauhorse.com; Estrada Governador Albano de Oliveira, Taipa; admission MOP$20) This has been the venue for horse racing since 1991. You can watch races from the five-storey, air-con grandstands on Saturday from 2pm and Tuesday from 7.30pm (in summer on Wednesday and Saturday from 7.30pm).

Macau Canidrome (Map pp532-3; ☎ 261 188, racing information hotline ☎ 333 399; Avenida do General Castelo Branco; admission from MOP$10) Some 16 greyhound races are held here on Monday, Thursday, Friday, Saturday and Sunday at 7.45pm. Admission to the Canidrome costs MOP$10. If you want to sit in the members' stands it costs MOP$80 Monday to Thursday and MOP$120 Friday to Sunday. Minimum bet is MOP$30.

SHOPPING

Macau's main shopping area is along the Avenida do Infante Dom Henrique and Avenida de Almeida Ribeiro. Also check out Rua da Palha, Rua do Campo and Rua Pedro Nolasco da Silva.

Around Macau's back lanes, you'll stumble across bustling markets and Chinese shops selling birdcages, dried herbs, medicines and mah jong sets. Try Rua de Madeira or Rua dos Mercadores, which lead up to Rua da Tercena and its **flea market**, a great place for old Macanese coins and jade.

Great streets for antiques, ceramics and curios are Rua de São Paulo, Rua das Estalagens and Rua de São António as well as the lanes leading off them. One of the best antique shops in Macau is **Asian Artefacts** (Map p538; ☎ 881 022; 9 Rua dos Negociantes; ☺ 10am-7pm) in Coloane Village.

The MGTO distributes a useful pamphlet called *Shopping in Macau*, which highlights neighbourhoods and their specific wares.

GETTING THERE & AWAY

Air

Ultra-modern **Macau International Airport** (Map p538; ☎ 861 111; www.macau-airport.gov.mo), which opened in 1995 on the east coast of Taipa, has only a small volume of passenger traffic so it's fast and efficient.

Air Macau (NX; Map pp532-3; ☎ 396 5555; www .airmacau.com.mo; ground fl, Dynasty Plaza Bldg, Avenida da Amizade) and several carriers of the **China National Aviation Corporation** (CNAC; Map p535; ☎ 788 034; fax 788 036; lat Teng Hou Bldg, Avenida de Dom João IV) fly to mainland China, with at least one flight a day to Běijīng, Fúzhōu, Guìlín, Hángzhōu, Kūnmíng, Shànghǎi, Shēnzhèn and Xiàmén. The same carriers also fly to/from Bangkok (five times a week), Kaohsiung (daily), Manila (twice a week), Singapore (three times a week) and Taiwan (daily).

Other airlines with flights from Macau to destinations in the region include:

AirAsia (FD; Hong Kong ☎ 3167 2299; www.airasia.com)

EVA Airways (BR; ☎ 726 848; www.evaair.com)

Silk Air (MI; ☎ 323 878; www.silkair.com)

Singapore Airlines (SQ; ☎ 861 321; www.singapore air.com)

Trans Asia Airways (GE; ☎ 701 556; www.tna.com.tw)

East Asia Airlines/Heli Hong Kong (☎ 727 288, Hong Kong ☎ 2108 9898; www.helihongkong.com) runs a 16-minute helicopter shuttle between Macau and Hong Kong (HK$1600 Monday to Thursday, HK$1700 Friday to Sunday) up to 27 times a day from 9am to 10.30pm (9.30am to 11pm from Hong Kong).

DEPARTURE TAX

Macau levies an airport tax of MOP$80/50 adult/child for destinations in China and MOP$130/80 for international destinations, including Hong Kong by helicopter. These are usually included in the quoted fare.

Boat

HONG KONG

Two ferry companies operate services to/ from Hong Kong, with frequent departures and boats running virtually 24 hours a day.

TurboJet (☎ 790 7039; Hong Kong ☎ 2859 3333 information, ☎ 2921 6688 bookings; www.turbojet.com .hk; economy/superclass Mon-Fri MOP$142/244, Sat & Sun MOP$154/260, night crossing MOP$176/275) runs three types of vessels that take between 55 and 65 minutes. From Hong Kong Island, departures are from the Macau ferry pier at

the **Shun Tak Centre** (☎ 2859 3359, 200 Connaught Rd, Sheung Wan), and in Macau from the **Macau ferry terminal** (Map pp532-3; ☎ 790 7240).

New World First Ferry (☎ 727 676, Hong Kong ☎ 2131 8181; www.nwff.com.hk) operates up to 22 high-speed catamarans a day from the Macau ferry terminal every half-hour or so between 7am and 8.30pm. In Hong Kong they leave the China ferry terminal (Canton Rd, Tsim Sha Tsui) up to 25 times a day, departing on the half-hour from 7am to 9pm or 10pm). The trip takes 65 to 75 minutes and tickets cost HK$140/175 on weekday days/nights (ie from 6pm to 9pm or 10pm from Hong Kong and 6.30pm to 8.30pm from Macau), and HK$155/175 on weekends and public holidays. Deluxe class is HK$245/275 on weekday days/nights and HK$260/275 on weekends and public holidays.

Tickets for both lines can be booked up to 28 days in advance and are available at ferry terminals, all CTS branches and many travel agents. There is also a stand-by queue before each sailing. On weekends and public holidays, book your return ticket in advance as boats are often full.

CHINA

A daily ferry run by the **Yuet Tung Shipping Co** (☎ 574 478; adult/child MOP$100/57) connects Macau with the port of Shékǒu in Shēnzhèn. The boat leaves at 10am, 2pm and 5.30pm and takes 1½ hours; it returns from Shékǒu at 8.15am, 11.45am and 3.45pm. Tickets (adult/child MOP$100/57) can be bought up to three days in advance from the point of departure, which is pier No 14 in Macau, just off Rua das Lorchas and 100m southwest of the end of Avenida de Almeida Ribeiro.

Sampans and ferries sail across the Inner Harbour to Wānzái (MOP$12) on the mainland from a small pier near where Rua das Lorchas meets Rua do Dr Lourenço Pereira Marques. They depart hourly between 8am and 4pm, returning a half-hour later.

DEPARTURE TAX

There's a departure tax of MOP$20 on anyone leaving by sea for China or Hong Kong. It's almost always included in the price of the ticket.

Bus

Macau is an easy gateway into China. Simply take bus No 3, 5 or 9 to the **Border Gate**

(Portas de Cerco; ☺ 7am-midnight) and walk across. A second, less busy crossing is the **Cotai Frontier Post** (☺ 9am to 8pm) on the causeway linking Taipa and Coloane and allows visitors to cross over the Lotus Bridge by shuttle bus (HK$4) to the Zhūhǎi SEZ. Bus Nos 15, 21 and 26 will drop you off at the crossing.

If you want to travel further afield in China, buses run by the **Kee Kwan Motor Road Co** (☎ 933 888) leave the bus station (Map p535) on Rua das Lorchas, 100m southwest of the end of Avenida de Almeida Ribeiro. Buses for Guǎngzhōu (MOP$55; 2½ hours) depart about every 15 minutes and for Zhōngshān (MOP$15; one hour) every 20 minutes. There are many buses to Guǎngzhōu (MOP$75) and Dōngguǎn (MOP$79) from Macau International Airport.

GETTING AROUND
To/From the Airport
Airport bus AP1 (MOP$3.30) leaves the airport and zips around Taipa before crossing the Macau–Taipa Bridge and heading to the Macau ferry terminal and the Border Gate, where it terminates. The bus stops at a number of major hotels en route and departs every 15 minutes from 6.30am to 12.10am. There's an additional charge of MOP$3 for each large piece of luggage. A taxi from the airport to the centre of town should cost about MOP$40.

Bicycle
Bikes can be rented in Taipa Village (p539). You are not allowed to cross the Macau–Taipa bridges on a bicycle though they are permitted on the causeway linking Taipa and Coloane.

Car & Motorcycle
Happy Rent A Car (Map pp532-3; ☎ 726 868; fax 726 888; rm 1025, Macau ferry terminal) has four-person Mokes, brightly coloured Jeep-like

convertibles, can be rented for MOP$500 per day. Renting from just 9am to 5.30pm costs MOP$250. You can also rent four/six-person Mokes from **Avis Rent A Car** (Map pp532-3; ☎ 336 789; www.avis.com.mo; ground fl, rm 1022, Macau ferry terminal) for MOP$450/500 Monday to Friday and MOP$500/500 on Saturday and Sunday.

Public Transport
Public buses and minibuses run on 40 routes from 6.45am till just after midnight, with destinations displayed in Portuguese and Chinese. Fares – MOP$2.50 on the peninsula, MOP$3.30 to Taipa, MOP$4 to Coloane Village and MOP$5 to Hac Sa Beach – must be paid into a box upon entry; there's no change.

The *Macau Tourist Map* (p530) has a full list of both bus companies' routes. The two most useful buses on the peninsula are Nos 3 and 3A, which run between the ferry terminal and the city centre, near the main post office. No 3 continues up to the border crossing with the mainland, as does bus No 5. From the ferry terminal, bus No 12 runs past the Lisboa Hotel and then up to the Lou Lim Ioc Garden and Kun Iam Temple.

The most useful buses to both Taipa and Coloane are Nos 21, 21A, 25 and 26A. Bus No 22 to and around Taipa only terminates at the Macau Jockey Club.

Taxi
The taxi flag fall is MOP$10 for the first 1.5km and MOP$1 for each additional 200m. There is a MOP$5 surcharge to go to Coloane; travelling between Taipa and Coloane is MOP$2 extra. Journeys starting from the airport incur an extra charge of MOP$5. Large bags cost an extra MOP$3. Taxis can be dispatched by radio by ringing ☎ 519 519 or ☎ 939 939.

Guǎngdōng
广东

HIGHLIGHTS

- Stroll through Guǎngzhōu's **Shamian Island** (p555) and admire the decaying colonial architecture
- Make the pilgrimage to revolutionary leader Sun Yatsen's birthplace in **Cuìhēng** (p571), north of Zhūhǎi
- Skim across the lake at **Zhàoqìng** (p564), with the Seven Star Crags as backdrop
- Watch the **Nanfeng Ancient Kiln** (p563) at Fóshān turn clay into porcelain some 500 years after it first went into operation
- Visit the impressive **Sea Battle Museum** (p571) at Hǔmén

Nanfeng Ancient Kiln
Shamian Island
Zhàoqing ★ ★ ★ Sea Battle Museum
Cuìhēng ★

■ POP: 75.9 MIL	■ AREA: 177,933 SQ KM	■ www.newsgd.com

Guǎngdōng's coastal location and its proximity to Hong Kong have made it a major gateway into China. In the 1970s the province was just an economic middleweight, but the high level of economic integration between the cities and towns of Guǎngdōng's Pearl River delta and Hong Kong over the past two decades have led to record economic growth. Today Guǎngdōng (formerly known as Canton) is the country's most affluent province and the industries that made Hong Kong so rich and so famous are now located here.

The Cantonese, as the people of Guǎngdōng are called, are regarded with a mixture of envy and suspicion by other Chinese. Guǎngdōng's topography, unique dialect and great distance from traditional centres of authority, coupled with long-standing contact with 'foreign barbarians', has created a strong sense of self-sufficiency and autonomy.

The Cantonese also spearheaded Chinese emigration to the USA, Canada, Australia and South Africa in the mid-19th century, spurred on by the gold rushes in those countries and by the wars and growing poverty in China. Bustling Chinatowns around the world are steeped in the flavours of Guǎngdōng cuisine and ring with the sounds of the Cantonese dialect and Canto-pop melodies. Indeed Dr Sun Yatsen, himself a native of Guǎngdōng, led the Chinese Revolution with the help of these 'overseas Chinese' and they continue to target the province for investment.

Guǎngdōng was a relative latecomer to the Chinese empire. Although it was integrated during the Qin dynasty (221–206 BC), it was not until the mid-12th century that large numbers of Han settlers, propelled by the invading Jurchen, ancestors of the Manchu, migrated to the province from northern China. Until that time Guǎngdōng was considered to be a barbaric borderland fit only for exiled officials.

In subsequent years, the province was the site of many rival national governments, which earned it a reputation for unruliness and revolt.

History

As China's southern gateway, Guǎngdōng has had contact with the outside world for over a millennium. A mosque was built in what is now Guǎngzhōu as early as the 7th century (p554) and specialised branches of handicrafts (such as Fóshān pottery, p562) developed producing goods for export.

Many important events that were to shape modern Chinese history, especially in the 19th century, took place within this province, including the two Opium Wars (1840–2; 1856–60) and the Taiping Rebellion (1848–64). Dr Sun Yatsen, leader of the revolution that overthrew the Qing dynasty in 1911, was a native of Guǎngdōng.

Climate

As Guǎngdōng lies on the northern edge of the tropical zone, its climate and vegetation can be called subtropical. Winters are mild and summers very hot and humid. The rainy season generally lasts from April/May to September and typhoons can be frequent from July/August to October. The province's average annual temperature varies from 19°C to 23°C, with January being the coldest month (9 to 16°C) and July the hottest (28 to 30°C). Rainfall amounts to between 1500mm and 2000mm annually.

Language

The vast majority of the people of Guǎngdōng speak Cantonese, a dialect distinct from Mandarin. Though it enjoys much

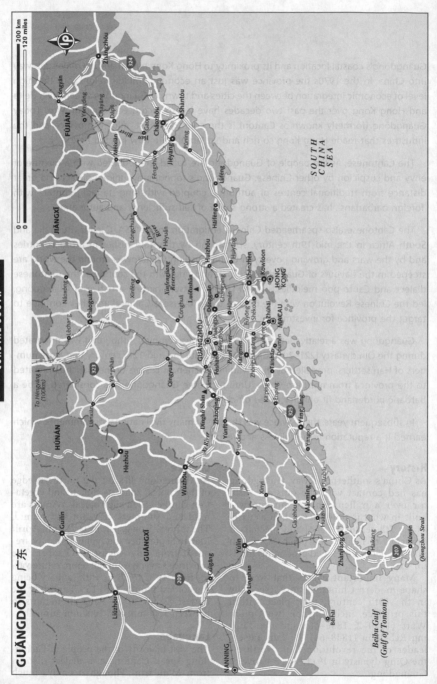

GUĂNGDŌNG 广东

less exalted status than the so-called national language, Cantonese is in fact older than Mandarin and classical poetry sounds much better when read using that dialect's pronunciation.

Getting There & Away

While Guăngdōng is accessible from such neighbouring provinces as Fújiàn and Guăngxī by bus and train, by far and away the easiest entry/exit point to/from the province is Hong Kong via the KCR East Rail line (see p525).

GUĂNGZHŌU 广州

☎ 020 / pop 3.24 million

Guăngzhōu, known for centuries as Canton, is the capital of Guăngdōng province and one of China's most prosperous cities. At first glance it may look not unlike an Asian Los Angeles, with kilometre after kilometre of ring roads and flyovers, skyscrapers and one shopping mall leading into the next. While it's true that the city is not overly endowed with essential sights, there is a surfeit of peaceful parks and a couple of world-class museums. What's more, wandering the busy streets filled with the newly rich shopping and gawping peasants up from the countryside offers an up-close look at the dichotomy that is modern China.

Those in search of the past should head for Shamian Island, a former foreign concession in the southwestern part of the city, where bits of 'old Canton' survive.

History

The legend of Guăngzhōu's founding by five genies riding goats down from heaven (see p553) notwithstanding, the first settlement on the site of the present-day city dates back to 214 BC when the so-called First Emperor of Qin sent his troops south to gain control of the sea. Among the first outsiders to make their way here were the Romans, who appeared as early as the 2nd century AD. By the Tang dynasty (618–907 AD), Arab merchants were visiting regularly and a sizeable trade with the Middle East and Southeast Asia had developed.

The Portuguese arrived in the 16th century in search of porcelain, tea and silk and were allowed to set up base downriver in Macau in 1557. They were followed by the Jesuits in 1582, who established themselves first at Zhàoqìng, west of Guăngzhōu, and later at Běijīng.

Attempts by the British in the early 17th century to muscle in on the trade with China were rebuffed, but by 1685 merchant ships from the East India Company's concessions along the Indian coast were calling at Guăngzhōu. In 1757 an imperial edict gave the *cohong*, a local merchants' guild, a monopoly on China's trade with foreigners, who were restricted to Shamian Island.

Trade remained in China's favour until 1773 when the British shifted the balance by unloading 1000 chests of Bengal opium at Guăngzhōu. Addiction swept China like wildfire and in 1839 the emperor appointed Lin Zexu commissioner of Guăngzhōu to stamp out the opium trade altogether (see the boxed text on p572). The Chinese war on drugs led to a British military reaction – the so-called First Opium War. As part of the Treaty of Nanking (1842), which brought an end to the conflict, Hong Kong Island was ceded to the British 'in perpetuity'.

Guăngzhōu was a hotbed of revolt in the 19th century. The leader of the antidynastic Taiping Rebellion (1848–64), Hong Xiuquan, was born in 1814 at Huaxian, 40km northwest of Guăngzhōu, and some of the early activities of the revolt centred on this area.

The city was also a stronghold of the republican forces after the fall of the Qing dynasty in 1911. Sun Yatsen (1866–1925), the first president of the Republic of China, was born at Cuìhēng village southeast Zhōngshān, and in the early 1920s he led the Kuomintang (Nationalist Party) in Guăngzhōu, from where the republicans mounted their campaigns against the northern warlords. Guăngzhōu was also a centre of activities for the fledgling Communist Party and Mao Zedong and other prominent Communist leaders were based here in 1925–26.

Since liberation, however, Guăngzhōu ('Broad Region') has put all its energies into the business of making money. Even when China had effectively cut itself off from most of the rest of the world, what was then called the Canton Trade Fair was the only forum in which the Middle Kingdom did business with the West.

Orientation

Central Guăngzhōu is bounded by semi-circular Huanshi Lu, literally 'circle-city

COASTAL SOUTH

GUĂNGZHŌU 广州

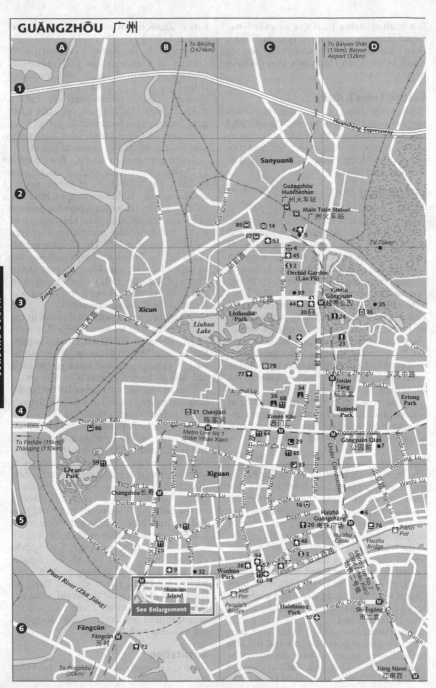

To Běijīng (2474km)

To Báiyún Shān (13km); Báiyún Airport (32km)

Huancheng Expressway

Sanyuanli

Guǎngzhōu Huǒchēzhàn 广州火车站

Main Train Station 广州火车站

85 □ ⊙ 14
87 □ 53

44 4
5

♦ 4
45

♦ 2
Orchid Garden (Lán Pǔ)

TV. Tower

Zengbu River

Huanshi Xilu

Xicun

Dongfeng Xilu

Guangyuan Lu

Zhanqian Lu

Zhanqian Lu

六花路

Liuhua Lu

Liuhualu Park

Liuhua Lake

Renmin Beilu

● 89
41
44 □
30 �📷

Yuexiu Gōngyuán 越秀公园

♦ 35
📷 36

🏛 24

23

8 ✚

Pantu Lu

Xinshi Zhonglu

Yuexiu

78

77 ♦

Jinghui Lu

26 68
34

Ximen Kǒu 西门口

Dongfeng Zhonglu 东凤中路

Jinián Táng 纪念堂

Yuehua Lu

Ertong Park

Jiefang Beilu

Renmin Park

🏛 21 Chénjiācí 陈家祠

Zhongshan Balu

□ 86

To Fóshān (19km); Zhàoqìng (110km)

Zhongshan Qilu

Metro Line No 1 (Dìtiě Yīhào Xiàn)

Huifu Xilu

64
🏛

Guangta Lu

Gōngyuán Qián 公园前

⊙ 7

Zhongshan Wulu

Zhongshan Wulu

Under Construction

Wende Lu

Weiming Lu

Renmin Zhonglu

Wenchang Beilu

Dinlu Lu

29

65

33

Huifu Xilu

Xiguan

Renmin Nanlu

Hazhu Nanlu

Dade Lu

16 ⊙

Daxin Lu

Wanfu Lu

Jiefang Zhonglu

Longjin Xilu

59

Liwan Park

Baoyuan Lu

Changshou Xilu

Changshou Lu 长寿

Duobao Lu

Enning Lu

Huangsha Dadao

Baohua Lu

Dalong Lu

Wenchang Nanlu

Changshou Lu

Xia Jiulu Shang Jiulu

61 🏛

Dishipu Lu

69

Qingping Lu

✚ 9

● 32

Wenhua Park

38
54 57
60 18

Haizhū Guǎngchǎng

20 海珠广场

Haizhu Circle

Hazhou Bridge

● 6

76 □

Tianzi Pier

Hazhou Guǎngchǎng

Yide Lu

✚ 46

3

37

Changdi Dalu

Yanjiang Xilu 沿江西路

Binjiang Xilu

Shi Èrgōng 市二宫

Metro Line No 2 (Dìtiě Èrhào Xiàn)

Pearl River (Zhū Jiāng)

Shamian Island
See Enlargement

Xidi Pier

People's Bridge

Haizhuang Park

10 ✚

Tongfu Donglu

Fāngcūn

Fāngcūn 芳村

72 □

To Pīngzhōu (20km)

Jiāng Nánxī 江南西

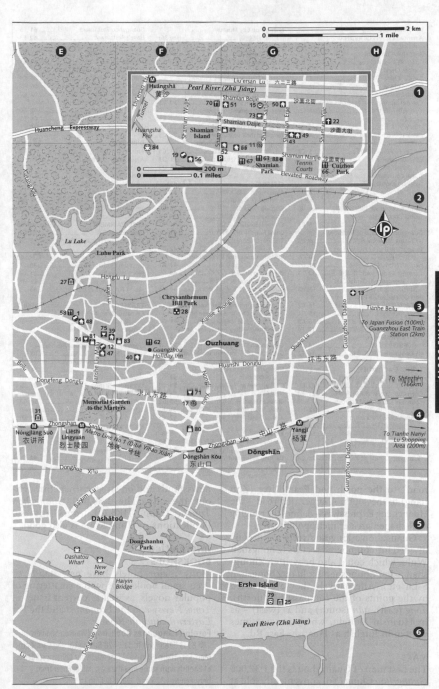

COASTAL SOUTH

road', to the north and Pearl River (Zhū Jiāng) to the south. A larger ring road – the Huancheng Expressway – defines the roughly oval-shaped greater metropolitan area.

Guǎngzhōu's longest streets are usually divided into numbered sectors (Zhongshan Wulu, which could also be written Zhongshan 5-Lu, Zhongshan Liulu or Zhongshan 6-Lu etc). Alternatively they are labelled by the points of the compass: *běi* (north), *dōng* (east), *nán* (south) and *xī* (west) – as in Huanshi Donglu, which is sometimes written in English as Huanshi East Rd.

MAPS
The best map of Guǎngzhōu is the 1:37,000 *Guangzhou China* (Y6) conveniently sold at newsstands and on street corners throughout the city. The 1:30,000 *Guangzhou Touring Map* (HK$20) from Universal Publications in Hong Kong is also good.

Information
BOOKSHOPS
Many major hotels have newsstands or even small bookshops with a smattering of popular novels, as well as current issues of *Time*, *Newsweek*, the *Economist* and the *Far Eastern Economic Review*.

Foreign Languages Bookshop (Wáiwén Shūdián; ☎ 8333 5185; 2nd fl, 326-328 Beijing Lu; ⏱ 9am-6pm Mon-Sat, 10am-6pm Sun) Essentially for Chinese students of English with some literature available. Enter from between Nos 326 and 328 of Beijing Lu.

EMERGENCY

Public Security Bureau (PSB; Gōngānjú; ☎ 8311 5800, 8311 5808; 155 Jiefang Nanlu; ☽ 8.30am-5pm) Between Dade Lu and Daxin Lu.

INTERNET ACCESS

China Telecom (Zhōngguó Diànxìn; ☎ 1000; 196 Huanshi Xilu; per hr Y6; ☽ 8am-6pm) There are computers on the 2nd floor with fast Internet access.

Henan Webmail (Hénán Wǎngluò; ☎ 8121 6061; Shamian Sanjie; ☽ 9am-11pm) This small Internet café on Shamian Island charges Y20 for the first hour and Y10 every half hour after that.

Shengzhan Internet (Shèngzhàn Wǎngluò; ☎ 8760 7153; 3rd fl, Yixing Bldg, 728 Dongfeng Donglu; per hr Y3; ☽ 8am-midnight) The city's biggest Internet café is also one of the cheapest.

MEDICAL SERVICES

Can-Am International Medical Centre (Jiāměi Guójì Yīliào Zhōngxīn; ☎ 8387 9057; 5th fl, Garden Tower, Garden Hotel, 368 Huanshi Donglu) Call this place to be sure you'll get an English-speaking doctor.

Global Doctor Clinic (Huánqiú Yīshēng Yīliào Zhōngxīn; ☎ 8104 5173; 7th fl, Ying Dong Treatment Centre, 1 Panfu Lu) For general treatment of non-emergencies, try this medical clinic for foreigners located in the complex of the Guangzhou No 1 People's Hospital (Dìyī Rénmín Yīyuàn).

Guangzhou Hospital of Traditional Chinese Medicine (Zhōngyī Yīyuàn; ☎ 8188 6504; 16 Zhuji Lu) This training hospital just north of Shamian Island and west of the Peaceful Market is the place to go for acupuncture and traditional herbal remedies.

Guangzhou Red Cross Hospital (Hóngshízìhuì Yīyuàn; ☎ 8441 2233; 396 Tongfu Zhonglu) Contact this large hospital on the other side of the Pearl River in an emergency.

Sun Yatsen Memorial Hospital (Sūn Yìxiān Jìniàn Yīyuàn; ☎ 8133 2199; 107 Yanjiang Xilu) This hospital on the riverfront and close to Shamian Island has good medical facilities and the prices are low.

Kai Yi International Dental Care (Kǎiyí Guójì Yákē Zhěnshì; ☎ 3387 4278; 5th fl, Ice Flower Hotel, 2 Tianhe Beilu; ☽ 9am-9pm) Staff here speak English.

MONEY

Most branches of the **Bank of China** (Zhōngguó Yínháng; ☎ 8334 0998; ☽ 9am-6pm Mon-Fri, 9am-4pm Sat & Sun) change travellers cheques and have ATMs linked to international money systems such as Cirrus, Maestro and Plus. There's a branch at the **Guangdong International Hotel** (ground fl, Main Tower, 339 Huanshi Donglu), next to the **Friendship Hotel** (698 Renmin Beilu), and opposite the **Furama Hotel** (316 Changdi Nanlu).

American Express Guangzhou (Měiguó Yùntōngā Guǎngzhōu; ☎ 8331 1611; fax 8331 1616; room 806, 8th fl, Main Tower, Guangdong International Hotel, 339 Huanshi Donglu; ☽ 9am-5.30pm Mon-Fri) can cash and sell Amex travellers cheques.

POST

Post office (yóujú; Huanshi Xilu; ☽ 8am-8pm) Adjacent to the train, this is known locally as the Liuhua post office (Liúhuā yóujú).

Courier Services

Private companies offering a courier service can deliver to and pick up from your hotel.

DHL International (☎ 800-810 8000)
Federal Express (☎ 800-830 2338)
UPS (☎ 8778 7108)

TELEPHONE

China Telecom (Zhōngguó Diànxìn; ☎ 1000; 196 Huanshi Xilu; ☽ 8am-6pm) The main branch is opposite the train station on the eastern side of Renmin Beilu.

TOURIST INFORMATION & TRAVEL AGENCIES

In addition to the agencies listed below, most hotels have travel desks open to all.

China International Travel Service Guangdong (CITS; Zhōngguó Guójì Lǚxíngshè; ☎ 8666 6889; 179 Huanshi Xilu; ☽ 9am-6pm) Helpful office just east of the main train station.

China Travel Service Guangzhou (CTS; Zhōngguó Lǚxíngshè; ☎ 8333 6888; 10 Qiaoguang Lu; ☽ 8.30am-6pm Mon-Fri, 9am-5pm Sat & Sun) Runs tours and books tickets air, train and boat tickets.

Sights & Activities

The vast majority of Guǎngzhōu's most important sights are in the western part of the city and easily accessible by bus and/or metro. Several noteworthy museums are in the eastern section.

YUEXIU PARK 越秀公园

This public **park** (Yuèxiù Gōngyuán; 13 Jiefang Beilu; metro line No 2 Yuèxiù Gōngyuán station, bus Nos 5, 24, 63 & 110; admission Y5; ☽ 6am-9pm) is Guǎngzhōu's largest, covering some 93 hectares. A short distance northwest of the main entrance is the **Five Rams Statue** (Wǔyáng Shíxiang), erected in 1959. Legend has it that, long ago, five rams (or goats) carrying an equal number of celestial beings, arrived in Guǎngzhōu from on high. Each of the immortals wore a different coloured robe and carried a stem of rice, which they presented to the people as a sign that the area would be forever free from famine. From this story Guăngzhōu gets its nickname: City of Rams (or just Goat City).

Five-storey **Zhenhai Tower** (Zhènhai Lóu) was built in the late 14th century and is the only part of the old city wall still standing. The tower was occupied by the British and French troops at the time of the First Opium War and the 12 cannons in front date from this time. The tower now houses the **Guangzhou City Museum** (Guăngzhōushì Bówùguăn; ☎ 8355 0627; admission Y10; ⏰ 9am-5.30pm), which displays some 700 exhibits tracing the history of the city and surrounding areas from Neolithic times until the early part of the 20th century. The upper storeys of the tower command a view of the city.

MUSEUM OF THE SOUTHERN YUE ROYAL MAUSOLEUM 南越王墓
Just opposite the main entrance to Yuexiu Park, this superb **museum** (Nányuèwáng Mù; ☎ 8666 4920; 867 Jiefang Beilu; adult/senior/student Y12/6/5, audioguide Y10; ⏰ 9am-5.30pm) stands on the site of the tomb of Emperor Wen, the second ruler of the Southern Yue kingdom, dating back to 100 BC. The Southern Yue kingdom is what the area around Guăngzhōu was called during the Western Han dynasty (206 BC–AD 8).

The museum is composed of five exhibition rooms plus the tomb itself, discovered in 1983 some 20m under **Xiànggăng Shān** (Elephant Hill), where you start your tour. Inside the tomb itself archaeologists found five funerary bodies – four concubines, four cooks and seven eunuchs – and more than 1000 sacrificial objects made of jade, including the dragon and phoenix 'ring', which has become the museum's symbol. The jade shroud covering the king's corpse is composed of almost 2300 pieces stitched together.

TEMPLE OF THE SIX BANYAN TREES 六榕寺
The trees that gave the name to this Buddhist **temple** (Liùróng Sì; 87-89 Liurong Lu; bus No 56; admission Y1; ⏰ 8am-5pm) have long since disappeared, but it remains a popular attraction for its octagonal **Huā Tă**, or 'Decorated Pagoda', built in AD 1098. At 54m, the pagoda stands in ornate contrast to the Guăng Tă

at the Mosque Dedicated to the Prophet (below) to the south. The pagoda, which appears to have only nine storeys from the outside but actually counts 17, is worth climbing.

The temple, which was founded in AD 479, contains several halls. In the main one you can see three Qing dynasty statues of the seated Buddha and one of Guanyin, the much revered goddess of mercy (see p499).

Liurong Lu has a colourful array of souvenir shops selling ceramics, jade and religious ornaments. Behind the temple, Cangqian Jie is a narrow street filled with stalls selling amulets, incense sticks and the like.

GUANGXIAO TEMPLE 光孝禅寺
The **'Bright Filial Piety Temple'** (Guāng Xiào Chán Sì; 109 Jinghui Lu; metro line No 1 Xīmén Kŏu station; admission Y4; ⏰ 6am-5pm), about 400m west of the Temple of the Six Banyan Trees, is one of the oldest (founded in the 4th century AD) temples in Guăngzhōu. It's a large complex with more than a half-dozen halls and temples, most of which date from after a major fire in the mid-17th century. Keep an eye open for the statue of the laughing Buddha and some impressive latticed windows.

MOSQUE DEDICATED TO THE PROPHET 怀圣寺
The original building on the site of this **mosque** (Huáishèng Sì; metro line No 1 Xīmén Kŏu station, bus No 56; ☎ 8333 3593; 56 Guangta Lu) is believed to have been established in AD 627 by an uncle of Mohammed, the first Muslim missionary to China, but the present ones date from the Qing dynasty. Inside the grounds is a 24m-tall minaret known as **Guāng Tă** ('Naked Tower' or 'Smooth Minaret') because of its unadorned appearance. The mosque keeps erratic hours (and may not be open to the public in any case).

TEMPLE OF THE FIVE IMMORTALS 五仙观
This Taoist **temple** (Wŭxiān Guàn; ☎ 8333 6853; Huifu Xilu; admission Y5; ⏰ 9am-5pm), due south of the mosque, is said to be where the five rams carrying celestial beings (see p553) first 'landed', and the large hollow in the rock in the first courtyard to the right is

said to be the impression of one of the immortal's feet.

The 5-tonne bell in the main tower is known as 'calamity bell' since it was rung as a warning of impending danger or disaster. Behind the tower are life-size statues representing four of the immortals, with four matching stone rams in the temple forecourt.

CHEN CLAN ANCESTRAL HALL 陈家祠
This enormous **compound** (Chénjiā Cí; ☎ 8181 4559; 34 Enlongji Lu; metro line No 1 Chénjiācí station, bus Nos 85 & 104; admission adult/senior over 60 & student Y10/5; ♥ 8.30am-5.30pm), part of the Guangdong Museum of Folk Art (Guǎngdōng Mínjiān Gōngyì Bówùguǎn), was built as the extended Chen family's ancestral hall in 1894. It encompasses 19 buildings of the traditional Lingnan style (combining traditional Chinese, Japanese and Western traditions) and numerous courtyards, and houses exquisite carvings, statuary and paintings.

CATHEDRAL OF THE SACRED HEART
石室教堂
The impressive twin-spired **Roman Catholic cathedral** (Shí Shì Jiàotáng; Yide Xilu; bus Nos 8, 82 & 86; ♥ 8am-6pm), built between 1863 and 1888, was designed by a French architect in the neo-Gothic style and built entirely of granite. The massive towers reach an impressive height of 48m. The four bronze bells were made in France as was the original stained glass, most of which has now disappeared.

QINGPING MARKET 清平市场
Just north of Shamian Island, what is translated as **Peaceful Market** (Qīngpíng Shìchǎng; Qingping Lu, btwn Liu'ersan & Dishipu Lu; metro line No 1 Huángshā station; ♥ 8am-6pm) was one of the first private markets to flourish as a result of Deng Xiaoping's radical economic reforms when it opened in 1979. While vast displays of medicinal herbs, dried mushrooms and other plants, live birds and tubs of squirming turtles, fish and frogs are now commonplace at markets throughout China, this was the trailblazer. In fact Qingping Market became so successful that vendors began trafficking in live monkeys, deer, dogs, owls, pangolins and other exotic creatures for human con-

sumption until a police crackdown in the late 1990s.

SHAMIAN ISLAND 沙面岛
Shamian Island (Shāmiàn Dǎo; metro line No 1 Huángshā station), connected to the mainland by several bridges, is a leafy oasis from the bustle of Guǎngzhōu. With its history and evocative architecture, it's an ideal place to wander around and visit the past.

Shamian Island ('Sand Surface Island') was little more than a sandbank when foreign traders were granted permission to set up their warehouses here in the middle of the 18th century. Land reclamation has increased its area to 800m from east to west and 350m from north to south. The island became a British and French concession after the two Opium Wars and shelters some 150 colonial buildings in varying states of decay.

The Roman Catholic **Church of Our Lady of Lourdes** (Tiānzhǔjiào Loùshèngmǔ Táng; Shamian Dajie; ♥ 8am-6pm), built by the French in 1892, is about the only real sight on the island. **Shamian Dajie**, the main boulevard on which it stands, is a gentle stretch of gardens, trees and old men playing Chinese checkers.

The reason why there are so many Westerners – particularly Americans – wheeling strollers and prams on the island is because they are in the process of adopting Chinese babies, a process that generally requires prospective parents to spend a month in Guǎngzhōu. The US consulate is on the island.

ART MUSEUMS
The **Guangzhou Museum of Art** (Guǎngzhōu Yìshù Bówùguǎn; ☎ 8365 9337; 3 Luhu Lu; bus Nos 10 & 63; adult/student Y20/10; ♥ 9am-5pm Tue-Fri, 9.30am-4.30pm Sat & Sun), which opened in 2000, houses an impressive collection of ancient and contemporary Chinese art and sculpture, including terracotta soldiers from Xī'ān and works by painters Guan Shanyue, Lai Shaoqi, and Lu Xiongcai. One wing of the museum houses a collection of works by Liao Bing Xiong, a political cartoonist exiled from China in 1958.

The even newer **Guangdong Museum of Art** (Guǎngdōng Měishùguǎn; ☎ 8735 1468; www.gdmoa.org; 38 Yanyu Lu; bus Nos 12, 18 & 89; adult/student Y15/7; ♥ 9am-5pm Tue-Sun), with 12 exhibition halls, is in a startling modern building at the eastern end of Èrshā Dăo (literally, 'Two Sands Island'). For the most part it has special exhibits.

REVOLUTIONARY SIGHTS

The **Peasant Movement Institute** (Nóngmín Yùndòng Jiăngxísuŏ; ☎ 8333 3936; 42 Zhongshan Silu; metro line No 1 Nóngjiăng Suŏ station; adult/student Y5/3; ⊗ 9am-4.30pm), housed in an impressive Ming-dynasty temple dating from 1370, was formerly a communist training centre set up in 1926 and chaired by Mao Zedong. The institute is now a revolutionary museum.

Chrysanthemum Hill Park (Huánghuāgăng Gōngyuán; ☎ 8769 4152; 79 Xianlie Zhonglu; bus Nos 11 & 65; adult/student Y8/4; ⊗ 6am-6.45pm) north of Huanshi Donglu is the site of the **Mausoleum of the 72 Martyrs** (Qīshíèr Lièshì Mù) dedicated to the six-dozen soldiers under the command of Sun Yatsen who fell here during the Chinese Revolution in 1911.

PEARL RIVER CRUISES 珠江游览船

The northern bank of Pearl River is one of the most interesting areas of Guăngzhōu – filled with people, markets and dilapidated buildings, and a wonderful place to stroll on a warm summer's evening.

The **Guangzhou Passenger Ship Company** (☎ 8333 0397) has up to five evening cruises on the Pearl River (Y38 to Y98, 1½ hours) between 6.30pm and 9pm. Boats leave from the **Tianzi Pier** (Tiānzi Mătóu; Beijing Nanlu; metro line No 2 Hăizhū Guăngchăng station), at the southern end of Beijing Nanlu just east of Haizhu Bridge (Hăizhū Qiáo), and head down the river as far as Ersha Island (Èrshā Dăo) before turning back.

Special Events

The invitation-only, 10-day **Guangzhou Trade Fair** (Zhōngguó Chūkŏu Shāngpĭn Jiāoyì Huì; ☎ 2608 8888; www.cantonfair.org.cn), also known as the Chinese Export Commodities Fair, has been held twice yearly, usually in April and October, since 1957 and attracts some 150,000 buyers from 200 countries. Apart from the Spring Festival (Chinese New Year) in late January/early February, this is the biggest event in Guăngzhōu and accommodation can be a real problem. The fair is held in complexes on Liuhua Lu opposite the Dong Fang and China Hotels and south of the river in the Pázhōu district.

Sleeping

Guăngzhōu is not a great place for budget hotels, but prices have dropped from the dizzy heights of a few years ago. In general most hotels open to foreigners here are in the mid-range and top-end price categories. A surfeit of rooms due to over-building have forced many places to offer up to 50% off their rack rates, depending on the season, so it's a good idea to get into the habit of asking for discounts (zhékòu). Top-end (and some mid-range) places add 15% service charge to the quoted room rate.

Accommodation of all types is centred in three principal areas: around the main train station in the north; along Huanshi Donglu in the northeast; and on Shamian Island and along the river in the south.

All rooms listed in this section have bathrooms and air-conditioning unless noted otherwise.

TRAIN STATION AREA

If you're arriving in Guăngzhōu at the main train station it might be worth checking out what's on offer from the galaxy of touts who will come rushing at you as you exit.

Budget

CITS Hotel Guangdong (Guăngdōng Guólǚ Jiŭdiàn; ☎ 8666 6889, ext 3812; fax 8667 9787; 179 Huanshi Xilu; s Y168-188, d Y228-318, tr Y240-378) The 149 rooms at this hotel by the main train station are no great shakes, but count on a 30% discount on the higher priced 'deluxe' rooms (ie ones with carpet and fridge).

Guangzhou City International Youth Hostel (Guăngzhōu Guójì Qīngnián Lǚguăndiàn; dm Y50, s without/with bathroom Y80/118, d Y130/178) This Hostelling International-affiliated property inside the CITS Hotel Guangdong has very cheap dorm accommodation for HI members.

Mid-Range

Art Hotel (Yìshù Bīnguăn; ☎ 8667 0255; fax 8667 0266; 698 Renmin Beilu; s & d Y268-328, ste from Y628) This 100-room hotel directly behind the Friendship Hotel has clean, bright rooms and is one of the better mid-range deals in this area. Discounts of 30% may be available.

Liuhua Hotel (Liúhuā Bīnguăn; ☎ 8666 8800; www.lh.com.cn; 194 Huanshi Xilu; s & d Y280-428, ste from Y498) This large hotel with some 500 rooms is just opposite the train station. The lobby is a great place to chill (literally) after a 36-hour train ride. Discounts of up to 60% are available.

Friendship Hotel (Yŏuyì Bīnguăn; ☎ 8667 9898; fax 8667 8653, 698 Renmin Beilu; s & d Y330-380, ste from Y480) This 112-room hotel is a mid-range alternative for those attending the Guangzhou Trade Fair.

Top End

Dong Fang Hotel (Dōngfāng Bīnguăn; ☎ 8666 9900; www.dongfanghotel-gz.com; 120 Liuhua Lu; s US$96, d US$140-160, ste from US$240) The 'Eastern' is as close to the Guangzhou Trade Fair's main hall as you'll get. It's a vast place, with 880 guestrooms and five restaurants. Discounts of up to 60% are available.

China Hotel (Zhōngguó Dàjiǔdiàn; ☎ 8666 6888; www.marriotthotels.com/canmc; Liuhua Lu; s & d US$98-168, ste from US$148) A long-standing favourite with international business travellers, this 1013-room luxury hotel is managed by the Marriott group and boasts some outstanding food outlets. Ask about discounts of up to 30%.

NORTHEAST AREA

The northeastern part of the city has the highest concentration of top-end hotels and is probably the best area for business travellers.

Mid-Range

Baiyun Hotel (Báiyún Bīnguăn; ☎ 8333 3998; www.baiyun-hotel.com; 367 Huanshi Donglu; s Y398-658, d Y508-728) The 706-room 'White Cloud', with a full dozen food and beverage outlets, is an excellent choice for the price. Count on discounts of about 20%.

Cathay Hotel (Guótài Bīnguăn; ☎ 8386 2888; fax 8384 2606, 376 Huanshi Donglu; s & d Y500-680, ste from Y1080) Rooms at this Hong Kong–owned hotel are a cut above for the price category though service is a bit frenetic. Discounts of up to 60% may be available.

Top End

Garden Hotel (Huāyuán Jiǔdiàn; ☎ 8333 8989; www.thegardenhotel.com.cn; 368 Huanshi Donglu; s & d US$160-180, ste from US$450) This elegant, five-star property has some lovely green spaces. Don't miss the enormous mural in the lobby.

Guangdong International Hotel (Guăngdōng Guójì Dàjiǔdiàn; ☎ 8331 1888; www.gitic.com.cn; 339 Huanshi Donglu; s & d US$140-170, ste from US$220) This 702-room hotel, once owned by the now bankrupt GITIC provincial investment company,

soldiers on independently. You'll see 40% knocked off the rack rates by just booking online.

SHAMIAN ISLAND & RIVERFRONT

Shamian Island is by far the quietest and most attractive area to stay in Guăngzhōu; you are much more likely to meet other travellers here and the nightlife options are decent. The riverfront area, with its busy streets and overpasses, is noisier but less expensive.

Budget

Guangzhou Youth Hostel (Shěngwàibàn Zhāodàisuǒ; ☎ 8121 8606; fax 8121 8298; 2 Shamian Sijie; dm Y50, s/d/tr Y150/180/240) This place wins the title of 'backpackers' headquarters' in Guăngzhōu. It has clean and comfortable rooms and there's a useful travel desk for booking train and plane tickets.

Guangdong Overseas Chinese Activity Centre (Guăngdōng Qiáobāo Huódòng Zhōngxīn; ☎ 8121 8218; fax 8121 8690; 31-33 Shamian Dajie; d/tr Y190/230) The friendly service compensates for the somewhat claustrophobic rooms at this small hotel on Shamian Island.

Mid-Range

Guangdong Victory Hotel (Shènglì Bīnguăn; ☎ 0121 6688; www.vhotel.com; 53 & 54 Shamian Beijie) There are two branches of the Victory Hotel on Shamian Island, an older one at 54 Shamian Beijie (enter from 10 Shamian Sijie) with rooms for between Y280 and Y360 and a newer wing at 53 Shamian Beijie with doubles/triples for Y380/580.

Shamian Hotel (Shāmiàn Bīnguăn; ☎ 8121 8288; www.gdshamianhotel.com; 52 Shamian Nanjie; s Y268-345, d 275-380, tr Y312-405, q Y420-520) This attractive and popular hotel on Shamian Island faces the sea and a little park.

Xinhua Hotel (Xīnhuá Dàjiǔdiàn; ☎ 8188 9788; fax 8186 8809; 2-6 Renmin Nanlu; s Y198-225, d Y248-320, tr Y450) This reasonably priced hotel is arguably the pick of the crop of the riverfront hotels. The Chinese-style suites (Y980) and those with their own sauna (Y680) are worth considering. Discounts of up to 30% are available.

Aiqun Hotel (Àiqún Dàjiǔdiàn; ☎ 8186 6668, 8188 3519; 113 Yanjiang Xilu; s Y250, d Y320-430, tr Y368, ste from Y538) The grand old 360-room 'Love the Masses' (whose name has nothing to do with what's on offer at the nearby cathedral) faces the Pearl River and dates back to 1937. Singles are an excellent deal, while the higher priced doubles offer views of the river.

Customs Conference & Reception Centre (Hăiguān Huìyì Jiēdài Zhōngxīn; ☎ 8110 2388; fax 8121 8552; 35 Shamian Dajie; d Y500, ste Y800) Housed in an old colonial building on Shamian Island's main drag, this hotel has 42 doubles and seven suites.

Furama Hotel (Fùlìhuá Dàjiŭdiàn; ☎ 8132 3288; www.furama.com; Changdi Nanlu; s & d Y450, ste from 900) Some of the upper rooms in this 360-room hotel have panoramic views of the river.

Baigong Hotel (Báigōng Jiŭdiàn; ☎ 8101 2213; www.baigong-hotel.com; 13-17 Renmin Nanlu; s Y268-388, d Y288-428, tr Y388-538) The 'White Palace' has been around in some form or another for 70 years and offers good, welcoming service.

New Asia Hotel (Xīnyà Jiŭdiàn; ☎ 8188 4722; fax 8188 3733; 10-12 Renmin Nanlu; s Y260-380, d Y320-420, tr Y430) This hotel founded in 1927 is close to the river and has clean and attractive rooms. The staff try hard to please. Discounts of 30% are available.

Top End

White Swan Hotel (Báitiān'é Bīnguăn; ☎ 8188 6968; www.whiteswanhotel.com; 1 Shamian Nanjie; s & d US$148-180, ste from US$240) This 843-room property is the best known (if not the best) hotel in Guăngzhōu, with an excellent range of rooms and outlets (a dozen restaurants and bars), all business facilities and a shopping arcade.

Eating

Some of Guăngzhōu's long-established Chinese restaurants are legendary. Nowadays just about any cuisine you can name is on offer in a city that often appears to live in order to eat.

CHINESE

Guangzhou Restaurant (Guăngzhōu Jiŭjiā; ☎ 8138 0388; 2 Wenchang Nanlu; dishes Y35-80; 7am-3pm & 5.30-10pm) This is probably the most famous restaurant in Guăngzhōu and spreads across three floors. Specialities include shark's fin soup with shredded chicken, crabmeat balls, braised pigeon and endless preparations of seafood.

Da Tung Restaurant (Dàtóng Jiŭjiā; ☎ 8188 8988; 71 Yanjiang Xilu; dim sum Y18-25; 7am-midnight)

This local favourite is in an eight-storey building that can seat 1600 diners so don't worry about not getting a table. Specialities include *dàtóng cuìpíjī* (crisp-fried chicken) and *kăo rŭzhū* (roast suckling pig).

Tao Tao Ju Restaurant (Táotáojū Jiŭjiā; ☎ 8139 6111; 20 Dishipu Lu; dishes from Y35; 6.45am-midnight) The dim sum at this restaurant, housed in an academy dating back to the 17th century, is particularly good. Specialities include the trademark *táotáo jiāngcōng jī* (tao tao ginger and onion chicken).

Moslem Restaurant (Huímín Fàndiàn; ☎ 8130 3991; 325 Zhongshan Liulu; dishes from Y25; 6.30am-midnight) This large restaurant with the imaginative name serves excellent Huí (Chinese Muslim) cuisine. Try the *shuàn yángròu* (boiled sliced mutton) or the *cuìpí huŏé* (crispy goose).

Nur Bostan Muslim Restaurant (Nŭĕr Bósītăn Cāntīng; ☎ 8187 4919; 43 Guangta Lu; dishes from Y20; 8.30am-10.30pm) This restaurant opposite the Mosque Dedicated to the Prophet serves halal food as prepared by the Uighur people of Xīnjiāng in northwest China. There's lots of lamb dishes and occasional live entertainment.

Banxi Restaurant (Bànxī Jiŭjiā; ☎ 8181 5718; 151 Longjin Xilu; dishes from Y15; 5am-9.30pm) This eatery is noted for its dumplings, roast pork, chicken cooked in tea leaves, and crabmeat and shark's fin soup. The famous dim sum is served daily from 5am to 5pm.

OTHER ASIAN

Pasar (Bāshā; ☎ 8121 5910; 7 Shamian Nanjie; dishes Y18-45; 11.30am-11.30pm) This wonderful restaurant, with outside tables overlooking the river, serves Malaysian, Singaporean and Indonesian favourites such as satay (barbecued meat skewers; Y18) and laksa (coconut-based prawn and noodle soup; Y28).

Japan Fusion (Zhōngsēn Míngcài Rìbĕn Liàolĭ; ☎ 3880 8118; 2nd fl, Metro Plaza, 358-378 Tianhe Beilu; dishes from Y35; 11am-10pm) This place claims to be the world's largest Japanese restaurant and after our trip to and from the toilet, we are believers. Everything from sushi and sukiyaki to sake.

Thai Zhen Cow & Bridge (Tàizhēn Niú Qiáo; ☎ 8121 9988; 54 Shamian Beijie; starters & salads Y25-35, mains Y58-78; 11am-11pm) This place with the crazy name serves just about the most authentic Thai food in Guăngzhōu. Helpful service too.

Banana Leaf Restaurant (Jiāoyè Fēngwèi Wū; ☎ 8359 7499; ground fl, Broadcasting & TV Hotel, 8 Luhu Lu; mains Y30-65; ⊗ 11am-midnight) This is a branch of a chain that serves Southeast Asian curries and other dishes.

Haveli Restaurant (☎ 8359 4533; Overseas Chinese Village, 2 Aiguo Lu; starters Y30-45, mains Y35-50, set lunch Y38; ⊗ 11am-2am) If you're in need of a fix of Indian curry or a tandoori dish, head for this charming restaurant with outside seating opposite the Guangzhou Holiday Inn.

WESTERN

La Seine (Sàinàhé Făguó Cāntīng; ☎ 8735 2531; 33 Qingbo Lu; soups Y40-68, starters Y48-138, fish & grills Y68-218; ⊗ lunch 11am-2.30pm, dinner 5.30pm-midnight) This excellent French-run restaurant on Ersha Island, sharing space with the Xinghai Concert Hall (see right), is especially popular at weekend brunch (Y78).

Lucy's (Lùsī Jiŭbā Cāntīng; ☎ 8121 5106; 3 Shamian Nanjie; Y28-40; ⊗ 11am-2am) A favourite of Americans on a mission (see p555), this Shamian landmark has decent burgers, fried chicken, pizza, and beer for Y16 a pint (happy hour is 4pm to 6pm daily). Service is especially welcoming.

Rose Garden Club (Méiguì Yuánjùlèbù; ☎ 8121 8008; 3 Shamian Nanjie; starters & pasta Y25, mains Y18-48; ⊗ 9.30-2am) Closer to the river than Lucy's but not as popular, this bar-restaurant has Western and Chinese dishes and *al fresco* seating.

VEGETARIAN

Shang Shi Zhai Vegetarian Restaurant (Shàngshízhāi Sùcàiguăn; ☎ 8108 0385; 38 Jinghui Lu; dishes Y16-34; ⊗ 6am-9.30pm) Just east of the Guangxiao Temple, this place serves simple vegetarian dishes and takeaway on the ground floor and dim sum on the 1st floor.

Drinking

BARS

Guăngzhōu has a number of international-style bars where, in addition to sinking chilled Tsingtaos and imported beers, you can you can scoff pizza or burgers, rice or noodles. One area especially popular with local people is **Baietan Bar Street** (Báiétán Jiŭbā; metro line No 1 Fāngcūn station, ⊗ approx 7pm-2.30am), a strip of some two dozen bars on the riverfront opposite Shamian Island. Reach it via the metro or the ferry (Y1)

from Hungsha Pier (Huángshā Mătóu), just west of the White Swan Hotel, which runs round the clock

Aiqun Hotel Jazz Bar (Àiqún Dàjiŭdiàn Juéshìba; ☎ 8186 6668, ext 298; 113 Yanjiang Xilu; ⊗ 11am-1am) What better venue for jazz than this old pile (see p557) dating back to the 1930s? Two-hour sessions start at 9.30pm.

Cave Bar (Mòxīgē Cāntīngjiŭbā; ☎ 8386 3660; 360 Huanshi Donglu; ⊗ 7pm-2am) This tequila-and-salsa bar serves Tex-Mex food (Y16 to Y55) as well as drinks. Happy hour is 7pm to 9.30pm daily.

Elephant and Castle (Dàxiàngbăo Jiŭbā; ☎ 8359 3309; 363 Huanshi Donglu; ⊗ 5pm-3am) This place is Guăngzhōu's most popular sports bar with decent pub grub (Y28 to Y35) and a happy hour from 5pm to 8pm daily.

CAFÉS

Cafés are sprouting up like mushrooms after rain in Guăngzhōu and, in addition to the predictable international chains, a number of home-grown varieties are represented.

Blenz Coffee (Băiyì Kāfēi; ☎ 8121 5052; 46 Shamian Dajie; ⊗ 7.30am-11.30pm) Canada's answer to Starbucks has several branches here, including this pleasant one on Shamian Island.

Seattle Espresso (Xīyătú Yìpàsū; ☎ 8339 7608; 2 Qiaoguang Lu; ⊗ 8am-11pm) In addition to excellent coffee (Y20), this Western-style café and bar serves reasonable breakfast and lunch/dinner combinations.

Entertainment

That's Guangzhou (www.thatsguangzhou.com), a free monthly entertainment guide, is an invaluable source of information for what's on in town. It's available at most of the major hotels and international-style bars and restaurants. **City Talk** (ismaygz@pub.guangzhou.gd.cn), another monthly freebie, is more of a 'scene and seen' 'zine and its listings are far less reliable.

Xinghai Concert Hall (Xīnghăi Yīnyuè Tīng; ☎ 8735 2766, 8735 3869; 33 Qingbo Lu), home to the Guangzhou Symphony Orchestra (GSO), this is the city's premier venue for classical music. It's on Ersha Island and has two concert halls that are said to have perfect acoustics.

CLUBS

The nightlife in Guăngzhōu moves fast, but it can be difficult to pin down venues.

Check *That's Guangzhou* for the latest hot spots.

Africain Bar (Fēizhōu Bā; ☎ 8762 3336; 2nd fl, Zidong Hua Bldg, 707 Dongfeng Donglu; ☷ 7.30pm-2am Mon-Fri, 7.30pm-4am Sat & Sun) If reggae and bongo is your thing, you may want to try this 'underground' place with the French name.

Face Club (Fēisī Jùlèbù; ☎ 8388 0688; basement, International Bank Tower, 191 Dongfeng Xilu; ☷ 8pm-2am) DJs from all over the world come to spin an eclectic mix of tunes, but karaoke threatens to take over.

Yes Disco (Yīnlè Gōngchàng; ☎ 8136 6154; 2nd fl, Liuhua Square, 132 Dongfeng Xilu; ☷ 8.30pm-2am) Strobe and sci-fi in your face at this almost-retro disco.

Shopping

Though not known as a mecca for shopping, Guăngzhōu's countless shops and shopping centres can deliver the goods. Two of the better malls are the **World Trade Mall** (Shìmáo Dàshà; ☎ 8778 9938; 371-375 Huanshi Donglu) and the nearby **Peace World Plaza** (Hăoshìjiè Guăngchăng; ☎ 8375 2800; 362-366 Huanshi Donglu).

One of the best places to shop is in and around Tianhe Nanyi Lu where you'll find any number of shops selling everything under the sun – from **clothing** and items for the home to **antiques** and **curios**.

The intersection of Beijing Lu and Zhongshan Lu, northeast of Haizhu Circle, was traditionally the principal shopping area in the city and is still a decent place to buy clothes and shoes if you can find the right size. A better street for **discount clothing**, including some of the better Hong Kong labels, might be Nonglin Xialu.

On Shamian Sijie at the western end of Shamian Island is a string of well-stocked **souvenir shops** selling paintings, clothes and calligraphy.

The large hotels have well-supplied tourist stores, but bear in mind that their prices can be up to 10 times the price on the streets.

Getting There & Away

AIR

China National Aviation Corporation (Zhōngguó Mínháng; CNAC) is represented by **China Southern Airlines** (Zhōngguó Nánfāng Hánglóng; CZ; ☎ 800-820 6666, 8668 2000; www.cs-air.com; 181 Huanshi Lu; ☷ 9am-6pm), arguably China's best-run airline. The office

is southeast of the main train station. The ticketing office on the 2nd floor is open round the clock. For general flight information ring ☎ 96060.

China Southern has five daily flights to Hong Kong (Y694 one way, 35 minutes). There are also flights to Shànghăi (Y1160) and Běijīng (Y1700). The domestic airport tax is Y50.

International destinations served by China Southern include Amsterdam, Bangkok, Ho Chi Minh City, Jakarta, Kuala Lumpur, Los Angeles, Melbourne, Osaka, Paris, Penang, Singapore and Sydney. The international airport tax is Y80.

Some foreign airlines with offices in Guăngzhōu:

Japan Air Lines (☎ 8666 5581; fax 8666 5603; room A201, China Hotel, Liuhua Lu)

Malaysia Airlines (☎ 8335 8868; fax 8335 8898; shop M04-05, Garden Hotel, 368 Huanshi Donglu)

Singapore Airlines (☎ 8335 8868; mezzanine, Garden Hotel, 368 Huanshi Donglu)

Thai Airways (☎ 3882 1818; fax 3882 1333; 7th fl, Times Square; Tianhe Beilu)

United Airlines (☎ 8333 8989, ext 3165; Garden Hotel, 368 Huanshi Donglu)

Vietnam Airlines (☎ 8386 7093, ext 10; room 924, East Bldg, Garden Hotel, 368 Huanshi Donglu)

BOAT

Guăngzhōu is a major port on China's southern coast but most ferry and catamaran services have been discontinued, victims of much improved land transportation. However, there are still services within the greater Guăngzhōu metropolitan area to/from Hong Kong and far-flung Hăinán. Tickets are available from CTS Guangzhou (see p553) and the travel desks at most top-end hotels.

High-speed catamarans, run jointly by **Nanhai Pinggang Passenger Transport Co** (☎ 8444 8218, 0757-8677 2417) and Hong Kong's **Chu Kong Passenger Transportation Co** (☎ 2858 3876; www .cksp.com.hk), make two trips a day from the port of Nánhăi in Píngzhōu, located about 23km southwest of Guăngzhōu, to Hong Kong. Boats depart from Nánhăi at 9.15am and 4pm and from Hong Kong at 8.05am and 2pm. The trip takes 2½ hours and costs Y170/160 in 1st/2nd class.

Ferries for Hăikŏu on Hainan Island (Hăinán Dăo) depart from the pier at **Huángpǔ** (☎ 8248 9839), located some 32km southeast of Guǎngzhōu, at 3.30pm on Tuesday, Thursday and Saturday. The trip takes 18 hours and prices range from Y150 in 5th class to Y450 in 1st class.

BUS

The easiest way to get to Hong Kong is by the deluxe buses that ply the Guǎngzhōu–Shēnzhèn freeway in 2½ hours. Most of the top-end hotels, including the Dong Fang, China and Guangdong International Hotels, have them, and tickets cost around Y100 (Y250 to Hong Kong International Airport).

Direct buses through Zhūhǎi to Macau (Y60, 2½ hours) leave from the China and Garden Hotels.

Deluxe buses to Shēnzhèn (Y60, two hours) leave frequently from two bus stations: the Liúhuā bus station (Liúhuā Chēzhàn) that straddles the chaotic mess of vehicles across Huanshi Xilu in front of the train station, and from the main **Guǎngdōng long-distance bus station** (Guǎngdōng Shěng qìchēzhàn; Huanshi Xilu) west of the train station. They leave every 12 minutes or so from 6am to 11pm. Buses depart every 15 minutes for Zhūhǎi (Y35 to Y55, 2½ hours) between 7am and 9pm.

Buses for other destinations leaving mostly from the long-distance bus station include: Fóshān (Y12–14, 45 minutes); Guìlín (Y150 to Y180, sleeper, 13 hours); Hǎikǒu (Y180 to Y280, sleeper, 16 hours); Nánníng (Y150 to Y180, sleeper, 15 hours); Shàntóu (Y90 to Y180, six hours); Zhàoqìng (Y30, 1¼ hours); and Zhōngshān (Y30 to Y35, two hours).

TRAIN

Guǎngzhōu's **main train station** (metro line No 2 Guǎngzhōu Huǒchēzhàn station), which is useful for short-distance destinations such as Zhàoqìng (Y24, 2½ hours), is a chaotic and seething mass of humanity. The **Guangzhou east train station** (metro line No 1 Guǎngzhōu Dōng Zhàn station), on the other hand, which serves more far-flung destinations, is a model of efficiency. Bus No 272 (Y2) links the two stations while bus No 271 goes between the Liuhua bus station and the Guangzhou east train station.

Travellers will find ticketing at the east station a fairly straightforward affair, with separate **ticketing booths** (🕙 7.30am-9pm) for

Hung Hom, in Hong Kong's Kowloon (Y253/210 HK$230/190 1st/2nd class, 1¾ hours), and Shēnzhèn (Y80, 55 minutes) on the border with Hong Kong. Signs are in English. There are four high-speed through trains per day to Shēnzhèn; local trains (Y70, two hours) depart every half-hour from about 6.30am to 10.20pm.

Hong Kong is served by a dozen fast trains a day from the east station between 8.35am and 9.23pm. Trains also head north from here to Shànghǎi (hard seat/soft seat/sleeper Y216/392/609, 21¼ hours) and Běijīng (Y253/452/708, 22¼ hours) as well as destinations all over the country.

Despite all the hassles at the main Guǎngzhōu train station, booking train tickets here is a lot easier than it used to be. There are two separate places to buy them at the station itself. A 24-hour ticketing office is in the hall to the left of the large clock as you face the station. Current, next-day and two-day advance tickets are sold in the white and silver building just east of the station, open daily from 5.30am to 10.30pm.

CITS Guangzhou (see p553) near the main train station will book train tickets up to five days in advance for a service charge of about Y20.

Getting Around

Greater Guǎngzhōu, as defined by the Huancheng Expressway, extends some 20km east to west and more than 10km north to south. Since most of the interesting sights are scattered throughout the city, seeing the place on foot not exactly practical. Metro line No 1 goes by many of the city's major sights along Zhongshan Lu and is also a convenient way to get to Shamian Island. Metro line No 2 is good for the main train station, many of the sights around Yuexiu Park and the riverfront hotels.

TO/FROM THE AIRPORT

Guǎngzhōu's new Baiyun International Airport (Báiyún Guójì Fēijīchǎng), which opened in June 2004, is 34km north of the city. There is an airport shuttle bus (Y13 to Y32, one hour) that leaves from a half-dozen locations around Guǎngzhōu, including the China Southern Airlines main office (see opposite) near the train station, every

15 to 30 minutes from 7am to 10pm. A taxi to/from the airport will cost about Y100.

BICYCLES

Rental bikes are usually available somewhere on Shamian Island; ask at your hotel for details. At the time of research there was a stall on Shamian Erjie in the northeast corner of Shamian Park (Shāmiàn Gōngyuán) with bicycles for rent for Y15 per hour (plus Y400 deposit).

BUS

Guăngzhōu has a large network of motor buses and electric trolley-buses (Y2 to Y5). Unfortunately the network is overstretched and the buses are usually very crowded.

METRO

Guăngzhōu's No 1 metro line, which opened in 1999, runs for 18.5km from Guăngzhōu east train station in the northeast and across Pearl River in the southwest. A second line, which opened in June 2003, goes essentially north–south for 23km from Pázhōu station in the south to Sānyuán Lǐ station in the northeast. The two lines intersect at one station: Gōngyuán Qián. Several more lines, including an extension to line No 2, are under construction

Depending on the line, the metro runs from about 6.20am to just before 11pm. Fares are Y2 to Y7, depending on the number of stops you travel (eg, Y5 for the 10 stops between the two train stations). You can pay with a plastic token sold at kiosks or machines in every station or with a stored-value Yang Cheng Tong (Yáng Chéng Tōng) card, which offers a 5% discount on all fares. The card costs Y80, including a refundable Y30 deposit, and can be recharged in increments of Y50 up to Y500.

TAXI

Taxis are abundant on the streets of Guăngzhōu but demand is great, particularly during the peak hours: from 8am to 9am and at lunch and dinner.

Taxis are equipped with meters, which are always used, and flag-fall is Y7. A trip from the main train station to Shamian Island should cost between Y15 and Y20; from Guangzhou east train station to the island is Y40 to Y45.

AROUND GUĂNGZHŌU

Báiyún Shān 白云山

Báiyún Shān (White Cloud Hills; admission Y5), in the northern suburbs of Guăngzhōu, are an adjunct to of the **Dayu Range** (Dàyǔ Lǐng), the chief group of mountains in Guăngdōng. In total there are more than 30 peaks that were once dotted with temples and monasteries. It's a good hike up to the top – or a leisurely walk down if you take the cable car – and a lovely respite from the polluted city below.

Star Touching Peak (Mōxīng Lǐng) at 382m is the highest point in the hills. Local people rate the vista from a precipice called **White Cloud Evening View** (Báiyún Wǎnwàng) as one of the eight greatest sights of Guăngzhōu.

Famous as a resort since the Tang and Song dynasties, the hills have been thematically restored to attract tourists and now boast a number of attractions including the **Mingchun Valley Aviary** (Míngchūngǔ Niǎoyuán; ☎ 3722 9528; admission Y25; ✪ 8.30am-5pm), which features a wide variety of bird species. The restored **Nengren Temple** (Néngrén Sì; admission Y5; ✪ 8am-6pm), a short walk from the cable car's upper station, is also worth a visit.

GETTING THERE & AWAY

The hills are about 15km from Guăngzhōu. Bus Nos 24 and 285 can take you from Dongfeng Zhonglu, just north of Rénmín Gōngyuán, to the cable car at the bottom of the hill near Luhu Park (Lùhú Gōngyuán). The trip takes between half and one hour, depending on traffic. The bus stops at the park entrance.

FÓSHĀN 佛山

☎ 0757 / pop 496,300

Fóshān, 19km southwest of Guăngzhōu, is remarkable for three things: its enormous ancestral temple, a beacon for southern Chinese for centuries; its pottery and ceramics industry, which has continued uninterrupted since the Song dynasty (AD 960–1276); and its martial arts grand master Huang Feihong (1847–1925), who was born here and about whom so much has been written and filmed.

The city's name – 'Buddha Hill' – is derived from three statues of the Lord Gautama that stood on a nearby hill under the Tang (AD 618–907), when Fóshān was an important religious centre.

Information

Foshan Municipal Government (www.foshan.gov.cn)
Has an excellent website on Fóshān.

Bank of China (Zhōngguó Yínháng; cnr Renmin &
Zumiao Lu; 8.30am-5pm Mon-Fri, 9am-4pm Sat)

China International Travel Service Foshan
(CITS; Zhōngguó Guójì Lǚxíngshè; ☎ 8363 6888; 75
Fenjiang Zhonglu; 8am-6pm) Very helpful branch in
the Foshan Hotel.

China Travel Service Foshan (CTS; Zhōngguó
Lǚxíngshè; ☎ 8223 3828; 14 Zumiao Lu; 8.30am-6pm
Mon-Fri, 9am-5pm Sat & Sun) This CTS at the Overseas
Chinese Hotel can book air, train and boat tickets.

Post office (yóujú; Qinren Lu; 8.30am-9.30pm)

Sights

ZÚ MIÀO 祖庙

This ancestral **temple complex** (☎ 8229 3723;
21 Zumiao Lu; admission Y20; 8.30am-7.30pm) was
originally built in the late 11th century
as a place of ancestor worship, but from
the mid-15th century it has enshrined a
2.5-tonne bronze statue of Beidi, the Taoist
god of water and all the creatures that live
in and around it. You'll see lots of carvings
of turtles and snakes that are meant to protect the city from flooding.

Some of the buildings here have the
'wok-handle' roofs distinctive to the region
as well as delightful ridge tiles covered with
ceramic figures and ornaments. The compound is part of the **Foshan Museum** (Fóshān
Bówùguǎn) and contains some excellent
collections, including an extensive one on
Cantonese opera and martial arts.

SHÍWĀN 石湾

Some 2km southwest of Fóshān, this township is celebrated for its porcelain and
ceramics. The highlight is a visit to the
Nanfeng Ancient Kiln (Nánfēng Gǔzào; ☎ 8271 1798;
6 Gaomiao Lu; admission Y15; 8am-6pm), which
contains two kilns from the early Ming that
are more than 30m long and have never
gone out since the day they fired up. Signs
(in English) explain the four-day process
from clay to glazed pot. You can visit the
workshop and there's a large shop selling
exquisite bowls and figurines. Some 200m
east on Gaomiao Lu are some traditional
buildings housing more shops.

OTHER SIGHTS

Around 400m north of the ancestral temple is the Buddhist **Renshou Temple** (Rénshòu

Sì; ☎ 8225 3053; 9 Zumiao Lu; admission free; 8am-
5pm), with its seven-storey pagoda built
in 1656.

Still north, **Liang's Garden** (Liáng Yuán; ☎ 8224
1279; Songfeng Lu; admission Y10; 8.30am-5.30pm) is –
along with Kěyuán in Dōngguǎn (see p573) –

considered to be one of the most beautiful gardens in Guǎngdōng. It's a walled oasis of ponds, pavilions, paths and bridges dating from the first half of the 19th century.

Sleeping & Eating

Foshan Hotel (Fóshān Bīnguǎn; ☎ 8298 6881; 75 Fenjiang Zhonglu; s & d Y638-738, ste from Y850) This 415-room five-star property is Fóshān's swishest and has excellent health and business facilities.

Foshan Overseas Chinese Hotel (Fóshān Huáqiáo Dàshà; ☎ 8222 3828; www.fshq-hotel.com; 14 Zumiao Lu; s Y478-528, d & tw Y528-648, ste Y1288) This 152-room hotel has one star less than its closest competitor but is closer to the main bus and train stations.

Rotating Palace Hotel (Xuàngōng Jiǔdiàn; ☎ 8296 6338; www.fsxuangonghotel.com; 1 Zumiao Lu; s & d Y320-360) This 109-room, mid-range hotel gets its name, not from a queen dervishing within, but from the revolving restaurant on the 18th floor. Some rooms have saunas.

Blue + White (Lán Bái; ☎ 8230 0577; 5 Zumiao Lu; small dishes Y5-8, set meals from Y15; ☼ 24hr) This branch of a popular Taiwan chain of café-restaurants offers solid dishes and set meals round the clock.

Getting There & Away

Frequent buses (Y12 to Y14, 45 minutes) link Fóshān's **Zǔmiào bus station** (Zǔmiào chē zhàn; Chengmentou Lu) with the main bus stations in Guǎngzhōu. Minibuses (Y8 to Y10) also go to Guǎngzhōu's **Guangfo Bus Station** (Guǎngfó Qìchē Zhàn; Zhongshan Balu).

Destinations served from Fóshān's **long-distance bus station** (Fóshān shěng qìchēzhàn; Fenjiang Beilu) include Shēnzhèn (Y70 to Y103) and Zhūhǎi (Y35 to Y60). To get to Hong Kong (Y106 to Y140, three hours) it's easiest to catch one of the five daily buses departing from the Foshan and Foshan Overseas Chinese Hotels.

Trains between Fóshān and Guǎngzhōu (Y13, 30 minutes) are faster than buses, but there are fewer daily departures. There is also a direct express train to Hung Hom in Hong Kong (Y240, 2½ hours), with a daily departure at 10.55am (2.20pm from Kowloon).

CITS Foshan (p563) provides a free shuttle to/from the port of Nánhǎi in Píngzhōu, from where high-speed catamarans depart for Hong Kong (see p560).

Getting Around

Bus No 1 (Y2) links the train station with Zǔ Miào. Bus No 1 is also good for Shíwān, as is No 9.

ZHÀOQÌNG 肇庆

☎ 0758 / pop 331,400

Zhàoqìng, lying on the Xī Jiāng some 110km west of Guǎngzhōu, is bordered to the north by lakes and a series of limestone formations that make up the Seven Star Crags (Qīxīng Yán). The Dǐnghú Shān (Mt Dinghu) protected area to the northeast is one of the most attractive scenic spots in Guǎngdōng.

Information

Bank of China (Zhōngguó Yínháng; Duanshou Wulu; ☼ 8.30am-5.30pm Mon-Fri, 9am-5pm Sat & Sun)

Post office (Yóujú; Jianshe Sanlu; ☼ 8am-8pm)

China Travel Service Zhaoqing (CTS; Zhōngguó Lǚxíngshè; ☎ 226 8090; Duanshou Wulu; ☼ 8am-9pm)

Sights

SEVEN STAR CRAGS PARK 七星岩公园

Central to this **island park** (Qīxīng Yán Gōngyuán; ☎ 227 7724, 238 7218; admission Y50; ☼ 8am-5.30pm), bounded by lakes, is a group of limestone towers. The crags conceal caves and grottos that you can explore; willow and kapok trees line the paths around **Star Lake** (Xīng Hú).

A motor boat (Y10/15 one way/return) will take you from Gateway Square (Páifáng Guǎngchǎng) at the southernmost tip of the lakes to a small bridge leading into the park.

OTHER SIGHTS

Nine-storey **Chongxi Pagoda** (Chóngxī Tǎ; Guta Nanlu; admission Y5; 8.30am-5pm), a red, green and white tower facing the river in the southeast, was badly damaged during the Cultural Revolution but has been restored to its original Song style and can be climbed. On the opposite bank of the river are two similar pagodas.

The oldest part of Zhàoqìng, an important port during the Qing dynasty, is surrounded by **old city walls** (gǔ chéng) complete with fortifications: **River View Tower** (Yuèjiāng Lóu; ☎ 223 2968; Jiangbin Zhonglu; admission Y8; ☼ 8.30am-5pm) to the southeast was rebuilt in 1959 and, to the northwest, the more flamboyant **Cloud Draped Tower** (Pīyú Lóu; Songcheng Xilu).

Sleeping

Duan Zhou Hotel (Duānzhōu Dàjiǔdiàn; ☎ 223 2281; fax 222 9228; 77 Tianning Beilu; s Y228, d Y268-368, tr Y328)

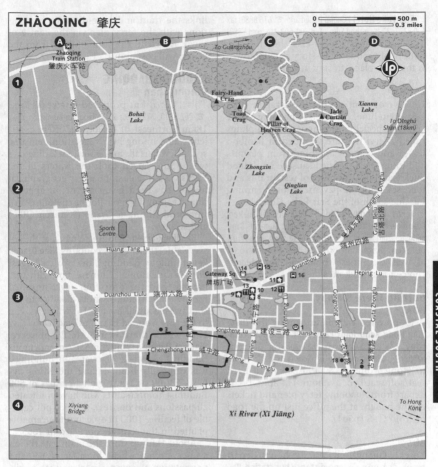

ZHÀOQÌNG 肇庆

This three-star hotel's rooms are quite attractive for the price. Some have lake views.

Dynasty Hotel (Huángcháo Jiǔdiàn; ☎ 223 8238; dynasty@pub.zhaoqing.gd.cn; 9 Duanzhou Wulu; s & d Y560-610, ste from Y950) This flashy new joint has Chinese, Western and Japanese restaurants.

Overseas Chinese Hotel (Huáqiáo Dàshà; ☎ 223 2952; fax 223 1197; 90 Tianning Beilu; s & d Y363-399, tr Y427, ste from Y848) Just next door to the Duan Zhou Hotel, this 200-room place has a stunning central garden-courtyard behind glass.

Star Lake Hotel (Xīnghú Dàjiǔdiàn; ☎ 616 8888; fax 619 3333; 37 Duanzhou Silu; s & d 500-600, ste from Y880) This near international-class hotel at the bottom of a modern, 31-story circular tower is the 'face place' to stay in Zhàoqìng.

Eating

Unless you visit during the Dragon Boat Festival in June, you'll miss Zhàoqìng's No 1 culinary speciality: glutinous rice dumplings called *zòngzi* that are wrapped in bamboo leaves and contain anything from peanuts and lotus seeds to dried sausage and salted duck egg yolk. A number of restaurants and food stalls fill the pavements of Wenming Lu, due south of the Star Lake Hotel.

Texas Cowboy Fastfood (Dézhōuniúzǎi Kuàicān; Duanzhou Wulu; Y6-25; 8.30am-midnight Mon-Sat, 8am-midnight Sun) This restaurant serves up fried chicken, pizza, hamburgers and French toast as well as Chinese food, and is a decent choice for a quick meal.

Getting There & Away
BOAT

A jet-powered catamaran run by the **Zhaoqing Hong Kong Joint Passenger Transport Company** (☎ 222 5736; www.zhaogang.com; Gongnong Nanlu; ☽9am-6pm) speeds down the Xī Jiāng to Hong Kong (Y180/190/200 for a hard seat/soft seat/bed, 3¾ hours) at 2pm. Boats depart from Zhàoqìng ferry pier and tickets can be bought at the office just up the road or from CTS (p564).

BUS

Buses to Guǎngzhōu (Y30, 1½ hours) depart from Zhàoqìng's **long-distance bus station** (Duanzhou Silu) opposite the lake every half-hour. A bus to Hong Kong (Y130, four hours) leaves from the Overseas Chinese Hotel daily at 4pm.

TRAIN

The fastest train to Guǎngzhōu takes two hours; hard seat tickets are Y24 (Y12 without air conditioning). Book tickets at CTS or major hotels for a Y5 service charge.

There is a direct express train to Hong Kong (Y240, 4½ hours), with a daily departure at 9.37am (2.20pm from Kowloon).

Getting Around

The **local bus station** (Duanzhou Silu) faces the lake just opposite Gateway Square. Bus No 12

links the train and long-distance bus stations with the ferry pier via the centre of town. A taxi to the train station from the centre will cost about Y15.

AROUND ZHÀOQÌNG
Dǐnghú Shān 鼎湖山

This 11.3 sq km protected **reserve** (Mt Dingu; ☎ 262 2510, 222 6386; 21 Paifang Lu; admission Y50), 18km northeast of Zhàoqìng, offers excellent walks among lush vegetation, temples, springs, waterfalls and pools, including one where Sun Yatsen took the waters in the 1920s. As is the custom, every geographical feature has been given a fanciful appellation: Leaping Dragon Pool (Yuèlóng Tán), Immortal Riding a Crane (Xiānrén Qíhè) and so on.

Baoding Garden (Bǎodǐng Yuán), at the reserve's northern edge, contains **Nine Dragon Vessel** (Jiǔlóng Bǎodǐng), the world's largest *dǐng*, a ceremonial Chinese pot with two handles and three or four legs, unveiled for the millennium. A short distance to the southwest a small boat (Y15) will ferry you to the tiny wooded island in **Ding Lake** (Dǐng Hú), where there is a butterfly preserve. **Qingyun Temple** (Qìngyún Sì), an enormous Buddhist complex of over 100 buildings, was originally built during the Ming dynasty. Don't miss the gilded statues of 500 Buddhist *arhats* (saints who have eradicated all passions and desires), the rice pot capable of feeding 1000 people and the camellia planted in the central courtyard in 1685.

About 1km up from the main gate there's a reserve office where, for a fee of Y30 and presentation of your passport, you can go **hiking** up the trail that follows the river's western bank. The hike takes about four hours and eventually ends up at Qingyun Temple.

Dinghu Summer Resort (Dǐnghú Sēnlín Jiànyáng Zhōngxīn; ☎ 262 1688, fax 262 1665; s & d Y288-308) This place has decent accommodation and a popular pool should you get stranded in the reserve after dark.

Mt Dinghu International Youth Hostel (Dǐnghú Shān Guójì Qīngnián Lǚguǎn; dm Y38, s & d Y138) Dinghu Summer Resort also runs this hostel with very basic rooms not far from the temple.

Bus No 21 (Y3.50) goes to Dǐnghú Shān from the local bus station in Zhàoqìng. From the reserve's main entrance you can follow the main road north on foot or you can catch one of the electric carts (Y10)

DĬNGHÚ SHĀN 鼎湖山

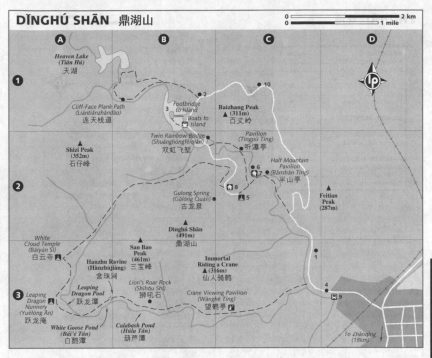

that make a loop around the reserve. A taxi from Zhàoqìng to the reserve will cost about Y60.

ZHŪHĂI 珠海

☎ 0756 / pop 460,600

Like Shēnzhèn to the northeast, Zhūhăi is a Special Economic Zone (SEZ). But 'Pearl Sea' has never reached the level of success – or excess – of its well-heeled step-sister across the Pearl River estuary. So much the better for residents and travellers, for this city just over the border from Macau is one of the cleanest and greenest metropolises in China. It is also an important university centre.

Zhūhăi is so close to Macau that a visit can be arranged as a day trip; alternatively, you can use Zhūhăi as an entry or exit point for the rest of China. Visas (MOP$150) valid for three days only are available at the **border** (⊙ 7.30am-midnight).

Orientation

The city of Zhūhăi is divided into three main districts. Gŏngbĕi, which abuts the Macau border, to the south of the city, is the main tourist district, with lots of hotels, restaurants and shops; Gongbei Port (Gŏngbĕi Kŏu'àn) is the large modern complex where visitors arrive from Macau. To the northeast is Jídà, the eastern part of which contains some large waterfront hotels and resorts as well as Jiuzhou Harbour (Jiǔzhōu Găng), where Hong Kong, Shēnzhèn and Guăngdŏng passenger ferries arrive and

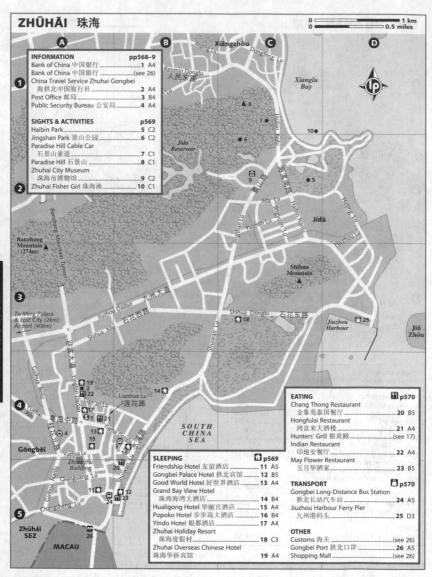

ZHŪHĂI 珠海

INFORMATION	pp568–9
Bank of China 中国银行	1 A4
Bank of China 中国银行	(see 26)
China Travel Service Zhuhai Gongbei	
海拱北中国旅行社	2 A4
Post Office 邮局	3 B4
Public Security Bureau 公安局	4 A4

SIGHTS & ACTIVITIES	p569
Haibin Park	5 C2
Jingshan Park 景山公园	6 C2
Paradise Hill Cable Car	
石景山索道	7 C1
Paradise Hill 石景山	8 C1
Zhuhai City Museum	
珠海市博物馆	9 C2
Zhuhai Fisher Girl 珠海渔	10 C1

EATING	p570
Chang Thong Restaurant	
金象苑泰国餐厅	20 B5
Hongfulai Restaurant	
鸿富来大酒楼	21 A4
Hunters' Grill 蔡黄殿	(see 17)
Indian Restaurant	
印地安餐厅	22 A4
May Flower Restaurant	
五月华酒家	23 B5

SLEEPING	p569
Friendship Hotel 友谊酒店	11 A5
Gongbei Palace Hotel 拱北宾馆	12 B5
Good World Hotel 好世界酒店	13 A4
Grand Bay View Hotel	
珠海海湾大酒店	14 B4
Hualigong Hotel 华丽宫酒店	15 A4
Popoko Hotel 步步高大酒店	16 B4
Yindo Hotel 银都酒店	17 A4
Zhuhai Holiday Resort	
珠海度假村	18 C3
Zhuhai Overseas Chinese Hotel	
珠海华侨宾馆	19 A4

TRANSPORT	p570
Gongbei Long-Distance Bus Station	
拱北长站汽车站	24 A5
Jiuzhou Harbour Ferry Pier	
九州港码头	25 D3

OTHER	
Customs 海关	(see 26)
Gongbei Port 拱北口岸	26 A5
Shopping Mall	(see 26)

depart. Xiàngzhōu is the northernmost part of Zhūhăi City and has many government buildings, housing blocks and a busy fishing port.

Information

Bank of China (Zhōngguó Yínháng; Gongbei cnr Yingbin Dadao & Yuehai Donglu; ☗ 8.30am-5pm Mon-Fri, 10am-4pm Sat & Sun; Gongbei Port branch ☗ 8.30am-5pm Mon-Fri, 10am-4pm Sat & Sun) One branch is just after customs and immigration coming from Macau and there's another next to the Yindo Hotel.

China Travel Service Zhuhai Gongbei (Zhōngguó Lǚxíngshè; CTS; ☎ 888 5777; 33 Yingbin Dadao; ☗ 8.30am-5pm Mon-Fri, 10am-4pm Sat & Sun) Next door to the Zhuhai Overseas Chinese Hotel.

Post office (yóujú;1041-1043 Yuehai Donglu; ☯ 8am-8pm)
PSB (Gōngānjú; ☎ 864 2114; Guihua Nanlu, Gongbei)

Sights

In Jídà, the **Zhuhai City Museum** (Zhūhǎshì Bówùguǎn; ☎ 332 4116; 191 Jingshan Lu; bus Nos 2, 20 & 26; admission Y10; ☯ 9am-5pm) is housed on two floors of a large building done up like a Ming dynasty compound. It contains a small but interesting collection of copperware (temple bells, figurines etc), some of which date back 5000 years; Tibetan art and artefacts, including gilded cups formed from human skulls; and scroll paintings and calligraphy.

Parks in Jídà include the waterfront **Haibin Park** (Hǎibin Gōngyuán; Haibin Nanlu; admission Y2; ☯ 8am-7pm), with hills on both sides, palm trees, statues and an amusement park, and **Jingshan Park** (Jǐngshān Gōngyuán; Haibin Beilu; admission Y2; ☯ 8am-7pm) noted for its 'boulder forest' covering **Paradise Hill** (Shíjǐng Shān) behind it and a **cable car** (Shíjǐng Shān Sùdào; ☎ 213 6477; return Y50) that will take you to the top.

In the bay between the two parks is the **Zhuhai Fisher Girl** (Zhūhǎi Yúnǚ), a large statue of a girl holding a pearl over her head and the symbol of the city.

A couple of kilometres northwest of Gǒngběi is **New Yuan Ming Palace** (Yuánmíng Xīnyuán; ☎ 861 0388; Jiuzhou Dadao & Lanpu Lu; bus Nos 13, 62 & 69; adult/child Y120/00; ☯ 9am-9pm), a massive theme park that is a reproduction of the original imperial Yuan Ming Palace in Běijīng destroyed by British and French forces during the Second Opium War. It is a huge adventure playground of reproduced scenic sights from around China and the world, including the Great Wall of China, European castles, halls, restaurants, temples and a huge lake. There are lavish 30-minute performances staged throughout the day. The entry fee includes admission to **Lost City** (Mènghuàn Shùichéng; ☎ 861 0388; ☯ 10.30am-6pm Mon-Fri, 9.30am-6.30pm Sat & Sun May, Jun, Sep & Oct, 9am-9pm Jul & Aug), a huge adventure and water park just next door.

Sleeping

Very few travellers stay in Zhūhǎi apart from people on business. There's relatively little demand for budget accommodation, so prices are generally mid-range to top end (though heavy discounting can blur the distinctions). Most hotels here add a 10% to 15% service charge to the bill. Expect higher prices at the weekend.

BUDGET & MID-RANGE

Friendship Hotel (Yǒuyì Jiǔdiàn; ☎ 813 1818; fax 813 5505; 2 Youyi Lu; s Y368-418, d & tw Y388-418, ste from Y568) This modern hotel, opposite the border crossing, will cut its quoted prices by half if you just ask.

Gongbei Palace Hotel (Gōngběi Bīnguǎn; ☎ 888 6833; fax 888 1900; 21 Shuiwan Lu; s Y280, d & tw Y280-380, tr 450-580, ste from Y680) Its advertised rates notwithstanding, this over-the-top 220-room hotel by the waterfront has singles/doubles for as low as Y180/230.

Good World Hotel (Hǎo Shìjiè Jiǔdiàn; ☎ 888 0222; fax 889 2061; 82 Lianhua Lu; s & d Y300, tr Y440, ste from Y550) This place offers reasonable rooms (180 in total) for a remarkable 'unquoted' rate of Y150 for a single or double.

Hualigong Hotel (Huálìgōng Jiǔdiàn; ☎ 813 1828; fax 813 1299; 116 Yuehua Lu; s Y368-438, d Y388-488, ste from 788) This small, centrally located hotel has bare-bones but clean rooms. Expect 50% off the asking price.

Popoko Hotel (Bùbùgāo Dàjiǔdiàn; ☎ 888 6628; fax 888 9992; 2 Yuehai Donglu; s & d Y368-468, ste from Y688) This 203-room hotel with rooms overlooking the waterfront is slightly worn around the edges.

Zhuhai Overseas Chinese Hotel (Huáqiáo Bīnguǎn; ☎ 888 6288; fax 888 5119; 35 Yingbin Dadao; s & d Y368-398, ste from Y498) This friendly, 196-room hotel is a block north of Yuehai Lu.

TOP END

Grand Bay View Hotel (Zhūhǎi Hǎiwān Dàjiǔdiàn; ☎ 887 7998; www.gbvh.com; Shuiwan Lu; s & d Mon-Fri Y860-1380, Sat & Sun Y980-1480, ste Mon-Fri from Y1480, Sat & Sun from Y1680) This 273-room hotel overlooking the sea but still close to the centre is a favourite of business travellers.

Yindo Hotel (Yíndū Jiǔdiàn; ☎ 888 3388; fax 888 3311; cnr Yingbin Dadao & Yuehai Lu; s & d Y860-1240, ste from Y1360) This 310-room hotel next to the main Bank of China is one of the best places to stay within striking distance of the border. Outlets include a decent Western restaurant called Hunters' Grill (see p570) and the **Tea Palace** (Chá Huángdiàn; ☯ 8am-5pm), which serves traditional Chinese brews and snacks.

Zhuhai Holiday Resort (Zhūhǎi Dùjiàcūn; ☎ 333 3838; www.zhuhai-holitel.com; 9 Shihua Dong Lu; s & d Y880-980, ste from Y1380) If you're looking for resort accommodation, visit this five-star complex with spacious grounds and sporting facilities near Jiuzhou Harbour.

COASTAL SOUTH

Eating

The area of Gǒngběi near the Macau border has restaurants, night markets and street hawkers; try Lianhua Lu for bakeries and a couple of basic restaurants serving Cantonese food.

Chang Thong Restaurant (Jìnxiàngyuàn Tàiguó Cāntīng; ☎ 815 9890; 87-97 Shuiwan Lu; dishes Y25-75; ❂ 11am-midnight) Don't expect Bangkok-style fare from this Thai place but the *tom yum gong* (spicy prawn soup) is a reasonable facsimile.

Hongfulai Restaurant (Hóngfúlái Dàjiǔlóu; ☎ 828 2693; 1138 Yuehai Donglu; meals from Y85; ☎ 7am-10pm) This enormous and very popular place serves up excellent seafood dishes as well as simple vegetable and meat ones.

Hunters' Grill (☎ 888 3388; 2nd fl, Yindo Hotel, cnr Yingbin Dadao & Yuehai Lu; meals from Y200; ❂ lunch 11am-2.30pm, dinner 5.30-10.30pm) This 'classic European' restaurant is celebrated for its steak and goose liver dishes.

Indian Restaurant (Yìndí'ān Cāntīng; ☎ 815 0615; 2100 Lian'an Lu; dishes Y26-78; ❂ 6-2am) No, not curries, but wigwams, tomahawks and waitresses dressed up like squaws. Lots of steaks and burgers. Little scalping.

May Flower Restaurant (Wǔyuèhuā Jiǔjiā; ☎ 323 0000, Shuiwan Lu; meals Y100; ❂ 11-3am) This place opposite the Gongbei Palace Hotel specialises in Cantonese seafood and clay pot dishes.

Getting There & Away

AIR

Zhūhǎi's airport serves destinations in China, including Běijīng (Y1940), Shànghǎi (Y1400) and Hángzhōu (Y1210). There are also daily flights to Guǎngzhōu (Y1050).

BUS

Air-conditioned buses for Guǎngzhōu (Y35 to Y55, 2½ hours) leave from **Gongbei long-distance bus station** (Youyi Lu), departing every 20 minutes between 6am and 9pm. Buses to other points in China depart from either this station or the one below the shopping centre at Gongbei Port. Destinations include Dōngguǎn (Y60, 2½ hours), Fóshān (Y35 to Y60, three hours), Hǔmén (Y40 to Y50, two hours), Kāipíng (Y40, 2½ hours), Shàntóu (Y160, seven hours), Shēnzhèn (Y80, 2½ hours), Zhàoqìng (Y55, 4½ hours) and Zhōngshān (Y15, one hour).

Most of the top-end hotels have bus services travelling to and from Hong Kong (Y150, 2½ hours).

BOAT

Jetcats between Zhūhǎi and Hong Kong (Y150, 70 minutes) depart six times a day between 8am and 5pm from **Jiuzhou Harbour** (☎ 333 3359; bus Nos 3, 12, 25 & 26) for the China ferry terminal in Kowloon and eight times a day from 9am to 9.30pm for the Macau ferry pier in Central.

A high-speed ferry operates between Jiuzhou Harbour and Shēnzhèn's port of Shékǒu (Y70, one hour). There are departures every half-hour between 8am and 6.30pm; they leave from Shékǒu at the same frequency between 7.30am and 6.30pm.

Getting Around

TO/FROM THE AIRPORT

Zhūhǎi's airport is 43km southwest of the city. An airport shuttle bus (Y20) runs reasonable frequently from outside the **Zhongzhu building** (Zhōngzhū Dàshà; cnr Yuehua Lu & Yingbin Dadao); ask CTS Zhuhai Gongbei (see p568) for the current schedule. A taxi will cost about Y130.

BUS

Zhūhǎi has a clean, efficient and cheap bus system, with fares pegged at Y2.

TAXI

Taxis have meters and flag-fall is Y10 for the first 3km, then Y0.60 for each additional 250m. From the Macau border to Jiuzhou Harbour costs around Y20.

AROUND ZHŪHǍI

Zhongshan Hot Springs 中山温泉

This **resort** (Zhōngshān Wēnquán; ☎ 0760-668 3888; www.zshs.com; admission Y108; ❂ 8.30-1.30am), about 25km northwest of Zhuhai near the town of Sānxiāng (三乡), has more than 30 indoor hot springs as well as a golf course. Dating back to the mid 1980s, the resort was one of the first foreign joint ventures in China and, frankly, the whole place is looking rather rundown. However, if you're a real enthusiast of either activity, you might want to take a dip, have a massage (including a two-hour foot massage for Y188) or even spend a night at the 313-room **Zhongshan Hot Springs Hotel** (Zhōngshān Wēnquán Bīnguǎn;

中山温泉兵馆; ☎ 668 3888; 6683888@zsha.com; s & d Y380-660, ste from Y720), whose higher-priced rooms (80 in total) have hot-spring tubs.

Buses to Zhōngshān from Zhūhăi can drop you by the entrance to the resort, from where it's a 500m walk along a tree-lined avenue to the hotel.

Cuìhēng 翠亨

This small village 33km north of Zhūhăi is the site of the **Dr Sun Yatsen Residence Memorial Museum** (Sūn Zhōngshān Gùjū Jìniànguǎn; 孙中山故居纪念馆; ☎ 0760-550 1691; Cuiheng Dadao; adult/child Y20/10; ☺ 9am-5pm), where the revolutionary hero was born in 1866 and returned to live with his parents for four years in 1892. A solemn place of pilgrimage for Chinese of all political persuasions, the museum recreates the house (the original was torn down in 1913) where Sun grew up and the village compound includes a remarkable collection of furniture and objects from everyday life. The main hall has exhibits examining his life and accomplishments, with signs and in English.

To reach the museum take bus No 10 from Yingbin Dadao in Zhūhăi to the terminus, walk 10 minutes past the gate to the next bus stop and board bus No 12.

Imperial Hot Springs 御温泉

This massive **resort** (Yù Wēnquán; ☎ 0756-579 7128; www.imperial-hot-spring.com) some 65km west of Zhuhai City in Dóumén (斗门) has a number of thermal open-air pools (Y128 to Y200 for two hours) as well as rooms with their own hot-spring tubs, where you can soak away the fatigue and grime of touring a Chinese SEZ or have one of three types of massage (Shanghai/Hong Kong/ Thailand–style at Y198/268/298).

Bus Nos 402 and 609 from Zhūhăi will take you to the resort in 80 minutes.

ZHŌNGSHĀN 中山
☎ 0760 / pop 334,100

The administrative centre of the county with the same name, 'Middle Mountain' is a surprisingly green industrial city but without a whole lot to detain most travellers. If you do get stranded here for a spell, walk east from the long-distance bus station (or catch any bus running) along Fuhua Dao for just over 2km, cross the Qijiang Bridge (Qíjiāng Qiáo; 岐江桥) and stroll along delightful

Sunwen Xilu (孙文西路), a commercial pedestrian street of restored pastel-coloured shopfronts and arcades built by overseas Chinese from Singapore in the late 19th and early 20th century. Some of these hybrid Asian/Western (called 'Zhongshan-style') structures retain their original stained glass.

Just north of Sunwen Xilu is **Zhongshan Park** (Zhōngshān Gōngyuán; 中山公园), scenic, pleasantly wooded and dominated by seven-story **Fufeng Cultural Pagoda** (Fùfēng Wéntǎ; 阜峰文塔) built in 1608.

As well as having buses to Guǎngdōng (Y35, 1½ hours), Shēnzhèn (Y50, two hours) and Zhūhăi (Y15, one hour), Zhōngshān is linked by boat with Hong Kong (Y180, 1½ hours) by boat. Ferries depart from the port at **Zhōngshāngǎng** (钟山港; ☎ 559 6350, 559 6379), some 20km northeast of Zhōngshān, nine times a day (10 on Sunday) between 8.30am and 8pm. Eight of the ferries go to the Macau ferry pier in Central while two (at 5pm and 8pm) go to the China ferry terminal in Kowloon. Ferries from Hong Kong head for Zhōngshān the same number of times per day between 8am and 8pm.

HŬMÉN 虎门
☎ 0769 / pop 142,900

Also known as Tàipíng (太平) 'Tiger Gate' is a small city on the Pearl River whose impact on China's – and the West's – history has been far greater than its present size would suggest. It was here that Commissioner Lin Zexu declared war on the opium trade in China (see the boxed text p572) by publicly burning shipments of the narcotic in two pits in what is now **Zhixin Park** (Zhíxìn Gōngyuán; 执信公园; Renmin Nanlu; admission Y6; ☺ 8am-5.30pm). The park's **Opium War Museum** (Yāpiàn Zhànzhēng Bówùguǎn; 鸦片战争博物馆; ☎ 551 2065; admission Y10; ☺ 8am-5.30pm) commemorating this heroic man's deeds and tracing the history of opium in China is full of dusty (and rusty) objects and not unreasonable diatribes against the West.

To the north and northwest of the centre are three batteries that figured prominently in the First Opium War, including the Bogue Fort (Shājiǎo Pàotái; 沙角炮台), now part of a closed military base. Just south of massive **Weiyuan Fort** (Wēiyuán Pàotái; 威远炮台) on Weiyuan Island (Wēiyuán Dǎo; 威远岛) is the superb **Sea Battle Museum** (Hǎizhàn Bówùguǎn; 海战博物馆;

☎ 550 0322; adult/child 20/10; ☺ 8am-5.30pm), which examines the navel battle fought during the First Opium War through scale models, dioramas, simulated battle scenes and massive artwork, most with explanatory notes in English. There are numerous other exhibits scattered through four large halls, including large artillery pieces and other relics, as well as an enlightening exhibition on drug addiction in China today.

Buses link Hǔmén's long-distance bus station on Yong'an Lu with Dōngguǎn (Y5, 30 minutes), Guǎngzhōu (Y30, 1½ hours), Shēnzhèn (Y30 to Y35, 1½ hours) and Zhūhǎi (Y40 to Y50, 1½ hours). Minibuses (Y7) also go directly from the bus station in Dōngguǎn to the Sea Battle Museum.

You can get to Hong Kong (Y148, 1½ hours) from Hǔmén by boat, with three departures a day from the **Taiping Port Pier** (Tàipínggǎng Mǎtóu; 太平港码头; ☎ 519 0888) southwest of Zhixin Park at 9.30am, 3.30pm and 5.35pm. They leave Hong Kong for Hǔmén at 9am, 1.45pm and 5.30pm.

DŌNGGUǍN 东莞
☎ 0769 / pop 380,700

Until recently Dōngguǎn was a medium-sized town sitting in the heart of southern China's premier lychee-growing area. Today it is a sprawling metropolis with industrial estates, wide boulevards, ring roads and tracts of new housing. Most of the factories here are owned or operated by Taiwan-based companies (thus the prepon-

---

DIRTY FOREIGN MUD

Although trade in opium had been banned in China by imperial degree at the end of the 18th century, the *cohong* (local merchants' guild) in Guǎngzhōu helped ensure that the trade continued, and fortunes were amassed on both sides. Imports of the drug increased further after 1834, when the British East India Company lost its monopoly on China trade, delivering some 40,000 chests of opium to China each year.

All this was supposed to change in June 1839 with the arrival of Lin Zexu, a mandarin of great integrity who had orders from Běijīng to stamp out the opium trade once and for all. It took Lin a week to surround the British in Guǎngzhōu and cut off their food supplies. The British held out for six weeks until they were ordered by the chief superintendent of trade, Captain Charles Elliot, to turn over more than 20,000 chests of the 'foreign mud'. Lin then had the shipment – some 2.3 million catties (or almost half a tonne) – publicly burned in central Tàipíng.

Elliott suspended all trade with China while he awaited instructions from London. The foreign secretary, Lord Palmerston, goaded on by Guǎngzhōu-based Scottish merchants William Jardine and James Matheson, ordered the Royal Navy to force a settlement in Sino-British commercial relations. An expeditionary force of 4000 men under Rear Admiral George Elliot, a cousin of Charles, was sent to exact reparations and secure favourable trade arrangements.

What would become known as the First Opium War began in June 1840 when British forces besieged Guǎngzhōu before sailing north and occupying a number of ports and cities along the Cháng Jiāng (Yangzi River) and the coast as far as Shànghǎi. To the emperor's great alarm, the force threatened Běijīng, and he sent his envoy (and Lin's successor) Qi Shan to negotiate with the Elliots. In exchange for the Britons' withdrawal from northern China, Qi agreed to the Convention of Chuenpi, which ceded Hong Kong Island to Britain (though neither side accepted the terms of the treaty).

In February 1841 Captain Elliot attacked the Bogue Fort (Shājiǎo Pàotái) in Hǔmén, took control of the Pearl River and laid siege to Guǎngzhōu, withdrawing only after extracting concessions from the merchants there. Six months later a powerful British force led by Elliot's successor, Sir Henry Pottinger, sailed north and seized Xiàmén (Amoy), Níngbō (Ningpo), Shànghǎi and other ports. With the strategic city of Nánjīng (Nanking) under immediate threat, the Chinese were forced to accept Britain's terms.

The Treaty of Nanking abolished the monopoly system of trade, opened five 'treaty ports' to British residents and foreign trade, exempted British nationals from all Chinese laws and ceded the island of Hong Kong to the British 'in perpetuity'. The treaty, signed in August 1842, set the scope and character of the unequal relationship between China and the West for the next half-century.

derance of restaurants serving Northern-style cuisine), and Dōngguǎn is the central depot for most of the rice shipped to the far corners of the Middle Kingdom.

In the centre of old Dōngguǎn, about 4km southeast of the long-distance bus station and across the Wàn Jiāng (万江), are traditional shopfronts and arcades not unlike those found in Zhōngshān but not yet renovated. To the northwest you'll find **Kěyuán** (可园; ☎ 222 3600; 32 Keyuan Lu; admission Y8; 8am-5.30pm), a delightful walled garden built in 1850. Like Liang's Garden in Fóshān (see p563), it's a mini paradise of vegetation, rockeries, bridges, grottoes and some 20 halls and pavilions filled with furnishings and artwork. Climb the four-story Hakka-style **tower** for lovely views over the garden and city.

Buses link Dōngguǎn with Guǎngzhōu (Y28, 1½ hours), Hǔmén (Y5, 30 minutes), Shēnzhèn Y38, 1½ hours), Zhōngshān (Y40, 1¾ hours) and Zhūhǎi (Y60, two hours).

Dōngguǎn is on the rail line linking Hong Kong with Guǎngzhōu, but the station is some 22km to the southeast in Chángpíng (常平). Trains head for Guǎngzhōu (Y45, 45 minutes) up to eight times a day between 8.36am and 9.21pm and up to nine times day (9.16am to 9.04pm) to Hong Kong (Y165, one hour)

Bus Nos 10 and 12 go to the train station from the bus station and a stop outside Kěyuán on Keyuan Lu.

SHĒNZHÈN 深圳

☎ 0755 / pop 752,200

Shēnzhèn, the 'Special Economic Zone' straddling the Hong Kong border, is China's richest city. It is a restricted zone and, in theory, Chinese nationals require a special pass even to enter it, much less live and work here. The majority of foreigners who come here are on business or looking for bargains at the innumerable factory outlets and shops.

If you buy your visa (HK$150) at the border with Hong Kong (*not* the recommended option due to the queues), your stay will be limited to the confines of the Shenzhen SEZ only and valid for just five days. Without a proper Chinese visa, you cannot travel north into the rest of China, not even to Guǎngzhōu. The border is open from 6.30am to midnight.

History

Shēnzhèn was no more than a tiny fishing village until it won the equivalent of the National Lottery and became a SEZ in 1980. Developers added a stock market, hotels and towering office blocks and the world as Shēnzhèn knew it came to an abrupt end. Indeed, the only fishnets you're likely to see here nowadays will be on the legs of the city's formidable hordes of whores.

Nowadays Shēnzhèn is a big shopping mall for Hong Kong residents, much to the chagrin of the Special Administrative Region's retailers. It's also a good place for cheap (legitimate and otherwise) massage and dim sum. It's true that Shēnzhèn is a commercial success, but it is devoid of culture or spirit. Most travellers give the place a wide berth, but it is a useful transportation hub if you're coming from Hong Kong.

Orientation

The name Shēnzhèn refers to three areas: Shenzhen City (Shēnzhèn Shì), opposite the border crossing at Lo Wu; the Shenzhen Special Economic Zone (SEZ); and Shenzhen County (Shēnzhèn Xiàn), which extends several kilometres north of the SEZ.

Information

www.visitshenzhen.com An excellent resource
www.shenzhenparty.com An expat-run site for entertainment options in Shēnzhèn

EMERGENCY
PSB (Gōngānjú; ☎ 2446 3999; 4018 Jiefang Lu)

MONEY
You can use either Chinese *yuán* or Hong Kong dollars in Shēnzhèn, but if you choose the latter make sure you get your change back in Hong Kong currency, which is worth about 6% more than RMB.
Bank of China (Zhōngguó Yínháng; 23 Jianshe Lu; ☺ 8.30am-5pm Mon-Fri, 9am-4pm Sat & Sun)
HSBC (Huìfēng Zhōngguó; Renmin Nanlu; ☺ 9am-5pm Mon-Fri) In the Century Plaza Hotel but on the east side.

POST
Post office (yóujú; 3002 Jianshe Lu; ☺ 9am-8pm)

TOURIST INFORMATION
Shenzhen Tourist Information Centre (Shēnzhèn Shì Yóukè Wénxùnchù; ☎ 8236 5043; ground fl, West Exit Hall, Luohu Train Station; ☺ 8am-6pm)

SHĒNZHÈN 深圳市

TRAVEL AGENCIES

China Travel Service Shenzhen (CTS; Zhōngguó
Lǚxíngshè; ☎ 2519 2595; 3023 Renmin Nanlu;
🕑 9am-6pm)

Shenzhen Grandland International Travel Agency
(Shēnzhènshì Jùbāng Guójì Lǚxíngshè; ☎ 2515 5555;
3085 Shennan Donglu; 🕑 8am-8pm) In the lobby of the
Shenzhen Hotel and good for plane tickets.

Sights

Shenzhen may not have *much* culture but it
is not totally devoid of it.

The **Shenzhen Museum** (Shēnzhèn Bówùguǎn;
☎ 8210 2993; Tongxin Lu; bus Nos 3 & 12; adult/
student Y10/5; 🕑 9am-5pm Tue-Sun), in Lychee Park
(Lìzhī Gōngyuán), contains some 20,000
jade, porcelain and bronze artefacts and has
halls devoted to ancient Shenzhen, zoology
and underwater life.

The **Shenzhen Art Galley** (Shēnzhèn Měishùguǎn;
☎ 2540 9307; Aiguo Lu; admission Y5, Fri free; 🕑 9am-
5pm Tue-Sun), within Donghu Park (Dōnghú
Gōngyuán) to the northeast, for the most
part hosts special exhibits and has shown

the work of Chinese artists Wu Changshuo, Zhang Daqian and Xu Beihong in the recent past. Bus Nos 3 and 351 are good for the gallery.

THEME PARKS

About 15km west of Shenzhen City and about halfway to the port of Shékǒu, you'll find several theme parks, with everything from a miniature Great Wall and an Eiffel Tower 'that stands erect' to a 'bird's view of thousands of years of Chinese culture'. They're naff in the extreme, but it's always a treat to watch other people having fun. They can be reached by catching bus No 101 and minibus No 423 from the centre. A taxi will cost about Y50.

Splendid China (Jǐnxiù Zhōnghuá; ☎ 2660 0626; www.chinafcv.com; admission Y120; ☽ 9am-9.30pm) is a hum-drum assembly of China's sights in miniature. Contiguous to Splendid China and included in the admission price, **China Folk Culture Villages** (Zhōngguó Mínzú Wénhuà Cūn) recreates two dozen ethnic minority villages and a number of dwellings. Famous monuments of the world are scrutinised at **Window of the World** (Shìjiè Zhīchuāng; ☎ 2660 8000; www.szwwco.com; admission Y120; ☽ 9am-10.30pm).

Sleeping

Hotels in Shenzhen discount deeply during the week, slicing as much as 50% off the regular rack rates, though you should ask for a discount at any time. This is also partially offset by the 10% or 15% tax/service charge levied by many hotels.

BUDGET & MID-RANGE

Petrel Hotel (Hǎiyàn Dàjiǔdiàn; ☎ 8223 2828; fax 8222 1398; Haiyan Bldg, Jiabin Lu; s & d Y336-456, ste from Y576) This hotel has 242 rooms spread over 14 floors of an office tower. Expect a 35% discount during the week.

Guangdong Hotel (Yuèhǎi Jiǔdiàn; ☎ 8222 8339; fax 8223 4560; 3033 Shennan Donglu; s & d Y888-1188, ste from Y1988) The 278 rooms at this three-star hotel are attractive and comfortable and a steal at 50% off the rack rate.

Gold Hotel (Fùlìhuá Dàjiǔdiàn; ☎ 8218 0288; fax 8217 7436; 2098 Shennan Donglu; s Y480, d & tw Y680-850, ste from Y1180) A discount of 35% off the published price makes what is actually a 230-room, top-end hotel a great deal.

Shenzhen Hotel (Shēnzhèn Dàjiǔdiàn; ☎ 8235 1666; fax 8222 4922; 3085 Shennan Donglu; s & d Y328-368,

tr Y368, ste from Y668) At the intersection of Jianshe Lu and Shennan Donglu, this central place isn't much to look at from the outside but has a nice interior with comfortable rooms. Discounts of 20% apply.

Wah Chung International Hotel (Huázhōng Guójì Jiǔdiàn; ☎ 223 8060; fax 222 1439; 3041 Shennan Donglu; s/d Y300/350) The Wah Cheung has a central location and 170 recently renovated rooms.

Yatwah Hotel (Rìhuá Bīnguǎn; ☎ 2558 8525; fax 2558 8530; 4006 Shennan Donglu; s & d Y228, tr Y268, ste from Y328) The 'Sunflower', with tattered but adequate room is one of the cheapest hotels in Shēnzhèn. Ask for 25% off the published rate.

TOP END

Century Plaza Hotel (Xīndū Jiǔdiàn; ☎ 8232 0888; www.szcenturyplaza.com; 1 Chunfeng Lu; s & d Y1320-1430, ste from Y1980) The 401-room Century Plaza is a better deal than the Shangri-La as it sometimes discounts up to 50% and has more comprehensive facilities, including Laurel.

Shangri-La Hotel (Xiānggélǐlā Dàjiǔdiàn; ☎ 8223 0888; www.shangri-la.com; 1002 Jianshe Lu; s Y1450-1650, d Y1600-1800, ste from Y2300) Despite all the competition this luxurious hotel still keeps its prices up there in the stars.

Eating

Laurel (Dānguìxuān; ☎ 8232 3888; 2nd fl, Century Plaza Hotel, 1 Chungfeng Lu; meals from Y150; ☽ 7am-11pm) This is one of the finest Chinese restaurants in town; expect to wait in the queue. Dim sum is served from opening till 3pm daily.

Ocean King Restaurant (Hǎishàng Huáng Jiǔjiā; ☎ 8223 9000; 1116 Jianshe Lu; meals from Y100; ☽ 7am-midnight) This is one of Shēnzhèn's best seafood restaurants and is always full.

Taj Indian Restaurant (☎ 8236 2782; ground fl, Lianhua Bldg, Renmin Nanlu; starters Y20-30, tandoori & curry Y20-45; ☽ 10am-11.45pm) If you need a fix of something spicy, head for this authentic curry house in the complex opposite the Century Plaza Hotel.

Friday Café (Xīngqīwǔ Kāfēi; ☎ 8246 0757; ground fl, Diwang Commercial Bldg, Jiefang Lu; dishes from Y25; ☽ 7am-10pm) This attractive café-restaurant is in one of the most striking modern buildings in Shēnzhèn.

Noodle King (Miàndiàn Wáng; ☎ 8205 8099; 4 Jiefang Lu; dishes Y10-15; ☽ 8am-midnight; branch ☎ 8222 2348; 3021 Renmin Nanlu) This popular budget place has a line-up of chefs from whom you request dumplings, noodles and vegetable dishes.

COASTAL SOUTH

Drinking

Most of the top-end hotels have international-style bars, including **Henry J Bean's Bar and Grill** (☎ 8233 0888, ext 8270; 2nd fl, Shangri-La Hotel, 1002 Jianshe Lu; ✆ 5.30pm-2am), a low-key sort of place with occasional live music, and **BJ'zz.com Bar** (☎ 8217 2288, ext 504, 3rd fl, Landmark Hotel, 3018 Nanhu Lu; ✆ 5.30pm-2am), with a resident jazz band playing nightly.

Further afield in the port of Shékǒu there are a number of bars frequented by locals and resident expats alike, including **McCawley's Irish Bar & Restaurant** (☎ 2668 4496; shop 118, Sea World, off Taizi Lu; ✆ 11.30am-2am), among the best pubs on town, and **Soho Restaurant & Night Club** (☎ 2669 0148; Taizi Lu; ✆ 11am-2am), a popular dance club.

You can reach Shékǒu from the city centre on bus Nos 204 or 226.

Shopping

Shoppers' first port of call should be **Luohu Commercial City** (Luóhú Shāngyè Chéng), which greets you as you emerge from customs and immigration. Here there are corridors after corridors of stalls selling ceramics, curios, knockoff handbags, clothing and DVDs.

Popular for tailored suits and skirts, electronic goods, custom-made drapes and cheap ready-to-wear is the area around **Dongmen market** (Dōngmén shìchǎng; Hubei Lu), which is just off Dongmen Lu. Be warned that this is pickpocket territory so keep your valuables safe.

An invaluable book to guide you is the recently updated *Shop in Shenzhen: An Insider's Guide* (HK$95/US$12) by Ellen McNally, available in bookshops throughout Hong Kong and on **Amazon** (www.amazon.com).

Getting There & Away

AIR

Shēnzhèn airport (Shēnzhèn Fēijīchǎng; ☎ 2777 6789; www.szairport.com) is now China's fourth busiest. There are flights to most major destinations around China.

BOAT

There are 13 jet-cat departures daily between the **port of Shékǒu** (☎ 2669 5599) and Hong Kong (Y108/125 day/night sailing, 50 minutes) between 7.45am and 9.30pm. Seven of these go to the Macau ferry pier in Central, with the balance heading for the China ferry terminal in Kowloon. The same number of boats leave Hong Kong for Shékǒu from 7.45am to 9pm.

There are six departures daily to Kowloon's China ferry terminal from the **Fuyong ferry terminal** (Fúyǒng kèyùnzhàn; Shenzhen airport) and three to the Macau ferry pier in Central between 9am and 8.30pm. Tickets cost Y171/271 in 2nd/1st class and the trip takes

---

TALLY, HO TAI TAI!

Mrs Ho is a tai tai. *Taitai* simply means 'Mrs', and every married Chinese woman is a tai tai. But tai tai in southern China – and especially Hong Kong – has a somewhat different connotation. Tai tai are the well-to-do, leisured wives of successful businessmen. They lunch leisurely, gossip with their friends (mostly via mobile phone) and play mah jong. And they shop, especially in Shēnzhèn. For tai tai – however wealthy – are always in search of a bargain.

Mrs Ho took us to Shēnzhèn the first time we visited. Well, not exactly… The incomparable *HK Magazine,* a monthly listings freebie, had recently run a cover story about a tai tai who would board the KCR East Rail for Lo Wu (Luóhú) in the morning at least once a week, spend the day shopping, nibbling and being pampered and return at the end of the day thoroughly relaxed, satiated and clothed – at half the price it would have cost her back home.

Mrs Ho 'led' us on a tour of the Luohu Commercial City, then for lunch at the Laurel and to her favourite massage parlour (legitimate *naturellement* – Mrs Ho is a married woman with children!) for an hour's worth of foot rubbing after pounding the pavements of the SEZ all day. We did stop short of following Mrs Ho into the manicurist's where, 'feeling particularly whimsical', she had tiny flowers, butterflies and birds painted on each fingernail. That was, we thought, far beyond the call of duty.

Some people are snide about tai tai, dismissing them as lazy, self-indulgent creatures whose main concern is the quality of the oolong and the price of the knock-off Hermès handbag. But we – and now you – know differently. Tai tai have got something to teach us all.

one hour and 10 minutes. Boats leave Hong Kong for Fúyŏng nine times a day between 7.30am and 5.30pm.

Three ferries a day link Shékŏu with Macau; for details see p544. You can also reach Zhūhǎi (Y70, one hour) from Shékŏu every half-hour between 7.30am and 6.30pm.

A boat leaves Shékŏu at 5pm on Monday, Wednesday and Friday for Hǎikŏu (Y150 to Y450, 18 hours), returning from there at 4pm Tuesday, Thursday and Saturday.

BUS

Intercity buses leave from Luohu bus station (Luóhú qìchēzhàn) under the shopping centre. There are regular services to Cháozhōu (Y130 to Y160, five hours), Guǎngzhōu (Y60, 1½ hours), Húmén (Y30 to Y35, one hour), Shàntóu (Y150, four hours) and Xiàmén (Y210, eight hours). For information on getting to/from Hong Kong, see p525.

TRAIN

There are frequent local trains (Y70, two hours) and high-speed trains (Y80, 55 minutes) between Guǎngzhōu and Shēnzhèn. The Kowloon–Canton Railway's East Rail offers the fastest and most convenient transport to Shēnzhèn from Hong Kong (see p525).

Getting Around
TO/FROM THE AIRPORT

Shēnzhèn's airport is 36km west of the city. Airport buses (Y20, 30 to 40 minutes) leave from the **Hualian Hotel** (Huálián Dàshà; Shennan Zhonglu), which can be reached on bus No 101. A taxi to the airport will cost Y130 to Y150.

Many of the top-end hotels, including the Guangdong Hotel, run shuttles to/from Hong Kong International Airport (Y180/320 one way/return).

BUS

Shēnzhèn has an efficient network of buses and minibuses (Y1 to Y3). From the train station, bus Nos 12 and 101 head north and then east, passing Lychee Park. Bus No 204 to Shékŏu leaves from a station north of the intersection of Jianshe Lu and Jiabin Lu.

METRO

Shēnzhèn's first two metro lines, stretching from the Luohu border crossing to the Windows of the World theme park, should be open by the time you read this.

TAXI

The axi flag-fall is Y12.5 (Y16 from 11pm to 6am). It's then Y0.60 for every additional 250m travelled.

SHÀNTÓU 汕头
☎ 0754 / pop 1.22 million

Shàntóu, Guǎngdōng's second most populous city after Guǎngzhōu, is – along with Shēnzhèn, Zhūhǎi, Xiàmén and Hǎinán Dǎo (Hainan Island) – one of China's five original Special Economic Zones. It's a port on the border with Fújiàn and seldom visited by travellers.

The people who live here are largely Chiu Chow. They speak a dialect they call Taejiu (Chaoshan in Mandarin, a combination of Cháozhōu and Shàntóu, the two most important cities here), which is completely different from Cantonese. It is the language of many of the Chinese in Southeast Asia, especially those who emigrated to Thailand.

History

As early as the 18th century, when today's Shàntóu was just a fishing village, the East India Company had a station on an island outside the harbour. By the mid-19th century it had grown into an important trading port known to the outside world as Swatow.

The port was officially opened to foreign trade in 1860 under the Treaty of Tientsin, which ended the Second Opium War. By 1870 foreigners were living and trading in the town itself. A few of the old colonial buildings remain, but most are extremely dilapidated.

Orientation

Most of Shàntóu lies on a peninsula, bounded to the south by the South China Sea and separated from the mainland to the west and the north by a river and canals. Most tourist amenities are in the southwestern corner of the peninsula.

Information

Bank of China (Zhōngguó Yínháng; 55 Changping Lu; ☎ 8.30am-noon & 2.30-5pm Mon-Sat, ☼ 8.30am-noon Sun)

China Travel Service Shantou (CTS; Zhōngguó Lǚxíngshè; ☎ 863 6332; 41 Shanzhang Lu; ☼ 8am-9.30pm) Bus and air tickets are sold at this office next to the Shantou Overseas Chinese Hotel.

Post office (yóujú; Waima Lu; ☼ 8am-6pm)

COASTAL SOUTH

SHÀNTÓU 汕头

INFORMATION
Bank of China (Main Branch)
中国银行...**1** D1
Bank of China 中国银行...................................**2** C1
CTS Shantou 汕头中国旅行社..................(see 5)
Post Office 邮局.......................................**3** B2

SIGHTS & ACTIVITIES p578
Stone Fort Park 石炮台公园.............**4** C2

SLEEPING p578
Qiaolian Hotel 侨联大厦.......................**5** C1
Shantou Harbour View Hotel
汕头海景酒店...**6** C2

Shantou International Hotel
汕头国际大酒店.......................................**7** C1
Shantou Overseas Chinese Hotel
汕头华侨大厦...**8** C1
Swatow Peninsula Hotel
鮀岛宾馆...**9** C1

EATING pp578-9
Chao Zhou Restaurant
潮州菜瓜...**10** C2
Food Stalls...**11** A2
Zhonglu Restaurant 中旅酒家..........**12** C1

TRANSPORT p579
City Bus Station 市汽车站...................**13** C1
Guangchang Ferry Pier 广场码头.....**14** B2
Long-Distance Bus Station
汽车客货运站..**15** B1
Xidi Ferry Pier 西堤码头....................**16** A2

Sights

If you're heading down memory lane most of what remains of Shàntóu's **colonial buildings** can be seen in the area bounded by Waima Lu, Minzu Lu and Shengping Lu.

The centrepiece of **Stone Fort Park** (Shí Pàotái Gōngyuán; Haibin Lu; admission Y10; 7.30am-11pm), which faces the sea and the breezy **embankment** running above the shore, is a castle-like **battery** with solid walls and loopholes built in 1874. The fort is surrounded by a moat.

Sleeping

Shantou Harbour View Hotel (Shàntóu Hǎijǐng Jiǔdiàn; 854 3838; sthvh@pub.shantou.gd.cn; 18 Haibin Lu; s & d Y668-788, ste from Y1400) This lovely hotel west of the Stone Fort and facing the water will bring standard singles and doubles down to Y200 and suites to Y420.

Shantou Overseas Chinese Hotel (Shàntóu Huáqiáo Dàshà; 862 9888; fax 825 2223; 41 Shanzhang Lu; s & d Y300-480, ste from Y580) This rambling, 300-room pile conveniently located south of the city bus station has both renovated and older rooms on which you can expect discounts of 30% to 45% respectively.

Shantou International Hotel (Shàntóu Guójì Dàjiǔdiàn; 825 1212; www.stih.com; 52 Jinsha Zhonglu; s & d Y598-888, ste from Y1488) This glitzy 350-room place, with a fitness centre and revolving restaurant on the 26th floor, offers generous discounts of 50% and more on all their rooms and suites.

Swatow Peninsula Hotel (Túodǎo Bīnguǎn; 831 6668; www.pihotel.com; 36 Jinsha Lu; s & d Y388-788, ste from Y988) The Thai- and Chinese-owned Swatow Pen offers pleasant rooms and huge discounts. You should be able to get a single or double for Y160.

Qiaolian Hotel (Qiáolián Dàshà; 825 9109, fax 825 0108; 39 Shanzhang Lu; s/d/tr with fan & shared bathroom from Y60/70/90; s & d with air-con & bathroom Y120-286, tr with air-con & bathroom Y150-390) This one-star property at the corner of Shanzhang and Changping Lu has basic but clean rooms.

Eating

Chiu Chow has a distinct cuisine that makes great use of seafood and accompanying sauces. A few specialities include: *chui jau lou sui ngoh* (Chiu Chow soy goose); *tim suen hung xiu ha/ha kau* (deep-fried shrimp/crab balls with honey sauce); and *chui jau yi min* (pan-fried egg noodles served over chives). And no meal here is complete without thimble-sized cups of strong and bitter *ti kwan yu,* a fermented oolong tea called 'Iron Buddha'.

Zhonglu Restaurant (Zhōnglù Jiǔjiā; ☎ 862 6207; 41 Shanzhang Lu; meals from Y60; ♥ lunch 11.30am-4pm, dinner 5.30-9pm) This friendly place in the courtyard between the Overseas Chinese Hotel and city bus station specialises in seafood.

Chao Zhou Restaurant (Cháozhōu Càiguǎn; ☎ 854 6498; 2 Changping Lu; meals from Y35; ♥ lunch 10.30am-4.30pm, dinner 5.30-10.30pm) This is an excellent place to try Chiu Chow specialities like prawn balls and crab noodles.

There's a positively frenetic **night market** (Fuping Lu) with an entire world of food stalls just west of Minzu Lu. If your Chinese isn't up to it, let your fingers do the talking.

Getting There & Away
AIR
Shàntóu airport, 20km northeast of the centre, has flights to Bangkok and Hong Kong (Y1334, twice daily). Domestic destinations include Běijīng, Fúzhōu, Guǎngzhōu (Y66), Guìlín, Hǎikǒu, Nánjīng and Shànghǎi. A taxi will cost about Y40 from the centre.

BUS
Buses arrive/depart from the **long-distance bus station** (Shàntóu Shěng Qìchēzhàn; Huoche Lu) and the more central city station behind CTS and the Overseas Chinese Hotel. Destinations include Fúzhōu (Y110-140, seven hours), Guǎngzhōu (Y180, six hours), Hong Kong (Y180, five hours), Shēnzhèn (Y150, four hours) and Xiàmén (Y90, four hours). Buses to Hong Kong (Y210) also leave from the Shantou International Hotel. Minibuses to Cháozhōu (Y10, one hour) leave from a small office just south of the city station.

TRAIN
There are overnight services between Shàntóu and Guǎngzhōu (hard seat Y92, hard/soft sleeper Y164/230, seven hours) and trains to Cháozhōu (Y10, 35 minutes). The station is 5km to the east of the centre.

Getting Around
Bus No 2 links the centre with the train station via Jinsha Lu. Pedicabs and motorbikes are plentiful; 'flag-fall' is at least Y5.

CHÁOZHŌU 潮州
☎ 0768 / pop 354,200

A much prettier city than Shàntóu, Cháozhōu is an ancient commercial and trading city dating back some 1700 years. It is situated on the Han River (Hán Jiāng) and surrounded on three sides by the Jīn Shān (Golden Hills) and Húlú Shān (Calabash Hills). It can be explored in a couple of hours and is best visited as a day trip from Shàntóu. While travelling between the two cities you'll pass a number of fortified Hakka villages chock-a-block with traditional houses and ancient temples.

Sights
Kaiyuan Temple (Kāiyuán Sì; admission Y5; ♥ 6am-5pm), built in AD 738 during the Tang dynasty to house Buddhist scriptures sent by Emperor Qianlong, was reduced almost to rubble during the Cultural Revolution. The first hall houses three Buddhas flanked by 18 gilded arhats (saints). Kaiyuan is an active temple and most of it is off-limits to outsiders.

Cháozhōu's **old city wall** (*gǔ chéng*), the ramparts of which offer great views of

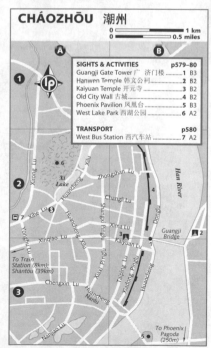

CHÁOZHŌU 潮州

0 ——— 1 km
0 ——— 0.5 miles

SIGHTS & ACTIVITIES	p579–80
Guangji Gate Tower 广 济门楼	1 B3
Hanwen Temple 韩文公祠	2 B2
Kaiyuan Temple 开元寺	3 B2
Old City Wall 古城	4 B2
Phoenix Pavilion 凤凰台	5 B3
West Lake Park 西湖公园	6 A2

TRANSPORT	p580
West Bus Station 西汽车站	7 A2

COASTAL SOUTH

the city, runs along the river for almost 2.5km and is interrupted by four ornate fortifications, including **Guangji Gate Tower** (Guăngjĭmén Lóu). From the wall look southeast to beyond the island and its modern **Phoenix Pavilion** (Fènghuáng Tái), to the much older **Phoenix Pagoda** (Fènghuáng Tă), a seven-story tower built in 1585. On the east bank of the Han and beyond **Guangji Bridge** (Guăngjì Qiáo), first erected in the Song dynasty, is **Hanwen Temple** (Hánwén Gōngsì), which commemorates the Tang dynasty poet and philosopher Han Yu, who was banished to 'far-flung' Guăngdōng for his outspoken views against Buddhism.

West Lake Park (Xīhú Gōngyuán; adult/child Y8/4; 5.30am-11.30pm), which extends up the hill beyond the eponymous lake, is a pleasant place to stroll, particularly in the early morning or evening.

Getting There & Away

Minibuses link Cháozhōu's west bus station with Shàntóu (Y10, one hour). Buses also depart from here for Guăngzhōu (Y160, 6½ hours), Shēnzhèn (Y130 to Y160, 4½ hours) and Xiàmén (Y80, 3½ hours).

Cháozhōu's train station is 8km west of the centre; there are two trains a day to Guăngzhōu (Y82, seven hours). A minivan taxi to the station will cost Y15.

Hǎinán 海南

COASTAL SOUTH

HIGHLIGHTS

- Body surf the beaches around **Sānyà** (p588) after escaping China's freezing north!
- Feel the tropical sweat dry as you ascend **Wǔzhǐ Shān** (p592), the island's highest mountain
- Run the macaque gauntlet at **Monkey Island** (p588)
- Stand in awe before the waterfall at **Báihuā Shān** (p592)
- Lick your fingers post-meal in **Wénchāng** (p587), a town famed for relaxed coconut plantations – and the most delectable chicken in China!

Wénchāng ★

Báihuā Shān ★

Wǔzhǐ Shān ★

Sānyà ★

★ Monkey Island

■ POP: 8.2 MIL   ■ AREA: 34,000 SQ KM   ■ www.hainandiscovery.com

Sun, surf, and sand – that's all you need to know about Hăinán, the large tropical island off the southern coast of China. For Middle Kingdom travellers, it is not unlike Hawaii in the US – a dreamy tropical getaway from the frigid north. With acres of beaches in the south (the best in China), balmy winds and lilting palm trees, Hăinán, once a place of banishment for disgraced officials, practises tourism with a capital 'T'.

Indeed, so much for exile. Today it withstands an annual friendly invasion of snowbirds; some 80% of the island's economy is washed ashore by tourism. Unless you wish to spend the Yuletide season cheek-by-jowl with the rest of China in pricey hotels, miss the rush and go between March and November when you can expect large discounts on hotel accommodation.

Hăinán is the country's largest island – technically comprising one main island with over 200 micro-sized dots spread out through the South China Sea – yet it's the smallest province, topping out at a mere 34,000 sq km in land area. The islands stretch 1800km north to south and over 900km east to west – factor in water area and it dwarfs other Chinese provinces. An equally small population (among the lowest in China) gives the place a much less hectic feel.

Hăinán tempts with the trappings of an island paradise: golden beaches, the promise of a deep tan and the thud of falling coconuts. Quite overlooked are the central highlands and their moderate temperatures, thick canopies of forest, and superb – if challenging – hiking.

Listen not to those who grouse about a preponderance of tour groups, most of whom never leave their few kilometres of beach. Read: there's a whole lot of unexplored here.

History

Historically, Hăinán was a backwater of the Chinese empire, a miserable place of exile and poverty. When Li Deyu, a prime minister of the Tang dynasty, was exiled to Hăinán he dubbed it 'the gate of hell'. Purportedly, only 18 tourists came to Hăinán of their own volition during the entire Song, Yuan and Ming dynasties (almost 700 years)! That's about the rate per second during winter nowadays.

The entire island of Hăinán was established as a Special Economic Zone (SEZ) in 1988, and quickly emerged as an enclave of free-market bedlam operating on the periphery of the law. Despite the once heady economic climate, the capital Hăikŏu's skyline today is punctuated with the shells of unfinished construction, testament to the fickleness of investors and financial overreaching.

Climate

Hăinán is the southernmost tip of China (Sānyà, in the south, is roughly on the same latitude as the southern reaches of Hawaii), and can be relied upon to be warm, even when the rest of China is freezing.

Even in winter, average temperatures of 21°C (69.8°F) prevail; the yearly average is 25.4°C (77.7°F). From as early as March through to November, the weather becomes hot and humid.

Typhoons can cripple all transport and communication with the mainland. They usually descend on the island between May and October, and there has been at least one every year for the last 50 years.

Language

Hainanese is a broad term for the baker's dozen local dialects of Hăinán Mĭn (it's known by many other names), most of which are also spoken in Guǎngdōng. It also has a large population of Hakka speakers.

Getting There & Around

Hăikŏu, the capital of Hăinán, and Sānyà, the beach capital, are the two major urban centres, at opposite ends of the island. Three highways link the towns: the eastern route via Wànníng (the fastest route); the central route via Túnchāng and Tōngzhá (also known as Tōngshí); and the less popular western route via Dānzhōu (also known as Nàdà), Bāsuǒ (Dōngfāng) and Yīnggēhǎi.

Most visitors take the eastern or western freeway routes from Hăikŏu to Sānyà. The central route (an expressway has been planned forever) requires patience and takes you through the highlands and near villages of the Li and Miao minority groups.

In November 2004, officials started a few experimental runs of a new train service from Guǎngzhōu to Hăikŏu. Trains back and forth will run in the evening via Sānshuǐ, Zhàoqìng, Màomíng and Zhànjiāng, and will literally cross the Qiongzhou Strait on a ferry, then arrive in Hăikŏu early to late morning. Train service on the island is not available.

HĂIKŎU 海口
☎ 0898 / pop 514,100

Hăikŏu, Hăinán's capital, lies on the northern coastline at the mouth of Nandu River

(Nándù Jiāng). This port town handles most of Hăinán's commerce with the mainland.

For most travellers, Hăikŏu is merely a transit point on the way to Sānyà. The city is attractive and folks are friendly; you'll find a sprinkling of temples and decaying colonial charm in the Sino-Portuguese architecture around Xinhua Lu.

Orientation

Central Hăikŏu has all the tourist facilities and most historical sights. To the northwest is the port area, one sight, and the city's own quite long and impressive beach zone.

Information

INTERNET ACCESS

Internet café (wǎngbā; Wuzhishan Lu; per hr Y3) You have to buy a membership.

Internet café (wǎngbā; 2nd fl, Haikou Worker's Cinema, Gōngrén Yíngjù Yùan; per hr Y2)

MONEY

There are three banks in Hăikŏu.

Bank of China (Zhōngguó Yínháng; 33 Datong Lu)

Bank of China (Zhōngguó Yínháng; opposite Huáqiáo Dàshà) Changes travellers cheques.

Bank of China (Zhōngguó Yínháng; cnr Haixiu Dadao & Haifu Dadao) Changes travellers cheques.

POST

Post & telecommunications office (Daying Lu) South of the long-distance bus station.

Post & telephone centre (Yóudiàn Dàlóu; Jiefang Xilu) Supposed to be 24 hours but it isn't.

TOURIST INFORMATION

China Travel Service (CTS; Zhōngguó Lǚxíngshè; ☎ 6675 7455; fax 6623 1585) In the same building as Huáqiáo Dàshà. Some of the staff speak English and are helpful. Tours can be cheaper than tackling it yourself. For an English-speaking guide you need a group. There are one- to four-day tours ranging from Y400 to Y1780 depending on the duration and the level of comfort. The usual package is three days and four nights, taking in Xīnglóng, Sānyà and back to Hăikŏu via the odd minority village. Prices include your transport, accommodation and meals (but ticket prices for sights are not included). Take the time to shop around (especially for hotels and plane tickets) if CTS is too pricey, as Hăikŏu has numerous travel agencies – every five feet you get hounded by agents' touts.

Public Security Bureau (公安局; PSB; Gōngānjú; ☎ 6859 3666, 6859 0746; 43 Jinlong Lu; ☼ 8am-noon & 2.30-5.30pm Mon-Fri) One of the friendliest PSBs is in the western part of the city. The easiest way to get there is by taxi for Y15 or bus No 12.

Sights & Activities

Pleasant palm tree-lined boulevards and a picturesque old quarter make strolling Hăikŏu nice, despite the heat.

The city's crumbling colonial remains can be viewed along Xinhua Lu. Take a couple of detours along Zhongshan Lu and then back to the city centre through the lively market street of Bo'ai Beilu.

Five Officials Memorial Temple (五公祠; Wǔgōng Cí; 169 Haifu Dao; admission Y15; ☼ 8am-6pm) is an attractive Ming temple (restored during the Qing dynasty) dedicated to five officials who were banished to Hăinán in earlier times. The famous Song dynasty poet, Su Dongpo, was also banished to Hăinán and is commemorated here. Take bus No 11 or 12 and get off one stop after the east bus station.

POPULATION & PEOPLE

Thirty-nine minority groups live on Hăinán, including the original inhabitants of the island, the Li and Miao, who live in the dense tropical forests covering Límǔlíng Shān (Mother of the Li Mountain Range). The Li probably migrated to Hăinán from Fújiàn 3000 years ago and today number one million on the island.

Despite a long history of rebellion against the Chinese, the Li aided the communist guerrillas on the island during the war with the Japanese. Perhaps for this reason the island's centre was made an 'autonomous' region post-communist takeover.

The Miao (H'mong) people spread from southern China across northern Vietnam, Laos and Thailand. In China they moved south into Hăinán as a result of the Chinese emigrations from the north, and now occupy some of the most rugged terrain on the island. Today there are some 60,000 Miao living on the island.

The coastal areas of the island are populated by Han Chinese. Since 1949, Chinese from Indonesia, Malaysia and, later, Vietnam have settled here.

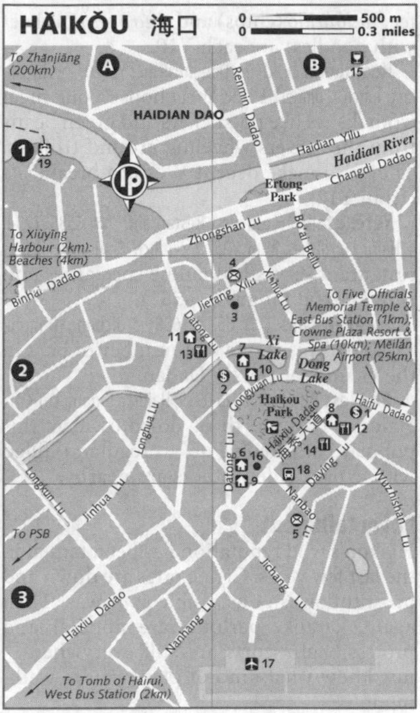

INFORMATION
Bank of China 中国银行 1 B2
Bank of China 中国银行 2 B2
Bank of China 中国银行 .... (see 6)
CTS 中国旅行社 .... (see 7)
Haikou Worker's Cinema 海口工人影剧院 3 B2
Internet Café 网吧 .... (see 12)
Internet Café 网吧 .... (see 3)
Internet Café 网吧 .... (see 5)
Post & Telephone Centre 中国电信 4 B2
Post & Telephone Office 邮局 5 B3

SLEEPING pp585–6
Haikou International Financial Centre 国际金融大厦 6 B2
Huáqiáo Dàshà 华侨大厦 7 B2
Hăikŏu Bīnguăn 海口宾馆 8 B2
Hăinán Mínháng Bīnguăn 海南民航宾馆 9 B2
Qiáoyŏu Dàshà 侨友大厦 10 B2
Yŏuyì Dàjiŭdiàn 友谊大酒店 11 A2

EATING p586
Forever Café 天长地久 12 B2
Fēnggé Kāfēidiàn 风阁咖啡店 13 A2
Kuàihuólín 快活林 14 B2
Yēfēngtáng 椰风堂 .... (see 8)

DRINKING p586
Red Jess Pub 15 B1

TRANSPORT pp586–7
China Southern Airlines 中国南方航空 16 B2
Former Haikou Airport 海口机场 17 B3
Long-Distance Bus Station 长途汽车站 18 B2
Xīngang Passenger Ferry Terminal 海口新港 19 A1

The attractive **Tomb of Hairui** (海瑞墓; Hăirui Mù; ☎ 6892 2060; Shugang Dadao, admission Y5; ⏲ 8am-6pm) was ravaged during the Cultural Revolution but restored in vibrant colour. Hairui was a compassionate and popular official who lived in the 16th century. The tomb is in western Hăikŏu, off Haixiu Dadao; take bus No 2 and watch for the west bus station or a turn-off marked by a blue sign in English and Chinese. From there it's a 1km-walk along the road heading south.

The city has kilometre after kilometre of smooth **sand beach** stretching west of Xiuying Harbour. From Haixiu Dadao bus No 40 (Y2) terminates smack in the middle.

Sleeping

BUDGET

Budget travellers have little to choose from; a couple of grubby places are near the Xīngăng passenger ferry terminal.

Qiáoyoŭ Dàshà (☎ 6676 6809; 18 Gongyuan Lu; s/d Y100/120; ❄) This hotel is at the corner of Datong Lu and Gongyuan Lu. Nice location but a somewhat gloomy atmosphere. Rooms (all with private bathroom) are tired but fine.

Yǒuyì Dàjiǔdiàn (Friendship Hotel; ☎ 6622 5566, fax 6621 8200; 2-1 Datong Lu; s/d Y138-158; ❄) Clean, standard rooms are a teensy bit threadbare and the 'hot' water is heated by passive solar rooftop bins – but all in all it's not a bad deal.

MID-RANGE

Most of Hăikŏu's hotels are mid-range to top end, but given competition, politely inquire about discounts *(zhékòu)*. Travel agents are often a good way to get an in.

Hăikŏu Bīnguăn (☎ 6535 1234; 4 Haixiu Dadao; r Y488; ❄) Do look at this hotel, which has undergone a thorough revamping. The rooms' cool minimalism is refreshingly non-generic; sliding screens, sybaritic beds and small balconies are lovely recent touches. The hotel's famed local food restaurant is worth a visit itself. Staff are over-the-top efficient and friendly.

Huáqiáo Dàshà (Overseas Chinese Hotel; ☎ 6670 8430; fax 6677 2094; 17 Datong Lu; s Y288-316, d Y360; ❄) This convenient, three-star hotel, the old standby, still sports great rooms and an irrepressibly cheery staff. Posted prices are debatably worthy, but they'll go down by half in low season, and close to that at times in high season.

Hǎinán Mínháng Bīnguǎn (Hainan Civil Aviation Hotel; ☎ 6677 2608; fax 6677 2610; 9 Haixiu Dadao; s/d Y468-518; 🔀) Another generally good option, though not as nice as the previous two. You can't beat the location and prices drop precipitously pretty much all the time now.

TOP END
These hotels offer 40% to 50% discounts in the low season.

Haikou International Commercial Centre (Hǎikǒu Guójì Shāngyè Dàshà; ☎ 6679 6999; fax 6677 4751; 38 Datong Lu; rm with kitchenette Y680-1080; 🔀 🔀 ▢). This modern structure, catering to business travellers, is in Hǎikǒu's prime location. It offers a health club, tennis courts, banks, shops and restaurants. The staff is beaver-busy and eager to please.

Crowne Plaza Resort and Spa (Huángguān Bīnhǎi Wénquán Jiǔdiàn; ☎ 6596 6888; www.crowneplazahainan.com; 1 Qiongshan Dadao; s & d Y1400-1600, ste Y2800; 🔀 🔀 🔁 ▢) This city-state-sized resort 15km east of town right on the beach is one of the most impressive facilities on the island. Kudos include being the largest resort in China, and having the largest indoor hot spring on the planet, and the place is spectacularly well run. Steep discounts from travel agents or online booking make it almost a steal.

Eating & Drinking
A well-known dish from Hǎinán is *wénchāng jī* (succulent chicken raised on a diet of rice and peanuts). The remaining triumvirate of island culinary specialties are *jiǎjī yā* (to-die-for roast duck from southeastern Hǎinán), *dōngshānyáng* (a black-woolled mountain goat fed camellias and orchids, and used in soups); and *hélè xiè* (juicy crab from Hélè, best eaten in autumn).

Plenty of street fruit sellers offer bananas, mangoes and sugar cane. Green coconuts, with their tops chopped off and straws poked in (Y2), are delicious as a refreshing drink.

Fēnggé Kāfēidiàn (☎ 6623 8890; 2nd fl, 4 Datong Lu; mains Y20-30; 😋 breakfast, lunch & dinner) Tasty, reasonable Western and Chinese meals are served in this pleasant café/restaurant. Cof-

fee, *tǔdòutiáo* (chips) and *niúròumiàn* (beef with noodles) are each Y10.

Kuàihuólín (1 Jichang Donglu; dishes Y5-20; 😋 breakfast, lunch & dinner) Pick and choose your meal from dishes like potstickers and green beans from the servers wheeling around trolleys. They also make decent Western breakfasts (from Y12).

Yěfēngtáng (Cocowind Restaurant; ☎ 6535 1234; 4 Haifu Lu; dishes from Y25; 😋 lunch & dinner) This restaurant serves Hainanese specialties and is in Hǎikǒu Bīnguǎn (p585).

Forever Café (☎ 6532 4658; 4 Jichang Donglu; 😋 dinner) This is one of a number of bars in the vicinity of Haixiu Dadao.

Red Jess Pub (☎ 6625 0939; Haidian Erdong Lu) On Haidian Dao, north of downtown, is this popular bar ('Red's Pub' to regulars), filled with expats. A few others are nearby.

Entertainment
Hǎikǒu's wild reputation has been tamed in the last few years. Crime rates are down and prostitution isn't as visible as it was. Then again, karaoke parlours are popular and professional escorts are still everywhere – just know what kind of place you're walking into.

Getting There & Away
AIR
Travel agents can scare up great deals. The **China Southern Airlines** (☎ 6534 9433) office is in a large building that houses Hǎinán Mínháng Bīnguǎn, from where the airport bus departs. There are regular flights between Hǎikǒu and cities including Běijīng (Y2190), Guǎngzhōu (Y650), Kūnmíng (Y1070), Nánníng, Shànghǎi (Y1630) and Shēnzhèn (Y640).

Daily flights travel between Hǎikǒu and Hong Kong (Y1510). China Southern Airlines has flights once a week to Bangkok (Y3344). Other international flights go weekly to Kaohsiung (Taiwan), Singapore, Kuala Lumpur and Macau. **Dragonair** (☎ 6855 0312) has a representative in the Hainan Mandarin Hotel (8 Wenhua Lu).

BOAT
Hǎikǒu has two harbours but most departures are from the Xīngǎng passenger ferry terminal. Minibus Nos 212 and 218 (or bus Nos 14 and 22) go to the harbour from the stop opposite Hǎikǒu Bīnguǎn. A taxi

costs around Y15. Bus No 3 goes to Xiuying Harbour.

Ferries depart roughly every 1½ hours from Xīngǎng for Hǎi'ān (Y32, 1½ hours) on Léizhōu Peninsula, where there are bus connections to Zhànjiāng (Y30, three hours) and Guǎngzhōu (Y130, 10 hours). Boats have stopped running directly to Zhànjiāng.

There are daily overnight boats from both harbours for Běihǎi in Guǎngxī, departing at 6pm. Tickets are sold at both harbours and cost between Y90 for a seat and Y230 for a cabin.

Slower boats to most destinations listed above leave from Xiuying Harbour. Boats leave every two days to Guǎngzhōu, and tickets start at Y150 and go up to Y305 (for a two-person cabin in 2nd class). The journey takes 20 to 25 hours. There's also a daily boat to Shékǒu, the harbour port near Shēnzhèn, which takes 17 hours. Tickets are Y138 for a seat, rising to Y366 for a cabin. Tickets for these departures can be bought in town at the Haikou Harbour passenger ferry ticket office at the corner of Haixiu Dadao and Haiful Dadao, directly under the pedestrian overpass. This office also books train tickets from Guǎngzhōu.

There's no passenger train service on Hǎinán, but it's possible to take a train to Guǎngzhou (p583).

BUS
The long-distance bus stations have combination ferry/sleeper buses going to Guǎngzhōu (Y256, 16 hours) and other mainland destinations (but not Zhànjiāng, for which you have to take a ferry to the mainland, then a bus). Note that the bus station in the centre of town does not have Sānyà buses; you must go to the east bus station.

The east bus station has buses to all major destinations on the island. (The west station also has buses, but it's not as convenient.) Frequent buses go to Wénchāng (with/without air-con Y16/13, 1½ hours), Tōngzhá (with/without air-con Y45/32, 5½ hours), Sānyà (with/without air-con Y49/70, three hours) and other destinations. To get to the east station take bus No 1 from Haixiu Dadao.

Getting Around
Hǎikǒu's Měilán airport is 25km southeast of the city centre. CAAC has an airport shuttle (Y20) that leaves every half-hour from in front of Hǎinán Mínháng Bīnguǎn on Haixiu Dadao. A taxi will cost about Y40.

Hǎikǒu's centre is easy to walk around, but there is also a workable bus system (Y1). Taxis are expensive, starting at Y10 for the first 3km.

WÉNCHĀNG 文昌
☎ 0898
Wénchāng is the home of a famous chicken dish and the Soong sisters, Meiling and Qingling, the wives of Chiang Kaishek and Sun Yatsen. For the traveller, however, it's the **Dōngjiāo Yēlín** (东郊椰林) coconut plantation, with cool, inviting pathways and glorious beaches that make Wénchāng attractive.

Minibuses heading to Gālōngwān, 10km from Wénchāng's bus station, depart from the riverside in Wénchāng and pass the turnoff to Qinglan Harbour (Qīnglán Gǎngwān). It's a five-minute motorbike ride to the harbour, where you can take a ferry (Y45) and motorbike (Y10) to the stands of coconut palms and mile after mile of beach. Another way is to take the direct bus to Dōngjiāo (Y16) from Hǎikǒu's east bus station.

The beaches in this area have been developed as resorts and accommodation prices can be high during the holiday season.

Frequent buses leave for Wénchāng from Hǎikǒu's east bus station between 7am and 7pm. Tickets are Y13, and Y16 for air-con.

XĪNGLÓNG 兴隆
Since 1952 more than 20,000 Chinese-Vietnamese and overseas Chinese refugees (mostly from Indonesia or Malaysia) have settled at a cultural park known as the **Xinglong Overseas Chinese Farm** (兴隆华桥村; Xīnglóng Huáqiáo Cūn; ☎ 6225 1888, ext 8811; admission Y38; ⏰ 7.30am-6pm). Tropical agriculture, rubber and coffee are important crops here; Xīnglóng coffee is famous all over China. Many residents speak English and may be able to organise transport to Miao villages. The interesting **Xinglong Tropical Botanical Garden** (兴隆热带植物园; Xīnglóng Rèdài Zhíwùyuán; ☎ 6225 5900; admission Y15; ⏰ 7.30am-6pm), 3km south of town, has tea- and coffee-tastings.

Otherwise, Xīnglóng has touristy hot spring resorts east of town (nothing to rave about). From the bus stop to the hotels it costs Y3 to go by motorbike, or Y5 by motortricycle. Trips out to the farm or the botanical garden from the city centre are Y5.

COASTAL SOUTH

DĂO: ISLAND

The simplified version of this character is readily identifiable as a bird sitting atop a mountain, with its feet tucked under its body. One can imagine the mountain being partly submerged under water, its peak forming an island in the sea. (The modern character leaves out more details of the bird.)

XĪNCŪN 新村

Xīncūn is populated almost solely by Danjia (Tanha) minority people, who are employed in fishing and pearl cultivation. The main attraction here is Monkey Island. It's home to a population of Guǎngxī monkeys (*Macaca mulatta*) and it makes a pleasant day trip from Sānyà. Buses travelling the eastern route from Hǎikǒu will drop you off at a fork in the road about 3km from Xīncūn. It should then be easy to get a lift on a passing minibus, or hitch or walk into Xīncūn. Frequent minibuses run to Xīncūn directly from Língshuǐ (15km away) and Sānyà.

Monkey Island 南湾猴岛

About a thousand macaque monkeys live on this hilly peninsula near Xīncūn. This **government research park** (Nánwān Hóudǎo; ☎ 6671 7080; admission Y20; ⏱ 8am-6.30pm) is under state protection and a wildlife centre has been established to investigate the monkey business. It sounds tacky and touristy, but the preserve is peaceful if you avoid the tourist groups.

The animals are tame and anticipate tourist arrivals for snacks of peanuts. It's all right to feed them but don't try to touch them. Keep a tight grip on your camera; these monkeys are wily!

Ferries (Y2) from Xīncūn's pier putt-putt to Monkey Island in 10 minutes, where a bus or hired car can take you to the park entrance. A cable car (Y45 return) also runs between Xīncūn and Monkey Island.

For best contact with the monkeys, visit in the morning or evening, otherwise you might have trouble spotting them in the foliage.

The mating season (February to May) is a more active time, however, the monkeys are, shall we say, over-hospitable and you may have to crowbar them off your leg.

SĀNYÀ 三亚

☎ 0898 / pop 440,600

Arriving in Sānyà, you'd swear the sleepy and modestly attractive city exists solely to efficiently transport tourist-folk to sunny strands. Indeed, it's surprising to see how, well, empty the city proper is, and the lion's share of buses are those roaring directly to the beaches!

On the western outskirts of Sānyà there's a community of around 5000 Hui, the only Muslim inhabitants of Hǎinán.

Orientation

Sānyà is oddly broken up. The bus stations and a few tourist facilities are situated in the two main peninsulas split between Sānyà Bay and Sānyà River; here Jiefang Lu is the main drag. The beaches are to the southeast.

Information

A **Bank of China** (中国银行; Zhōngguó Yínháng) in Dàdōnghǎi changes travellers cheques and another one in Sānyà (⏱ 8.30am-5.30pm) sits near the Gangmen Lu bridge.

There's a **post and telecommunications building** (Jiefang Lu) in Sānyà and one in Dàdōnghǎi, at the eastern end of Yuya Dadao. Also in Dàdōnghǎi, south of Chuānyà Bīnguǎn, are two **Internet cafés** (wǎngbā; per hr Y2).

The area around Dadonghai Beach (Dàdōnghǎi Hǎitān) is full of travel agencies. Try **Dragon Travel Agency** (☎ 821 3526; 11 Luling Lu), who can arrange tickets and tours, and may be able to rustle up a couple of bicycles.

Visas can only be renewed in Hǎikǒu.

Sights & Activities

Yalong Bay, Dàdōng-hǎi, Luhuitou Peninsula and Tiānyá Hǎijiǎo are popular beaches. The sun is intense from March onwards; take high sun-factor lotion.

Superb is **Yalong Bay** (亚龙湾; Yàlóng Wān; Asian Dragon Bay), to the east of Sānyà, featuring a 7km strip of sand. Roam about for hours and find your own postcard view. Take the infrequent bus No 102 (Y5) from Yuya Dadao.

The crescent-shaped beach at **Dàdōnghǎi** (大东海) is around 3km southeast of Sānyà and is easily reached by the unnumbered large green buses (Y1), which shuttle between Jiefang Lu and the beach. Dàdōnghǎi is a logical base camp, but the beach is smaller, more developed and crowded.

COASTAL SOUTH

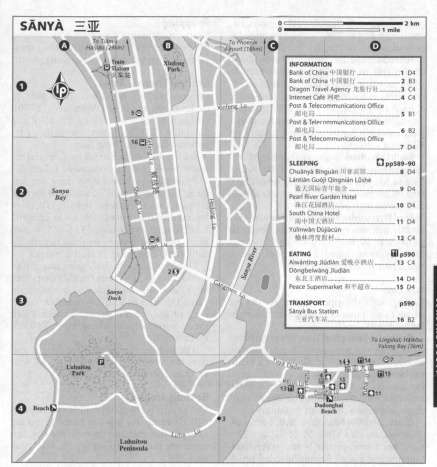

SĀNYÀ 三亚

0 _____ 2 km
0 _____ 1 mile

To Tiānyá
Hǎijiǎo (24km)

To Phoenix
Airport (18km)

Train
Station
火车站

Xinfeng
Park

Xinfeng Lu

Sanya
Bay

Hedong Lu

Xinjian Lu

Sanya River

Shengli Lu

Jiefang Lu

Mǎ Lu

Gangmen Lu

Sanya
Dock

Sanya
Dock

To Língshuǐ; Hǎikǒu;
Yalong Bay (3km)

Luhuitou
Park

Yuya Dadao

Haiyun Lu

Yuya Dadao

Y'hai Lu

Beach

Donghui Lu

Dadonghai
Beach

Lutiú Lu

Luhuitou
Peninsula

INFORMATION
Bank of China 中国银行 1 D4
Bank of China 中国银行 2 B3
Dragon Travel Agency 龙旅行社 3 C4
Internet Café 网吧 4 C4
Post & Telecommunications Office
邮电局 5 B1
Post & Telecommunications Office
邮电局 6 B2
Post & Telecommunications Office
邮电局 7 D4

SLEEPING 🛏 pp589–90
Chuānyà Bīnguǎn 川亚宾馆 8 D4
Lántiān Guójì Qīngnián Lǚshè
蓝天国际青年旅舍 9 D4
Pearl River Garden Hotel
珠江花园酒店 10 D4
South China Hotel
南中国大酒店 11 D4
Yúlínwān Dùjiàcūn
榆林湾度假村 12 C4

EATING 🍴 p590
Aiwǎntíng Jiǔdiàn 爱晚亭酒店 13 C4
Dōngbéiwáng Jiǔdiàn
东北王酒店 14 D4
Peace Supermarket 和平超市 15 D4

TRANSPORT p590
Sānyà Bus Station
三亚汽车站 16 B2

COASTAL SOUTH

The beaches on **Luhuitou Peninsula** (鹿回头)
are poor but they're uncrowded!

The beach at **Tiānyá Hǎijiǎo** (天涯海角; literally 'edge of the sky, rim of the sea'; admission Y50), 24km
northwest of Sānyà, swells with tourists
crowding around the stone featured on the
Y2 note to have their photo taken. You can
also catch a boat (Y120) from the dock here
to a small island 10 minutes off the coast
to do some snorkelling. Catch any minibus
(Y2, 45 minutes) heading north along the
coast road from the No 2 or 4 northern
terminus. These buses also go to **Nánshān
Dòngtiān Gōngyuán** (南山洞天公园; Nanshan
Park; admission Y70), further west – get a look
at the 108m-tall Buddha being constructed
in the ocean!

Sleeping
BUDGET
Lántiān Guójì Qīngnián Lǚshè (Blue Sky International
Youth Hostel; ☎ 8818 2320; sy-youthhostel@163.com; s/d
with private bath Y80/100-125; 🖳) Finally, a youth
hostel in Dàdōnghǎi. Rooms are spotless
(no dorms – yet) and the staff are friendly
in this laid-back gem. It's a bit tough to spot
off Haiyun Lu (look for the blue HI sign).

Chuānyà Bīnguǎn (☎ 8822 7333; fax 8821 3568; Yuya
Dadao; d/tr Y268/300; 🖳) Near the youth hostel,
this standby generally offers discounts. It is
basic but clean and the staff are welcoming.

MID-RANGE
Most hotels in Dàdōnghǎi are mid-range.
High-season rates start at Y350 for a double

(more in winter). Outside peak periods, negotiating a 30% to 50% discount is common; or book online or through travel agencies.

Yúlínwān Dùjiàcūn (Yulin Bay Holiday Resort; ☎ 8822 7188; fax 8821 2536; Lulin Lu; s/d Y300/410; 🏶) This place (with a thatched roof reception area) is a decent, if fading, mid-range option; try bargaining for a 50% discount during the low season. The staff are rather indifferent but for these quoted prices (not higher) it's decent.

South China Hotel (Nánzhōngguó Dàjiǔdiàn; ☎ 8821 9888; www.southchinahotel.com; Yuhai Lu; d Y980; 🏶 🛋) One of Sānyà's longstanding hotels. You'll find Western/Chinese restaurants, a pool and rooms with ocean views.

Pearl River Garden Hotel (Zhūjiāng Huāyuán Jiǔdiàn; ☎ 8821 1888; www.prgardenhotel.com.cn; Donghai Lu; s/d Y800/1100; 🏶 🛋) This four-star hotel is a more luxurious option; it has a pool, private beach and several restaurants.

TOP END

Yàlóng Bay's sybaritic five-star resorts are where to go if money is no object. See right for transport details.

Holiday Inn Yalong Bay (Yàlóng Hǎiwān Jiàrì Jiǔdiàn; ☎ 8856 5666; www.sixcontinentshotels.com; d standard/ocean-view Y1308/1708; 🗙 🏶 🖳 🛋) On a beautiful stretch of beach, this top choice is good for families as they have great kid-centred activities. Facilities include a beachside pool, disco and several bars and restaurants.

Gloria (Sānyà Kǎlái Dùjiā Jiǔdiàn; ☎ 8856 8855; www.gloriaresort.com; s & d Y1380; 🗙 🏶 🖳 🛋) This hotel has a semi-private beach, several restaurants and a pool. Rooms have balconies. Service at the Holiday Inn has a slight edge.

Eating

Sānyà swarms with restaurants, most outdoor and boisterously casual. Inexplicably, local delicacies aren't easy to find.

Dōngbĕiwáng Jiǔdiàn (King of the Northeast Restaurant; ☎ 8821 2192; Yuya Dadao; mains Y8-40; 🕑 lunch & dinner) By far one of the best restaurants in Dàdōnghǎi, it features delicious (not at all pricey) dishes from northern China and has great service (and an English menu).

Aìwăntíng Jiǔdiàn (☎ 8821 3278; 61 Luling Lu; mains Y20-45; 🕑 lunch & dinner) This famous restaurant serves up spicy Húnán specialties. It also has a branch in Shànghǎi.

Peace Supermarket (Hépíng Cháoshì; ☎ 8821 3011; 30 Yuya Dadao) Excellent for self-caterers.

Shopping

Southern Hăinán is famous for its cultured pearls, but don't be duped into paying spectacularly high prices for fine-looking plastic.

Getting There & Away

Phoenix airport has domestic flights to destinations including Shēnzhèn (Y730), Guǎngzhōu (Y670), Běijīng (Y1950) and Shànghǎi (Y1570). There are daily international flights to Hong Kong.

Dàdōnghǎi is full of travel agencies and the major hotels can also book plane tickets.

From Sānyà's bus station there are frequent buses and minibuses to most parts of Hǎinán. Deluxe buses to Hǎikǒu (Y70, three hours) depart frequently. Buses to Tōngzhá leave roughly every hour (Y14 to Y20, two to 2½ hours) and there are three departures daily for Qióngzhōng (Y23, five hours).

One minibus, No 102, goes directly to Yàlóng Bay (Y5). It runs roughly every half hour, and you can catch it at bus stops on Yuya Dadao. Or, hail any minibus heading east and see if it goes to Tiándú. From there, a motorcycle sidecar costs Y10 out to Yàlóng.

The railway line is used for freight and does not have a passenger service. All boat services operate from Hǎikǒu.

Getting Around

The airport is 18km north of Sānyà. Reportedly a shuttle bus is going to start running along Dàdōnghǎi and through the city, but currently there is no service. A taxi averages Y50.

Motorcycle sidecars cruise the streets. The real fare is usually half the asking price (Y5 to most places).

Given that Sānyà's attractions are so spread out, it's worth getting together with a few people and hiring a vehicle and driver. The minibuses by the long-distance bus station charge Y200 for a full-day, six-destination excursion.

AROUND SĀNYÀ

Two islands, **Xīmaò Zhoū** and **Dōngmaò Zhoū** are visible off Sānyà's coastline. Only Xīmaò Zhoū (西帽州) is open to visitors. At 2.6 sq km, it's fairly small, but you can hike around or go snorkelling. The Peace Supermarket in Dàdōnghǎi hires out a boat for Y450 return and the trip takes about two hours.

Speedboats from the beach take 30 minutes, but are expensive. A small homestay on the island offers basic accommodation for Y80 per night.

Jiānfēnglǐng Nature Reserve (尖峰岭自然保护区; Jiānfēnglǐng Zìrán Bǎohùqū) is 115km from Sānyà. This lush area is high above the humidity of the coastal plain and is home to many different species of plants and insects. To really get a feel for the place, it's best to stay overnight and spend the day walking in the reserve and the surrounding area.

Tiānchí Shānzhuāng (天池山庄; d with bath Y80) This place has basic accommodation in folksy huts in the middle of a man-made lake.

Tiānchí Bìshǔ Shānzhuāng (☎ 8572 0162; d with bath Y120-180) Nestled up in the hill west of the lake, this place has pristine rooms.

Getting to Jiānfēng by public transport tries your patience. Buses going to Bāsuǒ from Sānyà's bus station will drop you off at the turn-off (there's an English sign). Tickets are Y15, or Y25 for air-con. From the turn-off it's a rough 10km-ride by motorcycle sidecar (Y10) or a public mini-truck (Y1) to the town of Jiānfēng, 16km from the reserve. From there a public bus leaves mid-morning (Y5) to go up the horrendous road to the mountain. Unfortunately, if you miss the bus you'll have to hire a vehicle for about Y70 or sleep in the village's very spartan guesthouse.

TŌNGZHÁ 通什
☎ 0898

Tōngzhá, also known as Tōngshí (and Wǔzhǐ Shān on maps), is the capital of the Li and Miao Autonomous Prefecture. It's a pleasant place, with a lively market on Jiefang Lu, a university and a **museum** (Mínzú Bówùguǎn; ☎ 862 2336; admission Y10; ☼ 8am-5.30pm) that displays Li and Miao artefacts. Tōngzhá is a good starting point for trips into the highlands to seek out real Li and Miao villages.

For hikes around Tōngzhá, head out in a northeasterly direction past Tōngzhá Lǚyóu Shānzhuāng, at the head of Shanzhuang Lu, or start climbing some of the hills behind the university past the bus station.

There's a **Bank of China** (中国银行; Zhōngguó Yínháng) near the intersection of Jiefang Lu and Xinhua Lu and the **post office** (yóujú) is across the main bridge, on the northeastern side of the river.

Sleeping

Cheap hotels (a few currently exist) keep closing down and the remaining one opposite the bus station seemed unsure if foreigners could stay.

Tōngzhá Lǚyóu Shānzhuāng (通什旅游山庄; Tongzha Resort Hotel; ☎ 8662 3188; fax 8662 2201; 38 Shanzhuang Lu; d from Y388-468; 🅿) This hotel is on the northeastern fringe of town and offers discounts of 60%. The rooms and facilities are elegant and have rustic, rattan furniture.

THE SPRATLY SPAT

Were it not such a contentious piece of real estate, few people would have heard of the Spratly Islands, and their neighbours the Paracel Islands. On a map, look for a parcel of dots in the South China Sea, hemmed in by Malaysia, Brunei, the Philippines, Vietnam and China to the north. They all claim the islands as their own.

Why the fuss over 53 specks of land, many of which are just reefs and shoals? The answer is oil, though none have ever been discovered and many experts say none ever will!

China, the most distant of the claimants, insists Han dynasty temples found on some of the islands validate its territorial rights. Vietnam has long been a disputant to this claim, and in 1933 the colonial French government of Vietnam annexed the islands, before losing them to Japan in 1939. Following Japan's WWII defeat, it was not until a Philippine claim in 1956 that the Taiwan-based Kuomintang government reasserted the traditional Chinese claim over the islands by occupying the largest of the islands, Taiping, where they remain. Vietnam thereafter hoisted a flag over the westernmost point of the islands. The Chinese struck back in 1988 by sinking two Vietnamese ships and forcibly occupying the islands. In 1996, though the Philippine navy destroyed a small Chinese-built radar base on Mischief Reef, China refused (and refuses) to be dislodged.

Given these countries' continuing military upgrades, the Spratly Islands remain one of the most potentially destabilising issues in Asia.

Getting There & Away

Minibuses depart regularly from the Sānyà bus station (Y14 to Y20, two to 2½ hours). Frequent buses travel on to Qióngzhōng (Y11, two hours) and Hǎikǒu (Y30, 5½ hours) from Tōngzhá. Air-con buses to Hǎikǒu travel a bit quicker and cost Y40.

To head deep into the highlands, catch the bus to Báishā (Y14, three hours), 94km northwest of Tōngzhá.

AROUND TŌNGZHÁ

Near Tōngzhá, at 1867m, is **Wǔzhǐ Shān** (五指山; Five Fingers Mountain), Hǎinán's highest mountain. A good time to visit is on the third day of the third month of the lunar calendar, when lots of Miao gather for a festival. The entrance ticket costs Y45 plus an additional Y10 for entrance to a 'preserve'. It's possible to stay at the bottom at **Wǔzhǐshān Bīnguǎn** (五指山宾馆). The rooms here cost between Y100 and Y500, depending on demand (seriously). It's also possible to stay even further from the mountain in Shuǐmàn (水满), a dusty little village with one **guesthouse** (☎ 8635 0116; s/d Y80).

Buses leave at 10am and 2pm (possibly one extra bus if demand warrants it) from the car park opposite the entrance to the main bridge, on the northeastern side of the river in Tōngzhá. Tickets are Y4 to the town of Wǔzhǐ Shān, 60km northeast of Tōngzhá.

From there it's another 5km by motorcycle (Y5) to reach the base of the mountain.

QIÓNGZHŌNG 琼中
☎ 0898

The route between Tōngzhá and Qióngzhōng passes through forested hills and small villages. It's certainly worth your while starting early in the day and getting off the bus at one of the villages, such as Hóngmáozhèn, taking a look around, then catching the next bus going through. Qióngzhōng is a small, rather ugly hill town but the surrounding countryside is beautiful. The nearby **waterfall** at Báihuā Shān (白花山) drops more than 300m and is about 7km from town. Motorcycles can take you up for about Y15, and it's a nice walk back.

In Qióngzhōng there are two hotels on the main street, on either side of the bus station.

Jiāotōng Dàshà (交通大厦; Traffic Bldg; ☎ 8622 2615; 119 Haiyi Lu; common s/d Y40/60, standard s/d Y100/120; 🖃) The rooms here are basic but clean.

Hòngxiāo Dàshà (☎ 8622 1446; 59 Haiyi Lu; d Y90-158; 🖃) A few stores west of Jiāotōng Dàshà, this hotel has slightly fancier rooms.

Besides the road through the central highlands linking Qióngzhōng and Hǎikǒu to the north, and Tōngzhá and Sānyà to the south, you can also take a bus nearer to the coast to Xīnglóng (Y11, two hours) and hook up to the coastal freeway.

Guǎngxī 广西

HIGHLIGHTS

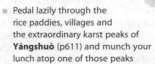

■ Explore the peak-dotted **riverine parks** (p616), some of China's most legendary

■ Drift along the **Li River** (Lí Jiāng, p611) from Guìlín, a superb river cruise from one of China's legendary tourist cities

■ Pedal lazily through the rice paddies, villages and the extraordinary karst peaks of **Yángshuò** (p611) and munch your lunch atop one of those peaks

■ Trek the **Dragon's Backbone Rice Terraces** (p618) near Lóngshèng and sleep in a Zhuang village

■ Enter Guìzhōu province via the 'back door' of **Sānjiāng** (p619) – a lush, isolated region of lovely villages, river ferries and wooden bridges

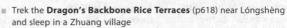

■ POP: 45.9 MIL   ■ AREA: 236,300 SQ KM   ■ www.gxi.gov.cn

SOUTHWEST CHINA

You've most likely seen Guǎngxī and not even known it. The riverine karst upthrusts of Guìlín and Yángshuò have graced endless coffee-table picturebooks and TV documentaries. Yet few travellers, like eons of Chinese before them, venture further afield.

All have missed out on a great deal. Guǎngxī roughly translates as 'vast, boundless west' – a counterpart to its equally broad east, Guǎngdōng province. (The overlooked province is no tiny pocket. Its 236,000 sq km rank it 9th in size nationally; with nearly 46 million denizens, it's 11th most populated in the country.) Whereas Guǎngdōng's vastness has always been recognised in terms of geography, population, and economy, Guǎngxī's historic backwater isolation has always, for the Chinese, impelled visions of a rough hinterland, an uneasy buffer of sorts to more savage places.

For centuries Guǎngxī's remoteness and challenging topography kept it poverty-stricken (a residual problem out of the main cities) and not far from a place of exile for banished officials. Yet these same features are modern draws for travellers looking for adventure and natural splendour. The topographically rough northern reaches of the province, bordering Guìzhōu, are home to spectacular rice terraces and villages with gorgeous wooden bridges and drum towers. In the south are the less-touristed rock paintings on Left River (Zuǒ Jiāng), a border crossing with Vietnam near the town of Píngxiáng, the binational Detian Waterfall, and China's best mainland beaches.

If you are a people person, you'll love this province. A mosaic of China's nationalities hails from here; in fact, nearly 75% of Guǎngxī is non-Han. Today the Zhuang are China's largest minority, with well over 15 million people concentrated in Guǎngxī. In 1955, Guǎngxī province was reconstituted as the Guangxi Zhuang Autonomous Region. (The Zhuang are, however, virtually indistinguishable from the Han Chinese.) Guǎngxī is also home to smaller numbers of Dong, Maonan, Mulao, Jing (Vietnamese Gin) and Yi peoples.

History

In 214 BC a Qin dynasty army finally conquered (on its third attempt) what is now Guǎngdōng and eastern Guǎngxī, overpowering the Zhuang people, who found sympathy in the northern regions with the Yao (Mien) and Miao (H'mong) people.

Unlike the Zhuang, who were ultimately immersed in Chinese customs and eventually assimilated, the Yao and Miao remained in the hill regions and were often cruelly oppressed by the Han. There was continuous conflict between the Chinese and the hill tribes, leading to uprisings in the 1830s and again during the Taiping Rebellion, which began in Guǎngxī. Compounding these conflicts was the rough land and its great distance from central power.

The Qin built China's first canal (Ling Canal), but could make little headway with it. A backwater until the 20th century, anti-Kuomintang forces began to modernise the province in the 1920s, but WWII devastated much of it. Herculean transport infrastructure laid down in the 1960s to supply Vietnam in their war against the US – and tourists flocking to Guìlín – have energised the province economically.

Climate

Latitudinally, Guǎngxī approximates balmy Florida in the US, but don't pack just a bathing suit. Tropical heat and humidity (average temperatures range from 13°C in January to 28°C in August) are the norm, but a north/south distinction exists. Northern Guǎngxī rises gradually into the Yúnnán plateau and, though still subtropical, highlands here are much more temperate, even in summer (and frost and snow are not unheard of in winter).

Much of the annual 150cm to 200cm of rain falls from June to August; less heavy (but more constant) early rains in March bring dismal, cold damp. Note that coastal regions can get hit by typhoons starting in summer. May, September and October are generally the best times to come.

Language

You'd best carry your Cantonese phrase-book, especially near the Guăngdōng border; traders and refugee-immigrants have carried Vietnamese to the southern coast and western regions. Among numerous minority languages are Yi, Miao and even some Hakka (and in these places Mandarin may be nonexistent). So assimilated are the Zhuang that the only thing you're likely to notice linguistically is the Zhuang Romanization system (quite different from standard pinyin but still understandable) employed on some signs.

Getting There & Around

The Nankun rail line into Yúnnán boasts China's most modern trains and tracks; Guìlín's airport is one of the nation's busiest and most efficient. Guăngxī also offers hydrophiles the chance to hop ferries to Hăinán Dăo.

An intra-provincial transport option is found in northern Guăngxī, where many minority villages are reached only by long-poled river ferries.

NÁNNÍNG 南宁

☎ 0771 / pop 1.3 million

As goes China, so goes Nánníng, the cap-ital that dents overgeneralised stereotypes of 'backwater' southwestern provinces and

---

THE DRAGON TO THE NORTH

Uneasy neighbours, China and Vietnam have been at odds for over 2100 years. Han dynasty armies conquered the first Vietnamese patriot, Tire Da, in the 2nd century BC. After dozens of attempts, Vietnam eventually threw off the yoke of imperialism in the 10th century AD.

After WWII, Western forces sent a 200,000-strong force of Chinese Nationalists to northern Vietnam to demobilise Japanese troops. The two nations have regularly been at war over since, apart from when China supported Vietnam during the (American) Vietnam War.

In 1979, open war broke out. The Chinese incursion was impelled (they say) after the Viet-namese signed a treaty with the Soviet Union – another border country with a Chinese love-hate relationship. Vietnam had also invaded Cambodia to topple the Khmer Rouge. Finally, and most importantly, Vietnam had seized the assets of and deported (or forced out) up to 250,000 huáqiáo (overseas Chinese), most of them to Yúnnán and Guăngxī.

The Chinese also claim Vietnamese forces crossed the border first. The Vietnamese of course deny this (most Western sources back their version). Over 16 days, scores of people were killed and five provincial border towns in Vietnam were heavily damaged. Bizarrely, both sides claimed to have won this battle.

Major battles erupted again in 1984 in several areas of Yúnnán and along much of Guăngxī's border. This time the Vietnamese used up to 10 expanded divisions to attack; while they didn't seize any land, they did inflict a humiliating lesson on China.

In 1997 Vietnam took its protests over China's selling of oil exploration rights in its waters to the Association of Southeast Asian Nations (ASEAN, which sided with Vietnam; this dispute continues to this day), and daily newspapers ran front-page banner headlines screaming about major Chinese border transgressions.

To everyone's surprise, China conceded on border issues, agreeing to clear landmines from 10 sq km. Cynics argue China did this as much to facilitate further trade – which had quad-rupled from 1992 to 1997 along the border – as to encourage friendly relations. Soon after, Běijīng greeted a high-level contingent of Vietnamese, and historic sites in Dōngxīng (Guăngxī) dating Sino-Viet ties to the 19th century were restored and opened to the public. Perhaps most symbolic: in mid-1999, direct postal links, which had previously gone through Singapore, were finally restored through Guăngxī.

GUÁNGXĪ 广西

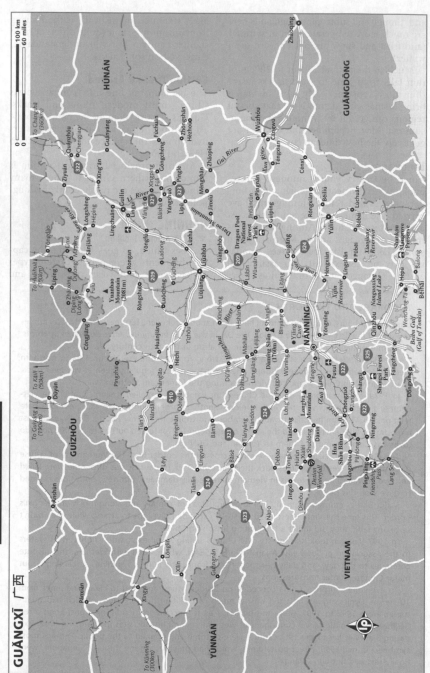

SOUTHWEST CHINA

makes for a warm welcome if you're coming from Vietnam. In recent years, most of the city's main streets and river banks have been beautifully landscaped and restored, yet backstreets retain a modicum of funkiness.

Nánníng became an important staging post for shipping arms to Vietnam in the 1960s. The thriving border trade that has sprung from Běijīng's increasingly friendly ties with Hanoi has now supplanted armaments. Nánníng is thus a good base for travellers wanting to leave or enter Vietnam; you can even arrange a Vietnamese visa here.

Orientation
In the north is the train station. Nánníng's main artery, Chaoyang Lu, runs roughly north–south towards Yong River (Yōng Jiāng), which bisects the city. Halfway down Chaoyang Lu is Chaoyang Garden.

MAPS
Hawkers around Chaoyang Garden sell the *Nanning Bilingual Street Map*.

Information
BOOKSHOPS
Xinhua Bookshop (Xīnhuá Shūdiàn; Xinhua Lu) One of the largest in China, with four levels jam-packed with books.

INTERNET ACCESS
Internet café (wǎngbā; per hr Y2) China Telecom's Internet café is on the 5th level of the Nanning Department Store; also check in the vicinity of Chaoyang Sq.

MONEY
Bank of China (Zhōngguó Yínháng; Minzu Dadao; ☉ 8am-noon & 2.30-6pm) Changes travellers cheques and gives credit card advances.

POST & COMMUNICATIONS
Post office (yóujú; ☉ 8am-8pm) This central full-service office is one long block southeast of the train station.

TRAVEL AGENCIES
China International Travel Service (CITS; Zhōngguó Guójì Lǚxíngshè; ☎ 280 4960; 40 Xinmin Lu; ☉ 8.30am-noon & 2.30-5pm) Its Family and Individual Traveller (FIT) department here has a friendly English-speaking staff and can help you get your hands on a one-month Vietnam visa (Y650). Expect a week's wait, minimum.
Guangxi Overseas Travel Service (Guǎngxī Hǎiwài Lǚxíngshè; ☎ 261 2553) One building over from CITS.

VISAS
Public Security Bureau (PSB; Gōngānjú; ☎ 289 1260; Keyuan Dadao; ☉ 8am-4pm Mon-Fri) The Foreign Affairs office of the PSB is northwest of the city centre, north of the zoo.

Sights & Activities
GUANGXI PROVINCIAL MUSEUM
广西省博物馆
This **museum** (Guǎngxī Shěng Bówùguǎn; 34 Minzu Dadao; admission Y8; ☉ 8.30am-noon & 3-6pm) offers a peaceful browse through 50,000 years of Guǎngxī history; the highlight is certainly the world's largest bronze drum collection. In the tree-filled rear garden sit several full-size examples of Dong and Miao houses and a nail-less bridge. Catch bus No 6 from the train station.

HEADING WEST?

In 1998 the government finally drove the last spike into the Nankun Railway, linking Kūnmíng with Nánníng and offering a crucial alternative transportation route between Guǎngxī, Guìzhōu and Yúnnán.

This extraordinary project is another perfect symbol of the New China 'can-do' spirit. The government poured over 20 billion *yuán* into the project, with a small army of workers toiling away nonstop for over seven years. The resulting all-electric railroad sports all the features they could cram in, including modern sensors built into the track to judge conditions and make adjustments.

Engineers had a field day with the geography; nearly one-third of the route is bridge or tunnel. The train passes through a rough jumble of around 900km of mountain ranges and steep valleys but, thanks to the designers, manages to bypass scenic waterfalls and other natural sights.

The government had a secondary motive for the railroad, which roars through some of the most 'backward' areas in China: already officials have touted that fresh fruit and vegetables are now available year-round in previously isolated villages. The government is also counting on tourism and, more particularly, mining, to boom in the region.

One other highlight of the train that will please travellers: hard-sleeper tickets are relatively easy to procure.

NÁNNÍNG 南宁

QINGXIU SHAN SCENIC AREA
青秀山风景区
A favourite summer retreat since the Sui and Tang dynasties, this 'scenic area' (Qīngxiù Shān Fēngjǐngqū) offers verdant woods, springs, lakes and landscaped gardens with modest but scenic peaks of up to 180m that can easily be scaled for a more elevated perspective.

Local bus No 10 heads to the park from the train station, but you still have a fair walk to the entrance. Tour buses to the park also depart from Chaoyang Garden.

GUANGXI MEDICINAL HERB BOTANICAL GARDEN 广西药用植物园
Far on the eastern outskirts of town, this fascinating **garden** (Guǎngxī Yàoyòng Zhíwùyuán; ☎ 561 7166; admission Y5) is the largest of its kind in China, with over 2400 species of medicinal plants (Guǎngxī alone has 5000 species). The botanical gardens will be especially impressive if you are lucky enough to tag along with one of the centre's few English speakers. It takes about 30 minutes to get there on bus No 101 or 102 from Chaoyang Garden.

Tours
Two-hour river tours (Y30) are scheduled to depart at 9.30am (and occasionally at 9.30pm) from a pier (near a lovely 500m-long footpath with teahouses) off Linjiang Lu, south of the Yong Jiang bridge. These may run only on weekends in low season.

Sleeping
Cháoyáng Fàndiàn (☎ 243 7688; fax 241 7132; Chaoyang Lu; common s/d Y35/50, with bathroom Y98/158;) A friendly (you'll probably be asked by the whole staff for help with English!) budget option is this one, opposite the train station, with clean rooms and efficient service.

Yínhé Dàjiǔdiàn (Milky Way Hotel; ☎ 211 6688; www.yhhotel.com; s & d Y188-550; 🅧) Also near the train station, this hotel has comfortable rooms and renovators were beaverishly whirring away with saws upgrading at last check. A dizzying parade of clients keeps the place hopping, but service is good.

Yǒngjiāng Bīnguǎn (☎ 280 0888; fax 280 0535; 41 Jiangdong Lu; s & d Y375-600; 🅧) Overlooking Yong River, this three-star hotel is underrated, and is arguably better value than the five-star monsters in town. Huge rooms (some with river views) and bathrooms and a good health club are pluses.

Xiángyún Dàjiǔdiàn (☎ 210 1999; xydjd@public .nn.gx.cn; 59 Xinmin Lu; s/tw Y375/430; 🅧) Less conveniently located, this three-star hotel offers 50% discounts outside summer months. The rooms were all given a face-lift in 2002 and still have a fresh feel.

Eating

Nánníng is famous for its *gǒuròu huǒguō* (dog hotpot), especially at the teeming **Canine Cuisine District** (Gǒuròu Qū), south of the Chaoyang Stream along Chaoyang Lu.

Zhongshan Lu, at the southern end of the city centre, is the most raucous street for other-than-dog (though still exotic) **food stalls**. Fare includes *juàntǒngfěn* (steamed noodle pancake wrap with pork and coriander filling, served in steaming broth), and *lǎoyǒumiàn* or *lǎoyǒufěn* (literally 'old friend' wheat or rice noodles).

Xiaǒdùlaí Shíjiē (Gong He Lu) This bustling, wander-point-choose restaurant is a great place to sample pan-provincial (and pan-Cathay) items, all in a casually upscale atmosphere. Items start at Y6, but it will cost around Y30 to eat your fill.

Getting There & Away
AIR

Domestic airlines fly everywhere, and there are multiple departures daily to almost all major cities, including Guǎngzhōu (Y660), Shànghǎi (Y1520), Shēnzhèn (Y710), Kūnmíng (Y580), Běijīng (Y1870), Guìyáng (Y570) and Hǎikǒu (Y560).

International flights include Hong Kong (Y1810) four times a week and Hanoi (Hénèi; Y810) twice a week; there is also a weekly flight to Bangkok.

Civil Aviation Administration of China (CAAC; Zhōngguó Mínháng; ☎ 243 1459; 82 Chaoyang Lu) is generally efficient though travel agencies often have lower prices.

BUS

Bus stations are sprinkled throughout Nánníng. The superefficient **Yíndōng Zhàn** is east of town along the expressway. Frequent express buses depart to: Běihǎi (Y50 to Y73, three hours), Guǎngzhōu (Y180, 10 hours), Guìlín (Y80 to Y117, four to 4½ hours), Guìpíng (Y50 to Y63, four hours), Liǔzhōu (Y50, three hours) and Wúzhōu (Y90 to Y110, six hours). Bus No 6 runs to the train station.

Northwest of the train station is the **Běidà Kèyùn Zhōngxīn**; anything to the north departs from here, including buses to Dàxīn (Y30, 2½ hours, 10 daily) or Jìngxī (Y50, seven hours). There is a direct bus to Detian Waterfall (Y50, four hours) but only in high season. Bǎisè (Y55, three to four hours) is also served best by this station; expressway construction should reduce travel times here. Bus No 52 links this station to the Yíndōng Zhàn via the train station.

Destinations south use the **Jiāngnán Zhàn**, south of Yong River. If you want to head southwest to Píngxiáng (Y60, 4½ hours), then consider the infinitely more convenient morning train. Bus No 41 runs along Chaoyang Lu to this station.

This means that the **Nanning Bus Station** (Nánníng Kèyùn Zǒngzhàn), the erstwhile main bus station (near the train station), is simply a ticket-dispenser (a shuttle bus runs to other stations).

TRAIN

Major direct rail links with Nánníng include Běijīng (T6 at 11.02am, 29 hours), Chéngdū (K142 at 6.57pm, 37 hours), Guǎngzhōu (K366 at 1.09am, 14 hours), Kūnmíng (K393 at 6.09pm, 14 hours), Shànghǎi (K197 at 8.37am, 30 hours), Xī'ān (K316 at 10.47am, 36 hours) and Guìlín (N802 at 8.22am, five hours).

The T6 for Běijīng also passes through Liǔzhōu (three hours), Guìlín (five hours), Wǔhàn (17 hours), Zhèngzhōu (22 hours) and Shíjiāzhuāng (26 hours). The K142 to Chéngdū passes through Guìyáng (19 hours) and Chóngqìng (29 hours).

The T905/M2 from Nánníng to Dong Dang (Tóngdēng) in Vietnam departs at 9.15pm, but think twice before hopping on. It takes forever with lengthy delays in Píngxiáng and at customs.

Getting next-day tickets at the train station doesn't seem to be too problematic. Foreigners can use any window though No 15 technically is supposed to be 'the one'; window No 16 is the place to go to change tickets.

Getting Around
TO/FROM THE AIRPORT
The most efficient way to reach the airport is by CAAC buses (Y15, 40 minutes), which depart regularly from the CAAC office on Chaoyang Lu (p599).

LOCAL TRANSPORT
You can hire **bicycles** (per hr Y0.6; ☺ 7am-11pm) at the southern end of Chaoyang Lu.

There are abundant taxis and motorcycle taxis plying the streets. Taxi rides usually start at Y10; motorcycle taxis are around Y5.

Buses generally run from 6am to around 11pm and fares start at Y1.

AROUND NÁNNÍNG
Yángmĕi 扬美
This beautifully preserved 17th-century town on the Yong River (26km west of Nánníng) has become a popular day trip from Nánníng. Guides will offer their services upon arrival; some speak some English.

The best way to get around the town is to hire an ox-cart for the half-day (Y10).

From Nánníng, boats depart from the ferry dock near the Yong Jiang bridge every Saturday and Sunday at 8.30am and return from Yángmĕi around 6pm (Y80, three hours), but they only depart with enough passengers. Buses leave from a bus stop just north of Chaoyang Garden or from a stop two blocks west of the train station, but only in high season.

Yiling Cave 伊岭岩
Twenty-five kilometres north of Nánníng, **Yiling Cave** (Yílíng Yán; admission Y25) is a bit of a tourist trap, but fun all the same with stalagmites and galactic lights. The surrounding countryside is also worth exploring.

Minibuses run from Chaoyang Garden on most weekends (especially during summer). Or, 7km north of the train station via You'ai Lu, is the Ānjí Zhàn bus station; bus No 41 runs here from Chaoyang Lu.

North of Yiling Cave is **Lingshui Springs** (灵水泉; Língshuǐ Quán), essentially a large outdoor mineral swimming pool. To reach the springs, continue on the bus past Yílīng to Wǔmìng, and catch a motorcycle taxi (Y3) the remaining few kilometres.

Dàmíng Shān 大明山
Some 90km northeast of Nánníng is **Dàmíng Shān** (admission Y8), an impressive mountain with an average elevation of over 1200m, and a maximum height of 1760m. With more than 1700 species of plants, the mountain is a provincially protected zone. The majority of the scenic spots are accessible within a day's hike, however most visitors organise a guide to show them around as paths are poorly marked.

Daming Shan Resort (大明山度假村; Dàmíng Shān Dùjiàcūn; ☎ 986 0902; dm Y25, tw with bathroom Y100) Here you'll find log cabins, a restaurant and prices that rise in summer. Out of season, it's best to ring ahead so they can make arrangements.

From Nánníng's Chaoyang Garden, there is one daily public bus (Y14, departing 3.10pm); another leaves in the morning from a stop a bit north, just south of the river and off Chaoyang Lu. Both terminate at **Dàmíngshān**, the small forestry town at the base of the mountain. This is where you'll find the ticket office, accommodation and a small shop. It is, however, another 27km from here to the top (and Daming Shan Resort) and the bus will only continue up if there are enough paying passengers.

Consider hopping off the bus 5km earlier in **Léijiāng**, where you can find a room and arrange a motorbike (Y50) to take you up to the top early the next day. You can also reach Léijiāng on any Dàhuà-, Mǎshān- or Liǎngjiāng-bound buses from Wǔmìng or Nánníng.

A bus returns to Nánníng from Dàmíng Shān daily at 7.30am with a second service at 2.30pm on weekends.

ZUO JIANG SCENIC AREA
左江风景区
A boat trip down Left River (Zuǒ Jiāng) to the Zuo Jiang Scenic Area (Zuǒjiāng Fēngjǐngqū) around 190km southwest of

Nánníng will take you through karst rock formations and offer glimpses of minority rock paintings.

The largest of 80 groups of paintings is in the area of **Huā Shān Bìhuà** (花山壁画; Flower Mountain; admission Y15), about three hours further south by boat. Here a fresco 170m high and 90m across depicts some 2000 figures of hunters, farmers and animals. It is now believed that the Luoyue, ancestors of the Zhuang minority, painted these cliffs around 2000 years ago.

Halfway to the site is the cheerful village of **Pānlóng** (攀龙) and the rough, explorable **Longrui Nature Reserve** (陇瑞自然保护区; Lóngruì Zìrán Bǎohùqū; admission Y6). The reserve is the only known home of the rare *báitóu yèhóu* (white leaf monkey).

The low-key tourist resort of **Hua Shan Ethnic Culture Village** (花山民族山寨度假村; Huā Shān Mínzú Shānzhài Dùjiàcūn; ☎ 862 8195; tw from Y120, meals Y25) is behind Pānlóng, and offers decent rooms in Dong-style wooden cabins, and traditional fare. Guides can be arranged.

Catch a morning Píngxiáng train (or bus) from Nánníng as far as Níngmíng. Tour operators in Níngmíng are unmissable. They offer Y100 boat tours for one or two people, and Y120 for three or four. Add Y50 if you want to stop overnight in Pānlóng. A new road runs along the river from Níngmíng to Pānlóng; a ride in a taxi (Y30) takes about 20 minutes.

PÍNGXIÁNG 凭祥

☎ 0771 / pop 100,000

The staging post for onward transport to Vietnam, Píngxiáng is a trading town rife with bustling markets but not much else.

Cheap hotels exist around the bus and train stations, but there is no real need to stay. By early morning bus or train from Nánníng, you will reach Píngxiáng around noon, from where you should be able to find transport to the Friendship Pass (Yǒuyì Guān) on the Vietnamese border. Minibuses and private vehicles run from near the bus and train stations and cost Y5 to Y20, depending on the number of passengers. From the Friendship Pass it's another 600m to the Vietnamese border post. Onward transport to Hanoi by train or bus is via the Vietnamese town of Lang Son (Liàngshān), 18km from the Friendship Pass. Remember that Vietnam is one hour behind China; at the time of writing the border post was open till 7pm Vietnam time.

If you're heading into China, catch one of the minibuses into Píngxiáng on the Chinese side of the border, from where you can catch a bus or train to Nánníng.

There are heaps of banks in Píngxiáng, so changing money is no problem.

DETIAN WATERFALL 德天瀑布

Located at the 53rd boundary marker between China and Vietnam, the Chinese have the earth-shaking majority of **Detian Waterfall** (Détiān Pùbù; admission Y30). The cascade drops only 40m, but makes up for it by a more than modest breadth. July is the best time to visit, although water levels will be fairly high from May through late September. While wandering around, be particularly careful that you don't accidentally cross the border into Vietnam – it's no laughing matter for them.

Sleeping & Eating

Just behind the ticket office is a **guesthouse** (one of two here) and **restaurant** (☎ 377 3570) with a fantastic view. If you want to stay here, be sure to book with its Nánníng (☎ 362 7088) or Dàxīn (☎ 262 4540) office for a discounted rate. If you just turn up at the door, twins/quads cost Y450/680.

If you get stuck in Shuòlóng, there are a few grubby **guesthouses** at the main intersection.

Getting There & Away

From Nánníng one infrequent direct bus to the falls leaves at or around 8.30am, but generally only during high season. Otherwise, from Nánníng or Píngxiáng, you will need to first head to Dàxīn. From Dàxīn, hop on a bus heading to Xiàléi and get off in Shuòlóng (Y8, 1½ hours). In Shuòlóng, you can catch a rattletrap minibus or motorbike taxi for the final 14km (Y3).

Leaving the falls, get back to Shuòlóng before late afternoon, as there isn't much movement on the main road in any direction after that. From here semiregular services run towards Dàxīn and Nánníng.

If you're heading for Jìngxī, either wait for a proper bus or leapfrog villages. First take a minibus (Y2) to Xiàléi, and then get another minibus (Y2) to Húrùn (pronounced Fúyuàn in these parts), from where you can get a 'proper' bus for the hour-long ride to Jìngxī. All up, the trip should take around two to three hours and you may enjoy a fun ride with pigs!

Jìngxī is a friendly town and home to the Jiuzhou Pagoda and a few cheap places to stay. From Jìngxī, take one of many buses to Bǎisè, the largest city in northwest Guǎngxī. The interesting **Baise Uprising Museum** (粤东会馆; Yuèdōng Huìguǎn) traces every movement of Deng Xiaoping and the Seventh Red Army during the 1920s and 1930s. From Bǎisè it's easy to head into Guìzhōu or Yúnnán via Xīngyì.

BĚIHǍI 北海
☎ 0779 / pop 560,000

No time for the beaches of Hǎinán? Head directly here, your next-best alternative. This friendly, tree-lined port community, 229km south of Nánníng, is the launching point for a ferry to Hǎinán but also has its own famed Silver Beach. Over 2000 years old, the city was once a major node on the ancient Marine Silk Route – the harbour area retains lovely old buildings. Pearl production later cemented its reputation. Thousands of Chinese-Vietnamese refugees landed here after the 1979 Sino-Viet conflict – look for them around the harbour.

Orientation & Information
The northern coast is home to the bus terminal, shops and most lodging options. The southern strip has the new International Ferry Terminal, hotels and that famous stretch of white sand.

Walking east from the main bus station along Beibuwan Lu, you'll pass by any number of **Internet cafés** (网吧; wǎngbā; per hr Y2). The **Bank of China** (中国银行; Zhōngguó Yínháng; Beihai Dado; ☏ 8am-noon & 2.30-5.30pm Mon-Fri) lies between Guizhou Lu and Sichuan Lu; an ATM is here.

Silver Beach 银滩
About 10km southeast of Běihǎi city, **Silver Beach** (Yíntān; admission Y25), has 1.6km of sparkling white sands (and few crowds, though the bodysurfing can't top Hǎinán's).

To get there from Běihǎi, walk west from the bus station, bear right at Woping Lu, which branches off behind the Běihǎi Yíngbīnguǎn, and catch bus No 3 at the corner of Jiefang Lu (Y2, 20 minutes).

Sleeping
Táoyuán Dàjiǔdiàn (桃园大酒店; ☎ 202 0919; s & d from Y100; 🖳) This great mid-range hotel (budget rooms exist, but usually not for you) is in an alley across the street from the bus station. Rooms are reasonably clean and there's a good restaurant. Rates include breakfast.

Běihǎi Yíngbīnguǎn (北海迎宾馆; ☎ 202 3511; d from Y100; 🖳) Once the premier hotel in town (a 10-minute walk east of the bus station on the opposite side of the street), don't give in to a grim feeling upon espying the capacious but empty grounds – this is likely the best choice *yuán* for *yuán*. The rooms are very clean and well maintained.

Shangri-la Hotel (香格里拉饭店; ☎ 206 2288; www.shangri-la.com; 33 Chating Lu; d Y840-1050; 🖳 🖳) Běihǎi's most luxurious, this hotel isn't well located but the service here is top-notch and rates are usually heavily discounted.

Good accommodation choices are available close to the beach; however, the cheapest dorms around start at around Y70.

Beach Hotel (海滩宾馆; Hǎitān Bīnguǎn; ☎ 388 8888; bhht@bh.gx.cninfo.net; d Y630; 🖳) This is your best option on the beach in the upper-mid to top end range. Rooms are comfy and offered at almost half-price outside summer. Plenty of amenities are offered.

Eating
Èrgēlǎojī Fàndiàn (二哥老鸡饭店) Around the corner from the bus station, this often rowdy place specialises in *huǒguō* (hotpot), *tángcù páigǔ* (sweet and sour pork ribs) and *bǎisījī* (a free-range chicken dish also referred to as *tǔjībǎn*).

Just west of the post office on Woping Lu, is a good little **teahouse** serving beverages and small snacks.

In the northern section of Yunnan Lu, close to the wharf, is Běihǎi's large **seafood market** (水产市场; shuǐchǎn shìchǎng). Near here, you will find **Waishā Dǎo** (外沙岛) an islandesque spit of land filled with boisterous seafood (among other) restaurants; you can eat for Y10 to Y120 per person here! Bus Nos 2 and 8 pass by from in front of the bus station.

Getting There & Away

There is a helpful **ticket office** (☎ 202 8618; ⏱ 8am-10pm) on the ground floor of the Shangri-la Hotel, selling boat, bus, train and plane tickets. There are also many other travel agencies around town.

AIR

There are daily flights between Běihǎi and Běijīng (Y1730), Guǎngzhōu (Y610), Guìyáng (Y700) and Hǎikǒu (Y350).

BOAT

The **International Ferry Terminal** (Guójì Kèyùn Mǎtou) serves Hǎikǒu on Hǎinán and the nearby island of Wéizhōu. Boats for the 11-hour journey to Hǎikǒu leave once daily (6pm). Tickets cost from Y90 for a seat to Y230 for a cabin, and can be bought at the terminal or just north of Beibuwan Zhonglu on Sichuan Lu; buy your ticket and await your shuttle bus.

BUS

Express buses connect Běihǎi with Dōngxīng (Y35, three hours), Guǎngzhōu (Y180, 9½ hours), Guìlín (Y92 to Y170, seven hours), Liǔzhōu (Y110, five hours) and Nánníng (Y50 to Y73, three hours). Another bus terminal lies about 15 minutes by foot east of the main bus station.

TRAIN

Train No 819 departs Běihǎi at 9.17am for Nánníng (three hours), from where you can connect to points beyond.

Getting Around
TO/FROM THE AIRPORT

Comfortable buses meet planes at the airport, 21km north of town (Y10, 30 minutes). A taxi should cost about Y50.

BUS

Most of Běihǎi's buses congregate on Jiefang Lu, north of Zhongshan Park. Here you can catch bus No 3 to Silver Beach and bus No 2 west to the ferry docks and seafood market. Local buses cost Y2.

GUÌPÍNG 桂平
☎ 0775

Midway between Nánníng and Wúzhōu, Guìpíng is known for its gorgeous **Xi Shan Park** (西山公园; Xī Shān Gōngyuán; admission Y15-30;

⏱ 8am-5pm), with a modest mountain climb of 880m. To get there, walk 15 to 20 minutes west of the public square along Renmin Xilu. Famed in the country is the mountain's Xī Shān tea.

Only 20km northwest of town is **Dragon Pool National Forest and Park** (龙潭国家森林公园; Lóngtán Guójiā Sēnlín Gōngyuán), which gives you the opportunity to delve into rustic wilderness and Guǎngxī's only remaining old-growth forest. Accommodation is available here for about Y25 per night.

Direct transportation to Dragon Pool Park doesn't exist. From Guìpíng, get the bus to Jīntiáncūn (Y2) and ask the driver to drop you off at the Dragon Pool Park access road (Longtan Lukou). Motorcycle taxis waiting at the intersection will take you to the park for about Y20. A two-day trip via the **Forestry Department** (☎ 338 0413) in Guìpíng, including guide, food, transport and accommodation, is about Y200.

Just 25km north of Guìpíng, **Jīntiáncūn** (金田村) is the birthplace of Hong Xiuquan, the schoolteacher who declared himself a brother of Jesus Christ and eventually led an army of over a million followers against the Qing dynasty in what came to be known as the Taiping Rebellion – one of the bloodiest civil wars in human history. A museum, **Qǐyì Jìniànguǎn** (起义纪念馆; admission Y3) now stands at the site of Hong's home.

To reach Jīntiáncūn from Guìpíng, take a green bus (Y2, 40 minutes) from inside the bus terminal gates. Backtrack 500m from the bus drop-off in Jīntiáncūn to the motorcycle taxis, from where the museum is a further 4km. The last bus back to Guìpíng departs Jīntiáncūn around 6pm.

Sleeping

Guìpíng Fàndiàn (桂平饭店; ☎ 338 2775; fax 338 3919; beds in common r Y20-45, standard d Y220; ❄) East of the public square along Renmin Zhonglu is the only central accommodation open to foreigners. There is a mind-boggling array of spartan but pleasant rooms.

Gōngdé Shānzhuāng (☎ 339 3399; fax 339 3618; d Y298; ❄) It's also possible to stay at Xī Shān – much more peaceful than in town but also costlier. Semi-posh rooms at this hotel are usually offered for a 20% discount, with impeccable service. A few basic inns nearby are not officially allowed to accept foreigners.

Getting There & Away

From Guìpíng, express buses leave for Nánníng every three hours (Y50 to Y63, four
hours). There are four express buses to
Wúzhōu (Y30, three hours) and one daily
to Guǎngzhōu at 1pm (Y90, six hours). If
you want to get to Guìlín or Liǔzhōu, head
to Guìgǎng (Y12) and change buses there.

WÚZHŌU 梧州

☎ 0774 / pop 330,000

For most travellers, Wúzhōu is a pit stop
on the road between Yángshuò and Guǎngzhōu. Consider lingering, as Wúzhōu has
some pleasant parks, street life (especially
markets), and one of Guǎngxī's more unusual sights: the Snake Repository.

Wúzhōu was a busy trading town in the
18th century. In 1897 the British arrived,
setting up steamer services to Guǎngzhōu,
Hong Kong and later Nánníng. An enormous urban gentrification project is creating a bustling, 24-hour riverfront area
while maintaining the city's traditional
architecture.

Orientation

Situated at the confluence of Gui River
(Guì Jiāng) and Xun River (Xún Jiāng),
the city is effectively divided in two, with
the modern and developed Héxī west of the
river and the more interesting Dōnghé on
the east bank.

Good maps of the city with bus routes
(though not in English) are available at the
shops inside both bus stations.

Information

Bank of China (Zhōngguó Yínháng) Just east of the
Internet café, on the corner of Zhongshan Lu.
Internet café (per hr Y2) Opposite Zhongshan Park.
Post & Telephone Office (Yóudiàn Dàlóu; Nanhuan Lu)
East of the bridge.

Sights

SNAKE REPOSITORY 蛇园

Wúzhōu has what it claims is the world's
largest **snake repository** (Shéyuán; with/without guide
Y10/5; ☯ 8am-6pm, snake restaurant until 10pm). More
than one million snakes are transported
each year to Wúzhōu for export to the
kitchens of Hong Kong, Macau and other
snake-devouring locales. To get there walk
along Shigu Lu for about 2km from the
Wúzhōu Dàjiǔdiàn. A warning: snake and

cat fights are sometimes staged for visiting
groups of tourists.

WESTERN BAMBOO TEMPLE 西竹园

Bordering Zhongshan Park, **Western Bamboo
Temple** (Xīzhú Yuán) overlooks the town
and is home to around 40 Buddhist nuns.
The temple's **vegetarian restaurant**, usually
open for lunch on weekends, is highly recommended. The restaurant doesn't keep
regular hours, but it seems the earlier you
get there, the better.

To reach the temple, continue straight up
Wenhua Lu to the top end of Sun Yatsen
Park. At the end on the left is a small path
that follows a brick wall all the way around
to the temple.

LÓNGMŬTÀI MIÀO 龙母太庙

Recently renovated, **Lóngmŭtài Miào** (Dragon
Mother Temple; admission Y3) was originally constructed during the Northern Song dynasty
to honour the dragon mother of a mythical female chieftain. A good time to visit
is during the temple's main festival, held
on the seventh and eighth days of the fifth
lunar month and the 15th day of the eighth
lunar month.

Sleeping

Jīnshān Jiǔdiàn (☎ 282 9265; s & d Y45-180; ⚡)
This budget stand-by opposite the bus station has a huge array of decent rooms, even
the cheaper ones have private bathroom.

Lóngmén Jiǔdiàn (☎ 202 0066; fax 203 8880; 64 Da-
dongshang Lu; s & d from Y150; ⚡) Low mid-range
prices and way-above-average rooms and
friendly service make this a good option.

Wúzhōu Dàjiǔdiàn (☎ 202 8888; www.wzhotel
.com.cn; 3 Xijiang Erlu; d Y220-340; ⚡) Recently
renovated, the rooms here are good value
and comfortable. The pricier ones have a
fridge. This hotel probably has the most
services offered in town.

Dōngxìn Bīnguǎn (☎ 283 8888; fax 282 5461; 28
Wenhua Lu; d/tw from Y380/410; ⚡) This is the
newest hotel in town and a solid mid-range
choice. Discounts of up to 50% are not unheard of here.

Eating & Drinking

Huālí Jiǔjiā is one of Wúzhōu's seafood palaces,
specialising in game meats and raw fish.

For more local flavours at more affordable prices, you could try the small, popular

WÚZHŌU 梧州

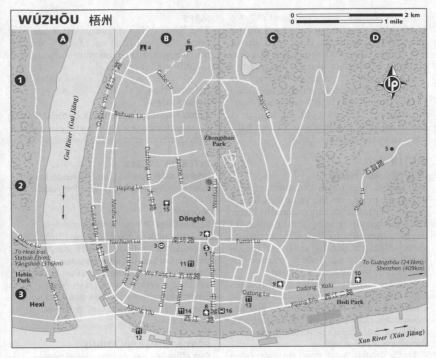

street restaurant on the corner of Juren Lu and Xijiang Yilu. Local fare is also available at the **snake repository restaurant** (opposite), though it's quite pricey.

For self-caterers, there are plenty of **fresh produce markets** along the backstreets.

Walking one street east of the post office on Nanhuan Lu, then north, you'll find a number of **bars** trying their hardest to be hip. A couple offer Western fare; none are cheap.

Getting There & Away

Wúzhōu has two bus stations: Hédōng and the main bus station in Héxī. In general, buses heading for smaller and closer destinations depart from Hédōng and those heading further afield depart from Héxī. A free shuttle bus (for ticketed passengers) runs between the two stations every 40 minutes. Bus Nos 2 and 12 also connect the stations (Y1.5, 20 minutes) or, if you're in a hurry, a taxi costs around Y20.

From Wúzhōu to Yángshuò expect a bumpy seven hours (Y70), and it's another 1½ hours to Guìlín (Y80 to Y90). Buses leave the Héxī station five times daily between 8.30am and 11pm. Only recently – and finally – have authorities broken ground on a new expressway to Guìlín.

For Guǎngzhōu, four expresses (Y97, 5½ hours) daily and more numerous slower buses cover the route (Y57, six hours); more expressway work should cut this dramatically. There are also regular express bus connections throughout the day for Liǔzhōu (Y90, seven hours) and Shēnzhèn (Y150, seven hours), and every half-hour for Nánníng (Y90 to Y110, six hours). A new expressway to Nánníng was about half-finished at the time of writing.

GUÌLÍN 桂林

☎ 0773 / pop 1,342,000

Say 'Guìlín' and watch the looks of rapture (and pride) on the faces of Chinese people. Dotted with supernaturally lovely karst topography gracing the Li River (Lí Jiāng) – these bizarre limestone upthrusts shape-shifting in dancing mists and haze – the city's beauty has been celebrated for generations by painters and poets.

While rapid economic growth and a booming tourist trade have diminished some of Guìlín's charm, it's still one of China's greener, more scenic cities. If you can handle the hectic traffic, most of Guìlín's peaks and parks are a short bicycle ride away.

Unfortunately, locals don't shy away from cashing in on Guìlín's popularity. Most tourist sights levy heavy entry fees and many travellers tell of being grossly overcharged at restaurants. Touts (some persistent) appear at every turn. Humid days create an opaque haze, obscuring even the closer peaks.

Orientation

Most of Guìlín lies on the west bank of Li River. The main artery is Zhongshan Lu, which runs roughly parallel to the river, on its western side. At the southern end (Zhongshan Nanlu) is Guìlín's train station. Zhongshan Zhonglu is a rapidly gentrifying stretch of tourist-class hotels, shops and expensive restaurants.

Closer to the centre of town, northeast of the lakes of Róng Hú and Shān Hú, is Guìlín's new Central Square (Zhōngxīn Guǎngchǎng) and the main shopping and eating district. Further along Zhongshan Beilu is the city's main commercial area.

Heading east on Jiefang Donglu and crossing over Liberation Bridge, will bring you to the large Qixing Park, one of the town's chief attractions.

MAPS

The *Tourist Map of Guilin* (Y4) is one of a few maps – nearly all out of date – sold by touts near the bus and train stations and including a bit of English.

Information
BOOKSHOPS
Xinhua Bookshop (Xīnhuá Shūdiàn; Zhongshan Beilu) Has a foreign-language section that carries a selection of English classics and photo-travel books on Guìlín.

INTERNET ACCESS
Internet cafés (wǎngbā; Y2 per hr) A number have sprouted up along the alley near the Jīnfēng Bīnguǎn.

MONEY
Bank of China (Zhōngguó Yínháng; Shanhu Beilu) This is the main branch. For changing money and travellers cheques, use the branches at the corner of Shanghai Lu and Zhongshan Nanlu next to the train station, and at Zhongshan Nanlu near Yinding Lu. Credit card advances at most branches are straightforward and you can expect ATMs friendly to foreign cards in at least the main branch by the time you read this. Most tourist hotels also have foreign exchange services.

POST & COMMUNICATIONS
Post office (yóujú) On the north corner of the large square in front of the train station. Several smaller offices are north along Zhongshan Lu.

TOURIST INFORMATION
CITS (Zhōngguó Guójì Lǚxíngshè; ☎ 286 1623; www .guilintrav.com; 41 Binjiang Beilu) Its FIT department has friendly and reasonably helpful staff offering a range of tours, including a half-day city tour (Y200) and a full-day Li River tour (Y460). Staff also organise longer trips, but prefer larger groups.
Tourist booths Bless the city for its eight city tourist booths to help you with directions and tour information, or even booking accommodation. Some staff speak a little English. The main office (☎ 280 0318 or 282 7491, toll-free ☎ 800 879 3318, tourism complaints ☎ 280 0315; www.guilin.com.cn; 14 Ronghu Beilu) is north of Róng Hú, near the park, and is the only one consistently open. Most travellers use those in front of the train station and inside the bus station. The city's website is outstanding for travel information.

VISAS
PSB (Gōngānjú; ☎ 582 9930; ⏰ 8.30am-noon & 3-6pm Mon-Fri) On the east side of Li River, south off Longyin Lu. They've been amazingly quick with visa extensions; be extra nice to them so it continues!

Sights

SOLITARY BEAUTY PEAK 独秀峰

This 152m **pinnacle** (Dúxiù Fēng; admission Y15) is in the centre of the town. The climb to the top is steep, but worth the effort for the splendid vistas.

At the foot of the peak is the 14th-century **Wáng Chéng**, a palace built by the nephew of a Ming emperor. The restored walls and gates of the palace surround the peak. It's also home to a theatre that holds nightly traditional minority performances (p610). You can reach the peak by bus Nos 1 or 2 from Guìlín's train station.

FÚBŌ SHĀN 伏波山

Close to Solitary Beauty Peak, **Fúbō Shān** (Wave-Subduing Hill; admission Y10) offers equally good views.

On the hill's southern slope is **Returned Pearl Cave** (Huánzhū Dòng). A 1000-year-old Buddha image is etched into the cave wall, along with more than 200 other images of the Buddha, most dating from the Song and Tang dynasties. Somewhere, too, is a portrait and autograph by Mi Fu, a famous calligrapher of the Song dynasty.

Nearby is **Thousand Buddha Cave** (Qiānfó Yán). The name's an exaggeration – a couple of dozen statues at most date from the Tang and Song dynasties.

Bus No 2 from the train station runs past the hill.

OTHER HILLS

North of Solitary Beauty Peak is **Diécǎi Shān** (Folded Brocade Hill; admission Y20). Climb the stone pathway that takes you through the cooling relief of Wind Cave, with walls decked with inscriptions and Buddhist sculptures. The hill climb can be skirted by taking bus Nos 1 or 2.

From Fúbō Shān there's a good view of **Lǎorén Shān** (Old Man Hill), a curiously shaped hill 2km to the northwest. The best way to get there is by bicycle, as buses don't go past it. At the southern end of town, one of Guìlín's best-known sights is **Xiàngbí Shān** (Elephant Trunk Hill; admission Y25), which actually does resemble an elephant dipping its snout into Li River.

QIXING PARK 七星公园

One of China's most picturesque city parks, with wending trails and lovely picnicking,

Seven Star Park (Qīxīng Gōngyuán; summer Y35, rest of year Y25; park ⏱ 7am-9.30pm, caves ⏱ 8am-5pm) is on the eastern side of Li River and covers 137 hectares (the seven peaks resemble the Big Dipper constellation). The park was one of the original tourist spots in southwest China, first opened to sightseers as far back as the Sui dynasty. The park's two highlights are **Seven Star Cave** (Qīxīng Yán), a capacious chamber filled with bizarre stalactites and stalagmites coloured by floodlights, and **Dark Dragon Cave** (Lóngyīn Dòng), with inscribed stelae dating back more than 1500 years.

To reach the park, walk across Liberation Bridge or catch bus Nos 10 or 11 from the train station. From the park, bus No 13 runs across Liberation Bridge, past Fúbō Shān and across to Reed Flute Cave.

REED FLUTE CAVE 芦笛岩

Some of the most extraordinary scenery – rock concert lights blazing at stalactites – Guìlín has to offer is underground at **Reed Flute Cave** (Lúdí Yán; admission Y60), 5km northwest of the city centre. At one time the entrance to the cave was distinguished by clumps of reeds used by the locals to make musical instruments, hence the name.

Inside, the Crystal Palace of the Dragon King alone can hold about 1000 people, although many more were crammed in during WWII when the cave was used as an air-raid shelter. Despite the high entrance price, the cave is worth visiting.

Take bus No 3 (Y1.5) from the train station or Zhongshan Zhonglu to the last stop. Otherwise, it's a pleasant bicycle ride. Follow Lijun Lu, which runs into Xishan Lu and then Taohua Jiang Lu. The latter parallels the small Taohua River (Táohuā Jiāng), and winds through fields and karst peaks. At Ludi Lu turn left and continue for another 1.2km back to Zhongshan Beilu.

RÓNG HÚ & SHĀN HÚ 榕湖, 衫湖

There are two lakes near the city centre, **Róng Hú** on the western side of Zhongshan Zhonglu and **Shān Hú** on the eastern side. Róng Hú is named after an 800-year-old banyan tree on its shore. The tree stands by the restored **South City Gate** (Nán Mén) originally built during the Tang dynasty. This area is one of the nicer neighbourhoods for a stroll.

SOUTHWEST CHINA

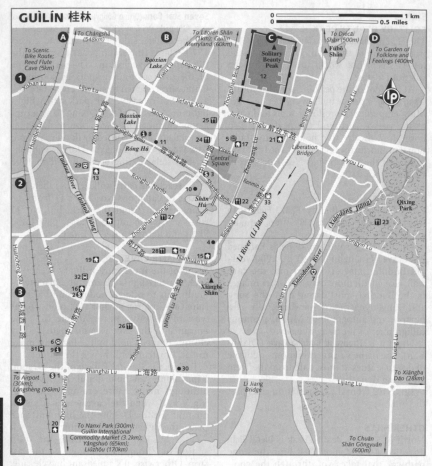

GUÌLÍN 桂林

Tours

There's no shortage of tour operators offering half- or full-day tours of Guìlín's major sights. They normally charge around Y35, not including entry tickets. The tour operators are usually outside the bus and train stations, and along Binjiang Lu.

Sleeping

BUDGET

It's something of a Guìlín tradition for budget travellers to trudge endlessly around the vicinity of the bus and train stations to politely finagle acceptance into a cheap local hotel. Good luck.

Overseas Chinese Hotel (Huáqiáo Dàshà; ☎ 383 5753, ext 2116; fax 382 0290; 13 Zhongshan Nanlu; dm Y70, standard d Y280-360; 🅰) This is an old backpackers' stand-by. It's a little inconveniently located, but it's the cheapest you'll find, and the rooms are clean.

MID-RANGE

A few mid-range spots with decent value for the price exist for those looking for something a bit cushier.

Měidù Fàndiàn (☎ 283 8268; fax 288 6698; 17 Nanhuan Lu; s/d from Y148/168; 🅰) A fresh place with friendly staff, the rooms are small (on the cheaper end) but a steal given the location.

Bǎilèmén Jiǔdiàn (☎ 282 5492; 42 Nanhuan Lu; s & d from Y168-188; 🅰) This place has large, well-maintained rooms; the cheaper ones always seem to be full.

Jīnfēng Bīnguăn (☎ 288 2793; tw & d from Y190; ※) Down a lane off Central Square, this place offers good mid-range rooms. Despite its prime location, outside of peak periods it will often offer substantial discounts, sometimes by one-third.

Huali Hotel (Huáli Jiŭdiàn; ☎ 383 6409; fax 382 7103; Zhongshan Nanlu; tw/d/tr from Y220; ※) This quiet and clean hotel was once a well-kept secret, but no longer. Rooms are often discounted to Y150 or less.

Golden Elephant (Jīnxiàng Dàjiŭdiàn; ☎ 280 8888; 36 Binjiang Lu; d Y330; ※) This three-star hotel has comfortable rooms, some with views of Li River and Xiàngbí Shān. You'll also find stylish traditional Korean *ondol* suites (Y960), a fine Korean restaurant, an Asiana Airlines office and even a Korean bathhouse.

Universal Hotel (Huánqiú Dàjiŭdiàn; ☎ 282 8228; htlunivs@public.glptt.gx.cn; 1 Jiefang Donglu; s & d from Y400; ✕ ※) This hotel is a little worn, yet the pleasant, if at times small, rooms offer nice river views. The walk-in prices (much higher than those listed here) may not be worth it, but huge discounts are offered outside peak seasons or through travel agents.

TOP END

There's no shortage of choice here, although only some of Guìlín's top-enders are worth it.

Osmanthus Hotel (Dānguì Dàjiŭdiàn; ☎ 383 4300; glosmh@public.glptt.gx.cn; Zhongshan Zhonglu; d from US$70; ※) This hotel is a popular target for tour groups. Rooms are nicely furnished (not to mention set for a face-lift) and are usually offered at a 40% discount, making them reasonable value.

Bravo Hotel (Guìlín Bīnguăn; ☎ 282 3950; www .glbravo.com; 14 Ronghu Nanlu; r US$110-120; ✕ ※

□ ※) This four-star hotel is arguably one of Guìlín's best, with the only swimming pool in town and good food available in the hotel's Chinese, Japanese and Western restaurants.

Eating

Guìlín is noted for its snake soup, wild cat or bamboo rat, washed down with snakebile wine. You could be devouring some of these animals into extinction, and we don't recommend that you do. The pangolin (a sort of armadillo) is a protected species but still crops up on restaurant menus. Other protected species include the muntjac (Asian deer), horned pheasant, mini-turtle, short-tailed monkey and gem-faced civet.

Mostly you'll find an infinite variety of *guìlín mĭfěn* (Guìlín rice noodles), generally eaten for breakfast and snacks. Strictly guarded recipes vary greatly from chef to chef; you'll find some not unlike Thai *pad thai,* and others smacking of a horse meat stew!

A Qing dynasty speciality, white fermented beancurd, is often used to make a sauce for dipping roast pork or chicken in. Sanhua wine, actually more like mellow rice firewater, is a favourite local drink, as is local oil tea (though it's actually quite salty, with flecks of rice in it).

North of Central Square along Yiren Lu you'll find a good variety of eateries including buffet-style caféterias, standard restaurants, trendy cafés and small hole-in-the-wall restaurants.

Good Aunt (Hăodàmā; Zhongshan Zhonglu; dishes from Y5) This theatre-sized food complex is on the 4th level of Bagui Mansion – an amazing smorgasbord of provincial specialities as

SOUTHWEST CHINA

well as some Western dishes and a Japanese sushi bar. Another local food plaza can be found at the **Nikodo Plaza** (187 Zhongshan Zonglu).

Coffee-Language 110 (Míngdiǎn; cnr Shantu Beilu & Zhengyang Lu; dishes from Y12) A trendy café with a variety of Chinese and Western food and beverages, prices here are reasonable but not cheap. A set breakfast is available.

Crescent Mansion (Yuèlèlóu) Located in Qixing Park, this is a good place for lunch, and offers lots of vegetarian fare. Try the local speciality, *gūzi miàn* (nun noodles).

Shèngfā Fàndiàn (Zishan Lu) This restaurant is very popular with locals who come here to eat *píjiǔyú* (beer fish; Y18), which is wok-fried on your table and usually knocked down with the local Liqun Beer. Noodles are added at the end to mop up the sauce.

Yíyuán Fàndiàn (Nanhuan Lu; ☯ 11.30am-2.30pm & 5.30-9.30pm) This outstanding Sichuanese restaurant is a longtime fave; two can eat well for Y70.

Tailian Hotel (Táilián Jiǔdiàn; ☯ noon-2pm & 6-8pm; set meals lunch/dinner from Y20/28) Considered to be the best place in town for a dim sum or yum cha buffet, you'll be hard-pressed to find an empty seat on weekends.

There are a number of **supermarkets** around town, the most convenient in the Nikodo Plaza basement.

Entertainment

In addition to the traditional minority shows at **Wáng Chéng** (tickets Y35; ☯ 7.30pm) – see also p607 – there are shows at **Garden of Folklore & Feelings** (Mínsú Fēngqíngyuán; tickets Y50; ☯ 8.30am, 2pm, 7.30pm & 8.30pm). Yet another venue is the **Guilin Children's Palace** (Guìlín Shàoniángōng; tickets Y80; ☯ 7.30pm).

On an island in the middle of Li River, **Xiāngba Dǎo** is a cultural theme park with traditional minority architecture, performances, crafts and cuisine.

Shopping

Guìlín and its back alley workshops are purportedly the source of many of southwest China's crafts for tourist consumption. One place you may wish to check out is the enormous **Guilin International Commodity Market**, in the far south of town. To get there, take bus No 11 from Zhongshan Zhonglu to its final stop and walk south towards the whirr and whine of small carving tools.

Getting There & Away

AIR

CAAC (☎ 384 7252; ☯ 7.30am-8.30pm) is at the corner of Shanghai Lu and Minzhu Lu. You'll find **Dragonair** (☎ 282 5588, ext 8895) in the Bravo Hotel.

Guìlín is supremely well connected to the rest of China (and beyond) by air. Destinations include Běijīng (Y1590), Chéngdū (Y900), Chóngqìng (Y670), Hǎikǒu (Y690), Guǎngzhōu (Y590), Guìyáng (Y500), Hong Kong (Y1661), Kūnmíng (Y740), Shànghǎi (Y1190) and Xī'ān (Y970). Seats *may* be available for next-day purchase; shop around travel agents for discount tickets.

International destinations include flights to Seoul (Hànchéng; Monday, Tuesday and Friday) and Fukoka, Japan (Fùgāng; Tuesday and Saturday). Tickets cost at least Y2800 one-way for either destination. Less frequent flights also go to Bangkok, Singapore and Kuala Lumpur; more and more international flights are being added.

BUS

For short local runs such as Yángshuò (Y10, one hour) and Xīng'ān (Y8 to Y12, two hours), buses depart from in front of the train station as well as from the main bus station.

Guìlín's **bus station** (Zhongshan Nanlu) is north of the train station. Hourly buses run to Lóngshèng (Y12 to Y15, three to four hours). There are several really slow buses to Sānjiāng (Y18.5) between 6am and 7.30pm and express buses (Y21) roughly every two hours. Expresses to Quánzhōu leave every hour (Y10, one hour). Frequent buses leave for Liǔzhōu every 20 minutes (Y29 to Y40, two to three hours) and to Nánníng (Y80 to Y117, four to 4½ hours) every 15 minutes.

To Guǎngzhōu and Shēnzhèn, express and sleeper buses are available, however the expresses are usually more reliable and smoother. Express buses head for Guǎngzhōu six times daily (Y150, eight hours) and to Shēnzhèn at 8pm and 9.30pm (Y180, 10 hours). Buses for Wúzhōu leave five times daily (Y75 to Y90, 6½ to eight hours).

TRAIN

Guìlín is not as convenient as Nánníng or Liǔzhōu for train connections (not much starts here) and tickets are harder to come by. Outside national holidays, you should have luck, but be prepared to wait an extra day or two for hard sleeper tickets.

Direct train services include train No T6 to Běijīng (3.06pm, hard sleeper Y449, 22 hours), No K36/7 to Guǎngzhōu (6pm, Y229, 11 hours), No K198 to Shànghǎi (2.08pm, Y400,25 hours) and train No K316 to Xī'ān (5.25pm, Y356, 25 hours). For Chóngqìng and Chéngdū, change trains at Guìyáng (or start in Nánníng or Liǔzhōu).

To Kūnmíng, train No 2055 departs at 8.54am and takes 22 hours (Y237); this is the only one which starts here, and the others can be tough to land tickets for. Consider a worthwhile trip to Nánníng to hop on the direct Nankun line (15 hours).

Getting Around

TO/FROM THE AIRPORT

Guìlín's international airport is 30km west of the city. CAAC runs buses from its **office** (cnr Shanghai Lu & Minzhu Lu) to the airport for Y20, leaving half-hourly from 6.30am. A taxi to the airport costs about Y80.

BICYCLE

One of the best ways to get around Guìlín is by bicycle. There are plenty of bicycle-hire shops. You'll find some near the bus and train stations and one next to the Overseas Chinese Hotel. Most charge Y10 to Y20 per day and require Y200 or your passport as security. Try to avoid handing over your passport.

BUS

Bus No 58 is a tourist freebie (anything that begins with '5' should be free) that runs to many local sights, including Xiàngbí Shān, Seven Star Park and Reed Flute Cave.

Otherwise, most of the city buses that stop in front of Guìlín's bus and train stations will get you to the major sights, but a bicycle is definitely better, especially in the searing summer heat. Bus No 2 runs from the train station through town, passing Xiàngbí Shān, Liberation Bridge, Fúbō Shān and Diécǎi Shān. Bus No 15 runs a circuit from the train station to the city's main tourist highlights. Local buses cost between Y1 and Y1.5.

TAXI

A taxi ride around town costs around Y20. Motorcycle taxis charge only Y5 per trip.

AROUND GUÌLÍN

Ling Canal 灵渠

The **Ling Canal** (Líng Qú) is in Xīng'ān County, about 70km north of Guìlín. It was built from 219 to 214 BC, to transport supplies to the armies of the first Qin emperor, and is considered to be one of the three great feats of Chinese engineering (the others being the Great Wall and the Du River – Dū Jiāng – irrigation system in Sìchuān). The 34km canal links Xiang River (Xiāng Hé), which flows into the Yangzi River (Cháng Jiāng), and Li River, which flows into the Zhu River (Zhū Jiāng), thus connecting two of China's major waterways.

Two branches of the canal flow through the market town of **Xīng'ān** (兴安), one at the northern end and one at the southern end.

From Guìlín, there are buses for Xīng'ān every half-hour until 6.30pm (Y8 to Y12, two hours) and hourly express buses to Quánzhōu (Y10, one hour).

Li River 漓江

Li River (Lí Jiāng) runs between Guìlín and Yángshuò; a phenomenally popular trip is the **boat ride** from Guìlín to Yángshuò. The price – which comes in at around Y500, including lunch and the bus trip back to Guìlín from Yángshuò – does hurt. Joining a Chinese tour group lets you pay a nominal Y180 for the same service, though *sans* English.

Boats (Y460) depart from Guìlín's tourist wharf opposite the Golden Elephant hotel (see Map p608) each morning at around 8am, although when the water is low you have to take a shuttle bus to Zhújiāng or Mópánshān wharf downriver. The ticket office is nearby, or you can book through many hotels. The trip lasts all day.

YÁNGSHUÒ 阳朔

☎ 0773 / pop 300,000

Ah, Yángshuò, that legendary backpacker hang-out just 65km south of Guìlín. Guìlín gets all the press, but Yángshuò, a great, laid-back base from which to explore other small villages in the nearby countryside, arguably surpasses it visually. It certainly beats it for the unrivalled opportunity to soak in strong local flavours on the cheap. Pedalling through the rice fields amid the splendid green-topped limestone peaks for a day, or three, is for many their top China experience.

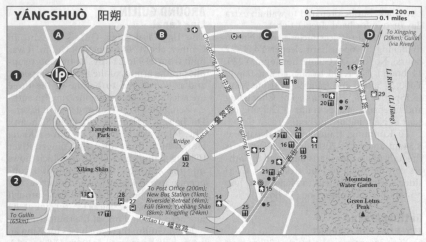

YÁNGSHUÒ 阳朔

Orientation

You'll probably only need to know two streets in Yángshuò. The first, Pantao Lu, forms the southwest perimeter of Yángshuò and is the main artery to and from Guilín. The second, Xi Jie, is known as 'Foreigner Street'. It runs northeast to Li River, and is lined with Western-style cafés, hotels and tourist shops. The further you go from Xi Jie or from Pantao Lu at its intersection with Xi Jie, the closer you get to Chinese group-tour reality. Xi Jie itself has been turned into a pedestrian mall (relatively) free from pesky wheels. Sadly, local authorities are knocking down buildings all around Xi Jie (and in its first block) to put in suspiciously modern looking edifices.

MAPS

A reasonably good street map of Yángshuò and surrounds is available throughout town

(Y2.5). The regional map isn't great but half the adventure is finding your way through the rice paddies!

Information

INTERNET ACCESS

One of the best Internet cafés (wǎngbā) you'll find anywhere in China is 20m north down an alley between Chengzhong Lu and Xi Jie. It has loads of DSL-connected computers (and scanners), all for a mere Y3 per hour.

MEDICAL SERVICES

There are a number of traditional medical clinics on the northern side of Pantao Lu offering therapeutic massage, acupuncture and traditional medicine. It is even possible to enrol in brief courses at some of these centres.

People's Hospital (Rénmín Yīyuàn) North of the main tourist centre, not far from the PSB.

MONEY

Bank of China (Zhōngguó Yínháng; Binjiang Lu; 8am-5pm) Will change cash and travellers cheques, give credit card advances and receive wire transfers, although the latter can take up to 15 days. Other banks on Xi Jie also cash travellers cheques.

POST & COMMUNICATIONS

Post office (yóujú; Pantao Lu; 8am-5pm) Has English-speaking staff and long-distance phone services. You can also purchase IP cards that only cost Y2.4 to Y3.6 per minute for international calls, rather than the standard Y12 on China Telecom IC cards.

EMERGENCY

PSB (Gōngānjú) This PSB is well versed in dealing with travellers. That said, staff do not give visa extensions. Also, always be calm if taking in a complaint about a local business; losing your cool will get you nowhere.

TOURIST INFORMATION

Everywhere you look: travel agents. *Choose carefully.* Surfacing constantly are reports of aggressive agents not providing the service they sell. Flimsy bicycles for rent are the most chronic headache. Train tickets will never be easy unless you hike to Guìlín and do it yourself. Ask other travellers if anything dodgy has recently appeared.

Dangers & Annoyances

While Yángshuò is relatively safe, it's important to keep your wits about you. Yuèliàng Shān (Moon Hill) is particularly popular with muggers who have wounded their victims with knifes; don't stray off alone. Yángshuò is also the scene of many rip-offs, from hotel 'deposits' to dodgy tours (see also Tourist Information, above).

Sights & Activities

The somnolent peaks are a lovely vista as you sip your cappuccino. Established parks with trails dot the town, though see also Dangers & Annoyances.

In the southeastern corner of town is Yángshuò's main peak, **Green Lotus Peak** (Bìlián Fēng; admission Y27). It's also called Bronze Mirror Peak (Tóngjìng Fēng) because it has a flat northern face that is supposed to look like an ancient bronze mirror. The peak is next to Li River, in the **Mountain Water Garden** (Shānshuǐyuán).

Yangshuo Park is in the western part of town, and here you'll find **Xīláng Shān** (Man Hill; admission Y9), which is supposed to resemble a young man bowing and scraping to a shy young girl represented by **Xiǎogū Shān** (Lady Hill). There's a further jungle of hills nearby: **Shīzi Qí Lǐyú Shān** (Lion Riding Carp Hill), **Lóngtóu Shān** (Dragon Head Hill) and the like.

Should you desire to hoof it up other hills solo, get advice from locals before you set off – there's no search and rescue service for foreigners stranded on a karst cliff face. A better bet is guided **rock climbing**. Neophyte Spiderfolks head directly to Xianqian Jie to find advice, gear and tours (of the 75 or so routes up the cliff faces) from shops and climbing-oriented cafés like the **Karst Café** (☎ 882 8482) and **Lizard Lounge** (☎ 881 1033).

Merry Planet Language Club (Xi Jie) offers brief courses in Chinese language, taichi or Chinese medicine. It is also possible to enrol in some of the courses offered by the **Buckland School** (Bākèlán Wài Yǔ Xuéxiào; ☎ 882-7555; www.bucklandgroup.org), which welcomes volunteer teachers in exchange for a bed and food.

A popular evening activity is to take part in one of the **cormorant fishing tours** that begin around 7pm. While it's entertaining, it's mainly a tourist attraction these days as the river supports an ever-diminishing supply of fish. Hotels and restaurants usually charge around Y25 per person.

Sleeping

It can at times take a fair bit of walking to nail down a dirt-cheap bed (in peak periods, any bed may be tough to find). Weekly rates seem universally available and you can even use credit cards at many of the cheapies now.

BUDGET

On arrival you will no doubt be met by touts wielding name cards and photo albums of their abodes. Finding a clean dorm bed for Y10 or Y15 or a single/double with private bathroom for Y50 to Y100 is relatively easy outside summer weekends and holidays.

The most popular places to stay are on Xi Jie. Many travellers complain that some of the older hostels suffer from the noise of the late-night revellers in the cafés below.

Yangshuo International Youth Hostel (Xījiē Guójì Qīngnián Lǚguǎn; ☎ 882 0933; hostel-ys@163.com; 102 Xi Jie; dm/tw from Y20/80;) Offering spotless YHA-standard dorm beds and rooms – with or without bathroom and balcony – this place is efficient if a bit busy for some. As always, an HI card gets discounts.

Lisa's Café (Lìshā Jiǔdiàn; ☎ 882 0217; lisa@public .glptt.gx.cn; 71 Xi Jie; dm Y15, s/d from Y60/80; ✕) One place earning the title of 'institution' is Lisa's, run by its namesake, oft-dressed in her Mao suit and memorable always for her quirky good humour. An array of rooms is available, all in tip-top shape, and you'll find the downstairs restaurant unrivalled for sipping refreshments and people-watching.

Bamboo House Inn & Café (Zhúlín Fàndiàn; ☎ 882 3222; bamboohouse23@hotmail.com; dm with private bathroom Y15, d/tr with bathroom & fan Y40/60, with bathroom & air-con Y70/90; ✕) Down a small lane off Xi Jie, this place is quiet and pleasant and the staff, though harried, are helpful. All rooms have good bathrooms.

Riverside Retreat (☎ 882 7708; www.abstraction .org/rr; s & d Y80; ⌨) On the road to Yuèliàng Shān, 4km from town, this quiet, family-run place is on the banks of Yulong River (Yùlóng Hé) with 24-hour hot water, clean, heated rooms, Internet access and excellent food.

MID-RANGE

Most budget places also offer slightly cushier rooms for more money. A huge number of mid-range places are found in town, most of them Chinese hotels found along Pantao Lu, west of Diecui Lu. All are decent, if unremarkable.

Hotel Explorer (Wénhuà Fàndiàn; ☎ 882 8116; jimmyqin@hotmail.com; s/d with bathroom & air-con from Y100; ✕) Renovations are ongoing to convert this already clean and well-run place into a replica ancient courtyard with wood trims, sliding doors and indoor gardens – retro tastefully done. However, expect prices to rise.

Morning Sun Hotel (Yángguāng Jiǔdiàn; ☎ 881 3899; www.morningsunhotel.com; s/d/tr Y160/190/250, d with balcony Y268; ✕) This is the freshest and certainly most welcoming, staff-wise, of all newcomers to the mid-range market. Dark, hard-wood flooring, well-chosen designs for amenities, and a relaxing atrium show that some thought went into this place. You simply won't find a more gracious and helpful staff.

TOP END

New Century Hotel (Xīnshìjì Jiǔdiàn; ☎ 882 9819; fax 882 9809; s/d US$60/75; ✕) This newish, three-star Chinese-style hotel has good-quality rooms and service. They usually discount by 20%.

Paradise Yangshuo Resort Hotel (Yángshuò Bǎilèlái Dùjià Fàndiàn; ☎ 882 2109; www.paradiseyangshuo.com; standard/luxury d US$48/110; ✕ ✉) Also sporting three stars, this hotel has a little more ambience and fantastic gardens. The hotel has recently caught the renovation craze and rooms are receiving a much needed face-lift. It has a laundry list of amenities, including a fitness centre, swimming pool, satellite TV, pool tables, a business centre, restaurants and lounges.

Eating & Drinking

Xi Jie teems with tiny cafés offering interesting Chinese/Western fusion cuisine as well as perennial travellers' favourites, such as banana pancakes, muesli and pizza; they woo travellers with Hollywood movies or, more and more often, live music. However, Xi Jie is now so full of tour groups and pestering touts that the possibility of a quiet evening of dining al fresco is pretty much gone.

Susannah's Off Xi Jie on a side street, this was the first Western restaurant in town and continues to draw a steady stream of customers. Do try the *zuì yā* (drunk duck), cooked in a sauce of local red wine.

Meiyou Café Promises 'mei you bad service, mei you warm beer' (*méiyǒu* means 'don't have'), and it's delivered seemingly forever.

Café Under the Moon (Yuèliàngxià Kāfeīguǎn) This place has lots of ambience, friendly service and tasty food. It also has tables on a cosy 2nd-level balcony.

Rosewood Café (Méiguīmù Xīcāntīng; ✕ ✕) Tucked away off Xi Jie in a quiet location, its outdoor seating is the quietest around. Wonderful Korean food is a mainstay here. Even better, it has a nonsmoking room with perhaps China's best air-con!

Le Vôtre Café (Lèdéfǎshì Cāntīng) While it appears a little grand, this café has won the praise of many travellers for its fine French cuisine and delectable bakery (and tastefully designed guest rooms).

MC Blues Bar (Lìshì Jiǔdiàn) This longtime traveller favourite has moved from its anchor position at the corner of Xi Jie and Pantao Lu to Xiangqian Jie, but still has great food, cold beer and outstanding music.

Don't forget you're in China: wander the labyrinth of back alleys and you'll discover many small markets and restaurants catering to locals and Chinese travellers.

Farmer's Trading Market (Nóngmào Shìchǎng; Pantao Lu) Through an archway, this place is open all day and late into the evenings. *Píjiǔyú* (beer fish; Y30 per kilogram) is Yángshuò's most famous dish and this may be the best and cheapest place to try it. Local Li River fish are cooked with chillies, spring onion, tomato, ginger and beer. A good winter alternative is *qīngshuǐyú huǒguō* (Li River catfish hotpot). For the more adventurous, there is also *lǎoshǔgān* (fried dried rat with chillies and garlic; Y20) or *sōngshǔgān* (fried squirrel; Y20). The local government, as part of its beaverish gentrification programme, was eyeing a new location for this market.

The **fresh produce market** (*shāngmào shìchǎng*) has delicious small snacks such as the winter fave *pyramid zòngzi* (green bean, pork and peanuts wrapped in a lotus leaf with tofu and chilli sauce; Y0.5). You can stock up on fresh or dried fruit.

A **night market** for larger meals starts up from 5.30pm on Diecui Lu. Tasty dishes include *tiánluóniàng* (stuffed field snails; Y15) and *niàng xiānggū* or *niàng làjiāo* (stuffed mushrooms or capsicum). On Xi Jie, about a quarter of the way to the river from Pantao Lu, is an evening **tent city** of outdoor grills and woks. Try the local speciality, *mǐfěn* (riceflour noodles), usually served with crispy fried soy beans and spicy sour pickles.

Shopping

Yángshuò is a good place to do souvenir shopping. Good buys include silk jackets, scroll paintings and batiks (from Guìzhōu). Name chops (carved seals) are available from Y10 to Y60, but you are expected to bargain (hard) for everything. Don't forget that Yángshuò is not simply Xi Jie; for comparison shopping, wander around the backstreets, especially north around the **tourist market** (Lǚkè Shìchǎng; Binjiang Lu).

If you are in the market for a chop, bear in mind that it is not the size of the stone that is important in determining a price, but the quality of the stone itself.

Getting There & Away

AIR

The closest airport is in Guìlín; the numerous CITS outlets and many cafés dispense air tickets relatively cheaply. See p610 for details on available flights. Cafés and hotels can organise taxi rides from Yángshuò directly to the airport (Y75, one hour).

BUS

Most travellers arrive in Yángshuò via Guìlín, from where there are good connections to both domestic and international destinations.

An ever-excruciating topic is the cost of the bus between Guìlín and Yángshuò. On all buses now are very official-looking schedules (in Chinese) with the official price (Y10) listed, and at which your driver will likely point. Confusingly, others are 'express' buses (Y13), though at times it's hard to tell the difference (and they aren't all that much faster). Most buses for Yángshuò also leave from in front of the train station, though the bus station also has a few. From the train station, buses run every five to 15 minutes.

Yángshuò officials plan to relocate the town's bus station to another location further to the east, then south along Kangzhan Lu, some 800m in all from its current location. Thus, when you get off your bus, if you see a peak (Xīláng Shān) to the north, you're at the old one.

Your other options include express buses to Guǎngzhōu (Y150, 7½ hours), Wúzhōu (Y90, six hours), Shēnzhèn (Y220, nine hours) and Hong Kong.

Ancient sleepers still ply most of these routes from the bus station, however though cheaper they're smoky, haphazard and excruciatingly slow. Plus, you'll probably have to hike up to the petrol station near the toll booths to flag one down.

TRAIN

The nearest train station is in Guìlín. Almost any café or travel outfit around Yángshuò will organise train tickets. Some offer hard sleepers for high-demand routes like Guìlín to Kūnmíng for around Y270. To get any of these tickets you'll have to book at least two to three days in advance – further ahead during holidays.

Getting Around

Yángshuò itself is small enough to walk around, but hiring a bicycle is perhaps the local must-do. Average prices are Y10 per day, plus a deposit. Absolutely check gears, brakes, tyres, handle bars and cranks. The farmer's paths around Yángshuò put all bikes to the test and could leave you stranded miles away from your deposit. There have also been some ugly situations when travellers have been accused of returning bikes 'broken'; if this happens, don't expect the PSB to side with you.

AROUND YÁNGSHUÒ

What's here is just a thumbnail sketch. Many of the 'sights' not here have been turned into bus-choked tourist traps.

In Yángshuò, there are several locals offering guided tours of Yuèliàng Shān, the caves and other famous spots, as well as their home villages. Some now cook lunch or dinner as well. These mini-tours have garnered rave reviews from some travellers and may be worth a try, although you may need to get at least three people. Prices vary wildly – figure on Y50 to Y70 for a full day.

Yuèliàng Shān 月亮山

The highway from Guìlín turns southward at Yángshuò and, after a couple of kilometres, crosses Yulong River. South of the river and just west of the highway is **Yuèliàng Shān** (Moon Hill; admission Y9), a limestone pinnacle with a moon-shaped hole. The views from the top (some 1251 steps up, so reports one focused Frenchman) are incredible! You can espy Moon Hill Village and the 1500-year-old **Big Banyan Tree**. To reach Yuèliàng Shān by bicycle, take the main road south out of town towards the river and turn right on the road about 200m before the bridge. Cycle for about 50 minutes – Yuèliàng Shān is on your right.

Black Buddha Cave & Water Cave
黑佛洞, 水岩

These **caves** (Hēifó Dòng & Shuǐ Yán; per cave Y60) have been opened up not far from Yuèliàng Shān. Both are worth a visit, although Water Cave is especially popular. It's easy to reach the caves by bike; if you head for Yuèliàng Shān, you will undoubtedly be intercepted by touts.

Chufa Tours at Yuèliàng Shān offers both independent and group tours of the caves. Tours aren't bargains (two to four hours costs from Y78 to Y108), but prices include transport, entry and equipment and all who partake say it's a good adventure.

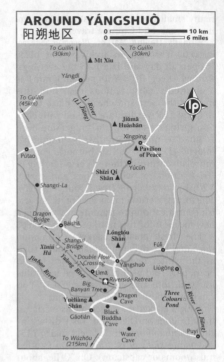

AROUND YÁNGSHUÒ
阳朔地区

If you're wanting to stay at Yuèliàng Shān, **Swallow's Guesthouse** comes highly recommended with new, basic rooms and hot showers.

Yulong River 遇龙河

Weeks worth of scenery along the Yulong River (Yùlóng Hé) rivals that of Li River and is the place that usually leaves the biggest impression on most visitors to Yángshuò – despite ongoing development.

It is possible to do a full-day tour of the river and neighbouring sights, including **Double Flow Crossing** (Shuāngliúdù), **Shangui Bridge** (Shànguì Qiáo), nearby **Xīniú Hú** (Rhinoceros Lake) and **Dragon Bridge** (Yùlóng Qiáo). This impressive last bridge was built in 1412 and is among Guǎngxī's biggest at 59m long, 5m wide and 9m high.

From Yángshuò, head towards Yuèliàng Shān. Before crossing the bridge over Yulong River, turn right down the dirt trail. It's possible to continue along this path all the way to Dragon Bridge and Báishā. Don't be tempted by the Báishā road as it is busy, noisy and dusty. A round trip to Dragon

Bridge takes a full day, but it's worth it. Pack a lunch and plenty of water.

River Excursions

Many villages close to Yángshuò are worth checking out. A popular riverboat trip is to the picturesque village of **Fúlì** (福利), a short distance down Li River, where you'll see stone houses and cobbled lanes. A couple of boats a day putter to Fúlì from Yángshuò for around Y40, although most people tend to cycle there – it's a pleasant ride and takes around an hour.

Another way to get to Fúlì is by inner tube, available for about Y10 per day. It takes around three or four hours to get to Fúlì this way. Several places also offer rafting trips and kayak hire, popular options in the warm summer months.

Many cafés and travel agents also organise boat trips to **Yángdī** (杨堤) and **Xīngpíng** (兴坪), about three hours upstream from Yángshuò. The mountain scenery around Xīngpíng is breathtaking and you'll spot many caves. Official prices for all boat trips are Y100 a ride though this has been dropping to around Y80 (or less), probably because few people are willing to fork out so much. Local boats charge Y2 for the same trip, but are deemed dangerous and the owners are not allowed to take foreigners.

A good alternative is to ride your bike to Xīngpíng and then put your bike on the boat coming back. Any number of places in Yángshuò or Xīngpíng can organise boat tickets (Y20 to Y45 per person). It's also possible to catch a local bus to Xīngpíng (Y5, one hour) from the minibus car park opposite the bus station in Yángshuò.

Another option is to spend the night in Xīngpíng where there are a growing number of budget (read: basic) accommodation and cuisine options.

River View Hotel (☎ 870 2276; beds in q Y25, tw Y80) Up the road from the river, this place is reasonably priced.

Bamboo Café Right on the river, this is a good spot for a meal and refreshing drink. Just up from the river is the wonderful **One World Café**.

Boat trips (Y25, 20 minutes) depart from Xīngpíng to **Yúcūn** (渔村), a picturesque ancient village with wonderfully preserved architecture. The problem is that boats only depart with enough people – never a given

in sleepy Xīngpíng. Other travellers simply prefer **bamboo rafting**.

From Xīngpíng, another intriguing option is to head towards Guìlín on the east side of the Li River, passing through a couple of traditional villages. However, no buses exist; local cafés can arrange vans for around Y300. Biking it is possible, but certainly not in one day and not on local clunkers.

Markets

The villages in the vicinity of Yángshuò are best visited on market days, which operate *roughly* on a three-day, monthly cycle. Thus, markets take place every three days starting on the first of the month for Báishā (1, 4, 7 etc), every three days starting on the second of the month for Fúlì (2, 5, 8 etc), and every three days starting on the third of the month for Yángshuò and Xīngpíng (3, 6, 9 etc). However, after every third market the next one is in four days, not three, but this doesn't happen in all towns. Confused? Definitely ask at your lodging or at cafés. There are no markets on the 10th, 20th, 30th and 31st of the month.

LÓNGSHÈNG 龙胜
☎ 0773 / pop 170,000

Three to four hours by bus (great road but not a few landslides) to the northwest of Guìlín, Lóngshèng is close to the border of Guìzhōu and is home to a colourful mixture of Dong, Zhuang, Yao and Miao cultures. Close by are the Dragon's Backbone Rice Terraces and a nearby *wēnquán* (hot spring).

Buses (Y5) to the hot spring pass through rolling hills sculptured with rice terraces and studded with Yao and Zhuang minority villages. It's possible to desert the bus around 6km from the hot spring and take off into the hills for some exploring. Other tourist sights around Lóngshèng include forest reserves and unusual stone formations.

When you return from the day's outing, Lóngshèng offers cheap to mid-range accommodation, and even cheaper food at its lively night market.

Information

Internet café (wǎngbā; per hr Y4; ⏱ 9am-midnight daily) Just 50m beyond the post office.
Longsheng Travel Service (Lóngshèng Lǚyóu Gōngsī; ☎ 751 7566) Next to the bus station, it should be able

to help you arrange transport, guides and tours to the surrounding sights.

Post & telephone office (Yóudiànjú; Gulong Lu)

Dragon's Backbone Rice Terraces
龙脊梯田

In the **Dragon's Backbone Rice Terraces** (Lóngjĭ Titián; admission Y30) feats of farm engineering reach all the way up a string of 800m peaks. A half-hour climb to the top delivers an amazing vista.

The 600-year-old Zhuang village of **Píng'ān** (平安), on the central main ridge of the back-bone, has become a small travellers' centre. It is still possible to avoid using the road as Píng'ān is only a half-hour's walk up a beau-tiful stone path from **Huángluò** (黄洛).

Píng'ān is a superb base camp. Walking possibilities include the one-hour circuit walk from the village to the clearly marked Viewpoint 1 and Viewpoint 2; pricier ac-commodation (Y70 for a room with simple private bathroom) is at each spot and has sublime views. More extensive day walks are also possible along the dragon's backbone and down to Héping, or over the ridge and down into the valley behind. Some travellers insist that the three-hour trek to the Yao vil-lage of **Dàzhài** (大寨) is the only place to 'get away' from the 'crowds' (an exaggeration, as Píng'ān remains eminently sleepy). Note that not all of these walks have established trails, so local guidance or at least advice is a good idea; it is not difficult to get lost.

Summer rains give the fields a sparkle, although some travellers have remarked at the beauty of the terraces covered in snow or in October, when the fields are stun-ningly golden. Winter and early spring bring heavy fogs and mist that often shroud the terraces.

Buses to the terraces leave five times daily from 7.30am to 3pm (Y4.5/6.5 to base/top) from Lóngshèng's bus station. Some buses will drop you off at the base of the ter-races and continue on to Shuānghékǒu, so ask where you'll be deposited. The trip is only about 20km, however some buses stop midway at the town of Héping to try to pull in more passengers, dragging the trip out to 1½ hours. Returning to Lóngshèng, buses usually depart from the car park near the beautiful covered bridge at the entrance to Píng'ān at 7.20am, 8.50am, 11am, 1pm, 3pm and 4.50pm.

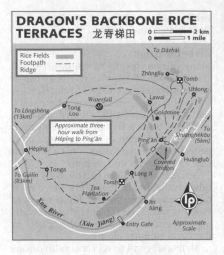

DRAGON'S BACKBONE RICE TERRACES 龙脊梯田

The entrance fee is collected on the main road along the valley bottom and checked just before the covered bridge.

Sleeping

Most accommodation is found in Píng'ān. Other villages in the area also offer basic lodging in traditional wooden homes. A basic dorm bed costs Y15 to Y20 in Píng'ān or Y10 to Y15 elsewhere; most also have rooms with private, though spartan, bath-rooms. Easiest to access in Píng'ān, with clean rooms and good food and service, is **Countryside Café & Inn** (乡村旅馆; Xiāngcūn Lǚguǎn; ☎ 758 3020; liyue_lu@hotmail.com).

In Lóngshèng, two options include:

Lǚyóu Bīnguǎn (旅游宾馆; ☎ 751 7206; Gulong Lu; d/tw/q with bathroom & air-con from Y80/100/160; 🔀) This is a very good mid-range option with clean, newly renovated rooms.

Riverside Hotel (凯凯旅舍; Kǎikǎi Lǚshè; dm Y10) Down the road to Guìlín, this exceedingly basic hotel is run by a sociable English teacher.

Eating

Longsheng Green Food Restaurant (绿色菜馆; Lùsè Càiguǎn) This place serves up decent local specialities. There is a photo board to help you order, but check the prices first as some dishes aren't cheap. Try hotpot (Y30 for the basic, plus extras) or the tasty *xiānggū ròupiàn* (beef strips with shitake mushrooms and red capsicum).

Up Shengyuan Lu, towards the PSB, is a pleasant, little traditional building with a **teahouse** inside that serves local teas and snacks.

Just past the bridge on Xinglong Xilu, **street stalls** appear around 8pm, offering point-and-choose meals.

Zhuang-Minority Flavours Restaurant This place offers a range of traditional Zhuang snacks, meals and drinks (none cheap). Traditional performances are also hosted in the restaurant on special occasions.

Getting There & Away

Buses leave the Lóngshèng bus station every 10 to 15 minutes for Guìlín (Y12, four hours) and express buses depart every two hours (Y15, three hours). Buses depart Lóngshèng for Sānjiāng hourly (Y8, two hours).

SĀNJIĀNG 三江

☎ 0772 / pop 330,000

Capital of the Sanjiang Dong Minority Autonomous County (Sānjiāng Dòngzú Zìzhìxiàn), the reason for coming here is to get out and explore (and for a worthy route into Guìzhōu). Approximately 20km to the north of town, Chengyang Wind and Rain Bridge and the wondrous patchwork of surrounding Dong villages are as peaceful and attractive as Sānjiāng is not.

Sights

CHENGYANG WIND & RAIN BRIDGE 程阳桥
Built in 1912, this 78m-long elegant **covered bridge** (Chéngyáng Qiáo; admission Y10) is considered by the Dong to be the finest of the 108 such structures in Sānjiāng County. The bridge is 78m-long and took villagers 12 years to build, theoretically without nails. Chéngyáng is a wonderful base to strike off into the surrounding countryside to numerous Dong villages.

From the Sānjiāng bus station, you can catch hourly buses to Línxī (Y3), which go right past the bridge. Otherwise, catch one of the frequent minivan taxis (Y3) that congregate outside the bus station.

Other villages and sights abound. Some can be accessed by trekking from the bridge (and some via long-poled ferry rafts), but it requires local advice; others may require backtracking to the Sānjiāng bus station.

Sleeping

Chengyang Bridge National Hostel (程阳桥招待所; Chéngyáng Qiáo Zhāodàisuǒ; ☎ 861 2444 or

858 2568; fax 861 1716; dm/d with shared bathroom Y20/60) Just to the left of the Chengyang bridge, on the far side of the river, this is easily the best abode in the area. The hotel is an all-wood, Dong-style building and the owners are friendly, informative and welcoming.

Chengyang Bridge Hotel (程阳桥宾馆; Chéngyáng Qiáo Bīnguǎn; d Y100; ☒) Down the street from the bus station in Sānjiāng, this place offers slightly more upmarket rooms; cheaper options exist but may not accept you.

Getting There & Away

Sānjiāng's bus station has several buses to Guìlín between 7am and 2pm (Y18.5, five hours; expresses Y21, 4½ hours) and to Liǔzhōu between 8am and 3pm (Y25, six hours). These should pass through Róngshuǐ (Y4.5), a scenic trip of 3½ hours. Buses to Lóngshèng (Y7) leave every 40 to 50 minutes between 6.30am and 5pm.

SĀNJIĀNG TO KĂILĬ

If you have time on your hands, it's worth entering Guìzhōu province through the back door. From Sānjiāng take the 6.40am or 2pm bus to Dìpíng (Lóng'é; Y10), which is just across the Guizhōu border. Though the journey is only approximately three hours, delays may leave you stranded in Dìpíng for the night. There are frequent buses departing Dìpíng for Lípíng (Y15, five hours).

The journey to Lípíng passes through some beautiful mountains, as well as the fabulous Dong village of Zhàoxīng (p640), the highlight of the trip and definitely worth a visit.

There are also frequent buses from Sānjiāng to Cóngjiāng in Guìzhōu. The road is new and improved but the route isn't as pretty. However, if you're in a hurry to reach Kǎilǐ, there are numerous onward connections from Cóngjiāng.

Another possibility is to take a train to Tōngdào in Húnán province and from there travel onward by bus to Lípíng. (But be careful where you stray in Húnán; between Tōngdào and Huáihuà lots of places are off limits to foreigners, and some travellers have been fined heavily.) Minibuses run every half-hour throughout the day to the train station, a few kilometres west of Sānjiāng.

LIǓZHŌU 柳州

☎ 0772 / pop 880,000

Liǔzhōu is the largest city on Willow River (Liǔ Jiāng) and is an important railway junction in southwest China. The place dates back to the Tang dynasty, when it was a dumping ground for disgraced court officials; today it's a modern, not unattractive town relatively unvisited by foreigners. Liǔzhōu is Guilín's poor cousin, with similar but less impressive karst scenery on the outskirts of town.

Information

Bank of China (Zhōngguó Yínháng) Has a couple of branches that can exchange travellers cheques.

Internet café (wǎngbā; per hr Y3) Next door to the post office. Another Internet café (per hr Y3) is on the 2nd floor of the building opposite Nánjiāng Fàndiàn.

Post & telephone office (Zhōngguó diànxìn; ☯ 8am-8pm) South of Liuzhou Square.

Ticket office (shòupiàochù; Longcheng Lu) Sells plane and train tickets.

Sights

Pleasant **Liuzhou Park** (Liǔzhōu Gōngyuán) has a lake and a small temple erected to the memory of Liu Zongyuan (AD 772–819), a famous scholar and poet. Bus Nos 2, 5 or 6 will get you there.

Along Fei'e Lu, near the main bus station, is **Yúfēng Shān** (Fish Peak Mountain), in Yufeng Park. At only 33m high, it derives its name from its resemblance to a 'standing fish'. Climb to the top for a smoggy vista of Guǎngxī's industrial city. You can also ride the cable car (return Y20), which is open until 8pm daily, from Yufeng Park up to the peak of neighbouring **Mǎ'ān Shān** (Horse Saddle Mountain), home to several temples and pavilions, and offering better views (in the mornings look for taichi aficionados atop this peak).

The pleasant **Bǎotǎ Shān** (admission Y3) is to the southeast of town with two beautiful seven-storey pagodas perched upon its peaks.

With Liǔzhōu's riverside parks recently landscaped, tourist boats now occasionally ply along Willow River during summer, departing from the wharf on the river.

Sleeping

Jīn'é Dàjiǔdiàn (☎ 361 1888, ext 2100; tw from Y50; 🏠) Next to the south bus station, this hotel is better than any of the grubby budget

INFORMATION
Bank of China 中国银行	1 B2
Bank of China 中国银行	2 A2
Internet Café 网吧	3 A2
Internet Café 网吧	(see 4)
Post & Telephone Office 中国电信	4 B1
Train & Plane Ticket Office 售票处	5 B2

SIGHTS & ACTIVITIES   p620
Yufeng Park 鱼峰公园	6 B2

SLEEPING   🏠 p620
Jīn'é Dàjiǔdiàn 金鹅大酒店	7 A2
Lìjīng Dàjiǔdiàn 丽晶大酒店	8 B2
Nánjiāng Fàndiàn 南疆饭店	9 A2

EATING   🍴 p621
Night Market 夜市	10 A2
Time Bar 时间酒吧	11 B1

DRINKING   🍷 p621
Popular Cafés & Bars 热闹的酒吧和餐厅	12 B1

TRANSPORT   p621
Ferry Dock 航运码头	13 B2
Liuzhou South Bus Station 柳州南站	14 A2
Main Bus Station 汽车总站	15 B2
Main Train Station 柳州火车站	16 A2
North Train Station 柳州北站	17 B1

options by the train station (though everybody's willing to take you).

Nánjiāng Fàndiàn (☎ 361 2988; fax 361 7575; d/tr Y268/368; 🛏) This mid-range three-star outfit has good comfy rooms – even nice family rooms. Despite the cleanliness of the rooms, the price is a bit stiff, so politely bargain.

Lìjīng Dàjiǔdiàn (☎ 280 8888; fax 280 8828; tw Y338-528; 🛏) This is Liǔzhōu's top-end hotel. Rooms are luxurious and well maintained. A 20% discount is usually available.

Eating & Drinking

Your best bet is the lively **night market** across from the main bus station. From around 8pm, numerous stalls serve tasty dumplings and noodles fried with a choice of fresh ingredients. The main train station area also has dumpling and noodle places.

Time Bar (Shíjiān Jiŭbā; Beizhan Lu) This is a Western-style bar with a few decent Western dishes and draught beer. A string of trendy and popular **cafés** and **bars** on Youyi Lu serve Western food and cocktails.

Getting There & Away
AIR
Fly from Guìlín; seriously – express buses from here even stop at the airport. Only one flight leaves for Guăngzhōu, and that's iffy. Tickets for flights departing from Guìlín and Nánníng can be purchased at window No 13 at the main bus station.

BUS
The Liŭzhōu south bus station is actually north of the main bus station, but let's not quibble. It's along Fei'e Lu and is much closer to budget lodgings and the train station, but it has mostly regional tiny towns for destinations. The main bus station is south of Yufeng Park and a fair hike from the train station.

From the main bus station, frequent express buses depart for Guìlín (Y40, 1½ hours) and hourly buses run to Sānjiāng (Y22, five hours). For Yángshuò, it's quicker to travel to Guìlín and change buses there.

TRAIN
Liŭzhōu is a main railway junction connecting Nánníng to Guìlín. There are good connections including Běijīng, Chángshā, Chéngdū, Guăngzhōu, Guìyáng, Shànghăi and Xī'ān.

Getting Around
Bus Nos 2 and 24 connect Liuzhou Sq with the train station. Bus Nos 10 and 25 run past the main bus station and go to Liuzhou Square and No 11 goes to the train station.

Guìzhōu 贵州

SOUTHWEST CHINA

HIGHLIGHTS

- Go underground in the striking **Zhijin Cave** (p634), the largest cavern in China
- Explore minority villages around **Chóng'ān** (p640), a peaceful getaway on the river
- Soak up the spray at **Huangguoshu Falls** (p634), China's premier cascade
- Enjoy the colourful **festivals** (p637) in the remote southeastern region, home to the Miao and Dong
- Brush up on your Communist Party history in the historical city of **Zūnyì** (p628)

★ Zūnyì
★ Chóng'ān
★ Zhijin Cave
★ Festivals
★ Huangguoshu Falls

■ POP: 38.1 MIL   ■ AREA: 227,420 SQ KM

Guìzhōu means 'precious land', a somewhat ironic name for a province that has ranked as one of the poorest in China for most of the 20th century. However, while Guìzhōu's economy might not be in great shape, it is a beautiful province and sadly one that visitors to China's southwest tend to neglect as they hurry on towards Sìchuān or Yúnnán. Brimming with dramatic landscapes, rich in minority culture and with a well-deserved reputation for a good ol' knees up, it's a province that would do well to feature on any traveller's itinerary.

Once outside the modern capital Guìyáng, the landscape appears almost otherworldly. Terraced fields creep up the sides of rolling mountains that eventually give way to wide, electric-green plateaus. Striking karst formations and crumbling stone punctuate the scenery and giant limestone caves stretch for miles beneath the earth. Dense green forests and cascading waterfalls appear unexpectedly and the overall impression leaves you wondering whether or not you've accidentally stumbled onto the set of a Peter Jackson movie.

Spread out among the colourful countryside lives a lively mix of people. Almost 35% of Guìzhōu's population is made up of over 18 different ethnic minorities including the Miao and the Dong. The traditional wooden homes on stilts of the Miao can be found in the mountainous areas of the province, often perched at precarious angles overlooking sloping rivers. The Miao are famous for their silverware, and come festival time you'll see the younger girls literally weighed down by their giant, elaborate headdresses and row upon row of necklaces and bangles. The Dong are respected architects and their lofty wooden drum towers and intricate wind and rain bridges – constructed without a single nail or bolt – characterise the south east region. Other minority groups include the Bouyi, Yi, Shui (Sui), Hui, Zhuang and Gejia, and together they all contribute to Guìzhōu's lively social calendar that enjoys more folk festivals than any other province in China.

History

Historically no one has really wanted much to do with Guìzhōu. Chinese rulers set up an administration in the area as far back as the Han dynasty (206 BC–AD 220) but merely in an attempt to maintain some measure of control over Guìzhōu's non-Chinese tribes. Chinese settlement was confined to the northern and eastern parts of the province and the western areas were not settled until the 16th century when rapid immigration forced the native minorities out of the most fertile areas.

It wasn't until the Sino-Japanese war when the Kuomintang made Chóngqìng their wartime capital that the development of Guìzhōu began: roads to neighbouring provinces were constructed, a rail link was built to Guǎngxī and industries were established in Guìyáng and Zūnyì. Most of this activity ceased with the end of the Sino-Japanese war and it wasn't until the communists began construction of the railways that industrialisation of the area was revived.

Nevertheless, Chinese statistics continue to paint a grim picture of underdevelopment and poverty for Guìzhōu. GDP per capita in Shànghǎi is 10 times higher than in Guìzhōu. The government is attempting to change all this, mostly by building roads in every possible place to enable travel to the Huangguoshu Falls and by promoting minority cultures as a local attraction.

Climate

Guìzhōu has a temperate climate with an annual average temperature of 15°C. The coldest months are January and February when temperatures dip to around 1°C.

Language
Mandarin Chinese is spoken by the Han majority, Thai and Lao is spoken by some and Miao-Yao (Hmong-mien) dialects by the Miao and Yao.

Getting There & Away
You can fly to more than 40 destinations within China from Guìyáng's airport, including all major Chinese cities. International destinations include Hong Kong and Bangkok.

Guìyáng and Chóngqìng are linked by an expressway. Yúnnán is accessible by bus via Wēiníng in the west or Xīngyì in the south of the province. From Xīngyì you can also cross into Guăngxī. Guăngxī can also be accessed through Cóngjiāng in the southeastern part of the province.

There are daily train departures to all major cities in China and sleepers to Chéngdū in Sìchuān or Kūnmíng in Yúnnán are popular options. Trains to Guìlín leave at awkward times and are painfully slow. If you're heading down this way your best bet is to take a train to Liŭzhōu in Guăngxī and change for a bus to Guìlín there.

GUÌYÁNG 贵阳
☎ 0851 / pop 1.7 million / elevation 1070m
Guìyáng is undergoing a face-lift, meaning the usual uncountable number of construction sites and mushrooming high-rises. Nevertheless, a few of the older neighbour-

GUÌZHŌU 贵州

hoods and temples have held on and some of the new areas, including the riverside and Renmin Square (Rénmín Guǎngchǎng), provide enjoyable areas to wander, mingle and relax. There's also some fantastic street food, lively markets and shopping areas, and a few interesting sights.

Guìyáng is built within a 30 sq km basin surrounded by 'forest clad hills' so the Chinese like to refer to the city as 'Forest City'.

Orientation

Guìyáng is somewhat sprawling but remains a manageable size and is easy enough to get around either on foot or by public bus. The main commercial district is found along Zhonghua Zhonglu and Zhonghua Nanlu. If you continue south you'll reach Zunyi Lu and Renmin Square. To the east of here is Jiaxiu Pavilion, a symbol of the city that hovers over Nanming River.

MAPS

There are no English maps of the city available but the Chinese tourist maps are helpful for navigating bus routes. These can be bought at newspaper kiosks or from Xinhua Bookshop.

Information
BOOKSHOPS
Foreign Languages Bookshop (Wàiwén Shūdiàn; Yan'an Donglu) Isn't particularly well stocked but does have a selection of maps.
Xinhua Bookshop (Xīnhuá Shūdiàn; Yan'an Xilu) Marginally better.

INTERNET ACCESS
Internet café (Wǎngbā; Jiefang Lu; per hr Y2-3) Opposite the bus station.

MEDICAL SERVICES
Guiyang Medical College (Guìyáng Yīshù Xuéyuàn; ☎ 689 3775; 4 Beijing Lu) The hospital attached to this college has a couple of English speaking doctors.
Ensure Chain Pharmacy (Yīshù Yàoyè Liásuǒ; cnr Zūnyì Lu & Jiefang Lu; ☺ 24hr) Near the train station.

MONEY
Bank of China (Zhōngguó Yínháng; cnr Dusi Lu & Zhonghua Lu) Has an ATM and will exchange money and travellers cheques and offers cash advances on credit cards. Another branch can be found on Zunyi Lu near the train station and another sits on the corner of Wenchang Beilu and Yan'an Donglu.

POST & TELEPHONE
China Post (Yóujú; 46 Zhonghua Nanlu) Offers a poste restante service. China Telecom is next door.

TOURIST INFORMATION
China International Travel Service (CITS; Zhōngguó Guójì Lüxíngshè; ☎ 581 4829; 20 Yan'an Zhonglu; ☺ 8.30-11am & 1-5pm Mon-Sat) The friendly English-speaking staff are helpful and can provide information and dates on local festivals.
Guìzhōu Overseas Travel Company (GOTC; Guìzhōu Hǎiwài Lüyóu Gōngsì; ☎ 586 4898; 28 Yan'an Zhonglu; ☺ 8.30-11am & 1-5pm Mon-Sat) Offers similar services and can arrange rafting trips down the Maling Gorge.
Public Security Bureau (PSB; Gōngānjú; ☎ 590 4509; Daying Lu; ☺ 8.30am-noon & 2.30-5pm Mon-Fri) The place to go to report lost or stolen items and for visa extensions.
Tourist complaint line (☎ 681 8436)

Dangers & Annoyances
Guìyáng has a reputation among Chinese as one of China's worst cities for theft. Be particularly careful in crowded areas such as the train station, busy streets and on local buses – the favoured haunts of pickpockets.

There has been one report (unconfirmed) of an attempted mugging by a hotel tout at the train station. Be careful, many of these cheaper hotels don't accept foreigners anyway.

Sights
PARKS 公园
Qianling Park in the north of the city is worth a visit both for its forested walks and **Hongfu Temple**, a 17th-century Qing dynasty temple perched near the top of 1300m Qiánlíng Shān. The monastery has a vegetarian restaurant in the rear courtyard. From the train station area take a No 2 bus.

PROVINCIAL MUSEUM 省博物馆
The **Provincial Museum** (Shěng Bówùguǎn; Beijing Lu; admission Y10) doesn't see many visitors, which is a shame because the displays are really interesting. Exhibits include various aspects of the province's minorities, such as traditional dress and customs from the Yelang kingdom; an ancient kingdom believed to have originated in the Warring States Period (475 BC–221 BC).

Also interesting is the small collection dating back to the 18th and 19th century

GUÌYÁNG 贵阳

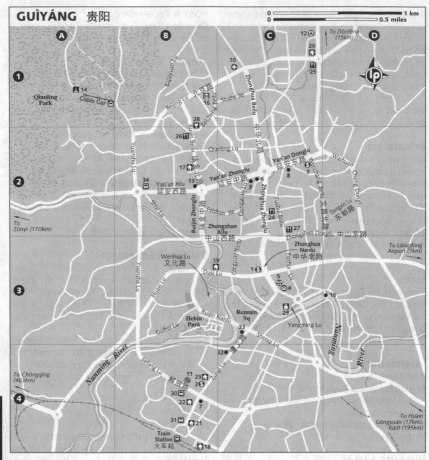

when the Miao staged a series of uprisings in protest against the rapid immigration of Han Chinese into Guìzhōu.

Tours

There are organised tours to Huangguoshu Falls and Longgong Caves that leave daily from the train station or the long-distance bus station. Many of the hotels also organise day tours as does the CITS and GOTC, although they are not as frequent off-season. Tours cost from Y250 per person and include transport and admission fees and sometimes lunch.

Festivals & Events

Guìzhōu plays host to hundreds of festivals every year. This might seem like an unfeasible number of parties but the minority groups here, in particular the Miao and Dong, always seem to have something to celebrate.

The major festivals are held on auspicious lunar dates and therefore vary from year to year in the Roman calendar. Most are annual events although some are held every few years and one, the Fertility Festival (鼓藏节; Gǔzàng Jié), is only celebrated every 13 years. Some of the larger and more popular annual festivals include the Lusheng Festival, Dragon Boat Festival and Sisters Festival. Celebrations are lively events that can last for days at a time and often include singing, dancing, horse racing and buffalo fighting.

A good starting point for festival forays is Kǎilǐ; a profusion of festivals is held in nearby minority areas (see p637 for more details).

Sleeping

BUDGET

Gōnglù Zhāodàisuǒ (☎ 599 2513; 101 Ruijin Beilu; dm Y50-70, d Y240) This is the best deal in town with recently renovated bright rooms, wooden floors and 24-hour hot water.

Tǐyù Bīnguǎn (Sports Hotel; ☎ 579 8777; fax 579 0799; cnr Jiefang Lu & Zūnyì Lu; d Y138-168, tr Y208) The staff here are lovely and speak some English. The rooms are a bit shabby and the beds on the small side but it's still a decent choice. You'll find the hotel on the grounds of the Guìzhōu stadium.

Míngzhū Fàndiàn (☎ 821 2600; 8 Sitong Jie; d Y128-168) On your right as you exit the train

station, the rooms here are old but clean enough. Have a look at a number of rooms as standards do vary.

MID-RANGE

Yùjūnyuán Bīnguǎn (☎ 597 0701; 71 Zūnyì Lu; s/d Y188/198) A modern hotel with enormous bedrooms and bizarre bathrooms. Staff are usually willing to give discounts.

Tōngdà Fàndiàn (☎ 821 3888; fax 579 0566; train station square; d Y160-208, tr Y300) The rooms are on the small side but not cramped. The main drawback is the noise of the train station but ask for a room on one of the top floors and you should be OK.

TOP END

Nénghuī Jiǔdiàn (☎ 589 8888; fax 589 8622; 38 Ruijin Nanlu; d Y520-696) In addition to good rooms this hotel offers some excellent facilities, including a well-equipped gym, sauna and an afternoon tea buffet.

Shénqí Dàjiǔdiàn (Miracle Hotel; ☎ 677 1888; 1 Beijing Lu; d plus 15% service charge Y800) Once part of the Holiday Inn chain, this hotel still offers high standards of rooms despite the change in management. The bakery and deli on the ground floor stock delicious banana bread, tins of baked beans and cans of Guinness.

Eating

Some of the best food in Guìyáng can be found at the night markets. At dusk countless stalls spring up near the train station, all stacked with a huge choice of veggies, tofu and meat. Point at what you like, grab a beer and watch it be cooked. If you're feeling really adventurous tuck into some steamed pig snout and trotters, a popular local choice. If not, try the local varieties of *shāguō fěn*, a noodle and seafood, meat or vegetable combination put in a casserole pot and fired over a flame of rocket-launch proportions.

Miao Nationality Restaurant (Miáojiā Fēngwèi Cānguǎn; cnr Beijing Lu & Yushan Beilu; dishes from Y10; ☯ 11am-9pm) You can try authentic Miao cuisine here, which involves lots of chilli and pickled vegetables. Follow the staircase down to a courtyard.

Júeyuán Cāntīng (☎ 584 1957; 11 Fushui Beilu; dishes from Y5; ☯ 7am-9pm) This Buddhist restaurant, originally constructed in 1862, forms part of the adjacent temple and promises meals 'free of worldly dust'. All food is strictly vegetarian.

SOUTHWEST CHINA

New Zealand Western Restaurant (Niǔxīlán Xǐcāntíng; ☎ 651 2086; 157 Ruijin Beilu; lunch buffet Y48, dinner buffet Y68; ☺ lunch buffet noon-2.30pm, dinner 6-9.30pm) What this restaurant has to do with New Zealand is anyone's guess but the lunch and dinner buffet is a good deal and the menu offers a decent selection of Western and Chinese dishes.

Drinking

UBC Coffee (UBC Shāngdǎo Kāfēi; 159 Ruijin Beilu) Next door to the New Zealand Western Restaurant is a branch of this well-known Taiwanese chain. There is a small food menu and an extensive coffee and tea menu that includes the ever popular *zhēnzhū nǎichá* (pearl milk tea).

London Bar (Lúndūn Jiǔbā; Ruijin Beilu) This is a swanky looking bar that sees the hip young Guiyangese lining up to enjoy the pricey cocktails.

Getting There & Away

AIR

Airline offices in Guìyáng include the **Civil Aviation Administration of China** (Zhōngguó Mínháng; CAAC; ☎ 597 7777; 264 Zūnyì Lu; ☺ 8.30am-9pm), which has helpful English-speaking staff and **China Southern Airlines** (☎ 582 8429; cnr Zūnyì Lu & Ruijin Nanlu).

Destinations include Běijīng (Y1570), Shànghǎi (Y1460), Guǎngzhōu (Y790), Guìlín (Y500), Chéngdū (Y570), Xī'ān (Y760), Kūnmíng (Y440), Chóngqìng (Y420), Mángshì (Y880) and Jǐnghóng (Y870).

International destinations include Hong Kong (Y1850) and Bangkok (Y1850).

BUS

There are three long-distance bus stations in Guìyáng. The main long-distance bus station is on Yan'an Xilu, quite a trek from the train station. They all have similar destinations at similar times and similar prices.

See box opposite for bus times.

TRAIN

Guìyáng's gleaming train station has a modern, computerised ticket office, making it one of the more pleasant places in China to buy a train ticket. However, you'll probably find that it's easier (and quicker) to travel within Guìzhōu by bus. You can buy tickets four days in advance. Prices listed here are for hard sleepers.

Destination	Price	Duration	Departs
Zūnyì	Y12	5hr	5pm
Kǎilǐ	Y29	3hr	8.10am
Liùpánshuǐ	Y35	4hr	10am
Chóngqìng	Y107	10hr	7pm
Chéngdū	Y193	19hr	3.38pm
Guǎngzhōu	Y166	24hr	12.15pm
Shànghǎi	Y326	30hr	11pm
Běijīng	Y490	29hr	7.50am
Kūnmíng	Y131	12hr	7.30pm
Guìlín	Y200	17hr	2am, 9.20pm
Liǔzhōu	Y93	16hr	9pm

Getting Around

TO/FROM THE AIRPORT

Airport buses depart from the CAAC office every 30 minutes (Y10, 8.30am to 6.30pm). A taxi from the airport will cost around Y50.

BUS

Bus Nos 1 and 2 do city tour loops from the train station, passing close to the long-distance bus station. Bus No 1 travels up Zhongshan Nanlu and heads westward along Beijing Lu. Buses cost Y1 and recorded announcements in Chinese and English let you know the name of the bus stops.

TAXI

Taxis charge a flat Y10 fare to anywhere in the city.

ZŪNYÌ 遵义

☎ 0852 / pop 4 million

Around 160km north of Guìyáng, Zūnyì is the site of the famous Zūnyì Conference and something of a mecca for those with an interest in Chinese Communist Party (CCP) history.

History

On 16 October 1934, hemmed into the Jiāngxī soviet by Kuomintang forces, the communists set out on a Herculean, one-year, 9500km Long March from one end of China to the other. By mid-December they had reached Guìzhōu and marched on Zūnyì. Taking the town by surprise, the communists were able to stock up on supplies and take a breather.

From 15 to 18 January 1935, the top-level communist leaders took stock of their situation in the now-famous Zūnyì Conference. At the meeting the leaders reviewed their

GUÌYÁNG BUS TIMETABLES

Buses from Guìyáng's Yan'an Xilu Bus Station include:

Destination	Price	Duration	Frequency	Departs
Zūnyì	Y25-45	3hr	half-hourly	7.30am-7.30pm
Ānshùn	Y15	2hr	every 20min	7am-7pm
Wēiníng	Y65	5hr	daily	9am
Chóngqìng	Y100	8hr	daily	1pm
Guìlín	Y108	10hr	daily	8pm
Guǎngzhōu	Y230	17hr	daily	1.30pm

Buses from the stand north of the train station:

Destination	Price	Duration	Frequency	Departs
Zūnyì	Y25-45	3hr	half-hourly	7am-10pm
Ānshùn	Y15-20	2hr	every 20min	6.10am-10pm
Xìngyì	Y60	5-7hr	hourly	9am-6pm
Kǎilǐ	Y30-40	2hr	every 40min	7am -6pm
Huangguoshu Falls	Y30-40	21/2hr	every 40min	7.10am-noon

Buses from the bus station on Jiefang Lu:

Destination	Price	Duration	Frequency	Departs
Kǎilǐ	YY30-40	2hr	every 30min	7.30am-7.30pm
Léishān	Y40	3hr	daily	3pm
Chóng'ān Jiāng	Y35	3hr	3 daily	12.30pm, 1.40pm, 3pm
Chóngqìng	Y80	9hr	daily	1.30pm

soviet-influenced strategies that had cost them their Jiāngxī base and caused them large military losses. Mao, who until this time had largely been overshadowed by his contemporaries, was highly critical of the communist's strategy thus far and the resolutions of the conference largely reflected his views. He was elected a full member of the ruling Standing Committee of the Politburo and Chief Assistant to Zhou Enlai in military planning. It would be another 10 years before Mao became the unrivalled leader of the Communist Party, but this event was a pivotal factor in his rise to power.

Information

Bank of China (Zhōngguó Yínháng; Minzu Lu) Has an ATM and can change cash, travellers cheques and offers cash advances on credit cards.
China Post (46 Zhonghua Lu; ☼ 8.30am-7pm) You can make international calls from a telephone office around the corner.

Internet café (wǎngbā; Zhonghua Lu; per hr Y3; ☼ 24hr) Next door to China Post.
PSB (Gōngānjú; Jinian Square; ☼ 8.30-11.30am & 2.30-5.30pm) Offers visa extensions.

Sights
COMMUNIST HISTORY SITES

The most celebrated communist history site is the **Zūnyì Conference Site** (Zūnyì Huìyì Huìzhǐ; Ziyin Lu; admission Y50; ☼ 8am-6.30pm) set within an old colonial-style house. The rooms are filled with CCP memorabilia as well as the meeting rooms and living quarters of the bigwigs.

The entrance fee includes admission to the other sites in town including the **Red Army General Political Department** (Hóngjūn Zǒngzhèngzhìbù; Ziyin Lu). The exhibition here is much more informative and there are interesting displays of photos and maps of the Long March and Zūnyì Conference, some with English captions.

ZŪNYÌ 遵义

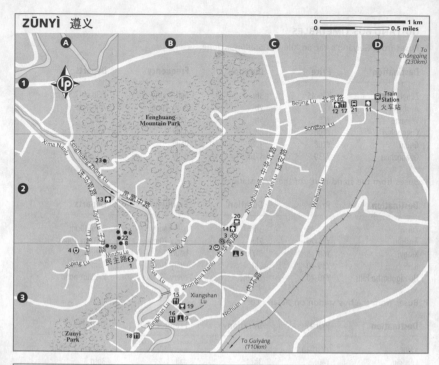

INFORMATION	
Bank of China 中国银行 1 B3	
China Post 邮局 2 B3	
Internet Café 网吧 3 C2	
PSB 公安局 4 A3	

SIGHTS & ACTIVITIES	pp629–30
Baiyun Temple 白云寺 5 C3	
Red Army General	
Political Department	
红军总政治部旧址 6 B2	
Residence of Bo Gu 博古旧居 7 B2	
State Bank of the Red Army	
红军银行 8 B2	
Xiangshan Temple 湘山寺 9 B3	
Zunyi Conference Site	
遵义会议会址 10 A3	

SLEEPING	pp630–1
Jīnghóng Dàjiǔdiàn	
金虹大酒店 11 D1	
Shīshān Dàjiǔdiàn	
狮山大酒店 12 D1	
Zájì Bīnguǎn	
遵义杂技宾馆 13 A2	
Zunyi Bīnguǎn	
遵义宾馆 14 C2	

EATING	p631
Grill Stalls 烧烤摊 15 B3	
Hotpot & Grill Restaurants	
火锅烧烤店 16 B3	
Hotpot & Grill Stalls	
火锅烧烤摊 17 D1	
Rénrén Jiǔjiā 人人酒家 18 B3	

DRINKING	p631
8150 Cháyuán Chàngbā	
茶缘唱吧 19 B3	
Baotong Disco	
宝通迪斯科广场 .... (see 19)	
Dingbùlā	
汀布拉茶馆 20 C2	

TRANSPORT	p631
Long-Distance Bus Station	
长途汽车站 21 D1	

OTHER	
Catholic Church 天主教堂 22 B2	
Monument to the Martyrs	
of the Red Army	
红军烈士纪念碑 23 A2	

Opposite is the **Residence of Bo Gu**, the general leader of the CCP Central Committee at the time of the Zūnyì Conference, and the former home of the **State Bank of the Red Army** (Huìyì Qījiān), now a bank.

TEMPLES
Also worth a visit are Zūnyì's two active Buddhist temples. Built in the 1920s, **Xiangshan Temple** is situated on a small hill in a lively part of town. **Baiyun Temple** is more run-down but still quite charming.

Sleeping
There's some reasonable accommodation to be found in Zūnyì.

Zájì Bīnguǎn (☎ 822 3335; 89 Zhonghua Nanlu; d Y158-208) Rooms here look like they've never been lived in and the staff are friendly.

Shīshān Dàjiǔdiàn (☎ 882 2978; fax 882 5861; 108 Beijing Lu; dm Y30-60, d with bath Y108-138) These are the cheapest rooms you'll find in Zūnyì and they're very clean too.

Jīnghóng Dàjiǔdiàn (Golden Rainbow Hotel; ☎ 319 1127; fax 882 3266; Shahe Lu; s/d/tr Y118/168/188 ⛺)

Opposite the train station the rooms here are in good condition but the location is noisy.

Zūnyì Bīnguǎn (☎ 822 4902, ext 8001; fax 822 1497; 3 Shilong Lu; s/d/tr Y108/148/166) This is Zūnyì's official three-star tourist hotel and it's set in a pretty shaded garden. Unfortunately it appears not as much work has been put into the rooms, the majority of them are old and overpriced.

Eating

Street food is your best bet in this town and there are some great hotpot, noodle and grill stalls to be found come dinner time. One of the best places to look is the alleys running southeast off Zhonghua Nanlu, or stroll down the lively Xiangshan Lu.

Rénrén Jiǔjiā (Zhongshan Lu; dishes from Y12) For something a bit more upmarket try this place, which serves decent food near the river.

Across the bridge south of Xiangshan Temple you'll find a large number of hotpot restaurants lining the riverfront.

Drinking

Dīngbùlā (Zhonghua Nanlu) A modern Taiwanese teahouse that also serves up local beers and bar snacks. It gets quite busy in the evening with a young student crowd.

8150 Cháyuán Chāngbā (Zhongshan Lu) This place is fun on a Saturday night when the karaoke crowd get going.

Baotong Disco (Xiangshan Lu) If dancing is more your thing then you have to try this disco, in Zūnyì's old cinema. It gets packed to the doors at the weekend with a young energetic crowd. Saturday night features the weekly 'Miss Zūnyì' dance competition, a spectacle in itself.

Getting There & Around

BUS

Useful local buses are No 9 and No 14 that run from the train station towards Minzu Lu and the Bank of China.

See box below for bus times.

TRAIN

There are regular trains for Guìyáng (Y12 to Y20, 3½ hours) but you're better off catching the bus. Other destinations include Chóngqìng (Y24 to Y40, five hours, 7am, 10.30am and 2.30pm) and Chéngdū (Y170, 15 hours, 7.30am, 2.30pm, 4.30pm and 6.30pm).

ĀNSHÙN 安顺

☎ 0853

In addition to giving you fairly easy access to Huangguoshu Falls and Longgong Caves, Ānshùn itself is set in a pleasant karst limestone region. Markets abound and are often host to minority entrepreneurs in traditional dress.

Once an important centre for tea and opium trading, Ānshùn remains the commercial hub of western Guìzhōu. Today it's most famous as a producer of batiks, kitchen knives and the lethal Ānjiǔ brand of alcohol. The nearby aviation factory is also well known, and recently diversified production from fighter planes to family hatchbacks.

Orientation

The long-distance bus and train stations are 3km and 4km south of downtown respectively. The main commercial and shopping area is found on Zhonghua Donglu, Minzhu Lu and Wangruofei Dadao Nanduan.

ZŪNYÌ BUS TIMETABLES

Buses from Zūnyì include:

Destination	Price	Duration	Frequency	Departs
Guìyáng	Y25-40	3hr	half-hourly	7am-9pm
Chóngqìng	Y50.5	8hr	daily	3pm
Fújiàn	Y290	30hr	daily	4pm
Guǎngzhōu	Y229.5	20hr	2 daily	1pm, 4pm
Kūnmíng	Y120.5	15hr	daily	4pm
Nánníng	Y180.5	12hr	daily	7pm
Wēnzhōu	Y260.5	36hr	daily	4pm

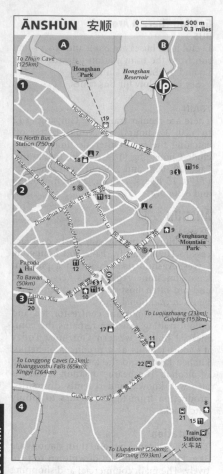

Information

Bank of China (Zhōngguó Yínháng; cnr Tashan Xilu & Nanhua Donglu) Changes cash, travellers cheques and offers cash advance on credit cards. There is also an ATM here.

China Post (Yóujú; cnr Zhonghua Donglu & Zhonghua Beilu) China Telecom is south of here.

China Travel Service (CTS; Zhōngguó Lǚxíngshè; ☎ 328 3168; Tashan Donglu; ☷ 8.30-11am & 1-5pm Mon-Sat) Fairly helpful although none of the staff speaks English.

Internet Café (Tashan Donglu; per hr Y3) South of Fēnghuángshān Dàjiǔdiàn. Another can be found on Zhonghua Donglu.

Sights

Ānshùn's main attraction is the huge **Sunday market** that takes over the centre of town with the most traditional part of it lying

along Shi Xilu. You can buy almost anything here – modern or traditional – from dried beef to human hair which the young Miao women use to boost their hairdos.

Donglin Temple is an active Buddhist temple, built in AD 1405 (during the Ming dynasty) and restored in 1668. The resident monks are very friendly and welcome visitors warmly. North of here, **Wén Miào** is a more recent concrete temple, which is dilapidated and deserted.

Sleeping

Ānjú Bīnguǎn (☎ 220 1359; dm Y10-20, d with bath Y100) You can't miss this bright pink building; it's on your right as you exit the train station. The hotel has recently been renovated and the rooms are basic but very clean, making this the best deal in town.

Xīxiùshān Bīnguǎn (☎ 221 2888; fax 221 1801; 63 Nanhua Lu; s/d Y288/328) Recent renovations have seen a hike in prices at this three-star hotel but if you're looking to treat yourself then the rooms overlooking the karst hills are worth the extra yuán.

Fēnghuángshān Dàjiǔdiàn (Golden Phoenix Mountain Hotel; ☎ 322 5663; 58 Tashan Donglu; d/tr Y198/268) Featuring a taste in bedroom décor that only your grandma could love, the chintzy rooms aren't the best in town but are a comfortable option.

Huáyóu Bīnguǎn (☎ 322 6020; Tashan Xilu; d Y120-180) The rooms are uninspired but the bathrooms are spotless.

Eating

Ānshùn is not bursting with culinary delights unfortunately. There are a handful of restaurants at the north of the Fēnghuángshān Dàjiǔdiàn on Tashan Donglu including a fantastic *jiǎozi* (Chinese ravioli) stall that makes delicious dumplings stuffed with a range of different fillings including a decent veggie selection.

There are a number of bakeries in town, the one on Wanruofei Dadao Nanduan is very popular. You'll find another decent one on Minzhu Lu.

In the evening a food market gets going down an alley off Nanhua Lu, just south of the Bank of China. Near the train station are a row of forgettable noodle stalls.

Be forewarned: dog is eaten in these parts – lots of dog. You'll see the skinned animals propped up outside restaurants as an enticement to come in for lunch.

Getting There & Around
BUS
The No 1 minibus is the most useful – it zips around town from the train station and up Tashan Donglu. Bus No 2 travels

between the train station and the north bus station. Buses costs Y1.

There are several bus stations in Ānshùn that are useful to travellers. The north bus station has buses to Zhījīn town (for Zhijin Cave) and the west bus station is useful for travelling to Longgong Caves.

The long-distance station on the corner of Nanhua Lu and Guihuang Gonglu has a handful of handy destinations, and the bus station in front of the train station has buses for provinces in the southeastern part of China.

See box below.

TRAIN
From Ānshùn, trains leave daily for Kūnmíng (Y130, 11 hours, 8.44am and 6.27pm) but it's virtually impossible to get sleeper reservations and you might decide to head back to Guìyáng. To Chóngqìng two trains leave daily (Y68, 12 hours, 9.38pm and 11.42pm). To Liùpánshuǐ (for Wēiníng) there are two trains daily at 10.52am and 11.34am (Y22, four hours). Four trains leave daily for Guìyáng (Y7 to Y12, two hours), although the bus is more convenient.

AROUND ĀNSHÙN
Longgong Caves 龙宫洞
About 23km south of Ānshùn, near the Bouyi settlement of Shítou Zhài, is a series of underground caverns called **Lónggōng**

BUS TIMETABLES

Buses from Ānshùn Long-Distance Bus Station:

Destination	Price	Duration	Frequency	Departs
Guìyáng	Y15	2hr	every 20min	6.50am-7.10pm
Xīngyì	Y51	5hr	hourly	7am-3.30pm
Kūnmíng	Y126	17hr	daily	1pm
Huángguǒshù	Y8	1hr	every 20min	7.20am-5pm

Buses from Ānshùn Long-Distance Bus Station to the Southeast:

Destination	Price	Duration	Frequency	Departs
Xiàmén	Y300	28hr	daily	noon
Fúzhōu	Y320	32hr	daily	noon
Guǎngzhōu	Y220	18hr	daily	noon
Fóshān	Y220	18hr	daily	noon
Shēnzhèn	Y220	18hr	daily	noon

(Lónggōng Dòng; Dragon Palace; admission Y50), which forms a huge network through 20 hills. At present only 1km of the cave system is open to tourists. While it's dolled up with recorded music and coloured spotlights, on a quiet day a glide through here in a hand-paddled boat can be an impressive and peaceful experience. Admission includes the boat ride.

A second, less impressive site has been opened 4km before Lónggōng, called **Guanyin Cave**. It's pleasant but not really worth the admission fee of Y25 (which also includes the boat ride).

GETTING THERE & AWAY

Local buses depart every hour from Ānshùn's west bus station (Y8, one hour). Returning, buses leave hourly until 5pm.

Minibuses run between Lónggōng and Huángguǒshù (Y20).

Zhijin Cave 织金洞

At around 10km long and up to 150m high, **Zhijin Cave** (Zhījīn Dòng; admission Y120) ranks as the largest in China and one of the biggest in the world. Located at the edge of a small village some 15km outside Zhíjīn, this place is impressive even if you're not a cave fanatic. Small passageways open up into giant rooms, where calcium deposits create an abstract landscape of spectacular shapes and spirals, often reaching from floor to ceiling.

Tickets to the site are steep but include a compulsory tour. If you're not travelling with a posse, this can mean a bit of a wait, as tours depart with a minimum of 10 people. While the tour itself is in Chinese only, you'll be glad to have someone around who knows the way back out of the maze of trails. The tour lasts for around three hours, possibly more.

GETTING THERE & AWAY

A trip to the cave can be made as a day trip from Ānshùn – just. Buses depart from Ānshùn's north bus station (Y18, three hours, every 25 minutes) for Zhíjīn town. Once there, hop on a motorised rickshaw over to the town's second bus station and catch one of the local buses that leave regularly for the cave (Y1; one hour). If you're in a group, consider getting a taxi (Y20).

Returning from the caves buses leave regularly. The last bus back to Ānshùn heads out of Zhíjīn at 5.30pm.

Huangguoshu Falls 黄果树大瀑布

Reaching a width of 81m and plunging 74m down into Rhinoceros Pool, it is not surprising that this huge cascade of water is Guìzhōu's No 1 tourist attraction. The Chinese explored this area in the 1980s, as a preliminary to harnessing the region's hydro-electric potential. They discovered about 18 falls, four subterranean rivers and 100 caves, many of which are now being gradually opened to visitors. The massive waterfall, cave and karst complex covers some 450 sq km, however the area near Huángguǒshù Village, home to the massive **Huangguoshu Falls** (Huángguǒshù Dà Pùbù; Yellow Fruit Tree Falls; admission Y150), is closer to 6km in length and easily explored in an afternoon.

The thunder of the waterfalls can be heard for some distance, and during the rainy season (May to October) the mist from the falls carries up to Huángguǒshù Village. The falls are most spectacular about four days after heavy rains. The dry season lasts from November to April and during March and April the flow of water can become a trickle.

There are three entrances to the main falls: at the top of the **cable car** (Y50), next to Huángguǒshù Bīnguǎn and just before Huángguǒshù Village. Once inside, you can get up close to the falls, both by trapezing across a stone path over **Rhinoceros Pool** and by visiting **Water Curtain Cave** where, for an extra Y10, you can walk through a tunnel behind the falls and view the water streaming past. During the rainy season, both of these explorations can turn into wades and prove treacherous. Good footwear and waterproof gear are necessary at any time of year.

There are a number of other waterfalls in the area that are included in the entry price for Huangguoshu Falls. One kilometre above the main falls and a couple of kilometres' walk north of town is **Steep Slope Falls** (Dǒupō Pùbù), 105m wide and 23m high. Eight kilometres below Huangguoshu Falls is the **Star Bridge Scenic Area** (Tiānxīng Qiáo Jǐngqū) known for its 'potted landscape'.

SLEEPING & EATING

You can do the falls in a day trip from Guìyáng at a push and it's an easy day trip from Ānshùn. There are accommodation options open to foreigners in Huángguǒshù Village but the hotels are fairly grim and very overpriced.

Huángguǒshù Bīnguǎn (黄果树宾馆; ☎ 359 2110; d Y380-480) Halfway between the bus stand and Huángguǒshù Village, this hotel has been redecorated but you still don't get much for your money. Rooms are somewhat musty and come with tiptoe views of the falls.

Huángguǒshù Gōngsāng Zhāodàisuǒ (黄果树贡桑招待所; ☎ 359 2583; d/tr Y180/220) This police run guesthouse is a little further up the road from Huángguǒshù Bīnguǎn; it has OK rooms. If they come with a discount then this is your best bet.

Along the main road in town are several restaurants with verandas at the back where you can eat and enjoy a great view of the falls.

GETTING THERE & AWAY

From Ānshùn, buses run every 20 minutes from the long-distance bus station (Y8, one hour, 7.20am to 5pm). Buses from Ānshùn to Xīngyì also pass by Huángguǒshù, leaving you about a 15-minute walk from the highway to the village.

From Guìyáng to Huángguǒshù buses leave every 40 minutes from the long-distance bus station (Y30 to Y40, 2½ hours, 7.10am to noon).

Heading out of Huángguǒshù buses for Ānshùn and Guìyáng run regularly between 7am and 7pm. Buses for Xīngyì leave in the morning.

Minibuses run the route between Longgong Caves and Ānshùn (Y20 per person).

WESTERN GUÌZHŌU

As the area most recently opened to tourists, Guìzhōu's west is rough and, at times, forbidding. The roads are poor and the bus journeys long but you will pass through some interesting minority territory, pretty countryside and get a unique look at rural life. The main attraction is the Nature Reserve at Cǎohǎi Lake. This route is for adventurers looking to get off the beaten track.

WĒINÍNG 威宁

☎ 0857

Wēiníng certainly isn't a pretty town, but what it lacks in aesthetics it makes up for in character. There's a real sense of reaching the end of civilisation (or at least the edge of

Guìzhōu) as your bus trundles up the main drag into the dusty, concrete town. There's not a lot to do here but the streets whir with a colourful mosaic of people, which makes it a fun place to wander for a day or two.

A large market is held here every three or four days. At other times there is a quieter market street in the old, eastern part of town. Evidence of the Hui includes a modern mosque in the northern part of town and several Muslim restaurants nearby.

The town's main draw is **Cǎohǎi Lake** (草海湖; Grass Sea Lake), one of China's premier birdwatching sites and only a 15-minute walk southwest of downtown Wēiníng. This 20 sq km freshwater wetland became a national nature reserve in 1992 and is an important winter site for many migratory birds, the most famous of which is the black-necked crane.

The lake has a fragile history, having been drained during both the Great Leap Forward and the Cultural Revolution with unfulfilled hopes of producing useable farmland. Refilled again in 1980, environmental problems remain and the government is enlisting locals in its attempts to protect the lake.

Trails wrap around the shore, but the best way to see the lake – and the birds – is by 'punts'. Don't worry about finding the boatmen: they'll find you. The best time to visit the lake is from December to March, when the birds are wintering. Bring warm clothes.

The official price for the boats is Y15 per person.

Sleeping & Eating

Cǎohǎi Bīnguǎn (草海宾馆; ☎ 622 1511; s/d/tr Y85/50/60) Close to the lake, this hotel is in a prime location but the rooms can be very cold and damp despite the electric blankets provided.

Diànlì Bīnguǎn (电力宾馆; ☎ 622 5450; dm Y50-60, s/d with bath Y130/110) Not long open, this place has good damp-free rooms. The shared bathrooms aren't great but they might be willing to offer discounts on the doubles.

Jiàngōng Bīnguǎn (建功宾馆; ☎ 622 9306; s Y90-150, d Y120-200) Rooms are musty but the hotel does have central heating, which kicks in each night at 8pm. Turn right out of the bus station and walk straight across the intersection. You will see the hotel on your left.

Cǎohǎi Cāntīng (草海餐厅; dishes from Y5) About 200m east of Cǎohǎi Bīnguǎn, this is a cheap and friendly restaurant.

There are a number of other good places to eat along this road. South of Xinhua Bookshop on the main street are several point and choose restaurants and you'll find a couple of Muslim restaurants near the mosque that serve tasty beef noodles.

Getting There & Away

The easiest way to reach Wēiníng is by bus from Guìyáng (Y65, eight hours, 8.30am).

Leaving Wēiníng you can backtrack to Guìyáng (8.30am daily) or take a bus south to Xiānwēi in Yúnnán (Y30, eight hours, five daily). If you catch the 7.30am bus to Xiānwēi then you'll arrive just in time to catch the last bus to Kūnmíng (Y40, eight hours) at 3.30pm, although it's a lot of travelling to do in one day. From Wēiníng, there is also a sleeper bus to Kūnmíng (Y90, 16 hours, 5.30pm).

Alternatively, take the morning bus to Zhāotōng (Y15, three hours; 7.30am) from where you can hop over to Xīchàng in southern Sìchuān and connect with the Kūnmíng–Chéngdū train line.

XĪNGYÌ 兴义
☎ 0859

Xīngyì is a rather unexciting town in the south of Guìzhōu on the border with Yúnnán. It's mainly a stopover for those travelling between Guìyáng and Nánníng or Kūnmíng and there is little to see in the town itself.

The surrounding countryside, however, is quite impressive and there's some beautiful karst scenery. The main attraction in the area is the 15km-long **Maling Gorge** (马岭河峡谷; Mǎlínghé Xiágǔ), which is well worth a visit if you are travelling down this way. With impressive scenery and fewer tour groups, many travellers find it more interesting than Huangguoshu Falls, and you can spend the better part of a day following the winding path into the lush gorge, across bridges and up to and behind high, cascading waterfalls. It's a good idea to bring waterproof gear, sturdy shoes and a torch (flashlight) to light your way through some of the caves. Buses to the Gorge run every 20 minutes from the east bus station (Y2, 7am to 7pm).

You can also raft on the river at several points; don't expect white-water rapids, this is a slow descent. Both **Xīngyì Outward Bound** (兴义旅游公司; Xīngyì Lǚyóu Gōngsī; ☎ 321 8019; 1 Guichun Lu) and **Mǎlíng Qīngshuǐhé Shēngtài Lǚyóu Gōngsì** (马岭清水河生态旅游公司; Maling Gorge Travel Company; ☎ 221 1488) organises rafting trips down the gorge.

Sleeping & Eating

Pánjiāng Bīnguǎn (盘江宾馆; ☎ 322 3456, ext 8118; 4 Panjiang Xilu; dm Y48, s/d/tr with bath Y106/108/Y98) This is the official tourist hotel and is often full. The rooms are comfortable and the staff friendly.

Shuìwù Bīnguǎn (税务宾馆; ☎ 322 3927; Dongfeng Lu; dm Y15, d with bath Y98) South of the east bus station, this hotel is convenient if you happen to arrive in town late at night. The rooms are decent.

There's a serious lack of restaurants in Xīngyì; try your luck with some of the point-and-choose places near the east bus station.

Getting There & Away

There are two bus stations in Xīngyì. Buses to Guìyáng (Y60-90, six to eight hours) leave every 40 minutes from the east bus station stopping at Huangguoshu Falls (Y40 to Y50) and Ānshùn (Y50) on the way.

From the west bus station a sleeper bus leaves daily at 8pm for Kūnmíng (Y60, nine hours). There are also regular minibuses to Luópíng (Y17.5, two hours, every 30 minutes until 6pm) from where you can change for a bus to Kūnmíng (Y30, four hours, half-hourly until 5pm).

EASTERN GUÌZHŌU

The rich minority areas of southeastern Guìzhōu are surprisingly unexplored by Western travellers. Technically, in the Qiandongnan Miao and Dong Autonomous Prefecture, over 13 different minorities live in the forested hillsides and river valleys of this region. Many of these minorities continue to hold epic weekly markets and annual festivals and retain a unique way of life relatively untouched by China's modernising mania.

It's easy to get out and explore the villages in this area; buses run frequently and you don't have to cover great distances to get anywhere. Particularly recommended are Chóng'ān, a gorgeous riverside Miao

(Hmong) hamlet and Xījiāng, China's largest Miao village with a colourful weekly market. The remote Dong village of Zhàoxīng, in the southeast, is also well worth a visit and can be incorporated into a back-door route into Guǎngxī.

Outside Kǎilǐ, there are no places to change money so bring plenty of cash Renminbi with you.

KǍILǏ 凯里
☎ 0855

About 195km almost directly east of Guìyáng, Kǎilǐ is the centre of the Miao silver culture and the gateway to the surrounding minority villages.

Information

Bank of China (Zhōngguó Yínháng; Zhaoshan Nanlu) Changes cash, travellers cheques and offers cash advance on credit cards. There is also an ATM here. A second branch on Beijing Donglu will also change cash.

China Post (Yóuyú; cnr Zhaoshan Beilu & Beijing Donglu) You can make international phone calls on the 2nd floor.

CITS (Zhōngguó Guójì Lǚxíngshè; ☎ 822 2506; www .cits-kaili.com; 53 Yingpan Donglu; ☷ 9am-5.30pm) One of the best in southwest China. Billy Zhang is particularly helpful and speaks excellent English. This is the place for information on minority villages, festivals and markets. The organised tours aren't cheap (from Y300 per person) but you're assured an excellent guide.

Internet Café (Wǎngbā; cnr Beijing Donglu & Wenhua Beilu; per hr Y3) A second one can be found on Yingpan Donglu.

PSB (Gōngānjú; ☎ 853 6113; 26 Yongle Lu; ☷ 8.30-11.30am & 2.30-5.30pm Mon-Fri) Deals with all passport and visa inquiries.

Sights

There's not much to see or do in Kǎilǐ other than a visit to **Dage Park** (Big Pagoda Park) or **Jinquanhu Park**, which has a Dong minority drum tower built in 1985. There is also a moderately interesting **Minorities Museum** (Zhōu Mínzú Bówùguǎn; Zhaoshan Nanlu; admission Y10; ☷ 9am-5pm), which might be open if somebody turns up to unlock the doors. Don't be deterred by what appears to be a furniture shop on the 1st floor; continue upstairs another flight to the museum.

Kǎilǐ also has a good **Sunday market** that swamps the streets with traders from nearby minority villages.

MARKETS

There are also a huge number of markets held in the villages surrounding Kǎilǐ. Xīnhuá has a huge market every six to seven days. Zhōuxī, Léishān and Táijiāng hold markets every six days.

Festivals & Events

Kǎilǐ and the areas around it host a large number of minority festivals. One of the biggest is **Lusheng Festival**, held all over the southeast in the spring. The *lúshēng* is a reed instrument used by the Miao people. Other important festivals include the **Dragon**

TRADITIONAL GARMENTS

The variety of clothing among the minorities of Guìzhōu provides travellers with a daily visual feast. Clothes are as much a social and ethnic denominator as pure decoration. They also show whether or not a woman is married and are a pointer to a woman's wealth and skills at weaving and embroidery.

Many women in remote areas still weave their own hemp and cotton cloth. Some families, especially in Dong areas, still ferment their own indigo paste as well, and you will also see this for sale in traditional markets. Many women will not attend festivals in the rain for fear that the dyes in their fabrics will run. Methods of producing indigo are greatly treasured and kept secret, but are increasingly threatened by the introduction of artificial chemical dyes.

Embroidery is central to minority costume and is a tradition passed down from mother to daughter. Designs include many important symbols and references to myths and history. Birds, fish and a variety of dragon motifs are popular. The highest quality work is often reserved for baby carriers, and many young girls work on these as they approach marrying age. Older women will often spend hundreds of hours embroidering their own funeral clothes.

Costumes move with the times. In larger towns, Miao women often substitute their embroidered smocks with a good woolly jumper (sweater) and their headdresses look suspiciously like mass-produced pink and yellow Chinese towels.

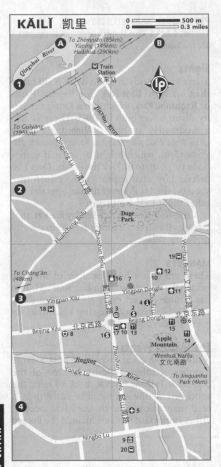

KǍILǏ 凯里

0 ——— 500 m
0 ——— 0.3 miles

Boat Festival, **Hill-leaping Festival** and the **Sharing the Sister's Meal Festival** (equivalent to Valentines Day in the West).

All minority festivals follow the lunar calendar and so dates vary from year to year according to the Roman one. The Miao New Year is celebrated on the first four days of the 10th lunar month in Kǎilǐ, Guàdīng, Zhōuxī and other Miao areas. CITS in Kǎilǐ can provide you with a list of local festivals and their dates.

Sleeping

Shíyóu Bīnguǎn (☎ 823 4331; 44 Yingpan Donglu; dm/d/tr Y20/Y100/69) The rooms here are good value, basic but clean. The shared bathrooms are very public (ie there are no doors).

Guótài Dàjiǔdiàn (☎ 826 9888; fax 826 9818; 6 Beijing Donglu; d Y258-288) This is a good value mid-range option and the fluffy white duvets alone are reason to stay. You can often get good discounts here.

Yíngpánpō Mínzú Bīnguǎn (☎ 823 4600; Yingpan Donglu) This hotel, in a lovely leafy setting opposite the CITS, was closed for renovation when we visited but it's worth checking the new rooms when you're there.

Eating

Kǎilǐ has some fantastic snack stalls lining its streets. Savoury crepes, potato patties, barbecues, tofu grills, noodles, hotpot, *shuǐjiǎo* (Chinese ravioli) and wonton soup overflow for extremely reasonable prices. Check out Beijing Donglu, east of China Post or Zhaoshan Beilu, especially its night market.

There is also a plethora of bakeries throughout town. The one on Beijing Donglu, across from the bank and behind a pedestrian overpass, sells instant hot drinks and cakes in a heated café.

Lǐxiǎngmiàn Shídiàn (Wenhua Nanlu; ⌚ 7.30am-7.30pm) This backpacker-friendly café has an English menu (with pictures!) and serves Chinese dishes along with some creative takes on Western food, including a pizza that'll stick to your ribs (Y2.5).

BUS TIMETABLES

Buses from the Kǎilǐ long-distance bus station:

Destination	Price	Duration	Frequency	Departs
Guìyáng	29	2hr	half-hourly	7.45am-7.15pm
Xijiāng	10	1hr	2 daily	1pm, 2pm
Léishān	9	1hr	half-hourly	7am-6pm
Róngjiāng	35-45	6hr	every 40 min	6.40am-4.40pm
Cóngjiāng	56-61	8hr	5 daily	7am-2pm

Getting There & Away

BUS

Kǎilǐ is served by three bus stations, the long-distance bus station on Wenhua Beilu has departures to most destinations but if you can't find what you're looking for try Wanbo bus station in the south of town near the museum or the local bus station on Yingpan Xilu.

See box above for bus times.

Destinations from the local and Wanbo bus stations include Lángdé (Y7), Chóng'ān (Y9, one hour), Májiāng (Y7), Huángpíng (Y12, 30 minutes), Dúshān (Y40) and Fúquán (Y17). Buses depart from both the local bus station and Wanbo bus station.

TRAIN

Kǎilǐ's train station is a couple of kilometres north of town but departures are infrequent and the train service slow, you're better off getting the bus. There are seven trains a day to Guìyáng (Y25) between 8am and 6.30pm. These take four or more hours.

For longer distances, it's worth stopping in Guìyáng to secure a reservation. Trains to Chóngqìng and to Kūnmíng pass through Kǎilǐ at 4.21am and 8.31pm respectively. You can't get a sleeper reservation in Kǎilǐ so you'll have to pray for intervention from a higher power (the conductor guard). The same advice is valid for east-bound services to Běijīng and Shànghǎi.

Getting Around

Bus fares cost Y0.5 in Kǎilǐ and almost all of the buses departing from the train station follow the same route up Qingjiang Lu, past the long-distance bus station, along Beijing Donglu and down Zhaoshan Nanlu to the museum. To the train station take bus No 2.

Taxis charge a flat rate Y5 for anywhere in the city and Y10 to the train station.

AROUND KǍILǏ

There are some beautiful places to visit in the area and it's easy to spend several weeks village-hopping around Guìzhōu's southeast. Base yourself at any of the following and go explore.

Xijiāng 西江

Hidden in the folds of the Leigong Hills, Xijiāng is thought to be the largest Miao village and is well-known for its embroidery and silver ornaments (the Miao believe that silver can dispel evil spirits). It's a superbly picturesque place, set in a natural basin and bordered by paddy fields, with wooden houses rising up the hillside.

There are also plenty of pleasant walks to be had in the surrounding countryside. For those of you looking for more than an afternoon stroll, there's a three day trek from here to Páiyáng (排羊), a Miao village north of Xijiāng. This trail winds its way through some remote minority villages and lush scenery. You will probably find accommodation with locals en route but you shouldn't expect it so come prepared with sleeping bags, food and camping equipment.

Simple accommodation in Xijiāng can be found at **Yóudiàn Zhāodàisuǒ** (邮电招待所; ☎ 334 8206; dm Y15) near the bus drop-off.

GETTING THERE & AWAY

From Kǎilǐ there are two buses a day to Xijiāng (Y10, one hour) at 1pm and 2pm. Returning to Kǎilǐ there are three buses a day at 6.30am, 7am and 8am. Alternatively, catch a bus to Léishān (Y8, 1½ hours, last bus 5pm) and from there head south towards Róngjiāng.

Chóng'ān 重安

Two hours north of Kǎilǐ by bus, this hamlet's claim to fame is its market, held every five days. Set along the river, Chóng'ān retains its village size and atmosphere as well as many of its wooden homes and buildings and is a charming place to base yourself while you explore the minority villages in the area.

Xiǎojiāngnán Lǚyóu Fàndiàn (小江南旅游 饭店; ☎ 235 1208; dm Y20) This is probably the best hostel you'll find in Guìzhōu. There are two buildings: one on the river and the other set among a fruit garden. Rooms are basic but both places have a lovely laid-back atmosphere and the owners are incredibly friendly. They have a hand-drawn map of the area and can recommend which villages to visit.

GETTING THERE & AWAY

Buses between Shībǐng, Huángpíng and Kǎilǐ all pass through Chóng'ān, which means there's a bus almost every half-hour in either direction. Buses to Kǎilǐ (Y11) run until around 6.30pm.

Lángdé 郎德

Only 20km outside Kǎilǐ this village has started to become a popular stop-off point on tours but don't let that put you off. This picture-postcard place is an excellent example of traditional Miao architecture; two- and three-storey wooden houses built on the hillside out of local cedar, black tiled roofs and surrounded by cobbled pathways. The village itself is 2km from the main road after which you can follow a 15km trail through several Miao villages along the Bala River.

GETTING THERE & AWAY

Buses on the Léishān–Kǎilǐ route run past Lángdé (Y4 to Y5) and it's easy to find a bus going in either direction.

Mátáng 麻塘

This village, 30 kilometres from Kǎilǐ, is home to the Gejia, a group that has been identified by the government as belonging to the Miao minority. The Gejia, who have different customs, dress and language, aren't particularly happy about this classification and nor for that matter, are the Miao. The Gejia are renowned batik artisans and their traditional dress often features batik and embroidery. Their hats (that look at bit like heavily starched napkins) are also made out

of batik. The village is incredibly friendly but be prepared for the army of women selling handicrafts who will pounce on you as soon as you arrive.

GETTING THERE & AWAY

The village is 2km from the main road and buses regularly run past the drop-off point in the direction of Chóng'ān (Y3) and Kǎilǐ (Y5). Just stand on the side of the road and flag down anything that comes your way.

Zhàoxīng 肇兴

Southeast of Kǎilǐ, the road climbs into the hills before finally descending into a subtropical basin. In the very south of this region is Zhàoxīng, a lively, traditional Dong minority village with a remarkable total of five drum towers and 700 households. Zhàoxīng still boasts its traditional wooden structures, including a number of wind and rain bridges and theatre stages. Many of the town's inhabitants continue to wear traditional clothing and speak only their native Dong language.

Wénhuàzhàn Zhāodàisuǒ (文化站招待所; dm Y20) East of the main drum tower, this is your best sleeping option. The hotel also gives tours of Zhàoxīng and the surrounding area for extremely reasonable rates.

Food options are limited in Zhàoxīng. Be sure to check on the meat of the day, as rat meat (*lǎoshǔ ròu*) is common in this area. If you plan to do some day walks, it might be a good idea to bring some snacks along.

GETTING THERE & AWAY

From Kǎilǐ you have to travel first to Cóngjiāng (Y56, eight hours) and change there for a bus to Zhàoxīng (Y15). Direct buses from Cóngjiāng aren't frequent however, so consider getting on a Lípíng bound bus and changing half-way (the bus driver will tell you) for a Dìpíng bus.

Alternatively, if you're looking to stretch your legs, take a Luòxiāng-bound bus from Cóngjiāng (Y12, two hours) and from Luòxiāng, it's a lovely 1½-hour walk along a dirt road to Zhàoxīng, passing through a number of smaller villages en route.

From Zhàoxīng, there is at least one Lípíng–Sānjiāng bus passing through each way. The trip to Sānjiāng, in Guǎngxī, takes about five hours. From there you can catch an onward bus to Guìlín (see p619).

(see p619)

Yúnnán 云南

SOUTHWEST CHINA

HIGHLIGHTS

- Step back through time in the narrow streets of Lìjiāng's **old town** (p669)
- Trek **Tiger Leaping Gorge** (p675), a breathtaking hike amid dramatic cliffs and waterfalls
- Cycle along the shoreline of **Ěrhǎi Hú** (p664), near the laid-back town of Dàlǐ
- Soak up the Southeast Asian atmosphere in tropical **Xīshuāngbǎnnà** (p685)
- Haggle for Burmese jade in the border town of **Ruìlì** (p702)

- POP: 42.1 MIL
- AREA: 394,000 SQ KM
- www.yunnantourism.net

Yúnnán is without doubt one of the most alluring destinations in China. It's the most varied of all of China's provinces, with terrain ranging from tropical rainforest to snow-capped Tibetan peaks. It's also the sixth-largest province and home to a third of all China's ethnic minorities (nearly 50% of the province is non-Han) and over half of all China's plant and animal species. If you can only get to one province in China, this might as well be it.

In the 1960s scientists discovered fragments of human-like teeth dating from 1.75 million to 2.5 million years ago, making 'Yuanmou' man the oldest human remains yet found in China. Yúnnán's other great anthropological discovery was of sophisticated Bronze Age cultures around Diān Chí (Lake Dian).

Important historical sites aside, Yúnnán is also well known for its mild climate year-round – its name means 'South of the Clouds'. The provincial capital, Kūnmíng, is similarly referred to as the 'Spring City'.

Despite the best government efforts, numerous pockets of the province have successfully resisted Chinese influence and exhibit strong local identities. Even Kūnmíng has a flavour all of its own that seems more than half a world away from Běijīng. Despite the rapid economic growth, Kūnmíng retains an individuality that has earned it a reputation for being one of the more cosmopolitan and relaxed cities in the southwest.

Nicknames are affixed to everything in China, and Yúnnán boasts more than its fair share. Since the province contains the nation's highest number of species of flora and fauna – including 2500 varieties of wild flowers and plants – it has been given monikers such as 'Kingdom of Plants (or Animals)', 'Garden of Heavenly Marvellous Flowers', and 'Hometown of Perfume'. Officials are less thrilled with the new tag 'Treasure House of Crude Drugs'.

History

Yúnnán has always been a bit of a renegade province. Throughout history its remote location, harsh terrain and diverse ethnic make-up have made it a difficult province to govern, and for centuries it was considered a backward place inhabited by barbarians.

Qin Shi Huang and the Han emperors held tentative imperial power over the southwest and forged southern Silk Road trade routes to Burma, but by the 7th century the Bai people had established their own powerful kingdom, Nanzhao, south of Dàlǐ. Initially allied with the Chinese against the Tibetans, this kingdom extended its power until, in the middle of the 8th century, it was able to challenge and defeat the Tang armies. It took control of a large slice of the southwest and established itself as a fully independent entity, domi-nating the trade routes from China to India and Burma.

The Nanzhao kingdom fell in the 10th century and was replaced by the kingdom of Dàlǐ, an independent state that lasted until it was overrun by the Mongols in the mid-13th century. After 15 centuries of resistance to northern rule, this part of the southwest was finally integrated into the empire as the province of Yúnnán.

Even so, it remained an isolated frontier region, with scattered Chinese garrisons and settlements in the valleys and basins, a mixed aboriginal population in the highlands, and various Dai (Thai) and other minorities along the Mekong River (Láncāng Jiāng).

During the Republican period, Yúnnán continued to exercise a rebellious streak. When Yuan Shikai tried to abandon the republican government and install himself

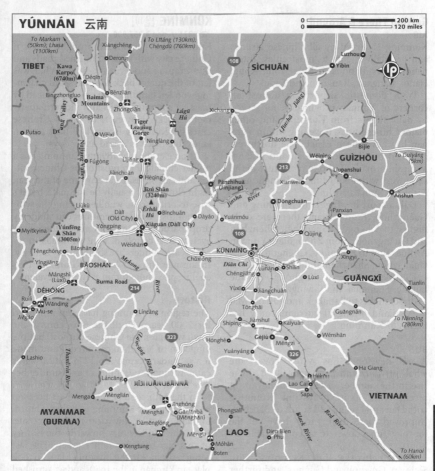

YÚNNÁN 云南

as emperor, military leaders in Yúnnán rebelled. One local military commander even renamed his troops the National Protection Army and marched them into Sìchuān, a stronghold for forces loyal to Yuan. Military forces elsewhere in China turned out in support and Yuan was forced to retreat.

Yúnnán, like the rest of the southwest, has a history of breaking ties with the northern government. During China's countless political purges, fallen officials often found themselves here, adding to the province's character.

Climate
Yúnnán has a climate as diverse as its terrain, with temperate, tropical and frigid zones; from the frozen northwestern region around Déqīn and Zhōngdiàn where winters reach chilling lows of -12°C and summer temperatures peak at highs of 19°C, to the subtropical climate of Jǐnghóng where the summer months soar to 33°C. Dàlǐ has an ideal temperature year-round, with temperatures never dipping below 4°C in the winter months or above 25°C in summer.

Language
In addition to Mandarin, the other major languages spoken in the Yúnnán province belong to the Tibeto-Burman family (eg the Naxi language), and the Sino-Tibetan family (eg the Lisu language).

Getting There & Around

AIR

Kūnmíng is served by all Chinese airlines and has daily flights to most cities. International destinations include Hong Kong, Hanoi, Bangkok, Rangoon and Seoul.

With domestic airports in almost all corners of Yúnnán province being served by daily flights from Kūnmíng and other major Chinese cities, travelling within Yúnnán has never been easier. The northwest is linked by Zhōngdiàn, Dàlǐ and Lìjiāng. Mángshì provides Déhóng prefecture in the southwest with an air link and Jǐnghóng is Xīshuāngbǎnnà's air link.

Dàlǐ airport has flights to Kūnmíng and Guǎngzhōu. From Lìjiāng there are daily flights to Chéngdū, Shànghǎi, Shēnzhèn and Guǎngzhōu. From Zhōngdiàn, Yunnan Airlines flies to Kūnmíng, Chéngdū, Lhasa, Guǎngzhōu, Shēnzhèn and Guìyáng.

Destinations from Jǐnghóng include Lìjiāng, Shànghǎi and Guǎngzhōu, as well as direct flights to Bangkok and Chiang Mai in Thailand. Mángshì currently only has flights to Kūnmíng.

BUS

A well-developed bus system covers the whole province and Yúnnán has seen a huge rise in the number of express highways in recent years. Expressways link Kūnmíng with Dàlǐ and Lìjiāng and south to Bǎoshān. Improved roads to Jǐnghóng have cut the journey time down to a comfortable 11 hours.

Road networks link Kūnmíng with Sìchuān, Guìzhōu and Guǎngxī and further on to Myanmar (Burma), Laos, Vietnam and Thailand.

TRAIN

Most travellers arrive in Yúnnán by train to Kūnmíng. However within the province trains are a less convenient, other than the popular overnight train from the capital to Dàlǐ. Development of the railways has been slower in Yúnnán than elsewhere in China; it was only in 1990 that the train line was extended out west to Dàlǐ, one of Yúnnán's most popular destinations. Railways link Yúnnán to Guìzhōu, Guǎngxī and Sìchuān.

The train line from Kūnmíng to Vietnam has been suspended indefinitely due to landslides.

KŪNMÍNG 昆明

☎ 0871 / pop 3,967,900

Kūnmíng has become a thoroughly modern Chinese city with wide palm-lined roads and sky-scraping modern buildings. What was left of the quaint back alleyways and charming wooden buildings have been replaced by massive shopping malls and modern apartment blocks. However, as far as Chinese cities go, Kūnmíng is very laid-back and an enjoyable place to spend a few days.

At an elevation of 1890m, Kūnmíng has a milder climate than most other Chinese cities, and can be visited at any time of the year. Light clothes will usually be adequate, but it's wise to bring some woollies during the winter months when temperatures can suddenly drop, particularly in the evenings; there have even been a couple of light snowfalls in recent years. Winters are short, sunny and dry. In summer (June to August) Kūnmíng offers cool respite, though rain is more prevalent.

History

The region of Kūnmíng has been inhabited for 2000 years. Until the 8th century, the town was a remote Chinese outpost, but the kingdom of Nanzhao captured it and made it a secondary capital. In 1274 the Mongols came through, sweeping all and sundry before them.

In the 14th century the Ming set up shop in Yúnnánfǔ, as Kūnmíng was then known, building a walled town on the present site. From the 17th century onwards, the history of this city becomes rather grisly. The last Ming resistance to the invading Manchu took place in Yúnnán in the 1650s and was crushed by General Wu Sangui. Wu in turn rebelled against the king and held out until his death in 1678. His successor was overthrown by the Manchu emperor Kangxi and subsequently killed himself in Kūnmíng in 1681.

In the 19th century the city suffered several bloodbaths. The rebel Muslim leader Du Wenxiu, the sultan of Dàlǐ, attacked and besieged the city several times between 1858 and 1868; it was not until 1873 that the rebellion was finally and bloodily crushed.

The intrusion of the West into Kūnmíng began in the middle of the 19th century from British Burma and French Indochina. By 1900 Kūnmíng, Hékǒu, Sīmáo and Měngzì had been opened to foreign trade. The French were keen on exploiting the region's copper, tin and timber resources, and in 1910 their Indochina train, started in 1898 at Hanoi, reached the city.

Kūnmíng's expansion began with WWII, when factories were established and refugees fleeing the Japanese poured in from eastern China. In a bid to keep China from falling to Japan, Anglo-American forces sent supplies to nationalist troops entrenched in Sichuān and Yúnnán. Supplies came overland on a dirt road carved out of the mountains from 1937 to 1938 by 160,000 Chinese with virtually no equipment. This was the famous Burma Rd, a 1000km haul from Lashio to Kūnmíng. Today, Renmin Xilu marks the tail end of the road.

In early 1942 the Japanese captured Lashio, cutting the supply line. Kūnmíng continued to handle most of the incoming aid from 1942 to 1945 when US planes flew the dangerous mission of crossing the 'Hump', the towering 5000m mountain ranges between India and Yúnnán. A black market sprang up and a fair proportion of the medicines, canned food, petrol and other goods intended for the military and relief agencies were siphoned off into other hands.

The face of Kūnmíng has been radically altered since then, with streets widened and office buildings and housing projects flung up. With the coming of the trains, industry has expanded rapidly, and a surprising range of goods and machinery available in China now bears the 'Made in Yúnnán' stamp. The city's produce includes steel, foodstuffs, trucks, machine tools, electrical equipment, textiles, chemicals, building materials and plastics.

Orientation

The jurisdiction of Kūnmíng covers 6200 sq km, encompassing four city districts and four rural counties. The centre of the city is the roundabout at the intersection of Zhengyi Lu and Dongfeng Xilu. East of the intersection is Kūnmíng's major north–south road, Beijing Lu. At the southern end is the main train station and the long-distance bus station.

MAPS

There's a great variety of maps available, some with a smattering of English names. The *Kunming Tourist Map* has street and hotel names in English and shows bus lines,

while the *Yunnan Communications and Tourist Map* has the names of nearly every town in the province – along with bordering countries – written in English.

Information

BOOKSHOPS

Mandarin Books & CDs (West Gate, Yunnan University) Has an excellent selection of Chinese, English and Dutch titles, including guidebooks, novels, magazines and a selection of travel writing.

Xinhua Bookstore (Nanping Jie) Has a decent selection of maps.

EMERGENCY & VISAS

Public Security Bureau (PSB; Gōngānjú; ☎ 571 7001; Jīnxīng Huáyuán, Jinxing Lu; ﾍ 9-11.30am & 1-5pm Mon-Fri) The Foreign Affairs Branch will issue visa extensions. The main entrance is off Erhuan Beilu. Bus Nos 3, 25 and 57 will get you here.

Tourist Complaint & Consultative Telephone (☎ 316 4961)

INTERNET ACCESS

China Telecom (cnr Beijing Lu & Dongfeng Donglu; per hr Y6; ﾍ 8.30am-5.30pm Mon-Fri, 9am-5.30pm Sat & Sun) Most hotels and cafés frequented by travellers also offer email for similar rates; try the Camellia Hotel (p649) and City Café (p650).

MEDICAL SERVICES

Shuanghe Pharmacy (Shuānghè Dàyàofáng; Tuodong Lu; ﾍ 24hr) Opposite Yúnnán Airlines.

Yanan Hospital (Yán'ān Yīyuàn; ☎ 317 7499, ext 311; 1st fl, block 6, Renmin Donglu) Has a foreigners' clinic.

MONEY

Bank of China (Zhōngguó Yínháng; 448 Renmin Donglu; ﾍ 9am-noon & 2-5pm) Changes travellers cheques and foreign currency and offers cash advances on credit cards. There is an ATM here. There are branches at Qingnian Lu, Dongfeng Xilu and Huancheng Nanlu.

POST & TELEPHONE

China Telecom (Zhōngguó Diànxín; cnr Beijing Lu & Dongfeng Donglu) You can make international calls here.

International Post Office (Guójì Yóujú; 231 Beijing Lu); branch office (Dongfeng Donglu) The main office has a very efficient poste restante and parcel service (per letter Y3, ID required). It is also the city's Express Mail Service (EMS) and Western Union agent.

TOURIST INFORMATION

Many of the popular backpacker hotels and some of the cafés can assist with travel

KŪNMÍNG 昆明

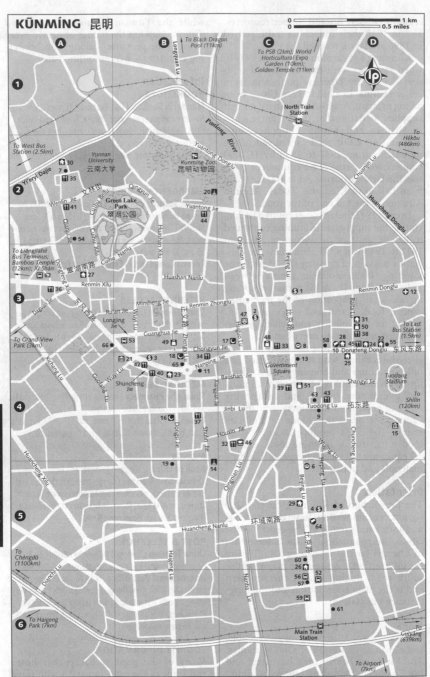

0 _____ 1 km
0 _____ 0.5 miles

To Black Dragon
Pool (11km)

To PSB (2km);
World
Horticultural Expo
Garden (10km);
Golden Temple (11km)

To
Hékǒu
(486km)

North Train
Station

Pánlóng River

To West Bus
Station (2.5km)

Yunnan
University
云南大学

Yi'eryi Dajie

Kunming Zoo
昆明动物园

Yuantong Donglu

Qingyun Jie

Green Lake
Park
翠湖公园

Yuantong Jie

Wenlin Jie

20

Yuantong Jie

44

To Liángjiāhé
Bus Terminus;
Bamboo Temple
(12km); Xī Shān

54

Huashan Xilu

Taoyuan Jie

Qingnian Lu

Beijing Lu

Renmin Donglu

12

Huancheng Donglu

Chuanjin Lu

Renmin Xilu

27

Huashan Nanlu

1

To Grand View
Park (3km)

Minsheng Jie

Renmin Zhonglu

31
50
38

To East
Bus Station
(1.5km)

Dianchi Jie

Ru'an Jie

Longjing
Jie

Guanghua Jie

47

48

58

28

45

22

24

55

Chongyun Jie

17

33

8

10 Dongfeng Donglu 东风东路

Xichang Lu

66

53

49

Zhengyi Lu

18

34

Nanping Jie

13

25

21

3

65

11

Baoshan Jie

Government
Square

Tuodong
Stadium

Wuyi Lu

42

23

40

Shuncheng
Jie

39

51

Shangyi Jie

To
Shílín
(120km)

63

43

Huancheng Xilu

16

37

Jinbi Lu

Tuodong Lu 拓东路

9

Chuncheng Lu

Dongsi Jie

Shizui Lu

Houxin Jie

32

46

15

19

14

Qingnian Lu

Beijing Lu

6

Wujing Lu

To
Chéngdū
(1100km)

Dianchi Lu

Haigeng Lu

Huancheng Nanlu

环城南路

29

4

5

64

60

26

52

56

57

Nanba Lu

59

61

To Haigeng
Park (7km)

Main Train
Station

To
Gùiyáng
(639km)

To Airport
(7km)

SOUTHWEST CHINA

INFORMATION	
Bank of China 中国银行	1 C3
Bank of China 中国银行	2 C3
Bank of China 中国银行	3 B4
Bank of China 中国银行	4 C5
CITS 中国国际旅行社	5 D5
International Post Office	
国际邮局	6 C5
Lao Consulate 老挝领事馆	(see 22)
Mandarin Books & CDs	
五华书苑	7 A2
Myanmar Consulate 缅甸领事馆	(see 22)
Post & Telephone Office 邮电	8 C3
Shuanghe Pharmacy 药店	9 C4
Thai Consulate 泰王国总领事馆	10 D3
Vietnamese Consulate 南领事馆	(see 64)
Xinhua Bookstore 新华书店	11 B4
Yanan Hospital 延安医院	12 D3

SIGHTS & ACTIVITIES	pp647–8
China Southern Airlines	
南航公司	13 C4
East Pagoda 东寺塔	14 B5
Kunming City Museum	
昆明市博物馆	15 D4
Mosque 清真寺	16 B4
Mosque 清真寺	17 C3
Nancheng Mosque	
南城清真古寺	18 B4
West Pagoda 西寺塔	19 B5
Yuantong Temple 圆通寺	20 D2
Yunnan Provincial Museum	
云南省博物馆	21 B4

SLEEPING	p649
Camellia Hotel 茶花宾馆	22 D3
Chúnchéng Jiǔlóu 春城酒楼	23 B4
City Café & Hostel	
厦门陈氏小吃和旅馆	24 D3
Holiday Inn Kunming	
樱花假日酒店	25 D4

King World Hotel 锦华大酒店	26 C5
Kunming Harbour Plaza	
昆明海逸酒店	27 A3
Kunming Hotel 昆明饭店	28 D3
Kūnhú Fàndiàn 昆湖饭店	29 C5
Yúndà Bīnguǎn 云大宾馆	30 A2
Yúnnán Jìxiè Bīnguǎn	
云南机械宾馆	31 D3

EATING	🍴 pp649–50
1910 La Gare Du Sud	
火车南站	32 C4
Brothers Jiang 江氏兄弟	33 C3
Cafe de Camel	
骆驼咖啡宫	(see 43)
Carrefour Supermarket	
家乐福超级市场	34 B4
City Cafe 厦门陈氏小吃	(see 24)
French Café 兰白红	35 A2
Happy Fish 幸福鱼	36 A3
Hump 驼峰酒吧	37 B4
Ma Ma Fu's 2 马马付	38 D3
Mengzi Across-the-Bridge Noodles	
Restaurant 蒙自过桥米线	39 C4
Muslim Restaurants 清真饭店	40 B4
Paul's 堡利	41 A2
Tropic Jungle Juice Shop	
复合热带概念饮品	42 B4
Wei's Pizzeria 哈哈餐厅	43 D4
Yuquanzhai Vegetarian Restaurant	
玉泉斋	44 B2
Zhènxìng Fàndiàn 振兴饭店	45 D3

DRINKING	🍸 p651
Upriver Club 河会馆	46 C4

ENTERTAINMENT	🎭 p651
Kunming Theatre 明剧院	47 C3

SHOPPING	🛍 p651
Climber Outdoors 攀登者	48 C3

Flower & Bird Market 花鸟市场	49 B3
Postar Outdoor & Equipment	
Collection	50 D3
Tian Fu Famous Teas 天福茗茶	51 C4

TRANSPORT	pp651–3
Bus Station 客运站	52 C6
Buses to Bamboo Temple	
往筇竹寺的车	(see 53)
Buses to Xī Shān	
往西山的车	53 B3
CAAC 中国民航	(see 63)
Dragonair 港龙航空	(see 64)
Fat Tyres Bike Shop	54 A2
JAL 日本航空公司	(see 25)
Ko Wai Lin Travel	
珠威霖旅游	(see 22)
Lao Aviation 老挝航空公司	55 D3
Long-Distance Bus Station	
长途汽车总站	56 C6
Sanye International Airline Company	
三叶国际航空服务有限公司	57 C6
Shanghai Airlines	
上海航空公司	58 D3
Singapore Airlines	
新加坡航空公司	(see 25)
Sleeper Bus Stand 铺汽车站	59 C6
Thai Airways 泰国国际航空	60 C5
Train Ticket Office	
火车站售票处	61 D6
Xiǎoxímén Bus Station	
小西门汽车客运站	62 A3
Yunnan Airlines 南航公司	63 C4

OTHER	
Kaīhuá Guǎngchǎng	
佳华广场酒店	64 C5
Kunming Department Store	
昆明百货大楼	65 B4
Mr Chen's Tours 陈先生旅游	(see 55)
Yúnnán Fàndiàn 云南饭店	66 A3

queries. The City Café (p650) and Camellia Hotel (p649) are both very good for booking tickets for your onward journey.

China International Travel Service (CITS; Zhōngguó Guójì Lǚxíngshè; ☎ 356 6730; 285 Huancheng Nanlu) can organise tours but is expensive.

Dangers & Annoyances

Kūnmíng is one of the safest cities in China but take special precaution near the train and long-distance bus stations as there have been reports of travellers having their bags razored in the train station or on Dàlǐ-bound buses.

Sights & Activities

TANG DYNASTY PAGODAS

To the south of Jinbi Lu are two Tang pagodas. **West Pagoda** (Xīsì Tǎ; Dongsi Jie; admission Y2; ⏱ 9am-9pm) is the more interesting. Attached is a compound that is a popular spot for older people to get together, drink tea and play cards and mah jong. You can even get a haircut and a shave at the base of the pagoda.

East Pagoda (Dōngsì Tǎ; Shulin Jie) was, according to Chinese sources, destroyed by an earthquake; Western sources say it was destroyed by the Muslim revolt. It was rebuilt in the 19th century, but there's little to see.

YUANTONG TEMPLE 圆通寺

This **temple** (Yuántōng Sì; Yuantong Jie; admission Y4; ⏱ 8am-5pm) is the largest Buddhist complex in Kūnmíng and a target for pilgrims. It is over 1000 years old and has seen many renovations. To the rear of the temple a new hall has been added, enshrining a **statue of Sakyamuni**, a gift from the king of Thailand. There's a great vegetarian restaurant (p650) across the main road from the temple entrance.

YUNNAN PROVINCIAL MUSEUM
云南省博物馆

This **museum** (Yúnnán Shěng Bówùguǎn; Wuyi Lu; adult/student Y10/5; ⏱ 9.30am-5.30pm) is divided into three sections covering the province's ancient bronze drums, Buddhist art and ethnic minorities. It's generally worth a visit. Bus No 5 goes here from the Camellia Hotel.

SOUTHWEST CHINA

KUNMING CITY MUSEUM 昆明市博物馆
The **museum** (Kūnmíngshì Bówùguǎn; Tuodong Lu; admission free; ☉ 10am-4pm Wed-Sun) focuses on the history of the Diān Chí area. Only one room has English translations, but a few rooms, despite the language barrier, offer interesting looks at the history of Kūnmíng; one room houses a scale model of the city.

GREEN LAKE PARK 翠湖公园
Near the university district this **park** (Cuìhú Gōngyuán; Cuihu Nanlu; admission Y2; ☉ 6am-6pm) is good for a stroll. Sunday sees it at its liveliest, when it hosts an English Corner, colourful paddleboats and hordes of families at play. The lakeside is lined with shops and cafés.

MOSQUES 清真寺
The oldest of the lot, the 400-year-old **Nancheng Mosque** (Nánchéng Qīngzhēn Gǔsì; 51 Zhengyi Lu), was ripped down in 1997 in order to build a larger version. The new mosque looks vaguely like a bad Las Vegas casino. Not too far away is a lively strip of Muslim restaurants and shops selling skullcaps, Arabic calligraphy and pictures of Mecca.

To get to the Muslim area from the Zhengyi Lu roundabout, walk west past Chūnchéng Jiǔlóu (Spring City Hotel) and then bear left a half-block to a small alley.

There's another **mosque** nearby, wedged between Huguo Lu and Chongyun Jie, and another **mosque** on the corner of Jinbi Lu and Dongsi Jie.

Tours
Several tour outfits cover Kūnmíng and its surrounding sights faster than public minibuses would, but you must be prepared to pay for them. They generally feature a lot of sights that most travellers find rather boring. Some tour operators refuse to take foreigners on their tours, claiming the language barrier causes too much trouble. More central sights like Yuantong Temple are just a short bicycle ride away – it hardly makes sense to join a tour to see them.

Mr Chen's Tour (☎ 318 8114; qijia@yahoo.com.cn; Room 3116, No 3 Bldg, Camellia Hotel, 154 Dongfeng Lu) can organise trips to almost anywhere you want to go, including flights and overland trips to Lhasa (see p652 for more details).

For more information about Shílín (Stone Forest), see p656.

YÚNNÁN'S MUSLIMS

Yúnnán's sizeable Muslim population dates back to the 13th century when Mongol forces swooped into the province to outflank the Song dynasty troops. They were followed by Muslim traders, builders and craftsmen. Yúnnán was the only region put under a Muslim leader immediately after Kublai Khan's armies arrived, when Sayyid Ajall was named governor in 1274.

All over China mosques were simultaneously raised with the new Yuan dynasty banner. A Muslim was entrusted to build the first Mongol palace in Běijīng and an observatory based on Persian models was also constructed here. Dozens of Arabic texts were translated and consulted by Chinese scientists, influencing Chinese mathematics more than any other source. The most famous Yúnnán Muslim was Cheng Ho, the famed eunuch admiral who opened up the Chinese sea channels to the Middle East.

Ethnically indistinguishable from the Han Chinese, the Hui, as ethnic Chinese Muslims are known, have had an unfortunate history of repression and persecution, a recent low point being the years of the Cultural Revolution. Heavy land taxes and disputes between Muslims and Han Chinese over local gold and silver mines triggered a Muslim uprising in 1855, which lasted until 1873.

The Muslims chose Dàlǐ (Xiàguān) as their base and laid siege to Kūnmíng, overrunning the city briefly in 1863. Du Wenxiu, the Muslim leader, proclaimed his newly established Kingdom of the Pacified South (Nánpíng Guó) and took the name Sultan Suleyman. But success was short-lived and in 1873 Dàlǐ was taken by Qing forces and Du Wenxiu was captured and executed. Up to a million people died in Yúnnán alone, the death toll rising to 18 million nationwide. The uprisings were quelled, but they also had the lasting effect of eliciting sympathy from Burma and fomenting a passion for culture among many of southwestern China's ethnic minorities, most of whom had supported the Hui.

Sleeping

BUDGET

Camellia Hotel (Cháhuā Bīnguǎn; ☎ 316 3000; fax 314 7033; 154 Dongfeng Donglu; dm Y30, d Y120-260) Long frequented by budget travellers, the Camellia is still a grand bargain. The doubles in the older wing have been spruced up and are a great deal. The hotel has bicycle hire, a foreign-exchange counter, *poste restante*, luggage and valuables storage, a free shuttle bus to the airport and a reasonably priced laundry service. To get here from the main train station, take bus Nos 2 or 23 to Dongfeng Donglu, then change to bus No 5 heading east and get off at the second stop.

City Café & Hostel (Shàmén Chéndī Xiǎochī Hé Lǔguǎn; 78 Dongfeng Donglu; s/d/dm Y40/20/20) This popular café has just opened up a small hostel with excellent-value rooms. There are only a handful of beds and the singles in particular are a steal. It's located just behind the City Café itself.

Yúnnán Jīxiè Bīnguǎn (Yunnan Machinery Hotel; ☎ 312 7606; fax 312 7379; 241 Baita Lu; d Y138-158, q Y150) This new hotel is set within a lovely garden. The rooms are excellent value for money, especially the quads which are enormous. There is also a laundry service, bicycle rental and a free shuttle bus to the airport and train station. Prices include breakfast.

Kūnhú Fàndiàn (☎ 314 3699; 202 Beijing Lu; dm Y25, d with bathroom Y80-120) Near the train and bus stations, the good dorm rooms and clean shared bathrooms here attract a good number of backpackers. Try to get a room at the back of the building so it won't be as noisy. The hotel is two stops from the main train station on bus Nos 2, 23 or 47, though it's easy enough to walk it. Prices include breakfast.

MID-RANGE

Chūnchéng Jiǔlóu (Spring City Hotel; ☎ 362 9586; fax 363 3191; 11-17 Dongfeng Xilu; dm Y54, d with bathroom Y98-128, tr with bathroom Y142-184) This is a good option. The dorms are bright and their shared bathrooms incredibly clean. Doubles might feel a bit small but they're still good value.

Yúndà Bīnguǎn (Yunnan University Hotel; ☎ 503 3624; fax 514 8513; d Y150-288) If you want to stay in the university area then the standard doubles here are a good choice. It's next to the university's west gate.

TOP END

Kunming Hotel (Kūnmíng Fàndiàn; ☎ 316 2063; www .kunminghotel.com.cn; 52 Dongfeng Donglu; d Y752) With a bar, disco, karaoke hall, tennis court and even a bowling alley on-site you may never want to leave. There are also several high-end restaurants, including Korean and Cháozhōu (the coastal region in eastern Guǎngdōng; light, tasty cuisine with an abundant use of vegetables) that enjoy good reputations.

Holiday Inn Kunming (Yìnghuā Jiàrì Jiǔdiàn; ☎ 316 5888; fax 313 5189; 25 Dongfeng Donglu; d incl breakfast Y1000 plus 15% tax) This super-luxury monster is opposite the Kunming Hotel. It has some excellent restaurants (Thai and southwestern American/Mexican, along with a popular breakfast/lunch buffet), a Western-style pub, a small health club and pool, and a disco.

Kunming Harbour Plaza (Hǎiyì Jiǔdiàn; ☎ 538 6688; www.harbour-plaza.com/hpkm; 20 Honghua Qiao; d Y1000 plus 15% tax) Part of the popular Hong Kong chain, this hotel provides reliable top-end service and rooms.

King World Hotel (Jīnhuá Dàjiǔdiàn; ☎ 6326 4000; 68 Beijing Lu; d incl breakfast Y464-1024) This luxury hotel features an expensive revolving restaurant (the highest above sea level in China, the hotel proudly points out) on the top floor and a complimentary shuttle between the airport and the hotel. Good discounts can often be had here.

Eating

Kūnmíng has some great food, especially in the snack line. Regional specialities are *qìguōjī* (herb-infused chicken cooked in an earthenware steam pot), *xuānwēi huǒtuǐ* (Yúnnán ham), *guòqiáo mixiàn* (across-the-bridge noodles), *rǔbǐng* (goat's cheese) and various Muslim beef and mutton dishes.

Gourmets with money to burn may perhaps be interested in a whole banquet based on Jizhong fungi (mushrooms) or 30 courses of cold mutton, not to mention fried grasshoppers.

Yúnnán's best-known dish is across-the-bridge noodles. You are provided with a bowl of very hot soup (stewed with chicken, duck and spare ribs) on which a thin layer of oil is floating, along with a side dish of raw pork slivers (in classier places this might be chicken or fish) and vegetables, and a bowl of rice noodles. Diners place all of the ingredients quickly into the soup bowl, where they are cooked by the steamy broth.

CHINESE

Happy Fish (Xìngfúyú; ⏲ 10.30am-10.30pm; dishes Y12-19) This is a fantastic self-service Yunnanese fast-food canteen, in a shopping centre just off Renmin Xilu. There is a huge range of food – from spring rolls and hotpot to fried shrimp and pigs trotters – and you can fill up your plate as many times as you like. The evening buffet price includes beer (as much as you can drink) and sees a big student crowd.

1910 La Gare Du Sud (Huǒchē Nánzhàn; ⏲ 316 9486; dishes from Y20) At the other end of the scale is this classy restaurant serving Yúnnán specialities in a pleasant neocolonial-style atmosphere. There's an English menu if you ask for it. It's hidden down an alley next to the Upriver Club, south of Jinbi Lu.

Mengzi Across-the-Bridge Noodles Restaurant (Méngzì Guòqiáo Mǐxiàn; Beijing Lu; noodles Y5-20) For Kūnmíng's favourite noodles, try this popular place that serves up some of the best in town.

Brothers Jiang (Jiāngshì Kèdì; Dongfeng Donglu; noodles Y5-20) This place has good across-the-bridge noodles that come with instructions on how to eat them. There are several branches throughout the city, all popular at lunchtime. Pay up-front first at the cash register.

Zhènxīng Fàndiàn (Yunnan Typical Local Food Restaurant; cnr Baita Lu & Dongfeng Donglu; ⏲ 24hr; dishes from Y5) You'll find a good range of dishes and snacks at this restaurant and it gets decent reviews from both locals and foreigners.

SELF-CATERING

Paul's (Bǎolì Shāngdiàn; ☎ 535 4210; Wenlin Jie) Specialises in Western gourmet and hard-to-find imports. It's located near the west gate of the university.

Carrefour (Jiālèfú; Dongfeng Xilu) This is a branch of the popular French supermarket chain.

SNACKS

In the vicinity of the long-distance bus station and in many of the side streets running off Beijing Lu are roadside noodle shops. Generally you get a bowl of rice noodles for around Y4 and a bewildering array of sauces with which to flavour the broth – most of them are hot and spicy.

Another place to go snack hunting is Shuncheng Jie, an east–west street running south of Dongfeng Xilu. Here you'll find literally dozens of Muslim restaurants, kebab stalls and noodle stands. Try *bānmiàn* (a kind of spaghetti) or Uighur *suoman* (fried noodle squares with peppers, tomato and cumin).

VEGETARIAN

Apart from the temples in and around town, most of the restaurants near Kūnhú Fàndiàn and the Camellia Hotel that cater to Westerners also have veggie selections.

Yuquanzhai Vegetarian Restaurant (Yùquánzhāi Cāntīng; Yuantong Jie; dishes from Y10) This outstanding vegetarian restaurant takes the practice of 'copying' meat-based dishes to a new level, with an encyclopaedic menu. The *tiěbǎn* (sizzling iron-pot) comes recommended. It's across the road from Yuantong Temple.

WESTERN

Literally dozens of friendly Western-style cafés can be found near the Camellia Hotel and Kūnhú Fàndiàn and the area surrounding Yunnan University, in particular Wenlin Jie.

Ma Ma Fu's 2 (Māmāfù Cāntīng; Baita Lu; dishes from Y5, pizzas from Y15) This legendary Lìjiāng café opened up around the corner east of the Camellia Hotel and is now run by the original Mama and Papa; it's still got the same freshly baked breads and mouth-watering apple pie.

City Café (Chéngshì Xiǎochī; 78 Dongfeng Donglu; dishes Y6-25) This place sees folk coming back night after night. Not only is the food very good but the staff are incredibly friendly. The menu has both Western and Chinese dishes, with a few Fújiàn specialities such as fishball soup (the owners are from Xiàmén).

Wei's Pizzeria (☎ 316 6189; Tuodong Lu; pizzas from Y25) If it's pizza you're after then you'll find the best wood-fired pizzas this side of Italy here. The menu also features very good Chinese dishes such as *qìguōjī* (medicinal-herb chicken in a pot). The restaurant is down an alley off Tuodong Lu.

French Café (Lán Bái Hóng; ☎ 538 2391; off Wenlin Jie; dishes from Y10) Especially popular with students, this place serves up sandwiches and salads and a decent selection of teas and coffees. There's a handy noticeboard useful for finding teaching jobs, language exchange partners or just the best place to go drinking.

Drinking

Any of the Western-style restaurants and cafés following double as drinking dens.

Upriver Club (Shànghé Huìguǎn; teas from Y20) This is a unique coffee/teashop-cum-art gallery hidden down an alley off Houxin Jie, south of Jinbi Lu. It's got a pleasant outdoor area and both permanent art displays and visiting exhibits.

Café de Camel (Tuodong Lu; 9am-late) A popular place with locals and foreigners, this restaurant/coffee shop/bar sees the tables moved to one side at the weekends and a DJ playing tunes until the early hours.

Tropic Jungle Juice Shop (Xiàhéshì Yǐnpǐn Gàiniàndiàn; Dongfeng Xilu) Serves up a huge range of freshly squeezed juices and shakes.

Hump (Tuófēng Kèzhàn; ☎ 364 4638, 364 4197; Jinbi Lu) Although not as popular as it used to be, this place still pulls in a good crowd at the weekend with regular drink specials and low-priced domestic beer.

Entertainment

The Song and Dance Ensemble of Yúnnán perform daily at the **Kunming Theatre** (Kūnmíng Jùyuàn; Qingnian Lu; tickets Y50-90; performance 8-9.40pm).

Shopping

You have to do a fair bit of digging to come up with inspiring purchases in Kūnmíng. Yúnnán specialities are marble and batik from Dàlǐ, jade from Ruìlì, minority embroidery, musical instruments and spotted-brass utensils.

Some functional items make good souvenirs: large bamboo water pipes for smoking angel-haired Yúnnán tobacco and local herbal medicines such as Yúnnán Báiyào (Yunnan White Medicine), which is a blend of over 100 herbs and is highly prized by Chinese throughout the world.

Yunnanese tea is also an excellent buy and comes in several varieties, from bowl-shaped bricks of smoked green tea called *tuóchá*, which have been around since at least Marco Polo's time, to leafy black tea that rivals some of India's best.

One teashop worth checking out is **Tian Fu Famous Teas** (Tiānfù Míngchá; cnr Shangyi Jie & Beijing Lu).

The **Flower & Bird Market** (Huāniǎo Shìchǎng; Tongdao Jie) seems to sell everything except flowers and birds, instead you'll find old coins and wooden elephants, tacky wall murals and so-called 'antiques'.

For real antiques it's better to look among the privately run shops on Beijing Lu and Dongfeng Donglu. Outside the Camellia Hotel you will probably be ambushed by women flogging their handiwork – bargain if you want a sane price.

For outdoor wear try **Climber Outdoors** (Pāndēngzhe Hùwài Luǎnxíng Yòngpǐn; ☎ 313 2783; 20 Dongfeng Donglu) or **Postar Outdoor & Equipment Collection** (Jíxīng; Baita Lu). Both stock outdoor clothing and equipment.

Getting There & Away

AIR

Yunnan Airlines/CAAC (☎ 316 4270, 313 8562; Tuodong Lu; 24hr) issues tickets for any Chinese airline but the office only offers discounts on Yunnan Airlines flights. Only the small ticket window on the left side of the building is open 8pm to 8am.

A good one-stop shop for booking flights is the **Sanye International Air Service** (Sānyè Guójì Hángkōng Fúwù Yǒuxiàn Gōngsī; ☎ 353 0773; fax 354 3370; 66-68 Beijing Lu), next door to the long-distance bus station. The office deals with more than 20 international carriers and all the national ones.

Other airline offices in Kūnmíng are **China Southern Airlines** (☎ 310 1831; 433 Beijing Lu) and **Shanghai Airlines** (☎ 313 8502; 46 Dongfeng Donglu).

Flights are scheduled to depart daily from Kūnmíng for Běijīng (Y1810), Chéngdū (Y700), Chóngqìng (Y710), Guǎngzhōu (Y1260), Guìyáng (Y440), Nánjīng (Y1750), Nánníng (Y580), Shànghǎi (Y1900) and Shēnzhèn (Y1240).

Flights to Qīngdǎo (Y1810) leave every day except Thursday and Saturday. Flights to Xī'ān (Y1050) leave four times a week. There is now a weekly flight to Lhasa (Y1960).

Within Yúnnán province you can fly to Bǎoshān (Y550), Jǐnghóng (Y650), Lìjiāng (Y530), Mángshì/Déhóng (Y660), Xiàguān/Dàlǐ (Y430) and Zhōngdiàn (Y700).

Several carriers have flights to Hong Kong (Y1870, daily), Hanoi (Y2230), Bangkok (Y1508), Chiang Mai (Y1344), Rangoon (Y1630), Mandalay (Y1450) and Seoul (Y5180).

Foreign airline offices in Kūnmíng include the following:

Dragonair (☎ 356 1208, 356 1209; 2/F Kaīhuá Guǎngchǎng; 157 Beijing Lu)

JAL (☎ 316 1230; Room 633, Holiday Inn Kunming, 25 Dongfeng Donglu)
Lao Aviation (Camellia Hotel, 154 Dongfeng Donglu)
Singapore Airlines (☎ 313 2334; Holiday Inn Kunming, 25 Dongfeng Donglu)
Thai Airways International (☎ 351 1515; 68 Beijing Lu) Next to the King World Hotel.

BUS
There seem to be buses leaving from everywhere in Kūnmíng and bus transport can be a little confusing at first. However, the long-distance bus station on Beijing Lu is the best place to organise bus tickets to almost anywhere in Yúnnán or further afield. Exceptions to this are more local destinations like Diān Chí; see Around Kūnmíng opposite for more details on transport to individual attractions close to the city.

See box below for bus details.

From the sleeper bus stand closer to the train station you can get sleeper buses to most of the same destinations. Buses here tend to be a bit older and so ticket prices are generally a bit cheaper.

For information on Shílín, see p657.

TRAIN
You can buy train tickets up to 10 days in advance, which is good news because at peak times, especially public holidays, tickets get sold out days ahead of departure.

At the time of writing, the train to Hekou in Vietnam had been suspended indefinitely due to landslides so you'll have to get the bus instead.

Rail options from Kūnmíng (all prices listed are for hard sleepers) include trains to Běijīng (Y578), Shànghǎi (Y519), Guìyáng (Y162), Guǎngzhōu (Y353), Xī'ān (Y258), Emei Town (Y209), Chéngdū (Y222) and Liùpánshuǐ (Y96). Several overnight trains run daily to Dàlǐ (Y95). Check at the train ticket office for times.

TO TIBET
It's now possible to fly to Lhasa from Kūnmíng. However, the situation is the same as in Chéngdū and you must have the requisite permit and travel as part of a group. Mr Chen's Tour (p648) can sort you out with the necessary permits and sign you onto a 'tour' with a bunch of people you'll never see again once you've landed in Lhasa. At the time of writing these packages cost around Y2500.

There are also flights from Zhōngdiàn to Lhasa and it's recently become possible to travel overland from Zhōngdiàn into Tibet (see p683). From Chéngdū Mr Chen can also organise overland travel to Tibet, although some travellers have reported his sales pitch to be better than his trips.

Getting Around
TO/FROM THE AIRPORT
Bus Nos 52 and 67 run between the centre of town and the airport. A taxi costs Y15 to Y20.

KŪNMÍNG BUS TIMETABLES
Some main bus services and fares from Kūnmíng:

Destination	Price	Duration	Frequency	Departs
Dàlǐ	Y104	5hr	frequent	8am-7pm
Dàlǐ (sleeper)	Y81	10hr	2 daily	9pm, 9.30pm
Lìjiāng	Y152	9hr	hourly	7.30-11.30am
Lìjiāng (sleeper)	Y119	10-12hr	2 daily	8pm, 8.30pm
Jǐnghóng	Y150-170	10hr	4 daily	9.30am, 6pm, 7.45pm, 8.30pm
Jǐnghóng (sleeper)	Y175	10hr	half-hourly	4-8pm
Zhōngdiàn	Y142-161	13-15hr	1-3 daily	8am, 4.30pm, 6pm
Zhōngdiàn (sleeper)	Y145-175	13-15hr	every 30min	4pm-8.30pm
Bǎoshān	Y132-152	7hr	4 daily	
Bǎoshān (sleeper)	Y118	12hr	2 daily	7.30pm, 8.30pm
Ruìlì	Y181	13hr	2 daily	10am, 6pm
Ruìlì (sleeper)	Y148	15hr	daily	8pm
Hékǒu	Y112	12hr	2 daily	9.45am, 1.30pm

BICYCLE

The Camellia Hotel and City Café carry a decent selection of bikes for hire (Y10 per day, deposit Y100).

Fat Tyres Bike Shop (☎ 530 1755; 61 Qianju Jie; per day Y20) has a large stock of bicycles including some very good mountain bikes. It also organises Sunday morning bike rides – you need to make reservations ahead of time.

BUS

Bus No 63 runs from the east bus station to the Camellia Hotel and on to the main train station. Bus No 23 runs from the north train station south down Beijing Lu to the main train station. Fares range from Y1 to Y4. The main city buses have no conductors and require exact change.

AROUND KŪNMÍNG

Most of the major sights are within a 15km radius of Kūnmíng. Local transport to these places is awkward, crowded and time-consuming; it tends to be an out-and-back job, with few crossovers for combined touring. If you wish to take in everything, it would take something like five return trips, which would consume three days or more.

The trips of main interest are Bamboo Temple (Qióngzhú Sì) and Xī Shān (Western Hills), both of which have decent transport connections. Diān Chí (Lake Dian) presents some engrossing circular-tour possibilities of its own. If you have more time, get your hands on a good map, hire a good bicycle and tour the area on two wheels (although there are some steep hills lurking out there…).

Bamboo Temple 筇竹寺

Twelve kilometres northwest of Kūnmíng, this **temple** (Qióngzhú Sì; admission Y4) dates back to the Tang dynasty. Burned down and rebuilt in the 15th century, it was restored from 1883 to 1890 when the abbot employed master Sichuanese sculptor Li Guangxiu and his apprentices to fashion 500 *luóhàn* (arhats or noble ones). These life-size clay figures are stunning – either very realistic or very surrealistic – a sculptural *tour de force*. Down one huge wall come some 70-odd incredible surfing Buddhas, riding the waves on a variety of mounts – blue dogs, giant crabs, shrimp, turtles and unicorns.

The statues have been constructed with the precision of a split-second photograph –

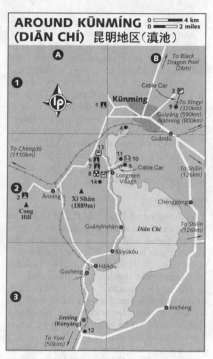

AROUND KŪNMÍNG (DIĀN CHÍ) 昆明地区（滇池）

SIGHTS & ACTIVITIES	pp653–6
Bamboo Temple 筇竹寺	1 A1
Cáoxi Si 曹溪寺	2 A2
Golden Temple 金殿	3 B1
Grand View Park 大观公园	4 B1
Haigenq Park 海埂公园	5 B2
Huating Temple 华亭寺	6 A2
Sānqīng Gé 三清阁	(see 8)
Taihua Temple 太华寺	7 A2
Tomb of Nie Er 聂耳墓	8 A2
World Horticultural Expo Garden 世界园艺博览园	9 B1
Yunnan Nationalities Museum 云南民族博物馆	10 B2
Yunnan Nationalities Village 云南民族村	11 B2
Zhenghe Park 郑和公园	12 A3

TRANSPORT	p655
Gāoyào Bus Station 高峣汽车	13 A2

OTHER	
Dragon Gate 龙门	14 A2

a monk about to chomp into a large peach (the face contorted almost into a scream), a figure caught turning around to emphasise a discussion point, another about to clap two cymbals together, yet another cursing a pet monster. So lifelike are the sculptures that they were considered in bad taste by Li Guangxiu's contemporaries (some of whom no doubt appeared in caricature),

SOUTHWEST CHINA

and upon the project's completion he disappeared into thin air.

Unfortunately you have to make do with peering your head round the door as the hall has been closed to visitors to stop local tourists throwing coins at the statues – an act that is thought to bring them good luck (it obviously didn't work). If the temple is quiet when you visit, then friendly monks might be persuaded to let you in for a peek inside.

Minibuses (one way/return Y10/20, 30 minutes) leave when full from opposite the Yúnnán Fàndiàn from 7am. Minibuses return regularly to Kūnmíng.

Diān Chí 滇池

The shoreline of Diān Chí (Lake Dian), to the south of Kūnmíng, is dotted with settlements, farms and fishing enterprises; the western side is hilly, while the eastern side is flat country. The southern end of the lake, particularly the southeast, is industrial.

The lake is elongated – about 40km from north to south – and covers an area of 300 sq km. Plying the waters are *fānchuán* (pirate-sized junks with bamboo-battened canvas sails). It's mainly for scenic touring and hiking, and there are some fabulous aerial views from the ridges at Dragon Gate in Xī Shān; see right).

Grand View Park 大观公园

This **park** (Dàguān Gōngyuán; admission Y5) is at the northernmost tip of Diān Chí, 3km southwest of the city centre. It covers 60 hectares and includes a nursery, a children's playground, rowboats and pavilions. A Buddhist temple was originally constructed here in 1862. The **Grand View Tower** (Dàguān Lóu) provides good views. Its façades are inscribed with a 180-character poem by Qing poet Sun Ranweng, rapturously extolling the beauty of the lake.

Bus No 4 runs to the park from Yuantong Temple via the city centre; bus No 52 departs from near the Kunming Hotel. At the northeastern end of the park is a dock where you may be able to get a boat (Y5, 40 minutes) to Longmen Village (Lóngmén Cūn) and Haigeng Park (Hǎigěng Gōngyuán). From Longmen Village you can hike up the trail to Dragon Gate and Xī Shān, and catch a minibus back into town from near the summit at the Tomb of Nie Er. From Haigeng Park, take bus No 44 to Kūnmíng's main train station.

Xī Shān 西山

This range, known as Xī Shān (Western Hills), spreads out across a long wedge of parkland on the western side of Diān Chí. Its hills are also called the 'Sleeping Beauty Hills', a reference to the undulating contours, which are thought to resemble a reclining woman with tresses of hair flowing into the sea. The path up to the summit passes a series of famous temples – it's a steep approach from the north side. The hike from Gāoyáo bus station, at the foot of the hills, to Dragon Gate takes 2½ hours, though most people take a connecting bus from Gāoyáo to the top section, or take a minibus direct to the Tomb of Nie Er. Alternatively, it is also possible to cycle to the hills from the city centre in about an hour – to vary the trip, consider doing the return route across the dikes of upper Diān Chí.

At the foot of the climb, about 15km from Kūnmíng, is **Huating Temple** (Huátíng Sì; admission Y4), a country temple of the Nanzhao kingdom believed to have been constructed in the 11th century, rebuilt in the 14th century, and extended in the Ming and Qing dynasties.

The road from Huating Temple winds 2km from here up to the Ming dynasty **Taihua Temple** (Tàihuá Sì; admission Y3). The temple courtyard houses a fine collection of flowering trees, including magnolias and camellias.

Further along the road, near the minibus and cable car terminus, is the **Tomb of Nie Er** (Nièěr Zhīmù; admission Y1). Nie Er (1912–36) was a talented Yúnnán musician who composed the national anthem of the People's Republic of China (PRC) before drowning in Japan en route for further training in the Soviet Union.

Sānqing Gé, near the top of the mountain, was a country villa of a Yuan dynasty prince, and was later turned into a temple dedicated to the three main Taoist deities.

From the tomb you can catch a **chairlift** (one way/return Y15/30) if you want to skip the fairly steep ascent to the summit. Alternatively a tourist tram takes passengers up to the Dragon Gate for Y2. You can also catch a **cable car** (one way/return Y30/50) from here down to Haigeng Park and the Yunnan Nationalities Village.

Further up, near the top of the mountain, is **Dragon Gate** (Lóng Mén; admission Y20). This is a group of grottoes, sculptures, corridors and pavilions that were hacked from the cliff between 1781 and 1835 by a Taoist monk and co-workers, who must have been hanging up there by their fingertips. At least that's what the locals do when they visit, seeking out the most precarious perches for views of Diān Chí. The tunnel along the outer cliff edge is so narrow that only one or two people can squeeze by at a time, so avoid public holidays and weekends! Entrance to the Dragon Gate area includes Sānqīng Gé. It's possible to walk up to the Dragon Gate along the cliff path and return via the back routes.

GETTING THERE & AWAY

Minibuses (one way/return Y10/20, one hour, 7.30am to 2pm) leave when full from opposite the Yúnnán Fàndiàn. The only trouble is you could be waiting for ages for the bus to fill up.

It's more reliable to use local buses: take bus No 5 from the Kunming Hotel to the terminus at Liǎngjiāhé, and then change to bus No 6, which will take you to Gāoyáo bus station at the foot of the hills. Minibuses (Y5) also leave from Liǎngjiāhé and drop passengers off at the Tomb of Nie Er.

To return to Kūnmíng take the bus or scramble down from the Dragon Gate area to the lakeside. Steps lead downhill a couple of hundred metres before Dragon Gate and the Sānqīng Gé area ticket office and end up in Longmen Village (Lóngmén Cūn), also known as Sānyì Cūn. When you reach the road, turn right and walk about 100m to a narrow spit of land leading across the lake. Continuing across the spit, you arrive at a narrow stretch of water and a small bridge. (You could also take the cable car across to Haigeng Park for Y30.) Walk through Haigeng Park's far entrance and catch bus No 44 to Kūnmíng's main train station. If you don't want to pay Y6 to cut through Haigeng Park, you'll have to walk 3km or so from the cable car to the entrance of the Yunnan Nationalities Village or take a taxi (Y10).

Alternatively, bus No 33 runs along the western lake shore through Longmen Village, or you can take a boat from Grand View Park.

Yunnan Nationalities Museum
云南民族博物馆

On the northeastern side of the lake, the **Yunnan Nationalities Museum** (Yúnnán Mínzú Bówùguǎn; adult/student Y10/4; ☺ 9am-4.30pm Tue-Sun) is worth a visit if you have an interest in China's minority nationalities. The museum doesn't see many visitors which is a shame because the exhibitions are really quite good. The eight halls display costumes, folk art, jewellery, handicrafts and musical instruments, as well as information concerning social structure and popular festivals on each of Yúnnán's 25 minority groups.

The museum has a couple of shops that sell some of the best examples of minority clothing that you'll find in southwestern China, though the prices are relatively high.

Yunnan Nationalities Village
云南民族村

Opposite the museum the local tourist authorities have cobbled together a string of mini-villages to form the **Yunnan Nationalities Village** (Yúnnán Mínzúcūn; adult/student Y70/35) that is supposed to represent all of Yúnnán's minorities. There are various song-and-dance performances throughout the day and guides dressed in traditional garb lead large groups around.

If you're at all averse to tourist-board fabrications of ethnic cultures, give the place a miss and spend an extra day in Xīshuāngbǎnnà or Déhóng, where you can see the real thing.

Bus No 44 runs to Haigeng Lu from one street north of the main train station.

Golden Temple 金殿

Hidden amid a pine forest on Phoenix Song Mountain is **Golden Temple** (Jīn Diàn; admission Y15), a Taoist temple that was the brainchild of General Wu Sangui. Wu was dispatched by the Manchus in 1659 to quell uprisings in the region but instead turned on the Manchus and set himself up as a rebel warlord, with the Golden Temple as his summer residence. The current structure dates back to 1671; the original Ming temple stood in the same spot but was carted off to Dàlǐ.

Bus Nos 10 or 71 run here from Kūnmíng's north train station or you can cycle. A cable car (Y15) runs from the temple to the World Horticultural Expo Garden.

World Horticultural Expo Garden
世界园艺博览园

This 218-hectare **garden complex** (Shìjiè Yuányì Bólǎnyuán; ☎ 501 2367; adult/student Y100/50; ☺ 8am-5pm, last entry at 4pm), about 10km northeast of

Kūnmíng near the Golden Temple, was built in April 1999 for the World Horticultural Exposition. The gardens are a mix of pleasant Disney-style topiary work and strangely pointless exhibits left over from the expo; the place is worth a visit if you are interested in gardens and plants, otherwise give it a miss.

Take bus No 10 to the terminal. A cable car (Y15) at the back of the gardens can take you to the Golden Temple.

Black Dragon Pool 黑龙潭

This is a rather mediocre **garden** (Hēilóng Tán; admission Y1), 11km north of Kūnmíng, with old cypresses, dull Taoist pavilions and no bubble in the springs. But the view of the surrounding mountains from the garden is inspiring. Within walking distance is the **Kunming Botanical Institute**, where the flora collection might be of interest to specialists.

Take bus No 9 from Kūnmíng's north train station.

Chénggòng County 呈贡县

This county (Chénggòng Xiàn) is an orchard region on the eastern side of Diān Chí. Flowers bloom year-round, with the 'flower tide' in January, February and March. This is the best time to visit, especially the diminutive Dòunán village nearby. Once one of Yúnnán's poorest villages, it now sells more than 400,000 sprays of flowers each day. The village's per capita income went from US$13 to US$415 in four years.

Many Western varieties of camellia, azalea, orchid and magnolia derive from southwestern Chinese varieties. They were introduced to the West by adventuring botanists who carted off samples in the 19th and 20th centuries. Azaleas are native to China – of the 800 varieties in the world, 650 are found in Yúnnán.

During the **Spring Festival** (January/February) a profusion of blooms can be found at temple sites in and around Kūnmíng – notably the temples of Tàihuá, Huátíng, Yuántōng and the Golden Temple, as well as at Black Dragon Pool.

Take bus No 5 heading east to the terminus at Júhuācūn, and change there for bus No 12 to Chénggòng.

Zhenghe Park 郑和公园

At the southwest corner of Diān Chí, this park (Zhènghé Gōngyuán) commemorates the Ming dynasty navigator Zheng He (known as Admiral Cheng Ho outside China). A mausoleum here holds tablets with descriptions of his life and works. Zheng He, a Muslim, made seven voyages to more than 30 Asian and African countries in the 15th century in command of a huge imperial fleet.

From Xiaoximen bus station take the bus to Jìnníng; the park is on a hill overlooking the town.

SHÍLÍN 石林
☎ 0871

Located around 120km southeast of Kūnmíng, **Shílín** (Stone Forest; ☎ 771 0316; adult/student Y80/55), is a massive collection of grey limestone pillars, the tallest 30m high, split and eroded by wind and rain water into their present fanciful forms. Marine fossils found in the area suggest that it was once under the sea. Legend has it that the immortals smashed a mountain into a labyrinth for lovers seeking privacy.

The maze of grey pinnacles and peaks, with the odd pond, is treated as an oversized rockery, with a walkway here, a pavilion there, some railings along paths and, if you look closely, some mind-bending weeds.

Most travellers find Shílín somewhat overrated on the scale of geographical wonders. The important thing if you venture here is to get away from the main tourist area – there are some idyllic, secluded walks within 2km of the centre and by moonlight it's otherworldly.

The villages in the Lùnán County vicinity are inhabited by the Sani branch of the Yi tribespeople. Considering that so many other ethnically interesting areas of Yúnnán are now open, you could be disappointed if you make the trip just to see the tribes people who live in this area. Sani women act as tour guides for groups. English-speaking guides cost Y80 for a 2½-hour tour.

There are actually several 'stone forests' in the region. About 8km northeast is the larger 300-hectare **Naigu Stone Forest** (Nǎigǔ Shílín Fēngjǐngqū; admission Y50), with karst caves, a large waterfall and an impressive causeway of black, volcanic blocks. The easiest way to get here is to take a microbus from Shílín (Y15).

Shílín can easily be done as a day trip from Kūnmíng. However if you decide to

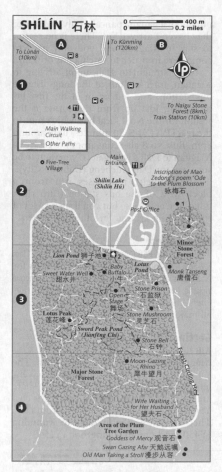

SHÍLÍN 石林

| 0 | 400 m |
| 0 | 0.2 miles |

drop you off, this new hostel offers the cleanest, best-value accommodation you will find in Shílín.

Shílín Bìshǔyuán Bīnguǎn (☎ 771 1088; d/tr Y300/360, discounted Y240/288) If you're looking to splash out then the rooms here are quiet and have some good views over Shílín, but you still don't get a lot for your money.

Several restaurants next to the bus stop specialise in duck, roasted in extremely hot clay ovens with pine needles. A whole duck costs Y40 to Y50 and takes about 20 minutes to cook – have the restaurant staff put a beer in their freezer and it'll be just right when the duck comes out.

Near the main entrance is a cluster of restaurants and snack bars that are open from dawn to dusk. Check all prices before you order, as overcharging is not uncommon.

Entertainment

Sani song-and-dance evenings are organised when there are enough tourists. Shows normally start at around 8pm at a stage next to the minor stone forest but there are sometimes extra performances, so ask at the hotels; performances are free.

There are also Sani performances during the day between 2pm and 3pm. During the **Torch Festival** (July/August), wrestling, bullfighting, singing and dancing is held at a natural outdoor amphitheatre by Hidden Lake at the back of Shílín.

Getting There & Away
BUS

Buses to Shílín (Y30 to Y40, two hours, every 30 minutes, 8am to noon) leave from the **bus station** (Beijing Lu, Kūnmíng) opposite the long-distance bus station. Make sure you don't get dragged onto one of the tourist

stay longer, then it's worth heading over to **Lùnán**, a small town about 10km north of Shílín. If you manage to time your visit with market day (Wednesday or Saturday), then you'll see Lùnán transform into a colossal jam of donkeys, horse carts and bikes. The streets are packed with produce, poultry and wares, and the Sani women are dressed in their finest.

Sleeping & Eating

Shílín doesn't have much in the way of accommodation and what it does offer is overpriced.

Stone Forest International Youth Hostel (Shílín Guójì Qīngnián Lǚguǎn; ☎ 771 0768; 4-bed dm Y50, s/d Y80/120) Directly opposite where the buses

buses, unless of course you want to spend the entire morning stopping off at various temples (a national obsession) and market stalls en route. In the afternoon there are minibuses waiting at Shílín's car park, leaving when full (Y10 to Y15).

Minibuses run between Lùnán and Shílín regularly (Y1, 10 minutes). At Shílín, they leave from a stand on the main road. Horse carts cost Y15. In Lùnán, flag down anything heading north of the main traffic circle. Minibuses to Kūnmíng (Y30, two hours) depart regularly from the western side of Lùnán's main roundabout until around 7pm.

TRAIN
At one time there was a high-speed tourist train that left Kūnmíng in the morning and arrived in Shílín in no time at all. But for some unknown reason, this convenient service has been stopped and getting to Shílín by train is even more time-consuming than catching a tour bus.

XIÀGUĀN 下关
☎ 0872
Xiàguān lies at the southern tip of Ěrhǎi Hú, about 400km west of Kūnmíng. It was once an important staging post on the Burma Road and is still a key centre for transport in northwest Yúnnán. Xiàguān is the capital of Dàlǐ prefecture and is also referred to as Dali City (Dàlǐ Shì). This confuses some travellers, who think they are already in Dàlǐ, book into a hotel and head off in

pursuit of a banana pancake only to discover they haven't arrived yet. There is no reason to stay in Xiàguān and you only need to come here in order to catch a bus or train.

To go straight to Dàlǐ, upon arriving in Xiàguān, turn left out of the long-distance bus station, and left again at the first intersection. Just up from the corner is the station for the No 4 local bus, which runs to the real Dàlǐ (Y1.5, 30 minutes) until around 8pm. Bus No 8 also runs from the centre of Xiàguān to Dàlǐ's west gate. If you want to be sure, ask for Dàlǐ Gǔchéng (Dali Old City).

Alternatively, minibuses run from a block west of the bus station (turn right out of the entrance) but you'll spend a lot of time waiting around for other passengers.

Information
The regional **PSB** (Gōngānjú; 21 Tianbao Jie; ☺ 8-11am & 2-5pm Mon-Fri) handles all visa extensions for Xiàguān and Dàlǐ. The **Bank of China** (Zhōngguó Yínháng; Jianshe Donglu) changes money and travellers cheques and has an ATM that accepts all major credit cards.

Getting There & Away
AIR
Xiàguān's airport is 15km from town. The Yunnan Airlines ticket office is inconveniently located near the train station. There are no public buses to the airport; taxis cost Y50 from Xiàguān or Y60 to Y80 from Dàlǐ. There are three flights daily to Kūnmíng (Y430) and one to Guǎngzhōu (Y1540).

XIÀGUĀN 下关

| 0 | 200 m |
| 0 | 0.1 miles |

To Dàlǐ (18km)
To North Bus Station
To Erhai Park (500m)
Cangshan Lu 苍山路
To Train Station, Yunnan Airlines (2km); Airport (15km); Jīzú Shān (110km)

Renmin Park
Post Office
Hospital
To Kūnmíng (399km)
Jianshe Lu
To Bāoshān (173km)
Longxi Lu

INFORMATION	
Bank of China 中国银行	1 B2
PSB 公安局	2 B1
TRANSPORT	pp658–9
Bus No 4 Terminus to Dàlǐ	
四路车到大理古城	3 B2
Bus Station 汽车客运站	4 C2
Long-Distance Bus Station	
汽车客运站	5 B2
Minibuses to Dàlǐ	
中巴车到大理古城	6 C2

SOUTHWEST CHINA

XIÀGUĀN BUS TIMETABLES

Buses from Xiàguān's long-distance bus station:

Destination	Price	Duration	Frequency	Departs
Kūnmíng	Y91-105	7hr	half-hourly	7.30am-6.30pm
Lìjiāng	Y50	3hr	4 daily	9am, 2pm, 4pm, 7pm
Bǎoshān	Y50	2½hr	daily	10.30am
Jǐnghóng	Y142	17hr	2 daily	2pm, 7.30pm
Mángshì (Lúxī)	Y90	6-8hr	2 daily	8.30am, 8pm
Ruìlì	Y100	10-12hr	2 daily	8.30am, 8pm
Téngchōng	Y72-82	6hr	2 daily	10am, 7.30pm
Nínglàng	Y45	8hr	daily	8.30am

BUS

Xiàguān has several bus stations, which throws some travellers. Luckily, the two main ones are both on the same side of the street, approximately two blocks apart. You might get dropped off at either one. Both have departures throughout the province, so if the long-distance bus station doesn't have a good departure time for you, wander over to the other one.

See box above for bus details.

For Zhōngdiàn (Y45 to Y58, eight to nine hours, every 20 minutes from 6.20am to 8pm) and local destinations you need to catch your bus from the north bus station. Minibuses to Lìjiāng also run regularly from Xiàguān.

Tickets for nearly all destinations can be booked in Dàlǐ.

TRAIN

The railway link between Kūnmíng and Xiàguān was finally opened in 1999. Overnight sleeper trains leave Kūnmíng's main train station at 10.10pm, arriving in Xiàguān at 6.45am. Hard sleepers are Y95. Returning to Kūnmíng, trains leave Xiàguān at 10.10am, 9.40pm, 10.40pm and 11pm.

Bus No 1 goes to the train station from the centre of town.

AROUND XIÀGUĀN
Jīzú Shān 鸡足山

This **mountain** (Chicken-Foot Mountain; admission Y60), 110km northeast of Xiàguān, is a major attraction for Buddhist pilgrims – both Chinese and Tibetan. At the time of the Qing dynasty there were approximately 100 temples on the mountain and somewhere in the vicinity of 5000 resident monks. The Cultural Revolution's anarchic assault on the traditional past did away with much that was of interest on the mountain, although renovation work on the temples has been going on since 1979.

Today it is estimated that more than 150,000 tourists and pilgrims clamber up the mountain every year to watch the sun rise. Jīndǐng, the Golden Summit, is at a cool 3240m so you will need some warm clothing.

SIGHTS & ACTIVITIES

Sights along the way include **Zhusheng Temple** (Zhùshèng Sì), the most important temple on the mountain, about an hour's walk up from the bus stop at Shāzhǐ.

Just before the last ascent is the **Magnificent Head Gate** (Huáshǒu Mén). At the summit is **Lengyan Pagoda** (Lèngyán Tǎ), a 13-tier Tang dynasty pagoda that was restored in 1927. There is basic accommodation at **Golden Summit Temple** (Jīndǐng Sì) next to the pagoda – a sleeping bag might be a good idea at this altitude.

A popular option for making the ascent is to hire a pony. Travellers who have done the trip claim it's a lot of fun. A **cable car** (admission Y30) to the summit is a good way to cheat, though the ride only starts halfway up.

SLEEPING & EATING

Accommodation is available at the base of the mountain, about halfway up and on the summit. Prices average Y10 to Y15 per bed. Food gets fairly expensive once you reach the summit so you may want to consider bringing some of your own.

SOUTHWEST CHINA

GETTING THERE & AWAY

From Xiàguān's north bus station take a bus to Bīnchuān (Y10, two hours), from where you'll have to change for a bus or minibus to Shāzhǐ at the foot of the mountain (Y10, one hour).

Wēishān

Wēishān is famous for the Taoist temples on nearby **Wēibǎo Shān** (Weibao Mountain), about 7km south of town. There are reportedly some fine Taoist murals here. It's 61km due south of Xiàguān, so it could be done as a day trip.

DÀLǏ 大理

☎ 0872

Dàlǐ is a perfect place to tune out for a while and forget about trains, planes and bone-jarring buses. The stunning mountain backdrop, the lovely Ěrhǎi Hú, the old city, cappuccinos, pizzas and the herbal alternative to cheap Chinese beer (you can pick it yourself) make it one of the few places in China where you can well and truly take a vacation from travelling.

History

Dàlǐ lies on the western edge of Ěrhǎi Hú at an altitude of 1900m, with imposing 4000m-tall Cāng Shān (Jade Green Mountains) behind it. For much of the five centuries in which Yúnnán governed its own affairs, Dàlǐ was the centre of operations, and the old city still retains a historical atmosphere that is hard to come by in other parts of China.

The main inhabitants of the region are the Bai, who number about 1.5 million. The Bai people have long-established roots in the Ěrhǎi Hú region, and are thought to have settled the area some 3000 years ago. In the early 8th century they grouped together and succeeded in defeating the Tang imperial army before establishing the Nanzhao kingdom.

The kingdom exerted considerable influence throughout southwest China and even, to a lesser degree, Southeast Asia, since it controlled upper Burma for much of the 9th century. This later established Dàlǐ as an end node on the famed Burma Rd. In the mid-13th century it fell before the invincible Mongol hordes of Kublai Khan.

The influx of Chinese tour groups is changing Dàlǐ's character. The southern part of town has been radically renovated to create a new 'old Dàlǐ', complete with original gates and renovated city walls. The wrecking balls have inched their way up Fuxing Lu, which is now lined with shops catering to Chinese tourists led around by guides dressed up in Bai costumes. The gentrification has been less successful than Lìjiāng's and some of the city's historical charm and authenticity has sadly been lost.

Orientation

Dàlǐ is a miniature city that has some preserved cobbled streets and traditional stone architecture within its old walls and its easy enough to get your bearings by just taking a walk for an hour or so. It takes about half an hour to walk from the South Gate (Nán Mén) across town to the North Gate (Běi Mén). You can also get a good overview of the town and its surroundings by walking around the town walls (renovated in 1998).

Huguo Lu is the main strip for cafés – locals call it Yangren Jie (Foreigner's St) – and this is where to turn to for your café latte, burritos, ice-cold beer and other treats.

MAPS

Tourist maps of Dàlǐ and Ěrhǎi Hú area are available at street stalls near the corner of Huguo Lu and Fuxing Lu. More useful ones can be picked up at **Mandarin Books & CDs** (Wǔhuá Shūyuán; Fuxing Lu), along with a great selection of guidebooks and novels in Chinese, English and Dutch.

Information

EMERGENCY

PSB (Gōngānjú; 21 Tianban Jie, Xiàguān; ☺ 8am-11am & 2-5pm Mon-Fri) Exhausted by a deluge of demands for visa extensions, the Dàlǐ PSB office has finally packed its bags and retreated to the relative safety of Xiàguān. To get there, take bus No 4 until just after it crosses the river in Xiàguān. The PSB office is a short walk south from here.

INTERNET ACCESS

China Telecom (cnr Fuxing Lu & Huguo Lu; per hr Y2; ☺ 8am-10pm) Most hotels also offer free Internet access for guests.

MONEY

Bank of China (Zhōngguó Yínháng; cnr Huguo Lu & Fuxing Lu) Changes cash and travellers cheques. There is also an ATM here that accepts all major credit cards.

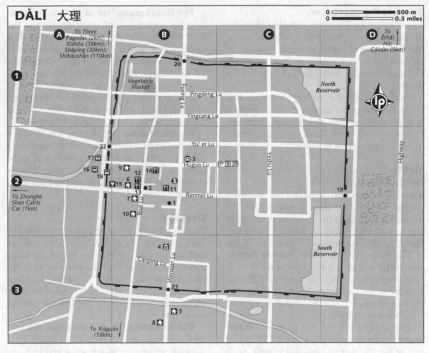

DÀLǏ 大理

0 —————— 500 m
0 —————— 0.3 miles

To Three Pagodas (2km); Xīzhōu (18km); Shāping (30km); Shibǎoshān (110km)

To Ěrhǎi Hú; Cáicūn (5km)

Vegetable Market

Pingdeng Lu

Yingcang Lu

Yu' er Lu

Huguo Lu 护国路

Renmin Lu

Canping Lu

North Reservoir

South Reservoir

Yeshu Lu

Highway

To Zhonghe Shan Cable Car (1km)

To Xiàguān (18km)

INFORMATION		
Mandarin Books & CDs 瓦片书兆		1 B2
Michael's Travel 迈克旅游		2 B2
Post & Telephone Office 邮电		3 B2

SIGHTS & ACTIVITIES	pp662
Dali Museum 大理博物馆	4 B3

SLEEPING	pp662–3
Friends Guesthouse 大理古城三友客栈	5 B3
Higherland Inn Booking Office 高地旅馆丁房局	6 B2
Jim's Tibetan Guesthouse 吉姆和平餐厅和饭店	7 B2

MCA Guesthouse	8 B3
No 3 Guesthouse 第三招待所	9 B2
Old Dali Four Seasons Inn 大理四季客栈	10 B2

EATING	pp663
Bamboo Café 紫竹屋	(see 11)
Buddha's Abode 妙香阁	11 B2
Jim's Peace Café 吉姆和平餐厅	(see 7)
Mr China's Son Cultural Exchange Café 中国之子	12 B2
Salvador's Coffee House 萨尔瓦多咖啡馆	13 B2
Tibet Café 西藏咖啡馆	14 B2

DRINKING	p663
Birdbar 鸟吧	15 B2

TRANSPORT	pp663–4
Bus Station 壮沙坪的公共汽车	16 A2
Buses to Train Station 八路车站往下关火车站	17 A2
Local Bus Station 汽车站	18 A2

OTHER	
East Gate 东门	19 D2
North Gate 北门	20 B1
South Gate 南门	21 B3
West Gate 西门	22 A2

POST

China Post (Yóujú; cnr Fuxing Lu & Huguo Lu; ⏰ 8am-8pm) The best place to make international calls as it has direct dial and doesn't levy a service charge.

TOURIST INFORMATION & TRAVEL AGENCIES

All the hotels offer travel advice and can arrange tours and book tickets for onward travel. There are also numerous travel agencies and cafés on Huguo Lu that offer a similar service. Day trips to Ěrhǎi Hú usually cost Y160 and include entrance fees, an English-speaking guide, lunch and transport.

Jim's Tibetan Guesthouse & Peace Café (see p662) Offers a long list of trips, including tours to Muslim markets and Yi minority markets, that come very highly rated by travellers. Jim and his wife Henriet also offer some more unusual trips including trekking in remote areas of Yúnnán and overland travel to Lhasa from Zhōngdiàn (per person from Y4500).

Michael's Travel (☎ 1398 855 4733; 68 Boai Lu) Michael can arrange calligraphy or tai chi lessons for Y40 per hour, as well as almost everything else you could think of, including horse rides and bus and train tickets.

Dangers & Annoyances

The hike up to Zhonghe Temple (Zhōnghé Sì) and along the mountain ridges is super, but there have been several reports of robbery of solo walkers, and in 1997 one German traveller was killed. Try to find a partner.

Be careful on the overnight sleeper bus from Kūnmíng as someone often finds a bag pinched or razored. Chain them securely and try cram them under the lower bunk as far back as possible.

Sights

THREE PAGODAS 三塔寺

Two kilometres northwest of Dàlǐ, standing on the hillside, the three pagodas (Sān Tǎ Sì) look particularly pretty when reflected in the nearby lake. They are among the oldest standing structures in southwestern China.

The tallest of the three, **Qianxun Pagoda**, has 16 tiers that reach a height of 70m. It was originally erected in the mid-9th century by engineers from Xī'ān. It is flanked by two smaller 10-tiered pagodas, each of which are 42m high.

The temple behind the pagodas, **Chongsheng Temple** (Chóngshèng Sì; admission Y10), is laid out in the traditional Yunnanese style, with three layers of buildings lined up with a sacred peak in the background. The temple has been restored and converted into a museum chronicling the history, construction and renovation of the pagodas.

DALI MUSEUM 大理市博物馆

The **Dali Museum** (Dàlǐ Shì Bówùguǎn; Wenxian Lu; admission Y5; 8.30am-6pm) houses a small collection of archaeological pieces relating to Bai history and has some moderately interesting exhibits on marble handicrafts. A number of marble stelae grace one wing.

Festivals & Events

If you don't mind crowds, the best time to be in Dàlǐ is probably during the **Third Moon Fair** (Sānyuè Jié), which begins on the 15th day of the third lunar month (usually April) and ends on the 21st day. The origins of the fair lie in its commemoration of a fabled visit by Guanyin, the Buddhist Goddess of Mercy, to the Nanzhao kingdom. Today it's more like an extra-festive market, with people from all over Yúnnán arriving to buy, sell and make merry.

The **Three Temples Festival** (Ràosān Líng) is held between the 23rd and 25th days of the fourth lunar month (usually May). The first day involves a trip from Dàlǐ's South Gate to Sacred Fountainhead Temple (Shèngyúan Sì) in Xīzhōu. Here travellers stay up until dawn, dancing and singing, before moving on to Jingui Temple (Jīnguì Sì) on the shore of Ěrhǎi Hú. The final day involves walking back to Dàlǐ by way of Majiuyi Temple.

The **Torch Festival** (Huǒbǎ Jié) is held on the 24th day of the sixth lunar month (normally July). Flaming torches are paraded at night through homes and fields. Other events include fireworks displays and dragon-boat racing.

Sleeping

There's a good choice of accommodation in Dàlǐ, even so, places tend to fill up quickly and those visiting during the peak summer months may find themselves trekking around town in search of that perfect bed on their first day. Most hotels offer laundry service, bicycle hire and free Internet access for guests.

MCA Guesthouse (☎ 267 3666; mcahouse@hotmail .com; Wenxian Lu; dm Y15, s/d/tr Y150/120/200) This popular place keeps on growing and offers a huge range of rooms. The dorm rooms are some of the nicest you'll find with hardwood floors and art on the walls. The newly built doubles and triples feature antique furniture, modern bathrooms and living rooms, making these some of the best rooms you'll find in Dàlǐ. You can also book overland trips to Tibet leaving from Zhōngdiàn here (see p683).

Jim's Tibetan Guesthouse (Jímù Hépíng Cāntīng Hé Fàndiàn; ☎ 267 1822; jimsguesthouse@hotmail.com; 63 Boai Lu; dm/d Y15/30, d with bathroom Y60-80) This is undoubtedly one of the friendliest guesthouses in Dàlǐ. It's so popular that Jim is in the process of building a new Tibetan-style hotel just outside the city walls called Jim's Peace Hotel. It promises to be quite spectacular with large rooms (some with kitchens), a garden and a roof terrace with stunning views of Ěrhǎi Hú. It should be up and running by the time you read this.

Friends Guesthouse (Dàlǐ Gǔchéng Sānyǒu Kèzhàn; ☎ 266 2888; dalifriends@sina.com; 1 Wenxian Lu; dm Y10, d/tr Y40/50) Opened last year, this hotel is fantastic value and has some of the cheapest rooms you'll find in Dàlǐ. You can hire bikes here – including tandems for all you lazy cyclists.

Old Dali Four Seasons Inn (Sìjì Kèzhàn; No 5 Guesthouse; ☎ 266 3925; fax 267 0382; 55 Boai Lu; dm Y10-30, s Y30-70, d Y50-70, d with bathroom incl breakfast Y120-150) This has long been a popular place for backpackers. The set-up, in an old converted school, is fun with lots of stairs and walkways leading to rooms and covered seating areas. Some travellers have complained about the cleanliness (or lack thereof) in the dorm rooms.

No 3 Guesthouse (Dìsān Zhāodàisuǒ; ☎ 266 4941; Huguo Lu; dm Y15-25) You'll find this friendly place set around a pretty garden. Rooms are simple but big and comfortable and there is a free laundry service. A good Korean restaurant is attached to the guesthouse.

Eating

Dàlǐ is overrun with restaurants. So many have opened up in the last couple of years that some reported a tenfold drop in business from one summer to the next. The best advice is to spread your patronage; you'll eventually find one you really like.

Jim's Peace Café (☎ 267 1822; jimsguesthouse@ hotmail.com; 63 Boai Lu) It's definitely worth coming here for the Tibetan banquet (Y25, minimum 10 people) where you can feast on at least 20 different dishes. Wash it all down with Jim's No 1 special and wonder the next morning how you got your hangover. See also Jim's Tibetan Guesthouse (opposite).

Tibet Café (Xīzàng Kāfēi; ☎ 266 2391; 42 Huguo Lu) This place has an extensive Tibetan menu as well as some Western and Chinese dishes, and a large outside seating area.

Salvador's Coffee House (Sāěrwàduō Kāfēiguǎn; ☎ 266 4146; 56 Boai Lu) Fresh coffee, homemade bagels and delicious home-made ice cream are just some of the reasons to make this a regular port of call while in Dàlǐ.

Buddha's Abode (Miàoxiāngé; ☎ 266 0032; 51 Renmin Lu) This place claims to be Dàlǐ's first vegetarian restaurant. Whether it is or not (another restaurant a few doors down claims the same title), the food is very good.

Bamboo Café (Zízhúwū; ☎ 267 1898; 71 Renmin Lu; dishes from Y8) This tiny restaurant only seats a handful of people at any one time and has a good menu featuring lots of Bai specialities.

Mr China's Son Cultural Exchange Café (Zhōngguó Zhīzǐ; ☎ 267 8234; http://cn.geocities.com/yndali/; 67-8 Boai Lu; dishes from Y8) Indulge in food for the body and food for the soul at this café run

by a fascinating gentleman who has penned an English-language account of his trials and tribulations during the Cultural Revolution. It's worth a visit alone for its thorough collection of maps and tips on Dàlǐ and environs – it's got a minor guidebook of its own.

Drinking

The Western-style restaurants mentioned above double as bars. Also worth trying is the **Birdbar** (Niǎobā; ☎ 266 1843; 22 Renmin Lu), a fun drinking den that doesn't shut until the last person leaves.

Shopping

Dàlǐ is famous for its marble, and while a slab of the stuff in your backpack might slow you down a bit, local entrepreneurs produce everything from ashtrays to model pagodas in small enough chunks to make it feasible to stow one or two away.

The city is also famous for it's blue-and-white batik printed on cotton and silk. A lot of the batik is still made in Dàlǐ and hidden behind many of the shopfronts sit vast vats of blue dye – it's worth asking around at some of the shops to see if you can have a look at how the batik is made.

Huguo Lu has become a smaller version of Bangkok's Khao San Rd in its profusion of clothes shops. Most shopkeepers can also make clothes to your specifications – which will come as a relief when you see some of the items of ready-made clothing on offer.

Most of the 'silver' jewellery sold in Dàlǐ is really brass. Occasionally it actually is silver, although this will be reflected in the starting price. The only advice worth giving is to bargain hard. For those roving sales ladies badgering you incessantly, don't feel bad to pay one-fifth of their asking price – that's what locals advise. For marble from street sellers, 40% to 50% is fair. In shops, two-thirds of the price is average. And don't fall for any 'expert' opinions; go back later on your own and deal.

Getting There & Away

AIR

Xiàguān's new airport has brought Dàlǐ to within 45 minutes' flying time from Kūnmíng (see p658). A taxi from Dàlǐ to the airport will cost Y60 to Y80. Alternatively, you can take a bus to Xiàguān and pick up a taxi from there (Y50).

BUS

The golden rule about getting to Dàlǐ by bus is to find out in advance whether your bus is for Dàlǐ or Xiàguān. Many buses advertised to Dàlǐ actually only go as far as Xiàguān. Coming from Lìjiāng, Xiàguān-bound buses tend to stop at the eastern end of Dàlǐ to let passengers off before continuing on to their final destination. From here it's a 20-minute walk to the main guesthouses or you can take a horse cart for around Y5.

For information on getting to Dàlǐ from Kūnmíng, see p652.

From the bus stop near the west gate in Dàlǐ there are daily buses to Zhōngdiàn (Y50, seven to eight hours, every 20 minutes, 7.30am to 11am) and express buses to Kūnmíng (Y106, 9am, 10am and 4pm). A slow bus for Kūnmíng also leaves daily at 8am (Y65). Express buses to Lìjiāng (Y105, three daily, 8.50am, 2.20pm and 7.20pm) and minibuses (Y35 to Y40, every 30 minutes, 7.30am to 6.30pm) also leave from here.

A bus leaves for Shāpíng every Monday morning (Y4, one hour, 9.30am) for the market. At all other times, local buses run regularly to Shāpíng, Xǐzhōu and other local destinations from opposite the bus station in Dàlǐ.

TRAIN

Probably the most popular means of getting to Dàlǐ is the overnight sleeper train from Kūnmíng (hard sleeper Y95). For more details see p659.

Getting Around

From Dàlǐ, a taxi to Xiàguān airport takes 45 minutes and cost around Y80; to Xiàguān's train station it costs Y30.

Bikes are the best way to get around (Y10 per day). Most of the guesthouses and several other places on Boai Lu rent bikes.

Bus No 4 runs between Dàlǐ and central Xiàguān (Y1.50, 30 minutes) every 15 minutes from 6.30am, which means that unless your bus leaves Xiàguān earlier than 7.30am you won't have to stay the night there.

Bus No 8 runs from Dàlǐ to Xiàguān's train station.

AROUND DÀLǏ
Markets

Usually markets follow the lunar calendar, but shrewd local operators have co-opted

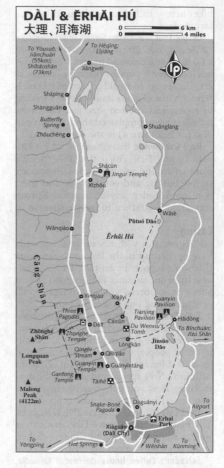

it into a regular scheme so that tourists have a market to go to nearly every day of the week. See opposite for information on the Monday Shāpíng market. Markets also take place in Shuānglǎng (Tuesday), Shābā (Wednesday), Yòusuǒ (Friday, the largest in Yúnnán) and Jiāngwěi (Saturday). Xǐzhōu and Zhōuchéng have daily morning and afternoon markets respectively.

Wāsè also has a popular market every five days with trading from 9am to 4.30pm. Many cafés in Dàlǐ organise transport for Y20 to Y30 per person.

Ěrhǎi Hú 洱海湖

This **lake** (Ear-Shaped Lake) is the seventh biggest freshwater lake in China at 1973m above sea level and covering 250 sq km. It's a 50-minute walk from town or a 10-minute downhill zip on a bike.

From **Cáicūn**, a pleasant little lake-side village east of Dàlǐ (Y2 on the No 2 minibus), there's a ferry at 4.30pm to **Wāsè** on the other side of the lake. You can stay overnight at the Wāsè Zhāodàisuǒ and catch a ferry back at 6am. Plenty of locals take their bikes over.

Ferries crisscross the lake at various points, so there could be some scope for extended touring. Close to Wāsè are **Pǔtuó Dǎo** (Putuo Island) and **Lesser Putuo Temple** (Xiǎopǔtuó Sì), set on an extremely photogenic rocky outcrop. Other ferries run between Lóngkān and Hǎidōng, and between Xiàguān and Jīnsuō Dǎo (Jinsuo Island). Ferries leave early in the morning (for the market) and return around 4pm; timetables are flexible and departures are somewhat unreliable.

Roads now encircle the lake so it is possible to do a loop (or partial loop) of the lake by mountain bike. A few intrepid travellers have leapfrogged these villages, made for Shāpíng's market, then continued all the way around the lake stopping at other markets on the way before boating themselves and their bicycles back to Dàlǐ. From Dàlǐ to Wāsè it's around 58km by road.

Plenty of cafés can arrange a horse-and-carriage ride to the lake, then a boat ride to Tianjing Pavilion and Guanyin Pavilion, then Jīnsuō Dǎo or whatever you dream up, for around Y50 per day.

Zhonghe Temple 中和寺
This **temple** (Zhōnghé Sì; admission Y2) is a long, steep hike up the mountainside behind Dàlǐ. This is a great day trip and offers fantastic vistas of Dàlǐ and Ěrhǎi Hú. You can cheat and take a new **chairlift** (one way/return Y50/80) up **Zhōnghé Shān** (Zhonge Mountain).

You could also hike up the hill, a sweaty hour for those in relatively good shape (see Dangers & Annoyances p662). No one path leads directly up the hill; instead, oodles of local paths wind and switch back through farm fields, local cemeteries, and even one off-limits military area (there is a sign in English here!). Walk about 200m north of the chairlift base to the riverbed (often dry). Follow the left bank for about 50m and you'll see lots of ribbony trails leading up. Basically, all roads lead to Rome from here,

just keep the chairlift in sight and when in doubt, bear left. You should eventually come upon a well-worn trail and, following that, some steps near the top.

Branching out from either side of the temple is a trail that winds along the face of the mountains, taking you in and out of steep, lush valleys and past streams and waterfalls. From Zhōnghé it's an amazing 11km up-and-down hike south to **Gantong Temple** (Gǎntōng Sì) or **Qingbi Stream**, from where you can continue to the road and pick up a Dàlǐ-bound bus.

Alternatively, you can spend some more time here and stay the night at **Higherland Inn** (☎ 266 1599; www.higherland.com; dm Y30) located just above Zhonghe Temple at 2590m. If you want to get away from the crowds in Dàlǐ then this is the place to do it. The hostel has fabulous views, regular barbecues and bonfire parties and only a handful of rooms (seven) which means it's an incredibly relaxing place to stay. You can reserve rooms at the booking office across from Salvador's Coffee House on Renmin Lu in Dàlǐ.

Xīzhōu 喜洲
Among the 101 things to do while you're in Dàlǐ, a trip to the old town of Xīzhōu would have to rate fairly high. Located 18km north of Dàlǐ, the Bai architecture here has been very well preserved. A local bus bound for Ěryuán would be the easiest option for getting here, but a bicycle trip with an overnight stop in Xīzhōu (there's accommodation in town) is also a good idea. From here, the interesting town of **Zhōuchéng** is 7km further north; it too has basic accommodation.

Shaping Market 沙坪赶集
Every Monday at Shāpíng, about 30km north of Dàlǐ, there is a colourful Bai **market** (Shāpíng Gǎnjí). The market starts to rattle and hum at 10am and ends around 2.30pm. You can buy everything from tobacco, melon seeds and noodles to meat, pots and wardrobes. In the ethnic clothing line, you can look at shirts, headdresses, embroidered shoes and moneybelts, as well as local batik. Expect to be quoted ridiculously high prices on anything you set your eyes on, so get into a bargaining frame of mind before you go.

Getting to Shaping Market from Dàlǐ is fairly easy. Some of the hotels and cafés in town run minibuses (Y15). They usually leave at 9am, although it's a good idea to ask around and book the day before. Alternatively you can walk up Huguo Lu to the main highway and catch the 9.30am bus to Shāpíng (Y4) from the local bus station.

Guanyin Pavilion 观音堂
This temple (Guānyīn Táng) is built over a large boulder that locals believe was placed there by Guanyin, the Buddhist Goddess of Mercy, disguised as an old woman in order to block the advance of an invading enemy. It is 5km south of Dàlǐ. If you follow the path uphill for 3km you will come across another temple, **Gantong Temple** (Gǎntōng Sì).

Shíbǎoshān 石宝山
About 110km northwest of Dàlǐ are the **Stone Treasure Mountain Grottoes** (Shíbǎoshān Shíkū). There are three temple groups: Stone Bell (Shízhōng), Lion Pass (Shīzī Guān) and Shadeng Village that include some of the best Bai stone carvings in southern China and offer insights into life at the Nanzhao court of the 9th century.

To get to Shíbǎoshān, take a bus to Jiànchuān, 55km north of Dàlǐ on the old Dàlǐ–Lìjiāng road. Get off at the small village of Diànnán, about 8km south of Jiànchuān, where a narrow road branches southwest to the village of Shāxī, 23km away. You'll just have to wait for a bus for this leg. The grottoes are close to Shāxī.

LÌJIĀNG 丽江
new town ☎ 08891 / old town ☎ 0888
About 160km north of Dàlǐ, the town of Lìjiāng is set in a beautiful valley and makes another great spot to while away a few days or weeks. Your initial response when your bus roars into town might well be: 'Get me out of here!'. It's not until you get into the old town – a delightful maze of cobbled streets, rickety old wooden buildings, gushing canals and the hurly-burly of market life – that you realise Lìjiāng is more than a boring urban sprawl in the middle of nowhere.

There are a number of interesting sights around Lìjiāng, some of which can be reached by bicycle, offering a week or more's worth of excursions.

Apart from the writings of botanist-explorer Joseph Rock (see the boxed text p674), another venerable work on Lìjiāng

that's worth reading if you can find it is the *Forgotten Kingdom* by Peter Goulart. Goulart was a White Russian who studied Naxi culture and lived in Lìjiāng from 1940 to 1949.

Beyond the Clouds is an excellent nine-hour documentary about Lìjiāng, made in 1994 by Britain's Channel 4, that is well worth seeking out.

In 1996 an earthquake measuring over seven on the Richter scale rocked the Lìjiāng area, killing more than 300 people – including one foreign tourist – and injuring 16,000. Damage was estimated at over half a billion US dollars. While much of newer Lìjiāng was levelled, the traditional Naxi architecture held up quite well. The Chinese government took note and sank millions of yuán into rebuilding most of Lìjiāng County with traditional Naxi architecture, replacing cement with cobblestone and wood. The UN was so impressed by the survival of Lìjiāng that it placed all of Lìjiāng County on its World Heritage Site list in 1999.

The town's reconstruction, coupled with the unveiling of Lìjiāng's new airport, has led to a huge increase in tourists. One indirect result has been a cluster of new tourist sights with fairly high fees. More worrying is the influx of Han Chinese entrepreneurs running tourist shops and restaurants for Han tourists, and souvenir sellers pushing out Naxi stalls. What used to be the preserve of hardy backpackers is now a major tourist destination.

Orientation
Lìjiāng is separated into old and new towns that are starkly different. The approximate line of division is Shīzī Shān (Lion Hill), the green hump in the middle of town that's topped by a radio mast and Looking at the Past Pavilion, a new pagoda. Everything west of the hill is the new town, and everything east is the old town.

The easiest way into the old town is from the north, along Dong Dajie. This area was largely reconstructed following the 1996 earthquake. From the long-distance bus station head east one block and follow an alley lined with snack bars heading north. The old town is a delightful maze of twists and turns – although it's small, it's easy to get lost in, which, of course, is part of the fun. Enjoy!

THE NAXI 纳西

Lìjiāng has been the base of the 286,000 strong Naxi (also spelt Nakhi and Nahi) minority for about the last 1400 years. The Naxi descend from ethnically Tibetan Qiang tribes and lived until recently in matrilineal families. Since local rulers were always male it wasn't truly matriarchal, but women still seem to run the show, certainly in the old part of Lìjiāng.

The Naxi matriarchs maintained their hold over the men with flexible arrangements for love affairs. The *azhu* (friend) system allowed a couple to become lovers without setting up joint residence. Both partners would continue to live in their respective homes; the boyfriend would spend the nights at his girlfriend's house but return to live and work at his mother's house during the day. Any children born to the couple belonged to the woman, who was responsible for bringing them up. The man provided support, but once the relationship was over, so was the support. Children lived with their mothers, and no special effort was made to recognise paternity. Women inherited all property, and disputes were adjudicated by female elders.

There are strong matriarchal influences in the Naxi language. Nouns enlarge their meaning when the word for 'female' is added; conversely, the addition of the word for 'male' will decrease the meaning. For example, 'stone' plus 'female' conveys the idea of a boulder; 'stone' plus 'male' conveys the idea of a pebble.

Naxi women wear blue blouses and trousers covered by a blue or black apron. The T-shaped traditional cape not only stops the basket worn on the back from chafing, but also symbolises the heavens. Day and night are represented by the light and dark halves of the cape; seven embroidered circles symbolise the stars. Two larger circles, one on each shoulder, are used to depict the eyes of a frog, which until the 15th century was an important god to the Naxi. With the decline of animist beliefs, the frog eyes fell out of fashion, but the Naxi still call the cape by its original name, 'frog-eye sheepskin'.

The Naxi created a written language over 1000 years ago using an extraordinary system of pictographs – the only hieroglyphic language still in use. The most famous Naxi text is the Dongba classic *Creation*, and ancient copies of it and other texts can still be found in Lìjiāng, as well as in the archives of some US universities. The Dongba were Naxi shamans who were caretakers of the written language and mediators between the Naxi and the spirit world. The Dongba religion, itself an offshoot of Tibet's pre-Buddhist Bon religion, eventually developed into an amalgam of Tibetan Buddhism, Islam and Taoism. The Tibetan origins of the Naxi are confirmed by references in Naxi literature to Lake Manasarovar and Mt Kailash, both in western Tibet.

Useful phrases in the Naxi language are: 'nuar lala' (hello) and 'jiu bai sai' (thank you).

Information

Lìjiāng's popular cafés and backpacker inns are probably your best source of information on the area. Most have noticeboards and travellers books full of useful tips and advice from other travellers on surrounding sights, especially the Tiger Leaping Gorge trek.

BOOKSHOPS

Xinhua Bookshop (Xīnhuá Shūdiàn; Xin Dajie) Has maps of the city and copies of *Hello Lìjiāng!* by Duan Ping-Hua and Ray Hilsinger which is a fairly useful guide to the local sights.

EMERGENCY

PSB (Gōngānjú; Fuhui Lu; 8.30-11.30am & 2.30-5.30pm) Reputedly very speedy and some travellers have reported same-day visa extensions.

INTERNET ACCESS

There are lots of places where you can go online in the old town.
Prague Café (see Eating p670; per hr Y5).

MONEY

Bank of China (Zhōngguó Yínháng; Xin Dajie) Changes cash and travellers cheques and offers cash advances on credit cards.
Bank of China (Zhōngguó Yínháng; Dong Dajie) This branch is in the old town and has an ATM machine.

POST & TELEPHONE

Many of the backpacker cafés in the old town have IDD lines.
China Post (Yóujú; Minzu Lu; 8am-8pm) Offers EMS (Express Mail Service), so your postcards might actually make it home before you do. Another post office is in the old town just north of the Old Market Sq.

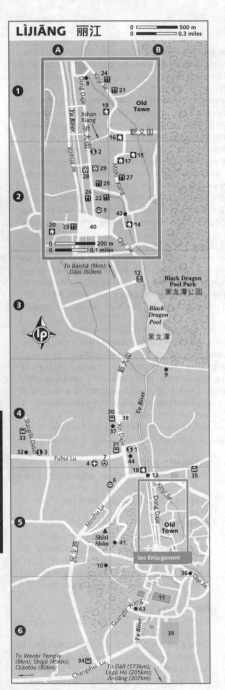

China Telecom (Minzu Lu) Next door to China Post; you can make international calls from here.

TOURIST INFORMATION & TRAVEL AGENCIES

You'll find many locals offering guide services. Those who have taken up these offers generally say that it's been worthwhile. If you're interested, ask around the backpacker hostels and cafés for recommendations.

CITS (Zhōngguó Guójì Lǚxíngshè; 3rd fl, cnr Fuhui Lu & Shangrila Dadao) Can arrange tours in and around Lìjiāng.

Tourist Reception Centre (Lǚyóu Jiēdài; ☎ 511 6666) At the entrance to the old town, you'll find the staff particularly helpful when you can't find your guesthouse (a common occurrence). They can also help with travel information and book tickets for your onward journey here.

Eco-tours (☎ 131-7078 0719; www.ecotourchina.com) Run by Zhao Fan at the Buena Vista Club (p675). He can organise tours to nearly anywhere you want to go in northern Yúnnán, as well as trekking and camping trips in less-well known areas. He has also produced his own map of cycling trails which is indispensable if you're planning on heading off to explore on two wheels.

Dangers & Annoyances

In 1997 two solo female travellers were robbed at knifepoint in separate incidents atop Xiàng Shān (Elephant Hill) in Black Dragon Pool Park (Hēilóngtán Gōngyuán). Both attacks occurred in broad daylight in the early afternoon, so keep your eyes sharp for people lurking behind you. It would obviously be a good idea to pair up with at least one other traveller.

Sights

Crisscrossed by canals, bridges and a maze of narrow streets, the old town is the reason why people come to Lìjiāng. The town's web of artery-like canals once supplied the city's drinking water. There are several wells and pools still in use around town. You can see one of the original wells opposite the Well Bistro.

The focus of the old town is the **Old Market Sq** (Sìfāng Jiē), full of Naxi women in traditional dress. Parrots and plants adorn the front porches, women sell griddle cakes in front of teahouses and players energetically slam down the trumps on a card table in the middle of the street. Unfortunately the Naxi traders are slowly being pushed out by tacky souvenir stalls. For all the controversy regarding what to preserve in the town and how, for now it is still extraordinary, but be prepared to share the experience with hundreds of other people.

Above the old town is a beautiful **park** that can be reached on the path leading past the radio mast. Sit on the slope in the early morning and watch the mist clearing as the old town comes to life.

Now acting as sentinel of sorts for the town, the **Looking at the Past Pavilion** (Wànggǔ Lóu; admission Y15) was raised for tourists at a cost of over one million yuán. It's famed for a unique design using dozens of four-storey pillars – unfortunately these were culled from northern Yúnnán old-growth forests. A path (with English signs) leads from the Old Market Sq.

MU FAMILY MANSION 木氏士司府
The former home of a Naxi chieftain, the **Mu Family Mansion** (Mùshì Shìsīfǔ; admission Y35; ☯ 8.30am-5.30pm) was heavily renovated (more like built from scratch) after the 1996 earthquake, with funds from the World Bank. Inside are some mediocre exhibitions of Naxi customs and culture. The mansion backs onto Shīzī Shān and you should be able to get access from here to Looking at the Past Pavilion.

BLACK DRAGON POOL PARK 黑龙潭公园
On the northern edge of town is the **Black Dragon Pool Park** (Hēilóngtán Gōngyuán; Xin Dajie; admission Y20). Apart from strolling around the pool – its view of Yùlóng Xuěshān (Jade Dragon Snow Mountain) is the most obligatory photo shoot in southwestern China – you can visit the **Dongba Research Institute** (Dōngbā Wénhuà Yánjiūshì) which is part of a renovated complex on the hillside.

At the far side of the pool are buildings used for an art exhibition, a pavilion with its own bridge across the water and the Ming dynasty **Five Phoenix Hall** (Wǔfèng Lóu).

Trails lead straight up **Xiàng Shān** (Elephant Hill) to a dilapidated gazebo and then across a spiny ridge past a communications centre and back down the other side, making a nice morning hike. See also Dangers & Annoyances on left.

At the northern entrance of the park is the **Museum of Naxi Dongba Culture** (Nàxī Dōngbā Wénhuà Bówùguǎn; ☯ 8.30am-5.30pm). Displays include Naxi dress and culture, Dongba script, information on Lìjiāng's old town and the dubious claim that the region is the 'real' Shangri-la.

Festivals & Events

The 13th day of the third moon (late March or early April) is the traditional day to hold a **Fertility Festival**.

July brings the **Torch Festival** (Huǒbǎ Jié), also celebrated by the Bai in the Dàlǐ region and the Yi all over the southwest. The origin

SOUTHWEST CHINA

of this festival can be traced back to the intrigues of the Nanzhao kingdom, when the wife of a man burned to death by the king eluded the romantic entreaties of the monarch by leaping into a fire.

Sleeping

There is no shortage of charming Naxi guesthouses in the old town. The new town boasts lots of modern hotels, but staying there kind of defeats the purpose of visiting Lìjiāng.

Wang Gu Youth Inn (Wànggǔlóu Qīngnián Kèzhàn; ☎ 512 9773; Xinhua Jie; dm Y20-60, d with bathroom Y100) On the path leading up to Looking at the Past Pavilion is this place with bright and breezy rooms. Some of the doubles are a little small but the location is quiet and there are some great views over town from the restaurant terrace.

Ancient Stone Bridge Inn (Gǔchéng Dàshíqiáo Kèzhàn; ☎ 518 4001; 71 Xingren Xiaduan; dm Y60-80, d with bathroom Y100-250) This is a small family-run inn in a lovely location. There are a couple of fabulous rooms right on the side of the canals with a shared bathroom and one good upper-floor double; apart from these, the rooms are average.

Dongba House (Dōngbā Háosī Bīnzhàn; ☎ 518 7630; dongbahouse@hotmail.com; 16 Xinyi Jie; dm Y15, d with bathroom Y60) You'll probably find better rooms elsewhere but the service here is very good. The place has an attractive sunlit café, Internet access and bike rental. The friendly Tibetan owner also owns the Tibet Café in Zhōngdiàn (and his brother owns the MCA Guesthouse in Dàli).

First Bend Inn (Dìyīwān Kèzhàn; ☎ 518 1688; 43 Mishi Xiang; s/d/tr Y80/80/90) This building is over 200 years old and is one of the old town's best-preserved buildings. The courtyard is gorgeous and the rooms very comfortable. The shared bathrooms are impeccable.

Ancient Town Youth Hostel (Gǔchéng Guójì Qīngnián Lǚguǎn; ☎ 510 5403; LjYouthhostels@yahoo.com.cn; 44 Mishi Xiang; dm Y20-30, d with bathroom Y60-120, tr with bathroom Y90-150) There are a big number of rooms to choose from here, all of a very good standard. The roof terrace is the perfect place to enjoy a beer and watch the sun set over Yùlóng Xuěshān.

Sānhé Nàxì Bīnguǎn (☎ 512 0891; Xinyi Jie; d high/low season Y560/320) This is a very swish mid-range option that has bathrooms of a quality more commonly found in the Hilton. Rooms

are elegant and very comfortable and set around a lovely traditional courtyard.

Grand Lijiang Hotel (Gélán Dàjiǔdiàn; ☎ 512 8888; fax 512 7878; Xinyi Jie; d Y480 plus 15% service charge) On your left as you enter the old town is this Sino-Thai joint venture which is your best luxury option.

Eating

Like Dàli, Lìjiāng has a legion of small, family-operated restaurants catering to travellers. The following run-down is by no means exhaustive.

There are always several 'Naxi' items on the menu, including the famous 'Naxi omelette' and 'Naxi sandwich' (goat's cheese, tomato and fried egg between two pieces of local bābā). Bābā is the Lìjiāng local speciality – thick flatbreads of wheat, served plain or stuffed with meats, vegetables or sweets. Try locally produced yinjiu, a lychee-based wine with a 500-year history – it tastes like a decent semi-sweet sherry.

INTERNATIONAL

Prague Café (☎ 512 3757; 18 Mishi Xiang; meals from Y10) An old favourite, this place is still popular and serves possibly the best breakfast in town. The rest of the menu is pretty good too with Japanese, Chinese and Naxi cuisine all on offer. The book-exchange shelves resemble a mini-library and they've got the biggest magazine collection you'll have seen since leaving home. You can access the Internet here (Y5 per hour).

Ma Ma Fu's (Māmāfǔ Cāntīng; Mishi Xiang; dishes from Y8) In a lovely location alongside a stream, this is one of Lìjiāng's stalwarts. Now run by a younger Mama Fu, it serves an excellent array of foods that includes Western and Chinese dishes.

Sakura Café (Dong Dajie) This popular and well-run café serves up excellent Korean and Japanese food (the cook is Korean and married to a local). The outstanding bimbap (rice, egg, meat and vegetables with hot sauce) set meal is enough for two. Also featured on the menu are a number of popular Western dishes.

Well Bistro (Jīngzhǔo Cānguǎn; Mishi Xiang) This lovely sunlit café has a large Western menu that includes a good range of vegetarian options and some pretty tasty desserts. The traveller's books here are good for picking up information.

NAXI & CHINESE

There are lots of snack bars and local restaurants to choose from. Some of these places cater specifically for Chinese tour groups and can be quite expensive; make sure you check prices before you order.

Lamu's House of Tibet (Xīzàngwū Xicǎntīng; ☎ 139-8704 9750; 56 Xinyi Jie; dishes from Y7) Away from the main drag, this place serves excellent food from a hugely varied menu. Try the *momo* (Tibetan dumplings) which come with a variety of fillings, but make sure you save room for the desserts – they're massive.

Naxi Family Café (Hónglóu Cānguǎn; 70 Xinyi Jie; dishes from Y10) For traditional Naxi food come to this family-run restaurant. Next door to Lamu's, the food is some of the best you will find in Lìjiāng; the Naxi ham and fried cheese are particularly good.

Monkey Bar (☎ 511 8817; dinner Y12; reservations must be made before 3pm) Tucked down an alley off Xinhua Jie is a Naxi house that belongs to Adam, a Lijianger who has decided to open up his home to guests. Everyone is invited to join him and his friends for dinner and the menu consists of whatever was available at the market that day. Dinner is served at a table in the courtyard which itself is a treasure trove of antiques, knick-knacks and odd bits of junk. Possibly the most fun you'll have eating dinner.

Entertainment

One of the few things you can do in the evening in Lìjiāng is attend performances of the **Naxi Orchestra** (Nàxi Gǔyuè Huì; Naxi Music Academy; tickets Y50-100; ☺ performances 8pm), located inside a beautiful building in the old town.

Not only are all 20 to 24 members Naxi, but they play a type of Taoist temple music (known as *dongjing*) that has been lost elsewhere in China. The pieces they perform are supposedly faithful renditions of music from the Han, Song and Tang dynasties, and are played on original instruments. In most of China such instruments didn't survive the Cultural Revolution; several of this group hid theirs by burying them

---

THE CONDUCTOR

The village schoolmaster was a chivalrous and energetic man with a shock of glinting blue-black hair, who lived with his childlike wife in a wooden house beside the Jade Stream.

A musicologist by training, he had climbed to distant mountain villages to record the folksongs of the Na-Khi tribe. He believed, like Vico, that the world's first languages were in song. Early man he said, had learnt to speak by imitating the calls of animals and birds, and had lived in a musical harmony with the rest of Creation.

His room was crammed with bric-a-brac salvaged, heaven knows how, from the catastrophes of the Cultural Revolution. Perched on chairs of red lacquer, we nibbled melon seeds while he poured into thimbles of white porcelain a mountain tea known as 'Handful of Snow'.

He played us a tape of Na-Khi chant, sung antiphonally by men and women around the bier of a corpse: Wooo…Zeee! Wooo…Zeee! The purpose of the song was to drive away the Eater of the Dead, a fanged and malicious demon thought to feast upon the soul.

He surprised us by his ability to hum his way through the mazurkas of Chopin and an apparently endless repertoire of Beethoven. His father, a merchant in the Lhasa caravan trade, had sent him in the 1940s to study Western music at the Kunming Academy.

On the back wall, above a reproduction of Claude Lorrain's *L'Embarquement pour Cythère*, there were two framed photos of himself: one in white tie and tails behind a concert grand; the other, conducting an orchestra in a street of flag-waving crowds – a dashing and energetic figure, on tiptoe, his arms extended upwards and his baton down.

'In 1949,' he said. 'To welcome the Red Army into Kūnmíng.'

'What were you playing?'

'Schubert's *Marche Militaire*.'

For this – or rather, for his devotion to 'Western culture' – he got 21 years in jail.

He held up his hands, gazing at them sadly as though they were long-lost orphans. His fingers were crooked and his wrists were scarred: a reminder of the day when the Guards strung him up to the roof-beams – in the attitude of Christ on the Cross…or a man conducting an orchestra.

Songlines (1987) by Bruce Chatwin

underground. This is a rare chance to hear Chinese music as it must have sounded in classical China. They also play plenty of Han Chinese music, so don't be surprised.

Xuan Ke usually speaks for the group at performances – speaks too much, some say – explaining each musical piece and describing the instruments. There are taped recordings of the music available; a set of two costs Y30. If you're interested, make sure you buy the tape at the show – tapes on sale at shops around town, and even in Kūnmíng, are often pirated copies.

You can usually turn up on your own and watch a performance, but you should book seats earlier in the day if you want a good seat.

The government-run **Dongba Palace** (Dong Dajie; tickets Y50-100; ☾ performances 8pm) has a less authentic song-and-dance show.

Getting There & Away
AIR
Lìjiāng's airport is 25km east of town. Tickets can be booked at the **CAAC** (Zhōngguó Mínháng; ☎ 516 1289; cnr Fuhui Lu & Shangrila Dadao; ☾ 8am-9pm). Most hotels in the old town also offer an air-ticket booking service.

From Lìjiāng there are 10 flights a day to Kūnmíng (Y530) and daily services to Chéngdū (Y880), Shànghǎi (Y2430), Shēnzhèn (Y1630) and Guǎngzhōu (Y1790).

BUS
Lìjiāng has three bus stations: one opposite Mao Sq; the main long-distance bus station in the south; and an express bus station to Kūnmíng and Xiàguān on Shangrila Dadao in the north of town. See box below.

From the express bus station there are daily departures to Kūnmíng (Y154, 8am, 9am and 11am) and Xiàguān (Y48 to Y53, 8am, 11.10am, noon, 2.10pm and 6.10pm).

Getting Around
Buses to the airport (Y10) leave from outside the CAAC 90 minutes before flight departures.

Taxis start at Y6 in the new town and are not allowed into the old town (the whole of the old town is pedestrianised).

Bike hire is available at Dongba House and the Ancient Town Youth Hostel (Y15 per day).

AROUND LÌJIĀNG
It is possible to see most of Lìjiāng's environs on your own, but a few agencies do offer half- or full-day tours, starting from

LÌJIĀNG BUS TIMETABLES
Buses from the Mao Sq bus station include:

Destination	Price	Duration	Frequency	Departs
Kūnmíng	Y119	12hr	daily	8pm
Xiàguān	Y31-40	3-4hr	half-hourly	7.30am-5.30pm
Zhōngdiàn	Y29	4-5hr	3 daily	7.50am, 9am, 11am
Nínglàng	Y23	5hr	3 daily	12.30pm, 1pm, 2pm
Jīnjiāng	Y44	8hr	3 daily	7am, 8am, 11am
Lúgū Hú	Y43	7-8hr	3 daily	8am, 9am, 10am

Buses from the long-distance bus station include:

Destination	Price	Duration	Frequency	Departs
Kūnmíng	Y151	12hr	hourly	8.20-11.20am
Kūnmíng (sleeper)	Y119	12hr	8 daily	6.30-8.30pm
Xiàguān	Y35-50	3-4hr	25 daily	7.10am-6.30pm
Zhōngdiàn	Y26-35	4-5hr	11 daily	7.30am-4pm
Nínglàng	Y23	5hr	hourly	7.50am-5pm
Qiáotóu	Y15	2	11 daily	7.30am-4pm

AROUND LÌJIĀNG & ZHŌNGDIÀN 丽江、中甸地区

Y150; it might be worth it if you take one that includes fees.

Monasteries

The monasteries around Lìjiāng are Tibetan in origin and belong to the Karmapa (Red Hat) sect. Most of the monasteries were extensively damaged during the Cultural Revolution and there's not much monastic activity nowadays. Nevertheless, it's worth hopping on a bicycle and heading out of town for a look.

PUJI MONASTERY 普及寺
This monastery (Pǔjì Sì) is around 5km northwest of Lìjiāng (on a trail that passes the two ponds to the north of town). The few monks here are usually happy to show the occasional stray traveller around.

FUGUO MONASTERY 富国寺
West of Báishā lies the remains of the **temple** (Fùguó Sì), once the largest of Lìjiāng's monasteries. Much of it was destroyed during the Cultural Revolution. To get there head west from the main intersection in

Báishā until you reach a small village. Turn right at the fork in the road and continue for around 500m before taking the next left that you come to. Walk up the hill for about 30 minutes and you will come to the monastery ruins.

JADE PEAK MONASTERY 玉峰寺
This small lamasery (Yùfēng Sì) is on a hillside about 5km past Báishā. The last 3km of the track require a steep climb. If you decide to leave your bike at the foot of the hill, don't leave it too close to the village below – the local kids have been known to let the air out of the tyres (or worse)!

The monastery sits at the foot of Yùlóng Xuěshān (5500m) and was established in 1756. The monastery's main attraction nowadays is the **Camellia Tree of 10,000 Blossoms** (Wànduǒ Shānchá). Ten thousand might be something of an exaggeration, but locals claim that the tree produces at least 4000 blossoms between February and April. A monk on the grounds risked his life to keep the tree secretly watered during the Cultural Revolution.

WENBI MONASTERY 文笔寺
To get to this monastery (Wénbǐ Sì) requires a steep uphill ride 8km to the southwest of Lìjiāng. The monastery itself is not that interesting, but there are some good views and pleasant walks in the near vicinity.

Frescoes

Lìjiāng is famed for its temple frescoes. Most travellers probably won't want to spend a week or so traipsing around seeking them out, but it may be worth checking out one or two.

Most of the frescoes were painted during the 15th and 16th centuries by Tibetan, Naxi, Bai and Han artists. Many of them were restored during the later Qing dynasty. They depict various Taoist, Chinese and Tibetan Buddhist themes and can be found on the interior walls of temples in the area. However, the Red Guards came through here slashing and gouging during the Cultural Revolution, so there's not that much to see.

In Báishā the best frescoes can be found in **Dabaoji Palace** (Dàbǎojī Gōng; admission Y8). Nearby, **Liuli Temple** (Liúlí Diàn) and **Dading Ge** also have some and in the neighbouring village of Lóngquán, frescoes can be found on the interior walls of **Dajue Palace** (Dàjué Gōng).

BÁISHĀ 白沙

Báishā is a small village on the plain north of Lìjiāng, near several old temples, and is one of the best day trips out of Lìjiāng, especially if you have a bike. Before Kublai Khan made it part of his Yuan empire (1271–1368), Báishā was the capital of the Naxi kingdom. It's hardly changed since then and offers a close-up glimpse of Naxi culture for those willing to spend some time nosing around.

The star attraction of Báishā will probably hail you in the street. Dr Ho (or He) looks like the stereotype of a Taoist physician and has a sign outside his door: 'The Clinic of Chinese Herbs in Jade Dragon Mountains of Lìjiāng'. The travel writer Bruce Chatwin

JOSEPH ROCK

Yúnnán was a hunting ground for famous, foreign plant-hunters such as Kingdon Ward and Joseph Rock. Rock lived in Lìjiāng between 1922 and 1949, becoming the world's leading expert on Naxi culture and local botany. More than his academic pursuits, however, he will be remembered as one of the most enigmatic and eccentric characters to travel in western China.

Rock was born in Austria, the son of a domineering father who insisted he enter a seminary. A withdrawn child, he escaped into imagination and atlases, discovering a passion for China. An astonishing autodidact – he taught himself eight languages, including Sanskrit – he began learning Chinese at 13 years of age. He somehow wound up in Hawaii, and in time became the foremost authority on Hawaiian flora.

Asia always beckoned and he convinced the US Department of Agriculture, and later Harvard University, to sponsor his trips to collect flora for medicinal research. He devoted much of his life to studying Naxi culture, which he feared was being extinguished by the dominant Han culture. He became *National Geographic* magazine's 'man in China' and it was his exploits in northwestern Yúnnán and Sìchuān for the magazine that made him famous.

He sent over 80,000 plant specimens from China – two were named after him – along with 1600 birds and 60 mammals. Amazingly, he was taking and developing the first colour photographic plates in his field in the 1920s! Tragically, container-loads of his collections were lost in 1945 in the Arabian Sea when the boat was torpedoed.

Rock's caravans stretched for half a mile, and included dozens of servants, including a cook trained in Austrian cuisine, trains of pack horses, and hundreds of mercenaries for protection against bandits, not to mention the gold dinner service and a collapsible bathtub.

Rock lived in Yùhú village (called Nguluko when he was there) outside Lìjiāng. Many of his possessions are now local family heirlooms.

The *Ancient Nakhi Kingdom of Southwest China* (Harvard University Press, 1947) is Joseph Rock's definitive work. Immediately prior to his death, his Naxi dictionary was also finally prepared for publishing. For an insight into the man and his work, take a look at *In China's Border Provinces: The Turbulent Career of Joseph Rock, Botanist-Explorer* (Hastings House, 1974) by JB Sutton, or Rock's many archived articles for *National Geographic*.

propelled the good doctor into the limelight when he mythologised Dr Ho as the 'Taoist physician in the Jade Dragon Mountains of Lìjiāng'. Chatwin did such a romantic job on Dr Ho that the doctor has subsequently appeared in every travel book (including this one) with an entry on Lìjiāng. Journalists and photographers from every corner of the world have since visited Báishā, and Dr Ho, previously an unknown doctor in an unknown town, has achieved worldwide renown. Look out for the John Cleese quote: 'Interesting bloke; crap tea'.

Almost directly opposite Dr Ho's clinic is **Café Buena Vista** (Nànà Wéisītǎ Jùlèbù; ☎ 131-7078 0719; info@ecotour.com) a lovely little café run by an artist, Zhao Fan, and his girlfriend. It also doubles up as an art gallery and is a good place to get travel information (see p669).

There are a couple of frescoes worth seeing in town and surrounding the area; see opposite for details.

Báishā is an easy bike ride from Lìjiāng. Otherwise take bus No 7 (Y2) from the corner of Minzu Lu and Fuhui Lu. The village is about 1km off the main road. From Báishā minibuses return to Lìjiāng regularly (Y5).

YÙLÓNG XUĚSHĀN 玉龙雪山

Soaring to 5500m, some 35km from Lìjiāng, is **Yùlóng Xuěshān** (Jade Dragon Snow Mountain; adult/ student Y80/60), also known as Mt Satseto. Its peak was first climbed in 1963 by a research team from Běijīng.

Three scenic spots have been developed for tourism: Dry Sea Meadow (Gānhǎizi), Cloud Fir Meadow (Yúnshānpíng) and Yak Meadow (Máoniúpíng). There is an entrance fee to the area around Yùlóng Xuěshān.

Dry Sea Meadow (甘海子; Gānhǎizi) is the first stop you come to if travelling by bus from Lìjiāng. A **chairlift** (Y160) ascends to a large meadow at 3050m which, according to geologists, was actually a lake 2000 years ago. At the bottom of the chairlift is the world's highest golf course at an altitude of roughly 3000m.

Cloud Fir Meadow (云杉坪; Yúnshānpíng) is the second stop and a **chairlift** (Y40) takes you up to 4506m where walkways lead to awesome glacier views. Horses can be hired here for Y70.

Around 60km from Lìjiāng is **Yak Meadow** (牦牛坪; Máoniúpíng) where yet another **chairlift** (Y60) pulls visitors up to meadows

at an altitude of 3500m. In the vicinity is Xuěhuā Hǎi (Snowflake Lake) and there are ample hiking opportunities around. If the weather is on your side, the views from here are breathtaking.

Watch out for the symptoms of altitude sickness here (see p932) – Chinese entrepreneurs sell bags of oxygen to chain-smoking Chinese tourists for around Y40. It can also get cold so bring warm clothing. Army overcoats are available for hire (Y20).

With golf courses and cable cars all over the place it's hardly surprising that building has started on some fancy resort-style hotels – expect them to be up and running by the time you read this. At the time of research, camping in the area was not prohibited but it's better to check when you get there as regulations have a tendency to change quicker than the cloud cover.

Bus No 7 (Y8 to Y15) leaves for all three spots from the intersection of Minzu Lu and Fuhui Lu and passes by Báishā on the way. Returning to Lìjiāng, buses leave fairly regularly but check with your driver to find out what time the last bus will depart.

If you enter the region from the north (Tiger Leaping Gorge) there's no ticket gate.

TIGER LEAPING GORGE 虎跳峡
☎ 0007

After making its first turn at Shígǔ, the mighty Yangzi River (at this point known as Jinsha River or Jīnshā Jiāng) surges between Hābā Shān (Haba Mountain) and Yùlóng Xuěshān, through one of the deepest gorges (Hǔtiào Xiá) in the world. The entire gorge measures 16km, and it's a giddy 3900m from the waters to the snowcapped mountaintops. The best time to come is May and the start of June, when the hills are afire with plant and flower life.

The hike through the gorge has gone from obscure adventure to the can't miss experience of northern Yúnnán, but you'll still probably only encounter several other travellers on the trail (unless it's peak season, in late summer). All up, plan on three to four days away from Lìjiāng doing the hike. You can do the walk in two days – one maniac walked it in a day – although some travellers, enchanted with Walnut Garden, have lengthened the hike to over a week.

The first thing to do is to check with cafés in Lìjiāng for the latest gossip on the

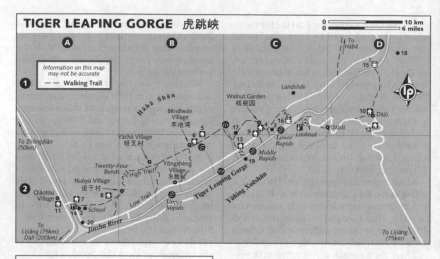

mini-trek, particularly the weather and its possibly lethal effects on the trail. Most cafés give away hand-drawn maps of the trek. They show paths, walking times and some places to stay, but remember that they aren't to scale.

Transport is easier than it once was. Finishing south in Qiáotóu allows for quicker transport back to Lijiāng, but heading north towards Dàjù gives you the option of continuing on to Báishuǐtái. Most people take a Zhōngdiàn-bound bus early in the morning, hop off in Qiáotóu, and hike quickly to stay overnight in Walnut Garden.

Development is taking its toll on the gorge. After three years of Herculean blasting and building, a road now leads all the way through the gorge from Qiáotóu to Walnut Garden and a dirt track swings north to Báishuǐtái, joining the road to Zhōngdiàn. Tour buses shuttle up and down the gorge and kitschy stop-off points are being constructed. Buses currently only reach as far as the upper rapids, about halfway through the gorge, but you can expect the fuss to slowly head downstream. This currently isn't too much of an annoyance for trekkers as the high path climbs way above all the activity.

This does mean that you can still see the gorge (if you don't want to trek) by taking a bus to Qiáotóu and then catching one of the ubiquitous microbuses that shuttle people to the main viewpoint 10km away (per person Y10 one way). You could even take a taxi (Y50) the 23km from Qiáotóu to Walnut Garden.

A second road has been built part of the way through the southern side of the gorge, though it remains to be seen what kind of development will follow.

There is an entry fee to the gorge of Y35, which many people have avoided by walking through at 5am or waiting for the guy to go to sleep in front of the TV. There are check posts about 600m after you cross the bridge at Qiáotóu and at the eastern end of Walnut Garden.

Dangers & Annoyances

The gorge trek is not to be taken lightly, particularly during the wet months of July and August – or any time it rains, really – when landslides and swollen waterfalls can block the paths, in particular on the low road. Half a dozen people – including a few foreign travellers – have died in the gorge. Most perished because they wandered off the trail, got lost and/or were unable to return to the trail, or fell. One hiker was buried while trying to scramble over a landslide and in 2004 a car was caught in a landslide on the low road and four people died. Two solo travellers have also reported being assaulted on the trail by locals, although this couldn't be officially confirmed.

On a less severe note, several travellers have reported becoming ill after eating in Qiáotóu or from drinking water along the trek. Speaking of water, one litre of water is not enough on this trek. You'll also want to bring plenty of sunscreen.

Sleeping & Eating

There are accommodation options at either end of the trek, and all the way in between.

QIÁOTÓU

Jane's Guesthouse (☎ 880 6570; janetibetgh@hotmail .com; dm/s/d Y10/15/15; ☐) Next to the school at the start of the trek, this is your best option in Qiáotóu. Jane can tell you everything there is to know about the gorge trek and it's worth talking to her even if you don't stay the night. There are left-luggage facilities and Internet access here.

Táoyuán Jiǔdiàn (☎ 880 6778; d/q Y50/80) If Jane's happens to be full then try this new hotel where the rooms are clean, but completely devoid of any character.

Gorged Tiger Café (☎ 880 6300) Run by an Australian woman Margo, this is another place you should stop by before starting your trek to get up-to-date information on the trail. It's also a good place to feed up before a trek or reward yourself after a long day's hike.

DÀJÙ

Snowflake Hotel (Xuěhuā Fàndiàn; beds Y10) A lovely courtyard and excellent food make this the best place in town. The hotel can arrange the 7.30am bus to Lìjiāng to pick you up at the hotel.

Tiger Leaping Gorge Hotel (Hǔtiào Xiágǔ Lǚguǎn; bed Y10) If for some bizarre reason the Snowflake is full then try this place by the central square where the buses pick up.

Activities
GORGE TREK

There are two trails – the higher (the older route, known as the 24-bend path, although it's more like 30), and the lower, the new road, replete with belching tour buses. Only the high trail is really worth hiking but as one traveller aptly points out, 'the high road leaves less time for drinking beer in Walnut Garden'. There are now yellow-and-red arrows – a godsend – pointing you along the upper path.

The following route starts at Qiáotóu.

To get to the high road, after crossing through the gate, cross a small stream and go 150m. Take a left fork, go through the schoolyard's football pitch, and join the tractor road. Continue until the track ends and then follow the yellow arrows to the right. It's six hours to Běndìwān or a strenuous eight hours to Walnut Garden. Guesthouses dot the trail which means you're usually never more than a few kilometres from a bed – good news for those not willing to start trekking at the crack of dawn. The following list is not exhaustive.

Naxi Family Guesthouse (Nàxī Kèzhàn; dm Y10) Eight kilometres into the trek, this place gets rave reviews from travellers.

Halfway Lodge (Zhōngtú Kèzhàn, Běndìwān; dm Y10-15) This is an excellent place. There are hot showers on request and some of the best food on the trek. A few years back the owner, a traditional medicine practitioner, was so regularly interrupted by exhausted, dehydrated travellers panicking in the dark outside his modest home that he just opened up a room. He and his ad hoc medicinal herb-and-plant tours proved so popular that he's now had to expand with additional rooms and showers and toilets.

Five Fingers Guesthouse (Wǔzhǐ Kèzhàn; dm Y10-15) Nearby is this new guesthouse that has also been receiving glowing praise from travellers. It offers hot showers and good food. Some of the rooms have fine views.

Tina's Guest House (Zhōngxiá Lǚdiàn; dm Y10) About 1½ hours from Běndìwān you descend to the road to this place – budget more time if you are ascending. Tina's is a

SOUTHWEST CHINA

THE END OF THE GORGE?

Tiger Leaping Gorge, one of the deepest canyons in the world and one of China's most spectacular natural attractions, could disappear in a matter of years if new plans to build eight dams along the upper reaches of the Yangzi River go ahead.

The proposed dams will stretch over 564km of river starting from Shígǔ near Lijiāng and ending in Pānzhīhūa, Sìchuān. Once completed, the dams will flood more than 13,000 hectares of prime farmland, force over 100,000 people to relocate and wash away local culture, history, unique architecture and indigenous plant and animal life.

Officials say the dams are a necessity and that hydropower can solve China's energy shortage problems. While the country's economy races ahead, power supplies are struggling to keep up and many coastal manufacturing hubs experience regular blackouts. The proposed dams will also divert water towards Kūnmíng and help ease urban water shortages. One of the project's major backers is a power company headed by Li Xiaopeng, the son of Li Peng, the former prime minister who pushed through the controversial Three Gorges Dam project (p458). Local authorities are also said to be backing the scheme which will produce an estimated US$50 million a year in tax revenue once power generation begins – double the current annual figure.

Although the central government has yet to grant final approval, Chinese media reports that preparatory work, including blasting, has already begun and proper construction on the dams is expect to begin by 2008. Local and international environmental groups are lobbying the government to halt plans but with such a pro-development economic policy in full swing, it's hard to believe that those in charge will take much notice.

friendly and convenient place to spend your first night from Dàjù. A good detour from here leads down 40 minutes to the middle rapids and Tiger Leaping Stone, where a tiger is once said to have leapt across the Yangzi, thus giving the gorge its name. The man who restored the path charges Y10 to take people down it (regardless of whether you want him to or not).

From Tina's to Walnut Garden it is a 40-minute walk along the road. A new alternative trail to Walnut Garden keeps high where the path descends to Tina's, crosses a stream and a 'bamboo forest' before descending into Walnut Garden.

Walnut Garden (Hútáoyuán; dm Y10-15) A bit beyond the halfway mark, this is one of the original gorge guesthouses and is still one of the most popular. With two buildings serving up great food, beer and dorm beds, some travellers find it so relaxing that they wind up spending several days here.

Sean's Spring Guesthouse (Shānquán Kèzhàn; ☎ 880 6300; www.tigerleapinggorge.com; dm Y10-15) This is one of the original guesthouses on the trail and still the spot for more lively evenings and socialising. Sean's has a free hot shower (Y5 for a hot bath!), electric blankets, mountain-bike hire (per hr Y10) and can organise camping, guides, and horse trips.

Chateau de Woody (Shānbáiliǎn Lǚguǎn; dm Y10-15) This is considered the quiet alternative but the ugly concrete annexe of cramped rooms takes away some of the charm. Woody's also has a free hot shower and Y5 hot bath.

Be aware that in peak times – particularly late summer – up to 100 people per day can make the trek, so bed space is short. Be prepared to sleep in a back room somewhere. Supplies of bottled water can be chancy; it's probably best to bring your own.

The next day's walk is slightly shorter at four to six hours. There are now two ferries and so two route options to get to Dàjù. After 45 minutes you'll see a red marker leading down to the new (winter) ferry (xīn dùkǒu; one way Y10); the descent includes one hairy section over planks with a sheer drop below. From here it's a hard climb to the car park where you should register with the Lìjiāng PSB (Gōngānjú). The PSB officer offers a car to take you into Dàjù for Y10, avoiding the dull 1½-hour's walk along the road.

The second, lesser-used option continues along the road from Walnut Garden until it reaches the permanent ferry crossing (Y10). From here paths lead to Dàjù.

If you're doing the walk the other way round and heading for Qiáotóu, walk north through Dàjù, aiming for the white pagoda at the foot of the mountains.

TIGER LEAPING GORGE TO BÁISHUĬTÁI

An adventurous add-on to the gorge trek is to continue north all the way to Hābā village and the limestone terraces of Báishuĭtái. This turns it into a four-day trek from Qiáotóu and from here you can travel on to Zhōngdiàn. From Walnut Garden to Hābā, via Jiāngbiān, it is seven to eight hours. From here to the Yi village of Sānbà is about the same, following trails. You could just follow the road and hitch with the occasional truck or tractor but it's longer and less scenic. Some hardy mountain bikers have followed the trail but this is really only fun from north to south, elevations being what they are. The best way would be to hire a guide in Walnut Garden for Y50 to Y100 per day, depending on the number of people. For Y100 to Y120 per day you should be able to get a horse and guide. Eventually buses will make the trip, but that is still some time off.

In Hābā most people stay at the **Haba Snow Mountain Inn** (Hābā Xuěshān Kèzhàn; beds Y10) which has toilets and showers. In Sānbà, the **Shānzhuāng Lǚguǎn** (bed Y10) is probably the most popular. From Sānbà there is an 8am bus to Zhōngdiàn (five hours), or you could get off at the turn-off to Bìtá Hǎi (Emerald Pagoda Lake) and hike there.

If you plan to try the route alone, assume you'll need all provisions and equipment for extremes of weather. Ask for local advice before setting out.

Getting There & Away

From Lìjiāng to Qiáotóu, buses run to Zhōngdiàn every hour or so from 7.30am to 4pm from the long-distance bus station and pass through Qiáotóu (Y15).

From Lìjiāng to Dàjù (Y23.50, four to five hours) buses leave fairly regularly from the long-distance bus station. From Dàjù to Lìjiāng one bus a day departs at 1.30pm.

Returning to Lìjiāng from Qiáotóu, buses start running through from Zhōngdiàn between 8am and 9am. The last one rolls through around 6pm (Y15). The last bus to Zhōngdiàn passes through at 4.30pm.

Eventually the new highway through the gorge will link Qiáotóu, Walnut Garden and the settlement across the river from Dàjù and then bend north to connect Báishuĭtái, allowing travellers to get to Zhōngdiàn from here.

LÚGŪ HÚ 泸沽湖
☎ 0888

This stunning lake overlaps the remote Yúnnán–Sìchuān border and is a centre for several Tibetan, Yi and Mosu (a Naxi subgroup) villages. The Mosu are the last practising matriarchal society in the world (see the boxed text, p681) and many other Naxi customs lost in Lìjiāng are still in evidence here. The lake, formed by two sinking faults, is fairly high at 2685m and is usually snowbound over the winter months. There are villages scattered around the lake but Luòshuĭ (洛水) is the one that has been heavily developed for tourism and this is where your bus will drop you off.

A better option is to head to Lǐgé (里格), a small village on the northeastern shore of the lake and by far a more tranquil setting.

The best times to visit the lake are April to May, and September to October, when the weather is dry and mild. Entrance to the lake is Y40.

Sights & Activities

From Luòshuĭ you can visit several islands on the lake by dugout canoe, which the Mosu call 'pig troughs' (zhūcáo). The canoes are rowed by Mosu who also serve as guides and usually take you out to **Lǐwùbǐ Dǎo** (里务比岛; per person Y25), the largest island. From here you can practically wade across to a spit of land in Sìchuān. The second largest island is **Hēiwàè Dǎo** (黑瓦俄岛; per person Y35). A trip to both islands will cost you Y40. Canoes leave from a beach area to the south of the hotel strip in Luòshuĭ. In Lǐgé any of the hostels can help arrange boat trips.

Near the bus stop in Luòshuĭ is the worthwhile **Mosu Folk Custom Museum** (摩俗民族博物馆; Mósú Mínsú Bówùguǎn; admission Y20). The museum is set within the traditional home of a wealthy Mosu family and the obligatory guide will show you around and explain how the matriarchal society functions. There is also an interesting collection of photos taken by Joseph Rock in the 1920s.

In the outskirts of nearby Yǒngníng is **Zhamei Temple** (Zhāměi Sì; admission Y1), a Tibetan monastery with at least 20 lamas in residence. A private mini van costs Y15 per person for the half-hour ride. A bus passes through Luòshuĭ to Yǒngníng for Y5, or you could opt to walk the 20km or so through pleasant scenery.

Sleeping & Eating

Hotels line the lakeside in Luòshuǐ.

Husi Teahouse (湖思茶屋; Húsī Cháwū; ☎ 588 1170; dm Y15; 🖥) One of the original backpacker hangouts, this place has very clean dorm rooms, Internet access and some indispensable local information, including some great trekking tips. It also has a good restaurant.

Mósūyuán (摩俗园; ☎ 588 1188; d with/without bathroom Y80/40) This old building has a modern annex with lots of standard doubles on offer.

There are lots of restaurants in Luòshuǐ, just walk along the lake and take your pick. Some of the traditional Mosu foods include preserved pig's fat and salted sour fish – the latter being somewhat tastier. Most restaurants offer a selection of Mosu dishes.

LǏGÉ 里格

This peaceful village set around a bay facing Lǐgé Dǎo (Lige Island) is the antithesis of it's neighbour Luòshuǐ. With only a handful of homes and guesthouses, it's a wonderful place to base yourself for a few days and explore the surrounding wilderness either by foot or by bike.

Sleeping & Eating

Yúnyóurén (云游人; ☎ 588 1075; dm Y10, d with bathroom Y60-80) This new guesthouse is so close to the lake you could almost dip your toes in. The doubles come with a balcony and unrivalled views and there is a great restaurant and well-stocked bar downstairs.

Bīnmǎ Kèzhàn (宾马客栈; ☎ 588 1181; dm Y15) Just next door to Yúnyóurén, you'll find simple, clean dorm rooms here.

Mósū Wǎngshì (摩俗往事; ☎ 588 1035; dm Y15) A few metres up the road is this cool little bar and restaurant that also has a handful of dorm beds. The building is over 200 years old and the owner is a great character – if a little eccentric. He regularly organises singing and poetry evenings and 'candle parties' for when the electricity cuts out.

Getting There & Away

From Lìjiāng's long-distance bus station there are hourly buses to Nínglàng (Y23, five hours, 7.50am to 5pm). A direct bus to the lake leaves three times a day from the bus station opposite Mao Sq in Lìjiāng (Y43, seven to eight hours, 8am to 10am). From Nínglàng there are two buses to Luòshuǐ (Y43, two to three hours, 1pm and 2.30pm). For Lǐgé you will have to change for a minibus in Luòshuǐ (Y5).

Leaving Luòshuǐ there are two daily buses to Nínglàng (Y43, 9am and 10.30am) and from Nínglàng buses run every half-hour to Lijiāng (7.30am to 4pm) and once a day, Xiàguān (Y48, 7.50am).

Some travellers have tried crossing over to Lúgǔ Zhèn (also known as Zuǒsuǒ), on the Sìchuān side, from where there is bus transport to Xīchàng on the Kūnmíng–Chéngdū line. But be warned: it's a remote route with no accommodation. You'll need to bring a tent, a warm sleeping bag and all provisions.

ZHŌNGDIÀN 中甸

☎ 0887 / elevation 3200m

Zhōngdiàn, 198km northwest of Lìjiāng, is the start of the Tibetan world. Principally a Tibetan town (its Tibetan name is Gyeltang or Gyalthang), a boom in Shangri-la–driven tourism has fuelled the construction of a bland Han Chinese town. What is left of the old town is interesting to wander around. The main reason to come here is to visit the monastery and to get a taste of Tibet if you can't make it to the real thing.

Zhōngdiàn is also the last stop in Yúnnán for more hardy travellers looking at a rough five- or six-day journey to Chéngdū via the Tibetan townships and rugged terrain of western Sìchuān.

In mid-June Zhōngdiàn plays host to a horseracing festival that sees several days of dancing, singing, eating and, of course, horseracing. Another new festival – usually in September – features minority artists of southwest China. Accommodation can be a bit tight around these times, so you may want to arrive a day or two early in order to secure a room.

Information

Agricultural Bank of China (Zhōngguó Nóngyè Yínháng; cnr Changzheng Lu & Xiangyang Lu; ⏱ 8.30am-noon & 2.30-5.30pm Mon-Fri) Can change cash, travellers cheques and give cash advances on credit cards.

PSB (Gōngānjú; Changzheng Lu; ⏱ 8.30am-12.30pm & 2.30-5pm) Issues on-the-spot visa extensions.

China Telecom (Changzheng Lu) There are two telephone offices along this road that offer cheap international phone calls.

WALKING MARRIAGE

The Mosu are the last practising matriarchal society in the world. This system, whereby kinship and clan names, and social and political positions are passed on through the female line, has fascinated visitors since the area was developed for tourism in the early 1980s. What's proved to be the biggest draw, however, is the Mosu tradition of a 'walking marriage' (zuò hūn).

Mosu women never marry nor cohabit; instead women are free to choose as many lovers as they like throughout their lives. Mosu women come of age when they reach 13, after which they no longer have to sleep in the communal living areas but are given their own bedroom. Her lover visits at night and leaves to return to his mother's home in the morning, hence the expression 'walking marriage'.

This idea of such free and easy love has been heavily publicised. Traditionally referred to as Nǚ Guó (Woman's Kingdom), the area of Lúgū Hú was renamed Nǚ'ér Guó (Girl's Kingdom) in order to spice up the romantic and exotic image of the local women.

It's a strategy that's worked. Thousands of tourists have ventured up to this remote area, resulting in the Mosu becoming the richest ethnic minority group in Yúnnán. But it's also had some damaging effects on their culture. 'Walking marriage' has become synonymous with 'one night stand' and many men, in particular Han Chinese, visit the area in the hope of having a walking marriage themselves. This in turn has seen a rise in prostitution in the area and brothels disguised as karaoke bars now sit on the edge of Luòshuǐ town; the ultimate proof, if it was ever needed, that there's no such thing as free love.

Tibet Café (Changzheng Lu; per hr Y12) Internet access is available here.

TOURIST INFORMATION & TRAVEL AGENCIES

Khampa Caravan (☎ 828 8648; www.khampacaravan .com; Heping Lu) Organises some excellent adventures, from day treks in the surrounding countryside to week-long treks in the remote wilderness. It can also arrange overland travel into Tibet (see p683), as well as flights and permits from Zhōngdiàn to Lhasa. The company also runs a lot of sustainable development programs within Tibetan communities. One of these projects, Trinyi Eco-lodge, is a couple of kilometres outside town and is easy to get to by bike.

Tibet Café (☎ 823 0282; www.shambala.org; Changzheng Lu) Another great place to go for travel information; it also organises overland travel to Tibet. A particularly worthwhile trip is a visit to its eco-farm, Shambala, 40km from Zhōngdiàn, where you can spend the evening with a Tibetan family (per person Y20). All money goes directly to the Tibetan community.

Dangers & Annoyances

Be careful in Zhōngdiàn's bus station, particularly on the early-morning Lìjiāng buses; there's been a spell of push-and-slash bandit bands.

Sights

About an hour's walk north of town is the **Ganden Sumtseling Gompa** (Sōngzànlín Sì; admission Y10; ☺ 7.30am-8pm), a 300-year-old Tibetan monastery complex with around 600 monks. The monastery is the most important in southwest China and is definitely worth the trip to Zhōngdiàn. Bus No 3 runs here from anywhere along Changzheng Lu (Y1).

Much closer to the centre of things, just south of town and overlooking the old town district, is another monastery with exceedingly friendly monks.

Hidden within the old town is the **Scripture Chamber** (Gǔchéng Cángjīngtáng; admission Y10), formerly a memorial hall to the Red Army's Long March. **Guishan Park** (Guīshān Gōngyuán; admission Y3) is nearby and has a temple at the top with commanding views of the area.

Sleeping & Eating

Zhōngdiàn has seen a deluge of modern hotels spring up in the town centre to accommodate the growing number of tourists wanting a taste of Shangri-la. Fortunately there are still some good backpacker-friendly places.

Dúkèzōng Jiǔdiàn (☎ 823 0019; Changzheng Lu; dm Y25, d Y80-120) Attached to the Tibet Café rooms here are spotless and look brand new. Bathrooms in the higher-end doubles are state of the art and have an endless supply of hot water. Shared bathrooms have hot water from 9pm to 11pm.

Tibetan Bed & Breakfast (藏家风味; Zàngjiā Fēngwèi; ☎ 822 7505; dm Y30) On the road leading

SOUTHWEST CHINA

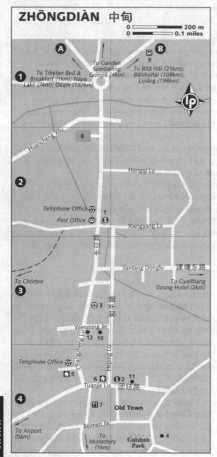

to the monastery is this lovely Tibetan house that has opened it's doors to visitors. Beds are either mattresses or Tibetan carpets on the floor. Washing facilities are basic – but there are plans to provide Internet access! Dinner with the family will cost you extra.

Shangri-La Traveller Club (Zàngdì Guójì Qīngnián Lǚshè; ☎ 822 8671; 98 Heping Lu; dm/d Y15/50; 🖥) This place has a lovely atmosphere and friendly staff and the dorms are very clean. You can rent bikes here (per day Y15) and go online (per hr Y6).

Gyalthang Dzong Hotel (Jiàntáng Bīnguǎn; ☎ 822 3646; www.coloursofangsana.com; d Y672, ste Y1600) This hotel has recently been taken over by the Angsana group (part of the Banyan Tree group) and is by far the most

luxurious hotel you'll find in this neck of the woods. Spa and massage treatments are also available.

Tibet Café (Xīzàng Kāfēiguǎn; Changzheng Lu; ☎ 822 7505; dishes from Y10) This friendly place does very good food (especially the breakfasts) and is a great place to get travel tips.

Have a look around the old town and on Tuanjie Lu for Tibetan and Western restaurants and cafés. Also look out for locally produced *Shangri-la* wine. French missionaries working in the Mekong area taught the Tibetans wine-producing techniques, a tradition which has fortunately carried on through to today. The wine produced is really very good – look for the bottle with a picture of a church on the label (Y30).

Getting There & Away
AIR
Yúnnán Airlines has flights to Kūnmíng (Y700), Chéngdū (Y980), Lhasa (Y1380), Guǎngzhōu (Y1750), Shēnzhèn (Y1860) and Guìyáng (Y1080). Direct flights to Běijīng and Shànghǎi will be up and running by the time you read this and plans for direct flights to Bangkok and Singapore are in the pipeline. Tickets can be bought at the **CAAC** (Zhōngguó Mínháng; ☎ 822 9901; Wenming Jie).

The airport is 5km from town and a taxi will cost from Y15 to Y20. Zhōngdiàn airport is sometimes referred to as Shangri-la, Díqìng or Deqen – there is currently no airport at Déqìn.

SOUTHWEST CHINA

BUS

The route that is now once again legal is the arduous bus-hopping trek to Chéngdū, in Sìchuān. If you're up for this you're looking at a minimum of five to six days' travel at some very high altitudes – you'll need warm clothes. The first stage of the trip is Zhōngdiàn to Xiāngchéng in Sìchuān. From Xiāngchéng, your next destination is Lǐtáng, though if roads are bad you may be forced to stay overnight in Dàochéng. From Lǐtáng, it's on to Kāngdìng from where you can make your way west towards Chéngdū. For more details on these towns see Western Sìchuān & the Road to Tibet (p735).

Note that roads out of Zhōngdiàn can be temporarily blocked by snow at any time from November to March. If you are travelling at this time bring lots of warm clothes and a flexible itinerary.

See box below for bus details.

For Bēnzǐlán you can also catch the Déqīn bus which passes through Bēnzǐlán on the way. See also individual local destinations for transport details.

TO TIBET

There are now flights from Zhōngdiàn to Lhasa, however the situation is much the same as in Kūnmíng and Chéngdū and travellers must be part of an organised 'group' and have the necessary permits in order to travel. There are three companies in Zhōngdiàn that sell 'packages' to Tibet (around Y2400 per person, including air ticket):

Khampa Caravan (☎ 828 8648; www.khampacaravan .com; Heping Lu)

Tibet Café (☎ 823 0282; www.shambala.org; Changzheng Lu)

Tibet Tourism Bureau (Xīzàng Lǚyóujù; ☎ 822 9028; yunnantibettour@yahoo.com.cn; Room 2206, Shangbala Hotel, 36 Changzheng Lu)

These same companies can also organise overland trips from Zhōngdiàn into Tibet via either the northern or southern highway to Lhasa. Likewise, you need official permits in order to do this and these trips don't come cheap (from Y700 per vehicle per day). You're also looking at an eight- to 12-day journey at high altitudes. That aside, the highway to Lhasa promises to be a spectacular adventure with some mind-blowing scenery.

The companies all offer slightly different trips so it's worth shopping around to see what best suits you. Remember that permits take five days to organise. The Tibet Café has arranged for travellers to start the permit process in Dàlǐ courtesy of the MCA Guesthouse. Traveller's can fax copies of their passports through to Zhōngdiàn from the MCA Guesthouse so by the time they arrive in Zhōngdiàn their permits will be ready to collect. Jim's Peace Café in Dàlǐ can also organise overland travel to Lhasa (see p661).

Getting Around

Bus Nos 1 and 3 zip between the monastery and town (Y1).

AROUND ZHŌNGDIÀN   Map p673

Some 7km northwest of Zhōngdiàn you'll find the seasonal **Nàpà Hǎi** (Napa Lake; admission Y15), surrounded by a large grass meadow.

SOUTHWEST CHINA

BUS TIMETABLES

Some bus services from Zhōngdiàn:

Destination	Price	Duration	Frequency	Departs
Kūnmíng	Y146	15hr	3 daily	11am, 1pm, 2pm
Kūnmíng (sleeper)	Y146	15hr	5 daily	4-7.30pm
Lìjiāng	Y29-43	5hr	hourly	7am-5pm
Xiàguān	Y45	8hr	hourly	7am-12.30pm
Xiàguān (sleeper)	Y65	10hr	2 daily	6.30pm, 7.30pm
Déqīn	Y37	6hr	hourly	7-11am
Xiāngchéng	Y68	8-9hr	daily	7.30am
Dōngwàng	Y43	7-8hr	daily	7.30am
Bǎishuǐtái	Y22	4hr	daily	7.50am
Bēnzǐlán	Y16	3hr	daily	2pm

Between September and March budding ornithologists will love the myriad rare species, including the black-necked crane. An entrance fee has recently been introduced.

Approximately 10km southeast of Zhōngdiàn is the **Tiansheng Bridge** (Tiānshēng Qiáo), a natural limestone formation, and further southeast, the subterranean **Xiagei hot springs** (admission Y5). If you can arrange transport, en route is the **Great Treasure Temple** (Dàbǎo Sì), one of the earliest Buddhist temples in Yúnnán.

Emerald Pagoda Lake 碧塔

Some 25km east of Zhōngdiàn, the bus to Sānbà (see Báishuǐtái, following) can drop you along the highway for **Bitǎ Hǎi** (Emerald Pagoda Lake; admission Y30), which is 8km down a trail. You can stay here in basic cabins for Y15 to Y30. There are lots of hiking options and ponies can be arranged at the lake. There is a second, southern entrance, from where it is 2km to the lake. It's possible to rent boats between the two ends of the lake.

Occasionally there is a bus that runs out here but it all depends on whether or not there are enough people. A taxi will cost Y250 to Y300 for the return trip.

Báishuǐtái 白水台

Báishuǐtái is a limestone deposit plateau 108km southeast of Zhōngdiàn with some breathtaking scenery and Tibetan villages en route. The terraces (admission Y30) are resplendent in sunlight, but can be tough to access if rainfall has made trails slippery. There are normally horses for hire.

A couple of **guesthouses** at the nearby towns of Báidì and Sānbà have rooms with beds from Y10 to Y15.

From Zhōngdiàn there are two daily buses to Báishuǐtái at 7.50am and 2pm (Y20 to Y30).

One option is to trek or hitch all the way from Báishuǐtái to Tiger Leaping Gorge; see p679 for information.

Bēnzìlán 奔子栏

This laid-back Tibetan village makes an excellent base to explore the wonderful **Dhondrupling Gompa** (东竹林寺; Dōngzhúlín Sì), 22km from Bēnzìlán, heading northwest along the main road.

Bēnzìlán has plenty of restaurants and small hotels. All offer decent beds for Y20.

Duōwén Lǚguǎn (bed Y10-20) is perhaps the best choice, around the bend in the northern end of town. This Tibetan-style place has a prayer wheel by the entrance and pleasant rooms.

To get to Bēnzìlán take any bus between Zhōngdiàn and Déqīn; buses pass through town between 11am and noon. A direct bus leaves Zhōngdiàn at 2pm (Y15). Returning to Zhōngdiàn, a bus leaves Bēnzìlán daily at 9am (two hours).

DÉQĪN 德钦

☎ 0887 / elevation 3550m

Some 187km northwest of Zhōngdiàn is the last outpost of Yúnnán before Tibet – Déqīn town and county (part of Díqìng Tibetan Autonomous Prefecture). The county is 80% Tibetan, though a dozen other minorities are found here, including one of the few settlements of non-Hui Muslims in China. For borderholics, east is Sìchuān, west is Tibet, and Myanmar lies southwest. Chinese authorities have christened Déqīn County 'Shangri-la' and claim James Hilton's classic *Lost Horizon* used the area for inspiration; they've decided to pump millions of *yuán* into tourism in coming years.

Getting here is possible on a bus but you're crossing some serious ranges along this route and at any time from mid-October to late spring heavy snows can close the road. Tibet beckons to be sure, but the road is currently closed to individual travellers.

Sleeping & Eating

Deqin Tibet Hotel (德钦楼; Déqīn Lóu; dm/d Y25/80) This place has clean toilets, friendly staff and some great views (particularly from room No 7). There is also a hot shower, a nice communal sitting area and an excellent map of the region on the wall. The owners can help arrange transport, such as to Feilai Temple (Fēilái Sì; Y40 return). You'll find this place 200m south of the bus station.

Trekker's Home (旅行者之家; Lǚxíngzhě Zhījiā; ☎ 841 3966; dm from Y20; 🖳) This is a very friendly place with good dorms, 24-hour hot water, public kitchen, Internet access and good local information.

Líshí Fàndiàn About 100m uphill from the Deqin Tibet Hotel, on your left, this doesn't look like much but it serves consistently good food.

Shuìyuán Cāntīng Opposite the Deqin Tibet Hotel, this restaurant has decent food and an outside eating area; look for the colourful canopy and pool table.

Getting There & Away

From Zhōngdiàn to Déqīn, buses leave at 8.20am, 9.20am and noon (Y24, five to six hours). Buses from Déqīn leave at the same time to return to Zhōngdiàn. For details on border crossings into Tibet, see p683.

AROUND DÉQĪN

Approximately 10km southwest of Déqīn is the small but interesting Tibetan **Feilai Temple** (Fēilái Sì).

A further 800m along the main road brings you to a row of **chörten** (stupas) and, weather permitting, breathtaking views of the Méili Xuěshān range, including the 6740m-high Kawa Karpo (also known as Méili Xuěshān or Tàizi Shān). The more beautiful peak to the south is the 6054m-high Miacimu (Shénnǚ in Chinese). Locals come here to burn juniper incense. To get here from Déqīn, get out on the road and flag down anything that moves.

Mingyong Glacier 明永冰川

Tumbling off the side of Kawa Karpo peak is the 12km-long **Mínqyóng Glacier** (Mínqyǒng Bīngchuān; admission Y63). For millennia the mountain and glacier has been a pilgrimage site.

Trails to the glacier lead up from Míngyǒng's central square marked by a new *chörten*. After 45 minutes a path splits off down to the scruffy toe of the glacier. Continuing on, after another 45 minutes you get to Tibetan **Tàizi Miào**, where there is a **guesthouse** (d Y100-120). A further 30 minutes along the trail is **Lotus Temple** (Liánhuā Miào), which offers fantastic views of the glacier framed by prayer flags and *chörten*. Horses can also be hired to go up to the glacier (Y80 to Y120).

SLEEPING

Beds in all guesthouses are around Y20 and toilet facilities are basic. Electricity is iffy so bring a torch or some candles.

Up some steps from Míngyǒng's main square, where the bus drops you off, is **Míngyǒng Shānzhuāng**, a government-run place with decent dorm rooms.

Heading back along the road towards Déqīn are the friendly, family-run **Nuòbù**

Sāngmù Kèzhàn and **Biānmǎdìngzhǔ Kèzhàn**, set in a lovely hamlet. Both offer beds for Y10 to Y15.

GETTING THERE & AWAY

From Déqīn, minibuses to Míngyǒng leave from the bridge near the market at the top end of town regularly (Y10 to Y15, one to two hours). Private cars will take you for about Y15. Returning buses run fairly regularly.

XĪSHUĀNGBĂNNÀ REGION 西双版纳

The region of Xīshuāngbǎnnà (usually called Bǎnnà) is in the deep south of Yúnnán, next to the Myanmar and Lao borders. The name is a Chinese approximation of the original Thai name, Sip Sawng Panna (12 Rice-Growing Districts). The place has a laid-back Southeast Asian feel and it's easy to watch the weeks slip by as you make your way around small villages and tropical forests.

In recent years Xīshuāngbǎnnà has become China's own mini-Thailand, and tourists have been heading down in droves for the sunshine, Dai minority dancing and water splashing festivals (held daily nowadays). But it's easy to get away from the crowds and explore the surrounding countryside and villages.

Environment

Xīshuāngbǎnnà is home to many unique species of plant and animal life. Unfortunately, recent scientific studies have demonstrated the devastating effects of previous government policies on land use; the tropical rainforest areas of Bǎnnà are now as acutely endangered as similar rainforest areas elsewhere on the planet.

The jungle areas that remain contain dwindling numbers of wild tigers, leopards, elephants and golden-haired monkeys. To be fair, the number of elephants has doubled to 250, up 100% from the early 1980s; the government now offers compensation to villagers whose crops have been destroyed by elephants, or who assist in wildlife conservation. In 1998 the government banned the hunting or processing of animals, but poaching is notoriously hard to control.

People

About one-third of the 800,000-strong population of this region are Dai; another third or so are Han Chinese and the rest is made up of conglomerate of minorities that include the Hani, Lisu and Yao, as well as lesser-known hill tribes such as the Aini (a subgroup of the Hani), Jinuo, Bulang, Lahu and Wa.

Xīshuāngbănnà Dai Autonomous Prefecture, as it is known officially, is subdivided into the three counties of Jǐnghóng, Měnghǎi and Měnglà.

Climate

The region has two seasons: wet and dry. The wet season is between June and August, when it rains ferociously almost every day. From September to February there is less rainfall, but thick fog descends during the late evening and doesn't lift until 10am or even later.

November to March sees temperatures average about 19°C. The hottest months of the year are from April to September, when you can expect an average of 25°C.

Festivals & Events

The **Water-Splashing Festival**, held around mid-April (usually from the 13th to the 15th), washes away the dirt, sorrow and demons of the old year and brings in the happiness of the new. The first day of this festival is devoted to a giant market. The second day features dragon-boat racing, swimming races and rocket launching. The third day features the water-splashing freakout – be prepared to get drenched all day, and remember, the wetter you get, the more luck you'll receive.

During the **Tanpa Festival** in February, young boys are sent to the local temple for initiation as novice monks. At approximately the same time (between February and March), **Tan Jing Festival** participants honour Buddhist texts housed in local temples.

The **Tan Ta Festival** is held during the last 10-day period of October or November, with temple ceremonies, rocket launches from special towers and hot-air balloons. The rockets, which often contain lucky amulets, blast off with a curious droning sound, like mini-space shuttles, before exploding high above; those who find the amulets are assured of good luck.

The farming season (from July to October) is the time for the **Closed-Door Festival**, when marriages or festivals are banned. Traditionally this is also the time of year that men aged 20 or older are ordained as monks for a period of time. The season ends with the **Open-Door Festival**, when everyone lets their hair down again to celebrate the harvest.

During festivals, booking same-day airline tickets to Jǐnghóng can be extremely difficult – even with 17 flights per day! You can try getting a flight into Sīmáo, 162km to the north, or take the bus. Hotels in Jǐnghóng town are booked solid, but you could stay in a nearby Dai village and commute. Festivities take place all over Xīshuāngbǎnnà, so you might be lucky further away from Jǐnghóng.

JǏNGHÓNG 景洪

☎ 0691

Jǐnghóng, the capital of Xīshuāngbǎnnà prefecture, lies beside the Mekong River. It's a laid-back but rapidly growing town; the streets are lined with picturesque palms that help mask the Chinese-built concrete boxes until they merge with the stilt-houses in the surrounding villages. For most travellers Jǐnghóng is more a base for operations than a place to hang out, although it's not without a certain relaxed charm.

THE DAI PEOPLE 傣族

The Dai are Hinayana Buddhists (as opposed to China's majority Mahayana Buddhists) who first appeared 2000 years ago in the Yangzi Valley and who were subsequently driven southwards by the Mongol invasion of the 13th century. The Dai state of Xīshuāngbǎnnà was annexed by the Mongols and then by the Chinese, and a Chinese governor was installed in the regional capital of Jinglan (present-day Jǐnghóng). Countless Buddhist temples were built in the early days of the Dai state and now lie in the jungles in ruins. During the Cultural Revolution, Xīshuāngbǎnnà's temples were desecrated and destroyed. Some were saved by serving as granaries, but many are now being rebuilt from scratch. Temples are also recovering their role as village schools where young children are accepted for religious training as monks.

The Dai live in spacious wooden houses raised on stilts, to keep themselves off the damp earth, with the pigs and chickens below. The most common Dai foods are sticky rice (khao nio in Dai) and fish. The common dress for Dai women is a straw hat or towel-wrap headdress, a tight, short blouse in a bright colour, and a printed sarong with a belt of silver links. Some Dai men tattoo their bodies with animal designs, and betel-nut chewing is popular. Many Dai youngsters get their teeth capped with gold, otherwise they are considered ugly.

Linguistically, the Dai are part of the very large Thai family that includes the Siamese, Lao, Shan, Thai Dam and Ahom peoples found scattered throughout the river valleys of Thailand, Myanmar (Burma), Laos, northern Vietnam and Assam. The Xīshuāngbǎnnà Dai are broken into four subgroups – the Shui (Water) Dai, Han (Land) Dai, Huayao (Floral Belt) Dai and Kemu Dai – each distinguished by variations in costume, lifestyle and location. All speak the Dai language, which is quite similar to Lao and northern Thai dialects. In fact, Thai is often as useful as Chinese once you get off the beaten track. The written language of the Dai employs a script that looks like a cross between Lao and Burmese.

In temple courtyards, look for a cement structure looking like a letterbox; this is an altar to local spirits, a combination of Buddhism and indigenous spirit worship. Some 32 separate spirits exist for humans.

Zhang khap is the name for a solo narrative opera, for which the Dai have a long tradition. Singers are trained from childhood to perform long songs accompanied by native flute and sometimes a long drum known as the elephant drum. Performances are given at monk initiations, when new houses are built, weddings, and on the birthdays of important people, and they often last all night. Even if you do understand Dai, the lyrics are complex – if not fully improvised. At the end, the audience shouts 'Shuay! Shuay!' which is close to 'Hip, hip, hooray!'. Even courtship is done via this singing. Some Dai phrases include doūzaŏ lǐ (hello), yíndií (thank you) and goīhán (goodbye).

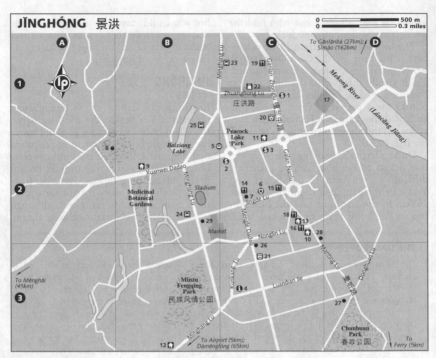

JĬNGHÓNG 景洪

The town's name means 'City of Dawn' in Dai.

Information

Check out the travellers' books at the Mei Mei, Forest and Mekong cafés for the most recent travel tips and for some very detailed trek notes.

INTERNET ACCESS

Internet cafés (wăngbā; Manting Lu; per hr Y2) There are literally dozens along this street.

MONEY

Bank of China (Zhōngguó Yínháng; Xuanwei Dadao); branch office (Ganlan Zhonglu) Changes travellers cheques and foreign currency, and has an ATM machine.
China Agricultural Bank (Zhōngguó Nóngyè Yínháng; Xuanwei Dadao) Changes travellers cheques and foreign currency, and has an ATM machine.

POST & TELEPHONE

China Post & Telecom (Yóudiàn; cnr Mengle Dadao & Xuanwei Dadao; ⏱ 8am-8.30pm) You can make international calls from here.

TOURIST INFORMATION & TRAVEL AGENCIES

CITS (Zhōngguó Guójì Lǚxíngshè; ☎ 663 8459; 2nd fl, Jĭnghóng International Travel Bldg; Luandian Jie) Can arrange several one-day tours from Y100. However, you're better off going to the Mekong Café and Mei Mei Café (see Eating p690), who will help with trekking information and put you in touch with English-speaking guides. Ask around for Sid, an Englishman living in Bǎnnà who is a great source of local information and can also help arrange trips.

VISAS

PSB (Gōngānjú; Jingde Lu; ☺ 8-11.30am & 3-5.30pm) Has a fairly speedy visa extension service.

Dangers & Annoyances

There have been two reports (unconfirmed) from travellers regarding drug-and-rob incidents (one successful, one not) on the Kūnmíng–Jĭnghóng bus trip. Like other countries in Southeast Asia, be careful who your friends are on buses, accept nothing, and leave nothing unattended when you hop off on breaks.

There have also been reports of an attempted mugging on the Dàménglóng to Bùlǎngshān trek (see the boxed text, p696) near the town of Bannanban. Don't carry any valuables if you do this trek and try not to walk alone.

Sights

TROPICAL FLOWER & PLANTS GARDEN
热带花卉园

The **botanical garden** (Rèdài Huāhuìyuán; ☎ 212 0493; 28 Jĭnghóng Xilu; admission Y40; ☺ 7.30am-6.30pm), west of the town centre, is one of Jĭnghóng's better attractions. Admission gets you into a series of gardens where you can view over 1000 different types of plant life. On the eastern side of the gardens there is a tropical rainforest area where it is easy to lose yourself for an hour or more under the canopy of trees. Take the path on the left-hand side as you enter the gardens. The gardens also house the **Zhou Enlai Memorial** (Zhōu Ēnlái Zǒnglǐ Jìniànbēi), a contemporary sculpture commemorating a 1961 visit by China's best-loved premier.

PEACOCK LAKE PARK 孔雀湖公园

This artificial lake in the centre of town isn't much, but the small park (Kǒngquè Hú Gōngyuán) next to it is pleasant. The English Language Corner takes place here every

---

Sunday evening, so this is your chance to exchange views or to engage with the locals practising their English.

Activities

Jĭnghóng's oft-recommended **Blind Massage School** (Mángrén Ànmó; ☎ 212 5834; cnr Mengle Dadao & Jingde Lu; ☺ 9am-1am) offers hour-long massages for Y40. There are also freelance masseurs around Peacock Lake Park. For a foot massage try the southeastern corner of the park, for back and shoulders try the western side.

Non-guests can use the swimming pool at the Crown Hotel (Y5).

Sleeping

Banna College Hotel (Bǎnnà Xuéyuàn; ☎ 213 8365; Xuanwei Dadao; dm Y10-15, d per person Y20-30; ✖) This newly opened guesthouse on the grounds of Bǎnnà's college has the best-value rooms in town. Higher-end doubles are carpeted.

Dai Building Hotel (Dǎijiā Huāyuán Xiǎolóu; ☎ 216 2592; 57 Manting Lu; dm Y25) People either love or hate this popular backpacker hang-out. All accommodation is in two- or four-bed bamboo bungalows on stilts. Some travellers have been less than impressed with the occasional rodent visitors and lack of privacy (the bamboo walls are definitely not soundproof!).

Wanli Dai Style Guesthouse (Wànlǐ Dàiwèi Cāntíng; ☎ 898 4496; Manting Lu; dm Y20) With only a handful of simple rooms, this place is basic but comfortable, although the rooms can get very hot in the summer months. There is a nice garden here and a good restaurant.

Jĭngyŏng Fàndiàn (☎ 212 3727; 12 Jinghong Donglu; d/tr Y60/80; 🌣) Beds in the Guìbīnlóu, the second building on your right as you enter the complex, are fantastic value. The rooms have all been recently renovated and have great big beds.

Tai Garden Hotel (Tàiyuán Jiŭdiàn; ☎ 212 3888; fax 212 6060; 8 Minghang Lu; d Y640 plus 15% tax; 🌣) Still the top option in town, this hotel is in the southern part of town towards the airport. It has quiet grounds replete with its own island, pool, sauna, gym and tennis court.

Eating

Manting Lu is lined with restaurants serving Dai food, the majority of which dish up Dai dance performances along with their culinary specialities. Dai women thump drums at the entrance and the restaurants are filled nearly every night with tourists generally being festive.

Dai dishes include barbecue fish, eel or beef cooked with lemongrass or served with peanut-and-tomato sauce. Vegetarians can order roast bamboo shoot prepared in the same fashion. Other specialities include fried river moss (better than it sounds and excellent with beer), spicy bamboo-shoot soup and *shāokăo* (skewers of meat wrapped in banana leaves and grilled over wood fires).

Mei Mei Café (Mĕimeī Kāfēitīng; Manting Lu roundabout; dishes from Y5) For good food, strong coffee, really cold beer and (you guessed it) banana pancakes, stop by this pleasant little Akha restaurant. Mei Mei was the first café to cater to foreigners and is still one of the most popular, with some of the best travel information you'll find in Jĭnghóng. This is the spot to rent a bicycle (Y20 per day).

Cold Drink Shop (Lĕngyĭndiàn; Mengle Dadao; juices from Y4, dishes from Y5) Next to the Blind Massage School, this breezy open-air restaurant and cold drinks shop serves simple Dai dishes and thirst-quenching fresh fruit juices – the coconut juice is particularly good.

Mekong Café (Méigōng Cānguăn; ☎ 216 2395; 111 Manting Lu) This is a great place, well-run and friendly, with sofas and cold beer. Food is generally excellent, with Hani, Western, Dai, Japanese and even Thai dishes on the menu. The upstairs balcony is a pleasant place to sit with a beer in the winter and read about the sub-zero temperatures in Bĕijīng.

Xīnguāng Jiŭjiā (☎ 212 4711; Ganlan Zhonglu) If you want Dai food in an unpretentious atmosphere, then try this restaurant run by one of Xīshuāngbănnà's best-known traditional singers.

Thai Restaurant (Tàiguó Cāntīng; ☎ 216 1758; Manting Lu) This hugely popular restaurant serves authentic Thai dishes, including a great *phad thai*. Wash it all down with some snake whisky if you're feeling brave.

There is a huge **night food market** by the new bridge over the Mekong where dozens of stalls serve up barbecued everything, from sausages to snails.

Entertainment

Mengbala Naxi Arts Theatre (Mĕngbālá Nàxī Yìshùgōng; Ganlan Zhonglu; tickets Y160; 🕑 8.30pm) This theatre has daily song and dance shows.

YES Disco (Mengle Dadao; admission free; 🕑 9pm-late) If you're in the mood for dancing yourself, then try this popular place, especially at the weekend. You'll probably want to fortify yourself with a few beers before you go however.

Shopping

The **Jade Market** (Zhuanghong Lu) in the north of town is fun to browse even if you're not particularly interested in the stuff. There are also a couple of shops selling Dai handicrafts, clothing and jewellery here.

Getting There & Away

AIR

More flights and bigger planes (Boeing 737s) mean that it's a lot easier to fly to Jĭnghóng from Kūnmíng than it used to be. In April (when the Water-Splashing Festival is held) you'll need to book tickets several days in advance.

There are several flights a day to Kūnmíng (Y650), and daily flights to Lìjiāng (Y760), Shànghăi (Y2250) and Guăngzhōu (Y1910). You can also fly to Bangkok (Y1200) and Chiang Mai (Y1200) from here.

Flights can be booked at **Yunnan Airlines** (☎ 212 7040; Jingde Lu; 🕑 8am-noon & 3-6pm).

BUS

The Jĭnghóng long-distance bus station (Minghang Lu) is the most useful for long-distance destinations. If you want to explore Xīshuāngbănnà, go to the No 2 bus station. See box opposite for bus details.

BĂNNÀ BUS TIMETABLES

Buses from Bǎnnà long-distance bus station:

Destination	Price	Duration	Frequency	Departs
Kūnmíng	Y156.50	11-12hr	2 daily	4pm, 7.30pm
Kūnmíng (sleeper)	Y145-169	12-16hr	20 daily	7.30am-7pm
Ruìlì	Y200	40hr	daily	9am
Bǎoshān	Y150	30-34hr	daily	noon
Xiàguān	Y152	18hr	daily	12.30pm

Bus services from the No 2 bus station:

Destination	Price	Duration	Frequency	Departs
Sānchàhé	Y10-11.50	1½hr	every 20min	6.15am-6.30pm
Mènyǎng	Y5.50	40min	half-hourly	8am-6pm
Měnglún	Y12.50	2hr	every 20min	7am-6pm
Měnglà	Y29	4-5hr	every 20min	7am-6pm
Gǎnlǎnbà	Y6	40min	every 20min	7am-6pm
Dàměnglóng	Y13	3-4hr	every 20min	6.30am-6.30pm
Měnghǎi	Y9.50	50min	every 20min	6.30am-6pm
Jǐngzhēn	Y11	2hr	every 20min	7am-6pm
Mènhùn	Y12.50	2hr	every 20min	7am-6pm
Sīmáo	Y30	5hr	every 15min	6.15am-6.30pm

Getting Around

The airport is 5km south of the city; CAAC minibuses (Y4) leave when full, across from the Yunnan Airlines booking office. A taxi will cost around Y20.

Jǐnghóng is small enough that you can walk to most destinations, but a bike makes life easier. The Mekong and Mei Mei cafés rent bikes for Y10 per day, or Y20 for a mountain bike. You can also rent bikes at the No 2 bus station.

AROUND JǏNGHÓNG

The possibilities for day trips and longer excursions out of Jǐnghóng are endless. Some travellers have hiked and hitched from Měnghǎi south to Dàměnglóng, some have cycled up to Měnghǎi and Měngzhē on mountain bikes (it's almost impossible on bikes without gears), and one French photographer hitched up with a local medicine man and spent seven days doing house calls in the jungle.

Obviously, it's the longer trips that allow you to escape the hordes of tourists and get a feel for what Xīshuāngbǎnnà is about. But even with limited time there are some interesting possibilities. Most destinations in Xīshuāngbǎnnà are only two or three hours away by bus, but generally they are not much in themselves – you need to get out and about. Note that to get to many villages, you'll often first have to take the bus to a primary village and stay overnight there, since only one bus per day – if that – travels to the tinier villages.

If you're a serious collector of local market experiences, there are plenty to be found in the region. Like anything else, markets are subjective things, but most people seem to prefer the Thursday market in Xīdìng, then Měnghùn, followed by Měnghǎi.

The best advice is to get yourself a bike or some sturdy hiking boots, pick up a map, put down this book and get out of town.

Nearby Villages

Before heading further afield, there are numerous villages in the vicinity of Jǐnghóng that can be reached by bicycle. Most of them you will happen upon by chance, and it's difficult to make recommendations.

On the other side of the Mekong are some small villages, and a popular jaunt involves heading off down Manting Lu – if you go far enough (about 5km) you'll hit a ferry crossing point on the Mekong (Y1), beyond which there are plenty of Dai temples and villages to explore.

Sanchahe Nature Reserve
三岔河自然保护区

This **nature reserve** (Sānchàhé Zìrán Bǎohùqù), 48km north of Jǐnghóng, is one of five enormous forest reserves in southern Yúnnán. This one has an area of nearly 1.5 million hectares.

The part of the park that most tourists visit is **Banna Wild Elephant Valley** (Bānnà Yěxiànggǔ; admission Y50), named after the 40 or so wild elephants that live in the valley; it's worth a visit if you want to see something of the local forest.

The reserve has two entrances. The main southern entrance has accommodation, displays on tropical birds and butterflies, and peacock shows. The other entrance has rather depressing 'wild' elephant performances for the throngs of shutterbug tourists. A 2km-**cable car** (one way/return Y40/60) runs over the treetops from the main entrance into the heart of the park. There is an elevated wooden walkway running through the jungle canopy and a number of dirt paths that run between the two main gates. It is only possible to get off the main paths with a guide and that will cost Y200 per day.

If you want to stay in the park there are **bungalows** (d/tr Y480/580) at the main entrance, although they are rather extortionate. Alternatively, you can stay in one of 22 Swiss Family Robinson-type **canopy treehouses** (d Y480) in the heart of the park, not that these are any cheaper. On the plus side, travellers who have stayed here have reported seeing elephants bathing in the stream beneath them at dawn. You might be able to get a discount.

Just about any bus travelling north from Jǐnghóng to Sīmáo will pass this reserve (Y10, one hour). Returning to Jǐnghóng there is a bus that leaves the north entrance daily at 2.30pm.

Měngyǎng 勐养

Měngyǎng is 34km northeast of Jǐnghóng on the road to Sīmáo. It's a centre for the Hani, Lahu and Floral-Belt Dai. Chinese tourists stop here to see the **Elephant-Shaped Banyan Tree** (Xiàngxíng Róngshù).

From Měngyǎng it's another 19km southeast to **Jīnuò**, which is home base for the Jinuo minority. Travellers have reported a cool reception here (some minorities dislike tourists), so if you want to overnight you'll probably have to stay in Měngyǎng.

Gǎnlǎnbà (Měnghǎn) 橄榄坝

Gǎnlǎnbà, or Měnghǎn as it's sometimes referred to, lies on the Mekong southeast of Jǐnghóng. In the past the main attraction of Gǎnlǎnbà was the boat journey down the Mekong from Jǐnghóng. Unfortunately, improved roads sank the popular boat trip (locals prefer to spend an hour on a bus to three hours on the boat), and the only way to travel down the river now is to charter a rubber dinghy **drift boat** (Y100) – an expensive and overrated trip.

However, Gǎnlǎnbà remains a wonderful retreat from hectic Jǐnghóng. The town itself comes alive in the evening when the streets fill up with locals eating, drinking, gossiping or just wandering the streets in an attempt to escape the heat indoors. The whole thing lends an almost carnival atmosphere to the town any day of the week.

It's worth coming by bike (or hiring one in Gǎnlǎnbà) as there's plenty of scope for exploration in the neighbourhood.

SIGHTS

The premier 'attraction' in Gǎnlǎnbà is the **Dai Minority Park** (傣族园; Dàizúyuán; ☎ 250 4099; Manting Lu; adult/student Y50/25), which is quite simply part of the town that has been cordoned off and had a ticket booth stuck at the entrance. Tourists can spend the night in villagers' homes and partake in water-splashing 'festivals' twice a day. While the 'park' and Dai architecture is beautiful, spending the night here can feel a bit like you're spending the night in a zoo, albeit a minority one. If you do stay overnight in the park, your ticket is valid for the following day.

There's a couple of old decaying temples on the road into town from Jǐnghóng, and nearby is a huge **produce market** (nóngyè shìchǎng), which sells all kinds of regional specialities including lots of weird tropical fruit.

Travellers recommend heading to the south of town, crossing the Mekong by ferry (Y2 with a bike), and then heading left (east). The last ferry returns at 7pm. Check the visitors' book in the Sarlar Restaurant for further ideas.

SLEEPING & EATING

There are a number of options. Beds in a Dai home within the park will cost Y20 per person. Beds are traditional Dai mats and are usually very comfortable. Most homes have showers and the owners will cook dinner for you. There are no restaurants within the park.

Yúnlì Bīnguǎn (运丽宾馆; ☎ 241 0204; Manting Lu; d/tr Y40/60) This is a modern hotel with spotless rooms that all come with private balconies.

Sarlar Restaurant (沙拉餐厅; Shālā Cāntīng; Jinlun Donglu; dm Y10) This friendly place has one 'room' (a corner of the restaurant partitioned off by a piece of wood) with Dai-style mats on the floor. Check whether the sheets are clean and don't expect to get to sleep early if people are socialising in the restaurant. This place is on the left-hand side of Jinlun Donglu, the main road travelling away from Jǐnghóng.

Dai Family Restaurant (傣家餐厅; Manting Lu) This place has an English menu on the wall and there are no prices listed, so check before you order as food is a little pricier than elsewhere.

You'll find a handful of Dai restaurants near the Dai Family Restaurant.

GETTING THERE & AWAY

Microbuses to Gǎnlǎnbà leave from Jǐng-hóng's No 2 bus station (Y6, every 20 minutes, 7am to 6pm). Minibuses depart Gǎnlǎnbà for Jǐnghóng and Měnglún (Y10) from the main intersection in the centre of town.

It's possible to cycle from Jǐnghóng to Gǎnlǎnbà in a brisk two hours or a leisurely three hours, and it's a pleasant ride.

GETTING AROUND

You can rent a mountain bike at the entrance to the Dai Minority Park (Y20 per day) or from one of several bicycle shops along Manting Lu (Y10 per day).

Měnglún 勐伦

Měnglún is the next major port of call east of Gǎnlǎnbà. The major attraction is the **Tropical Plant Gardens** (热带植物园; Rèdài Zhíwùyuán; adult/student Y60/40). The gardens are nicely laid out and it's a pleasant enough

---

THE JINUO PEOPLE 基诺族

The Jinuo, sometimes known as the Youle, were officially 'discovered' as a minority in 1979. The women wear a white cowl, a cotton tunic with bright horizontal stripes and a tubular black skirt. Earlobe decoration is an elaborate custom – the larger the hole and the more flowers it can contain the better. Teeth are sometimes painted black with the sap of the lacquer tree, which serves the dual dental purpose of beautifying the mouth and preventing tooth decay and halitosis.

Previously, the Jinuo lived in long houses with as many as 27 families occupying rooms on either side of the central corridor. Each family had its own hearth, but the oldest man owned the largest hearth, which was always the closest to the door. Long houses are rarely used now and the Jinuo sadly seem to be quickly losing their distinctive way of life.

---

place to commune with nature, but you'd have to be a keen botanist to fork out the steep entrance fee.

To get here, turn left out of the bus station and walk to the first corner. Walk one block and turn left again. You'll come to market hawkers, and a road leading downhill to the right side. Follow this until you reach a footbridge across the Mekong. The ticket booth is just in front of the bridge.

The **Bus Station Hotel** (车站招待所; Chēzhàn Zhāodàisuǒ; dm Y15) is the best-value option. Beds are comfortable doubles and there's a clean shared bathroom and shower down the hall.

Just before the park entrance is this very nice hotel, **Chūnlín Lǚshè** (春林旅社; ☎ 871 5816; dm Y20, d & tr with bathroom Y60-80; 🖳), set on four levels around a small garden. Dorms are simple but clean, high-end doubles are almost luxurious.

The **Friendship Restaurant** (友谊餐厅; Yǒuyì Cāntīng; Main Hwy) has lots of dishes made from strange vegetables, ferns and herbs only found locally.

From Jǐnghóng's No 2 bus station there are buses to Měnglún (Y12.50, two hours, every 20 minutes, 7am to 6pm). The buses pass through Gǎnlǎnbà. Some travellers have cycled here from Gǎnlǎnbà.

From Měnglún, there are buses to Měnglà (Y20, 2½ hours, 8.30am to 7.30pm) and Jīnghóng every 30 minutes.

Měnglà 勐腊

Měnglà sees an increasing number of travellers passing through en route to Laos via the border crossing at Móhān. As the bus journey from Jīnghóng, or even Měnglún, will take the better part of the day, you will probably have to stay overnight here.

There is a **Bank of China** (中国银行; Zhōngguó Yínháng; ☺ 8-11.30am & 3-6pm Mon-Fri) in the southern half of town that changes cash and travellers cheques but won't give cash advances on credit cards. To change Renminbi back into US dollars, you'll need your original exchange receipts.

Rooms at the new **Jīnqiáo Dàjiǔdiàn** (金桥大酒店; ☎ 812 4946; d/tr Y50/60; ☒) are nothing special, but it's convenient for the north bus station just up the hill on the left.

Měnglà Bīnguǎn (勐腊宾馆; ☎ 812 2168; dm/d Y10/40) is set within a pretty shaded garden. The dorm beds are very basic but the doubles are clean and have their own balcony. It's near No 2 bus station; ask a local to point you in the right direction.

There are loads of restaurants along Mengla Jie where you can get dishes for Y5.

Měnglà has two bus stations: the northern long-distance bus station and No 2 bus station in the southern part of town. Buses from Měnglà are listed as follows:

Destination	Price	Frequency	Departures
Kūnmíng	Y169	hourly	8.30-11.30am
Jīnghóng	Y31	every 20min	6.20am-6pm
Měnglún	Y20	every 20min	6.20am-6pm
Yáoqū	Y10	4 daily	8.30am, 10.30am, 2.30pm, 4.30pm
Móhān	Y12	2 daily	8am, 9am

From No 2 bus station there are buses to Móhān every 20 minutes (Y12, 1½ hours, 8am to 5.40pm), as well as a few departures to Jīnghóng.

TO LAOS

The good news is that you can now get an on-the-spot visa for Laos at the border (Y240). From Měnglà there are buses to Móhān every 20 minutes or so from 8am. No matter what anyone says, there should be no 'charge'

to cross. Once your passport is stamped (double-check all stamps) and you've waved goodbye to the border guards, you can jump on a tractor or truck to take you 3km into Laos for around Y3. Whatever you do, go early. Although the border doesn't officially close until 5.30pm Běijīng time (and don't forget that Laos is an hour ahead), things often wrap up earlier on the Lao side. There are guesthouses on both the Chinese and Lao sides; change money on the Lao side.

DÀMĚNGLÓNG 大勐龙

Dàměnglóng (written just 'Měnglóng' on buses) is about 70km south of Jīnghóng and a few kilometres from the Myanmar border and is a good base for hikes around the surrounding hills. The sleepy village itself is not much (it rouses itself somewhat for the Sunday market), but the surrounding countryside, peppered with decaying stupas and little villages, is worth a couple of days' exploration. You can hire bikes at Dàměnglóng Zhàodàisuǒ for Y15 per day.

The town's laid-back feel may change in the next few years, however. The border crossing point with Myanmar (poetically named 2-4-0) has been designated as the entry point for a planned highway linking Thailand, Myanmar and China. If and when it does open, things should definitely pick up here.

Sights

WHITE BAMBOO SHOOT PAGODA
曼飞龙塔

This **pagoda** (Mànfēilóng Tǎ; admission Y5), built in 1204, is Dàměnglóng's premier attraction. According to legend, the temple was built on the spot of a hallowed footprint left by Sakyamuni Buddha, who is said to have visited Xīshuāngbǎnnà – if you're interested in ancient footprints you can look for it in a niche below one of the nine stupas. Unfortunately, in recent years a 'beautification' job has been done on the temple with a couple of cans of white paint.

If you're in the area late October or early November, check the precise dates of the Tan Ta Festival. At this time White Bamboo Shoot Pagoda is host to hundreds of locals whose celebrations include dancing, rocket launchings, paper balloons and so on.

The pagoda is easy to get to: just walk back along the main road towards Jīnghóng for 2km until you reach a small village with a temple on your left. From here there's a path up the hill; it's about a 20-minute walk. There's an entry fee, but often there's no-one around anyway.

BLACK PAGODA 黑塔
Just above the centre of town is a Dai monastery with a steep path beside it leading up to the Black Pagoda (Hēi Tǎ) – you'll notice it when entering Dàměnglóng. The pagoda itself is actually gold, not black. Take a stroll up, but bear in mind that the real reason for the climb is the superb views of Dàměnglóng and the surrounding countryside.

Sleeping & Eating
Plenty of cheap options are available for foreigners.

Lai Lai Hotel (来来宾馆; Láilái Bīnguǎn; d/tr Y20/10) Right next to the bus station you'll see the English sign for this place. It has simple rooms and the owner is lovely and meticulous about cleanliness.

Dàměnglóng Zhàodàisuǒ (大勐龙招待所; dm Y10) Formerly the only place for foreigners, beds here are basic and the bathrooms are fragrant but passable. To get here, walk uphill from the main highway to where the local government building sits. The hotel is in the grounds to the left, just past some ornamental frogs. Bicycles can be rented here (Y15 per day).

Cáizhèngsuǒ (财政所; d Y30) A better option is this new hotel on the right-hand side of the same government grounds. All doubles come with a modern bathroom and TV.

There are a couple of decent restaurants down from the bus station, near the steps leading up to the Black Pagoda; the Chinese signs proclaim them to be Dai restaurants.

Getting There & Away
There are buses to Dàměnglóng (Y13, three to four hours, every 20 minutes, 6.30am to 6.30pm) from Jǐnghóng's No 2 bus station. Remember that the 'Da' character won't be painted on the bus window. Buses for the return trip run regularly between 6am and 6pm.

AROUND DÀMĚNGLÓNG
Xiǎojiē 小街
The village of Xiǎojiē, about 15km north of Dàměnglóng, is surrounded by Bulang,

Lahu and Hani villages. Lahu women shave their heads; apparently the younger ones aren't happy about this any more and hide their heads beneath caps. The Bulang are possibly descended from the Yi of northern Yúnnán. The women wear black turbans with silver decorations; many of the designs are of shells, fish and marine life.

There's plenty of room for exploration in this area, although you're not allowed over the border.

MĚNGHǍI 勐海
This modern town, 50km west of Jǐnghóng, serves as a centre for trips into the surrounding area rather than as a destination in itself. If you're passing through, it's worth visiting the huge daily produce market that attracts members of the hill tribes. The best way to find it is to follow the early morning crowds. North of Měnghǎi are many pagodas and interesting villages that make for some fine exploring on bicycle.

Buses run from Jǐnghóng's No 2 bus station to Měnghǎi (Y9.50, one hour, every 20 minutes, 6.30am to 6pm). From Měnghǎi's flashy new bus station there are buses to Bùlǎngshān (Y15, 9am and 2pm), Xīdìng (Y9, 10.40am and 3.30pm), Měngmǎn (Y9.50, 10am, 3.30pm and 4pm) and Kūnmíng (Y155 to Y170, hourly, 11.30am to 4.30pm), among other destinations. Buses return to Jǐnghóng every 20 minutes until 7pm.

AROUND MĚNGHǍI
Měnghùn 勐混
This quiet little village, about 26km southwest of Měnghǎi, has a colourful **Sunday**

market. The town begins buzzing around 7am and the action lingers on through to noon. The swirl of hill tribespeople with the women sporting fancy leggings, headdresses, earrings and bracelets alone makes the trip worthwhile. Měnghùn also a good place to buy local handicrafts for much cheaper prices than you would find in Kūnmíng (don't haggle too much, these women have yet to learn the idea of overcharging foreigners).

White Tower Hotel (白塔饭店; Báitǎ Fàndiàn; dm Y10) is basic but secluded and looks out over a lily pond. From the main intersection, take the road uphill, walk through the archway, then bear left across the basketball court and follow a small path heading downhill; around the corner is the hotel.

Liángwáng Cānting (粮王餐厅; ☎ 542 4378; dm Y10) is up from the bus station and has clean, basic rooms. Getting to the toilets (also clean) is an adventure in itself as you

---

TREKKING IN XĪSHUĀNGBĂNNÀ

Treks around Xīshuāngbǎnnà used to be among the best in China – you'd be invited into a local's home to eat, sleep, and drink *báijiǔ*. Increasing numbers of visitors have changed this in places. Don't automatically expect a welcome mat and a free lunch just because you're a foreigner, but don't go changing the local economy by throwing money around either. Also take care, it's a jungle out there, so go prepared, and make sure somebody knows where you are and when you should return. In the rainy season you'll need to be equipped with proper hiking shoes and waterproof gear. At any time you'll need water purification, bottled water or a water bottle able to hold boiling water, as well as snacks and sunscreen.

Dàměnglóng to Bùlǎngshān Trek

The most popular walk is this 48km trek through Dai, Hani, Bulang and Lahu villages. It can be done in either direction. This is a poor area but the people are friendly and the jungle is relatively pristine. If you do get invited into someone's home, try to establish whether payment is expected. If it's not, leave an offering of around Y10 or leave modest gifts such as candles, matches, rice etc – even though the family may insist on nothing.

Start by taking a bus to Dàměnglóng. From there it's roughly a 10km walk or hitch a ride on a tractor to the Dai village of Manguanghan. One bus per day should leave Dàměnglóng at noon but this is neither certain nor necessary. Take the path to the right, 200m beyond the end of Manguanghan. It's a steady 12km walk (three to four hours) to Manpo, a Bulang village. As you cross through Guangmin, an Aini village en route, look out for a temple. After staying overnight in a villager's home in Manpo, the next day is a 24km (six hours) walk to Weidong via Nuna (Bulang people), Songeer (Lahu people), and Bannankan (Lahu). In Manpo ask for the right path to Weidong (the path goes down). There are three or four places where you may get off the track and have to backtrack but that's part of the fun. Stay overnight in Weidong and the next day is another leisurely 10km (three hours) to Bùlǎngshān on a good road. If you want to just spend one night on the trail, a family in Songeer offers accommodation and two meals for Y20 per person. From Manpo to Songeer it's a three-hour walk.

From Bùlǎngshān there are minibuses back to Měnghǎi (via Měnghùn) at 8am and 2.30pm. There is a truck stop/karaoke place in Bùlǎngshān with dorm beds, but you'll probably be kept awake by drinking truckers offering you smokes. Try and find a local to put you up.

If you're short of time, it is possible to trek from Manpo to Bùlǎngshān in one go but it's an epic day of trekking. Those in shape can probably finish in nine hours.

If you time it right you could stop over at Měnghùn's Sunday market (p695) on the way back to Jǐnghóng, or start the trek in Bùlǎngshān and visit the market en route to the town.

Guides

One of the main advantages of taking a guide is to communicate with villagers en route; you won't hear much Mandarin Chinese on the trail, let alone any English. Ask at Mei Mei or Mekong cafés (p690) for guides; they cost around Y200 per day.

have to negotiate your way past the chickens, ducks and a pig before you get there. Make sure you bring a torch (flashlight). There is also a restaurant here that serves good, cheap food.

Buses departing from Jǐnghóng for Měnghùn (Y12.50, two hours, every 20 minutes, 7am to 6pm) run from Jǐnghóng's No 2 bus station.

From Měnghùn, minibuses run regularly to Měnghǎi (Y5), Xīdìng (Y9.50, 1½ hours, 7.10am and 4pm) and throughout the day to Jǐnghóng.

Unless you have a very good bike with gears, cycling to Měnghǎi and Měnghùn is not a real option. The road up to Měnghǎi is so steep that you'll end up pushing the bike most of the way. Cycling from Měnghùn back to Jǐnghóng on the other hand, is almost entirely downhill.

Xīdìng 西定
This sleepy hillside hamlet comes alive every Thursday for it's weekly market, reputedly one of the best in the region. At other times you'll find it almost deserted. To get here by public transport you can either catch one of the two direct buses from Měnghǎi (Y9, 10.40am and 3.30pm) or travel via Měnhùn and change for a bus to Xīdìng. If you want to see the market at its most interesting, you'll really have to get here the night before. The small guesthouse at the bus station has beds for Y15. Buses from Xīdìng leave twice a day (Y9.50, 7.20am and 1pm) for Měnghùn. If you miss the bus you can always get a ride on a motorbike (Y30), a spectacular if not hair-raising experience, from the only bike shop in town.

Jǐngzhēn 景真
In the village of Jǐngzhēn, about 14km northwest of Měnghǎi, is the **Octagonal Pavilion** (八角亭; Bājiǎo Tíng; admission Y10), first built in 1701. The original structure was severely damaged during the Cultural Revolution but renovated in 1978 and the ornate decoration is still impressive. The temple also operates as a monastic school. The paintings on the wall of the temple depict scenes from the *Jatatka*, the life history of Buddha.

Frequent minibuses from the minibus centre in Měnghǎi go via Jǐngzhēn.

THE HANI (AKHA) PEOPLE 哈尼族

The Hani (also known in adjacent countries as the Akha) are of Tibetan origin and related to the Yi, but according to folklore they are descended from frogs' eyes. They stick to the hills, cultivating rice, corn and the occasional poppy and are famed for their intricate rice terraces.

Hani women (especially the Aini, a subgroup of the Hani) wear headdresses of beads, feathers, silver rings and coins, some of which are turn-of-the-century French (Vietnamese), Burmese and Indian coins.

BĂOSHĂN REGION 保山

Travellers who pass through the Bǎoshān area tend to do so quickly on the way to or from Ruìlì, but the area, in particular Téngchōng, is worth a bit more time that that. There are some worthwhile historical sights and many distinctive minority groups. The old quarters of Téngchōng are worth browsing before they disappear entirely and the Téngchōng area is rich in volcanic activity, with hot springs and volcanic peaks.

As early as the 4th and 5th centuries BC (two centuries before the northern routes through central Asia were established), the Bǎoshān area was an important stop on the southern Silk Road – the Sìchuān–India route. The area did not come under Chinese control until the Han dynasty when, in AD 69, it was named the Yongchang Administrative District. In 1277 a huge battle was waged in the region between the 12,000 troops of Kublai Khan and 60,000 Burmese soldiers and their 2000 elephants. The Mongols won and went on to take Pagan.

TÉNGCHŌNG 腾冲
☎ 0875
Not many travellers get to this town on the other side of Gāolígòng Shān (Gaoligong Mountain) range, but it's an interesting place. There are about 20 volcanoes in the vicinity and lots of hot springs (p700). It's also prime earthquake territory, having experienced 71 earthquakes measuring over five on the Richter scale since 1500.

The town has some interesting backstreets with the kind of traditional wooden architecture that used to be commonplace in many towns and cities in Yúnnán. Unfortunately these are under threat from modernisation and work has already started on tearing them down.

Information

Bank of China (Zhōngguó Yínháng; cnr Fengshan Lu & Yingjiang Xilu) Will change cash and travellers cheques. There's also an ATM here.

China Post & Telecom (Yóudiàn; Fengshan Lu)

Internet café (wǎngbā; Feicui Lu; per hr Y2)

PSB (Gōngānjú; Yingjiang Xilu; 8.30-11.30am & 2.30-5.30pm Mon-Fri) Can help with visa extensions.

Xinhua Bookstore (Xīnhuá Shūdiàn; Nanmen Jie) Sells maps of Téngchōng.

Sights & Activities

The best places for a random wander are the backstreets running off Yingjiang Xilu. There are a couple of small markets with plenty of colour and activity in the mornings. Walking along Fengshan Lu from Feicui Lu, the first side street on the left has a small **produce market**. Further down on the right is a large, covered **jade market** where you can sometimes see the carving process. Walk east along Yinjiang Xilu and you will come across a larger **produce market** on your right.

On the western edge of town is the **Laifeng Shan National Forest Park** (Láifēng Shān Guójiā Sēnlín Gōngyuán; admission Y10; 8am-7pm). You can walk through lush pine forests to **Laifeng Temple** (Láifēng Sì) or make the sweaty hike up to the summit where a pagoda offers fine views. There are lots of further hiking possibilities.

In the southwestern suburbs of town, **Xianle Temple** (Xiànlè Sì; admission Y5) is beside the small **Dieshui Waterfall**, which makes a good place for a picnic. The area makes a nice destination for a bike ride and you could easily combine it with a trip to Héshùn (opposite), a picturesque village 4km outside Téngchōng.

Sleeping & Eating

Téngchōng's accommodation options are fairly spread out.

Línyè Dàshà (Forestry Bldg; ☎ 516 4058; fax 516 4057; Dongfang Lu; d Y60, d/tr with bathroom Y80/120) It's not in the most convenient location but the rooms are enormous and the views over the hills are great.

Yínhé Bīnguǎn (☎ 513 5813; fax 513 8172; 25 Nanmen Jie; d Y80) The posters pinned up in the corridors urging guests to make sure they 'use a condom' makes you wonder what kind of regular clientele comes here. But the rooms are very clean and while the bathrooms could do with some stronger light bulbs, the central location makes this a winner.

Fúzhuāngchǎng Zhāodàisuǒ (Fengshan Lu; dm Y10) This is as cheap (and as basic) as you'll find in Téngchōng. Rooms are divided by thin plywood and you'll do well to have your own sleeping bag. There's a basic shared wash area.

Your best option for lunch and dinner is the **food court** (cnr Feicui Lu & Laifeng Dadao), where you'll find half a dozen restaurants serving up delicious food from morning to night. There's a huge choice of delicious dishes here including *shāokǎo* (barbecue), grilled fish and chilli crabs.

Getting There & Away

There are two bus stations in Téngchōng: the shiny new long-distance bus station in the south of town and the old local bus station on Dongfang Lu. In general, for destinations north of Téngchōng, head to the long-distance bus station, and for all locations south of town head to the local bus station.

The local bus station has daily buses to Ruìlì (Y36, six hours, 7.40am, 8.30am, 10.40am and 11.40am) and Mángshì (Y36, 4½ hours, 7.40am, 10.20am and 1pm), and frequent departures to local destinations.

The long-distance bus station has sleeper buses to Kūnmíng (Y158 to Y170, 13 hours, hourly, 1.30pm to 7.50pm). An express bus also leaves for Kūnmíng at 8am (Y163). Buses to Bǎoshān (Y28 to Y35, five hours, 7.30am to 5.30pm) leave every 30 minutes and depart two to four times a day for Xiàguān (Y83, eight hours). Check for times when you arrive.

Buses going to local destinations north of Téngchōng, such as Mǎzhàn, Gùdōng, Ruìdián, Diántān or Zìzhì either leave

from, or pass through, Huoshan Lu in the northeast of town.

Getting Around

Téngchōng is small enough to walk around, but a bicycle is helpful for getting to some of the closer sights outside town – the surrounding scenery alone justifies a ride. You can hire a bike from a shop on Guanghua Lu (Y1 per hour).

Bus No 2 runs from the town centre to the long-distance bus station.

AROUND TÉNGCHŌNG

There's a lot to see around Téngchōng but getting out to the sights is a bit tricky. Catching buses part of the way and hiking up to the sights is one possibility, while some of the closer attractions can be reached by bicycle.

Your other option is a hired van, which may be affordable if there are several of you; head down to the minibus stand just off the northern end of Huoshan Lu or to the minibus stand for the Sea of Heat in the southwest of town.

Some highlights of the region are the traditional villages that are scattered between Téngchōng and Yúnfēng Shān (Cloudy Peak Mountain). The relatively plentiful public transport along this route means that you can jump on and off minibuses to go exploring as the whim takes you.

Héshùn 和顺

Southwest of town is the village of Héshùn which is well worth a visit. It has been set aside as a retirement village for overseas Chinese, but it's of more interest as a quiet, traditional Chinese village with cobbled streets. There are some great old buildings in the village, providing lots of photo opportunities. The village also has a small **museum** (博物馆; *bówùguǎn*) and a famous old **library** (图书馆).

Minibuses leave from the corner of Feicui Lu and Laifeng Xiang (Y1.50) in Téngchōng or you can hop on bus No 3 that passes nearby. It's an easy bicycle ride out to the village but the ride back is an uphill slog.

Yúnfēng Shān 云蜂山

Yúnfēng Shān (Cloudy Peak Mountain; admission Y10), 47km north of Téngchōng, is a Taoist mountain dotted with 17th-century temples and monastic retreats. Most people take the **cable car** (one way/return Y30/50), from where it's a 20-minute walk to **Dàxióngbǎo Diàn** (大雄宝殿), a temple at the summit. **Lǔzǔ Diàn** (鲁祖殿), the temple second from the top, serves up great vegetarian food at lunchtime. It's a quick walk down but it can be hard on the knees.

To get to the mountain, go to Huoshan Lu where you can flag down a bus to Ruìdián or Diántán and get off at the turnoff to Yúnfēng (Y8). Alternatively, take a bus to Gùdōng (Y6) and then a microbus from here to the turn-off (Y2). From the turn-off you have to either hitch, or you can choose to take the lovely walk past the village of Heping to the pretty villages just before the mountain. Hiring a vehicle from Téngchōng to take you on a return trip will cost about Y300.

Volcanoes

Téngchōng County is renowned for its volcanoes, and although they have been behaving themselves for many centuries the seismic and geothermal activity in the area indicates that they won't always continue to do so. The closest one to town is **Mǎ'ān Shān** (马鞍山; Saddle Mountain), around 5km to the northwest. It's just south of the main road to Yíngjiāng.

Around 22km to the north of town, near the village of Mǎzhàn, is the most accessible cluster of **volcanoes** (admission Y20). The main central volcano is known as **Dàkòng Shān** (大空山; Big Empty Hill), which pretty much sums it up, and to the left of it is the black crater of **Hēikòng Shān** (黑空山; Black Empty Hill). You can haul yourself up the steps for views of the surrounding lava fields (long dormant).

Minibuses run frequently to Mǎzhàn (Y5) from along Huoshan Lu, or take a Gùdōng-bound minibus. From Mǎzhàn town it's a 10-minute walk or take a motortricycle (Y5) to the volcano area.

Sea of Heat 热海

This is a cluster of hot springs, geysers and streams about 12km southwest of Téngchōng. In addition to the usual indoor baths, the **Sea of Heat** (Rèhǎi; adult/student Y30/20, with pool access Y100; 7.30am-11pm) features a couple of outdoor hot springs and a nice

warm-water swimming pool. If the steep entrance fee puts you off swimming then you can pay Y30 for a quick dip in the **Měinǚ Chí** (Beautiful Lady Pool) instead. Some of the springs here reach temperatures of 102°C.

The site is a popular local resort and there are several hotels.

Rehai Grand Hotel (热海大酒店; Rèhǎi Dàjiǔdiàn; ☎ 515 0366; d Y280) has two branches, one within the park and the other just outside the main entrance.

The basic rooms at **Rèhǎi Zhāodàisuǒ** (热海招待所; ☎ 515 0306; d & tr Y80) are a bit damp but come with free access to the hotel's very own bathing pool (not such a bonus once you've seen it). This place is to the left of the park entrance.

Microbuses leave for Sea of Heat (Y5) when full from the Dongfang Lu turn-off in the south of town.

DÉHÓNG PREFECTURE
德宏州

Déhóng Prefecture (Déhóng Lìsù) and Jingpo Autonomous Prefecture, like Xīshuāngbǎnnà, borders Myanmar and is heavily populated by distinctive minority groups, but hasn't yet captured travellers' imaginations as 'Bǎnnà' has. It's in the far west of Yúnnán and is definitely more off-the-beaten track than Xīshuāngbǎnnà.

Most Chinese tourists in Déhóng are here for the trade from Myanmar that comes through the towns of Ruìlì and Wǎndīng – Burmese jade is a popular commodity and countless other items are spirited over the border. The border with Myanmar is punctuated by many crossings, some of them almost imperceptible, so be careful if you go wandering too close.

The most obvious minority groups in Déhóng are the Burmese (normally dressed in their traditional sarong-like *longyi*), Dai and Jingpo (known in Myanmar as the Kachin, a minority long engaged in armed struggle against the Myanmar government). For information on etiquette for visiting temples in the region see the boxed text, p689.

Around Déhóng are signs in Chinese, Burmese, Dai and English. This is a border region getting rich on trade – in the markets you can see Indian jewellery, tinned

MÁNGSHÌ (LÙXĪ) 芒市 (潞西)

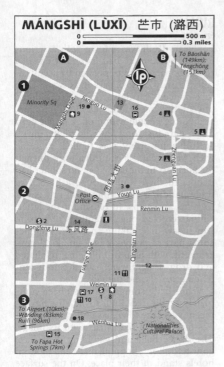

fruits from Thailand, Burmese papier-mâché furniture, young bloods with wads of foreign currency, and Chinese plain-clothes police.

MÁNGSHÌ (LÙXĪ) 芒市 (潞西)
☎ 0692
Mángshì is Déhóng's air link with the outside world. It's a large, sprawling town and there's little to see here. Most travellers simply pass through on their way to Ruìlì. If you fly in from Kūnmíng there are mini-buses running direct from the airport to Ruìlì and your best bet is to jump into one of these and head south.

If you're planning to fly out of Mángshì then you might have to stay overnight here, in which case there are enough things to keep you occupied for an afternoon or so. There are a couple of **markets** in town that are fun to wander around, and a number of temples including **Puti Temple** (Pútí Sì), **Five Clouds Temple** (Wǔyún Sì) and **Foguang Temple** (Fóguāng Sì) that have managed to survive (just about) the onslaught of concrete around them.

Halfway along Youyi Lu, in a school playground, is the 200-year-old **Embracing Tree Pagoda** (Shùbāo Tǎ; admission Y5), so named because over the years it has fused with the surrounding tree.

Around 7km south of town are the **Fapa Hot Springs** (Fǎpà Wēnquán), which get good reports from travellers.

The **Bank of China** (Zhōngguó Yínháng; Dongfeng Lu) changes cash and travellers cheques and gives cash advances on credit cards. There is an ATM machine around the corner from the southern bus station on Weimin Lu.

Sleeping & Eating
Chángjiāng Bīnguǎn (☎ 228 6055; Weimin Lu; s/d Y60/50, with bathroom Y80/100; ☒) This is one of those rare hotels where the cheaper rooms are actually nicer than their more expensive counterparts. Check the rooms before you hand over your cash as one or two smell a bit musty, but they're generally good value.

Zhōngyù Bīnguǎn (☎ 213 3188; Mangshi Dajie; d Y150) The beds in this hotel are reason enough to spend one night in Mángshì – they're enormous! Situated opposite Minority Sq (Mínzú Guǎngchǎng), you can watch the oldies practising taichi in the morning.

Mángshì is strangely lacking in restaurants. You'll find some point-and-choose restaurants along Qingnian Lu and in the vicinity of the long-distance bus station. Otherwise try the small **noodle restaurant** (Tuanjie Dajie) near the southern bus station where you can get a big plate of fried noodles for Y5.

The Zhōngyù Bīnguǎn has a good coffee shop, **Yunjoy Coffee** (Yúxǐ Kāfēi; ☉ 9am-midnight) that serves frothy cappuccinos and stiff whiskies.

Getting There & Away

AIR

The airport is 10km from the city. There are daily flights between Mángshì and Kūnmíng (Y660). Buses sometimes leave from Mángshì airport to the town centre (Y2), although you might have no choice but to negotiate with the taxi sharks at the airport (Y10 to Y20). Minibuses to Ruìlì (Y30, two hours) usually wait at the airport for incoming flights. Buses leave the Mángshì **Yunnan Airlines** (Wenhua Lu; ☉ 8.30am-noon & 2.30-6pm) office for the airport around an hour before flight departures.

BUS

There are several bus stations in Mángshì. Both the long-distance bus station in the north of town and the southern bus station offer similar destinations at similar prices and schedules. If you don't find your bus at one, trudge along to the other.

See box below for bus details.

A bus stand a block southwest of the southern bus stand has the most frequent departures to Wǎndīng (Y15) and Ruìlì (Y20, 7am to 8pm). Minibuses leave when full so be prepared to wait.

RUÌLÌ 瑞丽
☎ 0692

For years Ruìlì was a town with a serious image problem. It had a reputation as a rough border town populated by seedy casinos, bawdy karaoke bars and discos where folk danced 'till dawn. It was considered one of the happening places in Yúnnán, and young people with money would head down here just for a few wild nights out.

Ruìlì's notoriety was fuelled by trade with Myanmar. The border only opened for business in the 1990s but no sooner had it opened than Ruìlì became a hotbed of trade handling everything from raw goods to gems and arms. In return for the latter, China received huge quantities of heroin, which saw drug-taking and trafficking become part of everyday life. The local government, with help from Běijīng, retaliated and drug dealers were hauled before sentencing panels and then executed.

While drug-smuggling hasn't been completely eradicated, Ruìlì's wild past has. In recent years the town has undergone a serious facelift in a bid to clean up its image. The dance halls and gambling dens have gone and shiny shopping malls and modern hotels stand in their place. On the surface there is little left to suggest that Ruìlì used to be a town of such ill repute.

However, despite the change in landscape, Ruìlì is one of the more interesting towns in southwest China. There's a great mix of Han Chinese, minorities and Burmese traders hawking jade, some lively local markets and a laid-back Southeast Asian feel.

There are some interesting minority villages nearby; the stupas are in much better condition than those in Xīshuāngbǎnnà,

---

MÁNGSHÌ BUS TIMETABLES

Bus services from Mángshì include:

Destination	Price	Duration	Frequency	Departs
Kūnmíng	Y171	13hr	3 daily	10.30am, 6.20pm, 9pm
Xiàguān	Y81	14hr	3 daily	11am, 7.20pm, 8pm
Lìjiāng	Y129	17hr	daily	5pm
Jǐnghóng	Y200	24hr	daily	11.30am
Téngchōng	Y22	4hr	7 daily	7.40am-4.20pm
Bǎoshān	Y31	5hr	10 daily	7.20am-3.30pm
Yinjiang	Y25	3hr	every 40min	7.30am-4.50pm

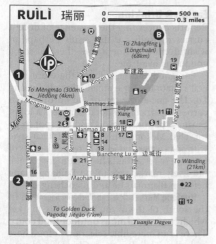

and it's worth getting a bicycle and heading out to explore. Travellers that do venture down here tend to linger longer than they intended, simply for the atmosphere, and it's only a matter of time before Ruìlì becomes the next 'must-visit' destination in Yúnnán.

Another draw for travellers is Myanmar, which lies only a few kilometres away from Ruìlì. Border-crossing restrictions are beginning to relax and although individual tourists are still not allowed to cross, organising permits to take you through the sensitive border area is becoming easier (see p705). New highways laid to facilitate border trade stretch all the way from the border to Mandalay, making what had been a horrible five-day journey much more sane. Soon, foreign travellers will be able to recreate the 'Southern Silk Route', of which Ruìlì and Mandalay were a part.

Information

BOOKSHOPS
Xinhua Bookshop (Xīnhuá Shūdiàn; Renmin Lu) Sells the useful *Ruili Tour Traffic Map*, published by the Ruili Tourism Bureau.

EMERGENCY & VISAS
PSB (Gōngānjú; Jianshe Jie; ☉ 8.30-11.30am & 2.30-5.30pm) Just up the road from Ruìlì Bīnguǎn.

INTERNET ACCESS
Internet café (wǎngbā; Mengmao Jie; per hr Y2-3)

MONEY
Bank of China (Zhōngguó Yínháng; Nanmao Jie) Provides all the usual services and will let you cash travellers cheques for US dollars in case you're headed to Myanmar.
Industrial Bank of China (ICBC; Zhōngguó Gōngchǎng Yínháng; Renmin Lu) Changes cash.

POST & TELEPHONE
China Post & Telecom (Yóudiàn; cnr Mengmao Lu & Renmin Lu) International calls can be made from here.

TOURIST INFORMATION & TRAVEL AGENCIES
Ruili Overseas Travel Company (Ruìlì Hǎiwài Lǚyóushì; ☎ 412 5980; 18 Jianshe Lu; ☉ 8-11.30am, 2.30-5.30pm & 7.30-10pm) The friendly staff here speak some English and can provide information on the local area.

Dangers & Annoyances
Despite Ruìlì's new look, old problems die hard and prostitution remains an enormous industry in Ruìlì. You don't have to look very hard to see the evidence: brothels disguised as hairdressers fill the town.

Another major problem is of the poppy-derived variety, Ruìlì being an entry point for Burmese opium headed to Hong Kong.

This has resulted in a serious IV drug-use problem in the Déhóng region, along with its pernicious sibling – HIV. The province, with Běijīng's help, has poured millions of *yuán* into anti-drug efforts along the border with Myanmar.

Sights

There is not a lot to see in Ruìlì itself, although it's a great town to wander around, and is small enough that you can cover most of it in an hour or so. The huge **market** in the west of town is most colourful by day, especially in the morning, when the stalls are lined with Burmese smokes, tofu wrapped in banana leaves, snack stalls and charcoal sellers. It's a great place to see the mosaic of ethnic groups that make up Ruìlì's diverse population, in particular the Burmese women with their painted faces.

At the other end of town, Ruìlì's **jade market** is worth a visit. Most of Ruìlì's sights are outside town, and you'll need a bicycle to get out and see them.

Sleeping

There are some good deals to be found in Ruìlì's hotels and all the accommodation is within easy walking distance of the main bus station.

Nányáng Bīnguǎn (☎ 414 1768; Nanmao Jie; d & tr Y60) In the centre of town this hotel has some great doubles in the new building. Triples are in the old building and are, well, older. Take a look before you decide.

Lìmín Bīnguǎn (☎ 414 2249; Nanmao Jie; dm Y15, d Y50-80; 🔀) This place has got the biggest selection of rooms, but while the dorm beds are cheap, they can get hot and stuffy and the shared bathrooms hum a bit. There is little to distinguish the doubles, so go for the cheaper ones.

Ruìlì Bīnguǎn (☎ 410 0899; 15 Jianshe Lu; d Y100) Just like the town itself, this hotel has cleaned up its act and is no longer the cheap option. Doubles are very comfortable although the wood panelling on the walls could make you feel like you were sleeping in a sauna.

New Kaitong International Hotel (Xīn Kǎitōng Guójì Dàjiǔdiàn; ☎ 415 777; fax 415 6190; 2 Biancheng Lu; d Y360, discounted d Y180; 🔀) This is the original luxury hotel in Ruìlì and offers good discounts which make it a worthwhile option. The outdoor swimming pool is perhaps the best feature and is open to non-residents for Y10.

Eating & Drinking

Reports concerning the existence of decent curries in Ruìlì are the result perhaps of wishful embellishment, but there is some good food available.

For good Burmese food, there are several restaurants in a small alley off Jiegang Lu. The one at the top of the northwestern corner is particularly good, and sees a lot of Burmese patrons. This is also the spot to go for Thai Mekong whisky, served Thai-style with soda water and ice. There are also lots of Cantonese restaurants here. At night a small but lively market sets up on Baijiang Xiang between Bianmao Jie and Biancheng Lu.

Huafeng Market (Huáfēng Shìchǎng; Jiegang Lu) In the south of town you'll find this market which has an enormous outdoor food court. There is an incredible selection of food here including Thai, Burmese, Chinese and even some Western dishes on offer.

Jo Jo's Cold Drinks Shop (Juéjué Lěngyǐndiàn; Jiegang Lu) One of the original backpacker hangouts, Jo Jo's has moved to the market and does some excellent fresh fruit juices, simple meals and delicious Burmese-style banana pancakes (fried and smothered in condensed milk).

Bo Bo's Cold Drinks Shop (Bùbù Lěngyǐndiàn; Baijiang Xiang) This place serves similar food and drinks to Jo Jo's.

Make sure you try a freshly squeezed lime juice (large/small Y3/2) from one of the numerous stands dotting the town.

Getting There & Away

AIR

Ruìlì has daily flight connections to Kūnmíng via Mángshì, which is a two-hour drive away. See p701 for details. You can buy tickets at **Yunnan Airlines** (☎ 414 8275; Renmin Lu; 🕑 8.30am-noon & 2.30-6pm). Minibuses leave daily for the two-hour trip to the airport from the office. Check that day's flight schedule to see what time the buses leave. You can also use the ticket office to book and reconfirm return flights – do so early as this is an increasingly popular flight.

BUS

There are two bus stations in Ruìlì, the long-distance bus station in the centre of town and the north bus station at the top of Jiegang Lu. The north bus station is useful if you're trying to get to Zhāngfēng (Y10)

RUÌLÌ BUS TIMETABLES

Buses from Ruìlì long-distance bus station are:

Destination	Price	Duration	Frequency	Departs
Téngchōng	Y36	6hr	every 40min	6.30-10.30am
Bǎoshān	Y47	7½hr	every 40min	6.30am-2.30pm
Xiàguān	Y100	11hr	hourly	4-8pm
Kūnmíng	Y181	16hr	hourly	8am-8pm
Jǐnghóng	Y222	36hr	daily	9am

but not much else; you're better off going to the long-distance station.

See box above for bus details.

Minibuses to Mángshì from Ruìlì (Y20), run all the time from 7am to 7.30pm from the long-distance bus station.

For local destinations, minibuses and vans leave from the minibus stand near the jade market, or you can just flag one down in the street. Destinations include Wǎndīng (Y5), the border checkpoint at Jiěgào (Y4), and the village of Nóngdǎo (Y8). Buses to Zhāngfēng (Y10, one hour) leave from Xinjian Lu.

TO MYANMAR

To cross from China into Myanmar, travellers must have the correct visa, travel permits and be part of an official 'group'. The group, which might consist entirely of yourself and no-one else, will be escorted from Jiěgào in China to Hsipaw in Myanmar, an eight-hour drive from the border. Once you reach Hsipaw you can wave good bye to your guide and are free to travel on your own further south to Mandalay, Rangoon and so on.

There are two companies that can organise these permit and group packages:

Ko Wai Lin Travel (Map p646; ☎ 0871-313 7555; myanmarwailin@yahoo.com; Room 221, Camellia Hotel, 154 Dongfeng Lu, Kūnmíng)

Way Thar Li Tour & Travel Company Ltd (☎ 928 2987; waytharli@mptmail.net.mm; 19 Zhuyu Jie, Ruìlì) At the time of research, both companies offered packages that included travel permits, guide (minder) and transportation from Jiěgào to Hsipaw for Y1350. Permits only take one day to organise. Remember it's not possible to organise a visa for Myanmar in Ruìlì and you will have to do this in Kūnmíng at the Myanmar consulate (see p893).

Getting Around

Ruìlì is easily seen on foot, but all the most interesting day trips require a bicycle. Lìmín Bīnguǎn rents bikes for Y10, with a Y200 deposit if you aren't staying at the hotel.

A flat rate for a taxi ride inside the city should be Y5, and up for negotiation from there. There are also cheaper motor and cycle rickshaws.

AROUND RUÌLÌ

Most of the sights around Ruìlì can be explored easily by bicycle. It's worth making frequent detours down the narrow paths leading off the main roads to visit minority villages. The people are friendly, and there are lots of photo opportunities. The *Ruili Tour Traffic Map*, published by the Ruili Tourism Bureau, shows the major roads and villages.

The shortest ride is to turn left at the corner north of the post office and continue out of the town proper into the little village of Měngmǎo. There are half a dozen Shan temples scattered about; the fun is in finding them.

Golden Duck Pagoda 弄安金鸭塔

In the outskirts of town to the southwest, on the main road, this pagoda (Nóng'ān Jīnyā Tǎ) is an attractive stupa set in a temple courtyard. It was established to mark the arrival of a pair of golden ducks that brought good fortune to what was previously an uninhabited marshy area.

Jiegao Border Checkpoint 姐告边检点

Continue straight ahead from Golden Duck Pagoda, cross the Myanmar bridge over Ruìlì Jiāng and you will come to Jiěgào, about 7km from Ruìlì. It's a little thumb of land jutting into Myanmar that serves as the main checkpoint for a steady stream of cross-border traffic (see left for more details). There's not a lot to see but you can still marvel at how laid-back everything seems on both sides of the – quite literally – bamboo curtain and indulge the perennial fascination with illicit borders. As with Ruìlì this place has seen its popular casinos and other dens of iniquity replaced by lemonade stands and cheap electronic shops.

Microbuses shuttle between the border and Ruìlì's long-distance bus station when full for Y4 or you can charter one for around Y20. Buses continue until late at night.

Wanding Border Checkpoint 湾丁边检点

West of Ruìlì lies Wǎndīng, a second checkpoint for crossing into Myanmar. It's not as busy here, nor is it as interesting as Jiěgào but if you're a serious borderholic then it's worth making the 30-minute drive here just so you can take a photo and say you've been.

Minibuses for Wǎndīng (Y5) leave Ruìlì when full, and vice versa.

Temples

Just past Golden Duck Pagoda is a crossroad and a small wooden temple. The road to the right (west) leads to the villages of Jiěxiàng and Nóngdǎo, and on the way are a number of small temples, villages and stupas. None are spectacular but the village life is interesting and there are often small markets near the temples.

The first major Dai temple is **Hansha Zhuang Temple** (Hánshā Zhuāng Sì), a fine wooden structure with a few resident monks. It's set a little off the road and a green tourism sign marks the turn-off. The surrounding Dai village is interesting.

Another 20 minutes or so further down the road, look out for a white stupa on the

hillside to the right. This is **Léizhuāngxiāng**, Ruìlì's oldest stupa, dating back to the middle of the Tang dynasty. There's a nunnery in the grounds of the stupa as well as fantastic views of the Ruìlì area. Once the stupa comes into view, take the next path to the right that cuts through the fields. You will see blue signs written in Chinese and Dai pointing the way through a couple of Dai villages. When you get to market crossroads at the centre of the main village, take the right path. You'll need to push your bicycle for the last ascent to the stupa. In all, it should take you about 50 minutes to cycle here from Golden Duck Pagoda.

About 2km past the town of Jiěxiàng is **Denghannong Zhuang Temple** (Děnghánnóng Zhuāng Sì), a wooden Dai temple with pleasant surroundings.

It's possible to cycle all the way to Nóngdǎo, around 29km southwest of Ruìlì. There's a solitary hotel in town that has cheap doubles or you can return to Ruìlì on one of the frequent minibuses.

Golden Pagoda 姐勒金塔

A few kilometres to the east of Ruìlì on the road to Wǎndīng is the Golden Pagoda (Jiělè Jīntǎ), a fine structure that dates back 200 years.

Bàngmáhè 棒麻贺

Another possible cycling route takes you west of Ruìlì, past the old town of Měngmǎo, now a suburb of Ruìlì. After 4km, just past the village of Jiědōng, a turn-off north leads to Bàngmáhè village, a Jingpo settlement with a small waterfall nearby.

Sìchuān 四川

SOUTHWEST CHINA

HIGHLIGHTS

- Catch the sunrise on the sacred mountaintop of **Éméi Shān** (p725)
- Travel the **Sichuan–Tibet Hwy** (p735) amid soaring snow-capped peaks, grasslands and Tibetan villages
- Take a ride on horse-back through alpine forests in **Sōngpān** (p749)
- Get up close to pandas at the Giant Panda Breeding Research Base in **Chéngdū** (p714)
- Scale the Grand Buddha, the world's largest Buddha statue, in **Lèshān** (p731)

Sōngpān ★

★ Sichuan–
Tibet Hwy

★ Chéngdū

Éméi Shān ★ ★ Lèshān

■ POP: 87.8 MIL | ■ AREA: 491,146 SQ KM

There is a popular saying in China, 'do not visit Sìchuān when you are young', the idea being that once you visit the province you will never want to leave. Sìchuān enjoys a number of similar maxims including the title of 'Heavenly Kingdom', a reference to the province's abundance of natural resources and cultural heritage.

The name Sìchuān (Four Rivers) refers to four of the more than 80 mighty rivers spilling across the province, weaving their way down through the soaring mountains of the northwest and across the Chuānxī plain in the east. Sìchuān's mountainous terrain, fast rivers and the foreboding Tibetan plateau have kept it relatively isolated until the present era and once prompted the Tang dynasty poet, Li Bai, to liken the journey to Sìchuān as being more difficult than the road to heaven.

The largest province in the southwest, Sìchuān is also one of the more interesting and its population displays as much diversity as its landscape. In the east, the fertile Sìchuān basin supports one of the densest rural populations in the world while in the west, the Tibetan plateau rises up in giant steps and houses less than 10% of the population. This is where green tea becomes butter tea, Confucianism yields to Buddhism and the soft, curved hills swell into jagged snow-capped peaks.

Stunning scenery and colourful culture aside, Sìchuān's cuisine is another reason visitors flock to the area. Famous for dishes laden with spice, Sìchuān's home cooking is not for the faint-hearted. The Sìchuān hot pepper – so fiery it will leave your lips tingling and your tongue numb – is believed to help reduce a person's internal dampness caused by the frequent high humidity and rainy weather.

Sìchuān is one of the wealthiest provinces in the southwest, and Chéngdū in particular is enjoying the spoils of economic reforms. The capital is one of the more prosperous, liberal and fashionable cities in the region and as such, supports a thriving contemporary art and music scene.

History

The Sìchuān basin was one of the first areas to be settled in China and records show that people have lived in the area since the 5th century BC. The province has been the site of various breakaway kingdoms throughout history. It was established as the capital of the Qin empire in the 3rd century BC and it was here that the Kingdom of Shu ruled as an independent state during the Three Kingdoms Period (AD 220–80). The Kuomintang (p43) spent its last days in Sìchuān before being vanquished and fleeing to Taiwan and most recently Chóngqìng split from Sìchuān when it was promoted to the status of Municipality in 1997.

Sìchuān became famous during the Warring States period (475–221 BC), when a famed engineer, Li Bing, managed to harness the Du River (Dū Hé) on the Chuānxī plain with his weir system, allowing Sìchuān some 2200 continuous years of irrigation and prosperity. The fertile land of 'Heaven's Granary', as Sìchuān became known, produced enough harvest to supply neighbouring provinces, and at the start of the last century was producing up to 11% of China's total output of grain and soybeans. When the Great Leap Forward (p46) was instituted, it dealt Sìchuān an especially cruel blow. While the exact figures of how many people died are not known, it's believed that one in 10 people starved.

SÌCHUĀN 四川

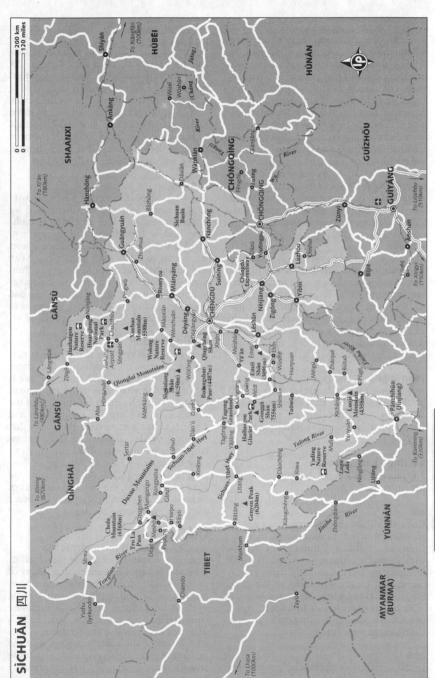

In 1975 Zhao Ziyang was appointed governor of Sìchuān and the province's first Communist Party secretary. Zhao was the driving force behind the agriculture and economic reforms that put Sìchuān back on map. His system (the 'Responsibility System'), whereby plots of land were let out to individual farmers on the proviso that a portion of the crops be sold back to the government, was so successful that it became the national model and was later applied to the industrial sector. Zhao, on the other hand, was not so fortunate. As one of the few leaders opposed to the use of troops against demonstrators in the Tiananmen Sq protests, he was sacked and has spent his years since 1989 under house arrest in Běijīng.

Climate

Sìchuān's weather varies significantly. Chéngdū and the east have a subtropical, humid monsoon climate with temperatures ranging from 3°C to 8°C in winter and 25°C to 29°C in summer. The Qinghai-Tibet plateau in the west experiences intense sunlight and low temperatures most of the year with temperatures dropping to -9°C in winter and reaching highs of only 17°C in summer.

Language

In addition to Mandarin, which is spoken by the Han and the Hui, the other major languages Sìchuān belong to the Tibeto-Burman family and are spoken by Tibetans and the Yi.

Getting There & Away

For more details about travelling between provinces see p916.

AIR

Chéngdū's Shangliu Airport is the largest international airport in southwest China. Air China and Sichuan Airlines link Chéngdū with all major Chinese cities and fly direct to Lhasa in Tibet. Currently there are international flights scheduled to Bangkok, Singapore, Hong Kong, Japan and Seoul.

There are plans to link Jiuhuang Airport in northern Sìchuān to other major cities in China in the near future.

BUS

In 2000 Sìchuān's provincial government decided to invest Y60 billion in highway development in the 10th Five-Year Plan, and the results can be seen today. High-speed expressways link Chéngdū with Chóngqìng and the construction of highways to link Chéngdū with Shànghǎi, Běihǎi in Guǎngxī province and Tibet are underway.

Travel to Gānsù is possible via Jiǔzhàigōu and Zöigê. To get to Yúnnán you can travel south via Lèshān, Éméi Shān and Pānzhīhuā on the border, or travel along the southern route of the Sichuan–Tibet Hwy through Lǐtáng and Xiāngchéng to Zhōngdiàn.

TRAIN

Jiuhuang Airport connects Chéngdū with Sōngpān and Jiǔzhàigōu. Chéngdū is an important railway hub in China's southwest and is linked to different parts of the country by major railway lines. Direct trains run to cities such as Běijīng, Xī'ān and Shànghǎi. Travel to Kūnmíng in Yúnnán by train tends to be the most popular option. Trains to Chóngqìng are slow and irregular, and to get to Gānsù you need to change in Hànzhōng, Shaanxi province.

Getting Around

New expressways connect the eastern part of the province, including a link from Chéngdū to Lèshān, and travel by bus is by far the quickest and most convenient way to travel. The buses on this side of the province are modern and comfortable and a much better option than the trains that tend to be older, slower and more irregular. Travel in the west of the province can only be done by bus (or hitching in logging trucks; see p920). But make sure you have enough time, the roads in this part of Sìchuān are in a terrible state and the buses are in an even worse condition.

CHÉNGDŪ 成都

☎ 028 / pop 4.1 million / elevation 500m

Chéngdū abounds with new-found affluence and is bent on modernising. Many of the city's older wooden buildings have been pushed aside and replaced with trendy, opulent department stores and high-rise commercial and residential blocks. This may well be a positive change for residents who associate the older buildings with the poverty of generations past and, despite the transformation, the city has surprisingly managed to retain much of its charm.

Although they're disappearing quickly, there are still some bustling side streets to explore, where you'll stumble upon markets, commercial districts, underground shopping malls, countless tiny restaurants specialising in Sìchuān snacks, and old men walking their song birds or hunched over a game of chess. You'll also encounter the city's artisans: small-time basket-weavers, cobblers, itinerant dentists, tailors, houseware merchants and snack hawkers who swarm the streets and contribute to Chéngdū's lively atmosphere.

For a capital city, Chéngdū is a manageable size and it's abundance of greenery and friendly characters make it one of China's more laid-back cities.

History
Built in 316 BC during the late Warring States period, Chéngdū boasts a 2300-year history which is linked closely with the arts and crafts trades.

Running through Chéngdū is Brocade River (Jǐn Jiāng), a reminder of the city's silk brocade industry which thrived during the Eastern Han dynasty (AD 25–220). The city's name eventually shifted from Jǐnchéng (Brocade City) to 'Lotus City', still used today by locals. The name 'Chéngdū' means Perfect Metropolis and by the time of the Tang dynasty (AD 618–907) the city had become a cornerstone of Chinese society. Three hundred years later, during the Song dynasty, Chéngdū began to issue the world's first paper money.

Like other major Chinese cities, it has had its share of turmoil. First, it was devastated by the Mongols in retaliation for the fierce resistance put up by the Sichuanese. From 1644 to 1647 it was presided over by the rebel Zhang Xiangzhong, who set up an independent state in Sìchuān, ruling by terror and mass executions. Three centuries later the city became one of the last strongholds of the Kuomintang.

The original city was walled and surrounded with a moat. Gates were built at the four points of the compass with the Viceroy's Palace (14th century) at the city's heart. The remains of the city walls were demolished in the early 1960s and the Viceroy's Palace was blown up at the height of the Cultural Revolution. In its place was erected the Russian-style Sìchuān

---

STREETWISE

Chéngdū is a true Asian city in its nonchalant disregard of systematic street numbering and naming. It's not unusual, when following street numbers in one direction, to meet another set coming the other way, leaving some places with five sets of numbers on their doors. Street names, also, seem to change every 100m or so – with very little apparent logic involved. Try to bear this in mind when you're looking for somewhere in particular, and rely more on nearby landmarks and relative locations on maps than on street numbers and names.

Exhibition Centre with a massive Mao statue outside, waving merrily down Renmin Nanlu.

Orientation
Ring roads circle the outer city: Yihuan Lu (First Ring Rd), Erhuan Lu (Second Ring Rd) and Sanhuan Lu (Third Ring Rd). These are divided into numbered segments (duàn). The main boulevard that sweeps through the centre of everything is Renmin Lu – in its north (běi), central (zhōng) and south (nán) manifestations.

The nucleus of the city is the square that interrupts Renmin Lu, with administrative buildings, the Sìchuān Exhibition Centre, a sports stadium and the colossal Mao. This is also where you'll find Tianfu Sq, a pedestrianised neon extravaganza and the main shopping district.

The area where Renmin Nanlu crosses Brocade River has become the city's backpacker ghetto.

MAPS
There are a number of tourist maps available in Chéngdū, including a handful of English-language ones. These can be bought at train and bus stations, and the South West Book Centre (see next section). One of the best maps around comes free with *Go West* magazine (see p713). City maps in Chinese can be useful for tracing bus routes, though not even the best ones can hope to fully capture the insanity that is Chéngdū's street naming (see Streetwise, above).

SOUTHWEST CHINA

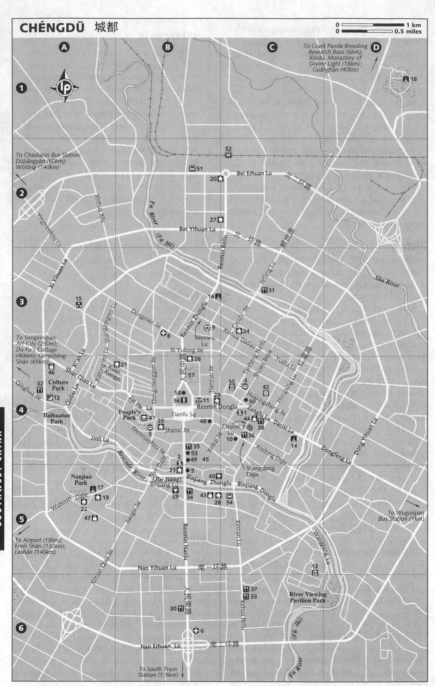

CHÉNGDŪ 城都

0 ▭▭▭▭▭ 1 km
0 ▭▭▭▭▭ 0.5 miles

To Giant Panda Breeding
Research Base (6km);
Xīndū, Monastery of
Divine Light (18km);
Guǎnghàn (40km)

🏛 18

To Chadianzi Bus Station;
Dūjiāngyàn (60km);
Wòlóng (140km)

🏠 51
52

20 🏠

Bei Erhuan Lu

北 一 环 路

27 🏠

Bei Yihuan Lu
北 一 环 路

Fu River (Fǔ Hé)

Renmin Beilu

Jiefang Lu

🏛 31

To Songxinqiao
Art City (250m);
Du Fu's Cottage
(400m); Qingchéng
Shān (65km)

15 🏠

Dongmen Jie

16 🏛

🔴 9

Wenwu Lu

🔴 8

Xi Yulong Jie

🏠 26

🏠 57

Renmin Zhonglu

Xinhua Dadao

Chadu Jie

🔴 24

Taisheng Nanlu

Shuwa Beijie

Yusha Lu

🔵 46

Shier Qiao Lu

🏠 21

Kuan Xiangzi

Xinhua Xilu

Qintai Lu

🔵 32

🔵 12

Culture
Park

Baihuatan
Park

58 🔴

56 🔴

Jin He Lu

4 🔵

Huaxingzheng Jie

55 🔵

42 🔵

50 🔵

🔴 29

🏠 11 Renmin Donglu

31 🔵

Zongfu Lu Dacisi Lu

Honglieng Jie

People's
Park

🔴 41

25 🔴

🏠 3

Shanxi Jie

Tianfu Sq

48 🔴

Chunxi 7 ☕
Lu 🔵 36

10 🔴

44 🔵

Yankai Jie

Xiadong Dajie

14 🏠

Dongfeng Lu

Dong Yihuan Lu

To Wuguiqiao
Bus Station (1km)

Jinli Lu

Wenmiaohou Jie

🏠 35

🔴 53

🔴 49 45

🔴 5

2 🏠

23 🏠

Brocade River

Binjiang Zhonglu

40 🔴

Binjiang Donglu

Shangdong
Dajie

Nanjiao
Park

🏛 17

🏠 19

22 🏠

47 🏠

Wuhouci Dajie

[Jin Jiang]
Binjiang Lu

39 🏠

34 🏠

43 🏠

28 🔴

54 🏠

Ximan Lu

To Airport (18km);
Éméi Shān (130km);
Lèshān (140km)

Nan Yihuan Lu   南 一 环 路

13 🏛

River Viewing
Pavilion Park

Renmin Nanlu

🏠 37

🏠 33

Kehua Beilu

Wangjiang Lu

30 🏠

🔴 6

Nan Erhuan Lu   南 一 环 路

To South Train
Station (1.5km)

Fu River (Fǔ Hé)

SOUTHWEST CHINA

Information

BOOKSHOPS

South West Book Centre (Xīnán Shūchéng; Xiadong Dajie) Has maps and a small selection of English titles.

INTERNET ACCESS

Chéngdū has countless Internet cafés; try the large one on Chunxi Lu. Most guesthouses such as Dragon Town Youth Hostel (p717) and Sam's Guesthouse (p717) and a lot of the Western cafés such as Highfly Cafe (p719) also offer Internet access. They all charge about Y2 to Y3 per hour.

INTERNET RESOURCES

Chengdu (www.chengdu.gov.cn) Operated by the provincial government, this website has an English version that provides information on the city and surrounding areas.

MEDICAL SERVICES

No 3 Hospital (Dongmen Jie) Helpful staff with a handful of English speakers.

Global Doctor Chengdu Clinic (☎ 8522 6058, 139-8225 6966; ground fl, Kelan Bldg, Bangkok Garden Apts, Section 4, 21 Renmin Nanlu; ⏱ 24hr) Has a 24-hour English-speaking helpline.

MONEY

Bank of China (Zhōngguó Yínháng; Renmin Nanlu; ⏱ 8.30am-6pm Mon-Fri, 8.30am-5pm Sat & Sun)

Can change money and travellers cheques and offer cash advances on credit cards. There is another branch on Renmin Donglu and a strategically placed ATM outside the Xinanmen bus station.

POST & TELEPHONE

The Traffic Hotel (p717) offers poste restante and will hold letters and parcels for 15 days. Items should be mailed care of the Traffic Hotel, 6 Linjiang Lu, Xinnanmen, Chéngdū 610041.

China Post (Yóujú; cnr Huaxingzheng Jie & Shuwa Beijie; ⏱ 8.30am-6pm) Close to the Cultural Palace in the centre of town. A smaller branch can be found on Dongchenggen Jie near People's Park.

Telecommunications Business Centre (Diànxìn Shāngchéng; Renmin Donglu) You can make reverse charge (collect) calls here.

TOURIST INFORMATION

The best source for up-to-the-minute restaurant, bar and entertainment listings is the free monthly magazine *Go West* which you can pick up at places like the Traffic Hotel and Dragon Town Youth Hostel.

That's National is a free monthly magazine that covers southwest China and often has some interesting travel articles.

Tourist hotline (☎ 8292 8555) Free hotline with English-speaking operators.

TRAVEL AGENCIES

The notice boards and notebooks in cafés and guesthouses are good places to look for travel tips and recommendations from travellers on tourist agencies; those you should choose and those that you should avoid.

The more useful travel agencies are located in and around the Traffic Hotel, within the Dragon Town Youth Hostel and at Sam's Guesthouse.

Tours include those to Hailuogou Glacier Park, Wolong Nature Reserve, Jiǔzhàigōu, Éméi Shān and Sōngpān. Also on offer are day trips to the Giant Panda Breeding Research Base and local Sìchuān opera performances. Prices depend upon the number of travellers but are generally good value.

Agencies can often arrange Yangzi River (Cháng Jiāng) cruise tickets, train and flight tickets and permits to Tibet.

You may also encounter Mr Lee who frequents the Renmin Teahouse. In addition to providing free information to travellers, he can arrange tours of everything from artists' quarters to silk factories to kindergartens.

China International Travel Service (CITS; Zhōngguó Guójì Lǚxíngshè; ☎ 8642 8212, 8666 4422; Renmin Nanlu) Arranges pricey tours including packages to Tibet. They can book train and plane tickets here although most guesthouses offer a similar, faster and often cheaper service.

VISAS

Public Security Bureau (PSB; Gōngānjú; ☎ 8640 7067; 136 Wenwu Lu; ☼ 9am-noon & 1-5pm Mon-Fri) The foreign affairs entrance is on Tianzuo Jie; this is where you can get visa extensions.

Dangers & Annoyances

There have been several reports of foreigners becoming targets for rip-offs and theft in Chéngdū. In particular there have been a couple of incidents on the riverside pathway between Jǐnjiāng Bīnguǎn and the Traffic Hotel. Take care late at night – it's best not to walk alone.

Take care if you hire a bike, some travellers have reported having things stolen out of their bicycle basket when cycling around the city.

Sights

GIANT PANDA BREEDING RESEARCH BASE
大熊猫繁殖研究中心

About 10km north of Chéngdū, the **Giant Panda Breeding Research Base** (Dàxióngmāo Fánzhí Yánjiū Zhōngxīn; admission Y30; ☼ 8am-6pm) is a research station and breeding ground for giant and lesser pandas. The base was established in 1987 and was first opened to the public in 1995.

About 40 giant pandas currently reside at the base, although you will be lucky if you see half that number on your visit. There is also a breeding centre that has been partially opened and where some of China's animal ambassadors are allowed to 'freely roam'. The result has been a number of baby pandas and if you visit in autumn, you may also have the opportunity to see tiny newborns in the 'nursery'.

Just past the entrance gate, the base museum has detailed exhibits on panda evolution, habits, habitats and conservation efforts, all with English captions.

Once the breeding area is completed and opened, the base will cover over 230 hectares. It's best to visit the base in the morning, feeding is around 9.30am and soon thereafter the pandas return to their other favourite pastime – sleeping.

Getting to the base is tricky. Cycling is not recommended, as you'll mainly be travelling along congested motorways. Bus No 10 runs out to Qinglong from where you'll have to change for bus No 1 to the terminus. From here, hop on a motorised rickshaw to the breeding centre.

Easier, faster and a lot less hassle are the tours run by Dragon Town Youth Hostel and Sam's Guesthouse for Y50 including the entrance fee.

WENSHU TEMPLE 文殊院

This Tang dynasty monastery is Chéngdū's largest and best-preserved Buddhist temple. **Wenshu Temple** (Wénshū Yuàn; Renmin Zhonglu; admission Y1; ☼ 8am-5.30pm) was originally known as Xinxiang Temple but was renamed after a Buddhist monk who lived there in the late 17th century.

Perhaps the best thing about the monastery is the bustling crowd of worshippers who flock to the place. Together with the exquisite relief carvings that decorate many of the buildings in the complex, they render the temple well worth a visit.

There's a vegetarian restaurant (p718) and two teahouses (p719).

The alley off Renmin Zhonglu, on which Wenshu Temple is located, is a curiosity in

THE ELUSIVE PANDA

Distributed almost entirely in the north and northwest of Sìchuān are the thousand or so giant pandas surviving in the wild. Living at high altitudes in mountainous regions, this endangered mammal is shrouded as much by mystery as by perpetual mist and cloud. Sightings are rare and our knowledge remains scant.

Some sources claim that the giant panda has existed for around 600,000 years while others date earliest remains of the panda back as far as the ice age, between one and three million years ago. Scientists have spent over a century debating whether pandas belong to the bear family, the raccoon family, or are a separate family of their own.

As good climbers and solitary animals, pandas are adept at evading observation. Yet despite their shy nature, the panda has been popularised as the emblem of the World Wide Fund for Nature, as the logo on Chinese cigarettes, and was once a popular present from the Chinese government to foreign governments. While Chinese literature has references to pandas (called *xióngmāo* or bear cats) going back over 3000 years, it wasn't until 1869 that the West found out about the panda, when a French missionary brought a pelt back with him to Paris. Now, in the 21st century, this stout, pigeon-toed animal is racing towards extinction.

An obvious factor in the depletion of the giant panda population is the encroachment of humans as China's massive population attempts to meet its land and resource needs. To counter this, the government has set up 11 reserves in the southwest for the panda.

Pandas are also threatened by their exclusive eating habits. They consume enormous amounts of food – up to 20kg a day each – with bamboo accounting for around 95% of their diet. They spend 10 to 16 hours a day munching on it, but will only eat around 20 of China's 300 species of bamboo. In the mid-1970s more than 130 pandas starved to death when one of these favoured species flowered and withered in Mín Shān, Sìchuān.

Perhaps the greatest difficulty faced by conservationists is the panda's slow reproductive rate. Pandas remain solitary throughout the year, except during their short, three-month mating season each spring. Then pandas not only have a tricky time finding one another, they're also rather particular about who they'll mate with.

Females generally give birth to only one cub, weighing about as much as an apple. When two cubs are born, the mother tends to leave one behind or crush it in its sleep, unable to care for both. For the first month after birth, she carries the cub in one of her paws at all times, even as she sleeps and eats.

Conservationists have had low success rates with breeding pandas in captivity. Chéngdū's Giant Panda Breeding Research Base (opposite) has seen the birth of a number of pandas but still remains unable to multiply the population to the level hoped for.

With world attention on the survival of the panda, Chinese laws now strictly forbid locals to hunt, fell trees or make charcoal in the habitats of the panda. Peasants in these areas are offered rewards equivalent to double their annual salary if they save a starving panda, and life sentences or public executions are imposed on convicted poachers. And despite a constant battle with budget deficits, China's central government maintains its funding to the Breeding Research Base, which continues in its struggle to preserve pandas and their habitats.

itself, filled with joss-stick vendors, foot-callus removers, blind fortune-tellers with bamboo spills, and flower and fireworks sellers.

TOMB OF WANG JIAN 王建墓

In the northwest of town, the **Tomb of Wang Jian** (Wángjiàn Mù; Yongling Lu; admission Y13; 7am-7pm) was, until 1942, thought to be Zhuge Liang's music pavilion (see Wuhou Temple, p716). Wang Jian (AD 847–918) was a Tang general who established the Former Shu kingdom in the aftermath of the collapse of the Tang in 907.

The tomb in the central building is surrounded by statues of 24 musicians all playing different instruments, and is considered to be the best surviving record of a Tang dynasty musical troupe. It is the only mausoleum excavated in China so far that features above-ground tomb chambers. Also on display are tomb relics including a jade belt, mourning books and imperial seals.

SOUTHWEST CHINA

ZHAOJUE TEMPLE 照觉寺

Zhaojue Temple (Zhàojué Sì; admission Y1; ☻ 7am-7pm) dates back to the 7th century although little remains of the original architecture. During the early Qing dynasty, it underwent extensive reconstruction under the supervision of Po Shan, a famous Buddhist monk who established waterways and groves of trees around the temple. The temple has since served as a model for many Japanese and Southeast-Asian Buddhist temples.

The temple went through hard times during the Cultural Revolution and has only been restored during the last decade. There's a vegetarian restaurant on the grounds (p718) and a teahouse next door.

Zhaojue Temple is about 6km northeast of Chéngdū city centre. Direct minibuses run to the nearby zoo from the north train station (běi chēzhàn). Cycling isn't advisable unless you don't mind arriving asphyxiated from riding along clogged motorways.

TEMPLE PARKS

West of the Mao statue is **Culture Park** (Wénhuà Gōngyuán; ☻ 7am-10pm), home to the **Green Ram Temple** (Qingyáng Gōng; admission Y5; ☻ 7am-6.30pm), the oldest and most extensive Taoist temple in the Chéngdū area. The story goes that Laotzu, the high priest of Taoism, asked a friend to meet him there. When the friend arrived he saw only a boy leading two goats on a leash – and in an impressive leap of lateral thinking realised the boy was Laotzu.

The goats are represented in bronze in the rear building on the temple grounds. If the one-horned goat looks slightly ungoatlike, it is because it combines features of all the Chinese zodiac animals. The other goat can vanquish life's troubles and pains if you stroke its flank.

In the centre of the temple grounds is an eight-sided pagoda, considered to be an architectural illustration of Taoist philosophy. There are no bolts or pegs holding the building together. Instead each piece fits into the next and the building balances as a whole.

Green Ram Temple can be combined with a visit to nearby **Du Fu's Cottage** (Dùfú Cǎotáng; 38 Qinghua Lu; admission Y30; ☻ 7am-7pm), erstwhile home of the celebrated Tang dynasty poet. Du Fu (AD 712–70) was born in Hénán but left his home province at the tender age of 20 to see China. After being captured by rebels following an uprising,

he eventually fled to Chéngdū, where he lived for four years in a humble cottage. He penned more than 200 poems here on simple themes around the lives of the people who lived and worked nearby. From the time of his death in exile (in Húnán), Du Fu acquired a cult status, and his poems have been a major source of inspiration for many Chinese artists.

The grounds here are huge (20 hectares) and dotted with bamboo gardens, pagodas and covered walkways that represent a much-enlarged version of Du Fu's original retreat.

Next to **Nanjiao Park** (Nánjiāo Gōngyuán; admission Y2; ☻ 6am-10pm) is **Wuhou Temple** (Wǔhòu Sì; Y30; ☻ 6.30am-8pm). Wǔhòu might be translated as 'Minister of War', the title given to Zhuge Liang, who was a famous military strategist of the Three Kingdoms period (AD 220–80) and immortalised in one of the classics of Chinese literature, *The Romance of the Three Kingdoms*.

Curiously, Zhuge Liang is not the main attraction of the temple. Instead, the front shrine is dedicated to Liu Bei, Zhuge Liang's emperor. Liu's temple, the Hanzhaolie Temple, was moved here and rebuilt during the Ming dynasty.

In the southeast of town, near Sichuan University, is **River Viewing Pavilion Park** (Wàngjiānglóu Gōngyuán; admission Y2; ☻ 6am-9pm). The pavilion itself is a four-storey wooden Qing structure overlooking Brocade River, and was built in memory of Xue Tao, a female Tang dynasty poet with a great love for bamboo. Nearby is a well where Xue Tao is believed to have drawn water to dye her writing paper.

The park is famous for its lush forests, boasting over 150 varieties of bamboo from China, Japan and Southeast Asia. They range from bonsai-sized potted plants to towering giants, creating a shady retreat in the heat of summer and a cold, damp one in winter.

PEOPLE'S PARK 人民公园

To the southwest of the city centre, **People's Park** (Rénmín Gōngyuán; admission Y2; ☻ 6am-8pm) is one Chinese park well worth visiting. The teahouse here is excellent (see p719).

A popular setting for wedding photo shoots, the park holds a bonsai rockery, a playground, swimming pools and the **Monument to the Martyrs of the Railway Protection Movement** (1911). This obelisk, decorated with shunting manoeuvres and railway tracks, marks an uprising of the people against officers who pocketed cash raised for the construction of the Chéngdū to Chóngqìng line. Since, at the time, People's Park was a private officer's garden, it was a fitting place to erect the structure.

Across the lake from the teahouse is the entry to an underground **funhouse** (admission Y5) that must count as one of Chéngdū's weirder experiences. The entry fee buys you a tour through a converted air-raid shelter where you can take a ride on a rickety shuttle-train through bizarre and aging scenes from the Wild West, space, the dinosaur age, Christmas and straight into the mouth of a shark.

SICHUAN UNIVERSITY MUSEUM
四川大学博物馆

Founded in 1914 by US scholar DS Dye, the **Sichuan University Museum** (Sìchuān Dàxué Bówùguǎn; Wanjiang Lu; admission Y20; ☯ 8.30-11.30am & 2.30-5.30pm Mon-Fri) is one of the better museums in the southwest. The collection is particularly strong in the fields of ethnology, folklore and traditional arts. The ethnology room exhibits artefacts from the Yi, Qiang, Miao, Jingpo, Naxi and Tibetan cultures. The Chinese painting and calligraphy room displays works from the Tang, Song, Yuan, Ming and Qing dynasties.

At the time of writing, a new museum big enough to display all 40,000 items in the collection at one time (they're currently displayed on a rotation basis) was being built. The new museum should be open by the time you read this.

Sleeping
BUDGET
There is no shortage of backpacker friendly hostels in Chéngdū.

Dragon Town Youth Hostel (Lóngtáng Kèzhàn; ☎ 8664 8408; www.dragontown.com.cn; 27 Kuan Xiangzi; dm Y25-35, s/d/tr per bed without bathroom Y60/60/35, d with bathroom Y120-160) Located down a narrow alley in a beautiful four-storey building that dates back to the Qing dynasty, this has to be one of Chéngdū's best budget options. The team that runs this place is fantastic and the rooms are clean, simple and comfortable. The higher-end doubles feature antique Chinese furniture.

Chengdu Dreams Travel International Youth Hostel (Chéngdū Mèngzhīlǚ Guójì Qīngnián Lǚshè; ☎ 8557 0315; www.dreams-travel.com/youthhostel; 242 Wuhouci Dajie; dm Y25-60) Situated in the Tibetan area of town, the dorm rooms here are good value and the roof terrace has fantastic views of the neighbouring park. There's even a kitchen where you can cook for yourself.

Traffic Hotel (Jiāotōng Fàndiàn; ☎ 8545 1017; fax 8544 0977, 6 Lijiang Zhonglu; dm Y30-40, s without bathroom Y50, d with bathroom Y200) The Traffic used to be the first choice for accommodation in Chéngdū but it's facing some stiff competition these days. Rooms are devoid of character but comfortable and the shared bathrooms are incredibly clean.

Holly's Hostel (Jiǔlóngdǐng Qīngnián Kèzhàn; ☎ 8554 8131; Hollyhotelcn@yahoo.com; 246 Wuhouci Dajie; dm Y15-30) This charming guesthouse can be found in the heart of the Tibetan quarter. The rooms look a bit old but they're large and clean, and the staff are friendly.

Sam's Guesthouse (☎ 8615 4179; samtour@yahoo .com; 130 Shanxi Jie; dm/d Y40/100) Sam's place is located in a wing of the Róngchéng Fàndiàn not far from the heart of downtown Chéngdū. Dorms are good value but the doubles look a bit tired.

MID-RANGE
There isn't much in the way of mid-range options in Chéngdū but fortunately many of the budget guesthouses have mid-range value doubles for bargain prices.

Jìndì Fàndiàn (☎ 8691 5339; 8691 7778; 89 Xinhua Dadao; s/d Y220/280; ▨) If a private bathroom is top of your wish list when choosing somewhere to stay then you won't go wrong with this hotel which offers decent value for money.

Chéngdū Dàjiǔdiàn (☎ 8317 3888; fax 8317 6818; 29 Renmin Beilu; d Y150-280) The permanent discounts offered here make this a good choice, although you might find the location a bit inconvenient.

Róngchéng Fàndiàn (☎ 611 2933; 130 Shanxi Jie; d Y240) This is the supposed upmarket neighbour to Sam's Guesthouse but the rooms are only mediocre and some travellers have reported nocturnal visitations by Mr Rat.

TOP END
With continuously growing competition, you may often get huge discounts (up to 40%) at top-end hotels during winter so it's worth shopping around. The prices listed are the posted rates and what you can expect to pay during high season.

SOUTHWEST CHINA

Tibet Hotel (Xīzàng Dàjiǔdiàn; ☎ 8318 3388; fax 8319 3838; 10 Renmin Beilu; s/d Y598/1180) The location is not the most convenient but the rooms here are beautifully decorated. This hotel has received a number of good reviews from travellers.

Jǐnjiāng Bīnguǎn (☎ 8550 6666; www.jjhotel.com; 80, Section 2, Renmin Nanlu; d Y880-1380) The rooms are somewhat overpriced, however they do offer the option of nonsmoking rooms. There are good views to be had from the rooftop Chinese restaurant here, but at a high price: beer and soft drinks are around Y30 each.

Yinhe Dynasty Hotel (Yínhé Wángcháo Dàjiǔdiàn; ☎ 8661 8888; 99 Xiaxi Shuncheng Jie; d Y1120-1440) These rooms are very luxurious and a good choice if you're looking for that top-end option.

Sheraton Chengdu Lido Hotel (Tiānfǔ Lìdū Xīláidēng Fàndiàn; ☎ 8676 8999; www.sheraton.com/Chengdu; Section 1, 15 Renmin Zhonglu; d Y1280-1920) The usual Sheraton standards can be found here. Plush rooms and a good selection of expensive restaurants make this a luxury escape from the outside world.

Eating
CHINESE

Sìchuān's cuisine is famous throughout China for being hot and spicy (see boxed text, opposite). It's also famous for it's *xiǎo chī* (little eats) and there are more places in Chéngdū than any other city in Sìchuān where you can get good, cheap snacks on the run.

Huǒguō (hotpot) is very popular in Chéngdū. You'll see lots of pavement hotpot operations in the older section of town, near the Qingshiqiao market. It's similar to a fondue affair: dip skewered meat and veggies into big woks filled with hot, spiced oil and then into little dishes of peanut oil and garlic. Be forewarned – hotpot can be very hot; even many Sichuanese can't take it. If you want something a little tamer, try asking for *báiwèi*, the hotpot for wimps. Peanut milk, sold in tins, will also stop you from breathing fire.

Equally as popular is *shāokǎo*, Sichuanese barbecue. Skewers of meat, veggies and smoked tofu are brushed with oil and chilli and grilled. Unlike hotpots, which generally don't appear until the sun goes down, *shāokǎo* is a popular lunch-time snack as well. You'll find roadside stalls all over the city as well as portable grills on bikes.

Lóngcháoshǒu Cāntīng (cnr Chunxi Lu & Shandong Jie; meals Y5-15) This is one little snack restaurant that is still going strong with sampler courses that allow you to dip into the whole gamut of the Chéngdū snack experience. The cheapest option gives you a range of sweet and savoury items, with each price bracket giving you the same deal on a grander and more filling scale. Unfortunately it hasn't much to offer vegetarians.

Shìqiáo Shǒumiàn (Hongxing Lu; dishes Y2) This place serves up excellent bowls of filling noodles that you can watch being made fresh on the premises. The friendly staff are happy to cater to vegetarians.

Chén Mápó Dòufu (Pockmarked Grandma Chen's Bean Curd; Jiefang Lu; dishes from Y5) *Mápó dòufu* is served here with a vengeance – soft, fresh bean curd with a fiery sauce of garlic, minced beef, salted soybean, chilli oil and fiery Sìchuān pepper. The 2nd floor has been redone to look like a typical Chinese banquet hall and carries a Y5 'seating charge'. Sit downstairs instead; don't worry about the grotty décor – those spices should kill any lurking bugs. This place is no longer an unknown cubbyhole and has franchised, with a second, more pleasant version across from Culture Park.

Bāguó Bùyī Fēngwèijiǔbù (Renmin Nanlu; dishes from Y10) This place is named after the traditional cotton clothing worn by peasants in an ancient state of eastern Sìchuān. Best described as country Sìchuān, the food is prepared all over its two storeys; you wander and point. Be careful – it isn't cheap.

VEGETARIAN

A special treat for vegetarians is to head out to the Wenshu Temple (p714) where there is an excellent vegetarian restaurant with an English menu (dishes Y6 to Y10).

Zhaojue Temple (p716) also serves up vegetarian dishes for lunch (from 11am to 3.30pm, dishes from Y8) and if you're really keen, you might ride out to Monastery of Divine Light (p722) in Xīndū, 18km north of Chéngdū, in time for lunch (11am to noon, dishes from Y7).

Most of the Western restaurants also feature vegetarian options on their menus.

WESTERN

The number of Western restaurants springing up in Chéngdū continues to grow and the following are just a few options.

Highfly Cafe (Gāofēi Kāfēi; ☎ 8544 2820; 18 Linjiang Zhonglu; dishes from Y12; ☒ 9am-late) Another old-timer, this place still serves great breakfast, pizzas and delicious calorie-laden fudge brownies.

Grandma's Kitchen & Deli (Zǔmǔ Dēchúfang; ☎ 8524 2835; 73/75 Kehua Beilu; mains from Y40) If you've been craving Western food, then this is the place to come for burgers, steaks, salads and delicious deserts. There is also a deli here where you can treat yourself to Western chocolate, cereal and even a can of Boddingtons beer. A second branch, **Grandma's Kitchen** (☎ 8555 3856; 22 Renmin Nanlu) serves up similar dishes but has a more limited menu.

Red Brick Café Pub & Pizzeria (Hóng Zhuān Xīcānting; ☎ 8521 4065; 77 Kehua Beilu; set meals from Y28) The pizzas baked in a stone oven here are excellent. Also on the menu are salads and sandwiches.

Drinking
TEAHOUSES
Teahouses have long played an important part in Chinese society and nowhere more so than in Sìchuān where the art of drinking tea dates back 3,000 years. Traditionally, the teahouse functioned as the centre of social life, a place where people had haircuts, watched opera performances, had their ears cleaned and gossiped about their neigh-bours. A bit like going to the pub today. While teahouses no longer play the same role, they're still wonderful places to while away an afternoon and Chéngdū has some excellent teahouses to choose from.

Renmin Teahouse (Rénmín Cháguǎn; People's Park; tea Y5-20; ☒ 10am-6pm) This is one of Chéngdū's finest. A most pleasant afternoon can be spent here in relative anonymity over a bottomless cup of stone-flower tea.

Another charming family type teahouse is in Wenshu Temple (p714), with an amazingly crowded and steamy ambience. This is in addition to the huge tea garden outside – one of the largest and most lively in Chéngdū. If you want to join in, sit on the west side of the path, closest to the main temple, where tea costs Y2. The tea must be greener on the other side of the path where it costs Y10. As well, try the teahouse in **Temple of Mercy** (Dàcí Sì; Dacisi Lu; Y1; ☒ 10am-6pm). The temple itself doesn't offer much to see, however, the grounds, with tables piled high with mah jong pieces and teacups, are a perfect place for a lazy afternoon in the sun.

PUBS & BARS
Like most Chinese cities, bars quickly open and close in Chéngdū and what is one week's happening spot is next week's old news. However, there are lots of bars out there and Chéngdū can be a very fun place to go out.

To find out what's new in town, get hold of a copy of *Go West* (see p713) or check with Billy at Dragon Town Youth Hostel who always seems to know where's 'in'.

Paul & Dave's Oasis (☎ 8950 0646; 21/1 Binjiang Zhonglu; ☒ 6pm-late) This is one of the original Western-style cafés and it's still popular. Large comfy sofas make this an easy place to kick back for the evening and enjoy

---

HOT & SPICY

The Chinese have a saying 'Shí zài Zhōngguó, wèi zài Sìchuān' (China is the place for food but Sìchuān is the place for flavour). And if you've ever tasted the spicy chillies and mouth-numbing-pepper at the heart of Sìchuān cuisine then you'll know the saying rings true. With such fiery food the Sichuanese themselves have a reputation for being a little hot-headed and the local women are even referred to as *là měizi* (spice girls). Local gourmets claim that the province boasts a repertoire of over 5000 different dishes. We'll just start with five of the most popular:

- *huíguō ròu* (boiled and stir-fried pork with salty and hot sauce; 回锅肉)
- *gōngbào jīdīng* (spicy chicken with peanuts; 宫保鸡丁)
- *shuǐzhǔ yú* (boiled fish in a fiery sauce; 水煮鱼)
- *gānbiān sìjìdòu* (dry-fried green beans; 干煸四季豆)
- *mápó dòufu* (pock-marked Mother Chen's beancurd; 麻婆豆腐)

The last two dishes can be made suitable for vegetarians, just ask them to leave out the meat 'bú fàng ròu' (不放肉).

a beer or two, which Dave claims is the cheapest in town. On weekends this place doesn't shut until the early hours.

Guan 9 (Jiǔhàoguǎn; ☎ 8555 1302; 9 Binjiang Lu ☯ 11.30am-2am) Popular with the local artist community, this is a cool little bar that features a great mezzanine area and a breezy terrace outside in addition to an extensive drinks menu.

Entertainment

Chéngdū is the home of Sìchuān opera, which has a 200-year tradition and features slapstick, eyeglass-shattering songs, men dressed as women and occasional gymnastics. Several opera houses are scattered throughout the older sections of town.

Mike (☎ 8626 6510) If you are interested in seeing a local Sìchuān opera, your best bet may be to contact Mike, a friendly, English-speaking local, after 8.30pm. He'll take you to a small, local opera house hidden in the depths of a market. The cast, costume and make-up is all very professional. You'll also get a backstage tour, tea and a taxi to and from the opera for around Y100 per person. The price is a little steep but all in all it is an entertaining and worthwhile experience. Try to go on the weekends when the performance is a combination of the highlights from a number of operas. Any of the guesthouses will be able to organise backstage tours for a similar price.

Jinjiang Theatre (Jǐnjiāng Jùyuàn; Huaxingzheng Jie) If you'd rather go on your own, one of the easier opera venues to find is the Jinjiang Theatre, which is a combination teahouse, opera theatre and cinema. High-standard Sìchuān opera performances are given here every Sunday afternoon (Y120 per person).

Shopping

The main downtown shopping area extends from the eastern end of Renmin Donglu south to Shangdong Dajie, and has taken on the look of most modern cities, with trendy clothing shops and department stores. If you delve into the narrow alleys between the main streets you'll find arcades of smaller shops and stalls selling similar items at cheaper prices.

Qingshiqiao Market (Qīngshíqiáo Shìchǎng; Xinkai Jie) This large market is one of the most interesting and busiest places to wander in town. Shops and stalls sell brightly coloured seafood, flowers, cacti, birds, pets and a thousand dried foods. Although fairly frantic itself, it's a nice change of pace from the commercialism of the department stores.

South of the river, on a street across from the entrance of the Wuhou Temple, is a small Tibetan neighbourhood. While it's not evident in the architecture, it is in the prayer flags, colourful scarves, beads and brass goods for sale. You won't find the variety of things (nor the bargains) that you'll find in the northwest of Sìchuān, but it still makes for an interesting wander.

Sòngxīnqiáo Art City (Qinghua Jie) Not far from Du Fu's Cottage (p716), this large covered market features a selection of stalls selling art and antiques. It's not cheap but worth a browse.

Arts & Crafts Service Department Store (Chéngdū Měishùpǐn Fúwùbù; 10 Chunxi Lu) Located in Chunxi Commercial District, this shop deals in such Sichuanese specialities as lacquerware, silverwork and bamboo products.

There are a couple of shops along Binjiang Lu that sell outdoor clothing and equipment. **Mountain Dak Outdoor Sports Club** (Gāoshān Hùwài Lǚyóu Tànxiǎn Yòngpǐn) is not far from the Traffic Hotel and **Airwolf** (Fēiláng Hùwài) is near Highfly Café.

Tóng Rén Táng (Tong Ren Tang Pharmacy; 1 Zongfu Lu) A traditional Chinese pharmacy over 260 years old, this is an intriguing place to visit even if you're not feeling under the weather.

Getting There & Away

AIR

There are daily flights to almost everywhere within China. Internal destinations include Běijīng (Y1440, 2¼hr), Chóngqìng (Y240, 45 minutes), Dàlián (Y1810, 3½hr), Shànghǎi (Y1660, two hours and 20 minutes), Guǎngzhōu (Y1300, one hour and 50 minutes), Kūnmíng (Y700, one hour) and Xī'ān (Y630, one hour and 20 minutes).

Within Sìchuān there are four flights a day to Jiuhuang Airport (Y700, 40 minutes), the new air link for Jiǔzhàigōu and Sōngpān in northern Sìchuān.

International destinations include Hong Kong (Y2204, 2½hr), Tokyo (Y2900, 6½hr), Singapore (Y2034, four hours and 20 minutes) and Bangkok (Y1834, two hours and 55 minutes).

CHÉNGDŪ BUS TIMETABLES

Buses from Xinanmen Bus Station:

Destination	Price	Duration	Frequency	Departs
Éméi	Y33	2hr	every 20min	6.40am-7pm
Dūjiāngyàn	Y17	1½hr	half-hourly	8-10.30am
Kāngdìng	Y101-122	8hr	hourly	7am-2pm
Lèshān	Y31	2hr	every 20min	7.50am-7.35pm
Lúdìng	Y88-98	6hr	hourly	7am-2pm

For northern destinations you will need to trek over to the Chadianzi Bus Station in the northwest of the city.

Destination	Price	Duration	Frequency	Departs
Dūjiāngyàn	Y8.5-16	1½hr	every 40 minutes	7am-8pm
Jiŭzhàigōu	Y79-92	10-12hr	4 daily	7.20am, 8am, 8.40am, 4pm
Sōngpān	Y50	8hr	3 daily	6.30am, 7am, 7.30am
Wòlóng	Y20	4hr	daily	11.40am
Xiăojīn	Y44.5	7hr	4 daily	6.30am, 7am, 7.30am, noon

For eastern destinations your best bet is to try the north bus station, near the north train station.

Destination	Price	Duration	Frequency	Departs
Bàogúo (Éméi)	Y30	2hr	half-hourly	6.30am-5.25pm
Chóngqìng	Y85.5	4½hr	hourly	7.30am-5pm
Dàzú	Y64.5	4hr	2 daily	9am, 12.30pm
Dūjiāngyàn	Y9.5	1½hr	every 20 min	7am-6pm
Lèshān	Y23.5	2hr	every 40 min	6.40am-7pm

Airline offices in Chéngdū include:

Air China (Zhōngguó Mínháng; ☎ 8666 1100; 41, Section 2, Renmin Nanlu ✆ 8am-7.30pm).

Sìchuān Airlines (Sìchuān Hángkōng Gōngsī; ☎ 8665 7163, 8665 4858; 31, Section 2, Renmin Nanlu)

Dragon Air (Gănglóng Hángkōng Gōngsī; ☎ 675 5555, ext 6105; Sìchuān Bīnguăn, 31 Zongfu Lu).

BUS

Transport connections in Chéngdū are more comprehensive than in other parts of the southwest. High-speed expressways from Chéngdū to both Chóngqìng and Lèshān have cut down travel time significantly.

Xinanmen Bus Station, next to the Traffic Hotel is the main bus station and has tickets to most places around Sìchuān.

See box above for bus times.

For Chóngqìng, the Wuguiqiao bus station, outside the 2nd ring road, has express buses leaving every half-hour (Y100, four hours) from 6.30am to 9.30pm.

TRAIN

Almost all the hostels can book train tickets for you although they'll tag on a service charge of around Y20. This might be useful if you're having trouble obtaining some of the more popular tickets – like hard sleepers to Kūnmíng – or if you simply can't be bothered to schlep up to the train station.

Daily departures include Kūnmíng (Y240, 18 hours), Yíbīn (Y50, eight hours), Zìgòng (Y40, six hours), Éméi (Y22, two hours), Chóngqìng (Y65, 11 hours), Běijīng (Y420, 26 hours) and Xī'ān (Y220, 18 hours).

TO TIBET

The most frequently asked question in Chéngdū must be 'Can I fly to Lhasa?'. If you're on your own without a permit, the official answer is 'No'. To get around this, travel agents in the Traffic Hotel, Sam's Guesthouse and elsewhere can sign you onto a 'tour', which usually includes a one-way ticket to Lhasa and a Tibet Tourism Bureau permit which you will probably never see. At the height of summer, you may have to book the two-hour transfer from Gongkar airport (95km from Lhasa) to Lhasa. The fact that members of the tour group have never seen each other prior to the flight and split up immediately after, is overlooked by the authorities.

At the time of writing these packages were priced at about Y1750 including flights and were the most cost-effective way of getting into Tibet. CITS runs its own four to six day tours (Y2000 to Y4000).

If you can arrange for a permit from a travel agency, you can try picking up a ticket from one of the airlines yourself; regulations change and travellers occasionally – no, rarely – get lucky. Just make sure you have the cash on hand to buy the ticket before they change their mind. Another trick is to ask for a 1st-class ticket.

Sìchuān's land borders into Tibet are still closed to foreigners. Some travellers attempt to sneak across but the majority are turned back and fined heavily. Don't believe anyone who says they can drive you to Lhasa; they can't. Stories of travellers being dumped off in the middle of nowhere once they've crossed the border into Tibet (minus their bags and money) are not uncommon.

Getting Around
TO/FROM THE AIRPORT
Shangliu Airport is 18km west of the city. Bus No 303 leaves from outside the Air China office on Renmin Nanlu. Sichuan Airlines provide a free shuttle from your hotel to the airport if you buy your ticket with them. A taxi will cost around Y40.

BICYCLE
Cycling is a great way to get around Chéngdū although the pollution can be terrible at times. Dragon Town Youth Hostel, Sam's Guesthouse and the Traffic Hotel all rent bikes for about Y10 per day. The bikes are in fairly good condition but the usual rules apply: check your bike before you cycle off and make an effort to park it

in a designated parking area. Bicycle theft is a problem here as in most Chinese cities and make sure you don't put anything valuable in the bicycle basket (see Dangers & Annoyances p714).

BUS
The most useful bus is No 16, which runs from Chéngdū's north train station to the south train station (nán chēzhàn) along Renmin Nanlu. Regular buses cost Y1, while the double-deckers cost Y2. Bus No 81 runs from the Mao statue to Green Ram Temple and Bus No 12 circles the city along Yihuan Lu, starting and ending at the north train station. Bus No 4 runs from the centre of town to Chadianzi bus station and Wuguiqiao bus station.

TAXI
Taxis have a flag fall of Y5 (Y6 at night), plus Y1.4 per kilometre. Motorised rickshaws also scuttle around the city and are cheaper, but slower, than cabs.

AROUND CHÉNGDŪ
Monastery of Divine Light 宝光寺
In Xindu County, 18km north of Chengdu, this is an active Buddhist temple with five halls and 16 courtyards surrounded by bamboo.

Founded in the 9th century, the **Monastery of Divine Light** (Bǎoguāng Sì; ☺ 8am-5.30pm) was destroyed and reconstructed in the 17th century. Among the treasures here are a white jade buddha from Myanmar (Burma), Ming and Qing paintings, calligraphy, a stone tablet engraved with 1000 Buddhist figures (AD 540) and ceremonial musical instruments. Unfortunately, most of the more valuable items are locked away and require special permission to be viewed – you may be able to get this if you can find whoever's in charge.

The **Arhat Hall**, built in the 19th century, contains 500 2m-high clay figurines of Buddhist saints and disciples – well, not all of them: among this spaced-out lot are two earthlings, the emperors Kangxi and Qianlong. They're distinguishable by their royal costumes, beards, boots and capes.

Buses run to the monastery from in front of Chéngdū's north train station and north bus station from around 6am to 6pm. The trip takes just under an hour.

On a Chinese bicycle, the round trip would be about 40km, or at least four hours cycling time.

Qīngchéng Shān 青城山

A holy Taoist mountain some 65km west of Chéngdū, with a summit of only 1600m, **Qīngchéng Shān** (Azure City Mountain; Y60) is an excellent day trip into the subtropics. It offers beautiful trails lined with gingko, plum and palm trees, picturesque vistas and plenty of atmospheric sights along its four-hour return route. In nasty weather it's a good alternative to Éméi Shān as its somewhat sturdier steps are stone rather than slate (and therefore less slippery) and the views here are less likely to be obscured by mist and cloud. It's also a far easier climb.

Situated outside the entrance gate, **Jianfu Temple** (Jiànfú Gōng) is the best preserved of the mountain's temples. Of the 500 or so Taoist monks resident here prior to liberation, there are still about 100 living here.

Further up the hill, both **Chaoyang Cave** (Cháoyáng Dòng) and **Taoist Master Cave** (Tiānshī Dòng) are temples built into hollows in the side of the mountain. In the courtyard of Taoist Master Cave are ancient twin gingko trees planted during the Han dynasty over 1000 years ago. Only 500m from the mountain's summit is **Shangqing Temple** (Shàngqīng Gōng), established in the Jin dynasty.

The most popular way of ascending Qīngchéng Shān is by gliding across Yuèchéng Hú (Yuecheng Lake) on a small ferry (Y5) and then ascending via the cable car (one way/return Y30/50) to within a 20-minute walk from Shangqing Temple. This removes most of the hard work and makes it very easy to fit Qīngchéng Shān into a day trip from Chéngdū. If you do walk only one way, the western trail past Chaoyang Cave and Taoist Master Cave offers the most sights and views. At the southern end of this route is the lush **Chunxian Mountain Path**, created early in the 19th century by headmaster Chunxian Peng who had each visitor to the mountain plant a tree along the path.

In a bid to bolster tourism, the local authorities have opened up **Qīngchéng Hòushān** (青城后山, Azure City Back Mountain) to trekkers. Its base lies about 15km northwest of the base of Qīngchéng Shān proper. With over 20km of hiking trails, this mountain of-

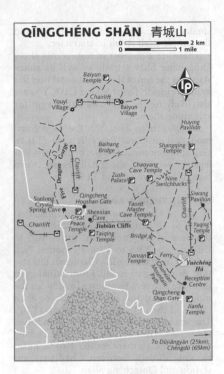

QĪNGCHÉNG SHĀN 青城山

fers a more natural environment than the slopes of Qīngchéng Shān strewn with temples and tour groups, with **Five Dragon Gorge** (Wǔlóng Gōu) offering dramatic vistas. Most travellers who come here spend several days and one Englishman enjoyed it so much he stayed several weeks. There is a cable car to help with part of the route, but climbing the mountain will still require an overnight stay; you won't want to rush the trip anyway.

SLEEPING & EATING

There are a number of pricey resort-style hotels on the road leading up to the Qīngchéng Shān's main gate but your best option is to stay in one of the temples on the mountain itself.

Shangqing Temple (Shàngqīng Gōng; dm Y36-60, d Y120) This charming wooden temple offers hotel-like facilities. Rooms are basic and clean and have common balconies that look out over the surrounding forests. The restaurant here serves up excellent food, their omelettes are especially good.

Taoist Master Cave (Tiānshī Dòng; d with/without bathroom Y80/50) The rooms here are very similar to those at Shangqing Temple and the temple itself is full of character.

There are a number of restaurants along Qīngchéng Shān's trails as well as snack stands at the top of the chairlift and noodles available inside Taoist Master Cave. You are also likely to find fruit and boiled eggs for sale along the way.

At Qīngchéng Hòushān there's accommodation in Great Peace Temple (Tài'ān Gé), at the mountain's base, or at Youyi Village (Yòuyī Cūn), about halfway up. Dorm beds at both are around Y15.

GETTING THERE & AWAY
To get to Qīngchéng Shān you must first travel to Dūjiāngyàn, a town 25km from the base of the mountain. Buses run to Dūjiāngyàn (Y8.5 to Y16, 1½ hours, 7am to 8pm) from Chéngdū's Chadianzi bus station, departing when full. From Dūjiāngyàn there are frequent minibuses leaving for the mountain, stopping first at Qīngchéng Shān (Y4) and then Qīngchéng Hòushān (Y10). The last bus returning to Dūjiāngyàn leaves Qīngchéng Hòushān around 7pm. During the high season there are likely to be buses running directly between Chadianzi bus station and Qīngchéng Shān.

Dujiangyan Irrigation Project
都江堰水利工程
Located some 60km northwest of Chéngdū, the **Dujiangyan Irrigation Project** (Dūjiāngyàn Shuǐlì Gōngchéng; admission Y60; ⏱ 6am-8pm) was undertaken in the 3rd century BC by famed prefect and engineer Li Bing to divert the fast-flowing Min River (Mín Hé) into irrigation canals. Min River was subject to flooding at this point, yet when it subsided, droughts could ensue. A weir system was built to split the force of the river and a trunk canal was cut through a mountain to irrigate the Chéngdū plain.

Li Bing's most brilliant idea was to devise an annual maintenance plan to remove silt build-up. Thus the mighty Mín was tamed, with a temple erected in AD 168 to commemorate the occasion. Located in Solitude Park (Líduī Gōngyuán), **Dragon-Subduing Temple** (Fúlóng Guàn) contains a tame gallery of propaganda photographs.

The project is ongoing; it originally irrigated over a million hectares of land and since Liberation (the communists' rise to power) this has expanded to three million hectares. Most of the present dams, reservoirs, pumping stations, hydroelectric works, bridgework and features are unsurprisingly modern. A good overall view of the outlay can be gained from **Èrwáng Miào** (Two Kings Temple), which dates from AD 494 and commemorates Li Bing and his son, Er Lang. Inside the temple is a statue of Li Bing, shockingly lifelike; in the rear hall is a standing figure of his son holding a dam tool.

While the whole idea of visiting a mocha-coloured, massive irrigation project may not be everyone's cup of tea, it's an interesting day trip from Chéngdū if you're interested in Chinese history or engineering.

GETTING THERE & AWAY
The bus station is located in the south of town. Buses run regularly to Dūjiāngyàn from the Chadianzi bus station in Chéngdū (Y8.5 to Y16, 1½ hours, 7am to 8pm). The last bus back to Chéngdū leaves around 8pm. There is also a direct bus from Dūjiāngyàn to Wòlóng (Y40.5, 2½hr) at 8am and 2pm.

Bus No 1 runs to the irrigation project from outside the bus station.

Wolong Nature Reserve
卧龙自然保护区
Wolong Nature Reserve (Wòlóng Zìrá'n Bǎohùqū; admission Y40) lies 140km northwest of Chéngdū, about four hours by bus (via Dūjiāngyàn). It was set up in the late 1970s and is the largest of the 16 reserves set aside by the Chinese government for panda conservation (of these 16 reserves, 11 are in Sìchuān). The UN has designated Wòlóng an International Biosphere Preserve.

The reserve is estimated to have some 4000 kinds of plants and covers an area of 200,000 hectares. To the northwest rises Sìgūniáng Shān (6250m); to the east the reserve drops as low as 155m. Pandas like to dine on fang cane and fountain bamboo in the zone from 2300m to 3600m, ranging lower in winter. Other animals protected here are the golden monkey, golden langur, musk deer and snow leopard.

There are currently 60 captive pandas, including nearly 20 babies born in the past four years. However, there is little chance of seeing a panda in the wild; the pandas have a hard enough time finding each other. In spring, the park is closed so that trekkers don't disturb the pandas' hunt for each other during their mating season.

If you're just out to commune with nature, Wòlóng can be pleasant. The rainy season, however, is a bad time to be here as leeches take over the park. Summer is the most popular time to visit, especially for Japanese tourists who are looking for the two rare types of azaleas that bloom here.

Trekking here is fairly tough and the trails are faint. The Park Administration Office in Wòlóng village (also called Shawan), at the centre of the reserve, can give information on hiking trails and researchers at the Conservation Centre (some of whom speak English) are good sources of info on conditions. Be sure to bring your own supplies, including warm clothing.

At the Conservation Centre, 6km from Wòlóng village, the **Panda Inn** (☎ 0837-624 3028; fax 0837-624 3014; d Y200) has clean, comfortable doubles with hot showers and heaters. There is also a restaurant in the hotel and barbecue stalls across the road.

GETTING THERE & AWAY

One bus leaves daily from Chéngdū's Chadianzi bus station to Wòlóng village (Y20, four hours, 11.40am). If you miss that bus then head over to Dūjiāngyàn from where buses to Wòlóng run twice daily (Y40.5, 2½hr; 8am and 2pm). If you want to get dropped at the Conservation Centre, rather than Wòlóng village, be sure to tell the bus driver.

Onward buses continue on from Wòlóng village over the 4487m Bulangshan Pass to Rìlóng and Xiǎojīn, from where you can catch buses to Kāngdìng. Schedules on these routes are irregular.

ÉMÉI SHĀN 峨眉山
☎ 0833 / elevation 3099m

Locked in a medieval time warp, Éméi Shān, 130km southwest of Chengdu, is dotted with monasteries and temples, many of which have their histories posted for visitors both in English and in Chinese.

Éméi Shān is one of the Middle Kingdom's four famous Buddhist mountains (the others are Pútuoshān, Wǔtái Shān and Jiǔhuá Shān). The original temple structures dated from as long ago as the advent of Buddhism itself in China; by the 14th century, the estimated 100 or so holy structures housed several thousand monks. Unfortunately, Éméi Shān has little of its original templework left. Glittering Jinding Temple (Jīndǐng Sì), with its brass tiling engraved with Tibetan script, was completely gutted by fire. A similar fate befell numerous other temples and monasteries on the mountain. War with the Japanese and Red Guard looting didn't help either.

After a Cultural Revolution hiatus, around 20 temples are now active, regaining traces of their original splendour. Since 1976 the remnants have been renovated, access to the mountain has been improved, hiking paths widened, lodgings added, and tourists permitted to climb to the sacred summit.

The pilgrims, tourists and hawkers that line the path on a sunny day during peak season may remove the chance of finding much solitude on the mountain but they do add to the atmosphere. The crowds hover largely around the monasteries; once away from them, the path is not lined so much with stalls as with the fir, pine and cedar trees that clothe the slopes. Lofty crags, cloud-kissing precipices, butterflies and azaleas together form a nature reserve of sorts. The mountain was added to Unesco's list of World Heritage Sites in 1996, joining Lèshān and Jiǔzhàigōu.

The major scenic goal of Chinese hikers is to witness a sunrise or sunset over the sea of clouds at the summit. On the rare afternoon there is also a phenomenon known as Buddha's Aureole where rainbow rings, produced by refraction of water particles, attach themselves to a person's shadow in a cloud bank below the summit. Devout Buddhists, thinking this was a call from yonder, used to jump off the Cliff of Self-Sacrifice in ecstasy, leading officials of the Ming and Qing dynasties to set up iron poles and chain railings to prevent further suicides.

Information
TICKETS

Tickets for Éméi Shān have soared up to a hefty Y120. This price includes having your mug shot scanned onto the ticket which is then laminated – think of it as ready-made present for someone back home. Entry to Declare Nation Temple and Crouching Tiger Monastery at the foot of the mountain do not require this ticket and have their own admission charge (see p728).

ÉMÉI SHĀN 峨眉山

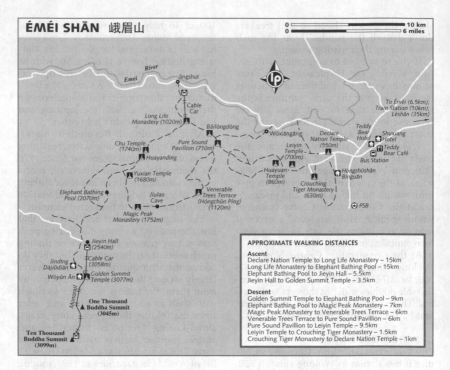

APPROXIMATE WALKING DISTANCES

Ascent
Declare Nation Temple to Long Life Monastery – 15km
Long Life Monastery to Elephant Bathing Pool – 15km
Elephant Bathing Pool to Jieyin Hall – 5.5km
Jieyin Hall to Golden Summit Temple – 3.5km

Descent
Golden Summit Temple to Elephant Bathing Pool – 9km
Elephant Bathing Pool to Magic Peak Monastery – 7km
Magic Peak Monastery to Venerable Trees Terrace – 6km
Venerable Trees Terrace to Pure Sound Pavillion – 6km
Pure Sound Pavillion to Leiyin Temple – 9.5km
Leiyin Temple to Crouching Tiger Monastery – 1.5km
Crouching Tiger Monastery to Declare Nation Temple – 1km

CLIMATE

The best time to visit Émēi Shān is between May and October. Visiting in winter is not impossible, but will present real trekking problems – iron soles with spikes can be hired to deal with encrusted ice and snow on the trails. Snowfall generally starts around November on the upper slopes. On the plus side the mountain will be virtually deserted leaving you to enjoy it all in peace. Try to avoid visiting during national holidays when the number of visitors to the mountain reaches epic proportions.

At the height of summer, which is scorching elsewhere in Sìchuān, Émēi Shān presents cool majesty. Temperate zones start at 1000m.

Cloud cover and mist are prevalent all year round at Émēi Shān and will most likely interfere with your view of the sunrise. If you're very lucky, you'll be able to see Gònggā Shān (Gongga Mountain) to the west; if you're not so lucky, you'll have to settle for the less appealing Telecom tower and the meteorological station.

Some average temperatures in degrees Celsius are:

Location	Jan	Apr	Jul	Oct
Émēi town	7	21	26	17
summit	6	3	12	-1

WHAT TO BRING

Definitely not your entire pack. Nevertheless, Émēi Shān is a tall one at 3099m, so the weather is uncertain and it's best to prepare for sudden changes without weighing yourself down – the steps are very steep. If you're staying at the Teddy Bear Hotel (p729), you can store your bags there for free. If not, staff will probably keep them for you anyway for a modest charge.

There is no heating or insulation in the monasteries, but blankets are provided and some even have electric blankets, a godsend in the winter. You can also hire heavy overcoats at the top. Heavy rain can be a problem, as even a light mist can make the slate steps slippery and extremely treacherous. A good pair of rough-soled shoes or boots is a must. When it does rain, flimsy, plastic bags with hoods are sold by enterprising vendors on the slopes. They appear to do the trick, at least for a little while.

Strange hiking equipment as it may sound, a fixed-length umbrella would be most useful – for the rain and as a walking stick. You should be able to find one in Émèi town for Y30 to Y45. If you want to look even more authentic, you can buy yourself a handcrafted walking stick (very cheap), for sale along the way. The Teddy Bear Café (p730) lends walking sticks out for free. A torch (flashlight) is important if you're spending the night or planning to hike at dawn. Food supplies are not necessary with food stalls along the way; nevertheless a pocket of munchies wouldn't hurt as long as you can keep it out of sight of the monkeys. Finally, don't forget toilet paper.

A few travellers have reported catching a serious case of conjunctivitis at guesthouses on the mountain. You can try to avoid this by bringing a towel or pillowcase to cover the pillow and then washing it before using it again. Other travellers have become sick from contaminated water supplies on the mountain; it's wise to drink only the bottled water available at stands along the way.

ROUTES
The most popular route for those planning to hike up and down the mountain is to ascend via Long Life Monastery, Chu Temple (Chū Sì), Elephant Bathing Pool and on to the summit. On the way down, take the path off towards Magic Peak Monastery after you reach Elephant Bathing Pool. This path will also lead you past Venerable Trees Terrace (Hóngchūn Píng) and Pure Sound Pavilion. The majority of hikers agree that the descent is superior in sights and views.

If you're short on time or energy, you can be carried up on the back of a porter. Or there are buses going up the mountain from the bus station in Bàoguó, next door to the Teddy Bear Cafe. Bus routes and prices are posted at the Bàoguó bus station and at the stops en route. A ride to the top costs Y30, to Wǔxiāngǎng costs Y10 and a return trip with a number of stops is Y60. Buses run half-hourly from approximately 6am to 5pm but you don't want to cut it too close on the way down – if you miss the last bus, it's a 15km walk down from Long Life Monastery.

There are numerous ways to tackle the mountain. One popular option is to take a bus to Wǔxiāngǎng and begin hiking from here. Alternatively stay on the bus until you reach Jìngshuǐ from where you can get a cable car (up/down/return Y40/30/60, 6am to 6pm) up to Long Life Monastery. From the top of the cable car you can join the route to the summit. Buses run as far up the mountain as Jieyin Hall (Jiēyǐn Diàn; two hours) from where it's a steep two-hour hike or five-minute cable car ride (one way/return Y40/50) to the top.

If for some reason you wish to conquer the whole mountain in one day, most hotels can book you on a bus leaving at 3.30am (!). This is supposed to get you to the summit in time to see the sunrise, and is a popular option with Chinese tourists. Unfortunately, so many buses make this early morning run now that there's usually an immense traffic jam at the entrance gate followed by an enormous queue of tourists crawling up the mountainside trying to reach Golden Summit Temple before sunrise – very few do.

These buses begin to head down from Jieyin Hall around mid-morning, stopping at various temples along the way and finally bringing you back to Bàoguó at around 5pm. The round trip costs about Y60 and will probably leave your head spinning. It's best to do it in segments; buy your bus ticket up (Y30) at the Teddy Bear Café the day before, so once you're up there you can decide if, when and how you'll return.

DURATION
It's difficult to estimate how long you will need to make it up and back down Émèi Shān by foot. While you don't require any particular hiking skills, it is nonetheless a tough climb. You will be quoted wildly differing times by locals and other hikers. It is possible to make it to the summit from Long Life Monastery and back down to Declare Nation Temple in two days but you must be willing to spend at least 10 hours hiking each day and hope for good weather. The altitude may also play havoc with your breathing and ascending too quickly will only increase this. Finally, you may well want to explore the many temples and monasteries en route and to enjoy the vistas. All up, it's wise to leave yourself three days for the trek.

SOUTHWEST CHINA

The approximate distances on the map will give you an idea of what is involved but remember, the entire route resembles a very steep staircase. To get an idea of how long it's going to take you, time yourself on the first kilometre or two and then average out your own probable climbing duration.

Sights

DECLARE NATION TEMPLE 报国寺
Constructed in the 16th century, enlarged in the 17th century by Emperor Kangxi and recently renovated, **Declare Nation Temple** (Bàoguó Sì; admission Y8) features a 3.5m-high porcelain Buddha that was made in 1415; it's housed near the Sutra Library. To the left of the gate is a rockery for potted miniature trees and rare plants.

CROUCHING TIGER MONASTERY 伏虎寺
The renovated **Crouching Tiger Monastery** (Fúhǔ Sì; admission Y6) is sunk deep within the forest. Inside is a 7m-high copper pagoda inscribed with Buddhist images and texts.

PURE SOUND PAVILION 清音阁
Named after the sound effects produced by rapid waters coursing around its surrounding rock formations, this **temple** (Qīngyīn Gé) is built on an outcrop in the middle of a fast-flowing stream.

There are several small pavilions from which to observe the waterworks and appreciate the natural music. It's possible to swim here although the water is only likely to be warm enough during the summer months.

LONG LIFE MONASTERY 万年寺
Reconstructed in the 9th century, **Long Life Monastery** (Wànnián Sì; admission Y10) is the oldest surviving Éméi temple. It's dedicated to the man on the white elephant, the Bodhisattva Puxian, who is the protector of the mountain. This 8.5m-high **statue** is dated from AD 980, cast in copper and bronze and weighs an estimated 62,000kg. If you can manage to rub the elephant's hind leg, good luck will be cast upon you.

The statue is housed in Brick Hall, a domed building with small stupas on it. When the temple was damaged by fire in 1945, Brick Hall was the only building left unharmed. There is also a graveyard to the rear of the temple.

MAGIC PEAK MONASTERY 仙峰寺
Somewhat off the beaten track, this **monastery** (Xiānfēng Sì) is backed by rugged cliffs, surrounded by fantastic scenery and oozing with character. The nearby **Jiulao Cave** is inhabited by big bats.

ELEPHANT BATHING POOL 洗象池
According to legend, **Elephant Bathing Pool** (Xǐxiàng Chí) is the spot where Puxian flew his elephant in for a big scrub, but today there's not much of a pool to speak of. Being almost at the crossroads of both major trails, the temple here is something of a hang-out and often crowded with pilgrims.

GOLDEN SUMMIT TEMPLE 金顶寺
This magnificent **temple** (Jīndǐng Sì) at the Golden Summit (Jīn Dǐng; 3077m) is as far as most hikers make it. It has been entirely rebuilt since being gutted by a fire several years ago. Covered with glazed tiles and surrounded by white marble balustrades, the temple now occupies 1695 sq metres. The original temple had a bronze-coated roof, which is how it got the name Jīn Dǐng (which can also mean 'Gold Top').

It's constantly overrun with tourists, pilgrims and monks, and you'll be continuously bumped and jostled. The sun rarely forces its way through the mists up here and the result is that it is usually impossible to see very far past your own nose.

From the Golden Summit it was once possible to hike to **Ten Thousand Buddha Summit** (Wànfó Dǐng) but pilgrims now take a monorail (a one-hour return ticket costs Y50).

Sleeping & Eating
ON THE MOUNTAIN
The old monasteries offer food, shelter and sights all rolled into one. While some travellers complain about the spartan and somewhat damp conditions, others find what may be as many as a thousand years of character a delightful change from the regular tourist hotels.

You won't often find a reception desk at the monasteries. Instead, find a monk or caretaker and ask to be pointed in the right direction. A few of the monasteries at key junctions have posted prices but at others you may well have to bargain with the monks. You can expect to pay between Y15 and Y40 for a bed in a dorm room, with

MONKEY ETIQUETTE

The monkeys have got it all figured out. If you come across a monkey 'tollgate', the standard procedure is to thrust open palms towards the outlaw to show you have no food. The Chinese find the monkeys an integral part of the Éméi trip, and many like to tease them.

The monkey forms an important part of Chinese mythology, and there is a saying in Chinese, 'With one monkey in the way, not even 10,000 men can pass' – which may be deeper than you think!

Some of these chimps are big, and staying cool when they look like they might make a leap at you is easier said than done. There is much debate as to whether it's better to give them something to eat or to fight them off.

One thing is certain, if you do throw them something, don't be too stingy. They get annoyed very quickly if they think they are being undersold.

plumbing and electricity provided in those at the higher end of the scale. The following should give you an idea as to where to head for the cheapest beds, but expect to pay more in the high season.

Declare Nation Temple (dm from Y20), **Pure Sound Pavilion** (dm Y15-20, d Y150), **Long Life Monastery** (dm Y10-40), **Elephant Bathing Pool** (dm from Y20), **Crouching Tiger Monastery** (dm from Y50), **Golden Summit Temple** (dm Y15-40), Magic Peak Monastery, Venerable Trees Terrace and Leiyin Temple (Léiyīn Sì) have monastery guesthouses. There's also a host of smaller lodgings at Chu Temple, Jieyin Hall, Yuxian Temple (Yùxiān Sì), Báilóngdòng (White Dragon Cave) and Huayuan Temple (Huáyuán Sì), among others. The smaller places will accept you if the main monasteries are full. Failing those, if night is descending, you can kip virtually anywhere – a teahouse, a restaurant.

During peak season, be prepared to backtrack or advance under cover of darkness, as key points are often full of pilgrims.

There are a growing number of guesthouses and hotels cropping up on Éméi Shān. Many of the cheaper places do not accept foreigners while others close in the off season. On average you can expect to pay between Y150 and Y300 for a room, depending on the availability of hot water and whether or not you opt for a private bath. Most of these guesthouses are clumped behind Golden Summit Temple, to the west.

Wòyún Ān (dm Y50) This ramshackle wooden building was once a nunnery and is now a popular place for pilgrims to stay. It's full of character: countless narrow corridors slant in all directions and the rooms have about as much insulation as a tent with no door. Electric blankets are provided, however, and you're in a perfect location to see the sun rise – if the sun doesn't make an appearance you can just roll over and go back to sleep.

Jìndǐng Dàjiǔdiàn (☎ 509 8088, 509 8077; s/d/tr Y380/480/600) This three-star hotel is located at the base of the cable car and offers the ultimate luxury, 24-hour hot showers.

Vegetarian meals are included with the price of a bed at many of the monasteries. You can often find a small food stall or shop near the monastery grounds as well, selling biscuits, instant noodles, peanuts and drinks – not to mention a wide variety of fungus.

You will also come across a large number of food stalls and restaurants along the route. Food becomes more expensive and less varied the higher you climb, due to cartage surcharges and difficulties. Be wary of teahouses or restaurants serving *shénshuǐ* (divine water), or any type of tea or food said to possess mystical healing qualities. Miracles are not guaranteed but the price of at least Y10 for the cup of water or tea is.

BAOGUO VILLAGE

The stretch of road leading up to Declare Nation Temple witnesses the rise and fall of many hotels. Most are nondescript and overpriced but will accept foreigners if you catch staff in the right mood. It's best to have a wander and check out a few options as prices and room conditions fluctuate.

Teddy Bear Hotel (☎ 559 0135; teddybearcafé@yahoo.com.cn; dm Y30, d Y80-150) This is still the most popular place in town. Rooms are spotless and the shared bathrooms sparkle. Other perks include a free laundry and left-luggage service and a massage when you make it back down the mountain. The hotel is just round the corner from the Teddy Bear Café.

Shuxiang Hotel (Shūxiāng Bīnguǎn; ☎ 559 0131; d/tr Y60/80) Next door to the Teddy Bear Hotel, this place makes a good alternative. Rooms are very nice and the owner is lovely.

Hóngzhūshān Bīnguǎn (☎ 552 5888; d Y350)
You might want to splurge on a room here.
Doubles in building No 7 are the best deal
and, while they may not appear particularly
special, the tranquil setting of lush forests
and the view on the edge of a pond makes
it feel like money well spent.

Teddy Bear Café (☎ 559 0135) Friendly staff
serve up Chinese and a few Western dishes
which you can order from an English menu.
You can also order a picnic to take up the
mountain.

The street leading up to Declare Nation
Temple is lined with restaurants including
huǒguō and *shāokǎo* stalls which begin to
appear as the evening approaches. There
are also a large number of shops along here
which stock food supplies for your trek up
the mountain.

Getting There & Away

Éméi town lies 6.5km from Éméi Shān and
is the main transport hub for travel to and
from the mountain. Buses from Chéngdū's
Xinanmen bus station run every 20 minutes
to Éméi town (Y33, two hours, 6.40am to
7pm) and every half-hour from Chéngdū's
north bus station to Bàoguó village (Y30,
two hours, 6.30am to 5.25pm).

BUS

See box below for bus details.

There is no direct public bus between
Bàoguó village and Éméi town. If you don't
want to catch a taxi (Y20) then take the
No 1 bus from outside the long-distance
bus station (Y0.5). Get off at the first stop,
cross the road and catch the No 5 (Y1) to
Bàoguó village.

Heading back to Éméi town, buses leave
every 10 minutes from outside Bàoguó's
long-distance bus station (Y1, 20 minutes, 7.30am to 7pm). You can also catch

a direct bus to Chéngdū (Y32, two hours,
hourly, 6.30am to 6pm), Lèshān (Y8, one
hour, hourly, 6am to 5pm) and Chóngqìng
(Y35, seven hours, 8.30am) from here.

TRAIN

Éméi train station is on the Chéngdū–
Kūnmíng line and lies 3.5km from the
centre of Éméi town. Bus No 4 (Y0.5) runs
between the train station and the long-
distance bus station. Éméi town has trains
to Chéngdū, Kūnmíng and Wūsīhé. Patricia at the Teddy Bear Cafe can help you out
with train times (they change frequently)
and booking tickets.

LÈSHĀN 乐山

☎ 0833 / pop 155,800

Once a sleepy counterpart to Éméi Shān,
Lèshān has taken off as a popular tourist destination thanks to its main claim to fame –
the towering Grand Buddha. Prospering
from increasing droves of Chinese tourists, Lèshān has revamped many of its old
quarters, levelling old residential districts
to make way for new apartment towers and
department stores. There is little else to see
in Lèshān other than the Buddha, nevertheless, the city has managed to retain a
friendly, relaxed atmosphere.

Information

Bank of China (Zhōngguó Yínháng; Renmin Nanlu)
Changes money and travellers cheques and offers cash
advances on credit cards. There is also an ATM here.

China Post (Yóujú; Yutang Jie) Next door is China
Telecom where you can make international phone calls.

Internet cafés (Wǎngbā; Baita Jie; per hr Y2) There are
two Internet cafés opposite Jiāzhōu Bīnguǎn.

Mr Yang (☎ 211 2046, 130-3645 6184; richardyang
min@163.net; Yang's Restaurant, 154 Baita Jie) Has long
been the guru of travel information in Lèshān. While he can
organise almost anything (a visit to a local doctor, a local

ÉMÉI BUS TIMETABLES

Buses from Éméi town:

Destination	Price	Duration	Frequency	Departs
Chéngdū	Y32	2hr	every 15 min	7am-6.30pm
Lèshān	Y5.5	40 min	every 15 min	7am-6.30pm
Yǎ'ān	Y23.5	3hr	4 daily	7.50am, 9.40am, 12.30pm, 2.10pm

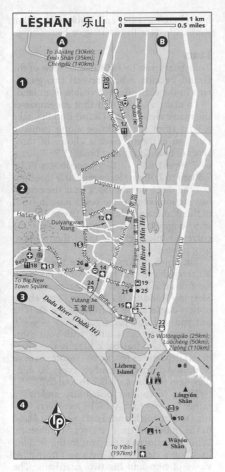

LÈSHĀN 乐山

family, nearby villages, calligraphy lessons), for a while now he has been getting mixed reviews from travellers who feel he has doled out dubious information in order to encourage them to patronise his services. The company he is affiliated with in Chóngqìng for Yangzi River cruise tickets has received a particularly bad rap. Have a chat with him by all means, he's a great source of information and an interesting character, but you might want to think about organising the boat trip yourself or going through a travel agency in Chóngqìng.

People's Hospital (Rénmín Yīyuàn; ☎ 211 9310, out of hr emergencies ☎ 211 9328; 76 Baita Jie) Has a couple of English-speaking doctors.

PSB (Gōngānjú; 236 Chunhua Lu; ✆ 9am-noon & 2-6pm Mon-Fri) Reputedly one of the speediest in China for visa extensions (same-day extensions are not uncommon).

Sam Zhang (☎ 299 5221) The new travel guide on the block with hopes of cashing in on some of Mr Yang's

success. He claims to offer similar services to Mr Yang and can also help find teaching jobs.

Sights

GRAND BUDDHA 大佛

Carved into a cliff face overlooking the confluence of Dadu River (Dàdù Hé) and Min River (Mín Hé), the **Grand Buddha** (Dà Fó) is an overwhelming 71m high. Qualifying as the largest Buddha in the world, his ears are 7m long, his insteps 8.5m broad, and you could picnic on the nail of his big toe – the toe itself is 8.5m long.

This mammoth project was begun in AD 713, engineered by a Buddhist monk called Haitong who organised fundraising and hired workers; it was finally completed 90 years after his death. Below the Grand Buddha was a hollow in the river where boatmen used to vanish; Haitong hoped that the Buddha's presence would subdue the swift currents and protect the boatmen. And the Buddha has done a lot of good, as the surplus rocks from the sculpting filled the river hollow.

Inside the body, hidden from view, is a water-drainage system put into place to prevent weathering, although the stone statue has had its fair share of it. A building once sheltered the giant statue, but it was destroyed during a Ming dynasty war.

Officials are worried about the possibility of collapse due to soil erosion; one suggestion that has not met with an enthusiastic response is to cover the buddha with a huge transparent shell.

It's worth looking at the Grand Buddha from several angles. While the easiest way to see him is to walk along the riverfront on Binhe Lu, you need to get closer to him to really appreciate his magnitude. You can go to the top, opposite the head, and then descend a short stairway to the feet for a Lilliputian perspective

THOUSAND BUDDHA CLIFFS 夹江千佛岩

About 30km north of Lèshān, 2.5km west of the train station at Jiājiāng, are the **Thousand Buddha Cliffs** (Jiājiāng Qiānfóyán; admission Y35; ◷ 8am-5pm). For once, the name is not an exaggeration: over 2400 Buddhas dot the cliffs, dating from as early as the Eastern Han dynasty. The statues show a few signs of wear and tear but, considering their age, are in fairly good condition.

Set in a rather pretty location along a riverbank and on the edge of the countryside, this site takes something of an effort to reach. Catch one of the many buses from Lèshān's long-distance bus station down the bumpy road to Jiājiāng (Y5; one hour). From Jiājiāng bus station, take a pedicab (Y10) or taxi (Y15) to the site. The last bus returning to Lèshān leaves Jiājiāng at 6pm.

OTHER SIGHTS

The boardwalk along Binhe Lu follows Dadu River from its confluence with Min River, up past Jiāzhōu Bīnguǎn. Popular for strolling in the evenings, if you follow it as far as Jiāzhōu Bīnguǎn, you'll see fan dancers, ballroom dancers and even tango lessons underway in a large square near the intersection with Baita Jie. You can also take bus No 6 out to the **Big New Town Square** where a 27m-high fountain attracts crowds of Leshanese in the evenings.

Travellers have recommended day trips to villages outside Lèshān, including **Luóchéng**, 50km southeast, famed for its old 'boat-house' architecture, and **Wǔtōngqiáo**, 25km south. Check with Mr Yang or Sam Zhong.

Tours

Tour boats pass by for a frontal view of the Grand Buddha, which reveals two guardians in the cliff side, not visible from land.

To make a round tour that encompasses the many views of the Grand Buddha, take a boat from the dockside along Binjiang Lu. You currently have a choice of three types of boat. Large tour boats (Y30, 7.30am to 7.30pm) and smaller speedboats (Y30, 7.30am to 7.30pm) leave regularly throughout the day from the dock near the central bus station. Both these boats pass in front of the Buddha and hover for five to 10 minutes, engines whirring madly against the current while everyone takes their obligatory photos.

The third option is to take the bargain Y3 ferry that leaves from a small dock not far from the Táoyuán Bīnguǎn next to the Sleeping Buddha Tea Pavilion. This cheap option doesn't stop in front of the Buddha but you will still get a good view – you'll just have to be extra quick with your camera. The only drawback here is the infrequent departures (every 90 minutes 7am to 5.30pm April to September; every 90 minutes 8am to 5pm October to March).

There is another possibility and it's a rather fun way to travel. The local ferry (Y1) runs to Lizheng Island, a narrow strip of land in the middle of the two rivers' confluence. While this doesn't take you to the Buddha itself, on a clear day it gives you unrivalled views of him and his two guardians. The ferry leaves regularly throughout the day from Lizheng Gate (look for a stone archway), not far from the Jiāzhōu Bīnguǎn.

The final destination for the boats leaving from the main docks is **Wuyou Temple** (Wǔyóu Sì; admission Y8; ◷ 8am-6pm). Like the Grand Buddha, this monastery dates from the Tang dynasty with Ming and Qing renovations. It commands panoramic views and is a museum piece containing calligraphy, painting and artefacts, many with English captions.

Wuyou Temple has a hall of 1000 terracotta *arhat* (Buddhist celestial beings, similar to angels) displaying an incredible variety of postures and facial expressions – no two are alike. The *arhat* are housed in the **Luohan Hall** which dates back to 1909.

Inside is also a fantastic statue of **Avalok-iteshvara**, the Sanskrit name of the Goddess of Mercy (Guanyin in Chinese).

If you get off the boat at Wuyou Temple, a visit through the temple will take you across Wūyóu Shān and down to a small bridge which crosses over to **Língyún Shān** (Towering Cloud Hill). Here you can visit **Oriental Buddha Park** (Dōngfāng Fódū Gōngyuán; admission Y37), a newly assembled collection of 3000 Buddha statues and figurines from all around Asia. The park's centrepiece is a 170m-long reclining Buddha, said to be the world's longest. Though touted by local tourist authorities as a major attraction, the park seems more of a hasty effort to cash in on Buddha-mania – the Hong Kong and Chinese sculptors raced to knock off the reclining buddha in a mere two years. Still it makes for an interesting walk.

Next door is the **Mahaoya Tombs Museum** (Máhàoyámù Bówùguǎn; admission Y5), which has a modest collection of tombs and burial artefacts dating from the Eastern Han dynasty (AD 25–220).

Continuing past the museum and up Língyún Shān brings you to the entrance gate of **Dafo Temple** (Dàfó Sì; admission Y40). This is where you can get right up close to the Grand Buddha, with views from a platform level with his head. You can also follow a narrow staircase down to reach his feet. Avoid visiting on public holidays or weekends when traffic on the staircase comes to a complete standstill. Nearby is the **Lingbao Pagoda** (Língbǎo Tǎ).

To return to Lèshān, you can either catch another boat from the ferry dock near the entrance to the Buddha or take bus No 13 which leaves from the same place and will drop you back at Lèshān's dock.

This whole exercise can be done in less than 1½ hours from the Lèshān dock; however, it's worth making a day of it.

Sleeping

Duìyángwān Bīnguǎn (☎ 501 0345, 336 7582; Middle Section, Duiyangwan Xiang; s/d Y100/168) This might not be the cheapest place in town but it's certainly the nicest. Newly opened, the rooms are great and the staff incredibly friendly and helpful.

Post & Telecommunication Hotel (Yóudiàn Bīnguǎn; ☎ 213 5450; 32 Yutang Jie; d/tr Y198/268 incl breakfast) The rooms here are nothing special

but they are clean and damp-free. In the off season huge discounts can be found, making this your best budget choice in town.

Táoyuán Bīnguǎn (☎ 210 1718; dm Y50, d Y198) Almost directly opposite Lèshān's docks, this hotel was once a backpacker favourite but has recently seen a steep slide in standards. The outside of the hotel has had a facelift but the rooms are damp and grotty.

Xiāndǎo Bīnguǎn (☎ 230 1848; fax 230 1352; 2 Wuyou Bei; d Y218-268; ☒) Conveniently located by the entrance for Wuyou Temple this hotel is handy for beating the crowds in the morning but the rooms are a bit overpriced. To get here take bus No 13 from the Lèshān dock to its terminus near the hotel.

Jiāzhōu Bīnguǎn (☎ 213 9888; fax 213 3233; 19 Baita Lu; s/d Y450/480) This is Lèshān's original three-star hotel. They are planning to redecorate soon so expect nicer rooms (and a hike in prices) by the time you read this.

Eating

There are lots of small restaurants hidden away on Lèshān's side streets. A good place to start your search is along the small roads near the dock, in particular Xuedao Jie, which is buzzing with culinary delights. You'll find a selection of noodle and dumpling eateries and an entire alley lined with cheap hotpot restaurants. Alternatively, there's a popular **hotpot restaurant** (huǒguō cāntīng; ☺ 11am-9pm) just north of the intersection of Jiading Zhonglu and Renmin Donglu.

Another good place to wander is Binhe Lu, where you'll find a number of restaurants and a handful of teahouses that serve up simple dishes.

Yangs' Restaurant (Yàngjiā Cāntīng; 154 Baita Jie; dishes Y15-25; ☺ 6-9pm) Run by Mr Yang the travel guru, this restaurant is in the living room of his home. His wife is the chef and serves good local food. Check prices before ordering as some travellers have complained of very expensive vegetable fried rice.

Getting There & Away

There are now expressways linking Lèshān to Chéngdū and Chóngqìng resulting in a triangular transportation conduit which is second to none in southwest China.

BUS

There are two bus stations in Lèshān. The main one for travellers is the Lèshān long-distance bus station, annoyingly located in the northern reaches of the city.

For Chéngdū, the bus station next to the Lèshān docks is the most convenient. Buses leave for Chéngdū's Xinanmen bus station every hour (Y31, two hours, 7.30am to 6.30pm). There are also frequent departures to Éméi town from here (Y7, 7am to 6pm). For all other destinations you'll have to go to the long-distance bus station.

There is a handy **ticket office** (☎ 227 1508; ⏰ 8.30am-5pm) across from the central bus station that sells bus tickets for Lèshān's long-distance bus station.

When catching your bus to Chéngdū make sure you get on a bus heading to the Xinanmen bus station otherwise you'll find yourself being dropped off at Shiyangchang bus station on the outskirts of the city, kilometres from the centre. If this does happen, bus No 28 runs into town.

See box below for bus info.

TRAIN

It doesn't matter what anyone says, there simply is no train service to Lèshān. Ticket sellers in other cities will swear blind they can sell you a ticket to Lèshān but in reality they will only sell you a ticket to Éméi Shān, or more likely Jiājiāng, both about an hour away by bus.

Getting Around

Bus Nos 1 and 8 run the length of Jiading Lu and connect the pier area with the long-distance bus station. Buses run from 6am to 6pm, at roughly 20-minute intervals. Bus No 13 runs from Lèshān dock to Wuyou Temple, passing the entrance to the Grand Buddha on the way.

On foot, it's about an hour's walk from one end of town to the other. A pedicab from the main long-distance bus station to Táoyuán Bīnguǎn should cost about Y5 and from the pier to Jiāzhōu Bīnguǎn about Y2. Pedicab operators in Lèshān all split up the fares, so don't be paranoid when one of them stops halfway and tells you to get on his buddy's pedicab. Just pay him half (or whatever) and pay the remainder when you arrive. Taxis in Lèshān start at a flat rate of Y3 for the first 3km.

Unfortunately there doesn't seem to be any bicycle hire in Lèshān – or many bicycles at all for that matter. But you probably wouldn't want to take them up and down the stairs at the Grand Buddha anyway.

WESTERN SÌCHUĀN & THE ROAD TO TIBET

The Sìchuān mountains to the north and west of Chéngdū rise above 5000m with deep valleys, vast grasslands and rapid rivers. To Tibetans, this area is part of the province of Kham which covers the eastern third of the Tibetan plateau. For travellers, it is an opportunity to visit Tibet without actually crossing the 'official' provincial border.

Tibetans and Tibetan-related peoples (Qiang) live here by herding yaks, sheep and goats on the high-altitude Kangba Plateau grasslands. The further out you go from Kāngdìng, the more evident the Tibetan customs and clothing become.

Towns in these areas experience cold temperatures, with up to 200 freezing days per year; summers are blistering by day

LÈSHĀN BUS TIMETABLES

Buses from Lèshān's long-distance bus station:

Destination	Price	Duration	Frequency	Departs
Chéngdū	Y31	2hr	every 20 min	6.30am-7.30pm
Chóngqìng	Y79-88	6hr	hourly	7am-5.10pm
Éméi	Y5.5	40min	every 15 min	7am-6pm
Kāngdìng	Y72-86	8hr	daily	9.30am
Yǎ'ān	Y26-30	4hr	hourly	7am-4.40pm
Yíbīn	Y49-52		5 daily	7am-3.10pm
Zìgòng	Y24-30		half-hourly	9am-5.10pm

and the high altitude invites particularly bad sunburn. Lightning storms are frequent from May to October, when cloud cover can shroud the scenic peaks.

The Sìchuān–Tibet Hwy, begun in 1950 and finished in 1954, is one of the world's highest, roughest, most dangerous and most beautiful roads. It splits into northern and southern routes 70km west of Kāngdìng. Much of this area was only opened to foreigners in 1999 and, as yet, there isn't much in the way of tourist facilities. For more information on Kham visit www.khamaid.org.

If you're planning to attempt to cross into Tibet from Bātáng or Dégé, you may want to reconsider. The PSB in both of these towns keep a close eye on foreigners, and as truck drivers are levied hefty fines and lose their driving licence for carrying foreigners across the border, they're unlikely to give you a lift. Some travellers have managed to bribe their way in but at costs that make flying from Chéngdū seem cheap. If you do reach Lhasa, you'll likely be fined and sent back. However, if you're arriving from Tibet into Sìchuān, nobody seems to give a damn.

Be forewarned: at the time of writing it was not possible to change money (except in Kāngdìng) or travellers cheques or to get advances on credit cards in Sìchuān's northwest. Bring your Renminbi with you.

KĀNGDÌNG (DARDO) 康定

☎ 0836 / pop 82,000 / elevation 2616m

Kāngdìng is a fairly large town nestled in a steep river valley at the confluence of the swift Zheduo and Yala Rivers, known as the Dar and Tse in Tibetan. Kāngdìng is famous throughout China for a popular love song that the town's surrounding scenery inspired. If you're en route to western Sìchuān, chances are you'll end up overnighting here and it's worth staying for a day to take in the sights and check out some of this dreamy scenery. Towering above Kāngdìng is the mighty peak of Gònggā Shān (7556m).

Arriving in Kāngdìng, there is a tangible sense that you've reached the end of the Chinese world and the beginning of the Tibetan. The town has been a trade centre between the two cultures for centuries with the exchange of wool, Tibetan herbs and, especially, bricks of tea from Yǎ'ān wrapped in yak hide. It also served as an important

KĀNGDÌNG 康定

staging post on the road to Lhasa, as indeed it does today. Kāngdìng was historically the capital of the local Tibetan kingdom of Chakla (or Chala) and later, from 1939 to 1951, the capital of the short-lived province of Xikang, when it was controlled by the opium-dealing warlord Liu Wenhui.

Today Kāngdìng is largely a Chinese town, though you'll still see plenty of

SOUTHWEST CHINA

Khambas down from the hills shopping or selling huge blocks of yak butter in the market. You'll also spot monks wandering around town in crimson robes.

Information

Agricultural Bank of China (Zhōngguó Nóngyè Yínháng; Xi Dajie; ☼ 9am-5pm Mon-Fri) Can change US dollars and UK pounds. They cannot change travellers cheques or offer cash advances on credit cards. There is no ATM in town.

China Telecom office (Yanhe Xilu) Offers cheap international phone calls; it's next to the Black Tent Guesthouse.

Internet cafés (Wǎngbā; Guangming Lu; per hr Y2-3; 8am-midnight) There is a telephone office with Internet service on Xi Dajie and you can also get online at Sally's Café (see right), which has a very speedy Internet service for Y3 per hour.

Kangding Tour Service (Kāngdìng Lüvyóu Fúwù Zhōngxīn; ☎ 283 4000; Xi Dajie) Offers information and tours of nearby sights. The Tibetan owner speaks English and can tailor tours to suit you.

PSB (Gōngānjú; ☎ 281 1415; Dongda Xiaojie; ☼ 8.30am-noon & 2.30-5.30pm) In the southern part of town.

Sights

There are several lamaseries in and around Kāngdìng. Just behind Black Tent Guesthouse, Anjue Temple (Ānjué Sì; Ngachu Gompa in Tibetan) dates back to 1652 and was built under the direction of the fifth Dalai Lama. These days it's fairly quiet with several monks and a few old prayer wheels.

Nanwu Temple (Nánwù Sì) belongs to the Gelugpa (Yellow Hat) sect of Tibetan Buddhism and is the most active lamasery in the area with around 80 lamas in residence. Set in the west of town on the northern bank of the river, it affords good views of Kāngdìng and the valley. Walk south along the main road, following its bend to the left for 2km. Cross the bridge at the southern end of town and continue on 300m. Next to a walled Han Chinese cemetery is a dirt path that follows a stream uphill to the lamasery.

You can also head up **Pǎomǎ Shān** for excellent views of Kāngdìng, the surrounding mountains and valleys and – if you're lucky – Gònggǎ Shān. The ascent takes you past oodles of prayer flags, several Buddhist temples and up to a white *chörten* (stupa). Take particular care when wandering around Pǎomǎ Shān and try to avoid hiking on your own. A British tourist was murdered here in the spring of 2000.

To reach the hill, bear left at the fork in the road just south of the bus station and

walk about 10 minutes until you reach a lamasery on the left; a stairway leads up the hill from here. A second, more direct route, heads up the hill further south, beginning above the staircase on Dongda Xiaojie.

In the south of town is **Jingang Temple** (Jīngāng Sì), a 400-year old monastery that was being gutted for renovation at the time of research. A taxi from the bus station will cost you Y5.

About 5km north of Kāngdìng are the **Erdao Bridge Hot Springs** (Èrdào Wēnquán; admission Y10), where you can have a half-hour bath in slightly eggy-smelling, warm, sulphur water. Take your own towel. You can reach the hot springs by taxi for about Y8.

In town, the **market** on Dongda Xiaojie is worth a look.

Festivals & Events

Kāngdìng's biggest annual festival, the **Walking Around the Mountain Festival** (Zhuànshānjié), takes place on Pǎomǎ Shān on the eighth day of the fourth lunar month to commemorate the birthday of the Historical Buddha, Sakyamuni. White-and-blue Tibetan tents cover the hillside and there's plenty of wrestling, horse racing and visitors from all over western Sìchuān. There's also a street fair that lasts for ten days making this a good time to visit Kāngdìng.

Sleeping

There are a surprising number of hotels in Kāngdìng and new ones are being built all the time.

Black Tent Guesthouse (Gònggàshān Lùshè; ☎ 886 2107; 28 Yanhe Xilu; dm/d Y20/25) Centrally located, this is a fantastic hostel. There are great dorm rooms, hot showers and a friendly Tibetan teahouse on the ground floor.

Sally's Café (Bēibāo Kèzhàn; ☎ 283 8377, 130-6007 5296; dm Y20) Next to Jingang Temple is this laid-back hostel and café. Washing facilities are basic and the hot water is temperamental (despite claims that it is available 24 hours). But the rooms are good and you can sleep in colourful carved wooden beds. There is a café and restaurant on the ground floor. A taxi from the bus station will cost you Y5.

Chángchéng Bīnguǎn (☎ 882 2956; Xinshi Qianjie; d Y40-50) Not far from the bus station, this hotel is a good option for those solo travellers looking for a cheap room of their own.

Kǎlākǎ Dàjiǔdiàn (☎ 282 8688; fax 282 8777; 5 Yanhe Donglu; d Y190) The entrance to this hotel is flanked by two awkward-looking plastic palm trees – one in orange and the other in green. The rooms aren't nearly as kitsch unfortunately. The hotel has connections with the Erdaoqio Hot Springs (Y35; 5km).

Love Song Hotel (Qínggē Dàjiǔdiàn; ☎ 281 3333; fax 281 3111; 156 Dongda Xiaojie; d Y580) This flashy hotel seems out of place in Kāndìng; it even has a cinema attached to it. Building of the Love Song Mall, a glossy shopping complex that will complement the hotel, is underway on the other side of the river.

Eating

For a rousing cup of yak butter tea, try the teahouse on the ground floor of the Black Tent. They also serve simple Tibetan dishes here such as *zanba* (roasted barley flour) and *momo* (Tibetan dumplings).

Qingkexiang Tibetan Restaurant (Qīngkèxiāng; dishes from Y20; ☯ 11am-8pm) Almost next door to the Black Tent is this upmarket restaurant that features a staggering number of yak-meat dishes on its menu. Fortunately it also does some very good *momo* filled with potato and vegetables. Walking north from the Black Tent, the restaurant is down the first alley you come to on your left; it's on the second floor.

Jíxiáng Fàndiàn (Dongda Xiaojie; dishes from Y7; ☯ 8am-9pm) This small restaurant has an English menu and the friendly owners serve tasty local cuisine at good prices. Try the potato pancake or the black bean fish.

There are a handful of point-and-choose restaurants near the bus station and a couple of noodle and *bāozi* (steamed stuffed buns) places in the market (great to take on bus journeys). In the evening, numerous covered stalls set up camp at the northern end of town with arguably the widest selection of skewered meat, veggies and fish in Sìchuān.

Drinking

Tibetan Dance Halls are the place to go for a night out in Kāngdìng and they make for a very entertaining evening. Traditional Tibetan and Chinese songs, including the famous Kāngdìng Love Song, are performed to ear-splitting techno beats and a very appreciative audience. Try the **Kangba Dancehall** (Kāngbā Dàwǔtái; ☎ 669 3255; Xidakai Lu; drinks from Y20) where you can get up and dance once the performances are finished.

Getting There & Away
BUS

Improved roads have made Kāngdìng far more accessible. The completion of the Èrláng Shān tunnel has cut the ride to Chéngdū down to a comfortable eight hours. The bus station is in the northeast of town.

See box below for bus details.

TAXI

Taxis congregate on Xinshi Qianjie, not far from the Chángchéng Bīnguǎn. Trips to Lúdìng cost around Y20.

AROUND KĀNGDÌNG

There are several mountain lakes and hot springs in the vicinity of Kāngdìng. Lying 21km to the north of town up the Yala Valley, **Mùgécuò Hú** is one of the highest lakes

KĀNGDÌNG BUS TIMETABLES				
Buses from Kāngdìng:				
Destination	**Price**	**Duration**	**Frequency**	**Departs**
Bātáng	Y138	2 days	daily	6.45am
Chéngdū	Y101-122	8hr	hourly	6am-4pm
Dānbā	Y36	4hr	daily	8am
Dégé	Y166	24hr	daily	7.15am
Gānzī	Y106	12hr	daily	6am
Lèshān	Y72-86	8hr	daily	7am
Lǐtáng	Y80	8hr	daily	7am
Tǎgōng	Y25-33	4hr	daily	6am
Xiāngchéng	Y115	14hr	daily	7.15am

SOUTHWEST CHINA

in northwestern Sìchuān, at 3700m. Locals also boast that it's one of the most beautiful. Trails around the lake lead to other smaller lakes such as the **Red Sea** (Hóng Hǎi). Also worth checking out is **Seven Colour Lake** (Qīsè Hǎi), which lies a few kilometres before Mùgécuò. It's best not to wander around these parts alone or to stray too far off the path. The area of 'Wild Men's Lake', as Mùgécuò means in Tibetan, is home to wolves and other wild beasts.

There are no buses running to Mùgécuò but idle taxi drivers will be more than pleased to shuttle you there and back for Y150 to Y200 (1½ hours). You can also talk to the Kangding Tour Service to see if it has any tours going there.

Mùgécuò Hú can easily be done as a day trip from Kāngdìng but if you choose to stay out there, both **Qīsèhǎi Bīnguǎn** and **Mùgécuò Bīnguǎn** have beds which you may be able to get for as low as Y30.

LÚDÌNG 泸定

☎ 0836 / **elevation 1310m**

Lúdìng is a small, bustling town about half-way between Kāngdìng and Móxī. As a major connection point for buses between western Sìchuān and Chéngdū, Lèshān and Móxī, you are likely to find yourself here. For those with a keen interest in China's communist history, it may be worth a brief stop.

Sights

Lúdìng is famous throughout China as the site of what is often regarded as the most glorious moment of the Long March which took place on the **Luding Bridge** (泸定桥; Lúdìng Qiáo; admission Y5), a 100m-long chain suspension bridge over Dadu River (Dàdù Hé).

On 29 May 1935 the communist troops approached Luding Bridge only to discover that Kuomintang troops had beat them to it, removed the planks from the bridge and had it covered with firepower. In response, 20 Communist troops crossed the bridge hand-over-hand armed with grenades and then proceeded to overcome the Kuomintang troops on the other side. This action allowed the Long March to continue before the main body of the Kuomintang forces could catch up with them.

The bridge is five minutes' walk from the bus station. Just follow the river into town and you'll find it. The original bridge

was first constructed in 1705 and was an important link in the Sìchuān–Tibet road. The Luding Bridge Revolutionary Artefacts Museum (泸定桥革命文物陈列馆; Lúdìng Qiáo Gémìng Wénwù Chénlièguǎn) used to be housed in a building in the centre of town and displayed a collection of some 150 items left behind by members of the Long March. It was torn down as part of Lúdìng's modernisation process and the collection was put into boxes. Plans are supposedly underway to build a new museum in the vicinity of the bridge and it could well be open by the time you read this.

You can also get a gander at some of Mao's calligraphy on a shelter near the Buddhist Temple on the hillside above town.

Sleeping & Eating

The hotel situation in Lúdìng was not brilliant to start with but the recent frantic demolition work has seen almost all the cheap hotels disappear.

Chēzhàn Lǚguǎn (车站旅馆; Bus Station Hostel; ☎ 139-9048 9606; dm Y15, d/tr Y30/60) If you do find yourself overnighting, this is your best bet. It is a relatively clean guesthouse attached to the bus station.

More upmarket accommodation options can be found in the new area of town across the river from the bus station. Try the **Lúdìng Qiáo Bīnguǎn** (泸定桥宾馆; ☎ 312 888; d Y480) where you can often get 50% discounts on rooms. It's the building with the large green dome on the roof.

Clustered around the bus station are a number of nondescript restaurants as well as a teahouse where you can while away your time until the next bus pulls into town.

Getting There & Away

From Lúdìng there are daily buses to Chéngdū (Y88-98, six hours, 6.30am, 10am and 1pm), Yǎ'ān (Y46, four hours, 7am and 2pm) and Shímián (Y20, three hours, 6am and noon). Minibuses run regularly to Kāndìng (Y20) and Móxī (Y20).

YǍ'ĀN 雅安

☎ 0835 / **pop 110,700**

Depending on what bus you catch to and from Chéngdū you might be forced to break your journey in Yǎ'ān. It is a communications centre near the crossing of two main routes: one running west to Kāngdìng and onto the Sìchuān–Tibet Highway and another running north–south from Chéngdū to the southwest. A friendly town during the day, Yǎ'ān really comes to life at nightfall with its **Music Square** (中桥花园; Zhōngqiáo Huāyuán). Visit the square during the day and find it deserted. Return in the evening and find the entire town out moving to the beat of Chinese and European dance music.

Be warned, however: as a foreigner, you may well become the object of interest to what can quickly become a frenzied mob of 12-year-olds, screaming for your signature on scraps of paper, their arms and T-shirts. At the very least you will be dragged up to dance, whether you want to or not. To find Music Sq, turn right out of the bus station and cross the bridge. Bus No 1 also runs here from outside the bus station.

Sleeping & Eating

Xīkāng Fàndiàn (西康饭店; ☎ 0835-263 3690; 84 Ximen Beilu; d Y80-100) The woman that runs this hotel will probably grab you as soon as you step off the bus. But on the off chance she's not there, turn left out of the bus station and cross over the road. You'll find the hotel down the first side street on your right-hand side. The rooms here are very new and modern and there's a washing machine so you can do your laundry.

Outside the bus station are a number of dumpling and noodle stalls. Slightly more upmarket restaurants line the riverbank near the bus station.

Getting There & Away

See box on below for bus times.

A second route between Éméi Shān and Lúdìng, without doubling back to Chéngdū, is south via Wūsīhé. There is usually one morning bus at 6am from Lúdìng to Wūsīhé (Y20) but if it doesn't appear, jump on the bus to Shímián from where there is frequent onward transport. Once you reach Wūsīhé you'll need to hop on a train to Éméi town. The train departs Wūsīhé in the afternoon meaning you shouldn't have to stay overnight here but should you need to, there are several cheap hotels around the train station. If you're headed south to Pānzhīhuā or Kūnmíng, be advised that you can only buy hard-seat tickets in Wūsīhé and very few onward trains stop here.

MÓXĪ 磨西

☎ 0836

Nestled in the mountains around 50km southwest of Lúdìng, this peaceful village's main attraction is Hailuogou Glacier Park (see the following section). However, with lots of character, Móxī itself is a fun place to explore.

Orientation

The village consists of two main roads and lots of narrow lanes running off them that hide crumbling buildings, vegetable gardens, the local school and some colourful characters.

Sights

Móxī's older, traditional wooden buildings are at the bottom of the village. Also at this end is a multicoloured **Catholic church** (天主教堂; admission Y1) where Mao camped out during the Long March. It's open to the public and you will be given an obligatory tour by the old men that look after the place. From here, the village climbs its way up a hill. If you follow the dirt road up, about 200m past the main crossroads, on

YĂ'ĀN BUS TIMETABLES

Buses from Yǎ'ān:

Destination	Price	Duration	Frequency	Departs
Chéngdū	Y40	8hr	half-hourly	6.30am-7pm
Chóngqìng	Y102	7hr	2 daily	8.30am, 11am
Kāndìng	Y60	5hr	5 daily	8.30am, 10.30am, 11.30am, 1.30pm, 3.30pm
Lúdìng	Y48	3½hr	3 daily	9.30am, 12.30pm, 2.30pm
Shímián	Y31.5	6hr	6 daily	8.30am-2.30pm

the right is **Guānyīnggǔ Gompa** (观音古寺), a 400-year-old Bön (Tibetan Buddhist sect) temple that is run by some delightful older women. Take a peek inside and they'll drag you in to show you around. In the courtyard is a mammoth, gnarled tree around which the temple has been built. Across the road from the temple is a small **pagoda** (塔) from where you can get a view of the surrounding scenery.

Sleeping & Eating

Bīngchuān Fàndiàn (冰川饭店; dm Y20) Opposite the entrance to the church is this wonderful wooden guesthouse run by the woman who sells tickets for the church. Old newspapers line the walls, mattresses are made out of straw and you have to brush your teeth at the sink outside – in front of the most amazing views of the glacier. While it may sound primitive, it really is one of the most charming places you'll stay in.

Xīnfēi Fàndiàn (鑫飞饭店; ☎ 326 6214; d Y70) Walking up the hill from the church you'll find this hotel on your right. It has good doubles that come with private bathrooms. There's also a small restaurant.

Hǎiluó Fàndiàn (海螺饭店; ☎ 326 6297; d Y60-80; 🏠) Just up the road from the Xīnfēi Fàndiàn, this place has recently been renovated so the rooms are in great condition. The rooftop terrace offers stunning views of the glacier providing the weather is on your side.

There are a number of restaurants, barbeque stalls and hotpot places along the main road and the road leading to the glacier park entrance. Check prices before ordering.

Móxī's shops and fruit stands are well stocked if you need to buy some supplies for a trip to Hǎiluógōu.

Getting There & Away

Most visitors to Móxī arrive on a tour bus and the public transport system is erratic if it runs at all. Most locals scoot around on motorbikes or catch a ride to Lúdìng (Y20) in one of the minibuses that ply the road between the two towns. These leave from the crossroads at the top end of town.

There is supposedly a 7am bus to Lúdìng (Y15; two hours) but don't count on it. The owner of the Bīngchuān Fàndiàn will be able to help you out with transport. Change at Lúdìng for Chéngdū, Yǎ'ān and Kāngdìng. If you're headed to Shímián, get off the

bus at Māozìpíng, on the other side of the bright-orange Rainbow Bridge. From here you can flag down a southbound bus.

To reach Móxī, get off your bus in Lúdìng from where you can grab a minibuses to Móxī (Y20). Travelling from the south via Shímián get off at Māozìpíng and flag down a minicab to Móxī from there. If you're coming from Yǎ'ān, get the driver to let you off at Gāngǔdì (干谷地), from where you can get a taxi (Y20, one hour).

HAILUOGOU GLACIER PARK
海螺沟冰川公园

Magnificent Hailuogou Glacier tumbles off the eastern slopes of Gònggā Shān to form the lowest glacier in Asia. **No 1 Glacier** (一号冰川; Yīhào Bīngchuān), the main glacier, is 14km long and covers an area of 16 sq km. It's relatively young as glaciers go: around 1600 years. The top of Hǎiluógōu can offer incredible vistas of Gònggā Shān and surrounding peaks, all above 6000m, but how much you actually see is entirely up to Mother Nature. Constantly framed with a backdrop of snowy peaks, the surrounding forests are also beautiful, with their ecosystems changing as you ascend the mountain.

The entrance to **Hailuogou Glacier Park** (Hǎiluógōu Bīngchuān Gōngyuán; admission Y80) lies in Móxī and the park was once a popular choice for trekking and camping. Today however, the park has fallen under the watchful eye of the government's tourist board and the atmosphere of the park has changed dramatically in recent years. It was once possible to ascend the mountain by foot or pony trek but these days there is not a neigh to be heard for miles. The road running from the park entrance to Camp No 3, via Camps No 1 and 2, has been paved over and most people travel to **Belvedere** (Guānjǐngtái; 观景台), 3km above Camp No 3, by minibus. From Belvedere the tour groups tend to continue their ascent to the base of No 1 Glacier via **cable car** (Y160; ⏰ 8.30am-4pm).

It is still possible to trek from Belvedere and it's a one- to two-hour walk up to No 1 Glacier. While the walk is not a tough climb, the walk is made more difficult as the path has been largely neglected and so at times is hard to follow. On a clear day, however, there are some beautiful views to be had and the trail passes through some lovely forest. En route to the base is the **Waterfall Viewing Platform**

(冰川观景台; Bīngchuān Guānjǐngtái) at 3000m. From here you can see the main glacier tongue, plus **No 2 Glacier** (二号冰川; Èrhào Bīngchuān) and **Golden Peak** (金银峰; Jīnyínfēng) at 6368m.

The entrance fee to the park includes a guide, compulsory for all tourists going out on the glacier and handy for keeping you away from deep crevices and melting points, as well as for pointing out wind tunnels and naming mountain peaks. Guides meet you at the base of No 1 Glacier and take you on a 30-minute tour of the glacier after which you are free to go off and explore the surrounding scenery.

The park has become incredibly commercial and will continue to do so with increased tour buses racing up and down the mountain and travellers hanging out of cable cars above the glacier. If you're looking for a real getaway into the wilderness, then sadly this is no longer it. But if your main interest is seeing and even walking across a glacier, then the park is still worth a visit. If you do plan to trek, come prepared with warm clothes and sunglasses. You'll also need to bring food and water, as you might not find much to buy en route until you reach Camp No 3 and its pricey restaurants. Maps of the park are available from the entrance gate; however, marked trails may be less than accurate and some may have disappeared.

The rainy season for this area spans July and August, although the locals say they get 200 days of rain a year. The best time to visit is between late September and November, when skies are generally clear. Autumn colours are particularly beautiful at this time, though it can be cold up at Camp No 3.

Sleeping & Eating

Accommodation options in the park tend to fall into one category; old and overpriced.

Camp No 1 (一号营地; Yīhào Yíngdì; dm Y100), at 1940m, still offers budget dorm beds but conditions are damp and dirty.

Camp No 2 (二号营地; Èrhào Yíngdì; dm Y150) sits at 2620m and has cramped, expensive dorm rooms although the price does include a dip into the hot springs.

Camp No 3 (三号营地; Sānhào Yíngdì) at 2940m is the highest camp and offers two resort-style hotels. The huge **Jīnshān Fàndiàn** (金山饭店; Golden Mountain Hotel; ☎ 326 6433; d Y150) and the new **Jīnshān Dàjiǔdiàn** (金山大酒店;

Golden Mountain Grand Hotel; ☎ 326 6383; d Y480) sit side by side and offer the best – and most expensive – accommodation within the park.

The park authorities frown upon camping and there isn't a great deal in the way of flat ground on the way up, in any case.

The camps sell some food and drinks although, out of season, you can only count on this at Camp No 3. Mineral water, soft drinks, beer and instant noodles are usually available. Prices are naturally higher than in Móxī and rise with the altitude.

Getting There & Away

The entrance to the park is in Móxī. Turn left at the main crossroads at the top of the hill and carry on to the ticket office, about 400m up the road. Móxī itself can be reached by minibus from Lúding (see opposite for details). Buses start running up the mountain from the park entrance gate at 7.30am and leave as soon as they have more than one passenger.

Minibuses (Y50 return, one hour) start running up the mountain from the park entrance gate at 7.30am and leave as soon as they have more than one passenger. The last bus leaves Belvedere around 7pm and stops at all three camps on the way down.

SICHUAN–TIBET HWY (NORTHERN ROUTE)

Of the two routes to Tibet, this is the less heavily travelled. This may be because at 2412km, it is 300km longer than the southern route, but it probably has more to do with the fact that it crosses Chola Mountain, the highest pass this side of Lhasa. The highway also crosses through the Tagong Grasslands (p742), with their blue-green rivers and velvety hills, studded with Tibetan prayer flags and watched over by gracefully soaring eagles.

For travellers, this highway leads to the border town of Dégé, with its internationally revered printing lamasery. It also takes you to the north where it is possible to work your way up to Qīnghǎi province via Sêrxu.

If you do come this way, be sure to bring some warm clothing; this area reaches high, frozen altitudes. Remember that bus service can be erratic – this is no place to be if you're in a hurry. It's also not possible to change money or travellers cheques up here so come prepared.

Tagong Grasslands 塔公草原

About 110km northwest of Kāngdìng lie the **Tagong Grasslands** (Tǎgōng Cǎoyuán), a vast expanse of green meadow surrounded by snow-capped peaks and dotted with Tibetan herdsmen and tents. An annual horse-racing festival *(saimǎhui)* features thousands of local Tibetan herdsmen and Tibetan opera.

The small village of **Tǎgōng** is a fantastic place to visit if you want to get a taste of Sìchuān's Tibetan Wild West. In the village, **Tagong Temple** (Tǎgōng Sì) blends Han Chinese and Tibetan styles and dates back to the Qing dynasty.

Local families will likely offer you cheap accommodation and meals. Ask in the small lamasery shop where a friendly monk may take you home to his folk's amazing little ornate guesthouse. If that fails, try **Tǎgōng Bīnguǎn** (dm Y5-15). To find the hotel, head south down the main street, away from the lamasery; it's on your right.

Buses to Tǎgōng village run daily from Kāngdìng (Y23, four hours, 6am) and drop you outside the lamasery. (During the horse festival buses are likely to be more frequent.) If you're heading to Gānzī, you can pick up the same bus the next day at about 10am as it passes through town. Returning to Kāngdìng, afternoon buses can be flagged down as they pass through Tǎgōng village. You can also catch a minibus on the main street that will take you to Yǎjiāng from where there are buses to Chéngdū or Lǐtáng.

Gānzī 甘孜

☎ 0836 / pop 61,400 / elevation 3394

The lively market town of Gānzī sits in a valley at 3800m, surrounded by the sleeping giants of Chola Mountain. Some 385km northwest of Kāngdìng, Gānzī is the capital of the Gānzī (Garzê) Autonomous Prefecture and is mostly populated by Tibetans and Khambas.

Now open to tourism, Gānzī sees a growing number of foreigners sojourning here as an intermediate stop between Sêrxu and Kāngdìng or on their way west to Dégé. It is a friendly place and it's easy to spend several days here exploring the beautiful surrounding countryside which is scattered with Tibetan villages and monasteries. Photo opportunities abound and it's impossible to take a bad picture here.

Gānzī is also good for shopping, in particular for Tibetan jewellery, antiques and clothing, although it isn't particularly cheap so make sure you bring enough cash with you.

INFORMATION

Dorjee Tsewang (☎ 139-9049 6777) If you're looking for a local guide, Dorjee Tsewang in the neighbouring town of Rongpatse can arrange hiking and horse-riding treks in the area. He speaks fluent English and is happy to cater tours to your needs.

SIGHTS & ACTIVITIES

Situated north of the town's Tibetan quarter you'll find **Ganzi Temple** (甘孜寺; Gānzī Sì; Garzê Gompa in Tibetan) a 540-year-old lamasery. Home to over 500 monks, this is the region's largest monastery and it glimmers with blinding quantities of gold. Encased on the walls of the main hall are hundreds of small golden Sakyamunis. In a smaller hall just west of the main hall is an awe-inspiring statue of Jampa (Maitreya or Future Buddha), dressed in a giant silk robe. The monks are very friendly and will invite you in to look around. If you arrive at lunch time, you might even get to peak in the kitchen where saucepans the size of Mini Coopers boil away furiously on wood-fuelled stoves.

To find the lamasery, take a left out of the bus station and head north for about 10 minutes until you reach the Tibetan neighbourhood. From there wind your way uphill, around the clay and wooden houses. You'll see the lamasery long before you reach it.

There are also a number of lamaseries in neighbouring towns that you might want to visit. **Beri Gompa** is about a half-hour drive west, on the road to Dégé. Also off this road, one hour from Gānzī, is **Dagei Gompa**. About 15km from here on a steep slope above the Yalong River sits **Hadhi Nunnery**, home to sixty or so nuns.

To reach Beri Gompa and Dagei Gompa, catch the morning bus to Dégé or one of the sporadic local buses heading west. A taxi costs around Y20.

Back in Gānzī, turn right out of the bus station and walk through the Tibetan housing until you reach a bridge festooned with prayer flags. There are endless possibilities for walks on the other side of the bridge.

SLEEPING & EATING

Accommodation options in Gānzī are limited as most of the hotels do not accept foreigners.

Hóngmófáng (红磨坊; ☎ 752 2676; d Y60, tr without bathroom Y45) This hotel's policy on accepting foreigners changes frequently. It was foreigner-friendly when we visited, however, we later heard reports of midnight visits by the police and travellers being kicked out of their rooms. Check when you arrive. The rooms are basic but comfortable. To find it, turn left out of the bus station, cross the main intersection, and continue up the road until you see the red-and-white sign (no English) of the hotel on your left.

Jīnmáoníu Jiǔdiàn (金牦牛酒店; ☎ 752 2353; dm Y30, d Y120-180) This place, attached to Gānzī's bus station, is your only other alternative. The cheap dorm beds are in the older building while the more expensive doubles can be found in the shiny new building opposite.

The food in Gānzī tends to be very good. Around the bus station are several dumpling and *bāozi* (steamed buns) stalls. For a more hearty meal, turn right at the main intersection as you come out of the bus station, and you will find a number of restaurants to choose from.

If you head west, up the hill at the main intersection, you'll find eateries pumping out fresh Tibetan flatbread.

Gyalten Rinpoche Guesthouse (dm Y30) Several kilometres west of Dagei Gompa. Set against white-capped mountains with no neighbours to be seen for miles, this is a truly relaxing place to rest for a day or two. The views from the rooftop are mind-blowing. Simple meals are available and you would be wise to bring a sleeping bag with you.

GETTING THERE & AWAY

Buses to Gānzī (Y106, 12 hours) leave Kāngdìng daily at 6am. A bus to Kāngdìng leaves Gānzī every morning at 6.30am. Buses to Dégé (Y60, eight to ten hours) run every two to three days. Check the schedule.

Private minivans to Dégé are available for hire (Y450), not a bad deal if there's a group of you.

You can head north from Gānzī to Xīníng in Qīnghǎi province via Sêrxu (Y90, nine hours). Buses to Sêrxu originate in Kāngdìng

every third day or so and pass through Gānzī around 6am.

MANIGANGO 马尼干戈
☎ 0836

Manigango lies halfway between Gānzī and Dégé and is the jumping-off point for Dzogchen Gompa and Yihun Lhatso. Manigango itself is a dusty one-street town that looks unmistakably like the movie set for a Tibetan Western. It's a glorious multicoloured scene with Tibetans on horseback, monks in crimson robes on motorbikes and tractors piled precariously high with pilgrims rattling down the road. It's worth stopping off just for the atmosphere. A horse-racing festival is usually held here in the summer.

The town is known in Chinese as Yùlóng or Mǎnígāngē but it's most commonly referred to by its Tibetan name Manigango.

Sights

DZOGCHEN GOMPA 竹庆佛学院
This important Nyingmapa **monastery** (Zhùqíng Fóxuéyuàn), 50km north of Manigango, has a stunning location at the foot of a glacial valley. The monastery was founded in 1684 and is the home of the Dzogchen school, the most popular form of Tibetan Buddhism in the West. Several important high Nyingmapa lamas, now exiled abroad, originate from nearby valleys.

The site includes the small town, 1.5km off the road, which has a few shops, *chörten* and a chapel with huge prayer wheels. Up the small gorge is the main monastery and 1km further is the college (*shedra*). The monastery was destroyed in the Cultural Revolution and reconstruction was nearing completion when we visited.

Buses to Yùshù and Sêrxu run daily past Dzogchen but in practice it's easier to hitch. If you do plan to hitch make sure you set out in the morning, as there is little traffic on the roads come the afternoon. If you want to hire a car and driver then it will cost Y250 for the return journey. Getting here you have to cross over the Muri La pass (4,633m) so make sure you have some warm clothes, especially if you're hitching in the back of a truck.

YIHUN LHATSO 新路海
Thirteen kilometres southwest of Manigango is **Yihun Lhatso** (Xīnlù Hǎi; admission Y20), a stunning holy alpine lake to rival any

found in Jiǔzhàigōu. The lake is bordered by *chörten* and dozens of rock carvings, and the shoreline is sprinkled in places with pure white sand. It's possible to walk an hour or two up the left (east) side of the lakeshore for glacier views. The lake has many great places to camp though you need to guard against the mosquitos. To get here you'll have to hitch on Dégé-bound traffic to the turn-off where there's a bridge and 1km trail to the lake.

Activities
The countryside surrounding Manigango is crying out to be explored and one good way to do it is on horseback. The folk at the Mǎnígāngē Shísùdiàn (see next section) can help you organise a horse and guide for trekking in the neighbouring areas. Prices usually run at Y200 per day (for horse and guide) but you can probably negotiate. If you plan to go off camping for several days you will be expected to provide meals for your guide as well. Make sure you have all the equipment and food you need as there's hardly anything available to buy in Manigango let alone once you've left town.

Sleeping & Eating
Manigango seems to have the biggest population of mangy dogs in southwest China and they all come out to play at night. Don't expect to get much sleep.

Yùlóng Shénhǎi Bīnguǎn (玉龙神海宾馆; dm Y15-30) Next door to the Mǎnígāngē Shísùdiàn, this hotel is more modern and has its own toilet – bonus! Look for the large red-and-white sign.

Mǎnígāngē Shísùdiàn (马尼干戈食宿店; dm Y10-20) This is where all the buses stop and has comfortable basic rooms. Ask for the toilets however and they'll point you half a mile up the road – make sure you bring a torch! The staff can help with travel information and bus timetables.

The restaurant at the Mǎnígāngē Shísùdiàn serves particularly tasty food and is very cheap. There is a good *niúròumiàn* (beef noodle) restaurant next door to the petrol station.

The college at Dzogchen Gompa offers beds for Y15 per night though you need a sleeping bag and your own food. There are a couple of well-stocked shops in the village below.

Getting There & Away
A daily bus passes through Manigango at 11am for Dégé (Y35, three to four hours). Coming from Dégé, a bus stops in Manigango at 11am and heads on to Gānzī (Y25, five to seven hours) and Lúhuò (Y50, five hours) where it overnights before heading on to Kāngdìng (Y130, overnight via Lúhuò) the following morning. A 9am bus leaves daily for Sêrxu.

DÉGÉ 德格
☎ 0836 / pop 58,300 / elevation 3270
Resting in a valley with Chola Mountain to the east and the Tibetan border to the west, Dégé (Dêgê) is steeped in tradition and sees little of the outside world, other than the truckers and few travellers who pass through. While the Chinese influence is evident in the newer, tiled buildings, the population is mainly Tibetan and the military presence that you might expect so near to the Tibetan border is not prevalent in the town itself.

Getting to Dégé is a long haul. En route you'll see the towering snowy peaks of Chola Mountain stretching up 6168m, and the Xinhua Glacier which comes down almost to the road at 4100m. Chola Mountain itself was first scaled in 1988 and you might begin to wonder if your bus driver is attempting the same, as the bus grumbles and inches its way uphill to the top of the peaks. At the Tro La (Chola) Pass of nearly 6000m, Tibetans on board will throw coloured prayer papers out the window and chant something that you can only hope will carry your bus to safety.

While the views from here are phenomenal, conditions can be treacherous on this narrow, ice-encrusted dirt road and it's a toss up as to whether you'll be more frozen from the icy blasts or fear. Overturned buses are not uncommon – you'll see them from your window. Altitude sickness is also a very real possibility up here. Once you descend from the mountains on the other side of the pass, you can breathe a sigh of relief as the bus heads through a beautiful farmed valley and gorge and enters Dégé at 4000m, some eight to 10 hours after leaving Gānzī.

Sights
BAKONG SCRIPTURE PRINTING LAMASERY
德格印经院
At the heart of Dégé is this **lamasery** (Dégé Yìnjīngyuàn; admission Y25; ☗ 8.30am-noon & 2-6.30pm).

While the present structure dates from 1744, the printing house has existed on this site for over 270 years with printing blocks dating from the early 18th century. The lamasery currently houses over 217,000 engraved blocks of Tibetan scriptures from the five Tibetan Buddhist sects, including Bön. Texts include ancient works on astronomy, geography, music, medicine and Buddhist classics. A history of Indian Buddhism, comprising 555 woodblock plates, is the only surviving copy in the world (written in Hindi, Sanskrit and Tibetan).

Built in the Qing dynasty by the 42nd prefect of Dégé, the lamasery is revered as one of the three most important Tibetan lamaseries (along with Sakya Monastery and Lhasa's Potala Palace) – not surprising when you consider that the material stored in Dégé makes up an estimated 70% of Tibet's literary heritage.

Within the lamasery hundreds of workers hand-produce over 2500 prints each day. A visit will give you the opportunity to witness this rare sight as ink, paper and brushes fly through the workers' hands at lightning speed. Upstairs, an older crowd of printers produce larger prints of Tibetan gods on paper or coloured cloth that later find their way to hills and temples as prayer flags. If you catch them with a free moment, they'll print you one of your choice for Y10.

You can also examine the storage chambers, lined floor to ceiling with bookshelves, as well as paper-cutting and binding rooms and the main hall of the lamasery itself, all of which are quite phenomenal. Protecting the monastery from fire and earthquake is a guardian goddess, a green Avalokiteshvara (Guanyin).

The entrance fee to the lamasery includes a tour guide who is excellent at communicating through pictures if your Chinese isn't up to scratch. The lamasery is closed holidays.

There are three other lamaseries in town, including a large one just behind the printing house, which is over 1000 years old.

To reach the printing house, turn left out of the bus station and right over the bridge. Continue up this road to the southeast of town and it will bring you to the lamasery's front door. You will usually see some of the town's many devotees circumambulating the building and spinning their prayer wheels.

Sleeping & Eating

There is only one place in town that is officially open to foreigners and it's not very nice.

Dégé Bīnguǎn (德格宾馆; ☎ 822 2157; dm Y10; d Y180) The dorm rooms are fairly grim and smelly but the doubles are overpriced. Take your pick.

Some travellers have managed to bag a bed at **Wùzī Zhāodàisuǒ** (物资招待所; dm Y20). Located directly opposite the bus station you'll recognise it from the multi-coloured bunting hanging outside.

There are several forgettable point-and-choose restaurants around the bus station.

Getting There & Away

A rickety old bus leaves Gānzī for Dégé (Y60, eight to 10 hours) every two to three days. Marginally more comfortable buses leave from Kāngdìng for Dégé daily at 7.15am (Y166, 24 hours), stopping overnight in Lúhuò.

From Dégé there is a daily bus for Kāngdìng that stops in Manigango (Y35, three to four hours), Gānzī (Y60, eight to 10 hours) and Lúhuò (Y86, 10 to 12 hours) on the way.

SICHUAN–TIBET HWY (SOUTHERN ROUTE)

A journey along this 2140km route takes you through vast, open landscapes with horizons of majestic peaks. Tibetan homes pepper the landscape like small stone castles. Huge vultures soar overhead while roaming yaks munch on frosty grass. Solitary Tibetans watch your bus pass from a distance and you may be miles down the road before you spot the black tents of these nomadic herdsmen.

With roads and transport improving and restrictions for foreign visitors lifted, it is no wonder that the southern route of the Sichuan–Tibet Hwy is seeing a considerable rise in the number of foreign tourists. In particular, the route Kāngdìng–Lǐtáng–Xiāngchéng–Zhōngdiàn has become a popular back-door trail into Yúnnán.

As with the rest of northwest Sìchuān, warm clothing is a must. Some travellers experience difficulties with the high altitudes here; be on the lookout for side effects (see p932) and if you're feeling unwell, head to somewhere lower. There are no money-changing facilities here.

Lǐtáng 理塘

☎ 0836 / pop 51,300 / elevation 4014m

Surrounded by snow-capped peaks and resting on open grassland at an altitude of 4014m, Lǐtáng will leave you breathless in more ways than one. Tibetan culture abounds here. Markets are filled with yak-skin coats, wooden and silver teacups and brightly coloured woven cloth. 'Tashi delek', the Tibetan greeting, is more commonly used than 'Nǐ hǎo' and traditional stone and dirt homes painted in a multitude of psychedelic colours fill the northern half of town.

Lǐtáng has a fantastically relaxed and friendly atmosphere. While there may not be much in the way of sights, you can easily fill your days hanging out with the local people under a blazing sun and starry night skies or exploring the spectacular walks into the surrounding hills. Advice on where to go (ie where isn't currently being used as grazing pastures or for sky burials; see Sky Burial, opposite) should be sought from locals. Be sure to allow yourself time to acclimatise to the altitude before you set out.

If you do find yourself suffering from altitude sickness and can't get out of town, there is a local treatment consisting of medicated pills and re-hydration drinks. The woman running Crane Guesthouse may be able to help you out; however, this shouldn't be considered a remedy and you should still descend to a lower altitude as soon as possible.

HISTORY

Lǐtáng is famed as the birthplace of the 7th and 10th Dalai Lamas. The area around the town has strong connections to the epic warrior Gesar of Ling. Lǐtáng was heavily bombed by Chinese troops in 1959 during a Khampa rebellion.

INFORMATION

China Post (Yóujú; 🕘 9am-11.30am & 2-5.30pm) On the main north–south street. Next door is a place to use Internet Phone (IP) cards.

Internet café (Wǎngbā; per hr Y5) On the third floor in a building diagonally across from the High City Hotel.

Public showers (Yuánxǐyù Zhōngxīn; 园洗浴中心; Y8) Can be found south of the main crossroads.

SIGHTS & ACTIVITIES

At the northern end of town is the large **Lǐtáng Chöde Gompa** (理塘长青春科尔寺; Lǐtáng Chángqīng Chūnkē Ěrsì), a Tibetan lamasery, built for the third Dalai Lama. Inside is a statue of Sakyamuni that is believed to have been carried from Lhasa by foot. Tibetan homes lead up to the lamasery and you are likely to encounter friendly monks en route who may offer to give you a tour.

On the eastern edge of Lǐtáng is **Qūdēnggābù**, a newly erected *chörten* which active worshippers seem to be perpetually circling, reciting mantras and spinning prayer wheels. Dozens of smaller *chörten* fill the courtyard which itself is edged with a corridor of prayer wheels.

There are **hot springs** (温泉; wēnquán; admission Y6-7) at the western edge of town, 4km from the centre. A taxi costs Y7 one way.

FESTIVALS & EVENTS

The annual Lǐtáng Horse Festival is known as one of the biggest and most colourful in Tibet and every five years they stage an even more spectacular event (the next one is coming up in 2005). The festival usually starts August 1st and lasts for ten days although it's worth checking at the hostels and travel agencies in Kāngdìng or Chéngdū before you head out here. The festival includes horse racing, stunt demonstrations on horseback, dance competitions and an arts-and-crafts festival and trade fair.

SLEEPING & EATING

Lǐtáng has decent food and lodging, making it a fine place to stay for a day or more. No hotels have hot water and electricity can be unreliable.

Crane Guesthouse (Xiānhé Bīnguǎn; 仙鹤宾馆; ☎ 532 3850; dm Y25) Cosy two- and three-bed dorms are a good deal here with electric blankets and heaters. The two Tibetan sisters who run the place will store luggage if you want to travel light for a while. Turn left out of the bus station and head about 350m east into town; it's on the right-hand side of the road.

High City Hotel (Gāochéng Bīnguǎn; 高城宾馆; d/tr Y100/120) This is a government-run hotel and the spacious rooms come with a heater, TV and squat toilet but no shower. The lobby has a killer karaoke unit, loaded and ready at all times.

Good Luck Guesthouse (Jíxiáng Bīnguǎn; 吉祥宾馆; ☎ 532 3688; d Y60, with toilet Y120) Another option with pretty good, spacious rooms. The reception is accessed from the back.

Lǐtáng has countless small restaurants, the most popular of which can be found on the south side of the main road a couple of hundred metres west of the Crane Hotel. Of these, **Lianmeixian Restaurant** (廉美县餐厅; Liánměixiàn Cāntīng; dishes Y8; ☻ 10am-8pm) has an English speaker.

GETTING THERE & AWAY

Lǐtáng's bus station is a chaotic place so double-check all times and prices. At the time of writing daily buses were leaving Lǐtáng for Kāngdìng (Y80, eight hours, 7am) and Bātáng (Y46 to Y50, six hours, 7.30am). One or two buses pass through Lǐtáng each day from Kāngdìng en route to Dàochéng and Xiāngchéng (Y60, five hours, 7am) and a ride to Sangdui (for Yading) costs Y35.

Lǐtáng to Zhōngdiàn

This is a back-door route to Yúnnán that takes you through 400km of spectacular scenery via Xiāngchéng to Zhōngdiàn (p683).

Buses from Kāngdìng and Lǐtáng head for Xiāngchéng (see p737 and above re-

spectively), where you'll have to spend the night. From Xiāngchéng you can catch a bus to Zhōngdiàn in Yúnnán province between 7am and 8am. Going the other way, buses from Xiāngchéng head back to Lǐtáng at around the same time. Try to buy your onward ticket on arrival in Xiāngchéng as the ticket office is not always manned before the first buses leave in the morning. Be forewarned: the road between Xiāngchéng and Zhōngdiàn is sometimes closed in the dead of winter due to heavy snow. You'd be wise to check before heading out from Lǐtáng.

Xiāngchéng is a small border town that is quickly expanding with the usual tiled buildings and blaring horns. A hike up to the Tibetan temple offers views over the valley and what's left of the town's traditional square stone houses. This lamasery itself is being completely rebuilt by hand and is worth a visit to watch carvers and painters at work.

The lamasery is at the opposite end of town from the bus station. To find it, follow the dirt track up on the left as you reach the edge of town.

SKY BURIAL

The white cloth is removed from the body while the Tomden (a religious master of ceremonies) sharpens his large knife. He circles a small Buddhist monument, reciting mantras all the while, and slices into the body lying before him on the stone slab. The flesh is cut into large chunks and the bones and brain are smashed and mixed with barley flour.

The smell of flesh draws a large number of vultures that circle impatiently above. Eventually the Tomden steps away and the huge birds descend into a feeding frenzy, tearing at the body and carrying it in pieces up to the heavens.

This is sky burial (tiānzàng), an ancient Buddhist-Tibetan burial tradition that performs both a spiritual and practical function. According to Buddhist beliefs, the body is merely a vehicle to carry you through this life; once a body dies, the spirit leaves it and the body is no longer of use. Giving one's body as food for the vultures is a final act of generosity to the living world and provides a link in the cycle of life. Vultures themselves are revered and believed to be a manifestation of the flesh-eating God Dakinis.

Practically, this form of burial provides an ecologically sound way to dispose of bodies in a terrain where wood is scarce and the ground is often frozen solid.

The Chinese banned sky burials in the 1960s and '70s. It wasn't until the '80s, as Tibetans regained limited religious rights, that the practice was once again legalised. However, most Han Chinese still regard sky burials as a primitive practice. The fact that one Buddhist sect has been known to keep the tops of the skulls to use as enlarged sacred teacups has often been touted as proof of Tibetan savagery.

In Lhasa, tourists require official permission to attend a sky burial; in the more remote areas of Sìchuān, however, you may well be told where and when the burials are to take place. Nevertheless, local Tibetans have been unsurprisingly offended by travellers who have turned these funerals into tourist outings. Common decency applies – if you aren't invited, don't go, and whatever you do, do not attempt to capture the moment on Kodak.

Bámùshān Bīnguǎn (dm/d Y25/200) is the only hotel in town with a permit to accept foreigners. Don't let its fancy exterior scare you – beds in clean, warm dorm rooms are a good deal. The hotel is the huge building on the right as you exit the muddy bus station.

Bātáng 八塘
☎ 0836 / elevation 2589

Lying 32km from the Tibetan border and 5½ bumpy hours down a dirt track from Lǐtáng, low-lying Bātáng is the closest town to Tibet that is open to foreigners. An easy-going and friendly place with lots of streetside barbecue grills and outdoor seating, the town itself is quite modern and the surrounding suburbs of ochre Tibetan houses are lovely. Bātáng is much lower than surrounding areas; when it's still the end of winter in Lǐtáng it's already spring in Bātáng.

Many travellers try to sneak into Tibet from Bātáng, so, unsurprisingly, the local PSB is a little suspicious of foreigners.

SIGHTS
The Gelugpa sect **Chöde Gaden Pendeling Monastery** in the southwest of town is well worth a visit. The monks (over 500) are friendly and active (they had just finished building a sand mandala during our visit). There are three rooms behind the main hall: a protector chapel, giant statue of Jampa and a 10,000 Buddha room. Up some stairs via a separate entrance is a room for the Panchen Lama, lined with photos of exiled local lamas who now reside in India. Most images here are new but one upstairs statue of Sakyamuni is claimed to be 2000 years old. An old Chinese hospital is now used as monk accommodation. Stop in the kitchen for butter tea before leaving.

There are some fine walks around town. Head north to a lovely Tibetan hillside village and then west to a riverside *chörten* and a few inevitable pilgrims. Alternatively, head south from the town centre over a bridge and then east to a hilltop covered in prayer flags and offering views of the town.

SLEEPING & EATING
Jīnhuì Bīnguǎn (金汇宾馆; ☎ 562 2700; dm Y10-15, d Y70, tr without bathroom Y60) This is a good option, in particular the doubles without bath although they are quite run down. Get a back-facing room for views of the surrounding Tibetan village and away from the street karaoke. The common hot-water showers are pretty good and there is lots of hot water for washing clothes. From the bus station continue into town and take the first right after the huge, hard-to-miss golden eagle; it's a block down on the left.

Bāwǔ Bīnguǎn (巴武宾馆; ☎ 562 2882; dm Y15-25, s/d without bathroom Y60/40, d with bathroom Y120) This central option is a decent budget bet, with pleasant doubles and common hot showers.

Government Hotel (迎宾楼; Yíngbīn Lóu; ☎ 562 1566; d Y266) The top place in town, frequented by visiting cadres. Smoky but comfortable rooms come with hot-water shower, a kettle and even a Western toilet. Rooms are often discounted as low as Y180.

There are plenty of Sichuanese restaurants around town. Local supermarkets stock everything from chocolate to French red wine.

GETTING THERE & AWAY
There are daily buses to Lǐtáng (Y59, six hours, 7am), Kāngdìng (Y135, two days via Lǐtáng) and Chéngdū (Y231, two days via Yǎjiāng). The road to Lǐtáng is under major construction until 2006 so expect serious delays. The bus station is a 10-minute walk from the town centre.

Headed west, there are buses at 2pm (Y44, four hours) and afternoon microbuses (Y50) to Markham, 138km away inside Tibet. Foreigners may have problems buying tickets to Markham as the town is officially closed.

From Kāngdìng, a bus leaves for Bātáng (Y135) each morning at 6.45am, overnighting in Lǐtáng. Buses from Lǐtáng to Bātáng (Y46 to Y59) leave daily at 7.30am.

NORTHERN SÌCHUĀN

With dense alpine forests and wide grasslands, northern Sìchuān is a great place to get out and commune with nature. Pony treks around Sōngpān and hiking in the stunning nature preserve of Jiǔzhàigōu have made this area increasingly popular with travellers.

Northern Sìchuān is home to the Ābà, Tibetan and Qiāng Autonomous Prefectures. In the extreme northwest, the region around Zöigê and Lǎngmùsì is the territory of the Goloks, nomads who speak their own dialect of Tibetan, distinct from the local

BILL WASSMAN

The 11th-century wooden pagoda Mù Tǎ
(p405) in Yìngxiàn, Shānxī

MARTIN MOOS

Xī'ān's city walls (p411), Shaanxi

Army of Terracotta Warriors (p418) outside Xī'ān, Shaanxi

JULIET COOMBE

HILARY SMI

Buddha statue in the Yungang Caves (p403), Shānxī

Huá Shān (p421) in Shaanxi

GRANT SOMF

BILL WASSMAN

Bell in Tayuan Temple (p400)
in Wǔtái Shān, Shānxī

Royal guards perform the evening changing of the guards in Xī'ān (p409),
Shaanxi

MATT DARBY

Amdo dialect. You'll see meadows speckled with their black-and-white tents and roaming yaks. While these Tibetan destinations are less visited, you can incorporate them into an alternative route into Gānsù.

Most of northern Sìchuān is between 2000m and 4000m in altitude so make sure you take warm clothing. The grassland plateau in the northwest averages more than 4000m and even in summer, temperatures can dip to 15°C at night. The rainy season lasts from June to August.

Beyond the Sōngpān–Jiǔzhàigōu route, roads in the region aren't always in the best condition. In worse condition are many of the buses. Roads are particularly hazardous in summer when heavy rains prompt frequent landslides; several foreigners were killed in the summer of 1995 when their bus got caught in a landslide and plunged into a river. You might want to think about planning this trip for the spring or autumn, when the weather is likely to be better.

One thing you are bound to see in the north are the countless logging trucks that shuttle up and down the Minjiang Valley (near Huánglóng), stripping the area of its forest. Some sources estimate that up to 40% of the region's forests have been logged in the last half decade, causing erosion, landslides and increased levels of silt heading downstream, eventually flowing into the Yangzi River (Cháng Jiāng).

While you're getting prepared, bear in mind that there is nowhere to change money in this region, so bring sufficient cash Renminbi.

SŌNGPĀN 松潘
☎ 0837 / pop 71,400

Although largely viewed as a base for horse treks or a stopover point on the road to Jiǔzhàigōu, Sōngpān itself is a lively town that is worth exploring. While the bustling downtown is filled with modern tourist shops selling Tibetan wares, old wooden buildings still line some of the side streets and residential areas although many of them are in the process of being knocked down.

The town sees far fewer tour groups than Jiǔzhàigōu and as such the atmosphere is much more relaxed.

On another note, be sure to bring a torch (flashlight) with you to Sōngpān, which is often plagued with faulty electricity.

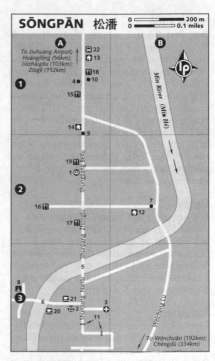

INFORMATION	
China Post 邮局	1 A2
China Telecom 中国电信	2 A3
Hospital 医院	3 A3
Public Showers 公用洗浴	4 A1

SIGHTS & ACTIVITIES	p750
Covered Bridge 古松桥	5 A3
Covered Bridge 古松桥	6 A3
East Gate 东门	7 B2
Guānyīn Gé 观音阁	8 A3
North Gate 北门	9 A1
Shun Jiang Horse Treks 顺江旅游马队	10 A1
South Gate 南门	11 A3

SLEEPING	p750
Shun Jiang Guesthouse 顺江自助旅馆	(see 10)
Sōngzhōu Lǚguǎn 松潘旅馆	12 B2
Sōngpān Jiāotōng Bīnguǎn 松州交通宾馆	13 A1
Tàiyáng Dàjiǔdiàn 太阳大酒店	14 A1

EATING	pp750–1
Emma's Kitchen 小欧洲西餐厅	15 A1
Hotpot Restaurant 火锅餐厅	16 A2
Muslim Restaurant 穆斯林餐厅	17 A2
Song in the Mountain	18 A1
Yùlán Fànguǎn 玉兰饭馆	19 A2

DRINKING	p751
Gǔchéng Cháyuán 古城茶园	20 A3
Teahouses 茶馆	21 A3

TRANSPORT	p751
Bus Station 客运汽车展	22 A1

SOUTHWEST CHINA

Information

China Post (Yóujú; Shungjian Lu; ☑ 9am-11.30am & 2-5.30pm) is on the main street about halfway between the north and south gates. Not far from the Min River (Mín Hé) and teahouses are a couple of China Telecom shops where you can make cheap international calls with Internet phone (IP) cards. Public showers (Y3) sit diagonally opposite the Shun Jiang Guesthouse and supposedly have hot water from noon to 11pm. Shun Jiang Horse Treks is planning to set up an Internet café which should be open by the time you read this.

Sights

The ancient gates from Sōngpān's days as a walled city are still intact and a couple of old wooden bridges cross over Min River. On the far eastern side of the river is **Guānyīn Gé**. Walking up to it will take you through a village-like setting and the small temple offers views over Sōngpān.

Activities

Several kilometres outside Sōngpān lie idyllic mountain forest and emerald-green lakes. One of the most popular ways to experience this is by joining up with a horse trek from Sōngpān. Guides can take you out through pristine, peaceful valleys and forests, all aboard a not-so-big, very tame horse. Many people rate this experience as one of the highlights of their travels in Sìchuān.

Treks are organised by **Shun Jiang Horse Treks** (Shùnjiāng Lüvyóu Mǎduì; ☎ 723 1201), located about 30m south of the bus station on your left. The guys here have been catering horse treks to backpackers for years and are extremely friendly and helpful. They can offer anything from one- to 12-day treks and are happy to tailor a trip to suit you.

One of the most popular treks is the four-day trip to **Ice Mountain** (雪玉顶; Xuěyùdǐng) a spectacular trip through as yet unspoilt scenery.

If you're feeling particularly adventurous (and particularly flush) you can make the trip north to Zöigê on horseback, a trek that takes around 12 days. Bear in mind that you will have to cover the cost of the horses on their return journey to Sōngpān which can make it quite an expensive way to travel.

Rates are very reasonable (from Y100 per day per person); you get a horse, three meals a day, tents, bedding, warm jackets and raincoats. The guides take care of everything: you won't touch a tent pole or a cooking pot unless you want to. The only additional charge is entrance to the different sites (Y20 to Y110 each), but you will be warned of these before you set out.

As food consists mainly of green veggies, potatoes and bread, you may want to take along some extra snacks for variety.

Sleeping

With Sōngpān's faulty electricity also comes a shortage of hot water (apparently the water pumps halt), something you might want to consider before splashing out on an expensive room with an en suite.

Shun Jiang Guesthouse (Shùnjiāng Zizhù Lûguǎn; ☎ 723 1201, 723 1064; Shunjiang Beilu; dm Y20) Run by the Shun Jiang Horse Trek company, this simple but clean guesthouse is situated right above their office which means you can literally roll out of bed and into the saddle.

Sōngzhōu Jiāotōng Bīnguǎn (☎ 723 1818, 723 1258; Shunjiang Beilu; dm Y20-40, d/tr Y180/150) Attached to the bus station, this sparkling new hotel has an enormous number of rooms to choose from. If you're travelling in a large group then this is a great place to stay.

Sōngpān Lûguǎn (dm Y20) With only a handful of beds and basic washing facilities, this small wooden hostel is down an alley not far from the east gate – look for the red arrows painted on the side of the buildings.

Taìyáng Dàjiǔdiàn (☎ 723 2888; Shunjiang Beilu; d Y280) Located beside the north gate this enormous hotel is one of the most upmarket in town. The rooms are lovely and the showers pump out hot water.

Eating

Sōngpān has an excellent assortment of breads for sale, made and sold fresh all day at small stalls along Shunjiang Zhonglu – big crusty loaves, dumplings, Tibetan flatbread and sweet breads.

There are also a huge number of restaurants along Shunjiang Zhonglu including hotpot and noodle shops. Many have English signs and menus. You'll find a large **hotpot restaurant** (hotpot from Y15; ☑ noon-9pm) in what was once the town's cinema, before the advent of DVD; it's opposite the west gate at the other end of the road.

Emma's Kitchen (Xiǎo Ōzhōu Xīcāntīng; ☎ 880 2958; mains from Y10; ⏱ 6.30am-late) Great food and atmosphere and some comfy sofas (which feel even more comfortable when you return from your horse trek) make this a popular place. Emma is very helpful and can sort out almost anything from laundry to travel information.

Song in the Mountain (☎ 723 3916; mains from Y10; ⏱ 7am-11.30pm) This small restaurant is run by the daughter of Fis Took Yang, 'the good guide with the bad eye' at the Shun Jiang Horse Trek. It's right next door to the office and serves up some decent food.

Yùlán Fànguǎn (Shunjiang Beilu; dishes from Y8; ⏱ 8am-8pm) This is Sōngpān's original hang-out for foreign travellers and remains popular today with excellent food and good ambience.

South of the intersection on Shunjiang Zhonglu is a recently refurbished **Muslim restaurant** (Mùsīlín Cāntīng; dishes from Y10) with fantastic food. Prices are a bit high and there's no English menu, but you can easily pick out what you want in the kitchen. The *yúxiāng qiézi* (fish-flavoured eggplant) is particularly good.

Drinking

Along Min River, on the western edge of town, are a number of teahouses where you can enjoy views of the covered wooden bridge, Guānyīn Gé and wooden houses. Try the **Gǔchéng Cháyuán** (Old Town Tea Garden; ☎ 723 3745), on the left before you cross over the bridge.

Getting There & Away

AIR

Jiuhuang Airport (九黄机场; Jiǔhuáng Jīchǎng) is located in Chuānzhǔsì, a small town almost halfway between Sōngpān and Jiǔzhàigōu.

Flights leave regularly from Chéngdū and cost a staggering Y700 one way. Returning to Chéngdū there are flights throughout the day. Plans are in motion to introduce other flight destinations from here.

Buses to Jiǔzhàigōu (Y45, 1½ hours) await flight arrivals and leave when full. Occasionally buses leave from here to Huánglóng (Y22, one hour) but only if there are enough people. There are no buses to Sōngpān so you'll either have to catch a taxi (around Y80) or go to Jiǔzhàigōu

first and catch the early morning bus to Sōngpān the following day.

BUS

Sōngpān's shiny new bus station is at the northern end of town. There are daily departures to Chéngdū (Y50, eight hours, three daily, 6am to 7am), Jiǔzhàigōu (Y26, two to three hours, 7am, 11am, 1.30pm), Hóngyuán (Y40, five hours, 7am) and Zöigê (Y46, six hours, 7am). You might also be able to grab a seat on a Chéngdū-bound bus from Jiǔzhàigōu or Zöigê that passes through Sōngpān between 8.30am and 10am every day. There are no direct buses to Huánglóng from here. For Lǎngmùsì you will need to change at Zöigê.

From Chéngdū's Chadianzi bus station there are three daily departures to Sōngpān (Y50, eight hours, 6.30am, 7am and 7.30am) and from Jiǔzhàigōu there is a morning departure to Sōngpān at 7.20am.

HUANGLONG NATIONAL PARK
黄龙景区

Designated a national park in 1983, **Huánglóng** (Huánglóng Jīngqù; Yellow Dragon Valley; www.huanglong .com; admission Y110; ⏱ 7am-6pm) is studded with waterfalls and terraced, coloured limestone ponds of blue, yellow, white and green. Consequently, it has earned the nickname Wǔcǎichí (Five-Coloured Pools). To see the pools in their full rainbow glory, the best time of year to visit is September and October.

Legend has it that 4000 years ago a yellow dragon helped the King of the Xia Kingdom, Xiayu, channel the floodwater into the sea thereby creating the Min River. The calcium carbonate mineral deposit patterns and the golden hue of the water supposedly look like a dragon's tail. In later years, a temple was built to honour the yellow dragon and the valley given its name.

The most spectacular ponds are located behind **Huanglong Temple** (黄龙寺; Huánglóng Sì), located deep in the valley, 7.5km from the road. A round trip along a footpath takes about four hours, with the trail returning through dense (and dark) forest. While some people rave about the valley's beauty and love the peace and quiet here, others find it disappointing and prefer an extra day at Jiǔzhàigōu. If you do visit, there are no vendors, so bring some water and supplies.

SOUTHWEST CHINA

A great time to visit is during the annual **Temple Fair** (庙会, Miào Huì). Held here around the middle of the sixth lunar month (usually July), it attracts large numbers of traders from the Qiang minority.

In the national park there are several small guesthouses with cheap beds – no frills, just hard beds and maybe a coal burner in the winter. Huánglóng Zhāodàisuǒ (黄龙招待所) has slightly more upmarket accommodation, with dorm beds in three-bed dorms (Y20) and standard doubles.

Around 56km from Sōngpān, Huánglóng is almost always included on the itinerary of the seven-day Jiǔzhàigōu tours that run out of Chéngdū, as well as on the horse-trekking tours out of Sōngpān. Unfortunately, unless you've signed up on a tour, the valley can be difficult to reach. There is one bus a day from Jiǔzhàigōu (Y41, three hours, 7.10am) but unless you manage to jump on a tour bus, be prepared to stay the night as the returning bus from Huánglóng departs in the morning.

JIUZHAIGOU NATURE RESERVE
九寨沟自然保护区

☎ 0837 / pop 62,000

Just inside Sìchuān's northern border lies **Jiuzhaigou Nature Reserve** (Jiǔzhàigōu Zìrán Bǎohùqū; Nine Village Gully; www.jiuzhaigouvalley.com; adult/student Y145/113; ⊙ 7am-6pm), a gorgeous alpine valley studded with dazzling turquoise lakes as clear and as bright as gemstones. Heavily forested and surrounded by snowy peaks, Jiǔzhàigōu is a national treasure reserve and home to protected takins, golden monkeys and pandas.

According to legend, Jiǔzhàigōu was created when a jealous devil caused the goddess Wunosemo to drop her magic mirror, a present from her lover the warlord God Dage. The mirror dropped to the ground and shattered into 118 shimmering lakes.

Jiǔzhàigōu, meaning 'Nine Village Gully' refers to the nine Baima Tibetan villages that can be found in the valley. The area is lightly sprinkled with Bön prayer flags, *chörten* and prayer wheels that spin anticlockwise, powered by the current of the rivers.

The park is in pristine condition; however, it has also been groomed for the rapidly increasing influx of tourists. Jiǔzhàigōu was first pinpointed for tourism in the 1970s and there are now enough resort-style hotels leading up to the park entrance to house 20,000 people. A scary thought. Furthermore visitors are no longer allowed to sleep within the park and even the original residents have been forced to move in order to 'protect' the park. What was once a place where you could escape for several days and commune with nature is now only possible as a day trip.

Orientation & Information

Buses from Chéngdū and Sōngpān will drop you outside the park reception centre and ticket office, just north of the park entrance. If you can produce something remotely resembling a student card you'll be given a discount. The price includes entrance to all areas of the park but does not include the bus (Y90) that ferries tourists around inside the park.

There is an ATM at the park entrance that accepts major credit cards.

Sights

The first official site inside the park is Tibetan **Zaru Temple** (Zārú Sì; Zaru Gompa in Tibetan). The bus is unlikely to take you there, but it's only a short walk down the first fork off the main road.

If you continue on the main road, you'll follow **Zechawa River** (Zécháwā Hé) as it runs past **Heye Stockade** (Héyè Cūn) to **Huǒhuā Hú** (Sparkling Lake). This is the first in a series of lakes filled by the **Shuzheng Waterfall** (Shùzhēng Pùbù). Keep your eyes open for trees growing unexpectedly out of the middle of the river, lakes and waterfalls. This is caused by fertile pockets of calcium in the waterways which create impromptu flowerpots.

A walking trail begins north of Sparkling Lake and runs along the eastern edge of the river as far as **Shuzheng Stockade** (Shùzhēng Zhài). Here it crosses back over, leading you to a number of water-powered prayer wheels. The trail then continues up to the Shuzheng Waterfall.

South from here, just past **Promising Bright Bay Waterfall** (Nuòrìlǎng Pùbù), the road branches in two, with the eastern road leading to **Long Lake** (Cháng Hǎi) and **Five-Coloured Pool** and the western road to **Swan Lake** (Tiānè Hǎi). If you're looking to stretch your legs and clear your lungs, you'd be better off heading along the western route where there are a number of scattered sights

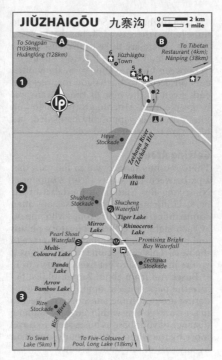

JIŬZHÀIGŌU 九寨沟

and a quiet forest trail leading from **Mirror Lake** (Jìnghǎi) to **Panda Lake** (Xióngmāo Hǎi). Views from this trail are particularly good, especially of **Pearl Shoal Waterfall** (Zhēnzhūtān Pùbù). If you continue past Panda Lake, you will leave the majority of the traffic behind.

The eastern route is almost better done by bus as the narrow road sees a great deal of traffic from one end to the other. Nevertheless, the two lakes at the far end are both well worth a visit.

From the park entrance to Promising Bright Bay Waterfall is about 14km. It's a further 17.5km along the western road to the primary forest and 18km down the eastern road to Long Lake.

Tours

During summer, various companies in Chéngdū operate tours to Jiǔzhàigōu and the surrounding area. Most of the trips are advertised for a certain day, but the bus will only go if full. If you are unlucky you may have to spend days waiting so it's best to try to register first and then pay before departure.

A standard tour includes Huánglóng and Jiǔzhàigōu, lasts seven days and starts from Y400 per person. Hotels, food and entry fees are not included in the price. Chéngdū travel agencies in the Dragon Town Youth Hostel, Traffic Hotel, Sam's Guesthouse, Jǐnjiāng Bīnguǎn (see p717 for these places) and CITS (p714) all offer tours. The latter two are the most expensive. Check around and compare prices.

A word of warning: several tour operators in Chéngdū have been blacklisted by travellers for lousy service, rip-offs and rudeness. Ask around among travellers to pinpoint a reliable agency and look in the travellers' notebooks in cafés and hostels.

Sleeping & Eating

There are literally dozens of top-end hotels and only a handful of budget ones. Expect a huge hike in prices during high season (July and August) and all national holidays. Rates quoted below are for the off season.

Jiǔtōng Bīnguǎn (☎ 773 9879; fax 773 9877; dm Y30, d Y100) Attached to the bus station, this is your best option for cheap accommodation. Dorms have concrete floors but are clean.

Héyè Yíngbīnguǎn (☎ 773 5555; fax 773 5688; d Y290) Just north of the park entrance, this hotel has lovely rooms with fancy marble bathrooms.

Látiān Bīnguǎn (☎ 877 8888; d Y120-398, tr Y100-200) In the off season these rooms are a great deal and come with great fluffy duvets rather than those horrible brown hotel blankets. This hotel is about 15-minutes' walk north of the park entrance.

Sheraton Jiuzhaigou Resort (☎ 773 9988; fax 773 9666; www.sheraton.com/jiuzhaigou; d Y1200) One of the biggest hotels on the block and also one of the poshest. Rooms are elegant and the service is impeccable.

There isn't a huge choice of restaurants in Jiǔzhàigōu as most tourists tend to eat in their hotels. There are several restaurants near the Lántiān Bīnguǎn that serve up simple Chinese dishes.

Alternatively there is a good **Tibetan Restaurant** (阿布鲁孜; Ābù Luzī; ☎ 889 7603, 844 8309; dishes from Y25; ☯ noon-9pm) that serves very good Chinese and Tibetan food. It's not cheap, but it's a nice place to treat yourself. The restaurant is not very conveniently located and you'll have to get a taxi here (Y10). It's next to Chángqīng Fàndiàn (长青饭店).

Inside the park eating options are even more limited, especially if you visit during the off season. You can also expect to pay slightly more for food inside the park.

Outside the park entrance you'll find cheap and tasty cold noodle stands set up at lunch time and in the evening.

Getting There & Away
AIR
The new Jiuhuang Airport (Jiǔhuáng Jīchǎng) means you can fly up to Sōngpān and Jiǔzhàigōu from Chéngdū in just 40 minutes. But tickets aren't cheap at Y700 one way. There are currently only flights to Chéngdū although more destinations are likely to be added in the near future.

Buses for Jiǔzhàigōu (Y45, 1½hr) wait at the airport for arrivals and leave when full. This means that you might have to wait around for a while, as most of your fellow passengers will be hopping off the plane and straight onto a tour bus.

Returning to the airport is much easier as a scheduled bus leaves from outside the Jiǔtōng Bīnguǎn; check the schedule in the ticket office opposite the entrance to the hotel.

BUS
With a new road from Sōngpān to Jiǔzhàigōu, the once horrid ride from Chéngdū can be done in 10 to 12 relatively painless hours. From Chéngdū's Chadianzi bus station there are four daily buses to Jiǔzhàigōu (Y79 to Y89, 7.20am, 8am, 8.40am and 4pm). If you're coming from Gānsù via Zöigê, you'll have to go through Sōngpān. From Sōngpān to Jiǔzhàigōu (Y26, three hours, three times daily), the road goes up and over some gorgeous scenery.

From Jiǔzhàigōu to Sōngpān (Y26, two to three hours) there is a daily bus that leaves at 7.20am. There are three to five buses a day to Chéngdū (Y79 to Y92, 10 to 12 hours).

Between October and April, snow often cuts off access to Jiǔzhàigōu for weeks on end. Even at the best of times, transport is not plentiful. Hitching to Jiǔzhàigōu on tour buses has supposedly happened, but it's a rare occurrence indeed.

Getting Around
There is a bus service within the park that zips between the sights (Y90) stopping at Nuorilang Bus Station in the heart of the park. Unfortunately, these buses are often commandeered by tour groups who hop off at each sight, take their obligatory photos and hop back on 15 minutes later to race to the next. This can become rather tedious if you're just trying to get from point A to B.

Buses run from about 7am until just before the park shuts at 6pm. If you're wandering around in the afternoon, it's best to make sure you're within an easy walking distance of your base as buses seem to travel more by the whim of their tour group than by any sort of schedule or route.

NORTHWEST ROUTE TO GĀNSÙ
This journey through the extreme northwest of Sìchuān has emerged as a popular back-door route into Gānsù province for many travellers. Even if you're not headed north beyond the Sìchuān border, this area offers an opportunity to explore more remote Tibetan towns and villages. At an average altitude of 3500m to 4000m, travel through this grassland bog is not recommended for those in a hurry – bus transport is slow and sporadic. If you plan to explore any of the towns or lamaseries on the way, you'll need a minimum of five days, more if you make a side trip to Jiǔzhàigōu.

In winter months, roads often become impassable and temperatures plummet way past the tolerance levels of most mere mortals. While still cold, early autumn sees little rain and many clear and sunny skies. If you are travelling in the autumn or winter, it's best to buy your onward tickets as soon as possible as, during these colder months, the nomadic Goloks stay closer to main roads and towns and do much of their travel by bus, leaving little room for you and your bags.

The first leg of this route is from Chéngdū to Sōngpān (see p751 for more details). Most travellers take a side trip from Sōngpān to Jiǔzhàigōu at this point. From Sōngpān you can travel 168km northwest to your next overnight stop in Zöigê, and from there it's worth heading to Lǎngmùsì, just inside the Sìchuān border, for a day or two before crossing into Gānsù.

Zöigê 若尔盖
☎ 0839 / pop 59,000

A dusty concrete town set amid the grasslands, Zöigê doesn't have much pull for travellers other than as a resting point en route to Lǎngmùsì and north to Gānsù province. It is easy enough to spend a day here sipping tea in the sun and at the northeastern edge of town is a **gompa** (寺院, sìyuàn) with pleasant, peaceful grounds. While the town's Chinese name is Ruòěrgài, it is most commonly referred to by its Tibetan name, Zöigê.

SLEEPING & EATING

Don't expect much in the way of washing facilities or hot water in Zöigê.

Liángjú Bīnguǎn (量具宾馆; ☎ 229 8360; dm Y25) This is the best option in town. Beds are a bit more expensive but it's quiet, clean and cheerful. And the central heating works! Head right as you come out of the western bus station, take the first left onto the main street and walk up about 15 minutes. This white-and-yellow hotel will be on your left.

Lìyuán Bīnguǎn (李园宾馆; ☎ 299 1885; dm Y20) Conveniently located across the road from the western bus station, the rooms here are fairly clean but rather bleak with toilets outside and temperamental central heating. The hotel also serves as the main guesthouse for truckers which means it is often noisy through to the wee hours as these big rigs pull into town.

Between Liángjú Bīnguǎn and the southwestern end of the main street are a number of small restaurants including hotpot and noodles shops.

Across from the ever-popular pool tables in the centre of town, **Gābāfǎngzhào Cháguǎn** (嘎巴仿照茶馆) is a teahouse where you can sit outside on the balcony, eat fresh bread and sip delicious eight-treasure tea.

There are also some small restaurants right next to the western bus station that sell fresh bread and dumplings in the mornings.

GETTING THERE & AWAY

Zöigê has two bus stations, one at the western edge of town and the other, on the same road, in the southeast. The more conveniently located western bus station has services to all destinations while the southeastern only has buses to Sōngpān. If you're heading to Sōngpān and can't get a ticket at the western station, it's worth trying at the southeastern one.

To Sōngpān there is a departure at around 6am (Y46, six hours). Buses to Lǎngmùsì also leave at 6am (Y56, four hours). This bus carries on to Hézuò in Gānsù province which is only a few hours from Xiàhé. From Xiàhé you have the option of travelling on to Lánzhōu or taking the more unusual option of heading to Xīníng in Qīnghǎi province, via Tóngrén.

Chóngqìng
重庆

CONTENTS

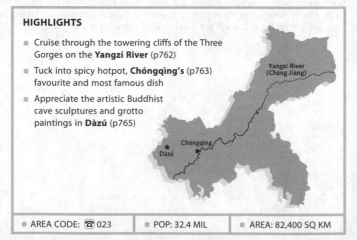

HIGHLIGHTS

- Cruise through the towering cliffs of the Three Gorges on the **Yangzi River** (p762)
- Tuck into spicy hotpot, **Chóngqìng's** (p763) favourite and most famous dish
- Appreciate the artistic Buddhist cave sculptures and grotto paintings in **Dàzú** (p765)

Yangzi River
(Cháng Jiāng)

Dàzú ★   ★ Chóngqìng

- AREA CODE: ☎ 023   - POP: 32.4 MIL   - AREA: 82,400 SQ KM

SOUTHWEST CHINA

Perched on the steep hills overlooking the confluence of the Yangzi River (Cháng Jiāng) and Jialing River (Jiālíng Jiāng), Chóngqìng is one of China's more unusual cities. Under a murky veil of fog, dusty tenements and gleaming office towers cling precariously to the steep hillsides that make up most of the city centre. Porters scurry up and down the steep stone steps that link the city together, carrying anything from vegetables and rice to furniture and TVs, strung on poles across their shoulders. Passenger boats and cargo ships sail relentlessly through the city centre and the docks heave with all walks of life, day or night.

Something immediately noticeable in Chóngqìng is the absence of bicycles; the hill climbs make it coronary country for any would-be rider. In their place you'll see motorbikes and cars fighting for space on the city's crowded streets and it comes as no surprise to learn that Chóngqìng is the second-largest producer of motorbikes and cars in the country. Despite this dependence on motor transport you may also notice a certain silence on the streets. In 1997 the city banned outright the use of car horns to reduce noise pollution on the congested peninsula, which means that while your bus journey might be a long one, it won't be too noisy.

Chóngqìng is a big city with even bigger plans, most of them connected with the hype surrounding the Three Gorges Dam (p766). It already rates as the chief industrial city of southwestern China with its production equal to a quarter of the industrial output of neighbouring Sìchuān. Cheap electricity from the dam and faster communications with Wǔhàn and Shànghǎi are set to boost the city's industries even further and kick-start economic growth throughout the entire southwest. Either that or it will place the city right at the end of the largest toilet in China.

HISTORY

In 1996 stone tools unearthed along the Yangzi River valleys showed that humans were found in this region two million years ago, a million years earlier than had been thought.

Chóngqìng (known in pre-pinyin China as 'Chungking') was opened as a treaty port in 1890, but not many foreigners made it up the river to this isolated outpost, and those who did had little impact.

An industrialisation program got underway in 1928, but it was in the wake of the Japanese invasion that Chóngqìng really took off as a major centre, when it became the Kuomintang's wartime capital from 1938 to 1945. Refugees from all over China flooded in, swelling the population to over two million. The bulk of Chóngqìng's sights are linked to this history.

In a city overpopulated and overstrained, with its bomb-shattered houses, these war-time residents must have found the name of their new home somewhat ironic: Chóngqìng means 'double happiness' or 'repeated good luck'. Originally named Gongzhou, Emperor Zhaodun of the Song dynasty renamed it in 1190 when he ascended the throne. As he had previously been made the prince of the city, he called it Chóngqìng in celebration of these two happy events.

It was in Chóngqìng, under the shadow of Kuomintang military leaders, that representatives of the Chinese Communist Party (CCP), including Zhou Enlai, acted as 'liaisons' between the Kuomintang and the Communists' headquarters at Yán'ān, in Shaanxi province. Repeated efforts to bring the two sides together in a unified front against the Japanese largely failed due to mutual distrust and Chiang Kaishek's obsession with wiping out the Communists, even at the cost of yielding Chinese territory to an invading army.

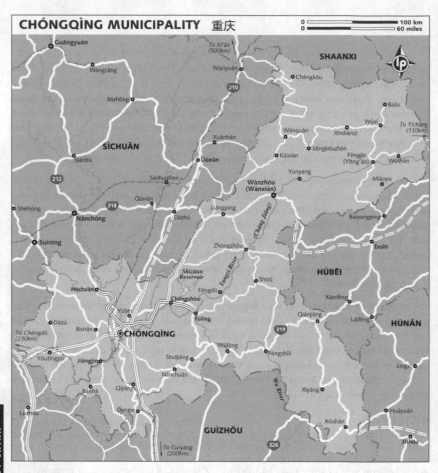

CHÓNGQÌNG MUNICIPALITY 重庆

For a long period the city lobbied for a special status akin to that of Shànghǎi. In 1997 what it got wasn't quite provincial status, but the three-county area separated from Sìchuān and became a 'special' municipality directly under central government control. It is hoped that Chóngqìng, now in many ways the largest city in China, will be the catalyst for economic development in the hitherto 'backwards' western provinces.

CLIMATE

Within China, Chóngqìng is famous for its searing summers when temperatures can exceed 40°C. This lovely climate has earned the city a place among the country's 'three furnaces', along with Wǔhàn and Nánjīng.

ORIENTATION

The heart of Chóngqìng spreads across a hilly peninsula of land wedged between the Jialing River to the north and the Yangzi River to the south. The rivers meet at the tip of the peninsula at the eastern end of the city.

For most visitors, the central focus of this congested peninsula is the now neon-shrouded Liberation Monument (Jiěfàng Bēi). Originally a wooden structure built to commemorate Sun Yatsen's death, the monument was rebuilt in 1945 to celebrate the end of China's war with Japan.

Chóngqìng is easy to explore on foot. The distances are manageable, and there's always an interesting alley to duck into.

SOUTHWEST CHINA

Maps

Good maps in Chinese and much less detailed ones in English are available from the massive **Xinhua Bookshop** (Minsheng Lu; ⊙ 9am-9pm), as well as from street vendors around the Liberation Monument area, and at the bus and train stations.

INFORMATION
Bookshops

Xinhua Bookshop (Xīnhuá Shūdiàn; Minsheng Lu) Good choice of Chinese maps of the city and surrounding areas and a handful of English ones. There is also a selection of English titles including guidebooks. A smaller Xinhua Bookshop can be found on Minzu Lu.

Internet Access

Xinhua Bookshop (Xīnhuá Shūdiàn; Minsheng Lu; per hr Y3) There is an Internet café on the 3rd floor of this bookshop.

Media

Go West is a free monthly magazine that covers Chéngdū and Chóngqìng, and has up-to-date bar, restaurant and entertainment listings. You can pick up a free copy from Westerner-friendly hotels, such as the Hilton.

Medical Services

There is a large pharmacy next door to the Peace Hotel on Minzu Lu.
Global Doctor Chóngqìng Clinic (☎ 8903 8837; Hilton Hotel; 139 Zhongshan Sanlu; ⊙ 24hr)

Money

Bank of China (Zhōngguó Yínháng; 104 Minzu Lu; ⊙ 9am-noon & 1.30-5pm Mon-Fri) Changes cash and travellers cheques, and offers cash advances on credit cards. Also has an ATM. Another branch with an ATM is located around the corner from Huìxiánlóu Bīnguǎn.

Post

Post office (yóujú; Minzu Lu; ⊙ 8.30am-9.30pm) Within walking distance of Huìxiánlóu Bīnguǎn. You can make international phone calls here.

Tourist Information & Travel Agencies

China International Travel Service (CITS; Zhōngguó Guójì Lǚxíngshè; ☎ 6903 7560; www.trekyangtze.com; 8f Zourong Sq, Liberation Monument) The helpful English-speaking staff are an excellent source of information, and also run interesting six-day treks along the Yangzi riverbank.
Yangzi River Three Gorges Travel Reception Centre (Cháng Jiāng Sānxiá Lǚyóu Jiēdài Zhōngxīn; ☎ 6387 2711, 6387 2722; fax 6387 2633; 165 Zhongshan

Sanlu) This is your one-stop travel shop; tickets for all modes of transport can be booked here.

Visas

Public Security Bureau (PSB; Gōngānjú; ☎ 6383 1830; 48 Wusi Lu; ⊙ 9am-noon & 1.30-5pm Mon-Thu, 9am-noon Fri) Issues visa extensions, but it has to be one of the slowest offices in the southwest. Wait until you get to Chéngdū or Lèshān.

DANGERS & ANNOYANCES

Chóngqìng is a relatively safe city, bit still take care around the bus and train stations and around the dock area, which are favourite haunts of pickpockets.

Be wary of touts meeting you at the bus and train stations with promises of cheap accommodation. Remember these folk only get paid to bring you to the hotel and aren't that interested in the rules. Most of these hotels don't accept foreigners, and those that do tend to be rather grim and unsafe.

SIGHTS & ACTIVITIES
Arhat Temple 罗汉寺

Built around 1000 years ago, this **temple** (Luóhàn Sì; admission Y5; ⊙ 8am-5pm) has since been sandwiched between the skyscrapers and apartments of the city. At its peak, this temple was home to 70 monks; there are only around 18 in residence these days. Nonetheless, the temple is still popular with local worshippers and it's worth a visit.

Luóhàn is the Chinese rendering of the Sanskrit *arhat*, which is a Buddhist term referring to people who have released themselves from the psychological bondage of greed, hate and delusion. Appropriately enough, there are 500 life-like, terracotta *arhat* sculptures inside the temple. You'll also find a large golden Buddha figure, behind which is an Indian-style *jataka* mural depicting Prince Siddhartha in the process of cutting his hair to renounce the world.

The temple's most remarkable feature is its long entrance flanked by rock carvings, many of which have survived the onslaught of time, the Cultural Revolution and the city's pollution amazingly well.

Ciqikou Ancient Town 磁器口古镇

Perched on a hill overlooking the Jialing River in the west of the city, Ciqikou Ancient Town (Cíqìkǒu Gǔzhèn) dates back to the late Ming dynasty. The buildings have

CHÓNGQÌNG CITY 重庆市

been restored and preserved for tourists, and the main drag is lined with shops and restaurants; but there is still an air of authenticity about the place, most probably because behind the shop fronts lies a living, breathing 'real' working village. There are several teahouses that feature daily performances of traditional Chinese music.

At one time there were five temples in town, but only **Bǎolún Sì** (admission Y5) remains today. The temple is in remarkable condition considering that it dates back to the Western Wei dynasty (535–56AD), over 1500 years ago.

Opposite the entrance to the temple is a small **museum** (admission Y3) dedicated to Chóngqìng's trackers, the coolies that used to haul ships up the Yangzi against the current. There are no English captions, but there is an interesting collection of photos taken by a German diplomat who lived in Chóngqìng in the early 1900s.

Bus No 215 runs out here from Liberation Monument. The ride takes about an hour.

Red Cliff Village 红岩村

During the Kuomintang-Communist alliance against the Japanese in WWII, this **village** (Hóngyán Cūn; admission Y10; ☻8am-5.30pm), outside Chóngqìng, was used as the offices and living quarters of the Communist representatives to the Kuomintang.

Among others, Ye Jianying, Zhou Enlai and Zhou's wife, Deng Yingchao, lived in Red Cliff Village. After the Japanese surrender in 1945, Mao Zedong also arrived in Chóngqìng –

at the instigation of US ambassador Patrick Hurley – to join in the peace negotiations with the Kuomintang. The talks lasted 42 days and resulted in a formal agreement that Mao described as 'words on paper'.

One of China's better revolutionary history museums now stands at the site and has a large collection of photos, although all of the captions are in Chinese only.

To get to Red Cliff Village, take bus No 104 from the bus stop on Beiqu Lu, just north of the Liberation Monument. The ride takes about an hour.

US-Chiang Kaishek Criminal Acts Exhibition Hall & SACO Prisons
中美合作所集中营旧址

In 1943, the USA and Chiang Kaishek signed a secret agreement to set up the Sino-American Cooperation Organisation (SACO), under which the USA helped to train and dispatch secret agents for the Kuomintang. As an extension of SACO, a number of prison camps were also built here. The chief of SACO was Tai Li, the notorious head of the Kuomintang military secret service; its deputy chief was a US Navy officer Commodore ME Miles. Both an **Exhibition Hall** and the **prisons** (Zhōngměi Hézuòsuǒ Jízhōngyíng Jiùzhǐ; admission Y20; ☻8am-7pm) have been opened to the public.

The Kuomintang never recognised the Communist Party as a legal political entity, although in theory it recognised its army as allies in the struggle against the Japanese invaders. Civilian communists remained subject to repressive laws and hundreds were kept captive as political prisoners by the Kuomintang in these prisons and others. According to the communists, many were also executed.

Unfortunately, the site has Chinese captions only. The exhibition hall has many photos on display; there are manacles and chains, but nothing too ghoulish.

To get there take bus Nos 215 or 217 just south of Zhongshan Sanlu, not far from the Jialing Bridge. It's about a 45-minute ride. Make sure that the driver knows where you want to get off, as the place is not obvious. The SACO Prisons are an hour's walk from the exhibition hall, or you can get a taxi for around Y20.

Stillwell Museum 史迪威将军旧居

This **museum** (Shǐdíwēi Jiāngjūn Jiùjū; admission Y5; 9am-6pm Mar-Dec) is something of a novelty in China, as it sheds a relatively positive light on the US involvement in WWII. The museum is housed in the former VIP guesthouse of the Kuomintang and residence of General Stillwell, who was Commander of the US forces in the China-Burma-India Theatre and chief of staff to Chiang Kaishek in 1942. On display is an extensive display of mostly US-supplied photos, documents, articles and the odd video that may be of interest to American history buffs.

Parks

Chóngqìng's two temple parks are neglected by many visitors, but they are a pleasant enough way to while away an afternoon. At 345m, **Pipa Mountain Park** (Pípá Shān Gōngyuán; admission Y5, plus Y3 for temple; 6am-10pm) marks the highest point on the Chóngqìng peninsula.

Along the Yangzi River, just east of the bus station, is **Coral Park** (Shānhú Gōngyuán; admission Y10), designed as a theme park and

opened in 1997. It's a pleasant place to wander or wait for your bus.

Cable Car Trips

A trip on a **cable car** (admission Y1.5; 7.30am-8.30pm) spanning both the Jialing and Yangzi rivers will carry you over the precipitously stacked housing and polluting industrial estates for a bird's-eye view of the murky waters. The ride over the Yangzi River links up to a series of lifts and Chiang Kaishek's old domicile. Both are within walking distance of the Liberation Monument.

Northern Hot Springs Park 北温泉公园

Fifty-five kilometres northwest of the city, at the foot of Jìnyún Shān and overlooking the Jialing River, the Northern Hot Springs (Běi Wēnquán Gōngyuán) are in a large park that is also the site of a 5th-century Buddhist temple. The springs have an Olympic-size swimming pool where you can bathe with an audience, or private rooms with big hot baths. Water temperature averages around 32°C. Swimsuits can be hired here – they're coloured red, symbolising happiness.

To get to the springs, take bus No 306 from the Liberation Monument.

River Tours

Chóngqìng looks better by night when the grey of the city is replaced by a kaleidoscope of neon, and what better way to enjoy the spectacle than from the water. River cruises (with/without dinner Y100/80) leave from Chaotianmen Dock, sailing around the peninsula and passing both the Jialing Bridge and the Yangzi River Bridge. The trip is from 7.30pm to 10pm, and tickets can be bought from almost anywhere in town, including most hotels, the Cháotiānmén Booking Hall or any of the Yangzi tour operators.

CHÓNGQÌNG IN ONE DAY

Start your day Chóngqìng style with a bowl of chilli noodles from any of the street stands near **Liberation Monument**. Wander over to **Arhat Temple** and watch the worshippers burn incense. Stroll down to the bustling **Chaotianmen Dock** area stopping at the various **street markets** for a browse along the way.

Jump on a bus and visit the old Ming dynasty town of **Ciqikou Ancient Town**, sip tea in a teahouse and enjoy a traditional Chinese music performance.

In the evening, ride a **cable car** over the **Yangzi River** and walk along Nanan Binjiang Lu, Chóngqìng's liveliest restaurant and bar strip. After a pre-dinner drink or two tuck into a fiery **hotpot**, the spicier the better.

SLEEPING

If you're thinking of splurging, Chóngqìng is the place to do it as there is next to nothing in the way of budget accommodation. Mid-range hotels tend to be relatively good value for money, while there is no shortage of quality top-end hotels. There are usually some good discounts floating around during the off-season.

Budget

Fúyuán Bīnguǎn (☎ 8903 3922; 38 Caiyuan Lu; tr Y148, d/tr with bath Y128/168) The location isn't great, but the rooms are excellent and this is the best budget accommodation in town. Unfortunately, all tour groups think the same and this place is often full. Book in advance.

Huìxiānlóu Bīnguǎn (☎ 6384 5101, ext 888; fax 6384 4234; 186 Minzu Lu; dm Y50, s with bath Y240, d with bath 260-320, with breakfast) For solo travellers this is your best choice, as the dorms offer good value for money. Doubles can be cramped, and cleaning practices are somewhat lackadaisical.

Chóngqìng Shípǐn Dàshà (☎ 6384 7300; 72 Shaanxi Lu; d/tr Y80/90, d/tr with bath Y180/200) This would have to be your last choice for budget accommodation. Dorms look like they've been housing visitors since pre-liberation.

Mid-Range

Yúdū Dàjiǔdiàn (☎ 6382 8888, ext 4101; fax 6381 8168; 168 Bayi Lu; s Y238, d Y280-360, tr Y398 plus 15% service charge) Centrally located with a gleaming marble lobby and green-capped bellboys to carry your bags, you could be forgiven for thinking you'd walked into a five-star hotel.

Milky Way Hotel (Yínhé Bīnguǎn; ☎ 6380 8585, ext 2001/2; fax 6381 2080; 49 Datong Lu; d Y280) This is another comfortable mid-range option, with good-sized rooms and a quiet location.

Peace Hotel (Hépíng Bīnguǎn; ☎ 6378 8315; fax 6380 9546; 128 Minzu Lu; d Y260-290) The Peace Hotel's standard rooms are very clean apart from the carpet, which could do with a serious scrubbing. Fortunately, free bedroom slippers are provided!

Rénmín Bīnguǎn (☎ 6385 6888; fax 6385 2076; Renmin Lu; d Y320, discounted Y250) This palatial-looking hotel was constructed in 1953 and comprises three wings separated by an enormous 65m-high circular concert hall that can seat 4000 people. The rooms aren't nearly as stately as the building, but the cool setting in leafy Rénmín Gōngyuán makes a wonderful retreat from the concrete jungle. From the train station, head up to Zhongshan Lu and catch bus Nos 401 or 405 to the traffic circle and then walk east down Renmin Lu.

Top End

Chongqing Guesthouse (Chóngqìng Bīnguǎn; ☎ 6384 5888; fax 6383 0643; 235 Minsheng Lu; old d Y260, VIP d Y405; 🏊) Rooms in the VIP wing are pure luxury; elegantly decorated with large, comfortable beds. The indoor swimming pool makes this an oasis in the heart of the city.

Harbour Plaza (Chóngxīhǎiyì Jiǔdiàn; ☎ 6370 0888; www.harbour-plaza.com/hpcq; Wuyi Lu; d Y1330; 🏊) Überchic rooms and enough extras to keep you occupied for a week, including an indoor swimming pool, ice-skating rink and bowling alley.

Hilton Hotel (Xīěrdùdùn Jiǔdiàn; ☎ 8903 8888; www .hilton.com/chongqing; 139 Zhongshan Sanlu; d Y660) You can never really go wrong with a Hilton and this one is no exception – great rooms, great restaurants and a great night's sleep.

EATING
Street Food

The central business district, in the eastern section of the city near the docks, abounds with small restaurants and street vendors. For tasty noodles and *baozi* (steamed stuffed buns), check out Xinhua Lu and Shaanxi Lu towards Chaotianmen Dock. There are some good night markets behind Huìxiānlóu Bīnguǎn, in the vicinity of Arhart Temple and near Yúdū Dàjiǔdiàn.

Hotpot

Chóngqìng's most famous dish has to be *huǒguō* (hotpot; see Hot and Spicy, p764). While it's usually cheap, it's a good idea to check prices as you go along. Hotpot can be found wherever there are street vendors or small restaurants. Wuyi Lu has the greatest variety and is locally known as Huǒguō Jiē (Hotpot St). Another good place to look is Minsheng Lu, or if you're looking for somewhere a bit more lively then try any of the hotpot eateries along Nanan Binjiang Lu.

Little Swan (Xiǎotiān'é Huǒguō; ☎ 6785 5328; 78 Jianxin Lu; meals from Y100) Up near the university district, this is reputedly Chóngqìng's best hotpot restaurant. It's self-service, which means it can get very expensive very quickly, but the hotpot is fantastic. Take bus Nos 411 or 902 from the Liberation Monument.

SOUTHWEST CHINA

Restaurants

Undoubtedly the best place to look for restaurants is along Nanan Binjiang Lu, the other side of the Yangzi River. This restaurant strip is absolutely heaving with outdoor restaurants and it's worth going for the atmosphere alone. On weekends street musicians add to the carnival feel and you can happily spend several hours here enjoying your food and the crowds.

Yízhìshí Cāntīng (Zourong Lu; dishes from Y12) Among the many larger, sit-down restaurants along Zourong Lu, this popular restaurant is an excellent place to feast on Sichuanese main courses. Sichuan-style pastries are served in the morning, and local specialties, like tea-smoked duck and dry-stewed fish at lunch and dinner.

Yángròu Guǎn (Lamb Restaurant; Minzu Lu; dishes from Y8) The dishes are spicy, but the kebabs aren't too punishing on the taste buds. The

surrounding neighbourhood is teeming with restaurants.

Pizza Almalfi (Āměifēi Bǐsà; ☎ 6381 7868; Minzu Lu; ☽ 9am-11pm; pizza from Y39) If you've had enough of spicy food, this place does fairly good pizza with a range of toppings. Takeaway is available. It's near Liberation Monument.

DRINKING

With more illuminations than Blackpool, Nanan Binjiang Lu is Chóngqìng's pride and joy, and it's a great place to go for bars as well as restaurants. Have a look for the **Fast Car Bar** (Kuàichē Jiǔbā; Nanan Binjiang Lu), which features live bands on Saturday nights.

South of Liberation Monument is **Celtic Man** (Àiěrlán Jiǔbā; Miquan Lu), an Irish pub (what else?) that serves Kilkenny and Guinness. Not far from here, on Xinhua Lu, is **Lǎojiēshí Bātīlóu**, a beautiful teahouse with wooden and bamboo décor, and old teapots, cups and photos on display.

Also near Liberation Monument you'll find **Noah's Ark** (Nuòyà Fāngzhōu; Zhonghua Lu), a cosy bar set over four floors. If it's coffee you're after, try **Sophia's Coffee House** (Sūfēiyà Kāfēiguǎn; Minsheng Lu), which serves simple Western meals in addition to the pots of freshly brewed coffee and tea.

New bars are opening up in Chóngqìng all the time. Check out *Go West* magazine for recommendations.

SHOPPING

Carrefour (Jiālèfú Cháojíshìchǎng; Cangbai Lu) is a great place to stock up on pre-boat trip supplies. The French supermarket chain has everything from Western toiletries to Chinese snacks and decent chocolate bars. The **New Century Department Store** (Xīnshìjiè Bǎihuò; Linjiang Lu) also has a decent supermarket.

GETTING THERE & AWAY
Air

Chóngqìng's Jiangbei airport is 25km north of the city centre. You can purchase tickets at **China Southwest Airlines** (☎ 6366 0444; Zhongshan Sanlu) and **Dragonair** (Holiday Inn Hotel; ☎ 6280 3380; 15 Nanpin Beilu). You can book flights at most hotels and in the numerous ticket offices around Liberation Monument.

There are daily flights to nearly everywhere in China, including Chéngdū (Y360), Kūnmíng (Y710), Guìyáng (Y490), Guǎngzhōu (Y1180), Wǔhàn (Y790), Shànghǎi

---

HOT AND VERY SPICY

Hotpot (*huǒguō*; literally 'fire pot') is Chóngqìng's most famous and favourite dish. It's eaten year-round, even in the summer months when the city itself resembles a furnace.

Born on the banks of the Yangzi River, hotpot was originally eaten by poor boatmen. Enterprising meat vendors would prepare a broth of chillies and Sìchuān pepper, and sell skewers of offal to cook in the spicy soup. Today, hotpot is no longer a poor man's dish and ingredients for dunking are not restricted to tripe. You can dip almost anything you like in your pot, from Chinese mushrooms and squid to tofu and lotus root.

Hotpot restaurants can be found all over Chóngqìng, not to mention all over China, but no one eats hotpot quite like a Chongqinger; the chillies they use are much, much hotter than the ones found in neighbouring Chéngdū.

If all this sounds like too much for your taste buds, ask for the *'yuānyáng'* version which is divided like a yin-yang symbol into a spicy side and a mild side (soup made of fish or chicken). Just tell the restaurateurs that you are *'pà là'* (scared of chilli spice). Don't be surprised if they laugh, however, you might as well be saying 'I'm a wimp'.

(Y1490), Běijīng (Y1560) and Shēnzhèn (Y1810).

International destinations include Hong Kong (Y1604), Seoul (Y2310) and Singapore (Y2310).

Boat

Zillions of boats make the run from Chóngqìng down the Yangzi River to Yíchāng. The ride is a popular tourist trip and worth doing before the Chinese government finishes its massive dam project and floods the Three Gorges (see The Damned Yangzi, p766). For details on Yangzi River trips, see Cruising Downriver (p768).

Travelling upriver by boat from Chóngqìng hasn't been a viable option since the government pulled its money out of the ferry business and put it all behind the expressway. You may find private boats selling tickets for Yíbīn or Lèshān in the summer; however, it's considered by locals to be a risky ride.

Bus

Buses from Chóngqìng depart from the two-storey long-distance bus terminal next to the train station. Destinations include:

Destination	Price	Frequency	Departs
Chéngdū	Y112	every 20 min	6.30am-9.30pm
Dàzú	Y45	hourly	9.50am-5.50pm
Éméi	Y95	twice daily	9am, 11am
Lèshān	Y80	hourly	7am-6pm

Train

Chóngqìng's enormous train station is inconveniently located in the southwest of the city.

See box below for details.

GETTING AROUND
To/From the Airport

The Civil Aviation Administration of China (CAAC; Zhōngguó Mínháng) bus service to the airport was suspended at the time of writing; check at the CITS to see if it has resumed. A taxi will cost around Y50.

Bus

Buses in Chóngqìng can be painfully slow and, since there are no bicycles, they're even more crowded than in other Chinese cities. Useful routes include: No 401, which runs between the Chaotianmen Dock and the intersection of Renmin Lu and Zhongshan Lu; No 405, running the length of Zhongshan Lu up to the Liberation Monument; and No 102, which connects the train station and Chaotianmen Dock.

Taxi

Taxi fares start at Y6, although they can be slightly higher depending on the size of the car. Expect to pay Y10 to Y15 from the city centre to the bus station. A plethora of one-way and 'no entrance' streets can make for some circuitous routing.

AROUND CHÓNGQÌNG

DÀZÚ COUNTY 大足县
pop 9.1 million

The grotto art of Dàzú County, 160km northwest of Chóngqìng, is rated alongside China's other great Buddhist cave sculptures at Dūnhuáng, Luòyáng and Dàtóng.

Historical records for Dàzú are sketchy. Scattered over 40-odd places across the

---

CHÓNGQÌNG TRAIN TIMETABLES

Trains travel daily to the following destinations:

Destination	Price	Duration	Frequency	Departs
Běijīng	Y430	33hr	2 daily	12.26pm, 8.31pm
Chéngdū	Y137	10hr	daily	9.08pm
Guǎngzhōu	Y391	30hr	3 daily	7.35pm, 9pm, 10.33pm
Guìyáng	Y103	10hr	daily	10.55pm
Kūnmíng	Y263	22hr	2 daily	12.40pm, 2.42pm
Shànghǎi	Y490	33hr	2 daily	12pm, 8pm
Xī'ān	Y117	14hr	daily	9.48am

THE DAMNED YANGZI

The Three Gorges Dam is China's biggest engineering project since the construction of the Great Wall. When completed in 2009, it will back the Yangzi River up for 550km, flood an area the size of Singapore and wash away the homes of up to two million people. It will rank as the world's largest dam – an epic show of communist might, definitive proof of man's dominance of capricious nature and the 21st century symbol of a new superpower.

Located at Sandouping, 38km upstream from the existing Gezhou Dam, the Three Gorges Dam is a cornerstone of government efforts to channel economic growth from the dynamic coastal provinces into what are considered the more backward western regions, somehow transforming hinterland into heartland. When completed the dam will measure 185m high and 2km wide, and will have a hydroelectric production capacity equivalent to 18 nuclear power plants.

The dam will improve navigation on the Yangzi River, which already transports 70% of the entire county's shipping, and will be instrumental in flood control, a problem that has claimed more than one million lives in the past 100 years alone.

However, the massive scale of the Three Gorges Dam project has caused disquiet among environmentalists, economists and human-rights activists, arousing some of the most outspoken criticism of government policy in China since 1989.

Construction of the dam is incredibly expensive, and the initial estimates of US$20 to US$30 billion have now risen to as high as US$75 billion. The social implications of the dam are enormous; an estimated 1.5 million people living in inundated areas will need to be relocated and, more importantly, given a new livelihood. Environmentalists are perhaps the most vocal in their concerns; it's thought that as the river slows, so will its ability to oxygenate. The untreated waste that pours into the river from over 40 towns and 400 factories, as well as the toxic materials and pollutants from industrial sites, could well create another world record for the dam; a 480km-long septic tank – the largest toilet in the world.

The dam will also disrupt the environments of such endangered species as the Yangzi River dolphin and Chinese sturgeon. The rising waters will cover countless cultural artefacts at over 8000 important archaeological sites. Despite an ambitious plan of relocation and preservation, only one-tenth of all historic sites and relics will be saved.

In 1999, 100 cracks were discovered running the full height of the up-stream face of the dam. Yet despite this, in June 2003 the reservoir was filled to a depth of 127m. Chinese engineers say such problems are common in large dams and that the cracks have been repaired. Others, ex-premier Zhu Rongji among them, are concerned that construction shortcuts have resulted in concrete with the strength of 'mashed tofu'.

Fears about the project were further heightened when information was released about two dams that collapsed in Hénán province in 1975. After 20 years as a state secret, it is now apparent that as many as 230,000 people died in the catastrophe. If a similar accident was to happen on the Yangzi River, the population of nearby Yíchāng would be dead within an hour.

Planners insist that the Three Gorges Dam will be constructed according to safety regulations that would make such disasters impossible. Still, the collapse of the walls holding back the world's largest storage reservoir in one of the world's most densely populated pieces of real estate is a scenario that must keep even the most gung-ho supporters of the Three Gorges Dam project awake at night.

county, the cliff carvings and statues (with Buddhist, Taoist and Confucian influences) amount to thousands of pieces, large and small. The main groupings are at North Hill (Běi Shān) and the more interesting at Treasured Summit Hill (Bǎodǐng Shān). They date from the Tang dynasty (9th century) to the Song dynasty (13th century).

North Hill 北山

According to inscriptions, this **site** (Běi Shān; admission Y5, plus Y50 for sculptures; ☯ 8am-5pm) was originally a military camp, with the earliest carvings commissioned by a general. The dark niches hold small statues, many in poor condition; only one or two really stand out.

Niche No 136 depicts Puxian, the patron saint (male) of Éméi Shān, riding a white elephant. The same niche has the androgynous Sun and Moon Guanyin. Niche 155 holds a bit more talent, the Peacock King.

North Hill is about a 30-minute hike from Dàzú town – aim straight for the pagoda visible from the bus station.

Treasured Summit Hill 宝顶山

Fifteen kilometres northeast of Dàzú town, the sculptures at this **site** (Bǎodǐng Shān; admission Y50; ☺ 8am-5pm) are definitely more interesting than those at North Hill. It is believed the sculptures were completed over 70 years, between 1179 and 1249.

The founding work is attributed to Zhao Zhifeng, a monk from an obscure yoga sect of Tantric Buddhism. A monastery with nice woodwork and throngs of pilgrims sits atop a hill; on the lower section of the hill is a 125m horseshoe-shaped cliff sculptured with coloured figures, some of them up to 8m high.

The centrepiece is a 31m-long, 5m-high reclining Buddha depicted entering nirvana, with the torso sunk into the cliff face. Next to the Buddha, with a temple built around her for protection, is a mesmerising, gold Avalokiteshvara (or Guanyin, the Goddess of Mercy). Her 1007 individual arms fan out around her, entwined and reaching for the skies. Each hand has an eye, the symbol of wisdom.

Statues around the rest of the horseshoe vary considerably: Buddhist preachers and sages, historical figures, realistic scenes (on the rear of a postcard one is described as 'Pastureland – Cowboy at Rest') and delicate sculptures a few centimetres high. Some of them have been eroded by wind and rain, some have lost layers of paint, but overall there is a remarkable survival rate.

Treasured Summit Hill differs from other grottoes in that it was based on a preconceived plan which incorporated some of the area's natural features – a sculpture next to the reclining Buddha, for example, makes use of an underground spring.

Minibuses (Y5, 45 minutes) travel to the site from 9am to 6pm, departing from the Dàzú bus station when full. A motorcycle taxi will take you there for Y20.

As you pass by on the bus, look out for solo sculptures on the cliff faces.

Sleeping & Eating

Most hotels don't take foreigners, leaving you with only two options in Dàzú, neither of which is particularly cheap.

Dàzú Bīnguǎn (大足宾馆; d Y160-350) Rooms are clean and comfortable, with good service. To find the hotel, turn left from the bus station, cross over the bridge and take the road branching to the right.

Běishān Bīnguǎn (北山宾馆; d Y150) Near the base of North Hill, this hotel is musty, unkempt and horrendously overpriced.

Finding a bite to eat in Dàzú is no problem. Shizi Jie (the first right after the roundabout) comes alive at night, with dozens of street stalls serving noodles, dumplings, hotpot and wok-fried dishes.

Getting There & Away

BUS

From Dàzú, there are four buses daily to Chéngdū (Y64.5, four hours) departing between 6.30am and 9.30am, and regular buses to Chóngqìng (Y45, two hours) depart between 6.30am and 5.30pm. In Chéngdū buses leave twice a day from the north bus station at 9am and 12.30pm. From Chóngqìng buses leave every hour between 9.50am and 5.50pm.

TRAIN

Travelling to Dàzú by train is impractical and time-consuming. You're much better off taking a bus down the new expressways.

Cruising Downriver

THE RIVER

The Yangzi River (Cháng Jiāng) is China's longest river and at 6300km is the third longest in the world. Originating in snow-covered Tánggǔlǎ Shān in southwestern Qīnghǎi, it cuts its way through Tibet and seven Chinese provinces before emptying into the East China Sea just north of Shànghǎi. Between the towns of Fēngjié, in Sìchuān, and Yíchāng, in Húběi, lie three great gorges, regarded as some of the great scenic attractions of China.

The dramatic scenery and rushing waters of China's greatest river were inspirational to many of China's painters and poets, and the distinct rock formations and breathtaking cliffs of the Three Gorges continue to inspire and excite visitors today.

The journey downriver itself is very enjoyable, not least because of the change of pace (and perspective) that travelling by boat provides. The Three Gorges are incredible, but they are just one part of the cruise, and if you set sail expecting to be dwarfed by towering peaks and mile-high cliffs for the entire journey, you will probably be quite disappointed.

During the high season (April to May and October to November) boats can get very busy and you might tire of fighting the crowds on deck. Off season, however, the trip downstream is a relaxing affair and a great opportunity to observe life on the river – even better if you bring some binoculars with you.

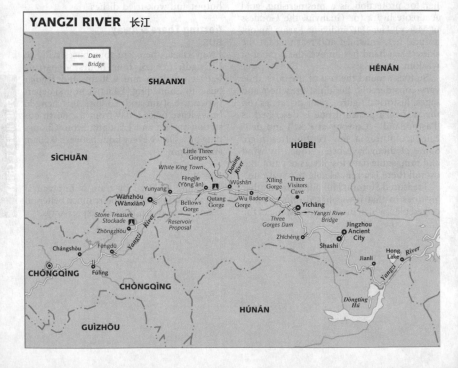

YANGZI RIVER 长江

Whether you like boats or not, it's worth considering the journey simply because it won't be long before the famed Three Gorges will be underwater. By 2009, when the mega-project Three Gorges Dam (Sānxiá Dàbà) is completed, the gorges will be part of history, 1.5 million people will have been displaced and southwestern China will never be the same. See The Damned Yangzi (p766) for more information.

TICKETS & FARES
In theory it's possible to buy your ticket on the day of travel; however, it's probably worth booking one or two days in advance, especially if you're picky about who you share a cabin with. Fares tend to be similar whether you buy them from an agency or direct from the ticket hall, but it's worth shopping around as there are often some good discounts available. Chóngqìng's budget travel agencies offer especially good deals.

In Chóngqìng the following companies enjoy a good reputation: **Chóngqìnggǎng Guójì Lǚxíngshì** (Chóngqìng Port International Travel Service; ☎ 023-6310 0553/711; www.cqpits.com.cn; 18 Xinyi Jie), with an office around the corner from the main ferry ticket hall, and friendly and very helpful English-speaking staff; and **Chóngqìng Sānxiá Guójì Jièdài Zhōngxīn** (Chóngqìng Three Gorges International Travel Centre; ☎ 023-6387 2711/22; 165 Zhongshan Sanlu), also good for booking tours downriver.

Once you've boarded your boat, a steward will exchange your ticket for a numbered, colour-coded tag that denotes your bed number. Hang on to the tag, since it must be exchanged for your ticket at the end of the voyage – without it you may not be allowed off the boat.

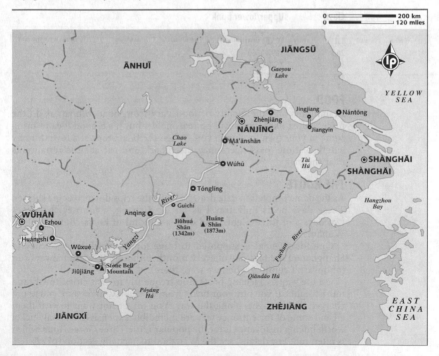

Boat

When it comes to choosing your boat you have three options. The most popular (and sensible) choices are the regular tourist boats that leave daily before noon and between 8pm and 10pm. Otherwise you can choose from a cheap cargo boat or an extortionate luxury cruise liner. The cargo boats might sound tempting but they're only worth it if you don't mind sailing through the gorges in the dead of night.

If you're in a rush, hydrofoils do the trip from Chóngqìng to Yíchāng in 11 hours.

Classes

If you're going to cruise the Yangzi, it's worth doing it in (relative) style and treating yourself to a 2nd- or even 1st-class cabin. While two days of travel might not sound like a long time, it can feel like two months if you're sharing a small living space with six chain-smoking, alcohol-swilling, karaoke-singing travel companions.

'Boats stop frequently to visit cities, towns and tourist sights'

The 1st-class cabins come with two beds, a private bathroom, a TV and air-con. Second-class cabins have two to four berths and a private bathroom. Third class has from six to 12 beds depending on the boat. Fourth class usually has eight to 12 beds, but on older vessels can have over 20 beds. Toilets and showers are shared and can be very grotty.

Travellers have complained that access to the outside decks is often restricted to what class your ticket is, although it's usually possible to argue your way to the upper decks. Nevertheless, this can be very annoying; just don't expect to have access to the outside decks all the time.

The following ticket prices are from Chóngqìng to Yíchāng:

Class	Upper/lower bunk
1st	Y1525
2nd	Y992/1060
3rd	Y620/656
4th	Y530/553

FOOD

Restaurants and the quality of food vary from boat to boat, as do the prices. Most likely costs will be reasonable, but it's a good idea to bring some of your own food with you. When the boat stops at a town for any length of time, passengers may disembark and eat at little restaurants near the pier.

THE ROUTE

As the dam completion date draws nearer, the trips downriver get shorter. These days boats only travel as far as Yíchāng, a journey that takes two days and three nights, and only a handful of boats continue on to Wǔhàn.

One tourist boat is supposed to leave for the week-long journey to Shànghǎi on the first day of every month, although it doesn't always run (and wasn't running when we were there).

On the way to Yíchāng boats stop frequently to visit cities, towns and tourist sights. If you buy your ticket from an agency, make sure you're not charged for the sights along the way. You might not want to visit them all and some of the entrance fees are incredibly expensive. The only ticket worth buying in advance is for the popular Little Three Gorges tour, which is often full. For details, see the Wànzhōu to Yíchāng section (p772).

When the boat stops make sure you find out when it's leaving again; it won't wait for latecomers.

Chóngqìng to Wànzhōu 重庆 – 万州
For the first few hours the river is lined with factories, although this gives way to some pretty, green terraced countryside with the occasional small town.

The first big town you pass is **Fúlíng**, overlooking the mouth of Wū Hé, which runs southwards into Guìzhōu and controls the river traffic between Guìzhōu and eastern Sìchuān.

Look for large white signs along the route indicating where the water level will rise to once the dam is completed. By 2009 water levels will have risen to 175m.

The next major town is **Fēngdū**, 170km from Chóngqìng. Nearby is the **Abode of Ghosts** (Guǐchéng; ☎ 7061 9114; admission Y120; ⏱ 6am-6pm), which is said to be the place of devils. Numerous temples containing sculptures of demons and devils have been built since the Tang dynasty, with heartening names like 'Bridge of Helplessness' and 'Palace of the King of Hell'. A cable car goes to the temples (Y15), but you can also walk up. The boat then passes through the county of **Zhōngzhōu**.

Soon after comes the **Stone Treasure Stockade** (Shíbǎo Zhài; ☎ 5484 0174; admission Y40; ⏱ 8am-4pm) on the northern bank of the river. This is a 12-storey 56m-high wooden temple built on a huge rock bluff, which is supposed to look something like a stone seal. Construction began during the early years of Emperor Kangxi's reign (1662–1722) in the Qing dynasty. It houses a statue of Buddha and inscriptions to commemorate its construction. It will all become an island when the water level reaches its full height after the completion of the dam.

Next is the large town of **Wànzhōu** (Wànxiàn), where most morning boats tie up for the night. It's one of the largest and most important ports on the Yangzi and is an interesting place to wander around while the boat is in port.

Wànzhōu to Yíchāng 万州 – 宜昌
Boats staying overnight at Wànzhōu generally depart before dawn. Before entering the gorges the boat passes by (and may stop at) the town

Traditional Chinese pavilion above Wūshān, overlooking the Yangzi River and the start of Wu Gorge

PHOTO BY MARTIN MOOS

of **Fēngjié** (Yǒng'ān). This ancient town overlooks the first of the three gorges, Qutang Gorge, and was the capital of the state of Kui during the Spring and Autumn and Warring States periods from 722 to 221 BC.

At the entrance to Qutang Gorge is **White King Town** (Báidichéng; ☎ 5673 1478; admission Y30), which lies on the river's northern bank. It was here that the dying King of Shu, Liu Bei, entrusted his son and kingdom to Zhu Geliang, as chronicled in the classic Chinese novel *Romance of the Three Kingdoms*. Plaster mannequins on display depict this historic event inside one of the temples.

The spectacular **Three Gorges** (Sānxiá), Qutang, Wu and Xiling, start just after Fēngjié and end near Yíchāng, a stretch of about 200km. The gorges vary from 300m at their widest to less than 100m at their narrowest. The seasonal difference in water level can be as much as 50m.

'The gorges vary from 300m at their widest to less than 100m at their narrowest'

Qutang Gorge (Qútáng Xiá) at 8km long is the smallest and shortest gorge, although the water flows most rapidly here and many travellers consider the scenery to be the most dramatic. On the northern bank is **Bellows Gorge** (Fēngxiāng Xiá). Nine coffins were discovered here high up in the cliffs, possibly put there by an ancient tribe whose custom was to place the coffins of their dead in mountain caves. Some of the coffins contained bronze swords, armour and other artefacts, believed to date back as far as the Warring States period.

Wu Gorge (Wū Xiá) is about 40km in length and the cliffs on either side rise to just over 900m, topped by sharp, jagged peaks on the northern bank, including Goddess Peak (Shénnǚ Fēng) and Peak of the Immortals (Jíxiān Fēng). If it's misty, and it very often is, you'll get a good idea of the inspiration behind Chinese traditional painting. **Bādōng** is a town on the southern bank of the river within the gorge.

In between Qutang and Wu gorges, most boats will stop for five or six hours so passengers can shift to smaller boats for tours of the **Little Three Gorges** (Xiǎo Sānxiá; admission Y300). Flanking Daning River (Dàníng Hé), these gorges are much narrower than their larger counterparts and, some people say, more impressive. The tour is expensive, but it's a great chance to get out and view the rock formations up close.

Xiling Gorge (Xīlíng Xiá), at 80km, is the longest of the three gorges. Just before you get to the end, the massive **Three Gorges Dam** (p458; Sānxiá Dàbà; admission Y240) looms up and boats stop so passengers can shuttle across to the dam observation deck for a bird's eye view of this mammoth project. Boats then pass through the locks of the **Gezhou Dam** (Gézhōu Bà) before terminating 30km downstream in Yíchāng.

Yíchāng (p458), which is regarded as the gateway to upper Yangzi River, was once a walled city dating back at least as far as the Sui dynasty. Near Yíchāng's train station you can take bus No 10 to the **Three Visitors Cave** (Sānyóu Dòng; admission Y15; ⏰ 8am-6pm) and walk through caverns with impressive stalactites and stalagmites. A cliff trail nearby overlooks the Yangzi River.

Yíchāng to Shànghǎi 宜昌 – 上海

Even if you do manage to hop on a boat continuing downstream from Yíchāng, there's isn't very much to see. The first place of any significance that you come across is **Jingzhou Ancient City** (Jīngzhōu Gǔchéng), the remains of an ancient town that is open to visitors.

After Jīngzhōu you're out on the flat plains of central China, the river widens immensely and you can see little of the shore. The boat continues downriver and eventually arrives at **Wǔhàn** (p450), which more or less marks the halfway point in the long navigable stretch of the Yangzi River from Chóngqìng to Shànghǎi.

The journey to the sea is even more mundane; the river broadens, and most of the towns and cities are industrial. Some of the more interesting towns along the way include **Jiǔjiāng** (p469) in Jiāngxī, home to **Shízhōng Shān** (Stone Bell Mountain), noted for its numerous Tang-dynasty stone carvings. Guìchí is of interest as you can get a bus to **Jiǔhuá Shān** (Nine Brilliant Mountains, p264) and spectacular **Huáng Shān** (Yellow Mountain, p259) from here.

Boats on the Yangzi River
PHOTO BY MARTIN MOOS

Crossing into Jiāngsū the first large city you pass is **Nánjīng** (p220), followed by **Zhènjiāng** (p231), then the port of **Nántōng** before turning down towards **Shànghǎi** (p266), where the Yangzi River empties into the East China Sea.

Xīnjiāng 新疆

HIGHLIGHTS

- Travel along the sandswept southern **Silk Road** (p796) or up the sheer **Karakoram Hwy** (p795)
- Get a taste of the Siberian taiga at **Kanas Lake** (p800)
- Bargain for carpets in **Kashgar** (p793), one of Asia's greatest crossroads
- Sleep in a Kazakh yurt at **Tiān Chí** (p784)
- Eat grapes, explore ruins and admire the **Flaming Mountains** (p788) around Turpan

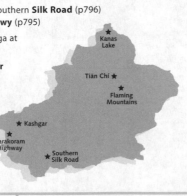

- POP: 19.25 MIL
- AREA: 1,600,000 SQ KM

SILK ROAD

Xīnjiāng is like a whole other country enclosed within China's borders. Gone are the trifling regional differences between Běijīng and Guǎngzhōu – here the language is not just a different dialect, it's a completely different linguistic family; it's no longer about whether you dip your dumplings in soy sauce or vinegar, it's how you want your mutton cooked. In times past, Xīnjiāng was known as Eastern Turkestan, these days it's the controversial Uighur Autonomous Region. However you look at it, the province is a world apart, more Central Asian than East Asian, but nevertheless with a fate that's always been inextricably tethered to the Middle Kingdom.

A huge, geopolitically strategic area, Xīnjiāng shares an international border with eight other nations, and is the largest province in China, comprising 16% of the country. The vast deserts here stretch for over a thousand kilometres before ending abruptly at the foot of towering mountain ranges, and its extreme climate has been a defining aspect of the culture throughout the centuries. Abandoned Buddhist cities lie along the treacherous trade routes of times past, while in newer oasis towns Islamic monuments point the way to the future.

For the Chinese, Xīnjiāng is one of those contradictory outer regions through which so much of their culture has filtered in. Home of the 'barbarians' to be sure, but also the birthplace of the immortal poet Li Po (Lǐ Bái), and source of much of the music, dance and fashion that defined China's golden age, the Tang dynasty.

Visitors shouldn't have as hard a time coming to grips with the province. Packed with history, ethnic variety, superb landscapes and a vibrant Central Asian culture, Xīnjiāng maintains your interest whether you're a connoisseur of the Silk Road, a student diving into the linguistic melting pot or a hardcore traveller looking for some serious adventure.

History
NOMADS & OASIS DWELLERS
The key to understanding the history of Xīnjiāng begins with the region's two principal groups: the pastoral nomads, north of the Tiān Shān range, and the sedentary oasis dwellers, skirting the Tarim Basin. The original nomads were the Xiongnu, while the earliest known oasis dwellers were an Indo-European group generally referred to as the Tocharians. Over the millennia, the ethnicities comprising these two groups have changed, however the groups themselves remained the basis of human civilization in Xīnjiāng up until the modern era.

SILK & HORSES
Although evidence of Hotanese jade in China indicates that trade must have existed as far back as 7000 years ago, signifi-

cant mention of the western regions doesn't appear in the Chinese annals until the Han dynasty.

In the 2nd century BC, in the hope of ending the devastating Xiongnu raids along their borders, the Chinese sought an alliance with the far off Yuezhi. Zhang Qian, the Chinese envoy charged with completing the mission, set out in 138 BC into the hitherto unexplored west. Immediately taken prisoner by the Xiongnu, he wasn't to escape until 10 years later, and in the end, failed to rally the support of the Yuezhi. Where Zhang Qian did succeed, however, was in discovering the northern and southern routes around the Taklamakan and into Central Asia, as well as the exceptional Ferghana horses.

While other goods were imported into China during this time, none took on the

SILK ROAD

XĪNJIĀNG 新疆

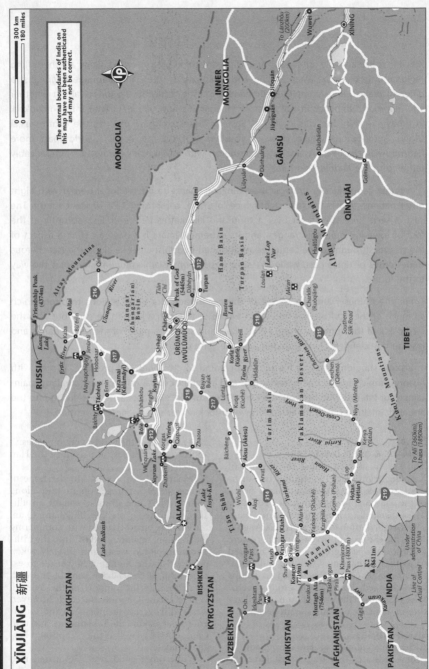

importance of the superior Central Asian steeds. By the end of the 2nd century BC, the Han had pushed their borders further west, military garrisons were established along the trade routes and silk flowed out of the empire in return for the 'Heavenly Horse'.

BUDDHISM

Along with goods from the west came ideas and languages, and by the 3rd century AD Buddhism had taken root throughout the Tarim Basin. A number of powerful Buddhist city-states arose, chiefly in Hotan, Kuqa and Turpan, leaving behind beautiful artwork that blended Kashmiri, Persian, Indian and even Greek styles. Much of this was attested to by the Chinese pilgrims Fa Xian and Xuan Zang, who passed through in the 5th and 7th centuries respectively on their way to India and the source of Buddhism.

In the 7th century, the Tang dynasty reasserted the imperial rule that had been lost following the collapse of the Han, and Chinese influence was once again felt in Xīnjiāng.

THE UIGHURS, ISLAM & THE MONGOLS

Tang control of Xīnjiāng came to an end in the 9th century with the arrival of the Uighurs from Mongolia, and the area was ruled by a succession of tribal kingdoms – Uighur, Kharakhanid and Kharakhitay – for almost 400 years. It was during Kharakhanid rule in the 11th and 12th centuries that Islam took hold in western Xīnjiāng; the religion didn't penetrate the eastern areas until the 14th century.

Yīlí (Ili), Hotan and Kashgar fell to the Mongols in 1219 (whose rule was the only period when the Silk Roads were controlled by a single, albeit factious, power), and Timur, coming from the west, sacked Kashgar again in the late 14th century. The area was under the control of Timur's descendants or various Mongol tribes until the Manchu army marched into Kashgar in 1755.

THE STRUGGLE FOR TURKESTAN

During the 1860s and 1870s, a series of Muslim uprisings erupted across western China, and after Russian troops were withdrawn from a 10-year occupation of the Yīlí region in 1881, waves of Uighurs, Chinese Muslims (Dungans) and Kazakhs fled into Kazakhstan and Kyrgyzstan.

In 1865 a Kokandi officer named Yaqub Beg seized Kashgaria, proclaimed an independent Turkestan and made diplomatic contacts with Britain and Russia. A few years later, however, a Manchu army returned, Beg committed suicide and Kashgaria was formally incorporated into China's newly created Xīnjiāng (New Frontier) province. With the fall of the Qing dynasty in 1911, Xīnjiāng came under the rule of a succession of warlords, over whom the Kuomintang (KMT; the Chinese Republic) had very little control.

The only real attempt to establish an independent state was in the 1940s, when a Kazakh named Osman led a rebellion of Uighurs, Kazakhs and Mongols. He took control of southwestern Xīnjiāng and established the Eastern Turkestan Republic in January 1945. The KMT, however, convinced the Muslims to abolish their new republic in return for a pledge of real autonomy.

With the consolidation of communist power in 1949, a Muslim league opposed to Chinese rule formed in Xīnjiāng. Conveniently for the PRC, a number of its most prominent leaders subsequently died in a mysterious plane crash on their way to hold talks in Běijīng. Organised Muslim opposition to Chinese rule collapsed, although the Kazakh Osman continued to fight until he was captured and executed by the communists in early 1951.

Since 1949 China's main goal has been to keep a lid on ethnic separatism while flooding the region with Han settlers. The Uighurs once comprised 90% of the Xīnjiāng population, today that number has dropped below 50%. Xīnjiāng's minorities make little secret of their dislike of China's policies and have staged sporadic protests over the past decades, some of them violent. Most recently, Běijīng took advantage of the events following 9/11 to further crackdown on Uighur nationalism by locking up or executing thousands of suspected 'Islamic terrorists' – with, ultimately, Washington's approval.

Climate

Like its geography, Xīnjiāng's climate is one of extremes. Turpan is the hottest spot in the country (it gets up to 47°C), and the Tarim and Jungar Basins aren't much better at the height of summer. As daunting as the heat may seem, spring (April and May) is

SILK ROAD

not a particularly good time to visit, with frequent sandstorms and clouds obscuring the landscape and making travel difficult. Unless you're up in the mountains or in the far north, the one thing you won't have to worry about is rain. Winters see the mercury plummet below zero throughout the province.

Language

Uighur, the traditional lingua franca of Xīnjiāng, is part of the Turkic language family and thus fairly similar to other regional languages you might come across such as Uzbek, Kazakh and Kyrgyz. The one exception is Tajik, which is related to Persian.

It would be hard not to notice the bilingual signs in Chinese and Arabic everywhere. In fact, the Arabic script (used phonetically – Uighur has no similarities to the Semitic languages) wasn't reinstituted until the era of Deng Xiaoping. From 1969 to 1983, Uighur was written with a Roman alphabet – phased out, it's said, because of the advantage this gave Uighurs in learning English. This may sound far fetched, until your neighbour on the bus leans over your shoulder and starts pronouncing the words in your book far more accurately than the average Chinese student.

Many Uighurs can't, or won't, speak Mandarin. Aside from the ethnic rivalries at work, the main reason is that there just aren't enough Chinese teachers in Xīnjiāng to go around. The job market implications stemming from this problem are quite serious, and the 'solution' announced in 2002, to discontinue university education in Uighur, is nothing short of wilful segregation.

That said, if you want to get the most out of travelling through Xīnjiāng, learning a little bit of Uighur will go a long way. Lonely Planet's *Central Asia Phrasebook* is a good place to start.

Getting There & Away

In addition to a host of domestic connections, you can fly to Ürümqi from a number of Central Asian cities, including: Almaty (Kazakhstan), Bishkek (Kyrgyzstan), Islamabad (Pakistan), Novosibirsk (Russia), Moscow and Tashkent (Uzbekistan). There's also

---

THE BEGINNING OR THE END?

Uighurs have, with good reason, always viewed Han Chinese as invaders, and relations between the two nationalities have never been good. However, ties have become far more strained since the early 1950s, when communist China began its policy of bolstering the Xīnjiāng population with Han settlers.

Although China has invested a fair amount of money in developing Xīnjiāng's economy and infrastructure, Uighurs frequently argue that all the good jobs and business opportunities are dominated by Han Chinese. A look through Xīnjiāng's towns and cities shows little integration between the two ethnicities, although there seems to be more Han-Uighur interaction in the capital, Ürümqi. Even there, however, it's possible to detect the underlying tension.

This long simmering Uighur resentment boiled over in February 1997 when Muslim separatists in the northern city of Yíníng started riots that led to a swift crackdown by Chinese security forces. At least nine people died and nearly 200 were injured, making the protest the most violent to date, according to the Chinese media.

Hundreds of Muslim residents were arrested for their roles in the riots: three were executed on the day of their trial, the rest were given life sentences. These arrests sparked several deadly responses. In late February separatists blew up three buses in Ürümqi, killing at least nine passengers and wounding many others.

The violence returned to Yíníng in April 1997, when a mob attacked prison vehicles transporting some of the convicted February rioters. Again, several people were killed or wounded. In 2001, Chinese secret police raided a number of Uighur underground mosques in Korla; one prominent leader and a handful of others were tried and executed. Uighurs in exile have vowed to continue the campaign of violent protest until Xīnjiāng gains its freedom from Běijīng. At the same time, Běijīng has clamped down heavily on separatist activities and is keeping a close watch on all of Xīnjiāng's Muslims. The question now is: were the February riots the start of a long march towards secession or the last gasp of a hopeless cause?

talk of a new flight to Lahore (Pakistan). Tashkent, Islamabad and Lahore may soon connect with Kashgar as well.

There are overland border crossings with Pakistan (Khunjerab Pass), Kyrgyzstan (Irkeshtam and Torugart Passes) and Kazakhstan (Korgas, Ālāshānkǒu, Tǎchéng and Jímùnǎi). Apart from Ālāshānkǒu, China's rail link with Kazakhstan, all of these borders crossings are by bus, though you can generally get a bike over. Remember that borders open and close frequently due to changes in government policy; additionally, many are only open when the weather permits. It's always best to check with the Public Security Bureau (PSB; Gōngānjú) in Ürümqi for the official line, or Lonely Planet's Thorn Tree to see what other travellers are saying. A new crossing, the Kulma Pass to Tajikistan, may open to foreign travel in the coming years.

Heading back into China, the obvious route is the train running through Gānsù. More rugged approaches are along the southern Silk Road from Charklik to Qīnghǎi, and Karghilik to Ali (Tibet).

Getting Around

The railway coming from Gānsù splits in two near Turpan, with one branch heading west through Ürümqi to Kazakhstan, and the other going southwest along the Tarim Basin to Kashgar. Apart from this, travel around Xīnjiāng involves a lot of sitting on buses.

Bear in mind that although flying around the province may seem like a time-saver, flights are sometimes cancelled due to 'bad weather', this usually means there aren't enough passengers. Frustrating as it is, there's really nothing you can do if this happens, except wait another 12 to 24 hours for the next flight – or get a refund on your ticket and take the bus instead. In the event that there really is a sandstorm, there is no choice but to wait it out.

ÜRÜMQI 乌鲁木齐
☎ 0991 / pop 2,800,000

As its name in Mongolian suggests, Ürümqi (Wūlǔmùqí or Wūshì) must once have been beautiful pastureland. Coming back from Tiān Chí (Heaven Lake) in spring, you'll see green plains running up against the Tiān Shān range, and if it weren't for the enormous capital and congested highways, you

could almost imagine the nomadic Kazakhs passing through with their herds of sheep.

Well, maybe not. The days of romanticised bucolic life are long gone from this increasingly teeming city – otherwise known as the furthest place in the world from an ocean (2250km). In the past decade Ürümqi has undergone a major facelift, with soaring skyscrapers, a hotwired economy and a steadily growing international population of Russian, Kazakh and Pakistani businessmen. Oil is a major source of revenue, and trainloads of migrant Han Chinese have all jumped on the western bandwagon, opening the new shops and businesses constantly appearing on the urban horizon.

Apart from the provincial museum and nearby Tiān Chí, there's little to see here. Ürümqi is basically a practical hub, from where you can make all the necessary preparations for various trips through Xīnjiāng, Central Asia or back towards China.

Orientation

Ürümqi is a sprawling metropolis and you'll need to take taxis or buses to get around. The city centre revolves around Minzhu Lu, Zhongshan Lu and Xinhua Beilu, where government offices, fancier hotels and department stores are located. Not far from here are the Xidaqiao and Hongshan intersections, both of which are important transport hubs. The train and long-distance bus stations are in the southwestern corner of the city.

Information
BOOKSHOPS
Foreign Languages Bookshop (Wàiwén Shūdiàn; ⊙ 10.30am-8.30pm) On Xinhua Beilu, just south of Minzhu Lu.

INTERNET ACCESS
Tóngxīn Wǎnglù (Xinhua Beilu; per hr Y2) An enormous Internet café directly to the right of the China Merchant's Bank. It's through the nondescript doorway and down a flight of stairs.

INTERNET RESOURCES
www.uygurworld.com Comprehensive introduction to the Uighur, with interesting links and an English-Uighur dictionary.
http://depts.washington.edu/uwch/silkroad One of the best online resources concerning the Silk Road. Of particular interest is the virtual art exhibit and related timeline.

WHICH TIME IS IT?

Xīnjiāng is several time zones removed from Běijīng, which prefers to ignore the fact. While all of China officially runs on Běijīng time *(Běijīng shíjiān)*, most of Xīnjiāng runs on an unofficial Xīnjiāng time *(Xīnjiāng shíjiān)*, two hours behind Běijīng time. Thus 9am Běijīng time is 7am Xīnjiāng time. Almost all government-run services such as the bank, post office, bus station and airlines run on Běijīng time. To cater for the time difference, government offices (including the post office and CITS) generally operate from 10am to 1.30pm and from 4pm to 8pm. Unless otherwise stated, we use Běijīng time in this book. To be sure, though, if you arrange a time with someone make sure you know which, as well as what, time.

www.silk-road.com Covers history, travel and culture along the Silk Road.

www.silkroadproject.org Focuses on the musical heritage of the Silk Road.

MONEY

Bank of China (中国银行; Zhōngguó Yínháng; cnr Jiefang Beilu & Dongfeng Lu; ☼ 9.30am-7pm Mon-Fri, 11am-5pm Sat & Sun) To date, no ATMs in Xīnjiāng accept foreign debit cards.

POST

Post office (yóujú; Hongshan intersection; ☼ 9.30am-8.30pm) The main branch handles all international parcels. There is also a post office on Zhongshan Lu, near the corner of Xinhua Nanlu.

TOURIST INFORMATION & TRAVEL AGENCIES

China International Travel Service (中国国际旅行社; CITS; Zhōngguó Guójì Lǚxíngshè; ☎ 230 5238; Xinhua Beilu; ☼ 10am-1.30pm & 4-7.30pm Mon-Fri) The Central Asian bureau is on the 4th floor of the Xīnjiāng Dàjiǔdiàn. It has information on Kazakhstan visas.

Ecol Travel (☎ 886 1578; Bógédá Bīnguǎn gate) This agency has the best rates around for trips to Kanas Lake, but all hotels are able to book tickets and trips.

VISAS

PSB (公安局; Gōngānjú; ☎ 281 0452, ext 3456; ☼ 10am-1.30pm & 4-6pm Mon-Fri) The PSB is planning to relocate to Nanhu Lu in the northeast of the city; you'll need to call ahead or ask your hotel to help with directions. Check here for information on border crossings.

Dangers & Annoyances

In addition to the usual problems of petty theft around the bus and train stations, there have also been reports of solo female travellers being sexually harassed in Ürümqi.

Sights

XINJIANG AUTONOMOUS REGION MUSEUM
新疆自治区博物馆

For those even remotely interested in the Silk Road, the provincial **museum** (Xīnjiāng Zìzhìqū Bówùguǎn; ☎ 453 6436; 132 Xibei Lu; admission Y25; ☼ 10am-1.30pm & 3.30-6.30pm) is a must. Prime exhibits are the preserved bodies and garments of nearly a dozen people discovered in tombs throughout Xīnjiāng. The most well known is the 4000-year-old 'Loulan Beauty' of Indo-European ancestry, who became something of a Uighur independence symbol in the 1990s. There are also excellent displays from all the major archaeological sites, including Niya, Loulan, Astana and Jiaohe. This is your best opportunity for learning about the lost cities of Xīnjiāng, as they're now all either bare or off-limits (in particular Loulan, near one of China's nuclear test sites). Some of the highlights include the Tang figurines and silk paintings from the Astana Graves, and a proto-boomerang discovered outside Hāmì from 1000 BC.

Major renovations have been ongoing for a number of years. Until final completion (estimated in 2006), only two rooms containing the museum highlights are open to the public. New exhibitions planned include Buddhist frescoes from the Kizil Caves (p789) and an introduction to grasslands culture. From the Hongshan intersection, take bus No 7 for four stops and ask to get off at the museum *(bówùguǎn)*.

PEOPLE'S PARK & HONGSHAN PARK
人民公园、红山公园

There are two major parks in the city. **People's Park** (Rénmín Gōngyuán; admission Y5; ☼ 7.30am-dusk) is the city's green oasis while **Hongshan Park** (Hóngshān Gōngyuán; admission Y10; ☼ dawn-dusk) is more of an amusement park, though it does have better views. Both have north and south entrances.

ERDAOQIAO MARKET 二道桥市场

This former Uighur market (Èrdàoqiáo Shìchǎng) is no better than a Chinese-run tourist trap these days, but the streets to

Kazakh women making felt with Tiān Shān (p804) in the background, Xīnjiāng

A camel caravan travels through the Taklamakan Desert (p799), Xīnjiāng

A Tajik camel driver on the Silk Road (p796), Xīnjiāng

The 44m-high Emin Minaret (p785) and adjoining mosque in Turpan, Xīnjiāng

Crowds gather at the Sunday Market (p791) in Kashgar, Xīnjiāng

An Uighur man in Turpan (p784), Xīnjiāng

Arid terrain reflected in Karakul Lake
(p796), Xīnjiāng

Snow on the Khunjerab Pass (p795), border between China and Pakistan,
Xīnjiāng

ÜRÜMQI 乌鲁木齐

0 _____ 1 km
0 _____ 0.5 miles

INFORMATION
Bank of China 中国银行	1 D4
CITS 中国国际旅行社	(see 19)
Ecol Travel 生态旅行社	(see 7)
Foreign Languages Bookshop 外文书店	2 C4
Main Post Office 邮局	3 B3
Post Office 邮局	4 C4
Tóngxīn Wǎnglù 同心网路	5 C4

SIGHTS & ACTIVITIES pp780–2
Xinjiang Autonomous Region Museum 新疆自治区博物馆	6 A2

SLEEPING p782
Bógédá Bīnguǎn 博格达宾馆	7 C3
Hǎidé Jiǔdiàn 海德酒店	8 D4
Jīngǔ Dàjiǔdiàn 金谷大酒店	9 C4
Kǒngquè Dàshà 孔雀大厦	10 B3
Yà'ōu Bīnguǎn 亚欧宾馆	11 A5

EATING pp782–3
Kraman 可拉曼餐厅	12 B5
Vine Coffeehouse 德曼咖啡屋	13 C4

TRANSPORT pp783–4
Buses to Tiān Chí 去天池的汽车	14 B3
China Southern/ China Eastern Booking 南方航空公司/东方航空公司	15 B3
Kazakh Train Booking Office	(see 11)
Kyrgyzstan Airlines/Huaqiao Binguan 华侨宾管	16 C6
North Bus Station 长途汽车站	17 A4
Siberian Airlines/Ramada Inn 屯河华美大酒店	18 B5

OTHER
Xījiāng Dàjiǔdiàn 新疆大酒店	19 C3

To Airport (14km)
To Kazakhstan Consulate (3.3km); Airport (15km)
To Almaty (Kazakastan) (1373km)
To Tiān Chí (115km)
To Turpan (142km); Liúyuán (780km)
To Nánjiāo Bus Station (800km)

Hongshan Park 红山公园
Hóng Shān
People's Park
Renmin City Square
Erdaoqiao Market 二道桥市场
Wuyi Night Market 五一夜市
Ürümqi Train Station 火车站

SILK ROAD

the north are still the centre of Ürümqi's Uighur community.

Sleeping

BUDGET & MID-RANGE

To the right of the train station as you exit are a number of inexpensive (albeit windowless) *lǚguǎn* (hostels). If you're on a shoestring, it's worth asking around.

Yà'ōu Bīnguǎn (☎ 585 6699; dm/tw Y40/120; 🞩) The Yà'ōu has the most reliable budget accommodation. Twins are overpriced, but you should be able to get a discount. Dorms have private bathrooms.

Kǒngquè Dàshà (Pea Fowl Mansion; ☎ 988 7777; 71 Youhao Nanlu; tw Y70-260, tr Y135-285) The pick of the bunch is this modern tower with good value rooms in excellent condition.

Jīngǔ Dàjiǔdiàn (☎ 282 6788; fax 283 3613; 84 Xinhua Beilu; tw Y280-380; 🞩) The staff don't win any points for friendliness, but its central location and luxurious rooms make up for it.

Bógédá Bīnguǎn (☎ 886 3910; fax 886 5769; 10 Guangming Lu; dm/tw Y20/388; 🞩) The Bogeda has pleasant three-star twins. It also has budget accommodation, but there are only 12 dorm beds in the entire hotel, so consider calling ahead. The travel agency here comes recommended.

TOP END

Hǎidé Jiǔdiàn (Hoi Tak Hotel; ☎ 232 2828; www .hoitakhotel.com; 1 Dongfeng Lu; tw Y1200-4180; 🞩) Five-star facilities make this Hong Kong establishment the place to stay in Ürümqi. Winter rates drop as low as Y518.

Eating

Ürümqi is unpredictably cosmopolitan when it comes to eating out. As well as being a good spot to try Uighur food, such as *nang* (flat bread) or *laghman*, there's also a decent selection of regional Chinese cooking. Jianshe Lu has the largest selection of restaurants,

---

UIGHUR FOOD

Uighur cuisine includes all the trusty Central Asian standbys such as kebabs, *polo* (pilaf) and *chuchura* (dumplings), but has benefited from Chinese influence to make it the most enjoyable region of Central Asia in which to eat.

Uighurs boast endless varieties of *laghman* (*lāmiàn* in Chinese), though the usual topping is combination of mutton, peppers, tomatoes, eggplant and garlic shoots. *Suoman* are noodles fried with tomatoes, peppers, garlic and meat. *Suoman gush siz* are the vegetarian variety. *Suoman* can be quite spicy so ask for *laza siz* (without peppers) if you prefer a milder version.

Kebabs are another staple and are generally of a much better standard than the ropey *kawaps* of the Central Asian republics. *Jiger* (liver) kebabs are the low-fat variety. *Tonor* kebabs are larger and baked in an oven *tonor* – tandoori style.

Nan (breads) are a particular speciality, especially when straight out of the oven and sprinkled with poppy seeds, sesame seeds or fennel. They make a great plate for a round of kebabs. Uighur bakers also make wonderful *girde nan* (bagels).

Other snacks include *serik ash* (yellow, meatless noodles), *nokot* (chickpeas with carrot), *pintang* (meat and vegetable soup) and *gang pan* (rice with vegetables and meat). Most travellers understandably steer clear of *opke*, a broth of bobbing goat's heads and coiled, stuffed intestines.

Samsas (baked mutton dumplings) are available everywhere but the meat-to-fat ratio varies wildly. Hotan and Kashgar offer huge meat pies called *daman* or *gosh girde*. You can even get *balyk* (fried fish).

For dessert try *maroji* (vanilla ice cream churned in iced wooden barrels), *matang* (walnut fruit loaf), *kharsen meghriz* (fried dough balls filled with sugar, raisins and walnuts) or *dogh* (sometimes known as *durap*), a delicious, though potentially deadly, mix of shaved ice, syrup, yoghurt and iced water. *Tangzaza* are triangles of glutinous rice wrapped in bamboo leaves covered in syrup.

Xīnjiāng is justly famous for its fruit, whether it be *uruk* (apricots), *uzum* (grapes), *tawuz* (watermelon), *khoghun* (sweet melon) or *yimish* (raisins). The best grapes come from Turpan; the sweetest melons from Hami.

Meals are washed down with *kok chai* (green tea), often laced with nutmeg or rose petals. Uighur restaurants usually provide a miniature rubbish bin on the table in which to dispose of the waste tea after rinsing out the bowl.

ranging from Uighur staples to affordable Cantonese. During July and August, markets are awash in fresh fruit.

Kraman (Kēlāmàn; Huanghe Lu) There aren't too many places where you can get a four-course Uighur meal for Y10, but Kraman is one of them. The speciality is *polo*, or rice pilaf (*zhuāfàn*), accompanied with pickled salad, yoghurt and fresh fruit.

Vine Coffeehouse (Démàn Kāfeīwū; ☎ 230 4831; 65 Minzhu Lu; from Y18; ❀ 1.30-11.30pm, closed Mon) Direct from Curacao, this agreeable café brings you fine cuisine, fruit shakes and a Caribbean atmosphere – not bad for the world's most landlocked city. It's down a side street on the left.

The animated night markets with shish kebabs and handmade noodles are also worth a gander. The most thriving by far is the **Wuyi night market**; bus No 902 runs nearby between the train station and Xidaqiao (tell the driver '*Wǔyī yèshì*').

Getting There & Away

AIR

In addition to domestic services, Ürümqi also has international flights to neighbouring Central Asian countries. Destinations include: Almaty (Kazakhstan), Bishkek (Kyrgyzstan), Hong Kong, Islamabad (Pakistan), Novosibirsk (Russia), Moscow and Tashkent (Uzbekistan). There's also talk of a new flight to Lahore (Pakistan). It's not uncommon for these flights to be suspended, especially during the winter months.

Domestic flights connect Ürümqi with Běijīng (Y2410), Chéngdū (Y1670), Chóngqìng (Y1830), Lánzhōu (Y1190), Guǎngzhōu (Y2840), Shànghǎi (Y2800) and Xī'ān (Y1600) among others.

Destinations within Xīnjiāng include Altai (Ālètài), Hotan (Hétián), Kashgar (Kāshí), Kuqa (Kùchē), Tǎchéng and Yīníng.

China Southern and China Eastern both have booking offices next to the Kǒngquè Dàshà, but hotel travel agents will consistently get you better prices. The travel agent in the post office also books tickets at a discount.

There are two international airline offices in town: **Siberian Airlines** (☎ 286 2326; Changjiang Lu) in the Ramada Inn and **Kyrgyzstan Airlines** (☎ 231 6333; Xinhua Nanlu) in the Huáqiáo Bīnguǎn.

BUS

There are two long-distance bus stations in Ürümqi, serving northern and southern destinations. The north bus station (*chángtú qìchēzhàn*) is on Heilongjiang Lu and has sleeper buses to Tǎchéng (Y100, 12 hours), Yīníng (Y100 to Y136, 11 to 14 hours) and Bù'ěrjīn (Y90 to Y100, 13 hours). If you have a Kazakh visa, you can also go to Alamaty in Kazakhstan via a sleeper bus to Korgas (Y106, 14 hours). From Korgas it's another 12 hours to Alamaty. A longer but more pleasant trip would be to travel to Alamaty via Yīníng. Bus No 2 runs from the train station to Hongshan, passing Heilongjiang Lu on the way.

The south bus station (*nánjiāo kèyùnzhàn*) is south of the city and has frequent departures for Turpan (Y29, 2½ hours), Kuqa (Y86 to Y132, 17 hours), Kashgar (Y152 to Y177, 24 hours) and Hotan (Y220 to Y325, 19 to 26 hours), the latter crossing the Taklamakan Desert. Bus No 1 runs between Xidaqiao and the Nanjiao station; bus No 109 will get you there from Hongshan.

TRAIN

There are numerous trains to Lánzhōu; the one shown in the following table is the best choice. The schedule of direct daily departures from Ürümqi is as follows:

Destination	Train	Duration	Departs
Běijīng	T70	45hr	2.19pm
Chéngdū	1014	53hr	11.35pm
Dūnhuáng	N950	13hr	7.44pm
Kashgar	N946	23hr	3.51pm
Kuqa	N946	14hr	3.51pm
Lánzhōu	T296	25hr	6.47pm
Shànghǎi	T54	48hr	2.55am
Xī'ān	1044	53hr	8.52pm

There are trains departing Ürümqi twice a week for Almaty, Kazakhstan on Monday and Saturday at midnight. The journey takes a slow 32 hours, six of which is spent at both the Chinese and Kazakh customs. Tickets start at Y480 and can only be purchased in the lobby of the Yà'ōu Bīnguǎn, at the **booking office** (❀ 10am-1pm & 3.30-6pm Thu-Mon). To undertake this journey, you will, of course, need a visa for Kazakhstan.

Getting Around
TO/FROM THE AIRPORT
The airport is 16km from the Hongshan intersection; a taxi costs about Y40. If you're in no hurry, bus No 51 runs between Hongshan intersection and the airport gate, but takes about an hour. From the gate you'll need to hire a three-wheeler.

BUS
Buses all cost Y1. Some of the more useful bus routes include No 7, which runs up Xinhua Lu through the Xidaqiao and Hongshan intersections, linking the city centre with the main post office; and No 2, which runs from the train station through the Hongshan intersection and way up along Beijing Lu. Bus No 1 goes from the south bus station through the city centre to Xidaqiao and the Bógédá Bīnguǎn, and No 109 goes from the Nanjiao bus station to Hongshan. Bus No 8 runs from the train station along Heilongjiang Lu to the Minzhu Lu traffic circle.

AROUND ÜRÜMQI
Tiān Chí 天池
Two thousand metres up in the Tiān Shān mountain range is **Tiān Chí** (Heaven Lake; admission Y60), a small, deep-blue lake presided over by the lofty 5445m Peak of God (Bógédá Fēng). Scattered across the spruce-covered slopes are the yurts (circular tents) of the Kazakh people who inhabit these mountains in the summer. Though heavily touristed, the scenery is still stunning, and there's plenty of backcountry to hike around and get away from it all. You can also take long horse treks up to the snow line, although these get mixed reviews.

In late May Kazakhs begin setting up their yurts around the lake for tourist accommodation (Y40 per person with three meals); Rashit is the most well known host. The yurts near the ticket office are authentic and take boarders (Y10), unfortunately you'll need to hitch a ride the rest of the way up. Alternatively, you can camp out.

Buses to the Tiān Chí car park leave Ürümqi from 9am to 9.30am from the north gate of People's Park and return between 5pm and 6pm. The return fare is Y50 and the trip takes about 2½ hours. The drivers may annoyingly charge you Y50 even if you plan on spending the night – if this

happens, try to arrange a pick-up time for the next day.

From the car park, there's a chairlift (Y15 return), bus (Y15 return) or you can hoof it an hour uphill. The path starts left of the chairlift.

Regardless of the temperature in Ürümqi, take warm clothes and rain gear, as the weather can be unpredictable.

DÀHÉYÁN 大河沿
Fifty-eight kilometres from the Turpan oasis is Dàhéyán (marked Tǔlǔfān on schedules), the nearest train station. Minibuses run from here to Turpan (Y7.5, 1 hour) once every 30 minutes throughout the day, starting at 6.30am. Shared taxis are Y10 per person.

Most travellers are interested in trains heading east or west, since people going to Ürümqi usually opt for the bus, which is much faster than trekking up here to catch a train. There are daily trains to Běijīng, Chéngdū, Lánzhōu (22 hours), Xī'ān and Kashgar (21 hours). Eastbound trains also pass through Dūnhuáng (eight hours) and Jiāyùguān (11 hours).

You can buy tickets at the station or through a travel agent in Turpan. It can be difficult to get a hard sleeper east, as many of these berths will have already been sold from Ürümqi. If worse comes to worse, buy a hard seat and try your luck with an upgrade.

TURPAN 吐鲁番
☎ 0995 / pop 56,000
Turpan (Tǔlǔfān) is one of those legendary Xīnjiāng names whose reputation precedes it. An oasis in the Turpan Basin, its various settlements have long been a stopover on the northern route of the Silk Road as well as a home to Indo-Europeans, Chinese and Uighurs. At 154m below sea level, it's perhaps even better known as the second lowest depression in the world (after the Dead Sea) and the hottest spot in China – the highest recorded temperature here was 49.6°C!

The drab communist architecture that has invaded most of Xīnjiāng is covered up with the occasional grapevine trellis, a visual treat and a godsend in the fierce heat of summer. With its stress-free atmosphere, Turpan is a good place to take it easy for a few days, and while the sights aren't overwhelming, there is enough here to keep you occupied.

History

There have been settlements in the Turpan Basin since before the Han dynasty; the inhabitants have ranged from Indo-Europeans (possibly Tocharians related to the mummies in Ürümqi's museum) to the Chinese and Uighurs. The original Han outpost was in Jiaohe, although the Tang city of Gaochang went on to replace it in prominence.

In the mid-9th century, the ancestors of the Uighurs were forced from their homeland in Mongolia, with one group eventually settling in Gaochang (Khocho). The city was the Uighur capital up to 1250, and saw the Uighurs transform from nomads to farmers, and Manicheans to Buddhists. Turpan was probably not settled until after the Uighurs convered to Islam in the 14th century.

Orientation

Turpan is not a hard place to get around in. You'll find the hotels, restaurants, market and long-distance bus station all in the centre and within easy walking distance. Most of the sights are scattered in the surrounding desert.

Information

The **Bank of China** (Zhōngguó Yínháng; Laocheng Lu; 9.30am-1pm & 4.30-8pm) can change cash and travellers cheques. Heading west down the same street brings you to the main **post office** (10am-8pm); another branch is across from the main square. There are a couple of Internet bars just north of the main square on Gaochang Lu charging Y2 per hour.

CITS (☎ 852 1352; 8am-9pm) has a branch in the Jiāotōng Bīnguǎn and can help book train and plane tickets, as well as arrange tours of local sights.

The **Public Service Bureau** (PSB; Gōngānjú; Gaochang Lu) is north of downtown; they'd rather you went to the capital for anything other than the most mundane requests.

Sights

EMIN MINARET 额敏塔

Emin Hoja, a Turpan ruler, founded this Afghan-style mosque and **minaret** (Émín Tǎ; admission Y20; dawn-dusk) in 1777. Also known as Sūgōng Tǎ, this is one of the prettiest structures you'll see in Xīnjiāng. The circular minaret was designed with simple brick motifs, and the austere, dark interior contrasts nicely with the lush green of the grape fields outside. You can climb to the mosque's roof, but cannot enter the minaret.

The dusty, tree-lined streets of old Turpan that lead to the mosque are evocative of how the entire town must have once looked, and make for a pleasant 3km walk or bike ride.

CITY MOSQUE 清真寺

There are several other mosques (Qīngzhēn Sì) in town. The most active of them is on the western outskirts about 3km from the town centre. You can get here by bicycle.

TURPAN MUSEUM 吐鲁番博物馆

Outside of a mummified Tang dynasty dumpling, there's not a whole lot in the local **museum** (Tǔlǔfān Bówùguǎn; Gaochang Lu; admission Y20; 9am-7.30pm). There are some small exhibits from Astana and Gaochang, however the majority of artefacts have been moved to the provincial museum in Ürümqi.

Sleeping

Jiāotōng Bīnguǎn (☎ 853 1320; 125 Laocheng Lu; dm/tr/tw Y25/34/160; 🔀) This hotel is in a noisy location, and hence the cheapest spot in town. All things considered though, the rooms here are fairly reasonable.

Gāochāng Bīnguǎn (☎ 852 3229; 330 Gaochang Lu; tw Y100-128, tr Y120; 🔀) While not at the heart of the action, the Gaochang is clean, quiet and has inexpensive twins and triples.

Tǔlǔfān Bīnguǎn (☎ 852 2301; lfhan-tl@mailxj .cninfo.net; 2 Qingnian Lu; dm/tw Y25/380; 🔀 🖳) This is Turpan's top hotel, with evening performances and even a swimming pool. The five-person dorms are a bit crowded, but it certainly has a more pleasant atmosphere than other hotels in town.

Oasis Hotel (Lüzhōu Bīnguǎn; ☎ 852 2491; www.the -silk-road.com; 41 Qingnian Beilu; tw Y338-728; 🔀) The Oasis tried commendably to incorporate local aesthetics into its hotel design, but for whatever reason (perhaps the unrefurbished rooms?), it's just not that enticing.

Eating

John's Information Café (Qingnian Nanlu; dishes from Y10; ☯ 7am-10pm) This place serves Western and Chinese meals in a shaded courtyard. The menu is in English, prices are fair and you can even get cold drinks with ice (much appreciated in Turpan's heat!).

For Uighur cooking, nothing beats the food court at the **Bazaar** (Shì Màoyì Shìchǎng), though finding the stalls – not the handful on the main alley – requires a bit of patience. The fresh 'pull noodles' (sozoup laghman) are excellent.

In addition to the lively market action surrounding the public square, dinner choices also include a string of hybrid Uighur-Chinese restaurants that set up tables under the trees on Qingnian Lu. Laghman and Chinese dishes run from Y5 to Y10.

Entertainment

A traditional Uighur music, song and dance show is staged at Tǔlǔfān Bīnguǎn in the courtyard nightly at 9pm in the high season (Y20). They're fun nights that usually end up with some of the audience being dragged out to dance with the performers.

Getting There & Away

The nearest train station is at Dàhéyán (p784), 58km north of Turpan. Minibuses to Dàhéyán (Y7.5, one hour) run approximately every 30 minutes between 8.30am and 8pm.

Buses to Ürümqi (Y25, 2½ hours) run every 20 minutes between 8am to 8pm. There is one daily bus at 11.30am to Kashgar (Y132, 26 hours) via Kuqa (Y65, 15 hours).

Getting Around

Public transport around Turpan is by taxi, minibus or bicycle. Bicycles, available from John's Café, are most convenient for the town itself.

AROUND TURPAN

There are a plethora of sights in the countryside around Turpan, some of which are fascinating and others that are a complete waste of time. The only way to see them is to sign up for a tour – you won't have to look for the drivers, they'll find you. Private 'tours' run by cabbies generally work out best as you can pick and choose what you want to see. In a group of four, figure on paying between Y50 and Y70 (depending on what you visit) per person. The CITS minibus is a reliable Y50 for eight sights, but you're pretty much locked into the standard programme.

You can definitely skip the **Astana Graves** (阿斯塔那古墓区; Āsītǎnà Gǔmùqū; admission Y20) and the **Bezeklik Caves** (柏孜克里克千佛洞; Bózīkèlǐkè Qiānfó Dòng; admission Y20), both of which are essentially empty. The latter is infamous

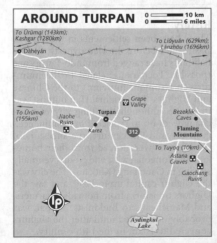

AROUND TURPAN
0   10 km
0   6 miles

To Ürümqi (143km);
Kashgar (1280km)

To Liǔyuán (629km);
Lánzhōu (1696km)

Dàhéyán

Grape
Valley

To Ürümqi
(155km)

Jiaohe
Ruins

Turpan

Karez

312

Bezeklik
Caves

Flaming
Mountains

To Tuyoq (10km)

Astana
Graves

Gaochang
Ruins

Aydingkul
Lake

KAREZ

The *karez* is a peculiarly Central Asian means of irrigation that can be found in Xīnjiāng, Afghanistan and Iran. Like many dry, arid countries Xīnjiāng has great underground reservoirs of water, which can transform otherwise barren stretches of land – if you can get the water up. This subterranean water is often so far underground that drilling or digging for it, with primitive equipment, is virtually impossible.

Long ago the Uighurs devised a better way. They dig a *karez*, known as the 'head well', on higher ground, where snowmelt from the mountains collects (in Turpan's case, the Bogda Mountains). A long underground tunnel is then dug to conduct this water down to the village farmland. A whole series of vertical wells, looking from above like giant anthills, are dug every 20m along the path of this tunnel to aid construction and provide access. The wells are fed entirely by gravity, thus eliminating the need for pumps. Furthermore, having the channels underground greatly reduces water loss from evaporation.

Digging a *karez* is skilled and dangerous work and the *karez-kans* are respected and highly paid workers. The cost of making and maintaining a *karez* was traditionally split between a whole village and the *karez* was communally owned.

The city of Turpan owes its existence to these vital wells and channels, some of which were constructed over 2000 years ago. There are over a thousand wells, and the total length of the channels runs to an incredible 5000km, all constructed by hand and without modern machinery or building materials.

for having many of its distinctive murals cut out of the rock face by German archaeologists in 1905. Some buses may stop at **Grape Valley** (葡萄沟; Pútao Gōu; admission Y20) for lunch, but outside of the September harvest it's hardly a must see.

Two possible additions to tours include a **karez** (以儿井; kǎněrjǐng; admission Y20) – though if you're travelling through Xīnjiāng, you'll have other opportunities to see less touristy ones – and **Aydingkul Lake** (艾丁湖; Àidīng Hú), the second lowest lake in the world. Be forewarned that it's more of a muddy, salt-encrusted flat than a lake.

You'll be gone for the day, so don't underestimate the weather. The desert sun is hot – damn hot. Essential survival gear includes a water bottle, sunscreen, sunglasses and a hat.

Tuyoq 吐峪沟

Set in a green valley fringed by the Flaming Mountains, this tiny grape-producing **village** (Tǔyùgōu; admission Y30) is an excellent place to explore traditional Uighur life and architecture. Tuyoq has been a pilgrimage site for Muslims for centuries, and the devout claim that seven trips here equal one trip to Mecca. The *mazar*, or symbolic tomb of the first Uighur Muslim, is the object of pilgrimage, and is within the earthen walls on the hillside above the village. Up the gorge are a series of Buddhist caves dating back to the 3rd century AD. Only four are open to the public, and though they've been defaced, it's an adventurous scramble up the cliff side.

Tuyoq is not yet on the standard tour, and private drivers may raise their prices slightly to include it.

Jiaohe Ruins 交河故城

During the Han dynasty, **Jiaohe** (Jiāohé Gùchéng; admission Y30) was established by the Chinese as a garrison town to defend the borderlands. The buildings are more obvious than the ruins of Gaochang, and you can walk through the old streets and along the roads. A main road cuts through the city; at the end is a large monastery with Buddhist figures still visible. If you only visit one desert city, make it this one.

The ruins are around 7km to 8km west of Turpan and stand on a plateau bound by two small rivers – thus the name Jiāohé, which means 'confluence of rivers'. During the cooler months you can cycle out here.

Gaochang (Khocho) Ruins 高昌故城

Founded in the 7th century during the Tang dynasty, **Gaochang** (Gāochāng Gùchéng; admission Y20), also known as Khocho, or sometimes Kharakhoja, became the Uighur capital in 850. A major staging post on the Silk Road, its ruins have provided much insight into the cosmopolitan population of Central Asia. Texts in classical Uighur, Sanskrit, Chinese and Tibetan have all been unearthed here, as well as evidence of a Nestorian church and a significant Manichean community – a dualistic Persian religion that borrowed figures from Christianity, Buddhism and Hinduism.

The city was divided into an outer city, inner city, palace and government compound. Today, though the earthen walls of the city (once 12m thick) are clearly visible, not much else is in good condition. You'll have to flex your imagination to visualise anything apart from the large Buddhist monastery in the southwest.

Flaming Mountains 火焰山

Around Bezeklik and Tuyoq are the Flaming Mountains (Huǒyàn Shān), whose midday appearance is compared to multicoloured tongues of fire. The Flaming Mountains were immortalised in the Chinese classic *Journey to the West* as a mountainous inferno that the monk Tripitaka had to pass through. Thankfully for Tripitaka, Sun Wukong (Monkey) managed to obtain a magic fan with which to extinguish the blaze. Though the story is far removed from the actual life of the Tang pilgrim Xuan Zang, who journeyed some 5000km to India and back in search of Buddhist scriptures, it's easy to see how the legend arose. You can clamber around in places, but only in the early morning – and don't forget your fan.

KUQA 库车
☎ 0997 / pop 63,500
The oasis town of Kuqa (Kùchē) was an important Buddhist city-state on the ancient Silk Road. It was here that Kumarajiva (AD 344?–413), the first great translator of Buddhist sutras from Sanskrit into Chinese, was born to an Indian father and Kuqean princess, before later being abducted to Dūnhuáng and then Cháng'ān to manage translations of the Buddhist canon. When the 7th-century monk Xuan Zang passed through, he recorded that two enormous 30m-high Buddha statues flanked Kuqa's western gate, and that the nearby monasteries held upwards of 5000 monks.

Though the numerous Buddhist caves and ruined cities bespeak of times past, sadly, modern-day Kuqa retains little of its former glory. It's now a bizarre juxtaposition of strip-mall architecture and traditional donkey cart life, and the main thing you'll get out of visit here is an accurate glimpse at how the Uighurs of today really live.

Orientation & Information
The main thoroughfare that connects the new and old parts of town is Tianshan Lu/ Renmin Lu (new town/old town). The bus station is east of town on Tianshui Lu, and the train station a further 5km southeast.

The **Bank of China** (中国银行; Zhōngguó Yínháng; ☻ 9.30am-8pm) is at 25 Tianshan Donglu. The Liántóng Wǎngbā on Youyi Lu just south of Wenhua Lu has Internet access on the second floor.

Sights
BAZAAR & MOSQUE 巴扎、清真寺
Every Friday a large bazaar (Lǎochéng Bāzā) is held about 2.5km west of town, next to a bridge on Renmin Lu. Traders come in from around the countryside to ply their animals, wares and foodstuffs. The bazaar is thus far largely a local affair, and is worth a visit.

About 150m further west from the bazaar is a small mosque (Qīngzhēn Sì) where large crowds of worshippers congregate on Friday afternoon. North of here through the old town is the Great Mosque (Qīngzhēn Dàsì), though it's less animated than its smaller counterpart.

To get here from the new town, take bus Nos 1 or 3 from Tianshan Lu.

QIUCI ANCIENT CITY RUINS 龟兹故城
These 'ruins' (Qiūcí Gùchéng) are all that is left of the capital of Qiūcí, one of several ancient feudal states. The ruins are on the main road, about a 20-minute walk northwest of the main intersection where Tianshan Lu forks in two.

Sleeping & Eating
Jiāotōng Bīnguǎn (交通宾馆; ☎ 712 2682; tw Y50-100; ✖) The old standby, the bus station hotel, comes through again. The more expensive twins have air-con and hot water after 10pm.

Kùchē Bīnguǎn (库车宾馆; ☎ 712 2901; 76 Jiefang Lu; tw Y120-188, tr/q Y138/160; ✖) Kuqa's main hotel has clean, renovated rooms near the city centre. It's easiest to catch a motorcab here.

The best place to get a bite to eat is under the shaded awnings at the **vegetable market** (菜市场; *cài shìchǎng*) south of the Youyi Lu and Tianshan Lu intersection. There are the usual kebabs, noodles and *samsas* (mutton dumplings) available for a few *yuán*.

Getting There & Away

AIR

The airport east of the city theoretically has flights to Ürümqi (Y590) three days a week. A taxi there costs Y10.

BUS

Leaving Kuqa by bus can be confusing, and it doesn't help that the bus station staff are as confused as you are. Heading east are a variety of sleepers to Ürümqi (Y100 to Y150, 10 to 15 hours) and five daily buses to Lúntái (Y12, 1½ hours), from where you can take the cross-desert highway to Hotan. West to Kashgar (Y120, 16 hours) is a bit more vague – you have to wait for a sleeper from Ürümqi to pass, and hope that it has free berths.

Once the snow melts (mid-May), there is also a daily bus to Yīníng (Y120, 22 hours), a spectacular trip crossing the Tiān Shān range. You can try to get off at the Mongolian village of Bayanbulak, the mid-way point, but at last check the area was closed to foreigners.

TRAIN

Moving on to Ürümqi or Turpan (Y175, 14½ to 16 hours) is generally not a problem. If you're going west to Kashgar (nine to 10 hours), however, sleeper tickets are not available – you'll need to try your luck with an upgrade. Bus No 2 runs along Tianshan Lu to the train station.

Getting Around

Taxi rides are a standard Y5 per trip, while motorcabs, tractors and donkey carts are generally Y1 to Y3, depending on the distance you want to travel.

AROUND KUQA
Kizil Thousand Buddha Caves
克孜尔千佛洞

In the field of Central Asian studies, the **Kizil caves** (Kèzǐěr Qiānfó Dòng; admission Y35) are an important site. Begun in the 3rd century, the patterns and motifs are strikingly different to what you see in the Mogao Caves at

Dūnhuáng, and contain no Chinese influence whatsoever.

Unfortunately, although there are more than 230 caves here, only eight are open to the public, and these are in pretty poor shape. One cave is entirely bare (stripped by Western archaeologists), while the others have been defaced by both Muslims and Red Guards.

More interesting than the caves is the hike through the desert canyon to the spring Qiānlèi Quán. If you forgo the caves, admission is only Y5, but it's a long way to drive just to go hiking. A taxi there will cost around Y160 and takes 1½ hours.

Ancient City Ruins 苏巴什故城

There are several ruined cities in the Kuqa region, but these consist of no more than a few crumbling walls. The most famous is **Sūbāshí** (temple admission Y15, city admission Y15) 23km northeast of Kuqa, while 20km to the south is Wushkat. A taxi to Sūbāshí and back costs about Y40.

LÚNTÁI 轮台

Lúntái is a homonym for the word 'tyre', which pretty much sums it up. The town stands amid oil fields near the start of the Cross Desert Hwy (p799), and is the link between Kuqa and Hotan. To Kuqa (Y12, 1½ hours) there are buses every half-hour starting at 9.30am. If you're interested in crossing the desert from the north, you'll either need to hitch to the crossroads (40km away) or take a share taxi for around Y10 per person. Buses from Ürümqi pass by at night, so you won't see too much of the desert. If you get stuck here, the dependable Jiāotōng Bīnguǎn next to the bus station has dorms (Y15) and twins (Y100).

SOUTHWEST XĪNJIĀNG – KASHGARIA

Kashgaria is the historical name for the western Tarim Basin. Despite its present isolation, Kashgaria was a major Silk Road hub and has bristled with activity for over 2000 years. A ring of oases lined with poplar trees and centred around weekly bazaars remain a testament to the mercantile tradition. The region remains the heartland of the Uighur.

KASHGAR 喀什

☎ 0998 / pop 340,000

Even in the 21st century, the name Kashgar (Kāshí) still sparks images of a remote desert oasis, the sole outpost of civilisation leading from the vast deserts of Xīnjiāng to the icy peaks of the Karakoram. Desert brigands, exotic bazaars and colourful silks spring to mind at the mention of China's westernmost city.

Kashgar is no longer so remote, and the modern age has certainly taken its toll (emphatically symbolised by the statue of Chairman Mao – one of the largest in China). Kashgar is only 1½ hours by plane from Ürümqi, or 24 hours by sleeper bus. The old town walls have been torn down, flashy green taxis with blaring horns congest the growing sea of pavement and Chinese super freeways encircle the beleaguered old town. In 1999 the railway link from Ürümqi was formally opened, sounding what has been the death-knell for traditional Kashgar. Indeed, in 2003 over a thousand homes were torn down in the old town, many to make way for a new shopping centre.

Even so, Kashgar retains an intoxicating air of the exotic, mainly due to its fascinating ethnic mix of Uighurs, Tajiks, Kyrgyz, Uzbeks and Han Chinese. Some things haven't changed since medieval times – metalworkers and cobblers use hand tools in the old quarter and the Id Kah Mosque draws the town's faithful as it has since 1442. Markets with rows of shimmering silks, knives and jewellery vie for your attention and narrow backstreets lined with earthen-walled homes beckon for exploration.

Kashgar has been a Silk Road trading centre for two millennia and traders from Kazakhstan, Kyrgyzstan, Pakistan and even Russia (along with travellers from around the globe) continue to fuel the city with impromptu street-corner negotiations, perpetual bazaars and hotel-room deals with Gilgit (in Pakistan) traders. Shifting geopolitics have reopened lines of communication and it's not hard to imagine a new high-tech Silk Road recrossing the Tarim Basin one day. Kashgar's future, it seems, lies firmly rooted in its past.

With all the trading activity, one couldn't call Kashgar 'laid-back', but it has a great atmosphere and is a good launching pad for trips along the southern Silk Road to Hotan, over the Torugart or Irkeshtam Passes to Kyrgyzstan or south up the stunning Karakoram Hwy to Pakistan.

Orientation

Official (Chinese) street names are given here. The town centre is a Tiānānmén-style square north of People's Park, dominated by a statue of Mao Zedong. The Uighur old town lies just north of here, bisected by Jiefang Beilu.

Information

INTERNET ACCESS

Though easy to find, Internet bars were not open to foreigners at the time of writing. For now, hotels are your only option.

LAUNDRY

There is a cheap laundry service (gānxǐ diàn) next to the Caravan Café.

MEDICAL SERVICES

People's Hospital (Rénmín Yīyuàn; Jiefang Beilu) North of the river.

Clinic (under CITS bldg in Chini Bagh compound) Can administer first aid and medicines. Some staff speak English.

MONEY

Bank of China (Zhōngguó Yínháng; main square; ☼ 9.30am-1.30pm & 4-7.30pm) Can change travellers cheques and cash; ditto with the branch west at 239 Renmin Xilu. You can also sell yuán back into US dollars at the bank's foreign exchange desk if you have exchange receipts; a good idea if you are headed to Tashkurgan, where the bank hours are erratic.

POST

Post office (yóujú; 40 Renmin Xilu; ☼ 9.30am-8pm) The second floor handles all foreign letters and packages.

TOURIST INFORMATION & TRAVEL AGENCIES

The **Caravan Café** (p793) and **John's Café** (p793) both organise bookings, transport and excursions and can link you up with other budget-minded travellers to help share costs.

Elvis (elvisablimit@yahoo.com) Otherwise known as Ablimit Ghopor, Elvis is another good contact to have. A local Uighur, Elvis' main business is buying and selling carpets (ask his advice if you're considering a purchase), but he also takes tourists on offbeat tours of the old town and lines up desert treks. He operates out of the Old City Restaurant across from the Seman Hotel.

KASHGAR 喀什

0 ———————— 1 km
0 ———————— 0.5 miles

INFORMATION
Bank of China 中国银行 1 A4
CITS 中国国际旅行社 ....(see 3)
CTS 中国旅行社 ....(see 19)
Former British Consulate
英国领事馆 2 B3
Health Clinic 诊所 3 B3
Laundry 干洗店 ....(see 19)
Main Bank of China 中国银行 4 B4
Old City Restaurant
喀地美协海尔饭店 5 A3
Post Office 邮局 6 A3
PSB 公安局 7 A3

SIGHTS & ACTIVITIES   pp791–3
Id Kah Mosque 艾提尕尔清真寺 ... 8 B3
Kashgar Regional Museum
喀什地区博物馆 9 D3
Mao Statue 毛泽东塑像 10 B3
Old Town Admission Gate 11 C3
Old Town Walls 12 A3
Tomb of Yusup Has
玉素甫哈斯哈吉甫陵墓 13 B4

SLEEPING   p793
Chini Bagh Hotel
其尼瓦克宾馆 14 B3
Kāshí Gáěr Bīnguǎn
喀什噶尔宾馆 15 D3
Noor Bish Hotel 脑北西饭店 ... 16 B3
Sēmǎn Bīnguǎn 色满宾馆 ... 17 A3
Tiānnán Fàndiàn 天南饭店 ... 18 C4

EATING   p793
Caravan Cafe 凯瑞咖啡 19 B3
Chinese Food Stalls 熟食馆 ... 20 A4
Intizar 银提扎尔餐厅 21 B3

John's Cafe 约翰中西餐厅 ....(see 17)
Night Market 夜市 22 B3
Uighur Teahouse 茶馆 23 B3

SHOPPING   pp793–4
Uyghur Musical Instrument Factory ... 24 B3

TRANSPORT   pp794–5
CAAC Office 中国民航公司 25 B4
International Bus Station
国际汽车站 26 B2
Long-Distance Bus Station 喀什汽车站 ...27 C4

To People's Hospital;
Airport (12km);
Irkeshtam Pass (215km);
Torugart Pass (312km);
Ürümqi (1180km);

To Abakh
Hoja Tomb (1.5km);
Ha Noi Ruins (35km)

Youmulakexia Lu
尤木拉克夏路

Seman Lu 色满路

色满路 Seman Lu

Renmin Xilu

Old Town

Old Town

Sunday Market

Aizirete Lu 艾孜热特路

Tawuguzi Lu

To Train Station (10km)

River

Tumin

Renmin Xilu 人民西路

Square

人民公园 Renmin Park

Tiyu Nanu Lu

Jiefang Beilu

Renmin Donglu 人民东路

Binhe Lu

Anisilahan Lu

Payinaru Lu

Dong Lake
东湖

Youmulakexia Lu

Kuli'keduowei Lu

Naru Nanlu 那如南路

Tuyu Lu

To Livestock Market

To Tashkurgan (240km);
Pakistani Border (1012km)

To Yarkand (175km);
Hotan (472km);
Tibet (600km)

CITS (Zhōngguó Guójì Lǚxíngshè; ☎ 298 3156) The main office is up one flight of stairs in a building just outside the Chini Bagh Hotel.

China Travel Service (CTS; Zhōngguó Lǚxíngshè; ☎ 283 2875) CTS has an independent office next to the Caravan Café.

VISAS
PSB (Gōngānjú 111 Youmulakexia Lu; 9.30am-1.30pm & 4-8pm) You can extend your visa here.

Dangers & Annoyances
Travellers have lost money or passports to pickpockets at the Sunday Market, in the ticket scrum at the bus station, and even on local buses, so keep yours tucked away.

Some foreign women walking the streets alone have been sexually harassed. The Mus-lim Uighur women dress in long skirts and heavy stockings like the Uighur women in Ürümqi and Turpan, but here one sees more female faces hidden behind veils of brown gauze. It is wise for women travellers to dress as would be appropriate in any Mus-lim country, covering arms and legs. This should be second nature for travellers who have come from Pakistan but it may come as a surprise if you've come from Kyrgyzstan, Kazakhstan or eastern China.

Sights
SUNDAY MARKET & LIVESTOCK MARKET
星期天市场、动物市场
Once a week Kashgar's population swells by 50,000 as people stream in to the Sunday

SILK ROAD

Market – surely one of the most mind-boggling bazaars in Asia, and not to be missed. By sunrise the roads east of town are a sea of pedestrians, horses, bikes, motorcycles, donkey carts, trucks and belching tuk-tuks, everyone shouting, 'Boish-boish!' (coming through!).

Southeast of the city is the Livestock Market (Mal Bazaar; Dòngwù Shìchǎng), where buyers can 'test-drive' horses or peer into sheep's mouths. A wonderful assortment of people gather here, with old men stopping to trim their beards and makeshift produce stalls set up on the ground outside the giant corral. The actual 'Sunday Market' itself (Yengi Bazaar; Xīngqītiān Shìchǎng) is open daily, and a little less crowded on weekdays. This is where you'll find carpets, clothing and boots, hardware and junk, tapes and boomboxes – and, of course, hats.

A taxi to the Sunday Market is Y5, and to the Livestock Market Y10. Otherwise, bus No 16 runs to the Livestock Market from the main square.

Kashgar's Sunday Market can get fairly touristy, but don't be discouraged, there are plenty of other lesser-known markets to visit. For starters, try the Sunday market at Hotan (p798), the Monday market in Upal (p796), the Tuesday market in Charbagh (p797) or the Friday market in Kuqa (p788).

OLD TOWN

Sprawling on both sides of Jiefang Lu are roads full of Uighur shops and narrow passages lined with adobe houses that seem trapped in a time warp. Despite gradually disappearing, the old town is still one of the most fascinating places in Xīnjiāng to take in the incredible ethnic diversity of Central Asia. Be warned that the residential area far to the east has been transformed into a money-maker – you have to pay Y10 just to enter! The Chinese-approved 'civilized homes' in this quarter are predictably drab, and you're much better off wandering through the lively 'uncivilized' areas west of here.

At the eastern end of Seman Lu stands a 10m-high section of the former town walls, which are at least 500 years old.

ID KAH MOSQUE 艾提尕尔清真寺

The yellow-tiled **Id Kah Mosque** (Ài Tígǎ'ěr Qīngzhēn Sì; admission Y10) is one of the largest in China, with a courtyard and gardens that

can hold 20,000 people during the annual Qurban Baiyram celebrations. It was built in 1442 as a smaller mosque on what was then the outskirts of town.

It's acceptable for non-Muslims to go into Id Kah. Local women are rarely seen inside but Western women are usually ignored if they're modestly dressed (arms and legs covered and a scarf on the head). Take off your shoes if entering carpeted areas, and be discreet about photos.

ABAKH HOJA TOMB 香妃墓

On the northeastern outskirts of town is the **Abakh Hoja Maziri** (Xiāngfēimù; admission Y15), covered in splendidly mismatched glazed tiles. The tomb supposedly holds the body of one of Emperor Qianlong's concubines, but is better known among Uighurs as the resting place of Abakh Hoja, one of Kashgar's more popular rulers, and is thus an important pilgrimage site.

There are/were other tombs scattered throughout Kashgar, but many of these have been inauspiciously ploughed under to make way for new housing complexes. The only ones remaining, such as the Tomb of Yusup Has, are in a state of disrepair.

KASHGAR REGIONAL MUSEUM 喀什地区博物馆

This **museum** (Kāshí Dìqū Bówùguǎn; 19 Tawuguzi Lu; admission Y6; ☿ 7.30am-noon & 4-8pm) is on the eastern edge of Kashgar. Despite half-hearted attempts to liven up the exhibits here, most travellers come away underwhelmed.

HA NOI RUINS & MOR PAGODA 罕诺依古城、莫尔佛塔

At the end of a jarring 35km drive northeast of town are the ruins of Ha Noi (Hǎnnuòyī Gùchéng), a Tang dynasty town built in the 7th century and abandoned in the 12th century. Little remains except a great solid pyramid-like structure and the huge Mor Pagoda (Mù'ěr Fótǎ) or stupa.

CITS will take you to Ha Noi for Y200 per 4WD or you can hire a car from the CTS for Y70 per person. John Hu, at John's Café, charges Y350 per car.

Tours

Both Asian Explorations (www.asianexplorations.com), an affiliate of the Caravan Café, and John's Café organise multiday trips. Some of the more popular destinations for trekking around Kashgar include the K2 base camp, Muztagh Ata and camel tours through the Taklamakan Desert. If you're looking for a challenge, you can also consider biking the Karakoram Hwy.

Sleeping
Accommodation can be tighter on the days preceding the Sunday Market than afterward. In low season you should be able to coax out some discounts.

Noor Bish Hotel (Nàobĕixī Lũshè; ☎ 282 3092; beds Y10) This is a small Uighur guesthouse 200m down the road that connects the Chini Bagh Hotel with Id Kah Sq. It's up an alley to the left, with basic rooms set around a plant-filled courtyard.

Tiānnán Fàndiàn (☎ 282 4023; 49 Renmin Donglu; dm Y12-20, tw Y238) Across from the long-distance bus station, the multi-building Tiannan is a convenient fall back in a pinch.

Sèmǎn Bīnguǎn (☎ 258 2129; fax 258 2861; 170 Seman Lu; dm Y20, tw Y60-680; 🖳) This hotel has various buildings of various quality, and is overall the cheapest accommodation in Kashgar. Around the back is the former Russian consulate, with seven rooms – despite the tacky décor, this is the must-stay choice for the well-heeled Great Game aficionado.

Chini Bagh Hotel (Qíníwǎkè Dìnguǎn; ☎ 298 2103; fax 298 2299; 93 Seman Lu; dm Y40, tw Y180-380; 🖳 🖳) Centrally located on the grounds of the former British consulate (now a restaurant), the Chini Bagh is the best all-around choice. The three-star International Building has some of the nicest rooms in Kashgar; the dorm rooms are in good shape as well.

Kāshí Gǎěr Bīnguǎn (☎ 265 2367; fax 265 4679; 57 Tawaguzi Lu; tw/ste Y288/888; 🖳) If you're looking for a quiet place to stay, this is it. Set in spacious gardens 3km east of the centre, the rooms here were renovated in 2004 and are the most comfortable in Kashgar. A taxi to the main square is Y5.

Eating
UIGHUR
Intizar (Yíntízǎěr; Renmin Xilu) A jam-packed Kashgar favourite, the classic dish here is *tohu gangpan* (jīròu mǐfàn), spicy chicken and potatoes with rice (Y5).

Another good spot to sample Uighur cooking is at the food stalls across from Id Kah Mosque. Vendors sell noodles, chickpeas, poached eggs, kebabs, breads and boiled goat heads; bring your own fork. For dessert there is watermelon by the slice, *tangzaza, kharsen meghriz* or simply a glass of hot milk and a pastry. In restaurants, *suoman, suoman gush siz* and *polo* are all recommended. See the boxed text on p782 for more about Uighur food.

For good views of the old town street life, make sure you pay a visit to the rickety second-floor teahouse (*chai hanna*), north of the music shop.

CHINESE
Chinese fast-food stalls serve oily but cheap lunches in an alley off Renmin Xilu, behind the Bank of China. This is a good option for vegetarians; just point and pay, a tray of ready-cooked food costs about Y5. Go at noon when the food is hot.

WESTERN
Caravan Café (☎ 298 1864; www.caravancafé.com; 120 Seman Lu; 🕙 9am-9.30pm Apr-Oct) This place is tops: great coffee, great pastries and even pizza, all served with panache. It's next to the Chini Bagh Hotel.

John's Café (☎ 258 1186; www.johncafé.net; in courtyard of Seman Hotel) This is another popular hang-out, offering both Western and Chinese dishes.

Shopping
SOUVENIRS
The citizens of Kashgar have been selling things for 2000 years, so be ready to bargain. For serious shopping go to the old town; but beware, Sunday Market prices tend to be higher. Hats, teapot sets, copper and brass ware and Uighur knives are among some of the souvenirs you'll find around town.

CARPETS
Most carpet dealers display their wares at the Sunday Market pavilion. The rugs here are made out of everything from silk to synthetics, so do your carpet homework if you plan on purchasing. The brightly coloured felt *shyrdakhs* from Kyrgyzstan are a good buy – you shouldn't pay more than Y350 for a large one. The best regional carpets were once made in Hotan, however the quality of a Hotanese rug today is dubious.

MUSICAL INSTRUMENTS

The family-run **Uyghur Musical Instrument Factory** is on the street north of the post office. Here you'll find long-necked stringed instruments running the gamut from souvenirs to collector's items. If any traditional performances are on, Mohammed (the owner) will know where to find them.

Getting There & Away

It's imperative when you buy tickets in Kashgar to verify what 'time' the person who's selling the tickets has set their watch to. Officially it's Běijīng time, but unsurprisingly, this isn't always the case.

AIR

There are three daily flights to Ürümqi (Y1230), which are sometimes cancelled due to poor turnout or sandstorms. Two new international routes are in the works: one from Delhi to Tashkent (Uzbekistan) via Islamabad (Pakistan) and Kashgar; the other from Lahore (Pakistan) to Ürümqi via Kashgar. The **Civil Aviation Administration of China office** (CAAC; Zhōngguó Mínháng; ☎ 282 2113; 95 Jiefang Nanlu; ☒ 10am-1pm & 4.30-8pm) will have more information.

BUS

To Kyrgyzstan

There are two passes into Kyrgyzstan, the Torugart, which leads to Bishkek, and the Irkeshtam, which goes to Osh. Getting to Osh (US$50, two days) is straightforward

enough, with a weekly bus leaving the **international bus station** (guójì qìchēzhàn; Jiefang Beilu) on Mondays at 10am. Another option is to hire a taxi up to the border, which should work out to be a similar price. Crossing the Torugart Pass, however, is a different matter (see below). For the record, a Chinese bus runs twice weekly from the international bus station to Naryn ($25) and Bishkek ($50).

To Pakistan

Buses to/from Sost (Y270 plus Y2 per bag, two days) in Pakistan leave the international bus station daily at 10am. The 500km trip takes two days, with an overnight at Tashkurgan. Bring water, snacks and warm clothes as nights can be cold all year. Sit on the left side for the best views.

Customs procedures are conducted at Tashkurgan. Drivers like luggage to go on the roof, though most people load up the back seats if there aren't too many passengers.

If buses have stopped for the season but you're desperate to cross the border, Pakistani traders may have space in a truck or chartered bus. You can also hire a taxi or a 4WD from one of the tour outfits.

Other Destinations

Other buses use the **long-distance bus station** (kāshí zhàn; Tiannan Lu). There have been instances of theft at the bus station, especially in the early morning crush, so keep a close watch on your bags.

OVER THE TORUGART PASS

Officially the Torugart Pass is a 'second grade' pass and therefore for local not international traffic. Except, of course, that it is. What you require on the Chinese side is a *xūkězhèng* permit from the PSB entry-exit section in Ürümqi. Most agents in Kashgar can get this (CTS claim in two working days), though no one will arrange a permit without transport (see opposite for prices).

It's unclear whether you can get into Kyrgyzstan without booking Kyrgyz transport. Officially the Chinese won't let you leave the arch without onward transport into Kyrgyzstan and Chinese travel agencies are reluctant to take you without booking onward transport. But it looks likely that the Chinese guards will let you cross if you can find a lift from the arch to the Kyrgyz border post. If you do manage to get to the Kyrgyz border post you will need to find onward transport to Naryn or Bishkek – though be forewarned, you could be in for a long wait. In the event there are taxi sharks at the crossing, they may open the bidding at US$200 or more to Bishkek (and may lead you to think that's for the vehicle, then later tell you it's per person), though US$50 for the car is a more realistic amount.

There are public buses to Kyrgyzstan over the Torugart Pass, but at the time of writing foreigners were not allowed to take these services. Without a permit, you'll most likely be thrown off the bus at the customs post. You must, of course, already have a Kyrgyzstan visa.

Making the 1480km trip to Ürümqi are nonstop, soft-seat or sleeper coaches (Y155 to Y225) that take about 24 hours. They leave frequently between 7.30am and 7.30pm.

Local buses to Tashkurgan leave daily at 10am (Y43, six hours) and charge the full fare to drop you off in Karakul.

There are seven buses for Hotan (Y51 to Y85, 10 hours) between 10am and 9pm, but it is more enjoyable to stop off in Yengisar (Y7, 1½ hours), Yarkand (Y22, three hours) or Karghilik (Y29, four hours). Buses to these last three towns run hourly.

For information on buses to Tajikistan see p912.

CAR
You can hire 4WDs (four to six passengers) and minibuses (eight to 12 passengers) from the Caravan Café, John's Café, CTS or CITS. At the time of research, rates for a 4WD to meet/drop you off at Torugart ranged from Y800 to Y1200, plus Y200 per person to arrange the requisite permits (minimum two-day wait). CITS and CTS offer the cheapest rates, but it pays to shop around. Food and lodging are extra, and the driver pays for his own.

HITCHING
You might be able to hitch a lift to Tashkurgan, but from there to Pakistan you'll probably have to wait for an empty seat on the bus. There are plenty of trucks crossing the Torugart Pass to Kyrgyzstan but it's likely that you'll have problems getting past the customs post.

TRAIN
Daily trains to Ürümqi depart at 9.30am and 4.50pm and take 30 and 23 hours respectively. Sleeper tickets will set you back Y177 to Y335.

Getting Around
TO/FROM THE AIRPORT
The airport is 12km northeast of the centre. A bus (Y10) leaves from the CAAC ticket office 2½ hours before all departures, and one bus meets all incoming flights. A taxi there should cost the same price.

BICYCLE
A bike is the cheapest and most versatile way to get around Kashgar. One-gear clun-

kers can be hired by the hour or the day at John's Café.

BUS
Useful bus routes are bus Nos 2 (Jiefang Lu to the airport), 10 (Renmin Lu to the Kashgar Hotel and Abakh Hoja Tomb), 9 (international bus station to the Chini Bagh and Sèmǎn Bīnguǎn), 16 (main square to the Livestock Market) and 28 (main square to the train station). The fare is Y1.

TAXI
A fleet of noisy, green taxis clog every street and alleyway, honking and congesting the city. It's Y5 everywhere within Kashgar and Y10 for the train station, airport, livestock market and Abakh Hoja Tomb.

KARAKORAM HWY 中巴公路
The Karakoram Hwy (Zhōngbā Gōnglù) over the Khunjerab Pass (4800m) is the gateway to Pakistan. For centuries this route was used by caravans plodding down the Silk Road. Khunjerab means 'valley of blood', a reference to local bandits who took advantage of the terrain to plunder caravans and slaughter the merchants.

Nearly 20 years were required to plan, push, blast and level the present road between Islamabad and Kashgar, and more than 400 road-builders died in the process. Facilities en route are being steadily improved, but take warm clothing, food and drink on board with you – once stowed on the roof of the bus, your baggage will not be easily accessible.

Even if you don't wish to go to Pakistan, it's worth doing the trip up to Tashkurgan. From Kashgar, you first cross the Pamir Plateau (3000m), passing the foothills of Kongur Mountain (Gōnggé'ér Shān), which is 7719m high, and nearby Muztagh-Ata Mountain (Mùshìtǎgé Shān) at 7546m.

The journey continues through stunning scenery – high mountain pastures with grazing camels and yaks tended by Tajiks who live in yurts. The last major town on the Chinese side is Tashkurgan at 3600m.

Officially, the border opens 15 April and closes 31 October. However, the border can open late or close early depending on conditions at Khunjerab Pass. Travel formalities are performed at Sost, on the Pakistan border; the Chinese border post is at Tashkurgan.

SILK ROAD

You'll need to get your papers in order ahead of time, as China doesn't let anyone out of the country if they don't have an onward visa, and you can't get one in Kashgar. If you're coming in from Pakistan, make sure you have enough cash on hand – the bank in Tashkurgan doesn't change travellers cheques.

Kashgar to Karakul Lake

If you'd like to see the Karakoram Hwy, Karakul Lake, a glittering mirror of glacial peaks, makes for a good destination. Spending the night is recommended – like Tiān Chí, it can get crowded here during the day, but evenings and mornings you'll have the place to yourself, and you can hike up into the hills or circumnavigate the lake. Most settlements as far as Karakul are Kyrgyz.

As you leave Kashgar the main attraction, rising up from the plain to the west, is the luminous rampart of the Pamir. An hour down the road is Upal (Wùpàĕr in Chinese), where the Kashgar-Sost bus normally stops for lunch. There's a weekly market here every Monday.

Two hours from Kashgar you enter the canyon of the Ghez River (Ghez Darya in Uighur), with wine-red sandstone walls at its lower end. Ghez itself is just a checkpost; photographing soldiers or buildings here can result in confiscated film. Upstream, the road is cut into sheer walls or inches across huge boulder fields. At the top of the canyon, 3½ hours above the plain, is a huge wet plateau ringed with sand dunes, aptly called Kumtagh (Sand Mountain) by locals.

The bus will drop you off after five or six hours next to the lake, ringed by magnificent ice mountains. There's only one hotel that has yurts (Y40) and rooms; camping is possible but not recommended. Travellers have warned of strong-arm tactics from local leaders who 'control' the area. If you don't want to battle with tour groups at the restaurant, bring your own food.

One bus daily leaves the long-distance bus station at 10am, takes five to six hours and costs Y45. The bus to Sost from the international bus station also stops off here. It's supposed to leave at 10am but usually doesn't (they have to overnight in Tashkurgan anyway so it doesn't matter when they leave) – you can often still get it around noon! Day-trippers can rent a taxi for as

little as Y400 (return). The official price is double this, but if you ask around, someone is always ready to bargain.

SOUTHERN SILK ROAD

The Silk Road east of Kashgar splits into two threads in the face of the huge Taklamakan Desert. The northern thread follows the course of the modern road and railway to Kuqa and Turpan. The southern road charts a more remote course between desert sands and the huge Pamir and Kunlun ranges. The ancient route is marked by a ring of abandoned cities deserted by retreating rivers and encroaching sands. Some cities, like Niya, Miran and Yotkan, remain covered by sand, others, like Yarkand and Hotan, remain important Uighur centres.

While there are no spectacular sights, the journey takes you about as far into Uighur heartland as you can get. It's possible to visit the southern towns as a multiday trip from Kashgar before crossing the Taklamakan Desert to Ürümqi, or as part of a rugged backdoor route into Tibet or Qīnghǎi.

YENGISAR 英吉沙

The tiny town of Yengisar (Yīngjíshā), 58km south of Kashgar, is synonymous with knife production. There are dozens of knife shops here (though prices are not much better than in Kashgar) and it's sometimes possible to visit the knife factory (小刀厂; xiǎodāochǎng in Chinese; pichak chilik karakhana in Uighur) in the centre of town to see the knives being made. Each worker makes the blade, handle and inlays himself, using only the most basic of tools. From the main highway walk east past Yīngjíshā Bīnguǎn (英吉沙宾馆) then turn left to the bazaar. The factory is just west of the bazaar. Try not to visit between the noon to 4pm lunchbreak.

Getting There & Away

Buses pass through the town regularly en route to Yarkand (Y13, 1½ hours) and Kashgar (Y7.5, 1½ hours). There's no bus station per se; ask a motorcab to take you to the drop off point (Y2).

YARKAND 莎车

Yarkand (Shāchē) is one of those Central Asian towns, like Samarkand and Kashgar, whose name still resonates deeply with Silk Road romance. At the end of a major trade route from British India, over the Karakoram Pass from Leh, Yarkand was for centuries an important caravan town and centre of Hindu tradesmen and moneylenders.

The intriguing old quarter still resounds with the clanging of blacksmith's hammers, the jangling of donkey bells and the incessant whine of grindstones. Apart from the cemetery, there's nothing in particular to search out, but Yarkand's craftsmen are still hard at work, a sight that is quickly evaporating from Uighur life elsewhere.

Orientation
Modern Yarkand is split into a Chinese new town and an Uighur old town. Heading right out of the bus station will bring you to the main avenue. Take a right here, and flag down any public bus (Y0.5), which will take you past the Shāchē Bīnguǎn, the Altyn Mosque and the old town.

Sights
Getting to the old town is slightly tricky – the best way to find it is to use the **Altyn Mosque complex** (阿勒电清真寺; Āqíndiàn Qīngzhēn Sì; admission Y10) as a landmark. The complex is on a smaller street off the main avenue. To get to the old town, take a left off the main avenue as if heading to the mosque, then take the first right down a dirt lane and keep going. To visit the town's sprawling, overgrown cemetery and *mazar* (pilgrimage site), take a left off this lane after five minutes. There is no charge to enter.

Other tombs out of town include Hajiman Deng Mazar, Sud Pasha Mazar and Hayzi Terper Mazar. There's plenty of scope here to take many interesting walks around the surrounding countryside.

Yarkand also has a Sunday Market, untouristed but smaller than the markets at Kashgar (p791) or Hotan (p798). The market is held a block north of the Altyn Mosque.

Sleeping & Eating
Finding a place to stay is a problem in Yarkand. Consider sleeping in Karghilik instead.

Shāchē Bīnguǎn (莎车宾馆; ☎ 851 2365; 4 Xincheng Lu; tw/tr 280/240) A run-of-the-mill Chinese hotel, this is the only place in Yarkand that currently takes foreigners.

The old town has tempting noodle shops with patrons sitting on kangs instead of chairs. For Chinese food, around the bus station is as good as it gets.

Getting There & Around
Buses leave half-hourly for Kashgar (Y22, three hours), Yengisar (Y14, 1½ hours) and Karghilik (Y6, one hour). There are two daily buses at 11am and noon to Hotan (Y29, six hours), and five daily to Ürümqi (Y170 to Y190, 24 hours).

From the bus station it's about 1.5km to Shāchē Bīnguǎn and the same again to the start of the old town.

KARGHILIK 叶城
Karghilik (Yèchéng) is a convenient place to break the long trip to Hotan. There are decent places to stay and you could enjoyably spend some time exploring the old town. Karghilik is also of importance to travellers as the springboard for the long overland trip to Tibet.

The main attraction to take in here is the 15th-century Friday Mosque (Jama Masjid) and covered bazaar out front. The traditional adobe-walled backstreets of the old town spread south behind the mosque.

The town of Charbagh, 10 minutes' drive towards Yarkand, has a large market on Tuesday.

Sleeping & Eating
Jiāotōng Bīnguǎn (交通宾馆; ☎ 728 5540; 1 Jiaotong Lu; dm Y30, tw Y80-100) Right by the bus station, this is actually the best place in town. Hot water can be temperamental on the upper floors.

There are busy Uighur eateries outside the Friday Mosque and 24-hour food stalls across from the bus station.

Getting There & Away
There are buses to Yarkand (Y6) and Kashgar (Y25) every half hour until 8.30pm and six buses to Hotan (Y24, five hours) between 11am and 8.30pm. There are also five daily sleeper buses to Ürümqi (Y173 to Y182, 25 hours).

TO TIBET
The 1100km-long road to Ali, in western Tibet, branches off from the main Kashgar–Hotan road 6km east of Karghilik.

SILK ROAD

Tibetan Antelope buses make the trip, but were only running thrice monthly at the time of writing, so you may have to hitch a ride with a truck. Ticket prices fluctuate wildly according to the severity of recent PSB crackdowns; count on paying anywhere between Y400 and Y1000, for either the bus or a truck. This is a very tough road with some passes over 5400m, and several foreigners have died, either from exposure or in traffic accidents. You should come equipped with warm clothes, enough food for a week (even if the trip to Ali can take as little as three days) and as a safety precaution, something to fend off nomads' dogs. Although this road is officially closed to foreigners, a number of travellers have been making it around the checkpoints in recent years – but not everyone. You may be fined upon arrival in Ali (Y300), and will need to pick up a Y50 permit. See Lonely Planet's *Tibet* guide for more details.

HOTAN 和田
☎ 0903 / pop 104,900

Merchants laden with jade have been departing Hotan (Hétián; also known as Khotan) for China since approximately 5000 BC, well before the desire for better horses spurred Chinese trade routes westward or the silkworm went on to steal the spotlight. Hotanese have proven to be formidable businessmen over the millennia: they uncovered the secret of Chinese silk by the 5th century AD and later established themselves as the region's foremost carpet weavers.

Modern Hotan is unfortunately less charismatic than its traditional wares. The main reason to haul yourself all the way out here today is to catch the fantastic Sunday Market, the largest and least visited in Xīnjiāng. There's still silk, carpets and jade, but these days they're hardly spectacular enough to warrant the 1980km trip from Kashgar. You can check out the local selection of jade, supposedly pulled from the muddy Jade Dragon Kashgar River, at the rows of stores and stalls along Beijing Lu.

For those setting off on the infrequently explored southern Silk Road, via Keriya (Yútián), Cherchen (Qiěmò), Charklik (Ruòqiāng) and on to Golmud, this is the last place to take care of important errands like changing money, stocking up on supplies or extending your visa.

Orientation
Beijing Xilu is the main east–west axis running past the enormous main square. The bank and PSB are to the east of the square, while the hotels and bus stations are north from here. The Jade Dragon Kashgar River runs several kilometres east of town.

Information
The **Bank of China** (中国银行; Zhōngguó Yínháng; ⏺ 9.30am-1.30pm & 4-8pm Mon-Fri) on Beijing Xilu cashes travellers cheques. Five minutes west is the **PSB** (公安局; Gōngānjú; 22 Beijing Xilu; ⏺ 9.30am-1.30pm & 4-7.30pm Mon-Fri), which will process visas in one day. There's an Internet café a few minutes north of the Hétián Yíngbīnguǎn.

CITS (Zhōngguó Guójì Lǚxíngshè; ☎ 202 6090; 23 Tamubake Xilu, 3f) far to the south off Wulumuqi Nanlu, arranges tours of the silk factory and expensive excursions with a car and guide to the ruins at Yuètègān and Málìkèwǎtè.

Sights
SUNDAY MARKET 星期天市场
Hotan's most attraction is its traditional weekly market, which rivals Kashgar's in both size and interest. The colourful market swamps the northeast part of town and reaches fever pitch between noon and 2pm Xīnjiāng time. The most interesting parts to head for are the *gillam* (carpet) bazaar, which also has a selection of atlas silks, the *doppi* (skullcap) bazaar and the livestock bazaar.

CARPET & SILK FACTORIES
地毯厂、丝绸厂
On the eastern bank of the Jade Dragon Kashgar River is a small carpet factory (*gillam karakhana* in Uighur). Even with up to 10 people working on the large looms, one square metre in a wool carpet takes 20 days to complete. The tour is interesting, although the carpets seem to have lost their lustre with the advent of communism – Kashgar is a far better place to shop. To get here, take minibus No 2 heading east, which leaves from the main crossroads downtown, and then change to minibus No 3 or walk 20 minutes over the bridge.

Past the carpet factory is the small town of Jíyǎxiāng, a traditional centre for atlas silk production. You can look around the fascinating **workshop** (atlas karakhana in Uighur; admission Y10) to see how the silk is spun, dyed and woven using traditional methods. A round trip in a taxi to the carpet and atlas factories costs Y30.

Hotan Silk Factory (Hétián Sīchóu Chǎng; ☼ 9am-1.30pm & 3.30-7.30pm Mon-Fri) uses a less traditional form of silk production, employing over 2000 workers. Staff at the office will give you a tour of the plant to see the boiling of cocoons and spinning, weaving, dyeing and printing of silk. If you don't speak at least some Chinese, you are better off arranging a visit through CITS. No photos are allowed in the factory. To get there, take minibus No 1 from outside the bus station to the end of the line and then walk back 150m.

HOTAN CULTURAL MUSEUM 和田博物馆
Far to the west of town on Beijing Xilu is the regional **museum** (bówùguǎn; admission Y7; ☼ 9am-2pm & 4-7pm). The main attractions are two Indo-European mummies, a 10-year-old girl and 35-year-old man, both of whom are now over 1500 years old. The museum has been undergoing major renovations and should be open by 2006. Take bus Nos 2 or 6 from the town centre to get here.

ANCIENT CITIES 故城
The deserts around Hotan are peppered with the faint remains of abandoned cities. Ten kilométres west of town are the **Yotkan Ruins** (Yuètègān Yízhǐ; admission Y10), the ancient capital of a pre-Islamic kingdom dating from the 3rd to 8th centuries AD.

The **Melikawat Ruins** (Mǎlìkèwàtè Gùchéng; admission Y10) are 25km south of town, and there are some temples and pagoda-like buildings a further 10km to the south. Hiring a taxi should cost about Y30 to Yoktan and Y75 to Melikawat. It's an additional Y5 to take photos.

Other ruins such as the Rawaq Pagoda and city of Niya (Endere) are currently off limits; though you can always check with CITS if you're interested.

Sleeping & Eating
Hétián Yíngbīnguǎn (和田迎宾馆; ☎ 202 2824; fax 202 3688; 4 Tanayi Beilu; dm Y20, tw Y90-180; ✷) The main building here is the nicest place to stay in Hotan, and the cheaper rooms in the old wing aren't bad either. To get here, take a taxi (Y5) from the bus station – just make sure you don't wind up at the depressing Hétián Bīnguǎn.

Happy Hotel (幸福旅社; Xìngfú Lǚshè; ☎ 202 4804; Guodao 315; bed Y30) This Uighur-style alternative is a couple of minutes' walk right from the bus station. Rooms are basic and there are hot showers in the 'Happy Bathroom'.

Jiāotōng Bīnguǎn (交通宾馆; ☎ 203 2700; Guodao 315; tw Y180) Next to the bus station, the Jiaotong is a last ditch convenience choice. They have cheaper rooms, but weren't letting foreigners in at last check. Bargain hard if you stay here.

For Sichuanese food and cold beer, head right out of the Hétián Yíngbīnguǎn. Uighur staples are found throughout the town.

Getting There & Away
AIR
In theory, there are daily flights between Hotan and Ürümqi (Y1250). The **CAAC office** (☎ 251 2178; Wulumuqi Nanlu) is west of the main square. The airport is 10km west of town; a taxi there costs Y15.

BUS
There are five daily buses from Hotan to Kashgar (Y58, 10 hours). These buses also pass through Karghilik (Y30, five hours) and Yarkand (Y37, six hours). Express buses to Kashgar (Y80, seven hours) leave at noon and 2pm.

CROSS-DESERT HWY
The 500km trans-Taklamakan highway was originally built to facilitate the extraction of oil from beneath a desert whose reputation, up until recently, was one of certain death. Grids of planted reeds are all that keep the rippling ocean of sand from constantly blowing over the road, and the slightest bit of bad weather can stop traffic for days. Before you even reach the desert, you'll see dust devils erupting in the distance like yellow geysers, and the snowy Kunlun Mountains towering forebodingly over the gravely plain.

If this sounds like your kind of trip, you'll need to catch the earliest bus to Ürümqi at 10am (Y220, 25 hours) or the express at 1pm (Y330, 20 hours) to make the most of it. There are six other buses throughout the day, which cross the desert at night. If you're interested in going to Kuqa, you can get off near Lúntái (Y130, 15 hours); buses also pass through Korla. Drivers work in shifts, so it's not a bad idea to reiterate your destination. Bring plenty of water and food in case of breakdowns or storms.

Getting Around
Bus No 10 runs from the bus station past the bazaar to the east bus station. Taxis in town cost a flat Y5; cycle rickshaws are Y2.

HOTAN TO GOLMUD 和田至格尔木
To continue east along the southern Silk Road, you'll need to catch the 10.30am bus to Cherchen (且末; Qiěmò), 580km away. The two-day trip costs Y72 and goes via the Uighur towns of Keriya (于田; Yútián) and Niya (民丰; Mínfēng). Buses leave from the east bus station (东站; dōng zhàn) in Hotan; bus No 10 runs here from the main bus station.

From Qiěmò, buses continue another 320km east to Charklik (若羌; Ruòqiāng). The trip takes anywhere from 13 to 16 hours under good conditions, and tickets are Y56. From Charklik you may be able to get a bus to Golmud, though it's more likely you'll have to resort to a combination of private jeep and minibus services to get you the nine hours to Huātǔgōu (花土沟; from Y150 to Y200). From here you can reportedly catch a public bus to Golmud (Y140, 17 hours). This route requires a few overnight stops, and roads in this area are plagued by washouts and landslides, so don't go this way if you're in a hurry.

NORTHERN XĪNJIĀNG

Until the 1990s, this region of thick evergreen forests, rushing rivers and isolated mountain ranges was a quiet backwater, closed off to foreigners due to the proximity of the Russian, Mongolian and Kazakhstan borders. The highlight of the area is beautiful Kanas Lake (Hānàsī Hú) and the surrounding valleys.

BÙ'ĚRJĪN 布尔津
☎ 0906 / pop 60,000
Bù'ěrjīn, meaning 'dark green water' in Mongolian, is named after the nearby Bu'erjin River, which is a tributary of the Ertix River. The Ertix is the only river in China to flow into the Arctic Ocean. Bù'ěrjīn, 620km north of Ürümqi, marks the end of the desert and the beginning of the grasslands and mountains to the north. The town's population is mainly Kazakh (57%), but there are also Han, Uighurs, Tuva Mongolians and Russians.

There isn't much to see in Bù'ěrjīn, especially on that long ride through the desert, but you may need to stay here if you're headed to Kanas Lake.

Orientation
Bù'ěrjīn's main street is Xingfu Lu, bisected by Wenming Lu. One block to the west of Wenming Lu is Xiangyang Lu, with the PSB, and further south, the night market.

Information
You can't change travellers cheques in Bù'ěrjīn, but the local Industrial & Commercial Bank (ICBC) can change major currencies. Should you need a permit for a closed area, the PSB is on the corner of Xiangyang Lu and Xingfu Lu.

Sleeping & Eating
Jiākèsī Jiǔdiàn (嘉客思酒店; ☎ 652 1716; 2 Xiangyang Nanlu; tw Y120-280) This place has nice rooms right by the night market, with hot water in the evening.

Jiāotōng Bīnguǎn (交通宾馆; ☎ 652 2643; Wenming Lu; dm/tw Y10/90) The most convenient and cheapest place to stay is at the bus station. There is often no hot water, but the staff are friendly.

For a hearty bowl of beef noodle soup, make a beeline for the **Yínchuān Huímín Fàndiàn** (银川回民饭店; Wenming Lu). It's at the corner on the end of Wenming Lu. Opposite Jiākèsī Jiǔdiàn is a tiny night market specialising in grilled fish and fresh yoghurt.

Getting There & Away
There are two buses to Ürümqi (Y104, 13 hours) at 11am and 7pm, and Jímǔnǎi (Y11, two hours) at 11am and 4pm.

If you'd like to fly up from Ürümqi, there is an airport nearby in Altai (Ālètài). Buses run to/from the city hourly (Y15, 1½ hours) between 9am and 7pm.

KANAS LAKE NATURE RESERVE
哈纳斯湖自然保护区
The most impressive sight in the Altai region is Kanas Lake, a long finger lake found in the southern-most reaches of the Siberian taiga ecosystem. The trip to the lake is

stunning, with beautiful vistas that range from desert to grasslands to alpine wilderness. Along the way you may pass semi-nomadic Kazakhs, who are either on their way up or down the valley, depending on the season. The forests, dominated by spruce, birch, elm and Siberian larch, provide a vivid backdrop of colours in autumn.

There are a couple of invigorating day hikes around Kanas Lake. The most popular trip is to the lookout point, Guanyu Pavilion (观鱼亭; Guānyú Tíng; 2030m). It's a long, ambling walk from the village, eventually leading up a series of never-ending steps. The effort is well rewarded though, as from the top are superb panoramas of the lake, Friendship Peak and the nearby grasslands. It's possible to return to the village via a circuitous scenic route down the eastern slope by following the dirt road, a loop that takes a lazy five hours. If you're short on time, a bus (Y30 return) drives to the Guanyu Pavilion steps from outside the village.

There are similar landscapes in the neighbouring valley of Hemu Kanas (Hémù Hānàsī) and the Bai Kaba (Báihābā) village. You'll need to rent a taxi from Bù'ěrjīn to get there.

Eighteen kilometres past the entrance to the **reserve** (Hānàsī Hú Zìrán Bǎohùqū; admission Y100) is a Tuva village, which now serves as the tourist centre. There is talk of creating a shuttle service that runs back and forth between the park entrance and the village. The area is only accessible from mid-May to mid-October, with ice and snow making transport difficult the rest of the year.

Sleeping & Eating
Officially, the only options for accommodation are the log cabins and wooden yurts situated around the village school (学校; xuéxiào). The going rates per bed are: yurts Y30, dorms Y60 and twins Y80. During the peak summer months, there are nightly barbecues accompanied by Kazakh and Mongolian dancing and a roaring bonfire.

While camping is off-limits, it's unlikely that anyone will come out looking for you – just remember the area is still unspoiled, so stay low impact. No matter where you sleep, food is extremely expensive and redundant. Bring your own supplies.

Getting There & Away
This is the hard part. During July and August there should be tourist buses (Y50) that head to the lake from Bù'ěrjīn's bus station. Unfortunately, it's impossible to count on them, because most tourists come up here with a tour group from Ürümqi. Your best bet is to hire a taxi to make the four-hour, 170km trip. The bidding starts at Y400, with Y250 being a reasonable target (one way).

You might also consider doing a tour. The four-day trip out of Ürümqi with Ecol Travel (p780) in the Bógédá Bīnguǎn is an excellent deal. For Y580 you get an air-con minibus (only 10 hours to Bù'ěrjīn), two nights in Bù'ěrjīn, a park entrance ticket, one night's lodging at the lake and a visit to the strange rock formations at Wuerhe Ghost Town, where the movie *Warriors of Heaven and Earth* was filmed. It's cheaper, easier and will give you the chance to make friends with Chinese tourists. The drawback is the emphasis on the 'group': you might freak out your trip leaders when you tell them you want to hike around by yourself.

FRIENDSHIP PEAK 友谊峰
Standing on the glacier-covered summit of Friendship Peak (Yǒuyì Fēng; 4374m) allows you to be in three nations at once. Presumably you won't need a visa for each one, but you will need a climbing permit, guide, ice axe, crampons and other appropriate mountaineering paraphernalia.

JÍMǓNǍI 吉木乃
The only reason to visit this town is if you're going to Kazakhstan. The border here is generally open, but come armed with a plan B in case you don't get through. The first major town in Kazakhstan is Maykapchigay, from where you can catch a taxi to Zaysan and then a bus to Semey (12 hours).

There are a couple of buses that depart from the bus station and the main intersection for Ürümqi between 4pm and 5pm daily. The trip takes 14 hours and costs Y52 for a seat or Y100 for a sleeper, although prices are negotiable with the private operators. There are two daily buses that make the dusty trip to Bù'ěrjīn (Y11, two hours).

There is no reliable public transport to the border, but a taxi will make the 30km trip for Y25. Coming the other way, you can share a taxi to Jímǔnǎi for Y5.

TĂCHÉNG 塔城

In a lonely corner of northwestern Xīnjiāng, Tǎchéng is a relatively obscure border crossing into neighbouring Kazakhstan. Now and then the gates are closed; if you do make it here and can't get through, don't despair, Tǎchéng is a pleasant enough place to relax before catching a bus south to Ālāshānkǒu or north to Jímǔnǎi.

Information

The post and telephone office (邮电大楼; Yóudiàn Dàlóu) is in the centre of town, on the corner of Xinhua Lu and Ta'er Bahetai Lu. The PSB is on Jianshe Jie. The Bank of China is south of here on Guangming Lu and can handle cash and travellers cheques.

Sleeping

Tǎchéng Bīnguǎn (塔城宾馆; ☎ 622 2093; Youhao Jie; dm Y35, tw Y100-140) This hotel, tucked away in the northwest of town, has beds in a Russian-style building. The twins are reasonable and the hotel has 24-hour hot water.

Getting There & Around

AIR

Daily flights operate between Ürümqi and Tǎchéng; you can purchase your tickets (Y390) from **CAAC** (中国民航; Zhōngguó Mínháng; ☎ 622 3428).

BUS

There are two daily buses to Tǎchéng (Y100, 12 hours) from Ürümqi, departing at 11am and 7pm. From Tǎchéng to Ürümqi the time and price are similar.

TAXI

Tǎchéng is small enough to get around on foot. If you're coming from Kazakhstan, take a shared taxi for Y5 into town.

YĪNÍNG 伊宁

☎ 0999 / pop 240,000

Also known as Gulja, Yīníng lies about 390km west of Ürümqi. The centre of the Ili Kazak Autonomous Prefecture, Yīníng is of primary interest as a stopover on the way to Kazakhstan.

Looking at the city today, you'd hardly know it was the scene of violent separatist riots in 1997. Yīníng has since gone the Sinicised way of most frontier towns in Xīnjiāng, and many of the original Kazakh and Uighur inhabitants seem to have been swallowed up without a trace.

Even though the Chinese appear to currently dominate the border regions, there's no doubt that the easily accessible Ili Val-

---

THE GREAT ENERGY GAME

China may be pledging to cut back on coal consumption, but there can be little doubt that raw energy is something the country will need increasingly more of, not less. Unsurprisingly, the vast oil and gas reserves in Central Asia are one of PetroChina's principle targets. Oil means politics, and as always, access to a brightly lit future is generally not something modern nations are willing to share with each other.

In March 2004 China and Kazakhstan finalised a deal to build a 3000km pipeline stretching from the Caspian Sea all the way through Ālāshānkǒu into Xīnjiāng. China's heavy investment in the Central Asian republics is generally regarded as an economic carrot, a two-pronged means of ensuring security both in and around the country's most unstable province. With the encroaching interests of neighbours Russia, India and Pakistan in the area, and a US base established in Uzbekistan (a mere 322km from the Xīnjiāng border) and military presence in Afghanistan, there can be little doubt that China is seen scrambling to establish itself as the big kid on the block.

And if you've begun to think Xīnjiāng is culturally and geographically more similar to a Central Asian state than China, you're not alone. Not only does Běijīng want to tie up the natural resources of its relatively new trading partners, it also wants promises from its neighbours to weed out Uighur separatist groups taking refuge beyond Chinese soil. The area's porous borders have previously seen large-scale migrations, and continuous persecution of the Uighurs has, at the very minimum, engendered little love for the PRC among your average Uzbek, Kyrgyz and Kazakh.

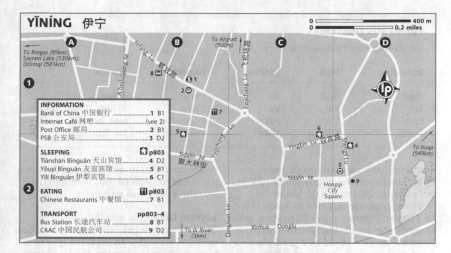

ley is a cause for concern. Yíníng was occupied by Russian troops from 1872 to 1881, and as recently as 1962 there were major Sino-Soviet clashes along the Ili River (Yīlí Hé). While the Russians no longer pose a threat, Beijing's major fear is that separatist elements from the neighbouring Central Asian republics will continue to provide fuel to an ever-restless 'Uighurstan'.

Information

The **Bank of China** (中国银行; Zhōngguó Yínháng; Jiefang Lu; ⏲ 10am-8pm Mon-Fri, 11am-4.30pm Sat & Sun), east of the bus station, changes cash and travellers cheques. The post office is opposite; Internet access (per hour Y2) is available on the 3rd floor. The **PSB** (公安局; Gōngānjú Sidalin Jie) is opposite Yīlítè Dàjiǔdiàn (Yilite Grand Hotel).

Sights

Just to the south of town is a long line of open-air restaurants and teahouses where you can sit and watch the Ili River slide by. To get there, hop on bus No 2 and get off at the last stop, just before the bridge over the river. They're only open when the weather is nice.

Sleeping & Eating

A taxi to any of the hotels below shouldn't cost more than Y5.

Tiānshān Bīnguǎn (☎ 802 22304; Shengli Lu; dm Y15-20, tw Y60) This small place is in excep-

tional condition and is the only budget accommodation accepting foreigners.

Yīlí Bīnguǎn (☎ 802 3799; fax 802 4964; 8 Yingbin Lu; tw Y100-400) The rooms here aren't always the fanciest, but the Yili certainly has character. The old Soviet buildings lost in a quasi-forest full of chirping birds make this hotel the top choice.

Yǒuyì Bīnguǎn (☎ 782 3111; fax 782 3222; 7 Sidalin Jie, 3 Xiang; tw Y210) Renovated in 2003, this is a comfortable mid-range hotel with international standards.

There are plenty of street markets that set up stalls in the evenings around town. The first street west of the main traffic circle is home to the city's expanding collection of Chinese restaurants.

Getting There & Away

AIR

There are daily flights between Ürümqi and Yíníng for Y740. The **CAAC office** (Zhōngguó Mínháng; ☎ 804 4328) is inside the Yīlítè Dàjiǔdiàn, opposite Hongqi City Sq (Hóngqí Guǎngchǎng). A taxi to/from the airport is Y20.

BUS

See box on p804 for bus times.

Buses leave Yíníng on Monday, Wednesday, Thursday and Saturday for Almaty in Kazakhstan; visas are not available here. To Ürümqi, there are three choices: soft seat, regular sleeper or express. The first leaves in the morning, the latter two in the

YĪNÍNG BUS TIMETABLES

Destinations from Yīníng include:

Destination	Price	Duration	Frequency	Departs
Almaty	US$30	10hr	4 weekly	8.30am
Bólè	Y36	4hr	3 daily	10.50am, 11.50am, 12.50pm
Kuqa	Y140	24hr	3 daily	noon, 3pm, 6pm
Ürümqi	Y100-136	11-14hr	8 daily	9am-9pm

afternoon. Although numerous buses pass by Sayram Lake (three hours), they all charge full price; the best deal is the bus to Bólè.

The spectacular bus ride to Kuqa (May to October) passes over Tiān Shān and through the small Mongolian village of Bayanbulak. This would be a good place to break the journey, but at last check the area was closed to foreigners. Amazingly, three daily buses also leave for Kashgar (Y246).

AROUND YĪNÍNG

Ili Valley 伊犁谷

The farmland of the Ili Valley (Yīlí Gǔ) is home to some 20,000 Xibe (Xībózú), who were dispatched by the Qing government to safeguard and colonise the region during the 18th century. This is the only place in China where you'll find a population capable of reading and writing Manchurian, which otherwise died out when the Manchus were assimilated into Chinese culture.

As intriguing as the Xibe sound, there's actually very little to see here. The Lamaist temple **Jingyuán Sì** (靖远寺; admission Y10), outside nondescript Qapaqal (Chábùchá'ěr), is hardly worth the admission fee, and generally speaking, the Xibe resemble the Han. If

you're interested nonetheless, you can catch a minibus to Qapaqal (Y3, 30 minutes) outside the Yīníng bus station.

Sayram Lake 塞里木湖

The vast Sayram Lake (Sàilǐmù Hú), 120km north of Yīníng, is an excellent spot to explore the Tiān Shān range. The lake is especially colourful during June and July, when alpine flowers blanket the ground.

It's not hard to access the more pristine mountainous areas, and you could conceivably stop here for just a day hike. However, if you want to spend significant time exploring, it's best to bring a tent. While there is some food around, the selection is limited and prices expensive, so take what you need. In the height of summer, there are also Kazakh yurts (about Y30 per night, with meals) scattered around the lake willing to take boarders, although the PSB has been cracking down on unauthorised homestays.

Buses from Yīníng to Sàilǐmù Hú take about three hours, and drop passengers off at the 'yurt village' (consisting of fake yurts) along the main road. All buses between Ürümqi and Yīníng pass by the lake, so just stand by the road and wave one down.

Gānsù 甘肃

CONTENTS

HIGHLIGHTS

- Step back into the origins of Chinese Buddhism in the **Mogao Caves** (p823)
- Stock up on good karma at Xiàhé's Tibetan **Labrang Monastery** (p813)
- Explore forgotten Silk Road remains around **Tiānshuǐ** (p825) and **Luòmén** (p828)
- Hike through hazy **Moon Canyon** (p828) or up the ridges of the **Qílián Shān range** (p817)
- Take the yak-inhabited back roads to Sìchuān via **Lángmùsì** (p816)

★ Mogao Caves

★ Qílián Shān

Labrang Monastery ★　Luòmén

Lángmùsì ★　★ Tiānshuǐ

★ Moon Canyon

SILK ROAD

■ POP: 26.3 MIL	■ AREA: 450,000 SQ KM

Threading its way through the mountains and deserts of Gānsù was the famed Silk Road, the well-trodden highway along which camel caravans once carried goods and ideas in and out of China. Travellers and merchants entered the Middle Kingdom using a string of oasis towns as stepping-stones, passing through the barren Hexi Corridor: a narrow strip of land hemmed in by rugged mountain ranges, which for millennia has been China's sole link with the lands to the west. While Gānsù is most known for its Silk Road legacy – the series of ancient Buddhist grottoes stretching from the eastern edge to western tip – what makes the province truly spectacular is the unexpected variety of landscapes and peoples within its elongated borders.

According to legend, Gānsù was the birthplace of the original Chinese patriarch, Fú Xī. In recent years, archaeologists have dated excavations made in the eastern part of the province back 10,000 years, suddenly giving flesh and bone to some of the earliest myths surrounding the people of the Yellow River.

Despite these illustrious beginnings, an unforgiving arid climate has made life hard here. Outside of the oases, most of the land west of the capital is barely habitable, and up until recently, Běijīng did little to relieve the area of its isolation. Even with the completion of the vital Lánzhōu–Ürümqi railway line in 1963 and the subsequent development of mining and industry, Gānsù remains one of China's five poorest provinces.

Nevertheless, for travellers Gānsù is the highlight of the northwest. The province contains an unimaginable trove of Buddhist paintings and sculptures, a fascinating glimpse of the vibrant Tibetan culture of Amdo and the idyllic, little-visited rural scenery in the southeastern corner. Some of the diverse people you might meet on your way include the Hui, Tibetans, Mongols, Dongxiang and Kazakhs.

Climate

Gānsù can be roughly divided into three climatic regions: the low-altitude green belt south of Tiānshuǐ; the arid Hexi Corridor extending from Lánzhōu to Dūnhuáng; and the alpine grasslands rising up along the borders of Qīnghǎi and Sìchuān. In the east and southwest, annual precipitation averages 80cm, with snow common in the latter area from winter to May. While the remainder of the drought-stricken province rarely sees rain, dust storms are not uncommon, particularly in the spring. Winters get pretty nippy and last from November to April.

Language

As in the rest of the country, Gānsù has its own group of regional Chinese dialects, loosely known as Gansuhua (part of the northwestern Lanyin Mandarin family). On the borders of Qīnghǎi and Sìchuān is a significant Tibetan population speaking the Tibetan Amdo dialect.

Getting Around

Foreigners travelling by bus in the southwest corner of the province will need PICC insurance (see box, opposite). In most places, you can get around the insurance fee by buying your ticket directly from the driver (for an extra charge, of course) once the bus leaves the station. Take heed, though – unless you read Chinese, it can be hard to confirm that the bus is actually going to the place that the touts say it's going to. If you're unsure, it's always better to buy your ticket inside the bus station.

It's also worth noting that buses in the above area rarely leave at their scheduled departure times. As a general rule, figure

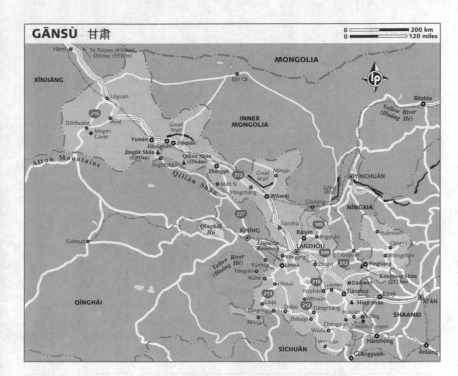

on trolling the streets for passengers for a half-hour minimum.

LÁNZHŌU 兰州
☎ 0931 / pop 2,804,600

The first major city along the Yellow River (Huáng Hé), Gānsù's capital has been an important garrison town since ancient times. Following the communist victory and the city's integration into the expanding rail network, Lánzhōu developed fairly quickly – perhaps too quickly, as it's now famous for being the most polluted city in the world.

Lánzhōu is a major transport hub, and the beginning of the epic overland journeys into Xīnjiāng and Tibet. While there are a number of great destinations surrounding the capital, there's little reason to linger here any longer than it takes to extend your visa.

Orientation

Geography has conspired to make Lánzhōu a city of awkward design. At 1600m above sea level, it's crammed into a narrow valley walled in by steep mountains, forcing it to develop westwards in a long, urban corridor that extends for more than 20km along the southern banks of the Yellow River. The most practical area to base yourself is in the east.

Information
BOOKSHOPS

Foreign Languages Bookshop (Wàiwén Shūdiàn; Zhangye Lu; ☽ 8.30am-6.30pm)

TRAVEL INSURANCE

Foreigners travelling by public bus in Gānsù are required to have *bǎoxiǎn* (insurance) with the People's Insurance Company of China (PICC), regardless of whether they have taken out their own travel insurance or not. Ironically, you couldn't actually collect anything from this policy if you were involved in some sort of accident – it is there to insure the government against lawsuits.

The regulation is only enforced in Lánzhōu and southern Gānsù, along the roads to Sìchuān and Qīnghǎi. You can buy the insurance at most bus stations for Y40, valid for a 20-day period.

LÁNZHŌU 兰州

INFORMATION		SLEEPING	pp809–10	DRINKING	p810
Bank of China 中国银行 1 D3		Huálián Bīnguǎn		Yiran Pottery Barn 依然陶吧 23 C2	
Chāofán Guódù 超凡国度 2 D3		华联宾馆 13 C3			
CITS 中国国际旅行社 3 D3		Lánshān Bīnguǎn		TRANSPORT	pp810–11
CITS 中国国际旅行社 4 D3		兰山宾馆 14 C3		Bus 111 to South Bus Station	
Foreign Languages Bookshop		Lánzhōu Fàndiàn		去汽车南站的公交车111 ...... 24 C2	
外文书店 5 C2		兰州饭店 15 D3		CAAC 中国民航 .... (see 25)	
Main Post Office 邮局 6 C3		Lánzhōu Fēitiān Dàjiǔdiàn		China Eastern Office	
Post Office 邮局 7 D3		兰州飞天大酒店 16 D3		东方航空公司 25 D3	
Post Office 邮局 8 A3		Yíngbīn Fàndiàn		East Bus Station 汽车东站 26 D3	
PSB 公安局 9 C2		迎宾饭店 17 D3		Lánzhōu Jiāotōng Lǚxíngshè	
Western Travel Service		Yóuyì Bīnguǎn 友谊宾馆 18 A3		兰州交通旅行社 27 D3	
西部旅行社 ....(see 15)				South Bus Station 汽车南站 28 A1	
		EATING	p810	Train Station 火车站 29 C3	
SIGHTS & ACTIVITIES	p809	Bakery 面包店 .... (see 16)		West Bus Station 汽车西站 30 B3	
Gansu Provincial Museum		Bǎisuìjī 百岁鸡 19 D3		West Train Station 火车西站 31 A3	
甘肃省博物馆 10 A3		Entrance to Hezheng Lu Night Market			
White Cloud Temple		和政路市场 20 D3		OTHER	
白云观 11 B1		Néngrénjù 能仁聚 21 D3		Dongfanghong Square 东方红广场 . 32 C2	
White Pagoda Temple		Sānyì Pénghuī Niúròumiànguǎn		Lanzhou University Entrance	
白塔寺 12 C1		三伊篷灰牛肉面馆 22 D3		兰州大学 33 D3	

EMERGENCY

Public Security Bureau (PSB; Gōngānjú; 482 Wudu Lu; ⏰ 8.30am-noon & 2.30-6pm Mon-Fri) The foreign affairs branch is located on the 2nd floor of a giant Orwellian tower. Visa extensions are generally granted the same day.

INTERNET ACCESS

Chāofán Guódù (Tianshui Lu; per hour Y2; ⏰ 8am-midnight)

MONEY

Bank of China (Zhōngguó Yínháng; Tianshui Lu; ⏰ 8.30am-noon & 2.30-6pm Mon-Fri) You can change travellers cheques and use the ATM here.

POST

Post Office (Yóujú; cnr Minzhu Lu & Pingliang Lu; ⏰ 8am-7pm) There is also a post office next to Lánzhōu's train station and another near the west bus station.

TOURIST INFORMATION & TRAVEL AGENCIES

China International Travel Service (CITS; Zhōngguó Guójì Lǚxíngshè; ☎ 881 9395; 11th fl, Tourism Bldg, Nongmin Xiang; ☻ 8.30am-noon & 2.30-6pm Mon-Fri) Located on the street running behind the hotel Lánzhōu Fàndiàn. A more accessible office is on Donggang Xilu, just west of Tianshui Lu.

Western Travel Service (Xībù Lǚxíngshè; ☎ 885 2929; 434 Donggang Xilu; ☻ 8.30am-noon & 2.30-6pm Mon-Fri) Located in the west wing of Lánzhōu Fàndiàn. It has English-speaking staff, and offers competitive-priced tours and ticket bookings.

Sights

GANSU PROVINCIAL MUSEUM
甘肃省博物馆

Gānsù's **museum** (Gānsù Shěng Bówùguǎn; Xijin Xilu; admission Y25; ☻ 9am-5pm Tue-Sun) is the one sight definitely worth visiting in Lánzhōu. Significant exhibits include Neolithic painted pottery taken from a site 300km southeast of here at Dàdìwān. Dàdìwān culture existed at least 10,000 years ago and is thought by some archaeologists to predate the better-known Yangshao culture.

Other displays dating from the Han dynasty (206 BC–AD 220) include inscribed wooden tablets used to relay messages along the Silk Road, and a graceful bronze horse galloping upon the back of a swallow. The latter, known as the 'Flying Horse of Wuwei', has become a popular symbol throughout northwestern China since its discovery in 1969. One piece that may set your mind pondering is a 2nd-century BC silver plate depicting Bacchus, the Greco-Roman God of Wine – it was unearthed 120km northeast of Lánzhōu.

Major renovations were ongoing at the time of writing, though the museum is expected be open by the time you read this.

WHITE CLOUD TEMPLE 白云观
This decrepit Qing-dynasty **Taoist temple** (Báiyún Guàn; ☻ 7am-6.30pm) comes complete with a former opera stage, fortune-telling monks and kite-eating trees. Overlooking the Yellow River, it's one of the city's few links to the past.

LANSHAN PARK 兰山公园
Rising steeply to the south of the city is the Lánshān mountain range, a cool repose in summer heat. The quickest and easiest way up is by **chairlift** (lǎnchē; one way/return Y10/18; ☻ May-Oct), accessible from **Wuquan Park** (Wǔquán Gōngyuán; admission Y6; ☻ 6am-10pm).

From the train station take bus No 31 or 34 five stops, get off and continue walking until you reach Jinchang Nanlu. Turn left here and walk about 500m to the Wǔquán Gōngyuán ticket office.

WHITE PAGODA HILL 白塔山
This **park** (Báitǎ Shān; admission Y5; ☻ 6.30am-9pm summer) is on the northern bank of the Yellow River. At its zenith is White Pagoda Temple (Báitǎ Sì), originally built during the Yuan dynasty (AD 1206–1368), from where there are good views across the city. There's a **chairlift** (one way/return Y12/16) spanning the river; the terminal is just to the west of Zhongshan Bridge. Bus No 34 comes here from in front of the train station on Tianshui Lu.

Sleeping

It's always worth asking for a discount in Lánzhōu – most hotels cut their rates considerably during the off season.

Huálián Bīnguǎn (☎ 499 2000; 7-9 Tianshui Lu; tr/tw Y30/90) Directly across from the train station, the Hualian has excellent-value rooms. The only drawback is the inspired karaoke next door. Hot water available from 7.30pm to 10am.

Lánshān Bīnguǎn (☎ 861 7211; 6 Tianshui Lu; s/tw/tr Y40/26/20 per bed) This old dinosaur is not yet extinct, but only those looking for bargain-basement beds will want to consider it. Hot water available from 8pm to 11pm.

Yíngbīn Fàndiàn (☎ 888 6552; 37 Tianshui Lu; tr Y51, tw Y80-150; ☒) Unfortunately, the dimly lit rooms here aren't quite as nice as the lobby; however, they're less noisy than at the Hualian.

Yǒuyì Bīnguǎn (Friendship Hotel; ☎ 233 3051; fax 233 0304; 16 Xijin Xilu; tw old wing Y60, new wing Y198-380; ☒) This long-standing hotel is a quiet place on the western side of town, handy if you're catching an early morning bus from the south or west bus stations.

Lánzhōu Fàndiàn (☎ 841 6321; fax 841 8608; 434 Donggang Xilu; tw Y190-480; ☒) This large, constantly renovated Sino-Stalinist edifice has cosy mid-range rooms.

Lánzhōu Fēitiān Dàjiǔdiàn (Lanzhou Legend Hotel; ☎ 853 2888; www.lanzhoulegendhotel.com; 529 Tianshui Lu; tw/d 800/880; ☒) This four-star hotel is the most comfortable hotel in the city, surpassing even the newer five-star hotels. Pluses include English-speaking staff and money-changing facilities.

Eating

Lánzhōu's big highlight is eating out. The Hezheng Lu night market, extending from Tianshui Lu to Pingliang Lu, is one of the best places to savour the flavours of the northwest. The mix of Hui, Han and Uighur stalls offers countless varieties of noodles and kebabs, as well as *ròujiābǐng* – mutton served inside a 'pocket' of flat bread.

Lánzhōu is also known for its *niúròumiàn*, beef noodle soup that's spicy enough to make you sweat, even in winter. Two handy phrases are *'jiā ròu'* (with beef) and *'búyào làjiāo'* (without chillies). A large bowl at **Sānyī Pénghuī Niúròumiànguǎn** (Yizhichuan Nanlu), located under a green and yellow sign, or anywhere else for that matter, costs Y4.

A bit more upscale, try **Bǎisuìjī** (hot pot for 2 people Y50), a spicy chicken hotpot chain just 50m to the west of Lánzhōu Fàndiàn. You'll need at least two people to finish the smallest serving *(xiǎo guō)*. Try adding *tǔdòu* (potato), *dòufu* (tofu) and *fěntiáo* (noodles).

Alternatively, there's **Néngrénjù** (Tianshui Lu; hot pot for 2 people Y50), south of the university, which serves mutton hotpot accompanied by a delicious peanut sauce.

Just next to Lánzhōu Fēitiān Dàjiǔdiàn is a small bakery that makes banana bread – great for day hikes.

Drinking

If the sight of the muddy Yellow River gets your creative juices flowing, the **Yiran Pottery Barn** (Yírán Táobā; Guangchang Nankou; ☼ 9-1am) has throwing wheels, and serves beer and tea. One hour of clay time is Y20.

Getting There & Away

AIR

China Eastern (Zhōngguó Dōngháng; ☎ 882 1964; ☼ 8.30am-9pm) has a booking office on Donggang Xilu. Just next door is the **Civil Aviation Administration of China** (CAAC; Zhōngguó Mínháng; ☎ 888 9666; ☼ 8.30am-9pm), with significantly cheaper prices for western destinations.

There are daily flights to Běijīng (Y1100), Chéngdū (Y860), Guǎngzhōu (Y1720), Ürümqi (Y1300) and Xī'ān (Y550). Other destinations include Jiāyùguān (Y910), Dūnhuáng (Y1030), Kūnmíng, Shànghǎi, Shēnzhèn, Fúzhōu, Hángzhōu, Nánjīng, Qīngdǎo, Shěnyáng, Xiàmén and Wǔhàn.

BUS

Lánzhōu has a south, west and east bus station. The south bus station *(qìchē nánzhàn)* is the most useful, see box below.

On Xijin Xilu, the west bus station *(qìchē xīzhàn)* handles departures to Xīníng (Y27,

---

LÁNZHŌU BUS TIMETABLES

The Lánzhōu south bus station has departures to:

Destination	Price	Duration	Frequency	Departs
Dūnhuáng	Y213	20hr	1 daily	6pm
Hézuò	Y32-44	5-6hr	half-hourly	7.30am-4pm
Línxià	Y27	3hr	hourly	8.30am-4pm
Xiàhé	Y32-44	6hr	3 daily	7.30am, 8.30am, 2pm
Zhāngyè	Y100	12hr	1 daily	6pm

The east bus station *(qìchē dōngzhàn)* on Pingliang Lu has departures to:

Destination	Price	Duration	Frequency	Departs
Gùyuán	Y90	8hr	1 daily	6.30am
Píngliáng	Y57-70	5hr	hourly	7.30am-6.30pm
Tiānshuǐ	Y49	4hr	hourly	7.30am-6.30pm
Xī'ān	Y120	14hr	1 daily	6.30pm
Yínchuān	Y85	12hr	1 daily	7pm

five hours) and Liújiāxiá (Y12, two hours), near Bǐnglíng Sì.

Lánzhōu is strict about foreigners purchasing PICC insurance. This can be done at ticket windows in the south and west bus stations; at the east bus station, you'll need to go to the Lánzhōu Jiāotóng Lǚxíngshè, 10m north on Pingliang Lu.

TRAIN

Trains run to: Ürümqi; Běijīng via Hohhot and Dàtóng; Golmud via Xīníng; Shànghǎi via Xī'ān and Zhèngzhōu; and Běijīng via Xī'ān and Zhèngzhōu. You can also head south to Chéngdū. Heading west, it takes about 10 hours to reach Jiāyùguān, 12 to 14 hours to Dūnhuáng, 22 hours to Turpan and 24 hours to Ürümqi. The most popular route west is to Ürümqi on train No T295 (hard sleeper Y326) and east is to Xī'ān on train No K120 (hard sleeper Y169). Express trains to Xīníng (hard seat Y33) take three to four hours.

As Lánzhōu is the major rail link between eastern and western China, buy your onward tickets as early as possible (up to five days in advance), especially if you want to guarantee a sleeper berth.

Getting Around

The airport is at Zhōngchuān, about 70km north of the city. Airport buses (Y30, one hour) leave from the CAAC office three hours before scheduled flight departures.

The most useful bus routes are Nos 1 and 31 running from the train station to the west bus station and Yǒuyì Bīnguǎn via Xiguan Shizi. Bus No 111 runs from Zhongshan Lu (at the Xiguan Shizi stop) to the south bus station. Bus Nos 7 and 10 run from the train station up the length of Tianshui Lu before heading west and east, respectively. Public buses cost Y1; flag fall for taxis is Y7.

AROUND LÁNZHŌU
Bǐnglíng Sì 炳灵寺

Due to its relative inaccessibility, Bǐnglíng Sì is one of the few Buddhist grottoes in China to survive the tumultuous 20th century unscathed. Over the past 1600 years, sculptors dangling from ropes carved 183 niches and sculptures into the porous rock along the canyon walls. Today the site is isolated by the waters of the Liujiaxia Reservoir (Liújiāxiá Shuǐkù) on the Yellow River.

Like other Silk Road grottoes, wealthy patrons, often traders along the route west, sponsored the development of Bǐnglíng Sì, which reached its height during the prosperous Tang dynasty. The star of the caves is the 27m-high seated statue of Maitreya, the future Buddha, but some of the smaller, sway-hipped bodhisattvas and guardians, bearing an obvious Indian influence, are equally exquisite. Across the canyon is a large sleeping Buddha, housed inside a temple. To climb the staircase to cave 169, you'll need to purchase a special ticket (Y300).

There are two admission fees: the first is for the Yellow River scenic area (Y20); and the second is for the caves (Y30).

TOURS

Taking a tour will save you some hassle. **Western Travel Service** (☎ 885 2929; 434 Donggang Xilu) in Lanzhou can organise a visit for two people for Y340 per person. Travel onwards to Línxià or Xiàhé can also be arranged.

GETTING THERE & AWAY

Bingling Sì is not a straightforward place to get to – you might want to consider the easier trips to Màijī Shān or Dūnhuáng instead. You can feasibly do it as either a long day trip from Lánzhōu or as a stop over en route to Línxià.

The 7.30am bus from Lánzhōu (Y12, two hours) runs past the Liujiaxia Reservoir, where you'll be dropped off in front of the Yellow River Travel Service. To the left of the travel service is the ticket office – to hire a boat, start here. Going rates for a covered speedboat (seating up to eight people; one hour) are Y400. Private operators near the dam will rent you an uncovered speedboat for Y200. For those with time, the ferry (May to October) is just Y30, but it's a pretty dreary seven hours return trip!

If you're heading on to Línxià after the caves, you can arrange for a speedboat to drop you off at Liánhuātái (莲花台) on the way back. From here, minibuses will taxi you on to Línxià (Y10, one hour). If you're returning to Lánzhōu, the last bus passes by the reservoir at 5pm. There's no food anywhere, so make sure you bring something to eat and drink.

LÍNXIÀ 临夏

☎ 0930 / pop 203,200

Línxià was once an important terminus on the Silk Road. Since then it's become a major centre for Hui Muslims, reflected by the large number of mosques both in and around the town. Línxià maintains a market crossroads atmosphere, and a fair share of swaggering Tibetans seem to be constantly passing through. Shops sell a variety of products from carved gourds, daggers, saddlery, carpets and wrought-iron goods to Muslim and Buddhist religious paraphernalia.

Surrounding Línxià are villages home to the Dongxiang minority. The Dongxiang speak an Altaic language, and are believed to be descendants of 13th-century immigrants from Central Asia, moved forcibly to China after Kublai Khan's Middle East conquest.

Information

The **Bank of China** (Zhōngguó Yínháng; ◷ 8.30am-noon & 2.30-6pm Mon-Fri) changes travellers cheques and cash. It's a five-minute walk north of the Shuǐquán Bīnguǎn on Jiefang Lu.

Sights

WÀNSHÒU GUÀN 万寿观

This cedar-scented **Taoist complex** (admission Y5; ◷ 8am-8pm) extends seven levels up the hillside outside of Línxià. Along the cliffs you can visit other surrounding temples overlooking the city. To get there, take bus No 6 to the west bus station; head for the nine-storey pagoda on the ridge opposite.

Sleeping & Eating

Shuǐquán Bīnguǎn (水泉宾馆; ☎ 631 4715; Sandao-qiao Guangchang; dmY15, tw Y36-50) At the intersection 200m to the right as you leave the south bus station, this is a lively hotel and attracts an array of mountain characters.

Línxià Fàndiàn (临夏饭店; ☎ 623 2100; 9 Hongyuan Lu; dm Y25, tw Y120-180) This is the nicest place to stay in Línxià, although it's smack in the middle of town – not the most exciting area.

Línxià is not a great place for eating, so don't knock yourself out looking for food. The Muslim restaurants near the Shuǐquán Bīnguǎn are a good bet.

Getting There & Away

There are two long-distance bus stations in Línxià, the south (nán zhàn) and the west (xī zhàn). There's no reason to go to the west station, though you may be dropped off here. Bus No 6 runs between the two.

See box below for details.

An interesting route is the bus to Xúnhuà via Dàhéjiā (Mengda Nature Reserve) in Qīnghǎi. You can buy PICC insurance at both bus stations.

XIÀHÉ 夏河

☎ 0941

Set in a beautiful mountain valley, Xiàhé is most definitely worth a visit, especially if you can't get to Tibet. It's the leading Tibetan monastery town outside of Lhasa and many Tibetans come here on pilgrimage dressed in their finest, most colourful clothing. Walking through the warrens and alleys of the huge Labrang Monastery (Lābǔléng Sì), side by side with the prostrating pilgrims and monks in fuchsia-coloured robes, feels like you've entered another world.

The religious focal point is Labrang Monastery, one of six major Tibetan monasteries of the Gelugpa order (Yellow Hat sect of Tibetan Buddhism). The others are Ganden, Sera and Drepung Monasteries near Lhasa; Tashilhunpo Monastery in Shigatse; and Kumbum (Tǎ'ěr Sì) near Xīníng, Qīnghǎi.

LÍNXIÀ BUS TIMETABLES

Departures from the south bus station include:

Destination	Price	Duration	Frequency	Departs
Hézuò	Y13	2½hr	half-hourly	6am-4pm
Lánzhōu	Y26.5	3hr	half-hourly	5.30am-4pm
Xiàhé	Y13.5	3hr	half-hourly	7am-4.30pm
Xīníng	Y38	9hr	1 daily	6am
Xúnhuà	Y15	4hr	1 daily	6am

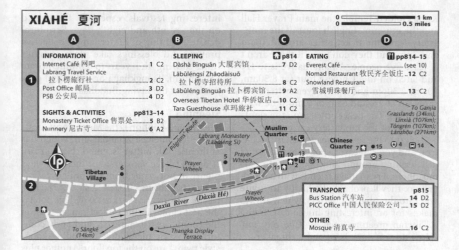

XIÀHÉ 夏河

Xiàhé is a microcosm of southwestern Gānsù, with the area's three principal ethnic groups represented. In rough terms, Xiàhé's population is 50% Tibetan, 40% Han and 10% Hui.

Orientation

At 2920m above sea level, the Daxia River (Dàxià Hé) flows for several kilometres through the valley of the same name. Labrang Monastery is roughly halfway along, and marks the division between Xiàhé's mainly Han and Hui Chinese eastern quarter and the Tibetan village to the west.

A 3km pilgrims' route, with long rows of prayer wheels (1174 of them!) and Buddhist shrines, encircles the monastery. There are some 40 smaller monasteries affiliated with Labrang in the surrounding mountains (as well as many others scattered across Tibet and China). If you're interested in hiking, you can follow the river up to Sāngkē or head up into the surrounding valleys, but carry a stick or a pocket full of rocks, as wild dogs can be a problem. Don't forget to take warm clothing and wet-weather gear.

Note that the Thangka Display Terrace on the south side of the Daxia River is sacred and shouldn't be climbed. Also, photograph respectfully; asking first and shooting later might get you a better picture.

Information

It is possible to change US dollars at the banks, otherwise try some of the small antique shops along the main street, who will give you a reasonable rate. Change travellers cheques before you arrive.

The post office is in the east of town, near the bus station. Internet cafés open and close frequently; the best place to look is across the street from the Muslim quarter. They generally charge Y3 per hour.

At last check, the PSB in Xiàhé did not handle visa requests; you'll need to go to Hezuò to get an extension.

Sights

LABRANG MONASTERY 拉卜楞寺

E'angzongzhe, the first-generation Jiamuyang (Living Buddha) from the nearby town of Ganjia, founded **Labrang Monastery** (Lābùléng Sì; admission Y21) in 1709. At its peak the monastery housed nearly 4000 monks, but their ranks were decimated during the Cultural Revolution. The numbers are recovering, and today there are about 1200 monks, drawn from Qīnghǎi, Gānsù, Sìchuān and Inner Mongolia.

In addition to the numerous temple halls, Living Buddha residences and living quarters for the monks, Labrang is also home to six 'colleges' or institutes: the Institute of Esoteric Buddhism; the Higher & Lower Institutes of Theology; the Institute of Medicine; the Institute of Astrology; and the Institute of Law.

The only way to visit the interior of these buildings is with a tour, which generally includes the Institute of Medicine, the Ser

SILK ROAD

Kung Golden Temple, the main Prayer Hall and the museum. English tours of the monastery leave the ticket office around 10am and 3pm, but they don't run if there aren't at least five people. An alternative is to try and latch on to a Chinese tour (at 8.30am, 10am, 2.30pm and 4pm); even better is to show up at around 6am or 7am to be with the monks. The ticket office is on the right-hand side of the monastery car park.

Access to the rest of the monastery area is free, and you can easily spend several hours just walking around and taking in the atmosphere. Try to make friends with a monk or two: they'll probably be happy to invite you into their living quarters, which always makes for an interesting house call. Using a Tibetan greeting, such as 'Cho day mo' (How do you do?), is a good icebreaker.

NUNNERY

Xiàhé also has a nunnery (nígūsì) on the hill above the Tibetan part of town. The nuns are insatiably curious and may pull you inside (assuming you're female) to visit. At dusk the hillside resonates with the throaty sound of sutras being chanted behind the wooden doors.

Festivals & Events

Festivals are important not only for the monks, but also for the nomads who stream into town in multicoloured splendour from the grasslands. Since the Tibetans use a lunar calendar, dates for individual festivals vary from year to year.

The **Monlam (Great Prayer) Festival** starts three days after the Tibetan New Year, which is usually in February or early March. On the 13th, 14th, 15th and 16th days of the month there are some spectacular ceremonies.

On the morning of the 13th a *thangka* (sacred painting on cloth) of Buddha, measuring over 30m by 20m, is unfurled on the hill facing the monastery. This is accompanied by processions and prayer assemblies.

On the 14th there is an all-day session of Cham dances performed by 35 masked dancers, with Yama, the lord of death, playing the leading role. On the 15th there is an evening display of butter lanterns and sculptures. On the 16th the Maitreya statue is paraded around the monastery.

During the second month (usually starting in March or early April) there are several interesting festivals, especially those held on the seventh and eighth days. Scriptural debates, lighting of butter lamps, collective prayers and blessings take place at other times during the year to commemorate Sakyamuni, Tsongkhapa or individual generations of the Living Buddhas.

Sleeping

The cheapest option is the Monastery Guesthouse (Lābǔléngsì Zhāodàisuǒ), which has authentic yak butter 'scented' beds (Y10). It doesn't have showers, but there's always plenty of hot water from the boiler.

Tara Guesthouse (Zhuōmǎ Lǚshè; ☎ 712 1274; t-dolma@yahoo.com; dm Y15-25, tw Y50-70) This hotel is the best choice in the budget range. Most of the rooms are Tibetan style and fairly comfortable – the nicest digs (including kang-style twins) are on the top floor. Another plus is the rooftop terrace, with fantastic views over the monastery and mountains. Hot water is available from 6.30pm to 10pm.

Overseas Tibetan Hotel (Huáqiáo Fàndiàn; ☎ 712 2642; othotel@public.lz.gs.cn; dm Y20, tw Y80-120, d Y200; ▣) The doubles on the 3rd floor are as luxurious as it gets in Xiàhé. The 2nd-floor twins are also a good choice, with similar decorations and paintings by local Tibetan artists.

Lābǔléng Bīnguǎn (☎ 712 1849; fax 712 1328; dm Y30, tw Y80-220, ste Y320) The location by the river outside of town is serene, but the rooms haven't been refurbished in years and are showing serious wear. You can get there by motor-tricycle for about Y5.

Dàshà Bīnguǎn (☎ 712 1546; dm Y25-38, tw Y100) This is a simple place, not bad in a pinch. Hot water is available in the evening.

Another potential place to stay is the popular Snowland Restaurant. Hotel construction was underway at the time of writing, so it's worth checking out. Otherwise, there are a few standard Chinese-style hotels with cheap rooms.

Eating

Popular Tibetan dishes that you'll find in Xiàhé are *momo* (boiled dumplings) and *tsampa*, a mixture of yak butter, cheese, barley and sugar that's eaten uncooked.

Nomad Restaurant (Mùmín Qíquán Fànzhuāng; dishes from Y5) Not only does it have a great location, but it also offers the best Tibetan cooking around. *Jaathik* (noodle soup) and boiled yak meat (better than it sounds) are two local dishes to try here. It's on the 3rd floor just before the monastery walls.

Everest Cafe Next door to the Overseas Tibetan Hotel, the Everest has quasi-Western breakfasts (Y6) and delicious Nepali curries (Y18).

Snowland Restaurant (Xuěyù Cāntīng; dishes from Y5) This is one of the more popular spots in town, with cheap Tibetan and Chinese eats. It's on the 2nd floor.

For Chinese or Hui food, try the restaurants around the bus station.

Shopping
You can pick up some Tibetan handicrafts in the shops along the main street, the pickings include daggers, fur-lined boots, colourful Tibetan shawls and tiny silver teapots. Prices are sometimes negotiable, sometimes not.

Getting There & Away
There are continual rumours of an airport being built here, but for the time being Xiàhé is accessible only by bus. Most travellers head on to either Lánzhōu or Sìchuān; the road less travelled takes you over the mountains to Tóngrén. Touts are pretty aggressive at the bus station, so hold on tight to your bags.

See box below for details.

If you can't get a direct ticket to/from Lánzhōu, take a bus to Línxià and change there (see p812 for details). Insurance is available from the PICC office across from the post office.

Getting Around
Most hotels and restaurants rent bikes for Y10 per day. Motor-tricycles cost about Y2 for a short trip.

AROUND XIÀHÉ
Sangke & Ganjia Grasslands
桑科、甘加草原
Around and beyond the village of Sāngkē, 14km up the valley from Xiàhé, are large expanses of open grassland, where the Tibetans graze their yak herds. In summer these rolling pastures are at their greenest and abound with wildflowers. Of Lower and Upper Sāngkē, the latter is preferable (admission Y3).

The road from Xiàhé rises gradually and you can cycle up in about one hour. You can also get there by taking a bus from Xiàhé to Sāngkē village (Sāngkē gōngshè) or hire a motor-tricycle for about Y25 return. There are horseback rides (Y20 per hour), but some travellers find them cheesy.

If you're willing to spend a little more, visit the Ganjia Grasslands (Gānjiā Cǎoyuán) instead, 34km from Xiàhé and much less developed. An additional half-hour from Ganjia are the Takkar Grasslands, famed for their enormous rock formations and a great place to camp.

The **Labrang Travel Service** (Lābǔléng Lǚxíngshè; 2nd fl; ☎ 712 5168) in Xiàhé runs tours to Ganjia and Takkar; a car for four people and an English-speaking guide is Y200 for the day. Otherwise buses pass by the Ganjia Grasslands; ask for Gānjiā Cǎoyuán.

Tarzang Lake
Approximately 25km from Xiàhé towards Lánzhōu is this small sacred Tibetan lake. It makes for a lovely picnic and you can walk around it in about 20 minutes. You can get here by bicycle or bus. When you see a white-on-blue sign above the road, take the next road up. It's a steep, rocky grade and will take up to an hour to get to the lake on foot.

XIÀHÉ BUS TIMETABLES
Buses from Xiàhé include:

Destination	Price	Duration	Frequency	Departs
Hézuò	Y9	1½-2hr	half-hourly	6.10am-5.40pm
Lánzhōu	Y32-44	5-6hr	4 daily	6.30am, 7.30am, 8.30am, 2.30pm
Línxià	Y13-18	2½-3hr	half-hourly	6am-5.30pm
Tóngrén	Y17	5hr	1 daily	7.30am
Xīníng	Y41	7hr	1 daily	6.30am

HÉZUÒ 合作

☎ 0941

The booming regional capital of Gānnán (southern Gānsù), Hézuò is a transit point for travellers plying the route between Gānsù and Sìchuān provinces.

To extend visas, walk 500m to your right as you exit the main bus station. The PSB is on the 3rd floor of an official-looking building.

About 2km from the bus station along the main road towards Xiàhé is the **Milarepa Palace** (Jiǔcéng Lóu; 九层楼; admission Y10; ☯ 9am-6pm), whose nine-storey interior is a patchwork of colours and sparkling golden thread. In addition to the elaborate quilted *thangkas*, there's also a sacred meteorite inside.

If you time your buses, you won't have to spend the night here. If not, stay at the hotel **Jīndū Bīnguǎn** (金都宾馆; ☎ 821 1135; 60 Tengzhi Jie; dm/tw Y30/90), to the left as you exit the main bus station, 75m down the road.

Getting There & Away

There are two bus stations in Hézuò, one government-run (the main bus station), the other private, and their schedules are much the same. To get from the private bus station to the main bus station, take a motor-tricycle for around Y3. You can buy PICC insurance at both bus stations.

Hézuò is the place where buses from Zöigê (Ruòěrgài), in Sìchuān, and Xiàhé meet. There are frequent buses to Xiàhé (Y9, 1½ to two hours), Línxià (Y12 to Y18, two to 2½ hours) and Lánzhōu (Y32 to Y744, five to six hours) from 6.30am to 4pm.

Going south is a different story. There are only two buses per day to Zöigê, leaving at 7.30am and 9am (Y36.5, seven hours). Buses to Lángmùsì leave at 8am and 11am (Y20, five hours). The new highway from Hézuò to Zöigê, under construction at the time of writing, should shorten these times.

LÁNGMÙSÌ 郎木寺

☎ 0941

Straddling the border between Sìchuān and Gānsù is Lángmùsì (Namu), a rural Tibetan village nestled among steep grassy meadows, evergreen forests and snow-clad peaks. An enchanting place, surrounded by countless red and white monastery buildings and with numerous possibilities for hikes and horse

treks, it's easy to spend a few relaxing days here. The hills surrounding this area are also traditional sites for sky burials (see p747)

The White Dragon River (Báilóng Jiāng) divides the town in two. On the Sìchuān side is the **Dachang Lamo Kerti Gompa** (admission Y15). Built in 1413 this lamasery is home to around 700 monks, who study medicine, astrology and esoteric traditions. The ticket is valid for three days, and grants admission to the monastery (visit in the morning) as well as several small grottoes further up the valley, where monks give thanks for the village's water source. On the Gānsù side, higher up on the hills, is the smaller **Sertri Gompa**. Both lamaseries belong to the Gelugpa school.

There's also a Hui mosque at the end of town. Check with Gompo at the Lángmùsì Bīnguǎn for horse treks.

Sleeping & Eating

Accommodation in Lángmùsì is basic.

Lángmùsì Bīnguǎn (郎木寺宾馆; dm/tw Y15/25 per bed) The English-speaking staff are extremely friendly; the main drawback is the noise. It's on a smaller road across from Lesha's Restaurant.

Dácāng Bīnguǎn (达仓宾馆; tr Y15, tw Y20-45 per bed) If you're a stickler for cleanliness, this is the hotel for you. It's a large, white-tiled building in the town centre.

Renchin Hotel (仁青宾馆; Rénqīng Bīnguǎn; dm/tw Y20/25 per bed) Though quiet, the Renchin doesn't get the best reviews from travellers. It's across from Kerti Gompa, 10 minutes' up the road from the town centre.

Lesha's Restaurant (☎ 667 1179) This tiny place is along the main road. Lesha whips up fresh apple pie, coffee (the real thing!), yak burgers and chips. Be warned – the servings are humungous! Lesha can also arrange travel to/from Sōngpān (in Sìchuān, p749).

Getting There & Away

Unless you take a direct bus to Lángmùsì from Hézuò, you can get here on one of the Hézuò/Xiàhé–Zöigê buses, which drop you off at an intersection 4km from the town. Motor-tricycles wait there to take passengers into town for Y2.

To get to Zöigê (Ruòěrgài) you'll need to catch one of the buses from Hézuò, which means catching a motor-tricycle out to the intersection with the main road to Sìchuān.

Buses to Zöigê generally pass by between 11.30am and 2pm. From Lángmùsì there are two daily buses to Hézuò (Y20) departing at 7am and 8am.

HEXI CORRIDOR

Bounded by the Qílián Shān range to the south and the Mazong, Longshou and Heli ranges to the north, this narrow strip of land, around which the province is formed, was once the sole western passage in and out of the Middle Kingdom.

ZHĀNGYÈ 张掖

☎ 0936 / pop 489,600

Zhāngyè is an agreeable place, with willow-shaded streets and a friendly, carefree atmosphere, making it decidedly nicer than other towns along the Hexi Corridor. The major reason to stop here is to visit China's largest sleeping Buddha and to do some hiking in the Qílián Shān range around Mǎtí Sì.

The **Great Buddha Temple** (Dàfó Sì; 大佛寺; ☎ 821 9671; admission Y21; ⏰ 7.30am-6.30pm) originally dates to 1098 (Western Xia dynasty) and contains a 35m-long sleeping Buddha, surrounded by deteriorating clay arhats and Qing dynasty murals. Take a good look at the main hall – it's one of the few wooden structures from this era still standing in China. One block north you'll find the **mù tǎ** (wooden pagoda; 木塔; admission Y5; ⏰ 7.30am-6.30pm), a brick and wooden structure that was first built in AD 528.

For orientation, the drum tower (*gǔlóu*, 鼓楼) stands in the centre of town; the Great Buddha Temple complex is on a Qing-style pedestrian street south of here.

Sleeping & Eating

Liángmào Bīnguǎn (粮贸宾馆; ☎ 824 0162; Dong Jie; dmY18, tw Y60-120) Five minutes' east of the drum tower is this seven-storey hotel, with clean, airy rooms.

For eating, head 300m west of the drum tower and look for an alley with colourful, wooden signs at the entrance and more faux-Qing architecture. There are dozens of clean, friendly restaurants here. English isn't spoken, so it's a perfect time to whip out the phrasebook and match up the dishes.

Getting There & Away

The town has three bus stations, in the south, east and west. The south station (*nán zhàn*), near the Great Buddha Temple, is the most convenient.

See box below for details.

While arriving by train is no problem, departures are another story. You're better off sticking to the bus.

AROUND ZHĀNGYÈ
Mǎtí Sì 马蹄寺

In the foothills of the icy Qílián Shān range lie the former Tibetan and Chinese Buddhist grottoes of **Mǎtí Sì** (admission Y35). While the area isn't actually a national park, it very well could be, with kilometres of trails rising up along the high ridges overlooking the Hexi Corridor. There are several good day hikes, including the five-hour loop through pine forest and talus fields to the Linsong Waterfall (Línsōng Pùbù; 临松瀑布) and back down past 'Sword Split Stone' (Jiànpīshí, 剑劈石). For unrivalled panoramas, take the elevator-like ascent of the ridge behind the white *chörten* (Tibetan stupas) at Sānshísāntiān

---

ZHĀNGYÈ BUS TIMETABLES

Destinations from Zhāngyè's south station include:

Destination	Price	Duration	Frequency	Departs
Dūnhuáng	Y80	12½hr	1 daily	5.30pm (sleeper)
Jiāyùguān	Y31-39	4-5hr	6 daily	8.20am-1.20pm
Lánzhōu	Y71	7hr	4 daily	7.50am, 10am, noon, 1pm
Lánzhōu	Y121	11hr	1 daily	8pm (sleeper)
Xīníng	Y45.5	7hr	4 daily	7am, 9am, 11am, 6.10pm

SILK ROAD

Shíkū (三十三天石窟). Unfortunately the temples here, built miraculously into the sandstone cliff face, have mostly been decimated inside and are now closed.

The **Wòlóng Shānzhuāng** (卧龙山庄; ☎ 889 1694; dm/tw Y20/100) is a good place to stay. If you're adequately prepared for camping, some overnight trips are also possible. Finding a decent noodle shop (Y5) is not a problem.

GETTING THERE & AWAY

Direct buses leave from the south bus station in Zhāngyè on weekends at 8.20am (Y8.5, 1½ hours) and return around 4pm. During the week you can take frequent buses to the village of Mǎtí Hé (Y7.5, 1½ hours), from where you can catch a minibus for the final leg. Weekly departures are also available from Mǎtí Hé.

JIĀYÙGUĀN 嘉峪关
☎ 0937 / pop 130,900

Following the construction of the Ming dynasty fort here in 1372, Jiāyùguān came to be known colloquially as the 'mouth' of China, while the narrow Hexi Corridor, leading back towards the *nèidì* (inner lands), was dubbed the 'throat'. Even today the metaphor remains lodged in the Chinese psyche, and Jiāyùguān continues to guard its symbolic location at the end of the Great Wall, and hence the western boundary of China proper.

Although a mandatory stop for tour groups, the city and its surrounding sights are not so amazing as to merit a special visit. However, if you're moving east or west at a leisurely pace, a stop here should prove interesting enough.

Information

The main **Bank of China** (Zhōngguó Yínháng; Xinhua Zhonglu; 🕑 9.30am-5.30pm Mon-Fri, 10am-4pm Sat & Sun) changes cash and travellers cheques. The **post office** (Yóujú; cnr Xinhua Zhonglu & Xiongguan Donglu; 🕑 8.30am-7pm Mon-Fri, 10am-6pm Sat & Sun) is at the traffic circle in the centre of town. Just next door is China Telecom's Internet Café, which charges Y2 per hour. There are also plenty of *wǎngbā* (Internet cafés) along Xinhua Zhonglu. The **PSB** (Gōngānjú; Yingbin Donglu; 🕑 8.30am-6pm Mon-Fri) is in the southern part of the city, diagonally opposite the stadium.

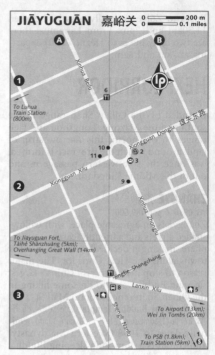

JIĀYÙGUĀN 嘉峪关

0	200 m
0	0.1 miles

Sleeping

Wùmào Bīnguǎn (☎ 628 0855; Shengli Nanlu; dm/tw Y30/100) Just west of the bus station, this is the only budget accommodation around.

Xióngguān Bīnguǎn (☎ 620 1116; fax 622 5399; 1 Xinhua Zhonglu; tr/tw Y78/280) This is a spotless mid-range choice. It also has cheaper triples (without bathrooms) available.

Tàihé Shānzhuāng (☎ 639 6616; Jiayuguan Fort; tw/ste Y80/120) This peaceful hotel has been designed to look like a Qing-era courtyard house. Better yet, it's located at Jiayuguan Fort (right) instead of in town. The ticket office at the fort can give you directions.

Eating

Restaurants are few and far between in Jiāyùguān. When in doubt, head for the Fuqiang Market (Fùqiáng Shìchǎng), north of the traffic circle.

Liuyuan Restaurant (Yuànzhōngyuàn Jiǔdiàn; Lanxin Xilu; dishes from Y5) Directly across from the bus station is this popular Sìchuān restaurant. The cooking is a notch above your standard fare, and there's a menu in English.

Getting There & Away

AIR

Jiāyùguān's airport only operates from May to October, when it offers daily flights to Lánzhōu (Y910) and Xī'ān (via Lánzhōu, Y1110). There are flights to Běijīng (Y1880) thrice weekly.

Book tickets at the **CAAC** (Zhōngguó Mínháng; ☎ 628 7788), located in the Jiāyùguān Bīnguǎn.

BUS

See box below for details.

TRAIN

Jiāyùguān lies on the Lánzhōu–Ürümqi railway line. From here it's three hours to Dūnhuáng, 14 to 17 hours to Ürümqi, two to three hours to Zhāngyè, 9½ hours to Lánzhōu and 20 hours to Xī'ān. Sleeper tickets to Lánzhōu and to Ürümqi are sometimes available, but don't count on it. Other destinations include Běijīng, Chéngdū, Zhōngwèi, Shànghǎi and Zhèngzhōu.

You can purchase tickets at the **train booking office** (huǒchē zhàn shòupiào tīng; Y5 commission; ⊙ 9.30am-5.30pm), left of the ICBC Bank on Xinhua Zhonglu.

The train station is 5km south of the town centre. Bus No 1 runs down Xinhua Zhonglu to the train station and charges Y1. A taxi there should cost no more than Y10.

Getting Around

TO/FROM THE AIRPORT

The airport is 13km northeast of the city; shuttles to/from the Jiāyùguān Bīnguǎn are Y10.

BICYCLE

Bikes are excellent for getting to some of the surrounding attractions. The gatekeeper at the Jiǔgāng Bīnguǎn rents them for Y6 per day.

TAXI

Motorbikes, taxis and minibuses congregate outside the main hotels and around the bus station. It is possible to hire a taxi and visit the Wei Jin Tombs, Jiayuguan Fort and the Overhanging Great Wall in half a day, which should cost you no more than Y100; if you just go to the fort and Overhanging Wall, figure on Y50. One way to the fort is about Y15.

AROUND JIĀYÙGUĀN
Jiayuguan Fort 嘉峪关城楼

One of the classic images of western China, the **Jiayuguan Fort** (Jiāyùguān Chénglóu; admission Y60; ⊙ 8.30am-6.30pm) guards the pass that lies between the snow-capped Qílián Shān peaks and Hēi Shān (Black Mountain) of the Mǎzōng Shān range.

Built in 1372, the fort was christened the 'Impregnable Defile Under Heaven'. Although the Chinese often controlled territory far beyond the Jiāyùguān area, this was the last major stronghold of the empire to the west.

JIĀYÙGUĀN BUS TIMETABLES

Destinations from Jiāyùguān include:

Destination	Price	Duration	Frequency	Departs
Dūnhuáng	Y45.5-66.5	5-7hr	4 daily	9am, 10.30am, 11.30am, 2.30pm
Lánzhōu	Y135	12hr	3 daily	2.30pm, 4.30pm, 6.30pm
Zhāngyè	Y30.5-37	4-5hr	4 daily	9.40am, 11.10am, 11.40am, 3pm

At the eastern end of the fort is the Gate of Enlightenment (Guānghuà Mén) and in the west is the Gate of Conciliation (Róuyuǎn Mén). Over each gate stand 17m-high towers with upturned flying eaves; on the inside are horse lanes leading up to the top of the wall.

Admission also includes an excellent museum, with photos, artefacts, maps and historical anecdotes related to the Great Wall and Jiāyùguān.

Only 5km west of town, it's possible to cycle here in about half an hour.

Overhanging Great Wall 悬壁长城

Linking Jiāyùguān with Hēi Shān, the **wall** (Xuánbì Chángchéng; admission Y9; 8.30am-dusk) is believed to have been constructed in 1539. It had since pretty much crumbled to dust, but was reconstructed in 1987. From the upper tower high on a ridge you get a sweeping view of the desert, the oasis of Jiāyùguān and the glittering snow-capped peaks in the distance.

The wall is 6km north of Jiayuguan Fort via the shortest route (a rough dirt road leading north towards the mountains) or 10km on the surfaced road.

Wei Jin Tombs 新城魏晋墓

These **tombs** (Xīnchéng Wèijìnmù; admission Y31; 8am-6.30pm) date from approximately AD 220 to 420 (the Wei and Western Jin periods) and contain brick wall paintings depicting various social activities, such as hunting, farming and banqueting. There are literally thousands of tombs in the desert 20km east of Jiāyùguān, but only one is currently open to visitors. You can also see some of the bricks and tomb contents at the fort museum.

July 1st Glacier 七一冰川

The July 1st Glacier (Qīyī Bīngchuān) sits at 4300m, high up in the Qílián Shān range. It is about 90km southwest of Jiāyùguān and is reached via the train (Y9) to the iron-ore town of Jìngtiěshān, which departs from Jiāyùguān's Luhua train station at 8.10am. It's a scenic three-hour train trip to Jìngtiěshān, where you can hire a taxi to the glacier. It is a further 20km to the glacier, and the return trip should cost about Y120. Hikers can walk a 5km trail alongside the glacier, but at that elevation it gets cold even in summer, so come prepared.

You could theoretically do this in one day, but it's better to stay the night in Jìngtiěshān. This leaves you with enough time the next morning to hire a taxi (Y50 return) up to Tiān'é Hú and the Tibetan village Qíqīng. There is a cheap and basic hostel (zhāodàisuǒ) in town.

LIǓYUÁN 柳园

☎ 0937

Liǔyuán, a forlorn little town on the railway line between Lánzhōu and Ürümqi, is the jumping-off point for Dūnhuáng, 130km to the south. The **Liǔtiě Fàndiàn** (柳铁饭店; ☎ 557 2102; dm/tw Y30/80) is to the right of the train station, but unless you're catching an early morning train, there should be no need to stay here.

There are six trains daily in each direction. Going east, it takes three hours to reach Jiāyùguān and 13 hours to Lánzhōu. To the west, it's eight to 10 hours to Turpan and 10 to 12 hours to Ürümqi. Train Nos N949 and T197 are good options west as they originate here; they depart at 7.41pm and 11.08pm respectively.

Tickets can be purchased up to three days in advance or at the booking office in Dūnhuáng. There are also daily departures to Běijīng, Chéngdū, Korla, Shànghǎi, Xī'ān and Zhèngzhōu.

Minibuses for Dūnhuáng (Y15, two hours) depart from in front of the train station when trains arrive. A shared taxi generally charges around Y30 per person.

DŪNHUÁNG 敦煌

☎ 0937

After travelling for hours towards Dūnhuáng, the monotonous desert landscape suddenly gives way to lush, green cultivated fields with mountainous rolling sand dunes as a backdrop. The area has a certain haunting beauty, especially at night under a star-studded sky. It's not so much the desert dunes and romantic nights that attract so many tourists to Dūnhuáng, but the superb Buddhist art at the nearby Mogao Caves.

Information
EMERGENCY
At the time of writing, the PSB in Dūnhuáng did not handle visa requests; you'll need to go to Jiāyùguān to get an extension.

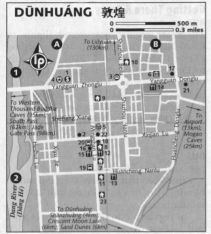

DŪNHUÁNG 敦煌

0 ————— 500 m
0 ————— 0.3 miles

To Liǔyuán
(130km)

To Western
Thousand Buddha
Caves (35km);
South Pass
(62km); Jade
Gate Pass (98km)

To
Airport
(13km);
Mogao
Caves
(25km)

To Dūnhuáng
Shānzhuāng (4km);
Crescent Moon Lake
(6km); Sand Dunes (6km)

Dang River
(Dāng Hé)

INTERNET ACCESS
Shíkōng Wǎngbā (Mingshan Lu; Y2 per hr; ☷ 8am-midnight).

INTERNET RESOURCES
http://idp.bl.uk Online database of digitalised manu-scripts from the Library Cave at Mogao. Geared towards

researchers, but with some good background information nevertheless.

LAUNDRY
Laundry (Gānxǐdiàn; Xinjian Lu) A central and cheap laundry service.

MONEY
Bank of China (Zhōngguó Yínháng; Yangguan Zhonglu; ☷ 8am-noon & 3-6.30pm) You can change travellers cheques or use the ATM here.

POST
Post Office (Yóujú; ☷ 8am-7pm) Located in the China Telecom building on the main traffic circle.

TOURIST INFORMATION & TRAVEL AGENCIES
Travel agencies are a dime a dozen in Dūnhuáng, although there's little reason to use them.
CITS (Zhōngguó Guójì Lǚxíngshè; ☎ 882 5584; Mingshan Lu) Located on the 2nd floor of the International Hotel, this office can set you up with an English-speaking guide.

Sights
COUNTY MUSEUM 县博物馆
Exhibits at the local **museum** (Xiàn Bówùguǎn; ☎ 882 2981; Yangguan Donglu; admission Y10; ☷ 8am-6pm) include Tibetan and Chinese scriptures uncovered from the Library Cave, and relics from the South Pass and the Jade Gate Pass.

Sleeping
Competition among Dūnhuáng's hotels is fierce, and you should get significant dis-counts outside of summer.

BUDGET
Fēitiān Bīnguǎn (☎ 882 2337; Mingshan Lu; dm Y30, tw Y260-320; ☷) This long-standing two-star hotel is in a good location. Dorms are clean and the air-conditioned twins comfortable.

Míngshān Bīnguǎn (☎ 882 2122; Mingshan Lu; dm Y25, tw Y120-360 ☷) Its dorms are a better deal than the twins, which are somewhat musty.

Yǒuhǎo Bīnguǎn (☎ 882 3072; Mingshan Lu; tw Y80-140, tr Y150-210) These are the best-value twins in town, some newly renovated.

MID-RANGE
Tàiyáng Dàjiǔdiàn (☎ 882 9998; www.dhsuntravel .com; 5 Shazhou Beilu; tw Y488-688; ☷) The Tàiyáng is as nice as it comes in town, with some Japanese touches and spacious rooms.

Jiàrì Dàjiǔdiàn (☎ /fax 882 5258; 18 Mingshan Lu; tw & d Y238; ❀) Opened in 2004, the Jiari is bright, clean and has a no-smoking policy.

TOP END

Dūnhuáng Shānzhuāng (Silk Rd Dunhuang Hotel; ☎ 888 2088; www.the-silk-road.com; tw US$100, ste US$150-1000; ❀) If you're going to splurge on one hotel in China, this would be a good choice. One kilometre from the Míngshā Shān sand dunes, the rooms match the desert landscape perfectly. Imagine Central Asian rugs, a cool stone floor and tasteful Chinese antiques. There's a taxi service (Y10) to/from town.

Eating

There are three Western cafés in town, all with similar food and prices: **Charley Johng's Cafe** (Mingshan Lu), **Shirley's Cafe** (Mingshan Lu) and **John's Information Cafe** (Fēitiān Bīnguǎn courtyard, Mingshan Lu). In addition to providing extra services, such as bike rental (Y1 per hour), these are good spots to exchange information with other travellers.

Dūnhuáng's night market is an extremely lively scene and worth a visit. Spilling out of a large courtyard off Yangguan Donglu, it houses scores of restaurants and kebab stands. For gastronomes, the town's strange speciality, *lǘròu huáng miàn* (noodles with donkey meat), can also be found here.

Another popular local dish is *dàpánjī*, a whole chicken cut up and stir-fried with noodles, onions and peppers, then drowned in a pool of chilli sauce. For an authentic meal, the raucous restaurant around the corner from the Yǒuhǎo Bīnguǎn is a sure bet. One serving will feed three people (Y30). For noodles and dumplings at Chinese prices, try the smaller restaurants on Shichang Xiang.

Getting There & Away

AIR

There are regular year-round flights to Lánzhōu (Y1030), Xī'ān (Y1680), Běijīng (Y1880) and Ürümqi (Y710). From July to October, there are flights to Chéngdū (Y1540) and Shànghǎi (Y2460). Seats can be booked at the **CAAC** (Zhōngguó Mínháng; ☎ 882 2389; Yangguan Donglu; ☽ 8.30am-noon & 2.30-6pm), or at the **China Southern Airlines** (Nánfāng Hángkōng Gōngsī; ☎ 882 9710) office along Mingshan Lu.

BUS

See box below for details.

Remember that if there's a sand storm blowing, the trip to Liǔyuán can take up to four hours.

The regular bus to Golmud leaves at 8am, and takes a rugged but scenic route that crosses the snow-covered Altun Mountains. There's also a sleeper bus in the evening. It's chilly up in the mountains, so keep some warm clothing handy, regardless of how hot it may have been in Dūnhuáng.

To get to Ürümqi or Turpan, you'll need to change buses in Hāmì.

TRAIN

More than one person has complained of getting ripped off by various 'booking agents' in town. The real **train booking office** (tiělù shòupiàochù; Y5 commission) is just to the right of a small Bank of China branch on Yangguan Donglu – this will definitely save you money. See p820 for train details.

Getting Around

You can rent bikes from the cafés or street stalls for Y1 per hour. Getting to some of the outlying sights by bike is possible, but not such a great idea at the height of summer.

DŪNHUÁNG BUS TIMETABLES

Direct buses to/from Dūnhuáng include:

Destination	Price	Duration	Frequency	Departs
Golmud	Y78-91	8hr	2 daily	8am & 7.30pm (sleeper)
Hāmì	Y60	7hr	1 daily	8am
Jiāyùguān	Y43.5-66	5-7hr	hourly	7am-10.30pm
Lánzhōu	Y214	17hr	2 daily	8.30am, 10.30am (both sleepers)
Liǔyuán	Y15	2hr	every 2 hours	7.30am-7.30pm

To charter a ride for the sights around town, the minibus stop across from the Jiàrì Dàjiǔdiàn on Mingshan Lu is the place to start the negotiations.

Dūnhuáng's airport is 13km east of town. A taxi there costs around Y20.

AROUND DŪNHUÁNG

Mogao Caves 莫高窟

The Mogao Caves (Mògāo Ku) are, simply put, one of the greatest repositories of Buddhist art in the world. Following the collapse of trade along the Silk Road after the Yuan dynasty, this vast series of grottoes – stretching 1700m along a canyon wall – lay forgotten for centuries amid the sands of the Gobi.

The traditional date ascribed to the founding of the first cave is AD 366. From this point onwards the site gradually developed into an important centre of Buddhist learning and worship, and at its peak housed 18 monasteries, over 1400 monks and nuns, as well as countless artists, translators and calligraphers. Wealthy traders and important officials were the primary donors responsible for creating new caves, and caravans heading in either direction would often make the long detour past Mogao to pray or give thanks for a safe journey through the treacherous wastelands to the west.

NORTHERN WEI, WESTERN WEI & NORTHERN ZHOU CAVES

The earliest caves are distinctly Indian in style. All contain a central pillar, representing a stupa (symbolically containing the ashes of the Buddha), which the devout would circle in prayer. Paint was derived from malachite (green), cinnabar (red) and lapis lazuli (blue), expensive minerals imported from Central Asia.

Historically speaking, this was the period when Buddhism began to take root in China. The fall of the Han dynasty in AD 220, coupled with invasions in the north by the Turkic-speaking Tuoba, sent the country into turmoil. The insecurity of life during this time made Buddhism's teachings of suffering, transience and rebirth particularly appealing.

The art of this period is characterised by its attempt to depict the spirituality of those who had transcended the material world

through their asceticism. The Wei statues are slim, ethereal figures with finely chiselled features and comparatively large heads. Paintings are of predominantly male figures, often in unusual postures. Don't be fooled by the thick, black modernist strokes – it's the oxidization of lead in the paint, not some forerunner of Picasso.

SUI CAVES

The Sui dynasty began when a general of Chinese or mixed Chinese-Tuoba origin usurped the throne of the Northern Zhou dynasty. Prudently putting to death all the sons of the former emperor, he embarked on a series of campaigns that by AD 589 had reunited northern and southern China for the first time in 360 years.

The Sui dynasty was short-lived, and very much a transition between the Wei and Tang periods. This can be seen in the Sui caves: the graceful Indian curves in the Buddha and Bodhisattvas figures start to give way to the more rigid style of Chinese sculpture.

TANG CAVES

During the Tang dynasty (AD 618–907), China pushed its borders westward as far as Balkhash Lake in today's Kazakhstan. Trade expanded and foreign merchants and people of diverse religions streamed into the Tang capital of Chang'an.

This was the high point of the cave art at Mogao. Painting and sculpture techniques became much more refined, and important aesthetic developments, notably the sex change (from male to female) of Guanyin and the flying apsaras, took place. The beautiful murals of Western Paradise offer rare insights into the court life, music, dress and architecture of Tang China.

Some 230 caves were carved during the Tang dynasty, including two impressive grottoes containing enormous, seated Buddha figures. The statue residing in cave 96 (believed to represent Empress Wu Zetian, who used Buddhism to consolidate her power) is a towering 34.5m tall.

POST-TANG CAVES

Following the Tang dynasty, the economy around Dūnhuáng went into decline, and the luxury and vigour typical of Tang painting began to be replaced by simpler drawing techniques and flatter figures. The mysterious

Xixia kingdom, who controlled most of Gānsù from 983 to 1227, made a number of additions to the caves at Mogao and began to introduce Tibetan influences.

ADMISSION

Entrance to the **caves** (admission Y120; ☉ 8am-5pm) is extremely rigid – it's impossible to visit them on your own. The general admission ticket grants you a two-hour tour of 10 caves, including the infamous Library Cave (No 17 – see Foreign Devils on the Silk Road, below) and a related exhibit containing rare fragments of manuscripts in classical Uighur and Manichean. The highly recommended Dunhuang Research Centre, with eight flawlessly reproduced caves, each representative of a different period, can be visited after the tour. Excellent English-speaking guides are always available, and you can generally arrange tours in many other European and Asian languages as well.

While there are certain caves that are justifiably more famous than others, don't get your hopes up too much for seeing (for example) Cave No 257 on the general tour. The 20 'open' caves are rotated fairly regularly, unfortunately, making recommendations useless. It is, however, possible to visit 12 of the more unusual caves for an additional fee. Prices cost Y100 (No 217, early Tang) to Y500 (No 465, Tantric art).

Most caves are lit only by indirect sunlight from outside, making a torch (flashlight) imperative. Your guide will have one, but if you're in a large group consider renting one at the gate (Y13) or bringing your own. Photography is strictly prohibited everywhere within the fenced-off caves area, and cameras and bags must be deposited at an office near the entrance gate (Y2).

Despite the high admission and the inconvenience of the guide system, don't be discouraged – entering your first cave will make it all seem worthwhile.

GETTING THERE & AWAY

The Mògāo Caves are 25km (30 minutes) from Dūnhuáng. A bus leaves at around 8am from in front of Fēitiān Bīnguǎn (one way Y10). Alternatively you can negotiate with minibus drivers who sit diagonally across from Dūnhuáng Fàndiàn; you should be able to get a seat for Y15.

Some people ride out to the caves on a bicycle, but be warned that half the ride is through total desert – hot work in summer.

Western Thousand Buddha Caves
西千佛洞

These **caves** (Xī Qiānfó Dòng; admission Y20), 35km west of Dūnhuáng, are cut into the cliff face of the Dǎng Hé gorge. The desolation of these caves stands in stark contrast to the

---

FOREIGN DEVILS ON THE SILK ROAD

Few things raise the ire of a Chinese intellectual faster than the subject of cultural relics destroyed or carted off by marauding Western imperialists. Near the top of the list of crimes is Dūnhuáng's Library Cave (No 17), where in 1900 the self-appointed guardian Wang Yuanlu discovered a hidden library filled with tens of thousands of immaculately preserved manuscripts and paintings, dating as far back as AD 406. It's hard to describe the exact magnitude of the discovery, but stuffed into the tiny room were texts in rare Central Asian languages, military reports, music scores, medical prescriptions, Confucian and Taoist classics, and Buddhist sutras copied by some of the greatest names in Chinese calligraphy – not to mention the world's oldest printed book, the *Diamond Sutra* (AD 868). In short, it was an incalculable amount of original source material regarding Chinese, Central Asian and Buddhist history. Exactly to whom this information should belong, however, went on to become something of a thorny issue.

Seven years after the discovery rival archaeologists Aurel Stein and Paul Pelliot – only two of the numerous European adventurers hauling away Central Asian Buddhist art from the old Silk Roads – together managed to get their hands on close to 20,000 of the cave's priceless manuscripts, smuggling them to museums in England and France respectively. Today defenders of the pair point to the widespread destruction that took place during the Cultural Revolution, and the defacing of Buddhist artwork by Muslim iconoclasts. But what really provokes the wrath of the Chinese is the amount the two 'donated' to Wang Yuanlu for their haul: in total, the paltry sum of UK£220.

intense tourist conveyer belt at Mogao – on a nice day you may find yourself here alone, with only the sound of the wind in the trees to keep you company.

There are currently 16 caves still intact, six of which are open to the public. The earliest caves date back to the Northern Wei dynasty and the most recent were carved during the Tang dynasty. While less impressive than Mogao, the advantage is that there are no time constraints here, and the atmosphere is much more conducive to appreciating the artwork. You can even wander off on a walk through the desert canyon.

The caves are best reached by taxi (Y60 return) or minibus. Alternatively catch a public bus from the intersection of Xiyu Jie and Yangguan Zhonglu (also known as Xi Dajie) in Dūnhuáng, which goes to Shāzǎoyuán. Just ask the driver to drop you off at the turn-off to the caves. It's a five-minute walk down to the caves. Bringing a torch is recommended.

Crescent Moon Lake 月牙泉
Six kilometres south of Dūnhuáng at Míngshā Shān (Singing Sands Mountain), the desert meets the oasis in dramatic fashion. At the base of the colossal mega dunes, whose highest peak stands at 1715m, lies a small pool, known as **Crescent Moon Lake** (Yuèyáquán; admission Y50).

The climb to the top of the dunes is sweaty work, but the view across the undulating desert sands and green poplar trees below makes it a spectacular sight. If your sole interest is in scaling the dunes, you can avoid the entrance fee – just keep going to the right until there's no more fence.

Recreational activities within the park include camel rides, 'dune surfing' (sand sliding) and paragliding (jumping from the top of high dunes with a chute on your back).

Most people head out here at about 5pm when the weather starts to cool down. You can ride a bike to the dunes in around 20 minutes. Minibuses (sitting diagonally across from Dūnhuáng Fàndiàn) cost Y3 when full, and taxis are Y15 one way.

Jade Gate Pass & South Pass
玉门关、阳关
Jade Gate Pass (Yùmén Guān) and South Pass (Yáng Guān) were originally part of the Han dynasty series of beacon towers

that extended to the garrison town of Loulan in Xīnjiāng. For caravans travelling westwards, Jade Gate Pass marked the beginning of the northern route to Turpan, while the South Pass was the start of the southern route through Miran.

Today there's not much left of either, and the absurd admission fees (Y30 and Y40 respectively) and long drive (over half a day to visit both) will probably deter all but the most serious history buffs.

EASTERN GĀNSÙ

The southeast of Gānsù holds some of the prettiest country in the northwest. Tamped earthen houses and terraced wheat and corn fields are interspersed with lush, forested hills, and the Silk Road remains at Tiānshuǐ and Luòmén are in relatively good condition compared with much of what you'll see to the west.

TIĀNSHUǏ 天水
☎ 0938 / pop 400,000
Located near one of the legendary cradles of Chinese civilization, Tiānshuǐ has two major sights: the Buddhist statues at Màijī Shān and the Fu Xi Temple in Qínchéng. Tiānshuǐ is technically the second-largest municipality in Gānsù, but it's not too overwhelming and is a pleasant first stop for those following the Silk Road west. Of note are the ancient cypress trees, some more than 1000 years old, growing in the temples of Qínchéng.

Orientation
Tiānshuǐ is in fact two separate towns connected by a long freeway – the gritty railhead sprawl, known as Běidào, and the central area to the west, known as Qínchéng. Bus Nos 1 and 6 run frequently between the two districts (Y2.4, 30 minutes). While Běidào is ultimately more convenient, Qínchéng is by far the nicer place to stay.

Màijī Shān is 35km south of Běidào. There are no direct public buses there, but minibuses leave when full from in front of the train station (Y10, one hour). You can also hire a taxi for Y100 return.

Information
In Běidào you can change cash and travellers cheques at the **Bank of China** (Zhōngguó Yínháng;

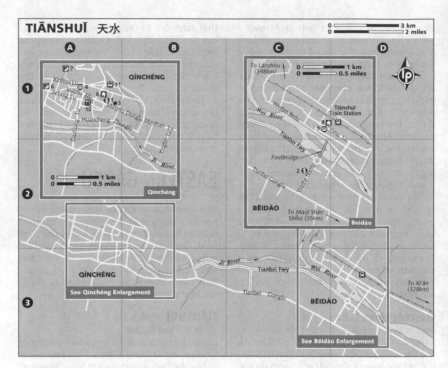

TIĀNSHUǏ 天水

🕑 8.30am–noon & 2.30–5.30pm) branch on Weihe Nanlu, 500m south of the intersection with Weibin Beilu. The main branch is on Minzhu Donglu in Qínchéng. The **post office** (Yóujú; 🕑 8am–6pm) is on Minzhu Xilu in Qínchéng, with a branch on Yima Lu in Běidào.

There is a **CITS** (Zhōngguó Guójì Lǚxíngshè; ☎ 821 3621) office in Qínchéng on Minzhu Donglu, 200m east of the Bank of China.

In Qicheng there are a few Internet cafés in the pedestrian Wénmiào Shāngchǎng (a bazaar).

Sights

MÀIJĪ SHĀN SHÍKŪ 麦积山石窟

These **grottoes** (Haystack Mountain; admission scenic area & caves Y54) are one of China's four largest temple groups; the others are at Dàtóng, Luòyáng and Dūnhuáng. The solitary rock formation, sticking up out of the verdant, rolling landscape like a giant haystack (kind of anyway), is adorned with niches and statues carved principally during the Northern Wei and Zhou dynasties (AD 386–581), though new grottoes were added continuously throughout the following fifteen centuries. Catwalks and steep spiral stairs have been built around the cliff face, so while the art is not as amazing as at Dūnhuáng, getting to it is more fun, and you have complete freedom to venture where you like.

Besides the hard-to-miss trio in various states of transcendence (No 13), the most accessible sculptures are along the upper walkways, where you pass the marvellous

SHÍKŪ: GROTTO

The top of the character *shí* (stone, rock) is like the corner of a rock or a cliff, whereas the bottom half is a cake of rock. The top of *kū* means a cave or an earth room. The bottom half sees someone bending to carry something into or out of the cave or room, which would usually have a very low ceiling.

Qīfó Gé (No 4). It's not certain just how the artists managed to clamber so high; one theory is that they created piles from blocks of wood reaching to the top of the mountain before moving down, gradually removing them as they descended. Stone was evidently brought in from elsewhere, since the local rock is too soft for carving, as at Dūnhuáng.

There are three competing *dānwèi* (work units) here, each with their hand in the honey pot. The first will charge you for entering the 'scenic area', the second for entering the grottoes and the third for the **botanical garden** (zhíwùyuán; admission Y17). The latter is not compulsory, but if you want to do some walking, the dense forest filled with the sound of whirring cicadas is the best place to do it. For great views, climb the stairs leading to the botanical garden (the opposite direction from the grottoes).

If you'd like a guided tour, you'll need to pay a visit CITS ahead of time. A guide charges Y150 for the day – the main advantage is that you might see several grottoes that are otherwise closed to the public. Maps (Y5) are available at the first ticket office.

FU XI TEMPLE 伏羲庙
This Ming dynasty **temple** (Fú Xī Miào; admission Y30; ☉ 8am-6pm) was begun in 1483. The main hall is one of the most elaborate structures in Gānsù, with intricate wooden door panels and original paintings of the sixty-four hexagrams (varying combinations of the eight trigrams used in the I Ching) on the ceiling. The city museum, a well-presented collection of regional artefacts and antique furniture, is in a side building.

One of the mythic progenitors of the Chinese people, leaf-clad Fú Xī was reputedly a Chenji local (present-day Tiānshuǐ) who introduced the domestication of animals, hunting and the eight trigrams to early Chinese civilisation. In other guises he appears as a half-dragon with his sister/wife Nǚ Wā, who created the human race from clay.

YUQUAN TEMPLE 玉泉观
On the hillside above Qínchéng is this seemingly infinite **Taoist complex** (Yùquán Guàn; admission Y10; ☉ 7.30am-7.30pm). Although the 'vicissitudes of life' have taken their toll, it's still a pleasant place to wander.

Sleeping & Eating
Tiělù Zhāodàisuǒ (☎ 493 9660; 26 Yima Lu; dm/tw Y20/50-100) This place has simple but cheap rooms. Turn right as you leave the square in front of the train station and continue for about 50m.

Any number of hotels on Yima Lu will have reasonable twins from Y80.

Jiànxīn Fàndiàn (☎ 498 5300; 91 Xinhua Lu; dm/tw Y20/100) The Jianxin has a few nice touches and a convenient location close to the bus station.

Alternatively, for a nicer setting, there are two hotels at Màijī Shān, which will give you a chance to hike in the surrounding area.

Màijī Shānzhuāng (麦积山庄; ☎ 1389 388 6500; dm/tw Y50/60 per bed) The cheaper of the two hotels, this is a slightly worn-down place about 500m before the main car park to the grottoes.

Zhíwùyuán Zhāodàisuǒ (植物园招待所; ☎ 223 1025; beds Y180) Occupies a fabulous spot in the middle of the botanical gardens. It's a hefty hike uphill from the car park, so be prepared.

In Qínchéng, there are scores of good restaurants to choose from in the pedestrian Wénmiào Shāngchǎng. Another option are the food stalls and cheap restaurants located around the Màijī Shān car park.

Getting There & Away
BUS
See the box on p829 for details.

There are also buses to Lánzhōu that depart throughout the day from in front of the train station at Běidào. If you miss the bus to Luòmén, try asking for Wǔshān.

TRAIN
Tiānshuǐ is on the Xī'ān–Lánzhōu railway line; there are dozens of daily trains in either direction, all of which stop here. If you arrive early, you can visit Màijī Shān as a day trip, avoiding the need to stay overnight in Tiānshuǐ.

From Tiānshuǐ it's four to six hours to either Lánzhōu or Xī'ān. There's also a 3pm train to Luòmén (one hour).

LUÒMÉN 洛门
A trip to the **Water Curtain Caves** (Shuǐlián Dòng; 水帘洞; admission Y12), 17km from Luòmén, is like visiting the China of your dreams. Eroding sandstone domes rise above lush canyon walls, and Taoist and Buddhist temples lie hidden in the cliffs, seemingly transported from a Song dynasty landscape painting. The main sight is Lāshāo Sì, an overhanging cliff sheltering a 31m-high figure of Sakyamuni (the historical Buddha), seated cross-legged upon a throne of lotus petals, lions, deer and elephants. The bas-relief carving and accompanying frescoes were completed in the Northern Wei dynasty (AD 386–534). Minibuses in Luòmén will take you to the Water Curtain Caves for Y60 return.

Luòmén is on the Lánzhōu–Xī'ān rail line; there are two trains per day that stop here in either direction. Local buses also run to/from Tiānshuǐ (three hours). Alternatively, catch the morning train (from Lánzhōu) or bus (from Tiānshuǐ) to nearby Wǔshān. From here it's a 20-minute bus ride (Y1.5) to Luòmén. The only place to stay is Luòmén **Bīnguǎn** (洛门宾馆; tw with/without bath Y60/30).

MOON CANYON 月亮峡
Though the Tang eccentric Hán Shān supposedly lived in southeastern China, you can just as easily imagine him eking out a hermit's existence amid the rocky escarpments and cascading streams at Moon Canyon (Yuèliàng Xiá). Part of the Three Beaches National Park (Sāntān Zìrán Bǎohùqū), this is a rare corner of the Middle Kingdom that still has some pristine wilderness. Day hikes along Moon River lead past moss-covered boulders, dense undergrowth and precipit-

ous cliffs to the far-off upper canyon. For those with camping equipment, a possible three-day trek to the purported old growth forest (yuánshǐ sēnlín, 原始森林) upstream.

It's best to pre-arrange transport through **Moon Canyon Retreat** (Yuèliàng Xiá Dùjiàcūn; 月亮峡度假村; www.threebeaches.com; ☯ Apr-Oct) from the nearby towns of Jiālíng or Huīxiàn. There are simple, low-impact lodges (Y120), tents (Y50; sleeping bags not available) and an excellent cook. 'Retreat' is the key word – tucked away inside the canyon, there aren't too many peaceful spots like this in China

Getting There & Away
Moon Canyon is on the Chéngdū–Xī'ān rail line near the village of Jiālíng (嘉陵). There is only one stop per day in either direction (both at around 1pm) – the closest major rail links are Guǎngyuán (Sìchuān) and Bǎojī (Shaanxi). A bus from Tiānshuǐ also runs to nearby Huīxiàn (徽县, Y25, three hours).

PÍNGLIÁNG 平凉
☎ 0933 / pop 106,800
Píngliáng is a quintessential northern town, with broken street lamps and the smell of coal dust in the air. The busy streets hardly seem like the sort of place a Taoist immortal would want to hang around, and, in fact, all of these folks have wisely retired to Kōngtóng Shān – the main reason for visiting the area.

Orientation & Information
The train station is in the northeastern part of town and the bus station in the far western part. The two stations are connected by Dàjiē, the main thoroughfare, home to the town's major hotels, restaurants and shops.

The **Bank of China** (Zhōngguó Yínháng; 17 Xidajie; ☯ 8.30am-noon & 2.30-5.30pm Mon-Fri) and the **post office** (yóujú; 91 Dongdajie; ☯ 8am-7pm) flank the main intersection, 200m apart. The ATM accepts foreign cards. Internet cafés are in the marketplace west of Gòngxiāo Bīnguǎn.

Sleeping & Eating
Píngliáng Bīnguǎn (平凉宾馆; ☎ 825 3988; 86 Xidajie; dm/tw Y60/188) Centrally located, with clean rooms and friendly staff.

Gòngxiāo Bīnguǎn (供销宾馆; ☎ 823 0834; 98 Xidajie; tr Y17-32, tw Y32-40 per bed) Several minutes' walk west of the Píngliáng Bīnguǎn, this place bears a marked resemblance to a Chinese student dorm.

QÍNCHÉNG BUS TIMETABLES

Departures from Qínchéng bus station include:

Destination	Price	Duration	Frequency	Departs
Huīxiàn	Y25	3hr	hourly	6.30am-6pm
Gùyuán	Y33.5	7hr	1 daily	7am
Lánzhōu	Y49	4hr	hourly	6.40am-6.30pm
Línxià	Y47	8hr	1 daily	6.30am
Luòmén	Y11.5	3hr	1 daily	6.30am
Píngliáng	Y34.5-40.5	5-6hr	4 daily	6am, 7am, 8am, noon
Yínchuān	Y65	12hr	1 daily	2.30pm

PÍNGLIÁNG BUS TIMETABLES

Departures from the Píngliáng bus station include:

Destination	Price	Duration	Frequency	Departs
Gùyuán	Y13	1½hr	hourly	8am-4pm
Lánzhōu	Y52-80	4½-5hr	hourly	5.30am-8.30pm
Tiānshuǐ	Y34.5-40.5	5-6hr	hourly	6am-noon
Xī'ān	Y35.5	6hr	hourly	5.30am-8.30pm
Yán'ān	Y81	9hr	1 daily	5.40am

Just west of the above two hotels is a marketplace with numerous restaurants.

Getting There & Away
BUS
See the box above for details.

TRAIN
Getting to Píngliáng is easiest by train. There is an overnight train to Lánzhōu (No N905, Y86) and two daily trains to Xī'ān (Y66, seven hours) via Bǎojī. There is also a 7.30am train to Yínchuān (11½ hours).

Getting Around
Bus No 1 runs from the train station to the bus station along Dajie. A taxi into town is Y5.

AROUND PÍNGLIÁNG
Kōngtóng Shān 崆峒山
On the border of Níngxià in the Liùpán Shān range, **Kōngtóng Shān** (admission Y60; ☯ 8am-6.30pm) is an important peak in the Taoist universe. It was first mentioned by the philosopher Zhuangzi (399–295 BC), and all sorts of immortal sages allegedly lived or made visits here, not least among them the Yellow Emperor himself. The highest summit is over 2100m and there are numerous small paths that lead to the dozens of picturesque temples and pagodas scattered across the mountain. If you'd rather not walk, a vertigo-inducing **cable car** (suǒdào; Y30 return) spans the reservoir to the top of the cliffs.

There is simple accommodation and food available on the mountain, at the **Kōngtóng Shānzhuāng** (崆峒山庄; dm/tw Y60/160; ☯ closed Nov-May).

GETTING THERE & AWAY
Kōngtóng Shān is 11km west of Píngliáng. There are regular minibuses departing from the opposite side of the park across from the bus station (Y5). A taxi to the base costs Y20/40 one way/return, including waiting time. Try to head back early as there are not many buses after 5pm.

If you interested in exploring the Liùpán Shān range further, there are a couple of buses that pass the park's main entrance on the way to Jīngyuán in Níngxià.

Níngxià 宁夏

HIGHLIGHTS

- Raft down the Yellow River past the sand dunes of the **Tengger Desert** (p838)
- Ponder the mysterious sights outside Níngxià's capital, **Yínchuān** (p835)
- Seek out the isolated Buddhist grottoes at **Xūmí Shān** (p839)

★ Yínchuān

★ Tengger Desert

★ Xūmí Shān

■ POP: 5.9 MIL   ■ AREA: 66,400 SQ KM

SILK ROAD

Níngxià resembles a leftover puzzle piece that doesn't quite fit between the neighbouring deserts and mountain ranges. Hanging precariously to the Yellow River (Huáng Hé) that runs along its northern border, the region was never solid ground for the Chinese, who began building earthen fortifications in the Liùpán Shān as early as the Warring States period (475–221 BC). Níngxià's brightest moment in history came under the Xixia (AD 1038–1227), a powerful kingdom that rose up around Xingqing (Yínchuān) and controlled an enormous swath of today's northwest.

In terms of age and size, the province is no more than a mere babe, belatedly formed as an autonomous region for the Hui in 1958. The Hui, descendants of Arab and Persian traders who began settling in China during the Tang dynasty, are in some respects one of the country's more unusual minority groups. Scattered throughout 14 provinces, their various communities generally have little in common, with the exception of cultural practices related to Islam. If the idea of a communist government using religion to define ethnicity seems like a paradox, even stranger is the fact that nearly 80% of the Hui live outside of their own designated autonomous region. In Níngxià itself, the Hui comprise one-third of the population, and live primarily in the poorer south.

Day-to-day existence here is anything but a bed of roses. Beyond the Yellow River and the ancient irrigation channels that run off it, there is little water to be found – bad news for a population that consists mainly of farmers. Poor land reform, little social aid and continuous droughts have turned many of the inhabitants into migrant workers, forced to venture out to big cities such as Lánzhōu and Hohhot in order to support their families.

Entirely off the beaten track, Níngxià remains a place of specific interests: the beautiful but intruding desert, remnants of the enigmatic Xixia and a look at how Islam functions in today's China.

Climate

Part of the Loess Plateau, Níngxià is comprised primarily of arid mountain ranges and highlands. Summer temperatures during the day can be baking, and precipitation is generally no more than a myth. During the long winter, it's not uncommon for the mercury to drop below zero.

Language

Níngxià's dialect is grouped together with the northwestern dialects of Gānsù and Qīnghǎi; an umbrella group known to linguists as Lanyin Mandarin.

YÍNCHUĀN 银川

☎ 0951 / pop 1,000,000

Sheltered from the deserts of Mongolia by the high ranges of Hèlán Shān to the west and abundantly supplied with water from the nearby Yellow River, Yínchuān occupies a favoured geographical position in otherwise harsh surroundings.

The city was once the capital of the Xixia, a powerful Buddhist kingdom founded during the 11th century. Today it's one of China's more pleasant, relaxed provincial capitals, with some interesting outlying sights and a lively market atmosphere.

History

The Xixia, or Tanguts, were descendants of a tribe forced to flee the Tibetan plateau towards the end of the 10th century. Although short-lived, at the kingdom's height it encompassed an area comprised of modern-day Gānsù, Níngxià, Shaanxi and western Inner Mongolia. The Xixia present such an enigma

NÍNGXIÀ

0 _____ 50 km
0 _____ 30 miles

To Bāotóu (461km);
Hohhot (594km)

INNER MONGOLIA

Hèlán Shān

Shízuǐshān

Huángqūqiáo

Pínglúo

Bayan Hot

Twin Pagodas
of Baisikou

Yellow River (Huáng Hé)

INNER MONGOLIA

Gǔnzhōngkǒu

Yínchuān
New City

Yínchuān

Western
Xia Tombs

Tengger Desert

Língwǔ

Qīngtóngxiá Shì

Wúzhōng

307

Qīngtóngxiá Zhèn
108 Dagobas

To Wǔwēi
(140km)

Qīngtóngxiá
Reservoir

Yánchí

Dìngbiān

Zhōngwèi

Gàntáng

Shāpōtóu

Zhōngníng

211

SHAANXI

To Lánzhōu
(210km)

Yellow River (Huáng Hé)

109

Tōngxīn

Huán River

Hǎiyuán

Huánxiàn

Jìngyuán

To
Qìngyáng
(30km)

GĀNSÙ

Nanhua
Mountain

Xumi Shan
Grottoes

Sānyíng

Qīngshuǐ River

Xījí

Gùyuán

GĀNSÙ

Lúpán Shān

Péngyáng

Xīfēngzhèn

Lóngdé

Dīngxī

Jìngyuán

Kōngtóng
Shān
(2123m)

Pingliáng

To Tōngwèi (10km)

To Bǎojī (110km)

SILK ROAD

today because nearly all traces of their civilisation disappeared in one fell swoop – thanks to the Mongols, who supposedly obliterated them in 1227. Nevertheless, if one were to believe Marco Polo, and more convincingly, archaeological evidence uncovered in Kharakhoto (near Ejin Qi, Inner Mongolia), it's possible that some form of Xixia culture existed for at least another hundred years.

Orientation

Yínchuān is divided into two parts. The new industrialised section, Xīxià Qū, is near the train station. The Old City (Xìngqìng Qū) is about 8km to the east and has most of the town's sights, hotels, restaurants and shops, and the long-distance bus station.

Information

BOOKSHOPS

Foreign Languages Bookshop (Wàiwén Shūdiàn; Jiefang Xijie)

INTERNET ACCESS

Lóngbā Wǎngbā (per hr Y2) This central Internet café is inside a courtyard off Xinhua Dongjie.

MONEY

Bank of China (Zhōngguó Yínháng; Jiefang Xijie; 8am-6.30pm) You can change travellers cheques and use the ATM at this main branch. At the branch on Xinhua Dongjie, just east of Minzu Nanjie, you can change travellers cheques, although the ATM is known to be fickle.

POST

Post office (yóujú; 8am-8pm; cnr Jiefang Xijie & Minzu Beijie)

TRAVEL AGENCIES

China International Travel Service (CITS; Zhōngguó Guójì Lǚxíngshè; ☎ 504 8006; 116 Jiefang Xijie; 8.30am-noon & 2.30-6pm) Has an office on the 3rd floor of the building here.

VISAS

Public Security Bureau (PSB; Gōngānjú; 472 Beijing Donglu; 8.30am-noon & 2.30-6.30pm Mon-Fri) This is the foreign affairs bureau. Take the No 3 bus from the Drum Tower.

Sights

NINGXIA PROVINCIAL MUSEUM

宁夏省博物馆

Níngxià's **museum** (Níngxià Shěng Bówùguǎn; 32 Jinning Nanjie; admission Y22; 8.30am-6pm) is in the old Chengtian Temple. Its collection includes an excellent exhibit of Xixia artefacts and writing (which deceptively resembles some sort of esoteric Chinese script), a mediocre sample of the Hèlán Shān rock carvings and a poor introduction to the Hui culture.

Within the leafy courtyard is **Chéngtiānsì Tǎ**, also known as Xī Tǎ (West Pagoda), which you can climb via 13 tiers of steepish stairs. Perhaps of more interest is the small **Reading Room** (Cānkǎo Yuèlǎnshì; admission Y1; 9am-8pm, closed Mon) around the back on Limin Jie. It has a good selection of current magazines in English as well as French and German.

HĀIBĂO TĂ 海宝塔

Also known as Běi Tǎ (North Pagoda), records of this **pagoda** (admission Y5; 8am-6pm) date from the 5th century. In 1739 an earthquake toppled the lot, but it was rebuilt in 1771 in the original style. It's set in the pleasant gardens of a working monastery, and you can still climb up the nine storeys for views of Hèlán Shān to the west and the Yellow River to the east.

There is no public transport here, so you'll have to take a taxi (Y5). It's a little over 3.5km from the Drum Tower.

NANGUAN MOSQUE 南关清真寺

Yínchuān's main **mosque** (Nánguān Qīngzhēnsì; Yuhuangge Nanjie; admission Y8; 8am-6pm) is a modern Middle Eastern–style structure that shows little Chinese architectural influence, with Islamic arches and domed roofs covered in green tiles. It was originally constructed in the Ming dynasty and rebuilt in 1981.

Sleeping

OLD CITY

Báigē Bīnguǎn (☎ 609 0718; Gulou Jie; dm Y30, tw Y108-200;) This hotel has everything you could want from a budget hotel: it's clean, quiet and has a perfect location. It's no surprise that such a good deal is potentially hard to find. Bus No 1 runs here from both the train station and the bus station: get off at the Drum Tower (Gǔlóu) stop, head south on the pedestrian street, and the hotel is hidden in a courtyard to the right.

Yīshèng Bīnguǎn (☎ 604 1888; 67 Nanxun Donglu; tw Y80-138) This brightly lit place has cheap

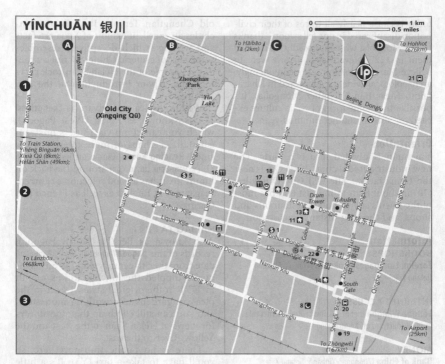

YÍNCHUĀN 银川

twins and a convenient location near the bus station.

Gǔlóu Fàndiàn (☎ 602 8784; fax 602 2573; 26 Jiefang Dongjie; tr Y150, tw Y138-198) The cosy Gulou is adorned with Chinese *huāniǎo* (bird and flower) paintings and some of the nicer rooms overlook the Drum Tower. Discounts of up to 25% are offered year-round.

Gōnghuì Dàshà (Labour Union Hotel; ☎ 601 6898; fax 602 4931; 1 Jiefang Dongjie; tw Y280-360, ste Y480; 🔁) This three-star exemplifies the Party's effortless transition from class struggle to luxury massage showers, which do, in fact, look pretty inviting.

NEW CITY

Yíhéng Bīnguǎn (☎ 396 5366; Xingzhou Lu; dm Y40, tw Y80-400; 🔁) Left out of the train station along the main road, this hotel is handy if you're leaving by train at some odd hour of the night. It's also the only decent place to eat in this part of town.

Eating

Yíngbīnlóu (Yingbinlou Restaurant; Jiefang Xijie; dishes from Y10) This is a fun place popular with the locals. The restaurant on the 2nd floor has excellent Chinese cooking while the 1st floor offers hotpot, yoghurt and ice cream.

SILK ROAD

Shāojīgōng (Jiefang Xijie; small dishes Y36) The specialty of this restaurant is a spicy chicken stew. You cook it yourself and can add various vegetables and noodles to the broth. A small serving is enough for two people.

Ālǐ Dàngāo (Ali Cake; 55 Minzu Beijie; snacks Y2) This is a pleasant place to sit down and have breakfast or write a few postcards. It has pastries and instant coffee.

Good for standard noodles and dumplings are the family-run restaurants around the long-distance bus station or on Zhongshan Nanjie.

Getting There & Away

AIR

Yínchuān's main ticket office of the **Civil Aviation Administration of China** (CAAC; Zhōngguó Mínháng; ☎ 691 3456; cnr Nanhuan Donglu & Shengli Beijie; ☒ 8am-6pm) is located south of the bus station. There are flights connecting Yínchuān with Běijīng (Y1090), Chéngdū (Y1010), Guǎngzhōu (Y1890), Shànghǎi (Y1500), Tàiyuán (Y450), Ürümqi (Y1350, three times a week) and Xī'ān (Y600) among other domestic destinations. Another **office** (36 Minzu Beilu) is across from Ālǐ Dàngāo.

BUS

The long-distance bus station is in the southeastern part of town on the square near the South Gate (Nán Mén). For some northern destinations you may be referred to the **northern bus station** (běimén zhàn); to get there from the long-distance bus station hop on a No 4 bus (Y1).

See box below for bus details.

The frequent kuàikè (express buses) to Zhōngwèi and Gùyuán are definitely worth the added expense.

TRAIN

Yínchuān is on the Lánzhōu–Běijīng railway line, which also runs via Bāotóu, Hohhot and Dàtóng. Express trains from Yínchuān take nine hours to Lánzhōu, 11 hours to Hohhot, 14 hours to Xī'ān and 19 hours to Běijīng. If you're heading for Lánzhōu or Xīníng, there is a handy overnight train (No N901) that leaves at 10.05pm. The train station is in the New City, about 9km west of the Old City centre.

There's a **booking office** (huòchē shòupiàochù; Xinhua Dongjie; commission Y5; ☒ 8am-7pm) in the Old City, in the ICBC Bank (Gōngshāng Yínháng), next to Dico's Burgers. You can purchase tickets at window No 1.

Getting Around

The airport is 25km from town; shuttle buses (Y15) leave from in front of the CAAC office. A taxi to the airport will cost around Y40.

Bus No 1 runs from the bus station in the Old City, along Jiefang Jie and then on to the train station in the New City. The fare is Y1. Minibuses (also No 1) cover the same route faster, and charge Y2. Count on 30 minutes minimum to shuttle between the two parts of town.

Taxis are fairly cheap, with flag fall at Y3. A taxi between the train station and the Old City will cost around Y15.

AROUND YÍNCHUĀN

Hèlán Shān 贺兰山

The Helan Mountains are clearly visible from Yínchuān. The range forms an important natural barrier against desert winds and invaders alike, with the highest peak reaching 3556m. Along the foothills of Hèlán Shān lie an array of various sights.

YÍNCHUĀN BUS TIMETABLES

Buses from the main station include:

Destination	Price	Duration	Frequency	Departs
Gùyuán	Y37-60	4½-7hr	hourly	7am-8.30pm
Lánzhōu	Y89	6½hr	1 daily	8am
Xī'ān	Y126	11-14hr	6 daily	7.40am-4.30pm
Yán'ān	Y78.2	8-12hr	3 daily	7.15am, 8.30am, 5.30pm
Zhōngwèi	Y19-28	2-3½hr	hourly	7.50am-5.45pm

SILK ROAD

About 54km northwest of Yínchuān's New City is the historic pass village of **Gǔnzhōngkǒu** (滚钟口; admission Y20), with walking trails up into the surrounding hills.

North of Gǔnzhōngkǒu are the **Twin Pagodas of Baisikou** (拜寺口双塔; Báisìkǒu Shuāngtǎ), which are 13 and 14 storeys high and decorated with Buddha statuettes. Just past the pagodas is a boulder-strewn gorge filled with **rock carvings** (贺兰山岩画; Hèlánshān Yánhuà; admission Y25) thought to date back 10,000 years. There are over 2000 carvings here, depicting animals, hunting scenes and faces, including one (so local guides like to claim) of an alien. The carvings are some of the only surviving remnants of the early nomadic tribes who lived in the steppes north of China. The gorge is a peaceful place, with potential for day hikes.

South of Gǔnzhōngkǒu is Níngxià's most famous sight, the **Western Xia Tombs** (西夏王陵; Xīxià Wánglíng; admission Y35). The tombs, consisting of large, earthen mounds, were begun by the first Xixia ruler, Li Yuanhao. The site is undergoing massive tourist development, but if you're up for a long walk, the best way to visit is to trek out to some of the more remote tombs scattered across the plains. As you can't actually enter them, it's more of a visual experience. The museum here contains an exhibit similar to the provincial museum.

No buses travel to any of these places; the only way to reach them is by taxi or through CITS (p833). A taxi to the four sights should cost no more than Y200 for the full day. CITS asks double this, but throws in an English-speaking guide for 'free'.

108 Dagobas 108 塔

These unusual **Buddhist dagobas** (Yìbǎilíngbā Tǎ; admission Y10), or stupas, are 83km south of Yínchuān, near the town of Qīngtóngxiá Zhèn. The 12 rows of white, vase-like structures date from the Yuan dynasty and are arranged in a large triangular constellation on the banks of the Yellow River. Why exactly they were erected is unknown.

A visit to the 108 Dagobas is a relaxing trip, and you may even stumble across an isolated stretch of the Great Wall not far from the town. To get here, jump on one of the frequent buses (Y9, 2½ hours) from the long-distance bus station to Qīngtóngxiá Zhèn (make sure you don't get off at the

larger town of Qīngtóngxiá Shì). Once you arrive you'll need to take a minibus or taxi to the river, and then a ferry across (Y15 return).

Bayan Hot 阿拉山左旗

Bayan Hot (Ālāshān Zuòqí) is a town just across the border in Inner Mongolia, some 105km from Yínchuān, and a worthy day trip. It lies surrounded by desert and has an outpost feel to it. In town is **Yanfu Temple** (延福寺; Yánfú Sì; admission Y2), a small Mongolian temple that dates back over 300 years; once populated by 200 lamas, it now houses around 30. You can see services here most mornings. From Bayan Hot ('Rich City') there's plenty to explore in the desert.

Halfway to Bayan Hot the road broaches crumbling, yet still mighty, remains of the Great Wall. You can hop off the bus here and wander along the wall into the foothills of the mountains from which it descended, although watch you don't accidentally wind up in a military zone.

GETTING THERE & AWAY

Frequent buses leave the Yínchuān long-distance bus station for Bayan Hot (Y15, 2½ hours). They slow in frequency in the late afternoon; the last bus leaves at 6pm.

ZHŌNGWÈI 中卫

☎ 0953

Zhōngwèi lies 167km southwest of Yínchuān on the Lánzhōu–Bāotóu railway, sandwiched between the sand dunes of the Tengger Desert (Ténggélǐ Shāmò) to the north and the Yellow River to the south. In addition to its unusual setting, Zhōngwèi has a fairly relaxed pace – a nice change from the rush of most Chinese cities.

Information

Bank of China (Zhōngguó Yínháng; ⏰ 9am-5pm) Across from the Drum Tower (Gǔlóu) roundabout, this also has a working ATM.

Desert Travel Service (Shāpōtóu Lǚxíngshè; ☎ 701 2961) This English-speaking service, at the entrance to the Zhōngwèi Bīnguǎn, can arrange some interesting trips to the sights out of town (see p838).

Fēitiān Wǎngbā (per hr Y2) Next to the Gulou Department Store, on the 4th floor inside a courtyard, is this Internet café.

Post office (yóujú; Gulou Xijie)

PSB (Gōngānjú; Gulou Xijie)

Sights
GĀO MIÀO 高庙
The main attraction in town is **Gāo Miào**
(Gulou Beijie; admission Y15; ⏰ 7am-6.30pm), an
eclectic, multipurpose temple that at one
time catered to the needs of Buddhism,
Confucianism and Taoism. It's still a
hodgepodge of architectural styles, but a
pantheon of refurbished Buddhist deities
have pushed out the original Taoists and
Confucians.

The main point of interest is the former
bomb shelter built beneath the temple
during the Cultural Revolution. The eerie
tunnels were at some point converted into
a Buddhist hell/haunted house, complete
with black lights, sound effects and gory
statues. Evildoers may very well find themselves trapped down here indefinitely.

Sleeping & Eating
A nicer alternative to staying in town is the
desert guesthouse at Shāpōtóu (see p838).

Xīngxiáng Bīnguǎn (☎ 701 9970; 61 Changcheng
Donglu; dm Y20, tw Y100-128) The rock-hard dorm
beds here are offset by heat lamps in the
common showers. The Chóngqìng-style
restaurant next door is excellent; they're
often willing to prepare smaller, cheaper
versions of dishes for solo travellers. For
slightly nicer twins, ask the restaurant
about the hotel around back.

Yìxīng Dàjiǔdiàn (☎ 701 7666; fax 701 9993;
2 Gulou Beijie; tw Y120-280, ste Y488-688) This is the
most upmarket place in town, overlooking
the Drum Tower. Rates include breakfast.

The best place to eat is the **night market**
(yèshì; Changcheng Xilu); it's a happening spot
with different types of local specialties. Two
favourites are *ròujiāmó* (fried pork or beef
stuffed in pita bread, sometimes with green
peppers and cumin) and *shāguō* (mini-
hotpot). Otherwise there are always kebabs
(Y0.30 each) and draught beer (Y2.50).

Getting There & Away
BUS
The **long-distance bus station** (*chángtú qìchēzhàn*) is 1km east of the Drum Tower, on
the southern side of Dong Dajie. A taxi here
is Y3. Regular buses to Yínchuān (Y19, three
hours) leave every half-hour from 6.30am
to 6pm; express buses (Y28, two hours)
make the trip at 9.30am, 1pm and 4.30pm.
A sleeper bus to Lánzhōu (Y50, five hours)
leaves from the Drum Tower at 10.30pm.
This unfortunately lands you in Lánzhōu at
a very inconvenient hour. To get to Gùyuán,
you'll need to change buses in Zhōngníng
(Y7, one hour).

TRAIN
From Zhōngwèi you can catch trains heading to the north, south and southeast. By express train it will take you 2½ hours to reach
Yínchuān (No K44; 9.36pm), six hours to
Lánzhōu (No K43; 9.32am) and 11 hours
to Xī'an (No 2586; 7.03pm). Other destinations include Běijīng, Chéngdū, Gùyuán,
Píngliáng, Shànghǎi and Hohhot.

AROUND ZHŌNGWÈI
The best thing about exploring this area is
the abrupt convergence of desert sand dunes,
the Yellow River and lush farm fields.

SILK ROAD

Shāpōtóu (沙坡头; main area Y30, botanical gardens & desert Y20), 10km west of Zhōngwèi, lies on the fringe of the Tengger Desert. It's based around the Shapotou Desert Research Centre (沙坡头沙漠研究所; Shāpōtóu Shāmò Yánjiùsuǒ), which was founded in 1956 to find a way to keep drifting sand dunes from covering the railway lines, and has since gone on to battle the ever-increasing problem of desertification in China's northwest.

Shāpōtóu has become something of a desert amusement park, with camel rides, speed boats, cable cars, sheepskin rafts and sand sleds. With its choice location at a bend in the Yellow River, it's not a bad place to spend the night. There are two entrances to the area, one at the guesthouse and the other at the top of the sand dunes, from where you can access the desert.

A traditional mode of transport on the Yellow River for centuries was the *yángpí fázi* (leather raft) made from sheep or cattle skins soaked in oil and brine and then inflated. An average of 14 hides are tied together under a wooden framework, making a strong raft capable of carrying four people. Touts at Shāpōtóu offer boat rides up to Shuāngshìshān for Y60 per person, from where you can raft back downstream.

Shui chē (water wheels) are another traditional element of Níngxià life. Mechanical pumps have now taken over, but there is still one working water wheel upstream from Shāpōtóu at Běichángtān, a small mountain village some 70km from Zhōngwèi. A day trip up the river by boat and back again on a sheepskin raft costs Y320.

Tours

The Desert Travel Service (see p836) offers several enticing river and desert trips. A three-day camel trek through the Tengger Desert with a visit to the Great Wall and camping in the dunes costs around Y300 per person per day for transport, guide and accommodation (minimum three people).

Another option is a one-day leather raft trip down the Yellow River, starting at the water wheel and ending at Mèngjiāwān. This costs Y250 per person, including transport to and from Zhōngwèi.

Sleeping

Shāpō Shānzhuāng (沙坡山庄; ☎ 768 9073; tr/tw per bed Y40/50) A pleasant option is a night or two at this guesthouse built around a garden courtyard on the bank of the river. There's a small restaurant on the premises.

Getting There & Away

From Zhōngwèi there are regular public minibuses to Shāpōtóu (Y3.5, 45 minutes). They leave from inside a courtyard opposite the long-distance bus station, stopping

---

THE WORLD ACCORDING TO MA YAN

Gender inequality and rural poverty are hardly breaking news in China, but rarely does one have the chance to view them first-hand through the eyes of a young girl. In 2001, 14-year-old Ma Yan found herself face-to-face with a future not uncommon to Chinese women: unable to pay the tuition fees for three children, Ma Yan's parents decided to pull her out of school, for the sake of her brothers' education.

Ma Yan's school diaries were later thrust upon a French journalist, at the time a last-ditch cry for help from a desperate mother, herself deprived of an education and married at 16. Reading them can be an unsettling experience – some days she has no more than a bowl of rice to eat, other days even less. But no other book will bring you closer to understanding just how hard it is to make ends meet in Níngxià, or the extremity with which the Communist Party has turned its back on its original *raison d'être*.

The subsequent translation and publication of extracts from the diary not only introduced the world to the people of Níngxià, it also changed the fates of hundreds of families. Readers sent in personal donations to keep Ma Yan in school, and continuing interest sparked the publication of the entirety of Ma Yan's diaries in book form. Royalties from sales and reader donations were put into a grass-roots fund to help provide tuition fees for children throughout the province. *The Diary of Ma Yan* has since been translated into 14 languages, and the organisation Enfants du Ningxia (www.enfantsduningxia.org) has helped ensure the right to an education for several hundred children in southern Níngxià – no small accomplishment for the diary of a teenage girl.

at the Gulou Beijie and Changcheng Xilu intersection.

Minibuses run half-hourly. The first bus departs Zhōngwèi at 7am; the last bus departs from the Shāpōtóu main entrance, near the Shāpō Shānzhuāng, at 6.30pm. A taxi costs Y30/50 one-way/return.

GÙYUÁN 固原

☎ 0954

Fifty kilometres northwest of Gùyuán, in southern Níngxià, is a relatively unknown set of Buddhist grottoes, **Xūmí Shān** (须弥山; admission Y20). Xūmí is the Chinese transliteration of the Sanskrit word *sumeru*, meaning 'treasure mountain'.

Cut into the five adjacent sandstone hills are 132 caves housing more than 300 Buddhist statues dating back 1400 years, from the Northern Wei to the Sui and Tang dynasties. The best statues are protected by the Yuanguan (caves 45 & 46; 6th century) and Xiangguo (cave 51; 7th century) Temples, where you can walk around the interior and examine the artwork up close – amazingly, the paint on several of the statues has yet to wear away. Cave 5 contains Xūmí Shān's largest statue: a colossal Maitreya (the future Buddha), standing 19m high. It remains remarkably well preserved, even though the protective tower has long since collapsed and left it exposed to the elements.

There is no regular transport to the caves, but you can catch a bus from Gùyuán directly to Sānyíng (Y10, one hour), on the main road 40km north of Gùyuán near the Xūmí Shān turn-off. From Sānyíng you can hop on a minibus to Huángduóbǎo (Y5 when full) and then a tractor (Y2) up to the caves. It's more likely, however, that you'll be the only customer, in which case you have to take the whole minibus for yourself. From Sānyíng to Xūmí Shān it's Y50 return.

Sleeping

Gùyuán Bīnguǎn (固原宾馆; ☎ 203 2479; Zhengfu Jie; dm Y25, tw Y120-226) Gùyuán's main hotel shares the block with plenty of restaurants. A taxi here from the bus station will cost Y3.

Liùpánshān Bīnguǎn (六盘山宾馆; ☎ 203 7014; 77 Zhongshan Jie; tw Y80) Five minutes to the right as you exit the bus station is this hotel's main building; from here they'll direct you to the dependable twins in the foreign-approved wing.

Getting There & Away

Gùyuán is on the Zhōngwèi–Bǎojī railway line and is served by trains from Xī'ān (eight hours), Zhōngwèi (3½ hours), Yínchuān (six hours) and Lánzhōu (10 hours). Keep in mind that sleeper tickets are near impossible to get, and the majority of trains depart in the middle of the night. To get to the train station you'll need to take a taxi (Y4).

Buses to Yínchuān (Y37 to Y60, 4½ hours) leave every half-hour between 8am and 5.30pm from the long-distance bus station. There are buses running once daily to Lánzhōu (Y90, eight hours) and Tiānshuǐ (Y70, seven hours) at 6am. There are also regular buses to Pínglíang and Jīngyuán (Y20, two hours).

Inner Mongolia
内蒙古

HIGHLIGHTS

- Explore the big-sky country or sample Russian food in **Mǎnzhōulǐ** (p852)
- Ride across the boundless **Mongolian steppes** (p847) on horseback at Xilamuren, Gegentala or Huitengxile
- Watch the Naadam festivities – horse racing, archery and wrestling – in **Hohhot** (p845)

★ Mǎnzhōulǐ

Mongolian
★ Steppes
★ Hohhot

■ POP: 24.4 MIL	■ AREA: 1,183,000 SQ KM

The nomadic tribes of the northern steppes have always been intrinsically at odds with the agrarian Chinese. Seeking an easier solution to the constant skirmishes with the numerous Xiongnu clans, the first emperor of the Qin dynasty (221–207 BC), Qin Shi Huang, began building the Great Wall for the express purpose of keeping them out. Traditionally, the untilled grasslands beyond the Wall marked the limits of the Chinese empire, but the actual line of control was nevertheless constantly in flux, at times even nonexistent, as one side subsumed the other. It was only under the Qing dynasty (1644–1911) that much of the Mongolian homeland came under Chinese rule for good, divided into the 'Inner' and 'Outer' regions – otherwise known to the Mongols as South and North Mongolia.

Inner Mongolia (Nèi Ménggǔ) today covers an enormous expanse of land, stretching some 2150km as the hawk flies, from the Gobi Desert in the west to the Argun River (É'ěrgǔnà Hé) along the Russian border in the northeast. For most people, the big attractions of Inner Mongolia are the rolling steppes, the horses and the Mongolian way of life. Just how much you can see of the Mongolian way of life in China is dubious, and the small Mongolian horse is unsurprisingly being phased out – herders now purchase motorcycles, and on some of the larger farms, helicopters and light aircrafts are used to spot and round up grazing herds.

While the province is comprised of some intriguing and desolate landscapes, keep in mind that much of Inner Mongolia is a sensitive border region and thus off limits to travellers. For those who are truly interested in learning more about the Mongols, their land and their culture, it's suggested that you visit Mongolia, the independent country to the north, instead. For more information, see Lonely Planet's *Mongolia* guide.

History

The nomads endured a rough life as shepherds and horse breeders in the grasslands beyond the Gobi. They moved with the seasons in search of pastures for their animals, living in transportable circular tents known as yurts (the Russian word) or *ger* (the Mongolian word).

Early on, much of 'Mongolia' was inhabited by various clans, beginning with the Xiongnu and later the Turkic Uighurs and Kyrgyz. The Mongols first began moving into present-day Mongolia from Manchuria sometime in the 10th century.

THE MONGOL EMPIRE

United by Genghis Khan and later led by his grandson Kublai Khan, the Mongols went on to conquer not only China but most of the Eurasian continent, founding an empire that stretched from Vietnam to Hungary. Begun in 1211, it was a conquest won on horseback: the entire Mongol army was cavalry, allowing rapid movement and deployment of the armies.

Despite the death of Genghis Khan in 1227, the Mongols lost none of their vigour. Successful campaigns thundered across Central Asia, Tibet, Persia and Russia, eventually reaching Europe's threshold. The subjugation of the West was only called off when Genghis Khan's successor, Ogadai, died in 1241.

The Mongols eventually moved their capital from Karakoram in Mongolia to Běijīng, and after conquering southern China in 1279, Kublai Khan became the first emperor of the Yuan dynasty. His empire was the largest nation the world has ever known. The Mongols improved the road system linking China with Russia, promoted trade throughout the empire and with Europe, instituted a famine relief scheme and expanded the canal system, which brought food from the countryside to the cities.

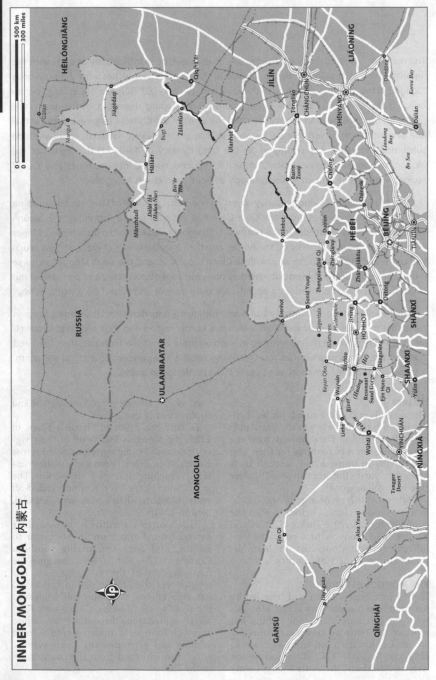

A series of incompetent rulers led to the disintegration of the Mongol Empire by the end of the 14th century, and the Mongols returned to the way of life they had known before Genghis Khan – again becoming a collection of disorganised roaming tribes, warring among themselves and occasionally raiding China, until the Qing emperors finally gained control in the 18th century.

RELIGION

At the mercy of their environment, the early Mongols based their religion on the forces of nature: the moon, sun and stars were all revered, as were the rivers. The gods were infinite in number, signifying a universal supernatural presence. Mongol shamans could speak to the gods and communicate their orders to the tribal chief, the khan.

With the establishment of the Yuan dynasty, the Mongols, particularly Kublai, began to express a growing interest in Tibetan Buddhism. It wasn't until after the collapse of the empire though, that the doctrine of the Gelugpa (Yellow Hat) school would radically alter Mongolian culture.

Critical in the conversion of his people was Altan Khan, who invited the Gelugpa Lama, Sonam Gyatso, to Qīnghǎi Hú (Lake Kokonor) in 1578. Altan conferred upon the Tibetan leader the new title of 'Dalai Lama' (*dalai* being the Mongolian translation of *gyatso*, or ocean), and thus was a powerful relationship between the two cultures rekindled. Lamaism swept Mongolia, influencing all aspects of society, from politics to art to demographics – up to 40% of the male population would enter the monastic life.

INNER MONGOLIA TODAY

Mongolians make up about 15% of the total population of Inner Mongolia. The other 85% are mostly Han Chinese with a smattering of Hui, Manchu, Daur and Ewenki.

Since 1949 the Chinese have tried hard to assimilate the Mongolians, although they have been permitted to keep their written and spoken language. The nomadic lifestyle, on the other hand, has been pretty much eradicated, along with Tibetan Buddhism.

Much of the Inner Mongolia region comprises vast areas of natural grazing land or desert. The far north is forested – the Greater Hinggan range contains about one-sixth of the country's forests and is an important source of timber and paper pulp. The southern borders tend to be heavily industrial, and it's there, in cities like Hohhot and Bāotóu, that the greatest concentration of people live.

Climate

The Mongolian climate tends towards extremes. Siberian blizzards and cold currents rake the plains from December to March and in winter you'll even witness snow on the desert sand dunes. Summer brings pleasant temperatures, but in the western areas it can get scorchingly hot during the day.

From June to September is the recommended time to visit, but pack warm clothing for spring or autumn. In the grasslands, make sure you have some sort of windbreaker handy.

Language

The Mongolian language is part of the Altaic linguistic family, which includes the Central Asian Turkic languages and the now defunct Manchurian. The vertical Mongolian script (written left to right) that adorns street signs is actually an adaptation

---

GONGXI FACAI?

A serious environmental threat to East Asia is the increasing desertification of much of Inner Mongolia. The raging dust storms that darken spring skies hundreds of kilometres away in Běijīng, Korea and even Japan have their origins here, in the swiftly disappearing loess soil of China's northwest. The major sources of the crisis are intensive sheep grazing, the transformation of steppe to farmland, and the harvesting of a peculiar grass known as *fácài*.

Fácài is responsible for binding the otherwise loose soil together, but more importantly for many Chinese – who have taken to importing and cooking mass amounts of the hair-like grass in soup – it's also a homonym for 'to get rich'. Although illegal, local governments tolerate the rampant harvesting of *fácài* by poor peasants as a short-term solution to rural China's economic woes. Běijīng has tried to counter the problem with a massive tree-planting campaign to wall in the desert, but thus far has met with little success.

INNER MONGOLIA

of classical Uighur. It's unlikely you'll need to learn any Mongolian, as just about everybody speaks standard Mandarin.

Getting There & Away

Inner Mongolia borders Mongolia and Russia. There are border crossings at Erenhot (Mongolia) and Mǎnzhōulǐ (Russia), which are stopovers on the Trans-Mongolian and Trans-Manchurian Railways respectively. You don't need to have a Běijīng–Moscow ticket to make the crossing though. If your sole interest is in visiting Mongolia, for example, it's perfectly plausible to catch a local train up to Erenhot, cross the border, and take another local train to Ulaanbaatar (with the appropriate visa).

HOHHOT 呼和浩特

☎ 0471 / pop 1.4 million

Altan Khan founded Hohhot (Hūhéhàotè or Hūshì) in the 16th century and, like other towns, it grew around its temples and lamaseries, most of which are now in ruins. Following the Manchurian conquests during the Qing dynasty, Hohhot developed into two towns: Mongols and Chinese in one quarter, Manchus in the other. Hohhot was named capital of Inner Mongolia in 1952, the old walls were torn down, and the two districts merged into a single city.

A relatively prosperous and cosmopolitan place, Hohhot serves as the main entrance point for tours of the grasslands, and is a good place to watch the summer Naadam festivities (opposite).

Hohhot literally means 'blue city' in Mongolian, although for some unfathomable reason, most of the Chinese tourist industry insists that it means 'green city'.

Information
BOOKSHOPS

Foreign Languages Bookshop (Wàiwén Shūdiàn; Xinhua Dajie) Adjacent to the Bank of China.

INTERNET ACCESS

Wenhuagong Jie is Hohhot's big Internet alley, with the highest concentration of web bars near the Xinhua Dajie intersection.

MONEY

Bank of China (Zhōngguó Yínháng; Xinhua Dajie; ⏲ 8am-noon & 2.30-5pm) You can change travellers cheques here. There is also an ATM, but it's only accessible

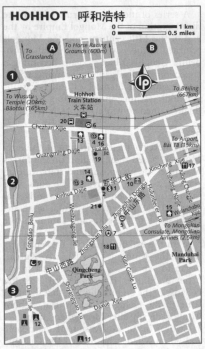

during opening hours. A 24-hour ATM is in the lobby of Nèi Ménggǔ Fàndiàn (p846), along with other money-changing facilities.

POST
Post office (yóujú; Zhongshan Donglu) There is another post office on the left-hand side of the square as you exit the train station.

TRAVEL AGENCIES
From the minute you arrive, you'll be assaulted by tour agents trying to sell you trips to the grasslands. The only benefit of this constant harassment is that you should be able to work out a very good deal.
China International Travel Service (CITS; Zhōngguó Guójì Lǚxíngshè; 2nd fl, Nèi Ménggǔ Fàndiàn)

VISAS
Public Security Bureau (PSB; Gōngānjú; 30 Zhongshan Xilu; ☼ 8.30am-noon & 2.30-5pm Mon-Fri) For visa extensions and other inquiries, the foreign affairs bureau of the PSB is to the left of the main building, outside the gated compound.

Sights
The old town in the southwestern corner of the city is where Hohhot's temples were once centred. These days there's little remaining, but you can still spend an enjoyable half-day visiting them.

WUTA PAGODA 五塔寺
The strikingly Indian **Wuta Pagoda** (Wǔtǎ Sì, Wutasi Houjie; admission Y15; ☼ 8am-6pm), completed in 1732, was originally part of the Xiao Zhao lamasery, since destroyed. Its main claim to fame is the Mongolian star chart around back, though the engraving of the Diamond Sutra, in Sanskrit, Tibetan and Mongolian, extending around the entire base of the structure, has weathered the years in much better condition. Bus No 1 runs by the pagoda.

DÀ ZHÀO & XÍLÌTÚ ZHÀO
大召、席力图召
The quiet **Dà Zhào** (Danan Jie; admission Y15; ☼ 8am-6.30pm) was formerly the city's largest lamasery. The main prayer hall retains a sacred atmosphere.

Across the main boulevard is the simpler **Xílìtú Zhào** (Danan Jie; admission Y10; ☼ 8am-6.30pm), the purported stomping ground of Hohhot's 11th Living Buddha (he actually works in an office elsewhere).

GREAT MOSQUE 清真大寺
North of the old town is the **Great Mosque** (Qīngzhēn Dàsì; Tongdao Beilu). Built in the Chinese style, it dates from the Qing dynasty with later expansions. You're free to visit the grounds, as long as you don't enter the prayer area.

INNER MONGOLIA MUSEUM 内蒙古博物馆
Well presented and definitely worth a visit, this **museum** (Nèi Ménggǔ Bówùguǎn; Hulunbei'er Lu; admission Y10; ☼ 9am-6pm) is perhaps the biggest attraction in town. The collection includes a large mammoth skeleton dug out of a coalmine near Mǎnzhōulǐ, dinosaur exhibits, a yurt and an excellent array of Mongolian dress, artefacts, archery equipment and saddles, as well as detailed introductions to the other ethnic groups in the province.

Festivals & Events
The summer festival known as **Naadam** features traditional Mongolian sports such as archery, wrestling, horse racing and camel racing, and in Hohhot takes place at the horse racing grounds (sàimǎchǎng; 赛马场) in the northern part of the city (on bus route No 13). Prizes vary from a goat to a fully equipped horse. The fair has its origins in the ancient Obo-Worshipping Festival (an *obo* is a pile of stones with a hollow space for offerings – a kind of shamanistic shrine). The Mongolian clans head for the fair on any form of transport they can muster, and create an impromptu yurt city.

The exact date of Naadam varies in China, but is usually between mid-July and mid-August, depending on when the grass is at its greenest.

Sleeping
Běiyuán Fàndiàn (☎ 226 4222; fax 696 4629; 28 Chezhan Xijie; dm Y15-25, tw Y60-120) This hotel is the best value in Hohhot and extremely convenient for both the bus and train station. Service is generally excellent.

Tōngdá Fàndiàn (☎ 696 8731; Chezhan Dongjie; dm/tw Y19/90) Also across from the train station, this place is more beat-up than the Běiyuán and a definite second choice.

Hūhéhàotè Tiělù Bīnguǎn (☎ 225 2001; 131 Xilin Guole Lu; tw Y70-110) This is a simple mid-range hotel with well-maintained and peaceful rooms. Rates include breakfast.

Nèi Měnggǔ Fàndiàn (Inner Mongolia Hotel; ☎ 693 8888; www.nmghotel.com; Wulanchabu Xijie; tw Y230, d Y500-1250; 🖳 🖵) This 14-storey high-rise doesn't look like much from the outside, but it's actually one of Hohhot's nicest hotels. The five-star services include money-changing facilities, a pool, health centre and an Italian restaurant.

Eating

Mongolia's most famous contribution to the culinary world is *huǒguō* (hotpot), a refined version, so the story goes, of the stew originally cooked in soldier's helmets. People generally add *yángròu* (mutton), *miàn* (noodles), *dòufu* (tofu) and *pínggū* (mushrooms) to the bubbling cauldron.

Xiǎoféiyáng (Xilin Guole Lu; for 2 people from Y40) The 'Little Fat Sheep' is the sophisticated choice for today's hotpot connoisseur – one taste of the garlic- and date-based broth and you'll see why.

Mǎlāqin Fàndiàn (Julong Changjie) This Hohhot institution offers a more traditional atmosphere. As well as the Mongolian hotpot (available for dinner) and roasted lamb, there are Chinese and vegetarian dishes, including *sùhézi* (an egg, spinach and noodle patty) and *chǎoxiānnǎi* (fried milk and egg with pine nuts). Prices are moderate (from Y10) and the menu is in English.

Tempting street stalls are located around the Great Mosque and in the yurts erected at the horse racing grounds, a popular spot for a night out on the town.

Getting There & Away

AIR

The **Civil Aviation Administration of China** (CAAC; Zhōngguó Mínháng; ☎ 696 4103; Xilin Guole Beilu) has an office here. There are regular flights to Běijīng (Y500), Guǎngzhōu (Y1880), Shànghǎi (Y1350), Hǎilāěr (Y1310, thrice

weekly) and Xilinhot (Y560, twice weekly) among others.

There are also flights to Ulaanbaatar two days a week with **Mongolian Airlines** (MIAT; ☎ 430 2026; 🕑 8.30am-7pm Tue, Wed, Fri & Sat) for Y1449 one-way. Its office is in the same building as the Mongolian consulate (Měnggǔ Lingshìguǎn).

BUS

See the box below for bus details.

TRAIN

Hohhot is on the Běijīng–Lánzhōu railway line that cuts a long loop through Inner Mongolia. Express trains go to Běijīng (11 hours), Dàtóng (4½ hours), Bāotóu (two hours) and Yínchuān (9½ hours). To Běijīng, the K90 leaving at 9.12pm is a convenient option. There is also a train to Erenhot (Èrliánhàotè; sleeper Y80, 11 hours) at the Mongolian border, leaving at 10.30pm.

You shouldn't have too much of a problem buying tickets here, although you're usually limited to the top berth for hard sleepers. If you want a lower berth, go through your hotel; the general commission is Y30.

Getting Around

Hohhot is reasonably small and there are several stalls hiring bicycles for a pittance. One rental place, charging a mere Y3 for the day, is near the train station on the corner of Xilin Guole Lu and Hua'an Jie.

Useful bus routes for travellers include No 1, which runs from the train station to the old part of the city in the southwest, via Zhongshan Xilu; No 33, which runs west on Xinhua Dajie from the train station; No 5, which plies the length of Xilin Guole Lu; and No 13 down Xilin Guole Lu to the horse racing grounds.

HOHHOT BUS TIMETABLES

Buses from Hohhot (the evening bus to Běijīng is a sleeper coach):

Destination	Price	Duration	Frequency	Departs
Bāotóu	Y17-26	2hr	half-hourly	6.40am-7.30pm
Běijīng	Y80-90	8-11hr	2 daily	8.30am, 6pm
Dàtóng	Y40	4hr	hourly	7.20am-5.40pm
Dōngshèng	Y29-47	3hr	hourly	7.40am-6pm

Hohhot's airport is 15km east of the city. The airport bus (Y5) leaves from the CAAC office, or you can catch a taxi for Y25 (flag fall Y6).

AROUND HOHHOT

About 20km west of Hohhot is the Sino-Tibetan **Wusutu Temple** (乌素图召; Wūsùtú Zhào; admission Y3). It's not much to look at, but the surrounding arid landscape is impressive. A taxi will cost about Y50 return from the train station.

About 15km east of Hohhot, just past the airport, is **Bái Tǎ** (白塔; White Pagoda), a seven-storey octagonal tower. The pagoda can be reached by a 20-minute train ride on No 6055 that leaves at 12.20pm; buy your ticket on the train. You'll probably have to get a taxi (Y35) back, as the train doesn't make the return journey until 4.18pm.

THE GRASSLANDS 草原

The *cǎoyuán* (grasslands) are what most travellers come to see in Inner Mongolia, but if you are after a more authentic experience, consider a trip to Mǎnzhōulǐ instead – or better still, Mongolia.

Tours

Organised tours to the grasslands, with lunch, endless rounds of *báijiǔ* (white spirit) and horseback riding across the steppes can be fun, just don't get your hopes up about learning a lot about Mongolian culture. At best you might pass a sheep strapped incongruously to the back of a motorcycle, or be badgered into a singing duel with your waitress after one too many drinks.

There are three areas targeted by most tours: Xilamuren (two hours from Hohhot), Gegentala (2½ to three hours from Hohhot) and Huitengxile (three to 3½ hours). Xilamuren, the closest one, is predictably the most developed. If you want to spend the night, aim for one of the latter two.

Travel agents lie in wait at the train station, the bus station and hotel lobbies, and depending on where you stay, they'll probably be calling your room before the massage girls even know you've checked in. While annoying, this has its benefits. Prices for a day trip to Xilamuren start around Y400, but if you can't get someone down to at least Y150, you're doing something wrong. Groups of four or more are in an even better

bargaining position. These tours generally include transportation and lunch; horseback riding is an extra Y50 per hour, with rates often doubling in the high season.

To get to Xilamuren independently, take the 8am bus to Zhàohé (Y15, two hours). From here you can arrange private tours including lunch and horseback riding for a good deal cheaper than in Hohhot. The bus back leaves at 3.30pm.

There are also taxi drivers around the train station who do self-styled grassland tours. The starting price is Y300 (extra if you stay overnight), but once again, exert your bargaining skills to the utmost. Be aware that these unofficial tours get very mixed reviews. Also, as you'll discover if you explore the Mongolian hinterland, sanitation is not a strong point, so watch what you eat and drink.

Another thing to remember is that grass is only green in summer – the rolling pasturelands turn a shrivelled shade of frost-coated brown from November to April. Make sure you take warm, windproof clothing, as there's a considerable wind-chill factor even in the middle of summer.

BĀOTÓU 包头

☎ 0472 / pop 2.4 million

Bāotóu lies on the bleak northernmost reaches of the Yellow River (Huáng Hé), to the west of Hohhot. Previously set in an area of undeveloped semidesert inhabited by Mongol herders, Bāotóu underwent a radical change when the communists came to power in 1949. Over the next decade, a 1923km-long railway line linking the town with Běijīng was extended southeast to Yínchuān, and roads were constructed to facilitate access to the region's iron, coal and other mineral deposits.

Today, Bāotóu is a grim industrial centre and the largest city in Inner Mongolia. The only reason to stop here is for its convenience as a transit point.

Orientation

Bāotóu is a huge town – 20km of urban sprawl separate the eastern and western parts of the city. It's the eastern district (Dōnghé) that most travellers visit because it's useful as a transit hub, although the western districts (Kūndūlún and Qīngshān) inconveniently have everything of practical value.

INNER MONGOLIA

The train station in the western area is Bāotóu Zhàn; in the eastern area it's Bāotóu Dōngzhàn.

Information
EMERGENCY
PSB (Gōngānjú; Gangtie Dajie; Map p849; 8.30-11.30am & 2.30-5pm Mon-Fri) In a futuristic tower well past the Bank of China in West Baotou.

INTERNET ACCESS
Internet Plaza (Liántōng Wǎngyuàn; Map p849; cnr Gangtie Dajie & Minzu Xilu; per hr Y2) In West Baotou.

MONEY
Bank of China (Zhōngguó Yínháng; Map p849; Gangtie Dajie; 8-11.30am & 2.30-5.30pm) You can exchange travellers cheques here in West Baotou. The ATM in the lobby of Bāotóu Bīnguǎn (right) sometimes works, but don't count on it. The Bank of China branch in East Baotou is way off on Bayan Tala Xidajie and only changes cash. You'll need to take bus No 5 to get there; ask the driver for Zhōngguó Yínháng.

POST
Post office (yóujú; Map p849; Linyin Lu) In West Baotou.

TRAVEL AGENCIES
CITS (Zhōngguó Guójì Lǚxíngshè; Map p849; 511 6824; cnr Shaoxian Lu & Shifu Donglu; 8.30-11.30am & 2.30-5pm Mon-Fri) In West Baotou, can arrange tours to the Steam Locomotive Museum.

Sights
STEAM LOCOMOTIVE MUSEUM
蒸汽火车博物馆
Baotou's 'sight' is this museum (Zhēngqì Huǒchē Bówùguǎn), which is targeted towards train buffs. It can only be visited on a CITS tour and the whole deal costs Y120, including transportation.

Sleeping
Jiāotōng Dàshà (Map p848; 418 7001; dm Y14, tw Y60-80) Across from the East Baotou train station, the Jiāotōng is one of those 'rock' hotels, with rock-hard beds at rock-bottom prices.

Xīhú Fàndiàn (Map p848; 418 7101; 15 Nanmenwai Dajie; dm Y30, tw Y158-188, ste Y418;) Also in East Baotou, this US-backed venture has basic twins and more upmarket suites. Try a bit of friendly bargaining on the standard rooms.

Yǒuyì Bīnguǎn (510 3888; 15 Youyi Dajie; dm Y30, tw Y120-168) This is the only budget option in West Baotou. It's fairly nice, although out in the middle of limbo. You'll need to take

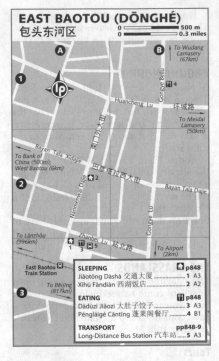

EAST BAOTOU (DŌNGHÉ)
包头东河区

SLEEPING	p848
Jiāotōng Dàshà 交通大厦	1 A3
Xīhú Fàndiàn 西湖饭店	2 A2
EATING	p848
Dàdùzi Jiǎozi 大肚子饺子	3 A3
Pénglǎigé Cāntīng 蓬莱阁餐厅	4 B1
TRANSPORT	pp848-9
Long-Distance Bus Station 汽车站	5 A3

bus No 1, a taxi or a motor tricycle from the train station.

Bāotóu Bīnguǎn (Map p849; 515 6655; 33 Gangtie Dajie; tw Y220-400;) This is the best accommodation in Bāotóu, with a range of options. In West Baotou, it's 8km from the main train station, so you'll have to take a taxi.

Eating
Pénglǎigé Cāntīng (Map p848; Gongye Beilu; dishes from Y5) This is one of East Baotou's most popular spots, with an assortment of delicacies.

Dàdùzi Jiǎozi (Map p848; Huoche Zhan; dishes from Y2) Just opposite East Baotou train station is this large canteen that serves a range of Chinese breakfast dishes, such as congee and steamed buns.

Tiānjīn Gǒubùlǐ Bāozidiàn (Map p849; Anshan Dao; dishes from Y3) This restaurant is popular with the West Baotou crowd for its Tiānjīn-style dumplings.

Getting There & Away
AIR
The **CAAC** (Zhōngguó Mínháng; Map p849; 513 0941; 26 Gangtie Dajie) ticket office is next to the Bank

of China in West Baotou. There are flights connecting Bāotóu with Běijīng (Y590) and Shànghǎi (Y1350).

BUS
See the box below for bus times.

The latter two destinations are in Shaanxi. From West Baotou, buses leave from the intersection of Tuanjie Dajie and Baiyun E'bo Lu.

TRAIN
There are frequent trains between Hohhot and Bāotóu that stop at both the east and west stations. The journey takes just under two hours on the express trains.

There are also trains to Běijīng (12 hours), Yínchuān (seven hours), Tàiyuán (14 hours) and Lánzhōu (15 hours).

Getting Around
TO/FROM THE AIRPORT
The airport is 2km south of East Baotou train station. In spite of the short distance, taxis ask around Y30 for the one-way journey.

BUS
Bus No 5 (Y2) takes 45 minutes to shuttle between Bāotóu's two districts. There are also express minibuses, which cost Y3 – you board these at the regular bus stops. Bus No 101

runs between the bus station and main train station.

AROUND BĀOTÓU
Wudang Lamasery 五当召
Built in 1749, this was once one of the largest lamaseries (Wǔdāng Zhào; admission Y30; ☉ 8am-6.30pm) in Inner Mongolia, housing 1200 monks belonging to the Gelugpa (Yellow Hat) sect of Tibetan Buddhism. Unfortunately it hasn't fared too well in the past several decades. The eighth, or current, Living Buddha has been mysteriously erased from temple history, and the overall atmosphere, with listless monks forced to punch holes in tourist tickets at every building, is one of underlying despair. The attractions are the beautiful Qing murals in the main

---

BAOTOU BUS TIMETABLES
Buses from East Baotou:

Destination	Price	Duration	Frequency	Departs
Hohhot	Y17-26	2-3hr	half-hourly	6.30am-6.30pm
Dōngshèng	Y22	1½hr	hourly	6.30am-7pm
Yúlín	Y50	5hr	4 daily	6.10am, 8.30am, 1pm, 2.30pm
Yán'ān	Y100	12hr	1 daily	1pm

prayer hall and the unusual surrounding landscape.

The monastery is 67km northeast of Bāotóu. Direct buses (Y7, two hours) leave from early morning to around noon – whenever they are full – from East Baotou's long-distance bus station.

Otherwise, bus No 7 (Y5, one hour), at the far left of the parking lot as you exit the long-distance bus station, goes to Shíguāi, 40km from Bāotóu. From Shíguāi you can hire a taxi to the monastery (Y50 return).

Meidai Lamasery 美岱召

This **lamasery** (Měidài Zhào; admission Y15) is much smaller than Wudang and rarely visited. It is halfway between Bāotóu and Hohhot, a 10-minute walk north of the old highway. Getting here is trickier since the construction of the new freeway, but you still should be able to find a Hohhot–Bāotóu bus that passes by. From Hohhot the fare is Y8 and from Bāotóu Y7. Like Wudang Lamasery, Meidai belongs to the Gelugpa sect.

Resonant Sand Gorge 响沙湾

Some 60km south of Bāotóu is this **gorge** (Xiǎngshāwān; admission Y50) filled to the brim with sand dunes reaching up to 90m high. Due to its inaccessibility, it's more of a stop-off for tour buses than individual travellers, but if this is your sole chance to see the desert, you can hire a taxi (Y200 return) out here from Bāotóu. Activities here include camel rides, parasailing and sand sliding.

DŌNGSHÈNG 东胜

☎ 0477 / pop 95,000

Dōngshèng is an uninspired town south of Bāotóu that serves as the stage for Genghis Khan's Mausoleum. If you get an early start, it's possible to come here from Hohhot or Bāotóu, visit the mausoleum and then move

on that afternoon, thus avoiding the need to stay here for the night.

Jiāotōng Bīnguǎn (交通宾馆; ☎ 832 1414; dm/tw Y15/60) This hotel is to the right of the bus station as you exit; the entrance is around the corner off the marketplace.

Hóngyè Bīnguǎn (宏业宾馆; ☎ 834 1518; s/tw Y80/150) For nicer rooms, turn right out of the bus station and walk several minutes down the main road.

Eating in Dōngshèng is pretty miserable. If you walk south from the bus station for 10 minutes, you'll see a small statue of a chicken on the right at the main intersection. This is the town's most popular hang-out, **Màikěnjī** (麦肯鸡; Hangjin Beilu), a cacophonic place serving Chinese buffet.

See the box below for bus times.

AROUND DŌNGSHÈNG
Genghis Khan's Mausoleum
成吉思汗陵园

The tribute to Mongolia's greatest leader is a bus ride from Dōngshèng, in the middle of nowhere. Visiting the **mausoleum** (Chéngjí Sīhán Língyuán; admission Y35; ☑ 7am-7pm) itself is already a surreal enough experience, but it's stepping off the rattletrap Chinese bus into the crowds of foreign tour groups that makes it even weirder. Unless you have a special predilection for Genghis Khan, consider that it's a long way to come to see very little.

The reason why this site is believed to be the final resting place of the Great Khan is unclear, as it contains no remains and few of the relics are actually attributed to the great leader. Nonetheless, the location's emblematic importance for Mongolians took root long ago. In keeping with nomadic culture, the original shrine was by no means a permanent structure. It wasn't until the relics were returned from hiding in Qīnghǎi in 1954 (to keep them out of the

DŌNGSHÈNG BUS TIMETABLES

Buses from Dōngshèng:

Destination	Price	Duration	Frequency	Departs
Bāotóu	Y13-20	1-2hr	half-hourly	6.30am-6.30pm
Hohhot	Y42-45	3hr	7 daily	8am-5.20pm
Xī'ān	Y128	18hr	1 daily	2.20pm
Yúlín	Y28-36	3-4hr	hourly	6.30am-4pm

hands of the Japanese) that construction of the present-day mausoleum was begun by the Chinese state.

Although there is little inside – a few historical artefacts and some weaponry – the mausoleum is an important sacred place for all Mongolians. Ceremonies are held four times a year (3/15, 5/15, 9/12 and 10/3 using the lunar calendar) to honour Genghis Khan's memory, and it's not unusual to see pilgrims from Outer Mongolia here. Butter lamps are lit, *khata* (ritual scarves) presented and entire roast sheep are piled high before the Khan's stone statue, while chanting is performed by Mongolian monks and specially chosen Daur elders. On the embankment beside the entrance is an *obo* festooned with prayer flags, also dedicated to the leader.

You can visit the temporary residence of the Khan on the same ticket. It's 1km down the dirt road to the right of the parking lot (when facing the mausoleum). Nearby is a **compound** (☼ summer) set in the grasslands, with horses, sheep and goats, plus some interesting buildings with traditional clothing, warrior outfits and riding equipment inside.

SLEEPING

Chéngjísīhán Bīnguǎn (成吉思汗宾馆; dm Y25, yurt & tw Y100) You can stay at the mausoleum if you like, but the location is not particularly appealing, with the yurts more or less set up in the parking lot.

GETTING THERE & AWAY

Buses from Dōngshèng to Shaanxi are supposed to run by the mausoleum hourly between 6.30am and 5pm, though in reality they aren't quite as frequent. The ride takes from one to two hours and costs Y8.5. The driver will let you off, but you won't be able to miss the blue-tiled dome as it comes into view. To be on the safe side, don't linger here too late into the afternoon.

HǍILĀĚR 海拉尔
☎ 0470 / pop 197,300

The northernmost major town in Inner Mongolia, Hǎilāěr is a base for visiting the surrounding Hulunbei'er Grasslands, a vast expanse of prairie that begins just outside the city.

CITS and other travel services in Hǎilāěr offer grasslands tours, but they generally consist of visits to tourist 'yurt camps', where you can eat, listen to traditional music, and sometimes stay the night, rather than places where Mongolians actually live. You may be able to arrange to visit a local family, particularly outside the July/August peak season.

If you fly, Hǎilāěr is a useful transit point to nearby Mǎnzhōulǐ. By train, you can go directly to Mǎnzhōulǐ if you prefer.

Information
Bank of China (中国银行; Zhōngguó Yínháng; ☎ 822 3721; 5 Shengli Sanlu; ☼ 8am-noon & 2.30-6pm summer, 8am-noon & 2-5pm winter) In Hédōng ('east of the river'), about a five-minute walk north from the roundabout at Shengli Jie, this office has a 24-hour ATM that accepts Plus, Cirrus, Visa and MasterCard.
CITS (中国国际旅行社; Zhōngguó Guójì Lǚxíngshè; ☎ 822 4017; 22 Shengli Sanlu) In Hédōng on the 2nd floor of Běiyuán Bīnguǎn.
Hailar Travel Service (海拉尔旅行社; Hǎilāěr Lǚxíngshè; ☎ 832 0075; 36 Zhongyang Dajie at Xingan Xilu) Next door to Běiěr Dàjiǔdiàn. The eager, helpful employees, who speak some English, arrange grasslands tours.
Internet café (网吧; wǎngbā; cnr Chen Barag Lu & Xing An Xilu; per hr Y2) Near the main square.
Post & Telephone Office (邮电大楼; Yóudiàn Dàlóu; Zhongyang Dajie) Opposite Běiěr Dàjiǔdiàn.
PSB (公安局; Gōngānjú; Shengli Sanlu) Opposite CITS in Hédōng.

Sleeping & Eating
Běiěr Dàjiǔdiàn (贝尔大酒店; Bei'er Hotel; ☎ 833 2511; fax 833 4960; 36 Zhongyang Dajie; s Y120-180, d Y180-380, incl breakfast; ☒) The enthusiastic staff at this central, mid-range hotel make up for the occasionally temperamental plumbing.

Yǒuyì Dàjiǔdiàn (友谊大酒店; Friendship Hotel; ☎ 833 1040; 10 Qiaotou Dajie; d & tr Y180-300 incl breakfast; ☒) Another good mid-range choice near the main square. The entrance is on the right of the market lane; the reception desk is hidden on the 2nd floor.

Both of these hotels have decent restaurants. On Xinfengbuxing Jie, a pedestrian street off Zhongyang Dajie, a **food market** houses vendors selling dumplings, fruit and other snacks.

Getting There & Away
CAAC (中国民航; Zhōngguó Mínháng; ☎ 833 1010; Qiaotou Dajie) is beside the bridge. There are direct flights between Hǎilāěr and Běijīng (Y1060) on Monday, Wednesday, Thursday, Saturday and Sunday, and to Hohhot (Y1310) on Tuesday, Friday and Sunday.

The **long-distance bus station** (长途汽车站; Chángtú Qìchēzhàn; Chezhan Jie) is southeast of the train station. There are regular buses to Mǎnzhōulǐ (four hours).

You can reach Hǎilāěr by train from Hāěrbīn (10 hours), Qíqíhāěr (seat/sleeper Y53/104, eight to nine hours) and Běijīng (27 hours). Several daily trains go to Mǎnzhōulǐ (Y25, three hours).

The train station is in the northwestern part of town. If you arrive by train, cross the tracks using the footbridge to the left of the station as you exit and get a bus or taxi from there.

Getting Around
The airport bus (Y3) leaves from the booking office. A taxi costs about Y20.

Bus No 1 runs from Hédōng to the train station. Taxi fares start at Y6.

MǍNZHŌULǏ 满洲里
☎ 0470 / pop 54,300
The border town where the Trans-Siberian Railway crosses from China to Russia, Mǎnzhōulǐ was established in 1901 as a stop for the train, although the area had long been inhabited by Mongolians and other nomads. This laissez-faire border community feels more Russian than Chinese. Russian-built log houses with filigree windows still dot the town, and many Russians cross the border from Siberia to purchase Chinese goods. Unless you look Asian, expect shopkeepers to greet you in Russian.

Vast grasslands surround Mǎnzhōulǐ, and there are huge coal deposits in the vicinity, including the open-pit mine in nearby Zālàinuò'ěr, which the Russians first developed in the early 1900s.

Orientation & Information
Mǎnzhōulǐ is small enough to get around on foot. The town centre sits between the train station in the south and Beihu Park in the north.

Bank of China (中国银行; Zhōngguó Yínháng; ☎ 622 3707; cnr Sandao Jie & Xinhua Lu; ⏰ 8am–noon & 2.30–5.30pm summer, 8am–noon & 2–5pm winter)

CITS (中国国际旅行社; Zhōngguó Guójì Lǚxíngshè; ☎ 622 4241; 35 Erdao Jie; ⏰ 8.30am–noon & 2.30–5pm Mon–Fri) On the 2nd floor of Guójì Fàndiàn (International Hotel). If you're heading for Moscow, you can purchase tickets here for the Trans-Siberian Railway.

Internet café (网吧; wǎngbā; 2nd fl, Xinhua Lu, btwn Erdao Jie & Sandao Jie; per hr Y3; ⏰ 24hr)

Post & Telephone Office (邮电大楼; Yóudiàn Dàlóu; cnr Haiguan Jie & Sidao Jie)

PSB (公安局; Gōngānjú; cnr Sandao Jie & Shulin Lu) East of the centre.

Xinhua Bookshop (新华书店; Xīnhuá Shūdiàn; cnr Sidao Jie & Xinhua Lu) Sells maps of Mǎnzhōulǐ (Y4).

Sights & Activities
GRASSLANDS 草原
If you're looking for big-sky country, Mǎnzhōulǐ is the place to come. Vast grasslands (cǎoyuán) surround the town – they're in verdant splendour from late June to August. Should you chance upon Mongolians living traditionally, you might be offered a cup of their milk tea. It's made of horse's milk and salt, and it's most impolite to refuse.

CITS arranges grasslands excursions, which might include a stay in a yurt with a Mongolian family, horseback riding and a Mongolian banquet. You may also be able to negotiate with a local taxi driver for a grasslands tour.

DÁLÀI HÚ 达赉湖
One of the largest lakes in China, **Dálài Hú** (admission per person/vehicle Y5/10), known as Hulun Nur in Mongolian, unexpectedly pops out of the Mongolian grasslands like an enormous inland sea. Located 39km southeast of Mǎnzhōulǐ, it's popular for fishing and bird-watching.

The easiest way to get to Dálài Hú is to hire a taxi (about Y150); they'll generally wait up to four hours. Or try to hitch a ride with one of the Russian or Chinese tour buses that often park on Xinhua Lu.

ZALAINUO'ER COAL MINE 扎赉诺尔煤矿
For train buffs, the steam locomotive storage and repair yards in Zālàinuò'ěr are some of the more impressive in China, as is the open-pit mine (Zālàinuò'ěr Méikuàng) that still uses steam engines to haul out the coal.

CITS arranges visits to the train yards and mine. To go on your own, take bus No 12 from Wudao Jie, just east of Xinhua Lu, to the town of Zālàinuò'ěr, where you can get a taxi to the mine.

You can also hire a taxi directly from Mǎnzhōulǐ (at least Y100 return).

Sleeping & Eating

Diànlì Shāngwù Dàjiǔdiàn (电力商务大酒店; ☎ 622 8718; cnr Sandao Jie & Shulin Lu; d Y100) Head to the eastern part of town to this good-value place with airy, comfortable rooms. At the time of writing, renovations were under way; look before you book.

Míngzhū Fàndiàn (明珠饭店; ☎ 622 7418; 4 Xin-hua Lu at Yidao Jie; d Y140-240) Many Russians stay at this lively hotel. For entertainment, sit in the lobby and watch the world go by.

Yǒuyì Bīnguǎn (友谊宾馆; Friendship Hotel; ☎ 622 3977; 26 Yidao Jie; d Y318-348, tr Y378, incl break-fast) These decent rooms with fridges go for Y200 or less, except in midsummer. Some rooms have been spiffed up, but others are a little mouldy.

There are several **Russian restaurants** (dishes Y10-20) on Erdao Jie, near Xinhua Lu and Zhongsu Lu. A Chinese **bakery-café** (cnr Sidao Lu & Xinhua Lu; dishes Y5-10) serves tasty noodle bowls, rice plates and gooey desserts.

Getting There & Away

You can reach Mǎnzhōulǐ by train from Hǎilāěr (Y25, three hours), Hāěrbīn (seat/sleeper Y104/193, 14 hours) or Qíqíhā'ěr (11 hours).

From the train station to the town centre, it's a 10- to 15-minute walk. Turn right immediately as you exit the station, then turn right again to cross the footbridge. Across the bridge, you'll come out near the corner of Yidao Jie and Zhongsu Lu, a block west of Míngzhū Fàndiàn and Yǒuyì Bīnguǎn.

A taxi from the station to the centre will cost about Y10; set a price before you get in.

Most of the Russians drive over the border (9km from town) in private vehicles, and you might be able to organise a lift across. A taxi to the checkpoint costs Y10. Naturally, you will need a Russian visa.

The Trans-Siberian to Moscow from Běijīng passes through town early Monday morning. CITS (opposite) sells tickets for Moscow; if you want to stopover here, confirm it when you buy your ticket in Běijīng.

Regular buses leave all day for Hǎilāěr (four hours) from the long-distance bus station on Yidao Jie, west of Míngzhū Fàndiàn.

XANADU 元上都

About 320km north of Běijīng are the remains of Xanadu (Yuánshàngdū), Kublai Khan's summer palace of legendary splendour. Over the centuries the deserted palace has crumbled back to dust, and hardly anything remains of the ancient city.

Xanadu was off limits at the time of writing. Check with the **PSB** (p845; ☎ 0471-669 0586) in Hohhot, or possibly **CITS** (☎ 010-6515 8566) in Běijīng.

In the event that the area opens in the future, the best way to get there is to take a bus directly to Duōlún or Zhènglánqí and proceed to Xanadu from there.

Tibet 西藏

CONTENTS

HIGHLIGHTS

- Join the pilgrims to marvel at the Potala Palace, Jokhang Temple and Barkhor pilgrim circuit in the holy city of **Lhasa** (p859)
- Ascend Gyantse's **Kumbum Chörten**, Tibet's architectural master piece (p868)
- Enjoy the colours of the Changtang plateau at scenic **Nam-tso lake** (p867)
- Gaze open-mouthed at the magnificent views of Mt Everest from **Rongphu Monastery** (p872)
- Take the rollercoaster Land Cruiser trip from **Lhasa to Kathmandu** (p857) over the plateau's high passes and down into the subcontinent

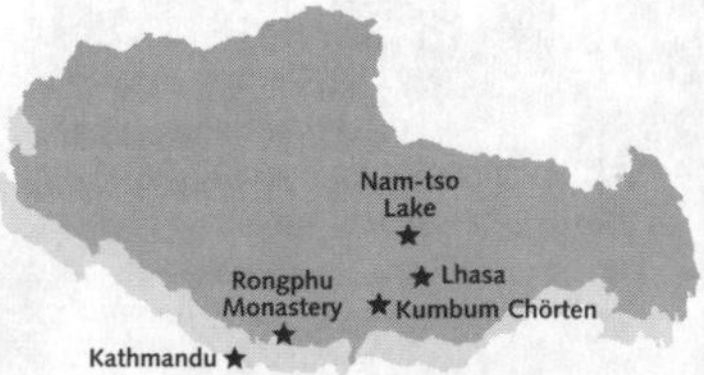

- POP: 2.7 MIL
- AREA: 1,220,000 SQ KM
- www.tibet.com

'Shangri-La', 'the Land of Snows', 'the Rooftop of the World': locked away in its mountain fortress of the Himalayas, Tibet (Xīzàng, or the 'Western Treasure House' in Chinese) has long exercised a unique hold on the imagination of the West.

Until recently few outsiders had laid eyes on the holy city of Lhasa and the other secrets of Tibet. It is more the pity that when Tibet finally opened to tourism in the mid-1980s, it was no longer the magical Buddhist kingdom that had so intoxicated early Western travellers.

Tibetans have never had it easy. Their environment is harsh, and human habitation has always been a precarious proposition. By necessity, Tibetans have become a tough and resilient people. Even in the face of the cultural attacks of the last 50 years, Tibetans have not only kept their culture and religion alive, but retained an inspiringly joyful outlook on life.

With a geographical area more than twice that of France, Tibet still manages a total population of only 2.7 million. There are more Tibetans outside of the Tibetan Autonomous Region (TAR) in the provinces of Qīnghǎi, Sìchuān, Gānsù and Yúnnán (over four million combined) than there are in the TAR.

Most of Tibet is made up of an immense plateau that lies at an altitude of 4000m to 5000m. The cultural heartland of Tibet is the fertile Yarlung Tsangpo (Brahmaputra) valley. On the uplands surrounding this and other valleys, the inhabitants are mainly seminomadic pastoralists, known as *drokpas,* who raise sheep, yaks and horses. Western Tibet is higher still, and its spiritual and geographical focal point is sacred Mt Kailash (Kang Rinpoche), in whose vicinity rise the sources of the Indus, Sutlej and Brahmaputra Rivers.

Since full-scale coverage of Tibetan regions would take a whole book, Lonely Planet has published a separate *Tibet* guidebook.

History

Recorded Tibetan history begins in the 7th century AD when the Tibetan armies were considered as great a scourge to their neighbours as the Huns were to Europe. Under King Songtsen Gampo, the Tibetans occupied Nepal and collected tribute from parts of Yúnnán.

Shortly after the death of Gampo, the armies moved north and took control of the Silk Road, including the great city of Kashgar. Opposed by Chinese troops, who occupied all of Xīnjiāng under the Tang dynasty, the Tibetans responded by sacking the imperial city of Chang'an (present-day Xī'ān).

It was not until 842 that Tibetan expansion came to a sudden halt with the assassination of the king, and the region broke up into independent feuding principalities.

Never again would the Tibetan armies leave their high plateau.

As secular authority waned, the power of the Buddhist clergy increased. When Buddhism reached Tibet in the 3rd century it had to compete with Bön, the traditional animistic religion of the region. Buddhism adopted many of the rituals of Bön, and this, combined with the esoteric practices of Tantric Buddhism (imported from India) provided the basis from which Tibetan Buddhism evolved.

The religion had spread through Tibet by the 7th century; after the 9th century the monasteries became increasingly politicised, and in 1641 the Gelugpa (Yellow Hat sect) used the support of the Buddhist Mongols to crush the Red Hats, their rivals.

The Yellow Hats' leader adopted the title of Dalai Lama (Ocean of Wisdom), given

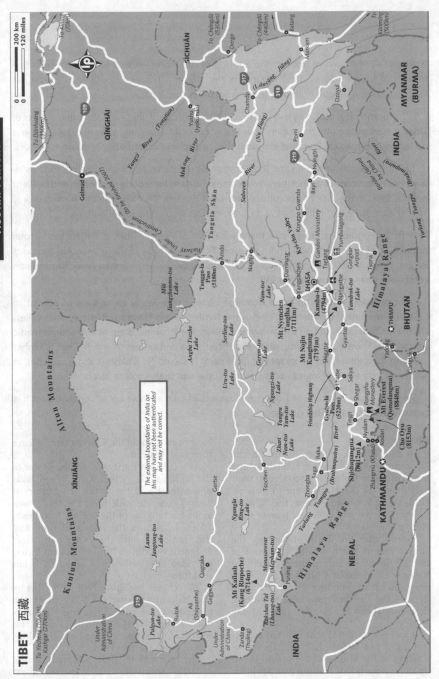

TIBET 西藏

The external boundaries of India on this map have not been authenticated and may not be correct.

to him by the Mongols; religion and politics became inextricably entwined, presided over by the Dalai Lama. Each Dalai Lama was considered the reincarnation of the last. Upon his death, the monks searched the land for a newborn child who showed some sign of embodying his predecessor's spirit.

With the fall of the Qing dynasty in 1911, Tibet entered a period of de facto independence that was to last until 1950. In 1950 a resurgent China invaded Tibet (the invasion was labelled a 'liberation'), making good a long-held Chinese claim on the strategically important high plateau.

It made no difference that the Chinese claim was based on highly dubious historical grounds: between 1950 and 1970 the Chinese 'liberated' the Tibetans of their independence, drove their spiritual leader and 100,000 of Tibet's finest into exile, caused 1.2 million Tibetan deaths and destroyed most of the Tibetans' cultural heritage.

Despite Chinese efforts to paint a rosy picture of life on the roof of the world, behind the scenes the picture is of a country under occupation. The Dalai Lama continues to be worshipped by his people, and his acceptance in late 1989 of the Nobel Peace Prize marked a greater sympathy on the part of the Western world for the plight of the Tibetan people.

The Dalai Lama himself has referred to China's policies as 'cultural genocide' for the Tibetan people. Unfortunately, China's great potential as a trading nation and as a market for Western goods makes many world leaders wary of raising the Tibet issue with China. Those who believe that pressure from Western governments will eventually force China to grant Tibet independence or true autonomy are probably being unduly optimistic. The Dalai Lama himself is now pushing for autonomy rather than independence.

For their part, the Chinese can't understand the ingratitude of the Tibetans. As they see it, China has built roads, schools, hospitals, an airport, factories and a budding tourist industry. The Chinese honestly believe that they saved the Tibetans from feudalism and that their continued occupation is a mission of mercy.

The Tibetans, who cannot forgive the destruction of their monasteries and attacks on their religion and culture, see things differently. Nor do the Tibetans get much joy from the continued heavy-handed presence of the Chinese police and military. Most damaging, a massive influx of Han settlers from surrounding provinces now threatens to make Tibetans a minority in their own 'autonomous region' and to swamp Tibetan culture with that of the Han Chinese. This trend can only intensify when the railway line finally connects Lhasa to the rest of China in 2007 (see p883).

Climate

Most of Tibet is a high-altitude desert plateau over 4000m and many passes exceed 5000m. Days in summer (June to September) are warm, sunny and dry, but temperatures drop quickly at night.

You can now buy warm clothing and low-grade trekking gear in Lhasa, but it is advisable to bring sunscreen, lip balm, deodorant, a water purification system and any medication you might need from home. Travellers will need to be particularly aware of acute mountain sickness (AMS); for a full discussion of prevention and treatment, see p932.

Getting There & Away

Although there are five major road routes to Lhasa, foreigners are officially allowed to use the Nepal and Qīnghǎi routes only.

NEPAL ROUTE

The 920km road connecting Lhasa with Kathmandu is known as the Friendship Highway. It's a spectacular trip over high passes and across the Tibetan plateau, the highest point being Gyatso-la pass (5220m) outside of Lhatse.

By far the most popular option for the trip is renting a Land Cruiser and driver through a travel agency in Lhasa (p866). A five-day Land Cruiser trip from Lhasa to the Nepalese border, via Shigatse, Everest Base Camp (EBC) and Tingri, costs about Y1200 per person. It's also possible to bus and hitch along the Friendship Highway. Public transport runs as far as Shegar (sometimes called new Tingri) and the occasional bus runs all the way from Shigatse to Zhāngmù.

When travelling from Nepal to Lhasa, foreigners must arrange transport and permits through travel agencies in Kathmandu

VISITING MONASTERIES & TEMPLES

Most monasteries and temples extend a warm welcome to foreign guests, and in remote areas will often offer a place to stay for the night. Please maintain this good faith by observing the following courtesies:

- Always circumambulate monasteries, chapels and other religious objects clockwise, thus keeping shrines and chörten (stupas) to your right.
- Don't touch or remove anything on an altar and don't take prayer flags or *mani* stones.
- Don't take photos during a prayer meeting. At other times always ask permission to take a photo, especially when using a flash. The larger monasteries charge photography fees, though some monks will allow you to take a quick photo for free. If they won't, there's no point getting angry, as you don't know what pressures they may be under.
- Don't wear shorts or short skirts in a monastery, and take your hat off when you go into a chapel.
- Don't smoke in a monastery.
- If you have a guide, try to ensure that he or she is a Tibetan, as Chinese guides invariably know little about Tibetan Buddhism or monastery history.

(see Travel Restrictions, right). You need to be particularly aware of the effects of altitude sickness in this direction as the gain in elevation is quite sudden.

At the time of writing, travel agencies in Kathmandu were offering budget tours to Lhasa from around US$130/150 for a five-day overland bus/jeep trip. Seven-day trips via Everest Base Camp cost around US$400 per person. For a flight to Lhasa you needed to buy a three-day tour for around US$360. This includes the flight ticket (US$273), airport transfer to Kathmandu and Lhasa, Tibetan Tourism Bureau (TTB) permits and dormitory accommodation for three nights in Lhasa.

QĪNGHǍI ROUTE

The 1754km road that connects Xīníng with Lhasa via Golmud crosses the desolate, barren and virtually uninhabited northern Tibetan plateau. The highest point is the Tanggu-la pass (5180m), but despite the altitude, the surrounding scenery can be quite monotonous.

Bus tickets from Golmud are officially only available from China International Travel Service (CITS) and cost around Y1600 for the Y250 ticket! In Lhasa you are free to purchase a ticket to Golmud without the need for any travel permits.

Reckon on around 24 to 30 hours from Golmud to Lhasa, and remember to take warm clothing, food and water on the bus, since your luggage is often not accessible during the trip.

OTHER ROUTES

Between Lhasa and Sìchuān, Yúnnán or Xīnjiāng provinces are some of the wildest, highest and most dangerous routes in the world. Unfortunately, they are officially closed to foreigners, though increasing numbers of travellers are making it through.

The lack of public transport on these routes makes it necessary to hitch, but that is also officially prohibited. The authorities sometimes come down very heavily on truck drivers giving lifts to foreigners, particularly on the Yúnnán and Sìchuān routes in or out of Tibet, so don't expect to find a ride easily. More importantly, be aware that you put any truck driver you ask a lift from at risk of fines and losing his license.

A few travel companies in Yúnnán have started to organise overland trips from Kūnmíng (p652) or Zhōngdiàn (p683) to Lhasa, but prices are high.

TRAVEL RESTRICTIONS

The current regulations (which could change tomorrow) state that all foreigners wanting to visit Tibet must be part of a group (though a 'group' can be only one person!). Only then can you obtain the TTB permit required to buy an air ticket into Tibet. During the high season (July to September) you may also need a return ticket to either Kathmandu, Chéngdū or Golmud, and perhaps a couple of nights' accommodation booked. These restrictions may change soon and are expected to be dismantled by 2007 if not before.

The reality is that most travellers buy a package through a budget travel agency. The cheapest way into Tibet is an air 'package' to Lhasa from Chéngdū for around Y1750, which includes the flight (Y1250), the semi-mythical TTB permit (which you'll never see) and transfer to Chéngdū airport. On arrival in Lhasa these temporary 'groups' disband; there are no permit checks in Lhasa. It is now also possible to fly to Lhasa from Zhōngdiàn in Yúnnán by first arranging the ticket and permits through a travel agency in Kūnmíng. See the Kūnmíng and Chéngdū sections for more details.

From Kathmandu, you will have to sign up for a tour to Tibet (p857) to get the TTB permit that will allow you to cross the border at Zhāngmù. Moreover, it's currently impossible to enter Tibet from Nepal on an independent visa, even if you have one in your passport. Travellers will have their Chinese visa cancelled and be put on a group visa, which comes as a separate piece of paper rather than a stamp in your passport. It is possible to get your own personal group visa (!), which is well worth asking for as you are then free to travel independently after the tour ends for the duration of your group visa, without the considerable hassle of having to split from a group visa. It is possible to extend a group visa, but not in Tibet; for this you need to go to Chéngdū or Xīníng. These restrictions change frequently and without warning.

Once in Tibet, entry to anywhere outside of Lhasa prefecture and the cities of Shigatse and Tsetang (ie to places such as Everest Base Camp, Samye, Sakya and Mt Kailash) technically requires you to procure a travel permit. To get a permit you again have to be a member of a tour group arranged through an authorised travel agency. Luckily, at the time of research Shigatse's Public Security Bureau (PSB) was issuing travel permits (Y50) to individual travellers for independent travel along the Friendship Highway to Nepal.

At the time of writing only one government-sponsored travel agency, known as Foreign Individual Traveller (FIT), was allowed to organise Land Cruiser trips and travel permits for individual travellers, though this may well change.

It's worth bearing in mind that Tibet (much more than the rest of China) is effectively a police state, and political discussions with local Tibetans can have serious consequences. It is illegal to bring pictures of the Dalai Lama or the Tibetan flag into Tibet. Incidentally, many of the secret police are ethnic Tibetans.

Getting Around

Transport can be a hurdle if you want to explore the backwaters.

Minibuses run around Lhasa prefecture, from Lhasa to the main towns of Shigatse, Tsetang and Ali, and along the Friendship Hwy as far as Shegar. Beyond this, Land Cruisers are the most common form of transport. They are pricey, but not impossible for non-budget travellers willing to split the cost among several people.

As for cycling – it's possible, but not without its hazards. Aside from hassles with the PSB, cyclists in Tibet have died from road accidents, hypothermia and pneumonia. Tibet is not the place to learn the ins and outs of long-distance cycling – do your training elsewhere. For experienced cyclists, the Lhasa–Kathmandu trip is one of the world's great rides.

LHASA 拉萨

☎ 0891 / pop 200,000 / elevation 3700m

The holy city of Lhasa is the heart and soul of Tibet, the abode of the Dalai Lamas, and an object of devout pilgrimage. Despite modernisation and the large-scale encroachments of Chinese influence, it is still a city of wonders.

As you enter the Kyi-chu Valley, either on the long haul from Golmud or from Gongkar airport, your first view of Lhasa will be of Chinese compounds and truck fumes, but you'll soon you get your first magical sight of the Potala Palace, a vast white and ochre fortress soaring over one of the world's highest cities.

TIBETAN PLATEAU

TIBET INTERNET RESOURCES

www.atc.org.au/travel Travel overview and other information from the Australia Tibet Council.
www.tibetmap.com Downloadable maps from the Tibet Map Institute.
www.tibet-tour.com Shanghai Branch of Tibet Tourism Bureau, with information on flights, festivals and more.
www.tibetinfo.net Pro-Tibetan news gathering service with a section on tourism.
www.tibet.com Background Information on Tibet from the Government in Exile.

TIBETAN PLATEAU

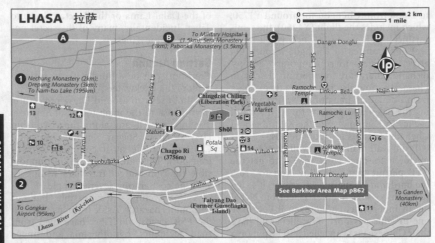

LHASA 拉萨

While the Potala Palace serves as a symbolic focus for Tibetan hopes for self-government, it is the Jokhang Temple, some 2km to the east of the Potala Palace, that is the spiritual heart of the city.

The Jokhang, a mix of sombre darkness, wafting incense and prostrating pilgrims, is the most sacred and active of Tibet's temples. Encircling it is the Barkhor, the holiest of Lhasa's devotional circumambulation circuits. It is here most visitors first fall in love with Tibet. The medieval push and shove of crowds, the street performers, the stalls hawking everything from prayer flags to jewel-encrusted yak skulls, and the devout tapping their foreheads to the ground is an exotic brew that few newcomers can resist.

Orientation

Modern Lhasa divides clearly into a Chinese section in the west and an increasingly fragile but immensely more interesting Tibetan old town in the east. For travellers who have arrived from other parts of China, the Chinese part of town harbours few surprises. Nestled at the foot of the Potala Palace and extend-

ing for kilometres westward is an uninspired muddle of restaurants, karaoke bars, administrative blocks and department stores.

The colourful Tibetan part of town, which envelops the Jokhang Temple, holds the best hotels and restaurants, and is the better area to be based.

Information

The best place for the latest on Tibetan individual travel these days is in the courtyards of one of the popular Tibetan hotels, or at a table in Tashi's restaurants (p864). The notice boards at some of the hotels can be very useful if you're looking for a travel partner or a used travel book.

INTERNET ACCESS

Internet access is available all over the place for around Y5 per hour. Popular places include the Snowlands and the Yak hotels.

LAUNDRY

The Kirey and Banak Shol hotels offer free laundry for its guests. The Pentoc Guesthouse charges Y20 for a large bag.

Snowlands Laundry (Map p862; Xuěyù Xǐyīdiàn; Mentsikhang/Zangyi Lu) Next to Snowlands Hotel, this laundry charges Y3 per piece.

MEDICAL SERVICES

In case of emergency you will probably be taken, or directed to, the People's Hospital on Linkuo Beilu, though the **Military Hospital** (Xīzàng Jūnqū Zhōngyīyuàn; ☎ 625 3120; Nangre Beilu) near Sera Monastery is by far a better option.

MONEY

Bank of China (Zhōngguó Yínháng; Map p860; ⊗ 9am-6.30pm Mon-Fri, 10am-3pm Sat & Sun) This main branch is west of the Potala Palace – turn right at the yak statues and look for it on the left. Come here on the weekends for credit-card advances, bank transfers and foreign exchange. It also has a 24-hour ATM.

Bank of China (Zhōngguó Yínháng; Map p862; Beijing Donglu; ⊗ 8.30am-1.30pm & 3.30-5.30pm Mon-Fri) This branch is located between the Banak Shol and Kirey hotels.

POST

China Post (Zhōngguó Yóujú; Map p860; Beijing Donglu; ⊗ 9am-8pm Mon-Sat, 10am-6pm Sun) East of the Potala Palace. Buy stamps from the counter in the far left corner as you walk through the main door.

TELEPHONE

China Unicom (Map p860; Zhōngguó Liántōng; Beijing Donglu; ⊗ 9am-8pm) Offers the cheapest long-distance rates.

Telecom Booths (⊗ 10am-11pm) There are several private phone booths near the Pentoc Hotel that offer cheap international calls.

TRAVEL AGENCIES

To trek or visit remote areas, you need to visit a travel agency to secure a permit, transport and (possibly) a guide. At the time of writing independent travellers had to arrange travel with Foreign and Independent Travellers (FIT), but regulations are expected to change so you may find that the other travel agencies or fixers have resurfaced.

FIT Snowlands Hotel (Map p862; ☎ 634 9239; 4 Zangyi Donglu), Banak Shol Hotel (Map p862; ☎ 634 4397; Beijing Donglu) The two branches operate independently and offer different prices. Contact Sonam at the Snowlands Hotel and Xiaojing at the Banak Shol Hotel. The Banak Shol branch is often cheaper.

VISAS

There are two Public Security Bureau (PSB; Gōngānjú) offices in Lhasa, although it's doubtful that either will prove to be of much use. The office (Map p860) at the eastern end of Beijing Donglu issues travel permits, but the staff are unwilling to issue these to individual travellers and will instead refer you to a travel agency.

The office (Map p860) on Linkuo Beilu occasionally grants visa extensions of up to seven days in an emergency. If you require a longer extension contact one of the travel agencies.

Sights

BARKHOR 八角

The **Barkhor** (Map p862, Bājiǎo) is essentially a *kora* (pilgrim circuit) that proceeds clockwise around the periphery of the Jokhang Temple. It is also a hive of market activity, an astounding pilgrim jamboree and a wonderful introduction to Tibet.

Lining the circuit are shops, stalls, teahouses and hawkers. There's a wide variety of items to gladden a Tibetan heart – prayer flags, block prints of holy scriptures, turquoise jewellery, Tibetan boots, Nepalese biscuits, yak butter and juniper incense.

Many of the Tibetans here are also visitors to the city. Khambas from eastern Tibet, who braid their hair with red yarn and stride around with ornate swords or daggers; and Goloks (Tibetan nomads) from the northeast wearing ragged sheepskins. Golok women display incredibly ornate braids and coral headpieces.

JOKHANG TEMPLE 大昭寺

The golden-roofed **Jokhang Temple** (Dàzhāo Sì; Map p862; admission Y70; ⊗ inner chapels 8am-noon & sometimes 3-5.30pm) is 1300 years old and is Tibet's holiest shrine. It commemorates the marriage of the Tang princess Wencheng to King Songtsen Gampo, and houses a pure gold statue of the Buddha Sakyamuni brought to Tibet by the princess.

You can follow the crowd of awestruck pilgrims through a hushed labyrinth of shrines, halls and galleries containing some of the finest and oldest treasures of Tibetan art. Some originals were destroyed during the Cultural Revolution and have been replaced with duplicates.

The Jokhang Temple is best visited early in the morning; during the afternoon you'll have to enter via the side door to the right of the main entrance and interior chapels

BARKHOR AREA 八角街

may be shut. There are often prayers led by monks on the roof around 6.30pm. The outer halls and the roof are effectively open from sunrise to sunset.

POTALA PALACE 布达拉宫

Lhasa's most imposing attraction is the **Potala Palace** (Bùdálā Gōng; Map p860; admission Y100; ☎ 9.30am-3pm before 1 May, 9am-3.30pm after 1 May, interior chapels close 4.30pm), once the seat of the Tibetan government and the winter residence of the Dalai Lamas. Each day a stream of chanting pilgrims files through this religious maze to make offerings of *khatak* (ceremonial scarves) and liquid yak butter at the innumerable chapels and shrines.

One of the architectural wonders of the world, this huge construction is 13 storeys tall and contains literally thousands of rooms. Construction of the present structure began during the reign of the fifth Dalai Lama in 1645 and took more than 50 years to complete. The first recorded use of the site dates from the 7th century AD, when King Songtsen Gampo built a palace here.

The layout of the Potala Palace includes the White Palace (the eastern part of the building), for the living quarters of the Dalai Lama, and the Red Palace (the central building rising above), for religious functions. The most stunning chapels of the Red Palace house the jewel-bedecked *chörten* tombs of previous Dalai Lamas. The apartments of the 13th and 14th Dalai Lamas, in the White Palace, offer a more personal insight into life in the palace. The roof gives marvellous views of Lhasa and it's surrounds. There are extra charges to get access to the roof and an exhibition room (both Y10).

At the time of research foreigners had to enter via the northwest entrance, accessible by road, thus exiting via the southern settlement of Shöl. Pilgrims visit in the other direction, and are most numerous on Monday, Wednesday and Friday when they are admitted free of charge. Photography is not allowed inside the chapels.

NORBULINGKA 罗布林卡

About 3km west of the Potala Palace is the **Norbulingka** (Luóbùlínkǎ; Jewel Park; Map p860; admission Y60; ⏰ 9am-1pm & 2.30-6pm), the former summer residence of the Dalai Lama. The pleasant park contains several palaces and chapels, the highlight of which is the **New Summer Palace**

(Takten Migyü Potrang), but it's hard to justify the high Norbulingka entry fee. Avoid the awful **zoo** (Y10). The best time to visit is during festivals or on public holidays.

Festivals & Events

If possible, try to time your visit to Lhasa to coincide with one of the city's festivals. The Losar and Saga Dawa festivals are particularly exciting, as thousands of pilgrims flood into town and the *koras* exude a party atmosphere.

Tibetan festivals are held according to the Tibetan lunar calendar, which usually lags at least a month behind the West's Gregorian calendar. Following is a brief selection of Lhasa's major festivals:

Losar Festival (New Year Festival) Taking place in the first week of the first lunar month, Tibetan new year is a colourful week of activities. There are performances of Tibetan drama, pilgrims make incense offerings and the streets are thronged with Tibetans dressed in their finest.
Lantern Festival Held on the 15th day of the first lunar month, huge yak-butter sculptures are placed around Lhasa's Barkhor circuit.
Mönlam (Great Prayer Festival) This is held midway through the first lunar month (officially culminating on the 25th). An image of Maitreya from Lhasa's Jokhang Temple is borne around the Barkhor circuit, attracting enthusiastic crowds of locals and pilgrims.
Saga Dawa (Sakyamuni's Enlightenment) The 15th day of the fourth lunar month (full moon) is an occasion for outdoor operas, and also sees large numbers of pilgrims at the Jokhang Temple, on the Barkhor circuit and climbing Gephel Ri, the peak behind Drepung Monastery.
Worship of the Buddha During the second week of the fifth lunar month, the parks of Lhasa, in particular the Norbulingka, are crowded with picnickers.
Shötun Festival (Yoghurt Festival) This is held in the first week of the seventh lunar month. It starts at Drepung Monastery and moves down to the Norbulingka. Operas and masked dances are held, and locals use the occasion as another excuse for more picnics.
Palden Lhamo The 15th day of the 10th lunar month has a procession around the Barkhor circuit bearing Palden Lhamo, protective deity of the Jokhang Temple.

Sleeping

BUDGET   Map p862
Banak Shol Hotel (Bālángxué Lǚguǎn; ☎ 632 3829; 8 Beijing Donglu; dm Y20, s Y30, d Y60, d with bathroom Y100-120) This is a popular budget stalwart, with a charming Tibetan-style courtyard, a free laundry service, a great restaurant, bicycles

for hire and a good notice board. The downside is that walls are paper thin, singles are pokey and some rooms face the noisy main road. The mid-range doubles are the best value in Lhasa.

Yak Hotel (Yàkè Bīnguǎn; ☎ 632 3496; 100 Beijing Donglu; dm Y20, d Y80, tr Y100, d with bathroom Y260; 🖳) This hotel has a range of options, from dark dorms to excellent twins with Tibetan-style décor. The rooms that face the rear courtyard are quietest, but can be dark. Renovations at the time of research may result in some new rooms. Hot showers are available in the morning and evening, and there's good Internet access.

Kirey Hotel (Jírì Lǚguǎn; ☎ 632 3462; 105 Beijing Donglu; dm Y20, d with/without bathroom Y100/50) The Y50 doubles offer the best value in this quiet, comfortable hotel; those with bathroom are looking a bit tired these days. It has reliable hot showers at the back (9am to 9pm), free laundry service and friendly staff. The Tashi II restaurant is located here.

Snowlands Hotel (Xuěyù Lǚguǎn; ☎ 632 3687; 4 Zangyi Lu; dm Y25, d Y80, tr Y90, d with bathroom Y260, deluxe Y360; 🖳) This place is now the least popular backpacker option, though it's location is unbeatable. Toilets can be 'fragrant' and the hot-water showers are unreliable.

Pentoc Guesthouse (Pānduō Lǚguǎn; ☎ 632 6686; www.pentoc.com; 5 Zangyi Lu; dm Y25, s/d Y40/65; 🖳) The Pentoc is friendly, clean and stylish, with nice touches, like free videos every night at 8pm, a café and individual bed lights in the three-bed dorms. Rooms overlooking the street can be noisy. The two singles get booked up in advance. Reservations are a good idea, though the system is inherently chaotic. The hot showers are a bit hit-and-miss.

MID-RANGE
During the last few years the backpacker hotels mentioned under Budget have built carpeted mid-range rooms with private hot-water bathrooms, which are far better value than staying at the more expensive hotels. The best options are currently the Yak and Banak Shol hotels. Most other places are Chinese style and cater to the growing numbers of Chinese tourists.

Hotel Kyichu (Lāsà Jiǔjù Fàndiàn; Map p862; ☎ 633 1541; fax 632 0234; 18 Beijing Zhonglu; s/d Y200/280, deluxe d Y320, all with bathroom; 🖳) A friendly, well-run and recommended hotel. There's

TIBETAN PLATEAU

a nice garden restaurant at the back and the rooms are pleasant. The location is great.

Dhood Gu Hotel (Dūngù Bīnguǎn; Map p862; ☎ 632 2555; dhoodgu@public.ls.xz.cn; s/d with bathroom Y320/480; 🖳) This Nepalese-run hotel is a good choice, with excellent Tibetan-style décor and a superb location in the old town. Rooms come with modern bathrooms and kettles, though the singles are cramped. The rooftop has fine Potala views.

Mandala Hotel (Mǎnzhài Jiǔdiàn; Map p862; ☎ 632 4783; fax 632 4787; 31 South Barkhor; s/d/tr with bathroom Y180/260/360) This place has a killer location just off the Barkhor; try for a room with a view of the pilgrims. The rooms are clean and comfortable, and there's a rooftop teahouse and Nepalese-style restaurant.

Flora Hotel (Hādáhuāshén Lǚguǎn; Map p862; ☎ 632 4491; flora@public.ls.xz.cn; Hobaling Lam; dm Y35, d/tr with bathroom Y180/228) A well-run Nepalese-owned hotel in the interesting Muslim quarter. There are nice touches like a minibar at local shop prices, a stock of foreign magazines and a laundry service. Decent three-bed dorms out the back offer a quiet alternative to Lhasa's backpacker hotels.

Himalaya Hotel (Xīmǎlāyǎ Fàndiàn; Map p860; ☎ 632 1111; fax 623 2675; 6 Linkuo Donglu; old block d/tr Y373/439, superior s/d Y456/648, deluxe d Y747; 🖳) The choice is between the tatty and overpriced old block and the much better superior rooms in the new block. Still, it's mostly trekking groups that get placed here. Discounts of 20% are normally available.

TOP END

Lhasa Hotel (Lāsà Fàndiàn; Map p860; ☎ 683 2221; fax 683 5796; 1 Minzu Lu; tr Y980, d Y1020-1328, Tibetan ste Y1555; 🖳) Standards have dropped considerably since the Holiday Inn pulled out in 1997, but it's still a group tour favourite. A discount of 30% is standard.

Tibet Hotel (Xīzàng Bīnguǎn; Map p860; ☎ 683 9999; fax 683 6787; 64 Beijing Xilu; old block d/tr Y880/980, discounted to Y580/680; 🖳) Best value are the four-star rooms in the old block, which are well worth the extra Y100. The location is fairly inconvenient.

Eating
Map p862

Lhasa offers a range of cuisine you won't find anywhere else in Tibet, including Chinese, Western, Tibetan, Nepalese and Indian, so enjoy it while you can.

FOOD

The staple diet in Tibet is *tsampa* (roasted barley meal) and *bö cha* (yak-butter tea). Tibetans mix the two in their hands to create dough-like balls. *Momo* (dumplings filled with vegetables or yak meat) and *thukpa* (noodles with meat) are usually available at small restaurants. Variations include *than-thuk* (fried noodle squares) and *shemre* (rice, yoghurt and yak-meat curry).

Tibetans consume large quantities of *chang*, a tangy alcoholic drink derived from fermented barley. The other major beverage is sweet milky tea, known as *cha ngamo*.

Tashi I Restaurant (cnr Zangyi Lu & Beijing Donglu; dishes Y8-15) This place deserves a special mention. It has been running for some time now, and despite increased competition continues to be a budget favourite. Special praise is reserved for the *bobi* (chapatti-like unleavened bread), which comes with seasoned cream cheese and fried vegetables or meat. The Western dishes are less authentic, but Tashi's cheesecake (Y6) is still a treat.

Tashi II (☎ 632 3462; 105 Beijing Donglu) In the Kirey Hotel, this has the same menu and food as Tashi I, but friendlier service.

Nam-tso Restaurant (☎ 632 1895; 8 Beijing Donglu; mains Y20, set breakfast Y20) In the Banak Shol Hotel, this is probably the most popular place in town. Prices are a little higher than at the Tashi restaurants, but the chicken sizzler (Y20) could well be the best meal in Tibet. The roof is a great place for a beer in summer. The restaurant's breakfasts (muesli brought in from Kathmandu, among other things) have also achieved a devoted following.

Snowlands Restaurant (☎ 632 3687; Zangyi Lu; mains Y25-35) This is a slightly more upmarket place that serves a mixture of Tibetan, Indian and Nepalese food in civilised surroundings. There's a 50% discount on the excellent cakes after 9pm.

Dunya Restaurant (☎ 633 3374; www.dunyarestaurant.com; 100 Beijing Donglu; dishes Y25-40) With sophisticated décor, excellent, wide-ranging food and interesting specials this foreign-run place feels like a 'real' restaurant. It's pricier than most other places in town, but it's popular with travellers who aren't on a shoestring. The homemade bread and soups and the Saturday brunch (Y25), served 11am to 2pm, are popular.

Tibet Café (Zangyi Lu; dishes Y12-22) This is probably the pick of the Nepalese restaurants and the place for all your Kathmandu favourites, plus Thai and Korean dishes. Prices are low, and service and food are good.

Āxìyà Cāntīng (Barkhor Square; noodles Y5-6) For cheap Muslim noodles and Chinese dishes, like *chǎo miànpiàn* (fried noodle squares) and *gànbàn*, a kind of stir-fried spaghetti bolognaise, try this Chinese-language-only place off the Barkhor.

Drinking   Map p862
Dunya (100 Beijing Donglu; bottled beer Y12) At Dunya Restaurant, the upstairs bar is popular with local expats and tour groups. The happy hour offers a Y2 discount between 7pm and 9.30pm.

Another Place (Biéchù Shūba; ☎ 627 3793) A cool Chinese-managed bar that plays DVDs and offers free Internet access. It's just down the alley off Beijing Donglu on the east side of the Yak Hotel.

Entertainment
Apart from the ubiquitous karaoke bars and video houses, entertainment is restricted to impromptu beers and tall tales at the Namtso and Tashi restaurants (see opposite).

Shopping
Whether it's prayer wheels, *thangkas* (Buddhist paintings), sun hats or muesli, you shouldn't have a problem finding it in Lhasa. The Barkhor circuit is especially good for buying souvenirs to fill up your pack, though you'll have to haggle hard for a sane price. Most of this stuff is mass-produced in Nepal.

Dropenling (Map p862; ☎ 633 0898; www.tibet craft.com; ⏱ 10am-7pm) Wander through the Tibetan old town to this excellent new initiative established by the Tibet Artisans' Fund to support local handicrafts. Quality and prices are top end, and well worth a look as you can watch local craftspeople at work on site.

Lhasa Department Store (Lāsà Bǎihuò Dàlóu; Map p860; Yutuo Lu) A good one-stop shop for most supplies, with a good supermarket, though it's a little more expensive than elsewhere.

There are now dozens of shops in Lhasa that sell Chinese-made Gore-Tex jackets, fleeces, sleeping bags, stoves, tents, mats and so on. **Outlook Outdoor Equipment** (Map p862; Kàn Fēngyún Biànhuàn Yuǎnjǐng; ☎ 634 5589; 11 Beijing Donglu) is probably the best and most convenient place, and it rents equipment.

It is still a good idea to come with your own film supplies, but slide film is now relatively easy to find in Lhasa. A profusion of photographic shops are clustered to the east of the Potala Square.

Getting There & Away
AIR
Lhasa has flights departing for Kathmandu (Y2290) two or three times weekly; to Chéngdū (Y1270) three times daily; to Zhōngdiàn (Y1380). Kūnmíng (Y1960) and Chóngqìng (Y1400) weekly; and to Xīníng (Y1390) four times a week. Flight connections continue to Xī'ān (Y1420), Běijīng (Y2040), Shànghǎi (Y2880) and Guǎngzhōu (Y2500). These tickets are often discounted by up to 20%

No matter where you fly in from, all tickets to Lhasa have to be purchased through a travel agency, which will arrange your TTB permit (see p858). Air China won't sell you a ticket without a permit.

Leaving Lhasa is a lot simpler, as tickets can be purchased without hassle from the **Civil Aviation Administration of China** (CAAC; Zhōngguó Mínháng; Map p860; ☎ 633 3446; 88 Niangre Lu; ⏱ 9am-8pm).

BUS
Tickets for buses from Lhasa to Golmud (Y250 sleeper bus, 24 to 30 hours) can be bought at the long-distance bus station in the southwest of town, near the Norbulingka. There are also sleeper buses that continue all the way to Xīníng (Y340), the capital of Qīnghǎi. Hard-core masochists might be attracted by the epic nonstop 3287km sleeper bus to Chéngdū (Y500, three days and four nights), via Golmud, though most sane people will take the plane.

Destinations around Tibet are a little trickier, as the long-distance bus station is currently refusing to sell tickets to foreigners. In case this changes, there are minibuses every 30 minutes to Tsetang (Y30) and Shigatse (Y38 to Y50), and daily departures to Nagqu (Y63). You can often buy tickets direct from drivers.

Private minibuses to Shigatse and Nagqu depart from the junction of Ramoche Lu and Beijing Donglu from 7am, though some travellers have been refused tickets as these buses are not officially allowed to take foreigners. There is also a government bus at 8.30am from the lot next to the Gang Gyen Hotel on Beijing Donglu. The easiest way to Gyantse is to change buses in Shigatse; there is very little public transport via Yamdrok-tso Lake.

Buses leave around 6.30am for Ganden Monastery (Y20 return, 1½ hours), 7am for Samye (桑耶; Y40, 3½ hours) and 7.30am for Tsetang (advertised as Shannan 山南, the Chinese name of the county; Y30, three hours) from the west side of Barkhor Square. Buses depart when full, so expect some hanging around.

There are no longer buses to the Nepalese border at Zhāngmù, though travel agencies occasionally advertise minibuses to the border. Seats cost Y250 to Y350 for the two-day trip.

CAR HIRE
The most popular way around Tibet in recent years is with a hired car. One of the best routes is a leisurely and slightly circuitous journey down to Zhāngmù on the Tibetan–Nepalese border, taking in Yamdrok-tso Lake, Gyantse, Shigatse, Sakya, Tingri and Everest Base Camp on the way. A six- to seven-day trip of this sort in a Land Cruiser costs around Y6000, including all necessary permits, driver, guide and car, and can be divided between four (five at a pinch) passengers. Look for trips advertised on the notice boards at the main backpacker hotels.

Other popular trips include Mt Kailash (17 to 21 days), Nam-tso Lake (three days) and various options to eastern Tibet.

At the time of writing, all Land Cruiser trips were supposed to be organised through FIT (see Travel Agencies, p861), though for trips around Lhasa prefecture (which require no permits) there is nothing to stop you talking direct to a driver or other travel agency.

Getting Around
TO/FROM THE AIRPORT
Gongkar airport is 95km from Lhasa. Airport buses (Y35, 90 minutes) leave at 6am for the morning flights to Kathmandu and

Chéngdū, and at several other times of day, from the courtyard in front of the CAAC building. Tickets are sold on the bus, so show up early to guarantee yourself a seat. Buses greet all incoming flights.

If you need to get to or from the airport more quickly, taxis cost around Y200, but you might find a shared taxi for Y25 per seat.

MINIBUS
Privately run minibuses travel frequently on and around Beijing Lu. There is a flat Y2 charge. This is a quick and convenient way to get across town. Minibus Nos 402, 200 and 204 run to the Norbulingka and the long-distance bus station. Minibus No 303 runs to Drepung Monastery from Beijing Donglu (there are also monastery minibuses from the west side of Barkhor Square), and minibus Nos 503 and 502 run to Sera Monastery from the junction of Duosenge Lu and Beijing Donglu.

TAXI
These are plentiful and charge a standard fare of Y10 to anywhere within the city. Few Chinese drivers know the Tibetan names for even the major sites.

BICYCLE
The best option is to hire a bike and peddle around yourself. They can be hired from the Banak Shol and Snowlands hotels for Y2 to Y3 per hour (Y20 per day).

AROUND LHASA
Drepung Monastery 哲蚌寺
This superb **monastery** (Zhébàng Sì; admission adult/student Y55/45; ⏱ 9am-5pm), 7km west of Lhasa, dates back to the early 15th century. In its time it was the largest of Tibet's monastic towns and, some maintain, the largest monastery in the world. Drepung, Sera and Ganden Monasteries functioned as the three 'pillars of the Tibetan state'.

Prior to 1959 the number of monks in residence here was around 7000. During the Cultural Revolution there was a concerted effort to smash the influence of the major monasteries and much of the monastic population was wiped out. Today around 700 monks reside here and in nearby **Nechung Monastery** (admission Y5; ⏱ 9am-4pm), a 10-minute walk downhill. Around

40% of the Drepung Monastery's structures have been destroyed.

The best way to see the chapels is to follow a group of pilgrims. Try to catch the lunch break when the monks feast on *tsampa* and yak butter tea. In the afternoons you can often see debating. There is an excellent 1½ hour long *kora* around the monastery.

Drepung Monastery is easily reached by bike, although most people take minibus No 303 (Y2) from Beijing Donglu or the monastery minibuses from the west side of Barkhor Square. There is a Y20 charge per chapel for photography.

Sera Monastery 色拉寺

About 5km north of Lhasa, this **monastery** (Sèlā Sì; admission adult/student Y55/35; ☉ 9am-5pm) was founded in 1419 by a disciple of Tsongkhapa.

About 600 monks are now in residence, well down from an original population of around 5000 monks. Debating takes place from 3.30pm to 5pm in a garden next to the assembly hall in the centre of the monastery. Like Drepung, there's a fine *kora* path around the monastery. Minibus Nos 502 and 503 run to Sera for Y2, or it's a 30-minute bicycle ride from central Lhasa. There is a Y30 fee per chapel for photography, and it's Y850 for video.

From Sera Monastery it's possible to walk northwest for another hour to **Pabonka Monastery**. Built in the 7th century by King Songtsen Gampo, this is one of the most ancient Buddhist sites in the Lhasa region and is well worth the walk.

Ganden Monastery 甘丹寺

About 40km east of Lhasa, this **monastery** (Gāndān Sì; admission Y25; ☉ dawn-dusk) was founded in 1417 by Tsongkhapa. During the Cultural Revolution the monastery was subjected to intense shelling, and monks were made to dismantle the remains.

Some 400 monks have now returned and extensive reconstruction is underway. The monastery remains an active pilgrimage site and has a stunning location, with an elevation of 4500m. There is a Y20 fee per chapel for photography, and it's Y1500 for video.

Pilgrim buses leave for Ganden Monastery (Y20 return) at 6.30am (and often at 7am) from the west side of Barkhor Square. You can buy tickets on the bus.

NAM-TSO LAKE 纳木错

An overnight stay at **Nam-tso** (Nàmùcuò; admission Y35), 195km north of Lhasa, has become a popular trip in recent years. The sacred, turquoise-blue lake is geographically part of the Changtang Plateau, bordered to the north by the Tangula Shan range and to the southeast by 7111m Nyenchen Tanglha peak – the scenery is breathtaking.

Accommodation is available at **Tashi Dor Monastery** (elevation 4718m), which is on the edge of the lake, or you can camp nearby. There are two **guesthouses** (dm Y25-35), but no toilets so bury your waste and burn all your toilet paper after use.

The closest public transport to Nam-tso Lake takes you to Damxung (Dāngxióng), a small town with a couple of guesthouses and Sichuanese restaurants, but the lake is still another 40km or more. The best option would be to organise a Land Cruiser in Lhasa, which should cost Y1200 to Y1600 for a two- or three-day trip.

Permits and guides are not necessary for the area. Nam-tso is 1100m higher than Lhasa so it's best to have been in Tibet for at least a week to avoid acute mountain sickness (AMS; see p932).

YARLUNG VALLEY 雅鲁流域

About 170km southeast of Lhasa, the Yarlung Valley (Yǎlǔ Liúyù) is considered to be the birthplace of Tibetan culture.

Samye Monastery 桑耶寺

Located about 30km west of Tsetang, on the opposite bank of the Yarlung Tsangpo (Brahmaputra) River, this **monastery** (Sāngyī Sì; admission Y40) was founded in AD 775 by King Trisong Detsen as the first monastery in Tibet. Getting there is complicated, but it commands a beautiful, secluded position.

To reach Samye, catch one of the morning buses from Barkhor Square. Buses leave at 7am, cost Y30 to Y40 and drop you at the Samye ferry crossing. There is sometimes a police check at the ferry crossing for valid permits, though there was no such check during our last visit. No-one is checked for weeks and then suddenly a bunch of travellers are fined. Before you leave Lhasa, ask around about the current situation.

The ferry leaves when full. The crossing costs Y3 but foreigners are often charged Y10. From the far shore, a bumpy lift in the

TIBETAN PLATEAU

back of a truck or tractor (Y3) will carry you the 9km to Samye Monastery. When river levels are low you may find buses running direct to the monastery via the bridge east of Tsetang.

Simple accommodation is available at the **Monastery Guesthouse** (dm Y30-40, d/tr Y100/150) or the **East Friendship Hotel** (d Y40), a cosy and basic family guesthouse outside Samye's east gate. The monastery restaurant serves cheap dumplings and noodles, but a better option is the **Friendship Snowland Restaurant** (meals Y8-18), also outside the east gate, which serves Chinese dishes, banana pancakes and mugs of milky tea.

Tsetang 泽当
☎ 0893 / elevation 3550m
The uninteresting modern town of Tsetang (Zédāng), about 180km from Lhasa, is mainly used as a jumping-off point for exploration of the Yarlung Valley area. You don't need a permit for the town itself but you do for the surrounding area, which can only be done by arranging a Land Cruiser and guide. The Tsetang PSB can be particularly unfriendly, so avoid it like the plague. Outside the town, keep a low profile if you don't have a permit.

Accommodation for foreigners is restricted to the following three overpriced hotels.

Yóudiàn Gōngyù (邮电公寓; Postal House Hotel; ☎ 782 1888, Naidong Lu; d Y188-318, ste Y666, extra bed Y88) While overpriced, the cheaper doubles are probably the best deal you'll get in Tsetang. Foreigners pay a 50% surcharge.

Shānnán Bīnguǎn (山南宾馆; ☎ 782 6168; Hunan Lu; d Y280-480, ste Y880) This mid-range hotel isn't bad, but the small less-expensive doubles are stained and overpriced. There are triple rooms for Y120, but foreigners aren't allowed to stay in these. All prices include breakfast.

Tsetang Hotel (泽当饭店; Zédāng Fàndiàn; ☎ 782 5666; fax 782 1855; 21 Naidong Lu; s/d/tr Y888/1680/1320, ste Y2200, extra bed Y300) This is the town's premier lodging.

GETTING THERE & AWAY
Buses for Tsetang leave Lhasa at 7.30am from Barkhor Square and every 30 minutes from Lhasa's long-distance bus station. Buses and minibuses heading back to Lhasa (Y27) depart from the bus station every

hour from 8.30am (the 8.30am bus travels nonstop) until about 5pm.

Yumbulagang
About 12km southwest of Tsetang on a dirt road, **Yumbulagang** (Yōngbùlākāng; admission Y15) is the legendary first building in Tibet. Although small in scale, it soars in recently renovated splendour above the valley and offers fine views.

On your way to Yumbulagang it's well worth stopping at **Trandruk Monastery** (昌珠寺; Chāngzhū Sì; admission Y30), 7km from Tsetang and 6km from Yumbulagang, one of Tibet's oldest Buddhist monasteries and a popular destination for pilgrims.

Bus No 2 runs from the Tsetang roundabout to Yumbulagang and Tranduk, or hike and hitch on a tractor.

YAMDROK-TSO LAKE 羊卓雍错
On the old road between Gyantse and Lhasa, dazzling Yamdrok-tso Lake (4488m) can be seen from the summit of the Kamba-la pass (4794m). The lake lies several hundred metres below the road, and in clear weather is a fabulous shade of deep turquoise. Far in the distance is the huge massif of Mt Nojin Kangtsang (7191m).

Nangartse is a small town along the way that has some basic accommodation and a couple of restaurants.

A 20-minute drive or a two-hour walk from Nangartse brings you to **Samding Monastery** (admission Y10), a charming place with scenic views of the surrounding area and lake.

GYANTSE 江孜
☎ 0892 / elevation 3950m
Gyantse (Jiāngzī) is one of the least Chinese-influenced towns in Tibet and is worth a visit for this reason alone. It's also one of southern Tibet's principal centres, although it's more like a small village.

Most people visit Gyantse as part of an organised tour down to the Nepalese border, but it's also possible to visit independently. Permits are normally available from Shigatse's PSB (opposite) for Y50, but many travellers risk going without one.

Sights
The **Pelkhor Chöde Monastery** (admission Y40; ☉ 8.30am-7pm), founded in 1418, is notable for its superb **Kumbum Chörten** (10,000 Images

Stupa), which has nine tiers and, according to the Buddhist tradition, 108 chapels. Take a torch (flashlight) to see the excellent murals.

Dzong (Old Fort; admission Y30; 🕙 8.30am-8.30pm) towers above Gyantse, and has amazing views of the neighbouring sights and surrounding valley. Entry is via the large gate at the main intersection.

Sleeping & Eating

Jianzang Hotel (建藏饭店; Jiànzàng Fàndiàn; ☎ 817 3720; www.jzjzhotel.com; tr with/without bathroom Y50/40 per bed, d Y180-200) Run by an English-speaking Tibetan doctor, this hotel gets our vote as the best in town. Some rooms have squat toilets, others Western seats. Staff are friendly (they'll do laundry for Y3 per piece) and there are shared hot showers for the cheaper rooms.

Wutse Hotel (☎ 817 2909; fax 817 2880; Yingxiong Nanlu; dm Y40, s/d/tr with bathroom Y220/286/320) A popular place set around a courtyard. Dorms are in musty quads and shared toilets are a bit rough, but there are clean showers and a decent restaurant. Discounts of 20% are available.

Zongshan Hotel (宗山饭店; Zōngshān Fàndiàn; ☎ 817 5555; 10 Weiguo Lu; s/d Y150/288) Catch this place while it still has that new hotel smell. The clean, carpeted rooms have 24-hour hot water. Cheaper rooms without bathroom (Y120) are planned. Discounts of 20% are standard.

Restaurant of Zhuang Yuan (庄园餐厅; Zhuāngyuán Cāntīng; Yingxiong Nanlu; dishes Y15-35) The owners are very keen to please and, though it's not the cheapest place in town, portions are large and prices flexible. The sweet and sour chicken (Y35) is legendary; make sure you are in the kitchen to see the pyrotechnics.

The **Wutse Restaurant** (Wutse Hotel; breakfast Y20, set Nepalese meal Y30, mains Y12-20) and **Yak Restaurant** (mains Y15-30) are Nepalese-run operations and offer vague approximations of Western food, like French toast (Y12), burgers and breakfasts.

Getting There & Away

The easiest way to Gyantse is via Shigatse, which gives you the chance to get a travel permit first. A minibus leaves every 30 minutes or so from in front of Shigatse's bus station (Y20, 90 minutes). Minibuses circle the main intersection in Gyantse looking for passengers.

SHIGATSE 日喀则

☎ 0892 / elevation 3900m

Shigatse (Rìkāzé) is the second-largest town in Tibet, and as the traditional capital of the central Tsang region has long been a rival with Lhasa for political control of the country. The Tsang kings and later governors exercised their power from the once imposing heights of the Shigatse Fortress – the present ruins only hint at its former glory. Since the Mongol sponsorship of the Gelugpa order, Shigatse has been the seat of the Panchen Lama, who is traditionally based in Tashilhunpo Monastery. The monastery is Shigatse's foremost attraction.

Information

INTERNET ACCESS

China Telecom Internet Bar (Zhōngguó Diànxìn Wǎngba Shandong Lu; per hr Y4; 🕙 24 hr)

MONEY

Bank of China (Zhōngguó Yínháng; Shanghai Zhonglu; 🕙 9am-1pm & 3.30-6.30pm Mon-Fri, 10am-5pm Sat & Sun, until 5pm in winter) Next door to the Shigatse Hotel, changes travellers cheques and cash and gives credit-card advances. There's a 24-hour ATM outside.

POST

China Post (Zhōngguó Yóujú; cnr Shandong Lu & Zhufeng Lu; 🕙 9am-noon & 4-7pm)

TELEPHONE

The cheapest places to make calls are the many private telecom booths around town.
China Telecom (Zhōngguó Diànxìn; Zhufeng Lu; 🕙 9am-6.30pm) You can send faxes and make international phone calls here.

VISAS

Shigatse itself is an open town, so a permit is not required to visit. If you want to travel in the closed areas of Tsang without the cost of a tour and Land Cruiser, you can ask for a permit at the Shigatse PSB. At the time of writing it was issuing 10- to 15-day permits (Y50) for all towns along the Friendship Highway to the border (including Everest Base Camp), and for Gyantse and Shalu Monastery. However, rules change like the wind.

PSB (Gōngānjú; Qingdao Xilu, signposted West Qingdao Lu; 🕙 9.30am-12.30pm & 3.30-6.30pm Mon-Fri)

TIBETAN PLATEAU

SHIGATSE 日喀则

0 — 500 m
0 — 0.3 miles

Old Town

Drolma Mountain
(Drölma Ri)

Tashilhunpo Kora

To Manasarovar
Hotel; Lhasa
(400km)

To Sakya (120km);
Lhatse (150km);
Nepal Border (450km)

Zhufeng Lu

Qingdao Lu

Shanghai Zhonglu

To Gyantse (120km);
Yamdrok-tso

LP

INFORMATION	
Bank of China 中国银行	1 B2
China Post 邮局	2 B2
China Telecom Internet Bar 中国电信网巴	3 B2
China Telecom 中国电信	4 B2
FIT	5 A2
People's Hospital 人民医院	6 B2
PSB 公安局	7 B1

SIGHTS & ACTIVITIES	p870
Shigatse Fortress 日喀则宗	8 B1
Tashilhunpo Monastery 扎什伦布寺	9 A1

SLEEPING	⌂ pp870–1
Holyland Hotel 圣康饭店	10 B2
Qomolongma Friedship Hotel	
珠峰友谊宾馆	11 A2
Shambhala Hotel 香巴拉饭店	12 B1
Shigatse Hotel 日喀则宾馆	13 B2
Tenzin Hotel 旦增宾馆	14 B1

EATING	🍴 p871
Galgye Tibetan Restaurant 格杰藏餐	15 B1
Songtsen Tibetan Restaurant 松赞餐厅	16 B2
Tashi Restaurant 扎西餐厅	17 B1
Tenzin Restaurant 天富餐	(see 14)
Tianfu Restaurant 天府餐厅	18 B1
Yuanfu Restaurant 迎宾餐厅	19 B1
Zhengxin Restaurant 正鑫饭馆	20 B1

TRANSPORT	p871
Bus Station 汽车站	21 B2
Minibuses to Lhasa	22 B1
Minibuses to Lhatse	23 A2

If you're lucky you might catch it open on the weekend also. It does not normally extend visas but may do so in an emergency.

Sights

Shigatse's main attraction is **Tashilhunpo Monastery** (Zhāshílúnbù Sì; admission Y55; ☻ 9am-noon & 3.30-6.30pm), the seat of the Panchen Lama. Built in 1447 by a nephew of Tsongkhapa,

the monastery once housed over 4000 monks, but there are now only 600.

Apart from a giant statue of Jampa (Maitreya) Buddha (nearly 27m high) in the Temple of the Maitreya, the monastery is also famed for its Grand Hall, which houses the opulent tomb (containing 85kg of gold and masses of jewels) of the fourth Panchen Lama. Photography inside the monastic buildings costs a whopping Y75 *per chapel*.

Little remains of the **Shigatse Fortress**, but the ruins on the skyline are imposing all the same. The best way to visit it to follow the *kora* around the monastery (clockwise) and then continue to the fortress (*dzong* in Tibetan) for good views of the town.

Sleeping

Tenzin Hotel (Tiānxin Lǚguǎn; ☎ 882 2018; 10 Bangjialin Lu; dm/tr Y30/35 per bed, d with/without bathroom Y200/120, deluxe Y260) This has long been the backpacker favourite, with a fine location in the old town. It was rebuilt and upgraded in 2002. The dorms are on the ground floor; the top floor triples are quieter for almost the same price. The very comfortable doubles with bathroom are often discounted to Y160. The shared bathrooms are excellent and have 24-hour hot water. The restaurant is pricey, but is a good place to hang out.

Shambhala Hotel (Xióngbālā Fàndiàn; cnr Qingdao Lu & Shanghai Lu; dm Y20-25, d Y70, d with bathroom Y120) If the Tenzin is full this is a decent budget choice. The dorms are clean and spacious (the 4th floor is quietest). There are communal squat toilets and sinks; hot showers cost Y5.

Qomolongma Friendship Hotel (Zhūfēng Yǒuyì Bīnguǎn; ☎ 882 1929; dm Y30, d Y200-258, tr Y288) This place is often used by budget tour companies from Nepal, though it's not really up to scratch. The dorm block at the back is basic, with pit toilets across the courtyard. Get a shower at the 'Bathroom of Clean Water' (Y5) on the main street, just outside the hotel's front door (to the left).

Manasarovar Hotel (Shénhú Jiǔdiàn; ☎ 883 2000; www.hotelmanasarovartibet.com; 20 Qingdao Lu; ordinary/ superior d Y480/280, tr Y320) This new three-star hotel is a bit of a hike from the action, but is probably the best mid-range place in town. Rooms are spacious and spotless, and the bathrooms have 24-hour hot water. Discounts of up to 50% are available.

Holyland Hotel (Shèngkāng Fàndiàn; ☎ 882 2922; 5 Shandong Lu; d Y360, discounted to Y180) This fresh hotel has clean bathrooms and hot water from 7pm to midnight. Upper floors have the better rooms.

Shigatse Hotel (Rìkāzé Fàndiàn; ☎ 882 2525; fax 882 1900; 13 Shanghai Zhonglu; d/tr Y300/360) This is a three-star tour group palace in the south of town. The Tibetan-style rooms are cosy, though the bathrooms are decidedly average. Doubles are often discounted to Y240.

Eating
There's a collection of tiny Chinese restaurants with foreign menus around the corner from the Tenzin Hotel. Names and owners change regularly, but the menus remain the same. All serve Sichuanese dishes for around Y10 for vegetable dishes or Y18 for meat dishes. Note that the English menus in these restaurants are 25% more expensive than the Chinese versions.

Places include Tianfu Restaurant and the Yuanfu Restaurant (also known as Yingbing and formerly known as Greasy Joe's). Further down is the Zhengxin Restaurant, which is good and has some breakfast foods, like pancakes and banana yoghurt.

Galgye Tibetan Restaurant (dishes Y10-15) A decent Tibetan restaurant serving dishes such as Tibetan noodles, curry potatoes and Lhasa beer (Y6).

For a break from Chinese food, the **Tashi Restaurant** (☎ 883 5969; dishes Y15-28) and **Songtsen Tibetan Restaurant** (☎ 883 2469; mains Y20-35) offer a wide range of Nepalese comfort food, from yoghurt and muesli to pizza. They are a little pricier than the Chinese and Tibetan restaurants.

Getting There & Away
BUS
Private minibuses to Lhasa (Y38, seven hours) leave from around 8am from a stand on Qingdao Lu on the eastern side of Shigatse. Taxis do the trip for around Y70 per person. You can also catch the similar public bus services that run from the bus station for the same price.

Minibuses to Gyantse (Y20, 1½ hours) run when full from outside the bus station from 10am until 8pm daily, but they can be reluctant to take foreigners. Taxis also run when full for Y20 per seat (Y80 for the taxi).

Headed west there are daily morning minibuses to Lhatse (Y30, five hours), Dingri (Y65) and occasional buses to Zhāngmù.

Those aiming for the Nepalese border may be better off inquiring at the Tenzin Hotel about minibuses or Land Cruisers heading out to the border to pick up tour groups (around Y250 per person). Otherwise, start hitching from Lhatse or Tingri.

CAR HIRE
Next to the Carpet Factory, this **FIT** (☎ 883 8068, 899 0505; Zhufeng Lu) branch office can arrange Land Cruiser hire along the Friendship Hwy (only). Sample prices are Y3400 per vehicle for a three-day return trip to Rongphu Monastery, or Y3300 for a three- to four-day trip to the Nepalese border.

You could also try to hire a Land Cruiser unofficially by talking to the drivers who park outside the Tenzin Hotel. Renting vehicles in Shigatse is more difficult than in Lhasa. Expect to pay Y2500 to Y3000 for a vehicle to Rongphu Monastery and the Nepalese border, but you'll have to arrange your own permits with the PSB.

SAKYA 萨迦
☎ 0892 / elevation 4280m
The monastic town of Sakya (Sàjiā) is one of Tsang's most important historical sights and, even more than Gyantse, is very Tibetan in character, making it an interesting place to spend a day or so. Sakya's principal attractions are its northern and southern monasteries on either side of the Trum-chu (Trum River). The fortress-like southern **monastery** (gompa; admission Y45; ⏰ 9.30am-1pm, 4pm onwards) is of most interest. The original, northern monastery has been mostly reduced to picturesque ruins, though restoration work is ongoing.

Sleeping & Eating
Manasarovar Sakya Hotel (神湖萨迦宾馆; Shénhú Sàjiā Bīnguǎn; ☎ 824 2222; 1 Gesang Xilu; dm Y30-40, d Y280, tr Y220-280) For modern comforts, choose this big shiny new hotel. One of the dorms comes with toilet and shower; the others have no access to a shower. Rooms are clean and fresh, and there are superb views from the roof. Discounts of 33% are available. Its restaurant (mains Y15 to Y25) is the best place for Western dishes, like chicken sizzler and breakfast foods.

Sakya Guesthouse (Sàjiā Zhāodàisuǒ; ☎ 824 2233; dm Y15-20) The rooms are basic but bearable if you have a sleeping bag, and there's a certain timeless feel about the place. Your minibus will probably pull in here; if not, look for the English sign saying 'Hotel'.

Sakya Monastery Restaurant (☎ 824 2267; dishes Y7-12) This restaurant belongs to the monastery and serves cheap Tibetan-style dishes.

Getting There & Away

There are daily minibuses departing from Shigatse's bus station to Sakya (Y32 to Y43, four hours) at around 8am and possibly also at 3.30pm. Minibuses return from the Sakya Guesthouse at around 11am. Another option is to take a Lhatse-bound bus to the Sakya turn-off and then hitch the remaining 25km. You'll most likely have to pay the full fare to Lhatse, though.

Most people arrange to see Sakya as an overnight stop when hiring a Land Cruiser to the border or to the Everest Base Camp.

RONGPHU MONASTERY & EVEREST BASE CAMP 绒布寺、珠峰

Before heading to the border, many travellers doing the Lhasa–Kodari trip take in Rongphu Monastery and Everest Base Camp (EBC; also known as Mt Qomolangma, or Chomolungma, Base Camp; 5200m).

Before you set off you'll need to stop in Shegar (or Tingri if coming from Nepal) to pay the Qomolongma National Park entrance fee of Y405 per vehicle, plus Y65 per passenger.

The walk from Rongphu Monastery to EBC takes about two hours, or 15 minutes in a Land Cruiser. The route is obvious, past a glacial moraine and across a sandy plain. In May there are usually dozens of tents belonging to various expeditions. Endowed with springs, EBC was first used by the 1924 British Everest expedition. The China Post kiosk here is the world's highest post box.

There is a **guesthouse** (dm Y25) next to Rongphu Monastery, with a restaurant that also sells simple supplies. It's possible to stay in **tent guesthouses** (dm Y25) at EBC.

TINGRI 定日

elevation 4390m

Tingri (Dìngrì) is a huddle of Tibetan homes that overlooks a sweeping plain bordered by the towering Himalayan peaks of Mt Everest (8848m) and Cho Oyu (8153m). It's where many travellers spend their first or last night in Tibet en route to/from Nepal.

Ruins on the hill overlooking Tingri are all that remain of the **Tingri Fortress**. This fort was not blown up by Red Guards, but rather destroyed in a late 18th-century Nepalese invasion. Many more ruins on the plains between Shegar and Tingri shared the same fate.

All the budget hotels have the same layout – a quad of rooms set around a dusty courtyard. Of these, the **Amdo Hotel** (Y25 per bed) is popular with budget Land Cruiser trips and has a hot shower. The **Lhasa Guest House** (dm Y25, Y35 or Y40), next door, is similar and has a good restaurant. Cheaper options include the friendly **Everest Guesthouse and Eatery** (bed Y15), which has a decent restaurant, and the basic **Himalaya Hotel** (bed Y10).

Snow Leopard Guest House (☎ 826 2711; d Y80-160) The all-brick rooms are the most comfortable in town, and the solar shower block (hot water 7pm to midnight) is spotless. There's also a cosy restaurant (dishes Y25) and sitting area, which doubles as reception. The cheapest doubles have saggy beds. Singles can pay per bed if things aren't that busy. It's about 400m east of the other hotels.

From Tingri it's four or five spectacular hours to the Nepalese border – up, up and up to the views from Tong-la (5120m) and then down, down, down via the town of Nyalam to Zhāngmù.

ZHĀNGMÙ 樟木

☎ 0892 / elevation 2300m

Zhāngmù (Khasa in Nepalese, Dram in Tibetan) is a remarkable town that hugs the rim of a seemingly never-ending succession of hairpin bends down to the customs area at the border with Nepal. After Tibet, it all seems incredibly green and luxuriant, the smells of curry and incense in the air are from the subcontinent, and the babbling sound of fast-flowing streams that cut through the town is music to the ears.

The **Bank of China** (Zhōngguó Yínháng; ☉ 9.30am-1.30am & 3.30-6.30pm Mon-Fri, 11am-2pm Sat & Sun) will change cash and travellers cheques into yuan and also yuan into US dollars, euros or UK pounds, if you have an exchange receipt.

Moneychangers change every combination of US dollars, yuan and Nepalese rupees.

Gang Gyen Hotel (☎ 874 2188; dm Y40-50, d Y150) This hotel is just up from Chinese immigration. The dorms are spacious, but sheets are a bit grubby and the communal bathrooms a little grim. Hot showers are available on the roof.

Zhangmu Hongqiao Hotel (樟木红桥宾馆; Zhāngmù Hóngqiáo Bīnguǎn; ☎ 874 2261; dm Y20-25, d Y100-120) For the cheapest beds in town this local hotel offers good value, though there's not much English spoken. Rooms are clean and bright; however, there's no privacy in the shared bathrooms. It's a five-minute walk uphill from the Gang Gyen Hotel.

ZHĀNGMÙ TO KODARI

After **Chinese immigration** (9.30am-6.30pm, sometimes closed 1.30-3.30pm), access to Nepal is via the Friendship Bridge and Kodari, around 8km below Zhāngmù. It's generally no problem to get a lift across this stretch of no-man's land (Y10). Occasional landslides mean that travellers may find themselves scrambling over debris in the places where vehicles can't pass.

It is possible to get a Nepalese visa at the border for the same price as in Lhasa (US$30 cash, plus one passport photo), though it would be sensible to get one beforehand in Lhasa just in case. There are a few hotels that offer rooms on the Nepalese side. For those planning to continue straight on to Kathmandu, there are a couple of buses a day from Kodari that leave whenever full. If you can't find a direct bus, you'll have to change halfway at Barabise. The other option is to hire a vehicle from near Nepalese immigration. A ride to Kathmandu (four to five hours) costs Rs 1500 to Rs 2000 per car, or around Rs 500 per person. There are currently around a dozen military checkpoints along the road. Bus passengers have to disembark at many of these, causing the trip to last around seven hours.

Nepal is 2¼ hours behind Chinese time.

Qīnghǎi 青海

TIBETAN PLATEAU

CONTENTS

HIGHLIGHTS

- Drop in on a local artist in **Tóngrén** (p880) and buy a *thangka* (Buddhist painting) direct
- Follow the Yellow River downstream to the lush **Mengda Nature Reserve** (p880)
- Rough it overland to Lhasa traversing the **Tibetan Plateau** (p882) via Golmud
- Visit Qīnghǎi's name-sake, the bird-watcher's delight of **Qīnghǎi Hú** (p879)

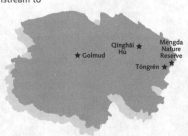

- POP: 5.3 MIL
- AREA: 720,000 SQ KM

Lying on the northeastern border of Tibet, Qīnghǎi is one of the great cartographic constructions of our time. For centuries this was part of Amdo in the Tibetan world; these days it's separated from the Tibetan Autonomous Region by nothing more than the colours on a Chinese-made map.

A relatively unknown province, Qīnghǎi may not immediately strike outsiders as cutting a particularly imposing figure. Think again though: this vast area is home to the headwaters of three of Asia's greatest rivers – the Yellow (Huáng Hé), Yangzi (Cháng Jiāng) and Mekong (Láncāng Jiāng) – as well as being the birthplace of some of Tibet's most important leaders. Chief among them are the current Dalai Lama, the 10th Panchen Lama and Tsongkhapa, founder of the Gelugpa (Yellow Hat) School of Tibetan Buddhism. Parts of the region's natural grasslands are still populated by seminomadic Tibetan herders.

Unfortunately, present-day Qīnghǎi has its demons to wrestle with. Since the founding of the PRC, it has served as a kind of Chinese Siberia, where large numbers of political and common criminals have been incarcerated, and even less glamorously as a nuclear waste dump. Poverty is rife, and a national study rated it number three on the list of China's poorest provinces.

All the same, it continues to draw visitors, primarily those attracted to the high mountains of Tibet. The normal route takes the intrepid across the Tibetan Plateau to Lhasa, but the areas along the eastern border are just as intriguing to explore, and may give you a better insight into traditional Tibetan culture.

As in times past, Qīnghǎi is populated by a mixture of different ethnic groups, including the Tibetans, Tu, Mongols, Salar and Hui. The Han, centred in Xīníng, comprise the majority of the population.

Climate
Qīnghǎi's climate is determined by the high altitude – wherever you go, it's likely to be cold and arid, though during the day the sun can get pretty intense.

The east and south are high, grassy plateaus, with elevations varying from 2500m to 3500m. Both the Tanggula Range along the border of Tibet and the Anye Maqen Mountains in the east have peaks over 6000m.

Northwestern Qīnghǎi is a large basin consisting mainly of barren desert, salt marshes and saline lakes. The Kunlun Mountains along the border with Xīnjiāng have summits that top out at a dizzying 6860m.

Language
Most of the population in Qīnghǎi speaks a northwestern Chinese dialect similar to

Gānsùhuà (part of the Lanyin Mandarin family). Tibetans speak the Amdo or Kham (near Sìchuān) dialects.

XĪNÍNG 西宁
☎ 0971 / pop 1.9 million
Xīníng is the only large city in Qīnghǎi and is the capital of the province. Long established as a Chinese city, it's been a military garrison and trading centre since the 16th century.

Nowadays Xīníng serves as a stopover for foreigners following the Qīnghǎi–Tibet route. Perched at an elevation of 2275m and positioned on the edge of the Tibetan plateau, the city itself is not the most aesthetic, though it is a convenient staging post for visiting Qīnghǎi Hú (p879) and Tǎ'ěr Sì (p879).

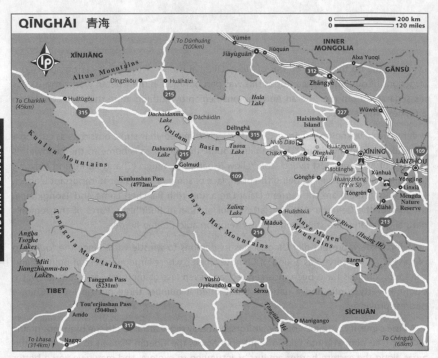

Information

BOOKSHOPS

Foreign Languages Bookshop (Wàiwén Túshūdiàn; Xiguan Dajie)

INTERNET ACCESS

There's a small *wǎngbā* (Internet café) in an alley off Jianguo Lu, on the 2nd floor across from a Bank of China.

Xīníng Shūchéng Wǎngbā (4th fl, Xīníng Shūchéng, Nan Dajie; per hr Y2) The Xining Bookstore, which is after the KFC, has an excellent Internet café.

LAUNDRY

Laundry (Gānxǐdiàn; Huzhu Lu) This inexpensive place is next door to the Post Hotel.

MONEY

Bank of China (Zhōngguó Yínháng; Dongguan Dajie; 8.30am-5.30pm Mon-Fri, 9.30am-4.30pm Sat & Sun) There's a smaller branch on Dong Dajie that also changes cash and travellers cheques.

POST

Post office (Yóujú; cnr Xi Dajie & Nan Dajie; 9am-7pm)

TOURIST INFORMATION & TRAVEL AGENCIES

China International Travel Service (CITS; Zhōngguó Guójì Lǚxíngshè; ☎ 813 0567; Huanghe Lu)

China Travel Service (CTS; Zhōngguó Lǚxíngshè; ☎ 817 0923; 1st fl, Lóngyuán Bīnguǎn, Jianguo Lu) Can get you to Qīnghǎi Hú for a decent price.

Wind Horse Adventure Tours (Xīhǎi Gōngmín Chūrùjìng Fúwùzhōngxīn; ☎ 824 7313; www.windhorse adventuretours.com; Nan Dajie) If you're interested in seeing any of the big peaks in Qīnghǎi, you'll need to go through a third party. This is a good agency, which can organize both trekking and cultural excursions. It's best to contact Betsy (American) or Phuntsok (Tibetan) first; they're not always in the office.

VISAS

Public Security Bureau (PSB; Gōngānjú; 35 Bei Dajie; 9am-6pm) This office can extend your visa in several days. Take bus No 14 or 24.

Sights

QINGHAI PROVINCIAL MUSEUM

青海省博物馆

This small **museum** (Qīnghǎi Shěng Bówùguǎn; admission Y15; 9am-5pm) has a Tibetan focus.

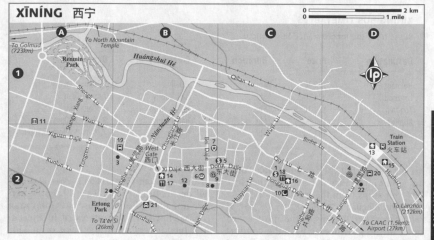

XĪNÍNG 西宁

Displays include Qing dynasty *thangkas* (Buddhist paintings), Buddhist sculptures and masks. To get there, take bus No 9, 25, 31, 16 or 104.

NORTH MOUNTAIN TEMPLE 北山寺
A 45-minute jaunt up the mountainside northwest of the city brings you to North Mountain Temple (Běishān Sì; admission Y5). The hike is pleasant and you'll be rewarded with a good view over Xīníng.

SHUIJING XIANG MARKET 水井巷商场
Xīníng's largest market (Shuǐjǐng Xiàng Shāngchǎng) occupies several streets and is an enjoyable place to browse and watch the crowds watch you. There is a good supply of snacks here if you need to stock up. It extends east from the West Gate (Xī Mén).

GREAT MOSQUE 清真大寺
The city's main **mosque** (Qīngzhēn Dàsì; 30 Dongguan Dajie; admission Y5) is one of the largest in China's northwest. There's little Middle Eastern influence here; the architecture reminds more of Běijīng than a place of Muslim worship. You can't enter the main building, but you can stroll the grounds. It was built during the late 14th century and has since been restored.

Sleeping
Post Hotel (Yóuzhèng Bīnguǎn; ☎ 813 3133; 138 Huzhu Lu; dm Y10-15, tw Y36-65) This long-time budget choice is still as reliable as ever. The hot water contraption in the rooms with showers is iffy, though.

Chēzhàn Bīnguǎn (☎ 814 9592; tr per bed Y30, tw per bed Y50-80) The only reason to come here is if they're all booked up at the Post Hotel. It's to the right of the train station.

Yǎháo Huáyuán Bīnguǎn (☎ 813 9307; fax 813 2514; 150 Dongguan Dajie; s/tw Y160/200) Rooms here

TIBETAN PLATEAU

XĪNÍNG BUS TIMETABLES

Buses from the long-distance bus station:

Destination	Price	Duration	Frequency	Departs
Hēimǎhé	Y25.30	4hr	7 daily	7.30am-2pm
Lánzhōu	Y26.30	5hr	half-hourly	7am-5.20pm
Tóngrén	Y29.30	5hr	half-hourly	7.30am-5pm
Xúnhuà	Y21	5hr	half-hourly	8.30am-3.30pm
Zhāngyè	Y43.30	9hr	3 daily	7.30am, 5.30pm, 6.30pm

are a bit snug, but they're much nicer than any other mid-range option. Take the No 1 bus four stops from the train station.

Jiànyín Bīnguǎn (☎ 826 1885; fax 826 1551; 55 Xi Dajie; s/tw Y298/398) This is the most lavish hotel in the province and for the comfort starved, it delivers. You can generally get discounted rooms.

Eating

Xiǎoyuánmén Shífǔ (188 Dongguan Dajie) This up-market Muslim restaurant has a good reputation among locals. Look for the hanging red lanterns.

Mǎlínhàn (Shuijing Xiang Market; dishes from Y5) If you're tired of the same old kebabs, Mr Ma and family also skewer veggies smothered in a special sauce. It's on the parallel alley west of the main stalls.

Around the train station at night, check out Jianguo Lu and the surrounding side streets for kebab stalls and places selling *shāguō* (a mini-hotpot of beef, mutton, vegetables, tofu and noodles).

Getting There & Away

AIR

There are flights from Xīníng to Běijīng (Y1450), Chéngdū (Y990), Guǎngzhōu (Y1650), Shànghǎi (Y1850, Monday), Ürümqi (Y1130, Monday), Golmud (Y840, twice weekly) and Xī'ān (Y650, thrice weekly). There is also a twice-weekly flight from Xīníng to Lhasa for Y1390, but you'll still need to go through CITS (p876) to purchase your ticket.

The **Civil Aviation Administration of China** (CAAC; Zhōngguó Mínháng; ☎ 818 9013; 34 Bayi Xilu; ☼ 8.30am-7.30pm) has a booking office on the eastern edge of town. To get there, take the eastbound bus No 25 to Bayi Lu, or bus No 28 from the train station.

BUS

The **long-distance bus station** (Jianguo Lu) serves all destinations except Tǎ'ěr Sì. Foreigners are not allowed on the buses to Golmud or Lhasa, but if you're interested in the latter, bus drivers are in the habit of making propositions anyway.

See box above for bus details.

From Tóngrén and Xúnhuà it's possible to take buses to Xiàhé and Línxià (in Gānsù) respectively (see p880).

If you're looking for an offbeat Tibetan experience, some travellers have made the journey from Xīníng to Chéngdū in Sìchuān by bus. The scenery is stunning and very Tibetan, but it's a rough trip that takes one week minimum. The route to Chéngdū is as follows: Xīníng to Mǎduō; Mǎduō to Xiēwú; Xiēwú to Sêrxu (Shíqú); Sêrxu to Kāngdìng; and Kāngdìng to Chéngdū.

Along the way there are cheap places to stay – the bus company will either put you up at its own hostels or direct you to another hotel. Another option would be to take a bus to Bānmǎ (two days), where you could then get a bus to Zöigê (one day), then to Sōngpān (eight hours) and on to Chéngdū (14 hours).

From Xīníng, buses to Mǎduō (Y75.30, 11 hours) leave daily at 9.30am; those to Bānmǎ (Y105.30, two days) depart at 9.45am on odd-numbered days. Neither of these buses are sleepers. If you're short on time, there are also two daily buses to the newly opened Yùshù (Y91 to Y133, 24 hours), bypassing the overnight in Mǎduō.

TRAIN

Xīníng has two express trains to Lánzhōu (Y33 to Y50, three hours) leaving at 7.23am and 12.12pm; there are also three overnight sleepers. There are three trains to Golmud taking from 14 to 16 hours. The 5701 (6.17pm) and the N903 (9.52pm) are both good bets. Hard sleepers start at Y117.

Getting Around

The airport is 27km east of the city. A CAAC shuttle bus (Y16) meets all flights.

AROUND XĪNÍNG

Tǎ'ěr Sì 塔尔寺

One of the six great monasteries of the Yellow Hat sect of Tibetan Buddhism, **Tǎ'ěr Sì** (admission Y30; ⌚ 8.30am-6pm), or Kumbum in Tibetan, is found in the town of Huángzhōng, 26km south of Xīníng. It was built in 1577 on sacred ground – the birthplace of Tsongkhapa, founder of the Yellow Hat sect.

The monastery is noted for its extraordinary sculptures of human figures, animals and landscapes carved out of yak butter. The art of butter sculpture probably dates back 1300 years in Tibet and was taken up here in the last years of the 16th century.

While of enormous historic significance, Tǎ'ěr Sì today seems to have been relegated to museum status by Běijīng. The artwork and architecture are redeeming, yet the atmosphere and scenery pale in comparison with other monasteries in Amdo.

Six temples are open, with admission tickets sold at the building diagonally opposite the row of stupas. Photography is prohibited inside the temples.

SLEEPING & EATING

Kumbun Motel (Chányuè Zhàn; tr/tw Y10/20) Just behind the row of stupas is this motel, situated in the old monks' quarters. Showers here cost Y3.

Tsongkha Hotel (Zōngkā Bīnguǎn; www.the-silk-road.com; tw Y680-880) One of the hotels in the Silk Road chain is also located here – unfortunately it's an overpriced letdown.

There are plenty of Muslim restaurants in town.

GETTING THERE & AWAY

Minibuses to Huángzhōng (Y4, 45 minutes) leave regularly from a private **bus station** (Xiguan Dajie) in Xīníng. To get here take bus Nos 22 or 29 – if you tell the driver 'Tǎ'ěr Sì', he'll know where to let you off. Catch the return minibus to Xīníng from the square 500m down the road from the monastery.

For a quicker ride, hail a taxi (Y20) at the traffic circle south of the West Gate (Xī Mén). Only certain taxis make the trip – they congregate inside a semi-hidden parking lot on the southeastern side.

QĪNGHĂI HÚ 青海湖

☎ 0970

Qīnghǎi Hú (Lake Kokonor) is a somewhat surreal-looking saline lake west of Xīníng. The lake has often served as the symbolic midway point between Tibet and Mongolia. It was here in 1578 that the Mongolian leader Altan Khan conferred upon Sonam Gyatso (then head of the Gelugpa School) the title of Dalai Lama, *dalai* being the Mongolian translation of *gyatso*, or ocean.

The main attraction is **Niǎo Dǎo** (鸟岛; Bird Island; admission Y58), located on the western side of the lake, and about 300km from Xīníng. It's a breeding ground for thousands of wild geese, gulls, cormorants, sandpipers, extremely rare black-necked cranes and other bird species. Perhaps the most interesting are the bar-headed geese. These hardy birds migrate over the Himalayas to spend winter on the Indian plains, and have been spotted flying at altitudes of 10,000m. You will only see great numbers of birds during the breeding season, which is between March and early June. Niǎo Dǎo is no longer an island, although it used to be before the lakeshore receded and made it part of the mainland.

If you're planning on doing some hiking, don't forget to bring warm clothing and water. You may meet some of the nomads living around the lake – most are friendly and will invite you in for a cup of tea in their tents.

Be aware that tourism here is depleting the native fish population, which the birds depend upon for survival. Stating that you don't eat fish *(wǒ bù chī yú)* well in advance of any meals is highly encouraged.

Tours

Between May and early September, tour buses run daily to Niǎo Dǎo (four hours). CTS in Xīníng (p876) charges Y150 to Y180, including admission, for a long day trip (8am to 5pm). Tours may include trips to Tǎ'ěr Sì and a brief stop at Sun Moon Pass (Rìyuè Shānkǒu) for a photo shoot. Some agencies head to the closer, uninteresting harbour (Y20) – double check to

TIBETAN PLATEAU

ensure that your bus is going to Niǎo Dǎo. Two-day trips are also available.

Sleeping & Eating

Niǎo Dǎo Bīnguǎn (鸟岛宾馆; ☎ 865 2447; dm/tw Y20/160). If you're not content with a day trip, you can stay here overnight. It's north of Hēimǎhé on the west side of the lake, and has a restaurant on the premises.

For those with a tent and a warm sleeping bag, camping out is also an option.

Getting There & Away

BUS

Unfortunately there are no public buses to Niǎo Dǎo. The closest you can get is to the small settlement of Hēimǎhé, 50km away. Getting from Hēimǎhé to Niǎo Dǎo will probably cost you another Y50 for a taxi, or less if you hitch. From Xīníng there are seven departures to Hēimǎhé (Y25.3, four hours) between 7.30am and 2pm; the return schedule is similar.

TÓNGRÉN 同仁

☎ 0973

Tóngrén (Repkong) is an amiable mid-sized town that looks like it was randomly plopped down in the midst of dry, dusty hills. The villages outside of town are famed for their artistically inclined inhabitants, who have been producing many of the thangkas and painted statues in the Tibetan world for several centuries now.

Visiting the monastery Wútún Sì not only gives you a chance to meet the artists, but also to purchase a painting or two, fresh off the easel. You can't change money here, so have a little extra Renminbi on hand, in the event that something strikes your fancy.

Sights

The villages surrounding the lamaseries are a mixture of Tibetans and Tu, distant cousins of the Mongols.

WÚTÚN SÌ 吾屯寺

Divided into an **Upper Monastery** (Shàng Sì; 上寺; Y10) and a **Lower Monastery** (Xià Sì; 下寺; Y10), this is the place to come if you're interested in Tibetan art. Generally the monks will offer to sell you some thangkas on a tour; if you want to look first, there's a gallery outside the Upper Monastery. These are no amateurs – commissions come in all

the way from Lhasa, and the prices, ranging from Y200 to Y800, are a good deal, especially considering that a small thangka takes a minimum of one month to paint.

If you want to visit an artist's studio, try asking for the monk Xiàwú Cáiràng (夏吾才让) at the Lower Temple, who comes from a family of painters that live just next door. No one speaks English, so you'll have to make do with Mandarin.

From Tóngrén, a motor tricycle can get you here for about Y5. You'll recognize the Lower Monastery from the eight large *chörten* (stupas) out front. It's best to visit in the morning.

GOMAR LAMASERY 郭麻日寺

A pleasant hike across the valley from Wútún Sì is the mysterious 400-year-old Gomar Gompa (Guōmàrì Sì), marked by an enormous gold and white chörten. The labyrinth-like paths here wind past chiming bells and fluttering prayer flags to seemingly deserted buildings. There are supposedly 130 monks in residence.

Festivals & Events

Besides the **Monlam Festival** (see Xiàhé, p814) at the beginning of the Tibetan New Year, Tóngrén is particularly famous for its five-day body-piercing **Lurol Festival**, beginning on the 21st day of the sixth lunar month (July or August).

Sleeping

Huángnán Bīnguǎn (黄南宾馆; ☎ 872 2293; 18 Zhongshan Lu; dm Y15, tw Y70-288) This is the main hotel in town, with dark but clean rooms.

Getting There & Away

See box opposite for details.

MENGDA NATURE RESERVE 孟达天池

This beautiful **natural park** (Mèngdá Tiān Chí; admission May-Oct Y26, Nov-Apr Y12) is located in the mountains above the Yellow River, 190km southeast of Xīníng. The highlight of the reserve is Heaven Lake (Tiān Chí), a sacred lake for both the local Salar Muslims and Tibetan Buddhists. The Salar speak an isolated Turkic language, but otherwise resemble the Hui.

The bus will drop you off at the turnoff to Heaven Lake, from where it is a 4km walk to the ticket office. From the ticket

TÓNGRÉN BUS TIMETABLES

Buses from Tóngrén include:

Destination	Price	Duration	Frequency	Departs
Línxià	Y27	3hr	1 daily	8am
Xiàhé	Y17	3hr	1 daily	8am
Xīníng	Y29	5hr	hourly	7.20am-4pm
Xúnhuà	Y13	2½hr	3 daily	8am, 1pm, 3pm

office, the road continues on for 2km until the car park; from there it's a final 800m stretch up to the lake. In total, the hike takes around 2½ hours. Once you reach the top it's possible to walk around the lake when the water level is low enough, or to head up into the surrounding peaks.

Sleeping & Eating

From May to October there are two options for accommodation: **tents** (per bed Y20), set up along the lakeshore, or the **hotel** (tw Y120). Food is limited; bringing your own is not a bad idea. You can camp out year-round.

You can also stay in the nearby town of Xúnhuà (循化) at the **Jiāotōng Bīnguǎn** (交通宾馆; dm Y13-30, tw Y90), next door to the bus station.

Getting There & Away

Mengda Nature Reserve is a spectacular one-hour bus ride from Xúnhuà. The road is cut into arid cliffs, following the coppery-green Yellow River as it snakes its way along below. Minibuses to Dàhéjiā pass the entrance, from where you can walk up to the lake. Depending on how many people are on board, you should be able to get there for about Y10. A taxi from Xúnhuà to the car park costs Y60.

From Xúnhuà there are six daily buses to Línxià (Y15, three hours); four daily buses to Tóngrén (Y13, 2½ hours); and frequent buses to Xīníng (Y21, five hours).

GOLMUD 格尔木

☎ 0979 / pop 200,000

Unless you're an engineer or an escaped convict on the run, the only reason to visit this strange outpost in the oblivion end of China is to continue into Tibet. While not a terrible place, you probably wouldn't want to stay around Golmud (Géěrmù) more than a day, and few visitors do. The town owes its existence to mining and oil drilling.

The eerie moonscape of the Tibetan plateau can be an inhospitable place – come prepared! At 2800m elevation, the days in summer can be very warm, but the nights are always cool. The daytime sun is incredibly bright – sunglasses and sunblock lotion are *de rigueur*.

Information

Bank of China (Zhōngguó Yínháng; cnr Kunlun & Chaidamu Lu; ⏰ 8.30am-6.30pm Mon-Fri, 10am-4pm Sat & Sun) You can change travellers cheques and cash here.

CITS (Zhōngguó Guójì Lǚxíngshè; ☎ 841 3003; ⏰ 8.30am-noon & 2.30-6pm Mon-Fri) CITS has offices on the 2nd floor of the Golmud Hotel and at the Tibet Bus Station. If you're planning to go to Lhasa legally, this is your first stop (see p882).

Internet Plaza (Liántōng Wǎngyuàn; China Unicom Bldg; per hr Y2) Access the Internet here.

Post office (Yóujú; Chaidamu Lu) There's also a smaller post office in front of the Golmud Hotel.

PSB (Gōngānjú; ⏰ 8am-noon & 2.30-5pm Mon-Fri; Chaidamu Lu) This office is east of the main post office.

Sleeping & Eating

Golmud Hotel (Géěrmù Bīnguǎn; ☎ 841 2061; fax 841 6484; 219 Kunlun Lu; dm Y25, tw Y100-300) This hotel has two buildings – the upmarket hotel *(bīnguǎn)* and the hostel *(zhāodàisuǒ)*. Considering Golmud's isolation, it's a pretty decent place.

The Hedong market (Hédōng Shìchǎng) has lots of open-air food vendors, some of which sell clay-pot stews. North of the Golmud Hotel is Ali Cake (Alǐ Dàngāo), with fresh bread and snacks. The underground **Jiale Supermarket** (Jiālè Chāoshì; cnr Kunlun & Bayi Lu) is a good place to stock up on food for the bus ride.

TIBETAN PLATEAU

GOLMUD 格尔木

Getting There & Away

AIR

Nobody actually flies to Golmud, but if you want to buck the trend, the city has two weekly flights to Qīngdǎo, Xī'ān and Xīníng.

BUS

The Golmud bus station is opposite the train station. The 524km trip from Golmud to Dūnhuáng departs twice daily, at 8am (Y78, eight hours) and 6pm (Y90, 12 hours); the latter is a sleeper. It's a scenic trip through the desert and mountains, but take a jacket as it can get cold at night. You may need to pick up an annoying permit at

the PSB (Y50) before you buy your ticket – remember they're closed weekends.

TRAIN

Express trains head to Xīníng (No 5702) or Lánzhōu (No N903). It's 14 hours to Xīníng and 18 hours to Lánzhōu; both trains leave in the evening. Avoid the slower local train (No 8760).

See The Lhasa Express for information on the railway being built from Golmud to Lhasa.

TO TIBET

CITS (p881) has an iron grip on foreign bus tickets from Golmud to Lhasa – all travellers must buy their tickets through the travel agency, and they pay dearly for it.

The Tibet Tourism Bureau officially requires every foreigner to have a Tibet Tourism Bureau permit, insurance, four days accommodation at the Kirey Hotel (p863) in Lhasa and a four-day tour. For all this, you will have the pleasure of handing over Y1700 (which doesn't include entrance fees). In comparison, the actual price of a sleeper ticket to Lhasa is Y200.

If you choose to go the CITS route, buses depart from the **Tibet Bus Station** (Xizang Lu) at 3pm and take anywhere from 20 to 25 hours, assuming the weather, traffic and bus engine cooperate. Once you arrive, you're free to stick with the 'tour' or strike off on your own.

The other option is to hang around the regular bus station (across from the train station) and make a deal with one of the drivers. They generally ask for about Y600 (bus) or Y800 (jeep); it's understood that this price includes a bribe for the PSB. There's definitely a risk involved, and there's no way to guarantee that you won't be fined and sent back. Some trucks are given the twice over, while others get through hassle free. It goes without saying that you shouldn't hand over any money until you're actually in a vehicle, and ideally the bulk of the payment should be made only once you've arrived.

It would be wise to stock up on a few necessities for the trip. People's Liberation Army (PLA) overcoats are available from Y75 at the market – consider getting one even if you wind up giving it away in Lhasa. It can easily get down to -10°C or lower in

THE LHASA EXPRESS

In 2001, after decades of dreams and indecision, the Chinese government proudly unveiled plans for its Herculean project: a 1118km-long, US$3.2 billion train line from Golmud (Qīnghăi) to Lhasa (Tibet), and what they hope isn't a Sisyphean venture.

The scope – no, 'megalomaniacal lunacy', spouted critics – of the job is hard to imagine. The government had sought international consultancy on numerous occasions, all of whom told them they were daft to attempt it; the Swiss, the world's best tunnel builders, said ice mountains made it impossible.

Undaunted, planners enthusiastically pushed the project through. Construction has been underway since late 2001, and the estimated completion date is now mid-2007 – just in time to have trains up and running for that other international esteem builder, the Olympics.

Consider the downsides though: four-fifths of the line will ride above 4000m (oxygen bars are planned for sleeper cars); over 60 medical clinics need to be built to deal with altitude-sickness problems; and more than half the distance will be atop permafrost. A radical Chinese-designed cooling system – questioned by many engineers – will be used for the rest of the way, to ensure that a track-buckling thaw will never take place. Of perhaps more concern is that the line encroaches on six national protected zones, home to endangered species such as the Tibetan antelope and black-necked crane.

Culturally, there will also be an impact. The government proudly states that railway development has created some 38,000 jobs for two of China's poorest provinces, yet an estimated 85% of employment is filled by migrant workers from outside regions. The few local Tibetans involved occupy the lowest rungs, working essentially as high-altitude ditch diggers. And while formerly 'destitute' Tibet will now be able to bring in supplies much more easily, another cargo will be riding alongside – thousands of Han Chinese, looking for new opportunities.

those mountain passes at night; although the buses are heated, you could be in serious trouble if you are ill equipped and there is a breakdown. Keep an eye on your possessions, there have been a couple of reports of thieves on the buses. Some travellers buy oxygen canisters (Y30) from the CITS office to help with the altitude sickness.

The official policy changes often, and the railway to Lhasa is expected to further revolutionize the whole permit system. The **Lonely Planet Thorn Tree** (http://thorntree.lonelyplanet.com) online forum is a good way to stay up to date on the latest rules and regulations.

Getting Around

The No 1 bus (Y1) runs from the train station to the Golmud Hotel. Taxis in town are Y5.

TIBETAN PLATEAU

Directory

DIRECTORY

CONTENTS

ACCOMMODATION

Overall, accommodation in China is quite humdrum and no cause for great excitement. Beyond Hong Kong and Macau, you won't find a classic hotel of real stature and pedigree like the Raffles Hotel in Singapore. Few historic hotels of character exist outside Hong Kong, Macau, Běijīng and Shànghǎi (and at a stretch Tiānjīn and Qīngdǎo). Lack of investment and management experience and an ingrained communist reluctance to excel drags many a hotel down.

Be warned that the star rating at China's hotels can be very misleading. Hotels are often awarded four or five stars, when they are patently a star lower in ranking. This might not be immediately obvious to guests approaching the reception desk (*zǒngtái*)

PRACTICALITIES

- There are four types of plugs – three-pronged angled pins (as in Australia), three-pronged round pins (as in Hong Kong), two flat pins (US style but without the ground wire) or two narrow round pins (European style). Electricity is 220 volts, 50 cycles AC.

- The standard locally published English-language newspaper is the *China Daily* (www.chinadaily.com.cn). China's largest circulation Chinese-language daily is the *People's Daily (Rénmín Rìbào)*. It has an English language edition on www.eng lish.peopledaily.com.cn. Imported English language newspapers such as the *Times*, the *International Herald Tribune*, the *Asian Wall Street Journal, The Financial Times* and the *South China Morning Post* can be bought from five-star hotel bookshops. Imported English-language international magazines such as *Time*, *Newsweek, Far Eastern Economic Review* and the *Economist* can be purchased at five-star hotel bookshops. Look out for expat English language magazines with local bar, restaurant and events listings in town. Magazines include *That's Beijing, That's Shanghai, That's Guangzhou, Red Star* (Qīngdǎo) and *Jin* (Tiānjīn).

- Listen to the BBC World Service (www .bbc.co.uk/worldservice/tuning/) or Voice of America (www.voa.gov). China Radio International (CRI) is China's overseas radio service and broadcasts in about 40 foreign languages. The national TV outfit, Chinese Central TV (CCTV), has an English language channel – CCTV9. CCTV4 also has some English programs. Your hotel may have ESPN, Star Sports, CNN or BBC News 24.

- China officially subscribes to the international metric system, but you are also likely to encounter the ancient Chinese weights and measures system that features the *liǎng* (tael, 37.5g) and the *jīn* (catty, 0.6kg). There are 16 *liǎng* to the *jīn*.

with high expectations, so take time to wander round and make a quick inspection of the overall quality or stick to chain hotels with recognisable names.

Some definitions of hotel terminology are in order. The vast majority of rooms in China are 'twins', which means two single beds placed in one room. A 'single room' (one bed per room) is a rarity, although they do exist. The Western concept of a 'double room' (a room with one double bed shared by two people) is also rare in China. In most cases, your choice will be between a twin room *(shuāng rén fáng)* or a suite *(tàofáng),* the latter being more expensive. However, in most cases two people are allowed to occupy a twin room for the same price as one person, so sharing is one good way to cut expenses.

The Chinese method of designating floors is the same as that used in the USA, but different from, say, Australia's. What would be the ground floor in Australia is the 1st floor in China, the 1st is the 2nd, and so on.

Most budget and mid-range hotels have an attendant *(fúwùyuàn)* on every floor, who keeps an eye on hotel guests and security.

The policy at every hotel in China is that you check out by noon to avoid being charged extra. If you check out between noon and 6pm there is a charge of 50% of the room price – after 6pm you have to pay for another full night.

Almost every hotel has a left-luggage room *(jìcún chù* or *xínglǐ bǎoguān),* and in many hotels there is one on every floor. If you are a guest in the hotel, use of the left-luggage room should be free.

In big cities, it's wise to phone first to check if there's a vacant room; the reception desk may not speak English. Ask the hotel operator for the *zǒng fúwù tái* or *zǒng tái* (service desk) and then ask *'Yǒu méiyǒu kōng fángjiān?'* (Do you have a vacancy?), to which they'll either reply *yǒu* (have) or *méiyǒu* (don't have).

Male guests regularly receive phone calls from prostitutes, who ask whether *ànmó* (massage) is required; if you don't want their services, unplug your phone, as they can be persistent.

Top End

Hotels with standard double rooms costing anything over around Y600 (and up to over US$300) are defined in this book as top end (four to five stars). Within this price range, standards in the top end bracket can vary considerably.

As China has few independent hotels of real distinction, it's advisable to select chain hotels that offer a proven standard of excellence and quality across the board when opting for top-drawer accommodation. Shangri-La, Marriott, Holiday Inn, Hilton, St Regis, Marco Polo and Grand Hyatt all have a presence in China and can generally be relied upon for high standards of service and comfort.

Some Chinese-owned hotels display five stars, when they are clearly four stars, so be warned. Five-star hotels should be equipped with top-notch sport (including swimming pool and tennis courts), recreational and shopping facilities, and there should be a wide selection of dining options and possibly ATMs that take international cards. Five-star hotel rooms should have kettle (and coffee sachets), safe, mini-bar, satellite or cable TV, broadband Internet connection, free newspaper (typically the *International Herald Tribune*) and nightly turndown. Superior comfort should also be available on executive floors, which typically provide free drinks upon arrival and in the afternoon, complimentary breakfast and business facilities. Service should be top-notch. Most top-end hotels usually list their room rates in US dollars, but you will have to pay in local currency. Practically all hotels will change money for guests and most mid-range and top end hotels accept credit cards. All hotel rooms are subject to a 10% or 15% service charge.

Mid-Range

Hotels with standard double rooms roughly costing between Y200 and Y600 are defined as mid-range in this book.

Mid-range hotels (three to four stars) offer comfort and a measure of style, but are often bland and unimaginative and housed in recently-built and sterile exteriors. You should find someone who can speak English, but language skills are rarely good and often problematic even at reception. When making a choice, opt for Sino-foreign joint-venture hotels over the Chinese-owned hotels, wherever possible. Furthermore, try to opt for the newer establishments as mid-range hotels rapidly get set in their ways and quickly lose their freshness. Apart from three-star hotels, Chinese mid-range hotels should have a Western restaurant and there may be a swimming pool and a bar. Rooms will all come with air-con, satellite or cable TV (or in-house movie channel, or just terrestrial stations) and telephone, and should also come with kettle (and coffee sachets), safe and mini-bar, and there could be broadband Internet connection. You may receive a free newspaper, but at best only the *China Daily*.

Budget
Any hotel or guesthouse that has rooms under Y200 is classed as budget in this book.

Budget rooms can be found in hotels rated as two stars or less. Expect basic facilities, grimy bathrooms, dirty carpets, flickering TVs, noisy neighbours, very basic or non-existent English language skills, a simple restaurant or none at all. Virtually all budget hotel rooms should come with air-conditioning and TV, but not all rooms have telephones (at youth hostels, for example), so ask beforehand.

In China's more developed regions along the eastern seaboard, it can be no cheaper than travelling in Europe or the USA. While more isolated regions like Inner Mongolia or Qīnghǎi are still pretty cheap, prices are rising everywhere. The government is aiming to develop the laggardly western regions, and this could lead to higher room prices. This trend could be offset by the opening up of cheap Chinese guesthouses to foreign travellers.

Where available, opt to stay at Hostelling International hostels (or other youth hostels), which are becoming more plentiful in large cities such as Běijīng, Shànghǎi and Xī'ān.

Foreign travellers have traditionally been steered away from ultra-cheap Chinese guesthouse accommodation towards Public Security Bureau (PSB)-approved lodgings that were invariably more expensive. This is beginning to change. It was announced in October 2003 that all hotels in Běijīng would henceforth accept foreigners and in other parts of China the situation has been relaxed. At the time of writing, however, most Chinese guesthouses in Běijīng were either unaware of the new ruling or still

unwilling to take foreign guests. By the time you visit, however, you may find that cheap Chinese guesthouses in Běijīng (or elsewhere) have indeed opened up to foreign travellers; so if ultracheap, ultrabasic and grubby accommodation is what you are after, try asking.

The pinyin and Chinese characters for guesthouses are:

zhāodàisuǒ	招待所
lǚdiàn	旅店
lǚguǎn	旅馆

Certain temples and monasteries (especially on China's sacred mountains) can provide accommodation. They can be very cheap, but extremely ascetic, with no running water or electricity.

Ask to see a room before taking it and check for smoke alarms (it is worth bringing your own anyway, as many smoke alarms are faulty). Hotel fires are quite common in China and conflagrations can get the upper hand because of the lack of smoke alarms and locked fire exits (check the exits on your floor and complain if they are locked).

UNIVERSITY ACCOMMODATION
In theory, university dormitories are for students, teachers and their guests, or others with business at the university (*dàxué*). In practice, universities are trying to make money, and they are simply entering into the hotel business just like many other state-run organisations.

Especially along China's east coast and in major cities, staying in a university dorm is often one of your cheapest options. Many universities will rent out vacant dorm rooms in the foreign student dormitory. Universities also sometimes have actual hotels, although the prices are usually on a par with regular budget hotels. On the negative side, university dormitories may have certain restrictions such as the main door locking early and a non-central location. On the positive side, many have 24-hour Internet cafés and are surrounded by decent restaurants and bars.

Reservations
It is always important to bargain for a room. Ask whether a discount (*dǎzhékòu*) is in force, as discounts on the rack rate are usually available. It is best to do this in person

at reception; if you book ahead, you can end up paying well over the odds. Apart from during the busy holiday periods (first week of May and October), hotels in China are rarely booked out. At reception, you should be able to get a discount of 10% to 50% off the tariff rate, but you may be able to secure a room for as little as 30% of the rack rate. Booking online is an excellent way to secure a good price on a room, and should be the first place you look. Often you actually get a discount by booking through an agency – and these can be substantial, up to 40% to 50% off the walk-in rate (although don't use Chinese online agencies which simply offer rates you can get from a hotel itself). Accommodation websites that could be useful for travellers booking accommodation include www.redflag.info, www.asia-hotels.com or www.sinohotel.com. Airports at major cities often have hotel-booking counters that offer discounted rates.

At check-in, you will need your passport and a registration form will ask what type of visa you have. For most travellers, your visa will be 'L'. For a full list of visa categories, see p904. A deposit (*yājīn*) is required at most hotels; this will be either a cash deposit, or your credit card details will be taken. If your deposit is paid in cash, you will be given a receipt which you should hold on to, for later reimbursement. Credit cards can usually be used for payment at three-star hotels and up, but always check beforehand.

ACTIVITIES

A whiff of the tourist dollar has sent Chinese entrepreneurs scrambling up the rock face of the adventure sport economy. Even in and around Běijīng there's a mushrooming choice, including paragliding, hang-gliding, rock climbing, diving with sharks, skiing, bungee jumping, horseback riding and more. Glance at the expat magazines in Běijīng, Guǎngzhōu and Shànghǎi for information on other activities such as running, mountain biking, football, cricket, swimming, ice skating, skateboarding and water-skiing.

Outfits in China itself, such as Wildchina (www.wildchina.com), offer a host of dramatic treks in remote parts of China.

Horse riding

Horse riding expeditions aimed at tourists can be found in Xīnjiāng, Gānsù, Inner Mon

golia, Sìchuān and beyond. Lángmùsì in Gānsù offers good horse trekking opportunities and horse riding around both Gānzī and Sōngpān in Sìchuān are popular.

In the big cities, a growing number of equestrian clubs can be found: check the classified pages of expat mags for details.

Skiing

It is not worth going to China for a skiing holiday, but if you are in China during the winter months, you can visit northeast China, which is the venue for downhill skiing (see p384 and p370).

Golf

Golf is an increasingly popular sport in China, with courses springing up everywhere. Běijīng has more than a dozen golf courses and others can be found throughout China, from Guǎngzhōu to Shànghǎi.

BUSINESS HOURS

China officially has a five-day working week. Banks, offices and government departments are usually open Monday to Friday, roughly from around 9am (some closing for two hours in the middle of the day) until 5pm or 6pm. Saturday and Sunday are both public holidays, but most museums stay open on weekends and sometimes make up for this by closing for one day during the week. Museums tend to stop selling tickets half an hour before they close. Travel agencies and foreign-exchange counters in tourist hotels have similar opening hours, but generally do not close for lunch and are usually open Saturday and Sunday as well (at least in the morning). Department stores and shops are generally open 10am-10pm, seven days a week. Note that businesses in China close for three week-long holidays (p895). Many parks, zoos and monuments have similar opening hours; they're also open on weekends and often at night. Internet café opening hours vary, but typically open at 8am and close between 10pm and midnight, while some are open 24 hours.

Chinese restaurants are generally open from around 10.30am to 11pm or midnight, but some shut at around 2pm and reopen at 5pm or 6pm. The Chinese are accustomed to eating much earlier than Westerners, lunching at around midday and having dinner in the region of 6pm.

DIRECTORY

CHILDREN

Children will feel more at home in the large cities of Hong Kong, Běijīng, Shànghǎi and Guǎngzhōu, but may feel out of place in smaller towns and in the wilds. Don't be surprised if a complete stranger picks up your child or takes them from your arms: Chinese people openly display their affection for children.

Practicalities

Baby food and milk powder is widely available in supermarkets, as are basics like nappies, baby wipes, bottles, medicine, dummies (pacifiers) and other paraphernalia. Practically no cheap restaurants have baby chairs and finding baby changing rooms is next to impossible. Ask a doctor specialised in travel medicine for information on recommended immunizations for your child.

Bear in mind that the simple convenience of family car travel is almost out of the question in China, except in large cities (see p919), so be prepared for long train and bus rides or plane journeys and the difficulties associated with them. Protesting infants on a long-haul train trip can make travel very stressful.

Admission prices to many sights and museums have children's rates, usually for children under 1.3m in height. Infants under the age of two fly for 10% of the full airfare, while tickets are generally 25% cheaper than the full airfare for children between the ages of two and 11.

Always ensure that your child carries a form of ID and a hotel card, in case they gets lost.

For more information on travelling with children, turn to the following:

■ *Travel with Children* (Maureen Wheeler, Cathy Lanigan; Lonely Planet)
■ *Travelling Abroad with Children* (Samantha Gore-Lyons; Arrow)
■ *Take the Kids Travelling* (Helen Truszkowski; Take the Kids series)
■ *Backpacking with Babies and Small Children* (Goldie Silverman; Wilderness Press)
■ *Adventuring with Children* (Nan Jeffrey; Avalon House Travel Series)

CLIMATE

See to p13 for advice on the best times to visit China's various regions. Spread over

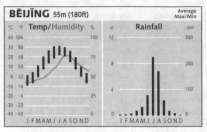

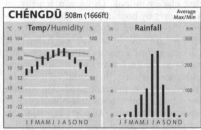

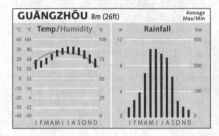

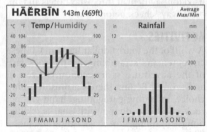

such a vast area, China is subject to the worst extremes in weather, from bitter cold to unbearable heat. The land can be roughly divided into the following climatic regions: north and northeast, northwest, central, south and Tibet.

Winters in China's north and northeast fall between November/December and March/April and are very cold. North of the Great Wall and into Inner Mongolia and Hēilóngjiāng, temperatures can drop

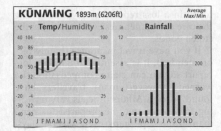

KŪNMÍNG 1893m (6206ft)

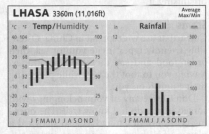

LHASA 3360m (11,016ft)

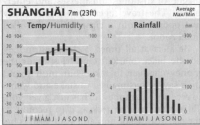

SHÀNGHĂI 7m (23ft)

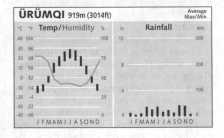

ÜRÜMQI 919m (3014ft)

to -40°C. Summer is hot and dry and falls roughly between May and August.

In central China – in the Yangzi River (Cháng Jiāng) valley area, including Shànghăi – the summers are typically uncomfortable, long, hot and humid. The three cities of Wǔhàn, Chóngqìng and Nánjīng are called the 'three furnaces', sweltering between April and October. Winters are short, wet and cold and the weather can be miserable.

Hăinán, Hong Kong and Guăngdōng province in the south are hot (temperatures can reach 38°C) and humid from April to September. This is also the rainy season, with typhoons liable to hit the southeast coast between July and September. Winters are short, between January and March; it's not nearly as cold as in the north (Hăinán is warm and, apart from the north of the province, Yúnnán is pleasant), but you will still need warm clothes as far south as Hong Kong.

China's northwest is very hot and dry in summer, while in winter, this region is as formidably cold as the rest of northern China. In Ürümqi, the average temperature in January is around -10°C, with minimums down to almost -30°C.

In Tibet, you can easily get the impression that all four seasons have been compressed into one day. Temperatures can be below zero during the evening and early morning, and can soar to a sizzling 38°C at midday, but it always feels remarkably cool in the shade. Winter brings intense cold and fierce winds. Tibet is arid, with rainfall scarcest in the north and west.

CUSTOMS

Chinese customs generally pay tourists little attention. There are clearly marked 'green channels' and 'red channels'. Duty-free, you're allowed to import 400 cigarettes or the equivalent, two bottles of wine or spirits and 50g of gold or silver. Importing fresh fruit and cold cuts is prohibited. You can legally only bring in or take out Y6000 in Chinese currency. There are no restrictions on foreign currency, however you should declare any cash exceeding US$5000 (or its equivalent in another currency).

Objects considered to be antiques require a certificate and red seal to clear customs. To get the proper certificate and red seal, your antiques must be inspected by the **Relics Bureau** (Wénwù Jiàndìng; ☎ 010-6401 4608, no English spoken). Basically anything made before 1949 is considered an antique and needs a certificate, and if it was made before 1795 it cannot legally be taken out of the country.

DANGERS & ANNOYANCES
Crime

Travellers are more often the victims of petty economic crime, such as theft, rather than serious crime. Foreigners are natural

SARS

The SARS health crisis in China (p930) put China on several countries' watch lists. For the latest travel advisories, check the following websites:

Australia (www.dfat.gov.au/travel)
Canada (www.voyage.gc.ca)
New Zealand (www.mft.govt.nz)
UK (www.fco.gov.uk/travel)
US (www.travel.state.gov/travel/warnings.html)

targets for pickpockets and thieves, but as long as you keep your wits about you and make it difficult for thieves to get at your belongings, you shouldn't have any problems. Certain cities and places are worse than others – Guǎngzhōu, Guìyáng and Xī'ān are notorious. Incidences of crime increase around the Chinese New Year.

High-risk areas in China are train and bus stations, city and long-distance buses (especially sleeper buses), hard-seat train carriages and public toilets. Don't leave anything of value in your bicycle basket.

Hotels are generally safe. Attendants are on each floor, keeping an eye on the rooms and safeguarding the keys. Dormitories obviously require more care. Don't be overly trusting of your fellow travellers – many of them are considerably less than honest. All hotels have safes and storage areas for valuables – use them. Don't leave anything you can't do without (passport, travellers cheques, money, air tickets etc) lying around in dormitories.

Carry just as much cash as you need and keep the rest in travellers cheques. Always take a money belt for larger sums of cash, along with your passport and credit cards.

A worrying trend is the increasing number of reports of foreigners attacked or even killed for their valuables, especially in more rural locations (a Western tourist was killed a few years ago on Moon Hill in popular Yángshuò); so be vigilant at all times. It's always advisable to travel with someone else or in a small group; individual travellers have to accept they are taking a risk.

LOSS REPORTS

If something of yours is stolen, you should report it immediately to the nearest Foreign Affairs Branch of the PSB. Staff will ask you to fill in a loss report before investigating the case and sometimes even recovering the stolen goods.

If you have travel insurance (highly recommended), it is essential to obtain a loss report so you can claim compensation. Be warned, however: many travellers have found Foreign Affairs officials very unwilling to provide one. Be prepared to spend many hours, perhaps even several days, organising it.

Scams

Con artists are widespread in China. Ostensibly friendly types invite you for tea, then order food and say they have no money, leaving you to foot the bill, while practising their English on you.

Don't leave any of your belongings with someone you do not know well. The opening economy in China has also spawned a plague of dishonest businesses and enterprises. The travel agent you phoned may just operate from a cigarette smoke-filled hotel room.

Be alert at all times if changing money on the black market. One trick is for the money-changer to take your money and then say he has made a mistake and wants to recount the money he has just given you. Taking the money back as if to recount it, the last you see of him and your cash is his heels moving at velocity down the road.

Lǎowài!

You will often hear calls or muttered whispers of 'lǎowài' when walking down the street. An excruciating 'Hellooooo', with ensuing hoots of laughter, often follows. Lǎowài means 'foreigner' and is used by one Chinese person to indicate to others the presence of someone non-Chinese. Lǎowài is used in conversation by all Chinese to refer to foreigners. Some travellers find it annoying to hear the words uttered by onlookers wherever they go. It is hardly ever said with anything but surprise and curiosity, however. Despite decades of foreign TV and films and ever increasing droves of Western travellers, the Chinese still find novelty in the sudden appearance of foreigners. Calls of lǎowài are far more common and more vocal in smaller towns than in the big cities. More neutral terms for foreigners are wàiguórén (foreigner) and wàibīn (foreign guest).

Pollution & Noise

Pollution is a serious problem in China and can make travel unpleasant for everyone, but especially if you have allergies, skin conditions, or chest, eye, nose and throat problems. According to the World Bank, China has 16 of the world's 20 most polluted cities.

In recent years the Chinese government has launched an anti–noise pollution campaign. The government is on a loser with this one, but a number of cities have banned the use of car horns within the city. The Chinese are generally much more tolerant of noise than most foreigners. People watch TV at ear-shattering volumes, drivers lean on the horn, and much of China seems to wake uncomplainingly to the sound of jackhammers and earth-moving vehicles. If it's peace and quiet you want, head for a remote part of China – try the desert in Xīnjiāng, or a mountain top in Tibet.

Spitting

When China first opened to foreign tourism, many foreign travellers were shocked by the spitting, which was conducted noisily by everyone everywhere. Campaigns to stamp out the practice have been reasonably successful in the major urban centres – there is less public spitting in Guǎngzhōu, Shànghǎi and Běijīng these days (some areas impose a Y50 fine), but in the country, the phlegm still flows.

Queues

In China a large number of people with a common goal (a bus seat, a train ticket, purchasing a mobile phone etc) generally form a surging mass, although elements of queuing are appearing. It is one of the more exhausting parts of China travel, and sometimes it is worth paying extra in order to be able to avoid train and bus stations. Otherwise, take a deep breath and leap in with everyone else.

DISABLED TRAVELLERS

China has few facilities geared for disabled travellers, but that doesn't necessarily put it out of bounds for those with a physical disability (and a sense of adventure). Most hotels have lifts, so booking ground-floor hotel rooms is not essential, unless you are staying in very budget accommodation.

Some hotels at the four- and five-star level have specially designed rooms for people with physical disabilities.

The roads and pavements make things very difficult for the wheelchair-bound or those with a walking disability. Pavements can often be crowded, in an appalling and dangerous condition and with high kerbs. People whose sight, hearing or walking ability is impaired must be extremely cautious of the traffic, which almost never yields to pedestrians. Escalators leading from subways in large cities like Běijīng frequently go up only. Travelling by car or taxi is probably the safest transport option.

Hong Kong is more user-friendly to the disabled than the rest of China, but it presents substantial obstacles of its own, such as the stairs at the subway stations, numerous overhead walkways and steep hills.

Get in touch with your national support organisation before leaving home. They often have travel literature for holiday planning and can put you in touch with travel agents who specialise in tours for the disabled.

In the USA, contact the **Society for Accessible Travel & Hospitality** (SATH; ☎ 212-447 7284; www.sath.org; Suite 601, 347 Fifth Ave, New York, NY).

In the UK, the **Royal Association for Disability & Rehabilitation** (RADAR; ☎ 020-7250 3222; www.radar.org.uk; 12 City Forum, 250 City Rd, London) produces three holiday fact packs for disabled travellers.

In France, try the **Comité National Français de Liaison pour la Réadaption des Handicapés** (CNFLRH; ☎ 01 53 80 66 66; 236 bis rue de Tolbiac, Paris).

You will find loads of information useful for wheelchair-bound travellers online at www.disabilitytravel.com.

EMBASSIES & CONSULATES
People's Republic of China Embassies & Consulates

For a full list of diplomatic representation abroad, go to the Ministry of Foreign affairs website at www.fmprc.gov.cn/eng/and click on Missions Overseas.

Australia Canberra (☎ 02-6273 4780, 6273 4781; www.chinaembassy.org.au; 15 Coronation Drive, Yarralumla, ACT 2600); Sydney consulate (☎ 02-9699 2216; http://sydney.chineseconsulate.org/eng); Melbourne consulate (☎ 03-9822 0604); Perth consulate (☎ 08-9321 8193)
Canada Ottawa (☎ 613-789 3434; www.chinaembassycanada.org; 515 St Patrick St, Ottawa, Ontario K1N 5H3);

Toronto consulate (☎ 416-964 7260); Vancouver consulate (☎ 604-736 3910); Calgary consulate (☎ 403-264 3322)
Denmark Copenhagen (☎ 039-625 806; Oregards Alle 25, 2900 Hellerup, Copenhagen)
France Paris (☎ 01 47 36 02 58; www.amb-chine.fr; 9 Ave V Cresson, 92130 Issy les Moulineaux, Paris)
Japan Tokyo (☎ 03-3403 3389, 3403 3065; 3-4-33 Moto-Azabu, Minato-ku, Tokyo) Consulates in Fukuoka, Osaka and Sapporo.
Malaysia Kuala Lumpur (☎ 03-242 8495; 229 Jalan Ampang, Kuala Lumpur) Consulate in Kuching.
Netherlands The Hague (☎ 070-355 1515; Adriaan Goekooplaan 7, The Hague)
New Zealand Wellington (☎ 04-472 1382; www.china embassy.org.nz; 2-6 Glenmore St, Wellington) Consulate in Auckland.
Singapore (☎ 65-734 3361; 70 Dalvey Rd)
Thailand Bangkok (☎ 02-245 7032/49; 57 Th Ratchadaphisek, Bangkok)
UK London (☎ 020 7636 8845, 24hr visa information ☎ 0891 880 808; www.chinese-embassy.org.uk; 31 Portland Place, London); Manchester consulate (☎ 0161-224 7480); Edinburgh consulate (☎ 0131-316 4789)
USA Washington (☎ 202-338 6688; www.china-embassy .org; Room 110, 2201 Wisconsin Ave NW Washington DC); Chicago consulate (☎ 312-803 0098); Houston consulate (☎ 713-524 4311); Los Angeles consulate (☎ 213-380 2508); New York consulate (☎ 212-330 7410); San Francisco consulate (☎ 415-563 9232)

Embassies & Consulates in China
EMBASSIES   Map pp102–3
There are two main embassy compounds in Běijīng – Jianguomenwai and Sanlitun. Embassies are open from 9am to 12pm and 1.30pm to 4pm Monday to Friday, but visa departments are often only open in the morning.

The following embassies are in the Jianguomenwai area:
India (☎ 010-6532 1908; fax 6532 4684; 1 Ritan Donglu)
Ireland (☎ 010-6532 2691; fax 6532 2168; 3 Ritan Donglu)
Japan (☎ 010-6532 2361; fax 6532 4625; 7 Ritan Lu)
Mongolia (☎ 010-6532 1203; fax 6532 5045; 2 Xiushui Beijie)
New Zealand (☎ 010-6532 2731; fax 6532 4317; 1 Ritan Dong Erjie)
North Korea (☎ 010-6532 1186; fax 6532 6056; Ritan Beilu)
Philippines (☎ 010-6532 1872; fax 6532 3761; 23 Xiushui Beijie)
Singapore (☎ 010-6532 3926; fax 6532 2215; 1 Xiushui Beijie)
Thailand (☎ 010-6532 1903; fax 6532 1748; 40 Guanghua Lu)

UK (☎ 010-6532 1961; fax 6532 1937; 11 Guanghua Lu)
USA (☎ 010-6532 3831; fax 6532 6057; 3 Xiushui Beijie)
Vietnam (☎ 010-6532 1155; fax 6532 5720; 32 Guanghua Lu)

The Sanlitun compound is home to the following embassies:
Australia (☎ 010-6532 2331; fax 6532 6957; 21 Dongzhimenwai Dajie)
Cambodia (☎ 010-6532 2790; fax 6532 3507; 9 Dongzhimenwai Dajie)
Canada (☎ 010-6532 3536; fax 6532 4072; 19 Dongzhimenwai Dajie)
France (☎ 010-6532 1331; fax 6532 4841; 3 Dongsan Jie)
Germany (☎ 010-6532 2161; fax 6532 5336; 17 Dongzhimenwai Dajie)
Italy (☎ 010-6532 2131; fax 6532 4676; 2 Sanlitun Dong Erjie)
Kazakhstan (☎ 010-6532 6182; fax 6532 6183; 9 Sanlitun Dong Liujie)
Laos (☎ 010-6532 1224; 11 Dongsi Jie)
Malaysia (☎ 010-6532 2531; fax 6532 5032; 13 Dongzhimenwai Dajie)
Myanmar (☎ 010-6532 1584; fax 6532 1344; 6 Dongzhimenwai Dajie)
Nepal (☎ 010-6532 1795; fax 6532 3251; 1 Sanlitun Xi Liujie)
Netherlands (☎ 010-6532 1131; fax 6532 4689; 4 Liangmahe Nanlu)
Pakistan (☎ 010-6532 2504/2558; 1 Dongzhimenwai Dajie)
Russia (☎ 010-6532 1381; fax 6532 4853; 4 Dongzhimen Beizhongjie) West of the Sanlitun Compound in a separate compound.
South Korea (☎ 010-6505 2608; fax 6505 3067; 3rd & 4th fl, China World Trade Center, 1 Jianguomenwai Dajie)
Sweden (☎ 010-6532 3331; fax 6532 2909; 3 Dongzhimenwai Dajie)

CONSULATES
Guǎngzhōu   Map pp550–1
Australia (☎ 020-8335 0909; fax 8335 0718; Room 1509, 15th fl, Main Tower, Guangdong International Hotel, 339 Huanshi Donglu)
Canada (☎ 020-8666 0569; fax 8667 2401; Room 801, Wing C, China Hotel, Liuhua Lu)
France (☎ 020-8330 3405; fax 8330 3437; Room 803, 8th fl, Main Tower, Guangdong International Hotel, 339 Huanshi Donglu)
Germany (☎ 020-8330 6533; fax 8331 7033; 19th fl, Main Tower, Guangdong International Hotel, 339 Huanshi Donglu)
Japan (☎ 020-8333 8999, ext 197; fax 8387 8835; 2nd fl, East Tower, Garden Hotel, 368 Huanshi Donglu)

Netherlands (☎ 020-8330 2067; fax 8330 3601; Room 905, 9th fl, Main Tower, Guangdong International Hotel, 339 Huanshi Donglu)
UK (☎ 020-8335 1354; fax 8332 7509; 2nd fl, Main Tower, Guangdong International Hotel, 339 Huanshi Donglu)
USA (☎ 020-8121 8000; fax 8121 8428; 1 Shamian Nanjie, Shāmiàn Dǎo)

Hohhot   Map p844
Mongolia (蒙古领事馆; Ménggǔ Língshìguǎn; ☎ 680 3540; 5 Dongying Nanjie; ☺ 8.30am-12.30pm Mon, Tue & Thu) It's possible to get a one-month visa for Mongolia here. Visas take a week to be issued (Y236) or there's an express 24-hour service for Y446; you'll need a letter of invitation from a travel agency to get one, though. US citizens do not need a visa to visit Mongolia.

Hong Kong
Australia (Map pp504-5; ☎ 0852-2827 8881; 23rd fl, Harbour Centre, 25 Harbour Rd, Wan Chai)
Canada (Map pp500-2; ☎ 0852-2810 4321; 11th-14th fl, Tower I, Exchange Sq, 8 Connaught Place, Central)
France (Map pp500-2; ☎ 0852-3196 6100; 26th fl, Tower II, Admiralty Centre, 18 Harcourt Rd, Exchange Sq, Admiralty)
Germany (Map pp500-2; ☎ 0852-2105 8744; 21st fl, United Centre, 95 Queensway, Admiralty)
Japan (Map pp500-2; ☎ 0852-2522 1184; 46th & 47th fl, Tower I, Exchange Sq, 8 Connaught Place, Central)
Netherlands (Map pp500-2; ☎ 0852-2522 5127; Room 5702, 57th fl, Cheung Kong Centre, 2 Queen's Rd, Central)
New Zealand (Map pp504-5; ☎ 0852-2877 4488, ☎ 2525 5044; Room 6508, 65th fl, Central Plaza, 18 Harbour Rd, Wan Chai)
South Africa (Map pp504-5; ☎ 0852-2577 3279; Room 2706-2710, 27th fl, Great Eagle Centre, 23 Harbour Rd, Wan Chai)
UK (Map pp500-2; ☎ 0852-2901 3000; 1 Supreme Court Rd, Admiralty)
USA (Map pp500-2; ☎ 0852-2523 9011; 26 Garden Rd, Central)

Kūnmíng   Map p646
Laos (☎ 0871-317 6624; Room N120, ground fl, Camellia Hotel, 154 Dongfeng Lu; ☺ 8.30am-noon & 1.30-4.30pm Mon-Fri)
Myanmar (☎ 0871-316 0003; www.mcg-kunming.com; 2nd fl, Camellia Hotel, 154 Dongfeng Lu; ☺ 9am-noon & 1-4.30pm Mon-Fri)
Thailand (☎ 0871-316 8916; fax 316 6891; ☺ 9-11.30am Mon-Fri) On the ground floor of the building next to the Kunming Hotel.
Vietnam (☎ 0871-352 2669; 2/F Kāihuá Guǎngchǎng; Kaihua Plaza, 157 Beijing Lu; ☺ 9am-noon & 2.30-5.30pm Mon-Fri)

Lhasa   Map p860
Nepal (☎ 0891-682 2881; fax 683 6890; ☺ 10am-12.30pm Mon-Fri for visa applications) On a side street between the Lhasa Hotel and Norbulingka. Visas are issued in 24 hours. The current fee for a 30-day visa is Y255. Bring a visa photo. It's also possible to obtain visas for the same cost at Kodari, the Nepalese border town, although you'd be wise to do this in an emergency only.

Qīngdǎo   Map pp204-5
South Korea (☎ 0532-288 8900/01; fax 288 8912; 3rd fl, Huiquan Dynasty Hotel, Nanhai Lu)

Shànghǎi
Australia (Map pp274-5; ☎ 021-5292 5500; www .aus-in-shanghai.com.cn; 22nd fl, CITIC Square, 1168 Nanjing Xilu)
Canada (Map pp274-5; ☎ 021-6279 8400; www .shanghai.gc.ca; Suite 604, West Tower, Shanghai Centre, 1376 Nanjing Xilu)
France (Map pp280-1; ☎ 021-6289 7414; www .consulfrance-shanghai.org; Room 1204, United Plaza, 1468 Nanjing Xilu)
Germany (Map pp274-5; ☎ 021-6217 2884; fax 6271 4650; 18th fl, Jing'an New Century Plaza, 188 Wujiang Lu)
Japan (Map pp270-1; ☎ 021-6278 0788; fax 6278 8988; 8 Wanshan Lu, Hóngqiáo)
New Zealand (Map pp280-1; ☎ 021-6471 1108; www .nzembassy.com; 15A, Qihua Tower, 1375 Huaihai Zhonglu)
Russia (Map pp274-5; ☎ 021-6324 2682; fax 6306 9982; 20 Huangpu Lu)
South Korea (Map pp270-1; ☎ 021-6219 6417; fax 6219 6918; 4th fl, International Trade Centre, 2200 Yan'an Xilu)
UK (Map pp274-5; ☎ 021-6279 7650; www.british consulate.sh.cn; 3rd fl, Room 301, Shanghai Centre, 1376 Nanjing Xilu)
USA (Map pp280-1; ☎ 021-6433 6880; www.us embassy-china.org.cn/shanghai; 1469 Huaihai Zhonglu) Entrance on Wulumuqi Lu. Another branch is in the West-gate Tower (Map pp274-5; ☎ 021-3217 4650, after-hours emergency number for US citizens ☎ 021-6433 3936; 8th fl, Westgate Tower, 1038 Nanjing Xilu).

Shěnyáng   Map p348
Japan (☎ 024-2322 7530; fax 2322 7490; 50 Shisi Wei Lu)
North Korea (☎ 8690 3451; fax 8690 3482; 37 Beiling Dajie) Visas are more likely to be obtained in Běijīng.
Russia (☎ 024-2322 3927; fax 2322 3907; 31 Nanshisan Wei Lu)
USA (☎ 024-2322 1198; fax 2323 1465; 52 Shisi Wei Lu; ☺ 1.30-4.30pm Mon-Wed & Fri)

Ürümqi   Map p781
Kazakhstan (Hāsàkèsītǎn Língshìguǎn; ☎ 383 2324; 31 Kunming Lu; ☺ 10am-1.30pm Mon-Thu) At the time

of writing you could get a three-week visitor visa here for US$30 to US$50 (price depends on nationality), plus a Y45 handling fee. A letter of invitation was not obligatory, but if one is required, CITS (p780) can help. The visa takes three days to be issued, but a week isn't unheard of. Show up early and don't expect calls to be taken. A taxi here will cost about Y30. If you take bus No 2 to Xiǎo Xī Gōu, turn right at the first intersection and then again five minutes later; this will put you on Kunming Lu. From there it's a five-minute walk. The Kazakhs are notorious for changing their visa requirements – check the Lonely Planet website for the latest.

FESTIVALS & EVENTS

February

Chinese New Year/Spring Festival (Chūn Jié) This starts on the first day of the first month in the lunar calendar. Many people take a week off work. Be warned: this is China's biggest holiday and all transport and hotels are booked solid. Although the demand for accommodation skyrockets, many hotels close down at this time and prices rise steeply. If you can't avoid being in China at this time, then book your room in advance and sit tight until the chaos is over. The Chinese New Year will fall on the following dates: 29 January 2006, 18 February 2007 and 7 February 2008.

Lantern Festival (Yuánxiāo Jié) It's not a public holiday, but it is very colourful. People make (or buy) paper lanterns and walk around the streets in the evening holding them. It falls on the 15th day of the first moon, and will be celebrated on the following dates: 13 February 2006, 5 March 2007 and 22 February 2008.

March/April

Guanyin's Birthday (Guānshìyīn Shēngrì) The birthday of Guanyin, the Goddess of Mercy, is a fine time to visit Buddhist temples, many of which have halls dedicated to the divinity. Guanyin's birthday is the 19th day of the second moon and will fall on the following dates: 18 March 2006, 6 April 2007, 26 March 2008.

April

Tomb Sweeping Day (Qīng Míng Jié) A day for worshipping ancestors; people visit and clean the graves of their departed relatives. They often place flowers on the tomb and burn ghost money for the departed. The festival falls on 5 April in most years, or 4 April in leap years.

Water-Splashing Festival (Pō Shuǐ Jié) Held in the Xīshuāngbǎnnà region in Yúnnán, this event is held mid-April (usually 13 to 15 April). The purpose is to wash away the dirt, sorrow and demons of the old year and bring the happiness of the new. The event is staged virtually daily for tourists.

April/May

Mazu's Birthday (Māzǔshēngrì) Mazu, Goddess of the Sea, is the friend of all fishing crews. She's called Mazu in Fújiàn province and Taiwan. She is also called Tianhou (pronounced 'Tin Hau' in Hong Kong) and Niangniang. Her birthday is widely celebrated at Taoist temples in coastal regions as far south as Vietnam. Mazu's birthday is on the 23rd day of the third moon; 20 April 2006, 9 May 2007, 28 April 2008.

June

Dragon Boat Festival (Duānwǔ Jié) This is the time to see dragon boat races and eat *zòngzi* (triangular glutinous rice dumplings wrapped in reed leaves). It's a fun holiday despite the fact that it commemorates the sad tale of Qu Yuan, a 3rd-century BC poet-statesman who hurled himself into the mythological Mi Lo river in Húnán to protest against the corrupt government. This holiday falls on the fifth day of the fifth lunar month; 11 June 2005, 31 May 2006, 19 June 2007, 8 June 2008.

August

Ghost Month (Guǐ Yuè) The devout believe that during this time the ghosts from hell walk the earth and it is a dangerous time to travel, go swimming, get married or move house. If someone dies during this month, the body will be preserved and the funeral and burial will be performed the following month. The Chinese government officially denounces Ghost Month as a lot of superstitious nonsense. Ghost Month is the seventh lunar month, or really just the first 15 days (usually from early August).

September

Birthday of Confucius (Kǒngzǐ Shēngrì) The great sage has his birthday on 28 September. This is an interesting time to visit Qūfù in Shāndōng, the birthplace of Confucius, although getting a hotel room may be tricky. A ceremony is held at the Confucius Temple starting around 4am, and other similar temples around China will observe the event.

September/October

Mid-Autumn Festival (Zhōngqiū Jié) This is also known as the Moon Festival, and is the time to gaze at the moon and eat tasty *yuè bǐng* (moon cakes); it's also a traditional holiday for lovers. The festival takes place on the 15th day of the eighth moon, and will be celebrated on the following dates: 18 September 2005, 6 October 2006 and 25 September 2007.

FOOD

Don't settle for that sweet Chinatown schlock any more, China is where it's at (see p80). Whether it's Xīnjiāng lamb kebabs, peppery Sìchuān hotpot, Hong Kong dim sum, Peking duck, Shànghǎi dumplings, Yúnnán across-the-bridge noodles, Lánzhōu *lāmiàn* (hand-pulled noodles), Tibetan *bobi* (chapatti-like unleavened bread), Dàlǐ banana pancakes, Macanese *galinha africana*

(African chicken), or international innovations from top restaurants in Hong Kong, Běijīng or Shànghǎi, food should be one of the main reasons you come to China in the first place. Although it depends where in China you travel, a meal for one at budget eateries should cost under Y30; mid-range dining options will cost between Y30 and Y80, and top end choices over Y80.

GAY & LESBIAN TRAVELLERS

In 2001 the Chinese Psychiatric Association no longer classified homosexuality as a mental disorder. Greater tolerance exists in the big cities than in the more conservative countryside. However, even in urban China it is not recommended that gays and lesbians be too open about their sexual orientation in public, even though you will see Chinese same-sex friends holding hands or putting their arms around each other. The situation is changing slowly as an increasing number of gay singers and actors in China are 'outed', but the police periodically crack down on gay meeting places.

On the other hand, there are many recognised gay discos, bars and pubs in the big cities that appear to function without official harassment, although they tend to keep a fairly low profile (see individual city entries for listings of these venues). Venues are listed for cities where gay and lesbian bars exist.

Check out www.utopia-asia.com/tips chin.htm for loads of tips on travelling in China and a complete listing of gay bars nationwide. Other links with useful information and pointers for gay travellers include www.mygayweb.com, www.gayguide.net, www.outandabout.com and www.gaytimes .co.uk. You can also contact the **International Gay and Lesbian Travel Association** (☎ +1-954-776 2626; fax 776 3303; www.iglta.com) in the USA.

Useful publications include the *Spartacus International Gay Guide* (Bruno Gmunder Verlag), a best-selling travel guide for gay travellers, currently in its 33rd edition.

HOLIDAYS

The People's Republic of China has nine national holidays, as follows (Hong Kong and Macau have different holidays):

New Year's Day 1 January
Chinese New Year (Spring Festival) usually February
International Women's Day 8 March
International Labour Day 1 May
Youth Day 4 May
International Children's Day 1 June
Birthday of the Chinese Communist Party 1 July
Anniversary of the Founding of the People's Liberation Army 1 August
National Day 1 October

The 1 May holiday is a week-long holiday, as is National Day on 1 October. Chinese New Year is also a week-long holiday for many. It's not a great idea to arrive in China or go travelling during these holidays as things tend to grind to a halt. Hotel prices all over China rapidly shoot up during the May and October holiday periods.

INSURANCE

A travel insurance policy to cover theft, loss, trip cancellation and medical problems is a good idea. Travel agents can sort this out for you although it is often cheaper to find good deals with an insurer on-line or from a broker. Some policies offer lower and higher medical expense options; the higher ones are chiefly for countries such as the USA, which have extremely high medical costs.

Some policies specifically exclude 'dangerous activities' such as scuba diving, skiing and even trekking. A locally acquired motorcycle licence is not valid under some policies. Check that the policy covers ambulances or an emergency flight home. You may prefer a policy which pays doctors or hospitals directly rather than you having to pay on the spot and claim later. If you have to claim, later make sure you keep all documentation. Some policies ask you to call back (reverse charges) to a centre in your home country where an immediate assessment of your problem is made.

Note that there is a choice of private medical care in large cities and booming towns such as Běijīng, Shànghǎi, Guǎngzhōu and Qīngdǎo, but in smaller towns and backwaters, facilities can be basic.

INTERNET ACCESS

Chinese may be the world's largest on-line language by 2007, but the authorities have closed scores of Internet cafés (*wǎngbā*) after a fire in a Beijing Internet café in 2002 killed 25 people. Internet cafés in some large cities such as Běijīng are not as plentiful as before, when authorities were startled to find online consoles appearing in hairdressers and even butchers. Before the fire, Internet operations were already under scrutiny by the government and in the summer of 2001, 2000 operations were closed and 6000 suspended. Cafés that are allowed to operate have to use filters to strain out irregular content. Rates at China's Internet cafés should be around Y2 to Y3 per hour for a standard, no-frills outlet, but comfier and smarter options naturally charge more (up to Y20 per hour). You may have to endure agonisingly slow connections in China's Internet cafés, especially on congested sites such as Hotmail.

Most travellers make constant use of Internet cafés and free web-based email such as Yahoo (www.yahoo.com) or Hotmail (www.hotmail.com). For information on websites with China content, see p16.

If you're travelling with a notebook or hand-held computer, be aware that your modem may not work once you leave your home country. The safest option is to buy a reputable 'global' modem before you leave home, or buy a local PC-card modem if you're spending an extended time in any one country. For more information on travelling with a portable computer, see www.teleadapt.com.

To access the Internet using a laptop from your hotel room (if it has no broadband Internet connection), free dial-up access can be made by hooking up through the phone line and using the local dial-up number (usually 163 or 169, but ask your hotel what the local number is). Use the same number as the account name and password, and you can get on-line.

LEGAL MATTERS

Anyone under the age of 18 is considered a minor, and the minimum age at which you can drive is also 18. The age of consent for marriage is 22 for men and 20 for women. There is no minimum age that restricts the consumption of alcohol or use of cigarettes. China's laws against the use of illegal drugs are harsh, and foreign nationals have been executed for drug offences (trafficking in more than 50g of heroin can result in the death penalty). The Chinese criminal justice system does not ensure a fair trial and defendants are not presumed innocent until proven guilty. Note that China conducts

more judicial executions than the rest of the world. If arrested, most foreign citizens have the right to contact their embassy.

MAPS

Top-quality maps of almost every Chinese city and many small towns are readily available in China. Many are detailed, illustrating bus routes (including names of bus stops) and the locations of hotels, shops and so on, and cost around Y2 to Y4. Unfortunately most maps are only in Chinese. They can be purchased from bookstalls or street vendors around train and bus stations, from branches of the Xinhua Bookshop or from hotel front desks. City and town road atlases can also be purchased from the same places, but again, they are largely in Chinese.

Tourist centres, hotel gift shops, Friendship Stores (Yǒuyì Shāngdiàn) and sometimes foreign-language bookshops in large cities stock English versions. Here you may also find Chinese- and English-language atlases of China. The Foreign Languages Bookstore (p97) in Běijīng has maps of other Chinese cities, but it's not comprehensive and is often out of stock.

Some of the most detailed maps of China available in the West are the aerial survey 'Operational Navigation Charts' (Series ONC). These are prepared and published by the Defence Mapping Agency Aerospace Center, St Louis Air Force Station, Missouri, USA. Cyclists and mountaineers have recommended these highly. In the UK you can obtain these maps from **Stanfords Map Centre** (☎ 020-7836 1321; www.stanfords.co.uk; 12-14 Long Acre, London), or from the **Map Shop** (☎ 0800 085 4080; www.themapshop.co.uk; 15 High St, Upton upon Severn, Worcestershire).

Australians can contact **Mapland** (☎ 03-9670 4383; www.mapland.com.au; 372 Little Bourke St, Melbourne) or the **Travel Bookshop** (☎ 02-9241 3554; 20 Bridge St, Sydney). In New Zealand, try **MapWorld** (☎ 0800 627967; www.mapworld.co.nz; 173 Gloucester St, Christchurch).

In France see **Ulysse** (☎ 01 43 25 17 35; 26 rue Saint Louis en l'Île) or **IGN** (☎ 01 43 98 80 00; 107 rue de la Boetie) in Paris.

In the United States, contact **Map Link** (☎ 1-800 962 1394; www.maplink.com; Unit 5, 30 S La Patera Lane, Santa Barbara, CA).

GeoCenter publishes an excellent map of China. Lonely Planet publishes *Beijing* and *Hong Kong* city maps. The *Hong Kong Guidebook* by Universal is a first-rate colour map of the city that is regularly updated. Nelles publishes good detailed regional maps of China, and Berndtson has an excellent detailed *Beijing* map.

MONEY

Consult the inside front cover for a table of exchange rates and refer to p14 for information on costs.

ATMs

ATMs (Automated Teller Machines) advertising international bank settlement systems such as GlobalAccess, Cirrus, Maestro Plus and others are common in Hong Kong and Macau. ATMs can be found in a limited, but growing, number of large banks (eg Bank of China, Agricultural Bank of China, and the Industrial and Commercial Bank of China) on the mainland where you can use Visa, MasterCard, Cirrus, Maestro, Plus and American Express (AmEx) to withdraw cash. The network largely applies to sizeable cities (such as Běijīng, Shànghǎi, Guǎngzhōu and Shēnzhèn), but occasionally appear in unlikely places (the summit of Huáng Shān). Useful ATMs include those at large airports such as at Beijing Capital Airport. Most other ATMs in China can only be used for withdrawing Renminbi in domestic accounts. Check the reverse of your ATM card to find which systems work with your card. The exchange rate on ATM withdrawals is similar to credit cards but there is a maximum daily withdrawal amount. If you plan on staying in China for a long period, it is advisable to open an account at a bank like the Bank of China with a nationwide network of ATMs.

For your nearest ATM, consult the ATM locator on www.international.visa.com/ps or www.mastercard.com/cardholderservices/atm; both have comprehensive listings. For those without an ATM card or credit card, a PIN-activated **Visa TravelMoney card** (US ☎ 1-877-394 2247) gives you access to pre-deposited cash through the ATM network. ATMs are listed in the Information sections (under Money) in destinations throughout this book.

Counterfeit Bills

Counterfeit notes are a problem in China. Very few Chinese will accept a Y50 or Y100 note without first checking to see if it's a fake. Old, tattered or torn notes are also sometimes hard to spend. You can exchange old notes for new ones at the Bank of China – counterfeits, however, will be confiscated.

Local Chinese have a variety of methods for checking notes, including checking the watermark, the drawn lines (more distinct in fake notes) and colour (more pronounced in counterfeit notes). The texture of a fake note also tends to be smoother than authentic notes. Examine large denomination notes if given to you as change by street vendors; they could well be dumping a forged banknote on you.

Credit Cards

Credit is not big in China: only one million or so of China's 1.3 billion strong population has a credit card. The Chinese don't like to be in debt, however short-term that debt may be. Foreign plastic is therefore of limited use through China, but cards that can be used include Visa, MasterCard, AmEx and JCB. Don't expect to be able to use them everywhere, and always carry enough cash. You should be able to use them at upmarket hotels and restaurants, supermarkets and department stores. Where they are accepted, credit cards often deliver a slightly better exchange rate than in banks. Money can also be withdrawn at certain ATMs (see left) on credit cards such as Visa, MasterCard and Amex in large cities. Credit cards can still not be used to buy train tickets, but Civil Aviation Administration of China (CAAC) offices readily accept international Visa cards for buying air tickets. Certain cards offer insurance and other benefits.

Credit card cash advances have become fairly routine at head branches of the Bank of China, even in places as remote as Lhasa. Bear in mind, however, that a 4% commission is generally deducted. The Bank of China does not charge commission on AmEx cash withdrawals.

Currency

The Chinese currency is the Renminbi (RMB), or 'People's Money'. Formally the basic unit of RMB is the *yuán*, which is divided into 10 *jiǎo*, which is again divided into 10 *fēn*. Colloquially, the *yuán* is referred to as *kuài* and *jiǎo* as *máo*. The *fēn* has so little value these days that it is rarely used.

The Bank of China issues RMB bills in denominations of one, two, five, 10, 20, 50 and 100 *yuán*. Coins come in denominations of one *yuán*, five *jiǎo*, one *jiǎo* and five *fēn*. Paper versions of the coins remain in circulation.

Hong Kong's currency is the Hong Kong dollar and Macau's is the *pataca*. Both currencies are worth about 7% more than Renminbi.

Exchanging Money

Renminbi is not convertible outside China, so you will have to wait till you reach China to exchange money. Foreign currency and travellers cheques can be changed at border crossings, international airports, branches of the Bank of China, tourist hotels, and some large department stores; hours of operation for foreign exchange counters are 8am to 7pm (later at hotels). Top end hotels will generally change money for hotel guests only. The official rate is given almost everywhere and the exchange charge is standardised, so there is little need to shop around for the best deal. See the exchange rate table on the inside front cover and consult a newspaper for the current rate of exchange.

Australian, Canadian, US, UK, Hong Kong and Japanese currencies and the euro can be changed in China. In some backwaters, it may be hard to change lesser-known currencies – US dollars are still the easiest to change.

Keep at least a few of your exchange receipts. You will need them if you want to exchange any remaining RMB you have at the end of your trip. Those travelling to Hong Kong can change RMB for Hong Kong dollars there.

BLACK MARKET

You can change money on the black market in major cities at lower rates than those offered by the banks. Ask a foreign resident or someone you trust for a recommendation on a 'reputable' moneychanger. Generally speaking, though, it's inadvisable to change money on the streets given the risk of short-changing, rip-offs and the abundance of counterfeit currency floating about.

Tipping

In China (including Hong Kong and Macau) almost no-one asks for tips. Tipping used to be refused in restaurants, but nowadays, many mid-range and top-end eateries include their own (often massive) service charge; cheap restaurants do not expect a tip. Taxi drivers throughout China do not ask for or expect tips.

Travellers Cheques

These are worth taking with you if you are principally travelling in large cities and tourist areas. Not only will they protect your money against theft or loss, but the exchange rate for travellers cheques is higher than for cash (around 2% higher). You can make a large saving, especially if you have paid no commission for your travellers cheques in the first place. They cannot be used everywhere however. You should have no problem cashing them at tourist hotels in China, but they are of little use in budget hotels and restaurants. As with credit cards, ensure that you always carry enough ready cash on you. If cashing at banks, aim for the larger banks such as the Bank of China or the CITIC Industrial Bank. Bear in mind that most hotels will only cash the cheques of guests. It's a good idea to change your money at the airport when you arrive as the rate there is roughly the same as everywhere else. Keep your exchange receipts so you can change your money back to its original currency when you leave. Cheques from most of the world's leading banks and issuing agencies are now acceptable in China – stick to the major companies such as Thomas Cook, AmEx and Visa. In big cities they are accepted in almost any currency, but in smaller destinations its best to stick to big currencies such as US dollars or UK pounds.

PASSPORTS

You must have a passport with you at all times; it is the most basic travel document (all hotels will insist on seeing it). The Chinese government requires that your passport be valid for at least six months after the expiry date of your visa. You'll need at least one entire blank page in your passport for the visa.

Have an ID card with your photo in case you lose your passport; even better, make photocopies of your passport – your embassy may need these before issuing a new one (a process that can take weeks). Also report the loss to the local PSB (Gōngānjú). Long-stay visitors should register their passport with their embassy. Be careful who you pass your passport to (eg dodgy bike-rental operators as a deposit), as you may never see it again.

POST
Sending Mail

The international postal service is efficient, and airmail letters and postcards will probably take around five to 10 days to reach their destinations. Domestic post is swift – perhaps one or two days from Guǎngzhōu to Běijīng. Intracity it may be delivered the same day it's sent.

Postage is no longer cheap. Postcards to overseas destinations cost Y4.20. Airmail letters up to 20g cost Y5.40 to Y6.40 to all countries except Hong Kong, Macau and Taiwan (Y2.50). Domestic letters cost Y0.80 and postcards Y0.30. Like elsewhere, China charges extra for registered mail, but offers cheaper postal rates for printed matter, small packets, parcels, bulk mailings and so on.

China Post operates an Express Mail Service (EMS) which is fast, reliable and ensures that the package is sent by registered post. Parcels sent to domestic destinations by EMS cost Y15 (up to 200g; Y5 for each additional 200g). International EMS charges vary according to country and sample minimum rates (parcels up to Y500g) include Australia (Y164), USA (Y181) and UK (Y224). Not all branches of China Post have EMS, so try larger branches.

Apart from local post offices, branch post offices can be found in major tourist hotels where you can send letters, packets and parcels, but you may only be able to post printed matter. Other parcels may require a customs form attached at the town's main post office and a contents check. Even at cheap hotels you can usually post letters from the front desk – reliability varies, but in general it's fine.

If you are sending items abroad, take them unpacked with you to the post office to be inspected and an appropriate box or envelope found for you. Most post offices offer materials (for which you'll be charged) for packaging, including padded envelopes, boxes and heavy brown paper. Don't take your own packaging as it will probably be refused.

If you have a receipt for the goods, put it in the box when you're mailing it, since it may be opened again by customs further down the line.

Customs inspections will retain anything suspected of being pirated and you will have to complete a customs declaration form. Post offices are very picky about how you pack things; don't finalise your packing until the item has got its last customs clearance.

Once the box is sealed, you go to another counter where you pay for the postage. Hang onto your receipt (the one for the postage of the item), as it could be useful for chasing misdirected goods, should this happen.

PRIVATE CARRIERS

There are a number of foreign private couriers in China that offer international express posting of documents and parcels. None of these private carriers are cheap, but they're fast and secure. In major cities these companies have a pick-up service as well as drop-off centres, so call their offices for the latest details.

The major players in this market are United Parcel Service, DHL, Federal Express and TNT Skypak.

Receiving Mail

There are fairly reliable *poste restante (cúnjú hòu)* services in just about every city and town, usually in the main post office. The collection system is not uniform, but the charge should be Y1 to Y2.30 for each item of *poste restante* mail you collect. Take your passport along for retrieving letters or parcels. Some larger tourist hotels will hold mail for their guests, but this is a less reliable option.

SHOPPING
Bargaining

Since foreigners are so often overcharged in China, bargaining is essential. You can bargain *(jiǎngjià)* in shops, markets and hotels, but not everywhere. In large shops and department stores where prices are clearly marked, there is usually no latitude for bargaining (although if you ask, the staff sometimes can give you a 10% discount). In small shops and street stalls, bargaining is expected, but there is one important rule to follow – be polite. Keep in mind that entrepreneurs are in business to make money – they aren't going to sell anything at a loss. Your goal should be to pay the Chinese price, as opposed to the foreigners' price – if you can do that, you've done well.

Where to Shop

The Friendship Stores you will encounter in China's larger cities are an anachronistic echo from an earlier epoch when imported luxury goods were hoarded under one roof for the privileged few. Some Friendship Stores can still be useful for English literature and magazines, and there are usually some members of staff who speak a little English. However, you are probably better off visiting markets or smaller shops.

Hotel gift shops should be avoided, except for newspapers, magazines or books. Don't ever buy paintings or antiques from such shops – visit local markets, otherwise you'll be hit with a vastly inflated price.

Five-star hotel arcades are often the place to go for top-brand-name shopping, but expect to pay a hefty whack. Also, some five-star hotels have attached residential apartment blocks (like the China World Trade Center in Běijīng) with their own multilevel shopping malls.

The explosion of shopping malls and department stores, feeding the consumer

revolution in China, has been a slap in the face to communist-era service standards. Market forces have jolted sleeping sales staff awake, but you may still meet a defiant clique of the old guard: slumped comatose on the counter or yacking to each other, oblivious to customers shrieking at them.

But the place to go to really roll up your sleeves and get to grips with local rock-bottom prices is the local markets. Blankets spread on the pavement and pushcarts in the alleys – this is where you find the lowest prices. In street markets, all sales are final; forget about warranties and, no, they don't take AmEx. Nevertheless, the markets are interesting, but be prepared to bargain hard.

While journeying the land, don't get too weighed down with souvenirs and trinkets – there's nothing worse than buying a replica Buddha statue in Dūnhuáng, only to spot exactly the same one in a Běijīng market the day before you fly home.

It's sensible to save your shopping for imported electronic consumer items for Hong Kong and Macau – import duties are still too high in the rest of China.

Some shopping tips: make sure you keep receipts and try and hang on to the bag of the shop where you bought each item in case you need to return the item. When returning something, try to return to the store where you bought it; be as firm as possible, as perseverance often pays off. If returning clothes, the sales tags should still be on them and there should be no signs that you have worn the item. Exchanging items is easier than getting a refund. Find out what the time limit is for returning goods bought at the store. Some stores, such as the clothing outlet Esprit, have a no-quibble refund policy; others won't refund or exchange goods.

Antiques

There are very few antiques of real worth left in China, apart from those which remain sealed in tombs, temples, in private hands or museums – basically beyond reach. Most of the antiques that you find in markets and shops around the land are replicas or ersatz. The quality of replication technology can be quite dazzling, but that monochrome Qing Guangxu imperial yellow bowl in your hands is far more likely to be a Jiang Zemin dynasty imitation. It's also worth bearing in mind that even auction

---

MORE THAN MEETS THE EYE...

Once upon a time in China you got what you paid for. If the sales clerk said it was top-quality jade, then it was top-quality jade. Times have changed, and cheap forgeries and imitations flood the market, from Tibetan jewellery to Qing coins, guidebooks, pirate DVDs to bogus Nike, Burberry, Gucci, train tickets and beyond. The reason why Chinese TV is stuck showing US and German films from the 1970s and '80s is probably because the pirate DVD market brings you the very latest, without the adverts in between.

Despite all the government's bluster and periodic CCTV footage of steamrollers grinding fake Rolexes and CDs, the pirating industry is in fine fettle. Fake goods just reappear in force after hitting the deck for a while. Wherever you voyage in China, you'll be cursing the number of forgeries, then snapping them up when you glance at the price tag. Just make sure your change doesn't include a counterfeit note. And if you are after genuine antiques, try to get an official certificate of verification – and make sure the ink is dry.

houses get caught out quite regularly, and experts assume that a considerable percentage of material that passes under the gavel is of dubious authenticity.

Street market are the best places to try your luck at antique shopping. Professional antique hunters will need to have a real nose for the business – you need to know the culture intimately. For your average traveller, take everything with a pile of salt.

Only antiques that have been cleared for sale to foreigners are permitted to be taken out of the country. When you buy an item over 100 years old it will come with an official red wax seal attached. However, bear in mind that this seal does not necessarily indicate that the item is an antique. You'll get a receipt of sale, and you have to show this to customs when you leave the country; otherwise customs will confiscate the antique.

Stamps & Coins

China issues quite an array of beautiful stamps that are generally sold at post offices in the hotels. Outside many of the post offices, you'll find amateur philatelists with books full of stamps for sale; it can be extraordinarily hard bargaining with these enthusiasts. Stamps issued during the Cultural Revolution make interesting souvenirs, but these rare items are no longer cheap. Check out www.cpi.com.cn/cpi-e, a website on Chinese philately. Old coins are often sold at major tourist sites, but many are forgeries.

Paintings & Scrolls

Watercolours, oils, woodblock prints, calligraphy – there is a lot of art for sale in China. Tourist centres like Guìlín, Sūzhōu, Běijīng and Shànghǎi are good places to look out for paintings. Convincing imitation oils of Níngbō-born artist Chen Yifei can be found everywhere, along with copies of other contemporary artists. Don't buy these from hotel shops, however, as you will be massively ripped off.

Much calligraphy is very so-so and some is downright bad; you will have to know your subject, and don't take anybody's word for the quality of the brushwork.

TELEPHONE

Both international and domestic calls can be easily made from your hotel room or from public telephones on the street. Local

---

ESSENTIAL NUMBERS

There are several telephone numbers that are the same for all major cities. However, only international assistance is likely to have English-speaking operators:

International assistance	☎ 115
Local directory assistance	☎ 114
Long-distance assistance	☎ 113/173
Police	☎ 110
Fire	☎ 119
Ambulance	☎ 120

---

calls from hotel-room phones are generally cheap (and sometimes free), although international phone calls are expensive and it is best to buy a phone card (p902) if calling abroad. Public telephones are plentiful, although finding one that works can be a hassle. The majority of public telephones take IC cards (see Phonecards) and only a few take coins. If making a domestic call, look out for public phones at newspaper stands (bàokāntíng) and hole-in-the-wall shops (xiǎomàibù); you make your call and then pay the owner (local calls are typically around four jiǎo). Domestic and international long-distance phone calls can also be made from main telecommunications offices.

Domestic long-distance rates in China vary according to distance, but are cheap. Card-less international calls are expensive (Y8.2 per minute or Y2.2 for calls to Hong Kong and Macau), but calls made between midnight and 7am are 40% cheaper; it's far cheaper to use an IP card.

If you are expecting a call to your hotel room, try to advise the caller beforehand of your room number as hotel operators and staff at reception (zǒngtái) frequently have trouble with foreign names. Otherwise, inform the receptionist that you are expecting a call and write down your name and room number.

The country code to use to access China is 86; the code for Hong Kong is 852 and Macau is 853. To call a number in Běijīng for example, dial the international access code (00 in the UK, 011 in the USA), dial the country code (86) and then the area code for Beijing (010), dropping the first zero, and then dial the local number. When calling China from Hong Kong or Macau, you also use the country code 86. For telephone calls within the same city, drop the international and area codes (qūhào). If calling internationally from China, drop the first zero of the area or city code after dialling the international access code, and then dial the number you wish to call.

Area codes for all cities, towns and destinations appear in the relevant chapters.

Mobile Phones

Mobile-phone shops (shǒujīdiàn) can sell you a SIM card which will cost around Y200; you then buy credits on the following denominations of cards: Y50, Y100, Y300 and Y500 (each valid for a limited period). The local per-minute, non-roaming city call charge for China Mobile is six jiǎo; intraprovincial calls are Y1.20 per minute, interprovincial calls Y1.40 per minute. It costs six jiǎo every minute to receive phone calls. Roaming charges cost an additional two jiǎo per minute, but the call receiving charge is the same. Overseas calls can be made for Y4.80 per minute plus the local charge per minute by dialling ☎ 17951, followed by 00, the country code then the number you want to call. Otherwise you will be charged the IDD call charge plus six jiǎo per minute.

Phonecards

A wide range of local and international phonecards exists in Běijīng.

Integrated Circuit (IC) cards (IC kǎ), available from kiosks, hole-in-the-wall shops, Internet cafés and from any China Telecom office, are prepaid cards that can be used in most public telephones, in telecom offices and in most hotels. IC cards come in denominations of Y20, Y50, Y100 and Y200, and appear in several varieties. Some cards can only be used in Běijīng (or locally, depending on where the card is purchased), while other cards can be used throughout China. If you want to call abroad, make sure the IC card can make international calls (dǎ guójì diànhuà), although international calls using IC cards are much more expensive than using Internet Phone (IP) cards. Purchasing the correct card can be confusing, as the instructions for use on the reverse of the card are usually only in Chinese.

If you wish to make international calls, it is much cheaper to use an IP card. International calls on IP cards (IP kǎ) are Y2.40 per minute to the USA or Canada, Y1.50 per minute to Hong Kong, Macau and Taiwan and Y3.20 to all other countries; domestic long-distance calls are Y0.30 per minute. You dial a local number, then punch in your account number, followed by a pin number and finally the number you wish to call. English-language service is usually available. IP cards come in denominations of Y50, Y100, Y200 and Y500 and substantial discounts are offered, so bargain (you should be able to buy a Y50 card for around Y30). Extra credits are also regularly included on IP cards. IP cards can be found at the same places as IC cards, and placards for vendors of both IC and IP cards are commonplace. Again, some IP cards can only be used locally, while others can be used nationwide, so it is important to buy the right card (and check the expiry date). If you want to use an IP card from a public telephone, you will need an IC card for the local call (you may find that the public telephone will not connect you, so you will have to use your hotel phone).

TICKETS

At some sights, such as temples and palaces, after you have bought an entrance ticket (ménpiào), you can be hit with further charges for drawcard halls or sights within the complex. A more expensive through ticket (tàopiào) can be bought at the entrance which will grant you access to all sights.

Tickets must be purchased for virtually every museum, temple, park or sight in China and you will find there is precious little you can do for free. Furthermore, ticket prices for many temples and historical monuments are increasing way ahead of inflation, which raises concerns about regulation. At the time of writing, entry to Huáng Shān was Y130 (in 2001 it was Y82), while entry to Wǔtái Shān was Y90, up from Y48 in 2001. At certain sights that carry heavy ticket prices, there is little attempt at either conservation or restoration, which makes you wonder where all the money goes.

TIME

The Chinese live by both the Gregorian and the lunar calendar. Time throughout China is set to Běijīng time, which is eight hours ahead of GMT/UTC. When it's noon in Běijīng it's also noon in far-off Lhasa,

Ürümqi and all other parts of the country. Since the sun doesn't cooperate with Běijīng's whims, people in China's far west follow a later work schedule so they don't have to commute two hours before dawn. There is no daylight saving time in China.

When it's noon in Běijīng the time in other cities around the world is:

Wellington	4pm
Sydney	2pm
Hong Kong	noon
Frankfurt	5am
Paris	5am
Rome	5am
London	4am
Montreal	11pm (previous day)
New York	11pm (previous day)
Los Angeles	8pm (previous day)

TOILETS

Travellers on the road relate Chinese toilet tales to each other like comparing old war wounds. Despite proud claims to have invented the first flushing toilet, China really does have some wicked loos. Large cities and towns have made a start on making their public toilets less of an assault course of foul smells and primitive appliances, but many are still pungent and sordid. Steer towards fast food outlets, hotels or department stores for cleaner alternatives. Toilet paper is rarely provided – always keep a stash with you. In some hotels, especially the old ones, the sewage system can't handle paper. In general, if you see a wastebasket next to the toilet, that's where you should throw the toilet paper, otherwise the loo could choke up and flood. Some public loos levy a small fee (around five máo) which you pay as you enter.

Rural toilets are ghastly snapshots of a scatological hell – just a hole in the ground or a ditch over which you squat and many cannot be flushed at all. Hyperventilate before tackling toilets on the older trains, or go in with a strong cigarette (eg Temple of Heaven brand).

Remember:

men	男
women	女

TOURIST INFORMATION

Outside Hong Kong (Hong Kong Tourism Board; www.discoverhongkong.com) and Macau (Macau Government Tourist Office; www.macautourism.gov.mo), tourist information facilities in China are largely rudimentary and of little use. Western travellers, used to relying on nationwide chains of helpful tourist information centres for free maps and useful info, will be disappointed. In the absence of a national tourism board, individual provinces, cities, towns and regions promote tourism independently. Large cities such as Běijīng and Shànghǎi have relatively better tourist information infrastructure, but even in Běijīng, the nation's capital, tourist information facilities are primitive. Elsewhere, you may have to fall back on the China International Travel Service (CITS; Zhōngguó Guójì Lǚxíngshè). Most towns and cities have a branch of CITS and addresses and contact details of offices are listed throughout this book. There is usually a member of staff who can speak English who may be able to answer questions and offer some travel advice, but the main purpose of CITS is to get you onto an expensive tour.

VISAS

A visa is required for the PRC, but at the time of writing visas were not required for most Western nationals to visit Hong Kong (p498) or Macau (p534).

For most travellers, the type of visa is an L, from the Chinese word for travel (lǚxíng). This letter is stamped right on the visa. The L visa can be either a multiple- or single-entry visa.

Visas are readily available from Chinese embassies and consulates in most Western and many other countries. A standard 30-day, single-entry visa from most Chinese embassies abroad can be issued in three to five working days. Express visas cost twice the usual fee. You normally pay up front for the visa, rather than on collection. You can get an application form in person at the embassy or consulate, or obtain one online from a consular website (try www.fmprc.gov .cn/eng/– click on About China, then Travel to China and then Visa Information). A visa mailed to you will take up to three weeks. Rather than going through an embassy or consulate, you can also make arrangements at certain travel agencies. Visa applications require at least one photo.

When asked on the application form, try to list standard tourist destinations such as Běijīng and Chéngdé; if you are toying with the idea of going to Tibet or western Xīnjiāng, just leave it off the form as it may raise eyebrows; the list you give is not binding in any way.

Three-day visas are available at the Macau–Zhūhǎi border (see p567 for details).

A 30-day visa is activated on the date you enter China, and must be used within three months of the date of issue. The 60-day and 90-day visas are activated on the date they are issued. While visas valid for more than 30 days were once difficult to obtain anywhere other than in Hong Kong, 90-day visas are now becoming easier to obtain abroad.

A Chinese visa covers virtually the whole of China, although some restricted areas still exist which will require an additional permit from the PSB. In addition to a visa, permits are also required for travel to Tibet (p858).

Be aware that political events can suddenly make visas more difficult to procure.

When you check into a hotel, there is a question on the registration form asking what type of visa you hold. The letter specifying what type of visa you have is usually stamped on the visa itself. There are seven categories of visas, as follows:

Type	Description	Chinese name
L	travel	lǚxíng
F	business or student	fǎngwèn (less than 6 months)
D	resident	dìngjū
G	transit	guòjìng
X	long-term student	liúxué
Z	working	rènzhí
C	flight attendant	chéngwù

Getting a China Visa in Hong Kong

Hong Kong is still the best place to pick up a visa for China. Any of the companies listed under Travel Agencies (p498) will be able to obtain one for you or you can apply directly to the **Visa Office of the People's Republic of China** (Map pp504-5; ☎ 3413 2300; 7th fl, Lower Block, China Resources Centre, 26 Harbour Rd, Wan Chai; ☯ 9am-noon & 2-5pm Mon-Fri). Visas processed here in one/two/three days cost HK$400/300/150. Double/six-month multiple/one-year multiple visas are HK$220/400/600 (plus HK$150/250 if you require express/urgent service). Be aware

that American passport holders must pay considerably more for their visas. You must supply two photos, which can be taken at photo booths in the MTR and at the visa office for HK$35.

Be aware that if you visit Hong Kong from China, you will need to be on a multiple-entry visa to re-enter China or else will have to get a new visa (p498).

Getting Other Types of Visas

LAOS

It is now possible to get a visa for Laos at the border (p694). Or visit the Laos consulate (p893) in Kūnmíng for a 15-day tourist visa. For Western European countries, Australia and New Zealand visas cost Y270 and for American, Japanese and German nationalities the cost is Y320. You must bring one passport photo with your application. Visas take three working days to process or you can pay a surcharge for next-day service.

MYANMAR

Travel to Myanmar is slowly getting easier. For a start, you no longer have to change US$200 prior to entering the country. The Myanmar consulate (p893) in Kūnmíng can issue 30-day tourist visas (Y185). Visas take three working days to process or you can pay a Y100 surcharge for same day processing and Y50 for next day processing. Overland travel into Myanmar is possible, although you must be part of a tour (p705).

THAILAND

Travellers from most countries won't need a Thai visa unless they're planning on staying in the country longer than 30 days. The Thai consulate (p893) in Kūnmíng can issue 60-day tourist visas for Y200. Visas take two days to process.

VIETNAM

Kūnmíng finally has a Vietnam consulate (p893) where you can pick up a 30-day tourist visa (Y400). Visas take three working days to process or you can pay an extra Y200 for the express service. You must bring along a passport photo with your application.

Residence Permit

The 'green card' is a residence permit, issued to English teachers, foreign expats and long-term students who live in China.

Green cards are issued for a period of six months to one year and must be renewed annually. Besides needing all the right paperwork, you must also pass a health exam (for which there is a charge). If you lose your card, you'll pay a hefty fee to have it replaced.

Visa Extensions

The Foreign Affairs Branch of the local PSB (Gōngānjú) – the police force – handles visa extensions.

First time extensions of 30 days are easy to obtain on single entry tourist visas, but further extensions are harder to get and may only give you a further week. Offices of the PSB outside of Běijīng may be more lenient and more willing to offer further extensions, but don't bank on it.

Extensions to single-entry visas vary in price, depending on your nationality. American travellers pay Y185, Canadians pay Y165, UK citizens pay Y160 and Australians pay Y100; prices can go up or down. Expect to wait up to five days for your visa extension to be processed.

The period of extension can differ from city to town. Travellers report generous extensions being decided on the spot in provincial towns and backwaters. If you have used up all your options, popping into Hong Kong to apply for a new tourist visa is a reliable option.

The penalty for overstaying your visa in China is up to Y500 per day. Some travellers have reported having trouble with officials who read the 'valid until' date on their visa incorrectly. For a one-month tourist (L) visa, the 'valid until' date is the date by which you must enter the country (within three months of the date the visa was issued),

not the date upon which your visa expires. Your visa expires the number of days that your visa is valid for after the date of entry into China. Sixty- and 90-day visas are activated on the day they are issued.

WOMEN TRAVELLERS

Principles of decorum and respect for women are deeply ingrained in Chinese culture. Despite the Confucianist sense of superiority accorded to men, Chinese women often call the shots and wield considerable clout (especially within marriage). Chinese males are not macho, and there is a strong sense of balance between the sexes. Nonetheless, in its institutions, China is a patriarchal and highly conservative country where virtually all positions of political and state authority are occupied by (old) men.

In general, foreign women are unlikely to suffer serious sexual harassment in China, but there have been reports of problems in Xīnjiāng. Wherever you are, it's worth noticing what local women are wearing and how they are behaving and making a bit of an effort to fit in, as you would in any other foreign country. Try to stick to hotels in the centre, rather than the fringes of town. Taking a whistle or alarm with you would offer a measure of defence in any unpleasant encounter. As with anywhere else, you will be taking a risk if you travel alone. If you have to travel alone, consider arming yourself with some self-defence techniques.

Tampons (wèishēng miántiáo) can be found almost everywhere, especially in supermarkets. It's best to take plentiful supplies of the pill (bìyùnyào) as the variant in China is locally made (rather than imported brands) and you may need a prescription. Condoms (male) are widely available.

Transport

GETTING THERE & AWAY

ENTERING THE COUNTRY

There are no particular difficulties for travellers entering China. The main requirement is a passport (valid for travel for six months after the expiry date of your visa; see p898), and a visa (see p903). As a general rule, visas cannot be obtained at the border. At the time of writing, visas were not required for most Western nationals to visit Hong Kong or Macau and some visa-free transits exist. For travel to Tibet, see p858. Chinese Immigration officers are scrupulous and, by definition, highly bureaucratic, but not difficult or overly officious. Travellers arriving in China will be given a health declaration form and an arrivals form to complete.

AIR

Airports & Airlines

Hong Kong, Běijīng and Shànghǎi are China's main international air gateways. Opened in 1998, **Hong Kong International Airport** (☎ 0852-2181 0000; www.hkairport.com) is the result of a HK$160 billion airport core programme and is located at Chek Lap Kok on Lantau Island in the west of the territory. Běijīng's **Capital Airport** (international arrivals & departures ☎ 010-6459 9567, domestic arrivals & departures ☎ 010-1689 6969) has benefited from considerable investment and a new terminal. Shànghǎi has two airports: **Hongqiao Airport** (☎ 021-6268 8899/8918) in the west of the city and **Pudong Airport** (☎ 021-6834 1000, flight information ☎ 021-3848 4500) in the east.

The best direct ticket deals are available from China's international carriers, such as China Eastern. Air China, China's national flag carrier, has a good safety record (managing a 46-year safe-flying record to 2001), and to date has only had one fatal crash. Air China should not be confused with China Airlines, the crash-prone Taiwan carrier.

Airlines flying to and from China:
Aeroflot Russian Airlines (www.aeroflot.org) Běijīng (☎ 010-6500 2412); Shànghǎi (☎ 021-6279 8033)
Air Canada (www.aircanada.ca) Běijīng (☎ 010-6468 2001); Shànghǎi (☎ 021-6375 8899)
Air China (www.airchina.com.cn) Běijīng (☎ 010-6601 7755); Shànghǎi (☎ 021-6269 2999)
Air France (www.airfrance.com) Běijīng (☎ 010-6588 1388); Shànghǎi (☎ 021-6360 6688)
Air Macau (www.airmacau.com.mo) Běijīng (☎ 010-6515 8988); Shànghǎi (☎ 021-6248 1110)
Air New Zealand (www.airnz.com) Hong Kong (☎ 852-2862 8988)
All Nippon Airways (ANA; www.ana.co.jp) Běijīng (☎ 010-6505 3311); Shànghǎi (☎ 021-6279 7000)
Asiana Airlines (www.us.flyasiana.com) Běijīng (☎ 010-6468 1118); Shànghǎi (☎ 021-6219 4000)
Austrian Airlines (www.aua.com) Běijīng (☎ 010-6462 2161); Shànghǎi (☎ 021-6340 3411)
British Airways (BA; www.british-airways.com) Běijīng (☎ 010-8511 5599)
China Eastern Airlines (www.ce-air.com) Shanghai domestic (☎ 021 6247 5953); Shanghai international (☎ 021 6247 2255)

THINGS CHANGE...

The information in this chapter is particularly vulnerable to change. Check directly with the airline or a travel agent to make sure you understand how a fare (and ticket you may buy) works and be aware of the security requirements for international travel. Shop carefully. The details given in this chapter should be regarded as pointers and are not a substitute for your own careful, up-to-date research.

China Northern Airlines (www.cna.com/cn) Běijīng (☎ 010 6601 7594), Shànghǎi (☎ 021 6350 6088);
China Southern Airlines (www.cs-air.com) Běijīng (☎ 010-6459 0539/6490, 6567 2203) Shànghǎi (☎ 021-6211 3604) Guǎngzhōu (☎ 020-8613 0873)
Dragonair (www.dragonair.com) Běijīng (☎ 010-6518 2533) Shànghǎi (☎ 021-6375 6375)
El Al Israel Airlines (www.elal.co.il) Běijīng (☎ 010-6597 4512)
Garuda Indonesia (www.garuda-indonesia.com) Běijīng (☎ 010-6505 2901)
Iran Air (www.iranair.com) Běijīng (☎ 010-6512 0047)
Japan Airlines (JAL; www.jal.com) toll-free in China (☎ 800 810 5553); Běijīng (☎ 010-6513 0888); Shànghǎi (☎ 021-6288 3000)
KLM (www.klm.nl) Běijīng (☎ 010-6505 3505); Shànghǎi (☎ 021-6884 6884)
Korean Air (www.koreanair.com; Běijīng ☎ 010-6505 0088; Shànghǎi ☎ 021-6275 2000)
Koryo Air Běijīng (☎ 010 6501 1557)
Laos Airlines (ground fl, Camellia Hotel, 154 Dongfeng Lu, Kūnmíng)
Lufthansa Airlines (www.lufthansa.com) Běijīng (☎ 010-6465 4488); Shànghǎi (☎ 021-5830 4400)
Malaysia Airlines (www.malaysia-airlines.com.my) Běijīng (☎ 010-6505 2681); Shànghǎi (☎ 021-6279 8579)
MIAT Mongolian Airlines (www.miat.com) Běijīng (☎ 010-6507 9297)
Northwest Airlines (www.nwa.com) Běijīng (☎ 010-6505 3505); Shànghǎi (☎ 021-6884 6884)
Pakistan International Airlines (PIA; www.piac.com.pk) Běijīng (☎ 010-6505 1681)
Qantas Airways (www.qantas.com.au) Běijīng (☎ 010-6467 4794); Shànghǎi (☎ 021-6279 8660)
Royal Nepal Airlines (www.royalnepal.com) Shànghǎi (☎ 021-3214 717)
Singapore Airlines (www.singaporeair.com) Běijīng (☎ 010-6505 2233); Shànghǎi (☎ 021-6289 1000)
Thai Airways International (www.thaiairways.com) Běijīng (☎ 010-6460 8899); Shànghǎi (☎ 021-5298 5090); Kūnmíng (☎ 0871-351 1515)

United Airlines (www.ual.com) Běijīng (☎ 010-6463 1111); Shànghǎi (☎ 021-3311 4567)
Uzbekistan Airways (www.uzbekistan-airways.com) Běijīng (☎ 010-6500 6442)
Virgin Atlantic (www.virgin-atlantic.com) Shànghǎi (☎ 021-5353 4600)

Tickets

The cheapest tickets to Hong Kong and China can often be found in discount agencies in Chinatowns around the world. Other budget and student travel agents offer cheap tickets, but the real offers are in agents that deal with the Chinese who regularly return home (travelling at festival times such as the Chinese New Year will be more expensive). A visit to your local Chinatown or a thumb through the *Yellow Pages* should unearth the lowest fares. Beyond Chinatown, firms such as **STA Travel** (www.statravel.com) with offices worldwide offer competitive prices to most destinations. The cheapest flights to China are with airlines requiring a stopover at the home airport such as with Air France to Běijīng via Paris or Malaysian Airlines to Běijīng via Kuala Lumpur. Air fares to China peak between June and September.

An increasing number of airlines fly to China, with Air China and China Eastern offering some of the cheapest fares. The cheapest available airline ticket is called an APEX (Advance Purchase Excursion) ticket, although this type of ticket includes expensive penalties for cancellation and changing dates of travel. Tickets listed below are tickets quoted by airline offices and you will be able to find cheaper rates through travel agencies.

For browsing and buying tickets on the Internet, try these online booking services:
www.bridgetheworld.co.uk Good for holiday bargains and speciality travel.
www.cheapflights.com No-frills website offering flights to numerous destinations.
www.expedia.com Offers discounted tickets.
www.lonelyplanet.com Use the Travel Services service to book multistop trips.
www.onetravel.com Offers some good deals.
www.travel.com.au A New Zealand version also exists (www.travel.co.nz).

To bid for last-minute tickets online, one site to try is **Skyauction** (www.skyauction.com). **Priceline** (www.priceline.com) aims to match the ticket price to your budget.

Discounted air courier tickets are a cheap possibility, but they carry restrictions. As a courier, you transport documents or freight internationally and see it through customs. You usually have to sacrifice your baggage and take carry-on luggage. Generally trips are on fixed, round-trip tickets and offer an inflexible period in the destination country. For more information, check out organisations such as the **Courier Association** (www .aircourier.org) or the **International Association of Air Travel Couriers** (IAATC; www.courier.org).

Australia

STA Travel (☎ 1300 733 035; www.statravel.com.au) has offices in all major cities and on many university campuses. **Flight Centre** (☎ 133 133; www.flightcentre.com.au) has offices throughout Australia.

From Australia, Hong Kong is a popular destination and is also the closest entry point into China. Although it's a shorter flight, fares from Australia to Hong Kong are generally not that much cheaper than fares to Běijīng or Shànghǎi. Low-season return fares to Shànghǎi or Běijīng from the east coast of Australia start at around A$1000, with fares to Hong Kong starting from A$910.

Cambodia

China Southern Airlines has two flights a week from Phnom Penh to Guǎngzhōu for US$350 one way or US$670 return.

Canada

Canadian discount air ticket sellers are also known as consolidators and their air fares tend to be about 10% higher than those sold in the USA. Check out travel agents in your local Chinatown for some real deals and browse agency ads in the *Globe & Mail,* the *Toronto Star,* the *Montreal Gazette* and the *Vancouver Sun.* **Travel CUTS** (☎ 800-667 2887; www.travelcuts.com) is Canada's national student travel agency and has offices in all major cities. For online bookings try www .expedia.ca and www.travelocity.ca.

From Canada, fares to Hong Kong are often higher than those to Běijīng. Air Canada has daily flights to Běijīng and Shànghǎi from Vancouver. Air Canada, Air China and China Eastern Airlines sometimes run supercheap fares. Return low-season fares between Vancouver and Běijīng start at around US$650.

Continental Europe

Generally there is not much variation in air fare prices from the main European cities. The major airlines and travel agents generally have a number of deals on offer, so shop around. **STA Travel** (www.statravel.com) and **Nouvelles Frontières** (www.nouvelles-frontieres.com) have branches throughout Europe.

Return fares to Běijīng from major Western European cities start at around €870 with Lufthansa, Air France and SAS. Flights to Hong Kong are slightly more expensive, return fares starting from around €1000.

FRANCE

France has a network of student travel agencies that can supply discount tickets to travellers of all ages. Recommended agencies include:

Anyway (☎ 0892 893 892; www.anyway.fr)
Lastminute (☎ 0892 705 000; www.fr.lastminute.com)
Nouvelles Frontières (☎ 0825 000 747; www.nouvelles-frontieres.fr)
OTU Voyages (www.otu.fr) This agency specialises in student and youth travellers.
Voyageurs du Monde (☎ 01 40 15 11 15; www.vdm.com)

GERMANY

Recommended agencies include:
Expedia (www.expedia.de)
Just Travel (☎ 089-747 3330; www.justtravel.de)
Lastminute (☎ 01805-284 366; www.lastminute.de)
STA Travel (☎ 01805-456 422; www.statravel.de) For travellers under the age of 26; branches in major cities.

ITALY

One recommended agent is **CTS Viaggi** (☎ 06 462 0431; www.cts.it), specialising in student and youth travel.

NETHERLANDS

One recommended agency is **Airfair** (☎ 020-620 5121; www.airfair.nl).

SPAIN

Recommended agencies include **Barcelo Viajes** (☎ 902 116 226; www.barceloviajes.com) and **Nouvelles Frontières** (☎ 902 170 979).

Hong Kong

Dragonair has eight flights a day from Běijīng to Hong Kong (single Y2800) and 12 daily flights from Hong Kong to Shànghǎi (Y1650 one way). It is cheaper to fly to

Guǎngzhōu or Shēnzhèn and then take the train or bus to Hong Kong.

Iran

Iran Air has twice weekly flights from Tehran to Běijīng (one way US$540, return US$800). China Southern also fly to Běijīng from Tehran.

Israel

El Al Israel Airlines has one flight a week between Běijīng and Tel Aviv (US$630).

Japan

There are daily flights operating between Tokyo and Běijīng, with one-way fares starting at around US$775. There are also regular flights between Osaka and Běijīng, with one-way fares at around US$600. Daily flights link Shànghǎi to Tokyo and Osaka, and there are also flights from Japan to other major cities in China, including Dàlián and Qīngdǎo.

Reliable travel agencies used to dealing with foreigners include:

No1 Travel (03-3200 8871; www.no1-travel.com)
STA Travel (www.statravel.co.jp) Tokyo (☎ 03-5485 8380); Osaka (☎ 06-262 7066)

Kazakhstan

Xīnjiāng Airlines is China's safest airline with a 48-year safe flight record. It has two flights per week between Ürümqi and Almaty. There is one flight per week between Běijīng and Almaty with Kazakhstan Airlines.

Laos

Laos Airlines has two flights a week from Wanxiang to Kūnmíng (one way Y740, return Y1265) and two weekly flights in the return direction (Wednesday and Sunday).

Macau

Air Macau has daily flights between Běijīng and Macau and several flights a day between Shànghǎi and Macau (one-way US$274, return US$520).

Malaysia

Malaysia Airlines operates five flights a week between Běijīng and Kuala Lumpur (US$839 return) and four flights a week between Shànghǎi and Kuala Lumpur (US$695 return).

Mongolia

MIAT Mongolian Airlines has five flights a week between Běijīng and Ulaanbaatar (one way US$210, return US$350) and two flights a week between Hohhot and Ulaanbaatar (Y1449 one way). Air China also flies between Běijīng and Ulaanbaatar. It can sometimes take a week to get a ticket and schedules are reduced in the winter months.

Myanmar (Burma)

Air China has two flights a week from Yangon to Běijīng, with a stopover in Kūnmíng (US$694 one way). There are two flights a week from Kūnmíng to Yangon (Y1630; Wednesday and Sunday) and three flights a week from Kūnmíng to Mandalay (Y1450; Monday, Wednesday and Friday). Air tickets and visas are available from the Myanmar consulate (p893) in Kūnmíng.

Nepal

Royal Nepal Airlines operates two flights per week between Kathmandu and Shànghǎi (US$200 one way, US$400 return) and three flights between Hong Kong (US$200/US$400 one way/return) and Kathmandu. There are also two or three flights a week from Lhasa to Kathmandu (Y2290). See the Tibet chapter for advice on travel to Tibet.

New Zealand

Both **Flight Centre** (☎ 0800 243 544; www.flight centre.co.nz) and **STA Travel** (☎ 0508 782 872; www .statravel.co.nz) have branches throughout the country.

International airlines such as Malaysia Airlines, Thai Airways International and Air New Zealand have return fares from Auckland to Hong Kong for around NZ$1500 during the low season. Return low-season fares to Běijīng start at around NZ$1600.

North Korea

There are four flights weekly between Běijīng and Pyongyang with Koryo Air and China Northern Airlines (one way US$160, return US$300).

Pakistan

Pakistan International Airlines operates two flights a week from Karachi to Běijīng (one way US$510, return US$950). Air China has a weekly flight to Karachi from Běijīng. There is one weekly flight between Ürümqi and Islamabad on Xinjiang Airlines (US$280 one way). A flight to Lahore from Ürümqi is a possible new route in future.

Russia

Aeroflot have daily direct flights connecting Běijīng and Moscow (Y8700) and five flights per week between Shànghǎi and Moscow (Y8700). Air China also have regular flights to Moscow from Běijīng and from Shànghǎi (via Běijīng). Moscow and Novosibirsk are also connected to Ürümqi by air.

Singapore

STA Travel (head office ☎ 737 7188; www.statravel.com.sg) has three offices in Singapore. Singapore, like Bangkok, has hundreds of travel agents offering competitive discount fares for Asian destinations and beyond. Chinatown Point Shopping Centre, on New Bridge Rd, has a good selection of travel agents.

Fares to Běijīng are about US$450 return, while fares to Hong Kong start at US$350; there are also daily flights to Shànghǎi.

South Korea

Discount travel agencies in Seoul include: Joy Travel Service (☎ 776 9871; fax 756 5342; 10th fl, 24-2 Mukyo-dong, Chung-gu, Seoul), directly behind City Hall; and discounters on the 5th floor of the YMCA building on Chongno 2-ga (next to Chonggak subway station).

Air China, Asiana Airlines and Korean Air have daily flights between Běijīng and Seoul (one way US$310, return US$593). Flights to Shànghǎi with China Eastern Airlines and Asiana Airlines are the same price. Seoul is also connected by air to Hong Kong, Shěnyáng and Qīngdǎo.

Thailand

Khao San Rd in Bangkok is the budget-travellers headquarters. Bangkok has a number of excellent travel agents but there are also some suspect ones; ask the advice of other travellers before handing over your cash. STA Travel (☎ 02-236 0262, www.statravel.co.th; Room 1406, 14th fl, Wall Street Tower, 33/70 Surawong Rd) is a good and reliable place to start.

One-way fares from Bangkok to Běijīng with Thai Airways or Air China are around US$320 one way or US$530 return. Other one-way fares from Bangkok include Hong Kong for around US$200, Chéngdū for US$255, Kūnmíng (Y1508) and Shànghǎi

(US$300). There are two flights a week between Kūnmíng and Chiang Mai (Y1344; Thursday and Sunday).

UK & Ireland

Discount air travel is big business in London. Advertisements for many travel agencies appear in the travel pages of the weekend broadsheet newspapers, in *Time Out*, the *Evening Standard* and in the free magazine *TNT*.

Travel agents in London's Chinatown that deal with flights to China include Jade Travel (☎ 0207-734 7726; www.jadetravel.co.uk; 5 Newport Place, London), Sagitta Travel Agency (☎ 0870-077 8888; fax 0870 075 2888; 9 Little Newport St, London) and Reliance Tours Ltd (☎ 0207-437 0503; 12-13 Little Newport St, London).

For further agents, look at www.china town-online.co.uk, which also includes a list of travel agents outside London that specialise in tickets to China.

From the UK, the cheapest low-season return fares to Běijīng start at around UK£350 with British Airways; flights to Hong Kong are a little bit pricier.

Recommended travel agencies include the following:

Bridge the World (☎ 0870-814 4400; www.b-t-w.co.uk)
Flightbookers (☎ 0870-814 4001; www.ebookers.com)
Flight Centre (☎ 0870-499 0040; www.flightcentre.co.uk)
North-South Travel (☎ 01245-608 291; www.northsouthtravel.co.uk) North-South Travel donate part of their profit to projects in the developing world.
Quest Travel (☎ 0870-442 3542; www.questtravel.co.uk)
STA Travel (☎ 0870-160 0599; www.statravel.co.uk) For travellers under the age of 26.
Trailfinders (☎ 0207-938 3939; www.trailfinders.co.uk)
Travel Bag (☎ 0870-814 4441; www.travelbag.co.uk)

USA

Discount travel agents in the USA are known as consolidators (although you won't notice a sign on the door saying Consolidator). San Francisco is the ticket-consolidator capital of America, although some good deals can also be found in Los Angeles, New York and other big cities. Consolidators can be found through the *Yellow Pages* or the travel sections of major daily newspapers.

From the US west coast, low-season return fares to Hong Kong or Běijīng start at around US$600. Fares increase dramatically during summer and the Chinese New Year. From New York to Běijīng or Hong Kong, low-season return fares start at around US$700.

STA Travel (☎ 800-781-4040; www.sta-travel.com), for travellers under the age of 26, has offices in most major US cities.

The following agencies and websites are recommended for online bookings:

- www.cheaptickets.com
- www.expedia.com
- www.flychina.com
- www.itn.net
- www.lowestfare.com
- www.orbitz.com
- www.sta.com
- www.travelocity.com

Uzbekistan

From Běijīng there are thrice-weekly flights to Tashkent with Uzbekistan Airways (one way US$450, return US$600) and there are also flights between Ürümqi and Tashkent.

Vietnam

China Southern Airlines and Vietnam Airlines fly between Ho Chi Minh City and Běijīng (one way US$180, return US$350). China Southern Airlines flights are via Guǎngzhōu. From Běijīng to Hanoi there are two flights per week with either China Southern Airlines or Vietnam Airlines (one way US$180, return US$350).

LAND

If you're starting from Europe or Asia, it's possible to travel all the way to China by land. Numerous interesting routes include the Trans-Mongolian and Trans-Manchurian Railway trek from Europe or the border crossings of China-Vietnam, Tibet-Nepal, Xīnjiāng-Pakistan, Xīnjiāng-Kyrgyzstan and Xīnjiāng-Kazakhstan.

Border Crossings

China shares borders with Afghanistan, Bhutan, India, Kazakhstan, Kyrgyzstan, Laos, Mongolia, Myanmar, Nepal, North Korea, Pakistan, Russia, Tajikistan and Vietnam. China also has official border crossings between its special administrative regions, Hong Kong and Macau. The borders with Afghanistan, Bhutan and India are closed. If planning an extensive trip to China overland, make sure you enter China within the given time after your visa is issued (see p904).

HONG KONG

Hong Kong is an excellent place to enter China and there is a variety of options for crossing over the border by land. See p525 for details on how to enter China from Hong Kong overland.

KAZAKHSTAN

A year-round road crosses from Ürümqi in China to Almaty via the border post at Korgas (see p783 for details); crossing the border shouldn't really be a problem as long as you have a valid Kazakhstan (obtainable in Běijīng) or China visa.

Two trains a week also run between Ürümqi and Almaty (see p783 for details).

There are two other China–Kazakhstan crossings further north, at Tǎchéng (p802; Bakhty in Kazakhstan) and Jímǔnǎi (p801; Maykapchigay on the Kazak side), although neither is particularly reliable.

KYRGYZSTAN

There is a weekly bus from Kashgar via Irkeshtam to Osh (see p794 for details). Ensure you have a valid Kyrgyzstan visa (available from Běijīng or Hong Kong). From June to September it's theoretically possible to cross the dramatic 3752m Torugart Pass (p794) on a rough road from Kashgar to Bishkek.

LAOS

From the Měnglà district in China's southern Yúnnán province it is legal to enter Laos via Boten in Luang Nam Tha province if you possess a valid Lao visa. From Boten there are morning and afternoon buses onward to the provincial capitals of Luang Nam Tha and Udomxai, three and four hours away respectively. See p694 for more information.

The majority of travellers from Kūnmíng go via Jǐnghóng to Měnglà and then on to the border at Mohan (which shuts a 5.30pm). As the bus journey from Jǐnghóng will take the better part of the day, you will probably have to stay overnight at Měnglà.

Lao visas can be obtained in Běijīng (p892); alternatively, the Lao consulate in Kūnmíng (p893) issues 15-day tourist visas (valid for two months from date of issue; visa extensions in Laos possible). You can also obtain a Laos visa at the border for US$30 (note that you cannot buy a China visa here). See p904 for more information on visas.

MACAU

See p544 for details on entering China by bus from Macau to Zhūhǎi.

MONGOLIA

As well as Trans-Mongolian Railway trains that run from Běijīng to Ulaanbaatar via Dàtóng (see p914), the K23 departs Beijing Train Station at 7.40am every Tuesday, reaching Ulaanbaatar at 1.15pm the next day. In the other direction, the K24 departs Ulaanbaatar every Thursday at 7.50am, reaching Běijīng the following day at 2.31pm. Two trains a week also run between Hohhot and Ulaanbaatar.

MYANMAR (BURMA)

Originally built to supply the forces of Chiang Kaishek in his struggle against the Japanese, the famous Burma Road runs from Kūnmíng, in China's Yúnnán province, to the city of Lashio. Nowadays the road is open to travellers carrying permits for the region north of Lashio, although you can legally cross the border in only one direction – from the Chinese side (Ruìlì) into Myanmar via Mu-se in the northern Shan State. Land crossings from China are only possible if you join an organised tour group from a Chinese travel agency (eg Ko Wai Lin Travel in Kūnmíng or Way Thar Li Tour & Travel Company Ltd in Ruìlì), who can arrange visas and permits. See the p705 for more details on journeying to Myanmar.

A second route, a little further northwest, from Lwaigyai to Bhamo, is also open in the same direction. You cannot legally leave Myanmar by either route.

NEPAL

The 920km road connecting Lhasa with Kathmandu is known as the Friendship Hwy. It's a spectacular trip across the Tibetan plateau, the highest point being Gyatso-la Pass (5220m). By far the most popular option for the trip is renting a 4WD through a hotel or travel agency and then organising a private itinerary with the driver (see p866).

Visas for Nepal can be obtained in Lhasa (p893), or even at the Nepalese border (see p873). When travelling from Nepal to Lhasa, foreigners must arrange transport through tour agencies in Kathmandu. If you already have a Chinese visa, you could try turning up at the border and organising a permit in Zhāngmù (p872) but transport out will be a problem and rules and regulations regularly change – it's far better to join an economy tour to Lhasa in Kathmandu. See p873 for further information, including transport from Kodari to Kathmandu.

NORTH KOREA

Visas are difficult to arrange to North Korea and at the time of writing it was impossible for US and South Korean citizens. Those interested in travelling to North Korea from Běijīng should get in touch with Nicholas Bonner at Koryo Tours (www.koryogroup .com), who can get you there (and back).

There are twice-weekly flights and four international express trains (K27 & K28) between Běijīng and Pyongyang.

PAKISTAN

The exciting trip on the Karakoram Hwy, over the 4800m Khunjerab Pass and what is said to be the world's highest public international highway, is an excellent way to get to or from Chinese Central Asia. There are daily buses from Kashgar for the two-day trip to Sost when the pass is open – normally May to early November. See p794 for more information.

RUSSIA

A twice-weekly train (N23 & N24, Monday and Friday) connects Haerbin East train station with Vladivostok. Also see Trans-Siberian Railway (opposite) for information on trains to Moscow from Běijīng. The Russian border 9km from Mǎnzhōulǐ is quite busy and reliable. Officially, the only public transport that crosses the border is the Trans-Manchurian, but there are also ample opportunities for picking up a lift in Mǎnzhōulǐ or at the border.

TAJIKISTAN

The Kulma Pass (4362m), linking Kashgar with Murghob (via Tashkurgan), opened in 2004, with three monthly buses making the trip. It's unsure when the pass will be officially opened for foreigners. Go to www .traveltajikistan.com/roadrail/road.html for the latest updates.

VIETNAM

Travellers can enter Vietnam overland from China and exit Vietnam to China on a standard visa. You cannot obtain visas at the border, but Vietnam visas can be acquired in Běijīng (p892) or Kūnmíng (p893). Chinese visas can be obtained in Hanoi. The Vietnam–China border crossing is open from 7am to 4pm, Vietnam time, or 8am to 5pm, China time. Set your watch when you cross the border – the time in China is one hour later than in Vietnam. There are currently two border checkpoints (following) where foreigners are permitted to cross between Vietnam and China.

Friendship Pass

The busiest border crossing is at the Vietnamese town of Dong Dang, an obscure town (nearest city is Lang Son 18km to the south) 164km northeast of Hanoi. The closest Chinese town to the border is Píngxiáng (p601) in Guǎngxī province, but it's about 10km north of the actual border gate. The only place in Guǎngxī where foreigners can cross is the Friendship Pass, known as Huu Nghi Quan in Vietnamese or Yǒuyì Guān in Chinese. Buses and minibuses on the Hanoi–Lang Son route are frequent.

There is a customs checkpoint between Lang Son and Dong Dang; expect long delays. There is a walk of 600m between the Vietnamese and Chinese border posts.

On the Chinese side, it's a 20-minute drive from the border to Píngxiáng by bus (Y5) or a shared taxi (US$3). Píngxiáng is connected by train to Nánníng, capital of China's Guǎngxī province, 220km away. Train No 5518 to Nánníng departs Píngxiáng at 3.20pm, arriving in Nánníng at 7.39pm. In the other direction, train No 5517 departs Nánníng at 7.58am, arriving in Píngxiáng at 12.07pm. There are more frequent buses (once every 30 minutes), which take four hours to make the journey and cost US$4.

A word of caution – because train tickets to China are expensive in Hanoi, some travellers buy a ticket to Dong Dang, walk across the border and then buy a train ticket on the Chinese side. This isn't the best way because it's several kilometres from Dong Dang to Friendship Pass, and you'll have to hire someone to take you by motorbike. If you're going by train, it's best to buy a ticket from Hanoi to Píngxiáng, and then in Píngxiáng buy a ticket to Nánníng or beyond.

There is also a twice-weekly international train that runs between Beijing West

train station and Hanoi, which stops at the Friendship Pass. You can board or exit the train at a number of stations in China. The entire Běijīng–Hanoi run is 2951km and takes approximately 55 hours, which includes a three-hour delay (if you're lucky) at the border checkpoint.

Schedules are subject to change, but at present train T5 departs Beijing West train station at 4.16pm on Monday and Friday, arriving in Hanoi at 6.50am Wednesday and Sunday, respectively. Going in the other direction, train T6 departs Hanoi at 6.50pm on Tuesday and Friday, reaching Beijing West train station at 1.38pm on Thursday and Sunday, respectively.

In China, the train stops at Shíjiāzhuāng, Zhèngzhōu, Hànkǒu (in Wǔhàn), Wǔchāng (Wǔhàn), Chángshā, Héngyáng, Yǒngzhōu, Guìlín North, Guìlín, Liǔzhōu, Nánníng and Píngxiáng.

Lao Cai–Hékǒu

A 762km metre-gauge railway, inaugurated in 1910, links Hanoi with Kūnmíng, although at the time of writing the twice-weekly international train service had been suspended due to floods and landslide damage. The border town on the Vietnamese side is Lao Cai, 294km from Hanoi. On the Chinese side, the border town is Hékǒu, 468km from Kūnmíng.

When operational, domestic trains run daily on both sides of the border. On the Chinese side, Kūnmíng–Hékǒu takes about 16 hours.

Mong Cai–Dōngxīng

Vietnam's third, but little known, border crossing is at Mong Cai in the northeast corner of the country, just opposite the Chinese city of Dōngxīng. Only Vietnamese and Chinese citizens may cross here.

Train

TRANS-SIBERIAN RAILWAY

The Trans-Siberian Railway and connecting routes comprise one of the most famous, romantic and potentially enjoyable of the world's great train journeys. Rolling out of Europe and into Asia, through eight time zones and over 9289km of taiga, steppe and desert, the Trans-Siberian makes all other train rides seem like once around the block with Thomas the Tank Engine.

There is some confusion here as there are, in fact, three railways. The 'true' Trans-Siberian line runs from Moscow to Vladivostok. But the routes traditionally referred to as the Trans-Siberian Railway are the two branches that veer off the main line in eastern Siberia to make a beeline for Běijīng.

Most readers of this book will not be interested in the first option since it excludes China – your decision is basically between the Trans-Manchurian or the Trans-Mongolian; however, it makes little difference. The Trans-Mongolian (Běijīng–Moscow, 7865km) is faster, but requires you to purchase an additional visa and endure another border crossing, although you do at least get to see the Mongolian countryside roll past your window. The Trans-Manchurian is longer (Běijīng–Moscow, 9025km).

Trans-Mongolian Railway

Train K3 leaves Běijīng on its five-day journey every Wednesday at 7.40am (arriving in Moscow on the following Monday at 2.19pm), passes through Dàtóng and travels north to the Mongolian border at Erenhot, 842km from Běijīng. The train continues to Ulaanbaatar before reaching the last stop in Mongolia, Sukhe Bator. From Moscow, train K4 leaves at 10.03pm every Tuesday, arriving in Běijīng on the following Monday at 2.31pm. Note that departure and arrival times may fluctuate slightly.

Trans-Manchurian Railway

Departing Běijīng Saturday at 10.56pm (arriving in Moscow the following Friday at 5.55pm), train K19 travels through Tiānjīn, Shānhǎiguān, Shěnyáng, Chángchūn and Hāěrbīn before arriving at the border post Mǎnzhōulǐ, 2347km from Běijīng. Zabaykal'sk is the Russian border post and the train continues from here to Tarskaya, where it connects with the Trans-Siberian line. Train K20 leaves Moscow every Friday at 11.58pm, arriving in Běijīng on the following Friday at 5.20am. Note that departure and arrival times may fluctuate slightly.

Visas

Travellers will need Russian and Mongolian visas if they take the Trans-Mongolian, as well as a Chinese visa. These can often be arranged along with your ticket by travel agents

such as China International Travel Service (CITS, Zhōngguó Guójì Lǚxíngshè). Mongolian visas come as two-day transit visas (three-day process US$30, express process US$60) or 90-day tourist visas (three-day process US$40, express process US$60). A transit visa is easy enough to get (just present a through-ticket and a visa for your onward destination). The situation regarding visas changes regularly, so check with a Mongolian embassy (p892) or consulate. All Mongolian embassies shut down for the week of National Day (Naadam), which officially falls around 11 to 13 July.

Russian transit visas (one-week process US$50, three-day process US$80, one-day process US$120; see p892) are valid for 10 days if you take the train, and will only give you three or four days in Moscow at the end of your journey. You will need one photo, your passport and the exact amount in US dollars. For a transit visa, you will also need a valid entry visa for a third country plus a through ticket from Russia to the third country.

Tickets

Intourist Travel (www.intourist.com) has branches in the UK, USA, Canada, Finland and Poland and offers a range of Trans-Manchurian and Trans-Mongolian tours and packages including flights to and from Moscow, 2nd-class travel, and accommodation in Moscow, Běijīng and Irkutsk.

White Nights (☎ /fax 916-979 9381; www.wnights .com; 610 Sierra Dr, Sacramento, CA) offers a range of trips including Trans-Manchurian tickets for US$311 (2nd class) or US$442 (1st class) and Trans-Mongolian tickets for US$330 (2nd class) or US$540 (1st class). The company also offers visa support and has contact addresses in Russia, Germany, Switzerland and the Netherlands.

Intours Canada (☎ 416-766 4720; fax 416-766 8507; www.tourussia.com; Suite 308, 2150 Bloor St West, Toronto, ON) offer tours and packages on the Trans-Siberian and Trans-Mongolian. A typical 13-day Moscow–Beijing Trans-Mongolian tour costs C$1099 (second/first class), including hotel accommodation.

The Russia Experience (☎ 020-8566 8846; www .trans-siberian.co.uk; Research House, Fraser Rd, Perivale, Middlesex) in the UK has a great choice of tickets and are in the know (they are also the people to get in touch with for trips to Mongolia and Russia). Full details and prices are in their downloadable website brochure.

Gateway Travel (☎ 02-9745 3333; www.russian -gateway.com.au; 48 The Boulevarde, Strathfield, NSW) in Australia can arrange tickets and tours.

Travel Service Asia (☎ 07351-373 210; www.tsa -reisen.de in German; Schmelzweg 10, Biberach/Riß) in Germany offers package tours and tickets on Trans-Mongolian and Trans-Manchurian routes.

Moonsky Star Ltd (Map pp506-7; ☎ 2723 1376; www .monkeyshrine.com; Flat 6, 4th fl, E block, Chungking Mansions, Nathan Rd) in Hong Kong arranges trips on the Trans-Siberian and have an informative website with a downloadable brochure. They have an info centre in Běijīng called **Monkey Business** (Map pp102-3; ☎ 6591 6519; www .monkeyshrine.com; Hidden Tree bar, 12 Dongdaqiao Xiejie, Chaoyang).

SEA
Hong Kong
Some ships still ply the waters between Hong Kong and the mainland, but numbers and destinations have been cut back and largely travel to destinations in Guǎngdōng. See p524 for details.

Japan
There are weekly ferries between Osaka and Shànghǎi (44 hours) and twice-monthly services between Kōbe and Shànghǎi (44 hours). Ticket prices to both destinations range from Y1300 to Y6500. See p301 for details.

From Tiānjīn, there is a weekly ferry to Kōbe in Japan (p162; Y1875, 48 hours). Check in two hours before departure for international sailings.

There are also boats from Qīngdǎo to Shimonoseki (Y1160) every two weeks.

Korea
Travelling from Korea, international ferries connect the South Korean port of Incheon with Wēihǎi, Qīngdǎo, Tiānjīn (Tánggǔ) and Dàlián.

The **Weidong Ferry Company** (☎ 822-3271 6713; www.weidong.com; 1005 Sungji Bldg, 10th fl, 585 Dohwa-dong, Mapo-gu, Seoul) runs boats on the routes to Wēihǎi (Y750; three per week in each direction) and Qīngdǎo (Y1180; two per week in each direction) in Shāndōng province. They can also be contacted at the **International Passenger Terminal** Incheon (☎ 8232-777 0490; 71-2 Hang-dong); Wēihǎi (☎ 0631-522 6173; 48 Haibin Beilu); Qīngdǎo (☎ 0532-280 3574; 4 Xinjiang Lu). Check their website for the latest timetables and prices.

In Seoul, tickets for any boats to China can be bought from the **International Union Travel Agency** (☎ 822-777 6722; Room 707, 7th fl, Daehan Ilbo Bldg, 340 Taepyonglo 2-ga, Chung-gu). Prices range from US$88 to US$300, and depending on the destination, boats leave anywhere from once a week to three times a week.

For the Tiānjīn ferry you can also get tickets in Seoul from **Taeya Travel** (☎ 822-514 6226), in Kangnam-gu by the Shinsa subway station. In China, tickets can be bought cheaply at the pier, or from CITS – for a very steep premium. The cheapest price is Y888 for a dorm bed.

To reach the International Ferry Terminal from Seoul, take the Seoul–Incheon commuter train (subway line 1 from the city centre) and get off at the Dongincheon station. The train journey takes 50 minutes. From Dongincheon station it's either a 45-minute walk or five-minute taxi ride to the ferry terminal.

INCHEON TO WĒIHǍI
There are three boat services a week between Incheon and Wēihǎi (2nd class Y750, 1st class Y1370, departs Tuesday, Thursday and Sunday at 7pm from Wēihǎi, 15 hours). See p217 for more details, and www.wei dong.com for an updated schedule.

TRANSPORT

INCHEON TO QĪNGDĂO

There are three boats a week between Qīngdăo and Incheon (from Y800, 15 hours). Phone the **passenger ferry terminal** (☎ 0532 282 5001; 6 Xinjiang Lu) to confirm days or consult www.weidong.com.

INCHEON TO TIĀNJĪN

There are two boats a week between Tiānjīn and Incheon (from Y1000, 24 hours). As with boats from Japan, the boat does not dock at Tiānjīn proper, but rather at the nearby port of Tánggū, where there are buses to speed you to either Tiānjīn or Běijīng. Boats to Tiānjīn are run by the Jinchon Ferry Company. They can be contacted in Seoul (☎ 822-517 8671); Incheon (☎ 8232-777 8260); and Tiānjīn (☎ 022-2331 1657). See p162 for more details.

INCHEON TO DÀLIÁN

A boat leaves for Incheon in South Korea on Monday, Wednesday and Friday at 3.30pm (Y850 to Y1469, 18 hours) from Dàlián; tickets can be bought at the ferry terminal. Boats leave Incheon for Dàlián on Tuesday, Thursday and Saturday at 4.30pm. Contact Da-In Ferry in Seoul (☎ 822-3218 6551), Incheon (☎ 8232-891 7100) or Dàlián (☎ 0411-8270 5082).

GETTING AROUND

AIR

While trundling around China in buses or chugging across the land by train is great on occasion, China is a country of vast distances. If you don't have the time or inclination for a long-drawn-out land campaign, take to the air.

China's air network is extensive and the country's rapid economic development means that its civil aviation fleet is expected to triple in size over the next two decades, with up to 2000 more airliners being added to the existing fleet by 2022. With predictions that China could become the world's most visited tourist destination by 2020, the nation is shaping up for a further upsurge in domestic air travel. Airports are being built and upgraded all over

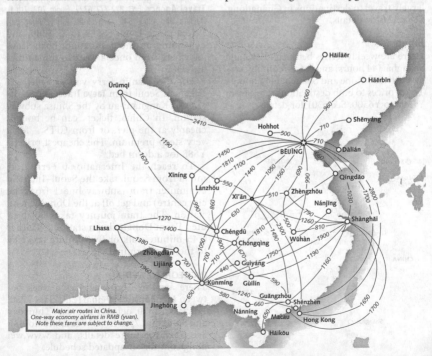

Major air routes in China.
One-way economy airfares in RMB (yuan).
Note these fares are subject to change.

the land, making air transport increasingly appealing, with new airports including Shànghǎi's Pudong Airport, Běijīng's new Capital Airport terminal and Hong Kong's spiffing Chek Lap Kok Airport. By 2005, it is expected that 150 of China's airports will have undergone some renovation.

The **Civil Aviation Administration of China** (CAAC; Zhōngguó Mínháng) is the civil aviation authority for numerous airlines, which include:

Air China (www.airchina.com.cn) Běijīng (☎ 010-6601 7755) Largely flies economically priced international routes.

China Eastern Airlines (www.ce-air.com) Shànghǎi (☎ 021-6268 6268) Range of international destinations, including London and Los Angeles, with flights out of Běijīng and Shànghǎi.

China Southern Airlines (☎ 020-8668 2000; www .cs-air.com) Guǎngzhōu based airline serving a number of international routes as well as a nationwide web of air routes including Běijīng, Shànghǎi, Xī'ān and Tiānjīn.

China Southwest Airlines Chéngdū (☎ 028-666 8080)

Some of the above also have subsidiary airlines; for example, subsidiaries of China Southern include Xiamen Airlines and Guangxi Airlines. Note that not all Chinese airline websites have English language capability. Airline schedules and airfares are listed within the relevant chapters.

CAAC publishes a combined international and domestic timetable in both English and Chinese in April and November each year. This timetable can be bought at some airports and CAAC offices in China. Individual airlines also publish timetables. You can buy these from ticket offices throughout China.

Tickets are easy to purchase as at most times there is an oversupply of airline seats (except during major festivals and holidays). Tickets can be purchased from branches of CAAC nationwide, other airline offices and travel agents or from the travel desk of your hotel. Ask around for discounts, which are generally available. Fares are calculated according to one-way travel, with return tickets simply costing twice the single fare. Shuttle buses often run from CAAC offices in towns and cities through China to the airport.

Children over 12 are charged adult fares; kids between two and 12 pay half-price. Toddlers under the age of two pay 10% of the full fare. You can use credit cards at most CAAC offices and travel agents.

> **DOMESTIC DEPARTURE TAX**
>
> Departure tax for domestic flights is Y50.

Cancellation fees depend on how long before departure you cancel. On domestic flights, if you cancel 24 to 48 hours before departure you lose 10% of the fare; if you cancel between two and 24 hours before the flight you lose 20%; and if you cancel less than two hours before the flight you lose 30%. If you don't show up for a domestic flight, you are entitled to a refund of 50%.

When purchasing a ticket, you may be asked to buy insurance (Y20). It's not compulsory and the amount you can claim is very low.

On domestic and international flights the free baggage allowance for an adult passenger is 20kg in economy class and 30kg in 1st class. You are also allowed 5kg of hand luggage, though this is rarely weighed. The charge for excess baggage is 1% of the full fare for each kilogram. Baggage reclamation facilities are rudimentary at the older airports and waits can be long; lost baggage compensation is Y40 per kilogram.

Planes vary in style and comfort. The more regularly travelled routes between cities employ Boeing or Airbus, more farflung regions still depend on Soviet-built passenger jets. You may get a hot meal, or just a small piece of cake and an airline souvenir. On-board announcements are delivered in Chinese and English if there are foreigners on board.

BICYCLE

Bicycles (zìxíngchē) are an excellent method for getting around China's cities or patrolling tourist sights.

Outdoor bicycle-repair stalls are found on every other corner in larger cities, and repairs are very cheap.

Despite the convenience of cycling, take care when you're on your bike. Helmets can be difficult to find in China as virtually no Chinese cycle with protection. Cycling at night can be hazardous, mainly because few Chinese bikes are equipped with lights. But your greatest concern will probably be China's pernicious traffic conditions and bad driving.

TRANSPORT

Hire

Bicycle hire outlets that cater to foreigners can be found in most traveller centres. Many hotels also rent out bicycles. Bikes can be hired by the day or by the hour and it's also possible to hire for a stretch of several days, so touring is possible. Rates for Westerners are typically Y2 per hour or Y10 to Y20 per day but you could pay as much as Y20 per hour at some tourist sights. Note that big hotels typically charge ridiculous rates so it's worth looking around.

Most hire places will ask you for a deposit of anything up to Y500 (get a receipt) and to leave some sort of ID. Sometimes the staff will ask for your passport. Give them some other ID instead, like a student card or a drivers' licence. In most large towns and cities bicycles should be parked for a small fee at designated places on the pavement.

Purchase

If you're planning to stay in one place for any length of time it may be worth buying your own bike and then selling it on. Bike shops are plentiful and prices should be clearly marked. The cheapest mountain bikes start in the region of Y400, but single-speed bikes are cheaper, starting at around Y250. It is important to buy a decent cable or U-lock as theft is commonplace. If you want to sell on your bike, advertising it on local university notice boards is a good idea, or in expat magazines such as *That's Beijing* or *That's Shanghai* (which often means you can advertise online – a good place also to look for second-hand bikes).

Touring

The legalities of cycling from town to town are open to conjecture. There is no national law in China that prohibits foreigners from riding bicycles. Basically, the problem is that of 'open' and 'closed' areas. It's illegal for foreigners to visit closed areas without a permit. Fair enough, but foreigners can transit a closed area – that is, you can travel by train or bus through a closed area as long as you don't exit the vehicle in this 'forbidden zone'. The question is: Should riding a bicycle through a closed area be classified as 'transiting' or 'visiting' it?

Chinese law is as clear as mud on this issue. Most of the time, the police won't bother you.

If you get caught in a closed area, it is unlikely to be while you are on the road. The law keeps firm tabs on transients via hotels. If you're staying overnight in an open place, but you are suspected of having passed through a closed area, the police may pull a raid on your hotel. You can be hauled down to the police station where you have to submit to a lengthy interrogation, sign a confession and pay a fine. Fines vary from Y50 to whatever they think you can afford. There is some latitude for bargaining in these situations, and you should request a receipt *(shōujù)*. Don't expect police to give you any tips on which areas are closed and which are open – they seldom know themselves – although such areas are usually near international borders or zones of a sensitive military nature, as well as much of Tibet.

BOAT

Boat services within China are limited. In coastal areas, you are most likely to use a boat to reach offshore islands like Pǔtuóshān or Hǎinán Dǎo. The Yāntái–Dàlián ferry will likely survive because it saves hundreds of kilometres of overland travel, despite the loss of more than 200 lives when a ferry on this route sank in heavy seas in 1999. For the same reason, the Shànghǎi–Níngbō service will probably continue to operate, but elsewhere the outlook for coastal passenger ships is not too good.

There are also several inland shipping routes worth considering, but these are also vanishing. For details of each trip see the appropriate sections in this book.

The best-known river trip is the three-day boat ride along Yangzi River (Cháng Jiāng) from Chóngqìng to Wǔhàn. Li River (Lí Jiāng) boat trip from Guìlín to Yángshuò is a popular tourist ride. You can also travel the Grand Canal from Hángzhōu to Sūzhōu on a tourist boat.

Hong Kong employs a veritable navy of vessels that connect with the territory's myriad islands and a number of popular boats run between the territory and other parts of China (principally Guǎngdōng province), including Macau, Zhūhǎi, Shékǒu (for Shēnzhèn) and Zhōngshān. See p524 for details.

Boat tickets can be purchased from passenger ferry terminals or through travel agents such as CITS.

BUS

Long-distance buses (*chángtú gōnggòng-qìchē*) are one of the best means of getting around. Services are extensive, main roads are rapidly improving and with the increasing number of intercity highways, bus journeys are getting quicker (often quicker than train travel). Another plus is that it's easier to secure bus tickets than train tickets and they are often cheaper. Buses also stop every so often in small towns and villages, so you get to see parts of the countryside you wouldn't see if you travelled by train, although breakdowns can be a problem.

On the down side, some rural roads and provincial routes (especially in the southwest, Tibet and the northwest) remain in shocking condition, dangerously traversed by bone-rattling hulks that shatter the nerves. Precipitous drops, pot holes, dangerous road surfaces and reckless drivers mean that accidents in black-spot areas such as parts of Sìchuān are common. Long-distance bus journeys can also be cramped and noisy, with Hong Kong films looped on overhead TVs and three dimensional sound. Drivers lean on the horn at the slightest detection of a vehicle in front.

Routes between large cities sport larger, cleaner and more comfortable fleets of private buses, such as comfy Volvos; shorter and more far-flung routes still rely on rattling minibuses into which the driver crams as many fares as is possible.

On popular long-haul routes, sleeper buses (*wòpù qìchē*) may cost around double the price of a normal bus service, but many travellers swear by them. Some have comfortable reclining seats, while others have two-tier bunks. Watch out for your belongings on them, however.

It's safe to estimate times for bus journeys on non-highway routes by calculating the distance against a speed of 25km/h. Also factor in driving techniques – drivers are loathe to change gears and appear to prefer to almost stop on a slope rather than changing from third into second.

If taking buses to high-altitude destinations in winter, make sure you take plenty of warm clothes. A breakdown in frozen conditions can prove lethal for those unprepared.

Bus journey times given throughout this book should be used as a rough guide only and do not factor in variables such as weather, breakdowns or bad traffic conditions.

Bus Stations & Ticketing

All cities and most towns across China have one or more long-distance bus stations (*chángtú qìchēzhàn*). Tickets are easy to purchase and it's usually just a case of turning up at the bus station and buying your ticket there and then, rather than booking them in advance. Wherever you are going, weigh up the options: besides that bone-rattling tin creature that you are being shoved onto by ticket operators, a plush, air-con (albeit slightly more expensive) coach could well be heading to the same destination. Bus drivers and ticket sellers at bus stations can press gang you aboard their vehicles; try to resist until you know what other choices exist.

CAR & MOTORCYCLE

For those who'd like to tour China by car or motorbike, the news is bleak. It's not like India, where you can simply buy a motorbike and head off. The authorities remain anxious about foreigners driving at whim around China, so don't plan on hiring a car and driving off wherever you want. Cars can be hired in Hong Kong, Macau, Shànghǎi, Guǎngzhōu and Běijīng for local use only. Furthermore, road conditions in China should abolish any remaining desire to get behind the wheel. Bilingual road signs may be making a slow appearance along some highways, but much remains to confuse would-be drivers from abroad.

Driving Licence

To hire a car, you will need to come armed with an International Driving Permit. If purchasing a vehicle as a resident, you will require a Chinese licence issued by the PSB, who will need to see your residency card, employment card, driving licence from your home country, or an International Driving Permit. You also have to perform a health examination. Foreigners can drive motorcycles if they are residents in China and have a Chinese motorcycle licence.

Hire

Although tourists are permitted to rent vehicles in Hong Kong, Macau, Běijīng, Guǎngzhōu and Shànghǎi, it's not worth the hassle and inconvenience. You will be restricted to driving around within the perimeters of each city. Although expat residents report little problem driving into provinces neighbouring the above locations, we cannot advise attempting to drive beyond these few cities as hire cars carry easily identifiable licence plates. Rates for hire cars start at around Y300 per day, with monthly rates from around Y5000; on most occasions, using taxis all day will work out much cheaper.

If you want to use a car, it's easy enough to book a car with a driver. Basically, this is just a standard long-distance taxi. Travel agencies like CITS or even hotel booking desks can make the arrangements. They generally ask excessive fees – the name of the game is to negotiate. If you can communicate in Chinese or find someone to translate, it's not particularly difficult to find a private taxi driver to take you wherever you like for less than half the CITS rates.

Purchase
Only legal residents of China can purchase a motor vehicle. Despite cheap petrol and the mushrooming car market (Volkswagen alone sold 700,000 vehicles in China in 2003), buying and running cars is an expensive business. Imported vehicles are very expensive indeed: the on-the-road price for a bottom-rung Porsche is around Y1.15 million (sorry, no road tests). The cheapest cars retail for around Y60,000 and the least expensive locally-made Volkswagen costs Y90,000, but you have to calculate in the licence plate fee. Large cities such as Běijīng and Shànghǎi only issue licence plates for astronomical sums, in a bid to control car ownership and ease the over congested roads. With Shànghǎi licence plates costing around Y40,000, it is possible to purchase licence plates from neighbouring Zhèjiāng or Jiāngsū, but the downside is that cars without Shànghǎi licence plates are barred from certain highways. Import duty on cars is very high, reaching around 300% of the vehicle purchase price. Highway tolls are also excessive in China: driving between Běijīng and Shànghǎi for example, will cost over Y500 in toll fees alone for an average four-seat car; then you've got to think of the petrol (Y3.5 a litre). You might as well take the train, it'll cost you less and it's much more fun. In fact, the cost of buying a car

is so high that you would have to spend around Y50 a day on taxis over seven years to equal the purchase cost of a vehicle and licence plate alone.

Road Rules
Cars in China drive on the right-hand side of the road. You're more likely to get fined for illegal parking than speeding. Indeed, with China's gridlock traffic, opportunities for speeding are swiftly vanishing, except on the highways. Even if you are a skilled driver, you will be unprepared for the performance on China's roads; cars lunge from all angles and chaos abounds. You see cars driving from minor onto major roads, their drivers totally ignoring oncoming vehicles. The figures make for grim reading: China tops the highway mortality charts with 300 people losing their lives daily on China's roads (a figure that is growing by 10% every year), despite there being fewer vehicles per head than in Western countries.

HITCHING
Hitching is never entirely safe in any country in the world, and we don't recommend it. Travellers who decide to hitch should understand that they are taking a small but potentially serious risk. People who do choose to hitch will be safer if they travel in pairs and let someone know where they are planning to go.

Many people have hitchhiked in China, and some have been amazingly successful. It's not officially sanctioned and the same dangers that apply elsewhere in the world also apply in China. Exercise caution, and if you're in any doubt as to the intentions of your prospective driver, say no.

Hitching in China is rarely free, and passengers are expected to offer at least a tip. Some drivers might even ask for an unreasonable amount of money, so try to establish a figure early to avoid problems later. Even when a price is agreed upon, don't be surprised if the driver raises it when you arrive at your destination and creates a big scene (with a big crowd) if you don't cough up the extra cash. Indeed, they may even pull this scam halfway through the trip, and if you don't pay up you get kicked out in the middle of nowhere.

In other words, don't think of hitching as a means to save money – it will rarely be any cheaper than the bus. The main reason to do it is to get to isolated outposts where public transport is poor. There is, of course, some joy in meeting the locals this way, but communicating is certain to be a problem if you don't speak Chinese.

The best way to get a lift is to head out to main roads on the outskirts of town. There are usually lots of trucks on the roads, and even postal trucks and army convoys are worth trying. There is no Chinese signal for hitching, so just try waving down the trucks.

LOCAL TRANSPORT

Long-distance transport in China is not really a problem – the dilemma occurs when you finally make it to your destination. While China boasts a huge and often inventive choice of local transport, vehicles can be slow and overburdened, and the transport network very confusing for visitors. Hiring a car is largely impractical or impossible and hiring a bike may be inadequate. Unless the town is small, walking is not usually recommended, since Chinese cities tend to be very spread out. On the plus side, local transport is cheap, although be on your guard against being overcharged.

Bus

Apart from bikes, buses are the most common means of getting around in the cities. Services are fairly extensive, buses go to most places and fares are inexpensive. The problem is that they are almost always packed. If an empty bus pulls in at a stop then a battle for seats ensues. Even more aggravating is the slowness of the traffic. You just have to be patient, never expect anything to move rapidly, and allow lots of time to get to the train station to catch your train.

Improvements in bus quality have been matched by increased congestion on the roads. Bus routes at bus stops are generally listed in Chinese only, without Pinyin, so navigation can be difficult. In larger towns and cities, more expensive private minibus operations follow the same routes as the larger public buses.

Good maps of Chinese cities and bus routes are readily available and are often sold by hawkers outside the train stations. When you get on a bus, point to where you want to go on the map, and the conductor (who is seated near the door) will sell you the right ticket. They usually tell you where to get off, provided they remember, but the bus stop may be quite a distance from your destination.

Metro

Going underground is highly preferable to taking the bus, as there are no traffic jams, but this transportation option is only possible in a handful of cities: Hong Kong, Běijīng, Shànghǎi, Guǎngzhōu, Tiānjīn and Shēnzhèn (which should be open by the time you read this).

By far the best and most comprehensive is Hong Kong's funky system; Běijīng's network is limited but is being expanded in preparation for the 2008 Olympics. Shànghǎi and Guǎngzhōu have new and efficient systems, while Tiānjīn's modest system is being extended.

Taxi

Many large Chinese cities endlessly sprawl and taxis (chūzū qìchē) are the best way to get around for first-time visitors. Taxis are cheap and plentiful and always on the lookout for customers, so finding one is rarely difficult. In fact, the ceaseless honking at or sidling alongside foreign travellers can be wearing. If you can't find a taxi, likely congregation points include the train station and long-distance bus stations. Some large cities also have taxi pickup points.

Taxi drivers speak little, if any English. If you don't speak Chinese, bring a map or have your destination written down in characters. It helps if you know the way to your destination; sit in the front with a map.

If you encounter a taxi driver you trust or who speaks a smattering of English, ask for his card (míngpiàn). You can hire them for a single trip or on a daily basis – the latter is worth considering if there's a group of people who can split the cost.

Taxi rates per kilometre are clearly marked on a sticker on the rear side window of the taxi; flag fall rates vary from city to city and also depend upon the size and quality of vehicle. Some cities such as Tiānjīn still employ small yellow minivans (miànbāochē), which are cheaper than standard taxis.

While most taxis have meters, they are often only switched on in larger towns and cities. If the meter is not used (on an

NAVIGATING CITIES

At first glance, Chinese street names can be a little bewildering, with name changes common every few hundred metres. The good news is that there is some logic to it, and a little basic Chinese will help to make navigating much easier.

Many road names are compound words made up of a series of directions that place the road in context with all others in the city. Compass directions are particularly common in road names. The directions are: *běi* (north), *nán* (south), *dōng* (east) and *xī* (west). So Dong Lu literally means East Rd.

Other words which regularly crop up are *zhōng* (central) and *huan* (ring, as in ring road). If you bring them together with some basic numerals, you could have Dongsanhuan Nanlu, which literally means 'east third ring south road' or the southeastern part of the third ring road.

excursion out of town for example), a price should be negotiated before you get into the taxi, and bargaining employed. Write the price down if you have to and secure an agreement, so that the price is not suddenly upped when you arrive. If you want the meter to be used, ask for *dǎbiǎo*. Try to remember to ask for a receipt *(fāpiào)*; if you leave something behind in the taxi, the taxi number is printed on the receipt so it can be tracked down.

Chinese cities impose limitations on the number of passengers a taxi can carry. The limit is usually four – though minibuses can take more – and drivers are usually unwilling to break the rules and risk trouble with the police.

It is practically impossible to find rear seat belts in China's taxi fleet, and the front passenger seat belt is so rarely used it is often grimy or locked solid. Even so, take the front seat if you are travelling alone and ignore protestations from taxi drivers that you don't need to wear a seat belt. Be prepared for bad driving. If sitting in the rear, try to position yourself so you don't lose an eye on one of the sharp corners and edges of the security cage the driver sits in if he suddenly halts (or crashes). Watch out for tired drivers – they work long and punishing shifts.

Other

An often bewildering variety of ramshackle transport options can be found throughout China, providing employment for legions of elderly Chinese. The motor tricycle *(sānlún mótuōchē)* – for want of a better name – is an enclosed three-wheeled vehicle with a driver at the front, a small motorbike engine below and seats for two passengers behind. They tend to congregate outside the train and bus stations in larger towns and cities. Some of these vehicles have trays at the rear with bench seats along the sides so that four or more people can be accommodated.

The pedicab *(sānlúnchē)* is a pedal-powered tricycle with a seat to carry passengers. Chinese pedicabs have the driver in front and passenger seats in the back. Gradually disappearing in China, pedicabs congregate outside train and bus stations or hotels in parts of China. In a few places, pedicabs cruise the streets in large numbers (Lhasa, for example).

In some towns you can get a ride on the back of someone's motorcycle for about half the price of what a regular four-wheeled taxi would charge. If you turn a blind eye to the hazards, this is a quick and cheap way of getting around. You must wear a helmet – the driver will provide one. Obviously, there is no meter, so fares must be agreed upon in advance.

Prices of all of the above can compare with taxis, however, check beforehand and bargain. Also note that none of the above offer decent protection in a crash, so taking a taxi is often the more sensible option.

TRAIN

Although crowded, trains are the best way to get around in reasonable speed and comfort. The network covers every province except Hǎinán Dǎo (limited) and Tibet (under construction). There is an estimated 52,000km of railway lines in China, most of which was built after 1949 and at any given time it is estimated that over 10 million Chinese are travelling on a train in China.

Travelling by train is an adventurous, fun and efficient way of getting around China and meeting the local people. A variety of classes means you can navigate as you wish: if you can endure a hard seat, getting from A to B is very cheap. Opting for a soft sleeper means things can get pricey.

RAIL DISTANCES

Distances are in kilometres

	北京 Běijīng	成都 Chéngdū	重庆 Chóngqìng	长沙 Chángshā	福州 Fúzhōu	广州 Guǎngzhōu	杭州 Hángzhōu	哈尔滨 Hāěrbīn	吉林 Jílín	昆明 Kūnmíng	青岛 Qīngdǎo	上海 Shànghǎi	乌鲁木齐 Ūrūmqi
Chéngdū 成都	2042												
Chóngqìng 重庆	2087	504											
Chángshā 长沙	1587	1923	1419										
Fúzhōu 福州	2334	2805	2301	985									
Guǎngzhōu 广州	2294	2527	2023	707	1588								
Hángzhōu 杭州	1664	2552	2315	1006	979	1609							
Hāěrbīn 哈尔滨	1288	242	3336	3381	3472	944	2727						
Jílín 吉林	1174	3235	3280	2798	3371	3505	2626	275					
Kūnmíng 昆明	3183	1100	1102	1595	2477	1595	2498	3588	4371				
Qīngdǎo 青岛	890	2412	2457	1957	2230	2549	1485	2028	1927	3512			
Shànghǎi 上海	1463	2351	2516	1207	1180	1810	201	2601	2500	2699	1359		
Ūrūmqi 乌鲁木齐	3768	3026	3530	3973	4957	4679	4065	5062	4961	4126	4138	4077	
Xī'ān 西安	1200	842	1346	1405	2389	2111	1635	2248	2352	1942	1570	1509	2568

TRANSPORT

The safety record of the train system is also good (despite the grim and graphic photographs displayed in train stations warning of the perils of transporting fireworks and explosives), but keep an eye on your belongings (see p889).

The new fleet of trains that run intercity routes is a vast improvement on the old models – they are much cleaner and equipped with air-con. The ultrafast maglev train that connects Pudong Airport to the Shànghǎi metro system is perhaps a sign of things to come. Trains nationwide are very punctual and leave on the dot.

Most trains have dining cars where you can find passable food. Railway staff also regularly walk by with pushcarts offering *miàn* (instant noodles), *miànbāo* (bread), *héfàn* (boxed rice lunches), *huǒtuǐ* (ham), *píjiǔ* (beer), *kuàng quán shuǐ* (mineral water) and *qìshuǐ* (soft drinks).

Many train stations require that luggage be X-rayed before entering the waiting area.

Virtually all train stations have leftluggage rooms (*jìcún chù*) where you can

safely dump your bags for about Y2 to Y4 (per day per item).

Classes

Train tickets are calculated simply according the kilometre distance travelled and, on longer routes, the class of travel.

Hard seat (*yìng zuò*) is actually generally padded, but the hard-seat section can be hard on your sanity – it can be very dirty, noisy and smoky, and painful on the long haul. Hard seat on tourist trains, express trains or newer trains is more pleasant, less crowded and air-conditioned.

Since hard seat is the only thing most locals can afford it's packed to the gills. You should get a ticket with an assigned seat number, but if seats have sold out, ask for a standing ticket (*wúzuò*), which at least gets you on the train, where you may find a seat or you can upgrade (see p924). Because hard-seat tickets are relatively easy to obtain, you may have to travel hard seat even if you're willing to pay for a higher class.

On short express journeys (such as Běijīng to Tiānjīn) some trains have soft-seat (ruǎn zuò) carriages. These trains have comfortable seats arranged two abreast and overcrowding is not permitted. Soft seats cost about the same as hard sleeper and carriages are often double-decker.

Hard-sleeper (yìng wò) carriages are made up of doorless compartments with half a dozen bunks in three tiers, and sheets, pillows and blankets are provided. It does very nicely as an overnight hotel. There is a small price difference between berths, with the lowest bunk (xiàpù) the most expensive and the top-most bunk (shàngpù) the cheapest. You may wish to take the middle bunk (zhōngpù) as all and sundry invade the lower berth to use it as a seat during the day, while the top one has little headroom and puts you near the speakers (tall passengers may prefer the top bunk, however, as the beds are short and passengers in the aisle bash into their overhanging feet). As with all other classes, smoking is prohibited in hard sleeper. Lights and speakers go out at around 10pm. Each compartment is equipped with its own hot-water flask (rèshuǐpíng), which is filled by an attendant. Hard-sleeper tickets are the most difficult of all to buy; you almost always need to buy these far in advance.

Soft sleeper (ruǎn wò) is luxurious travel, with four comfortable bunks in a closed compartment, with wood panelling, potted plants, lace curtains, teacups, clean washrooms, carpets and air-con. Soft sleeper costs twice as much as hard sleeper (the upper berth is slightly cheaper than the lower berth), so it is usually easier to purchase soft rather than hard sleeper; however, more and more Chinese are travelling this way.

If you get on the train with an unreserved seating ticket, you can find the conductor and upgrade (bǔpiào) yourself to a hard-sleeper, soft-seat or soft-sleeper if there are any available.

Reservations & Tickets

The vast majority of tickets are one-way (dānchéng) only. Buying hard seat tickets at short notice is usually no hassle, but you will not always be successful in getting a reserved seat. Tickets can only be purchased with cash.

Tickets for hard sleepers can usually be obtained in major cities, but with more difficulty in quiet backwaters. Don't expect to obtain a hard-sleeper ticket on the day of travel. Plan ahead and buy your ticket two or three days in advance, especially if you are heading to popular destinations. As a general rule there is a five-day, advance-purchase limit, but in large cities such as Běijīng or Shànghǎi you may find you can book further ahead.

If you try to buy a sleeper ticket at the train station and the clerk says méi yǒu (not have), turn to your hotel travel desk or travel agent (such as CITS) who can sell you a ticket for a service charge of around Y20. Telephone booking services exist, but they only operate in Chinese. Many towns and cities also have ticket offices dotted around town where you can obtain train tickets (again for a surcharge); such outlets are listed in the relevant chapters.

Buying hard-sleeper tickets in train stations can be trying. Large stations like Beijing Train Station have special ticket offices (also called VIP lounges or guìbīnshì) for foreigners where procuring tickets is straightforward. Purchasing your ticket from the main ticket hall (shòupiàotīng or shòupiàochù) – typically accessed by a separate entrance from the departure hall – can be a trial of endurance, especially at the larger train stations. Some stations are surprisingly well run, but others are bedlam. On a few rare routes (such as Běijīng to Tiānjīn) cash-taking automatic ticket machines exist (with instructions for use in Chinese only). There are windows at large train stations for partial refunds on unused tickets.

Touts swarm around train stations selling black-market tickets; this can be a way of getting scarce tickets, but foreigners frequently get ripped off. If you purchase a ticket from a tout, carefully check the departure date and the destination. As with air travel, buying tickets around the Chinese New Year and the 1 May and 1 October holidays can be hard and prices increase on some routes.

Timetables

Paperback train timetables for the entire country are published every April and October, but they are available in Chinese only (Y8). Even to Chinese readers, working one's way through their Byzantine layout is taxing. Thinner versions listing the major train services from Běijīng can be bought at train stations for about Y2 – again in Chinese only. An English translation of the timetable is provided by Duncan Peattie, listing the most important routes for travellers. The timetable is available in either printed form or electronically as two pdf files. In English, the timetable covers services to and from

more than 850 stations in China and is organised in a tabular form; a quick reference version is also available. Contact chinatt@eudoramail.com for details on how to get hold of a copy. Also consult www.travelchinaguide.com/china-trains/ which allows you to enter your departure point and destination, and gives you the departure times, arrival times and train numbers of trains running that route.

Health Dr Trish Batchelor

CONTENTS

Overall China is a reasonable healthy country to travel in, but there are a number of health issues worthy of your attention. Pre-existing medical conditions, such as heart disease, and accidental injury (especially traffic accidents), account for most life-threatening problems. Becoming ill in some way, however, is not unusual. Outside of the major cities medical care may be inadequate and food and waterborne diseases are common. Malaria is still present in some parts of the country and high altitude sickness can be a problem, particularly in Tibet.

In case of accident or illness it's best just to get a taxi and go to hospital directly – try to avoid dealing with the authorities if possible.

The following advice is a general guide only and does not replace the advice of a doctor trained in travel medicine.

BEFORE YOU GO

Pack medications in their original, clearly labelled, containers. A signed and dated letter from your physician describing your medical conditions and medications (using generic names) is also a good idea. If carrying syringes or needles, be sure to have a physician's letter documenting their medical necessity. If you have a heart condition, bring a copy of your ECG taken just prior to travelling.

If you take any regular medication bring double your needs in case of loss or theft. In China you can buy many medications over the counter without a doctor's prescription, but it can be difficult to find some of the newer drugs, particularly the latest antidepressant drugs, blood pressure medications and contraceptive methods. In general it is not advised to buy medications locally without a doctor's advice.

Make sure you get your teeth checked before you travel, and if you wear glasses take a spare pair and your prescription.

INSURANCE

Even if you are fit and healthy, don't travel without health insurance – accidents do happen. Declare any existing medical conditions you have – the insurance company *will* check if your problem is pre-existing and will not cover you if it is undeclared. You may require extra cover for adventure activities such as rock climbing. If you're uninsured, emergency evacuation is expensive (bills of over US$100,000 are not uncommon).

Make sure you keep all documentation related to any medical expenses you incur.

RECOMMENDED VACCINATIONS

Specialised travel-medicine clinics are your best source of information; they stock all available vaccines and will be able to give specific recommendations for you and your trip. The doctors will take into account factors such as past vaccination history, the length of your trip, activities you may be undertaking and underlying medical conditions, such as pregnancy.

Most vaccines don't produce immunity until at least two weeks after they're given, so visit a doctor six to eight weeks before departure. Ask your doctor for an International Certificate of Vaccination (otherwise known as the yellow booklet), which will list all the vaccinations you've received.

RECOMMENDED VACCINATIONS

The World Health Organization (WHO) recommends the following vaccinations for travellers to China:

Adult diphtheria and tetanus Single booster recommended if none in the previous 10 years. Side effects include sore arm and fever.

Hepatitis A Provides almost 100% protection for up to a year; a booster after 12 months provides at least another 20 years protection. Mild side effects such as headache and sore arm occur in 5% to 10% of people.

Hepatitis B Now considered routine for most travellers. Given as three shots over six months. A rapid schedule is also available, as is a combined vaccination with Hepatitis A. Side effects are mild and uncommon, usually headache and sore arm. In 95% of people lifetime protection results.

Measles, mumps and rubella Two doses of MMR recommended unless you have had the diseases. Occasionally a rash and flu-like illness can develop a week after receiving the vaccine. Many young adults require a booster.

Typhoid Recommended unless your trip is less than a week. The vaccine offers around 70% protection, lasts for two to three years and comes as a single shot. Tablets are also available; however, the injection is usually recommended as it has fewer side effects. Sore arm and fever may occur.

Varicella If you haven't had chickenpox discuss this vaccination with your doctor.

The following immunisations are recommended for long-term travellers (more than one month) or those at special risk:

Influenza A single shot lasts one year and is recommended for those over 65 years of age or with underlying medical conditions such as heart or lung disease.

Japanese B encephalitis A series of three injections with a booster after two years. Recommended if spending more than one month in rural areas in the summer months.

Pneumonia A single injection with a booster after five years is recommended for all travellers over 65 years of age or with underlying medical conditions that compromise immunity such as heart or lung disease, cancer or HIV.

Rabies Three injections in all. A booster after one year will then provide 10 years' protection. Side effects are rare – occasionally headache and sore arm.

Tuberculosis A complex issue. High-risk adult long-term travellers are usually recommended to have a TB skin test before and after travel, rather than vaccination. Only one vaccine is given in a lifetime. Children under five spending more than three months in China should be vaccinated.

Pregnant women and children should receive advice from a doctor specialised in travel medicine.

The only vaccine required by international regulations is yellow fever. Proof of vaccination will only be required if you have visited a country in the yellow fever zone within the six days prior to entering China. If you are travelling to China directly from South America or Africa, check with a travel clinic as to whether you need yellow fever vaccination.

MEDICAL CHECKLIST

Recommended items for a personal medical kit:

- Antibacterial cream, eg Muciprocin
- Antibiotic for skin infections, eg Amoxicillin/Clavulanate or Cephalexin
- Antibiotics for diarrhoea, including Norfloxacin, Ciprofloxacin; or Azithromycin for bacterial diarrhoea; or Tinidazole for giardia or amoebic dysentery.
- Antifungal cream, eg Clotrimazole
- Antihistamine – there are many options, eg Cetrizine for daytime and Promethazine for night-time
- Antiseptic, eg Betadine
- Anti-spasmodic for stomach cramps, eg Buscopan
- Decongestant, eg Pseudoephedrine
- DEET-based insect repellent
- Diamox if going to high altitudes
- Diarrhoea – consider an oral rehydration solution (eg Gastrolyte), diarrhoea 'stopper' (eg Loperamide) and anti-nausea medication (eg Prochlorperazine)
- Elastoplasts, bandages, gauze, thermometer (but not mercury), sterile needles and syringes, safety pins and tweezers
- Ibuprofen or another anti-inflammatory
- Indigestion tablets, such as Quick Eze or Mylanta

- Iodine tablets (unless you are pregnant or have a thyroid problem) to purify water
- Laxative, eg Coloxyl
- Paracetamol
- Permethrin to impregnate clothing and mosquito nets
- Steroid cream for allergic/itchy rashes, eg 1% to 2% hydrocortisone
- Sunscreen and hat
- Thrush (vaginal yeast infection) treatment, eg Clotrimazole pessaries or Diflucan tablet
- Ural or equivalent if prone to urinary infections

INTERNET RESOURCES

There is a wealth of travel health advice on the Internet. For further information, Lonely Planet (www.lonelyplanet.com) is a good place to start. The World Health Organization (WHO; www.who.int/ith/) publishes a superb book called *International Travel & Health,* which is revised annually and is available online at no cost. Another website of general interest is MD Travel Health (www.mdtravelhealth.com), which provides complete travel health recommendations for every country and is updated daily. The Centers for Disease Control and Prevention (CDC; www.cdc.gov) website also has good general information.

FURTHER READING

Lonely Planet's *Healthy Travel – Asia & India* is a handy pocket size and packed with useful information including pretrip planning, emergency first aid, immunisation and disease information and what to do if you get sick on the road. Other recommended references include *Traveller's Health* by Dr Richard Dawood and *Travelling Well* by Dr Deborah Mills – check out the website (www.travellingwell.com.au).

HEALTH ADVISORIES

It's usually a good idea to consult your government's travel-health website before departure, if one is available:

Australia (www.dfat.gov.au/travel/)
Canada (www.travelhealth.gc.ca)
New Zealand (www.mfat.govt.nz/travel)
UK (www.doh.gov.uk/traveladvice/)
US (www.cdc.gov/travel/)

IN TRANSIT

DEEP VEIN THROMBOSIS (DVT)

Deep vein thrombosis occurs when blood clots form in the legs during plane flights, chiefly because of prolonged immobility. Though most blood clots are reabsorbed uneventfully, some may break off and travel through the blood vessels to the lungs, where they may cause life-threatening complications.

The chief symptom of DVT is swelling or pain of the foot, ankle or calf, usually but not always on just one side. When a blood clot travels to the lungs, it may cause chest pain and difficulty in breathing. Travellers with any of these symptoms should immediately seek medical attention.

To prevent the development of DVT on long flights you should walk about the cabin, perform isometric compressions of the leg muscles (ie contract the leg muscles while sitting), drink plenty of fluids, and avoid alcohol and tobacco.

JET LAG & MOTION SICKNESS

Jet lag is common when crossing more than five time zones; it results in insomnia, fatigue, malaise or nausea. To avoid jet lag try drinking plenty of fluids (nonalcoholic) and eating light meals. Upon arrival, seek exposure to natural sunlight and readjust your schedule (for meals, sleep etc) as soon as possible.

Antihistamines such as dimenhydrinate (Dramamine), promethazine (Phenergan) and meclizine (Antivert, Bonine) are usually the first choice for treating motion sickness. Their main side effect is drowsiness. A herbal alternative is ginger, which works like a charm for some people.

IN CHINA

AVAILABILITY OF HEALTH CARE

There are now a number of good clinics in major cities catering to travellers. Although they are usually more expensive than local facilities, you may feel more comfortable dealing with a Western-trained doctor who speaks your language. These clinics usually have a good understanding of the best local hospital facilities and close contacts with insurance companies should you need evacuation.

Self-treatment may be appropriate if your problem is minor (eg traveller's diarrhoea), you are carrying the relevant medication and you cannot attend a clinic. If you think you may have a serious disease, especially malaria, do not waste time – travel to the nearest quality facility to receive attention.

Buying medication over the counter in China is not recommended, as fake medications and poorly stored or out-of-date drugs are common.

To find the nearest reliable medical facility, contact your insurance company or your embassy.

INFECTIOUS DISEASES
Avian Influenza (Bird Flu)
'Bird flu' or Influenza A (H5N1) is a subtype of the type A influenza virus. This virus typically infects birds and not humans; however, in 1997 the first documented case of bird-to-human transmission was recorded in Hong Kong. Since that time there have been a number of further cases of confirmed bird-to-human transmission, but so far there has been no direct human-to-human transmission. Infected birds shed the virus in their urine, faeces and saliva. It is believed that the cases of bird flu in humans occurred as a result of direct contact with infected poultry or surfaces contaminated with their urine or faeces. Travellers to countries with documented H5N1 outbreaks should avoid poultry farms, contact with animals in live food markets and surfaces contaminated with faeces or urine from poultry. In 2004 avian influenza was documented in Chinese birds but thus far there have been no human cases.

Dengue
This mosquito-borne disease occurs in some parts of southern China. It can only be prevented by avoiding mosquito bites – there is no vaccine. The mosquito that carries dengue bites day and night, so use insect avoidance measures at all times. Symptoms include high fever, severe headache and body ache (previously dengue was known as 'break bone fever'). Some people develop a rash and diarrhoea. There is no specific treatment – just rest and Paracetamol. Do not take aspirin and see a doctor to be diagnosed and monitored.

Hepatitis A
A problem throughout China, this food and waterborne virus infects the liver, causing jaundice (yellow skin and eyes), nausea and lethargy. There is no specific treatment for hepatitis A, you just need to allow time for the liver to heal. All travellers to China should be vaccinated.

Hepatitis B
The only sexually transmitted disease that can be prevented by vaccination, hepatitis B is spread by contact with infected body fluids, including via sexual contact. The long-term consequences can include liver cancer and cirrhosis. All travellers to China should be vaccinated

HIV
HIV is transmitted via contaminated body fluids. Avoid unsafe sex, blood transfusions and injections (unless you can see a clean needle being used) in China. The Chinese government is finally starting to take AIDS seriously, as the country is said to be on the brink of a major epidemic. Always use condoms if you have sex with a new partner and never share needles.

Influenza
Present particularly in the winter months, symptoms of the flu include high fever, muscle aches, runny nose, cough and sore throat. It can be very severe in people over the age of 65 or in those with underlying medical conditions such as heart disease or diabetes – vaccination is recommended for these individuals. There is no specific treatment, just rest and painkillers.

Japanese B Encephalitis
This is a rare disease in travellers; however, vaccination is recommended if spending more than a month in rural areas during the summer months. There is no treatment available and one-third of infected people will die, while another one-third suffer permanent brain damage.

Malaria
For such a serious and potentially deadly disease, there is an enormous amount of misinformation concerning malaria. Before you travel, seek medical advice to see if your trip warrants taking anti-malaria medication

HEALTH

and if it does, to ensure you receive the right medication and dosage for you.

Malaria has been nearly eradicated in China and is not generally a risk for visitors to the cities. It is found mainly in rural areas in the southwestern region – principally Hǎinán, Yúnnán and Guǎngxī bordering onto Myanmar, Laos and Vietnam. There is more limited risk in remote rural areas of Fújiàn, Guǎngdōng, Guǎngxī, Guìzhōu, Sìchuān and Tibet. Generally medication is advised if you are visiting rural Hǎinán or Yúnnán.

Malaria is caused by a parasite transmitted by the bite of an infected mosquito. The most important symptom of malaria is fever, but general symptoms such as headache, diarrhoea, cough or chills may also occur. Diagnosis can only be made by taking a blood sample.

Two strategies should be combined to prevent malaria – mosquito avoidance, and anti-malaria medications. Most people who catch malaria are taking inadequate or no anti-malarial medication.

You should always take general insect avoidance measures, to help prevent all insect-borne diseases, not just malaria. Travellers are advised to prevent mosquito bites by taking these steps:

- Use a DEET-containing insect repellent on exposed skin. Wash this off at night, as long as you are sleeping under a mosquito net. Natural repellents such as Citronella can be effective, but must be applied more frequently than products containing DEET.
- Sleep under a mosquito net impregnated with permethrin.
- Choose accommodation with screens and fans (if not air-conditioned).
- Impregnate clothing with permethrin in high-risk areas.
- Wear long sleeves and trousers in light colours.
- Use mosquito coils.
- Spray your room with insect repellent before going out for your evening meal.

Rabies

This is a common problem in China. This uniformly fatal disease is spread by the bite or lick of an infected animal – most commonly a dog. You should seek medical advice immediately after any animal bite and commence post-exposure treatment. Having pretravel vaccination means the post-bite treatment is greatly simplified. If an animal bites you, gently wash the wound with soap and water, and apply an iodine-based antiseptic. If you are not prevaccinated you will need to receive rabies immunoglobulin as soon as possible, followed by a series of five vaccines over the next month. Those prevaccinated require only two shots of vaccine after a bite. Contact your insurance company to find the nearest clinic that stocks rabies immunoglobulin and vaccine.

SARS

In mid-March 2003 the world's attention was drawn to the outbreak of a new and serious respiratory illness that subsequently became known as SARS. Since the outbreak, 8500 cases have been confirmed, resulting in 800 deaths. The peak of disease activity was in early May 2003, when over 200 new cases were being reported daily. The outbreak commenced in the Chinese province of Guǎngdōng in November 2002. By mid-March 2003, numerous cases of an unusually virulent respiratory virus were being reported in Hong Kong, Vietnam, Singapore and Canada. The symptoms of SARS are identical to many other respiratory infections – high fever and cough. There is no reliable quick test for SARS, and no specific treatment available; death from respiratory failure occurs in around 10% of patients. Although many of those dying were elderly or had underlying medical conditions, a significant number of previously fit and healthy young people also succumbed. There were four cases of SARS reported from China in 2004; however, these were all in laboratory workers who had direct exposure to the virus. As opposed to the initial outbreak, this time the Chinese authorities acted swiftly and efficiently to ensure the outbreak was rapidly contained.

Schistosomiasis

Also known as bilharzia, this disease is found in the central Yangzi River (Cháng Jiāng) basin. It is carried in water by minute worms which infect certain varieties of freshwater snails found in rivers, streams, lakes and particularly behind dams. The worm enters through the skin and attaches itself to your intestines or bladder. The infection often causes no symptoms until the disease is well established (several months to years after exposure) and damage to internal organs irreversible.

Avoiding swimming or bathing in fresh water where bilharzia is present is the main method of prevention. A blood test is the most reliable way to diagnose the disease, but the test will not show positive until a number of weeks after exposure. Effective treatment is available.

STDs

Sexually transmitted diseases most common in China include herpes, warts, syphilis, gonorrhoea and chlamydia. People carrying these diseases often have no signs of infection. Condoms will prevent gonorrhoea and chlamydia but not warts or herpes. If after a sexual encounter you develop any rash, lumps, discharge or pain when passing urine seek immediate medical attention. If you have been sexually active during your travels have an STD check on your return home.

Tuberculosis

Medical and aid workers, and long-term travellers who have significant contact with the local population, should take precautions against TB. Vaccination is usually only given to children under the age of five, but adults at risk are recommended pre- and post-travel TB testing. The main symptoms are fever, cough, weight loss, night sweats and tiredness.

Typhoid

This serious bacterial infection is spread via food and water. Symptoms are a high and slowly progressive fever, headache and it may be accompanied by a dry cough and stomach pain. Be aware that vaccination is not 100% effective so you must still be careful with what you eat and drink. All travellers to China should be vaccinated.

TRAVELLER'S DIARRHOEA

Traveller's diarrhoea is by far the most common problem affecting travellers – between 30% to 50% of people will suffer from it within two weeks of starting their trip. In most cases, traveller's diarrhoea is caused by a bacteria (there are numerous potential culprits), and therefore responds promptly to treatment with antibiotics. Treatment with

antibiotics will depend on your situation – how sick you are, how quickly you need to get better, where you are etc.

Traveller's diarrhoea is defined as the passage of more than three watery bowel-actions within 24 hours, plus at least one other symptom such as fever, cramps, nausea, vomiting or feeling generally unwell.

Treatment consists of staying well hydrated; rehydration solutions like Gastrolyte are the best for this. Antibiotics such as Norfloxacin, Ciprofloxacin or Azithromycin will kill the bacteria quickly.

Loperamide is just a 'stopper' and doesn't get to the cause of the problem. It can be helpful, for example if you have to go on a long bus ride. Don't take Loperamide if you have a fever, or blood in your stools. Seek medical attention quickly if you do not respond to an appropriate antibiotic.

Amoebic Dysentery

Amoebic dysentery is actually rare in travellers but is often misdiagnosed. Symptoms are similar to bacterial diarrhoea, ie fever, bloody diarrhoea and generally feeling unwell. You should always seek reliable medical care if you have blood in your diarrhoea. Treatment involves two drugs: Tinidazole or Metronidazole to kill the parasite in your gut, and then a second drug to kill the cysts. If left untreated complications such as liver or gut abscesses can occur.

Giardiasis

Giardia is a parasite that is relatively common in travellers. Symptoms include nausea, bloating, excess gas, fatigue and intermittent diarrhoea. 'Eggy' burps are often attributed solely to giardia, but work in Nepal has shown that they are not specific to giardia. The parasite will eventually go away if left untreated but this can take months. The treatment of choice is Tinidazole, with Metronidazole being a second option.

Intestinal Worms

These parasites are most common in rural, tropical areas. Some may be ingested on food such as undercooked meat (eg tapeworms) and some enter through your skin (eg hookworms). Infestations may not show up for some time, and although they are generally not serious, if left untreated some can cause severe health problems later. Consider

HEALTH

having a stool test when you return home to check for these and to determine the appropriate treatment.

ENVIRONMENTAL HAZARDS
Altitude Sickness

There are bus journeys in Tibet, Qīnghǎi and Xīnjiāng where the road goes over 5000m. Acclimatising to such extreme elevations takes several weeks at least, but most travellers come up from sea level very fast – a bad move! Acute mountain sickness (AMS) results from a rapid ascent to altitudes above 2700m. It usually commences within 24 to 48 hours of arriving at altitude and symptoms include headache, nausea, fatigue and loss of appetite (it very much feels like a hangover). If you have altitude sickness the cardinal rule is that you must not go higher as you are sure to get sicker and could develop one of the more severe and potentially deadly forms of the disease. These are high altitude pulmonary oedema (HAPE) and high altitude cerebral oedema (HACE). Both of these forms of altitude sickness are medical emergencies and there are no rescue facilities similar to those in the Nepal Himalaya here, so prevention is the best policy. AMS can be prevented by 'graded ascent' – it is recommended that once you are above 3000m you ascend a maximum of 300m daily and have an extra rest day every 1000m. You can also use a medication called Diamox as a prevention or treatment for AMS after discussion with a doctor experienced in altitude medicine. Diamox should not be taken by people with a sulphur drug allergy.

If you have altitude sickness you should rest where you are for a day or two until your symptoms resolve. You can then carry on, but ensure you follow the graded ascent guidelines. If symptoms are getting worse you must descend immediately before you are faced with a life-threatening situation. There is no way of predicting who will suffer from AMS but certain factors predispose you to it – rapid ascent; carrying a heavy load and working hard; and having a seemingly minor illness such as a chest infection or diarrhoea. Make sure you drink at least 3L of noncaffeinated drinks daily to stay well hydrated. The sun is intense at altitude so take care with sun protection and ensure you have adequate clothing to

---

DRINKING WATER

- Never drink tap water.
- Bottled water is generally safe – check the seal is intact at purchase.
- Avoid ice.
- Avoid fresh juices – they may have been watered down.
- Boiling water is the most efficient method of purifying it.
- The best chemical purifier is iodine. It should not be used by pregnant women or those with thyroid problems.
- Water filters should also filter out viruses. Ensure your filter has a chemical barrier such as iodine and a small pore size, eg less than four microns.

---

avoid hypothermia – temperatures drop rapidly once the sun goes down and winds can be intense.

Food

Eating in restaurants is the biggest risk factor for contracting traveller's diarrhoea. Ways to avoid it include eating only freshly cooked food, and avoiding food that has been sitting around in buffets. Peel all fruit, cook vegetables, and soak salads in iodine water for at least 20 minutes. Eat in busy restaurants with a high turnover of customers.

Heat Exhaustion

Dehydration or salt deficiency can cause heat exhaustion. Take time to acclimatise to high temperatures, drink sufficient liquids and do not do anything too physically demanding.

Salt deficiency is characterised by fatigue, lethargy, headaches, giddiness and muscle cramps; salt tablets may help, but adding extra salt to your food is better.

Hypothermia

Too much cold can be just as dangerous as too much heat. If you are trekking at high altitudes or simply taking a long bus trip over mountains, particularly at night, be aware. In Tibet it can go from being mildly warm to blisteringly cold in a matter of minutes – blizzards have a way of just coming out of nowhere. If you're out walking, cycling or hitching, this can be dangerous.

It is surprisingly easy to progress from very cold to dangerously cold due to a combination of wind, wet clothing, fatigue and hunger, even if the air temperature is above freezing. It is best to dress in layers; silk, wool and some of the new artificial fibres are all good insulating materials. A hat is important, as a lot of heat is lost through the head. A strong, waterproof outer layer (and a space blanket for emergencies) is essential. Carry basic supplies, including food containing simple sugars to generate heat quickly and fluid to drink.

Symptoms of hypothermia are exhaustion, numb skin (particularly the toes and fingers), shivering, slurred speech, irrational or violent behaviour, lethargy, stumbling, dizzy spells, muscle cramps and violent bursts of energy.

To treat mild hypothermia, first get the person out of the wind and/or rain, remove their clothing if it's wet and replace it with dry, warm clothing. Give them hot liquids – not alcohol – and some high-calorie, easily digestible food. The early recognition and treatment of mild hypothermia is the only way to prevent severe hypothermia, which is a critical condition and requires medical attention.

Insect Bites & Stings

Bedbugs don't carry disease but their bites are very itchy. They live in the cracks of furniture and walls and then migrate to the bed at night to feed on you. You can treat the itch with an antihistamine. Lice inhabit various parts of your body but most commonly your head and pubic area. Transmission is via close contact with an infected person. They can be difficult to treat and you may need numerous applications of an anti-lice shampoo such as permethrin. Pubic lice are usually contracted from sexual contact.

Ticks are contracted after walking in rural areas. Ticks are commonly found behind the ears, on the belly and in armpits. If you have had a tick bite and experience symptoms such as a rash at the site of the bite or elsewhere, fever or muscle aches you should see a doctor. Doxycycline prevents some tick-borne diseases.

WOMEN'S HEALTH

Pregnant women should receive specialised advice before travelling. The ideal time to travel is in the second trimester (between 14 and 28 weeks), when the risk of pregnancy-related problems is at its lowest and pregnant women generally feel at their best. During the first trimester there is a risk of miscarriage and in the third trimester complications such as premature labour and high blood pressure are possible. It's wise to travel with a companion. Always carry a list of quality medical facilities available at your destination and ensure you continue your standard antenatal care at these facilities. Avoid rural travel in areas with poor transportation and medical facilities. Most of all, ensure travel insurance covers all pregnancy-related possibilities, including premature labour.

Malaria is a high-risk disease in pregnancy. WHO recommends that pregnant women do *not* travel to areas with Chloroquine-resistant malaria.

Traveller's diarrhoea can quickly lead to dehydration and result in inadequate blood flow to the placenta. Many of the drugs used to treat various diarrhoea bugs are not recommended in pregnancy. Azithromycin is considered safe.

Supplies of sanitary products may not be readily available in rural areas. Birth control options may be limited so bring adequate supplies of your own form of contraception. Heat, humidity and antibiotics can all contribute to thrush. Treatment is with antifungal creams and pessaries such as Clotrimazole. A practical alternative is a single tablet of Fluconazole (Diflucan). Urinary tract infections can be precipitated by dehydration or long bus journeys without toilet stops; bring suitable antibiotics.

TRADITIONAL MEDICINE

Traditional Chinese medicine (TCM) views the human body as an energy system in which the basic substances of *qì* (vital energy), *jīng* (essence), *xuè* (blood, the body's nourishing fluids) and *tǐyè* (body fluids; blood and other organic fluids) function. The concept of Yin and Yang is fundamental to the system. Disharmony between Yin and Yang or within the basic substances may be a result of internal causes (emotions), external causes (climatic conditions) or miscellaneous causes (work, exercise, sex etc). Treatment modalities include acupuncture, massage, herbs, diet and *qìgōng* and aim to bring these elements back into balance. These therapies are particularly useful for treating chronic diseases and are gaining interest and respect in the Western medical system. Conditions that can be particularly suitable for traditional methods

include chronic fatigue, arthritis, irritable bowel syndrome and some chronic skin conditions.

Be aware that 'natural' doesn't always mean 'safe', and there can be drug interactions between herbal medicines and Western medicines. If you are utilising both systems ensure you inform both practitioners what the other has prescribed.

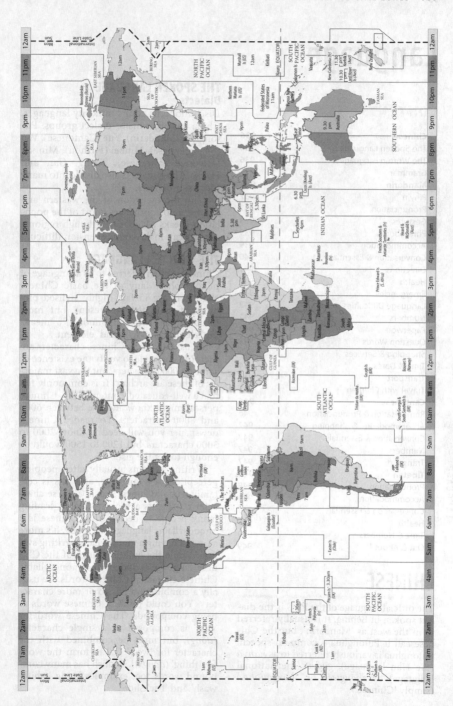

Language

CONTENTS

CHINESE

The official language of the PRC is the dialect spoken in Běijīng. It is usually referred to in the west as 'Mandarin', but the Chinese call it Putonghua – common speech. Putonghua is variously referred to as *hànyǔ* (the Han language), *guóyǔ* (the national language) or *zhōngwén* or *zhōngguóhuà* (simply 'Chinese').

THE SPOKEN LANGUAGE
Dialects

Discounting its ethnic minority languages, China has eight major dialect groups: Putonghua (Mandarin), Yue (Cantonese), Wu (Shanghainese), Minbei (Fuzhou), Minnan (Hokkien-Taiwanese), Xiang, Gan and Hakka. These dialects also divide into many more sub-dialects.

With the exception of the western and southernmost provinces, most of the population speaks Mandarin, although regional accents can make comprehension difficult.

THE WRITTEN LANGUAGE

Chinese is often referred to as a language of pictographs. Many of the basic Chinese characters are in fact highly stylised pictures of what they represent, but most (around 90%) are compounds of a 'meaning' element and a 'sound' element.

So just how many Chinese characters are there? It's possible to verify the existence of some 56,000 characters, but the vast majority of these are archaic. It is commonly felt that a well-educated, contemporary Chinese person might know and use between 6000 and 8000 characters. To read a Chinese newspaper you will need to know 2000 to 3000 characters, but 1200 to 1500 would be enough to get the gist.

Writing systems usually alter people's perception of a language, and this is certainly true of Chinese. Each Chinese character represents a spoken syllable, leading many people to declare that Chinese is a 'monosyllabic language.' Actually, it's more a case of having a monosyllabic writing system. While the building block of the Chinese language is indeed the monosyllabic Chinese character, Chinese words are usually a combination of two or more characters. You could think of Chinese words as being compounds. The Chinese word for 'east' is composed of a single character (*dōng*), but must be combined with the character for 'west' (*xī*) to form the word for 'thing' (*dōngxī*). English has many compound words too, examples being 'whitewash' and 'backslide'.

Theoretically, all Chinese dialects share the same written system. In practice, Cantonese adds about 3000 specialised characters of its own and many of the dialects don't have a written form at all.

Simplification
In the interests of promoting universal literacy, the Committee for Reforming the Chinese Language was set up by the Běijīng government in 1954. Around 2200 Chinese characters were simplified. Chinese communities outside China (notably Taiwan and Hong Kong), however, continue to use the traditional, full-form characters.

Over the past few years – probably as a result of large-scale investment by overseas Chinese and tourism – full-form or 'complex' characters have returned to China. These are mainly seen in advertising (where the traditional characters are considered more attractive) and on restaurant, hotel and shop signs.

GRAMMAR
Chinese grammar is much simpler than that of European languages. There are no articles (a/the), no tenses and no plurals. The basic point to bear in mind is that, like English, Chinese word order is subject-verb-object. In other words, a basic English sentence like 'I (subject) love (verb) you (object)' is constructed in exactly the same way in Chinese. The catch is mastering the tones.

MANDARIN

PINYIN
In 1958 the Chinese adopted a system of writing their language using the Roman alphabet. It's known as *pīnyīn*. The original idea was to eventually do away with characters. However, tradition dies hard, and the idea has been abandoned.

Pinyin is often used on shop fronts, street signs and advertising billboards. Don't expect Chinese people to be able to use Pinyin, however. There are indications that the use of the Pinyin system is diminishing.

In the countryside and the smaller towns you may not see a single Pinyin sign anywhere, so unless you speak Chinese you'll need a phrasebook with Chinese characters.

Since 1979 all translated texts of Chinese diplomatic documents, as well as Chinese magazines published in foreign languages, have used the Pinyin system for spelling names and places. Pinyin replaces the old Wade-Giles and Lessing systems of Romanising Chinese script. Thus under Pinyin, 'Mao Tse-tung' becomes Mao Zedong; 'Chou En-lai' becomes Zhou Enlai; and 'Peking' becomes Běijīng. The name of the country remains as it has been written most often: 'China' in English and German, and 'Chine' in French – in Pinyin it's correctly written as Zhōngguó.

Now that Hong Kong (a Romanisation of Cantonese for 'fragrant harbour') has gone over to China, many think it will only be a matter of time before it gets renamed Xiānggǎng. For more on Pinyin, see p938.

PRONUNCIATION
Vowels
a	as in 'father'
ai	as in 'aisle'
ao	as the 'ow' in 'cow'
e	as in 'her', with no 'r' sound
ei	as in 'weigh'
i	as the 'ee' in 'meet' (or like the 'oo' in 'book' after **c, ch, r, s, sh, z** or **zh**)
ian	as the word 'yen'
ie	as the English word 'yeah'
o	as in 'or', with no 'r' sound
ou	as the 'oa' in 'boat'
u	as in 'flute'
ui	as the word 'way'
uo	like a 'w' followed by 'o'
yu/ü	like 'ee' with lips pursed

Consonants
c	as the 'ts' in 'bits'
ch	as in 'chop', but with the tongue curled up and back
h	as in 'hay', but articulated from farther back in the throat
q	as the 'ch' in 'cheese'
r	as the 's' in 'pleasure'
sh	as in 'ship', but with the tongue curled up and back
x	as in 'ship'
z	as the 'dz' in 'suds'
zh	as the 'j' in 'judge' but with the tongue curled up and back

The only consonants that occur at the end of a syllable are **n, ng** and **r**.

PINYIN

While there are many dialects across China, the one thing all Chinese speakers have in common is their written language. Efforts have been made over the last 100 years to reform the written language, and a system called Pinyin (literally meaning 'spell sound') was invented last century as the standard for spelling Chinese characters. While Pinyin started life as a communist ploy to unite the peoples and popularise Mandarin within China, in its short life it has become the United Nations standard for 'spelling' Chinese characters, and for transliterating the names of people, places and scientific terms. Taiwan initially promulgated a different system of Romanisation, but recently announced that it was switching to the communist-designed Pinyin system, falling into line with the rest of the world.

Pinyin was not the first foray into spelling out Chinese characters. As early as the 17th century, foreign missionaries sought effective ways to spread the word and various spelling systems arose; even the Bible was reproduced in such scripts. In the late 19th century the Chinese themselves started to explore the issue of phonetic spelling systems. In 1933 the communists worked with a Russian and designed what they called Latinised New Script. This was based on Mandarin pronunciation and in 1958 the communist government implemented this as the official system, coinciding with its decision to adopt Mandarin as the official language of China. This new script came to be known as Pinyin. The government's prime purpose for adopting a Roman alphabet pronunciation of Chinese characters was to promote Mandarin throughout the nation. Although Mandarin was the the language of government, it had previously only enjoyed the same status as numerous other dialects spoken in China. A secondary purpose was to enable non-Chinese ethnic groups in China to create or reform their languages with a common base.

Another, less important, aim of Pinyin was to assist foreigners to learn Chinese. As foreign language learners will tell you, Pinyin is a fantastic tool, particularly at the beginning of a quest on the road to fluency. Unlike English, once you learn the Pinyin pronunciation system it is completely consistent. However, once the pronunciation system is learnt, problems start to arise: for one, Pinyin does not itself indicate tones (Mandarin has four tones) and there may be dozens of characters represented by one Pinyin word: for example there are about 80 dictionary entries for the word pronounced and written *yi*. Luckily, context and grammatical structure, as well as the formation of compound words when *yi* combines with other sounds, usually give a few clues as to which of the 80 possibilities is meant. To assist travellers, this book has used tones throughout for towns, cities, sights, hotels, restaurants and entertainment venues.

Pinyin has permeated some groups in Chinese society, but most ordinary Chinese cannot use it very effectively, and some people argue that Pinyin is for foreigners. For those travelling in China using either this book or the Lonely Planet *Mandarin Phrasebook*, the ability to use Pinyin and the government's regulation that all signs be in Pinyin and characters, will be a blessing.
Charles Qin

In Pinyin, apostrophes are occasionally used to separate syllables in order to prevent ambiguity, eg the word *píng'ān* can be written with an apostrophe after the 'g' to prevent it being pronounced as *pín'gān*.

Tones

Chinese is a language with a large number of words with the same pronunciation but a different meaning; what distinguishes these 'homophones' is their 'tonal' quality – the raising and lowering of pitch on certain syllables. Mandarin has four tones – high, rising, falling-rising and falling, plus a fifth 'neutral' tone which you can all but ignore. To illustrate the importance of getting tones right, look at the word *ma*, which has four different meanings according to tone:

high tone	mā (mother)
rising tone	má (hemp, numb)
falling-rising tone	mǎ (horse)
falling tone	mà (scold, swear)

Mastering tones is tricky for newcomers to Mandarin, but with a little practice it can be done.

GESTURES

Hand signs are frequently used in China. The 'thumbs-up' sign has a long tradition as an indication of excellence. Another way to

CHINESE SAYINGS

Chinese is an extremely rich idiomatic language. Many sayings are four-character phrases that combine a great balance of rhythm and tone with a clever play on the multiple meanings of similar-sounding characters. Perhaps most interesting is how many phrases have direct English equivalents.

缘木求鱼 (yuánmù qiúyú)
Like climbing a tree to catch fish (a waste of time)

问道于盲 (wèndào yú máng)
Like asking a blind man for directions (another waste of time)

新瓶装旧酒 (xīnpíng zhuāng jiùjiǔ)
A new bottle filled with old wine (a superficial change)

坐井观天 (zuòjǐng guāntiān)
Like looking at the sky from the bottom of a well (not seeing the whole picture)

水落石出 (shuǐluò shíchū)
When the tide goes out the rocks are revealed (the truth will out)

守株待兔 (shǒuzhū dàitù)
Like a hunter waiting for a rabbit to kill itself by running into a tree (trusting to dumb luck)

临阵磨枪 (línjùn móqiāng)
To not sharpen your weapons until the battle is upon you (to do things at the last minute)

热锅上的蚂蚁 (règuōshàng demǎyǐ)
Like ants on top of a hot stove (full of worries)

殊途同归 (shūtú tóngguī)
Different roads all reach the same end

同床异梦 (tóngchuáng yìmèng)
To sleep in the same bed but have different dreams (different strokes for different folks)

削足适履 (xiāozú shìlǚ)
Like trimming the foot to fit the shoe

种瓜得瓜 (zhòngguā déguā)
If a man plants melons, so will he reap melons

酒肉朋友 (jiǔròu péngyou)
An eating and drinking friend (fair-weather friend)

晴天霹雳 (qíngtiān pīlì)
Like thunder from a blue sky (a bolt from the blue)

沐猴而冠 (mù hóu ér guàn)
A monkey dressed in a tall hat (a petty official)

燃眉之急 (ránméi zhījí)
A fire that is burning one's eyebrows (extremely urgent)

---

indicate excellence is to gently pull your ear lobe between your thumb and index finger.

PHRASEBOOKS

Phrasebooks are invaluable, but sometimes seeking help by showing a phrase to someone can result in them wanting to read every page! Reading place names or street signs isn't difficult, since the Chinese name is usually accompanied by the Pinyin form; if not, you'll soon learn lots of characters just by repeated exposure. A small dictionary with English, Pinyin and Chinese characters is also useful for learning a few words.

Lonely Planet's *Mandarin Phrasebook* has script throughout and loads of useful phrases – it's also a very useful learning tool.

ACCOMMODATION

I'm looking for a ...
Wǒyào zhǎo ... 我要找 . . .
  camping ground
  lùyíngdì 露营地
  guesthouse
  bīnguǎn 宾馆

hotel
lǚguǎn 旅馆
tourist hotel
bīnguǎn/fàndiàn/jiǔdiàn 宾馆/饭店/酒店
hostel
zhāodàisuǒ/lǚshè 招待所/旅社
youth hostel
qīngnián lǚshè 青年旅舍

Where is a cheap hotel?
Nǎr yǒu piányì de lǚguǎn?
哪儿有便宜的旅馆?
What is the address?
Dìzhǐ zài nǎr?
地址在哪儿?
Could you write the address, please?
Néngbúnéng qǐng nǐ bǎ dìzhǐ xiě xiàlái?
能不能请你把地址写下来?
Do you have a room available?
Nǐmen yǒu fángjiān ma?
你们有房间吗?

I'd like (a) ...
Wǒ xiǎng yào ... 我想要 . . .
  bed
  yí ge chuángwèi 一个床位

single room
yìjiān dānrénfáng 一间单人房
double room
yìjiān shuāngrénfáng 一间双人房
bed for two
shuāngrén chuáng 双人床
room with two beds
shuāngrénfáng 双人房
economy room (no bath)
pǔtōngfáng (méiyǒu yùshì) 普通房(没有浴室)
room with a bathroom
yǒu yùshìde fángjiān 有浴室的房间
standard room
biāozhǔn fángjiān 标准房间
deluxe suite
háohuá tàofáng 豪华套房
to share a dorm
zhù sùshè 住宿舍

How much is it ...?
... duōshǎo qián ...多少钱?
per night
měitiān wǎnshàng 每天晚上
per person
měigerén 每个人

May I see the room?
Wǒ néng kànkan fángjiān ma?
我能看看房间吗?
Where is the bathroom?
Yùshì zài nǎr?
浴室在哪儿?
Where is the toilet?
Cèsuǒ zài nǎr?
厕所在哪儿?
I don't like this room.
Wǒ bù xǐhuān zhèijiān fángjiān.
我不喜欢这间房间
Are there any messages for me?
Yǒu méiyǒu rén gěi wǒ liú huà?
有没有人给我留话?
May I have a hotel namecard?
Yǒu méiyǒu lǚguǎn de míngpiàn?
有没有旅馆的名片?
Could I have these clothes washed, please?
Qǐng bǎ zhè xiē yīfu xǐ gānjìng, hǎo ma?
请把这些衣服洗干净, 好吗?
I'm/We're leaving today.
Wǒ/Wǒmen jīntiān líkāi.
我/我们今天离开

CONVERSATION & ESSENTIALS

Hello. *Nǐ hǎo.* 你好
Nín hǎo. (pol) 您好
Goodbye. *Zàijiàn.* 再见
Please. *Qǐng.* 请

CHINGLISH

Help!
Initially you might be puzzled by a sign in the bathroom that reads 'Please don't take the odds and ends put into the nightstool'. In fact this is a warning to resist sudden impulses to empty the contents of your pockets or backpack into the toilet. An apparently ambiguous sign with anarchic implications like the one in the Lhasa Bank of China, 'Question Authority', is really just an economical way of saying 'Please address your questions to one of the clerks'.

On the other hand, just to confuse things, a company name like the 'Risky Investment Co' means just what it says. An English-Chinese dictionary proudly proclaims in the preface that it is 'very useful for the using'. And a beloved sign in the Liangmao Hotel in Tài'ān proclaims:

Safety Needing Attention!
Be care of depending fire
Sweep away six injurious insect
Pay attention to civilisation

If this all sounds confusing, don't worry. It won't be long before you have a small armoury of Chinglish phrases of your own. Before you know it, you'll know without even thinking that 'Be careful not to be stolen' is a warning against thieves; that 'Shoplifters will be fined 10 times' means that shoplifting is not a good idea in China; that 'Do not stroke the works' (generally found in museums) means 'No touching'; and that you 'very like' something means that you like it very much.

The best advice for travellers in China grappling with the complexities of a new language is not to set your sights too high. Bear in mind that it takes a minimum of 15 years of schooling in the Chinese language and a crash course in English to be able to write Chinglish with any fluency.

Thank you. *Xièxie.* 谢谢
Many thanks. *Duōxiè.* 多谢
You're welcome. *Búkèqi.* 不客气
Excuse me, ... *Qǐng wèn, ...* 请问, ...

(When asking a question it is polite to start with the phrase *qǐng wèn* – literally, 'may I ask?' – this expression is only used at the beginning of a sentence, never at the end.)

I'm sorry.
Duìbùqǐ. 对不起

May I ask your name?
Nín guìxìng? 您贵姓?

My (sur)name is ...
Wǒ xìng ... 我姓...

Where are you from?
Nǐ shì cōng nǎr lái de? 你是从哪儿来的?

I'm from ...
Wǒ shì cōng ... lái de. 我是从...来的

I like ...
Wǒ xǐhuān ... 我喜欢...

I don't like ...
Wǒ bù xǐhuān ... 我不喜欢...

Wait a moment.
Děng yíxià. 等一下

Yes & No

There are no specific words in Mandarin that specifically mean 'yes' and 'no' when used in isolation. When asked a question the verb is repeated to indicate the affirmative. A response in the negative is formed by using the word 不 *bù* (meaning 'no') before the verb. When *bù* (falling tone) occurs before another word with a falling tone, it becomes *bú* (ie with a rising tone).

Are you going to Shanghai?
Nǐ qù shànghǎi ma? 你去上海吗?

Yes.
Qù. ('go') 去

No.
Bú qù. ('no go') 不去

No.
Méi yǒu. ('not have') 没有

No.
Búshì. ('not so') 不是

DIRECTIONS

Where is (the) ...?
... zài nǎr? ...在哪儿?

Go straight ahead.
Yìzhí zǒu. 一直走

Turn left.
Zuǒ zhuǎn. 左转

Turn right.
Yòu zhuǎn. 右转

at the next corner
zài xià yíge guǎijiǎo 在下一个拐角

at the traffic lights
zài hónglǜdēng 在红绿灯

map
dìtú 地图

SIGNS		
入口	*Rùkǒu*	Entrance
出口	*Chūkǒu*	Exit
问讯处	*Wènxùnchù*	Information
开	*Kāi*	Open
关	*Guān*	Closed
禁止	*Jìnzhǐ*	Prohibited
有空房	*Yǒu Kòngfáng*	Rooms Available
客满	*Kèmǎn*	No Vacancies
警察	*Jǐngchá*	Police
警察局	*Jǐngchájú*	Police Station
厕所	*Cèsuǒ*	Toilets
男	*Nán*	Men
女	*Nǚ*	Women

Could you show me (on the map)?
Nǐ néng bunéng (zài dìtú shang) zhǐ gěi wǒ kàn?
你能不能(在地图上)指给我看?

behind	*hòubianr*	后边儿
in front of	*qiánbianr*	前边儿
near	*jìn*	近
far	*yuǎn*	远
opposite	*duìmiànr*	对面儿
beach	*hǎitān*	海滩
bridge	*qiáoliáng*	桥梁
island	*dǎoyǔ*	岛屿
main square	*guǎngchǎng*	广场
market	*shìchǎng*	市场
old city	*lǎochéng*	老城
palace	*gōngdiàn*	宫殿
sea	*hǎiyáng*	海洋

HEALTH

I'm sick.
Wǒ bìngle. 我病了

It hurts here.
Zhèr téng. 这儿疼

I need a doctor.
Wǒ děi kàn yīshēng. 我得看医生

Is there a doctor here who speaks English?
Zhèr yǒu huì jiǎng yīngyǔ de dàifu ma?
这儿有会讲英语的大夫吗?

I'm ...
Wǒ yǒu ... 我有...

asthmatic
xiàochuǎnbìng 哮喘病

diabetic
tángniàobìng 糖尿病

epileptic
diānxiánbìng 癫痫病

EMERGENCIES

Help!
Jiùmìng a! 救命啊!
emergency
jǐnjí qíngkuàng 紧急情况
There's been an accident!
Chūshìle! 出事了!
I'm lost.
Wǒ mílùle. 我迷路了
Go away!
Zǒu kāi! 走开!
Leave me alone!
Bié fán wǒ! 别烦我!
Could you help me please?
Nǐ néng bunéng bāng 你能不能帮
wǒ ge máng? 我个忙?
Call ... !
Qǐng jiào ...! 请叫...!
  a doctor
  yīshēng 医生
  the police
  jǐngchá 警察

I'm allergic to ...
Wǒ duì ... guòmǐn. 我对...过敏
  antibiotics
  kàngjūnsù 抗菌素
  aspirin
  āsīpǐlín 阿司匹林
  bee stings
  mìfēng zhēcì 蜜蜂蜇刺
  nuts
  guǒrén 果仁
  penicillin
  qīngméisù 青霉素

antidiarrhoea medicine
zhǐxièyào 止泻药
antiseptic cream
xiāodúgāo 消毒膏
condoms
bìyùn tào 避孕套
contraceptive
bìyùnyào 避孕药
diarrhoea
lā dùzi 拉肚子
headache
tóuteng 头疼
medicine
yào 药
sanitary napkins (Kotex)
fùnǚ wèishēngjīn 妇女卫生巾

sunscreen (UV) lotion
fángshàiyóu 防晒油
tampons
yuèjīng miánsāi 月经棉塞

LANGUAGE DIFFICULTIES

Do you speak English?
Nǐ huì shuō yīngyǔ ma?
你会说英语吗?
Does anyone here speak English?
Zhèr yǒu rén huì shuō yīngyǔ ma?
这儿有人会说英语吗?
How do you say ... in Mandarin?
... zhōngwén zěnme shuō?
... 中文怎么说?
What does ... mean?
... shì shénme yìsi?
... 是什么意思?
I understand.
Wǒ tīngdedǒng.
我听得懂
I don't understand.
Wǒ tīngbudǒng.
我听不懂
Please write it down.
Qǐng xiěxiàlai.
请写下来

NUMBERS

0	*líng*	零
1	*yī, yāo*	一, 幺
2	*èr, liǎng*	二, 两
3	*sān*	三
4	*sì*	四
5	*wǔ*	五
6	*liù*	六
7	*qī*	七
8	*bā*	八
9	*jiǔ*	九
10	*shí*	十
11	*shíyī*	十一
12	*shí'èr*	十二
20	*èrshí*	二十
21	*èrshíyī*	二十一
22	*èrshí'èr*	二十二
30	*sānshí*	三十
40	*sìshí*	四十
50	*wǔshí*	五十
60	*liùshí*	六十
70	*qīshí*	七十
80	*bāshí*	八十
90	*jiǔshí*	九十
100	*yìbǎi*	一百
1000	*yìqiān*	一千
2000	*liǎngqiān*	两千

PAPERWORK

name	*xìngmíng*	姓名
nationality	*guójí*	国籍
date of birth	*chūshēng rìqī*	出生日期
place of birth	*chūshēng dìdiǎn*	出生地点
sex (gender)	*xìngbié*	性别
passport	*hùzhào*	护照
passport number	*hùzhào hàomǎ*	护照号码
visa	*qiānzhèng*	签证
extension	*yáncháng*	延长

Public Security Bureau (PSB)
gōng'ānjú	公安局

Foreign Affairs Branch
wàishìkē	外事科

QUESTION WORDS

Who?	*Shuí?*	谁?
What?	*Shénme?*	什么?
What is it?	*Shì shénme?*	是什么?
When?	*Shénme shíhou?*	什么时候?
Where?	*Zài nǎr?*	在哪儿?
Which?	*Něige?*	哪个?
Why?	*Wèishénme?*	为什么?
How?	*Zěnme?*	怎么?

SHOPPING & SERVICES

I'd like to buy ...
Wǒ xiǎng mǎi ...   我想买...

I'm just looking.
Wǒ zhǐshì kànkan.   我只是看看

How much is it?
Duōshǎo qián?   多少钱?

I don't like it.
Wǒ bù xǐhuan.   我不喜欢

Can I see it?
Néng kànkan ma?   能看看吗?

I'll take it.
Wǒ jiù mǎi zhèige.   我就买这个

It's cheap.
Zhè bùguì.   这不贵

That's too expensive.
Tài guìle.   太贵了

Is there anything cheaper?
Yǒu piányi yìdiǎn   有便宜一点
de ma?   的吗?

Can I pay by travellers cheque?
kěyǐ fù lǚxíng zhīpiào   可以付旅行支票吗?
ma?

Do you accept ...?
... shōu bushōu?   收不收...?
  credit cards
  xìnyòngkǎ   信用卡

travellers cheques
lǚxíng zhīpiào   旅行支票

more	*duō*	多
less	*shǎo*	少
smaller	*gèng xiǎo*	更小
bigger	*gèng dà*	更大
too much/many	*tài duō*	太多

Excuse me, where's the nearest ...?
Qǐng wèn, zuìjìnde ... zài nǎr?
请问, 最近的... 在哪儿?
I'm looking for a/the ...
Wǒ zài zhǎo ...   我在找...
  automatic teller machine
  zìdòng guìyuánjī   自动柜员机
  bank
  yínháng   银行
  Bank of China
  zhōngguó yínháng   中国银行
  chemist/pharmacy
  yàodiàn   药店
  city centre
  shìzhōngxīn   市中心
  ... embassy
  ... dàshǐguǎn   ...大使馆
  foreign affairs police
  wàishì jǐngchá   外事警察
  foreign exchange office/currency exchange
  wàihuì duìhuànchù   外汇兑换处
  hospital
  yīyuàn   医院
  hotel
  bīnguǎn/   宾馆/
  fàndiàn/   饭店/
  lǚguǎn   旅馆
  market
  shìchǎng   市场
  museum
  bówùguǎn   博物馆
  police
  jǐngchá   警察
  post office
  yóujú   邮局
  public toilet
  gōnggòng cèsuǒ   公共厕所
  telephone
  diànhuà   电话
  telephone office
  diànxùn dàlóu   电讯大楼
  the tourist office
  lǚyóujú   旅游局

change money
huàn qián   换钱

LANGUAGE

telephone card
  diànhuà kǎ   电话卡
international call
  guójì diànhuà   国际电话
collect call
  duìfāng fùfèi diànhuà   对方付费电话
direct-dial call
  zhíbō diànhuà   直拨电话
fax
  chuánzhēn   传真
computer
  diànnǎo   电脑
email (often called 'email')
  diànzǐyóujiàn   电子邮件
internet
  yīntèwǎng   因特网
  (more formal name)
  (hùliánwǎng)   (互联网)
online
  shàngwǎng   上网

Where can I get online?
Wǒ zài nǎr kěyǐ shàngwǎng?
我在哪儿可以上网?
Can I check my email account?
Wǒ chá yíxià zìjǐ de email hù, hǎo ma?
我查一下自己的email户, 好吗?

TIME & DATES
What's the time?
  Jǐ diǎn?   几点?
... hour ... minute
  ... diǎn ... fēn   . . .点. . .分
3.05
  sān diǎn líng wǔ fēn   三点零五分
When?
  Shénme shíhòu?   什么时候?

now   *xiànzài*   现在
today   *jīntiān*   今天
tomorrow   *míngtiān*   明天
yesterday   *zuótiān*   昨天
in the morning   *zǎoshang*   早上
in the afternoon   *xiàwǔ*   下午
in the evening   *wǎnshang*   晚上
weekend   *zhōumò*   周末

Monday   *xīngqīyī*   星期一
Tuesday   *xīngqī'èr*   星期二
Wednesday   *xīngqīsān*   星期三
Thursday   *xīngqīsì*   星期四
Friday   *xīngqīwǔ*   星期五
Saturday   *xīngqīliù*   星期六
Sunday   *xīngqītiān*   星期天

January   *yīyuè*   一月
February   *èryuè*   二月
March   *sānyuè*   三月
April   *sìyuè*   四月
May   *wǔyuè*   五月
June   *liùyuè*   六月
July   *qīyuè*   七月
August   *bāyuè*   八月
September   *jiǔyuè*   九月
October   *shíyuè*   十月
November   *shíyīyuè*   十一月
December   *shí'èryuè*   十二月

TRANSPORT
Public Transport
airport
  fēijīchǎng   机场
long-distance bus station
  chángtú qìchē zhàn   长途汽车站
subway (underground)
  dìtiě   地铁
subway station
  dìtiě zhàn   地铁站
train station
  huǒchē zhàn   火车站

What time does ... leave/arrive?
  ... jǐdiǎn kāi/dào?   . . .几点开/到?
the boat
  chuán   船
intercity bus; coach
  chángtú qìchē   长途汽车
local/city bus
  gōnggòng qìchē   公共汽车
minibus
  xiǎo gōnggòng qìchē   小公共汽车
microbus taxi
  miànbāochē, miàndī   面包车, 面的
the plane
  fēijī   飞机
train
  huǒchē   火车

I'd like a ...
  Wǒ yào yíge ...   我要一个. . .
one way ticket   *dānchéng piào*   单程票
return ticket   *láihuí piào*   来回票
platform ticket   *zhàntái piào*   站台票
1st class ticket   *tóuděngcāng*   头等舱
2nd class ticket   *èrděngcāng*   二等舱
hard-seat   *yìngxí/yìngzuò*   硬席/硬座
soft-seat   *ruǎnxí/ruǎnzuò*   软席/软座
hard-sleeper   *yìngwò*   硬卧
soft-sleeper   *ruǎnwò*   软卧

LANGUAGE

When's the ... bus?
... bānchē shénme shíhou lái?
... 班车什么时候来?

first	*tóu*	头
last	*mò*	末
next	*xià*	下

I want to go to ...
Wǒ yào qù ...
我要去...

The train has been cancelled/delayed.
Huǒchē tuīchí le/qǔxiāo le.
火车推迟了/取消了

CAAC ticket office
zhōngguó mínháng shòupiào chù
中国民航售票处

boarding pass	*dēngjī kǎ*	登机卡
left-luggage room	*jìcún chù*	寄存处
platform number	*zhàntái hào*	站台号
ticket office	*shòupiào chù*	售票处
timetable	*shíkèbiǎo*	时刻表

Private Transport
I'd like to hire a ...
Wǒ yào zū yíliàng ...
我要租一辆...

car	*qìchē*	汽车
4WD	*sìlún qūdòng*	4轮驱动
motorbike	*mótuōchē*	摩托车
bicycle	*zìxíngchē*	自行车

How much is it per day?
yìtiān duōshǎo qián? 一天多少钱?

How much is it per hour?
yíge xiǎo shí duōshǎo 一个小时多少钱?
qián?

How much is the deposit?
yājīn duōshǎo qián? 押金多少钱?

Does this road lead to ...?
Zhè tiáo lù dào ...? 这条路到...?

road	*lù*	路
section	*duàn*	段
street	*jiē/dàjiē*	街/大街
No 21	*21 hào*	21号

Where's the next service station?
xià yíge jiāyóuzhàn zài nǎr?
下一个加油站在哪儿?

Please fill it up.
Qǐng jiāmǎn yóuxiāng.
请加满油箱

I'd like ... litres.
Wǒ yào ... gōngshēng.
我要...公升

减速让行	*Jiǎnsù Mànxíng*	Give way
绕行	*Ràoxíng*	Detour
不得入内	*Bùdé Rùnèi*	No Entry
不得超车	*Bùdé Chāochē*	No Overtaking
不得停车	*Bùdé Tíngchē*	No Parking
入口	*Rùkǒu*	Entrance
保持畅通	*Bǎochí Chàngtōng*	Keep Clear
收费	*Shōufèi*	Toll
危险	*Wēixiǎn*	Danger
减速慢行	*Jiǎnsù Mànxíng*	Slow Down
单行道	*Dānxíngdào*	One Way
出口	*Chūkǒu*	Exit

diesel	*cháiyóu*	柴油
leaded petrol	*hánqiān qìyóu*	含铅汽油
unleaded petrol	*wúqiān qìyóu*	无铅汽油

How long can I park here?
Zhèr kěyǐ tíng duōjiǔ? 这儿可以停多久?

Can I park here?
Zhèr kěyǐ tíngchē ma? 这儿可以停车吗?

Where do I pay?
Zài nǎr fùkuǎn? 在哪儿付款?

I need a mechanic.
Wǒ xūyào jīxiūgōng. 我需要机修工

We need a mechanic.
Wǒmen xūyào jīxiūgōng 我们需要机修工

The car has broken down (at ...)
Qìchē shì (zài ...) huài de. 汽车是(在...)坏的

The car won't start.
Qìchē fādòng bùqǐlái. 汽车发动不起来

I have a flat tyre.
Lúntāi biě le. 轮胎瘪了

I've run out of petrol.
Méiyou qìyóu le. 没有汽油了

I had an accident.
Wǒ chū shìgù le. 我出事故了

TRAVEL WITH CHILDREN
Is there a/an ...?
Yǒu ... ma? 有...吗?

I need a/an ...
Wǒ xūyào ... 我需要...

baby change room
yīng'ér huànxǐshì 婴儿换洗室

baby food
yīngér shípǐn 婴儿食品

baby formula (milk)
pèifāngnǎi 配方奶

baby's bottle
nǎipíng 奶瓶

child-minding service
tuōér fúwù   托儿服务
chidren's menu
értóng càidān   儿童菜单
(disposable) nappies/diapers
(yícìxìng) niàopiàn   (一次性)尿片
(English-speaking) babysitter
(huì shuō yīngwén de) (会说英文的)
  yīng'ér bǎomǔ   婴儿保姆
highchair
yīng'ér gāojiǎoyǐ   婴儿高脚椅
potty
yīng'ér biànpén   婴儿便盆
pusher/stroller
yīng'ér tuīchē   婴儿推车

Do you mind if I breastfeed here?
Wǒ kěyǐ zài zhèr wèi nǎi ma?
我可以在这儿喂奶吗？
Are children allowed?
Yǔnxǔ értóng ma?
允许儿童吗？

CANTONESE

What a difference a border makes. Cantonese is still the most popular dialect in Hong Kong, Guǎngzhōu and the surrounding area. It differs from Mandarin as much as French differs from Spanish. Speakers of both dialects can read Chinese characters, but a Cantonese speaker will pronounce many of the characters differently from a Mandarin speaker. For example, when Mr Ng from Hong Kong goes to Běijīng the Mandarin-speakers will call him Mr Wu. If Mr Wong goes from Hong Kong to Fújiàn the character for his name will be read as Mr Wee, and in Běijīng he is Mr Huang.

For a more detailed guide to Cantonese, with script throughout, loads of phrases, and information on grammar and pronunciation, get a copy of Lonely Planet's *Cantonese Phrasebook*.

ROMANISATION & PRONUNCIATION

Unfortunately, several competing systems of Romanisation of Cantonese script exist and no single one has emerged as an official standard. A number have come and gone, but at least three have survived and are currently used in Hong Kong: Meyer-Wempe, Sidney Lau and Yale. In this language guide we use the Yale system. It's the most phonetically accurate and the one generally preferred by foreign students.

Vowels
Note that the examples given below for the pronunciation of vowels reflect British pronunciation.

a	as in 'father'
ai	as the 'i' in 'find', but shorter
au	as the 'ow' in 'cow'
e	as in 'let'
ei	as the 'a' in 'say', but without the 'y' sound
eu	similar to the 'ur' in 'urn' with lips pursed, but without the 'r' sound
i	as in 'marine'
iu	similar to the word 'you'
o	as in 'not'; as in 'no' when at the end of a word
oi	as the 'oy' in 'boy'
oo	as in 'soon'
ou	as the word 'owe'
u	as in 'put'
ue	as the 'u-e' in 'suet'
ui	as 'oo-ee'

Consonants
In general, consonants are pronounced as in English. Three that may give you a little trouble are:

g	as in 'go'
j	as the 'ds' in 'suds'
ng	as in 'sing'

Tones
Cantonese has seven tones (although you can easily get by with six). In the Yale system used in this language guide, six basic tones are represented: three 'level' tones, which do not noticeably rise or fall in pitch (high, middle and low), and three 'moving' tones, which either rise or fall in pitch (high rising, low rising and low falling).

Remember that it doesn't matter whether you have a high or low voice when speaking Cantonese as long as your intonation reflects relative changes in pitch. The following examples show the six basic tones. Note how important they can be to your intended meaning:

high tone: represented by a macron above a vowel, as in *fōo* (husband)

middle tone: represented by an unaccented vowel, as in *foo* (wealthy)

low tone: represented by the letter 'h' after a vowel, as in *fooh* (owe); note that 'h' is only pronounced if it occurs at the start of a word; elsewhere it signifies a low tone

middle tone rising: represented by an acute accent, as in *fóo* (tiger)

low falling tone: represented by a grave accent followed by the low tone letter 'h', as in *fòoh* (to lean)

low rising tone: represented by an acute accent and the low tone letter 'h', as in *fóoh* (woman)

ACCOMMODATION & SHOPPING
Do you have any rooms available?
　yáhùh mó fóng a?
　有冇房呀？
I'd like a (single/double) room.
　ngóh séuhng yiùh yāt gāàhn (dāàhn yàhn/sèùhng yàhn) fóng
　我想要一間（單人／雙人）房？
How much per night?
　gēih dōh chín yāt máhàhn a?
　幾多錢一晚呀？
How much is this?
　nī goh gēih dōh chín a?
　呢個幾多錢呀？
That's very expensive.
　hó gwaìh
　好貴
Can you reduce the price?
　pèhng dī dāk m dāk a?
　平啲得唔得呀？
I'm just looking.
　ngóh sīn táìh yāt táìh
　我先睇一睇

CONVERSATION & ESSENTIALS
Hello, how are you?
　néhìh hó ma?
　你好嗎？
Fine, and you?
　gēih hó, néhìh nē?
　幾好，你呢？
Good morning.
　jó sàhn
　早晨
Goodbye.
　bàāhìh baàhìh/joìh gin
　拜拜／再見
Thank you very much.
　dōh jē saàhìh/ m gòih saàhìh
　多謝哂／唔該哂
Thanks. (for a gift or special favour)
　dōh jē
　多謝
Thanks. (making a request or purchase)
　m gòih
　唔該
You're welcome.
　m sáìh haàhk hēìh
　唔使客氣

Excuse me. (calling someone's attention)
　m gòih
　唔該
I'm sorry.
　m hó yi si
　唔好意思
What is your surname? (polite)
　chéng mahn gwaìh sìng?
　請問貴姓？
My surname is ...
　síuh sing ...
　小姓...
Is it OK to take a photo?
　hóh m hóh yíh yíng séuhng a?
　可唔可以影相呀？
Do you speak English?
　néhìh sìk m sìk góng yìng mán a?
　你識唔識講英文呀？
I don't understand.
　ngóh m mìhng
　我唔明

Pronouns
I	*ngóh*	我
you	*néhìh*	你
he/she/it	*kúhìh*	佢
we/us	*ngóh dēìh*	我哋
you (plural)	*néhìh dēìh*	你哋
they/them	*kúhìh dēìh*	佢哋

NUMBERS
0	*lìhng*	零
1	*yāt*	一
2	*yìh (léhùhng)*	二（兩）
3	*saāhm*	三
4	*sēih*	四
5	*ng*	五
6	*luhk*	六
7	*chāt*	七
8	*baàht*	八
9	*gáùh*	九
10	*sahp*	十
11	*sahp yāt*	十一
12	*sahp yìh*	十二
20	*yìh sahp*	二十
21	*yìh sahp yāt*	二十一
100	*yāt baàhk*	一百
101	*yāt baàhk lìhng yāt*	一百零一
110	*yāt baàhk yāt sahp*	一百一十
120	*yāt baàhk yìh sahp*	一百二十
200	*yìh baàhk*	二百
1000	*yāt chīn*	一千
10,000	*yāt màhàhn*	一萬
100,000	*sahp màhàhn*	十萬

TRANSPORT
airport	*gēih chèhùhng*	機場
bus stop	*bā sí jàhàhm*	巴士站
pier	*máh tàhùh*	碼頭

USEFUL PORTUGUESE

A few words in Portuguese will come in handy when travelling in Macau. Portuguese is still common on signs (along with Cantonese script) and where opening and closing times are written.

Monday	segunda-feira		22	vint e dois
Tuesday	terça-feira		30	trinta
Wednesday	quarta-feira		40	quarenta
Thursday	quinta-feira		50	cinquenta
Friday	sexta-feira		60	sessenta
Saturday	sábado		70	setenta
Sunday	domingo		80	oitenta
			90	noventa
1	um/uma		100	cem
2	dois/duas		1000	mil
3	três			
4	quatro			
5	cinco		Entrance	Entrada
6	seis		Exit	Saída
7	sete		Open	Aberto
8	oito		Closed	Encerrado
9	nove		No Smoking	Não Fumadores
10	dez		Prohibited	Proíbido
11	onze		Toilets	Lavabos/WC
20	vint		Men	Homens (H)
21	vint e um		Women	Senhoras (S)

---

subway station	dēìh tit jahàhm	地鐵站
north	bāk	北
south	nàhàhm	南
east	dūng	東
west	sāìh	西

I'd like to go to ...
ngóh séùhng huìh ...   我想去...
Where is the ...?
... hàih bìn doh a?   ...喺邊度呀?
Does this (bus, train etc) go to ...?
huìh m huìh ... a?   去唔去...呀?
How much is the fare?
gêih dōh chín a?   幾多錢呀?
Please write down the address for me.
m gòih sé goh dēìh jí   唔該寫個地址俾我
bēìh ngóh

TIBETAN

PRONUNCIATION
Tibetan has its fair share of tricky pronunciations. There are quite a few consonant clusters, and Tibetan makes an important distinction between aspirated and unaspirated consonants.

Lonely Planet's *Tibetan Phrasebook* has script throughout and is an excellent tool for those wishing to learn the language in greater depth.

Vowels
The following pronunciation guide reflects standard British pronunciation.

a	as in 'father'
ay	as in 'play'
e	as in 'met'
ee	as in 'meet'
i	as in 'big'
o	as in 'go'
oo	as in 'soon'
ö	as the 'u' in 'fur', with no 'r' sound
ü	as in 'flute'

Consonants
With the exception of those listed below, Tibetan consonants should be pronounced as in English. Where consonants are followed by an 'h', it means that the consonant is aspirated (ie accompanied by an audible puff of air). An English example might be 'kettle', where the 'k' is aspirated and the 'tt'

is unaspirated. The distinction is fairly important, but in simple Tibetan the context should make it clear what you're talking about even if you get the sounds muddled up a bit.

ky	as the 'kie' in 'Kiev'
ng	as the 'ng' in 'sing'
r	produced with a slight trill
ts	as the 'ts' in 'bits'

ACCOMMODATION

guesthouse	dhön-khang
hotel	drü-khang/fan-dian
Do you have a room?	kang mi yöpe?
How much is it for one night?	tsen chik la katsö ray?
I'd like to stay with a Tibetan family.	nga phöbe mitsang nyemdo dendö yö

CONVERSATION & ESSENTIALS

Hello.	tashi dele
Goodbye. (to person leaving)	kale phe
Goodbye. (by person leaving)	kale shoo
Thank you.	thoo jaychay
Yes, OK.	la ong
I'm sorry.	gonda
I want ...	nga la ... go
Do you speak English?	injeeke shing gi yö pe?
Do you understand?	ha ko song-ngey?
I understand.	ha ko song
I don't understand.	ha ko ma song
How much?	ka tsö ray?
It's expensive.	gong chenpo ray
What's your name?	kerang gi ming lakary zer gi yö?
My name is ...	ngai ... ming la
... and you?	... a ni kerang zer gi yö?
Where are you from?	kerang lungba ka-nay yin?
I'm from ...	nga ...-nay yin

I	nga
you	kerang
he/she	khong
we	nga-tso
you all	kerang-tso
they	khong-tso

HEALTH

I'm sick.	nga bedo mindu
Please call a doctor.	amchi ke tongda
altitude sickness	lâdu na
diarrhoea	troko she
fever	tsawa
hospital	menkang

TIME & NUMBERS

What's the time?	chutsö katsö ray?
hour/minute	chutsö/karma
When?	kadü?
now	thanda
today	thiring
tomorrow	sangnyi
yesterday	kesa
morning	shogay
afternoon	nying gung gyab la
evening/night	gonta

Note: to form compound numbers, add the appropriate number for one to nine after the word in brackets, eg 21 is *nyi shu tsa chig*, 32 is *sum shu so nyi*.

1	chig
2	nyi
3	sum
4	shi
5	nga
6	troo
7	dün
8	gye
9	gu
10	chu
11	chu chig
20	nyi shu (tsa ...)
30	sum shu (so ...)
40	shi chu (shay ...)
50	nga chu (ngay ...)
60	doog chu (ray ...)
70	dun chu (don ...)
80	gye chu (gya ...)
90	gu chu (go ...)
100	chig gya
1000	chig tong

OUT & ABOUT

I want to go to ...	nga ... la drondö yö
I'll get off here.	nga phap gi yin
What time do we leave?	ngatso chutsö katsö la dro gi yin?
What time do we arrive?	ngatso chutsö katsö la lep gi yin?
Where can I rent a bicycle?	kanggari kaba ragi ray?
How much per day?	nyima chik laja katsö ray?
Where is the ...?	... kaba yo ray?
I'm lost.	nga lam khag lag song

airport	namdrutang
bicycle	kanggari
bus	lamkhor

right	yeba
left	yönba
straight ahead	shar gya
north	chang
south	lo
east	shar
west	noop
porter	dopo khur khen
pack animal	skel semchen

Geographical Terms

cave	trapoo
hot spring	chuzay
lake	tso
mountain	ree
river	tsangpo
road/trail	lam
valley	loong shon
waterfall	papchu

LANGUAGE

Glossary

(C) Cantonese; (M) Inner Mongolian; (T) Tibetan; (U) Uighur

A

adetki mashina (U) – ordinary bus
ali mashina (U) – soft-seat coach
amah – a servant who cleans houses and looks after the children
apsaras – Buddhist celestial beings, similar to angels
aptoos biket (U) – long-distance bus station
arhat – Buddhist, especially a monk who has achieved enlightenment and passes to nirvana at death

B

báijiǔ – literally 'white alcohol', a type of face-numbing rice wine served at banquets and get-togethers
bāozi – steamed savoury buns with tasty meat filling
běi – north; the other points of the compass are *nán* (south), *dōng* (east) and *xī* (west)
biānjiè – border
biéshù – villa
bīnguǎn – tourist hotel
bìxì – mythical, tortoise like dragon
Bodhisattva – one worthy of nirvana but who remains on earth to help others attain enlightenment
Bön – the pre-Buddhist indigenous faith of Tibet, pockets of which survive in western Sichuān
bówùguǎn – museum

C

CAAC – Civil Aviation Administration of China
cadre – Chinese government bureaucrat
cāntīng – restaurant
cǎoyuán – grasslands
catty – unit of weight, one catty (*jīn*) equals 0.6kg
CCP – Chinese Communist Party, founded in Shànghǎi in 1921
chang (T) – a Tibetan brew made from fermented barley
Chángchéng – the Great Wall
chau (C) – land mass, such as an island
cheongsam (C) – originating in Shànghǎi, a fashionable tight-fitting Chinese dress with a slit up the side
chí – lake, pool
chim (C) – sticks used to divine the future. They're shaken out of a box onto the ground and then 'read'
chop – see *name chop*
chörten – Tibetan stupa, see *stupa*

CITS – China International Travel Service; deals with China's foreign tourists
cohong – a local merchants' guild
CTS – China Travel Service; originally set up to handle tourists from Hong Kong, Macau, Taiwan and overseas Chinese
cūn – village
CYTS – China Youth Travel Service

D

dàdào – boulevard
dàfàndiàn – large hotel
dàjiē – avenue
dàjiǔdiàn – large hotel
dānwèi – work unit, the cornerstone of China's social structure
dǎo – island
dàpùbù – large waterfall
dàqiáo – large bridge
dàshà – hotel, building
dàshèngtǎ – pagoda
dàxué – university
déhuà – a type of white-glazed porcelain
dìtiě – subway
dōng – east; the other points of the compass are *běi* (north), *nán* (south) and *xī* (west)
dòng – cave
dòngwùyuán – zoo
dòufu – tofu

E

értóng – children

F

fàndiàn – a hotel or restaurant
fēng – peak
fēngjǐngqū – scenic area
feng shui – geomancy, literally 'wind and water'; the art of using ancient principles to maximise the flow of qì, or universal energy
Fifth Generation – a generation of film directors who trained after the Cultural Revolution and whose political works revolutionised the film industry in the 1980s and '90s
fó – a Buddha
Fourth Generation – a generation of film directors whose careers were suspended by the Cultural Revolution

G

gǎng – harbour
Gang of Four – members of a clique, headed by Mao's

GLOSSARY

wife, Jiang Qing, who were blamed for the Cultural Revolution

gé – pavilion, temple

ger (M) – the Mongolian word for a circular tent made with animal skin or felt; see *yurt*

godown (C) – a warehouse, usually located on or near the waterfront

gompa (T) – monastery

gōng – palace

gōngyuán – park

gōu – gorge, valley

gù – previous, earlier

gǔ – valley

guān – pass

guānxì – advantageous social or business connections

gùchéng – ruins

gùjū – house, home, residence

gwailo (C) – a foreigner; literally meaning 'ghost person' and interpreted as 'foreign devil'

H

hǎi – sea

hǎitān – beach

Hakka – a Chinese ethnic group

Han – China's main ethnic group

hé – river

hong (C) – a company, usually engaged in trade; often refers to Hong Kong's original trading houses, such as Jardine Matheson or Swire

hú – lake

huáqiáo – overseas Chinese

Hui – ethnic Chinese Muslims

húndùn (C) – wontons

huǒguō – hotpot

huǒshānqún – volcano

hútòng – a narrow alleyway

J

jiāng – river

jiǎo – see *máo*

jiàotáng – church

jiǎozi – stuffed dumpling

jiē – street

jié – festival

jīn – see *catty*

jīngjù – Beijing opera

jìniànbēi – memorial

jìniànguǎn – memorial hall

jìniàntǎ – monument

jiǔdiàn – hotel

jū – residence, home

junk – originally referred to Chinese fishing and war vessels with square sails; now applies to various types of boating craft

K

kadimi shahr (U) – the old part of town; see also *yangi shahr*

kaido (C) – a small- to medium-sized ferry that makes short runs on the open sea, usually used for non-scheduled service between small islands and fishing villages

kǎoyādiàn – roast duck restaurant

kapala – a kind of skull cup, generally from Tibet

karakhana (U) – workshop, factory

karst – denotes the characteristically eroded landscape of limestone regions, such as the whimsical scenery of Guìlín and Yángshuò

KCR – Kowloon-Canton Railway

Kham – traditional name for eastern Tibet, encompassing western Sichuān

kūnjù – a regional form of classical opera developed in the cities of Sūzhōu, Hángzhōu and Nánjīng

KMB – Kowloon Motor Bus

kora (T) – pilgrim circuit

kuài – colloquial term for the currency, *yuán*

Kuomintang – Chiang Kaishek's Nationalist Party, the dominant political force after the fall of the Qing dynasty; now Taiwan's major political party

L

lama – a Buddhist priest of the Tantric or Lamaist school; a title bestowed on monks of particularly high spiritual attainment

lǎobǎixìng – common people, the masses

lǎowài – foreigners

liǎng – see *tael*

lín – forest

líng – tomb

lìshǐ – history

lóu – tower

LRT – Light Rail Transit, in Hong Kong

lù – road

lǚguǎn – hotel

lúnchuán mǎtou – passenger ferry terminal

luóhàn – Buddhist, especially a monk who has achieved enlightenment and passes to nirvana at death; see also *arhat*

lúshēng – a reed pipe that features in many festivals in Guìzhōu

M

mah jong – popular Chinese card game for four people, played with engraved tiles

Mandate of Heaven – a political concept where heaven gives wise leaders a mandate to rule and removes power from those who are evil or corrupt

máo – colloquial term for *jiǎo*, 10 of which equal one *kuài*

mǎtou – dock

mén – gate
Miao – ethnic group living in Guìzhōu
miào – temple
motor tricycle – an enclosed three-wheeled vehicle with a small motorbike engine, a driver at the front and seats for two passengers in the back
MTR – Mass Transit Railway, in Hong Kong
mù – tomb

N
name chop – a carved name seal that acts as a signature
nán – south; the other points of the compass are *běi* (north), *dōng* (east) and *xī* (west)

O
obo (M) – a pile of stones with a hollow space for offerings, a kind of shaman shrine
oolong (C) – high-grade Chinese tea, partially fermented

P
páilou – decorative archway
pedicab – pedal-powered tricycle with a seat to carry passengers
piǎolū – rafting trip
Pinyin – the official system for transliterating Chinese script into roman characters
pípá – a plucked string instrument
PLA – People's Liberation Army
Politburo – the 25-member supreme policy-making authority of the CCP
PRC – People's Republic of China
PSB – Public Security Bureau/Police; the arm of the police force set up to deal with foreigners
pùbù – waterfall
púsa – Bodhisattva
Putonghua – the standard form of the Chinese language used since the beginning of this century, based on the dialect of Běijīng

Q
qarvatlik mashina (U) – sleeper coach
qì – vital energy (life force) or cosmic currents manipulated in acupuncture and massage
qiáo – bridge
qìgōng – exercise that channels *qì*
qīngzhēnsì – mosque
quán – spring

R
rénmín – people, people's
Renminbi – literally 'people's money', the formal name for the currency of China; shortened to RMB
ROC – Republic of China, also known as Taiwan

S
sampan (C) – a small motorised launch, too small for the open sea
sānlún mótuōchē – motor tricycle
sānlúnchē – pedal-powered tricycle
SAR – Special Administrative Region
savdo dukoni (U) – commercial shops
sēnlín – forest
shān – mountain
shāngdiàn – shop, store
shāokǎo – barbecue
shěng – province, provincial
shì – city
shí – rock
shìchǎng – market
shìjiè – world
shíkū – grotto
shuǐkù – reservoir
sì – temple, monastery
sìhéyuàn – traditional courtyard house
special municipality – the name given to centrally administered regions such as Běijīng, Tiānjīn, Chóngqìng and Shànghǎi
stele (stelae) – a stone slab or column decorated with figures or inscriptions
stupa – usually used as reliquaries for the cremated remains of important *lamas*

T
ta – pagoda
tael – unit of weight; one tael *(liǎng)* equals 37.5g; there are 16 tael to the *catty*
taichi – the graceful, flowing exercise that has its roots in China's martial arts; also known as *tàijíquán*
taipan (C) – boss of a large company
tán – pool
Tanka – a Chinese ethnic group who traditionally live on boats
thangka – Tibetan sacred art
tíng – pavilion
triads – secret societies; originally founded to protect Chinese culture from the influence of usurping Manchurians, their modern-day members are little more than gangsters
tripitaka – Buddhist scriptures

W
walla walla – a motorised launch used as a water taxi and capable of short runs on the open sea
wān – bay
wēnquán – hot springs

X
xī – west; the other points of the compass are *běi* (north), *nán* (south) and *dōng* (east)
xī – small stream or brook

xiá – gorge
xiàn – county
xiàng – statue
xuěshān – snow mountain

Y
yá – cliff
yán – rock or crag
yangi shahr (U) – the new part of town, usually Han-dominated; see also *kadimi shahr*
yēlín – coconut plantation
yóujú – post office
yuán – the Chinese unit of currency; also referred to as Renminbi or RMB

yuán – garden
yurt (M) – the Russian word for a circular tent made with animal skin or felt; see *ger*

Z
zhào – lamasery
zhāodàisuǒ – basic lodgings, a hotel or guesthouse
zhāpí – a pint (of beer)
zhékòu – discount, eg off room price
zheng – a 13- or 14-stringed harp
zhíwùyuán – botanical gardens
zhōng – middle
zìrán bǎohùqū – nature reserve
zǔjū – ancestral home

Behind the Scenes

THIS BOOK

This 9th edition of *China* was written by a team of authors led by Damian Harper. The team consisted of Steve Fallon, Katja Gaskell, Julie Grundvig, Carolyn B Heller, Thomas Huhti, Bradley Mayhew, Korina Miller, Christopher Pitts and Dr Trish Batchelor. Damian also coordinated the 8th edition, and Caroline Liou coordinated the 7th.

THANKS from the Authors

Damian Harper Heartfelt thanks, hugs and kisses as ever to my wife and two children. Special thanks also to the entire Dai clan for their help and support, you have all been amazing. Thumbs up to the hearty residents of Shānhǎiguān, a slap on the back to China's innumerable *yángròuchuàn* chefs and a raised glass to the brewery at Qīngdǎo for making CCTV almost endurable. Last but not least, *gānbēi* to the merry folk of China who always ensure a visit to their land is fun and fascinating.

Steve Fallon A number of people helped in the updating of the Hong Kong, Macau and Guǎngdōng chapters of China. In Hong Kong, once again I am grateful to Rocky Dang of Phoenix Services Agency, Margaret Leung of Get Smart and Rob Stewart of Bloomberg for their generous assistance. As always, thanks to Teresa Costa Gomes of the Macau Government Tourist Office for her help and to Anita Lauder and Warren Rook for their hospitality on Coloane Island. I would not have found my way round Guǎngzhōu as easily as I did without the efficiency of Katherine Lipsher. Thanks too to husband Larry for putting me in touch with her in the first place. As is the custom, I'd like to dedicate my efforts to my partner, Michael Rothschild, whose memory of Dàlù is long and knowledge of Chinese cuisine equal to none.

Katja Gaskell A big thank you to all the people that helped me out along the way – the bus drivers, ticket collectors, hotel staff, monks, restaurant owners, fellow travellers and everyone else who was willing to answer my questions. Thank you in particular to Billy Zhao and his great team (Chéngdū), Patricia and Angela (Éméi Shān), Dakpa and Yeshi (Zhōngdiàn), Jim and Henriet (Dàlǐ), Zhao Fan (Lìjiāng), Cindy and Grace (Chóngqìng), and Sid and Lili (Bǎnnà). To Michael Day, Rebecca Chau, Damian Harper, Corinne Waddell and the rest of the Lonely Planet team involved in putting this book together. To Hilde, Vanessa and Emre for always being the perfect hosts. My family and friends for their incredible support and encouragement, their periodic phone calls and for always making me laugh. To my great travelling companions John and Cyril who kept me company at various stages of the journey. And finally a very special thank you to my mum who proved that it's still possible to look glamorous even when you're living out of a backpack.

Julie Grundvig Special thanks to Yipeng for all his encouragement and help while on the road. In Běijīng, a big thank you to Holly Guo, Tang Ruiqiang

---

THE LONELY PLANET STORY

The story begins with a classic travel adventure: Tony and Maureen Wheeler's 1972 journey across Europe and Asia to Australia. There was no useful information about the overland trail then, so Tony and Maureen published the first Lonely Planet guidebook to meet a growing need.

From a kitchen table, Lonely Planet has grown to become the largest independent travel publisher in the world, with offices in Melbourne (Australia), Oakland (USA) and London (UK). Today Lonely Planet guidebooks cover the globe. There is an ever-growing list of books and information in a variety of media. Some things haven't changed. The main aim is still to make it possible for adventurous travellers to get out there – to explore and better understand the world.

At Lonely Planet we believe travellers can make a positive contribution to the countries they visit – if they respect their host communities and spend their money wisely. Every year 5% of company profit is donated to charities around the world.

and Sun Yajing for helpful tips and advice. I'm also indebted to Lu Tengsheng and Li Ren for the home-cooked meals and hospitality and to Zheng Ling for the fun times in Hángzhōu. Thanks also to the hardworking staff of Lonely Planet who worked on this book.

Carolyn B Heller Many thanks to Lynn Bryant for always wanting to sleep in a yurt and for cheerful companionship despite quirky plumbing, rock-hard beds and elusive bus schedules. My gratitude to Zhu Jia Wei and family in Qíqíhā'ěr (delicious dumplings!); the Hailar Travel Service; Shen Yu (Linda), Jiang Jian Guo, Wang Hongzhi and the staff at Wudalian Chi Volcano Mineral Spring Co.; the Jílín English teachers, especially Dave and Claire for the insiders' tour; David Kay (Běijīng), Renee at CITS in Dàlián, Liu Xiuli (Jǐnzhōu), and the countless others who offered tips, information and smiles. For advice, contacts and helping hands, thank you Tomoko Sandhar, Cathy Pattinson, Andrew Mason, Tracey Orr-Dean, Ruth Tobias, Haven To-bias, Zhitao (Sunni) Sui, Monica Gruder Drake and Yu-ling (Jazz) Hsueh. And I wouldn't have gotten home without Mark Hacker's able assistance. My appreciation to Lonely Planet colleagues Rebecca Chau, Michael Day, Katja Gaskell, Julie Grundvig, Damian Harper, Corinne Waddell, and Korina Miller (the original wonder woman). Special thanks to Audrey Heller, Ken Heller, Lucy Albert, and Richard Manning for keeping things running smoothly at home; to Talia and Michaela for 45 hugs and kisses; and to Alan for being my anchor and inspiration, wherever I go.

Thomas Huhti Foremost thanks go to the wonderful people of China, whose curiosity and friendliness (and superhuman helpfulness) make what can be a tough slog so enriching and enjoyable. The Chinese who aided me along the way are too numerous to list, but Rose Luo (Hǎikǒu) and the inimitable Jim Beam (Xī'ān) must be noted. Along the many roads and paths (and bus rides), Rudi Geerdink and Susanne Broh (Netherlands), Michael Barnes and Christena Veach-Barnes (USA), and James Santi and Alex Kim (Mexico) garnered karma for their outstanding companionship and advice. Chris Miller and Kevin Caldwell (and respective families) gave admirable assistance (and bed space). A special shout out to all the readers who take the time to write us; trust this author – it does help. On the home front, my family have always been a rock of support (thanks sis for Bobositting!), as have my second family at WESLI (thanks Jasmine Jia, for all your local expertise!). Thanks Ra

for watching the home front. Special thanks to the Ownbys – Meredith, Gabby, Leo and Eva – for their invaluable friendship.

Bradley Mayhew Best wishes to Amy Frey and Matt McGarvey from TPAF; all the best with your projects in Tibet. Thanks to Sonam, our great driver Dawa and the ever-grinning Namse for a fine trip out to Kailash. Thanks also to Eva Gerlach for keeping me up to date with events in Lhasa and to Katherine Thornton for hotel updates. Cheers to Cheyney 'Hughass' Steininger for info on his vagabonding overlanding trips through all places forbidden and thanks to David Jennings for joining me on a frozen trip out to remotest Sichuān.

Korina Miller Big thank-yous to Michael Day for the opportunity and to Rebecca Chau and my co-authors for answering my calls for help. Thanks and love to Paul for his limitless support and for watching countless Chinese films with me. And a big hug to Simone for letting Mummy get her work done.

Christopher Pitts Thanks to Michelle Luo for her wonderful gift, Anne and Pierre Barroux for their hospitality in Běijīng, Meng Zhe for saving my Mandarin from oblivion, and Zhang Lanzhu for answering pre-trip queries. On the road special thanks go to all the farmers, monks, nuns and entrepreneurs who shared their fruit and kept me company with opinionated conversation, as well as the omnipresent Roderik and Tamara for relating many of their experiences along the road to Tibet. Gratitude is also due to Tom, Bradley, Korina and Damian, who all shared their insights, Caroline Kyberd for her generosity, the Pavillards for providing a quiet room to work in (among numerous other things), my family for their endless support despite my continued absence, and of course Perrine, who won't ever get enough thanks.

CREDITS

This title was commissioned by Michael Day; Korina Miller wrote the brief. Rebecca Chau and Cathy Lanigan assessed the manuscript and Rebecca also helped develop this title. Coordinating editor Barbara Delissen was assisted by Carly Hall, Holly Alexander, Cinzia Cavallaro, Monique Choy, Piers Kelly, Anne Mulvaney, Kristin Odijk, Charlotte Orr, Katrina Webb and Helen Yeates. Coordinating cartographer Tadhgh Knaggs was assisted by Hunor Csutoros, Jenny Jones, Emma McNicoll and Jody Whiteoak. The book was laid out by Kaitlin Beckett (coordinator), Jacqueline McLeod, Adam Bextream and John Shippick, who also created the colour pages. Julie Rovis and Brendan Dempsey designed the cover and Wayne Murphy designed the back-cover map. Project manager Fabrice Rocher kept an eye on the project.

Thanks to Quentin Frayne for the language chapter, to Nicholas Stebbing and Mark Germanchis for technical support, and to Rebecca Lalor for her tireless assistance and invaluable advice on all things Chinese. Thanks also to Anthony Phelan and the managers involved: Martin Heng (editorial), Corinne Waddell (cartography), and Adriana Mammarella, Kate McDonald and Sally Darmody (layout). Thanks to Anna Ji and James Zhang for their last minute Chinese help.

THANKS from Lonely Planet
Many thanks to the following travellers who used the last edition and wrote to us with helpful hints, useful advice and interesting anecdotes.

A Jeff & Tammy Abare, Karly Abery, Keith Acker, Bernadette Ackermans, Veerle Ackerstaff, Gale Acuff, Chris Adams, Connie Adams, Tanveer Ahmed, Gabriel Keahi Aki, Dave Alcock, Fraser Alexander, RE Alexander, Daniel Alton, Alvaro Amejeiras, Lisa Andersson, Sally Anderson, Frida Andrae, Mark Andrews, Raymond Ang, Monika Angst, Micah Arbisser, David Arbuz, Edward Archibald, Traci Arkinstall, Nancy Arleen, Jacob Arnbjerg, Tom Arnold, Kormoczi Aron, Rhea Ashmore, David Atkinson, Majorie Atkinson, Hadas Avidor, Fatima Awwad, Maria Jose Azevedo **B** Nick Bailey, Steven Bailey, Rachel Baker, Sunchita Balachandran, Jon Baldwin, Tim Balensiefer, David Balfour, Rachel Ball, Claus Balslev, Wayne Bao, Issi Barbash, James Barber, Ines Barbieri, Jim Barbush, Yilmaz & Astrid Baris, Don & Karen Barnes, Jerry Barnes, Sylvia Barnes, Nicky Barnett, Dennis Barrier, Ian Barry, Geoff Barton, Melvin Bashner, Katarina Bastamow, Jan Bayer, Jonathan & Penelope Bayl, Bridgit Beasley, Roger Beaud, RV Beck, Aliza Beckett, Tom & Deborah Beierle, Rachel Beit-Aryeh, Mira Benes, Theresa Benner, Karl Benson, Philip Benusa, Wouter Jan Berends, Sven Berger, Joachim Bergmann, Mark Berkovich, Alex Bernikoff, Grahame Bernoth, Christopher Berresford, Keith Berry, Oran Bertelsen, Gareth Bibby, Rodrigo Bibiloni, Roger Bielec, Aart Biewenga, Brandon Biggs, Graham Binder, Matthew Bisley, Bjorn GS Bjornsson, Justin Blanckaert, Karin Blokziel, Laura Blom, Michel Bochu, Kate Boddington, Avi Bodha, HJ Bogaard, Edwin Bogh, Joseph Bolger, Boonchana Boonrasri, Shir Borenstine, Tom Bos, Kate Botkin, Reg & Pam Bottrill, Carmen Boudreau-Kiviaho, Jean-Pierre Boudrias, Raphael Bousquet, China Boy, David Boyall, Meretta Boyer, Harald Hjalmar Braakman, Keith & Fran Bradley, Danielle Bram, Paul Brand, Eric Brandt, Natasha Brault, Daniela Bredenbroeker, A Bregman, Marco Bresciani, Rebecca Brice, Samuel Brien, Peter Briggs, Jan Brinkmann, Graeme Brock, Nancy Broderick, Heather Bronson, Leah Brooke, Lynda Brooker, Candice & Nick Kilpatrick Broom, Marcel Brosens, Alan Brown, Anthony Brown, Chris Brown, Gerold Bruning, Bela Buchner,

Renate Buergler, Leanne Bugeja, Sandra Bulling, Jacquelien Bunt, Leslie Burhoe, Penny Burke, Tara Burke, Lisa Burton, Suzan Burton, Jeremy Butler, Marie Butson, James Butterfield, Marin Buyco **C** Elina Cabrera, Jenny Cai, Peter Callaghan, Paul Cammaert, Andy Campbell, Nigel Campbell, Nigel Canavan, Mary Frances Cappiello, Andy Carn, Jason Carpenter, Matt Carr, Steve Carr, Beatrice Carroli, Derek Carter, Phil Carter, Marcella Cassiano, Magnus Caullvine, Tody Cezar, Will Chadwick, Tiffany Chan, Tye Kuang Chan, Frances Chang, Alejandro Chaoul, Flaminia Chapman, Rod Chapman, Bob Chard, Gavin Chart, Ed Chen, Jinfeng Chen, Gregory Cheung, JF Cheung, Gabriel Chew, Elizabeth Chiang, Caroline Child, Lawrence Chin, Lili Chin, Patrick Chin-Dahler, Karen Chiu, HeaJung Choi, Chungwah Chow, Eva Christiansen, TK Chu, Dmitry Chumakov, Ekaterina Chumakova, Neil F Clancy, Jemetha Clark, Simon Clark, Dean Clarke, Ingo Claus, Rhonda Clegg, Nienke Coehoorn, Liz Coghill, Eamon Coleman, Tate Collin, Sharon Collins, Warren Collits, Creighton Connolly, Tim Connor, Ryan Cook, Susan Cook, Jock & Hazel Cooper, Lindsay Cooper, Peter Cooper, Cliff Cordy, Charlie Cornelius, Robert Cosgrove, Mike & Sonoko Cowie, Paul Cragg, Oliver Craig, Elizabeth Craven, Karen Crawford, Tony Creedy, Alison Cribbs, Collin Crowell, Ian Cruickshank, Chris Cummins, Charles Cunningham, Brian Curtis, Robert Cuzner, Paul Cyr **D** Tal Dagan, Gavin Daly, Lori Dam, Trinh Dang, Michael Dann, Laura D'Antonio, Katherine Davey, Uri Davidovich, Lynsey Davies, Geoffrey Davis, Les Davis, Michael Dawson, Alaric de Arment, David de Bhal, Mark de Boer, Chris de Fries, Aukje de Gier, Dorothy de Kiewiet, Heidi de Koninck, Christa de Kort, Hans de Rouw, Rupert & Jemma de Smidt, Marianne de Swart, Barry de Vent, Philip & Kerry Dean, Matthew & Jo Dear, Alaric DeArment, Caroline Defrance, Andrew DeFrancis, Thomas Degnan, Matthias Dehner, Andrea Dekkers, M Delange-Wang, Scott Delany, Laura Demetris, Bach Demian, John Dent, Graham Denyer, Catherine & Richard Desomme-Koch, Nathan Dhillon, Giuseppina Di Cicco, Paul Di Stefano, Joe Diamond, Andrea Dickson, Mark Diesendorf, Judy Dimter, Feng Ding, Francesco Diodato, Diane Ditcham, Steffi Doering, Hans Heinrich Doermann, Stephen Dolphin, Kelly Dombroski, John Donaldson, Wayne Donaldson, Sarah Dopp, WF Doran, Robert Doub, Daniel Dourneau, Michael Dowad, Tony Dragon, John Drake, Mark Drake, Christine du Fresne, Charles Dudley, Doug Durst, Daniel Duy Fogarty, Peter Dwyer, Robin Dwyer-Hickey, Sean Dyde, Matthew Dyke **E** John Easterbrook, Daniel Eaton, Yael Edrey, Jay Edwards, Nicky Efron, David J Ehredt, Dan Ehrman, Otto Eichman, Michael Eiselt, Amy Eisner, Omri Elaad, Mikael Elenfors, Sara Elinson, Daanish Ellias, Emily J Elliott, Mary Ann Ellis, Steve Emms, Paul Engels, David M Engum, Jeff David Entner, Reinhard Erb, Khosrow Esfahani, Meriam Espela, J Evans, Derek Evans, Edwin Evers **F** Michel Faas, Paul Facer, Angela Faerber, Trevor Faggotter, David Falkenstern, Catherine Fan, L Faze, Matthew Featherston, Ilan Feine, Ansgar Felbecker, Elinor Feldman, Michael Fenghua, Sebastien Ferenczi, Josep-Emili Ferrer, Dina Fesler, Kate Fewins, James Fichter, Nick Field, Michel Findhammer, Darren Findlay, J Patrick Fischer, Margaret & David Fitzgerald, Thomas Fleming, Pia Fobian, Matthew Fong, Ruth Forbes, Del Ford, Daniel Forger, Craig

Forman, John Fortune, Kyle Foster, Stefan Fouquet, Madeleine Fournier, Patrick Fournier, Doug Fowler, Lucy Fowler, Paul Fowler, Barry & Trish Fox, Aymeric Fraise, Diodato Francesco, Tom Frawley, David Fregona, Laura French, George Friedman, Stig Magne Frone, Jenny Frost, Christian Fuchs, Maggi Fuchs, Margret Fuchs, Markus Fuessel, Dave & Lina Fuller, Yonnie Fung **G** Justin Gallagher, Maureen Gallagher, Mike Galvin, John Gardner, Jan Garvelink, Thomas Gay, Martin & Maggie Gebbelt, Michael Gee, Naftali Gefen, Sean Geiger, Joern Geisselmann, Boni Suzanne Gelfand, Jim Gennrich, Anne Geursen, C David Gibbons, Jo Gibson, Christina & Scott Gifford, Walter Gillies, Anne Gilliland, Paul Gioffi, Johan Gjarum, Johannes Glas, David Glashan, Brad Gledhill, Yvonne Gluyas, Ran Gluzman, Elizabeth Godfrey, Jamie Godfrey, Bob & Eunice Goetz, Guy Goldberg, Mary D Goldsmith, Sam Golledge, Nieves Gonzalez Ramon, Diane B Goodpasture, Martin Gough, Lisa Grady, Matthew Grandage, Linda Grannas, Stu Grant, Kevin Green, Jay Greenberg, John Greenhow, Bryhanna Greenough, Pen Greenwood, James Greg, Alan Gregg, Anne-Marie Gregory, Karleen Gribble, Ed Griffith, Ivette Groenendijk, Bela Grolshammer, Rosanne Groom, Howard & Jean Groome, Anett Grusser, Anna Gurnhill, Linnea Gvransson **H** Vassily Haakon, Minna Haapanen, Kirsten Hafkemeyer, Ella ND Haim, Joe Hake, Matthew Hall, Richard & Jenny Hall, Patricia Halter, Laurence Hamels, Jesselyn Hamilton, Ji-Yeon Han, Ron Hannah, Amy Hanser, Carola Hantelmann, Peter Hardie, Tobias Hardy, Eyal Harel, Rose Harland, Cecilia Harlitz, John Harrill, Mark Harris, Manfred Hartmann, Stephan Hartry, Peter Harvey, John Hastings, Andrew Hatfield, Jian Ye Hau Yuan, Frances Haung, Johan Hausen, Lene Havgaard, James Hawkins, Vanessa Hayes, Xavier Hazenbosch, Kaihao He, Geraldine Healy, Peter Heath, Robert & Tura Heckler, Moritz J Heidbuechel, Thomas Heimberg, Wolfgang Heisel, Jan Henckens, Nate Henderson, Donald Henson, Moritz Herrmann, Achim Herzog, Matthias Hess, Nicolai Hesse, Ben Hewitt, Jessica Hexter, Sarah Heyer, Alf Hickey, Thng Hui Hien, David Higgs, Art Hilado, Ben Hill, Cara Hill, Crispin Hill, Thea Hill, Hagay Hochman, Christine Hoddie, Valerie Hoeks, Elizabeth Hoffman, Jenny Hogg, Robert Hoke, JJJ Hollander, Andrew Holmes, Chris Holmes, Pamela Holt, Tan Kor Hoon, Anthony Hopfe, Jeanie Hore, Alfonso Arias Hormaechea, Daniel Horn, David Horn, Richard Hoskin, Mike Howard, H Matthew Howarth, Aaron Howell, Rhodri Howell, Petr Hruska, Thomas Hudson, Mark Hughes, Kang Beng Hui, Dixson Huie, Robin Hujie, Judith Hunger, Malcolm Hunt, Carolyn & Jarrod Hunt-Wackett, John Hutton **I** Michelle Ingram, Lorenzo Iori, Henrietta Irving, David Irwin, Malcolm Irwin, Nadler Ishay, Fred Isler, Leejun Ivie **J** Dave Jackson, Glyn Jackson, Danny Jacqmot, Karen Jaffe, Anne Jahn, Kathrin Jaki, Ronald James, Steven James, Lana Jamieson, Laticia Jammes, Erica Jarnes, Tony Jenkins, Chua Yun Jia, Andrew Johns, Berit Johns, Helen Johnson, Hugh H Johnson, Jimmy & Anja Johnson, Ross Johnson, Tony Johnston, Riikka Jokihaara, Bonnie Jones, Harold Jones, Jason Jones, John Jose, Tom Joseph, Michelle Josselyn, Mathias R Jud, Chris Jules, Annelie Jung, Bomee Jung **K** Lynn Kagan, Barry Kaiser, Lau Ka-kin, Christine Kammer, Charlotte Kan, Robert Kaping, Judith Karena, Pius Karena, Rony Katz, Geoffrey Keating,

David Kelly, Jane Kelly, Patricia Kelly, Pim Kemps, Samantha Kempshall, Cameron Kennedy, Thom Kenrick, David Kerkhoff, Eva Kerzel, Thomas Kerzel, Anja Kessler, Alicia Khaw, Brian Kichler, Tim Kiehne, C Kim, Eugene Kim, Elad Kimchi, Charis King, Siu King, Lucie Kinkorova, Matti Kinnunen, Lisa Kirsebom, Nikolai Klemm, Nick Klensch, Pete Knust, Catherine Koch, Geertje Koeman, Wiebke & Matthias Koenig, Amy Kohrman, Kenneth Koo, Sheng-Cheng Koo, Alex Koolhof, Jolanda Koopmans, Remko Koppius, Jure Kos, Adam Kosack, Jan Kovac, Maya Kovskaya, Andrew Kowala, Edyta Krakowiecka, Annett Kraske, Oliver Krause, Marieke Krijnen, Frank Kroeger, Kathrine Kroijer Hoested, Alex Kryska, Mateusz Krzyzosiak, Karolina Kuberska, Agnieszka Kula, Simon Kull, George Kulstad, Linda Kung, Stefan & Charlotte Kunz, Shiamin Kwa, Aston Kwok, Boyoung Kwon, Charles Kydd **L** Leo Lacey, Richard Lambourne, Helen Lancashire, Nina Laney, Anat Langer, Petra Lapkova, William Laracy, Erik Laridon, Roderick Latham, Winnie Lau, Alexander Laue, Jolanda Laurijsen, Felix Lavoie, Davina Law, Mark Lawford, Stephen Lawson, Patricio Lecuona, Darlene Lee, Ee-Lian Lee, Henry Lee, Michelle Lee, Samuel Lee, Yin Lee, Thomas Leeb, Michael Lees, Ville Leino, Derek Leivers, Karen Leivers, Regitse Leleur, Jasper Lensen, Lucas & Vanessa Leonardi, Mikelson Leong, Yurika Leong, Rosa Levin, Sharon Lew, Jean & Colin Lewis, Philip Lewis, Dirk Leysen, Guo Zhao Li, Nathan Liang, Jesper Lidstrom, Liberty Lidz, Mike Lieven, Jo-Ann Lim, Justin Lim, Peter Lindgren, Mikael Lindqvist-Ottosson, Caroline Liou, Mei Jiun Liu, Omer Livay, Philip Livingstone, Oscar Ljungqvist, Adrian Lloyd, Mikael Lo, Charles Locher, Brent Lodding, Johanna Lofvenius, N Logan, Salvatore Loi, Mike Longley, Andy Loo, Karl Loring, Adam Lotery, Marie & Denis Louvegnies, Royce Lowe, Artur Loza, Khai Lu, Matt Lucas, Kip Luce, Ingrid K Lund, Martin Lundgren, Johann Lundström, Martin Lutterjohann, Jason Lynn **M** Gary Ma, Suzanne Maas, Ronan Mac-Aongusa, Julia Mackenzie, Pawel Maczel, Rafael Madrid, Diana Maestre, Masaki Magai, Raimund Magis, Laura Magliano, Alexandre Maier, Cedric Maizieres, Antony Makepeace, Shona Malcolm, Erika Malitzky, Don Mallory, Bertrand Maltaverne, Dan Manning, Phil Manson, Martin Maranus, Ato Mariano, Celia Mark, Eric Markowitz, Jonathon Marsden, Ruben Martherus, Caroline Martin, David Martin, Elandriel Martin, Glynn Martin, Jay Martin, Andre Martino, Jean Martino, Tom Jorgen Martinussen, Steve Martz, Deann Masin, Fran Mason, Paul Mason, Benedicte Masse, Iain Masterton, Jeffrey Mather, Erica Mathias, Jay Mattner, Kent Maxwell, Maralyn Mayayo, Annette Mayerbacher, Piotr Mazurkiewicz, Neil McCarthy, Stuart McClelland, Callum McConnell, Bronwyn Mc-Ewen, Seamus McGinley, Pat McGuire, Dave McKay, John & Robyn McKenna, Nina McKenna, Walter McKenzie, Malcolm McKinnon, Matt McLaughlin, Ross McLeish, Ann McMillan, Joanna McMillan, Gary McMurrain, Shane McNamara, Fri McWilliams, Daniel Meier-Behrmann, Marieke Meijer, Piet Meijer, Martin Mellish, Victoria Mellor, Monica Mengoli, Andrea Mensing, Vincent Mercier, Stephanie Messanger, Laura Messenger, Yves Mestric, Jon Metcalf, Scott Meyer, Ceciel Meys, Greg Michaels, Peter Micic, Gerie Mienes, Robin Miles, Sabrina Mileto, John Millbank, Allison Miller, Jon Miller, Simon Miller,

Wolfram Miller, Helen Mills, Robert Mills, Andrew Milne, Eric Minikel, Ariane Minnaar, Michael Miske, Jo Mitchell, Rob Mitchell, Kjell Mittag, Etienne Monin, Antonella Montironi, Lieuwe Montsina, Beth Moody, Peter Moorfield, Chris & Sandy Morgan, Francois Morvan, Astrid Muelli, Patrick Muhlen-Schulte **N** Eva Nagy, Wee Kee Nah, Chip Nakagawa, Ratna Nandakumar, Ranjit Narula, Kerwee Neau, Meira Neggaz, Steve Nelson, Tom Nelson, Elaine Ng, Angela Ngan, Trung Dung Nguyen, Kim Rene Nielsen, Hanneke Niesten, Karen Nikakis, Alex Nikolic, Tovit Nizer, Michelle Nochomovitz, Paul North, Bill Northby, Cindy Norum, Kiara Nowlan, Sebastian Nowozin, Rip Noyes, Loutfi Nuaymi, Anna-Lotta Nystrom **O** Debbie O'Bray, Roderick O'Brien, Jarlath O'Carroll, Kelly O'Hara, Shannon O'Laughlin, Viktoria Olausson, Mikko Ollikainen, Willem Oorschot, Michiel Opgenoort, Holden Osborne, Ingvild & Jan Helge Ostensen, Eoin O'Sullivan, Jonathan Owen, Jenna Owens **P** Julien Pagliaroli, Stacy Palestrant, Vicky Palmer, Lorraine Pang, Andrea Panzoni, Felix Parker, Philip Parker, Marcia Parrish-Siggelkow, Debaere Pascal, Nadia Pastouna, David Patel, Mario Pavesi, Ruth Payne, Catherine Peacock, John Peacock, Josh Pearlman, Duncan Peattie, Lukasz Pekacki, Renate Pelzl, David Penton, Mark Pepper, Bawanthi Perera, Bernard Peres, Raymund Perez, Eduardo Peris, Matthew Perrement, David Perrin, Matt Peterson, Mikko Pettila, Judy Pex, Helene Pfeiffer, Eric Phan-Kim, Ng Keng Phoy, Jerry Pi, Francie Picknell, Matthew Piercy, Brian C Pierini, Pat Piskulich, Dennis Plink, Steven Plummer, Mitja Podreka, Jacques Poitras, Daniel Polci, Daniel Poon, Aase Popper, Matthew Post, John & Wendy Preston, Igor Pribytkov, Torben Prokscha, Yuwanee Prommaporn, Francois Puech, Sue Purdon **Q** Liu Qianqian, Mark Quartley, Bernadette Quin, Philippe Quix **R** Kate Radford, Kim Radford, Stephen Radford, Katalin Rakoczi, Rami Rakovitzki, John Ransom, Alice Rawdon-Mogg, Karen Rayle, Phil Reavley, Brett M Reichert, David Reid, Fitzcarl Reid, Zqraggen Reto, Lane Rettig, Mark Reuber, Jurrian Reurings, Robert Rex-Waller, Stephan Rey, Mary Rezek, Sylvia Rhau, Samia Riaz, Deborah Ann Rice, Martin Rice Smith, Gene Richards, Bianca Rieckmann, Thomas Riedenbauer, Matthew A Rifkin, Helen Rigby, Tenzin Rinchen, Sven Ring, Virginia Risso, Dick Roberts, Scott Robertson, Nick Robey, Fraser Robinson, Dick Rochester, Viviane Rochon, Allison Rodman, Else-Marie Rombouts, Robert Rosenberg, Julia Ross, Paul Ross, Peter Ross, Tanya Ross, Gernot Roth, Daniel Rovai, Al Rowley, Ravi C Roy, Shannon Roy, Jay Ruchamkin, Carol Ann Rueckert, Rachael Ruegg, Angry Russell, Davina Russell, Craig Rutland, Lorna Ryan **S** Evelyn Saal, Anna-Leena Saarela, Amanda Saari, Zuzana Sadkova, Claire Saeki, Verena Sailer, John Sall, Emma Samuelsson, Fredrik Sand, Richard Sanders, Louisa Sanfey, Inbal Sansani, Ashish Sareen, Susan Sawczuk, Andrew Sayegh, Thomas Schafer, Christian Scheirmann, Bernd Schepers, Ed Schlenk, Christian Schlierkamp, Kristin Schmid, Thomas Schmidt-Doerr, Britta Schmitz, Heidrun Schmitz, Ernst Albert Schneider, Elizabeth Schoenfeld, David Schoolnik, Alex Schrama, Simon Schreiber, Walbert Schulpen, Birte Schulz, James Schumann, W Schuurman, Gerd Schwandner, Kolya Schweppe, Ralph Schwer, James Scotford, Elizabeth Searles, Ian Seccombe, Guy Seguin, Bart Seliger, Michael Serup,

Claire Sharratt, Christine & Carrie Shaw, Robert Shaw, MT Shea, Tu Shengbin, Paul Shepard, Wu Shi, Francis Shillitoe, Robin Shostack, Nolan Shulak, Xiem Weh Shun, Dan Siebers, Susan Simerly, Cynthia Simmons, Maxine Simmons, Craig Simons, Clive Simpson, Don Simpson, JFP Simpson, Lyndsee Simpson, Barrie Sims, Paul Sinclair, Annabelle Singer, Lim Wei Siong, Julian Sirull, Ryan Skeie, Max Slade, Al Slagle, Jeroen Slikker, Herbert Smit, Bernard Smith, CR Smith, Casey Smith, Daniel I Smith, Edward Smith, Jamie Smith, Malcolm Smith, Sue Smith, Jacco Snoeijer, Floris Snuif, Jaz Sohdi, Maik Solt, Helena Sopwith, Dawn Sorenson, David Speary, Saskia Spee, Roland Stabler, Johan Staes, Nikola Stankovic, Carl Stapleton, Ron Startek, Pat Stebleton, Ben Steele, Edwin Steele, Loa Stefansdottir, Nizza & Yaron Stein, Christoph Steinhardt, Moritz Steinhilber, Nick Stephen, Simon Stevens, Anika Stokkentre, Magnus Stomfelt, Alessia Stradella, David Straub, Rob Street, Pablo Strormann, Merav Suissa, Kate Sullivan, Nora Sun, Johan Sundblad, Kristy Surak, Chris Sutor, Hugh Sutton, Ivan Swater, Jan Swearingen, Fauzi Syed, John Szalus, Peter Szikinger **T** Craig Tafel, Wilson Tai, Alvaro Amejeiras Taibo, Naoko Takahashi, Christine Tam, Andrew Tamblyn, Boon In Tan, Jianguo Tang, Kun Won Tang, Hugh Tansley, Jiang Tao, Marie Stefanie Taschereau, Mark Taylor, Michel Mark Te, Genevieve Tearle, Damon Tedford, Claus Tempelmann, Anna Tenzing, Ines Teschke, Ben W Tettlebaum, Suet Lan Tham, Bill Thames, Barbara Theiler, Shanice Thia, David Thomas, Lucy Thomas, Simon Thorpe, Lucy Tickell, Allan Tighe, Martijn Tillema, PA Tillman, Andreas Tindlund, Kathy Tipler, EP Tissing, Nick & Rose Todd Brown, Derek Tokashiki, Fiona

Tomlinson, Mitzi Toney, S Tontian, Sissel Topple, Christophe Tourrenc, David Towers, Simon Tries, Peter Trippy, Prue Trollope, Annelies Troost, Sam Trousdale, William Tse, Ned & Denise Turcinov, Charlotte Turner, Ian Turner, Scott Tuurie, Debora & Laura Tydecks **U** Toshiko Ueda, Manolis Ulbricht, Debra J Underwood, Rob Unsworth, Elanah Uretsky, Darlene Joy Uy **V** Jenny & Cor Valk, Tom Sanpaworn Vamvanij, Ruud van Ammers, Peter van Buren, Arno van de Graaf, Robert van de Graaff, Timo van de Lagemaat, Marco van de Sande, David van Driessche, Erwin van Engelen, Ester van Kippersluis, Lotte van Laatum, Elles van Loo, Sandra van Osch, Erik van Raaij, Alan van Raalte, Richard van Schip, Mieke van 't Hoog, Andrew Vardon, Renata Zupanc Varsek, Sophie Ruth Vaughan, Greet Verbist, Andrea Vergara, Edegar Vergara, Ryan Verge, Rodolphe Verhaegen, Dimitri Verhoeven, Jos Verschaeren, Dirk Vetter, Clem Vetters, Diane Villa, Frank Villante, Marc Vincent, Jack Vittersum, Bernard Vixseboxse, John Vogel, Katharina Vogt, Gian Mario Volpe, Sabine von Imhoff, Florian von Oppenheim, Tobias von Platen, Francoise Vooren, Christina Vrakettas, Tomi Vuorela, Lilian Vyth **W** Steven Wagner, Chew Hiu Wah, Jessica Wahlberg, Shabnam Walji, Jessica Walker, Brandon Wall, Ben Walter, Daniel Wang, David Wang, Joseph Wang, Wenyuan Wang, Thomas Ward, Donna Waselyshen, Judy Watson, Georg Weber, Xuess Wee, Jesse Weiner, Julie Weiss, Bryce William Wentworth, Andreas Wenzlaff, Jane Werner-Aye, Jonas Wernli, Lydia Westbrook, Gudrun Westerlund, Andrew Whitby, Camilla White,

Libby Whitmore, Fiona Whittenbury, Michiel Wijers, Nishy Wijewardane, Siw Wikstrom, Nicole Wild, Kate & Owen Wilder, Chris Willcox, Lloyd Willemsen, Joan Willey, Andrew Williams, Ross Williams, Anna Willmer, Katherine Wilson, Kathy & Rick Wilson, Mark Wilson, Alexander Winter, Aleksandra & Georg Winterberger, Chris Winters, Erik Woltjen, Colin Wolverson, Ann Yukha Wong, Chow Wah Wong, Joanna Wong, J Woo, John Woo, Darryl Wood, Kathryn Wood, Michael Woodhead, Stephen Woodley, Jared Woolstenhulme, Jan Wostyn, John Wotherspoon, Isabel Wright, Tony & Jean Wright, Jessi Wu, Justin Wu, Wei Wu, Yidan Wu, Louisa Wumin, Ron Wurzer **X** Carlos Xavier, Qi Xian **Y** Karno Yan, David Yang, Michael Yang, Joseph Yin, Stacy Yoshioka, Roland Young, Simon Yu, Nitzan Yudan **Z** Tony Z, Shami Zain, Estela Zarate, Jack Zeng, Tymoteusz Zera, Jonathan Zhang, Tony S Zhou, Cornelia Zhu, Martin Ziegler, Maike Ziesemer, Henrik Zillmer, Adrian Zimmermann, Trayah Zinger, Maurus Zink, Naomi Zola, Sara Zolfaghari, Patrick Zoll

ACKNOWLEDGMENTS

Extract from *The Songlines* by Bruce Chatwin published by Jonathan Cape. Used with permission of The Random House Group Limited and Gillon Aitken Associates Limited.

Globe on back cover © Mountain High Maps 1993 Digital Wisdom, Inc.

Index

INDEX

INDEX

INDEX

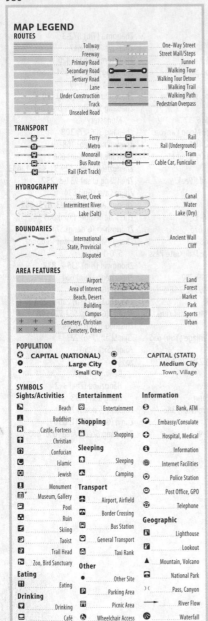

MAP LEGEND
ROUTES

Tollway	One-Way Street
Freeway	Street Mall/Steps
Primary Road	Tunnel
Secondary Road	Walking Tour
Tertiary Road	Walking Tour Detour
Lane	Walking Trail
Under Construction	Walking Path
Track	Pedestrian Overpass
Unsealed Road	

TRANSPORT

Ferry	Rail
Metro	Rail (Underground)
Monorail	Tram
Bus Route	Cable Car, Funicular
Rail (Fast Track)	

HYDROGRAPHY

River, Creek	Canal
Intermittent River	Water
Lake (Salt)	Lake (Dry)

BOUNDARIES

International	Ancient Wall
State, Provincial	Cliff
Disputed	

AREA FEATURES

Airport	Land
Area of Interest	Forest
Beach, Desert	Market
Building	Park
Campus	Sports
Cemetery, Christian	Urban
Cemetery, Other	

POPULATION

CAPITAL (NATIONAL)	CAPITAL (STATE)
Large City	Medium City
Small City	Town, Village

SYMBOLS

Sights/Activities
- Beach
- Buddhist
- Castle, Fortress
- Christian
- Confucian
- Islamic
- Jewish
- Monument
- Museum, Gallery
- Pool
- Ruin
- Skiing
- Taoist
- Trail Head
- Zoo, Bird Sanctuary

Eating
- Eating

Drinking
- Drinking
- Café

Entertainment
- Entertainment

Shopping
- Shopping

Sleeping
- Sleeping
- Camping

Transport
- Airport, Airfield
- Border Crossing
- Bus Station
- General Transport
- Taxi Rank

Other
- Other Site
- Parking Area
- Picnic Area
- Wheelchair Access

Information
- Bank, ATM
- Embassy/Consulate
- Hospital, Medical
- Information
- Internet Facilities
- Police Station
- Post Office, GPO
- Telephone

Geographic
- Lighthouse
- Lookout
- Mountain, Volcano
- National Park
- Pass, Canyon
- River Flow
- Waterfall

LONELY PLANET OFFICES

Australia
Head Office
Locked Bag 1, Footscray, Victoria 3011
☎ 03 8379 8000, fax 03 8379 8111
talk2us@lonelyplanet.com.au

USA
150 Linden St, Oakland, CA 94607
☎ 510 893 8555, toll free 800 275 8555
fax 510 893 8572, info@lonelyplanet.com

UK
72–82 Rosebery Ave,
Clerkenwell, London EC1R 4RW
☎ 020 7841 9000, fax 020 7841 9001
go@lonelyplanet.co.uk

Published by Lonely Planet Publications Pty Ltd
ABN 36 005 607 983

© Lonely Planet 2005

© photographers as indicated 2005

Cover photographs: Replicas of ancient terracotta warriors, Keren Su/ APL Corbis (front); People on bicycles at rush hour, Nicholas Pavloff/ LPI (back). Many of the images in this guide are available for licensing from Lonely Planet Images: www.lonelyplanetimages.com.